FINANCE

An Integrated Global Approach

FINANCE

An Integrated Global Approach

Anand G. Shetty
Francis J. McGrath
Irene M. Hammerbacher
Hagen School of Business
Iona College

AUSTEN PRESS

IRWIN
Burr Ridge, Illinois
Boston, Massachusetts
Sydney, Australia

Publisher: William Schoof
Production Manager: Bob Lange
Marketing Manager: Ron Bloecher

Development, design, and project management provided by Elm Street Publishing Services, Inc.

Compositor: Elm Street Publishing Services, Inc.
Typeface: 10/12 Goudy
Printer: R. R. Donnelley & Sons Company

Library of Congress Cataloging-in-Publication Data

Shetty, Anand G.
Finance: an integrated global approach / Anand G. Shetty, Francis J. McGrath, Irene M. Hammerbacher.
p. cm.
Includes index.
ISBN 0-256-15302-7
1. Finance. I. McGrath, Francis J. II. Hammerbacher, Irene M. III. Title
HG173.S513 1995
332—dc20 94-33047

Printed in the United States of America
1 2 3 4 5 6 7 8 9 0 DOC 9 8 7 6 5 4

Address editorial correspondence:
Austen Press
18141 Dixie Highway
Suite 111
Homewood, IL 60430

Address orders:
Richard D. Irwin, Inc.
1333 Burr Ridge Parkway
Burr Ridge, IL 60521

Austen Press
Richard D. Irwin, Inc.

- PICK-UP CHECK
- 20 JOE - 10 SHAWN
- 15 DARREN
- 160 MIKE
- WASH CLOTH
- CALL BOBBY
- PACK

This book is dedicated to

Barbara and Kamala Irene
Rosa, Patia, and Nuria
Lillian, Jerry, and Tom

Preface

Many introductory finance texts focus on the single area of financial management, ignoring the interdependent areas of financial markets and institutions and investments. This approach not only leaves many topics uncovered, it also fails to offer the student the comprehensive foundation a first course in finance should offer.

Finance: An Integrated Global Approach integrates the three subdivisions of financial management, financial markets and institutions, and investments through their common core of knowledge rather than treating them as separate topics. It emphasizes their similarities, and its simplicity of style enhances the student's understanding.

Finance: An Integrated Global Approach presumes the student has no prior knowledge of economics or finance. Because some familiarity with accounting and the forms of business organization will be helpful, Appendixes A and B at the end of the text provide the necessary material.

DISTINCTIVE FEATURES

Finance: An Integrated Global Approach, while covering all the material a first course requires, approaches its topics in several distinctive ways.

- Most introductory texts treat international finance in a single chapter. In *Finance: An Integrated Global Approach*, these international aspects of finance are thoroughly integrated throughout the text. This integrative approach corresponds to the internationalization of business. Financial institutions and markets in the United States are no longer treated as independent of those in Europe and Asia. Investments in multinationals and foreign securities are commonplace today. Exchange rates as well as the basic principles of investment must be understood. Globalized financial management must now consider the consequences of import and export decisions in both the cash and capital budgets. Financial managers must be able to evaluate foreign subsidiaries for acquisition. They must also be able to consider the ramifications of foreign corporations seeking to acquire their own firms.
- Each chapter moves from simple concepts to complex decision making. International similarities and variations are always noted. Furthermore, no

attempt is made to force one mathematical model or theory to fit every situation.

- A special chapter discusses the interrelationships among interest rates, inflation rates, and exchange rates. The text explains the interdependence of these areas and integrates them into all decision-making processes, unlike most other texts.
- In keeping with the significance of small business in today's world, the entrepreneurial aspects of many topics are covered. A company with one owner and five employees may do a cash budget on the back of an envelope, keep accounts receivable in a shoebox or under the cash register, and consider the purchase of one 91-day T-bill a major investment decision, but the principles of finance still apply to that company. The text specifically applies financial decision making directly to entrepreneurial enterprises.
- The text is practice oriented. Numerous exhibits containing real-world illustrations appear throughout the text. Each chapter includes several Focus on Finance boxes, where real financial events are discussed. A Focus on Careers box in each chapter also introduces students to financial occupations within their reach.
- *Finance: An Integrated Global Approach* discusses many terms and concepts not generally included in other introductory finance texts. Each term is made part of the text discussion, giving a clear understanding of its meaning and use. They are also defined in the marginal glossary. These and other terms are included:

hedging, arbitraging, and speculating in foreign currency markets
ERISA
Monday T-bill auctions
tax anticipation T-bills
international factoring
the consequences of not collecting on receivables
inventory disposal costs
the ABC model of inventory control
a midstream annuity problem
the rule of 72
the similarity between capital budgeting and security valuation
cash flow estimation for foreign projects
the problems that may be encountered when using the IRR
the cash flow relationship of changes in net working capital
interest rate and exchange rate swaps
international leases

multinational cash flow management

division of the underwriting spread

foreign securities exchanges

common-size and common-base financial statement analysis

- Many topics in *Finance: An Integrated Global Approach* are covered more extensively, clearly, and in more detail that in competing texts:

currency markets

inflation and its causes and consequences

commercial paper, T-strips, and federal agency issues

the qualitative aspects of working capital management, such as variations in compensating balance agreements, hedging strategies for exchange rate risk, the consequences of changing credit terms, and factoring

why interest rates differ

the workings of compound interest

determining the return on foreign investments

convertible issues

cumulative voting

foreign financing

- The emphasis on cash and its management through the cash budget is carried throughout the text. The student needs to understand the importance of cash management in all areas of finance, and that businesses live or die by their ability to pay, not by their accounting profitability.
- *Finance: An Integrated Global Approach*, above all, is relevant. The text stresses realism, not abstraction. The student is provided with a true "working knowledge of finance."

PEDAGOGICAL FEATURES

The text discussion in *Finance: An Integrated Global Approach* is supported by several pedagogical features appropriate to the first course in finance.

Each chapter begins with **learning objectives**, as well as an introduction to the material contained in the chapter. These introductory elements identify the relevance and scope of the topics discussed. They are also a brief summary of the chapter's contents.

The more quantitative chapters have numerous **examples** that demonstrate the procedures being discussed. These chapters also contain **Self-Test Problems** and step-by-step solutions that help the student understand the mechanics involved. Appendixes following Chapters 8, 9, 10, and 12 show how to use Lotus 1-2-3 to solve the chapter examples. Furthermore, Chapter 8 has a second appendix that shows how to use the HP12C financial calculator to solve the chapter examples.

A **marginal glossary** defines the text's bold-faced **key terms** when they are used for the first time. The key terms are listed at the end of each chapter. An **end-of-book glossary** contains all marginal glossary definitions in alphabetical order.

Numerous **exhibits** throughout the text clearly illustrate the discussion. They provide both hands-on application of the text material and examples of finance in action.

The **Focus on Finance** boxes, designed specifically to connect the text with media headlines and "newsbites," are refreshing, thought-provoking breaks throughout each chapter. Each presents a financial event, chosen to pique the students' interest. The boxes keep the students focused and make them aware of real financial events and their consequences.

Providing a clear answer to "why do I need to study this," the **Focus on Careers** boxes give students a glimpse of the many career opportunities available in finance. The student will realize the many directions a career path in finance may take.

Each chapter ends with a detailed **summary** of the covered material. For those chapters containing numerous equations, the summary also provides a list of all **equations** used.

Students will increase their understanding of the chapter material by answering the **Self-Study Questions** at the end of each chapter. The questions are presented in the order that the material is discussed in the text. The answers to these questions are incorporated into the *Study Guide*.

The end-of-chapter **Discussion Questions** stretch the students' understanding of the material. These questions frequently require informed-judgment responses and can trigger spirited classroom discussion.

The end-of-chapter **Problems** represent various degrees of difficulty. They test the students' ability to reason and deduce answers.

Most chapters suggest three or four **Topics for Further Research**. These questions or projects require library reference material or other external sources of information. They make excellent homework assignments or group discussion projects, requiring more in-depth understanding and research on the topics covered in the chapter. (Answers to the Discussion Questions and the Problems, and sources and approaches for Topics for Further Research, are provided in the *Instructor's Manual.*)

The end-of-book **Appendixes** supplement the student's basic understanding of accounting and business forms, and also include the time value of money tables for easy reference.

ORGANIZATION

Although *Finance: An Integrated Global Approach* is intended to be taught chapter by chapter, some professors may prefer to follow a different order in their introductory course. Consequently, each chapter is self contained, with cross-references to relevant material in other parts of the book. The instructor can easily change the order in which the chapters are covered.

Four chapter sequences should be followed as written because of the logic used in their development:

1. Chapter 6, Developing the Cash Budget, should precede Chapter 7, Working Capital Management.
2. Chapter 8, Time Value of Money, must precede both Chapter 9, Return, Risk, and Valuation, and Chapter 10, Capital Budgeting.
3. Chapter 13, Cost of Capital and Capital Structure Policy, should follow Chapter 11, Debt and Preferred Stock as Long-Term Sources of Funds, and Chapter 12, Leases, Common Stock, and Retained Earnings as Long-Term Sources of Funds.
4. Chapter 14, Investment Banks and Their Services, should precede Chapter 15, Secondary Markets for Securities.

An instructor preferring an institutional approach could follow this sequence:

Chapter 1, Introduction to Finance

Chapter 2, Factors in Financial Decision Making: Inflation Rates, Interest Rates, and Exchange Rates

Chapter 3, Financial Institutions

Chapter 4, Securities and Their Characteristics

Chapter 14, Investment Banks and Their Services

Chapter 15, Secondary Markets for Securities

Chapter 5, Financial Planning

Chapter 16, Financial Analysis

Chapter 6, Developing the Cash Budget

Chapter 7, Working Capital Management

Chapter 11, Debt and Preferred Stock as Long-Term Sources of Funds

Chapter 12, Leases, Common Stock, and Retained Earnings as Long-Term Sources of Funds

Chapter 13, Cost of Capital and Capital Structure Policy

Chapter 8, The Time Value of Money

Chapter 9, Return, Risk, and Valuation

Chapter 10, Capital Budgeting

Chapter 17, Strategic Intervention in the Corporate Life Cycle

An instructor preferring to cover all basic concepts before teaching applications could use this sequence:

Chapter 1, Introduction to Finance

Chapter 2, Factors in Financial Decision Making: Inflation Rates, Interest Rates, and Exchange Rates

Chapter 8, The Time Value of Money

Chapter 9, Return, Risk, and Valuation

Chapter 3, Financial Institutions

Chapter 4, Securities and Their Characteristics

Chapter 14, Investment Banks and Their Services

Chapter 15, Secondary Markets for Securities

Chapter 5, Financial Planning

Chapter 16, Financial Analysis

Chapter 6, Developing the Cash Budget

Chapter 7, Working Capital Management

Chapter 10, Capital Budgeting

Chapter 11, Debt and Preferred Stock as Long-Term Sources of Funds

Chapter 12, Leases, Common Stock, and Retained Earnings as Long-Term Sources of Funds

Chapter 13, Cost of Capital and Capital Structure Policy

Chapter 17, Strategic Intervention in the Corporate Life Cycle

An instructor preferring to teach capital budgeting before cash budgeting could use this sequence:

Chapter 1, Introduction to Finance

Chapter 2, Factors in Financial Decision Making: Inflation Rates, Interest Rates, and Exchange Rates

Chapter 5, Financial Planning

Chapter 8, The Time Value of Money

Chapter 9, Return, Risk, and Valuation

Chapter 10, Capital Budgeting

Chapter 11, Debt and Preferred Stock as Long-Term Sources of Funds

Chapter 12, Leases, Common Stock, and Retained Earnings as Long-Term Sources of Funds

Chapter 13, Cost of Capital and Capital Structure Policy

Chapter 14, Investment Banks and Their Services

Chapter 15, Secondary Markets for Securities

Chapter 3, Financial Institutions

Chapter 4, Securities and Their Characteristics

Chapter 6, Developing the Cash Budget

Chapter 7, Working Capital Management

Chapter 16, Financial Analysis

Chapter 17, Strategic Intervention in the Corporate Life Cycle

CHAPTER CONTENT

Chapter 1 examines the scope of finance and identifies the three principal subdivisions—financial institutions and markets, managerial finance, and investments—while emphasizing the need for an integrated study. It also identifies the goals relevant to various financial managers and discusses careers in finance. Chapter 2 examines inflation rates, interest rates, and exchange rates and their role in the decision-making process. The importance of forming expectations and coping with changes in these rates is also examined.

In Chapters 3 and 4, domestic and foreign financial institutions and markets are discussed in greater detail. The reader is presented with information about types of financial services, the institutions providing these services, how and to what extent the institutions are regulated, and the return and risk characteristics of various securities traded in the financial markets. Published information about the institutions and markets is explained and interpreted.

Chapters 5 and 6 examine the financial manager's tools of the trade—preparing pro forma statements and developing cash and capital budgets to achieve the planned goals. Since the construction and revision of a cash budget require an understanding of financial markets and how they work, the appropriate integration is included. These chapters also examine how changes in short-term asset or liability management policies will affect the cash budget.

Chapter 7 introduces the current practices of short-term financial management. Cash, accounts payable, accounts receivable, and inventory management practices are covered. The time value of money and its relationship to interest rates and discount rates are examined in Chapter 8. The compounding tools used to calculate future values and the discounting tools used to analyze future cash flows are included. These tools are then used for amortization, asset valuation, calculation of net present value, comparison of assets with different features, and the funding of future obligations. Chapter 9 examines different concepts of return and explains their measurement. It defines risk and discusses its measurement and sources Finally, the relationship between risk and return is analyzed.

Capital budgeting involves both the selection of assets for investment and raising of funds to procure desirable assets. Chapter 10 applies the time value of money and the risk and return concepts to corporate asset selection. Chapters 11 and 12 analyze the various long-term sources of funds. They examine special features of alternative securities from the issuing company's point of view. Costs, legal obligations, restrictions on the company, and bankruptcy implications are compared. Chapter 13 shows that the cost of capital is derived from the value of the firm and is dependent upon the risk adjusted return investors expect to receive. The chapter also discusses how the corporation chooses which type of security to issue.

Chapter 14 discusses the details of the security issuance process, the role of investment banks, and the design and marketing of new issues. It also discusses stock rights offerings and their valuation. Chapter 15 takes the investor's point of view in examining securities markets and those who participate in them. Security performance is paramount and indicators of security performance are evaluated. Finally, the different motives of investors are considered.

Chapter 16 provides the tools for financial analysis of firms and the rationale for such analysis. The final chapter, Chapter 17, discusses epochal financial events—mergers and acquisitions, divestitures, reorganizations, and bankruptcies—that interrupt the corporate life cycle.

SUPPLEMENTAL MATERIALS

Finance: An Integrated Global Approach has several ancillaries created to assist the instructor and student.

Study Guide. The *Study Guide* will enhance students' understanding of the material. For each chapter of the text, it generally contains:

- A skeletal framework of what the chapter is about
- A list of all important terms and concepts, with definitions and text page reference
- A detailed chapter outline
- A list of all equations used in the chapter
- A problem illustrating the application of each equation
- Answers to the Self-Study questions
- Supplemental questions and problems with detailed answers
- Application examples relating to the more challenging topics.

Instructor's Manual. The *Instructor's Manual* provides additional material to assist the instructor in preparation and testing. For each chapter, it generally contains:

- A summary of the chapter
- A list of the key terms used in the chapter with text page references
- Expanded learning objectives
- A list of all equations used in the chapter
- A detailed chapter outline
- Extra Problems, with answers
- Answers to chapter Discussion Questions
- Answers to chapter Problems
- Questions and problems relating to boxed material, where appropriate
- Topics for Further Research: helpful suggestions
- Referrals for supplementary handouts

Test Bank. Prepared by Professor Marianne Westerman of the University of Colorado at Denver, the *Test Bank* contains approximately 500 questions. The questions include multiple choice, true/false, problems, and essay formats. They are ranked according to degree of difficulty, with a 40/40/20 mixture of relatively easy, reasonably difficult, and hard questions. The *Test Bank* is also available on a computer disk.

Transparency Masters. Prepared by David J. Dreyfuss of the RAND Corporation, the *Transparency Masters* illustrate key concepts, outline the lecture material for the student, and present step-by-step solutions to problems.

ACKNOWLEDGMENTS

The authors wish to thank their reviewers for their many constructive criticisms of the various drafts of this manuscript. They especially wish to thank Marianne Westerman of the University of Colorado at Denver, David J. Dreyfuss of the RAND Corporation, Dean Drenk of Montana State University, Stephen N. Dike of Southeastern University in Washington, D.C., and Howard R. Whitney of Franklin University.

Deserving special thanks are Robert Strittmatter of Iona College for editing Appendix A, Rosa Silva McGrath for her work in compiling Appendix 8B, John Raleigh of Fleet Bank and Paul Tedesco of Chemical Bank for assistance with several of the Focus on Careers boxes, and George Mangiero of Iona College for streamlining our procedures on the HP12C. Special thanks also go to Charles F. O'Donnell, Dean of the Hagan School of Business, Iona College, for his encouragement and support of this undertaking. Diane Monachelli, our student assistant, has earned our undying gratitude for her invaluable help in undertaking last-minute research assignments and for her willingness to perform numerous clerical operations efficiently and pleasantly.

We also wish to thank Gerald Mentor of Richard D. Irwin for believing in this project and for his encouragement; Bill Schoof of the Austen Press for listening, understanding, and appreciating what it was that we wanted to do and for making it possible for us to do it; and Michele Heinz, our Developmental and Project Editor, and the rest of the staff at Elm Street Publishing for their assistance and suggestions.

Anand G. Shetty

Francis J. McGrath

Irene M. Hammerbacher

October 1994

Brief Contents

Contents

CHAPTER 6

Developing the Cash Budget 158

CHAPTER 7

Working Capital Management 197

CHAPTER 9

Return, Risk, and Valuation 284

CHAPTER 10

Capital Budgeting 328

Note to the Instructor

Austen Press texts are marketed and distributed by Richard D. Irwin, Inc. For assistance in obtaining supplementary material for this and other Austen Press titles, please contact your Irwin sales representative or the customer service division of Richard D. Irwin at (800) 323-4560.

CHAPTER 1

Introduction to Finance

LEARNING OBJECTIVES

This chapter is intended to provide an overview of finance and to identify the goals of financial decision makers. Consequently, at the conclusion of this chapter, the reader should:

1. *Have a basic understanding of the scope of finance and the process of financial decision making*
2. *Understand the traditional subdivisions of finance and their interrelationships*
3. *Be able to identify the goals of financial decision makers*
4. *Know the primary sources of financial information and be able to find pertinent information on securities (like stocks and bonds), financial institutions, and issues*
5. *Begin to understand the range of employment opportunities available in finance*

Finance and financial decisions are routine parts of daily life. Every aspect of economic or commercial interaction in society has financial implications. For example, finance involves the examination of money and the monetary needs of government, businesses, and individuals. It includes analyzing how decisions are made about using credit, making investments, managing funds, and obtaining capital. Finance can be viewed as the operational or practical side of economics.

DEFINING *FINANCE*

It is the breadth of finance that makes it fascinating. Finance encompasses issues as diverse as the cost in Japanese yen or French francs of dinner at Windows on the World (a restaurant at the top of the World Trade Center in New York City), the U.S. Treasury's decision to restructure its debt toward the short term, and IBM's decision to downsize.

In fact, the study of finance encompasses so much that the field has tended to become fractionalized, with three major subdivisions emerging as separate areas of specialization. Thus, (1) financial markets and institutions, (2) financial management, and (3) investments have become virtually independent disciplines. This text introduces and discusses each of these areas of specialization. It also integrates them to permit the reader to view the whole picture.

Financial Markets and Institutions

The network of business enterprises dedicated to the movement of financial assets, combined with the environment within which they transfer these assets, provides the institutional framework for the study of finance. Today's financial markets and institutions are designed to meet today's needs. They have evolved over time and are continually changing to accommodate new economic and financial circumstances. Thus, many of today's markets and institutions may well be obsolete early in the 21st century. Both to assist the orderly evolution of markets and institutions and to protect less sophisticated participants, government regulation has played a significant role in this evolutionary process.

Financial Markets. Financial markets result from individuals', governments', and businesses' needs for funds in excess of their own resources and their desire to put idle financial resources to work. If individuals purchased homes only for cash, if the government spent money only as it received tax payments, if corporations purchased inventory or planned expansions on the basis of the available cash from sales, then there would be no need for financial markets. Similarly, no financial markets would exist if every holder of cash in excess of current needs simply stashed it in a safe place and left it there untouched until a need for the funds arose. These scenarios do not describe the way the world works. Consequently, the world needs financial markets.

Financial markets include not only the major exchanges such as the New York Stock Exchange (NYSE) and the Tokyo Stock Exchange, but also the electronic markets where traders exchange corporate bonds, bankers' acceptances, currencies, and just about every other financial instrument one can conceive. Financial markets may be primary or secondary markets. In the **primary market,** issuers offer new securities for sale. For example, a corporation that wishes to raise additional funds may offer stocks and bonds for sale in the primary market. The corporation receives the proceeds of these sales, less any commissions or fees associated with the offering.

primary market
The market where newly issued securities are offered and sold by the issuers or their representatives.

secondary market
The market in which holders of outstanding securities offer them for resale.

In the **secondary market**, the holder of previously issued securities offers them for resale. The issuing corporation is no longer involved; the proceeds from the sale go directly to the seller. Perhaps the best known example of a secondary market is the trading floor of the NYSE. In every NYSE transaction, one holder transfers shares of outstanding stock to another. The corporation whose stock is being exchanged (traded) has no control over who purchases it or the price at which it sells; the corporation simply is no longer involved. Without the secondary market, however, the primary market would be very limited. The liquidity provided by the secondary market reduces the risk for the investor purchasing in the primary market, making new securities more attractive.

Financial markets may also be classified as money markets or capital markets, based upon the length of time that financial instruments traded in those markets are expected to remain outstanding. The **capital market** generally is considered to be composed of corporate equity issues (common and preferred stock), corporate and government long-term debt, and their derivatives.

capital market
The market for corporate equity securities and their derivatives, and corporate and government long-term debt securities.

In the **money market,** investors trade debt instruments with original maturities of one year or less. For example, the U.S. Treasury sells Treasury bills that mature in one year or less; these instruments are said to be offered in the money market. On the other hand, the Treasury also sells debt instruments that mature in 30 years; these Treasury bonds are considered part of the capital market.

money market
The market for debt instruments with original maturities of less than one year.

Both the capital and money markets have primary and secondary market elements. These classifications are not mutually exclusive. For example, original issue Treasury bills are part of the primary market, but all resales of these instruments take place in the secondary market. Likewise, newly issued common stock trades in the primary market, but any resales take place in the secondary market.

Financial Institutions. The growth of financial markets stimulates the growth of financial institutions, and the need to regulate both the institutions and the markets. More sophistication in the financial market increases the need of many participants for specialists to perform their transactions for them. Financial institutions are specialists that perform functions that individuals or businesses could perform themselves if they had the time, knowledge, and inclination. As specialists, financial institutions have accumulated expertise that could be misused to take advantage of the naive. Therefore, regulation becomes necessary.

Financial institutions have always arisen out of need. Money-changing houses originated in 17th-century Europe when interregional trade in goods necessitated currency conversion. Similarly, business needs dictated the origin of depository institutions as far back as the founding of the Bank of Amsterdam in 1609. Lloyd's of London, the oldest British insurance company, was created primarily to protect the interests of the East India Trading Company. Other financial institutions likewise have emerged specifically to meet particular needs or crises.

depository institution
An institution where customers leave money in checking, time deposit, or savings accounts. Such institutions include commercial banks and thrifts.

Although the distinctions are often blurred, three broad categories of financial institutions are currently identified: (1) depository institutions, (2) nondepository institutions, and (3) other financial service institutions. **Depository institutions** are so named because individuals, corporations, and other depositors leave their funds on deposit with the institutions, either in checking accounts or in time deposit or savings accounts. These deposits are liabilities of the receiving institutions and serve as their primary source of funds. Depository institutions include commercial banks and thrift institutions (savings banks, savings and loan associations, and credit unions). These institutions offer slightly different services to their customers, but all offer the depositor access to the payments system, a source of borrowed funds, and a safe haven for invested funds. Federal agencies such as the Federal Depository Insurance Corporation (FDIC) provide depositor protection up to $100,000.

nondepository institution
A financial company, such as a life insurance company or an investment company, that pools funds from many participants to fund investments.

Nondepository institutions are companies that obtain funds from participants and then pool these funds for investment purposes. Included in this group are such institutions as life insurance companies, pension funds, and investment companies. Nondepository institutions also include firms such as mortgage banks and finance companies, which use investors', rather than depositors', funds. Unlike depository institutions, nondepository institutions often invest for long-term gains, quite frequently through secondary market asset acquisition. Additionally, the funds provided to nondepository institutions are not protected against loss by federal agencies.

Other financial service institutions function as agents and advisors; these include investment banks, venture capital firms, and brokerage houses. While some of these institutions provide or guarantee long-term funding for business activities, they also act as agents for both users and suppliers of funds. Brokerage houses, for instance, act as agents for investors who wish to acquire long-term debt or equity assets. Investment banks act as agents or guarantors for corporations that want to raise long-term debt or equity financing. Some institutions, such as Merrill Lynch, function as both brokerage houses and investment banks.

Regulation of Financial Markets and Institutions. Regulation of financial markets and institutions comes from many sources. The federal government, through the Securities and Exchange Commission (SEC), regulates both the stock exchanges and the disclosure of information about securities to the public. The U.S. Treasury, through the Comptroller of the Currency and the Office of Thrift Supervision, regulates specific types of financial institutions.

The Federal Reserve System is a quasi-governmental organization empowered to set rules and regulations that affect a significant portion of U.S. commercial banks. The Federal Deposit Insurance Corporation, as the agency responsible for guaranteeing insured deposits in commercial banks and thrifts, has the authority to regulate the activities of insured institutions. Most states regulate both depository and nondepository institutions in their efforts to protect investor funds. International organizations such as the Bank for International Settlements also can influence U.S. financial institutions through international agreements of which the United States is part.

Regulation varies from agency to agency. The SEC requires corporations to submit documents relating to primary market securities sales, and it regulates the behavior of traders and other participants on the exchanges; it does not set min-

FOCUS ON FINANCE

Operating on Both Sides of the Market: Merrill Lynch

Brokerage houses can act either as retailers of investments, serving the needs of individuals to purchase or sell stocks, bonds, and derivative securities, or as wholesalers engaged in investment banking activities for corporate clients. Most large firms, notably Merrill Lynch, are key players in both arenas.

Merrill Lynch is the world's largest retail brokerage house, as well as the leading underwriter of debt and equity issues worldwide. At the retail level, as of the end of 1992, Merrill had over $475 billion of assets in client accounts and earned nearly $2.4 billion (17.9 percent of gross revenue) from commissions on listed securities trading and mutual fund activity. It had 12,700 registered representatives among its more than 40,000 employees and operated 460 retail offices.

Meanwhile, its investment banking activity accounted for nearly $1.5 billion in income (11.1 percent of gross revenue). It helped corporations raise more than $91 billion of domestic capital in 1992. Principal transactions (swaps, derivatives, fixed-income, unlisted equity, and foreign exchange activity on behalf of clients) accounted for an additional $2.1 billion (16.0 percent of gross income). Overall, Merrill earned nearly $900 million for its shareholders in 1992.

Other large brokerage houses, while not nearly the size of Merrill, generate similar percentages of income from their retail and investment banking units. Bear Stearns, for example, earned $2.7 billion in 1992 (compared to Merrill's $13.4 billion), of which 14 percent came from retail commissions and nearly 12 percent from investment banking. In contrast, none of Charles Schwab's $909 million income came from investment banking, and Morgan Stanley earned only 4.2 percent of its $8.3 billion gross income from commissions.

imum capital or asset requirements for those it regulates. The regulators of depository institutions do set minimum capital requirements and they do restrict the acquisition of assets by institutions that they regulate.

State regulation is predominant in the insurance industry, limiting the acceptable types of investments and generally prohibiting rate competition. Pension fund asset management is subject to both state and federal regulation, with rules designed to limit risk. Little activity in financial markets and institutions escapes regulation today.

Financial Management

The typical corporate finance function involves the acquisition of funds and the direction of these funds into projects that promote progress toward the goals of the enterprise. Financial management spans the development of planning tools (the cash budget, the capital budget, and pro forma statements), the forecasting of cash inflows and outflows, the selection of assets, and the acquisition of long-term sources of funds. Likewise, its domain includes the management of cash, accounts receivable, and inventories, along with the development of working capital policy. Financial management is concerned, therefore, with everything that affects the performance and survival of the firm.

Planning Tools. To survive, a firm must have sufficient cash available to meet its current obligations. In this context, the amount of cash is important, but its source is not. The cash budget summarizes the firm's anticipated cash inflows and outflows, permitting management to evaluate its need for short-term borrowing, plan short-term investment strategies, or take steps to procure funds from more permanent sources.

Working capital management is facilitated by the development of a cash budget. This effort leads the firm to continuously reexamine its policies for:

1. Cash management (the collection, disbursement, and investment of cash)
2. Accounts payable
3. Accounts receivable (including credit-granting standards, bad debt collection policy, and terms of trade)
4. Inventory accumulation

Forecasting. Whether for cash or capital budgeting, a firm needs to be able to predict the amounts and timing of its cash inflows and outflows. This allows the firm to determine its ability to meet obligations as they come due, the profitability of its investment opportunities, and the success of its capital market ventures. Good forecasting can reduce the uncertainty associated with the cash flows.

Asset Selection. The capital budgeting process relates to asset selection. The firm must decide what assets to acquire, sell, and lease. To make each decision, it must determine an asset's profitability. Consequently, the firm must develop an appropriate measure of asset profitability.

Several measures have become quite popular, including the payback period (PBP), the net present value (NPV), the internal rate of return (IRR), and the profitability ratio (PR). NPV, IRR, and PR depend on discounting and the time value of money. All four measures require the firm to evaluate future cash flows for the planned investment, a process which is subject to the uncertainties of estimation. Consequently, asset selection requires the firm to deal with risk.

An extension of the asset selection process relates to mergers and acquisitions. Merger and acquisition decision making involves the same evaluation of cash flows as ordinary asset selection, only the forecasting is more complicated and subject to greater uncertainty. Still, there is no conceptual difference, for example, between acquiring a new piece of equipment and acquiring a competing firm. For that matter, many firms have found that the best method of expansion is acquisition, rather than internal growth.

Long-Term Resources. Asset selection is linked to the firm's long-term existence. The firm must decide what it wants to do: grow, remain stable, or downsize. Whatever it decides, asset selection is an integral part of the process. The decision to expand generally involves finding sources of long-term funds. Thus, the financial manager must explore leases, debt, stock, and retained earnings to fund growth. Each of these sources has its own advantages and disadvantages and management's choice may very well depend on current economic conditions. Furthermore, the appropriate mix of these sources should minimize the firm's overall cost of funds. Consequently, financial management requires the firm to develop a capital structure appropriate for its goals.

Financial management thus examines all aspects of the firm's operations. The key ingredients of this analysis are return and risk. Every decision made by the financial manager is designed to enhance return at an acceptable level of risk. Risk arises from the uncertainty associated with forecasting economic conditions, market conditions, and public perceptions.

Investment

The third subdivision of finance is investment. Investment may be described as a process involving evaluation of investment opportunities, selection of a portfolio of assets, and management of the portfolio. The objective of the process is to preserve and foster growth in wealth. Thus, it encompasses the actions of three classes of market participants: (1) individuals who wish to accumulate wealth and perhaps retire to live in luxury; (2) government financial managers who want to increase the net assets of the trust funds of federal, state, and other government agencies; and (3) corporate financial managers who want to maximize the market values of their corporations. Any of these three parties may consult with professional portfolio managers, or turn over its entire investment function to them.

Regardless of who is managing the portfolio, the objective is the same. The goal of the manager is to earn a return on investment at least sufficient to compensate for the passage of time, inflation, and risk. This immediately raises three major themes: the time value of money, return, and investment risk.

Time Value of Money. Money has a time value because a dollar received today is worth more than a dollar received tomorrow. Since investments promise future cash flows in exchange for current cash outlays, the portfolio manager must evaluate the present worth of these future cash flows before investing. Specifically, the manager must discount the future cash inflows at some interest rate that reflects the time value of money. In practice, this is the rate that funds invested today could reasonably be expected to earn in a similarly risky investment. After evaluating all available investment opportunities in the same way, the portfolio manager is better able to choose among alternatives. Simply stated, all investments are judged on the basis of their present values.

Investment Return. The return on an investment is the difference between the funds committed to it and the cash flows received from it. That difference can be either positive or negative, resulting in either a gain or a loss. Returns are usually measured on an annual basis, either in terms of dollars or as percentages of the amounts originally invested. The portfolio manager judges investments in terms of their returns and degrees of risk. Most managers establish minimum returns that investments must yield to be considered. The minimum return typically consists of the rate that a risk-free investment would earn, plus a premium to compensate for risk.

Investment Risk. The possibility that an investment's actual return will differ from its expected return is investment risk. While such a deviation may result in a higher return than expected, investor concern focuses on the possibility that the return will be lower. Both changing economic conditions and firm-specific events can generate investment risk.

systematic risk
Return uncertainty caused by overall economic developments.

unsystematic risk
Return uncertainty caused by firm-specific developments.

Factors broad enough to affect the general movement of the market generate **systematic risk**. Such risk-generating factors include changing interest rates, exchange rates, inflation rates, or general business conditions. Changing firm-specific factors, such as operating conditions or the firm's financial structure, generate **unsystematic risk**. Users of funds must offer compensation to entice investors to accept risk.

In order to make appropriate investment decisions, the portfolio manager must first develop methods of analysis, evaluation, and selection. The first step in analysis is to create and monitor indicators of the financial health of the firm, its industry, and the economy. Detailed examination of financial statements is essential, along with construction and evaluation of numerous financial ratios.

optimal portfolio mix
The portfolio mix that provides the highest return for the risk the investor is willing to bear.

The evaluation and selection of investments focuses on their risk and return characteristics. Since many securities behave similarly relative to overall economic activity, the manager must strive to diversify the portfolio to reduce risk. Portfolio diversification requires the financial manager to select assets from diverse firms, industries, geographic regions, countries, security types, and maturity classes. The portfolio manager's ultimate objective is to achieve the **optimal portfolio mix**: the portfolio that provides the highest return for the risk the investor is willing to bear.

Integration of Financial Areas

While it is interesting to study each of the subdivisions of finance separately, this disjointed effort ignores much. For example, a study of the operation of the stock market as part of the financial markets also helps one to understand how a corporation can obtain long-term financing as part of its financial management function; an integrated analysis also helps to explain how the presence of the market reduces the risk associated with investment. To give another illustration, examining the effect of the Federal Reserve's monetary policy on the marketplace helps one to understand the financial manager's decision making process and the risk–return relationship for the investor. Segmented analysis has the advantage of simplification, but it also limits one's viewpoint.

Consequently, this text will integrate all aspects of finance. For example, it will discuss the cash budgeting process not only from the viewpoint of the corporation creating the budget, but also from the perspective of the investor who provides the funds, and the market process that facilitates the transfer of these funds. The book views commercial banks as leading suppliers of short-term funds, as places for the temporary investment of cash, and as key players in the market for short-term government securities. The book examines financial institutions, not merely from the viewpoint of their history and development, but rather as parts of a dynamic system of financial management and investment decision making.

FOCUS ON FINANCE

FINANCIAL INTEGRATION

The simple world of the past, when the corporate treasurer had to predict only interest rates, currency movements, inflation rates, and probably product prices, has become far more complex. In an effort to hedge against unanticipated movements in these variables, more and more corporate treasurers are turning to derivative securities.

Derivatives are hybrid financial arrangements that involve securities and financial transactions whose prices move in opposite directions in reaction to a change in an underlying variable. They can reduce certain types of risk and may well save the corporation money. Derivatives do, however, possess their own unique risks. A derivative's counterparty (the party on the other side of the transaction) may default.

The corporation itself may overstep the bounds of hedging and speculate on derivatives. This deviation from hedging to speculation can happen when corporate treasurers become besieged by both commercial and investment bankers, who market derivatives quite aggressively. It can also happen because the corporation's own employees have some success at hedging, and, in a fit of market fever, attempt to demonstrate just how great their talents are.

Corporate treasurers need to understand, not only the traditional domestic and foreign securities markets, but also the opportunities and pitfalls of the derivatives markets. They must protect themselves and their firms from unscrupulous bankers, and from overenthusiastic or greedy employees. For example, no corporation willingly writes naked option contracts (contracts that call for the delivery of securities or commodities that the contract writers do not own). However, the pressure and temptation to write such contracts is enormous and the ease with which they can be written is incredible.

Common themes run through all three subdivisions of finance. The concepts of return, risk, and the time value of money are pervasive. Each participant in a financial transaction, from the financial institution to the investor to the borrower, is concerned with balancing return against risk. Underlying every decision is the role of the time value of money. Without an evaluation of the present values of future cash flows, investment decisions risk being suboptimal. Similarly, the financial manager must evaluate the present cost of alternative sources of funds to make intelligent borrowing decisions.

GOALS OF THE FINANCIAL MANAGER

Every financial manager needs to state goals, whether he or she works for a corporation, for a financial institution, for the government, or independently. Goals keep one focused and provide benchmarks against which to measure progress. Economic theory provides the foundation for all financial goals. Specifically, the economic goals of maximization of profit and maximization of satisfaction are crucial in finance.

Refining Economic Goals

Refining these theoretical economic goals into concrete financial goals is, however, a big step. To begin with, economic goals do not specify time or risk, and they lack the precision of expression required of financial decision makers in today's complex environment.

Time Dimension for Financial Goals. Specifying a time dimension for a firm's goals involves more than the valuation of the firm's assets. Valuation requires determining the present value of an asset's future earning potential. Basically, a firm may be viewed as nothing more than an accumulation of assets, so its value should be equivalent to the sum of the present values of its assets. Conceptually, one must estimate the future earning potential of each asset and then analyze what the investor could earn by investing the funds in an alternative asset. In essence, the value of an asset is measured by its **opportunity cost**, or the value of the income lost by not investing in an alternative.

opportunity cost
The benefit of the best alternative course of action given up as part of a decision.

This becomes complicated because the sum of the potential earning power of a set of assets is not necessarily equivalent to the earning potential of the collection of assets together. A discrepancy could be caused by such factors as synergy and diminishing returns to scale. Synergy could increase the earning potential for the firm as a whole, whereas diseconomies of scale would have the opposite effect.

A further complication relates to the alternative return concept. Just what should the financial manager consider as an alternative investment outlet for the funds? Should the firm be compared with its competitors, with a risk-free investment opportunity, or with some idealized norm? The selection of the alternative return is critical in any analysis involving the present value of an investment's future cash flows.

Risk Dimension for Financial Goals. Measuring return without evaluating the degree of risk is meaningless in finance. Take, for example, a U.S. Treasury security that promises a 6 percent, tax-free rate versus a bond issued by the Westinghouse Corporation that promises a 6 percent, after-tax return. Which is the better investment? They both promise the same percentage yield, but the question remains whether or not the probabilities of receiving that yield and getting back the principal are the same for both investments. The Treasury security would be considered the better investment because of its lower risk. Normally a higher return accompanies greater risk. The investor must decide whether or not the return is worth an investment's risk. The problem becomes more difficult when trying to decide between a Treasury security at 6 percent and a Westinghouse bond with a 7 percent, after-tax yield.

Terminology. The precision of the term *maximization of profit* is questionable because both the accounting methodology employed and the methods of financing used can dramatically change the recorded profit. Different accounting methods for inventory valuation and depreciation can drastically change a firm's reported net income. Even the financial choice of leasing assets instead of purchasing them, or using bond financing instead of common stock financing, can alter balance sheet and income statement values. Thus, any measure of profit that relies strictly on the financial statements of the firm is without merit.

Without a clear meaning for *profit maximization*, a measure of the degree of risk associated with an investment, and the time value of potential returns, economic theory is of little use in defining operating goals for the financial manager. The process depends on a goal or set of goals that are financial in nature, precise enough to be quantified, and generally acceptable.

Goals of Different Entities

Each financial entity, be it a corporation, institution, unit of government, or individual, must refine general economic goals into specific operational goals. While the process is basically similar for all, the outcome is unique to the entity. The goals of various entities often clash. For example, a corporation may enhance its profit goal by reducing its work force. This would conflict with the goals of both the individuals who face termination and the government units that would lose payroll taxes and other tax receipts. Goals can also coincide. This would be true if a corporate goal were to lead to plant expansion resulting in potential profit to the corporation, new jobs, and enhanced tax receipts.

Corporate Goals. The primary goal of a corporation is to maximize shareholder wealth. Specifically, this means that the corporate financial manager must maximize the market value of the firm's common stock. Maximization requires management to consider the return and risk factors associated with corporate decisions.

How do financial managers know whether their decisions are good or bad? The market provides signals. Stockholders who are not pleased with the actions of management may well sell their stock. Should a significant number of stockholders become dissatisfied, then the market value of the stock will fall. This provides managers with a clear indication of the inappropriateness of their decisions and reminds them of the tenuous nature of their employment.

The decision maker's efforts to maximize stock value may be further constrained by community interests. The community includes the company's employees and their families; residents of neighborhoods affected by the company's operations; local governments and institutions; the company's creditors, suppliers, and competitors; international communities affected by the company's decisions; and even management itself. Thus, the concept of stockholder is sometimes expanded to **stakeholder**, and the company's goal is redefined as maximizing stakeholder wealth.

stakeholder
Anyone affected by a firm's decisions.

In defense of this broader objective, consider, for example, the role of public interest groups. Does a cosmetics company test its products on animals? If it does, bad publicity and boycott activities of various animal rights groups may depress its market price. With reference to public interest groups then, the firm must be, or it must at least give the perception of being, socially and politically responsible.

FOCUS ON FINANCE

Expressions of Stockholder Dissatisfaction

Generally when stockholders are dissatisfied with the performance of management, the most they do is sell their stock in the corporation. However, when the stockholder is an institutional investor, such as Lehman Brothers, Inc., then the reaction to inadequate management performance is likely to be quite different.

Take, for example, the case of Computervision Corporation, a $1.07 billion software and computer services company located in Bedford, Massachusetts. John J. Shields failed to generate consistent profits as he downsized the company during his more than two years as CEO. Lehman Brothers, which owned a 22 percent stake in the corporation, believed that Mr. Shields was too slow to generate greater productivity. Their opinion was instrumental when Computervision's board of directors decided to replace him with a new CEO.

Other corporations with substantial institutional investors, such as IBM and Westinghouse, likewise took strong action when their earnings reports began to show losses. In these cases, however, the outgoing CEOs were handsomely compensated for their tenures.

When they consider layoffs and plant closings, today's corporations are discovering that more and more communities are legislating away the prerogatives of the firm. Government entities, in trying to protect their tax bases as well as local employees, often require advanced notice, retraining benefits, and feasibility studies before allowing any corporate downsizing. Such legislation makes it harder to consolidate unprofitable operations, spin off undesirable units, and otherwise react to an ever changing market. This increases the cost of doing business, and stock prices generally react negatively.

Management may even have a different perspective than stockholders. Management's objective may be to keep itself in command. It may be able to promote this goal by spreading profits over a period of years rather than taking all available profits immediately, or it may take greater risk than the shareholders desire merely to enhance its own stature and collect profit-related bonuses. The conflict between managers and stockholders is described as the **agency problem**. The agency problem forces stockholders to incur costs to oversee the activities of management. The solution could be as simple as hiring an accounting firm to audit the corporation's books and actions, or as complex as providing a management compensation package tied to indicators of shareholder wealth.

agency problem
The conflict between managers and stockholders over the firm's objectives and the acceptable level of risk.

Institutional Goals. While all institutional goals have maximization objectives, the operational goals are as diverse as the institutions themselves. The goal of a commercial bank or a stockholder-owned brokerage firm is identical to that of any nonfinancial corporation—to maximize shareholder or stakeholder wealth. For an institution with no stockholders, for example, a mutual insurance company, the goal may be less obvious. Theoretically, the goal of the financial

FOCUS ON FINANCE

PERFORMANCE REWARDS

What is believed to be the largest stock award in corporate history was given to Roberto C. Goizueta, chairman and CEO of Coca-Cola Co., in 1992. The award, 1 million shares of stock valued at $81 million, was granted on the condition that Mr. Goizueta remain with the firm for an additional four years.

While the award drew criticism as overly generous from the United Shareholders Association, an advocacy group based in Washington, other complaints were sparse because of Coca-Cola's financial performance. It has been estimated that during Mr. Goizueta's more than ten years with the firm, it created over $50 billion of shareholder value. Furthermore, in the year preceding the award (1991), net income gained 17 percent while the company's stock gained close to 73 percent in market value.

Mr. Goizueta has certainly been rewarded for good performance.

manager of a mutual company should be to maximize the value of the interest of the mutual participants. However, the agency relationship is much looser in the mutual environment and, thus, management has more freedom to adjust operating goals to its liking.

Pension fund managers and other portfolio managers have as their goal the maximization of the return on the portfolio relative to risk. The pension fund should seek to preserve principal and produce income adequate to pay retirement benefits. Mutual fund managers, however, can seek to achieve a number of stated objectives, depending on the nature of the fund. A low-risk mutual fund may emphasize investments in high-quality, fixed-income securities that provide the best available returns without endangering principal. On the other hand, a fund that promises high returns must concentrate on growth stocks and, consequently, assume a high degree of risk. In each case, the objective is similar: to maximize return relative to risk; however, differences in risk tolerances of the participants require different operating goals.

Government Goals. Government agencies have the goal of maximizing the efficiency of the organizations they oversee. Thus, the SEC seeks to make the financial markets more efficient for the average investor. The Federal Reserve System can claim as its goal the smooth operation of the economy, especially with reference to inflationary pressures. These agencies are judged on their effectiveness by evaluating how well they achieve their objectives. Congressional hearings and the constant threat of tighter legislative control combine to minimize the agency problem.

Government must also manage numerous trust funds. These range from the Federal Highway Trust Fund and the Social Security Administration Trust Fund to state and local government employee pension funds. In this work, the goal of the financial manager is to increase the net asset value of such a fund so to fulfill its assigned purpose. A public sector pension fund manager is generally responsible to an oversight board consisting of the state Comptroller and union representatives.

Personal Goals. There is little debate over maximization of wealth as a goal for an individual investor. Any debate that does arise concerns the acceptable degree of risk. That is an individual choice based on three sets of factors: personal, social, and economic factors. These factors provide the basis for all financial planning decisions.

Personal factors such as age, family income, household size, and attitudes toward spending and saving have the most influence on one's degree of risk exposure. The combination of personal factors with events such as divorce, retirement, death of a spouse, or a career change determine a person's life situation. A personal financial plan should suit one's current life situation, yet be flexible enough to adapt to change.

Social and economic factors influence an individual's working and investing opportunities and, therefore, his or her financial objectives. Government-mandated health care will reduce the need for personal long-term health care planning, but it will raise businesses' operating costs and, thus, restructure the work environment. Demographic factors, such as an aging population, will expand opportunities for investment and also require any financial plan to place greater emphasis upon retirement income. Every change, every decision involves a trade-off—an opportunity cost. Personal financial planning can thus be viewed as maximizing personal wealth during both working and retirement years through a series of decisions designed to minimize the costs of lost opportunities.

CAREERS IN FINANCE

In the United States today, it is estimated that 6.7 million people, more than 6 percent of the work force, are employed in banking, insurance, and real estate. If the number of people performing financial functions in other industries were to be added to this total, then it is estimated that 10 percent of the employed population is involved in finance. The Japanese economy employs slightly more than 4 percent of its work force in banking, insurance, and real estate; Great Britain employs only 3.3 percent in these areas.

Careers in finance vary as widely as the scope of finance itself. Some of these career paths require extensive, highly specialized knowledge and advanced degrees. Others begin with entry level positions open to enthusiastic, hard-working individuals regardless of their undergraduate majors. An understanding of and an appreciation for finance certainly helps. Brief vignettes describing different careers in finance are distributed throughout the text.

FOCUS ON FINANCE

Investment Strategy Is Age Dependent

Early Years. Individuals in their 20s or early 30s are unlikely to be thinking about retirement, although they should. They are generally more concerned about planning families and purchasing houses. Such a person's investment strategy is multifaceted. Saving for a house generally involves conservative investments, possibly CDs or other highly secure liquid assets with three-year to five-year investment horizons. They also need highly liquid reserves to meet unforeseen emergencies such as temporary job losses or income losses due to child bearing.

Retirement investments should focus on stocks. Not only has the return been greater than that earned on bonds, but stock investors have suffered an overall decline in asset value in only two rolling five-year periods since 1945.

Earlier planning for retirement increases the benefits from compounding (earning interest on interest). An individual who set aside only $100 per month beginning at age 25, would have amassed by age 65 over $576,000, assuming an annual return of 10.3 percent (the average annual return earned on stocks since 1925). Even inflation (assuming historical rates) would not seriously erode this nest egg since the return on stocks has exceeded the rate of inflation by 7.2 percent per annum. Someone who waited until age 40 to begin saving would have to be set aside $466 per month to accumulate the same amount at retirement. Begin now!

These early years are also a time for risk taking. Investments in high-technology, small-company, and even foreign stocks should be considered. A portfolio mix with 75 to 80 percent stock is desirable. Even some junk-bond investments may be worthwhile.

Middle Years. Mid-life produces many crises, not the least of which are financial. Putting children through college, taking care of elderly parents, and preparing for retirement make this a time of stress. College tuition and eldercare can ruin any financial plan. Generally the house ends up with a second mortgage and retirement funds are depleted.

Many individuals may have no alternative. However, if one does have the means, this is the time to seek tax-sheltered returns and to expand the retirement fund. While *growth* is still the catchword for investing, greater consideration should be given to safety. Consequently, the portfolio mix should be modified to only 60 to 65 percent stock, with the remainder heavily invested in bonds (including tax-exempt issues).

Care should be taken not to underestimate retirement needs. If one does not want to decrease principal during retirement, then additional funding will be required to maintain current living standards. Assume, for example, that a retirement portfolio earns an average of 8 percent per year. If one is used to living on $50,000 per year, then the retirement account needs a balance of $625,000.

Retirement. Without paychecks, retirees live on the income generated by their investments, combined with their Social Security checks. In 1994, the maximum Social Security benefit for a worker retiring at age 65 was $1,147 per month or $13,764 per year. However, the average monthly Social Security benefit for all retired workers was only $674 per month or $8,088 per year. Retirees need another source of income.

Given the uncertainties of interest income, retirees should not limit their portfolios to bonds. A retiree's portfolio should be managed to achieve a total return (interest and dividend income combined with capital appreciation). A retiree today can anticipate living to 80 or 90 years old. Retiring at 65 means that 15 to 25 years remain in which to generate growth from the portfolio. Thus, a good strategy would be to keep 40 to 45 percent of the portfolio in stocks and much of the remainder in good-quality bonds or bond funds. The objective of this portfolio strategy is to be able to spend the income generated by the bonds and money market instruments without worrying about a declining standard of living. The stock portion of the portfolio should retain sufficient value to keep pace with inflation.

Careers in Institutions and Markets

Entry level positions in financial institutions and markets can include everything from bank teller to credit trainee. A person with a strong finance background would probably begin as an administrative assistant to a loan officer, or as a junior financial analyst in either the credit department or the research department of a depository institution. Positions such as customer service representative or mortgage servicing specialist in an insurance company or a mortgage banking company, respectively, are generally staffed by people with limited finance backgrounds. More experienced individuals would be eligible for loan officer, branch manager, or senior analyst positions.

Careers in Financial Management

Entry level positions for those with associate degrees and limited experience in finance include data processing clerks, investor relations specialists, and accounts payable staff positions. Finance majors find entry level positions as junior accountants in cost or financial accounting departments, budget analysts, or financial planners.

Promotion opportunities generally lead to managerial positions such as cash manager, credit manager, or financial accounting manager. Senior financial management positions include CFO, corporate comptroller, and treasurer.

Exhibit 1.1 illustrates the typical structure of a corporate finance unit. In practice, many additional organizational arrangements are possible, most commonly with the managers of financial analysis and financial planning reporting to the controller.

Careers in Investments

Generally it is the investment area that attracts people to finance. They see an appealing opportunity to control multimillion dollar investment portfolios, or to be part of an investment banking institution engaged in mergers and acquisitions. Most brokerage houses, however, provide entry level positions as registered representatives (for those who qualify by passing specific NASD examinations), or as investment or industry analysts. Clerical and assistant positions are always available with the major brokerage houses for those with limited experience, but excellent self-motivational skills. Senior employment opportunities include portfolio manager, senior investment analyst, and investment counselor.

Sources of Career Information

Interspaced throughout the text are more detailed discussions of particular career opportunities. Each opportunity relates to the topic under discussion and explains the educational background or other qualifications necessary for the position. It should be remembered that these are merely representative opportunities, and not the only employment options available in each respective area.

Several excellent information sources describe a myriad of such opportunities, including *Careers in Finance*, published by the Financial Management Association, *Careers in Banking and Finance*, published by the American Institute of Banking,

EXHIBIT 1.1

Sample Organizational Chart for a Finance Department

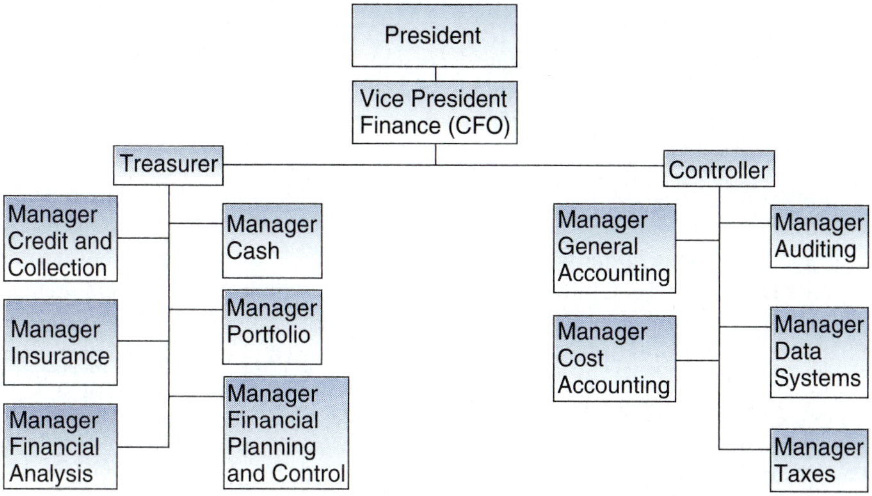

and *Business and Finance Career Directory*, published by Career Press, Inc. Each of these excellent reference books should be readily available in local libraries.

After examining the range of opportunities and evaluating the qualifications for each position, the next step is to learn where to seek specific jobs. The classified pages of *The Wall Street Journal*, the *Los Angeles Times*, the *Washington Post*, the *Chicago Tribune*, and other major, regional newspapers provide the primary source of information about job openings. Publications such as the *CPC Annual*, published by the College Placement Council, provide listings of corporations that offer jobs in specific areas of finance. Mailing resumes to the personnel managers or the heads of the finance departments in these major corporations has proven to be beneficial for many candidates. Sources such as college career placement centers or offices of alumni relations should also be investigated for possible opportunities or leads.

SOURCES OF FINANCIAL INFORMATION

Rational financial decisions depend on information. Consequently, it is necessary to know where to find appropriate financial data. Daily, business-related newspapers such as *The Wall Street Journal* and the *Financial Times* publish a wealth of information traversing the entire field of finance. They report the latest corporate crises, international events, or corporate leadership changes. They analyze the impacts of economic and political decisions and review the hottest ideas in investment strategy. These newspapers also provide valuable databases. They report daily quotes for the most recent prices of stocks and bonds, government securities, mutual funds, futures, and options, along with exchange rate quotations. Interest rate data and central bank statistics also appear here, as available.

While some of the information in these two newspapers is similar, each has its own emphasis. *The Wall Street Journal* concentrates on the U.S. economy. The *Financial Times* is decidedly British and much more interested in the European continent. Together they provide an excellent survey of happenings in trans-Atlantic commerce and world events.

Other general financial publications include *Fortune*, *Forbes*, *The Economist*, and *Business Week*. Each of these magazines covers general interest issues, but in varying degrees of depth. Additionally, each provides economic indicators and some evaluation of economic conditions. They may well provide useful general business and financial knowledge, but their limited publication schedules make them unattractive as data resources, except with reference to their proprietary indices.

Each subdivision of finance has its own specialized publications. For information on the financial markets and institutions, the leading newspaper is the *American Banker*, while the primary data sources include the *Federal Reserve Bulletin*, the *Survey of Current Business*, and *International Financial Statistics* of the International Monetary Fund. Other primary references would include the *Treasury Bulletin*, monthly or quarterly reports of the individual Federal Reserve Banks, and briefings published by individual financial institutions.

Financial management information appears in such publications as *Dun's Review*, Standard & Poor's *Industry Surveys*, and Moody's Investor Service's manuals. In addition, each corporation must regularly file Form 10K with the Securities and Exchange Commission to provide fundamental, publicly available data on industries and individual corporations. Magazines such as *Euromoney* keep financial managers abreast of international events. The *Financial Times Surveys* provide detailed information on transnational industries, international capital markets, and specific countries.

A myriad of information is available about investments. In addition to the Moody's and Standard & Poor's materials listed above, along with several other valuable publications from these services, the Fitch and Value Line services also provide good statistical information on individual corporations. *Institutional Investor* and *Investment Dealer's Digest* are among the best weekly publications that discuss investment strategies and analyze current market trends. Those interested in comparative analysis of industries can find an assortment of useful statistical information in *Key Business Ratios* published by Dun & Bradstreet, *Annual Statement Studies* published by Robert Morris Associates, and the *Almanac of Business and Industrial Financial Ratios* published by Prentice-Hall. The *Commercial and Financial Chronicle*, *Wall Street Transcript*, and *Investor's Business Daily* are three of the best newspaper-format publications available.

Investments professionals can also tap electronic sources to gather extensive information. At the inexpensive end of the spectrum, *Prodigy* provides real-time stock quotations, and *Tickdata* provides historical data on the commodities market. More advanced systems include *TradeStation*, *Trading Recipes*, and *SuperCharts*.

These advanced software systems enhance their real-time information with charting capabilities and even automatic trading strategies. Those investors who must know what is happening in the markets even when they are not tied to their computers can carry pocket pagers that beep and automatically display relevant information whenever predesignated securities change price.

Most good business libraries subscribe to the printed material listed, and that should be only the beginning of any information search. To find additional information about a particular industry, the best source would be the trade association representing that industry. For example, the American Iron and Steel Institute plays an prominent role in informing people about steel producers. The public relations departments of most firms generally are only too willing to send annual reports to anyone who requests them.

OVERVIEW OF CURRENT FINANCIAL TRENDS

Each decade has it own peculiar financial flavor. The high-flying days of the 1980s were characterized by vigorous stock market growth, a dramatic crash, and a rapid recovery. However, they may also be remembered as the era of junk bonds. The decade saw the largest mergers in history, financed by low-grade, highly speculative debt securities. The sagging economy toward the end of the decade made much of this debt worthless, bankrupting numerous individuals and financial institutions. The 1980s also produced the savings and loan industry crisis, insider trading scandals, and the highest rate of corporate bankruptcy in history.

The 1990s began on a dismal note with a worldwide economic downturn and a recovery that just wouldn't take hold. Interest rates were the lowest in 20 years, yet homebuilding remained sluggish. Corporations lengthened the terms of their debt structures by replacing notes with bonds, while the U.S. Treasury did the exact opposite. Commercial bank profits soared, yet commercial loan generation was dismal. All told, the early 1990s were free of financial crises. However, the groundwork of several major developments was being laid. Capital restructuring and internationalization became key forces.

As a wave of conservatism sweeps the financial community, corporations worldwide are reassessing the capital structure mixes they acquired during the 1980s. The trend is leading corporations to retire outstanding debt and expand their equity bases. The merger movement has given way to a divestiture movement. Major corporations are more likely to want to spin off units that are unrelated to their core businesses than they are to diversify their product mixes. The trend seems to be leaning back to basics. This movement has resulted in downsizing by many corporations, IBM and Citicorp for example. It has caused other firms to rethink merger plans, and leveraged buyouts (LBOs) are now looked upon as relics of the past.

On the other hand, finance is going international as institutions, markets, investment opportunities, and corporate financial management all cross borders. It is no longer possible to consider the U.S. economy in isolation. Federal Reserve monetary policies that have been designed solely to influence the domestic economy are now

FOCUS ON FINANCE

Bank of Credit and Commerce International

The Bank of Credit and Commerce International (BCCI) was chartered in Luxembourg, but it operated worldwide. Although its principal base of operations was London, it had offices in Bahrain, Jordan, Yemen, Germany, Netherlands, United Arab Emirates, Mauritius, Japan, and Cyprus. Its subsidiary organization, BCCI Overseas, Ltd. based in the Cayman Islands, was even more geographically diversified, operating offices in more than 50 nations. Other subsidiary enterprises included the National Bank of Georgia (USA), the Metropolitan Bank, Ltd. (Hong Kong), and the Gokal Shipping Company (Pakistan).

BCCI was founded by Agha Abedi of Pakistan and principally owned by Shiek Zayed al-Nahyan of Abu Dhabi. Its internationalization, combined with its myriad of holding companies and shell enterprises (corporations that existed only on paper) permitted it to operate beyond the laws of any one nation. No government took action against it, despite widespread concern about its lack of management controls, possible money laundering activities, involvement in drug dealings, financing of petty dictators (Manuel Noriega, Ferdinand Marcos, and Saddam Hussein), arms dealing, espionage, and fraudulent ownership of First American Bankshares (in Washington, D.C.). Only when the Bank of England refused to permit its London operations to continue due to lack of liquidity in July 1991 did the extent of BCCI's fraud and corruption become public.

The outcome of the crisis, in addition to the political intrigue and corruption investigations, was the agreement among members of the Bank for International Settlements to designate the chartering nation as the authority responsible for regulating a multinational bank's dealings.

---

forced to incorporate international reactions. For example, if the Fed keeps interest rates too low, it will stifle foreign capital investment. With the supply of available investment funding reduced, corporations may well find it impossible to borrow.

Even the regulation of U.S. depository institutions must now accommodate international considerations. Take, for instance, the minimum capital requirements imposed on domestic depository institutions. These requirements are the result of the Basel Accord of 1988, which was arranged in cooperation with the Bank for International Settlements. Such international standards are necessary because the growth of multinational depository institutions has outstripped the ability of any one nation to regulate all operations of such institutions, as evidenced by the BCCI scandal.

American depository receipts (ADRs)
Receipts that represent shares of a foreign corporation's stock held in trust by a bank. The receipts then trade alongside domestic stock shares.

International portfolio diversification has long been considered desirable for all investors. Consequently, U.S. brokerage houses have developed **American Depository Receipts (ADRs)** to simplify investments in foreign stocks. ADRs represent shares of a foreign corporation's stock that are held in trust by a bank. The ADRs are priced in U.S. dollars and trade similarly to the stocks of U.S. corporations. ADR trading, while a first step toward international diversification, leaves that process incomplete in that ADR volatility mimics the U.S. market rather than the foreign markets. Thus, the ever-increasing demand for foreign stock ownership by U.S. investors is forcing brokerage houses to operate globally. In spite of the additional risk factors that affect foreign stock purchases, U.S. investors are now actively trading on international exchanges. International diversification of the markets has gone so far as to permit serious consideration of 24-hour, worldwide trading in the stocks of major corporations.

Just as investors are considering the international markets as alternatives to the U.S. markets, multinational corporations are considering them as viable alternative sources of financing. Consequently, corporations such as McDonald's Inc. have sold bonds in Europe, denominated in British pounds, to finance their worldwide operations. Commercial banks have been tapping the Eurocurrency market for years to acquire additional reserves whenever the Federal Reserve's tightening of the domestic money supply has impeded their lending ability.

Internationalization is not new; it has simply come into its own in the 1990s, aided by advances in communications technology. Anyone involved in finance today must be cognizant of international activity.

SUMMARY

The scope of finance has increased so much over the past decade that the field is generally subdivided into three parts. Financial markets and institutions, financial management, and investments are commonly considered to be separate disciplines. The study of financial markets and institutions focuses on those public and private institutions engaged in granting loans, accepting deposits, facilitating securities transfers, raising corporate funds, and regulating both the economy (domestic and global) and its financial institutions.

Financial management is concerned with how firms acquire and allocate funds. It examines how firms obtain short-term and long-term funds and how these funds are spent to acquire selected assets. Decisions regarding dividend policies, merger and acquisition activities, and leasing, all fall within the realm of the capital budget. Financial management also emphasizes the cash budget and management of its components.

Investment analysis focuses on how individuals or portfolio managers select appropriate financial and real assets. It examines the markets within which fund raising and security trading take place. It explores the methodologies used by investors, providing insights into criteria for analyzing companies and industries, as well as generating norms of behavior. The study of the markets for stocks and bonds, stock and index options, warrants, and commodities and financial futures are all part of the investments area.

The separation of the three areas of finance, however helpful it may be at limiting the scopes of advanced textbooks, does a disservice to the financial novice. So many common elements and such overlapping of ideas make it imperative for an introductory finance textbook to consider them as integrated parts of a whole. Consequently, this textbook does not merely explain the operation of the stock market, it explains how the market benefits both the investor and the financial manager and how the roles of these interested parties are interrelated.

All participants in the world of finance have goals. While these goals may be grounded in the economic concepts of maximization of profit and maximization of satisfaction, they need to be much more specific to be useful in financial decisions. The financial manager of a corporation, for example, generally considers maximization of stockholder wealth to be the firm's primary goal. Other competing goals, combined with legislative restrictions, tend to favor a goal of maximization of stakeholder wealth. Consequently, it is not unreasonable to say that bondholders, employees, community residents, and even environmentalists need to interact with the corporation in the pursuit of mutual interests.

Institutional financial managers, like their corporate counterparts, are torn between personal goals and constituent goals. These managers also find limits on their flexibility from legal constraints imposed by regulatory agencies. Similarly, government financial managers are legally constrained in their actions and must work to maximize the efficiency of financial operations relative to these constraints.

Individual investors, serving as their own financial managers, would love to be completely free to maximize their wealth. However, they quickly find that certain activities, such as insider trading, are frowned upon by the U.S. judicial system. It should be obvious that the goal of the individual investor and that of other financial managers are closely interrelated.

The principal trends in finance today are corporate restructuring and the internationalization of finance. Restructuring was forced upon an unwilling corporate world by a recession and an anemic economic recovery. Consequently, such words as *downsizing* or *rightsizing* entered the corporate vocabulary, and conservatism in financial matters has come to predominate. The internationalization process has developed gradually over time, but the increasing complexity of trade and the continuing growth of multinational corporations has made it a keystone of finance in the 1990s. Hence, all future financial decisions must now contend with this new dimension.

Major sources of financial information include:

The Wall Street Journal

Almanac of Business and Industrial Financial Ratios

American Banker

Annual Statement Studies Ratios

Business Week

Commercial and Financial Chronicle

Dun's Review

The Economist

Euromoney

Federal Reserve Bulletin

Financial Times
Financial Times Surveys
Forbes
Fortune
Standard & Poor's *Industry Surveys*
Institutional Investor
International Financial Statistics of the IMF
Investment Dealer's Digest
Investor's Business Daily
Dun & Bradstreet's *Key Business Ratios*
Survey of Current Business
Treasury Bulletin
Value Line Investment Survey
Wall Street Transcript

Key Terms

agency problem
American depository receipts (ADRs)
capital market
depository institution
money market
nondepository institution
opportunity cost
optimal portfolio mix
primary market
secondary market
stakeholder
systematic risk
unsystematic risk

Self-Study Questions

1. What are the three areas of specialization within finance?
2. What is the primary market for securities?
3. Why are commercial banks considered to be depository institutions?
4. In general terms, what are the functions of the Securities and Exchange Commission?
5. What are the financial planning tools of the corporation?
6. What are the methods used to determine asset profitability?
7. What is the objective of an investment?
8. What is the ultimate objective of the portfolio manager?
9. What is meant by the *optimal portfolio mix*?
10. What factors influence an individual's personal financial objectives?

Discussion Questions

1. What are the advantages of examining finance as a single field of study rather than as three separate areas of specialization?

2. Does the issuing corporation receive money from a secondary market sale of its stock?
3. Distinguish between the primary and secondary markets for securities.
4. To issue common stock, in what market(s) would a corporation operate?
5. What distinguishes the money market from the capital market?
6. Why do we need market regulation?
7. Distinguish between a depository institution and a nondepository institution.
8. In addition to depository and nondepository institutions, another class of institutions serve as agents. What are some of these institutions, and what service do they perform?
9. Is the need to regulate financial institutions and markets a product of the declining moral standards of the 1990s?
10. What is the concern of financial management?
11. Why is there an inverse relationship between return and risk?
12. Why is it meaningless to measure return without examining risk?
13. Why can the corporation not simply adopt the economist's concept of maximization of profit as its goal?
14. Describe the potential for conflict between the interests of stockholders and those of management.
15. How can one claim that the goals of the financial manager are the same, whether that manager works for a corporation, an institution, or the government, or independently?
16. What is meant by *opportunity cost*, and what role does it play in finance?
17. Why should corporate goals be redefined to include stakeholders?
18. Who are the stakeholders of a typical corporation?
19. How could one find information about careers in finance?
20. Does one need an advanced degree to qualify for a career in finance?

CHAPTER 2

Factors in Financial Decision Making: Inflation Rates, Interest Rates, and Exchange Rates

LEARNING OBJECTIVES

This chapter defines and discusses the inflation rate, interest rates, and exchange rates. It explains how to measure changes in these rates, as well as the effects these changes have on each other and on financial decisions. Since every country regulates these rates as a matter of policy, the chapter explores the methods and significance of this regulation. At the conclusion of this chapter, the reader should:

1. *Know what the terms* inflation rate, interest rate, *and* exchange rate *mean and how these rates are measured*
2. *Understand the causes and consequences of changes in the rates*
3. *Understand the nature of the interrelationships among the rates*
4. *Appreciate the importance of regulating the rates*
5. *Understand the difficulties and the politics of changing the rates*

Inflation rates, interest rates, and exchange rates affect the outcomes of business and financial decisions made by all economic agents. These rates change all the time, and they are often considered as barometers of business conditions. A rational decision should be based on some prior expectations about these rates and provisions to deal with any unexpected changes.

To illustrate how changes in inflation rates, interest rates, and exchange rates affect the outcome of a business decision, assume that a U.S. dealer in electronic toys imports Nintendo games from a Japanese supplier for the Christmas holiday season, and that the dealer has six months to pay for the import. The dealer's prospects for profit hinge on two factors: consumer spending during the holiday season and the dollar cost of settling the account payable in six months.

Consumer spending is affected primarily by confidence about the economy and by interest rates. The cost of settling the account payable is affected by the exchange rate between the U.S. dollar and the Japanese yen. If economic conditions are deteriorating and interest rates are high, consumer spending will be low and so will the dealer's sales. If the exchange value of the dollar falls in the meantime, it will raise the cost of settling the account payable. These developments may result in a loss for the dealer.

INFLATION RATES

inflation
A persistent rise in the general level of prices.

disinflation
A falling inflation rate.

zero inflation
No change in the general level of prices.

hyperinflation
A rapidly rising inflation rate, often reaching hundreds of percentage points within a few months.

deflation
The opposite of inflation, in which the general level of prices declines.

stagflation
A simultaneous increase in both the inflation rate and the unemployment rate.

Everyone is familiar with the way prices of goods and services behave in the marketplace. They usually go up. The phenomenon of rising prices is called **inflation.** Since the economy includes multitudes of prices, and all do not rise or fall at the same time, it is convenient to use the concept of an average price and describe *inflation* as a continuing rise in the level of the average price, or the general price level.

The inflation rate is the rate of change (or the percentage change) in the general price level over a specified time period, usually a year. An increase in the inflation rate means that prices are rising at a faster rate. A decrease in the inflation rate means that prices in general are not rising as quickly as before; it does not mean that prices are falling. The term **disinflation** is often used to describe a declining inflation rate. If prices in general do not change, a situation of **zero inflation exists.**

Rapidly rising prices may lead to a situation called **hyperinflation.** Many countries have experienced hyperinflation, some very recently, with inflation rates reaching hundreds of percentage points in a matter of months.

Although there is nothing to keep prices in general from going down, most people have experienced rising prices. This is because economic process has favored prices going upward in recent years.

However, older people who lived through the Great Depression of the 1930s are sure to have a more diversified view of price changes. Prices actually fell by 25 percent between 1929 and 1933. A major slowdown of the economy in the future could bring about a similar decline in prices. The phenomenon of falling prices is known as **deflation.** It is the opposite of inflation.

Economies have also experienced a situation known as **stagflation.** This occurs when a high rate of inflation is accompanied by a high level of unemployment. This presents a dilemma for policy makers, as attempts to cure one problem invariably make the other one worse. The cherished goal of every country has been to keep both problems under control to avoid the heavy costs they inflict on people.

FOCUS ON FINANCE

Hyperinflation in Bolivia

When prices rise by 329 percent in one year, 2,700 percent in the next year, and 12,500 percent in the year after that, the economy suffers from hyperinflation. This is what happened in Bolivia between 1983 and 1985. To generate such a rate of inflation, prices must rise by the hour; they did in Bolivia. A bar of chocolate could sell for 35,000 pesos at one time, and for 50,000 pesos five minutes later. The stack of pesos needed to buy a chocolate bar weighed more than the chocolate. The amount of money needed to buy a luxury Toyota in 1982 bought just three boxes of aspirin in 1985.

According to *The Wall Street Journal*, the Bolivian peso bought so little in 1985 that pocket money had to be carried in suitcases. Housewives had to take their maids along to the market to carry the bales of cash needed to buy things they could carry home easily on their own. Each peso cost more to print than it purchased. To meet the demand for pesos, the government had to bring planeloads of them twice a week from printers in Germany and Britain. These purchases of pesos cost Bolivia more than $20 million, making currency the third largest import in 1984.

Measuring Inflation

purchasing power of money
The amount of goods and services a unit of money can command in the market.

price index
A numerical device used to measure changes in prices.

consumer price index (CPI)
A measure of inflation based on a theoretical market basket of consumer goods. It is compiled by the U.S. Department of Labor and published monthly.

Inflation and the **purchasing power of money** are inversely related. Inflation causes the purchasing power of money to fall. The purchasing power of money (also known as the *value of money*) is the amount of goods and services that one unit of money can buy. When prices rise, the same goods cost more in terms of dollars, and the dollar's value in terms of those goods falls.

Inflation is commonly measured with the aid of a **price index**. A price index is a statistical device to measure price changes between a base period and a subsequent period. Economists use many different price indices. The **consumer price index (CPI)** is the most popular index for tracking inflation in the United States. The CPI measures the average change in the prices paid by urban consumers for a fixed basket of goods and services. The statistics for this index are compiled by the Bureau of Labor Statistics of the U.S. Department of Labor, which publishes them monthly. The behavior of the CPI for the United States for a selected number of years is presented in Exhibit 2.1.

Causes and Consequences of Inflation

Why do prices begin to rise, and what propels them to rise continuously? One can answer these questions by examining how prices are determined and the causes of price changes. Prices are determined by demand and supply conditions in the market. Demand and supply conditions are influenced by a number of economic forces. When these economic forces change, they transmit their effects to prices, making prices a barometer of such changes. Economists have analyzed the relationship between prices and economic forces to produce a number of theories (or

EXHIBIT 2.1

Historical CPI[a]

	CPI	Percentage Change from Previous Year		CPI	Percentage Change from Previous Year
1915	10.1	1.0	1970	38.8	5.7
1920	20.0	15.6	1975	53.8	9.1
1925	17.5	2.3	1980	82.4	13.5
1930	16.7	−2.3	1982	96.5	6.2
1935	13.7	2.2	1984	103.9	4.3
1940	14.0	0.7	1985	107.6	3.6
1945	18.0	2.3	1986	109.6	1.9
1950	24.1	1.3	1988	118.3	4.1
1955	26.8	−0.4	1990	130.7	5.4
1960	29.6	1.7	1992	140.3	3.0
1965	31.5	1.6			

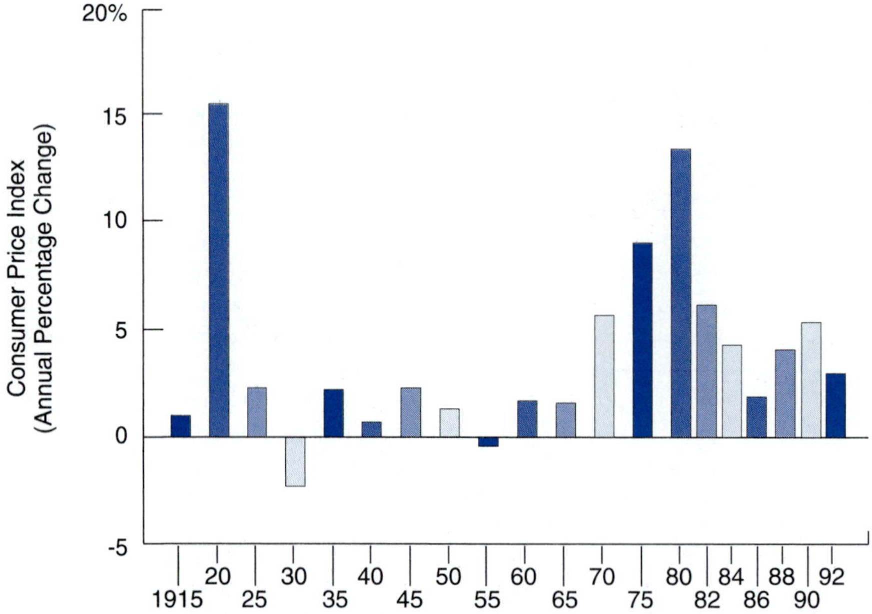

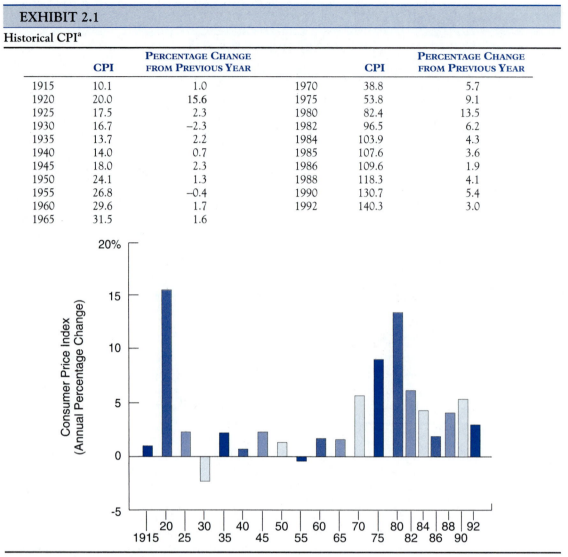

[a]All urban consumers (CPI-U), 1982–1984=100.
Source: Bureau of Labor Statistics, U.S. Department of Labor.

demand-pull theory
A theory that identifies excessive demand for goods and services as the primary cause of inflation.

models) of inflation. The forces that operate from the demand side of the market have been enshrined in what are called **demand-pull theories** of inflation. The forces that affect the supply side of the market process have been labeled **cost-push theories** of inflation.

Causes of Inflation. One economic force that operates on the demand side of the market with strong and direct impact on prices is the **money stock**. A simple

EXHIBIT 2.1 *continued*

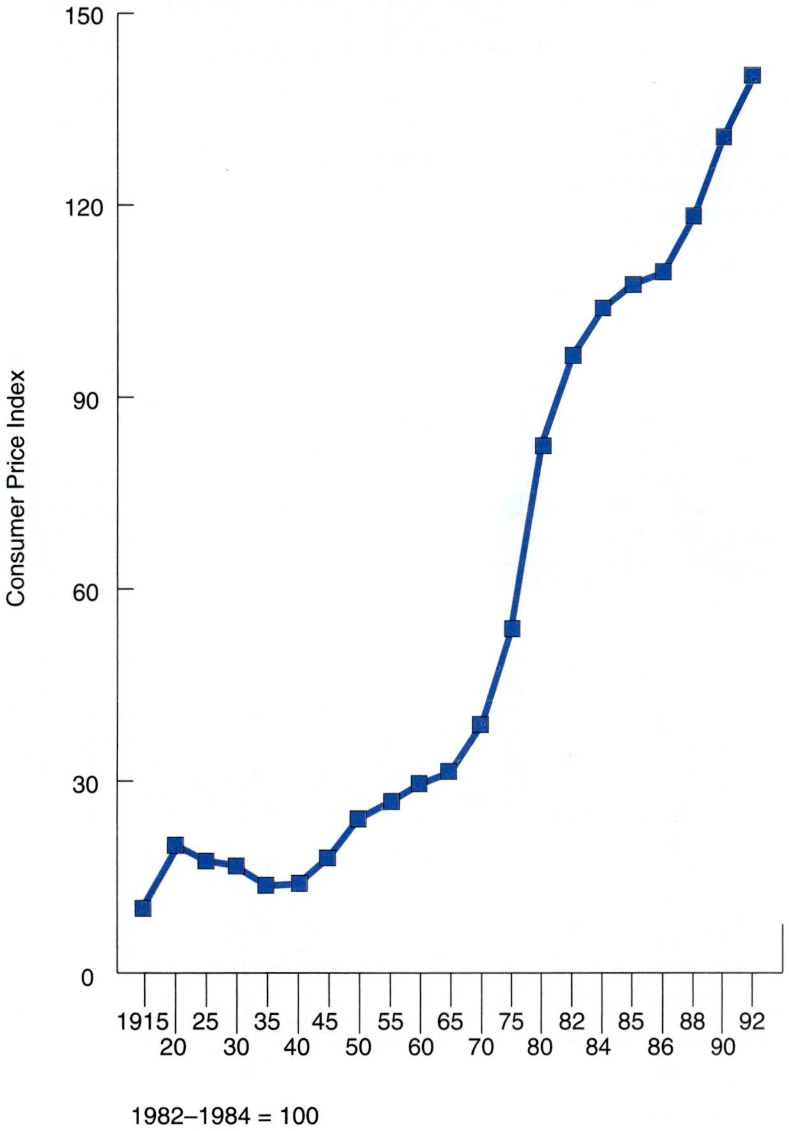

cost-push theory

A theory that holds institutional factors responsible for inflation.

money stock

The amount of money held by the nonbank public.

explanation shows how changes in money stock affect prices: an increase in the stock of money increases total expenditures on goods and services; the resulting increase in the demand for goods and services, in turn, causes prices to rise proportionally, if other things remain unchanged, including the supply of goods and

FOCUS ON FINANCE

Construction of a Price Index

The construction of a price index can be simple or complex. The simplest price index is a ratio of two prices, called the *price relative*. This type of index measures changes in the price of an item over time relative to its price in the base period. A price index that can measure changes in the overall prices paid by consumers must be based on a selected number of consumer goods. The first step in the construction of such an index is to select a base year and a basket of consumer goods, called the *market basket*. The next step is to calculate price index values for various years using a method of averaging.

The construction of a price index called the *simple average of relatives* is illustrated below. The price relative of an item in the basket of goods for period i can be represented as:

$$PR_i = (P_{t+i}/P_t)100$$

A simple average of price relatives is:

$$I_i = \sum_{i=1}^{i=n} PR_i / n$$

where t = base year

P_t = base year price of an item

P_{t+i} = price of the item in the ith year following the base year

PR_i = price relative of the item for period i

n = number of items in the basket

I_i = price index for period i with base year t

To illustrate the method numerically, assume that the market basket consists of two commodities, A and B, and the base year is 1989. Using hypothetical values for the prices, price index values are as shown below.

Year-to-year changes in price indices are usually expressed as percentage changes rather than changes in index points. Percentage changes are free from the influence of the level of the index in relation to its base period, whereas index points are not. In the above illustration, the increase in the prices during 1990 was 8.5 index points, which is also 8.5 percent. During 1991 the increase was 10.5 index points, but only (10.5/108.5)×100 = 9.68 percent.

Simple Average of Relatives

	P_t		PR_i		
t	A	B	A	B	I_i
1989	4.5	10.0	(4.5/4.5)×100	(10.0/10)×100	(100+100)/2=100.0
1990	5.5	9.5	(5.5/4.5)×100	(9.5/10)×100	(122+95)/2=108.5
1991	6.0	10.5	(6.0/4.5)×100	(10.5/10)×100	(133+105)/2=119.0

velocity of money
The rate at which money changes hands during a given period or the rate of turnover of money.

services, the speed at which money turns over (called the **velocity of money**), and the cost of production. A classic description of inflation propelled by a change in the money stock is that "too much money is chasing too few goods."

The historical data on U.S. inflation do not give strong support for the proportional relationship between the money stock prices. The United States has had many periods of inflation when the proportional relationship between prices and the money stock did not hold. For example, during the 1940s, a 200 percent increase in the money stock was followed by only a 70 percent increase in prices,

FOCUS ON FINANCE

Federal Reserve Money Stock Measures

♦ ♦ ♦

M1 includes (1) currency outside the U.S. Treasury, Federal Reserve Banks, and the vaults of depository institutions, (2) traveler's checks of nonbank issuers, (3) demand deposits at all commercial banks other than those owed to depository institutions, the U.S. government, and foreign banks and official institutions, less cash items in the process of collection and Federal Reserve float, and (4) other checkable deposits (OCDs), consisting of negotiable order of withdrawal (NOW) and automatic transfer service (ATS) accounts at depository institutions, credit union share draft accounts, and demand deposits at thrift institutions.

M2 includes everything in M1 plus (1) overnight (and continuing contract) repurchase agreements (RPs) issued by all depository institutions and overnight Eurodollars issued to U.S. residents by foreign branches of U.S. banks worldwide, (2) savings deposits (including MMDAs) and small, time deposits (time deposits—including retail RPs—in amounts of less than $100,000), and (3) balances in both taxable and tax-exempt general-purpose and broker–dealer money market funds. M2 excludes individual retirement accounts (IRAs) and Keogh balances at depository institutions and money market funds. It also excludes all balances held by U.S. commercial banks, money market funds (general purpose and broker–dealer funds), foreign governments, commercial banks, and the U.S. government.

M3 includes M2 plus (1) large, time deposits and term RP liabilities (in amounts of $100,000 or more) issued by all depository institutions, (2) term Eurodollars held by U.S. residents at foreign branches of U.S. banks worldwide and at all banking offices in the United Kingdom and Canada, and (3) balances in both taxable and tax-exempt, institution-only money market funds. M3 excludes amounts held by depository institutions, the U.S. government, money market funds, and foreign banks and official institutions. It also excludes the estimated amount of overnight RPs and Eurodollars held by institution-only money market funds.

Source: *Federal Reserve Bulletin*, Table 1.10.

while in the 1950s, a 25 percent increase in the money stock accompanied exactly a 25 percent increase in prices. When the rate of increase in the money stock is different from that of prices, it means that other factors have not remained constant. The level of output, the velocity of money, or the cost of production may have changed. However, most periods of inflation, especially hyperinflation, can be attributed primarily to changes in money stock.

An increase in the money stock may not lead to inflation if the other factors mentioned above change to counteract the effect of the increase. For example, an increase in the production of goods or a reduction in the velocity of money may offset the inflationary effects of an increased money stock. At the same time, the demand for goods and services cannot increase continuously and bring about inflation unless it is supported by increases in the money stock. All this means that an increase in the money stock is a necessary condition for inflation, but perhaps not a sufficient condition by itself.

On the supply side of the market, resource shortages, wage hikes, and rising costs of imports can push the cost of production and prices upward. This can add to inflationary pressure under given demand conditions. For example, the oil embargo imposed in 1973 and 1974 by the Organization of Petroleum Exporting Countries (OPEC) caused a precipitous increase in the price of oil, making it a major factor in the worldwide inflation of the 1970s. Resource shortages may result from human effort (as in the case of the oil embargo) or natural calamities such as droughts, floods, and earthquakes. The inflationary impact of a severe natural calamity can be substantial.

Consequences of Inflation. The consequences of inflation are well-known. Among the consequences that are most worrisome are:

1. Redistribution of income and wealth
2. Loss of confidence on the part of savers and investors
3. Fear that inflation may turn into hyperinflation
4. Impact on the country's exports and imports
5. Impact on the country's exchange rate

People's income and wealth represent their purchasing power, and purchasing power depends on the prices of goods and services. Under inflationary conditions, purchasing power falls if income and wealth increase less rapidly than prices. Some groups of people see their income and wealth rise more quickly than the inflation rate, while others suffer as their income and wealth lag behind the inflation rate.

Wage earners and those who live on fixed incomes, such as pensioners, may not enjoy proportionate increases in their incomes during periods of inflation. Businesses usually enjoy incomes that rise faster than inflation. The incomes of creditors who lend at fixed interest rates can lag behind inflation. Investors whose assets appreciate more quickly than the inflation rate benefit, and others whose assets do not appreciate as quickly lose. This creates a redistribution of income and wealth during inflation from wage earners and fixed-income groups to businesses, from creditors to debtors, and from those whose assets appreciate in price more slowly to those whose assets appreciate more rapidly.

Inflation creates price uncertainty when it cannot be correctly anticipated or forecasted. Under such conditions, economically inefficient decisions are made, investment choices tend to be speculative, and the allocation of resources gets distorted. Inflation encourages investment in less productive activities such as speculation on business inventory and real estate purchases, and it discourages investment in physical assets that add to the productive capacity of the economy.

Inflation tends to feed on itself, and it can easily turn into hyperinflation if left uncontrolled. The fear of hyperinflation may lead to a loss of confidence in a nation's monetary system and replacement of a country's currency. Hyperinflation may force people to abandon the existing monetary system and suffer the inefficiency and cost of exchanging goods and services for other goods and services under a **barter system**.

barter system

A system of trade in which goods are exchanged for goods.

FOCUS ON FINANCE

Federal Reserve's Position on Inflation

Ever since the early 1980s, the Fed has taken a determined stand on inflation control. The 7 governors and 12 district presidents (five of whom are part of the policy-making group at any given time) have pledged time and again their unwavering commitment to restrain inflation. The policy makers disagree, however, on the inflation rate that the Fed should target. Some among them even embrace the concept of zero inflation. When Congressman Stephen Neal sponsored a resolution in 1990 requiring the Fed to eliminate inflation over the next five years and maintain price stability thereafter, he received wholehearted support from this group. Some policy makers, however, are opposed to the idea of zero inflation because of its high cost in terms of unemployment and lost output.

All statements and policy actions coming out of the Fed suggest that it will do whatever it deems necessary to contain inflation. Its recent policy actions have aimed at forestalling any inflationary pressure that would be generated by an economic recovery. One immediate consequence of this approach has been violent gyrations in security prices.

The effect of inflation on a country's international trade and financial transactions is shaped by complex interactions among exchange rates and domestic and foreign interest rates. A discussion of the effects of inflation on exchange rates follows the section on exchange rates, later in this chapter.

Predicting and Coping with Inflation

The spending and saving decisions of individuals, the investment decisions of domestic and multinational firms, and the budget decisions of governments are all affected by the levels of present and future prices. These decisions need some solid basis in reasonable expectations or forecasts of future prices. Contractual commitments such as loans and wage contracts are exposed to the risk of loss of purchasing power due to inflation. Interest rates on loans and wage rates need to be adjusted (or indexed) to compensate for such losses. The calculation of such compensation is based on expected inflation during the contract period.

How does one form inflation expectations? Inflation expectations are formed on the basis of one's understanding of the economic process and knowledge of the underlying causes of inflation. A large number of models, some simple and some complex, have been built to explain and forecast inflation. A simple model might forecast future inflation rates by extrapolating from the past trend. One could go a step further and forecast inflation by forecasting future trends in underlying causes. This involves the construction of a model based on established relationships between underlying causes and inflation. This is called the *structural* (or *fundamental*) *approach* to forecasting inflation.

Inflation forecasting models, however sophisticated they may be, do not guarantee perfect forecasts. Expected rates of inflation often turn out to differ from actual inflation rates. This may result in investors, creditors, and wage earners being less than fully compensated for their loss of purchasing power due to inflation. This possibility is commonly known as **inflation risk**, and most economic and financial decisions are exposed to it because of the difficulty of forecasting inflation accurately. It is possible, however, to hedge against such inflation risk, through mechanisms provided in the financial markets.

inflation risk
The possibility of the actual inflation rate being different from the expected inflation rate.

Government Control of Inflation

The key to dealing with inflation effectively lies in a correct understanding of its causes. The policy adopted by a country to deal with inflation is influenced by the inflation theory that the policy makers in that country support and their view of inflation as an economic problem. In Germany, for example, inflation has long been perceived as the biggest economic problem. The Germans' fear of inflation goes back to their experience of the devastating effects of inflation caused by two world wars. This was especially true in 1923 when the inflation rate reached 10 billion percent (10,000,000,000 percent).

In the United States, the attitude toward inflation changes with the party in power, Republicans or Democrats. A Republican administration seems to worry more about inflation than a Democratic administration. Democrats traditionally pay more attention to unemployment, on the theory that it hurts their grassroots supporters more than inflation does.

Although both inflation and unemployment are serious problems faced by any society and deserve equal attention from policy makers, the either–or approach for dealing with these problems results from a policy conflict. The economics of these problems mean that policies adopted to control inflation tend to aggravate the unemployment problem (at least in the short run), and vice versa.

If policy makers in a country see inflation as their biggest problem and the primary cause of inflation as an increase in the money stock, then they will try to control inflation by reducing the money stock or its growth rate. In recent years, such a perception is clearly indicated by the policy pursued in Germany, and to a lesser extent by the policy pursued in the United States. The connection between tight monetary policy and inflation reduction is a simple one. A reduction in money stock leads to higher interest rates and reduced spending. The reduced spending, in turn, lowers the inflation rate and increases the unemployment rate.

International Differences in Inflation Rates

Inflation experiences among countries have been and continue to be different. The reasons for these differences are found in variations in the structures and sizes of economies, the economic (monetary, fiscal, and **balance of payments**) policies pursued by their governments, and whether or not they perceive inflation as a primary problem. In comparison to developed countries, for example, inflation rarely receives the same attention as unemployment in less developed countries. Recent inflation rates in selected countries are presented in Exhibit 2.2.

balance of payments
The accounts of a country's transactions in goods, services, and financial assets with the rest of the world.

Although inflation rates are different in various countries, the economic dependence among countries may cause exportation of inflation from one country to

EXHIBIT 2.2

Inflation in Selected Countries[a]

	United States	Canada	Mexico	Germany	Japan	United Kingdom
1980	76.6	69.6	9.3	82.7	87.3	70.7
1981	84.5	78.6	11.9	87.9	91.6	79.1
1982	89.7	87.1	19.0	92.5	94.1	85.9
1983	92.6	02.2	38.3	95.6	95.8	89.8
1984	96.6	96.2	63.4	97.9	98.0	94.3
1985	100.0	100.0	100.0	100.0	100.0	100.0
1986	101.9	104.2	186.2	99.9	100.6	103.4
1987	105.7	108.7	431.7	100.1	100.7	107.7
1988	109.9	113.1	924.6	101.4	101.4	113.0
1989	115.2	118.7	1,109.6	104.2	103.7	121.8
1990	121.4	124.4	1,405.4	107.0	106.9	133.4
1991	126.6	131.4	1,723.8	110.7	110.4	141.2
1992	130.4	133.4	1,991.2	115.2	112.3	146.4

[a]Consumer price index (1985=100).
Source: International Financial Statistics Yearbook, 1993, IMF.

Bretton Woods System
The system of fixed exchange rates that prevailed from 1946 until 1973.

another under certain conditions. The international transmission of inflation used to be a common problem when countries were operating under a fixed exchange rate arrangement called the **Bretton Woods System**. This system was introduced after World War II to establish monetary stability and promote growth in international trade. It was given up in 1973 when it ceased to be a feasible system. In the late 1960s, when the United States was experiencing high inflation, the exchange rate system was blamed for exporting the inflation to other countries. High U.S. inflation turned out to be one of the main reasons for ending the Bretton Woods System as some trading partners—West Germany, Japan, and France, in particular—refused to accept the U.S. inflation.

It is easy to see how inflation gets exported from one country to another under the fixed exchange rate system. If a country suffers from a higher rate of inflation than its trading partners, foreign goods become cheaper in that country at the existing exchange rate. As the country switches to cheaper imports, it will experience balance of payments deficits. The trading partners of this country will enjoy balance of payments surpluses. These surpluses will translate into increases in their money stocks unless their governments act to eliminate the monetary impacts of the surpluses. These increases in money stock will put pressure on prices and push inflation rates up.

INTEREST RATES

Lending durable goods to others to use has always been part of the economic process. Lending usually involves a payment from the borrower to the lender as compensation for the lender's sacrifice in giving up the present use of the loaned goods. The amount of this payment is determined by what the lender expects for compensation and by what the borrower is willing to pay. The compensation expected by the lender reflects a fair price for the sacrifice plus a premium to cover any risk associated with lending. The amount that the borrower is willing to pay reflects the usefulness of the goods borrowed.

The compensation received by lenders is known by different names depending on the type of goods involved. When goods such as land, buildings, and other physical assets are loaned, the compensation is called *rent*. Compensation for lending money is called **interest**, and it is usually expressed as an annual percentage of the amount loaned.

interest
Compensation paid to the lender for the use of loaned money.

Interest as Return and Cost

Borrowers and lenders of money during any period may include all three economic agents—individuals, businesses, and government agencies. They borrow to meet deficits in their budgets, and they lend to earn income from their surpluses. Individuals are the dominant lenders, and businesses and government agencies are the dominant borrowers. For a borrower, the interest payment constitutes a cost, the cost of using the services of money. For a lender, interest is a source of income. Individuals may receive income from many sources: wages, rent on property, dividends on investments, and interest on loans. For some individuals, the income from interest may constitute a major part of personal income.

Determination of Interest Rates

In a free-market system such as the economy in the United States, interest rates are ultimately determined in the marketplace by the interaction of borrowers and lenders. Such interaction results in an **equilibrium interest rate** when the preferences of borrowers and lenders are successfully matched. An equilibrium interest rate is acceptable to both parties to the transaction, and it is the rate at which the loan transaction is completed.

equilibrium interest rate
An interest rate established by the interaction of demand and supply forces.

Matching preferences and determination of an equilibrium interest rate is difficult because the factors that influence the preferences of the two groups are diverse and mostly unrelated. Lenders seek adequate compensation for:

1. Postponing the use of their money
2. Taking on any risk that may be associated with lending
3. Any decline in the value of money because of inflation

The preferences of borrowers are determined by the productivity of the money in the use for which it is borrowed. A free market performs the preference matching function very efficiently.

The level of an interest rate determined in the market depends on the characteristics of the lender–borrower group that agrees to loans at that rate. These characteristics include the time preferences of lenders, default risk, inflation, the duration of the loan, any collateral, liquidity, and the demand for money. For example, when a bank (a financial intermediary) lends money, the rate it charges will reflect current conditions on both the demand (borrower) and supply (lender) sides of the market, including an anticipated inflation rate. There are as many market interest rates as there are lender–borrower groups. Mortgage rates, money market rates, Treasury bill rates, certificate of deposit rates, commercial lending rates, and Eurodollar rates are some examples of market interest rates.

Fisher Effect

Interest on loan transactions is usually specified in nominal terms, that is, in current dollars. For example, if a bank lends money at an annual interest rate of 8 percent, it means that the interest due at the end of the year amounts to $8 for every $100 borrowed. The 8 percent is the nominal rate of interest. In practice, the term *nominal* is usually left out.

Fisher effect
The incorporation of an anticipated inflation rate into the nominal interest rate.

Nominal interest rates are expected to fully incorporate anticipated inflation rates. This is known as the **Fisher effect**. The Fisher effect is easily explained by representing a risk-free interest rate as a sum of two parts: the real interest rate and the anticipated inflation rate. (A detailed derivation of the Fisher effect appears in Chapter 8.) Expressed as an equation:

$$i = i_r + q \tag{2.1}$$

where i = nominal risk-free interest rate

i_r = real interest rate

q = anticipated inflation rate

The risk-free interest rate is the rate of interest, free from all risks except inflation risk. The real interest rate is the compensation for parting with money.

The anticipated inflation rate, q in Equation 2.1, is called the *inflation premium* component of the nominal rate, and it represents the Fisher effect. If the market expects the inflation rate to fall in the future, all market interest rates will be pushed to lower levels by the amount of the expected decline in the inflation rate. If the market expects the inflation rate to rise in the future, all market interest rates will be pushed to higher levels by the amount of the expected rise in the inflation rate.

Changes in Interest Rates

Changes in interest rates are linked to many domestic and foreign factors such as money stocks, output levels, exchange rates, and inflation rates. Some factors operate on the demand side and others on the supply side of the market for loans.

The domestic money stock has perhaps the most direct and closest link to the interest rate. This link is established by the lending and money creating activities of banks. Checkable deposit balances held at various depository institutions are a major component of the money stock, known as *deposit money*. When banks lend, they add to the deposit money component of the money stock as bank loans

EXHIBIT 2.3

Interest Rates in Selected Countries[a]

	United States	Canada	Mexico	Germany	Japan	United Kingdom
1980	13.36%	18.96%	—	9.1%	10.93%	15.62%
1981	16.38	12.82	—	11.3	7.43	13.12
1982	12.26	10.38	45.86%	8.7	6.94	11.36
1983	9.09	9.07	57.51	5.4	6.39	9.09
1984	10.23	10.05	49.94	5.5	6.10	7.62
1985	8.10	9.84	62.44	5.2	6.46	10.78
1986	6.81	8.16	88.01	4.6	4.79	10.68
1987	6.66	8.50	95.59	3.7	3.51	9.66
1988	7.61	10.35	69.01	4.0	3.62	10.31
1989	9.22	12.06	47.43	6.6	4.87	13.88
1990	8.10	11.62	37.36	7.9	7.24	14.68
1991	5.70	7.40	23.58	8.8	7.46	11.75
1992	3.52	6.79	18.87	9.4	4.58	9.55

[a]Money market rates (percent per annum).
Source: International Financial Statistics Yearbook, 1993, IMF.

become new deposits for borrowers. While an increase in bank lending raises the level of the money stock, competition in the loan market lowers interest rates.

Interest rate changes may also be affected by the demand side of the interest rate market. Seeing fewer profitable investment opportunities during a recession, or a downswing of the economy, borrowers may demand fewer funds and cause interest rates to decline. The opposite may happen during an upswing in the economy. Traditionally, therefore, interest rates tend to move with the business cycle, rising during an upswing and falling during a downswing.

Maintaining interest rates at a level that supports steady growth and full employment in the economy is one of the objectives of the economic policy of a country. To achieve this goal, policy makers exploit the connection between the money stock and interest rates. When they perceive a need to lower interest rates, a common policy strategy is to increase the money stock. At other times, they may decrease the money stock or slow its growth in order to halt a downward slide in interest rates. This strategy is also followed when excess money stock threatens to increase inflationary pressures in the economy.

To deal with the impact of foreign economic variables on domestic interest rates (and inflation), countries usually seek the cooperation of foreign governments, particularly those that have close economic ties to the domestic economy. The governments of the so-called *Group of 7*, or G-7, countries (the United States, United Kingdom, Japan, Germany, France, Canada, and Italy) have made a practice of meeting regularly for this purpose. In these meetings, they attempt to iron out their differences and coordinate their policies to minimize the adverse cross-border effects of their policies and to promote growth in the world economy.

Predicting and Coping with Interest Rate Changes

In a volatile financial market, interest rates change all the time in response to news about changes in the domestic and foreign factors that affect their levels. For example, bad news about inflation or good news about employment and output would cause interest rates to rise almost immediately. In fact, the mere expectation of an increase in the inflation rate or the employment level is enough to push current interest rates upward.

Participants on both sides of the interest rate market form their expectations about future interest rates and base their financial decisions such as when to borrow, lend, and invest on these expectations. For example, people planning to buy homes with mortgage financing may postpone their purchases if they expect interest rates to fall. They may speed up their purchases to lock in the present lower rate if they expect interest rates to rise. Bond investors will buy bonds if they expect interest rates to fall, as bond values move in the opposite direction of interest rates.

It is interesting that expectations can change quickly in response to information about events related to future interest rates. In an efficient market, such as the interest rate market, information travels quickly, and events that affect interest rates occur all the time. This is one of the reasons why interest rates change so frequently. Moreover, if the expectation formed at any time about a future event turns out to be true, then the interest rate may not respond to the event when it occurs. Interest rates may have already adjusted to reflect the impact of the event as soon as its expectation was formed.

International Interest Rates

Both the levels of and movements in interest rates tend to differ among countries, just as inflation rates do. These differences reflect the differences in inflation rates, borrower and lender characteristics, economic conditions of the countries, and movements in their exchange rates. Inflation rates, interest rates, and exchange rates of countries are linked though their commodity market and financial market activities. This relationship will be explained later in the chapter. Exhibit 2.3 shows the differences in interest rate levels and interest rate movements among selected countries.

EXCHANGE RATES

When residents of one country trade with residents of another country, they must generally convert funds between the currencies of the two countries to facilitate payments. Currency conversion requires a rate to define the value of one currency in terms of another currency. This rate is the **exchange rate**.

exchange rate
The value of a currency expressed in terms of another currency.

Defining *Exchange Rate*

Stated in simple terms, an exchange rate is the price of one unit of a currency expressed in units of another currency. For example, an exchange rate between the

EXHIBIT 2.4

Exchange Rate Quotes

EXCHANGE RATES

Monday, June 20, 1994

The New York foreign exchange selling rates below apply to trading among banks in amounts of $1 million and more, as quoted at 3 p.m. Eastern time by Bankers Trust Co., Dow Jones Telerate Inc. and other sources. Retail transactions provide fewer units of foreign currency per dollar.

	U.S. $ equiv.		Currency per U.S. $	
Country	Mon.	Fri.	Mon.	Fri.
Argentina (Peso)	1.01	1.01	.99	.99
Australia (Dollar)	.7391	.7350	1.3530	1.3605
Austria (Schilling)	.08885	.08829	11.26	11.33
Bahrain (Dinar)	2.6522	2.6522	.3771	.3771
Belgium (Franc)	.03035	.03017	32.95	33.15
Brazil (Cruzeiro real)	.0004235	.0004314	2361.05	2318.03
Britain (Pound)	1.5370	1.5353	.6506	.6513
30-Day Forward	1.5362	1.5345	.6510	.6517
90-Day Forward	1.5347	1.5332	.6516	.6522
180-Day Forward	1.5330	1.5317	.6523	.6529
Canada (Dollar)	.7189	.7188	1.3910	1.3912
30-Day Forward	.7178	.7180	1.3932	1.3928
90-Day Forward	.7146	.7160	1.3994	1.3966
180-Day Forward	.7099	.7127	1.4086	1.4031
Czech. Rep. (Koruna)				
Commercial rate	.0349235	.0344994	28.6340	28.9860
Chile (Peso)	.002438	.002423	410.24	412.64
China (Renminbi)	.115221	.114943	8.6790	8.7000
Colombia (Peso)	.001212	.001201	825.21	832.90
Denmark (Krone)	.1592	.1582	6.2824	6.3196
Ecuador (Sucre)				
Floating rate	.000463	.000465	2160.01	2149.01
Finland (Markka)	.18696	.18582	5.3488	5.3815
France (Franc)	.18282	.18175	5.4700	5.5020
30-Day Forward	.18263	.18155	5.4755	5.5082
90-Day Forward	.18232	.18130	5.4849	5.5158
180-Day Forward	.18198	.18113	5.4950	5.5209
Germany (Mark)	.6209	.6209	1.6105	1.6105
30-Day Forward	.6205	.6206	1.6115	1.6114
90-Day Forward	.6202	.6202	1.6123	1.6123
180-Day Forward	.6204	.6205	1.6118	1.6117
Greece (Drachma)	.004131	.004111	242.10	243.25
Hong Kong (Dollar)	.12939	.12937	7.7285	7.7300
Hungary (Forint)	.0097838	.0096609	102.2100	103.5100
India (Rupee)	.03212	.03212	31.13	31.13
Indonesia (Rupiah)	.0004613	.0004613	2168.02	2168.02
Ireland (Punt)	1.5073	1.5073	.6634	.6634
Israel (Shekel)	.3281	.3277	3.0480	3.0520
Italy (Lira)	.0006317	.0006317	1583.13	1583.13
Japan (Yen)	.009809	.009723	101.95	102.85
30-Day Forward	.009826	.009741	101.77	102.66
90-Day Forward	.009869	.009785	101.33	102.20
180-Day Forward	.009936	.009854	100.64	101.48
Jordan (Dinar)	1.4767	1.4599	.6772	.6850
Kuwait (Dinar)	3.3695	3.3568	.2968	.2979
Lebanon (Pound)	.000595	.000594	1682.00	1682.50
Malaysia (Ringgit)	.3854	.3856	2.5950	2.5935
Malta (Lira)	2.6846	2.6178	.3725	.3820
Mexico (Peso)				
Floating rate	.2970444	.2962963	3.3665	3.3750
Netherland (Guilder)	.5577	.5541	1.7931	1.8048
New Zealand (Dollar)	.5955	.5927	1.6793	1.6872
Norway (Krone)	.1437	.1430	6.9576	6.9944
Pakistan (Rupee)	.0327	.0327	30.61	30.61
Peru (New Sol)	.4705	.4694	2.13	2.13
Philippines (Peso)	.03774	.03765	26.50	26.56
Poland (Zloty)	.00004405	.00004419	22700.00	22629.00
Portugal (Escudo)	.006006	.005965	166.51	167.65
Saudi Arabia (Riyal)	.26667	.26667	3.7500	3.7500
Singapore (Dollar)	.6547	.6538	1.5275	1.5295
Slovak Rep. (Koruna)	.0307314	.0307314	32.5400	32.5400
South Africa (Rand)				
Commercial rate	.2748	.2740	3.6393	3.6503
Financial rate	.2107	.2105	4.7458	4.7500
South Korea (Won)	.0012402	.0012402	806.30	806.30
Spain (Peseta)	.007497	.007499	133.39	133.35
Sweden (Krona)	.1297	.1288	7.7080	7.7618
Switzerland (Franc)	.7404	.7378	1.3507	1.3553
30-Day Forward	.7404	.7378	1.3507	1.3553
90-Day Forward	.7407	.7383	1.3501	1.3545
180-Day Forward	.7418	.7396	1.3481	1.3521
Taiwan (Dollar)	.036969	.036958	27.05	27.06
Thailand (Baht)	.03981	.03971	25.12	25.18
Turkey (Lira)	.0000323	.0000322	30958.02	31012.95
United Arab (Dirham)	.2723	.2723	3.6725	3.6725
Uruguay (New Peso)				
Financial	.201613	.202429	4.96	4.94
Venezuela (Bolivar)				
Floating rate	.00583	.00607	171.50	164.80

SDR	1.43622	1.42231	.69627	.70308
ECU	1.19220	1.19220	....	....

Special Drawing Rights (SDR) are based on exchange rates for the U.S., German, British, French and Japanese currencies. Source: International Monetary Fund.

European Currency Unit (ECU) is based on a basket of community currencies.

Source: The Wall Street Journal, June 21, 1994.

U.S. dollar and the Canadian dollar of $1.00 = C$1.25 means that the price of one U.S. dollar is 1.25 Canadian dollars. It can also be stated as C$1.25/$.

To a Canadian, one U.S. dollar costs C$1.25. To a U.S. citizen, this expresses the price of the home currency in terms of a foreign currency (the Canadian dollar in this case). To the Canadian, it expresses the price of a foreign currency (the U.S. dollar in this case) in terms of the home currency.

The same exchange rate between the U.S. dollar and the Canadian dollar can be stated as C$1 = $0.80 or $0.80/C$. This is another acceptable way of stating the same exchange rate between the two currencies. Here, the price of a Canadian dollar is expressed in terms of U.S. dollars. To residents of the United States, this represents the cost of obtaining one Canadian dollar. To a Canadian, it is the price of the home currency in terms of a foreign currency; to the U.S. citizen, it is the price of a foreign currency in terms of the home currency.

EXHIBIT 2.5

Key Currency Cross Rates

Key Currency Cross Rates Late New York Trading June 20, 1994

	Dollar	Pound	SFranc	Guilder	Peso	Yen	Lira	D-Mark	FFranc	CdnDlr
Canada	1.3906	2.1374	1.03046	.77587	.41307	.01365	.00088	.86967	.25429	....
France	5.4685	8.405	4.0522	3.0511	1.62439	.05369	.00347	3.4199	....	3.9325
Germany	1.5990	2.4577	1.1849	.89215	.47497	.01570	.00101	....	.29240	1.1499
Italy	1577.4	2424.5	1168.88	880.10	468.56	15.487	....	986.49	288.45	1134.3
Japan	101.85	156.54	75.472	56.826	30.254	....	.06457	63.696	18.625	73.24
Mexico	3.3665	5.1743	2.4946	1.8783	....	.03305	.00213	2.1054	.6156	2.4209
Netherlands ..	1.7923	2.7548	1.3281	....	.53239	.01760	.00114	1.1209	.32775	1.2889
Switzerland ...	1.3495	2.0742	....	.75294	.40086	.01325	.00086	.84396	.24678	.9704
U.K.	.65062	....	.48212	.36301	.19326	.00639	.00041	.40689	.11898	.46787
U.S.	....	1.5370	.74102	.55794	.29704	.00982	.00063	.62539	.18287	.71911

Source: The Wall Street Journal, June 21, 1994.

In practice, exchange rates are considered both ways. The Europeans and the Japanese tend to think of the exchange rate as the price of a foreign currency, whereas in Britain and in the United States, it is treated as the price of the home currency.

European and American Terms of Quotation

European terms

A system expressing the exchange rate of the U.S. dollar in terms all foreign currencies.

American terms

A system expressing exchange rates of all foreign currencies in terms of U.S. dollars.

Two widely used systems of quoting exchange rates are known as **European terms** and **American terms** of quotation. In European terms, the value of the U.S. dollar is expressed in terms of all other currencies. In American terms, the values of all foreign currencies are expressed in terms of U.S. dollars. American terms of quotation are commonly used in many retail currency transactions. In their dealings among themselves, banks use European terms of quotation except for quotes on the British pound, the Irish punt, the Australian dollar, and the New Zealand dollar. These currencies have been traditionally quoted in American terms.

The Wall Street Journal reports daily exchange rates in both European terms and American terms. Exhibit 2.4 illustrates this.

Cross Rates

cross rate

The exchange rate between two foreign currencies.

Exchange rates between pairs of currencies that do not involve the U.S. dollar, such as the rate between the German mark and the Swiss franc, are known as **cross rates**. The common practice of quoting exchange rates in either European or American terms requires an additional calculation to obtain cross rates from these quotations.

Consider the following quotes (in European terms) of Deutschemarks and Swiss francs against the U.S. dollar:

DM1.6240/$ and SF1.4625/$

The cross rate of the DM against the SF is obtained by dividing the DM/$ rate by the SF/$ rate, as shown below:

$$\text{DM/SF} = (\text{DM/\$})/(\text{SF/\$}) = 1.6240/1.4625 = \text{DM}1.1104/\text{SF}$$

This cross rate indicates that one Swiss franc is worth 1.1104 Deutschemarks. *The Wall Street Journal* also reports cross rates for a selected number of currencies, as shown in Exhibit 2.5.

Foreign Purchasing Power

foreign purchasing power
The purchasing power of a currency measured in terms of foreign goods and services.

The prices of goods and services within a country are expressed in terms of that country's currency. Prices are expressed in terms of U.S. dollars in the United States, in terms of Canadian dollars in Canada, in terms of yen in Japan, and so forth. In general, prices reflect the purchasing power of the currency in terms of which those prices are expressed. The purchasing power of a currency is measured by the reciprocal of the domestic price level. The exchange rate, being the price of one currency in terms of another, represents the **foreign purchasing power** of a currency.

If the price of a McDonald's Big Mac in the United States is $2.00, then the purchasing power of one U.S. dollar in terms of Big Macs is one-half of a Big Mac. If the price of a Big Mac in Canada is C$2.00, then the purchasing power of the Canadian dollar in terms of a Big Mac is also one-half of a Big Mac. Given these respective measures of domestic purchasing power, the foreign purchasing power of each of the Canadian and U.S. dollars is defined by their exchange rate. For example, at an exchange rate of $1 = C$1.20, the foreign purchasing power of one U.S. dollar in terms of Canadian Big Macs is three-fifths (C$1.20/C$2.00) of a Big Mac, and the foreign purchasing power of one Canadian dollar in terms of U.S. Big Macs is two-fifths (C$0.80/$2.00) of a Big Mac.

Foreign Exchange Market

foreign exchange (forex) market
An institutional and communications network for currency trading.

The **foreign exchange market** (*forex market*, for short) is an institutional and communications network like any other financial market. Its main functions include:

1. Facilitation of trading in currencies
2. Determination of exchange rates between currencies by the interaction of demand and supply forces
3. Facilitation of international fund transfers
4. Facilitation of trading in instruments for hedging currency risk

Transactions between two currencies, such as the U.S. dollar and the Canadian dollar, constitute a currency market. There are as many currency markets as pairs of currencies.

The market performs its trading function when it brings together buyers and sellers and facilitates the exchange of currencies. Buyers of a foreign currency typically include:

FOCUS ON CAREERS

CURRENCY TRADER

No specific academic discipline prepares one for a career in currency trading, although most employers insist that a prospective trader possess at least a bachelor's degree. The position requires ambition, self-motivation, and immense confidence under pressure. Exceptional ability to calculate and formulate profitable trading strategies quickly is essential.

Currency traders operate in the spot and forward markets for a wide range of currencies. Employed primarily by banks and other large currency dealers, they trade in currencies as hedgers, as speculators, or merely as agents carrying out the buy and sell orders of their clients.

Beginners gain experience by apprenticing themselves to veteran traders and observing. Salary is usually minimal, but the opportunity to earn commissions is excellent. It is not uncommon for a currency trader, especially one who works for a major dealer, to gross in six and even seven figures. The head currency trader for Salomon Brothers earned an estimated $28 million in1993, while Salomon's CEO earned only $7 million.

Currency trading is generally considered to be "life in the fast lane." The money is good, the pressure enormous, and the burnout rate very high. As with most aspects of finance, high return goes with high risk.

1. Importers (including travelers) who need the currency to settle payments denominated in the currency
2. Investors buying assets denominated in the currency
3. **Arbitragers** who simultaneously buy and sell currencies in different markets to profit from exchange rate differences
4. **Hedgers** who want to protect the value of their liabilities denominated in the currency
5. **Speculators** who seek to profit from a gain in the value of the currency.

arbitrager
Someone who buys and sells currencies to profit from exchange rate and interest rate differences.

hedger
Someone who buys and sells currencies to protect the value of assets and liabilities denominated in foreign currencies.

speculator
Someone who buys or sells currencies in the hope of profiting from their future changes.

Buyers of foreign currencies also act as sellers of their home currencies in the same market. For example, a U.S. resident who imports goods from Japan and needs yen to complete the transaction is a buyer of yen and seller of dollars in the yen–dollar market. Similarly, a U.S. resident who buys stock on the Frankfurt Stock Exchange becomes a buyer of Deutschemarks and a seller of dollars in the Deutschemark–dollar market. A Canadian who invests in yen, expecting its value to improve against the Canadian dollar, is a buyer of yen and a seller of Canadian dollars in the yen–Canadian dollar market.

Sellers of a foreign currency include:

1. Exporters who want to convert the proceeds of sales denominated in that currency into their currency
2. Investors who have sold assets denominated in the currency
3. Arbitragers
4. Hedgers who want to protect the values of assets denominated in the currency
5. Speculators who seek to profit from declines in the value of the currency

Sellers of foreign currencies also act as buyers of their own currencies in the same market. A U.S. resident who exports goods to Japan and wants to convert the yen receipts into dollars is a seller of yen and a buyer of dollars in the yen–dollar market. When Toys R Us sells toys in Japan for yen, it will be a seller of yen in the yen–dollar market. A Japanese investor who buys stocks listed on the New York Stock Exchange will be a seller of yen in the yen–dollar market.

Exchange Rate Determination. The completion of every international transaction in goods, services, or financial assets invariably calls for currency conversions and exchange rates. Historically, exchange rates have been determined either completely freely by the forces of demand and supply in the foreign exchange (forex) market, fixed by national governments, or determined by market forces with governments influencing their direction. The system that lets exchange rates respond freely to the interaction of demand and supply forces in the forex market is known as the **flexible-rate** or **floating-rate** system. The system that sets exchange rates by actions of official agencies (such as central banks and exchange authorities) of the individual countries is known as the **fixed-rate** system. The system that allows exchange rates to react primarily to market forces, although changes are actively managed by national governments, is known as the **managed-float system**.

flexible-rate (floating-rate) system
A system in which exchange rates depend entirely on the forces of demand and supply.

fixed-rate system
A system in which governments fix the exchange rates of their countries' currencies.

managed-float system
A system in which governments actively manage market-driven changes in the exchange rates of their currencies.

Exchange rates in a flexible-rate system are subject to extreme fluctuation because of frequent changes in underlying demand and supply conditions. If the demand for yen, for example, exceeds the supply in the yen–U.S. dollar market, then the exchange value of yen rises in terms of U.S. dollars, causing the yen to appreciate. An increase in the value of yen means a decline in the value (or depreciation) of the U.S. dollar. When one currency appreciates against another, the other currency must always depreciate against the first. Exchange rates under a fixed-rate system change infrequently, only when governments decide to lower (in a **devaluation**) or raise (in a **revaluation**) the values of their countries' currencies.

devaluation
A government act to reduce the external value of a currency.

revaluation
A government act to raise the external value of a currency.

The currency system that prevails in the world today is a mixture of floating-rate and fixed-rate systems. One group of countries operates under the floating-rate system, although some allow only limited flexibility. Another group of countries have pegged their currencies to one or more foreign currencies. The member countries of the European Community operate under a cooperative arrangement by pegging their currencies to other EC currencies.

International Funds Transfers. Settlements of payments in foreign currencies and international transfers of funds through the forex market do not involve physical exchanges of currencies. The forex market carries out these functions electronically with the support of two communication systems: the Society for Worldwide Interbank Financial Telecommunication (SWIFT) and the Clearinghouse Interbank Payment System (CHIPS). SWIFT is a Belgian not-for-profit cooperative that links banks and currency traders all over the world. The CHIPS is a network developed by the New York Clearing House Association and links about 140 banks located in New York City. It is mostly involved with transfers of international dollar payments.

FOCUS ON FINANCE

Brief History of the Exchange Rate System

Prior to 1914, every major currency was on a gold standard. Under this system, each country declared the value of its currency in terms of a specified amount of gold (a relationship called gold parity) and maintained this value within a narrow range. A fixed *gold parity* for each currency automatically establishes a system of fixed exchange rates among currencies. For example, the declared value of the U.S. dollar under the gold standard was $20.67 per ounce, and that of the British pound was £4.2474 per ounce. This implied a fixed exchange rate between the dollar and the pound of $20.67/£4.2474, or $4.8665/£.

World War I disrupted trade and the flow of gold, forcing the United States and the European countries to abandon the gold standard and switch to a floating-rate system in which currency values were determined by the market forces of demand and supply. However, excessive fluctuations in exchange rates caused by international speculation and inexperience in managing a floating-rate system had convinced most countries to return to the gold standard by 1925.

Because the gold parities were haphazardly chosen and resulted in unreasonable exchange rate patterns, this return to the gold standard was short-lived. In 1931, Britain was forced to suspend gold payments and revert back to floating rates. Other countries soon followed.

The floating-rate system that emerged in the 1930s was different from that of the 1920s, principally because governments actively controlled the movements of exchange rates instead of leaving them to the mercy of market forces. This approach, later termed *managed float,* relied heavily for its success on policy cooperation among trading nations. Such cooperation was tenuous during the difficult years that followed. Clashes occurred and the world had a taste of monetary chaos.

In 1944, just before World War II ended, the Allied nations signed an agreement at the Bretton Woods Conference to establish an international monetary system based on fixed rates. Each member nation agreed to establish a par value for its currency in terms of other currencies. This parity was to be maintained within 1 percent of par value through official intervention in the currency markets by buying and selling currencies or gold.

The U.S. dollar was designated as the key currency for maintaining reserves and undertaking official market interventions. This meant that member countries would fix the values of their currencies in terms of the U.S. dollar. By protecting the dollar parities of their currencies, individual countries could then stabilize their exchange rates with other currencies. Member countries could change these parities only with the approval of the International Monetary Fund (IMF) and only in response to fundamental changes in their economies.

Through a separate agreement, the United States government agreed to fix the value of its dollar at $35 per ounce of gold, and to buy and sell gold at this rate. With the U.S. dollar pegged to gold, every currency pegged to the U.S. dollar was indirectly pegged to gold at a price determined by its dollar parity.

The Bretton Woods System played a key role in promoting monetary stability and economic growth in the late 1940s and 1950s. It was not until the dollar became very unstable in the late 1960s that the system started breaking down. President Nixon suspended the convertibility of the dollar into gold on August 15, 1971, to stop the massive outflow of gold from the United States. Subsequent efforts to save the system through a realignment of currencies failed, and most countries allowed their currencies to float.

By the beginning of 1973, it was clear that the Bretton Woods fixed-rate system was no longer workable. It was replaced by a hybrid of floating-rate and fixed-rate systems.

If a New York resident sends British pounds to a resident of London, for example, no British pound notes actually move from New York to London. Instead, a U.S. bank sends instructions through SWIFT to a bank in London to credit the British pounds to the account of the receiver. The London bank credits the account of the receiver, and, at the same time, debits the account of the U.S. bank.

Dealers. Commercial banks are the major participants in the forex market. They act as dealers in foreign exchange by selling foreign currencies to buyers and buying foreign currencies from sellers. A U.S. resident heading for Japan can buy yen without worrying about locating a seller of yen. The transaction simply requires locating a bank that deals in currencies. Individuals as well as commercial users such as exporters, importers, and multinational corporations all depend on banks for their foreign exchange needs. Banks also buy and sell foreign exchange among themselves, and the sizes of these interbank transactions far outweigh the banks' transactions with their commercial customers. In addition to commercial banks, a small number of nonbank currency dealers also operate in the forex market.

Bid–Ask Format. Currency dealers such as banks quote rates to each other in a bid–ask format. A bid price is the rate at which a dealer is willing to buy a currency, and an ask price is the rate at which a dealer is willing to sell a currency. If a bank's quote for an exchange of DM against the U.S. dollar is DM1.6040–DM1.6100/$, it means that the bank is willing to buy dollars at DM1.6040, and it is willing to sell dollars at DM1.6100.

Note that the ask price is always higher than the bid price. A banks typically quotes a single rate when it deals with a commercial customer. It quotes a bid rate or an ask rate depending on whether the customer is a seller or a buyer.

The bid–ask spread can vary widely across currencies depending on the activity in the currency market. The spread between the ask and the bid is a source of profit for the dealer. Currency dealers do not charge each other separate fees for buying and selling currencies.

Types of Forex Market Transactions

The forex market provides for the buying and selling of currencies for both immediate and future delivery. It serves both individuals and businesses.

spot transaction
Buying or selling a currency for immediate delivery.

spot rate
The exchange rate charged for the immediate delivery of a foreign currency.

Spot Transactions. If a market participant enters into a trade for the delivery of a foreign currency within two business days, this is classified as a **spot transaction**. The exchange rate at which a spot transaction takes place is called the **spot rate**. When a couple of foreign tourists walk into a bank in Miami to buy U.S. dollars, they are participating in the spot market for dollars. Spot transactions between dealers and their commercial customers are usually settled by immediate delivery. Dealer-to-dealer (interbank) spot transactions may take longer to settle, especially if the parties are located in different parts of the world. The settlement of spot transactions among dealers is usually completed by exchanging bank deposits in the respective currencies. A spot buyer or seller of a currency may be a commercial user, hedger, arbitrager, or speculator.

Forward Transactions. If a market participant enters into an agreement with a bank to take or make delivery of a foreign currency on a future date at a predetermined exchange rate, this is classified as a **forward transaction**. A bank is always one party in a forward transaction, and the predetermined exchange rate is called a **forward rate**. Forward rates are quoted in European terms. Most forward contracts are written for periods ranging from 1 to 12 months, and they are confined to about 20 actively traded currencies.

forward transaction
Buying and selling currency for delivery at a future date.

forward rate
The exchange rate for delivery of a foreign currency at a future date under a forward contract.

Making a forward contract that requires taking delivery of currency at a future date is called *buying currency forward*. An agreement to deliver currency at a future date is called *selling currency forward*. A forward contract is settled by taking or making delivery of the currency in question at the end of the specified period. No money changes hands when the contract is written.

Forward market participants typically include interest rate arbitragers, hedgers, and speculators. These arbitragers buy and sell currencies simultaneously in spot and forward markets to profit from interest rate differences. A dealer might buy Deutschemarks in the spot market and sell Deutschemarks forward at the same time to lock in a sure profit in an arbitrage transaction.

Hedgers participate in the forward market to protect the domestic-currency values of their assets and liabilities that are denominated in foreign currencies. If a U.S. importer of wines has an account payable in French francs due in three months, this account payable constitutes a short-term foreign currency liability of the importer. The dollar cost of settling this liability in three months is open to **exchange rate risk**.

exchange rate risk
The possibility that the value of an asset or a liability denominated in a foreign currency will change due to a change in the exchange rate.

If the French franc appreciates against the dollar, the dollar cost of the wine rises; if it depreciates against the dollar, the dollar cost falls. The importer may want to protect the dollar cost of this liability against such uncertainty. Buying a three-month forward contract in French francs allows the importer to lock in the dollar cost of the wine at the current forward rate. Forward contracts in currencies are widely used to hedge against exchange rate risk in this way.

Forward contracts are also used for speculation. If a dealer buys British pounds forward from another dealer with the hope of making profits from the future appreciation of the British pound, it is a speculative transaction in the forward market. Speculative transactions in forward contracts generally occur in the dealer market. Banks do not encourage commercial customers to use forward contracts for speculation.

Currency Futures and Options Markets

The International Monetary Market (a division of the Chicago Mercantile Exchange) introduced currency futures contracts in 1972. The Philadelphia Stock Exchange initiated currency option contracts in 1983 and they spread to other exchanges in later years. These instruments have provided additional tools for speculation and hedging in the currency market.

futures rate
The exchange rate specified for delivery of a foreign currency at a future date under a futures contract.

marking to market
A procedure that adjusts an account balance for the daily gain or loss from a futures transaction.

strike price
The price of the underlying asset at which an option contract is exercised.

call option
A contract between a buyer and a writer that gives the buyer a right, but not an obligation, to buy a certain quantity of an underlying asset at a predetermined price on (or perhaps before) a certain date.

put option
A contract between a buyer and a writer that gives the buyer a right, but not an obligation, to sell a certain quantity of an underlying asset at a predetermined price on (or perhaps before) a certain date.

Currency Futures. A currency futures contract promises delivery of a specific quantity of a currency at a predetermined exchange rate (called the **futures rate**) on a set future delivery date. Participants in the futures market are required to maintain margin accounts with brokers and pay brokerage fees.

The buyer of a futures contract acquires a long position in currency futures; the seller acquires a short position. The settlement of the futures contract follows a method known as **marking to market**. Under this method, profit and loss are determined on a daily basis. If the futures rate rises on a given trading day, the holder of a long position is credited with the profit and the holder of a short position is debited for the loss.

A futures position is usually closed out by taking an opposite position on or before the expiration date. Less than 5 percent of contracts are settled by delivery of currencies. Thus, about 95 percent of currency futures amount to bets on the future directions of exchange rates, rather than contracts for delivery of specific quantities of currencies. Someone who buys a currency futures contract (goes long) one is betting that the exchange rate of that currency will go up; someone who sells a currency futures contract (goes short) is betting that the exchange rate will go down. If the exchange rate goes up, the buyer (the long position) makes money and the seller (the short position) loses money. If the exchange rate falls, the buyer loses and the seller gains.

Traders buy and sell currency futures only on government-regulated exchanges with the help of brokers. The sizes and maturities of the futures contracts are standardized by the exchanges that trade them. The two U.S. exchanges that trade in currency futures are the International Monetary Market and the New York Futures Exchange (a subsidiary of the New York Stock Exchange).

Hedging with currency futures is similar to hedging with forward contracts. If one has assets denominated in a foreign currency and wants to protect or lock in their domestic currency values, one sells foreign currency futures. If one has liabilities denominated in a foreign currency and wants to protect their domestic currency values, one buys foreign currency futures. When hedged this way, a decline (or rise) in the domestic currency value of the asset because of a depreciation (or appreciation) of the foreign currency is offset by the gain (or loss) on the futures contract.

Speculation in the currency futures market involves buying when one expects the futures rate to rise and selling when one expects the futures rate to fall. This market is open to all interested parties.

Currency Options. Currency option contracts confer on the buyer a right, but not an obligation, to buy or sell a given quantity of a spot currency or a currency futures contract at a predetermined price (called the **strike price**) on or before a specified date. A **call option** contract gives the owner a right to buy; a **put option**

option premium
The market price of an option contract.

European option
An option contract that can be exercised only on the expiration date.

American option
An option contract that can be exercised on or any time before the expiration date.

gives a right to sell. The option buyer pays the seller (the option writer) a price (called the **option premium**) for the contract. The spot currency or futures contract specified in an option is known as the *underlying asset*. An option is a **European option** or an **American option**, depending on whether it can be exercised only on a specific date or at any time up to a specific date.

Options on spot currencies are traded both over the counter and on exchanges. Options on currency futures contracts are traded only on the exchanges. The currency amounts and expiration dates are standardized for exchange-traded options; these terms are negotiated for over-the-counter options. In the United States, spot currency options are traded on the Philadelphia Stock Exchange (PHLX), and options on currency futures contracts trade on the Chicago Mercantile Exchange (CME).

Hedging with option contracts follows the same principles as techniques that use forward and futures contracts. One takes an option position opposite to the position one wants to hedge. Someone with assets denominated in a foreign currency would buy a put option, a right to sell foreign currency at a predetermined exchange rate. Someone with liabilities denominated in a foreign currency would buy a call option, a right to buy foreign currency at a predetermined exchange rate. In this way, one can offset the loss (or gain) in the value of the asset due to a depreciation (or appreciation) in the foreign currency with a gain (or loss) on the option contract.

Option contracts give the hedger one major advantage: when the exchange rate moves in favor of the hedger (i.e, the foreign currency appreciates when an asset is hedged, or the foreign currency depreciates when a liability is hedged), the hedger can take advantage of the favorable rate without exercising the option. This is not possible when one uses forward or futures contracts for hedging. A forward contract locks in the rate and the contract to exchange currencies is binding. When the exchange rate moves favorably, a futures contract can only be sold at a loss. The gain from the favorable rate change will be wiped out by the loss.

A speculator in the options market would buy a call option if the spot exchange rate were expected to rise above the strike price; the speculator would buy a put option if it were expected to fall below the strike price. If the expectation proves correct, the speculator profits from the difference between the spot rate and strike price. This profit possibility is theoretically unlimited. If the expectation is wrong, the speculator has the choice of selling the option and minimizing the loss, or letting the option expire and limiting the loss to the premium cost.

Effect of Inflation on Exchange Rates

As mentioned before, the exchange rate represents a currency's foreign purchasing power. If foreign prices rise and the exchange rate does not change, then the foreign purchasing power of the home currency declines. The Big Mac example sets the foreign purchasing power of the U.S. dollar in terms of Canadian Big Macs at three-fifths of a Big Mac when the exchange rate was $1 = C$1.20 and Big Mac prices in the United States and Canada were $2.00 and C$2.00 respectively.

EXHIBIT 2.6

Inflation Rates and Exchange Rates (end of period)

	United States		Germany		Japan	
	Inflation Rate	Exchange Rate SDR*/$	Inflation Rate	Exchange Rate DM/$	Inflation Rate	Exchange Rate ¥/$
1980	13.48%	0.7841	5.48%	1.9590	7.77%	203.00
1981	10.31	0.8591	6.29	2.2548	4.92	219.90
1982	6.15	0.9065	5.23	2.3765	2.73	235.00
1983	3.23	0.9552	3.35	2.7238	1.81	232.20
1984	4.32	1.0202	2.41	3.1480	2.30	251.10
1985	3.52	0.9104	2.16	2.4613	2.04	200.50
1986	1.90	0.8175	0.10	1.9408	0.60	159.10
1987	3.73	0.7049	0.20	1.5815	0.09	123.50
1988	3.97	0.7431	1.30	1.7803	0.69	125.85
1989	4.82	0.7609	2.76	1.6978	2.27	143.45
1990	5.38	0.7029	2.69	1.4940	3.09	134.40
1991	4.28	0.6991	3.46	1.5160	3.27	125.20
1992	3.00	0.7273	4.07	1.6140	1.72	124.75

*The value of the SDR is a weighted average of the values of a basket of currencies comprised of the U.S. dollar, the Deutschemark, the French franc, the British pound, and the Japanese yen.
Source: *International Financial Statistics Yearbook*, IMF.

What happens if the price of a Canadian Big Mac rises to C$3.00 due to inflation, and the exchange rate does not change? The domestic purchasing power of the Canadian dollar is reduced from one-half to one-third (C$1/C$3.00) of a Big Mac, and its foreign purchasing power in terms of U.S. Big Macs is unchanged. As a result, one Canadian dollar now buys more Big Macs in the United States than it does in Canada. The foreign purchasing power of the U.S. dollar is reduced from three-fifths to two-fifths (C$1.20/C$3.00) of a Canadian Big Mac at the prevailing exchange rate.

At a given exchange rate between the U.S. dollar and the Canadian dollar, inflation in Canada will make U.S. goods cheaper for Canadian buyers and Canadian goods more expensive for U.S. buyers. Under the flexible exchange rate system, these market forces will put pressure on the exchange rate. As Canadians increase their imports of cheaper U.S. goods, the demand for U.S. dollars will increase in the currency market. As United States residents reduce their imports of expensive Canadian goods, the supply of U.S. dollars will decrease in the currency market. The Canadian dollar will depreciate and the U.S. dollar will appreciate, unless there is an offsetting change in the demand and supply of U.S. dollars resulting from financial transactions between Canada and the United States. The opposite result will follow if inflation raises prices in the United States relative to those in Canada.

In general, the relationship between inflation and the exchange rate is such that the home currency tends to appreciate when the inflation rate abroad rises, and it tends to depreciate when the inflation rate at home rises. If both foreign and domestic prices rise simultaneously, the exchange rate may remain unaffected. Exhibit 2.6 illustrates the relationship between U.S., German, and Japanese inflation rates and exchange rates.

Effect of Interest Rates on Exchange Rates

Changes in domestic and foreign interest rates affect exchange rates just as changes in domestic and foreign inflation rates do. The connection between domestic and foreign interest rates and the exchange rate is established primarily by arbitrage transactions between the two financial markets.

Variations in interest rates may create opportunities to move funds between two currency markets to lock in a gain by taking advantage of the differences. This is known as *interest rate arbitrage*. These opportunities also depend on the spot and forward exchange rates that prevail at the time. A typical arbitrage transaction locks in a higher return from investing in another currency market by simultaneously buying that currency in the spot market and selling the same currency in the forward market.

Interest rate arbitrage involves borrowing in one currency, buying another currency in the spot market, investing the proceeds in the second currency market, and selling the expected proceeds of the investment immediately for the original currency in the forward market. All four activities are carried out simultaneously. The investor can calculate the outcome of this transaction immediately based on readily available information on the spot rate, the forward rate, and the interest rates.

The following example illustrates how such an opportunity is exploited. Assume that spot and one-year forward rates between the Deutschemark and the U.S. dollar (DM/$) are DM1.6040/$ and DM1.6250/$, respectively. Also assume that lending/borrowing rates in the dollar and Deutschemark markets are 5 percent and 8 percent, respectively. Since the German interest rate is higher than the U.S. interest rate by 3 percent, borrowing money in the dollar market and lending it in the Deutschemark market should generate a 3 percent profit. One cannot jump to that conclusion, however, without considering the exchange rates in the spot and forward markets. Though the Deutschemark interest rate is higher, the true return for a U.S. investor in the Deutschemark market is the balance that remains after adjusting for the loss or gain in the forward market currency exchange.

In this example, investing in the Deutschemark market brings 3 percent more return than that obtained from investing in the dollar market. To compute the dollar return, one must adjust the Deutschemark return for the loss in the exchange value of Deutschemarks when they are converted to U.S. dollars in the forward market. In the spot market, a U.S. dollar fetches 1.6040 Deutschemarks, but when Deutschemarks are sold in the forward market, a U.S. dollar costs DM1.6250. This makes the dollar return from investing in the Deutschemark market smaller than the Deutschemark return. The determination of the dollar return from investing in the Deutschemark market using a hypothetical amount of $1,000 is illustrated below:

Proceeds from converting dollars into Deutschemarks at the spot rate of DM1.6040/$	DM1,604.00
Proceeds from lending in the Deutschemark market (DM1,604×1.08)	DM1,732.32
The proceeds from converting Deutschemarks to dollars in the forward market (DM1,732.32/1.6250)	$1,066.04
Dollar rate of return from investing in the Deutschemark market {[($1,066.04 – $1,000)/$1,000]×100}	6.60 percent

Note that the gain from lending funds in the Deutschemark market instead of the dollar market is only 1.6 (6.60 – 5.00) percent compared to the interest rate difference of 3 percent. This is the result of the depreciation of Deutschemarks in the forward market.

If the forward rate had been much higher than DM1.6250/$, say DM1.6550/$, then the transaction would have resulted in a lower dollar return. If the Deutschemark interest rate had been 6 percent instead of 8 percent, the transaction would also have resulted in a lower dollar return. This analysis suggests that the possibility of locking in a sure gain by moving funds between two currency markets depends on the difference between interest rates in the two markets and the spread between spot and forward exchange rates.

Movements of funds between currency markets in search of higher returns will eventually end as the exchange rates and the interest rates respond to such movements and eliminate the opportunity to lock in a gain. In the above example, as funds moved from dollars to Deutschemarks, they would put pressure on both exchange rates and interest rates. The spot rate would be pushed downward (dollars would depreciate and Deutschemarks would appreciate) as the demand for spot Deutschemarks rose; the forward rate would be pushed upward (forward dollars would appreciate and forward Deutschemarks would depreciate) as the supply of Deutschemarks rose. This would increase the spread between spot and forward exchange rates.

On the interest rate side, dollar interest rates would rise as more dollars moved abroad and the prices of dollar-denominated securities fell because of reduced demand. Deutschemark interest rates would fall as prices of Deutschemark-denominated securities rose because of increased demand. This would narrow the difference between dollar and Deutschemark interest rates. The exchange rates and the interest rates would eventually form a configuration that would eliminate any gain from moving funds between currency markets.

The preceding discussion suggests a definite relationship between exchange rates and interest rates in the respective currency markets. If interest rates in one currency market rise relative to interest rates in another currency market, the movement of investable funds between the markets will cause the currency whose interest rates have risen to appreciate in the spot market and depreciate in the forward market against the currency of the other country. In general, countries with rising interest rates will have depreciating currencies and vice versa, if funds are allowed to move freely between markets.

Predicting and Coping with Changes in Exchange Rates

Changes in exchange rates result from the interactions of demand and supply forces in currency markets under the flexible rate system, and from official devaluations or revaluations under the fixed rate system. Spot and future rates are interrelated, with future rates either higher or lower than the spot rate. As exchange rates change over time, they affect the outcomes of investment and business decisions that involve assets, liabilities, and cash flows denominated in foreign currencies.

If a U.S. investor has purchased bonds traded in the Tokyo market, the movement in the dollar–yen rate will affect the return on this investment. In general, exchange rate changes make the returns from foreign investments uncertain and expose them to exchange rate risk. The foreign exchange market provides a number of instruments through which investors and asset owners can protect (hedge) their returns and asset values against exchange rate risk.

In the absence of accurate foresight about future exchange rates, market participants have to rely on expectations. They form exchange rate expectations on the basis of currently available information. Forming expectations or forecasting future exchange rates is an essential part of the financial and economic decision making process. Commercial users of foreign exchange such as exporters, importers, and multinational corporations, as well as bank and nonbank currency dealers, use currency forecasts in their business decisions. They often use forward market rates as forecasts of future spot rates for those currencies that have forward markets.

Suppose that a U.S. currency dealer has bought more Deutschemarks than it sold on a given day in its dealings with commercial customers. The dealer is left with Deutschemarks, which may lose or gain value over time, exposing the dealer to exchange rate risk. The dealer has two choices: to get rid of the excess Deutschemarks in the interbank market and eliminate the currency risk, or to hold onto them. The dealer's decision will be influenced by the expected future Deutschemark rate. If the dealer feels strongly that the Deutschemark will appreciate in the future, it may take no action and maintain the Deutschemark balance. This is a purely speculative strategy.

Different market participants often form different expectations about future exchange rates based on their views of future economic conditions. It is, in fact, the presence of differing views of the future that explains much of the trading in the currency market. Better-informed market participants will make better forecasts and, hence, higher profits.

SUMMARY

Inflation rates, interest rates, and exchange rates represent fundamental forces in the economy that influence the outcomes of business and financial decisions, and hence the direction of economic activities. The phenomenon of continuously increasing prices is called *inflation*. The inflation rate is the percentage change in the general price level over a specified period of time. Inflation reduces the purchasing power of money and other assets denominated in monetary units. Changes in inflation are tracked by a measure known as a *price index*.

Inflation is caused by changes in a number of economic factors. These factors include the money stock, the level of output, interest rates, labor productivity, and the exchange rate. The far-reaching effects of inflation include redistribution of income and wealth, influence on a country's international trade and financial activities, and general uncertainty and loss of confidence. Governments usually try to control inflation by manipulating their money stocks.

The compensation paid for lending money is called *interest*. The interest rate is the percentage of the loan amount paid as compensation. Interest is a source of income to the lender and a cost to the borrower. In a free-market system, interest rates are determined by the interaction of demand and supply forces. The level of interest rates is affected by changes in economic factors such as the money stock, output, the inflation rate, and exchange rates. Governments try to control interest rate changes primarily by manipulating the money stock.

An exchange rate is the price of one currency expressed in terms of another currency. Exchange rates are commonly quoted either in European terms or American terms. In European terms of quotation, the value of a U.S. dollar is expressed in terms of all other currencies. In American terms of quotation, the values of all other currencies are expressed in terms of U.S. dollars.

Historically, exchange rates have been determined either by the market forces of demand and supply (the floating-rate system), by official government agencies (the fixed-rate system), or by a combination of the two (the system of managed float).

The foreign exchange market is the network that brings buyers and sellers of currencies together and facilitates exchanges of currencies. Each pair of currencies has a market of its own. The rate quotation in the forex market uses a bid–ask format. Major currencies are traded for both spot and forward delivery in the forex market. Futures and option contracts trade in a limited number of currencies on official exchanges and over the counter.

Exchange rates, interest rates, and inflation rates are interrelated. Changes in one can cause the others to change. The relationships between these rates can be summarized briefly:

1. Increases in inflation rates cause interest rates to rise via the Fisher effect.
2. Countries with higher inflation will have depreciating currencies; countries with lower inflation will have appreciating currencies.
3. Countries with higher interest rates will have depreciating currencies; countries with lower interest rates will have appreciating currencies.

The outcomes of business decisions are affected by the future values of these rates. Therefore, business decision makers must base their decisions on expectations of future values of these rates. Expectations formed by individual decision makers may differ depending on the information available to them, and on their perceptions of the future. The frequent observed changes in these rates result in part from changing expectations.

Key Terms

American option
American terms
arbitragers
balance of payments
barter system
Bretton Woods System
call option
consumer price index
cost-push theory
cross rate
deflation
demand-pull theory
devaluation
disinflation
equilibrium interest rate
European option
European terms
exchange rate
exchange rate risk
Fisher effect
fixed-rate system
flexible-rate (floating-rate) system
foreign exchange market
foreign purchasing power
forward transaction
forward rate
futures rate
hedger
hyperinflation
inflation
inflation risk
interest
marking to market
managed-float system
money stock
option premium
price index
purchasing power of money
put option
revaluation
speculator
spot rate
spot transaction
stagflation
strike price
velocity of money
zero inflation

Self-Study Questions

1. Define *inflation*, *disinflation*, *hyperinflation*, and *deflation*.
2. Explain the relationship between the money stock and inflation. Does it always hold?
3. How does inflation affect fixed-income recipients? Creditors?
4. Why do borrowers pay and lenders demand the payment of interest?
5. Why do interest rates change? Why is it important to regulate the level of interest rates?
6. Who are the buyers and sellers of currencies in the forex market?
7. Discuss the role of commercial banks in the forex market.
8. What is hedging? Who uses the currency market for hedging?
9. You want to secure the U.S. dollar value of an asset denominated in Australian dollars using a forward contract. What forward market strategy will you follow?
10. What are currency futures? Name two U.S. markets in which currency futures are traded.

Self-Test Problems

1. Calculate the inflation rates for 1988, 1989, and 1990 from the CPI data given below:

YEAR	CPI[a]
1987	115.4
1988	120.5
1989	126.1
1990	133.8
1991	137.9

[a](Base years 1982–1984 = 100)

2. If a nominal interest rate is 5 percent and the anticipated inflation rate is 3 percent, what is the real rate of interest?
3. On June 29, 1993, *The Wall Street Journal* reported the exchange rates of the Swiss franc and the Deutschemark against the U.S. dollar as SF1.5065/$ and DM1.6985/$. What is the implied cross rate of the Swiss franc with respect to the Deutschemark?
4. Suppose the exchange rate between the Canadian dollar and the U.S. dollar is C$1.25/$, and the price of a pound of ham is $1.00 in the United States and C$1.25 in Canada.
   (a) What is the foreign purchasing power of the U.S. dollar in terms of Canadian ham?
   (b) If the price of ham in the United States rises, what happens to the foreign purchasing power of Canadian dollars in terms of U.S. ham? (Assume that the exchange rate does not change.)
5. What should arbitragers do if the following interest rates and exchange rates prevail in the market? What is the arbitrage gain?

Swiss interest rate (annual)	6.5%
U.S. interest rate (annual)	5.5%
Spot U.S. dollar rate	SF1.4350
180-day forward U.S. dollar rate	SF1.4225

Discussion Questions

1. Explain what is meant by *inflation*. How is it measured?
2. Identify and discuss the main causes of inflation.
3. What is disinflation? Identify a post-World War II period during which the United States has experienced disinflation. (Refer to Exhibit 2.1.)
4. What are the consequences of inflation? Why do some countries treat inflation as their primary problem?
5. Explain what is meant by *inflation risk*. Give an example of exposure to inflation risk.
6. How and under what condition(s) is inflation exported from one country to another?

7. Explain why an increase in the money stock is a necessary condition for inflation.
8. Interest payments are a form of compensation. Discuss.
9. Identify the economic factors that generally affect interest rates.
10. What is the relationship between the nominal interest rate and the expected inflation rate?
11. If bond investors expect interest rates to go up in the future, what investment strategy should they follow?
12. Describe the functions of the foreign exchange market.
13. Identify two potential buyers of yen in the yen–dollar market. How would an increase in the U.S. income level affect the demand for yen in the yen–dollar market?
14. Identify two potential sellers of yen in the yen–dollar market. How would a decline in the Japanese stock market affect the supply of yen in the yen–dollar market?
15. A dealer gives the following bid–ask quote for the U.S. dollar in terms of the Deutschemark: DM1.6843–DM1.6900. Identify and explain the bid and ask prices.
16. Why is the ask price higher than the bid price in a bid–ask quotation?
17. What is interest rate arbitrage? Describe one such arbitrage transaction.
18. Discuss the uses of currency futures and option contracts.
19. A lot of time and effort is spent forecasting inflation rates, interest rates, and exchange rates. Why is it necessary to forecast these rates?
20. What are the expected relationships between (1) the inflation rate and the exchange rate and (2) the interest rate and the exchange rate?

Problems

1. Using the CPI data in Exhibit 2.1, calculate the inflation rates for 1981, 1983, 1989, and the period from 1981 to 1990.
2. Nancy Lockwood's family income rose from $45,000 in 1985 to $60,000 in 1993. The CPI rose from 107.6 (1982–1984 = 100) to 140.3 during the same period. Is Nancy Lockwood's family better off in 1993 than it was in 1985?
3. If lenders wanted a 2 percent real rate and the expected inflation rate were 3.5 percent, what risk-free nominal rate would they charge?
4. If a dollar is worth DM1.7120, what is the dollar value of a Deutschemark?
5. If the DM/$ rates at the end of two consecutive days are DM1.658/$ and DM1.645/$, which currency is depreciating and which is appreciating? What is the percentage change?
6. If the exchange rates of the Canadian dollar and the Deutschemarks against the U.S. dollar are C$1.20/$ and DM1.65/$ respectively, what is the cross rate between the Canadian dollar and the Deutschemark (C$/DM)?
7. An investor expects the C$/$ rate to go up by 20 percent in one year. The current one-year yield on a Canadian certificate of deposit is 8 percent

while a similar security in the United States yields 6 percent. Should the investor buy Canadian certificates of deposit? Explain your answer.

8. A U.S. firm needs \$1 million for one year. It could borrow in the U.S. market at 7 percent per annum, or in the U.K. market at 7.75 percent per annum. If spot and one-year forward exchange rates between the dollar and the pound sterling are \$1.4850/£ and \$1.4650/£, respectively, where should the firm borrow?
9. Using the information given below, determine the return that you can lock in by moving funds:
   (a) From the dollar market to the British pound market
   (b) From the British pound market to the dollar market

British pound–dollar spot rate	£0.6680/\$
British pound–dollar six-month forward rate	£0.6750/\$
U.S. interest rate (annual)	6.00 percent
British interest rate (annual)	7.50 percent

10. Global Property Management Co. has assets in Brussels worth 10 million Belgian francs. Assume that the spot and the one-year expected future spot exchange rates between the Belgian franc and the U.S. dollar are BF35.75/\$ and BF37.50/\$, respectively.
    (a) What is the current dollar value of Global Property Management's assets?
    (b) What is expected to happen to the dollar value of these assets in the next year if their value in Belgium francs remains the same?
    (c) What could Global Property Management do to protect the current dollar value of its assets?

Topics for Further Research

1. Select two countries and collect monthly data on their CPIs and exchange rates over a one-year period. Determine the percentage change in the foreign purchasing power of each country's currency in terms of the other's goods. (Possible source of data: *International Financial Statistics*)
2. Obtain exchange rate or interest rate forecasts for some past forecasting periods and compare the forecasts with the actual change in the exchange rate or the interest rate.
3. Collect price data for two consecutive trading days on a British pound futures contract and calculate the profit/loss on a long position. (Source: *The Wall Street Journal*)

Answers to Self-Test Problems

1. Inflation rates:

$$1988: [(120.5/115.4) - 1]\times 100 = (1.0442 - 1)\times 100 = 4.42 \text{ percent}$$

$$1989: [(126.1/120.5) - 1]\times 100 = (1.0465 - 1)\times 100 = 4.65 \text{ percent}$$

$$1990: [(133.8/126.1) - 1]\times 100 = (1.0611 - 1)\times 100 = 6.11 \text{ percent}$$

2. Real rate of interest = Nominal rate – Expected inflation rate

   = 0.05 – 0.03 = 0.02 or 2 percent

3. DM/SF = (DM/$)/(SF/$) = DM1.6985/SF1.5065 = DM1.1274/SF
4. (a) Since one U.S. dollar is worth C$1.25 and the price of Canadian ham is C$1.25 per pound, the foreign purchasing power of the U.S. dollar is one pound of Canadian ham.
   (b) The foreign purchasing power of Canadian dollars in terms of U.S. ham falls.
5. Strategy 1: Borrow in the Swiss market and invest in the U.S. market. Assume that SF100 is borrowed.

Proceeds from converting Swiss francs into U.S. dollars at the spot rate of SF1.4350/$	$69.69
Proceeds from lending $69.69 for 180 days in the U.S. market: $69.69[1+(0.055/2)]	$71.61
Proceeds from converting U.S. dollars to Swiss francs in the forward market: $71.61(1.4225)	SF101.86
Cost of settling the Swiss loan: SF100[1+(0.065/2)]	SF103.25
Gain (loss)	(SF1.39)
or	(1.39%)

Strategy 2: Borrow in the U.S. market and invest in the Swiss market. Assume that $100 is borrowed.

Proceeds from converting U.S. dollars into Swiss francs at the spot rate of SF1.4350/$	SF143.50
Proceeds from lending SF143.50 for 180 days in the Swiss market: SF143.50[1+(0.065/2)]	SF148.16
Proceeds from converting Swiss francs to U.S. dollars in the forward market: $148.16/1.4225	$104.15
Cost of settling the U.S. loan: $100[1+(0.055/2)]	$102.75
Gain (loss)	$1.40
or	1.40%

Arbitrage capital will move from the U.S. market to the Swiss market to reap a gain of 1.40 percent.

CHAPTER

3

Financial Institutions

LEARNING OBJECTIVES

This chapter introduces various types of financial institutions and explains what they are, what services they offer, and how they are regulated. At the conclusion of this chapter, the reader should:

1. *Recognize differences among depository, nondepository, and other financial institutions*
2. *Choose the appropriate financial institution to provide needed financial service*
3. *Understand the functions of regulatory agencies*
4. *Identify the regulatory agency that has authority over a given segment of the financial system*
5. *Understand the international dimensions of the activities of U.S. financial institutions*
6. *Understand the purposes and functions of the major international financial institutions*

People need many financial services from childhood through old age, and their familiarity with these services usually develops gradually. The first financial institution most children contact is the local bank and the first financial service they use (perhaps unwillingly) is usually a savings account. Exposure to other bank services follows, as adolescents discover checking accounts, tuition loans, credit cards, and car loans, though not necessarily in that order. A driver's license is often the impetus for one's first contact with another financial institution, an insurance company. Employment brings awareness of health insurance and investment services provided by brokers, mutual funds, and pension funds. Marriage and potential home ownership may introduce savings and loan associations, real estate agencies, mortgage bankers, life insurance companies, and trust fund managers.

A business firm deals with banking institutions, lenders, insurance companies, investment advisors and managers, and the myriad services provided by Wall Street from the time it is established. A financial manager needs to know about all of these financial institutions and services, and more, to make intelligent decisions regarding their use.

U.S. FINANCIAL INSTITUTIONS

transactions balance
Cash balance kept in anticipation of needs to pay for future purchases goods and services.

precautionary balance
Cash balance set aside to meet unexpected needs.

investment opportunity balance
The retention of investment funds as cash in anticipation of better future investment opportunities. Also called speculative balance.

financial institution
A company whose principal business involves selecting, holding, or transferring financial assets. Not all financial institutions are financial intermediaries.

depository institution
A company that accepts deposits, makes loans, transfers funds, obtains needed currency supplies, manages investments, and provides custodial services.

Corporations and individuals accumulate cash for several reasons:

1. They anticipate needs to pay for future purchases of goods and services. Cash balances that are put aside for such purposes are referred to as **transactions balances**.
2. They are concerned that they might need money unexpectedly. Cash balances that are reserved "for a rainy day" are referred to as **precautionary balances**.
3. Their incomes exceed their expenses. They usually accumulate excess cash balances and then invest them to produce additional returns. These balances are referred to as **investment opportunity balances** or speculative balances.

Where should these balances be kept? The standard, impulsive answer is almost always "in a bank." A generic, but more technically correct, response would be "in a financial institution." A **financial institution** is a company whose principal business involves selecting, holding, or transferring financial assets while matching the diverse needs of lenders and borrowers. In the United States, three types of financial institutions hold cash balances: depository, nondepository, and other financial service institutions.

Depository Institutions

Depository institutions are companies that accept deposits, make loans, transfer funds, obtain needed currency supplies, manage investments, and provide custodial services. The four types of depository institutions include commercial banks, savings and loan associations, savings banks, and credit unions. The distinctions among them are subtle today, but they have been significant in the past. Although each of these four types of depository financial institutions has a different history and background, all have come to offer very similar services to the public. Each type has lobbied Congress for the legal right to compete with the other three while protecting its own exclusive market. As a result, the rights of all have been expanded to encroach on each others' territories.

Commercial Banks. Commercial banks take all types of deposits in the forms of savings, checking, time, and special-purpose accounts (tax deposit accounts for corporations and Christmas/Chanukah Club accounts for individuals). They make

EXHIBIT 3.1

Assets of All Commercial Banks ($ billions)[a]

Real estate loans	$ 915.9	24.8%
Securities held for investment	850.1	23.0
Commercial and industrial loans	585.7	15.8
Loans to individuals	379.0	10.3
Other assets	322.1	8.7
Other loans	277.8	7.5
Cash assets	222.0	6.0
Interbank loans	145.3	3.9
Total Assets	$3,697.9	100.0%

[a]As of September 29, 1993.
Source: *Federal Reserve Bulletin* 79, no. 12 (December 1993), p. A20.

all kinds of loans: unsecured loans or loans secured by assets, loans to be paid off the next day or in the next decade, and/or loans to be repaid according to schedule, ability to repay, or on demand by the bank. Commercial banks also invest money, manage portfolios of securities, and bring some types of new securities to the public. They exchange foreign currencies on the spot and write forward contracts that promise deliveries of foreign currencies at future dates. Historically, banks have preferred to deal only with corporations and wealthy individuals, but today they aggressively compete to offer their services to everyone. Exhibit 3.1 summarizes the assets of commercial banks by category.

Savings and Loan Associations and Savings Banks. Savings and loan associations and savings banks, two kinds of thrift institutions, have evolved to develop such similar methods of doing business that they are now distinguishable only by their names. Historically, savings and loan associations have accepted only savings deposits from local individuals who chose to join the associations by becoming depositors. Only association members (depositors) could borrow from an association, and most of these loans were home mortgages. Saving banks were set up in the same fashion but the depositors were the owners of a savings bank. The principal distinction between S&Ls and savings banks was geographic. Citizens of the New England states preferred the savings bank form; citizens in the rest of the United States preferred the savings and loan association form.

Current law allows both kinds of thrift institutions to accept all types of deposits and make all types of loans and investments. On average, these institutions tend to be significantly smaller than commercial banks and oriented more toward their local geographic areas. Both continue to hold significant percentages of their assets in home mortgages.

Credit Unions. Credit unions traditionally have accepted deposits from members of a group (teachers, sailors, employees of one company, and so forth), lending only to their depositors for short-term, personal needs. Not all credit unions restrict their membership today, and many will lend money to their members for such long-term reasons as home buying or financing new businesses.

Nondepository Institutions

Corporations and individuals need more financial services than depository institutions provide. Federal law has prohibited banks and other depository institutions from diversifying into other types of financial services since the 1930s. Other types of financial institutions have been created to fill these needs. The nondepository financial institutions that are most important to financial managers include insurance companies, investment companies, money market funds, pension funds, real estate investment trusts, finance companies, and mortgage bankers. These institutions, like depository institutions, are all **financial intermediaries** because they collect funds from those who have surpluses and channel the funds efficiently to those who have deficits.

financial intermediary

An institution that collects funds from those who have surpluses and channels the funds efficiently to those who have deficits. All financial intermediaries are financial institutions.

insurance premium

Regular, small payment made to an insurance company to pay for a policy that will compensate the policyholder for an irregular, large loss.

Insurance Companies. Insurance companies are financial intermediaries that collect regular, relatively small payments called **insurance premiums** from many policyholders in order to make relatively large payments to compensate the few policyholders who actually suffer irregular losses against which they are insured: death, accident, illness, fire, crime, or some natural disasters. While insurance companies cannot predict who is going to encounter a financial loss, they employ actuaries (mathematicians highly trained in statistical analysis techniques) to estimate how many members of a carefully defined group will be affected, based on historical data.

The insurance company invests premiums paid on policies to produce income and preserve capital so that it can make cash payments as needed. The investment strategies of life insurance companies differ from those of fire and casualty insurance companies because the payouts on life insurance policies are more predictable in both amount and timing than the payouts on fire and casualty policies. Therefore, life insurance companies can select investments that are less liquid, or less marketable, and higher-yielding than investments selected by fire and casualty insurance companies.

Investment Companies. Investment companies are financial intermediaries that pool relatively small amounts of investors' money to finance large portfolios of investments that justify the cost of professional management. These companies can be set up in two ways. A closed-end investment company issues a fixed number of shares, which it sells to the public to raise money to purchase investments. These shares trade in the open market like the shares of any corporation, and their price varies with demand. Open-end investment companies, also called *mutual funds*, issue new shares whenever someone wants to buy them and repurchase shares whenever an investor wants to sell them.

The price of a mutual fund share equals the net value of the portfolio divided by the number of shares outstanding at that time. If the net value of the fund's portfolio of securities were $42 million and the fund had four million shares outstanding, the price of one share would be $42,000,000/4,000,000, or $10.50. This price is usually calculated twice a day, using the value of the securities in the portfolio at noon and the value at the close of the market each day. Shares traded in the interval between calculations are bought and sold at the most recently calculated price.

Each investment company focuses on a specific investment goal. Some provide the investor with monthly income in the form of interest and dividend distributions. Others provide the investor with capital gains by selecting securities that are expected to increase substantially in value. Some funds invest in the securities of specific industries, others in new companies, and still others in particular types of securities such as bonds or foreign stocks. Money market funds, the most popular special-purpose mutual funds, invest in very short-term securities—the average time to maturity of a money fund's holdings is measured in days. They may even allow their shareholders limited check writing privileges.

Pension Funds. Pension funds are set up to accumulate funds to provide retirement, disability, and/or lump-sum death benefit payments to the employees of companies or to labor union members. The company or union makes periodic payments to the fund and the fund managers invest the money in a portfolio of securities that they expect to generate enough money to make the benefit payments. A pension plan may be a **defined-contribution plan** or a **defined-benefit plan**. In the former case, the company makes payments to the fund as a fixed percentage of salaries and the size of the retiree's benefit payment depends on the investment success of the fund manager. In the latter case, the company promises a fixed benefit payment to the employee, which is usually related to the size of the employee's salary and the number of years of service; actuaries estimate the interest that the portfolio will earn and the expected life span of the employee, then they calculate the sizes of the periodic payments the company must make to fulfill its promise.

defined-contribution pension plan
The sponsor of the plan makes fixed contributions to the plan. The retiree's benefit varies.

defined-benefit pension plan
The sponsor of the plan promises a fixed benefit to the employee upon retirement or disability. The sponsor's contribution varies.

Real Estate Investment Trusts. Real estate investment trusts (REITs) operate like closed-end investment companies, but they invest in real estate rather than stocks or bonds. These trusts were very popular during the 1970s and early 1980s, but many went bankrupt after the real estate market began collapsing in 1987. The current re-emergence of enthusiasm for buying real estate has renewed REITs' popularity.

Finance Companies. Finance companies are important financial intermediaries. In fact, they are the second-largest provider of installment credit to consumers, as shown in Exhibit 3.2. Initially financed by manufacturing corporations, they subsequently borrow from the public and from banks in order to lend customers money to purchase expensive items such as automobiles, jet engines, major appliances, and boats. Most finance companies are wholly owned subsidiaries of the corporations that manufacture the products that they finance.

EXHIBIT 3.2

Consumer Installment Credit ($ billions)[a]

Installment credit extended by	
Commercial banks	$331.9
Finance companies	117.1
Credit unions	97.6
Savings institutions	43.5
Retailers	42.1
Gasoline companies	4.4
Others	120.4
Total installment credit	$757.0

[a]Year-end 1992.

Source: Survey of Current Business 73, no. 12 (December 1993), p. S–14.

Mortgage Banks. Mortgage banks do not accept deposits, but they do make loans. They offer first and second mortgages on commercial property, multifamily residential housing, and (since 1986) one-family and two-family houses. They are frequently privately owned corporations that are willing to make risky loans that banks reject.

Other Financial Institutions

Customers of the financial institutions discussed so far sometimes perceive them to be protectors or enhancers of wealth. Other financial institutions act as agents or advisors, especially in more sophisticated financial matters. These specialists offer expertise that is as important to their customers as their ability to collect and disburse funds. These institutions include investment banks, venture capitalists, brokerage houses, and securities exchanges.

Investment Banks. The term *investment bank* illustrates the tendency in the financial world to assign many meanings to one word. Investment banks are not banks in the generally understood sense of the word; they neither take deposits nor make loans. Investment bankers sell stocks and bonds based on a comprehensive understanding of recent past, current, and foreseeable future conditions in the securities markets. They advise corporations that wish to sell new issues of stocks and bonds to the public. They are authorities on designing new security issues that will give the public just what it wants when the issue hits the market.

Usually an investment bank buys new securities from the issuing company and resells them to the public in a matter of days. This process is known as **underwriting** a security issue. The bank may also support the issue in the aftermarket, which means that if the security's price starts to fall shortly after the issue has been sold to the public, the underwriter will buy back enough shares to stabilize the price. The corporation, of course, pays extra for this service, which is called **making a market** in the issue.

underwriting
A process in which an investment banker buys a new security issue from a company and resells it to the public.

making a market
A function of a brokerage house or investment banker in which it carries an inventory of a company's securities and quotes prices at which it is willing to buy or sell.

FOCUS ON FINANCE

GENERAL MOTORS ACCEPTANCE CORPORATION

General Motors set up the first successful captive finance company, General Motors Acceptance Corporation (GMAC), as a wholly owned, unconsolidated subsidiary in 1919. The original purpose of GMAC was to lend consumers money to buy General Motors cars. A potential customer whose auto loan application might be rejected by a bank would be evaluated more favorably by GMAC, because profits could be made on both the sale of the car and the interest on the loan. The enterprise was so successful that by 1987, General Motors had set up additional, unconsolidated subsidiaries to finance car sales in Australia, Austria, Canada, Chile, Colombia, England, France, Greece, Italy, Mexico, Netherlands, New Zealand, South Africa, Spain, and Switzerland.

Other companies copied General Motors' innovation. Aerospace, automotive, trucking, and big-ticket consumer appliance manufacturers decided that such an arrangement would boost their sales, too. Some large retail stores decided to offer their own credit cards and created financial subsidiaries to do the associated data processing. These decisions led to the creation of captive finance companies such as:

Chrysler Financial Corporation (1926)

May Department Stores Credit Company (1945)

Mack Financial Corporation (1946)

Fruehauf Finance Company (1948)

International Harvester Credit Corporation (1949)

Eaton Credit Corporation (1953)

General Electric Credit Corporation (1953)

Clark Equipment Credit Corporation (1954)

Sperry Rand Financial Corporation (1954)

Trailmobile Finance Company (1955)

Allis-Chalmers Credit Corporation (1956)

Sears Roebuck Credit Corporation (1956)

John Deere Credit Company (1958)

Ford Motor Credit Company (1959)

Massey-Ferguson Credit Corporation (1960)

Montgomery Ward Credit Corporation (1960)

Allied Stores Credit Corporation (1961)

Macy Credit Corporation (1961)

Singer Credit Corporation (1961)

Honeywell Finance, Inc. (1967)

McDonnell-Douglas Finance Corporation (1968)

Associated Dry Goods Credit Corporation (1969)

J. C. Penney Financial Corporation (1969)

FMC Finance Corporation (1971)

Carter Hawley Hale Credit Corporation (1974)

UT Credit Corporation (1974) (a division of United Technologies)

Since finance company employees had banking and financial expertise, some of the companies naturally branched out into other financial areas such as leasing and insurance during the 1970s and early 1980s. General Motors, for example, lost no time in creating leasing subsidiaries, insurance subsidiaries, and mortgage bank subsidiaries both in the United States and overseas.

The investment bank cannot always convince the issuing corporation to offer a new security on terms the public will accept at the moment. When this happens, the investment bank will not underwrite the issue. Instead, it will agree only to act as an agent and exert its best efforts to sell the security. A **best efforts sale** agreement usually contains a clause specifying that if a significant portion of the issue (10 to 30 percent) is not sold, the offer will be withdrawn and the new issue canceled.

best efforts sale
The process in which an investment banker acts as an agent, helping to sell a newly issued security to the public.

Venture Capitalists. Venture capitalists are individuals and institutions that pursue the rewards associated with high risk in the securities markets. They buy original stock issues of new companies, expecting to make enough profits on one successful issue to outweigh the complete losses experienced on two other, unsuccessful issues. Venture capitalists usually cannot resell their securities to the public for a few years, and they buy enough shares to acquire significant or controlling interests in new corporations. The issuing corporations, incidentally, need not be brand-new businesses. They may be individually owned or family owned businesses that need more capital than the owners can borrow.

Brokerage Houses. The fundamental function of a brokerage house is to buy and sell securities for its clients while completing all the documentation each transaction requires. Small discount brokers act only as agents for investors who trade stocks and bonds. Larger discount brokers also purchase and sell other types of securities: contracts for future deliveries of commodities such as agricultural crops, metals, petroleum products, foreign currencies, or bundles of securities, and option contracts that give the contract holders the right to buy or sell financial assets at fixed prices for limited periods of time.

Discount brokers charge small commissions to handle purchases and sales of securities because their overhead expenses are minimal. Full-service brokers charge larger commissions because, in addition to facilitating securities trades, they maintain research departments that supply investors with information and trading advice. Large, full-service brokerage houses may take on other functions as well, including investment banking, market making, venture capital, portfolio management, trust management, real estate, mortgage banking, and insurance.

Securities Exchanges. Securities exchanges are voluntary associations of brokerage houses that were originally formed to provide organized, indoor marketplaces for trading in securities. Over the last 60 years, they have formulated standards for trading activities; among other requirements, they specify how much information must be disclosed by companies who list their securities on the exchanges. The exchanges regulate the trading practices of their broker members to maintain reasonably fair and orderly markets and they encourage participation in the market by small investors.

In the United States, 9 exchanges handle trading of stocks, bonds, and option contracts, and 11 exchanges offer trading in commodity futures contracts. Large domestic and international companies list their securities on either of the two

FOCUS ON FINANCE

ARIZONA STOCK EXCHANGE

The Arizona Stock Exchange is a computer network launched by R. Steven Wunsch in 1989 with privately raised funds and a $700,000 loan from the state of Arizona. It has about a dozen employees and 100 customers, all of them institutional investors from the United States and Canada.

The exchange opens for business for one hour each day, at 4 p.m. New York time. Investors can see all the orders placed through the exchange via an on-line system. They can place their own buy/sell orders, changing them or withdrawing them as they wish, as long as the exchange is open. At 5 p.m. the exchange closes and the computer matches as many buy and sell orders as possible. On a typical day, the system may handle orders to trade more than 12 million shares, of which it can match orders for only about 500,000 shares. Unmatched orders are cancelled. The prices of trades are usually very close to the closing prices on the NYSE, but the traders pay commissions that are only about 15 percent of the NYSE's.

Source: William P. Barrett, "A Gnat Grows in Phoenix," *Forbes*, February 1, 1993, p. 54.

national exchanges—the New York Stock Exchange ("the Big Board") or the American Stock Exchange ("the Amex"). It is not cost-efficient to list the same security on both. Companies listed on the Big Board tend to be older and larger with more widely distributed shares than those on the Amex. Seven regional stock exchanges focus on the needs of their local markets, including the Boston, Philadelphia, Midwest (Chicago), Salt Lake City, Spokane, Cincinnati, and Pacific (San Francisco) Stock Exchanges. Stocks can be dual listed on the national and regional exchanges. Securities also change hands on small, fully licensed exchanges, such as the Honolulu Stock Exchange, and on privately owned, limited-volume exchanges that are exempt from full registration, such as the Arizona Stock Exchange.

The stocks and bonds of companies that are not listed on a stock exchange trade over the counter (OTC). Brokers match the buy and sell orders for popular OTC stocks using a computer network that continually lists orders, or by contacting any one of several market makers. A market maker is a brokerage house that carries an inventory of shares in a company; it publicly quotes the prices at which it is willing buy and sell these shares. Brokers execute buy and sell orders for a less popular stock by contacting the single market maker for that stock.

The National Association of Securities Dealers (NASD) has established an electronic network through which all brokerage houses can access price quotations on OTC securities: the NASD Automated Quotation system. Selections or complete listings of these NASDAQ prices are printed in many daily newspapers and displayed on some cable TV channels along with listed stock quotations.

An individual investor with a computer and modem can buy a service that gives access to listed and NASDAQ stock prices. The costs of stock price quotation services differ substantially, depending on whether the investor wants instantaneous access or is willing to accept quotations that are delayed by 15 minutes. Naturally, an investor who wants quotations on more stocks must pay a higher price for the service.

Financial Intermediation

Financial institutions have proliferated and provided new types of services during this century to meet ever increasing needs. Steadily rising standards of living in economically developed countries have given many individuals surpluses of cash. Prosperity has also made them feel secure enough to invest these surpluses in many different instruments instead of hoarding them.

A steady growth in commercial activity has accompanied and fostered this rising standard of living. Business expansion requires reinvestment of corporate profits as well as substantial amounts of additional capital from outside the business. These funds must frequently be raised quickly, in large amounts, and at auspicious times.

Financial intermediaries collect small amounts of capital from many individuals, aggregate them, and channel the sums efficiently to the corporations and industries that need them. They also provide effective ways to transmit the profits earned on this capital back to individual savers. Exhibit 3.3 illustrates this process.

If a corporation had to make a house-to-house appeal for cash, each attempt to raise money would be very expensive and time consuming. Obtaining $100 million (a modest sum by corporate standards) could require negotiation of 100,000 separate deals for $1,000 each! Finding these 100,000 investors and working out financial contracts with each would keep an army of corporate employees busy, and it would require extensive legal and financial sophistication on the part of investors. Further, if any of the investors needed to liquidate their investments before maturity, they would have no way to terminate their deals unless the company were willing and prepared to search for substitute investors.

Financial institutions have standardized the terms under which corporations can raise money, while creating enough diversity in characteristics of securities to meet the different needs of all companies. They have also created markets through which individual investors can quickly and conveniently enter into and exit from almost any investment.

REGULATION OF FINANCIAL INSTITUTIONS AND MARKETS

Most federal financial regulatory agencies were established to curb abuses or avert crises that threatened either the stability of the economy or the public's continued acceptance of the financial institutions. Regulation of the banking system began in 1913 following a century during which the monetary system collapsed approximately every 20 years. With each disaster worse than the one before it, the public's trust of the banking system was rapidly disappearing. Regulation of Wall Street followed the great stock market crash of 1929, and was designed primarily

EXHIBIT 3.3

Participants in the U.S. Financial Markets

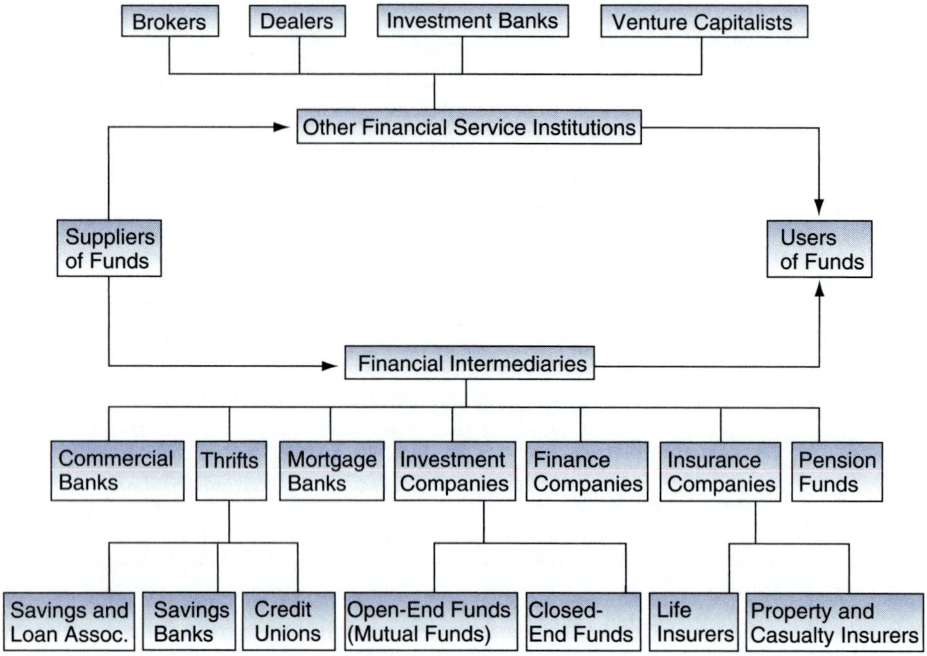

to restore public confidence in the markets. Regulation of pension plans in 1974 followed the exposure of mismanagement that cast doubt on the retirement incomes of more than a million union members.

Federal Reserve System

Established in 1913, the Federal Reserve System (the Fed) serves as the central bank for the United States. As a quasiindependent unit of government, its principal function is to formulate monetary policy. To carry out that function, the Fed regulates the banking activities of the principal commercial banks.

There are three major subdivisions of the Federal Reserve System: the Board of Governors, the Federal Open Market Committee (FOMC), and the 12 regional Federal Reserve Banks. The Board of Governors consists of seven officials who are appointed to 14-year terms by the president of the United States with the advice and consent of the Senate. These long terms of office are staggered; one governor's term expires every two years. This arrangement was designed to keep the board independent of political interference. It has two major responsibilities: making policy decisions that affect the money supply, and collecting financial data to evaluate the effectiveness of these decisions. The chairman of the Board of Governors serves as spokesperson for the Federal Reserve, and answers to Congress should monetary policy be ineffective.

Policy decisions are carried out primarily by the FOMC, which is composed of the 7 governors and 5 of the 12 Federal Reserve Bank presidents. This committee acts directly to influence the volume of money in the economy and indirectly to manipulate interest rates. The objective of this influence is to achieve the employment, price stability, and growth goals that the committee associates with a healthy economy.

The regional Federal Reserve Banks implement the commercial banking regulations drafted by the board and oversee the activities of the commercial banks within their respective districts. As each Federal Reserve Bank president participates in rotation on the FOMC, the bank interjects regional needs of its district into the policy making process.

To implement U.S. monetary policy, the Federal Reserve has three major tools: it can change the required reserve ratio on deposits, it can buy and sell securities in the open market, and it can change the discount rate.

Reserve Requirements. Every depository institution must keep a percentage of its transaction deposits (1) as vault cash, (2) on deposit at a correspondent bank, or (3) as a deposit in a noninterest-bearing account at the Federal Reserve. This percentage is the **required reserve ratio**. Congress changed the basic reserve requirement structure in 1980 when it enacted the Depository Institutions Deregulation and Monetary Control Act. Under this act, after a fixed 3 percent rate on the basic amount of transaction deposits, the Fed may set the rate anywhere between 8 and 14 percent on the remainder. Presently, the Federal Reserve requires a rate of 10 percent.

required reserve ratio

The percentage of a deposit that the Federal Reserve requires a bank to hold either as cash or on deposit at the Fed. The current ratio is 10 percent.

This means that when an individual or a corporation deposits $1 million into a checking account, the bank must keep 10 percent, or $100,000, of the deposit in reserves. Consequently, the deposit increases the lending ability of the bank by $900,000. A higher reserve requirement reduces the loans the bank can make based on a given deposit. Thus, if the Federal Reserve wishes to curtail money expansion, it can increase the reserve requirement.

In practice, the Federal Reserve is reluctant to do this. According to the *Federal Reserve Bulletin*, banks held $756.1 billion in transaction deposits in December 1992. Even a slight change in the reserve requirement would significantly influence loan volume.

Open Market Operations. The Federal Reserve seeks to influence the money supply primarily by purchasing and selling securities in the open market. *Open market* is merely another name for the secondary securities market. The securities purchased and sold are generally U.S. Treasury securities.

When the Federal Reserve buys a Treasury security from a dealer or broker in the open market, it writes a check payable to the seller. When the check is deposited into the seller's checking account, the funds available to the seller's bank increase. After setting aside the required reserves, the commercial bank can then expand its lending. In effect, purchases of Treasury securities expand banks' loanable reserves and, thus, the supply of money in the economy.

When the Federal Reserve sells Treasury securities from its portfolio, the buyers write checks against their commercial bank checking accounts. When the Fed cashes these checks, the funds available to the banks decline. This reduces the banks' lending abilities and the supply of money.

The Discount Rate. A depository institution with insufficient reserves in relation to its transaction deposits may borrow from the Federal Reserve. The Fed's interest rate for this loan is termed the *discount rate*. When the commercial bank receives the proceeds from the loan, its reserves are increased and it no longer has to curtail its loan activity.

Changes in the discount rate result from policy decisions of the Federal Reserve. Increasing the rate makes it more expensive for depository institutions with insufficient reserves to continue lending. Thus the banking system will be more reluctant to grant loans to its customers. Summarized briefly, if the Federal Reserve wishes to reduce lending activity and the supply of money, it raises the discount rate. Conversely, if it wishes to stimulate lending, it lowers the rate.

Since borrowing from the Federal Reserve is a relatively insignificant source of funds for the banking community, a change in the discount rate really can not have a significant impact upon bank loan activity. Changes in the rate still draw attention, however, because they signal changes in Federal Reserve policy. Thus, an increase in the discount rate really means that the Federal Reserve is warning the banking community to reduce its lending activities or else the Fed will use other means (probably open market operations) to slow down loan expansion and money supply increases.

Nonmonetary Activities. In addition to wielding its policy tools, the Federal Reserve performs numerous functions unrelated to monetary policy. Chief among these is the supervision of large commercial banks. All nationally chartered commercial banks and a substantial number of state banks are subject to Federal Reserve regulations. While these regulations are not substantially different from those of the Comptroller of the Currency or the Federal Deposit Insurance Corporation, they do impose another layer of regulation on the activities of affected banks.

The Fed operates the nation's largest check-clearing system and the only commercial bank wire transfer system. Control of these clearing activities permits the Federal Reserve to keep tabs on the level of financial activity and, thus, obtain a better reading of economic activity.

The Federal Reserve issues all paper currency currently in use in the United States. It also acts as the fiscal agent for the U.S. Treasury, providing the Treasury with both commercial banking and investment banking services. One additional activity carried out by the Federal Reserve is gathering data on the U.S. financial system. It reports this data monthly in the *Federal Reserve Bulletin*.

Federal Deposit Insurance

Bank failures more than tripled in the years following the stock market crash in 1929. People were afraid to deposit money in banks, and those who were brave enough to make deposits would withdraw them at the slightest rumor that their banks had financial problems. These panic reactions were frequently sufficient cause to close a bank that was both profitable and solvent. Very few banks could raise enough fast cash to satisfy a **bank run**—a surge of depositors demanding to withdraw all of their money simultaneously.

bank run
A panic situation in which large numbers of bank depositors attempt to withdraw their money simultaneously.

Federal Deposit Insurance Corporation. The Federal Deposit Insurance Corporation (FDIC) was created in 1934 to end this panic psychology and assure people that their deposits in commercial and savings banks were safe. Initially, the FDIC insured deposits up to $2,500, but by 1980 this amount had increased to $100,000.

The soothing effect of FDIC insurance was so powerful that the government subsequently created the Federal Savings and Loan Insurance Corporation (FSLIC) in 1934 to insure deposits in savings and loan associations and the National Credit Union Share Insurance Fund (NCUSIF) in 1970 to insure the deposits of credit union members.

Deregulation of the Thrifts. During the late 1970s and early 1980s, thrift institutions found themselves holding fixed-yield assets while they had to pay ever higher interest rates to attract deposits. They were unable to acquire deposit funds at their prevailing maximum allowable interest rates on time and savings deposits and, consequently, could not continue funding their asset structures. This forced the thrifts to sell off their relatively low-yielding mortgage loans in a depressed market at punishing losses. Furthermore, the thrifts found their profitability limited by regulations that prevented them from investing in higher-yielding commercial loans.

In an attempt to produce equality among depository institutions and to permit them to be more profitable, Congress enacted the Depository Institution Deregulation and Monetary Control Act of 1980 (DIDMCA). This act standardized reserve requirements, permitted institutions to pay interest on transaction accounts (NOW accounts), and began to phase out of the interest rate ceiling on deposit accounts. The act also permitted savings and loan institutions to reduce their dependence on mortgage lending by allowing expanded nonmortgage lending.

While well-intentioned, the act did little to assist the thrift industry. Consequently, in 1982 Congress enacted the Depository Institutions Act, also known as the Garn–St. Germain Act. This act permitted thrifts to establish reserve-free money-market deposit accounts (MMDA), and it eliminated the remaining interest rate ceilings on all time and savings accounts. Interestingly, the act also granted commercial bank holding companies the right to acquire financially troubled thrifts both in their home states and nationwide. The Garn–St. Germain Act exacerbated the thrift problem. Basically it deregulated the sources of funds, permitting thrifts to pay more for the funds they needed to acquire, but it did nothing to enhance the returns the thrifts earned on the assets they held.

Savings and loan associations began to fail in large numbers during the late 1980s. The FSLIC closed the weakened thrifts and did its best to pay all insured deposits, but by 1987 it had run out of funds. In order to prevent a return to public panic like that during the 1930s, Congress passed the Financial Institution Reform, Recovery, and Enforcement Act (FIRREA) in 1989. This act eliminated the FSLIC, turning its insurance functions over to the FDIC and providing over $50 billion to pay insured deposits in failing thrifts. FIRREA also created two new agencies: the Office of Thrift Supervision (to be discussed later) and the Resolution Trust Corporation.

Resolution Trust Corporation. The responsibility of selling the assets of the failed thrifts to recoup the funds paid out to depositors fell to the newly established Resolution Trust Corporation (RTC). The RTC was to use $50 billion provided by Congress under FIRREA to acquire the assets of failed thrifts, sell them, and then acquire more assets from additional failed thrifts. Congress intended the $50 billion as a loss reserve; the proceeds of asset sales were supposed to permit the RTC to continue to purchase failed thrift assets from the FDIC. Unfortunately, the market reality left the RTC holding foreclosed real estate that it could not readily sell. In order to raise money, it engaged in widely criticized "fire sales," divesting assets at fractions of their book values. This quickly depleted the $50 billion, and by late 1993, Congress again found itself funding the RTC, this time to the tune of $18 billion. The RTC was initially intended to fade out of existence by 1993, but the continuing effects of the thrift problem have forced its authority to extend into 1995.

FDIC Insurance Funds. Today the FDIC operates two separate insurance funds: the Savings Association Insurance Fund (SAIF) and the Bank Insurance Fund (BIF). The SAIF has replaced the FSLIC. All premiums paid by savings and loan associations go directly into this account, and any future failures of these thrifts will be covered by the assets of this fund. Should the fund balance become precariously low, the savings and loan associations will be assessed even larger premiums.

The BIF is the old FDIC fund for commercial banks. It was kept separate to appease commercial bankers, who did not want their premiums distributed to depositors in savings and loan associations. Since the fund is separate, commercial bank premiums are based on this fund's balance. Since 1992, the inflow of premiums has exceeded the need to pay depositors of failed institutions. Consequently, the FDIC has considered reducing commercial bank premiums.

Comptroller of the Currency

The office of Comptroller of the Currency was established by the National Bank Act of 1863 as part of the U.S. Treasury Department. The comptroller is appointed to a five-year term by the president of the United States, with the advice and consent of the Senate.

U.S. commercial banks operate under charters issued by either the federal government or individual states. Those with federal charters, called *national banks*, fall in the jurisdiction of the Comptroller of the Currency. The comptroller is responsible for issuing charters, approving expansions (by acquisition, merger, or open-

FOCUS ON CAREERS

Bank Examiner

Operating as part of a team, a bank examiner is responsible for enforcing the laws and regulations that govern the establishment, operations, and solvency of depository institutions. Specifically, the examiner: (a) assesses the financial condition of the institution and the character of its management, (b) searches for any unsafe and unsound practices, (c) reviews the adequacy of internal controls and procedures, and (d) determines the institution's compliance with all laws and regulations.

An examiner can be a federal government employee working for the Federal Deposit Insurance Corporation, the Office of Thrift Supervision, the Comptroller of the Currency, or one of the Federal Reserve Banks. The banking departments of most states also employ examiners.

Most trainee examiners join regulatory institutions immediately after earning their bachelor's degrees. The best opportunities for employment are available to individuals who have earned degrees in business administration, finance, accounting, economics, or marketing, with at least six semester hours of accounting and overall grade point averages of 3.5 or higher.

The salaries of examiners in federal service are determined by government grade (GG) level. Entry level staffers usually start out at GG-5 with promotion to GG-7 after a one-year probationary period. Advancement through higher levels depends on individual performance; an examiner with one to three years of experience normally reaches GG-12. At this level, a federal employee can take charge of an independent examination of a financial institution.

The job requires extensive travel, especially if the assignment is outside a large metropolitan area, since examinations are conducted on site. When not traveling, the examiner may be required to review applications for mergers, acquisitions, branch openings and closings, and various other institutional activities.

ing new branches), declaring insolvencies, establishing and enforcing operating regulations, and conducting bank examinations.

Office of Thrift Supervision

As part of the conditions attached to the congressional bailout of the thrift industry, in 1989 Congress eliminated the quasiindependent Federal Home Loan Bank Board, which up to that time had exercised regulatory authority over the thrift industry. In its place, Congress created the Office of Thrift Supervision (OTS). The OTS is a part of the U.S. Treasury as the Comptroller of the Currency is, which allows direct control by the executive branch. Its duties are also fairly similar to the Comptroller's. It charters federal savings associations (the new name for federally chartered savings and loan associations) and supervises their operations.

Securities and Exchange Commission

The stock market crash of 1929 changed the government's attitude toward regulating the securities industry. Before the crash, U.S. authorities assumed that anyone interested in the market would take the trouble to learn how it worked before parting with cash, and that those taking the investor's money (brokers, dealers, and corporations) would either operate properly or fail. The financial markets were ruled by the principle from biology of the survival of the fittest and the economic principle of laissez-faire.

The crash revealed that some people were willing to buy any stock if the certificates looked genuine. Some corporations considered it an invasion of privacy to reveal anything more than the company president's name, no matter how many stockholders and bondholders they had. Further, naive potential brokers and dealers tried to get rich by watching successful securities traders working on the sidewalks of lower Manhattan and copying whatever they saw (or thought they saw) being done. The crash also revealed that brokers and dealers played by their own rules, which could differ significantly from one firm to another.

Securities Act of 1933. To bring order and stability to the stock market, and to restore investors' trust in the safety of securities transactions, Congress passed the Securities Act of 1933. This law required companies to register new securities before selling them to the public. As part of this registration process, the act also required them to disclose relevant information about company operations and security provisions.

Securities Exchange Act of 1934. The Securities Exchange Act of 1934 created the Securities and Exchange Commission (SEC) with the power to approve or reject security registration applications. The basis for the commission's decision was (and still is) the truth or fraudulence of the facts in the registration statement. Approval does not signify that the issue is a good investment. It merely indicates that the SEC:

1. Did not find any evidence of fraud in the information disclosed
2. Deemed that enough information was provided to allow a rational investor to judge the quality of the issue

The 1934 act also gave the SEC authority over organized stock and bond exchanges, the OTC market, brokers, dealers, and outstanding security issues. The SEC's power was extended to cover trade associations of securities dealers in 1938, investment companies and investment advisors in 1940, and computer networks in the securities markets in 1975. At present, the only financial market not supervised by the SEC is the commodity futures market, which is self-regulated by the Commodity Futures Trade Commission (CFTC). The wisdom of this arrangement is currently being debated.

Securities Investor Protection Act of 1970. The Securities Investor Protection Act of 1970 established the Securities Investor Protection Corporation (SIPC) to insure investors against losses when a brokerage firm fails. The SIPC insures brokerage accounts for up to \$500,000 in securities and cash (though the maximum insurance on cash is \$100,000). The SIPC does not insure against declines in the market values of securities. It is not a government agency, but is supervised by the SEC.

Additional Regulations. In addition to these federal laws, each state has a set of laws designed to regulate securities trading as that state's government deems necessary. While these laws share many similar features, no two states have exactly the same set of laws.

Belief in the efficiency of self-regulation remains strong in the securities markets. The organized exchanges require more detailed disclosure by their members and listees than the SEC requires. Most large brokerage houses have formulated ethical practices policies, although the strictness of enforcement varies from firm to firm. Generally, an appeal for redress of grievances can be taken up the company's chain of command; if it is not satisfactorily resolved, it can be taken to the NASD or the appropriate exchange. All exchanges impose standards of practice and other policies that, when violated, can result in reprimands, suspensions, or disassociations of offenders. The SEC is the investor's last resort, but investors rarely need to carry their cases that far.

Employees Retirement Income Security Act

The Employees Retirement Income Security Act (ERISA) was passed in 1974; pension funds had been essentially unregulated before then. The standards prescribed by the act were so complex that it took the U.S. court system over ten years to determine exactly what was required of employers and mandated for employees.

vesting
Having the right to keep accumulated pension benefits.

Vested Benefits. The single most important concept involved in pension fund regulation is **vesting**. When employees are fully vested, none of their accumulated pension benefits can be taken away from them. When they are partially vested, they cannot lose the vested percentages of their accumulated benefits. If employees quit or are fired, their vested pension benefits may stay with the old employer or union, be transferred to the new employer or union, or be paid out in a lump sum to the employee, but they cannot be eliminated. If an employer or union terminates an old pension plan and starts a new one, the new one must provide for all of the old vested benefits.

ERISA established the minimum standards for vesting and gave the employer or union three options. Subsequent amendments to ERISA have shortened the time it takes both to become vested initially and to become completely vested. Pension plan sponsors now have two options:

1. The employee must be fully vested after five years
2. The employee must be 20 percent vested after three years, with the percentage increasing 20 percent each subsequent year. Under this graduated vesting option, the employee is fully vested after seven years.

Funding Pension Plans. Before ERISA, employers could choose to fund pension plans any way they wished. A company did not have to put any money aside to pay future benefits if it did not want to do so. It could simply pay benefits to its current retirees out of its current income. This works only so long as the company grows and is profitable. If the company stagnates or fails, little or no money may be available to pay pensioners. ERISA tried to prevent such situations in two ways: it required the company to make minimum contributions to a pension fund (whether the company managed that fund itself or hired a bank, an insurance company, or a professional investment manager to do the job) and it provided a guarantee that pensions would be paid.

Insuring Pension Benefits. ERISA established the Pension Benefits Guarantee Corporation (PBGC) to insure vested benefits in case an employer or union declared bankruptcy. The PBGC pays off any unfunded pension liabilities, and is compensated by the Bankruptcy Court from the liquidation of the company's assets before the claims of the general creditors. Unfortunately, Congress chose to put an upper limit on the extent of this compensation: the PBGC cannot put such a super-senior debt claim on more than 30 percent of the bankrupt company's net worth. This quirk in the legislation prevents the PBGC from fulfilling its purpose. It lacks sufficient funds to pay off the insurance claims of the pension funds of the companies now in bankruptcy.

Regulation of International Operations

U.S. financial institutions have provided financial services outside the United States for a long time. Commercial banks were the first financial institutions to explore foreign markets for financial services. Today, almost all types of U.S. financial institutions cross international borders to pursue their respective areas of specialization. Some U.S. investment banking institutions and brokerage houses have earned dominant positions in the world financial community, and they serve eager customers all over the world. U.S. mutual funds, pension funds, and insurance companies have expanded their portfolios to include assets traded in foreign financial markets. International diversification is the buzzword heard throughout today's investment environment.

Though the first overseas branch of a U.S. commercial bank was established in 1887, the real beginning of international banking activities by U.S. commercial banks occurred after the passage of the Federal Reserve Act in 1913. Until then, national banks were prohibited from operating foreign branches and accepting bills of exchange originating from foreign trade. Only state chartered commercial banks would operate foreign branches. The Federal Reserve Act permitted national banks to operate foreign branches and participate in trade financing.

The international banking activities of U.S. banks accelerated during World War I and the postwar period. Since World War II, U.S. international banking has seen enormous growth in terms of the number of branches opened, transaction volume, and geographic coverage. The factors responsible for this growth include the increase in world trade, post-World War II reconstruction efforts by the United States, and the role of the dollar as a world currency.

Today, U.S. financial institutions pervade the world financial markets. They provide a wide range of services, including accepting deposits, financing trade, dealing in foreign exchange, managing cash for multinational corporations, lending, financial advising, underwriting securities, and providing international custody services. They conduct their international operations through foreign branches, representative offices, agencies, subsidiaries, affiliates, joint ventures, correspondent banks, Edge corporations, and international banking facilities (IBFs). An individual bank can choose among these organizational setups to establish the form that best suits its needs. Several factors influence this decision:

1. The extent of its involvement in international banking activities
2. Its ability to finance these activities
3. Legal restrictions from home or host countries (Some countries do not permit foreign banks to own and operate branches, or to own subsidiaries.)

A foreign branch may meet the needs of a bank that wants to offer a full range of banking services and have full access to foreign financial markets. As an extension of the main office, a foreign branch provides name recognition. A branch is, however, expensive to run, and it must deal with problems related to staffing and political hostages. A representative office can only collect information and develop foreign contacts. An agency resembles a branch office, except that it cannot accept deposits from the general public. A subsidiary or affiliate provides local name recognition and can draw on the expertise of local institutions. An IBF is a special arrangement allowed by the Federal Reserve System for a bank to conduct Eurocurrency business without having to establish branches abroad. (A **Eurocurrency** is any currency held as a time deposit in a bank outside that currency's home country.) An Edge corporation, created under the Edge Act of 1919, deals specifically with trade financing and trade-related activities.

Eurocurrency
Any currency on deposit in a bank outside that currency's home country.

INTERNATIONAL FINANCIAL INSTITUTIONS

Financial institutions facilitate the flow of funds from those who have money to those who need it. This function is not restricted by national boundaries. Various institutions have been created to facilitate and regulate the international flow of funds and financing for international trade. Some emerged from global cooperation to address international concerns. Others were created by individual governments to operate in the global marketplace. None is exempt from the process of evolution. The older these institutions are, the more they differ from their original designs if they are functioning successfully.

International Monetary Fund

In 1944 representatives of the Allied nations met in Bretton Woods, New Hampshire, to deal with monetary and financial issues expected to arise in the post-World War II period. Three issues were foremost in their minds: reconstruction in war-torn nations, establishing a suitable world monetary system, and providing financing for developing nations.

The agreement reached at Bretton Woods committed member countries to a fixed exchange rate system. The articles of agreement also provided for the creation of two international financial institutions, the International Monetary Fund (IMF) and the World Bank Group, which consists of:

1. The International Bank for Reconstruction and Development, popularly known as the *World Bank*
2. The International Development Agency (IDA)
3. The International Finance Corporation (IFC).

All of these institutions have headquarters in Washington, D.C.

The IMF was entrusted with several responsibilities:

1. Overseeing the operation of the international monetary system
2. Monitoring the exchange rate system to avoid excessive volatility
3. Assisting member nations that face economic problems, especially balance of payments problems, by providing funds and facilitating the adjustment process
4. Encouraging international cooperation on foreign exchange matters
5. Encouraging elimination of exchange restrictions and fostering free flows of capital among countries
6. Permitting and supervising currency devaluations by member countries that experience long-term balance of payments difficulties

Membership in the IMF has grown from the original 44 countries to over 150 members in 1994. Each member country is assigned a quota or subscription to the capital fund of the IMF, and this capital is the primary source of funds for the IMF's lending activities. A member country's quota is determined by its economic characteristics, such as the size of its gross domestic product. This quota then determines the member country's voting rights, its access to IMF resources, and its allocation of SDRs.

special drawing rights (SDRs)
An accounting unit constructed as the weighted average of the U.S. dollar, the German mark, the French franc, the British pound, and the Japanese yen to serve as an international currency standard.

In 1969, the IMF created reserve assets called **special drawing rights (SDRs)** to help member nations supplement their reserve assets. SDRs are exchanged only in transactions between the central banks of member nations. The SDR itself is not currency; it is a unit of account in which central banks can settle their nations' obligations. The value of the SDR was originally set at parity with the U.S. dollar. In 1974, it was redefined to represent the daily weighted average of 16 major currencies. After another revision in 1981, the SDR now represents the daily weighted average of five currencies—the U.S. dollar, the Deutschemark, the Japanese yen, the French franc, and the British pound. The weight of each currency is adjusted every few years to reflect the relative importance of that currency in world export trade.

The IMF has played its assigned role rather effectively throughout its existence. Its main concern has always been balance of payments difficulties of its member countries. It has also helped member nations meet their specialized needs. It created the Structural Adjustment Facility (SAF) and the Enhanced Structural Adjustment Facility (ESAF) to provide concessions and other assistance to low-income member countries faced with serious balance of payments difficulties. It established the Compensatory and Contingency Financing Facility (CCFF) to help member countries who were dependent on primary exports to stabilize their incomes.

FOCUS ON FINANCE

LITTLE LOANS FROM THE WORLD BANK

In 1993, the World Bank lent about $25 billion to national governments, most of it classified as economic reform loans. Recognizing that these loans have provided few benefits to the poor in developing nations, the bank announced on November 30, 1993, that it would donate $2 million to a special fund designed to help individuals start small businesses in developing nations. The fund, created by the Grameen Bank of Bangladesh, has already helped some of the planet's poorest people (mostly women) borrow amounts as small as $50.

The World Bank

The World Bank is another international financial institution established in 1944. Its official title is the International Bank for Reconstruction and Development, but that label receives little recognition these days.

The World Bank is a profit-oriented agency that is empowered to borrow money anywhere it can, from individuals and corporations as well as from governments, and to lend that money to developing countries and their government agencies. Borrowers must demonstrate some ability to pay back their loans and the loans themselves must be expected to enhance economic development. World Bank interest rates are pegged to a weighted average of the interest costs to the treasuries of the major industrial nations.

The World Bank has developed many innovative ways of fulfilling its goals. It has created Structural Adjustment Loans which it extends to developing countries that want to improve their trade balances by enhancing economic productivity. It has entered into **co-financing agreements**, joining with other lenders such as government foreign aid agencies, export credit agencies, and commercial banks, to provide large blocks of funds to finance capital-intensive projects in developing countries. This sharing-the-loan approach spreads the risk of financing expensive projects among lenders. In 1988, the World Bank established the Multilateral Investment Guarantee Agency (MIGA) which, rather than lending money to a needy country itself, guarantees loans made directly to developing countries. This is a form of political risk insurance, protecting the lender against losses caused by the actions or attitudes of governments and influential groups in the borrowing countries.

co-financing agreement

A combination of two or more lenders to share the costs, risks, and profits of a loan.

International Development Association. The International Development Association (IDA) was established in 1960 as a not-for-profit affiliate of the World Bank. It was created to provide funds at low or zero interest rates to the governments of poor nations that could not qualify for or afford loans from the World Bank. The IDA imposes a service charge of 1.0 to 1.5 percent to help cover its administrative costs. The repayment periods of its loans range from 35 to 50 years, with initial grace periods up to 10 years.

Regional versions of the World Bank also operate internationally. The Inter-American Development Bank raises money primarily in North America for loans in Central and South America. The Asian Development Bank and the African Development Fund promote development on those continents. The European Bank for Reconstruction and Development helps Eastern bloc countries convert to free market economies.

International Finance Corporation

The International Finance Corporation (IFC) was formed in 1956 as a unit of the World Bank Group. Membership in the World Bank is a precondition for membership in the IFC. Its main functions are to promote private investment and assist individual enterprises in developing countries. It does this by providing equity and loan funds, technical assistance, and finance-related services. It often works in association with international banks to provide funds to private enterprises in developing countries.

The resources of the IFC come from several sources. Each member nation is required to contribute to its capital. In addition, the IFC can borrow from member countries, from the World Bank, and in world capital markets. The IFC also raises funds by selling shares in a mutual fund it created and manages: the Emerging Markets Growth Fund. Established in 1986, this fund invests in listed securities of companies in developing nations. It is well-diversified, investing a maximum of 20 percent of its assets in any one country and a maximum of 5 percent of its assets in any one company.

The IFC has a set of criteria for selecting the projects it will finance. The projects must satisfy a wide range of conditions that include benefits to the local economy, availability of private capital to supplement IFC efforts, and immediate or eventual local participation. It invests in projects covering a broad range of activities such as manufacturing, mining, utility development, agriculture, financial services, and tourism.

Though the IFC has set no rigid policy on the proportion of its participation, it usually limits its investment risk by providing no more than 15 percent of the funds needed by an enterprise. It offers loans in all major currencies and some minor currencies, with an occasional option allowing the borrower to switch currencies at a later date. It offers both variable-rate loans and fixed-rate loans. Clauses in some fixed-rate loans allow the rates to be reset every five years. IFC loan terms usually range from 7 to 12 years.

Export–Import Bank of the United States

The Export–Import Bank of the United States (ExImBank) was created in 1934 for the original purpose of facilitating trade between the United States and the Soviet Union. Subsequent world events dictated a change in its goals. Today the ExImBank serves to finance and facilitate exports of U.S. goods and services and to help maintain the competitiveness of U.S. companies in foreign markets. It has a mandate to supplement private sources of funds and is forbidden to compete with these sources. As an independent agency of the U.S. government, it carries out two separate programs—import financing and export financing.

Import Financing. The ExImBank helps foreign importers obtain intermediate-term loans from commercial banks to pay for purchases of U.S. goods. The ExImBank guarantees repayment to the commercial bank up to 85 percent of the amount of the loan and a portion of the interest, should the importer default for political and commercial reasons. The importer pays the ExImBank a fee for this service. The size of the fee depends on the riskiness of the importer's country, the riskiness of the importing company, and the term of the loan (which ranges from one to seven years).

Alternatively, the ExImBank finances large loans (at least $10 million) over long terms (more than seven years to maturity) at fixed rates to foreign buyers to purchase U.S. products that compete with officially subsidized foreign products. The ExImBank lends the money to a commercial bank at a below-market rate, and the bank relends the money to the importer at a specified higher rate.

Export Financing. The ExImBank helps U.S. exporters obtain working capital loans from commercial banks to finance production and sale of exportable goods. If the exporter defaults on the bank loan, the ExImBank repays the commercial bank up to 90 percent of the loan principal along with a portion of the accumulated interest. To get this guarantee, the exporter pays a fee and pledges its net working capital as collateral for the loan. The ExImBank does not protect the exporter if the foreign importer cannot pay for shipped goods; the exporter must absorb such a loss.

The ExImBank also helps to insure the foreign accounts receivable of U.S. exporters. The Foreign Credit Insurance Association (FCIA) was formed in 1961 by a group of private insurance companies to sell insurance policies to U.S. exporters and lenders to protect them from the risk of nonpayment by foreign importers. Most of the insurance companies left the FCIA in the 1980s because of heavy losses, so the ExImBank currently underwrites all FCIA policies. If the foreign importer defaults for business reasons such as insolvency, the FCIA reimburses the U.S. exporter or the lending bank up to 90 percent of the value of the invoice or loan. If the foreign importer defaults for political reasons such as an exchange blockage, embargo, or war, the FCIA reimburses the U.S. exporter or lending bank 100 percent of the value of the invoice or loan. Some restrictions apply to importers in specific countries.

The Private Export Funding Corporation (PEFCO) was established in 1971 by a consortium of commercial banks and industrial companies to mobilize nonbank funds to finance U.S. exports. It raises funds by issuing long-term bonds and lends this money to foreign buyers to finance large projects that use products of U.S. companies. These loans mature in 5 to 25 years and are guaranteed by the ExImBank. In addition to its regular loan program, PEFCO purchases the debt obligations of foreign importers that have been guaranteed by the ExImBank from banks and other lending institutions without recourse.

Bank for International Settlements

The Bank for International Settlements (BIS) provides assistance to countries that experience financial crises. It was created in 1930 to act as trustee in the settlement of German reparations and other debts from World War I. Headquartered in Basel, Switzerland, the BIS is guaranteed immunity from taxation and expropriation. Its membership includes the central banks of nearly all European countries, as well as Canada, Japan, Australia, and South Africa. The United States has never exercised its right to appoint a member of the Board of Directors.

Since the 1950s, the BIS has acted as a forum for consultation and collaboration among central banks; it has sometimes been called the "central bank's central bank." Among its powers, it can:

1. Discount, rediscount, purchase, or sell short-term obligations of prime liquidity, including government issues
2. Buy and sell foreign exchange
3. Buy and sell negotiable securities other than equities
4. Accept deposits from central banks, regional or national government bodies, the United Nations and its agencies, as well as the European Economic Community and its various funds
5. Act as a trustee or agent to settle international transactions
6. Conclude special agreements with central banks to facilitate settlements of international transactions

SUMMARY

The four types of depository financial institutions include: commercial banks, savings and loan associations, savings banks, and credit unions. These institutions have more characteristics in common than differences, but they are still legally distinct. All take deposits, make loans, transfer funds, exchange currencies, and perform investment management services and custodial services. Commercial banks, however, have historically done business with corporations and wealthy individuals. Savings and loan associations and savings banks have traditionally serviced the individual and residential mortgage markets. Credit unions were formed to serve the financial needs of specific groups of people.

Nondepository financial institutions are all financial intermediaries. They accumulate money in relatively small amounts from those who have surplus funds and channel money in relatively large amounts to those who have deficits. This greatly enhances the diversity of securities available to the suppliers and users of funds. The principal function of other financial service institutions is to act as agents and/or advisors in financial matters. They provide quick and convenient entries into and exits from almost all types of investments.

The financial markets have not always been able to practice successful self-regulation to eliminate major economic disruptions caused by abuses of the financial system. The Federal Reserve System regulates banking activity in the United

States and establishes monetary policy. The Securities and Exchange Commission guards against fraud in the securities industry and sets minimum disclosure standards for companies that issue securities to the public. Federal insurance corporations have been set up to protect individuals (and sometimes businesses) from failures by banks, thrifts, credit unions, brokerage houses, and pension funds.

U.S. financial institutions have provided financial services outside the United States since the first overseas branch of a U.S. commercial bank opened in 1887. Today, U.S. commercial banks can provide international financial services through almost a dozen different operational arrangements. U.S. investment banks and brokerage houses serve customers all over the world. U.S. investment companies, pension funds, and insurance companies have invested in foreign financial and tangible assets.

International financial institutions facilitate the flow of funds across national boundaries. The International Monetary Fund attempts to enhance the system of exchange rates among the currencies of its member nations and helps to resolve their balance of payments problems. Various international banks attempt to improve the economic conditions of their member nations by making or guaranteeing productivity-enhancing loans to developing countries.

Key Terms

bank run
best efforts sale
co-financing agreement
defined-benefit pension plan
defined-contribution pension plan
depository institution
Eurocurrency
financial institution
financial intermediary
insurance premium
investment opportunity balance
making a market
precautionary balance
required reserve ratio
special drawing rights (SDRs)
transactions balance
underwriting
vested benefit

Self-Study Questions

1. Name three reasons why corporations and individuals accumulate cash.
2. List five functions performed by commercial banks.
3. Which financial institutions other than commercial banks accept deposits and make loans?
4. Suppose you had invented a machine that would tend home aquariums and feed the fish automatically for up to two weeks. If you needed money to manufacture a large number of these machines, and to produce a half-hour infomercial and broadcast it on cable TV nightly for months, would you seek financing from a commercial bank, a mortgage bank, an investment bank, or a venture capitalist?
5. If you wanted to know the Nike Corporation's share of the market for sneakers, could a discount broker tell you? Why or why not?
6. Name the three major policy tools of the Federal Reserve System.

7. List any three of the five major nonpolicy functions of the Federal Reserve System.
8. How much deposit insurance do you have if your bank is a member of the FDIC?
9. Can a U.S. tourist convert U.S. dollars to SDRs and spend them in any country in Europe?
10. How does the ExImBank help U.S. exporters?

Discussion Questions

1. What effect might the proliferation of credit cards have on the sizes of transactions balances and precautionary balances held by individuals in the United States?
2. Suppose your neighborhood savings bank considers you a poor credit risk and refuses to lend you mortgage money for the house you want to buy; a mortgage bank decides to lend you the money, however. Would you expect the mortgage bank to charge a higher or lower interest rate than the savings bank?
3. Which type of insurance company has more predictable cash flows? Why?
4. Why is insurance for airline in-flight accidents cheaper than automobile accident insurance?
5. What is the essential difference between closed-end and open-end investment companies?
6. If you were the unrestricted manager of an unregulated pension fund that was intended to provide retirement and disability benefits for 10,000 people, would you choose securities with high returns and high risk or low returns and low risk? Why?
7. What is the difference between security underwriting and a best efforts sale?
8. You started a highly successful company that plans virtual reality scenarios. You have borrowed every dollar the banks are willing to lend and your family and friends have invested every dollar they can spare, but you still need money for expansion. Which financial institution should you consult now?
9. Changing reserve requirements is the policy tool the Federal Reserve System is least likely to use. Why?
10. Why do total reserves decline if the FOMC sells securities?
11. What is the Federal Reserve trying to do when it raises the discount rate?
12. The FDIC, the SAIF, and the BIF are all federal insurance for depository institutions. How are they different?
13. Is it safe to deposit money in a modern savings bank?
14. If the SEC regulates the securities markets, why is SIPC insurance necessary?
15. ERISA set many standards for pension fund management. Name some choices that pension fund managers are still free to make.
16. If a commercial bank is interested in doing business internationally, why would it consider any operating form other than setting up foreign branches?

17. What is an SDR and how is it used?
18. What lending innovations has the World Bank created?
19. What lending innovations has the International Finance Corporation created?
20. How does the ExImBank facilitate imports of foreign products and services into the United States?

Topics for Further Research

1. Throughout the 19th century (1800–1899), the U.S. banking system collapsed with distressing regularity. Look up any two financial crises during this time period. What conditions and/or events preceded the crises? Could such conditions or events reoccur today? Why or why not?
2. Look in your phone book's Yellow Pages for credit unions. Judging by their names, what groups were they founded to serve?
3. Identify the characteristics of the stock market in the 1920s that might have contributed to the crash of 1929. Were any of these characteristics apparent before the stock market crash in October 1987?
4. Analyze the recent history of any developing nation. Which international financial institutions have been active in that country? Are their efforts recognized as successful or ineffectual? Why?

CHAPTER

4

Securities and Their Characteristics

LEARNING OBJECTIVES

At the conclusion of this chapter, the reader should be able to:

1. *Understand the relationship between risk and return*
2. *Identify many of the securities available for investment*
3. *Understand the different characteristics of securities, such as maturity, type of income produced, potential for capital gains, and tax status*
4. *Interpret financial reporting by newspapers about different securities*
5. *Select appropriate types of securities for investors with different goals*

security
A paper or electronic document created as evidence of some financial transaction.

Securities are paper or electronic documents created as evidence of financial transactions. They are financial assets to those who hold them and financial claims against those who issue them. Historically, all money market securities have represented short-term loans, and capital market securities represented either long-term debt or ownership claims. This distinction between money and capital markets has become academic because many new types of securities have been invented and variations of old security types have proliferated.

Encyclopedic knowledge of all available securities is required only of those whose jobs involve daily management of security portfolios. A financial manager with other financial responsibilities needs only a basic understanding of the different categories of securities and an awareness of the factors that affect their expected rates of return.

All finance personnel should appreciate the wide range of risks associated with investing in securities. They can avoid some types of risk and minimize other types, but they must simply accept a few types of risk. The market generally compensates the owners of less risky securities with lower, but more certain, returns.

RETURN AND RISK

Security returns may consist of income or price appreciation or both. Suppose, for example, that an investor buys a bond issued by Desi Co. for $1,000. The bond promises to pay $30 interest every six months for 25 years. If the investor holds the bond for the full 25 years, the company should return the $1,000 principal value for the bond at maturity, in addition to the periodic interest payments. The annual rate of return on this bond is $60/$1,000, or 6 percent. The entire return is income; there is no price appreciation.

Another investor might buy a promissory note that pays no interest. Suppose a note from Luci Co. promises to pay $1,000 after one year. The price of this note now is $943.40. If the investor holds the note for the full year, the profit on the note is $1,000 minus $943.40 or $56.60. This gives the note a rate of return of $56.60/$943.40, or 6 percent. The entire return comes from price appreciation.

One more investor might buy a stock that pays dividends quarterly and whose price fluctuates constantly. Suppose an investor buys $1,000 worth of stock in Mertz Co. Every three months, a dividend check for $10 arrives in the mail. At the end of a year, the investor sells the stock for $1,020. The investor's profit on the stock is:

$$(4 \times \$10) + (\$1{,}020 - \$1{,}000) = \$40 + \$20 = \$60$$

This rate of return of $60/$1,000, or 6 percent, is a combination of 4 percent from income and 2 percent from price appreciation.

Regardless of the components in the calculations, the investors in these three illustrations earn rates of return of 6 percent. Are the three investors equally happy? Probably not. A few of the obvious reasons are:

1. The bond investor has to wait 25 years to get the $1,000 back; the other two have their money after one year.
2. The $1,000 payments from Desi Co. and Luci Co. are definite legal obligations. The selling price of the Mertz Co. stock, however, could easily have been $1,021 or $1,019 if the sale had taken place five minutes later.
3. Nothing has been said about the three companies' cash positions. They may not be equally able to make the expected payments.
4. The investor in Mertz Co. starts earning a return in three months; the investor in Desi Co. has to wait six months, while the investor in Luci Co. has to wait for a whole year for an all-or-nothing payment.

These reasons are all components of the concept of risk. Investors who take greater risks expect higher returns from their investments. Assuming that the companies have equally good cash positions, the return on the Desi Co. bond

EXHIBIT 4.1

Avoiding or Minimizing the Risks Associated with Securities

Type of Risk	Action to Be Taken by a U.S. Investor
	To avoid risk:
Default risk	Invest in U.S. Treasury securities
Illiquidity risk	Invest in U.S. Treasury bills
Interest rate risk	Hold any security to maturity
Call risk	Avoid securities with call features or sinking funds
Expiration risk	Avoid warrants, futures, options
Exchange rate risk	Invest in U.S. dollar-denominated issues
	To minimize risk:
Purchasing power risk	Invest in common stock for the long term
Country risk	Invest in securities of developed countries
Market risk	Cannot be avoided

should be higher than the return on the Luci Co. note because the investor has to wait 24 more years to get the $1,000 back. Under the same assumption, the return on the Mertz Co. stock should be higher than either of the other two securities because the return is protected by no legal obligation.

All investors must weigh the risks and returns associated with different securities. When comparing two securities with different returns, it is necessary to answer a fundamental question: is the extra return worth the extra risk?

TYPES OF RISKS

risk
The probability that an investor will not receive the expected return from an investment for one reason or another.

Risk can be defined as the probability that an investor will not receive the expected return from an investment, for one reason or another. Because returns can vary for many reasons, the market recognizes many specific types of risk. The reasons for variations in returns involve such possibilities as defaults on expected payments, lack of interest in particular securities by other investors, unanticipated inflation, fluctuating interest rates, news events, the terms of specific security issues, changes in foreign exchange rates, and international political events.

Some types of risk can be avoided by careful selection of securities and some types of risk can be minimized. Exhibit 4.1 summarizes the actions investors should take if they are risk averse.

Domestic Risks

The types of risk associated with domestic securities include default risk, the risk of illiquidity, purchasing power risk, interest rate risk, market risk, and call or expiration risk. Any increase in any or all or these will cause investors to demand a higher rate of return on a security.

default risk
The probability that a borrower will not pay interest or repay principal when due.

Default Risk. **Default risk** is the most obvious type of risk. It is the probability that the security issuer (borrower) will not pay interest or repay principal when due. Default risk can increase due to deteriorating economic conditions, financial difficulties experienced by the issuing company, or character flaws in the humans managing the issuing company. Investors (lenders) usually try to anticipate these probabilities and adjust the interest rate they demand to directly reflect this risk. Higher default risk leads investors to require more compensation, it increases the rate of interest on the security.

illiquidity risk
The probability that investors cannot buy or sell their securities quickly without disturbing the market price.

Illiquidity Risk. **Illiquidity risk** is the probability that investors cannot buy or sell their securities quickly without disturbing the market price. A security documents the original transaction with the issuing company; the investor may sell this claim to another investor, who may resell it so the security can change hands again and again. The original transaction that creates the security is said to occur in the *primary market*; all subsequent sales occur in the *secondary market*.

A liquid security can be sold quickly and easily in the secondary market, without the individual investor's decision to buy or sell affecting the market price and rate of return of the security. An investor who tries to buy a relatively illiquid security may push its market price upward and lower the yield he or she earns. An investor who tries to sell a relatively illiquid security may drive its market price downward, also reducing her or his own yield. Therefore, if investors perceive a security to be less liquid, this perception raises the expected return that it must pay to induce them to buy it in the first place.

purchasing power risk
The probability that investors can buy less with the principal and interest they receive from an investment than they could have bought with their principal at the time they made the investment.

Purchasing Power Risk. **Purchasing power risk** is the probability that investors can buy less with the principal and interest they receive from an investment than they could have bought with their principal at the time they made the investment. It exists because the actual inflation rate may be greater than the expected rate of inflation that is a component of the interest rate.

Suppose that an investor lends $1,000 at 10 percent for one year. At the time the loan is made, the price of a loaf of bread is $1.00, so the investor could have used the money to buy 1,000 loaves of bread. If the price of a loaf of bread is expected to rise to $1.05 in the coming year, the investor expects that the total of repaid principal and interest of $1,100 will buy $1,100/$1.05, or 1,047 loaves of bread. If, after one year passes, however, a loaf of bread costs $1.19, the investor's standard of living is lower than expected. After receiving the expected dollar return from the loan, $1,100, the investor can afford to buy only $1,100/$1.19 or 924 loaves of bread.

To protect themselves fully from inflation risk, investors would have to buy securities whose interest rates would vary with the inflation rate. In the short run, no U.S. securities have such variable rates, so it is impossible to avoid purchasing power risk, even by careful security selection. In the long run (over five years or more), the stock market is the only securities market that has produced returns higher than the inflation rate.

interest rate risk
The probability that current market rates of interest will change, making the prices of outstanding securities change in the opposite direction.

Interest Rate Risk. **Interest rate risk** is the probability that current market rates of interest will change, making the prices of outstanding securities change in the opposite direction. Interest rate risk has no real impact on an investor who buys a security and holds it to maturity; the return received will be the return expected. Interest rate risk affects only those investors who sell their securities before maturity because it influences the prices of those secondary market transactions.

Suppose a $1,000 security has a 12 percent annual rate and matures in one year. Interest of $120 is to be paid at maturity, although it is earned at $120/12, or $10 per month. Common practice in the securities markets pays an investor who sells a security before maturity the interest earned to the date of sale. Someone who buys the security after one month will pay $1,010 for it. The investors who holds the security when it matures will receive $1,120 no matter what the purchase date.

If interest rates did not change throughout the year, the investor could sell the 12 percent, $1,000 security described above for $1,010 after one month, or $1,040 after four months, or $1,110 after 11 months, and so forth.

Money market interest rates actually change from day to day. Suppose that, after two months, interest rates have fallen and the annual rate for a security with ten months to maturity is now 10 percent. Newly issued securities now earn interest at $100/12, or $8.33 per month. The old 12 percent security looks good compared to the new securities since it still earns $10 per month. Investor demand must push its market price higher than $1,020, so the seller's annual return rises above 12 percent. The buyer's annual return will be 10 percent if the security is held to maturity.

On the other hand, suppose that interest rates have risen and the annual rate for a security with ten months to maturity is now 15 percent. Newly issued securities now earn interest at $150/12, or $12.50 per month. The old 12 percent security now compares poorly with the new securities since it still earns only $10 per month. Weak demand must drive its market price below $1,020. The seller's return falls below12 percent annually, but the buyer still earns 15 percent if the security is held to maturity.

Interest rate risk occurs because the market prices of outstanding securities fall when current interest rates rise and those prices rise when current interest rates fall. Because companies rarely change their dividends every time interest rates change, common stock prices usually move in the same direction as bond prices, so stockholders are also subject to interest rate risk.

market risk
The probability that news events will depress general market prices on the day an investor wants to sell, or inflate prices on the day an investor wants to buy.

Market Risk. Sometimes called *psychological risk*, **market risk** is the probability that news events will depress general market prices on the day an investor wants to sell, or inflate prices on the day an investor wants to buy. All securities markets are sensitive to some degree to current events and changes in expectations about future events. Economically significant news items that surprise the markets can make them rise or fall dramatically on any given day. This is the element of pure luck that everyone who trades any kind of security must accept.

call risk
The probability that an issuer will retire a long-term debt security before its maturity date.

Call Risk. Some debt securities can be called, or repaid early, by the borrower. **Call risk** is the probability that an issuer will retire a debt security before its maturity date.

If a note or bond is designated as callable when it is first issued, the borrower can pay off the entire issue at will, giving the investor the face value of the security, the interest due to the date of the call, and any additional payment, called a *call premium*, specified in the original security agreement. Issuers usually call securities when interest rates have declined significantly, allowing them to replace the existing issue with a new, cheaper issue. The investor's only available opportunity is to reinvest the proceeds in a security that offers a lower return for the same level of risk that the called security offered.

Some notes and bonds require the company to establish a sinking fund, which pays off a fraction of the debt each year. This is another source of call risk, as the issuer must either purchase a number of securities sufficient to satisfy this commitment in the market or call randomly selected securities. Whichever way the issuer acquires these securities, they are retired and the remaining outstanding claims against the issuer have a reduced risk of default. The security holder whose note or bond is called to satisfy a sinking fund requirement usually receives only the face value of the security and the interest due up to the date of the call.

It is worth noting that not all bond sinking funds require real cash outflows. Accounting standards require that all bonds have sinking funds on the books. This means that, on paper, the company sets aside funds every year to provide for the repayment of principal when the bond matures. In practice, most companies replace maturing bonds with new ones, so the accounting rules do not require actual cash transfers and do not generate call risk.

Expiration Risk. Some securities, such as warrants and put and call options, can expire worthless. The investor who holds such a security on the expiration date can do nothing with it. Its value is zero when the market closes on that day. This creates **expiration risk.** As a matter of fact, during the last few days before expiration, the market price of such a security may deteriorate to the extent that it cannot be sold because the commission on the sale would exceed the proceeds from the sale.

expiration risk
The probability that certain types of securities will expire worthless.

International Risks

Foreign securities impose two additional risks on the investor: foreign exchange risk and country risk. Increases in either or both of these will cause investors to demand higher rates of return for international investments.

Exchange Rate Risk. To purchase a foreign security, an investor must convert domestic currency into the appropriate foreign currency. When the investment matures, the investor must convert the foreign currency payment back into the domestic currency. The exchange rate when the investment matures is likely to be different from the exchange rate when the investment starts. Thus, **exchange rate risk** is the probability that the domestic-currency return to the investor may be higher or lower than the rate realized on the foreign investment itself.

exchange rate risk
The probability that the domestic-currency return to an investor may be higher or lower than the rate realized on the foreign investment itself due to changes in currency exchange rates.

country risk

The probability that an investor will not earn the expected return on a foreign investment because of foreign political, economic, social, accounting, legal, or regulatory changes.

Country Risk. When investors purchase foreign securities, their investments may not produce the expected returns for many reasons. **Country risk** summarizes many sources of variations in returns:

1. The safety of a foreign investment depends on the stability of the government in power in the foreign country.
2. The return on a foreign investment depends on the economic conditions existing in the foreign country.
3. The return on a foreign investment may be affected by a change in social conditions in the foreign country.
4. Foreign accounting practices and standards may change during the time the investment is held.
5. Legal and regulatory requirements may change, tightening or easing restrictions on cross-border movements of capital.

In brief, investing in foreign securities requires far greater knowledge and financial sophistication than investing in U.S. securities.

YIELD CURVE

yield curve

A line that depicts the relationship between a security's time to maturity and its yield (rate of return).

The return an investor receives on a security is a function of two factors: risk and the yield curve. The **yield curve** is a line that depicts the relationship between the time it will take a security to reach maturity and the yield (rate of return) that the security offers. The yield curve is derived by plotting the yields to maturity for a set of debt securities on the vertical axis, or Y-axis, of a graph and their times to maturity on the horizontal axis, or X-axis.

A security's yield to maturity (YTM), expressed in words, is the:

$$\frac{\text{Annual interest} \pm \text{Average annual capital gain (loss)}}{\text{Average annual investment}}$$

Yield to maturity is approximated by the following equation:

$$YTM = [rF + (F - P)/n] \,/\, [(F + P)/2] \tag{4.1}$$

where r = fixed interest rate on the security

F = face (or maturity) value of the security

P = current market price of the security

n = number of years to maturity

EXHIBIT 4.2

The Treasury Yield Curve

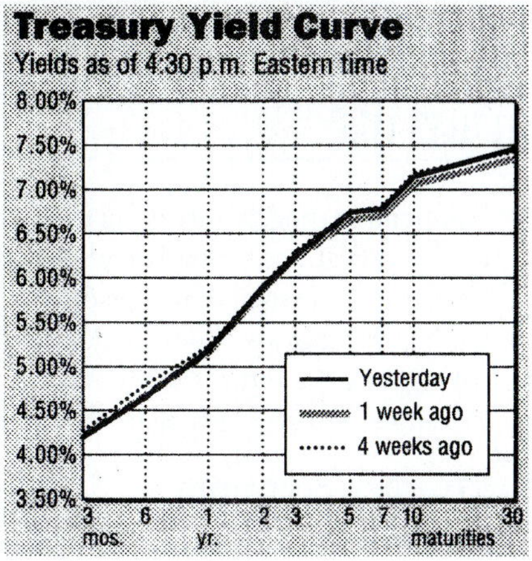

Source: The Wall Street Journal, February 15, 1994, p. C20.

❖ EXAMPLE 4.1

A bond issued with an interest rate of 11 percent is currently selling in the market for \$900. If it has a \$1,000 face value and matures in 15 years, its yield will be 12.3 percent.

$$YTM = \frac{(0.11)(\$1{,}000) + (\$1{,}000 - \$900)/15}{(\$1{,}000 + \$900)/2}$$

$$= \frac{\$110.00 + \$6.67}{\$950.00}$$

$$= 12.3 \text{ percent}$$

This bond would be plotted as ($X = 15$, $Y = 0.123$). Similar points could be obtained for many bonds with the same default risk and the graph would eventually display the yield curve. The yield curve for Treasury securities is illustrated daily in *The Wall Street Journal*, as shown in Exhibit 4.2. ❖

The yield curve is not a straight line; it rises relatively quickly for short maturities and relatively slowly for long maturities. Under normal market conditions, securites with longer times to maturity have higher returns. Occasionally, in response to expectations about impending changes in the level of interest rates, the yield curve takes on a negative slope. When the yield curve is inverted, long-term interest rates temporarily fall below short-term rates.

Economists differ about the causes of the exact shape that the yield curve takes at a specific point in time. In general, they believe that the level and slope of the curve are influenced by:

1. Risk
2. Expectations about future interest rates and future levels of risk
3. Expectations about government policies that affect the money supply
4. Existing and expected amounts of securities traded in the market

DOMESTIC SECURITIES

Financial managers surveying the vast array of domestic securities available for corporate investment usually try to control their degree of exposure to default risk by focusing on a particular type of issuer, either units of government, banks, or nonbank corporations. They decide on desirable maturities by balancing interest rate risk against the returns offered by the yield curve. They then examine specific securities, weighing return against remaining risks.

Treasury Securities

For more than 30 years, the U.S. government has spent more money annually than it has collected in taxes and fees. It has borrowed the difference—more than $4 trillion ($4,000,000,000,000.00) to date. The large majority of this debt (80 percent) is short-term; it matures in one year or less.

The U.S. Treasury is the official borrower of the U.S. government. The securities it issues when it borrows, called *bills*, *notes*, and *bonds*, are considered by the market to be virtually free of default risk. The federal government has the power to tax, so theoretically it can raise taxes to collect enough money to pay off its debt in full. If it did, however, it would cause a massive recession. Since this is not politically feasible, Treasury securities are described as *virtually* free of default risk.

Congress has legislated that a Treasury bill (also called a *T-bill*) matures in one year or less, a Treasury note (called a *T-note*) matures in one to ten years, and a Treasury bond (called a *T-bond*) matures in more than ten years. These maturity classes are not imposed on debt instruments issued by other borrowers.

treasury bill
A $10,000 discounted security issued by the U.S. Treasury that matures in one year or less.

Treasury Bills. A **Treasury Bill** (T-bill) is a discounted security with a $10,000 face value. The buyer pays a price less than $10,000, then receives exactly $10,000 when the bill matures. The difference is taxed as interest income by the federal government. This interest is not taxed at all by state and local governments, except in Tennessee.

The Treasury issues T-bills worth billions of dollars every Monday, mostly to raise the money to pay off maturing bills. Because so many T-bills are outstanding and they are held by almost all financial institutions, most corporations, many individuals, and some foreign governments, T-bills are considered to be free of the risk of illiquidity. This means that it is almost impossible for one investor to trade enough T-bills at one time to significantly influence their market price.

Tax Anticipation Bills. The Treasury occasionally sells additional issues of T-bills on weekdays other than Monday. After forecasting how much it will receive

FOCUS ON FINANCE

MONDAY AUCTION OF TREASURY BILLS

Two series of Treasury bills are auctioned every Monday. If Monday is a holiday, the auction may be held the preceding Friday or the following Tuesday. The auction closes at 1:30 p.m. (EST) and the results are announced via an electronic network within hours and major newspapers the next day. The results of the February 14, 1994, auction, as published in *The Wall Street Journal*, are shown in the clipping.

Published Results of a Treasury Bill Auction

	13-Week	26-Week
Applications	$58,559,455,000	$54,681,946,000
Accepted bids	$12,213,977,000	$12,276,380,000
Accepted at low price	20%	23%
Accepted noncompet'ly ...	$1,269,679,000	$955,768,000
Average price (Rate)	99.171 (3.28%)	98.266 (3.43%)
High price (Rate)	99.176 (3.26%)	98.271 (3.42%)
Low price (Rate)	99.171 (3.28%)	98.266 (3.43%)
Coupon equivalent	3.35%	3.54%
CUSIP number	912794K60	912794M84

Both issues are dated Feb. 17. The 13-week bills mature May 19, 1994, and the 26-week bills mature Aug. 18, 1994.

Source: *The Wall Street Journal*, February 15, 1994, p. C20.

Investors submit applications (called *tenders*) for the amounts of bills they want to buy. The reproduced form on the following page illustrates the tender for a 13-week T-bill auction. The minimum acceptable dollar amount for a tender is $10,000; higher tenders must be stated in multiples of $5,000. Competitive bidders specify the discount rates they want, which determine the prices they pay if their tenders are accepted. Most individual investors submit noncompetitive applications, agreeing to pay a price equivalent to the weighted average of the accepted competitive bids. Noncompetitive tenders from any single bidder may not exceed $5 million. Investors applied for more than $58 billion of 13-week bills on February 14, 1994.

The Treasury normally accepts all noncompetitive tenders. On February 14, received tenders worth more than $1.2 billion in 13-week bills. These investors paid $9,917.10 for each $10,000 bill, which represents a 3.28 percent annual discount rate. This rate is based on the $10,000 par value of a T-bill, and assumes 360 days in a year.

Next, the Treasury accepts competitive tenders, beginning with those that bid the lowest discount rate (the highest price). It accepts successively higher rates (lower prices) until it sells enough to raise the amount it had planned to borrow. On February 14, 1994, it accepted over $12.2 billion in competitive bids on 13-week bills. Bids at the highest discount rate (lowest price) are prorated. Thus, investors who bid between $9,917.60 and $9,917.20 per $10,000 bill got all the bills they wanted to buy, but investors who bid $9,917.10 got only 20 percent of the bills they wanted to buy.

The coupon equivalent rate of the discounted yield is based on the average purchase price of the bills and assumes 365 days in a year. Totalling the competitive and noncompetitive bills issued in both series, the Treasury borrowed $26,715,804,000 on St. Valentine's Day, 1994. As always, it issued the bills the following Thursday, February 17.

in corporate income tax payments on March 15, June 15, September 15, and December 15, it then borrows that money in advance by issuing special T-bills that mature on March 19, June 19, September 19, or December 19. These tax anticipation T-bills can be attractive to a corporation. Suppose that a firm plans to pay, say, $2 million in estimated taxes on June 15. It can (1) buy 200 tax anticipation T-bills in advance, all at once or a few at a time, paying less than

Tender for 13-Week Treasury Bill Auction

FORM PD 5176-1
(January 1986)

OMB No. 1535-0069
Expires 01-31-92

TREASURY DIRECT

TENDER FOR 13-WEEK TREASURY BILL

TENDER INFORMATION

AMOUNT OF TENDER: $ ______

BID TYPE (Check One) ☐ NONCOMPETITIVE ☐ COMPETITIVE AT __ . __ %

ACCOUNT NUMBER ___ - ___ - ___

INVESTOR INFORMATION

ACCOUNT NAME

ADDRESS

CITY STATE ZIP CODE

TAXPAYER IDENTIFICATION NUMBER

1ST NAMED OWNER ___ - ___ - ___ SOCIAL SECURITY NUMBER OR ___ - ___ EMPLOYER IDENTIFICATION NUMBER

TELEPHONE NUMBERS

WORK ( ) - HOME ( ) -

FOR DEPARTMENT USE

TENDER NUMBER
912794

CUSIP

ISSUE DATE

RECEIVED BY

DATE RECEIVED

EXT REG ☐

FOREIGN ☐

BACKUP ☐

REVIEW ☐

CLASS ☐

PAYMENT ATTACHED

TOTAL PAYMENT: $ ______

CASH (01): $ ______ CHECKS (02/03): $ ______

SECURITIES (05): $ ______ $ ______

OTHER (06): $ ______ $ ______

NUMBERS

DIRECT DEPOSIT INFORMATION

ROUTING NUMBER

FINANCIAL INSTITUTION NAME

ACCOUNT NUMBER

ACCOUNT NAME

ACCOUNT TYPE (Check One) ☐ CHECKING ☐ SAVINGS

AUTOMATIC REINVESTMENT

1 2 3 4 5 6 7 8 Circle the number of sequential 13-week reinvestments you want to schedule at this time

AUTHORIZATION

For the notice required under the Privacy and Paperwork Reduction Acts, see the accompanying instructions.

I submit this tender pursuant to the provisions of Department of the Treasury Circulars, Public Debt Series Nos. 1-86 and 2-86 and the public announcement issued by the Department of the Treasury.

Under penalties of perjury, I certify that the number shown on this form is my correct taxpayer identification number and that I am not subject to backup withholding because (1) I have not been notified that I am subject to backup withholding as a result of a failure to report all interest or dividends, or (2) the Internal Revenue Service has notified me that I am no longer subject to backup withholding. I further certify that all other information provided on this form is true, correct and complete.

______ SIGNATURE ______ DATE

$2 million in total for them, (2) earn interest every day for as long as it holds each T-bill, and then (3) turn them in as a full $2 million tax payment on June 15 even though four more days remain to maturity. This raises the yield a little, because the company obtains four extra days' interest.

The face value of T-bills used to pay taxes cannot exceed the tax bill, however. If the company owed only $1,997,000 in taxes, it could turn in only 199 T-bills. It would have to pay $3,000 in cash and continue to hold one T-bill. Surplus tax anticipation bills may be sold in the market or held four more days until they mature.

repurchase agreement
A very short-term contract between an investor and a bank or broker fixing the sale and repurchase prices of T-bills to guarantee the investor a profit.

Repurchase Agreements. **Repurchase agreements** (usually referred to as *repos* or *RPs*) were created by brokerage houses and popularized by commercial banks. Suppose a large investor has money to invest overnight or over a weekend, but it is concerned that T-bill prices will fall before it sells them. The investor can always find a bank or dealer willing to sell the desired number of T-bills and commit to buying them back later at a specified price. The purchase and sale prices are set to guarantee the investor a profit.

If interest rates fall or remain unchanged during the day(s) the investor holds the T-bills, the rate of profit on the repo will be slightly less than the rate that the investor could have earned by buying and selling T-bills in the open market. This difference, plus the fee charged for the transaction, constitutes the bank's or dealer's profit. If interest rates rise, however, the investor still gets the guaranteed profit and the bank or dealer absorbs the loss.

Treasury Notes and Bonds. T-notes and T-bonds are not discounted. They are sold in denominations of $1,000, $5,000, $10,000, $100,000, and $1 million and make semiannual interest payments. Notes that mature in less than four years are exceptions; they have $5,000 minimum denominations.

The U.S. Treasury announces that it will be offering a certain amount of T-notes or T-bonds for sale one week prior to the auction. The public and registered government securities dealers submit bids to buy the issue. These T-notes and T-bonds are registered issues, which means that the U.S. Treasury records the name and address of the current holder of each security and credits the bank account of the owner of record for accrued interest every six months.

Many major daily newspapers list price quotes for T-notes and T-bonds at the close of trading on the previous market day. Such a listing from *The Wall Street Journal* appears in Exhibit 4.3. A simulated entry during June 1994 appears below, followed by instructions for interpreting the information:

RATE	MATURITY	BID	ASK	CHANGE	ASK YIELD
$9\frac{5}{8}$	August 99n	101:03	101:05	+1	9.35

***Rate* = $9\frac{5}{8}$.** This means that a $1,000 security pays $96.25 interest per year. The security holder receives a check for $48.12 every February and a check for $48.13 every August.

EXHIBIT 4.3

Treasury Bonds, Notes, and Bills

TREASURY BONDS, NOTES & BILLS

Monday, June 20, 1994

Representative Over-the-Counter quotations based on transactions of $1 million or more.

Treasury bond, note and bill quotes are as of mid-afternoon. Colons in bid-and-asked quotes represent 32nds; 101:01 means 101 1/32. Net changes in 32nds. n-Treasury note. Treasury bill quotes in hundredths, quoted on terms of a rate of discount. Days to maturity calculated from settlement date. All yields are to maturity and based on the asked quote. Latest 13-week and 26-week bills are boldfaced. For bonds callable prior to maturity, yields are computed to the earliest call date for issues quoted above par and to the maturity date for issues below par. *-When issued.

Source: Federal Reserve Bank of New York.

U.S. Treasury strips as of 3 p.m. Eastern time, also based on transactions of $1 million or more. Colons in bid-and-asked quotes represent 32nds; 101:01 means 101 1/32. Net changes in 32nds. Yields calculated on the asked quotation. ci-stripped coupon interest. bp-Treasury bond, stripped principal. np-Treasury note, stripped principal. For bonds callable prior to maturity, yields are computed to the earliest call date for issues quoted above par and to the maturity date for issues below par.

Source: Bear, Stearns & Co. via Street Software Technology Inc.

GOVT. BONDS & NOTES

Rate	Maturity Mo/Yr	Bid	Asked	Chg.	Ask Yld.
5	Jun 94n	100:00	100:02	....	2.12
8½	Jun 94n	100:03	100:05	....	1.37
8	Jul 94n	100:08	100:10	....	2.97
4¼	Jul 94n	100:00	100:02	....	3.61
6⅞	Aug 94n	100:12	100:14	- 1	3.83
8⅝	Aug 94n	100:21	100:23	....	3.67
8¾	Aug 94	100:21	100:23	....	3.79
12⅝	Aug 94n	101:08	101:10	- 1	3.62
4¼	Aug 94n	100:00	100:02	+ 1	3.87
4	Sep 94n	99:28	99:30	....	4.19
8½	Sep 94n	101:04	101:06	....	4.03
9½	Oct 94n	101:16	101:18	- 1	4.38
4¼	Oct 94n	99:28	99:30	....	4.40
6	Nov 94n	100:16	100:18	....	4.53
8¼	Nov 94n	101:12	101:14	....	4.52
10⅛	Nov 94	102:04	102:06	- 2	4.47
11⅝	Nov 94n	102:22	102:24	....	4.52
4⅝	Nov 94n	99:31	100:01	....	4.54
4⅝	Dec 94n	99:28	99:30	....	4.75
7⅝	Dec 94n	101:12	101:14	- 1	4.81
8⅝	Jan 95n	102:00	102:02	- 1	4.87
4¼	Jan 95n	99:19	99:21	- 1	4.83
3	Feb 95	97:20	98:20	- 1	5.18
5½	Feb 95n	100:10	100:12	....	4.91
7¾	Feb 95n	101:23	101:25	- 1	4.93
10½	Feb 95	103:16	103:18	- 1	4.87
11¼	Feb 95n	104:01	104:03	....	4.78
3⅞	Feb 95n	99:07	99:09	....	4.94
3⅞	Mar 95n	99:02	99:04	....	5.04
8⅜	Apr 95n	102:15	102:17	- 1	5.17
3⅞	Apr 95n	98:29	98:31	....	5.12
5⅞	May 95n	100:18	100:20	....	5.15
8½	May 95n	102:26	102:28	- 1	5.18
10⅜	May 95	104:18	104:20	- 1	5.04
11¼	May 95n	105:11	105:13	....	5.02
12⅝	May 95	106:21	106:25	- 1	4.82
4⅛	May 95n	98:31	99:01	- 1	5.19
4⅛	Jun 95n	98:28	98:30	....	5.21
8⅞	Jul 95n	103:22	103:24	- 1	5.21
4¼	Jul 95n	98:26	98:28	- 1	5.31
4⅝	Aug 95n	99:05	99:07	- 2	5.33
8½	Aug 95n	103:13	103:15	- 1	5.35
10½	Aug 95n	105:21	105:23	- 2	5.31
3⅞	Aug 95n	98:08	98:10	- 1	5.36
3⅞	Sep 95n	98:03	98:05	- 1	5.39
8⅝	Oct 95n	103:28	103:30	- 1	5.48
3⅞	Oct 95n	97:27	97:29	- 1	5.50
5⅛	Nov 95n	99:14	99:16	- 1	5.50
8½	Nov 95n	103:28	103:30	- 1	5.53
9½	Nov 95n	105:07	105:09	- 2	5.52
11½	Nov 95	107:29	108:01	- 4	5.45
4¼	Nov 95n	98:05	98:07	- 2	5.55
4¼	Dec 95n	97:31	98:01	- 2	5.62
9¼	Jan 96n	105:08	105:10	- 2	5.65
4	Jan 96n	97:14	97:16	- 2	5.65
7½	Jan 96n	102:23	102:25	- 1	5.67
4⅝	Feb 96n	98:08	98:10	- 2	5.71
7⅞	Feb 96n	103:10	103:12	- 1	5.70
8⅞	Feb 96n	104:27	104:29	- 2	5.72
4⅝	Feb 96n	98:07	98:09	- 2	5.71
7½	Feb 96n	102:24	102:26	- 2	5.73
5⅛	Mar 96n	98:28	98:30	- 1	5.76
7¾	Mar 96n	103:08	103:10	- 1	5.76
9⅜	Apr 96n	105:31	106:01	- 2	5.83
5½	Apr 96n	99:12	99:14	- 2	5.82
7⅝	Apr 96n	103:01	103:03	- 2	5.84
4¼	May 96n	97:03	97:05	- 2	5.85
7⅜	May 96n	102:19	102:21	- 4	5.88
5⅞	May 96n	99:31	100:01	- 2	5.86
7⅝	May 96n	103:04	103:06	- 3	5.86
7⅞	Jun 96n	103:23	103:25	- 4	5.86
7⅞	Jul 96n	103:21	103:23	- 3	5.93
7⅞	Jul 96n	103:23	103:25	- 2	5.94
4⅜	Aug 96n	96:26	96:28	- 2	5.94
7¼	Aug 96n	102:15	102:17	- 3	6.00
7	Sep 96n	102:00	102:02	- 3	6.02
8	Oct 96n	104:03	104:05	- 2	6.05
6⅞	Oct 96n	101:23	101:25	- 3	6.05
4⅜	Nov 96n	96:07	96:09	- 3	6.06
7¼	Nov 96n	102:16	102:18	- 3	6.09
6½	Nov 96n	100:27	100:29	- 3	6.09
6⅛	Dec 96n	100:03	100:05	- 3	6.06
8	Jan 97n	104:08	104:10	- 3	6.16
6¼	Jan 97n	100:06	100:08	- 2	6.14
4¾	Feb 97n	96:18	96:20	- 3	6.15
6¾	Feb 97n	101:10	101:12	- 3	6.19
6⅞	Mar 97n	101:20	101:22	- 3	6.20
8½	Apr 97n	105:22	105:24	- 3	6.24
6⅞	Apr 97n	101:19	101:21	- 3	6.23
6½	May 97n	100:21	100:23	- 3	6.23
8½	May 97n	105:26	105:28	- 3	6.25
6¾	May 97n	101:08	101:10	- 3	6.25
5½	Sep 97n	97:15	97:17	- 4	6.35
8¾	Oct 97n	106:29	106:31	- 4	6.38
5¾	Oct 97n	98:02	98:04	- 3	6.38
8⅞	Nov 97n	107:12	107:14	- 4	6.40
6	Nov 97n	98:21	98:23	- 4	6.42
6	Dec 97n	98:19	98:21	- 4	6.43
7⅞	Jan 98n	104:13	104:15	- 3	6.45
5⅝	Jan 98n	97:08	97:10	- 3	6.47
8⅛	Feb 98n	105:07	105:09	- 4	6.48
5⅛	Feb 98n	95:17	95:19	- 2	6.49
5⅛	Mar 98n	95:12	95:14	- 2	6.51
7⅞	Apr 98n	104:14	104:16	- 3	6.52
5⅛	Apr 98n	95:06	95:08	- 3	6.54
9	May 98n	108:10	108:12	- 4	6.53
5⅜	May 98n	95:29	95:31	- 3	6.55
5⅛	Jun 98n	94:27	94:29	- 4	6.59
8¼	Jul 98n	105:26	105:28	- 3	6.58
5¼	Jul 98n	95:05	95:07	- 3	6.60
9¼	Aug 98n	109:14	109:16	- 4	6.60
4¾	Aug 98n	93:07	93:09	- 4	6.61
4¾	Sep 98n	93:04	93:06	- 4	6.61
7⅛	Oct 98n	101:25	101:27	- 6	6.63
4¾	Oct 98n	92:29	92:31	- 4	6.63
3½	Nov 98	92:00	93:00	- 4	5.31
8⅞	Nov 98n	108:11	108:13	- 5	6.64
5⅛	Nov 98n	94:06	94:08	- 4	6.64
5⅛	Dec 98n	94:01	94:03	- 4	6.66
6⅜	Jan 99n	98:26	98:28	- 5	6.66
5	Jan 99n	93:13	93:15	- 4	6.67
8⅞	Feb 99n	108:20	108:22	- 5	6.67
5½	Feb 99n	95:10	95:12	- 4	6.66
5⅞	Mar 99n	96:20	96:22	- 5	6.70
7	Apr 99n	101:05	101:07	- 4	6.70
6½	Apr 99n	99:03	99:05	- 5	6.71
9⅛	May 99n	109:30	110:00	- 6	6.70
6¾	May 99n	100:02	100:04	- 4	6.72
6⅜	Jul 99n	98:15	98:17	- 5	6.72
8	Aug 99n	105:13	105:15	- 5	6.73
6	Oct 99n	96:18	96:20	- 5	6.77
6⅜	Jan 00n	98:01	98:03	- 6	6.79
7⅞	Feb 95-00	101:17	101:21	....	5.25
8½	Feb 00n	107:28	107:30	- 6	6.79
5½	Apr 00n	93:28	93:30	- 6	6.78
8⅞	May 00n	109:31	110:01	- 4	6.78
8⅜	Aug 95-00	102:24	102:28	- 2	5.76
8¾	Aug 00n	109:10	109:12	- 5	6.86
8½	Nov 00n	108:08	108:10	- 3	6.87
7¾	Feb 01n	104:12	104:14	- 4	6.91
11¾	Feb 01	125:21	125:25	-11	6.86
8	May 01n	105:21	105:23	- 5	6.94
13⅛	May 01	133:20	133:24	- 7	6.89
7⅞	Aug 01n	104:31	105:01	- 3	6.97
8	Aug 96-01	103:20	103:24	+ 6	6.11
13⅜	Aug 01	135:26	135:30	- 8	6.92
7½	Nov 01n	102:24	102:26	- 6	7.01
15¾	Nov 01	150:07	150:11	-10	6.94
14¼	Feb 02	142:20	142:24	- 8	6.95
7½	May 02n	102:22	102:24	- 6	7.04
6⅜	Aug 02n	95:22	95:24	- 3	7.07
11⅝	Nov 02	128:10	128:14	- 5	7.08
6¼	Feb 03n	94:13	94:15	- 4	7.12
10¾	Feb 03	123:05	123:09	- 4	7.10
10¾	May 03	123:15	123:19	- 3	7.12
5¾	Aug 03n	90:20	90:22	- 4	7.15
11⅛	Aug 03	126:09	126:13	- 4	7.14
11⅞	Nov 03	131:24	131:28	- 4	7.16
5⅞	Feb 04n	91:02	91:04	- 4	7.16
7¼	May 04n	100:21	100:23	- 4	7.15
12⅜	May 04	136:04	136:08	- 5	7.19
13¾	Aug 04	146:13	146:17	- 3	7.21
11⅝	Nov 04	131:24	131:28	- 7	7.21
8¼	May 00-05	104:25	104:29	- 9	7.21
12	May 05	135:07	135:11	- 6	7.25
10¾	Aug 05	126:08	126:12	- 4	7.26
9⅜	Feb 06	116:10	116:14	- 5	7.26
7⅝	Feb 02-07	101:08	101:12	- 5	7.39
7⅞	Nov 02-07	102:29	103:01	- 3	7.38
8⅜	Aug 03-08	106:14	106:18	- 5	7.38
8¾	Nov 03-08	109:03	109:07	- 4	7.37
9⅛	May 04-09	112:04	112:08	- 3	7.36
10⅜	Nov 04-09	121:22	121:26	- 6	7.34
11¾	Feb 05-10	132:00	132:04	- 7	7.35
10	May 05-10	119:19	119:23	- 6	7.34
12¾	Nov 05-10	141:02	141:06	- 7	7.35
13⅞	May 06-11	151:05	151:09	- 1	7.34
14	Nov 06-11	153:00	153:04	- 6	7.38
10⅜	Nov 07-12	124:02	124:06	- 6	7.48
12	Aug 08-13	138:28	139:00	- 8	7.48
13¼	May 09-14	151:06	151:10	- 2	7.48
12½	Aug 09-14	144:23	144:27	- 6	7.50
11¾	Nov 09-14	138:12	138:16	+ 2	7.49
11¼	Feb 15	137:29	137:31	- 1	7.58
10⅝	Aug 15	131:20	131:22	- 1	7.59
9⅞	Nov 15	123:28	123:30	....	7.59
9¼	Feb 16	117:09	117:11	....	7.60
7¼	May 16	96:11	96:13	+ 1	7.59
7½	Nov 16	98:29	98:31	- 1	7.60
8¾	May 17	112:05	112:07	+ 1	7.61
8⅞	Aug 17	113:18	113:20	....	7.61
9⅛	May 18	116:16	116:18	+ 2	7.61
9	Nov 18	115:08	115:10	+ 2	7.61
8⅞	Feb 19	113:28	113:30	- 3	7.61
8⅛	Aug 19	105:21	105:23	- 3	7.61
8½	Feb 20	109:30	110:00	- 4	7.61
8¾	May 20	112:25	112:27	- 5	7.61
8¾	Aug 20	112:27	112:29	- 4	7.61
7⅞	Feb 21	103:02	103:04	- 4	7.60
8⅛	May 21	105:31	106:01	- 4	7.60
8⅛	Aug 21	106:03	106:05	- 4	7.59
8	Nov 21	104:27	104:29	- 4	7.57
7¼	Aug 22	96:14	96:16	- 4	7.55
7⅝	Nov 22	100:26	100:28	- 4	7.55
7⅛	Feb 23	95:04	95:06	- 3	7.54
6¼	Aug 23	85:21	85:23	- 3	7.46

U.S. TREASURY STRIPS

Mat.	Type	Bid	Asked	Chg.	Ask Yld.
Aug 94	ci	99:14	99:14	....	3.76
Nov 94	ci	98:06	98:06	....	4.62
Nov 94	np	98:05	98:05	- 1	4.70
Feb 95	ci	96:29	96:29	- 1	4.89
Feb 95	np	96:28	96:29	- 1	4.92
May 95	ci	95:17	95:18	- 1	5.13
May 95	np	95:18	95:18	- 1	5.11
Aug 95	ci	94:05	94:06	- 1	5.28
Aug 95	np	94:05	94:06	- 1	5.29
Nov 95	ci	92:22	92:23	- 2	5.49
Nov 95	np	92:21	92:22	- 1	5.51
Feb 96	ci	91:02	91:03	- 1	5.73
Feb 96	np	91:02	91:03	- 2	5.74
May 96	ci	89:19	89:21	- 1	5.85
May 96	np	89:18	89:19	- 2	5.88
Aug 96	ci	88:05	88:06	- 2	5.93
Nov 96	ci	86:19	86:21	- 2	6.06
Nov 96	np	86:17	86:18	- 2	6.11
Feb 97	ci	84:31	85:01	- 3	6.21
May 97	ci	83:14	83:17	- 3	6.31
May 97	np	83:14	83:17	- 3	6.31
Aug 97	ci	81:31	82:01	- 3	6.38
Aug 97	np	81:30	82:00	- 4	6.40
Nov 97	ci	80:17	80:19	- 3	6.45
Nov 97	np	80:17	80:20	- 4	6.45
Feb 98	ci	79:00	79:03	- 3	6.53
Feb 98	np	79:02	79:05	- 3	6.51
May 98	ci	77:18	77:20	- 3	6.60
May 98	np	77:18	77:20	- 3	6.60
Aug 98	ci	76:04	76:07	- 4	6.65
Aug 98	np	76:03	76:06	- 4	6.66
Nov 98	ci	74:26	74:29	- 4	6.68
Nov 98	np	74:25	74:28	- 4	6.70
Feb 99	ci	73:13	73:16	- 5	6.74
Feb 99	np	73:13	73:16	- 4	6.74
May 99	ci	72:04	72:07	- 5	6.76
May 99	np	72:03	72:06	- 5	6.76
Aug 99	ci	70:26	70:30	- 5	6.78
Aug 99	np	70:25	70:28	- 5	6.80
Nov 99	ci	69:18	69:21	- 4	6.81
Nov 99	np	69:17	69:20	- 4	6.82
Feb 00	ci	68:05	68:09	- 5	6.87
Feb 00	np	68:05	68:09	- 5	6.87
May 00	ci	66:31	67:03	- 2	6.88
May 00	np	66:30	67:02	- 5	6.89
Aug 00	ci	65:22	65:26	- 3	6.92
Aug 00	np	65:17	65:21	- 5	6.96
Nov 00	ci	64:15	64:19	- 2	6.95
Nov 00	np	64:09	64:12	- 5	7.00
Feb 01	ci	63:05	63:09	- 3	7.00
Feb 01	np	63:05	63:09	- 3	7.00
May 01	ci	61:30	62:01	- 3	7.04
May 01	np	61:28	62:00	- 3	7.05
Aug 01	ci	60:23	60:27	- 3	7.07
Aug 01	np	60:23	60:27	- 3	7.07
Nov 01	ci	59:18	59:22	- 3	7.10
Nov 01	np	59:18	59:22	- 3	7.10

TREASURY BILLS

Maturity	Days to Mat.	Bid	Asked	Chg.	Ask Yld.
Jun 23 '94	1	3.82	3.72	+0.11	3.77
Jun 30 '94	8	3.45	3.35	-0.05	3.40
Jul 07 '94	15	3.71	3.61	+0.14	3.67
Jul 14 '94	22	3.75	3.65	+0.05	3.71
Jul 21 '94	29	3.74	3.70	+0.02	3.76
Jul 28 '94	36	3.86	3.82	+0.01	3.89
Aug 04 '94	43	3.87	3.83	+0.02	3.90
Aug 11 '94	50	3.88	3.84	+0.02	3.91
Aug 18 '94	57	3.88	3.86	-0.04	3.94
Aug 25 '94	64	3.96	3.94	-0.02	4.02
Sep 01 '94	71	4.02	4.00	+0.01	4.09
Sep 08 '94	78	4.07	4.05	-0.03	4.14
Sep 15 '94	**85**	**4.12**	**4.10**	....	**4.20**
Sep 22 '94	92	4.17	4.15	....	4.25
Sep 29 '94	99	4.19	4.17	....	4.28
Oct 06 '94	106	4.24	4.22	+0.01	4.33
Oct 13 '94	113	4.26	4.24	....	4.36
Oct 20 '94	120	4.31	4.29	+0.01	4.41
Oct 27 '94	127	4.32	4.30	....	4.43
Nov 03 '94	134	4.38	4.36	+0.02	4.49
Nov 10 '94	141	4.40	4.38	....	4.52
Nov 17 '94	148	4.45	4.43	+0.01	4.57
Nov 25 '94	156	4.46	4.44	....	4.59
Dec 01 '94	162	4.47	4.45	....	4.60
Dec 08 '94	169	4.49	4.47	+0.01	4.63
Dec 15 '94	**176**	**4.50**	**4.48**	**+0.01**	**4.64**
Jan 12 '95	204	4.60	4.58	+0.02	4.76
Feb 09 '95	232	4.69	4.67	+0.01	4.86
Mar 09 '95	260	4.78	4.76	+0.04	4.96
Apr 06 '95	288	4.87	4.85	+0.03	5.07
May 04 '95	316	4.92	4.90	+0.03	5.14

Source: The Wall Street Journal, June 21, 1994, p. C17.

***Maturity* = *August 99n*.** This means that this security matures in August 1999 and is a note. If it were a bond, the *n* would not appear after the date. (In Exhibit 4.3, notice that the securities are listed in order of maturity.)

market order

An order for a broker to buy or sell a security at the current market price.

limit order

An order for a broker to buy (or sell) a security that sets an upper (or lower) limit on the price to be paid (or accepted).

***Bid* = 101:03.** This takes a bit of explaining. A potential investor can place either a market order or a limit order to buy securities. A **market order** tells the broker to buy the security at the current market price. Only after the order is executed does the investor find out the price paid. A **limit order** tells the broker to buy the security, but sets an upper limit on the price to be paid. If the current market price of the security does not fall to that limit, the purchase cannot be made and the order remains unfilled on the broker's books until it is canceled. The highest unfilled limit order on the books at the close of the trading day is listed as the bid price.

In capital market jargon, prices of all notes and bonds are listed as if their face values were $100. Further, $1 is fractured into 1/2, 1/4, 1/8, 1/16, or 1/32 of a dollar. The paper prints prices using 1/32. Because 1/32 of a dollar equals $0.03125, the bid price of 101:03 equals 101 and 3/32, or $101.09375. Since the T-note has an actual face value of $1,000, this figure is multiplied by 10. The highest unfilled limit order to buy on the broker's books at the close of the market specifies a price of $1,010.94.

***Ask* = 101:05.** This has an analogous interpretation. A limit order tells the broker to sell the security, but sets a lower limit on the price the security holder will accept. Since the T-note has a face value of $1,000, the lowest unfilled limit order to sell on the broker's books at the close of the market specifies a price of 101:05, which equals $1015/32, or $101.15625. This gives an ask price for the note of $1,011.56.

***Change* = +1.** This means that the closing ask price quoted, 101:05, is 1/32 higher than the closing ask price on the previous trading day.

***Ask Yield* = 9.35.** Finally, this means that an investor who buys the T-note in June at the ask price, $1,011.56, will earn an annual rate of return of 9.35 percent by holding the note to maturity (in five years and two months, or 5.16 years). Equation 4.1 demonstrates why 9.35 percent is an average annual yield:

$$\text{YTM} = \frac{\$96.25 - (\$11.56/5.16)}{(\$1{,}000 + \$1{,}011.56)/2}$$
$$= \frac{\$96.25 - \$2.24}{\$1{,}005.78}$$
$$= 9.35 \text{ percent}$$

flower bond

A treasury bond that pays a very low rate but can be used by an individual investor to pay estate taxes.

Flower Bonds. Flower bonds are normal T-bonds that became victims of timing. They were issued the last time interest rates were at the bottom of their cycle, about 20 years ago. As interest rates rose, the market prices of these bonds fell drastically. To remedy this deep discount, Congress passed laws designating issues such as the 3 percent bonds maturing in February 1995 and November 1998 (review Exhibit 4.3) as bonds that individual investors could use to pay estate taxes. This increased the demand for these issues and raised their prices.

Flower bonds are useless to financial institutions, corporations, and foreign governments because these entities are not subject to estate taxes. The limited market raises their risk of illiquidity. Flower bonds appeal only to wealthy individuals who are terminally ill (or think they are). Their expected rate of return has two components: a lower-than-normal yield to the pessimistic investor and a large capital gain to the investor's estate if he/she dies relatively soon after investing. One of Elvis Presley's biographers reported that the King of Rock and Roll owned $2 million in flower bonds when he died.

Flower bonds are also referred to in the trade as *funeral bonds* and *undertaker's bonds*. The euphemism *flower bonds* is preferred when dealing with the public, although the association of flowers with funerals makes this term only slightly less morbid.

treasury strip

One of the two theoretical securities created when a brokerage house sells the principal and the interest payments on a Treasury note or bond separately.

Treasury Strips. When the income tax laws were revised in 1986 and amended in 1987, brokerage houses created **Treasury strips** and found them to be both popular with the investing public and very profitable for themselves. The brokers bought T-notes and T-bonds and then theoretically separated each security into two pieces: the face value and the stream of future interest payments. (The name *Treasury strips* comes from the concept of stripping a bond of its interest payments.) An investor who wants capital gains and no annual income can buy the face value piece at a deep discount, and get $1,000 at maturity. An investor who needs annual income and no lump sum payment at maturity can buy the stream of interest payments. The sum of the current market prices of the two pieces will be the current market price of the whole bond, less brokerage charges for the extra service. In Exhibit 4.3, the entries featuring the letters *ci* represent streams of interest payments; the entries featuring the letters *np* refer to T-notes stripped of their interest payments; the entries featuring the letters *bp* refer to T-bonds stripped of their interest payments.

T-notes and T-bonds are free of the risk of default. T-strips are subject to the default risk of the brokerage house, mitigated by any insurance the house carries. (See Chapter 3.) Because each T-note, T-bond, and T-strip is a separate issue, with different outstanding amounts, rates, and maturities, these securities are not free of the risk of illiquidity.

Federal Agency Securities

When the country faces a national social problem that the federal government believes can be minimized or solved by spending money, a federal agency is usually created to implement policy and manage the flow of funds. During the Great Depression in the 1930s, the nation faced two pressing social problems: the lack of mortgage money for homeowners and the lack of money and credit for U.S. farmers. The Federal National Mortgage Association, usually known by its acronym FNMA, or Fannie Mae, was created to provide funds for the residential mortgage market. Several agencies—the Federal Land Bank, the Federal Farm Credit Bank, and the now-obsolete Federal Bank for Cooperatives—were established to provide financial relief to farmers.

Fannie Mae is no longer a federal agency. It was created as a federal corporation, with all of its stock held by the U.S. Treasury. In 1947, half of this stock was sold to the general public; in 1969, the other half followed. Today, Fannie Mae is a publicly held corporation, just like General Motors, but the social service it provides and the political power it represents keep its notes and bonds listed in the federal agency section. In addition, the federal government still appoints members to the FNMA board and scrutinizes Fannie Mae's borrowing.

In subsequent years, the Government National Mortgage Association, or Ginnie Mae, was created to provide money for FHA- backed and VA-backed mortgages. The Housing and Urban Development Administration similarly began to provide money for cities, the Inter-American Development Bank began to provide money for economic development projects in Central and South America, and the Student Loan Marketing Corporation, or Sallie Mae, began to provide money for college student loans.

While all federal agencies can borrow money by issuing notes and bonds, none of them has the power to tax. Therefore, their debt carries some risk of default. It is generally believed, however, that the U.S. Treasury and Congress would intervene if any of these agencies were to get into financial difficulty. The financial markets therefore consider the default risk of federal agency securities to be slight.

However, the different federal agencies bear different risks of illiquidity. Generally, an agency with more securities outstanding generates greater market interest in all of its issues and its securities become more liquid. Exhibit 4.4 shows that the securities of Fannie Mae and the Federal Home Loan Mortgage Corporation, or Freddie Mac, are shown to have the least risk of illiquidity; the Federal Land Bank and the Farm Credit Financial Assistance Corporation have the most.

Municipal Securities

municipal security
A note or bond issued by a unit of state or local government or its affiliate.

State and local governments and their affiliates issue **municipal securities**, as both notes and bonds (also called *munis*). The accounting practices of state and local governments vary tremendously because these units of government are not mandated by federal law to follow practices approved by the Financial Accounting Standards Board.

Investors have to rely on ratings furnished by bond-rating companies to assess the default risks for munis. These securities have a high risk of illiquidity because very few issuers can bear debt burdens large enough to make their securities readily marketable. Some municipal bonds are callable and therefore expose investors to call risk. Muni yields are usually low because they enjoy normally tax-free status. An investor living in the same state as the issuer usually pays no federal, state, or local income taxes on the interest. An investor living in a state other than the issuer's usually pays no federal tax on the interest. There are two types of municipal securities: general obligation and revenue bonds.

General Obligation. If a state, county, city, town, school district, sewer district, or other government authority that borrows funds has the power to tax,

EXHIBIT 4.4

Government Agency and Similar Issues

GOVERNMENT AGENCY & SIMILAR ISSUES

Monday, June 20, 1994

Over-the-Counter mid-afternoon quotations based on large transactions, usually $1 million or more. Colons in bid-and-asked quotes represent 32nds; 101:01 means 101 1/32.

All yields are calculated to maturity, and based on the asked quote. * -- Callable issue, maturity date shown. For issues callable prior to maturity, yields are computed to the earliest call date for issues quoted above par, or 100, and to the maturity date for issues below par.

Source: Bear, Stearns & Co. via Street Software Technology Inc.

FNMA Issues

Rate	Mat.	Bid	Asked	Yld.
7.45	7-94	100:04	100:08	2.62
8.90	8-94	100:15	100:19	4.28
10.10	10-94	101:13	101:17	4.87
9.25	11-94	101:16	101:20	4.88
5.50	12-94	100:04	100:08	4.98
9.00	1-95	101:28	102:00	5.23
11.95	1-95	103:11	103:15	5.41
11.50	2-95	103:23	103:27	5.20
8.85	3-95	102:13	102:17	5.18
11.70	5-95	105:03	105:07	5.54
11.15	6-95	105:02	105:06	5.58
4.75	8-95	98:25	98:29	5.73
10.50	9-95	105:10	105:14	5.80
8.80	11-95	103:25	103:29	5.81
10.60	11-95	106:04	106:08	5.82
9.20	1-96	104:23	104:29	5.84
7.00	2-96	101:16	101:22	5.89
9.35	2-96	104:30	105:04	6.01
8.50	6-96	104:14	104:20	5.97
8.75	6-96	104:29	105:03	5.96
8.00	7-96	103:18	103:24	6.03
7.90	8-96	103:12	103:18	6.09
8.15	8-96	103:28	104:02	6.09
8.20	8-96*	100:14	100:20	3.57
7.70	9-96	103:03	103:09	6.09
8.63	9-96	105:00	105:06	6.08
7.05	10-96	101:25	101:31	6.11
8.45	10-96	104:28	105:02	6.08
6.90	11-96*	100:15	100:21	5.14
7.70	12-96	103:03	103:09	6.24
8.20	12-96	104:14	104:20	6.18
6.20	1-97*	99:05	99:11	6.48
7.60	1-97	102:30	103:04	6.25
7.05	3-97*	100:28	101:02	5.50
7.00	4-97*	100:29	101:03	5.57
6.75	4-97	100:27	101:01	6.34
9.20	6-97	107:10	107:16	6.38
8.95	7-97	106:19	106:25	6.46
8.80	7-97	106:08	106:14	6.47
9.15	9-97*	100:23	100:29	4.80
9.55	9-97	107:05	107:11	6.96
5.70	9-97*	96:28	97:02	6.73
5.35	10-97*	95:31	96:05	6.66
6.05	10-97*	97:23	97:29	6.76
6.05	11-97	98:03	98:09	6.62
9.55	11-97	108:12	108:18	6.68
7.10	12-97*	101:04	101:10	6.67
8.60	12-97*	101:16	101:22	4.89
9.55	12-97	108:16	108:22	6.70
6.30	12-97*	98:12	98:18	6.77
6.05	1-98	97:27	98:01	6.68
8.65	2-98	106:00	106:06	6.70
8.20	3-98	104:08	104:14	6.82
5.30	3-98*	94:26	95:00	6.84
5.25	3-98	94:26	95:00	6.78
9.15	4-98	107:17	107:23	6.80
8.38	4-98*	102:01	102:07	5.61
8.15	5-98	104:19	104:25	6.73
5.25	5-98*	94:02	94:08	6.96
5.40	5-98*	94:10	94:16	7.02
5.38	6-98	94:27	95:01	6.82
5.10	7-98*	93:07	93:13	6.98
8.20	8-98*	102:14	102:20	5.76
5.35	8-98*	94:13	94:19	6.87
4.70	9-98*	91:31	92:05	6.87
7.85	9-98	103:29	104:03	6.72
4.95	9-98*	92:20	92:26	6.92
4.88	10-98*	92:00	92:06	7.00
5.05	11-98	93:13	93:19	6.76
5.30	12-98*	93:21	93:27	6.93
7.05	12-98*	100:23	100:29	6.81
7.05	12-98*	99:09	99:15	7.19
5.55	2-99*	94:13	94:21	6.91
7.50	3-99*	98:12	98:20	7.85
9.55	3-99	110:10	110:18	6.88
8.70	6-99	107:16	107:24	6.83
9.20	9-00	110:30	111:06	6.95
8.25	12-00	105:26	106:02	7.07
8.63	4-01*	103:11	103:19	6.47
8.70	6-01*	103:18	103:26	6.60
8.88	7-01*	104:10	104:18	6.46
7.80	12-01*	100:18	100:26	5.93
7.20	1-02*	97:21	97:29	8.12
7.50	2-02	101:14	101:22	7.21
7.90	4-02*	100:28	101:04	7.44
7.55	4-02	101:07	101:15	7.30
7.80	6-02*	98:26	99:02	7.96
7.30	7-02*	96:26	97:02	7.80
7.00	8-02*	96:02	96:10	7.61
6.93	8-02*	95:09	95:17	7.67
6.95	9-02*	96:15	96:23	7.49
7.30	10-02*	97:24	98:00	7.63
6.80	10-02*	94:23	94:31	7.62
7.05	11-02	97:28	98:04	7.35
6.80	1-03	96:02	96:10	7.39
6.40	3-03*	91:25	92:01	7.66
6.63	4-03*	93:06	93:14	7.66
6.45	6-03*	92:00	92:08	7.66
6.20	7-03*	90:14	90:22	7.64
6.25	8-03*	90:18	90:26	7.66
5.45	10-03	86:22	86:30	7.42
6.20	11-03*	89:29	90:05	7.69
5.80	12-03	88:27	89:03	7.42
6.40	1-04*	91:09	91:17	7.66
6.90	3-04*	94:03	94:11	7.74
6.85	4-04	95:25	96:01	7.43
7.60	4-04*	98:00	98:08	7.86
7.65	4-04*	98:10	98:18	7.86
7.55	6-04*	98:12	98:20	7.75
0.00	7-14	19:22	19:30	8.21
10.35	12-15	127:10	127:18	7.70
8.20	3-16	103:15	103:23	7.84
8.95	2-18	112:24	113:00	7.74
8.10	8-19	102:18	102:26	7.84
0.00	10-19	13:13	13:21	8.03
9.65	8-20*	102:20	102:28	9.35
9.50	11-20*	102:10	102:18	9.24

Tennessee Valley Authority

Rate	Mat.	Bid	Asked	Yld.
8.25	10-94	100:30	101:02	4.26
4.38	3-96*	97:12	97:18	5.90
8.25	11-96	104:08	104:14	6.22
4.60	12-96*	96:09	96:15	6.16
6.00	1-97*	99:03	99:09	6.31
6.25	8-99*	96:19	96:27	6.99
8.38	10-99	106:09	106:17	6.87
7.45	10-01*	100:08	100:16	7.36
6.88	1-02*	96:17	96:25	7.44
6.88	8-02*	96:11	96:19	7.44
8.75	10-19*	105:16	105:24	3.72
7.63	9-22*	94:02	94:10	8.14
7.75	12-22*	94:09	94:17	8.25
8.63	11-29*	101:18	101:26	8.46
8.25	4-42*	99:30	100:06	8.23
7.25	7-43	87:30	88:06	8.24
6.88	12-43*	83:25	84:01	8.21

Inter-Amer. Devel. Bank

Rate	Mat.	Bid	Asked	Yld.
13.25	8-94	101:09	101:13	3.49
11.63	12-94	102:26	102:30	4.80
11.38	5-95	104:26	104:30	5.38
7.50	12-96	102:13	102:19	6.35
9.50	10-97	107:27	108:01	6.75
8.50	5-01	106:00	106:08	7.32
12.25	12-08	138:05	138:13	7.78
8.88	6-09	111:11	111:19	7.57
8.50	3-11	105:29	106:05	7.83

Resolution Funding Corp.

Rate	Mat.	Bid	Asked	Yld.
8.13	10-19	103:27	104:03	7.75
8.88	7-20	112:24	113:00	7.71
9.38	10-20	118:00	118:08	7.74
8.63	1-21	109:22	109:30	7.74

Federal Home Loan Bank

Rate	Mat.	Bid	Asked	Yld.
7.50	6-94	100:01	100:05	0.00
8.60	6-94	100:02	100:06	0.00
8.63	6-94	100:02	100:06	0.00
8.30	7-94	100:11	100:15	3.07
6.70	8-94	100:07	100:11	4.62
8.60	8-94	100:18	100:22	4.51
6.58	9-94	100:07	100:11	5.16
8.30	10-94	100:28	101:00	5.25
4.75	11-94	99:21	99:25	5.26
5.89	11-94	100:05	100:09	5.19
8.20	11-94	101:01	101:05	5.38
8.05	12-94	101:08	101:12	5.28
5.45	1-95	99:31	100:03	5.28
8.40	1-95	101:21	101:25	5.28
5.94	2-95	100:09	100:13	5.31
8.60	2-95	102:00	102:04	5.35
6.45	3-95	100:21	100:25	5.38
7.88	3-95	101:24	101:28	5.32
9.00	3-95	102:18	102:22	5.34
6.04	4-95	100:11	100:15	5.45
8.88	6-95	103:03	103:07	5.55
10.00	6-95	104:14	104:18	5.30
10.30	7-95	104:22	104:26	5.68
4.60	8-95	98:17	98:21	5.79
4.50	9-95	98:07	98:11	5.88
5.00	10-95	98:26	98:30	5.83
5.38	11-95	99:11	99:15	5.76
9.50	12-95	105:02	105:06	5.86
8.10	3-96	103:10	103:16	5.96
9.80	3-96	106:03	106:09	5.97
6.68	4-96	101:01	101:07	5.96
4.36	4-96*	97:00	97:06	5.99
7.75	4-96	102:28	103:02	5.96
8.25	5-96	103:28	104:02	5.99
8.25	6-96	104:05	104:11	5.92
4.41	7-96*	96:16	96:22	6.16
8.00	7-96	103:20	103:26	6.03
7.70	8-96	103:04	103:10	6.05
8.25	9-96	104:09	104:15	6.09
7.10	10-96	102:00	102:06	6.08
8.25	11-96	104:20	104:26	6.08
6.85	2-97	100:31	101:05	6.37
7.65	3-97	103:02	103:08	6.34
9.15	3-97	106:25	106:31	6.35
6.99	4-97	101:14	101:20	6.35
6.34	6-97	99:28	100:02	6.32
9.20	8-97	107:08	107:14	6.56
5.26	4-98*	94:09	94:15	6.92
9.25	11-98	108:25	108:31	6.86
9.30	1-99	109:01	109:09	6.90
5.43	2-99	94:00	94:08	6.89
8.60	6-99	106:19	106:27	6.96
8.45	7-99	106:04	106:12	6.94
8.60	8-99	106:27	107:03	6.94
8.38	10-99	105:22	105:30	7.02
8.60	1-00	107:01	107:09	7.00
9.50	2-04	113:05	113:13	7.52

Federal Farm Credit Bank

Rate	Mat.	Bid	Asked	Yld.
3.32	7-94	99:31	100:03	0.00
3.60	7-94	99:31	100:03	0.00
3.65	7-94	100:00	100:04	0.00
3.26	8-94	99:27	99:31	3.51
3.64	8-94	99:27	99:31	3.87
4.19	8-94	100:00	100:04	3.02
3.40	9-94	99:20	99:24	4.67
3.77	9-94	99:24	99:28	4.38
4.31	9-94	99:25	99:29	4.74
4.48	9-94	100:00	100:04	3.81
8.63	9-94	100:19	100:23	4.72
13.00	9-94	101:13	101:17	4.75
3.43	10-94	99:16	99:20	4.75
4.00	10-94	99:25	99:29	4.30
3.48	11-94	99:14	99:18	4.70
4.63	11-94	99:28	100:00	4.60
3.62	12-94	99:11	99:15	4.84
4.94	12-94	100:00	100:04	4.64
11.45	12-94	102:19	102:23	5.12
3.61	1-95	99:02	99:06	5.19
8.30	1-95	101:17	101:21	5.33
3.53	2-95	98:31	99:03	5.06
6.38	4-95	100:20	100:24	5.36
4.43	4-95	99:09	99:13	5.21
5.16	5-95	99:26	99:30	5.23
5.47	6-95	100:03	100:07	5.22

Student Loan Marketing

Rate	Mat.	Bid	Asked	Yld.
8.50	7-94	100:05	100:09	1.22
7.50	7-94	100:04	100:08	2.67
8.10	7-94	100:07	100:11	3.39
8.30	9-94	100:21	100:25	5.00
7.54	10-94	100:20	100:24	4.95
0.00	11-94	98:08	98:12	4.61
8.55	2-95	101:23	101:27	5.40
5.28	2-95	99:27	99:31	5.32
7.63	3-95	101:17	101:21	5.24
9.50	9-97*	100:24	100:30	4.99
8.75	8-00*	100:11	100:19	5.01
9.80	9-00*	104:29	105:05	5.44
7.00	12-02	97:13	97:21	7.38
0.00	5-14	17:11	17:19	8.93
0.00	10-22	10:13	10:21	8.08

GNMA Mtge. Issues a-Bond

Rate	Mat.	Bid	Asked	Yld.
6.00	30Yr	86:20	86:28	8.12
6.50	30Yr	90:02	90:10	8.10
7.00	30Yr	93:16	93:24	8.12
7.50	30Yr	96:25	97:01	8.12
8.00	30Yr	99:22	99:30	8.13
8.50	30Yr	102:09	102:17	8.12
9.00	30Yr	104:13	104:21	8.02
9.50	30Yr	106:09	106:17	7.96
10.00	30Yr	107:23	107:31	7.84
10.50	30Yr	109:22	109:30	7.72
11.00	30Yr	111:08	111:16	7.58
11.50	30Yr	112:04	112:12	7.75
12.00	30Yr	113:04	113:12	7.49

World Bank Bonds

Rate	Mat.	Bid	Asked	Yld.
11.63	12-94	103:02	103:06	4.83
8.63	10-95	103:11	103:15	5.75
7.25	10-96	101:25	101:31	6.30
8.75	3-97	105:24	105:30	6.31
5.88	7-97	98:23	98:29	6.27
9.88	10-97	109:08	109:14	6.62
8.38	10-99	106:02	106:10	6.92
8.13	3-01	105:06	105:14	7.09
6.75	1-02	99:22	99:30	6.76
12.38	10-02	129:24	130:00	7.46
8.25	9-16	103:05	103:13	7.92
8.63	10-16	106:26	107:02	7.94
9.25	7-17	113:15	113:23	7.94
7.63	1-23	97:13	97:21	7.83
8.88	3-26	110:03	110:11	7.97

Financing Corporation

Rate	Mat.	Bid	Asked	Yld.
10.70	10-17	130:02	130:10	7.84
9.80	11-17	120:19	120:27	7.84
9.40	2-18	116:12	116:20	7.84
9.80	4-18	120:22	120:30	7.84
10.00	5-18	122:27	123:03	7.84
10.35	8-18	126:22	126:30	7.84
9.65	11-18	119:08	119:16	7.84
9.90	12-18	122:00	122:08	7.84
9.60	12-18	118:24	119:00	7.84
9.65	3-19	119:10	119:18	7.84
9.70	4-19	119:28	120:04	7.84
9.00	6-19	112:11	112:19	7.84
8.60	9-19	107:29	108:05	7.85

Farm Credit Fin. Asst. Corp.

Rate	Mat.	Bid	Asked	Yld.
9.38	7-03	112:11	112:19	7.44
9.45	11-03*	108:03	108:11	7.21
8.80	6-05	108:25	109:01	7.57
9.20	9-05	106:14	106:22	8.27
5.50	12-95	99:14	99:18	5.82
5.08	1-96	98:18	98:24	5.93
6.65	5-96	101:00	101:06	5.96
4.55	2-97*	95:15	95:21	6.38
5.12	3-97*	96:20	96:26	6.42
11.90	10-97	115:19	115:25	6.54
5.27	2-99*	93:12	93:20	6.91
5.79	3-99*	95:04	95:12	6.96
8.65	10-99	107:05	107:13	6.95
7.95	4-02*	98:14	98:22	8.18

Source: The Wall Street Journal, June 21, 1994, p. C17.

general obligation
Municipal note or bond backed by a state or local government unit's power to tax.

the notes and bonds it issues that are backed by this power are called **general obligations**. They are considered relatively safe because the market believes that the issuers can always raise tax rates a little higher to raise money to service outstanding debt. Oddly enough, general obligations issued by local governments that do not already have a tax in place are considered to be slightly more risky than those issued by local governments that already levy taxes. The market considers the political difficulty of imposing a new tax to be greater than the political difficulty of raising an existing tax, no matter how high the existing tax rate might be.

revenue bond
A municipal security issued to pay for a specific project and backed by the revenues from that project.

Revenue Bonds. **Revenue bonds** are debt instruments issued to pay for specific projects—bridges, tunnels, parks, World Fairs, and so forth. The government unit that issues the bonds may or may not have the power to tax, but it cannot use general tax money to pay interest and repay principal on revenue bonds. These funds must come from revenue generated by the project. If fewer than the expected number of people cross the bridge, drive through the tunnel, or visit the park or fair, the borrowers have no way to raise money to service the debt, so the risk of default on revenue bonds is generally considered to be high.

Bank Securities

Commercial banks contribute two unique types of securities to the market: negotiable certificates of deposit and bankers' acceptances.

Negotiable Certificates of Deposit. The most common denomination for a negotiable certificate of deposit (CD) is $100,000, but they are normally traded in units of $1 million. The investor deposits this amount or some multiple of it, and recovers that deposit plus interest at maturity.

If an investor cannot hold a negotiable CD until the specified maturity, it does not have to be returned to the bank for early withdrawal, which would entail significant interest penalties. Instead, the CD could be sold in the secondary market at a price that would give the buyer the current market yield to maturity. If interest rates rise after the CD is issued, the seller gets a lower price (and rate of return) than originally expected. If interest rates fall, the seller gets a higher price (and rate of return) than originally expected.

Negotiable CDs are insured, like normal bank deposits, up to $100,000. They still expose the investor to default risk if the bank that holds the deposit fails; the investor who holds CDs worth more than $100,000 loses the excess.

bankers' acceptance
A time draft drawn on and accepted by a bank.

Bankers' Acceptances. A **bankers' acceptance** is a security created by a bank to help traders and other customers raise funds to pay for current purchases and other trade-related activities using the bank's credit. It is, therefore, a credit instrument that gives the borrower access to the funds in the banking system as well as funds outside the banking system.

Though the bankers' acceptance has traditionally financed imports and exports, it is not limited to these transactions. It may also finance shipments of goods within a country and between two countries, storage of readily marketable goods, and other trade-related activities. An importer can use it to raise funds to pay for imports, and an exporter can use it to finance goods until it receives payment for the exports. A foreign oil importer who needs dollars to pay for the imports can use a bankers' acceptance to finance the transaction.

time draft
An order to pay at a specified future date.

As a document, a bankers' acceptance is a time draft drawn on and accepted by a bank. A **time draft** is an order to pay at a specified future date. A bankers' acceptance involves three parties: the drawer, the drawee, and the payee. The features of a bankers' acceptance are best explained by illustrating two specific uses: import financing and financing a shipment of goods between two countries.

letter of credit
A conditional promise from a bank to pay an exporter at a specified future time, after the bank is assured that the goods have been received by the importer, and their value is verified.

In import financing, the bankers' acceptance is used in conjunction with a **letter of credit**. Assume that a U.S. wine distributor wants to import German wine worth $100,000 on three-month credit terms. The importer applies to a U.S. bank to open a three-month letter of credit in favor of the German exporter of wines. This letter states that the bank will pay the exporter three months after the bank receives assurance that the wine has been received by the importer, and its value is verified. (A letter of credit is not a money market security; it is just a conditional promise from the bank.) The bank sends the letter of credit to the exporter. Based on the letter of credit, the German exporter ships the merchandise and draws a three-month time draft on the U.S. bank for $100,000. The exporter sends the draft along with shipping documents to the U.S. bank for acceptance. After making sure that the papers are in order, the bank signs *accepted* across the face of the draft. The time draft becomes a bankers' acceptance, and it is sent to the exporter.

The exporter now has two choices: to hold onto the bankers' acceptance and submit it for payment to the U.S. bank (the accepting bank) on the maturity date, or to sell the paper in the secondary market at a discount. If the exporter sells the acceptance in the secondary market to an investor, it receives less than the face value of the security. After three months, the accepting bank sends payment for the full amount to the exporter or to the investor—whoever submits the security for payment. Note that in this case either the exporter or the investor finances the import. The drawer of the draft is the exporter, the drawee is the U.S. bank, and the payee is either the exporter or the investor. This is an example of three-party paper.

The use of a bankers' acceptance in the dollar financing of a shipment of goods between two foreign countries usually involves a U.S. bank and a foreign bank. Suppose a Korean importer of oil needs dollars to pay for a shipment from Saudi Arabia. The importer draws a time draft on a Korean bank for the dollar-cost of the oil. The Korean bank simultaneously draws a dollar time draft on a U.S. bank. The U.S. bank accepts the draft and pays the Korean bank from its own funds, or discounts the draft with a broker and pays the proceeds to the Korean bank (after deducting the acceptance commission). The Korean bank then pays the Saudi Arabian supplier.

At the maturity of the draft, the Korean bank collects the Korean won equivalent of the dollar amount at the prevailing exchange rate from the importer. The Korean bank buys U.S. dollars and repays the U.S. bank. The U.S. bank, in turn, uses the proceeds to cover its loan (if it used its own funds)

EXHIBIT 4.5

Money

MONEY

Federal Funds:	
High:4¼ Low:4 3/16 Close:4¼	
Broker Call Loans	6.00
Primary Offerings by N.Y.C. Banks:	
30 day	3.39
90 day	3.67
180 day	3.98
***Bankers Acceptances:**	
30 day	4.23
90 day	4.39
180 day	4.70
Certificates of Deposit Secondary Market:	
30 day	4.27
90 day	4.43
180 day	4.80

Source: Telerate Systems Inc.

Eurodollar Time Deposits:	
Overnight	4.18
30 day	4.18
90 day	4.43
180 day	4.75
London Interbank Offered Rate:	
90 day	4.56
180 day	4.93
***Dealer Placed Commercial Paper:**	
30 day	4.33
***Financial Co. Commercial Paper:**	
15 day	4.25
30 day	4.27
60 day	4.35

*Discount rate.

Source: New York Times, June 21, 1994, p. D18.

or to pay the investor who provided the funds. Note that in this case the U.S. bank or U.S. investor finances Korean imports of oil from Saudi Arabia. The importer bears the exchange risk in this transaction. This is an example of four-party paper.

Bankers' acceptances usually have short-term maturities, perhaps extending up to 180 days. On occasion, a bank may create an acceptance with a longer maturity to meet the credit needs of a large borrower such as a foreign government. The time limit for such a bankers' acceptance is two years, and the transaction generally involves a **syndicate** of banks. This syndicate is a temporary legal association of banks formed to manage a security issue too large for any one of them to manage comfortably alone.

syndicate
A temporary legal association of financial institutions formed to manage a security issue too large for any one of them to manage comfortably alone.

The secondary market for bankers' acceptances is very large and active in the United States. Trading involves dealers and brokers. Various holders may discount an acceptance several times before it matures. The yields available on bankers' acceptances and CDs are approximately equivalent in the current market; both instruments have higher yields than Treasury bills. The yields available on bankers' acceptances and CDs of various maturities are published daily in the *New York Times* in a column labeled "Money" (see Exhibit 4.5) and in *The Wall Street Journal* in a column labeled "Money Rates."

Corporate Securities

Corporations raise money in the securities markets in three ways: they borrow for the short term by issuing commercial paper, they borrow for the long term by issuing notes and bonds, and they sell ownership shares by issuing preferred and common stock. There are enormous differences in the risks and returns associated with these three types of securities, even if they are all issued by the same firm.

commercial paper
Unsecured, discounted, corporate debt obligations, that mature in up to 270 days, with no conditions attached to the promise to repay.

Commercial Paper. Corporations issue two types of **commercial paper**: dealer paper and direct (finance company) paper. Both are unsecured, discounted debt instruments that mature in up to 270 days, with no conditions attached to the promise to repay. Most companies consult an investment banker when they wish to borrow short-term funds from the public (see Chapter 3). The investment bank acts as a dealer who buys the paper from the company and resells it to the public. This so-called *dealer paper* is payable to bearer at maturity. Dealer paper is rated with respect to default risk by the Standard & Poor's, Moody's, and Fitch services. The safest commercial paper is generally referred to as prime or A-1/P-1 paper. A-1 is the highest rating awarded by Moody's and P-1 is the highest rating awarded by Standard & Poor's.

Some finance companies, such as General Motors Acceptance Corporation, Chrysler Acceptance Corporation, General Electric Capital Corporation, and Westinghouse Capital Corporation, are subsidiaries of corporations that produce expensive consumer items. They were set up to help their parent companies sell their products by arranging for consumer financing. Since the volume of paper issued by these corporations generally exceeds $1 billion per month, it is financially advantageous for them to employ their own salespeople to sell their commercial paper directly. Such paper may be sold through direct negotiation between the buyer and the seller, or it may be offered to the customers of a commercial bank, with the issuer paying a small commission to the bank. Virtually all direct paper is rated A-1/P-1. Typical rates appear in the "Money" column, as shown in Exhibit 4.5.

The role of commercial banks in commercial paper dealings has steadily increased over time. Originally their only involvement was to offer commercial paper as an investment option to their corporate clients. Later they began to offer their own commercial paper both to their clients and through public auction.

Commercial banks also issue letters of credit, guaranteeing the commercial paper of their clients. Actually this amounts to selling their A-1/P-1 credit ratings to clients for fees (often as high as 2 percent of the face value of the paper). Since the default rate for commercial paper is very small, the bank collects the fee without significantly increasing its risk exposure. The client gets a higher rating on its paper than its own credit would earn and, therefore, is able to acquire needed funds at a lower rate. In the process, the commercial bank keeps its customer happy without really losing a commercial loan opportunity. Since it expends no funds, the bank still has the opportunity to lend to other customers who do not wish to borrow in the commercial paper market.

Today commercial banks also underwrite commercial paper through subsidiary corporations. This activity has been approved by the Federal Reserve so long as the underwriting does not constitute a "significant part of the subsidiary's profit." Commercial bank involvement has supported rapid growth in the commercial paper market so it is fast becoming the primary source of short-term funding for many corporations, usually at rates lower than they would pay to borrow from a bank.

Notes and Bonds. Corporations usually issue notes with maturities of 10 or 15 years and sell them privately to institutional investors. Corporations usually

FOCUS ON FINANCE

COMMERCIAL BANKS AND COMMERCIAL PAPER

When some commercial banks' short-term credit ratings were lowered from A-1/P-1 to A-2/P-2 during 1989 and 1990, it had an adverse impact on the ability of large banks to issue commercial paper. Investors were less willing to buy these securities and the SEC considered limiting money market funds' holdings of A-2/P-2 rated commercial paper.

In six months, major U.S. banks dramatically scaled back their average daily balances of commercial paper outstanding:

It is noteworthy that even after the cutbacks, these three banks together had more commercial paper outstanding than the amount of new 13-week bills the U.S. Treasury was issuing on Mondays.

Source: Kelley Holland, "Reliance on Commercial Paper Waning," *American Banker*, September 13, 1990, p. 32.

	DAILY BALANCE DURING FOURTH QUARTER, 1989	DAILY BALANCE DURING SECOND QUARTER, 1990	PERCENTAGE DECREASE
Citicorp	$8.17 billion	$6.50 billion	20.4%
Bankers Trust	4.87 billion	4.44 billion	8.8
Chemical Bank	1.82 billion	1.31 billion	28.0
Total	$14.86 billion	$12.25 billion	

issue bonds with maturities of 20, 25, or 30 years and they may sell the bonds to the general public or privately to institutional investors. Both types of securities usually have denominations of $1,000.

A corporate bond's default risk is based on its rating from Moody's and Standard & Poor's, or on the fact that it is not rated at all. The risk of illiquidity depends on the size of the issue and the marketplace in which it trades: the exchanges or the OTC market. A corporate bond's call risk is determined at the time it is issued; the issuing company must decide whether to make an issue callable or not, and set the terms of any call feature. Corporate notes and bonds are discussed in greater detail in Chapter 11.

Preferred Stock. Preferred stock is a hybrid security: some features make it resemble bonds and some features make it look like common stock. The quarterly dividend that preferred stock pays to shareholders of record is fixed when the stock is first issued, like a bond's interest payments, but the company's board of directors must meet and declare that the dividend is to be paid. If they decide not to declare a dividend, the preferred stockholders have no legal recourse. Because preferred stock is a fixed-income security, its market price fluctuates above and below the price at which it was first issued (usually $50 or $100 per share). If interest rates rise, preferred stock prices fall, and vice versa. The risk of illiquidity is determined by the size of the issue and the market in which the stock trades. Preferred stock can be callable, if the company desires. Preferred stock is discussed in detail in Chapter 12.

Market data on preferred stock issues appear in the columns headed either "New York Stock Exchange Composite Transactions," "American Stock Exchange Composite Transactions," or "NASDAQ National Market Issues" in *The Wall Street Journal*, depending on where the stock trades. Exhibit 4.6 is an excerpt from the "NYSE Composite Transactions" column. A simulated entry in this column appears below. The text that follows explains how to interpret the data.

52 Weeks					Vol				Net
Hi	Lo	Stock	Div	Yld %	100s	Hi	Lo	Close	Chg
99	81	Citicorp pf	7.00	7.2	14	97 ½	96 ¾	97	–1

***52 Weeks Hi* = 99.** This means that the stock price rose as high as $99 per share in the last 52 weeks.

***52 weeks Lo* = 81.** This means that the stock price fell as low as $81 per share in the last 52 weeks.

***Stock* = *Citicorp pf*.** This means that Citicorp issued the stock. The *pf* means that it is preferred stock. If the quote omits the *pf*, the issue is common stock. A corporation may have more than one issue of preferred stock outstanding. If so, each publicly traded issue will be entered on a separate line.

***Div* = 7.00.** This means that the stock pays an annual dividend of $7.00 per share, or $1.75 every three months.

***Yld %* = 7.2.** This means that the $7.00 dividend amounts to 7.2 percent of the stock's closing price of $97.

***Vol 100s* = 14.** This means that 1,400 shares of this stock changed hands during the day.

***Hi* = 97 ½.** This means that the highest price the stock reached during the trading day was $97.50 per share.

***Lo* = 96 ¾.** This means that the lowest price the stock reached during the trading day was $96.75 per share.

***Close* = 97.** This means that the price at which the stock traded at the end of the day was $97.00 per share.

***Net Chg* = –1.** This means that the closing price of $97.00 was $1.00 lower that the closing price on the previous trading day.

Common Stock. A share of common stock represents ownership of a portion of the issuing company. The size of the dividend, if any, that the firm will pay to its shareholders of record is determined by the board of directors quarterly. Because the common stockholders are technically the owners of the earnings generated by the company, most common stock prices reflect the market's expectations about the future earnings potential of the company. Therefore, no upper limit restrains a common stock's price. This is the only security with the long-term potential to

EXHIBIT 4.6

New York Stock Exchange Composite Transactions

NEW YORK STOCK EXCHANGE COMPOSITE TRANSACTIONS

	52 Weeks Hi	52 Weeks Lo	Stock	Sym	Div	Yld %	PE	Vol 100s	Hi	Lo	Close	Net Chg
	10½	8⅞	AllncGlblEnv	AEF		...	...	175	9⅝	9½	9⅝	...
n	16¼	12	AllianceWrld II	AWF	1.42a	11.0	...	1855	13¼	12¾	12⅞	− ⅜
▼	22½	13⅞	**AllianceWrld**	**AWG**	**1.68a**	**12.4**	...	**2730**	**14½**	**12¾**	**13½**	**−1**
	30	21¾	AlliantTech	ATK		...	9	84	29	28⅞	29	− ¼
	27⅝	21⅝	AlldIrishBk	AIB	1.06e	4.8	...	15	22½	22¼	22¼	− ¼
	29¼	25½	AlldIrishBk pf		2.97e	10.7	...	73	27⅞	27¾	27⅞	...
	17⅜	9½	AlliedPdts	ADP		...	10	346	14⅜	13⅞	14	− ⅜
s	40⅝	32⅛	AlliedSgnl	ALD	.67	1.9	15	3389	36⅜	35½	35½	−1
s	22⅛	15	AllmrPC	APY	.16	.9	9	125	17⅛	17	17⅛	+ ⅛
	12¼	10	Allmerica	ALM	.84a	7.9	...	30	10¾	10⅝	10⅝	...
	10¾	9⅝	AllmonTr	GSO	.48e	4.9	...	97	9¾	9⅝	9¾	+ ⅛
	34¼	22⅝	Allstate	ALL	.72	2.9	15	1049	25	24¾	24¾	− ¼
s	31¼	24	ALLTEL	AT	.88	3.4	18	734	26⅛	25⅞	26⅛	+ ⅛
	6⅛	3⅞	Allwaste	ALW		...	23	535	5⅞	5⅝	5⅞	...
n	27¾	16¾	Alumax	AMX	1.00p	...	...	587	26	25⅝	25⅞	− ⅛
	82	64¼	Alcoa	AA	1.60a	2.2	dd	2220	74½	73¼	73½	−1⅛
	30¾	19¼	Alza	AZA		...	55	778	25⅞	25½	25¾	− ¼
	10½	6	AmaxGold	AU	.06j	...	dd	1209	8⅛	7⅞	7⅞	− ¼
	49¾	35¾	Ambac	ABK	.48	1.1	8	379	42¼	41⅞	41⅞	− ⅜
	25⅞	16⅝	AmcastInd	AIZ	.48	2.3	13	218	21½	21⅛	21¼	− ⅜
	3	1⅞	Amdura	ADU		...	23	50	1⅞	1⅞	1⅞	...
	54¾	42⅜	AmerHess	AHC	.60	1.1	dd	4109	52¼	50⅝	52¼	+ ⅞
n	25½	20⅞	Amerco pfA		2.13	9.3	...	33	23	22⅝	23	+ ⅜
	10	8⅞	AmAdjTerm95	ADJ	.43e	4.8	...	75	9	8⅞	8⅞	− ⅛
	9¾	8¼	AmAdjTerm96	BDJ	.50e	6.0	...	404	8½	8⅜	8⅜	− ⅛
	9¾	8	AmAdjTerm97	CDJ	.56e	6.8	...	385	8¼	8⅛	8¼	...
	9¾	7⅞	AmAdjTerm98	DDJ	.58e	7.1	...	431	8⅛	8	8⅛	+ ⅛
	9¾	7⅞	AmAdjTerm99	EDJ	.59e	7.3	...	229	8⅛	8	8⅛	+ ⅛
	11	7⅞	AmAnnuity	AAG	.05e	.5	9	46	9⅝	9⅝	9⅝	...
	31	20⅜	AmBarrick	ABX	.10f	.4	30	11166	24⅝	24¼	24¼	− ¼
	35⅞	29⅜	AmBrand	AMB	2.00f	5.9	12	2603	33¾	33¼	33⅝	+ ¼
	28¾	18¾	AmBusnPdts	ABP	.80	3.9	13	15	20⅝	20½	20½	− ⅛
▼	21¼	17½	AmCapBdFd	ACB	1.54	8.7	...	124	17¾	17⅜	17¾	− ⅛
	24	19¾	AmCapCvSec	ACS	1.08a	5.2	...	1	20⅝	20⅝	20⅝	...
	8⅜	6⅝	AmCapIncTr	ACD	.65	9.3	...	138	7⅛	7	7	...
	56⅞	42¼	AmCyanmd	ACY	1.85f	3.5	dd	2286	53⅜	52¾	53	− ½
n▼	11	10	AmEagle	FLI		...	...	56	10	9¾	10	− ⅛
	40⅜	27¼	AmElecPwr	AEP	2.40	8.3	13	2490	29¼	28¾	28⅞	− ⅛
s	32⅛	23⅛	AmExpress	AXP	1.00	3.6	9	9561	27⅞	27⅜	27½	− ⅝
n	45¼	36¾	AmExpressDECS	AXD	2.30	5.6	...	23	41⅞	41⅜	41⅜	− ¾
	36½	24⅞	AmGenerl	AGC	1.16	4.1	23	3686	29⅛	28⅜	28⅝	+ ⅛
	9⅞	6⅝	AmGvIncFd	AGF	.77a	10.6	...	292	7⅜	7⅛	7¼	...
	12¼	8¼	AmGvIncoP	AAF	.96a	11.0	...	342	8⅞	8¾	8¾	...
	10¾	8½	AmGvTermTr	AGT	.78	8.2	...	40	9½	9½	9½	...
	29	24¼	AmHlthProp	AHE	2.27e	8.9	15	200	25⅞	25⅜	25½	− ⅜
	25⅛	16¾	AmHeritgLf	AHL	.66	3.6	11	6	18⅞	18½	18½	− ⅛
	66⅞	55⅝	AmHomePdts	AHP	2.92	4.9	12	2611	59¼	58⅝	59⅛	...
	28¼	22⅜	AmIncHldg	AIH	.32	1.2	12	71	26⅝	26½	26⅝	− ⅛
	28¼	19	BkrsLife	BLH	.60	3.1	8	91	19¾	19⅝	19⅝	− ¼
	84⅝	64½	BankTrst	BT	3.60	5.2	6	1842	69⅝	69	69¼	− ¾
n	25⅝	24¾	BkTrst dep pfQ		.27p	...	...	1100	25 1/16	25	25 1/16	− ⅛
	27¼	23⅝	BankTrst un		2.14	8.4	...	31	25⅜	25¼	25⅜	+ ½
	1½	9/16	BanyanMtgInv	VMG		...	20	245	13/16	¾	13/16	+ 1/16
	39	27¼	Barclays	BCS	1.13e	3.4	...	156	34	33½	33½	− ¾
	27¾	25½	Barclays pr		2.78	10.5	...	48	26½	26¼	26½	+ ¼
	27¾	25¼	Barclays prB		2.72	10.5	...	141	26⅛	26	26	...
	31	26⅝	Barclays pfD		2.88	10.4	...	59	27⅞	27½	27¾	− ⅛
	27	21¼	Barclays prE		2.00	8.8	...	233	22⅞	22⅝	22¾	− ⅛
	30¾	26⅜	Barclays pfC		2.81	10.2	...	28	27¾	27¼	27½	+ ⅛
	30½	20½	Bard CR	BCR	.56	2.3	22	541	24⅜	23 63/64	24¼	− ⅛
n	34	20	BarnesNoble	BKS		...	...	640	23¾	23⅜	23¾	− ⅛
	37¾	29½	BarnesGp	B	1.40	3.8	26	4	37¼	37	37	− ¼
	48⅞	37⅜	BarnettBks	BBI	1.64f	3.7	10	2558	44¾	44⅜	44½	− ¼
	99	80¾	BarnettBks pfA		4.50	5.2	...	315	87¼	86⅜	86⅜	−1⅛
	72½	61½	BarnettBks pfC		4.00	6.0	...	160	67⅝	66⅛	66⅛	− ⅞
	18½	13½	Bass	BAS	.78e	5.0	...	51	15⅞	15⅝	15¾	+ ⅛
	12⅝	7¼	BattleMtn	BMG	.05	.5	dd	2558	10¾	10½	10½	− ⅛
	70½	53⅝	BattleMtn pf		3.25	5.2	...	70	63¾	63	63	− ⅜
	53⅞	39½	BauschLomb	BOL	.98f	2.5	15	3165	40⅜	39½	39¾	− ¼
	29⅜	20	BaxterInt	BAX	1.00	3.9	dd	5177	25⅞	25⅜	25½	− ¾
n	22¾	20	BayApartmt	BYA		...	...	313	21⅜	20¾	21	− ⅜
	32	23⅜	BayStGas	BGC	1.46f	5.8	14	93	25	24⅝	25	+ ¼
n	18½	17¼	BeaconProp	BCN		...	...	488	17⅞	17½	17⅝	− ¼
▼	24¾	17½	BearStearns	BSC	.60b	3.4	5	1742	17¾	17⅜	17½	− ¼
	26⅝	21⅞	BearStearns pfB		1.97	8.2	...	29	24⅛	23⅞	24⅛	+ ⅜
n	25½	21⅝	BearStearns pfC		1.90	8.1	...	52	23⅞	23⅜	23½	− ¼
	50¼	48⅜	BearStearns pf		2.77e	5.6	...	25	49¾	49¼	49¼	− ½
n	24¾	20¾	BearStnEPICS pfA		2.00	8.9	...	72	22⅜	22¼	22⅜	...
	37½	21⅛	BearingsInc	BER	.64	2.0	22	145	32	31⅞	31 15/16	+ ⅛
n	18¾	13¾	BeazerHm	BZH		...	...	158	15½	15¼	15¼	− ⅛
	28¾	19⅝	BeckmanInstr	BEC	.40	1.5	dd	84	26½	25¾	26⅛	− ¼
	40¾	34	BectonDksn	BDX	.74	1.9	14	1818	39¾	39½	39⅝	− ⅜
n	20¼	14¼	Belden	BWC	.10e	.6	...	88	18¼	18	18	− ¼
	69⅛	49	BellAtlantic	BEL	2.76f	4.9	16	4764	56½	54¾	55⅞	+ ⅝
	19¾	12½	BellIndus	BI	.40b	2.3	14	174	17¼	16¾	17¼	+ ¼
	63⅞	53	BellSouth	BLS	2.76	4.5	25	3288	61½	60⅞	61	− ⅛
	55	44	Belo AH A	BLC	.60	1.3	21	69	47¾	47½	47¾	+ ¼
	25⅛	19⅞	Bemis	BMS	.54	2.3	25	241	23¾	23¼	23⅝	− ⅛
s	40⅞	34½	Beneficial	BNL	1.52	4.1	10	667	37	36	37	+ ½
	67¾	58	Beneficial pfA		4.50	7.5	...	z20	60	60	60	−1
	69	57¼	Beneficial pfB		4.30	7.2	...	1	59½	59½	59½	− ½
	37½	32	Beneficial pfV		2.50	7.4	...	z60	33¾	33¾	33¾	− ½
	36⅞	23⅜	Benetton	BNG	.47e	1.6	...	23	29¾	29¼	29¾	−1
	1⅜	13/16	Benguet	BE		...	...	281	1	⅞	⅞	− 1/16
	19⅞	14⅛	BergnBruns	BBC	.48	2.7	24	691	17½	17	17½	...
	17800	14000	BerkHathwy	BRK		...	25	z140	16455	16150	16150	−300
n	26	12⅛	BoydGaming	BYD		...	...	194	12⅝	12⅜	12½	+ ⅛
	17½	11	Bradlees	BLE	.60	4.4	10	387	13½	13½	13½	− ⅛
	31¾	15⅞	BrazilFd	BZF	1.01e	4.3	...	366	23⅞	23	23¾	+ ⅛
	26¼	11½	BrazEqtyFd	BZL	.08e	.4	...	294	19¼	18½	19	+ ⅛
	44	10¾	BreedTech	BDT		...	26	2175	30⅞	30	30¼	− ⅞
	90¼	61	BriggsStrat	BGG	1.84	2.5	12	272	73	72⅜	72½	−1
	23⅝	9⅜	BrillAuto	CBA	.08	.6	...	178	12⅝	12⅛	12⅝	− ⅛
s	33⅝	21⅜	BrinkerInt	EAT		...	27	5391	23⅝	22⅝	22⅞	− ⅞
	62¼	50	BrisMyrsSqb	BMY	2.92	5.3	14	5877	55¾	55¼	55⅜	− ¼
	74⅛	44	BritAir	BAB	.59e	1.0	...	625	60½	60	60½	− ⅛
	54¼	39¾	BritGas	BRG	2.76e	6.9	...	312	40⅜	40	40¼	− ⅞
	75⅛	51⅜	BritPetrol	BP	1.96e	2.6	39	4952	74⅝	74	74	− ⅞
	23⅛	12⅞	BritSteel	BST	.28e	1.3	...	1251	21½	21	21¼	+ ⅝
n	49½	35⅞	BritishTele 2nd	BTYP		...	...	2124	38⅛	38	38	− ½
	74⅞	53⅞	BritishTele	BTY	3.01e	5.3	...	7631	56⅜	56⅛	56⅜	− ⅝
	16⅜	8¼	BrdwyStore	BWY		...	dd	85	9½	9⅜	9½	+ ⅛
	5⅝	2⅛	**BrdwyStore wt**			...	...	3	2¼	2⅛	2⅛	− ⅛
	56	37¼	BrokenHill	BHP	1.18e	2.2	...	27	53⅞	53¾	53¾	− ⅝
s	6	1¼	BrookeGp	BGL		...	dd	7	1⅝	1⅝	1⅝	− ⅛
s	28⅞	22⅛	BklynUnGas	BU	1.35	5.5	15	389	24¾	24¼	24¾	+ ¼
	8⅝	5¾	BrownShrp	BNS		...	dd	28	6	5⅞	6	+ ⅛
	38⅞	29¾	BrownGp	BG	1.60	4.2	dd	179	38⅜	37¾	38¼	+ ½
s	30⅛	23⅛	BrownFormn A	BFA	.95	3.5	13	33	27¼	26¾	27	− ⅛
s	30½	24¼	BrownFormn B	BFB	.95	3.5	14	219	27½	26⅝	27½	+ ¾
	32¼	20⅞	BrownFer	BFI	.68	2.2	25	4698	30¾	30⅛	30¾	+ ¼
	25⅜	12½	Brunswick	BC	.44	1.9	38	1886	23⅞	23⅜	23⅝	− ¼
	18⅝	11⅜	BrushWell	BW	.20	1.2	24	247	16¾	16⅜	16⅝	− ⅛
	41⅝	32⅝	BuckeyePtr	BPL	2.80	7.5	10	75	37½	37⅛	37⅛	− ⅛
	49¼	22½	BuenosAires	BAE	.46p	...	...	469	34⅝	33¾	34⅜	+ ⅛
n	54¾	22½	BufetInd	GBI		...	...	5	29	28¾	28¾	− ⅜
	17⅜	14⅛	BurgerKgInv	BKP	1.56f	9.3	19	48	17	16¾	16¾	− ⅛
s	28⅜	13⅛	BurlgtnCoat	BCF		...	14	175	19	18⅝	18⅞	− ⅛
	17⅛	12⅝	BurlgtnInd	BUR		...	12	1640	13⅝	13	13	− ½
	66⅝	48⅝	BurlgtnNthn	BNI	1.20	2.2	18	1654	55½	54⅝	55⅛	+ ¼
	75	60½	BurlgtnNthn pfA		3.13	4.9	...	175	64⅜	63½	63⅞	− ½
	26½	19¾	BurlngtnRes	BRU	2.30e	10.6	...	414	21⅞	21⅝	21⅝	− ⅛
	53⅞	40¼	BurlgtnRes	BR	.55	1.2	23	1368	44¾	44⅛	44⅝	+ ⅛
	20⅞	16⅛	BurnhmPacif	BPP	1.40	7.9	21	235	17¾	17⅝	17¾	...
n	16⅝	15¼	BushBoake	BOA		...	...	1100	16¼	16	16⅛	− ¼
			-C-C-C-									
	35⅞	23⅝	CBI Ind	CBH	.48	1.8	dd	923	27¾	26⅞	26⅞	−1⅛
n	21	17⅝	CBL Assoc	CBL	1.50	7.5	...	1063	20⅝	20	20⅛	− ⅝
	326½	214	CBS	CBS	2.00	.8	12	555	266¼	262¼	264	+1
	32⅝	18⅞	CCP Insur	CCP	.08	.4	6	1149	22¼	22	22⅛	− ⅛
	15	7⅜	CDI	CDI		...	25	31	14⅛	14	14	− ¼
	73¾	56½	CIGNA	CI	3.04	4.2	17	1889	71¾	70¾	71¾	− ⅜
	1⅝	⅜	CarolcoPic	CRC		...	dd	463	7/16	13/32	13/32	− 1/32
	14¾	9¼	CarolFrght	CAO	.15j	...	dd	201	10½	10¼	10¼	− ½
	34⅝	23	CarolPwr	CPL	1.70	7.2	11	967	24	23½	23½	− ½
	66⅜	49⅜	CarpTech	CRS	2.40	3.9	15	157	61¼	60¾	61⅛	− ⅜
n	15⅝	5½	CarrGottstn	CGF		...	17	101	5¾	5¾	5¾	− ⅛
	26	20	CarrRlty	CRE	1.75	7.7	...	78	23	22⅝	22⅝	− ⅜
	33⅞	17⅞	CarterWal	CAR	.33	1.7	33	1938	19½	19	19¼	− ⅜
s	19½	14	CascadeNG	CGC	.96	6.2	27	32	15⅜	15⅛	15⅜	− ⅛
	10⅛	7	CashAmIntl	PWN	.05	.6	16	135	8⅛	8	8	− ⅛
	15¾	10	Castle&Cooke	CKI		...	33	22	11⅞	11¾	11⅞	...
	53⅞	29	CatalinaMktg	POS		...	37	378	45½	45⅛	45¼	− ¼
	9⅛	6⅛	CatellusDev	CDX		...	dd	158	7¼	7	7¼	...
	63⅞	46¼	CatellusDev pfA		3.75	7.3	...	46	52¼	51⅛	51½	− ½
	121½	71⅞	Caterpillar	CAT	1.20f	1.1	13	3941	107⅞	106¼	106⅜	−2⅜
	36⅝	27	CedarFair	FUN	2.00	6.0	12	106	33⅝	33⅜	33⅜	− ¼
▼	18⅞	10¼	CentrEngy	CX	.80	7.8	dd	2128	10⅜	10⅛	10¼	...
n	14⅜	9½	CentexConstr	CXP		...	...	794	12	11⅝	12	+ ¼
	45¾	23¾	Centex	CTX	.20	.7	10	2340	27	26¼	26⅞	− ⅝
	33⅞	21	CentlSoWest	CSR	1.70	8.0	13	2061	21½	21¼	21¼	− ¼
	35¾	25¾	CentlHudGE	CNH	2.06	7.5	10	273	27½	27⅜	27⅜	− ¼
	27⅛	21¼	CentlLaElec	CNL	1.46f	6.0	13	258	24⅞	24¼	24½	− ¼
	24	10⅝	CentlMePwr	CTP	.90	7.7	9	452	11¾	11⅝	11⅝	− ½
	105	81⅝	CentlMePwr pfA		7.88	9.5	...	1	82⅞	82⅞	82⅞	+ ⅜
x	30	23	CentlNews	ECP	.48	1.7	21	91	29½	28⅞	28⅞	− ¼
▼	24¾	15½	CentlVtPS	CV	1.42	9.3	11	133	15¾	15⅛	15¼	− ⅜
	22⅛	18	CenturaBk	CBC	.72	3.4	10	360	21⅜	21	21⅜	+ ½
	31⅝	21⅞	CenturyTel	CTL	.32	1.2	19	230	26¼	25⅞	26	− ¼
	25⅝	14	Ceridian	CEN		...	dd	1047	24⅞	24½	24⅝	− ⅛
n	61	49⅝	Ceridian dep pf		2.75	4.7	...	15	59½	59	59	−1
	36	28	ChampInt	CHA	.20	.6	dd	826	33¾	33⅛	33¼	− ⅜
	12¼	7⅞	ChaparlStl	CSM	.20	2.1	39	15	9½	9⅜	9⅜	− ⅛
	15¾	6⅝	ChartHousEnt	CHT		...	19	446	10¼	9¾	10¼	+ ¼
	9⅝	3⅜	ChartInd	CTI	.28	8.0	...	63	3½	3½	3½	+ ⅛
	40	29½	ChaseManh	CMB	1.32	3.5	7	12524	38⅜	37⅜	37¾	− ⅞
	51¼	49¾	ChaseManh pfF		3.16e	6.3	...	4	50⅛	50⅛	50⅛	...
	31⅝	26¾	ChaseManh pfG		2.63	9.3	...	7	28¼	28	28¼	+ ¼
	30¼	25¼	ChaseManh pfH		2.44	8.7	...	8	28	27⅞	28	+ ¼
	32½	28¼	ChaseManh pfI		2.71	9.1	...	27	29⅞	29⅝	29⅞	...
	28⅛	24¾	ChaseManh pfJ		2.27	8.7	...	16	26	25⅞	26	...
	27½	23⅜	ChaseManh pfK		2.13	8.4	...	67	25½	25¼	25⅜	...
	27⅜	23⅝	ChaseManh pfL		2.08	8.3	...	30	25⅛	24⅞	25⅛	− ⅛
	27⅝	23⅞	ChaseManh pfM		2.10	8.3	...	19	25⅜	25¼	25¼	− ⅛
n	25½	24⅝	ChaseManh pfN		.22p	...	...	2559	25	24 45/64	24 45/64	− ⅛
n	**10⅛**	**5**	**ChaseManh wt**			...	...	**149**	**8½**	**8**	**8⅛**	− ½
nx	24¼	18⅝	ChateauProp	CPJ	1.40	6.1	...	118	23⅜	22⅞	22⅞	− ⅝
	3¾	**1⅝**	**Chaus**	**CHS**		...	**dd**	**276**	**1⅞**	**1⅞**	**1⅞**	− ⅛
	17	8⅛	CheckptSys	CKP		...	cc	99	16⅜	16¼	16¼	− ¼
n	30½	25	Chelsea GCA	CCG	1.22e	4.6	...	759	26½	25¾	26½	+ ¼

Source: The Wall Street Journal, June 21, 1994, p. C3.

increase at a rate higher than the rate of inflation. Again, the risk of illiquidity depends on how many shares of stock are outstanding and on the market in which the stock is traded. An issuer cannot call common stock. Common stock is discussed in depth in Chapter 12.

Reports of most common stock data in *The Wall Street Journal* follow the same format as preferred stock data, shown in Exhibit 4.6. However, a column called the "NASDAQ Small-Cap Issues" covers stocks of small companies that may or may not be actively traded. Traders exchange these stocks through a system of market makers rather than through exchange-based transactions. Exhibit 4.7 contains excerpts from small-stock price listings. A simulated entry appears below; the text that follows explains how to interpret it.

ISSUE	DIV	VOL 100s	LAST	CHG
Hijack	.40	76	11 5/8	+3/8

***Issue* = *Hijack*.** This means that the name of the company issuing the stock is *Hijack*.

***Div* = .40.** This means that the stock is paying an annual dividend of $0.40, or ten cents per quarter, per share.

***Vol 100s* = 76.** This means that 7,600 shares were traded on the day for which the price is quoted.

***Last* = 11 5/8.** This means that the stock last traded on the day of the quote at $11.625 per share. The half-cent is not a problem because most stock trades are made in **round lots** (blocks of 100 shares) instead of **odd lots** (anything less than 100 shares at a time).

round lot
A trade involving exactly 100 shares of stock.

odd lot
A trade involving less than 100 shares of stock.

***Chg* = +3/8.** This means that the closing price was $0.375 higher than the closing price on the previous trading day.

Warrants. A company may want to issue bonds that it suspects will not be completely acceptable to the market because the interest rate is too low or the terms under which the bond is issued are biased against the potential investor. To sweeten the issue, it may attach warrants to the bonds. A **warrant** allows the holder to buy common stock in the company at a price above the current market price of the stock, but below its expected future market price.

warrant
A security attached to a bond that allows the holder to buy common stock in the issuing company at a price above the current market price but below the expected future market price.

Warrants usually have one to four years until expiration when issued, but they can be issued in perpetuity (with no expiration dates). Some warrants can be sold separately, or detached, from the bonds, a feature meant to appeal to the dealer that brings the bond to the public; others cannot. Nondetachable warrants are expected to increase the return to the bondholders.

Detachable warrants with expiration dates are relatively illiquid because the amounts outstanding are usually small. A sizable issue of warrants from a strong company can, however, be listed on a stock exchange, improving liquidity substantially. Companies that issue detachable warrants in perpetuity usually flood the market with them, so these securities have the image of being a cheap trick and are usually worth pennies, at best.

EXHIBIT 4.7

NASDAQ Small-Cap Issues

NASDAQ SMALL-CAP ISSUES

Issue	Div	Vol 100s	Last	Chg
A&A Fd g		20	15/16	- 3/64
ACTV		114	5 1/4	+ 1/8
ADM Tr		66	15/32	...
AGBag		232	1 1/8	...
AGP &Co		919	1 5/16	...
APA		40	3 3/4	- 1/4
ASA Int		5	1 1/4	...
ATC Env		228	9 7/8	- 1/2
ATC wt B		35	3	- 3/4
ATC EnC		250	1	- 1/4
ATC Inc		655	3/32	...
AberRs		1153	8 1/8	+ 1
AcresGm		248	5 21/64	- 11/64
AcreG wt		5	1 1/4	- 29/64
AcreG un		2	5 3/4	- 1/4
ActnPr		40	1 1/2	...
Activisn		3	5 3/4	+ 1/4
Actrade		99	2	...
Acuity		552	7 1/4	+ 1/4
AdapSol		243	3 3/8	...
AdapSl wt		27	1 1/2	+ 1/4
Admar		81	1 13/16	+ 1/8
AdvCre		796	2 3/8	...
AdvDep		94	3 5/8	- 1/8
AdvDp wt		43	7/16	...
AdvEnv		411	9/16	...
AdvMam		4	4 1/8	- 3/8
AdvMat		40	2	+ 1/16
AdvMedP		1	1 1/16	...
AdvOxy s		20	1 5/8	...
AdvSu wt		330	3/4	...
AdvanLfe		264	9/16	+ 1/32
AdvntTc		206	19/32	- 3/32
Aerial		30	3 3/4	- 1/4
Air LA		184	2 3/4	- 1/8
AirCure		110	3 1/2	- 1/8
AirInt		50	5/32	...
Ajay		4	3/8	...
AladnKn		182	5 5/8	- 3/8
Alamar		214	2 3/8	...
Alamr wt		40	1/2	- 1/8
Alanco		289	2 7/16	- 3/32
AlbionBc		20	13 5/8	+ 1/8
Alcde pf		4	1 3/4	- 1/4
Alden		26	2 3/4	...
AllACm		10	8 1/4	...
AllPrd un		46	8	...
AllQuote		30	2 5/8	- 1/8
AldCAdv		17	3 5/8	- 11/64
AlphHsp		75	7 3/4	...
AlphH wt		22	2	- 3/32
AlphaSo		1135	1/8	- 1/32
Alpnet		1109	13/16	- 1/32
AlterSal		420	1 1/32	...
Ameral		95	3 13/16	+ 1/16
vjAWAirl		2305	3 11/16	- 1/8
AmBiom		359	3/4	- 9/32
ABsCpt		311	1 15/16	+ 1/16
AmCasn		70	1 1/16	- 3/32
AmCine		147	7	+ 1/4
AmCin wt		32	2 1/2	...
AmDentl		7	1 1/2	- 1/8
AmFbre		18	1/16	...
AMdAlt		5	2 5/16	- 1/16
AmMdTc		95	29/32	- 1/32
AmNtEn		617	7 3/8	...
APacBk		5	1 1/8	...
AmResCp		423	5 7/8	- 3/8

Issue	Div	Vol 100s	Last	Chg
Bonso		8	1 7/16	- 1/16
BntyGp		73	3 1/2	- 1 1/2
BrandtT		2	6 1/8	+ 5/8
BrntwFn	.60a	2	25	- 1
Briolnd		59	4 1/8	- 3/8
BroadN pf	.85	3	12 1/4	- 5/8
BrshCr s		16	1 5/8	- 1/8
BldrWre		35	2 1/4	+ 1/8
ButlrNt		22	4 7/16	+ 5/16
BPreiss		321	5 5/8	...
BPreis wt		432	2 1/8	...
CAM Dt		330	3 3/16	- 3/32
CAPX		3	2 5/8	...
CB Bcp s		99	13 3/4	+ 1/2
vjCBL		564	1/4	...
CBT Cp	.88	44	39 1/2	...
CCAIR		202	2 1/4	- 1/8
CEC In		23	2	- 1/8
CEL Cm		25	1/2	...
CSL Lgt		270	4 1/2	- 1/4
CblCar		1247	13/16	...
Cabre s		10	5	...
Cadiz		636	5 9/16	- 7/16
Caledon		208	5 1/16	- 5/16
CalFedl wt		2410	21/32	- 1/32
CalQurtz		668	1 15/16	- 1/8
CalQu wt		120	1/2	...
Calnetcs		60	3 1/8	- 1/8
Camelot		1071	1 15/32	+ 1/16
Camiz		152	8 1/2	- 1/4
CndyTor		24	3 5/32	...
CapAcq		297	2 5/8	- 1/8
CaptlGm		2289	6 3/8	- 1/8
CapMult		27	8 3/4	- 1/8
Capucin		284	7/16	- 1/32
Caraco		86	4 1/2	- 1/4
CareCon	.15e	30	9/16	...
Caretnd		854	2 1/4	...
CaroF pf	1.88	11	26 1/2	...
CaroFt pf	.46e	24	26 1/2	...
CascBcp		19	13 1/8	- 3/8
CascSB s		2	17	- 1
Cavco		3	16 1/2	- 5/8
CecoEnv		115	2 3/4	- 1/8
CedarGp		2007	5 3/4	+ 1/8
CelebEnt		56	3 1/4	...
CelEnt wt		31	5 3/4	- 1 1/4
CelEnt pf		106	10 1/4	- 2
Cellex		90	13/32	+ 1/32
Cellex un		82	5 5/8	- 1/8
Celltch s		30	5	...
CellCm s		583	28 1/2	- 1 3/4
Centcre		26	31/32	- 1/32
CntMne		336	2 11/32	- 3/32
CentCas		47	2 1/4	- 11/64
Cerprbe	.03e	39	5 1/4	- 1/2
ChalInt		8	2 5/8	...
ChmpSp h		2420	11/32	+ 5/32
Chantal		535	1 1/16	...
ChtBnc	.24	17	14 1/4	- 1/4
ChkEx wt		92	4	+ 1/2
ChefsInt		28	2 1/4	...
Chmx wt94		100	3/32	...
Chemex		20	1	...
Cherokee		339	1	- 5/8
Chrk wtA		31	1/8	- 1/8
Chrk wtB		134	1/8	...
Chrk wtC		132	1/32	...

Issue	Div	Vol 100s	Last	Chg
DMI Frn		2	2 1/2	...
DMI Inc		50	5/8	...
DSI Ind		54	11/32	...
Danngr		200	3 7/8	...
Dtamap		84	2 5/8	+ 1/4
DavWht		7	9 1/2	+ 3/8
DawnTch		80	7/8	+ 1/8
DeNovo		63	7/16	- 1/16
Decora		853	1 1/32	...
DnsePc		222	1 5/16	+ 1/16
DeprAn		22	1 7/8	- 1/4
DermaSci		5	5 3/8	+ 3/8
DetCan	.50	5	26 3/4	- 3 1/4
DevRsc		10	2	...
DiagH wt		2	1/4	...
DiagHlt		2	1 11/16	+ 1/16
Dickinsn		10	4	+ 1/8
DigtlSol		302	2 11/32	- 1/16
Diplomat		86	7 3/8	- 3/8
Diplm wt		42	4 1/2	...
DrctCon		500	23/32	+ 3/32
DrcCn wt		40	15/16	- 1/32
Diversfx		45	2 11/16	- 3/16
Divers wt		100	1/2	- 1/8
DixieN		5	29/32	...
DocuCn		124	5/8	...
DocImg		137	7	+ 1/2
DocIm wt		50	1 3/4	+ 3/8
Dolco		2	19 3/4	...
DolrTme		710	1	...
DblEgl		50	7/8	...
DrugScrn		160	1 15/16	+ 1/16
DustyM		113	4 5/8	- 3/16
DwyerGp		18	5 1/4	- 1/4
DynaGp		137	7/8	+ 1/16
Dynacq		29	2	...
Dynagn		161	13/16	- 1/16
Dyng wtA		140	5/16	...
DynOil		203	1 7/16	- 1/16
DyntrCp		40	2 1/8	...
E&B Mar		1	9 1/2	- 1
ECO2		406	3 3/8	- 5/16
ERC Ind		35		...
EV Env		70	3 3/4	...
EVRO		1601	1	+ 1/32
EarthSc		50	1 13/16	- 1/16
Eastco		35	1 13/16	- 3/32
Eastco un		189	2 3/16	...
Edac		3	1 1/8	- 1/4
Edmark		4	10 1/4	- 1/2
ElCondor		281	3 3/4	- 3/32
ElBrain		357	1 1/4	- 3/16
ElCath		2	1 1/4	...
ElClear		563	9/16	- 1/16
Elctsrc		1080	4	+ 3/8
ElepCstl		152	5 5/8	...
ElmrSv	.64	22	15	- 3
Eltrax		39	61/64	+ 5/64
EmplySl		161	8	...
EngyRsh		26	11	...
EnvirIn		1382	4 1/8	- 3/8
Envrg un		100	4 1/16	- 1/16
Envmt un		257	16 1/2	+ 1/2
EnTUSA h		576	15/16	- 1/32
EqtFedl		4	14 1/2	+ 1/4
EqtAU		440	3/32	- 1/32
Equivst		40	2 1/16	...
Equivsn		17	4 1/8	- 3/8

Issue	Div	Vol 100s	Last	Chg
GrnMtn		9	5 5/8	- 5/8
GrnstRs		25	1 5/8	+ 7/64
GrnstR		110	1/2	- 1/32
GrntrSf s		125	2 3/8	...
GManning		163	2 13/16	...
GMann wt		259	13/16	...
Grifith		54	11 3/4	+ 3/4
GthEnvr		16	4 5/8	+ 3/16
GthFn	.38t	50	9 3/4	...
Gulfwest		5	3	- 1/2
GuntInt		100	4 1/8	- 3/8
GunIn wt		20	1 1/8	...
GunIn un		100	5 1/4	- 1/4
HERC		210	5 5/8	- 1/8
HMG Wd		2	7 3/8	...
HamPlsR		78	2 1/4	- 7/64
HamP wtA		7	1	...
HamP wtB		7	3/4	...
Hansen		44	2 3/8	+ 1/4
HarcorE		14	3 3/4	- 1/16
Haristn		402	6 1/4	- 3/8
HarmBrk		28	2 1/2	...
HrmHld		509	2 7/8	- 1/4
HarmPd		10	2 1/2	+ 1/4
HarveyC		257	11	...
HarveyU		73	1 1/2	...
HwkEn		2	1 1/2	...
Hawks		100	3/32	- 1/32
HltIm un		25	2	- 1/4
HltcrTc		2491	2 7/16	- 1/16
Hltplx		336	2 5/8	+ 3/8
Hlthw wtA		7	1/32	...
Hlthw wtB		15	1/32	...
Hlthwtc s		223	1 37/64	- 19/64
HlthPln		163	8 1/4	- 3/8
HrtLabs		65	3	- 1/8
HemaC		85	5 1/4	...
HemdlCm		2	1 1/2	- 1/4
HillsBed		2307	1 1/32	+ 5/32
HillBd wt		20	11/32	+ 5/32
HollyPd		181	5 7/8	- 3/8
HlyPd wt		5	1 1/8	...
HFSB WA		19	19 1/2	- 1/2
HmeThea		2771	5 27/32	- 3/16
H&S wt		100	3/16	- 1/32
Hmcall		5	3	+ 1/16
Hughes		43	15/16	- 1/16
HungTelc		81	12	- 3/4
HungTel		722	15 7/8	- 7/8
Hymedix		111	4 1/4	...
HypmdCm		33	7 1/2	- 3/16
ICC Tch		4621	5 5/16	+ 1/4
ID Biom		47	9 3/8	+ 7/8
IDM Env		607	5 1/2	...
IDM wt		451	2	- 1/2
IDM un		64	7 1/2	...
I-Flow		10	1 7/16	+ 1/8
ILX Inc		214	2	- 1/16
IMRE wt		50	1 1/8	+ 1/16
IMRE		120	2 5/8	+ 1/8
IPI Inc		70	4	...
IRATA un		316	5 1/4	- 1/16
IbisTech		28	4 3/4	...
IbisTc wt		87	3/4	...
IdanSft		690	1/2	- 3/32
Ikos		59	1 1/2	...
ImgMgt		115	11/32	- 3/32
Imex		70	3/4	- 1/16

Issue	Div	Vol 100s	Last	Chg
Jordan wt		140	3/16	...
Judicte s		6	1 1/8	...
JuniprF		515	15/32	+ 1/32
KLH Eng		135	7/32	- 1/16
KellyRus		10	4 5/8	...
KdyWils		245	1 7/8	+ 1/8
KiddePr	.17	1	15	+ 3/4
Kinert un		41	7 7/8	- 5/16
Kineret		365	5	...
Kinert wt		73	1 19/32	- 1/32
KingCty		3	25 1/2	...
KooKR		899	6 1/2	- 3/8
Krantor		443	4 3/4	- 1/16
LF Bcp	.30e	36	18	+ 1/4
LSB SC	.68	79	37 5/8	- 1 1/8
LaTeko		1670	2 3/8	+ 1/16
LaMan		139	1 9/16	+ 1/16
Lafay un		10	7 1/2	...
Lambert		20	3/8	- 1/16
LncrOrt		50	1/4	+ 1/16
LarDav		279	3 9/16	...
LasVDsc		2	11/16	+ 1/16
LasVEnt		420	1 3/4	- 1/32
LasVEE wtB		70	7/16	- 1/16
LasVMai		50	4 7/16	- 1/16
LVMai wt		240	1 3/32	+ 3/32
LaserFr		183	3 3/8	- 5/64
LsrSght		183	4 1/4	- 1/4
Lasrtch		11499	2	+ 3/16
LsrVide		2316	3 7/16	+ 1/8
LsrVis		257	6	+ 1/4
LsrVs wt		210	1 1/4	- 1/16
LatexRs		817	31/32	- 1/32
Latex wt		15	1/8	- 1/32
Latex un		21	13/16	- 3/16
Leadvle		10	7/8	+ 1/8
LeakX		203	4 1/8	...
Leak X wt		524	3 1/8	- 1/8
Leggons		26	1 1/8	- 1/4
LeisMkt		3	1 7/8	- 1/8
LetchInd	.40	2	22 3/4	+ 1/2
Licon		180	5/16	- 3/32
LfeMed		180	3 3/8	- 1/8
LfMd wtA		175	1	...
LfeMd un		66	5	- 1/4
Lifecell		560	2 1/2	- 5/8
Lifeway		6	1 1/2	+ 1/4
Lifschlt		905	5/16	- 1/32
LightSav		60	1 27/32	+ 1/32
LincSnk		232	1 1/2	- 1/8
LindasCh		25	4 1/4	- 1/2
Linda un		833	6	- 1/8
Linium		255	11/32	- 1/32
LiveEn pf	.50	1	7 3/4	...
LneStar		336	2 3/8	+ 1/8
LouG 5pf	1.25	9	16 3/4	+ 1/2
LucileFr		122	3 13/16	- 7/16
Lucile wt		10	1 3/8	...
LukMed		2	2 1/8	+ 1/8
Lunnl		5	1	+ 1/16
LuthMed		144	3 1/2	+ 1/4
Luxcel		160	13/16	- 1/8
Luxcl wt		66	5/16	- 3/16
M-SysFD		173	3 5/8	- 1/4
MBF		295	1 9/16	...
MCDC		96	2 5/8	- 1/4
MCDC wt		47	3/4	+ 1/16
MCDC un		107	3 1/4	- 1/4

Issue	Div	Vol 100s	Last	Chg
NRP		878	2 7/16	...
NTN		51	8 5/8	- 1/8
Nytest		73	5/8	...
Nastech		48	3 1/8	- 3/8
Natec		185	15/16	+ 1/32
NatEng		5	1 5/8	- 1/8
NtHlthE		22	4 3/8	- 3/8
NatlReg		146	3 7/8	+ 1/4
NtlTire		21	2 3/8	...
NtlWire		52	8	...
Natnmrt		153	1 3/4	- 1/4
NatEart		286	3 7/8	+ 1/8
NatEa wt		63	1 9/16	+ 1/16
NatrElm		47	3 1/2	...
NatEl wt		85	13/16	+ 3/16
Neogen		121	6 7/8	...
Neolens		371	3/4	...
NwkFS		295	13/32	- 3/64
NtwkLng		261	8	+ 1/4
NevEngy		179	1 9/16	+ 1/4
NewDay		48	2 1/8	- 3/8
NewDy wt		120	1 1/2	+ 3/8
NewDy un		5	5	- 1
NwVision		9	6 5/8	- 5/8
NwWEye		132	5 5/16	- 1/16
NwCm wt		202	3/32	...
NewsCm		265	3	- 1/8
NwCm un		25	4 1/4	...
NexusTel		960	3 63/64	- 1/64
NexT wtA		50	3/4	...
NexusT un		250	9 1/4	- 1/4
NexT wtB		50	1	...
NobelEd		10	1 1/4	- 3/64
NobleR		20	6 3/8	- 3/8
NonIMnt		51	5/16	...
Nona s		155	2 7/8	+ 1/8
NordPc s		10	15/16	...
NorrisC		548	4 1/4	- 1/16
NAPall		261	5 3/8	- 1/4
NAmTch		140	3 3/4	- 1/8
NthCstE	.24t	8	1 3/4	- 1/8
NE Ins		10	1 3/4	- 1/16
NthLily		405	7/32	- 1/32
NestU wt		50	1 3/8	...
Nvmtx un		65	8 3/4	- 1/4
Noxso		283	3 3/4	- 3/8
NutrMgt		5	2 7/8	...
NutrMg wt		123	1/2	- 1/16
OCG		2	5/32	- 1/32
OIS		2701	5 3/8	+ 3/8
OakhCap		13	3 1/8	...
OceanB	†	21	2 5/8	- 1/4
OceanOpt		22	4 1/8	- 1/8
Octagn un		50	19 13/16	+ 13/16
Octus		141	4 3/8	- 1/16
Octus wt		20	1 1/16	- 1/8
Odwalla		3	12 1/2	+ 1/4
OfCounsl		7	3	- 3/4
OfCou wt		204	5/8	- 3/8
OfCou un		35	4 1/4	- 1 1/4
Ofceland		4	3/8	...
OklaSvg		137	19 1/4	- 3/4
OldYork		198	4 3/4	- 1/4
OliverTr		52	4	- 1/4
OlivrT wt		207	1 1/16	- 3/16
OmgaHl		5	4 1/2	- 1/2
OmniUSA		5	3 3/4	...
Omnicp		209	17/32	+ 1/32

Issue	Div	Vol 100s	Last	Chg
ProtPoly		7	1 1/8	...
PrvAm		1	2 3/8	- 1/8
Proxymd		7	8	- 5/8
PsycCp		218	3 9/16	+ 1/8
PubcoC		4	5	...
PulaskiB		42	13 3/8	+ 1/8
Purflw		1	1 5/16	+ 1/16
Q Steak		2	4 3/4	- 1/4
Q Med		120	1 1/8	...
Qsound		52	2 7/8	...
Qdrax		808	3/8	- 1/32
QuantLr s		1362	1 21/32	+ 1/32
Questa		10	3 7/8	...
Questch		2	3 7/8	- 1/8
Quiznos		12	4	...
RCM		104	21/32	+ 1/32
RT Inds		154	1 1/2	...
RTI		83	1/2	...
RailAm		2	1 7/8	+ 1/4
Rail wtA		6	3/16	- 1/8
Ramtrn pf		300	4	- 1/8
RandC s		10	7 1/4	+ 7/8
RawsnKo		67	3 1/16	- 5/16
ReaGld		51	1 17/32	+ 1/32
ReconvTc		130	2 3/4	...
ReddiBrk		116	4 7/8	+ 1/16
RenGlf		292	2 1/4	...
RenGlf wt		106	1/2	...
RntWay		78	9 7/8	+ 3/8
Rentch		190	1 21/32	+ 3/32
RepubBk		1	13 1/2	+ 1/2
RschFrt s		139	7 7/8	- 5/16
RschF wt		42	3 1/2	- 1/4
Response		83	1	+ 1/8
ReunRsc		60	6 3/4	...
RichCst		66	1 13/16	- 1/16
RideSnw		777	5 15/16	- 5/16
RideS wt		288	1 9/16	- 1/16
RideS un		158	13 5/8	- 1/2
Rimag un		1	7 1/4	- 1/8
Robomtx		132	2 1/32	+ 1/32
RkMCh		3	13 1/4	+ 3/4
RotaryPw		244	5 3/8	...
RoyGld		44	8 1/8	- 1/4
RoylInv	.85	70	9 1/4	...
RoycLb s		208	3 5/8	+ 1/8
RyanMu		295	9/16	...
RynM wt		300	3/32	...
Ryka		327	1	+ 1/32
SA Hold		237	2 5/8	...
SBS En		10	4 1/2	+ 1/8
SCS		31	1 1/2	...
SI Diam		573	5 3/4	- 1/4
SSE Tl		58	6 5/8	- 1/4
S2 Glf		6	2	+ 1/4
Saliva		440	2	...
SancWod		175	3	...
SanFeFn		16	20 3/4	+ 3/4
SartgBd s		468	1 3/8	...
SaratgSp		112	5 1/4	- 1/2
Saztec		370	1 5/16	...
ScanGr		20	19/32	...
ScanSrce		146	7 7/8	+ 1/4
ScanSr wt		10	2 15/16	- 7/64
Scanfrm		10	2 3/16	...
Scorpn s		762	3/8	- 1/32
SellrPol		152	2 7/8	- 1/16
Selvac		7	9/32	...

Issue	Div	Vol 100s	Last	Chg
Thrmdy		39	5/32	...
3 CI		21	2 3/8	- 1/8
3Net Sy		267	1 1/2	+ 1/8
TitleWve		128	2 1/8	+ 1/8
Topro		51	3 3/4	+ 3/8
Topro wt		37	1/2	...
TotalRs		69	1	- 1/16
TchApd s		362	3 5/8	- 1/8
TowrTch		23	5	...
TracrPt		21	1 9/16	...
TA Wst un		z25	650	- 40
Transcor		92	3 1/4	+ 3/16
TwldH un		10	10	- 1/2
TriCnty	.10e	15	12 1/4	+ 1/4
Tubbys		47	3/8	- 1/32
TurfPar	.10	9	12 3/4	+ 3/8
Tyrex		2	7/32	...
UFP Tch		100	3 1/4	+ 1/4
US LAN		5	2 15/16	...
USMed un		471	3 3/4	...
US Wats	.48	410	2	+ 1/4
USA Hl un		343	7/16	- 1/16
USPRI	.24	8	3 1/8	...
UltElct		246	10 1/4	- 1 1/8
Unapix		417	2 7/8	...
Unpx wtA		15	21/32	- 3/32
UniCmp		16	3 5/8	- 1/4
UnicoDE		80	15/16	+ 1/8
Unign wtB		460	1/2	...
UPlntr pf	2.59	1	24 5/8	- 7/8
Uniqust		145	15/16	+ 1/16
UnitC wt		250	7/16	- 1/16
UnBnOH s	.32	3	22	...
UFedS	.04e	5	7 1/2	- 3/8
UtdFnBc	.30	7	19 3/8	- 1/8
UHrtg		478	7/16	+ 1/16
UtdRest		75	2 1/2	- 1/8
UtdRst un		96	3 1/2	...
USvAd pf		49	4 3/4	+ 1/8
USExpInc		247	1 5/8	- 3/16
US Gold		7	11/16	...
US Tech		166	3/4	+ 3/32
US Trn s		137	1 1/8	- 1/8
UnSyTc		300	3/64	+ 1/64
UtdVsn		667	3	- 3/8
UtdVs wt		53	1	...
UnvSelf		542	3	+ 1/4
UnSlf wtA		25	9/16	- 5/32
Urethane		7	4	- 1/8
VIP Glbl		5	2 7/8	- 1/2
VSI Ent		454	1/2	- 1/16
Vaalco		77	2 1/2	- 1/2
VlyFrg		24	3 1/8	- 1/8
Vari-L Co		62	4 1/2	...
Vari-L un		10	5 1/4	- 1/8
VctA 96wt		200	5/32	- 1/32
VctAer		90	21/32	- 1/32
VegasChp		9	2 1/8	+ 3/8
Velcro	1.00a	9	58 1/2	+ 1
VentEn		370	1 3/8	+ 1/16
VermPu		25	3 1/2	- 1/4
Vernt pf	†	12		...
VersTc		300	1 5/16	- 1/16
Veru wt		15	1/16	...
Vertexl		34	2 1/16	- 5/16
VidJuke		405	1 3/4	+ 1/8
VideoLab		70	3 1/2	...
Vimrx		333	29/32	+ 3/32

Source: *The Wall Street Journal*, June 21, 1994, p. C8.

FOCUS ON CAREERS

Registered Representative

Brokerage firms always welcome an energetic individual who has a knack for selling. They usually recruit young people on college campuses and place them in six-month apprenticeship programs. During this training period, they are expected to become familiar with brokerage house operations, the basics of securities trading, and the fundamentals of securities regulation.

Their duties include assisting registered representatives by placing cold calls to prospective clients. Cold calling involves telephone solicitation of individuals and institutions with the objective of convincing those contacted to engage in securities trading with the caller. The names of those called may come from mailing lists, personal contacts, or simply right out of the telephone book. All new accounts generated are assigned to more experienced individuals.

During this probationary period, the trainee generally draws a straight salary of $5 to $10 per hour. By the end of the training period, the brokerage firm has weeded out the less productive callers. (In unscrupulous firms, there may be no survivors.) The firm then agrees to sponsor those whom it intends to retain for the Series 7 and 14 examinations given by the National Association of Securities Dealers (NASD). The Series 7 exam tests a broker's knowledge about the mechanics of the market; a prospective broker must pass this exam in order to earn a license. To trade securities, the NASD mandates that the individual be knowledgeable in the product he or she sells, the protections afforded the investor, and recordkeeping. Passing the appropriate examination provides certification that the individual is registered to sell securities.

After passing the examination, the new broker can then solicit business for himself or herself. The firm may assign the beginner to handle new clients who walk into the office off the street or phone the office after perusing the Yellow Pages. Salary at this point is generally paid as a straight commission, or a minimal draw against commission.

Knowledgeable, enthusiastic, and talented salespeople eventually become account executives, specializing in certain types of investors, securities, or trading strategies. Their potential earnings are excellent. Every brokerage house has its vice presidents whose outstanding personalities have helped them to accumulate lists of wealthy, actively trading investors. These people earn six-figure or seven-figure salaries, and they benefit from a cadre of trainees making cold calls to generate new clients.

Warrant holders earn no income in the form of interest or dividends. They do, however, enjoy the potential for substantial price appreciation. The value of a warrant increases when the market price of its underlying stock rises. Because warrants are very inexpensive, even small increases in their prices produce huge rates of return. (A 25-cent increase in the price of a $2 warrant represents a 12.5 percent return.) This potential appeals to the gambling instincts of many investors. Market data on warrants are shown in both Exhibits 4.6 and 4.7.

Derivative Securities

Derivative securities represent rights and obligations to trade other financial or real assets; hence, their values are derived from the underlying assets. The two major types of derivative securities are commodities futures contracts and option contracts. Commodities futures contracts derive their trading values from the present and expected future prices of the underlying commodities. The volatility of these prices makes futures contracts attractive to risk-tolerant investors. Option contracts derive their trading values from present and future prices of securities, either individually or grouped into indices. The uncertainty and volatility of these prices can make option contracts appealing, as well. The return on derivative securities is mostly a function of market risk.

futures contract
A contract that promises delivery of a standardized quantity and quality of some commodity on the third Friday of a specified month.

Commodities Futures Contracts. The first **futures contracts** were created during the U.S. Civil War, when farmers sold their corn crops to animal feed and grain companies before the corn was harvested. The farmers got badly needed cash; the companies bought their future corn supplies at discounts. Wholesalers entered these transactions as intermediaries after the war, holding inventories of harvested corn and buying and selling contracts for future delivery to speculators. The value of the contracts fluctuated with news about the condition of the corn crop (their value dropped on good news and surged on bad news) and with news about expected future demand for corn (their value rose on good news and fell on bad news).

These fluctuations in contract values were so large and so frequent that they attracted the attention of investors who had no interest in the corn crop itself, but were looking for new ways to make a profit. The contracts developed standardized terms for quantity (5,000 bushels of corn, or one railroad boxcar full), quality, and delivery date. Banks and brokerage houses began facilitating purchases and sales of these contracts, and eventually an organized exchange was set up in Chicago to trade them.

The profits made in contracts for future delivery of corn were so large that markets developed in other agricultural crops: wheat, rye, cotton, beef, pork, coffee, orange juice concentrate, and many others. Investors accepted the huge market risk involved because the potential profits were larger than even the stock market's. In recent years, new commodities futures contracts have been based on metals, oil, Treasury securities, some foreign currencies, and even common stocks. It is estimated that over 90 percent of traders in commodities futures contracts are not interested in the underlying commodities; they are seeking spectacular returns from very short-term changes in the values of the contracts.

Exhibit 4.8 displays the daily listing of futures contracts from *The Wall Street Journal.* A simulated listing appears below and the following text explains how to interpret it.

Eggs (CBT) 10,000 doz., prices in cents per dozen

Delivery Month	Open	High	Low	Settle	Lifetime High	Lifetime Low	Open Interest
July	110	112	109	111	120	98	11,250

CBT. This means that contracts for the future delivery of eggs are traded on the Chicago Board of Trade, the leading futures exchange.

EXHIBIT 4.8

Futures Prices

FUTURES PRICES

Monday, June 20, 1994

Open Interest Reflects Previous Trading Day.

GRAINS AND OILSEEDS

	Open	High	Low	Settle	Change	Lifetime High	Lifetime Low	Open Interest
CORN (CBT) 5,000 bu.; cents per bu.								
July	274	276	271¼	271¼	−12	316½	241	79,721
Sept	271	272	267	267	−12	292¼	240½	43,312
Dec	265	267½	263	263	−12	277	236½	116,657
Mr95	270	273	268½	268½	−12	282½	248¾	12,712
May	273½	276	271¾	271¾	−12	285	253	2,121
July	274½	277½	272¾	272¾	−12	285¼	254	3,682
Sept	263	263	258	259	−11	270½	255	119
Dec	258	258	251	252¾	−8¼	263	243	3,602
Est vol 47,000; vol Fri 78,701; open int 261,926, +8,697.								
OATS (CBT) 5,000 bu.; cents per bu.								
July	130½	134	130	134	−3¼	161¼	112½	6,282
Sept	132	132	128¼	129¾	−6¼	154½	117¼	3,972
Dec	135½	136	132¼	134½	−6¼	157¼	124½	3,241
Mr95	143	137	136	137	−6¾	152¾	130	159
Est vol 5,000; vol Fri 5,016; open int 13,665, −137.								
SOYBEANS (CBT) 5,000 bu.; cents per bu.								
July	690	692½	681	681	−30	750	594½	38,320
Aug	690	691	678¼	678¼	−30	735	628	20,716
Sept	676	682½	670½	670½	−30	708½	617	10,218
Nov	673	675	665	665	−30	699	581½	78,596
Ja95	674	679	669	669	−30	704	613	6,111
Mar	674	682	672¾	672¾	−30	704½	618	2,857
May	680	683	674	674	−30	705½	621	2,071
July	680½	686	674	674	−30	706½	624	2,047
Nov	626	626	619	622	−12½	645	592	1,456
Est vol 45,000; vol Fri 70,105; open int 162,392, +5,357.								
SOYBEAN MEAL (CBT) 100 tons; $ per ton.								
July	200.00	200.50	196.00	196.70	−9.30	230.00	185.20	23,582
Aug	198.50	201.00	197.00	197.10	−9.90	225.00	185.00	18,572
Sept	196.90	200.50	196.90	196.90	−10.00	210.00	183.10	13,958
Oct	196.20	199.50	196.20	196.20	−10.00	207.50	180.00	6,617
Dec	196.30	199.90	196.30	196.30	−10.00	209.00	178.80	21,624
Ja95	196.50	200.00	196.40	196.40	−10.00	207.50	178.80	1,590
Mar	196.70	200.00	196.70	196.70	−10.00	207.50	181.00	1,833
May	199.00	199.20	195.70	195.70	−10.00	207.00	181.00	723
July	200.00	200.00	195.00	195.00	−10.00	206.00	182.00	356
Est vol 20,000; vol Fri 25,085; open int 88,855, +2,930.								
SOYBEAN OIL (CBT) 60,000 lbs.; cents per lb.								
July	27.65	27.75	27.18	27.24	−.89	30.82	21.55	18,067
Aug	27.45	27.75	27.18	27.26	−.86	30.65	21.65	15,332
Sept	27.50	27.70	27.14	27.22	−.84	30.34	22.40	12,002
Oct	27.25	27.50	26.88	26.93	−.86	29.54	22.10	8,643
Dec	27.00	27.27	26.62	26.70	−.86	28.87	22.00	22,687
Ja95	27.15	27.15	26.68	26.68	−.84	28.55	22.65	2,793
Mar	26.80	27.10	26.50	26.57	−.83	28.30	24.70	2,554
May	26.80	26.80	26.40	26.48	−.84	28.05	24.62	1,267
July		....	....	26.43	−.83	27.85	24.65	361
Est vol 16,000; vol Fri 15,539; open int 83,729, +1,278.								
WHEAT (CBT) 5,000 bu.; cents per bu.								
July	331	333	321¼	322	−13¼	356	296	18,808
Sept	337½	339½	327	327¼	−14¾	357¼	302	13,723
Dec	350	351	338	338½	−14¾	365	309	24,207
Mr95	352	352½	342	342	−14½	364	327	3,425
July	330	330½	320	320	−10	342¾	311½	309
Est vol 27,000; vol Fri 14,016; open int 60,751, −242.								
WHEAT (KC) 5,000 bu.; cents per bu.								
July	339	339½	330½	331¼	−11½	355	297	12,437
Sept	339	340¾	332	332¾	−11¼	355	302½	7,736
Dec	347	349	340	340¼	−11¼	360	312½	6,834
Mr95	349	349½	341	341	−10½	359½	326½	1,207
Est vol 9,506; vol Fri 5,173; open int 28,289, +198.								
WHEAT (MPLS) 5,000 bu.; cents per bu.								
July	347	348¾	339	340	−11	369½	299½	4,444
Sept	339	341¼	330½	331½	−12¾	358	300	5,283
Dec	347½	347½	337	337½	−12¾	360	304	2,787
Est vol 1,120; vol Fri 1,870; open int 12,631, −162.								
RICE-ROUGH (MCE) 2000 cwt; $ per cwt								
July	6.900	7.000	6.810	6.860	−.240	13.150	6.470	812
Sept	6.550	6.550	6.320	6.320	−.280	10.100	6.070	1,417
Nov	6.400	6.400	6.250	6.250	−.200	9.650	5.950	692
Ja95		....	....	6.400	−.200	9.700	6.270	313
Mar		....	....	6.550	−.200	9.630	6.340	9
Est vol 125; vol Fri 186; open int 3,339, +18.								
CANOLA (WPG) 20 metric tons; Can. $ per ton								
Aug	479.30	479.30	479.30	479.30	−10.00	514.50	321.50	6,832
Sept	395.70	397.50	392.00	392.00	−10.00	412.00	315.00	7,592
Ja95	98.25	98.25	95.50	97.25	+.70	132.00	95.20	3,201
Mar	99.50	100.00	99.00	99.25	+.75	124.25	97.50	1,298
Est vol 4,500; vol Fri 2,876; open int 23,985, +172.								

METALS AND PETROLEUM

	Open	High	Low	Settle	Change	Lifetime High	Lifetime Low	Open Interest
COPPER-HIGH (CMX)—25,000 lbs.; cents per lb.								
June	111.00	112.15	111.00	112.15	−1.40	113.70	74.10	418
July	111.70	112.45	110.70	112.15	−1.45	113.70	74.20	24,070
Aug	112.00	112.00	111.20	111.20	−1.50	112.60	75.30	702
Sept	112.00	112.60	111.00	112.30	−1.55	113.90	74.90	24,607
Oct	111.10	111.10	110.20	111.25	−1.40	111.10	75.20	275
Nov		....	....	111.20	−1.30	92.00	77.75	239
Dec	109.60	111.00	109.30	110.50	−1.20	111.70	75.75	7,744
Ja95		....	....	110.00	−1.10	108.00	76.90	292
Feb		....	....	109.70	−1.10	107.00	87.85	210
Mar	108.30	109.00	108.20	109.15	−1.05	110.00	76.30	2,091
May	108.00	108.00	108.00	108.15	−.95	108.00	76.85	789
July	107.50	107.50	107.50	107.30	−.95	107.50	78.00	706
Sept		....	....	106.55	−.95	105.00	79.10	567
Dec		....	....	105.85	−.95	105.50	88.00	752
Est vol 8,000; vol Fri 15,243; open int 63,597, +1,072.								
GOLD (CMX)—100 troy oz.; $ per troy oz.								
June	391.00	391.00	389.60	388.90	−2.70	417.20	339.40	791
Aug	394.90	395.40	390.50	390.90	−2.80	415.00	341.50	81,287
Oct	398.50	398.50	393.80	393.90	−2.80	417.00	344.00	5,307
Dec	401.00	401.80	396.70	397.10	−2.80	426.50	343.00	25,199
Fb95	404.80	404.80	401.00	400.60	−2.80	411.00	363.50	6,314
Apr	405.20	405.20	404.30	404.10	−2.80	425.00	385.50	6,868
June	409.50	409.50	407.90	407.70	−2.80	430.00	351.00	8,654
Aug	412.00	412.50	412.00	411.40	−2.80	412.50	380.50	1,480
Oct		....	....	415.30	−2.80	413.30	410.20	1,052
Dec		....	....	419.30	−2.80	439.50	358.00	4,518
Fb96		....	....	423.30	−2.80	424.50	412.50	533
Apr	430.00	430.00	430.00	427.40	−2.80	430.00	430.00	217
June		....	....	431.70	−2.70	447.00	370.90	2,006
Dec		....	....	444.70	−2.70	447.50	379.60	2,256
Ju97		....	....	458.30	−2.60	441.00	436.00	1,038
Dec		....	....	472.50	−2.50	477.00	402.00	1,337
Ju98		....	....	487.10	−2.40	489.50	483.90	1,201
Dec	503.00	503.00	503.00	502.30	−2.40	505.00	468.00	1,234
Est vol 42,000; vol Fri 54,463; open int 151,292, +10,875.								
PLATINUM (NYM)—50 troy oz.; $ per troy oz.								
July	na	413.00	405.10	406.50	−4.60	437.00	357.00	11,019
Oct	na	416.00	408.00	409.40	−4.60	435.00	368.00	10,829
Ja95	nl	416.50	416.50	411.60	−4.60	429.50	374.80	1,218
Apr	418.00	418.00	418.00	413.70	−4.60	428.00	390.00	1,167
Est vol 4,809; vol Fri 6,113; open int 24,233, +576.								
PALLADIUM (NYM) 100 troy oz.; $ per troy oz.								
June		....	....	138.25	−1.50	142.50	114.00	60
Sept	141.00	141.00	138.50	138.75	−1.50	142.00	113.00	3,842
Dec	140.00	139.50	139.50	138.95	−1.50	141.75	122.50	826
Est vol 302; vol Fri 194; open int 4,729, +96.								
SILVER (CMX)—5,000 troy oz.; cents per troy oz.								
June	546.5	546.5	546.5	547.0	−11.7	568.0	515.5	0
July	559.0	561.0	544.5	547.5	−11.8	586.5	372.5	63,867
Sept	563.5	566.0	550.0	552.4	−11.9	590.5	376.5	27,871
Dec	573.0	575.0	557.0	559.9	−11.9	597.0	380.0	18,091
Mr95	575.0	575.0	566.5	568.1	−11.9	604.0	416.5	5,902
May	578.0	578.0	573.0	573.6	−11.9	606.5	418.0	3,261
July	585.0	585.0	581.0	579.6	−11.9	610.0	403.0	1,257
Sept		....	....	585.7	−11.9	615.0	493.0	439
Dec		....	....	594.9	−11.9	628.0	434.0	2,085
Jl96		....	....	618.3	−11.9	630.0	524.0	943
Dec		....	....	636.4	−11.9	670.0	454.0	1,226
Jl97		....	....	662.7	−11.9	655.0	588.0	383
Dec		....	....	683.2	−11.9	695.0	502.0	307
Dc98		....	....	731.2	−11.9	710.0	710.0	105
Est vol 23,000; vol Fri 39,202; open int 125,773, −925.								
SILVER (CBT)—1,000 troy oz.; cents per troy oz.								
June	550.0	550.0	541.0	547.0	−11.0	582.0	375.0	9
July	554.0	554.0	546.0	547.0	−11.0	576.0	508.0	109
Aug	561.0	561.0	545.0	548.0	−11.0	586.0	390.0	744
Dec	572.0	572.0	555.0	559.0	−11.0	596.0	414.0	3,960
Ap95		....	....	569.0	−11.0	605.0	521.0	146
June		....	....	574.0	−11.0	605.0	538.0	153
Est vol 400; vol Fri 415; open int 5,171, +40.								
CRUDE OIL, Light Sweet (NYM) 1,000 bbls.; $ per bbl.								
July	20.89	20.89	20.35	20.75	+.04	20.80	14.15	37,018
Aug	19.50	19.78	19.45	19.71	−.08	20.78	14.35	92,034
Sept	na	19.27	18.97	19.21	−.03	20.78	14.50	58,225
Oct	na	18.98	18.70	18.92	−.02	20.73	14.65	30,458
Nov	na	18.75	18.55	18.72	−.02	20.69	14.82	24,128
Sept	162.25	162.75	161.50	162.50	+2.00	178.25	139.00	8,736
Oct	166.25	165.00	164.25	165.75	+2.50	167.00	142.50	8,233
Nov	164.25	167.50	166.25	167.50	+2.25	167.50	144.50	5,320
Dec	168.50	169.50	168.50	169.25	+2.25	173.00	146.00	13,862
Ja95	168.00	169.50	168.00	169.50	+2.50	169.50	147.25	5,124
Feb	167.00	167.25	167.00	167.25	+2.00	167.25	148.00	1,516
Mar	165.25	165.25	165.25	165.25	+2.00	172.00	147.25	1,848
Apr		....	....	163.50	+2.00	157.75	155.00	250
June	160.50	160.50	160.50	160.50	+1.00	160.50	146.00	1,080
Est vol 13,032; vol Fri 10,494; open int 88,352, −6,113.								

INTEREST RATE

	Open	High	Low	Settle	Change	Lifetime High	Lifetime Low	Open Interest
TREASURY BONDS (CBT)—$100,000; pts. 32nds of 100%								
June	103-29	104-12	103-12	103-28	−2	119-29	94-26	18,369
Sept	103-00	103-13	102-12	102-28	−3	118-26	90-12	373,434
Dec	102-08	102-22	101-24	102-05	−5	118-08	91-19	37,345
Mr95	101-08	102-00	101-08	101-16	−5	116-20	99-14	2,912
June	....	....	....	100-28	−6	113-15	98-31	1,186
Sept	....	....	....	100-10	−6	112-15	99-00	184
Est vol 325,000; vol Fri 510,541; op int 433,504, +12,799.								
TREASURY BONDS (MCE)—$50,000; pts. 32nds of 100%								
June	103-13	104-11	103-13	104-00	+3	118-31	101-04	361
Sept	102-18	103-13	102-13	103-00	+2	115-20	100-10	10,708
Est vol 4,700; vol Fri 6,724; open int 11,090, +1,229.								
TREASURY NOTES (CBT)—$100,000; pts. 32nds of 100%								
June	105-09	105-25	105-09	105-18	−2	115-21	102-18	34,535
Sept	104-14	104-18	104-00	104-10	−3	115-01	101-18	216,732
Dec	103-03	103-16	103-03	103-09	−3	114-21	100-25	1,408
Est vol 70,007; vol Fri 94,119; open int 252,748, −2,898.								
5 YR TREAS NOTES (CBT)—$100,000; pts. 32nds of 100%								
June	05-125	105-14	05-065	05-095	−5.0	11205	03075	24,592
Sept	104-14	04-165	04-065	104-12	−4.5	10195	10212	159,754
Est vol 39,500; vol Fri 54,663; open int 184,434, −3,303.								
2 YR TREAS NOTES (CBT)—$200,000, pts. 32nds of 100%								
June	03-195	03-215	03-187	03-195	−2¼	10600	02205	4,592
Sept	102-30	03-025	102-30	03-005	−2	10431	10204	27,984
Est vol 2,000; vol Fri 3,109; open int 32,576, +839.								
30-DAY FEDERAL FUNDS (CBT)-$5 million; pts. of 100%								
June	95.77	95.77	95.77	95.77	+.01	96.72	95.54	2,106
Jly	95.64	95.64	95.63	95.63	−.02	96.65	95.25	1,541
Aug	95.50	95.51	95.49	95.50	−.02	96.58	95.05	983
Sept	95.28	95.30	95.28	95.29	−.02	96.44	94.81	1,214
Oct	95.13	95.15	95.13	95.13	−.02	95.63	94.63	236
Nov	....	....	....	94.97	−.01	95.04	94.50	120
Est vol 777; vol Fri 291; open int 6,200, +66.								

TREASURY BILLS (CME)—$1 mil.; pts. of 100%

	Open	High	Low	Settle	Chg	Discount Settle	Discount Chg	Open Interest
June	95.81	95.83	95.81	95.83	....	4.17	....	4,298
Sept	95.32	95.37	95.32	95.35	−.01	4.65	+.01	22,000
Dec	94.68	94.76	94.68	94.74	+.01	5.26	−.01	7,686
Mr95	94.46	94.49	94.44	94.46	−.01	5.54	+.01	1,109
Est vol 4,808; vol Fri 2,360; open int 35,093, +394.								
LIBOR-1 MO. (CME)—$3,000,000; points of 100%								
July	95.50	95.52	95.50	95.51	−.01	4.49	+.01	22,262
Aug	95.31	95.32	95.30	95.31	−.03	4.69	+.03	10,147
Sept	95.14	95.15	95.13	95.14	−.01	4.86	+.01	2,556
Oct	94.97	94.97	94.96	94.97	−.01	5.03	+.01	1,482
Nov	94.81	94.82	94.80	94.81	−.01	5.19	+.01	1,817
Dec	....	....	....	94.04	−.01	5.96	+.01	893
Ja95	....	....	....	94.41	−.02	5.59	+.02	345
Mar	....	....	....	94.13	−.02	5.87	+.02	101
May	....	....	....	93.88	−.02	6.12	+.02	200
Est vol 3,751; vol Fri 2,981; open int 39,943, +87.								

MUNI BOND INDEX (CBT)-$1,000; times Bond Buyer MBI

	Open	High	Low	Settle	Chg	High	Low	Open Interest
June	92-04	92-25	92-03	92-09	−7	104-07	87-06	8,498
Sept	90-12	91-04	90-04	90-24	−1	95-17	86-13	21,493
Est vol 4,500; vol Fri 5,338; open int 29,992, +375.								
The index: Close 92-16; Yield 6.64.								

EURODOLLAR (CME)—$1 million; pts of 100%

	Open	High	Low	Settle	Chg	Yield Settle	Yield Chg	Open Interest
Sept	94.89	94.92	94.88	94.90	−.01	5.10	+.01	442,384
Dec	94.18	94.20	94.13	94.17	−.01	5.83	+.01	403,420
Mr95	93.91	93.96	93.88	93.92	−.02	6.08	+.02	289,669
June	93.60	93.67	93.59	93.62	−.03	6.38	+.03	214,776
Sept	93.35	93.41	93.34	93.38	−.03	6.62	+.03	197,252
Dec	93.12	93.17	93.11	93.14	−.04	6.86	+.04	138,795

	Open	High	Low	Settle	Change	Lifetime High	Lifetime Low	Open Interest
Dec	91.46	91.71	91.46	91.61	−.07	95.76	90.85	22,234
Mr95	91.23	91.37	91.15	91.29	−.09	95.56	91.05	10,249
June	90.80	90.95	90.80	90.92	−.09	95.33	90.80	4,351
Sept	90.70	90.70	90.65	90.65	−.13	95.11	90.65	1,791
Dec	90.40	90.50	90.40	90.37	−.13	94.79	90.24	1,705
Mr96	....	....	....	90.13	−.13	92.27	89.99	1,705
June	....	....	....	90.04	−.13	90.65	90.25	125
Est vol 7,703; vol Fri 6,064; open int 72,521, −504.								
10 YR. CANADIAN GOVT. BONDS (ME)—C$100,000								
June	....	....	....	97.85	−.85	115.25	99.55	2,153
Sept	96.55	97.60	96.45	97.14	−.80	102.60	96.45	26,754
Est vol 6,263; vol Fri 3,744; open int 28,907, +475.								
10 YR. FRENCH GOVT. BONDS (MATIF) FFr 500,000; 100ths of 100%								
Sept	112.40	112.96	111.60	112.84	−0.94	119.40	111.60	120,081
Dec	111.54	111.90	111.00	111.94	−0.94	118.44	111.00	8,756
Est vol 300,652; vol Fri 296,883; open int 128,837, +3,489.								

CURRENCY

	Open	High	Low	Settle	Change	Lifetime High	Lifetime Low	Open Interest
JAPAN YEN (CME)—12.5 million yen; $ per yen (.00)								
Sept	.9810	.9884	.9795	.9880	+.0101	1.0017	.8942	54,201
Dec	.9895	.9952	.9895	.9947	+.0103	1.0070	.9525	2,125
Mr95	....	....	....	1.0018	+.0104	1.0125	.9680	368
Est vol 28,930; vol Fri 24,787; open int 56,767, +913.								
DEUTSCHEMARK (CME)—125,000 marks; $ per mark								
Sept	.6207	.6258	.6195	.6246	+.0037	.6258	.5600	77,872
Dec	.6254	.6259	.6230	.6249	+.0038	.6259	.5590	1,514
Mr95	.6250	.6250	.6250	.6257	+.0038	.6250	.5798	661
Est vol 46,026; vol Fri 54,620; open int 80,104, +9,258.								
CANADIAN DOLLAR (CME)—100,000 dlrs.; $ per Can $								
Sept	.7143	.7156	.7108	.7145	+.0002	.7740	.7068	36,057
Dec	.7075	.7108	.7060	.7102	+.0002	.7670	.7038	2,649
Mr95	.7030	.7062	.7030	.7063	+.0002	.7605	.7020	644
June	.6990	.7015	.6990	.7020	+.0002	.7600	.6990	156
Est vol 6,880; vol Fri 7,651; open int 39,547, +159.								
BRITISH POUND (CME)—62,500 pds.; $ per pound								
Sept	1.5314	1.5384	1.5288	1.5352	....	1.5360	1.4440	38,695
Dec	1.5350	1.5356	1.5310	1.5332	....	1.5356	1.4400	299
Est vol 9,472; vol Fri 19,364; open int 39,011, +5,378.								
SWISS FRANC (CME)—125,000 francs; $ per franc								
Sept	.7375	.7450	.7356	.7414	+.0030	.7459	.6590	47,945
Dec	.7407	.7462	.7407	.7425	+.0030	.7462	.6885	1,042
Est vol 23,182; vol Fri 26,854; open int 48,997, +2,212.								
AUSTRALIAN DOLLAR (CME)—100,000 dlrs.; $ per A.$								
Sept	.7370	.7395	.7366	.7388	+.0048	.7412	.6645	7,058
Est vol 856; vol Fri 513; open int 7,086, −162.								
U.S. DOLLAR INDEX (FINEX)—1,000 times USDX								
Sept	91.19	91.25	90.66	90.78	−.36	98.55	90.66	12,066
Dec	91.55	91.35	91.00	91.04	−.37	99.00	91.00	3,041
Est vol 4,500; vol Fri 5,002; open int 15,110, +3,176.								
The index: High 91.22; Low 90.40; Close 90.45 −.52								

INDEX

S&P 500 INDEX (CME) $500 times index

	Open	High	Low	Settle	Chg	High	Low	Open Interest
Sept	459.60	460.00	455.70	456.75	−3.05	485.20	436.75	186,772
Dec	460.00	460.60	458.10	459.20	−3.10	487.10	438.85	8,754
Mr95	462.30	463.60	461.80	462.55	−3.10	479.00	441.45	1,830
Est vol 80,964; vol Fri 6,542; open int 255,425, +2,981.								
Indx prelim High 458.45; Low 458.46; Close 455.41 −3.04								
S&P MIDCAP 400 (CME) $500 times index								
Sept	169.00	169.50	168.15	168.75	−2.10	186.70	165.70	10,883
Est vol 722; vol Fri 597; open int 13,850, −16.								
The index: High 170.19; Low 167.69; Close 167.86 −2.33								
NIKKEI 225 STOCK AVERAGE (CME)—$5 times index								
Sept	21220.	21220.	21030.	21060.	−610.0	21775.	16240.	19,617
Est vol 1,532; vol Fri 1,339; open int 19,645, +179.								
The index: High 21515.68; Low 21125.63; Close 21152.83 −350.47								
GSCI (CME)—$250 times GSCI nearby prem.								
Aug	183.30	183.30	181.70	182.20	−1.50	183.80	167.00	4,831
Oct	182.10	182.50	182.10	182.40	−1.40	183.80	171.90	921
Est vol 278; vol Fri 156; open int 5,758, −26.								
The index: High 184.39; Low 181.85; Close 182.49 −1.88								
MAJOR MARKET INDEX (CME)—$500 times index								
July	381.10	382.00	379.80	381.15	−2.35	386.70	363.75	3,344
Dec		....	....	383.15	−2.50	400.45	361.75	4,253

Ja95	392.00	394.00	388.50	388.50	- 10.00	399.00	317.50	9,164
Mar	390.50	390.80	390.50	390.80	- 9.70	399.50	331.00	8,477
June		....	....	395.10	- 9.90	405.00	360.00	1,567

Est vol 1,725; vol Fri 3,669; open int 54,087, -1,106.

WHEAT (WPG) 20 metric tons; Can. $ per ton

July	109.30	109.40	108.80	109.20	- .80	118.50	94.40	4,148
Oct	107.20	107.30	106.50	106.80	- 1.60	115.00	101.00	4,071
Dec	106.70	106.80	106.50	106.60	- 1.40	112.80	101.00	2,721
Mr95	108.00	108.00	107.80	107.80	- 1.70	115.50	102.50	561
May		....	....	109.00	- 1.50	111.20	102.80	285
Jly		....	....	109.30	....	111.20	109.30	100

Est vol 560; vol Fri 441; open int 11,886, -41.

LIVESTOCK AND MEAT

CATTLE–FEEDER (CME) 50,000 lbs.; cents per lb.

Aug	73.87	73.87	72.55	73.32	+ .80	83.00	71.10	7,009
Sept	73.25	73.25	72.10	73.02	+ 1.02	81.70	71.00	2,737
Oct	73.10	73.10	72.20	72.97	+ .90	82.35	70.95	2,467
Nov	74.25	74.50	73.50	74.12	+ .70	81.85	72.40	1,851
Ja95	75.00	75.00	74.35	74.85	+ .65	80.95	72.95	609

Est vol 3,012; vol Fri 1,590; open int 14,844, +329.

CATTLE–LIVE (CME) 40,000 lbs.; cents per lb.

June	65.35	65.65	64.60	64.95	- .15	75.27	62.30	3,372
Aug	64.85	64.90	63.30	64.20	+ .22	73.87	62.15	32,061
Oct	68.50	68.50	67.15	67.97	+ .35	74.10	65.70	16,342
Dec	69.95	69.95	68.50	69.15	- .12	74.30	67.20	10,904
Fb95	70.60	70.70	69.40	69.90	- .27	74.25	67.90	7,505
Apr	71.40	71.60	70.50	70.97	- .25	75.10	69.40	3,454
June	68.67	68.70	67.67	67.90	- .25	72.50	66.90	633

Est vol 16,207; vol Fri 9,414; open int 74,271, +1,255.

HOGS (CME) 40,000 lbs.; cents per lb.

June	49.02	49.02	48.40	48.82	- .20	56.77	45.20	967
July	48.92	49.10	48.05	48.47	- .45	55.37	45.30	7,393
Aug	48.70	48.70	47.12	47.62	- .67	53.40	44.50	8,779
Oct	44.85	45.00	44.10	44.45	- .27	49.75	42.45	4,257
Dec	44.85	44.85	44.25	44.67	- .02	50.50	43.05	3,275
Fb95	44.40	44.50	44.12	44.27	- .10	50.80	43.10	813
Apr	43.25	43.25	43.00	43.10	- .15	48.80	42.30	427
June	48.80	48.00	48.10	48.40	- .20	51.55	47.40	271

Est vol 6,631; vol Fri 5,030; open int 26,237, -964.

PORK BELLIES (CME) 40,000 lbs.; cents per lb.

July	44.40	44.40	43.15	43.47	- .47	62.00	39.30	3,610
Aug	44.00	44.20	43.00	43.35	- .37	59.50	38.75	3,945
Fb95	48.80	49.00	48.20	48.27	- .27	60.05	47.25	491

Est vol 1,886; vol Fri 2,144; open int 8,129, -319.

FOOD AND FIBER

COCOA (CSCE) – 10 metric tons; $ per ton.

July	1,378	1,385	1,332	1,338	- 27	1,466	999	1,038
Sept	1,419	1,424	1,365	1,370	- 32	1,485	1,020	41,758
Dec	1,455	1,463	1,405	1,411	- 30	1,507	1,045	11,741
Mr95	1,485	1,489	1,453	1,441	- 30	1,540	1,077	8,027
May	1,505	1,510	1,484	1,460	- 30	1,570	1,111	2,941
July		....	....	1,482	- 30	1,593	1,225	2,346
Sept		....	....	1,502	- 30	1,340	1,265	1,170
Dec	1,540	1,540	1,540	1,535	- 30	1,570	1,290	3,377

Est vol 9,518; vol Fri 7,423; open int 72,401, +306.

COFFEE (CSCE) – 37,500 lbs.; cents per lb.

July	132.25	132.70	128.70	129.85	- 4.85	145.50	64.90	6,994
Sept	132.00	133.20	129.25	131.85	- 3.35	142.50	68.50	28,066
Dec	130.00	131.50	128.00	129.55	- 3.35	140.00	77.10	12,786
Mr95	127.75	129.25	125.25	128.10	- 2.00	136.60	78.90	7,948
May	126.75	128.00	126.75	127.50	- 1.75	134.50	82.50	1,108
July	125.50	128.00	126.50	128.00	- .25	130.00	85.00	194

Est vol 11,315; vol Fri 12,761; open int 57,134, -15.

SUGAR–WORLD (CSCE) – 112,000 lbs.; cents per lb.

July	12.31	12.34	12.01	12.06	- .30	12.60	9.15	25,933
Oct	12.26	12.35	12.02	12.07	- .35	12.60	9.42	74,759
Mr95	11.87	11.90	11.72	11.75	- .31	12.10	10.56	28,718
May	11.87	11.87	11.70	11.71	- .31	12.06	10.57	4,240
July	11.77	11.70	11.70	11.67	- .31	12.02	10.57	1,852
Oct	11.71	11.70	11.70	11.59	- .31	11.90	10.57	809

Est vol 25,540; vol Fri 11,309; open int 136,360, +419.

SUGAR–DOMESTIC (CSCE) – 112,000 lbs.; cents per lb.

Sept	22.44	22.45	22.44	22.46	+ .02	22.45	21.80	2,197
Nov	22.17	22.19	22.17	22.19	+ .02	22.19	21.82	3,236
Ja95	22.00	22.03	22.03	22.03	....	22.03	21.86	598
Mar	21.96	21.97	21.96	21.97	- .01	21.98	21.82	1,212
May	22.00	22.00	22.00	22.00	....	22.02	21.88	451
July		....	....	22.08	+ .10	22.08	22.02	220
Sept		....	....	22.08	+ .13	22.08	22.04	60

Est vol 252; vol Fri 575; open int 7,974, +31.

COTTON (CTN) – 50,000 lbs.; cents per lb.

July	79.85	79.90	77.66	77.66	- 2.00	84.15	58.30	7,090
Oct	77.40	77.60	75.72	76.38	- 1.34	78.60	59.51	7,294
Dec	76.30	76.45	74.60	75.13	- 1.44	77.25	59.48	30,843
Mr95	77.28	77.30	75.69	76.12	- 1.43	78.15	64.00	3,830
May	77.40	77.40	76.10	76.40	- 1.47	78.55	64.00	2,033
July	77.60	77.60	76.85	76.85	- 1.37	78.75	70.50	675
Oct		....	....	73.82	- .30	74.70	74.00	147

Est vol 12,000; vol Fri 4,233; open int 52,002, -251.

ORANGE JUICE (CTN) – 15,000 lbs.; cents per lb.

July	90.50	91.50	88.75	89.90	+ .40	135.00	88.00	7,559
Sept	93.75	94.50	91.50	92.55	+ .30	134.50	90.50	9,794
Nov	95.50	96.50	94.00	94.50	- .25	134.00	93.00	2,080

Ja95	na	18.50	18.36	18.51	- .03	20.12	15.15	16,842
Feb	na	18.40	18.32	18.44	- .03	19.60	15.28	10,990
Mar	na	18.35	18.26	18.38	- .03	20.66	15.42	12,320
Apr	na	18.30	18.23	18.34	- .03	19.68	15.55	8,522
May	na	18.30	18.20	18.32	- .04	19.23	15.69	9,189
June	na	18.31	18.22	18.33	- .04	21.21	15.73	20,796
July	18.25	18.28	18.22	18.34	- .04	18.28	16.28	4,881
Aug	18.25	18.25	18.25	18.35	- .04	18.25	16.90	3,519
Sept		18.25	18.25	18.36	- .04	19.84	16.28	7,075
Oct	18.25	18.25	18.25	18.37	- .04	18.25	16.42	1,495
Nov	18.25	18.33	18.25	18.38	- .05	18.33	17.15	2,696
Dec	na	18.33	18.30	18.40	- .05	20.80	16.50	10,601
Mr96		....	....	18.48	- .05	17.67	17.15	1,951
June		....	....	18.56	- .05	20.40	17.22	11,756
Dec		....	....	18.79	- .05	20.40	17.65	19,207
Ju97	na	19.00	18.90	19.07	- .05	19.10	18.55	2,353

Est vol 119,718; vol Fri 158,908; open int 421,499, -7,533.

HEATING OIL NO. 2 (NYM) 42,000 gal.; $ per gal.

July	.5202	.5202	.5110	.5147	- .0055	.5700	.4170	30,035
Aug	na	.5210	.5160	.5184	- .0051	.5617	.4270	27,584
Sept	na	.5270	.5230	.5246	- .0045	.5717	.4380	14,644
Oct	na	.5355	.5325	.5336	- .0045	.5730	.4490	9,836
Nov	na	.5450	.5420	.5421	- .0040	.5830	.4600	7,190
Dec	na	.5530	.5490	.5501	- .0040	.5900	.4680	15,820
Ja95	na	.5585	.5545	.5551	- .0035	.5850	.4745	10,988
Feb	.5540	.5565	.5530	.5526	- .0030	.5875	.4795	5,637
Mar	.5395	.5415	.5395	.5401	- .0025	.5750	.4700	4,723
Apr		....	....	.5286	- .0025	.5500	.4525	1,602
May		....	....	.5201	- .0025	.5185	.4700	1,694
June		....	....	.5161	- .0025	.5120	.4679	2,123
July	.5175	.5190	.5175	.5181	- .0025	.5190	.4785	2,407
Aug		....	....	.5241	- .0025	.5175	.4740	914
Sept		....	....	.5331	- .0025	.5060	.4845	544

Est vol 28,471; vol Fri 30,650; open int 135,756, +2,764.

GASOLINE-NY Unleaded (NYM) 42,000 gal.; $ per gal.

July	.5520	.5520	.5435	.5465	- .0055	.6050	.4410	31,999
Aug	.5501	.5532	.5460	.5485	- .0047	.6000	.4390	30,286
Sept	.5445	.5485	.5425	.5456	- .0041	.5505	.4390	11,584
Oct	.5250	.5340	.5265	.5286	- .0036	.5340	.4310	4,868
Nov	na	.5200	.5160	.5181	- .0031	.5200	.4275	4,662
Dec	na	.5650	.5600	.5621	- .0031	.5650	.5080	2,952
Ja95	.5560	.5560	.5560	.5566	- .0031	.5560	.5080	1,261
Feb		....	....	.5566	- .0031	.5453	.5110	901

Est vol 23,626; vol Fri 32,713; open int 88,513, +1,528.

NATURAL GAS (NYM) 10,000 MMBtu.; $ per MMBtu's

July	2.090	2.135	2.070	2.126	+ .041	2.320	1.590	12,328
Aug	2.145	2.170	2.120	2.155	+ .016	2.360	1.715	18,172
Sept	2.155	2.165	2.145	2.162	+ .007	2.395	1.940	12,098
Oct	2.175	2.185	2.170	2.180	+ .006	2.500	1.955	10,299
Nov	2.245	2.255	2.245	2.250	+ .006	2.595	2.090	11,431
Dec	2.350	2.355	2.340	2.346	+ .006	2.740	2.220	14,626
Ja95	2.241	2.350	2.341	2.349	+ .006	2.720	2.190	10,530
Feb	2.250	2.250	2.241	2.247	+ .006	2.460	2.070	5,750
Mar	2.177	2.185	2.177	2.183	+ .006	2.360	2.010	4,049
Apr	2.128	2.135	2.128	2.134	+ .006	2.310	1.980	3,278
May	2.135	2.137	2.135	2.136	+ .006	2.275	1.975	4,371
June	2.134	2.140	2.134	2.140	+ .006	2.245	1.975	2,133
July		....	....	2.143	+ .006	2.214	1.978	2,589
Aug	2.150	2.150	2.150	2.156	+ .006	2.234	2.068	2,864
Sept		....	....	2.185	+ .006	2.267	2.129	2,353
Oct		....	....	2.231	+ .006	2.280	2.170	2,122
Nov		....	....	2.311	+ .006	2.360	2.260	2,127
Dec	2.420	2.420	2.420	2.424	+ .006	2.444	2.370	1,789

Est vol 13,666; vol Fri 16,697; open int 122,909, -151.

BRENT CRUDE (IPE) 1,000 net bbls.; $ per bbl.

Aug	17.20	17.57	17.18	17.46	+ .05	18.12	13.27	73,900
Sept	17.08	17.40	17.04	17.35	+ .08	17.79	13.62	29,024
Oct	17.02	17.33	16.99	17.33	+ .12	17.33	13.59	12,253
Nov	16.98	17.27	16.97	17.20	+ .05	17.27	13.76	6,242
Dec	16.96	17.25	16.93	17.24	+ .06	17.25	13.90	9,874
Ja95	17.02	17.22	16.99	17.21	+ .11	17.22	14.60	2,812
Feb	17.01	17.15	16.97	17.18	+ .09	17.15	15.50	1,665
Mar	16.98	17.16	16.97	17.17	+ .09	17.16	15.60	1,925
Apr	16.85	17.04	16.85	17.15	+ .08	17.04	15.68	1,425
May		....	....	17.13	+ .07	16.61	15.05	166
June		....	....	17.12	+ .03	16.61	15.73	860

Est vol 40,383; vol Fri 33,822; open int 140,146, +3,285.

GAS OIL (IPE) 100 metric tons; $ per ton

July	159.25	159.75	158.25	159.25	+ 2.00	169.75	135.25	30,111
Aug	161.00	161.50	160.00	161.50	+ 2.25	167.05	137.00	12,272

EXCHANGE ABBREVIATIONS
(for commodity futures and futures options)

CBT-Chicago Board of Trade; CME-Chicago Mercantile Exchange; CSCE-Coffee, Sugar & Cocoa Exchange, New York; CMX-Commodity Exchange, New York; IPE-International Petroleum Exchange; KC-Kansas City Board of Trade; LIFFE-London International Financial Futures Exchange; ME-Montreal Exchange; MCE-MidAmerica Commodity Exchange; MPLS-Minneapolis Grain Exchange; CTN-New York Cotton Exchange; NYM-New York Mercantile Exchange; PBOT-Philadelphia Board of Trade; WPG-Winnipeg Commodity Exchange.

June	92.96	93.01	92.96	92.98	- .04	7.02	+ .04	100,105
Sept	92.86	92.90	92.85	92.88	- .04	7.12	+ .04	92,251
Dec	92.67	92.72	92.67	92.71	- .04	7.29	+ .04	71,997
Mr97	92.65	92.69	92.65	92.69	- .03	7.31	+ .03	64,017
June	92.55	92.59	92.54	92.58	- .03	7.42	+ .03	52,178
Sept	92.48	92.52	92.46	92.50	- .03	7.50	+ .03	48,336
Dec	92.31	92.37	92.31	92.35	- .03	7.65	+ .03	42,957
Mr98	92.32	92.37	92.31	92.35	- .03	7.65	+ .03	32,966
June	92.24	92.29	92.23	92.27	- .03	7.73	+ .03	29,908
Sept	92.18	92.23	92.16	92.20	- .03	7.80	+ .03	21,907
Dec	92.04	92.09	92.02	92.06	- .03	7.94	+ .03	17,372
Mr99	92.05	92.10	92.03	92.07	- .03	7.93	+ .03	12,178
June	91.96	92.02	91.96	91.99	- .03	8.01	+ .03	7,833
Sept	91.90	91.94	91.90	91.91	- .03	8.09	+ .03	6,444
Dec	91.79	91.81	91.77	91.78	- .03	8.22	+ .03	6,499
Mr00	91.81	91.83	91.79	91.80	- .03	8.20	+ .03	6,546
June	91.74	91.78	91.74	91.75	- .03	8.25	+ .03	4,859
Sept	91.68	91.72	91.67	91.69	- .03	8.31	+ .03	5,892
Dec	91.58	91.62	91.57	91.59	- .03	8.41	+ .03	4,822
Mr01	91.63	91.67	91.62	91.64	- .03	8.36	+ .03	6,188
June	91.60	91.63	91.59	91.61	- .03	8.39	+ .03	3,423
Sept	91.53	91.59	91.53	91.57	- .02	8.43	+ .02	1,959
Dec	91.45	91.51	91.45	91.49	- .02	8.51	+ .02	1,711
Mr02	91.50	91.56	91.50	91.55	- .02	8.45	+ .02	1,617
June	91.50	91.56	91.50	91.55	- .02	8.45	+ .02	1,694
Sept	91.50	91.54	91.50	91.54	- .02	8.46	+ .02	1,380
Dec	91.42	91.47	91.42	91.46	- .02	8.54	+ .02	1,135
Mr03	91.48	91.52	91.48	91.52	- .02	8.48	+ .02	1,289
June	91.46	91.50	91.46	91.50	- .02	8.50	+ .02	887
Sept	....	....	....	91.48	- .02	8.52	+ .02	909
Dec	91.43	91.43	91.38	91.42	- .02	8.58	+ .02	1,234
Mr04	....	....	....	91.47	- .02	8.53	+ .02	978

Est vol 320,444; vol Fri 338,716; open int 2,467,829, +28,458.

EURODOLLAR (LIFFE) – $1 million; pts of 100%

	Open	High	Low	Settle	Change	Lifetime High	Lifetime Low	Open Interest
Sept	94.88	94.88	94.88	94.89	- .02	96.20	93.76	2,268
Dec	94.13	94.13	94.13	94.15	- .04	95.71	93.66	1,855
Mr95	93.90	93.91	93.90	93.91	- .05	95.56	93.42	1,056
June	....	....	....	93.61	- .07	95.76	93.21	305

Est vol 207; vol Fri 152; open int 5,536, -37.

STERLING (LIFFE) – £500,000; pts of 100%

Sept	94.29	94.33	94.26	94.32	- .05	95.25	90.10	109,647
Dec	93.65	93.74	93.61	93.70	- .05	95.23	90.10	147,801
Mr95	92.98	93.05	92.87	93.00	- .08	95.10	90.70	61,450
June	92.27	92.38	92.22	92.35	- .10	94.93	91.73	46,362
Sept	91.77	91.87	91.67	91.84	- .09	94.81	91.46	39,924
Dec	91.38	91.40	91.24	91.39	- .09	94.66	91.14	31,054
Mr96	91.03	91.09	90.92	91.08	- .08	94.61	90.82	22,032
June	90.83	90.89	90.72	90.88	- .08	94.25	90.60	18,435
Sept	90.61	90.69	90.53	90.68	- .06	93.64	90.40	9,565
Dec	90.42	90.49	90.36	90.48	- .09	93.50	90.20	10,506
Mr97	90.15	90.27	90.15	90.27	- .07	93.33	90.05	8,471
June	90.01	90.09	89.92	90.04	- .09	90.09	89.92	414

Est vol 207; vol Fri 152; open int 5,536, -37.

LONG GILT (LIFFE) – £50,000; 32nds of 100%

June	100-06	100-08	99-14	99-26	- 1-06	119-20	99-14	10,275
Sept	99-02	99-11	97-31	98-19	- 1-06	111-17	97-31	118,456

Est vol 74,967; vol Fri 65,553; open int 128,798, -2,822.

EUROMARK (LIFFE) – DM 1,000,000; pts of 100%

Sept	95.00	95.05	95.00	95.04	+ .01	95.54	91.81	192,481
Dec	94.78	94.81	94.75	94.78	- .03	95.73	91.83	200,670
Mr95	94.50	94.51	94.40	94.45	- .07	95.83	92.45	201,234
June	94.11	94.11	93.99	94.06	- .08	95.91	93.15	103,836
Sept	93.81	93.81	93.69	93.75	- .09	95.83	93.62	67,098
Dec	93.50	93.53	93.43	93.47	- .11	95.74	93.43	39,492
Mr96	93.30	93.33	93.25	93.28	- .11	95.62	93.25	27,799
June	93.10	93.12	93.05	93.08	- .10	95.45	93.05	15,753
Sept	92.86	92.91	92.82	92.88	- .08	94.26	92.82	8,119
Dec	92.66	92.67	92.61	92.66	- .08	94.10	92.61	9,363
Mr97	92.49	92.50	92.45	92.48	- .11	93.99	92.45	6,072
June	92.33	92.33	92.31	93.32	- .11	92.62	92.31	2,046

Est vol 146,554; vol Fri 82,297; open int 873,463, -5,277.

EUROSWISS (LIFFE) – SFr 1,000,000; pts of 100%

Sept	95.50	95.50	95.40	95.46	- .04	96.75	95.37	30,781
Dec	95.18	95.24	95.14	95.18	- .07	96.80	95.14	9,757
Mr95	94.86	94.87	94.80	94.85	- .05	96.15	94.80	8,013
June	94.50	94.52	94.42	94.47	- .06	94.59	94.42	896

Est vol 6,243; vol Fri 7,518; open int 49,447, +2,171.

GERMAN GOVT. BOND (LIFFE)
250,000 marks; pts of 100%

Sept	90.41	90.73	89.91	90.33	- .78	97.25	89.91	155,479
Dec	89.51	90.00	89.52	89.65	- .81	93.23	89.52	2,043

Est vol 169,929; vol Fri 139,462; open int 157,522, +1,331.

ITALIAN GOVT. BOND (LIFFE)
ITL 200,000,000; pts of 100%

Sept	100.00	102.23	99.60	101.75	+ .15	114.30	99.60	66,136
Dec	....	....	....	100.00	+ .15	....	....	100

Est vol 64,248; vol Fri 47,941; open int 66,236, +2,164.

FT–SE 100 INDEX (LIFFE) – £25 per index point

Sept	2985.	2989.	2930.	2973.	- 40.0	3550.	2918.	49,947
Dec	....	....	....	2982.	- 40.0	3176.	3018.	952

Est vol 20,695; vol Fri 16,592; open int 50,899, +3,707.

CANADIAN BANKERS ACCEPTANCE (ME) – C$1,000,000

Sept	91.98	92.21	91.96	92.10	- .11	95.96	91.27	30,360

NYSE COMPOSITE INDEX (NYFE) 500 times index

Sept	252.70	253.00	251.40	252.05	- 1.85	267.00	241.00	3,064

Est vol 3,835; vol Fri 2,460; open int 3,192, +21.
The index: High 253.29; Low 250.95; Close 251.40 -1.89

TORONTO 35 INDEX (TFE) – $500 times index
NOT AVAILABLE

CAC-40 STOCK INDEX (MATIF) – FFr 200 per index pt.

June	1893.	1900.	1848.	1889.	- 34.	2123.	1848.	50,849
July	1890.5	1895.	1847.	1885.	- 34.5	2120.5	1847.	8,527
Sept	1906.	1910.	1863.5	1901.	- 35.	2127.	1863.5	15,646
Dec		....	....	1930.5	- 34.	2159.	2159.	7,531
Mr95	1963.	1963.	1963.	1957.5	- 34.	2190.5	1963.	1,779

Est vol 52,013; vol Fri 28,306; open int 84,382, +2,877.
The index: High na; Low na; Close na

OTHER FUTURES

Settlement prices of selected contracts. Actual volume (from previous session) and open interest of all contract months.

	Vol.	High	Low	Close	Net Change	Lifetime High	Lifetime Low	Open Interest
ANHYDROUS AMMONIA (CBT) 100 tons; $ per ton								
Sep	33	....	....	142.00	....	146.00	135.00	94
BARLEY (WPG) 20 metric tons; Can. $ per ton								
Aug	171	95.00	94.90	94.90	- 1.30	106.50	91.20	8,981
BRITISH POUND (MCE) 12,500 pounds; $ per pound								
Sep	117	1.5386	1.5336	1.5356	+ .0002	1.5386	1.4530	494
CANADIAN GOVT. BONDS (CBT) C$100,000; $ per C$								
Sep	73	97.45	97.00	97.12	- .88	102.78	97.00	1,647
CATTLE-LIVE (MCE) 20,000 lb.; ¢ per lb.								
Aug	66	64.90	63.30	64.20	+ .22	74.55	62.15	225
CORN (MCE) 1,000 bu.; cents per bu.								
Jly	2,378	276	271¼	271¼	- 12	316¼	241	6,356
DEUTSCHEMARK (MCE) 62,500 marks; $ per mark								
Sep	406	.6259	.6227	.6244	+ .0035	.9588	.5780	634
DEUTSCHEMARK (PBOT) 125,000 marks; ¢ per mark								
Sep	574	.6250	.6199	.6242	n.a.	.6250	.6199	470
DIAMMONIUM PHOSPHATE (CBT) 100 tons; $ per ton								
Sep	71	....	....	149.30	- .20	152.50	139.50	592
DM ROLLING SPOT (CME) $250,000; DM per U.S. $								
Sep	253	1.6045	1.5970	1.5993	- .0097	1.6717	1.5970	556
EURODOLLAR (MCE) $500,000; pts. of 100%								
Sep	6	94.91	94.88	94.90	- .01	96.11	94.13	307
EUROMARK (CME) DM 1,000,000; pts. of 100%								
Sep	0	....	....	95.04	+ .01	95.50	94.30	176
EUROTOP 100 INDEX (CMX) – $100 times index								
Sep	222	1145.1	1162.0	1158.7	- 32.00	1286.0	1162.0	1,756
The index: High 1136.00; Low 1162.60; Close 1148.40 -31.80								
FLAXSEED (WPG) 20 metric tons; Can. $ per ton								
Jly	373	273.40	272.70	272.70	- 6.00	295.40	251.00	3,945
FRENCH FRANC (CME) 500,000 FF; $ per franc								
Sep	488	.18264	.18210	.18240	+ .0080	.18264	.16484	2,006
GOLD-NY (MCE) 33.2 fine troy oz.; cents per troy oz.								
Jly	89	....	....	389.50	- 2.80	386.00	386.00	997
GOLD-KILO (CBT) 32.15 troy oz.; $ per troy oz.								
Aug	360	395.50	390.50	391.60	- 2.70	420.10	373.50	717
HOGS (MCE) 20,000 lb.; ¢ per lb.								
Jly	54	49.10	48.05	48.47	- .45	56.40	45.30	441
JAPANESE YEN (MCE) 6.25 million yen; $ per yen (.00)								
Sep	137	.9884	.9838	.9879	+ .0097	1.0003	.9090	282
KC MINI VALUE LINE (KC) – 100 times index								
Sep	289	449.40	446.60	447.50	- 5.00	478.00	434.20	399
KC VALUE LINE INDEX (KC) – 500 times index								
Sep	202	449.40	446.70	447.40	- 5.20	472.50	435.80	572
The index: High 451.45; Low 446.79; Close 447.16 -4.28								
KR-CRB INDEX (NYFE) – 500 times index								
Jly	688	237.50	234.80	234.90	- 4.65	239.70	218.00	2,677
The index: High 239.35; Low 234.84; Close 234.87 -4.51								
LUMBER (CME) 160,000 bd. ft., $ per 1,000 bd.ft.								
Jly	612	370.50	364.30	365.30	- 8.00	468.50	280.00	1,840
OATS (MCE) 1,000 bu.; ¢ per bu.								
Jly	43	133¾	130½	134	- 3¼	161¼	112½	153
PLATINUM (MCE) 25 troy oz.; cents per troy oz.								
Jly	8	....	....	406.50	- 4.60	429.00	376.30	483
PROPANE (NYM) 42,000 gal.; ¢ per gal.								
Jly	107	29.35	29.35	29.35	....	30.80	24.25	1,275
RUSSELL 2000 INDEX (CME) $500 times index								
Sep	28	249.00	246.40	247.00	- 3.40	274.00	243.40	2,164
SILVER (MCE) 1,000 troy oz.; cents per troy oz.								
Jly	57	561.0	544.5	547.5	- 11.8	586.5	372.5	1,965
SILVER (CBT) 5,000 troy oz.; cents per troy oz.								
Aug	4	....	....	548.0	- 11.0	560.5	390.0	448
SOYBEANS (MCE) 1,000 bu.; cents per bu.								
Jly	4,572	692½	681	681	- 30	750	594½	17,013
SOYBEAN MEAL (MCE) 20 tons; cents per ton								
Jly	29	200.50	196.00	196.70	- 9.30	230.00	185.20	365
SWISS FRANC (MCE) 62,500 francs; $ per franc								
Sep	166	.7448	.7398	.7414	+ .0028	.7448	.6879	429
10–YEAR T.NOTES (MCE) 50,000; pts. 32nds of 100%								
Sep	29	104-11	104-01	104-11	- 2	108-18	102-01	1,079
WHEAT (MCE) 1,000 bu.; cents per bu.								
Jly	477	333	321¼	322	- 13¼	356	296	2,072
WHITE WHEAT (MPLS) 5,000 bu.; cents per bu.								
Jly	50	368	364	365	- 6	373½	340	1,310

Source: *The Wall Street Journal*, June 21, 1994, p. C14.

Delivery Month = July. This means that the contract will expire on the third Friday in July. Whoever holds a contract when the market closes on that day will own 10,000 dozen eggs. The investor will not have to take delivery. The eggs will be held in a refrigerated warehouse until arrangements are made for their disposal or use, and the investor will be billed for warehousing costs.

Open = 110. This means that the first contract traded on the day of the quote specified a price of $1.10 per dozen. This gave the contract a value of $1.10 times 10,000 or $11,000. A large investor usually buys a futures contract on a 10 percent margin, which means that the investor puts up 10 percent of the purchase price, $1,100, and borrows the remaining 90 percent, $9,900, from the broker. Since the investor has no intention of taking delivery of the eggs at the end of the contract, the purchase of the contract and the loan are just book entries.

High = 112. This means that the highest price of the contract during the day of the quote was $1.12 per dozen, or $11,200 per contract. Most futures exchanges set limits on the amount a price can fluctuate in a day, usually five or ten cents. (Different commodities have different limits.) If news or rumors put pressure on the price to move beyond those limits, the market closes for the day and trading resumes the next morning.

Low = 109. This means that the lowest price of the contract during the day of the quote was $1.09 per dozen, or $10,900 per contract.

Settle = 111. This means that the last contract traded on the day of the quote at a price of $1.11 per dozen, or $11,100 per contract. If an investor had bought the contract at the open and sold it at the close, the day's profit would have been $100 on an $1,100 investment, or a daily rate of return of 9 percent before commissions.

Lifetime High = 120. This means that the highest price for egg futures since the contract first began trading has been $1.20 per dozen, or $12,000 per contract.

Lifetime Low = 98. This means that the lowest price for egg futures since the contract first began trading has been $0.98 per dozen, or $9,800 per contract.

Open Interest = 11,250. This means that 11,250 contracts were in existence at the end of the trading day before the day of the quotation. In other words, Wednesday's paper shows Tuesday's prices and Monday's open interest. As a conservative estimate, only about 1,000 of these contracts probably involved chicken farmers who had eggs to deliver or food companies that wanted to buy eggs. The rest of the contracts were book entries that would disappear as traders made offsetting transactions before the delivery date.

For commodities futures in general, the risk of default is the risk that the market for a particular commodity will collapse suddenly. This risk is considered to be small, although years ago, the potato futures market collapsed suddenly as the result of a scandal. An investor can get an impression of the relative risk of illiquidity by looking at open interest. A larger number of contracts outstanding increases the liquidity of a specific contract. Market risk is the critical element of risk for a commodities futures contract; the contract prices are extremely sensitive to news, rumors, and trader psychology.

call option
A contract that gives its holder the right, but not the obligation, to buy 100 shares of stock at a fixed price for a limited period of time.

put option
A contract that allows the holder to sell 100 shares of stock at a fixed price for a limited period of time.

Put and Call Stock Options. A **call option** is a contract that gives its holder the right, but not the obligation, to buy 100 shares of common stock at a fixed price for a limited period of time. A **put option** is a contract that allows its holder to sell 100 shares of common stock at a fixed price for a limited period of time. The fixed price is called the *striking price*, the *strike price*, or the *exercise price*. The market price of the contract itself is called the *premium*.

Exhibit 4.9 displays an excerpt from the daily listing for option contracts in *The Wall Street Journal*. A simulated listing appears below and the following text explains how to interpret it.

COMPANY	MARKET	STRIKE	CONTRACT	VOLUME	MONTH	PREMIUM
XYZ	53 1/2	50		102	June	4 1/4
XYZ	53 1/2	50	p	11	June	1/8
XYZ	53 1/2	55		138	June	7/16
XYZ	53 1/2	55	p	47	June	1 3/4

***Company* = *XYZ*.** This means that the contract allows the holder to buy or sell 100 shares of XYZ Corporation stock.

***Market* = *53 1/2*.** This means that the last trade of XYZ stock on the day of the quote specifies a price of $53.50 per share.

***Strike* = *50*.** This means that the contract holder can buy 100 shares of XYZ at $50 a share any time until the contract expires.

***Contract* = *(Blank)*.** This means that the contract is a call option; if a *p* appears in this column, the contract is a put. Therefore, the first and third lines refer to call contracts, the second and fourth to put contracts.

***Volume* = *102*.** This means that traders exchanged 102 contracts on the day of the quote.

***Month* = *June*.** This means that the contract expires on the Saturday after the third Friday in June. When the market closes on that Friday, the contract is worthless and whoever holds it has lost 100 percent of the premium paid.

***Premium* = *4 1/4*.** This means that the last contract traded on the day of the quote had a price of $4.25 per share, or $425 per contract. The premium has two components: the intrinsic value and the time/expectations value. The intrinsic value for a call is the difference between the market price of the stock and the strike price of the contract: $53.50 minus $50.00, or $3.50 per share. If the difference is less than zero, as in the $55 call on the third line, the intrinsic value is said to be zero; the market does not recognize negative intrinsic values. The time/expectations value, the remainder of the premium, increases with investors' demand for the contract and with the time remaining to expiration. Time value is never zero; for the $50 call it is $4.25 minus $3.50, or $0.75 per share; for the $55 call on the third line, it is 7/16 or $0.4375 per share.

Since a put contract involves the opposite transaction, its intrinsic value is the difference between the strike price of the contract and the market price of the stock. The $50 put has zero intrinsic value and a time value of 1/8 or $0.125 per share. The

EXHIBIT 4.9

Listed Option Quotations

LISTED OPTIONS QUOTATIONS

Monday, June 20, 1994

Composite volume and close for actively traded equity and LEAPS, or long-term options, with results for the corresponding put or call contract. Volume figures are unofficial. Open interest is total outstanding for all exchanges and reflects previous trading day. Close when possible is shown for the underlying stock on primary market. CB-Chicago Board Options Exchange. AM-American Stock Exchange. PB-Philadelphia Stock Exchange. PC-Pacific Stock Exchange. NY-New York Stock Exchange. XC-Composite. p-Put.

MOST ACTIVE CONTRACTS

Option/Strike				Vol	Exch	Last	Net Chg	a-Close	Open Int
AMedHI	Jul	30		6,488	PB	1¼	+ ⅛	25⅞	13,378
TelMex	Jul	60		4,392	XC	1 3/16	− 5/16	57⅞	9,413
GenDyn	Aug	45		3,504	CB	1⅛	− ½	43⅜	5,226
GenDyn	Aug	42½		3,500	CB	2¼	− 1⅛	43⅜	5,220
AMedHI	Jul	25		2,720	PB	2⅞	− 1/16	25⅞	10,600
MicrTc	Jul	35		2,718	XC	1⅛	− 9/16	32¾	5,342
I B M	Jul	65		2,693	CB	9/16	− 3/16	61⅞	23,228
Compaq	Jul	33⅜		2,691	PC	1⅝	+ 3/16	33½	8,887
Citicp	Jul	40		2,605	CB	1⅛	− ⅝	39¾	10,727
TelMex	Jul	55	p	2,503	XC	⅞	+ 1/16	57⅞	3,746
Sprint	Jul	40		2,501	PB	3/16	− 3/16	35⅝	2,310
GeoTek	Feb	7½	p	2,500	XC	1 3/16	...	8⅜	...
Compaq	Jul	30		2,249	PC	4	+ ⅛	33½	2,329
G M	Jul	55		2,249	CB	⅞	− 5/16	53¼	11,962
I B M	Jul	60	p	2,127	CB	¾	+ ⅛	61⅞	8,163
Glamis	Sep	7½		2,004	CB	13/16	+ ¼	7⅛	1,583
Chryslr	Jul	50		1,962	CB	⅞	− ⅜	47¾	14,034
US Hlth	Jul	45		1,846	AM	1¼	+ ⅜	43⅛	4,089
Motrla	Jul	45	p	1,785	AM	1¼	+ ¼	46	5,378
EchoB	Jul	12½		1,749	PC	3/16	− 1/16	11	7,471
Compaq	Jul	35		1,717	PC	15/16	+ ⅛	33½	14,584
QuakrO	Jul	80		1,701	PB	6½	+ ⅞	82	2,793
Sybase	Dec	60		1,600	PC	3½	− 1⅜	49½	7
Ph Mor	Jul	50	p	1,567	AM	¾	− 3/16	50⅞	5,699
Disney	Jan	45		1,554	XC	3⅝	− ⅜	44⅝	331
I B M	Jul	60		1,407	CB	2 13/16	− 7/16	61⅞	15,384
Citicp	Oct	45		1,359	CB	⅞	− ⅜	39¾	4,984
Buffets	Jul	17½	p	1,300	CB	1⅝	+ 1¼	16⅜	40
TelMex	Jul	65		1,259	XC	3/16	− 1/16	57⅞	16,526
RJR Nb	Dec	7½		1,257	XC	5/16	...	5¾	1,308
Disney	Jul	40		1,233	XC	4⅝	− ⅜	44⅝	3,343
CaesrW	Aug	40	p	1,209	AM	4⅝	+ ⅞	36¾	176
OutStk	Nov	30		1,203	XC	1 7/16	− 1 7/16	25¾	27
FedExp	Jul	80		1,194	CB	1⅞	...	78⅝	315
G M	Jul	55	p	1,180	CB	2⅜	+ ¼	53¼	4,509
I B M	Jul	70		1,178	CB	⅛	− 1/16	61⅞	7,731
I B M	Oct	60		1,174	CB	5	− ⅜	61⅞	12,844
ViacmB	Jul	30		1,163	CB	1½	− ¼	30⅝	3,276
USXUSS	Jul	35		1,160	AM	1	− 1½	35⅛	4,742
AuraSy	Sep	10		1,157	CB	⅜	− 1/16	8 7/16	2,449

Option/Strike		Exp.	Call Vol.	Call Last	Put Vol.	Put Last
ADC Tel	40	Jul	33	1 3/16	...	...
ADT	10	Dec	78	15/16	...	...
AL Lab	15	Sep	30	¾	...	...
ALC Cm	30	Sep	15	1¾	51	3⅜
27½	30	Dec	60	2⅞	5	5
A M R	50	Jul	...	...	50	1/16
58⅝	60	Jul	83	1⅛	153	2½
58⅝	60	Aug	114	2	15	3⅜
58⅝	65	Aug	33	11/16	...	...
58⅝	70	Aug	99	3/16	...	...
A S A	40	Jul	100	5⅛	100	⅛
44⅞	40	Aug	90	5½	13	7/16
44⅞	40	Nov	...	...	30	1⅜
44⅞	45	Jul	455	1¼	2	1½
44⅞	45	Aug	110	2 1/16	56	2 3/16
44⅞	45	Nov	37	3⅜	14	3¼
44⅞	50	Jul	108	¼	2	5½
44⅞	50	Aug	40	⅝	...	...
44⅞	50	Feb	25	2¼	...	...
AST Rs	15	Jul	4	½	45	1 7/16
14	15	Aug	10	1 1/16	115	1¾
14	15	Nov	35	2	5	2¼
14	17½	Aug	30	5/16	...	...
AT&T	50	Jul	37	5¾	...	...
55⅞	50	Jan	30	7⅛	...	...
55⅞	55	Jul	467	1 7/16	207	11/16
55⅞	55	Aug	...	...	110	1
55⅞	55	Oct	38	3⅛	25	1⅝
55⅞	55	Jan	...	...	40	2⅜
55⅞	60	Jul	249	⅛	...	...
55⅞	60	Oct	172	⅞	10	4⅝
55⅞	60	Jan	147	1⅞	...	...
55⅞	70	Jan	25	¼	...	...
Abbt L	30	Jul	165	½	5	1 1/16
29⅝	30	Aug	53	1	...	...
Aclaim	15	Jul	142	1⅞	35	⅞
15⅞	17½	Jul	60	¾	...	...
Actava	10	Dec	29	1	...	...
Adaptc	15	Jul	...	...	430	¾
15⅞	20	Oct	200	⅞	...	...
AdobeS	22½	Jul	...	...	51	⅝
25½	25	Jul	158	1¾	82	1⅛
25½	30	Jul	50	⅜	2	4
25½	35	Jul	36	⅛	...	...
A M D	22½	Jul	3	3	52	⅛
25½	22½	Aug	...	...	44	½
25½	25	Jul	161	1½	299	1 1/16
25½	25	Aug	...	...	29	1½
25½	25	Oct	64	3⅜	...	...
25½	30	Jul	120	¼	10	4⅝
25½	30	Aug	48	½	...	...
25½	30	Oct	44	1⅜	...	...
AdvTis	5	Sep	30	1	...	...
5¼	5	Dec	49	1⅜	...	...
Agnico	7½	Nov	80	4¾	...	...
12	10	Nov	...	...	30	⅝
12	12½	Jul	24	⅜	...	...
12	12½	Aug	345	¾	...	...
12	12½	Nov	50	1⅜	...	...
12	15	Aug	200	5/16	...	...
AirPd	45	Dec	50	1 11/16	...	...
Airtch	25	Jul	35	7/16	10	1 7/16
24⅛	25	Aug	38	1 1/16	...	...
24⅛	25	Oct	23	1 11/16	...	...
Albtsn	30	Sep	44	9/16	...	...
Alcatl	30	Sep	25	⅛	...	...
BausLm	40	Jul	15	1⅛	50	1 3/16
Baxter	25	Nov	50	2¼	2	1⅛
25½	30	Nov	43	7/16	...	...
BedBth	25	Jul	40	3¼	10	½
27⅜	30	Jul	30	½	10	2⅞
BellAtl	55	Jul	52	1⅜	...	...
55⅞	55	Jan	31	3½	...	...
55⅞	60	Jul	213	⅛	...	...
55⅞	60	Oct	203	⅞	...	...
BellSpt	25	Jul	290	1 5/16	5	1 3/16
BellSo	55	Oct	50	6¾	...	...
61	65	Jan	52	1⅞	...	...
BestBuy	20	Jul	...	...	50	3/16
28½	22½	Jul	...	...	543	¼
28½	25	Jul	363	4	757	9/16
28½	30	Jul	578	1	93	2⅝
28½	30	Aug	24	1⅞	35	3⅜
28½	30	Sep	107	2½	25	3¾
28½	30	Dec	33	3¾	24	5
28½	32½	Sep	239	1⅝	...	...
28½	35	Jul	47	3/16	2	6⅜
28½	35	Dec	242	2	...	...
Beth S	17½	Jul	100	2⅞	2	¼
20⅛	17½	Oct	...	...	50	11/16
20⅛	20	Jul	283	⅞	210	¾
20⅛	20	Oct	11	2	50	1⅜
Bevrly	15	Jul	44	⅛	...	...
Biogen	25	Jul	...	...	75	⅝
29	30	Jul	34	1¼	344	2¼
29	35	Jul	355	¼	300	6¼
29	35	Oct	174	1 7/16	1	6⅞
Biomet	10	Jul	91	3/16	10	7/16
9⅝	10	Oct	90	11/16	...	...
9⅝	10	Jan	45	15/16	...	...
9⅝	12½	Jan	28	7/16	...	...
Block	45	Jul	65	⅝	3	2¼
Blkbst	25	Sep	102	4¼	10	½
28⅝	25	Dec	6	5⅛	50	1⅛
28⅝	30	Jul	111	½	165	2
28⅝	30	Aug	105	1 1/16	...	...
28⅝	30	Sep	254	1⅜	...	...
28⅝	30	Dec	165	2⅜	...	...
Boeing	45	Aug	62	3¾	279	⅝
47¾	50	Jul	173	⅜	145	2⅝
47¾	50	Aug	123	⅞	28	3
47¾	50	Nov	105	2	5	3⅝
47¾	55	Aug	36	⅛	...	...
47¾	55	Feb	64	1¼	...	...
BoltBr	12½	Jul	175	¾	...	...
12⅜	12½	Aug	100	15/16	...	...
Bombay	12½	Jul	...	...	32	7/16
13⅝	15	Jul	70	½	...	...
Boomtn	22½	Sep	62	9/16	...	...
BordCh	15	Aug	23	9/16	...	...
...	15	Nov	64	15/16	...	...
Borind	7½	Aug	110	2⅛	...	...
9	10	Jul	161	⅜	...	...
9	10	Oct	45	1 3/16	...	...
BostCh	30	Oct	...	...	25	⅝
36⅛	35	Jul	1	2 5/16	25	11/16
36⅛	40	Jul	2	11/16	95	3⅜
36⅛	45	Jan	30	2 3/16	...	...
BostTc	10	Aug	35	5/16	...	...
BoxEnB	12½	Jan	80	7/16	...	...
BredTc	30	Jul	34	2¼	77	1⅞
30¼	35	Jul	158	⅝	10	5½
Citicp	35	Jul	74	5	15	3/16
39¾	35	Oct	98	5¾	25	¾
39¾	35	Jan	25	6¾	820	1 5/16
39¾	40	Jul	2605	1⅛	43	1 5/16
39¾	40	Oct	25	2¾	117	2⅝
39¾	40	Jan	20	3⅝	102	3⅛
39¾	45	Jul	35	⅛	200	5¼
39¾	45	Aug	60	⅜	...	...
39¾	45	Oct	1359	⅞	3	5¾
39¾	45	Jan	18	1¾	100	5¾
ClairS	12½	Nov	49	1⅜	...	...
ClerCd	5	Jul	25	⅛	...	...
Coke	35	Jul	51	5⅛	...	...
40⅜	35	Feb	...	...	51	13/16
40⅜	40	Jul	528	1⅛	177	11/16
40⅜	40	Aug	293	1 11/16	299	1
40⅜	40	Nov	291	2½	30	2
40⅜	40	Feb	71	3	48	2⅜
40⅜	45	Aug	49	⅛	...	...
40⅜	45	Nov	37	9/16	...	...
CoeurM	25	Aug	120	¼	...	...
ColgPl	60	Aug	30	9/16	...	...
Colign	17½	Jul	50	1½	...	...
18	20	Nov	107	1½	...	...
ColuGs	22½	Nov	...	...	30	⅜
28⅜	35	Nov	30	¾	...	...
ColHsp	30	Aug	...	...	100	¼
38	35	Aug	...	...	160	1
38	35	Nov	20	5⅞	105	1⅝
38	40	Jul	...	...	200	2 3/16
38	40	Aug	237	1⅜	25	2⅝
38	45	Jul	30	⅛	...	...
38	45	Nov	115	1⅛	...	...
Cmc sp	17½	Jul	300	1	...	...
Cmw Ed	25	Aug	...	...	40	1⅝
23⅞	25	Feb	30	1¼	...	...
CPsy	15	Jan	145	⅞	...	...
CmpUSA	12½	Nov	60	⅝	...	...
8⅞	15	Jul	...	...	250	6⅛
ChileT	90	Jul	...	...	50	3½
91⅝	95	Jul	31	2½	...	...
91⅝	100	Jul	53	1⅛	...	...
91⅝	100	Aug	25	2 11/16	...	...
Compaq	28⅜	Jul	...	...	243	¼
33½	30	Jul	2249	4	884	½
33½	30	Aug	184	4½	23	1 3/16
33½	31⅝	Jul	170	2 9/16	546	15/16
33½	31⅝	Jan	156	5¼	3	3¼
33½	33⅜	Jul	2691	1⅝	404	1 7/16
33½	33⅜	Oct	74	3½	7	3⅛
33½	35	Jul	1717	15/16	631	2⅜
33½	35	Aug	342	1⅝	...	...
33½	35	Oct	139	3⅛	40	3⅞
33½	35	Jan	209	4	7	5
33½	36⅝	Jul	364	½	83	3⅝
33½	36⅝	Oct	110	2	3	5¼
33½	38⅜	Jul	340	¼	15	6
33½	38⅜	Oct	37	1⅞	2	6¼
33½	38⅜	Jan	169	2¾	...	...
33½	40	Jul	82	⅛	10	6¾
33½	40	Oct	224	1⅛	1	8⅛
33½	40	Jan	167	2 3/16	7	8½
33½	41⅝	Jul	165	1/16	2	9¼
CmprsL	15	Oct	25	7/16	...	...
CmpAsc	35	Oct	...	...	40	1½
40⅛	40	Jul	78	1¾	5	1 13/16
11	12½	Aug	35	⅜	...	...
11	12½	Oct	205	¾	...	...
11	12½	Jan	99	1⅛	...	...
11	15	Oct	63	¼	...	...
11	15	Jan	80	⅝	...	...
EleArt	15	Jul	27	1¼	15	¾
15⅜	17½	Jul	30	⅜	2	2⅞
15⅜	25	Sep	27	⅜	3	9¾
EmrsEl	60	Dec	81	3	...	...
Emplca	22½	Aug	170	2 9/16	...	...
23¾	22½	Oct	230	3½	...	...
23¾	25	Jul	...	...	150	1⅞
ELaMd	25	Jan	40	3⅝	...	...
Enron	30	Jul	54	3⅞	...	...
33⅞	35	Jul	1000	7/16	...	...
Entrgy	25	Dec	25	2	10	⅞
EnzoBi	10	Jul	361	¾	10	¾
10	10	Aug	56	1 3/16	...	...
10	12½	Aug	38	7/16	...	...
Epitpe	15	Jul	85	1 13/16	52	1
15⅜	15	Oct	42	2¾	10	1⅞
15⅜	17½	Jul	...	...	25	2½
15⅜	17½	Oct	25	1⅞	20	3¾
15⅜	20	Oct	70	1¼	...	...
Equifx	25	Jul	50	4	...	...
29	30	Jan	100	1 7/16	...	...
EqtCos	20	Jul	100	1	100	½
20½	22½	Jul	2	5/16	40	2⅛
Exxon	55	Jul	25	3⅝	20	¼
58½	55	Aug	...	...	52	9/16
58½	60	Jul	130	½	48	1⅞
58½	60	Aug	31	⅞	70	2¾
58½	65	Jul	99	1/16	...	...
58½	65	Oct	25	7/16	...	...
Fastenl	35	Aug	250	1 9/16	...	...
FedExp	70	Oct	...	...	75	1 9/16
78⅝	75	Jul	102	5⅛	43	1 1/16
78⅝	80	Jul	1194	1⅞	23	3⅛
78⅝	80	Oct	45	5¼	...	...
78⅝	85	Jul	30	⅝	...	...
FHLB	55	Jul	107	5¼	...	...
60⅛	60	Jan	100	4⅝	...	...
60⅛	65	Jul	360	¼	...	...
F N M	80	Jul	25	6½	6	5/16
85⅝	85	Jul	72	2½	104	1 7/16
85⅝	90	Jul	238	½	14	4⅝
85⅝	90	Sep	29	1⅝	...	...
85⅝	95	Dec	27	1⅝	...	...
FedPap	25	Jul	50	9/16	...	...
24¼	25	Jan	25	1⅞	...	...
Fldcrs	25	Dec	26	2	...	...
FileNt	22½	Aug	100	1⅜	...	...
20	25	Jul	5	¼	100	4¾
FilBsm	10	Nov	1	1 7/16	56	1 5/16
9⅞	12½	Aug	18	¼	50	2 13/16
FstChi	45	Jul	47	4	232	5/16
48½	50	Jul	73	1	5	1 15/16
48½	55	Jul	175	⅛	...	...
48½	55	Oct	152	1 3/16	...	...
48½	60	Oct	110	9/16	...	...
FFB	50	Sep	40	11/16	...	...
FtFnMg	65	Jul	...	...	50	7½
Fintste	70	Oct	...	...	35	2⅝
75	75	Jul	138	2	...	...
75	75	Aug	...	...	200	3⅛
75	80	Jul	150	½	96	5⅛
FstUSA	30	Aug	...	...	30	¼
FUnion	45	Jul	51	1⅜	...	...
45⅞	50	Oct	25	⅝	10	4½
Ford	55	Jul	...	...	100	⅜
59	55	Sep	...	...	80	1½
59	60	Jul	433	1 3/16	137	2
59	60	Aug	116	2	5	2⅞
59	60	Sep	65	2 9/16	35	3⅝
59	65	Jul	532	3/16	501	5⅞
59	65	Aug	57	11/16	...	...
59	65	Sep	111	1	...	...
59	65	Dec	38	2⅛	65	7⅝
ForstL	45	Jul	25	2¼	12	1⅛
46	50	Jul	25	5/16	...	...
FramTc	10	Jul	30	⅝	...	...
FrnkRs	35	Jul	...	...	30	⅜
39⅝	40	Aug	...	...	97	3⅛
39⅝	45	Jul	...	...	30	5¾
FM Cop	25	Dec	14	2	37	2⅝
FrMcRP	20	Dec	90	7/16	...	...
GP Fnl	22½	Jul	200	¾	...	...
G T E	30	Jul	...	...	25	3/16
31¼	30	Aug	...	...	55	7/16
31¼	30	Sep	37	2 1/16	188	⅝
31¼	30	Dec	2	2⅝	124	1 3/16
31¼	35	Sep	30	¼	10	3½
31¼	35	Dec	248	7/16	...	...
Galoob	7½	Aug	60	7/16	...	...
6½	10	Aug	...	...	43	3½
Gannett	55	Oct	182	1½	...	...
Gap	35	Dec	...	...	32	2
38½	40	Jul	252	15/16	52	2⅜
38½	40	Aug	3	1⅝	544	3
38½	45	Sep	101	¾	1	6¾
38½	45	Dec	43	1 11/16	...	...
38½	50	Sep	118	5/16	...	...
Gtwy2000	12½	Jul	30	1⅜	25	11/16

Source: *The Wall Street Journal*, June 21, 1994, p. C11.

$55 put on the fourth line has an intrinsic value of $55.00 minus $53.50, or $1.50 per share; it has a time value of $1.75 minus $1.50, or $0.25 per share.

An investor who believes that a stock's price will rise can buy a call or write (sell) a put. An investor who believes that a stock's price will fall can buy a put or write a call. Buying an option gives the investor the potential for an unlimited return and the risk of losing the entire premium, the cost of the contract. Since the investor cannot lose more than the amount invested, the market advertises this threat as "limited risk." Writing an option gives the investor a fixed return, the premium received, but exposure to infinite risk. Chapter 15 will discuss two strategies that involve these contracts: investing in options and using them to hedge investments in stocks.

index option

An option contract that gives its holder the right, but not the obligation, to buy or sell a stock market index at a fixed price for a limited period of time.

Other Options. **Index options** are option contracts that allow the holders to buy or sell stock market indices such as the Standard & Poor's index of the 100 largest companies (S&P 100), the S&P index of the 500 largest companies (S&P 500), the NYSE index of all listed stocks, an index of Japanese stocks, indices of one-industry stocks such as banks, pharmaceuticals, or public utilities, and so forth. Index options function the same way as stock options, except that they allow the investor to bet on movements in a segment of the stock market instead of movements in individual stocks. The bulk of investor interest centers on the first two indices mentioned above.

futures option

A contract that gives its holder the right, but not the obligation, to buy a commodities futures contract at a fixed price for a limited period of time.

Futures options are option contracts that give the holders the right, but not the obligation, to buy commodities futures contracts at fixed prices for limited periods of time. They can serve as direct investments or can be used to hedge an investment in futures contracts.

Investors also trade options on foreign currencies, interest rates (based on 5-year, 10-year, or 30-year U.S. Treasury securities), and insurance premiums.

INTERNATIONAL SECURITIES

The search for increased returns at acceptable levels of risk has led many investors to cross national boundaries. Some securities that have proven popular with U.S. investors are Eurocurrency deposits and Eurobonds.

Eurocurrency

A time deposit held outside a home country, but denominated in the home country's currency.

Eurocurrencies. **Eurocurrencies** are time deposits held outside a home country, but denominated in the home country's currency. These deposits may range in maturity from one day to ten years. The market offers at least 16 Eurocurrency choices. The Eurodollar, Eurodeutschemark, Euroyen, and Eurolira deposits are some examples of Eurocurrencies. The banks that accept these deposits are known as *Eurobanks*.

A Eurobank is usually a division of a national bank involved in international banking. The Eurocurrency market is concentrated in certain regions of the world. In Europe, London, Paris, and the Channel Islands are the key centers of Eurobanking. In the Caribbean, the Cayman Islands and the Bahamas are the key centers of Eurobanking.

Eurocurrencies are not legal tender money. They are created when the ownership of demand deposits held at a domestic bank is transferred to a Eurobank. Suppose that a U.S. resident sends a check for $1,000 drawn on a bank in the United States to a firm in Paris to pay for a shipment of perfumes. If the French firm deposits the check in a Eurobank account, the ownership of the $1,000 is transferred from the U.S. importer to the Eurobank by the U.S. bank, and the transaction ends up creating 1,000 Eurodollars. If the French firm had deposited the check in its domestic bank, however, no Eurodollars would have been created.

When Eurodollar rates are significantly higher than CD rates in the United States, U.S. investors make arrangements with their domestic banks to have funds temporarily deposited in a Eurobank account. These transactions usually involve multiples of a million dollars and cannot be liquidated before maturity.

Eurobond

A bond denominated in the domestic currency of the issuing corporation but generally sold outside its country of origin.

Eurobonds. Eurobonds are bearer bonds denominated in a designated currency by the issuing corporation, but not registered in that issuer's country. Eurobonds are most frequently denominated in U.S. dollars, Japanese yen, Deutschemarks, Swiss francs, and Dutch guilders. Eurobonds are generally sold outside their countries of origin and they escape the regulation imposed on domestic bond issues. A typical Eurobond issue is underwritten and sold in various national markets simultaneously by a syndicate of banks.

The Eurobond market is self-regulated. The Association of International Bond Dealers (AIBD) holds itself responsible for monitoring and maintaining stability in the market. The Eurobond market is generally accessible to multinational corporations with recognized names and good credit ratings. Investors are attracted to this market because of its anonymity, high yield, and general ability to avoid income taxes.

SUMMARY

Individual, corporate, and institutional investors can choose among many types of securities. The returns vary with risk, which is the probability that the return an investor receives will not match the expected return when the investment was made.

Five types of risk affect all securities. Default risk is the probability that the borrower will not pay interest or repay principal when due. Illiquidity risk is the probability that the investor will not be able to buy or sell a security quickly without disturbing the market price. Purchasing power risk is the probability that the investor will be able to buy less with the principal and interest received from an investment than the principal would buy at the time the investment was made. Interest rate risk is the probability that current market rates of interest will change, making the prices of outstanding securities change in the opposite direction. Market risk is the probability that news events will force general market prices downward on the day an investor wants to sell, or upward on the day an investor wants to buy.

Four types of risk are specific to certain securities. Call risk is the probability that an issuer will retire a long-term debt security before its maturity date. Expiration risk is the probability that a warrant, put, or call will expire worthless. Exchange rate risk is the probability that the return to a U.S. investor may be lower than the rate realized on the foreign investment due to a change in currency exchange rates. Country risk is the probability that a U.S. investor will not get the expected return from a foreign investment because of a foreign political, economic, social, accounting, legal, or regulatory change.

The actual return an investor receives on a security is a function of the security's risk and the market's yield curve. This curve relates the security's yield to its time remaining until maturity. The yield on a specific security is a function of the income and price appreciation it produces, as well as the amount invested in it.

The U.S. Treasury issues T-bills, which mature in either 13 or 26 weeks every Monday; it issues tax-anticipation T-bills, which mature near corporate tax-payment deadlines, as necessary. It also issues T-bills that mature in 52 weeks on a monthly basis. All T-bills are $10,000 discounted securities free of the risks of default and illiquidity. Commercial banks have created repurchase agreements to protect the very short-term investor in T-bills from market risk and interest rate risk, as well.

Treasury notes and bonds are fixed-rate securities free of the risk of default. Brokerage houses have created Treasury strips by buying T-notes and T-bonds and reselling their principal and interest payments separately.

The federal government taps the capital markets in another way by permitting federal agencies to issue notes and bonds. This money finances attempts to solve economic and social problems that are perceived to have some political significance.

State and local governments finance some of their operations and most of their special projects by selling general obligation and revenue bonds, respectively. The risks on these municipal issues vary widely.

Commercial banks issue their own money market securities: negotiable certificates of deposit and bankers' acceptances. The yields on these classes of instruments are about equal, but they are higher than the yields on T-bills because the securities are riskier.

Corporations issue commercial paper, either directly or through dealers, at yields that reflect the probability that the issuing companies will default. Corporations raise most of the external funds they need by issuing notes, bonds, preferred stock, and common stock. A few companies also issue warrants to increase the returns to their potential bondholders.

A commodities futures contract promises delivery of a commodity at a future date; a put or call option allows the sale or purchase of a security at a fixed price until a future date. Market risk is the dominant influence on the returns for both of these derivative securities.

Internationally, the search for higher returns at acceptable levels of risk has stimulated the growth of the Eurocurrency and Eurobond markets.

Key Terms

bankers' acceptance
call option
call risk
commercial paper
country risk
default risk
Eurobond
Eurocurrency

exchange rate risk
expiration risk
flower bond
futures contract
futures option
general obligations
illiquidity risk
index option
interest rate risk
letter of credit
limit order
market order
market risk
municipal security
odd lot
purchasing power risk
put option
repurchase agreement
revenue bond
risk
round lot
security
syndicate
time draft
treasury bill
treasury strip
warrant
yield curve

Self-Study Questions

1. What is a security?
2. List the nine types of risk and define each.
3. Explain the differences among a T-bill, a T-note, and a T-bond. Are they equally risky?
4. Which municipal security should have the higher yield: a general obligation bond or a revenue bond? Why?
5. Name three uses of a bankers' acceptance.
6. Explain the difference between direct commercial paper and dealer paper.
7. Explain why calling a bond is usually not beneficial to the bond holders.
8. What does a commodity futures contract promise?
9. Explain the difference between a put and a call option.
10. What is a Eurobond?

Self-Test Problems

1. A $100,000 T-bond that matures in 25 years has an 8 percent rate and a current market price of $99,000. What is its YTM?
2. A $1,000 corporate bond with a 7.5 percent rate and ten years to maturity is selling at a market price that will give investors a 6 percent yield if they hold the bond to maturity. What is this bond's price?

Discussion Questions

1. An investor who is analyzing a security issued by a company that is headed for bankruptcy should be concerned primarily with what type of risk?
2. Explain the relationship between the liquidity of a security and its yield.
3. Suppose that an investor has money available to invest for one year. If interest rates are near their historical lows, why is it a bad idea to buy a long-term, fixed-rate security?
4. Explain the following U.S. Treasury security listing:

RATE	MATURITY	BID	ASK	CHANGE	ASK YIELD
11 7/8	November 03	134:26	139:25	+17	7.42

5. Suppose that a company has $1 million cash to invest on a Friday afternoon and it needs the funds Monday morning. What are the advantages and disadvantages of investing in a repo over the weekend?
6. Why is a flower bond unsuitable as an investment for a corporation?
7. Explain the difference(s) in risk between Treasury securities and federal agency securities.
8. What makes a negotiable CD different from the CDs that banks offer to individual depositors?
9. Why would an investor choose to buy a company's preferred stock rather than its common stock?
10. Explain the following stock listing:

52 WEEKS HI	52 WEEKS LO	STOCK	DIV	YLD %	VOL 100S	HI	LO	CLOSE	NET CHG
45	31	Ajax pf	4.80	13.3	20	37 1/8	34	36	+2

11. Which characteristic of a corporation generally has the most influence on the price of its common stock?
12. Why do companies issue warrants?
13. Why would an investor who neither owned nor wanted to own cows trade a beef futures contract?
14. Explain the following futures listing:

Coffee (CSCE) 37,500 lbs., prices in cents per pound

DELIVERY MONTH	OPEN	HIGH	LOW	SETTLE	LIFETIME HIGH	LIFETIME LOW	OPEN INTEREST
March	78.80	79.45	78.70	79.05	107.50	78.30	28,760

15. An investor who buys a call option expects the price of the underlying security to do what?
16. What happens at the expiration of an option?
17. Explain the following option listing:

COMPANY	MARKET	STRIKE	CONTRACT	VOLUME	MONTH	PREMIUM
ABC	42 7/8	40	p	62	July	1/2

18. Those who speculate in the option market frequently claim that it is easier to judge prospects for index options than for corporate stock options. Do you think this claim is justified? Why or why not?
19. The world market includes more than 100 different currencies. Only about 16 of them are acceptable to Eurobanks as Eurocurrencies. What characteristics might these 16 currencies share that the others lack?

20. Why would a U.S. corporation issue a Eurobond?

Problems

1. A $1,000 bond that matures in 17 years has a 10 percent rate and a market price of $950. What is its YTM? Would the YTM be higher or lower if the market price were $1,050?
2. A $10,000 bond that matures in 20 years has a 9 percent rate and its YTM is 10 percent. What is its current market price?

Topics for Further Research

1. Suppose that an investor has already done adequate research to make an intelligent decision about buying General Motors stock. If that investor were also considering buying stock in the following corporations, what additional information would be useful?
   (a) Volkswagen (Germany)
   (b) Volvo AB (Sweden)
   (c) Fiat (Italy)
   (d) Toyota (Japan)
   (e) Daimler-Benz (Germany)
2. Pick a T-bond with several years left to maturity. Compare the yields on that T-bond, a T-strip, and every federal agency issue with the same maturity. How would you account for the differences in yield?
3. What are BANs, Bunds, Gilts, JGBs, OATs, PNs, RANs, and TANs? (Hint: All these terms are explained in Marcia Stigum's book, *The Money Market*, 3d ed. (Homewood, Ill.: Dow-Jones Irwin, 1990).

Answers to Self-Test Problems

1.
$$\text{YTM} = \frac{\$8{,}000 + \$1{,}000/25}{(\$100{,}000 + \$99{,}000)/2}$$
$$= \$8{,}040/\$99{,}500$$
$$= 0.0808\text{, or } 8.08 \text{ percent}$$

2. Solve Equation 4.1 for P.

$$0.06 = \frac{\$75 + (\$1{,}000 - P)/10}{(\$1{,}000 + P)/2}$$
$$= \frac{\$75 + \$100 - 0.1P}{\$500 + 0.5P}$$

Multiply both sides of the equation by ($500 + 0.05$P$).

$$0.06(\$500 + 0.5P) = \$175 - 0.1P$$
$$\$30 + 0.03P = \$175 - 0.1P$$
$$0.13P = \$145$$
$$P = \$1{,}115.38$$

CHAPTER

5

Financial Planning

LEARNING OBJECTIVES

This chapter examines the four financial statements that managers can use as planning tools. At the conclusion of this chapter, the reader should be able to:

1. *Describe each of the four financial statements*
2. *Recognize the unique purpose each statement serves in financial planning*
3. *Understand how the four statements are related and together comprise the company's financial plan*
4. *Appreciate the differences between financial statements for small and large domestic companies*
5. *Comprehend some of the special problems that complicate the preparation of these financial statements for multinationals*

Planning a company's future is the primary responsibility of its top management. Planning at this level includes:

1. Determining the company's goals, such as maximizing shareholder wealth or the market for its products
2. Establishing a timetable for achieving these goals, such as the next year or the next decade
3. Choosing courses of action most likely to accomplish these goals, such as marketing, financing, and production strategies
4. Selecting yardsticks by which to measure the degree of success in accomplishing these goals, such as stock price or market share

After deciding upon the firm's courses of action, financial managers must plan their companies' financial strategies. They use projected income statements, projected balance sheets, cash budgets, and capital budgets as planning tools.

The general principles under which these financial statements are prepared are the same for all companies, but variations in company size significantly affect the degree of complexity involved in statement preparation. When discussing financial planning, therefore, it is useful to distinguish three company size categories:

1. Small companies, such as Polaroid, whose operations are completely domestic, although they may import some supplies and export some finished goods
2. Large companies, such as Eastman Kodak, with multiple domestic subsidiaries and at least one consolidated foreign subsidiary
3. Multinational corporations, such as Coca-Cola, that operate around the world. For many multinationals, their identification with a home country is mostly nostalgic.

INCOME STATEMENTS AND BALANCE SHEETS

The financial statements that have been in use for the longest time are the income statement and the balance sheet. Crude statements of accounts (partial balance sheets) have been found on ancient Sumerian clay tablets. The Romans clarified the concept of an income tax as distinct from a property tax, thereby laying the foundations for an income statement. It took the U.S. stock market crash of 1929, however, to bring about the standardization and publication of financial statements. To avoid subsequent losses of such magnitude, analysts demanded information about a business and its operations that they could compare to previous information about the same company and comparable information about other companies.

Historical Statements

An income statement and a balance sheet can be prepared on the back of an envelope for a small business, or they can fill many pages for a large company with international operations. Whatever their length, the amount of detail must be adequate for the purposes of many different users.

Income statements and balance sheets provide information to stockholders about the status and performance of their collective investment in a company. These statements provide information to existing and potential creditors about the risk of default on their loans to the company. They satisfy the disclosure requirements of various regulatory agencies. They allow managers and other interested analysts to evaluate the results of past decisions, and they provide management with information on which to base future decisions.

Exhibit 5.1 provides a sample income statement and balance sheet. These relatively brief examples highlight the components of greatest financial interest. Appendix A explains these statements in more detail.

EXHIBIT 5.1

Sample Financial Statements

Easter Grass Company
Balance Sheet
December 31, 19XX
($000)

ASSETS		**LIABILITIES AND OWNERSHIP**	
Cash	$ 2,000	Accounts payable	$ 9,000
Marketable securities	1,000	Short-term debt	44,000
Accounts receivable	8,000	Long-term debt	100,000
Inventory	72,000	Minority interest	5,000
Plant and equipment	217,000	Stock	92,000
Total assets	$300,000	Accumulated retained earnings	51,000
		Currency translation adjustment	(1,000)
		Total capital	$300,000

Easter Grass Company
Income Statement
January 1, 19XX to December 31, 19XX
($000)

Net Sales	$100,000
– Labor	–37,000
– Materials	–28,000
– Overhead	–10,500
– Depreciation	–9,000
Operating revenue (EBIT)	15,500
– Interest	–5,000
Taxable income (EAIBT)	10,500
– Taxes	–3,500
Net income after taxes (EAT)	7,000
– Dividends	–2,000
Retained earnings	$ 5,000

The income statement in Exhibit 5.1 includes some frequently encountered acronyms: *EBIT* refers to earnings before interest and taxes; *EAIBT* (pronounced YAB-bit and sometimes abbreviated to an unpronounceable EBT) refers to earnings after interest before taxes; *EAT* refers to earnings after taxes.

Income Statements, Balance Sheets, and Company Size

Different-sized companies prepare income statements and balance sheets some what differently. All companies apply the same accounting principles, but the information they disclose and the amount of work required to prepare the statements vary considerably among small companies, large domestic companies, and multinational companies.

Small Companies. For a U.S. company with only one operating facility, the preparation of an annual income statement and balance sheet follows textbook accounting practices. The company's ledgers, bank statements, and prior financial statements provide all the information the preparer needs.

Large, Domestic Companies. For a U.S. company with multiple operating facilities, possibly including a foreign subsidiary, the preparer's task is more complex. Each subdivision and subsidiary usually prepares its own statements and submits them to headquarters, where they are consolidated into companywide statements.

When consolidating the balance sheets, tangible assets like inventory or plant and equipment can simply be summed. The same rule applies to some financial assets and liabilities like cash, accounts receivable, accounts payable, and bank loans. The only extra work in this phase of the process arises from foreign operations and statements of amounts in foreign currencies. The Financial Accounting Standards Board has established Rule 52 to guide the conversion of foreign currencies to U.S. dollars. If the required conversion of a foreign subsidiary's currency values to U.S. dollars produces a gain or loss on paper, it must be recorded as a currency translation adjustment to equity. This is not a normal profit or loss subject to taxation.

Other balance sheet items must be handled very carefully; they cannot simply be totaled. For example, one subunit of a company may have temporary surplus cash at a time when another is temporarily in need of cash. If they agree on an appropriate interest rate, one can lend the necessary funds to the other. The lender's balance sheet shows a short-term asset; the borrower's shows a short-term liability. Neither of these amounts should show on the parent's consolidated balance sheet. Another possibility is that subsidiaries may be required to "invest" by transferring surplus cash to the parent company and to "borrow" by obtaining funds from the parent company. These transactions show up on the subsidiaries' statements, but not on the consolidated statements. Whether negotiated or mandated, no interest received or paid between different units of the company would show on the consolidated corporate reports.

Another complication may appear on the right-hand side of some balance sheets. Some common stock will remain outstanding for an acquired subsidiary that is not 100 percent owned by the parent company. The consolidated balance sheet, however, can show only the parent company's outstanding common stock. If the parent company owns more than 50 percent of a subsidiary, it is allowed to report 100 percent of that subsidiary's assets and liabilities on its own balance sheet, but it must report the value of that portion of the subsidiary that it does not own as a separate item, **minority interest**. See Exhibit 5.1.

minority interest
A balance sheet item reporting the value of that portion of a subsidiary that the parent company does not own.

Consolidating income statements follows the same principles. The components from sales down to net income after taxes report U.S. dollar totals from all parts of the company, net of any intracompany transactions. If some foreign currency from operations abroad is converted into U.S. dollars and transferred to the parent company, any gain or loss on the currency conversion is reported as a normal operating gain or loss, subject to taxation. This and many other items should be part of the overhead component in Exhibit 5.1.

Multinational Companies. A multinational corporation generates a substantial portion of its revenues from international operations. It may operate facilities in dozens of countries and function with almost as many currencies. It may borrow money in whatever bond market offers the lowest interest rates at the moment, and its stockholders may reside in over a hundred different countries. To a casual observer, McDonald's, Mitsubishi, and Fiat may appear to be American, Japanese, and Italian companies, respectively, but the managers of these companies no longer consider their firms anything less than global.

The financial statements of a multinational reflect this diversity. They are prepared in multiple versions, using the accounting practices and perspectives of each country that hosts a significant segment of the company.

Like a large domestic corporation, the components of a multinational's income statement and balance sheet destined for use in the United States give U.S. dollar totals net of any intracompany transactions. Analysts outside the company see only the overall picture, and evaluate the profit performance of a multinational relative to its overall assets. The multinational's manager must contend, however, with quota laws and restrictions on cash flows that some host countries impose. These obstacles may have a significant impact on the way different subsidiaries appear to perform based on internal data.

Pro Forma Financial Statements

Corporate financial planners use historical income statements and balance sheets as starting points. However, they recast this past data to develop *pro forma* income statements and *pro forma* balance sheets. ***Pro forma* statements** substitute calculated numbers into these statements to represent projections of future values instead of historical values. Since planning, not reporting, is the principal purpose of *pro forma* statements, these documents are not normally released to the public.

***pro forma* statement**

A financial statement that projects future data instead of reporting historical data.

The forecaster may perceive the company as either a sales-driven firm or an asset-based firm. The projection procedure for a sales-driven firm starts with the *pro forma* income statement. The analyst first estimates future sales, then determines the level of assets required to support those sales, the funds needed to acquire any necessary additions to assets, and the expenses to be incurred in generating the sales. The procedure terminates with calculations of expected profits and cash flows. Service and financial companies tend to see themselves as sales-driven firms. Companies with excess capacity also tend to forecast sales first.

On the other hand, if the forecaster sees the company as an asset-based firm, the projection procedure starts with the *pro forma* balance sheet and estimated level of assets. Capital-intensive companies, such as manufacturers, tend to base their forecasts on assets. A company operating at or near its maximum capacity almost always uses asset-based forecasting.

No matter which statement the forecaster starts with, it is impossible to finish one statement without doing some work on the other statement. They are too

FOCUS ON FINANCE

PepsiCo: Internal and External Growth

During the last two decades, PepsiCo has changed its long-term plan for growth. During the 12-year period from 1973 through 1984, it grew internally. Of only three acquisitions, two (Pizza Hut and Taco Bell) were attempts to increase sales by expanding the market for the company's soft drinks. During the eight-year period from 1985 through 1992, Pepsico grew both internally and externally. It acquired 12 other companies or subdivisions of other companies. Its assets more than quadrupled during each of those periods: from \$1.2 billion in 1973 to \$4.9 billion in 1984, then to \$21.0 billion in 1992.

YEAR	TOTAL ASSETS ($ BILLION)	ACQUISITION AND COST
1973	$1.2	—
1974	1.4	—
1975	1.4	—
1976	1.8	Lee Way Motor Freight[a]
1977	2.1	Pizza Hut Inc.[a]
1978	2.4	Taco Bell, $148 million
1979	2.9	—
1980	3.3	—
1981	4.0	—
1982	4.1	—
1983	4.4	—
1984	4.9	—
1985	5.9	Bottling subsidiary of Allegheny Beverage Corp., $160 million
1986	8.0	MEI Corporation, $591 million
		7-Up International, $246 million
		Kentucky Fried Chicken, $41 million
1987	9.0	—
1988	11.1	Calny Inc.[a]
		Grand Metropolitan Inc., $705 million
1989	15.1	Bottling subsidiary of General Cinema Corp., $1.77 billion
		Smiths Crisps Ltd. and Walkers Crisps Holding Ltd., $1.34 billion
1990	17.1	Empresas Gamesa, Mexico (70%), $300 million
1991	18.8	Hostess Frito-Lay, Canada (50%)[a]
1992	21.0	Fovarosi Asvanyviz es Uditoipari Reszvenytarsasag, Hungary[a]
		Evercrisp Snack Productas de Chile, $12.6 million

[a]Cost not available.

interdependent to be treated as completely separate forecasts. Simply for the sake of clarity, the following discussion starts with the *pro forma* balance sheet.

***Pro Forma* Balance Sheet.** The *pro forma* balance sheet is a snapshot of the company at some point in the future (usually one year ahead). It can illustrate either of two points of view:

1. The way management *wants* the company to look, in which case the statement is a target
2. The way management *expects* the company to look, in which case the statement is a forecast

If the *pro forma* balance sheet is prepared to reflect management wishes, or targets, the preparer starts with desired level of total assets, determined by the rate of growth management intends to foster. This growth may be external or internal. **External growth** is achieved by acquiring other companies or subdivisions of other companies. **Internal growth** is achieved by expanding the market for the company's products, increasing the company's share of the existing market, and/or diversifying into new products or services.

external growth

An increase in assets achieved by acquiring other companies or subdivisions of other companies.

internal growth

An increase in assets achieved by expanding the market for the company's products, increasing the company's share of the existing market, and/or diversifying into new products or services.

Once the target level of total assets is determined, the analyst estimates the various components of this total. If the company is growing by acquisition, the analyst combines the components of the balance sheets of the new companies, and then adjusts the combined figures for the changes management intends to make.

If the company is growing internally, many factors determine the relative sizes of the balance sheet components, such as:

1. The nature of the company's industry—labor intensive or capital (plant and equipment) intensive
2. The degree of capacity utilization that is considered to be efficient, given the type of business the company does
3. The existing degree of capacity utilization
4. The cost of holding inventory and the losses incurred from running out of stock
5. The dependability of raw materials deliveries
6. The amount of credit extended to customers and the expected timeliness of their payments
7. Management's policy regarding the appropriate degree of liquidity to be maintained

Regardless of their place in time—past, present, or future—all balance sheets must balance. Therefore, the target level of total assets (the left side of the *pro forma* balance sheet) must equal the target level of total capital (the right side of the *pro forma* balance sheet). Estimation of some of the components of total capital follows automatically from the work of estimating assets. For instance, once the analyst determines the desired inventory level and estimates materials purchases on credit, these values determine the accounts payable component. The cost of financing the targeted level of plant and equipment helps to determine the long-term debt and stock components.

In contrast, the accumulated retained earnings component requires a calculation that depends on a completed *pro forma* income statement. When this is done, the projected retained earnings are added to the retained earnings accumulated in the past. Finally, in this first pass at projection, the estimated short-term debt is the "fudge factor"—the component that the analyst adjusts to make total capital equal to total assets.

If the *pro forma* balance sheet is simply a forecast of the company's position at a future date, the method of projection becomes paramount. The analyst can choose among many forecasting techniques, ranging from very simple guesstimates to statistically sophisticated extrapolations of past trends. Four techniques are especially popular:

1. In the sustained growth technique, the preparer assumes that all components of the *pro forma* statements will grow at the same rates they have grown in the recent past. The forecasts simply apply the familiar growth rates to the most recent historical numbers.
2. In the sustained growth and proportionate composition technique, the preparer calculates all the projections based on some assumptions:
   (a) Total assets and net sales will grow at the same rates they have grown in the recent past.
   (b) All balance sheet components will represent the same percentages of total assets that they have represented in the recent past.
   (c) All income statement components will represent the same percentages of net sales that they have represented in the recent past.
3. In the extrapolation technique, the preparer fits a trend line to historical data on total assets and net sales; after extending these trend lines to the next period, the preparer calculates the components of the balance sheet and income statement as percentages of total assets and net sales, respectively.
4. In the economic model technique, the preparer statistically relates some or all of the statement components to economic and/or industry variables, then forecasts these variables and uses the relationships to forecast the statement components.

***Pro Forma* Income Statement.** The *pro forma* income statement summarizes the company's projected business performance over a period of time, as measured in dollar amounts. It accumulates the proceeds from expected sales during the period, deducts expenses to be accrued during the period, and shows the anticipated distributions of the company's operating revenue, or EBIT, to its creditors (interest), various units of government (taxes), stockholders (dividends), and itself (retained earnings).

If the *pro forma* income statement is being developed as a target along with a target *pro forma* balance sheet, then its components must reflect the company performance that is necessary to achieve management's goals. After management sets the net sales target, the analyst calculates the labor, materials, and overhead expenses either in their customary relationships to net sales, or in more efficient target relationships. Depreciation rates, as set by U.S. tax laws, are applied to the projected levels of plant and equipment. The interest expense is a function of the levels of short-term debt and long-term debt indicated by the *pro forma* balance sheet.

Changes in tax rates and dividend rates are not overnight surprises. Proposed changes are debated well in advance. If the debate remains unsettled when the *pro forma* statements must be prepared, the preparer usually develops two or more versions of the statements. Each version incorporates one possible outcome of the debate.

If the *pro forma* income statement reflects a forecast, rather than a target, then the preparer has the same choice of forecasting methods. The only stipulation is to employ consistent techniques.

Pro Forma Financial Statements and Company Size

Anyone who has never prepared a financial forecast is likely to assume that the smaller the company, the easier the task. This assumption in not quite true. Obviously, more complex statements present more opportunities to make forecasting errors, but the analyst must accommodate many additional considerations, as well.

Small Companies. On the plus side, the forecaster for a small company has easy access to top management and its plans; in a very small company, the forecaster may actually be a member of top management. Either way, the forecaster is familiar, and possibly intimately acquainted, with the business and the factors that affect its success or failure. Any small business can draw on a network of other companies and their managers for reality checks about the state of the industry. Historical bookkeeping data in a small company generally reflect real revenues, expenses, and cash flows rather than allocations among divisions that may be misleading. Finally, a forecast for a smaller company must cover fewer details.

On the minus side, a mistake in forecasting can have disastrous results for a small company. The forecaster may have only limited time and assistance. Subsequent reviews of actual outcomes versus forecasted outcomes may significantly affect the forecaster's future with the company. This last disadvantage tends to make small-company forecasters very conservative, overestimating projections of costs and underestimating projections of revenues.

Large Domestic Companies. The workload of projecting financial statements for domestic companies grows exponentially as they add subsidiaries and subdivisions. Each unit creates its own set of *pro formas*, which usually reconcile parent company guidelines and its own management's targets or chosen forecasting techniques. It then submits its idea of what its statements should be to headquarters for consolidation.

The financial managers of the parent company review each division's submission and evaluate it in terms of the overall forecasts and goals of the company. They may either dictate or negotiate changes in each subunit's plans before

FOCUS ON FINANCE

SUSTAINED GROWTH AND PROPORTIONATE COMPOSITION *PRO FORMA* STATEMENTS

To illustrate how the sample income statement and balance sheet in Exhibit 5.1 could be projected using the sustained growth and proportionate composition technique, the following information is needed:

1. Total assets and net sales will grow at 5 percent and 8 percent, respectively, the same rates at which they have been growing in the recent past.
2. All balance sheet components will be the same percentage of total assets that they were in the recent past. These percentages are shown below.
3. All income statement items will be the same percentage of net sales that they were in the recent past. These percentages are shown below.

Given all this information, the first step is to project:

Total assets = $300,000,000 × 105%
= $315,000,000

Net sales = $100,000,000 × 108%
= $108,000,000

The next step is to apply the proportionate composition percentages to these numbers to derive the *pro forma* balance sheet and income statements.

Easter Grass Company
Balance Sheet as a Percentage of Total Assets
December 31, 19XX

ASSETS		LIABILITIES AND OWNERSHIP	
Cash	0.67%	Accounts Payable	3.00%
Marketable securities	0.33	Short-term debt	14.67
Accounts receivable	2.67	Long-term debt	33.33
Inventory	24.00	Minority interest	1.67
Plant and equipment	72.33	Stock	30.67
Total assets	100.00%	Accumulated retained earnings	17.00
		Currency translation adjustment	(0.33)
		Total capital	100.00%

continued on next page

preparing the consolidated statements. (Negotiation is preferred by managerial theorists, but practicing managers frequently ignore this advice.) Occasionally, unanticipated problems become apparent during this process, and new policies and decisions formulated to cope with them may require alterations in the parent company's *pro formas*, some or all of the subunits' *pro formas*, or both.

A firm with a foreign subsidiary must forecast exchange rates for the time period covered by the *pro forma* statements. Any expectation of an unfavorable

Easter Grass Company
Income Statement as a Percentage of Net Sales
January 1, 19XX to December 31, 19XX

Net Sales	100.00%
– Labor	–37.00
– Materials	–28.00
– Overhead	–10.50
– Depreciation	–9.00
Operating revenue (EBIT)	15.50
– Interest	–5.00
Taxable income (EAIBT)	10.50
– Taxes	–3.50
Net income after taxes (EAT)	7.00
– Dividends	–2.00
Retained earnings	5.00%

Easter Grass Company
Pro Forma Balance Sheet
December 31, 19X(X+1)

ASSETS		LIABILITIES AND OWNERSHIP	
Cash	$ 2,110,500	Accounts payable	$ 9,450,000
Marketable securities	1,039,500	Short-term debt	46,210,500
Accounts receivable	8,410,500	Long-term debt	104,989,500
Inventory	75,600,000	Minority interest	5,229,000
Plant and equipment	227,839,500	Stock	96,610,500
Total assets	$315,000,000	Accumulated retained earnings	53,550,000
		Currency translation adjustment	(1,039,500)
		Total capital	$315,000,000

Easter Grass Company
Pro Forma Income Statement
January 1, 19X(X+1) to December 31, 19X(X+1)

Net Sales	$ 108,000,000
– Labor	–39,960,000
– Materials	–30,240,000
– Overhead	–11,340,000
– Depreciation	–9,720,000
Operating revenue (EBIT)	$ 16,740,000
– Interest	–5,400,000
Taxable income (EAIBT)	$ 11,340,000
– Taxes	–3,780,000
Net income after taxes (EAT)	$ 7,560,000
– Dividends	–2,160,000
Retained earnings	$ 5,400,000

shift in currency values encourages the company to devise strategies to minimize potential damage. Similarly, changes in foreign laws regarding cross-border cash transfers, import quota restrictions, taxes, employee compensation, or use of local managerial talent should be anticipated and incorporated into plans at this time.

Multinational Companies. To construct the *pro forma* statements of a company that does a substantial amount of international business, the analyst focuses on the overall performance of the parent. The factors that generate this performance differ slightly from those that affect other firms. For instance, the sizes of cash balances lose some importance when judging the liquidity of a multinational; maintaining adequate lines of credit and overdraft privileges in various currencies is significant. The firm can pool short-term cash surpluses into one currency or several, or leave them to individual units to manage. The firm can earn extra profits by pooling surpluses and investing in securities denominated in currencies that produce the highest returns, but this gain must be weighed against the extra cost of converting the funds into the pooled currencies and back again.

In-house analysis of the performance of the company's various budget units must take into account differences in the conditions under which the managers of those units must operate. For instance, a multinational with units in many countries faces a spectrum of tax rates on earnings. If taxes in the host country of one unit are high relative to taxes in the host countries of other units, the multinational may respond by implementing several policies.

First, it might allocate overhead costs more heavily to higher-taxed subsidiaries, reducing their taxable profits. The parent might even locate all of its research and development operations, or its computer or communications center, in the high-tax country, charging all the costs to that subsidiary but distributing the benefits through all the budget units in the company.

transfer pricing policy
The establishment of prices on sales between subsidiaries, which may or may not reflect market prices.

Second, it might establish a **transfer pricing policy** that favors its low-tax subsidiaries. If the subsidiaries buy and sell a lot among themselves, the parent company may direct them to charge each other prices that vary from market prices. Suppose that subsidiaries A and B buy nails from each other worth the equivalent of US$0.50 on the market. The multinational may develop a pricing policy that requires subsidiary A, located in a high-tax country, to pay the equivalent of US$1.00 for every nail it buys from subsidiary B, while B, located in a low-tax country, pays the equivalent of US$0.25 for every nail it buys from A. As a consequence, Subsidiary A will show depressed sales, taxes, and profits, and inflated cost of goods sold and inventory levels. Subsidiary B will show inflated sales, taxes (at the lower rate), and profits, and depressed cost of goods sold and inventory levels. Since the effects of the intracompany transactions cancel one another out on the consolidated statements, the parent company will show only higher after-tax profits. Note that some high-tax countries prohibit this practice.

As a third response to differences in tax rates, the multinational might arrange for a subsidiary located in a high-tax country to do most or all of the borrowing for the whole corporation, because interest is a tax-deductible expense. Additionally,

FOCUS ON CAREERS

CHIEF FINANCIAL OFFICER

A larger company needs more financial managers who do more specialized jobs. However, a company has only one Chief Financial Officer (CFO). This executive is responsible for the performance of all the financial managers within the company and must have a comprehensive understanding of how the company raises and uses money.

The CFO determines the financial policies the company follows. The understanding and skills employed in formulating these policies influence the firm's forecasting, budgeting, fund raising, investments, asset composition, recordkeeping, pricing, credit rating, risk management, incentive programs, mergers and acquisitions, spinoffs, stock price, and, ultimately, its very lifespan.

For a large corporation, this means that the CFO must be familiar with the financial management techniques and financial markets in this country and many foreign countries. This person must hold a master's degree (preferably an M.B.A.) and supplement this training with updating seminars and courses.

The CFO may fill the position of company treasurer, controller, or financial vice president, depending on the size and organization of the company. The position usually entails a six-figure salary and may include annual and/or performance bonuses.

the parent can charge a profitable foreign subsidiary a management fee and thus move before-tax income to the lower-taxed parent.

Whatever tax-minimizing techniques the firm choses, top management must take care to judge the performance of its subsidiaries fairly. It must take these techniques into consideration when comparing its subsidiaries' rates of return.

CASH BUDGETS

After creating the *pro forma* income statement and balance sheet, the financial manager constructs a cash budget. This is a detailed, month-by-month prediction of expected cash inflows and outflows during the forthcoming year. The process begins with calculation of the firm's net cash flows, and it continues with analysis of their effect on the company's cash balances. Thus, a cash budget predicts:

1. Whether a company will have to borrow or can invest
2. How much money is involved in each decision to borrow or invest
3. The timing and duration of these loans and investments

Exhibit 5.2 illustrates the format of a cash budget by presenting data for four months. For simplicity's sake, the exhibit omits the interest paid on the loans taken out in April and May, and the interest received on the investments made in June and July. Chapter 6 explains the process of creating a detailed cash budget.

After assessing the company's cash needs, the financial manager can shop for the most advantageous way of borrowing. If the company's credit is strong enough to obtain an unsecured, short-term loan, the manager has time to find the bank

EXHIBIT 5.2

Sample Cash Budget ($000)

	APRIL	MAY	JUNE	JULY
Collections from:				
Sales	$9,000	$6,000	$9,000	$7,500
Royalties	20	20	20	20
Interest	0	0	0	400
New stock	0	0	50,000	0
Asset sale	0	0	0	62
Tax refund	6	0	0	0
Total inflow	9,026	6,020	59,020	7,982
Payments for:				
Labor	2,000	2,400	3,100	3,000
Materials	2,000	3,200	3,400	3,600
Utilities	1,525	1,600	1,700	1,900
Dividends	4,000	0	0	4,000
Interest	175	200	250	100
Taxes	0	0	500	0
New assets	0	0	0	40,000
Total outflow	9,700	7,250	8,950	52,600
Net cash flow	(674)	(1,230)	50,070	(44,618)
Cash balance	1,000	1,000	1,000	1,000
Loans	674	1,230	(1,904)	0
Total loans	674	1,904	0	0
Investments	0	0	48,166	(44,618)
Total investments	0	0	48,166	3,548

that offers the least costly terms. If the company will need enough money to make issuing commercial paper practical, the manager has time to negotiate the best deal possible with either an investment bank or a commercial bank. If the company will have to pledge some of its assets as collateral for the loan, the manager has time to set up acceptable security arrangements.

When the company expects to have surplus funds to invest temporarily, the financial manager can devise an appropriate portfolio strategy that includes a combination of investments that will produce a satisfactory return at an acceptable level of risk. This analysis must include a forecast of interest rates so that the firm can minimize interest rate risk exposure through careful selection of maturity dates.

Reconciling the Cash Budget with the *Pro Formas*

After completing the cash budget, the financial manager must reconcile it with the *pro forma* financial statements. Few of the numbers on the *pro forma* statements will match the numbers in the cash budget because the *pro forma* statements are pre-

accrual basis
An accounting method that recognizes transactions when they are made, not when their cash consequences are felt.

cash basis
An accounting method that recognizes transactions when their cash consequences are felt.

pared on an **accrual basis** (recording transactions when they happen) and the cash budget is prepared on a **cash basis** (recording transactions when the firm spends or receives cash). In addition, some special items will need further adjustment.

The net sales component of the *pro forma* income statement will not match the collections from sales component of the cash budget. There are two reasons for this:

1. Some customers always pay later than the due dates on their invoices, so accrued sales for the year will not match cash collections from sales.
2. Some customers fail to pay at all and company policy may turn these credit sales over to collection agencies (none of whom have 100 percent success rates) or write them off as bad debts only after many months.

The interest components of the *pro forma* income statement (both receipts and payments) reflect lump-sum projections, not the detailed estimates calculated in the cash budget. The *pro forma* income statement's projection of the tax payments reflects the taxes the firm will owe for the fiscal year; the cash budget estimates taxes for the year, and adjusts this figure for a refund or additional payment that may occur the following spring.

Some forecasts should match exactly:

1. The cash component of the *pro forma* balance sheet should match the cash balance component of the cash budget.
2. The figure for marketable securities on the balance sheet should equal the cash budget's figure for total investments.
3. The *pro forma* balance sheet's accounts receivable amount should match the amount for collections from sales that are not yet recorded in the cash budget when its time period ends.
4. The balance sheet's accounts payable should match payments for materials that are not yet recorded on the cash budget when its time period ends.

Finally, the *pro forma* balance sheet's fudge factor, short-term debt, should be replaced with the number shown on the cash budget for total loans.

Cash Budgets and Company Size

Preparation of a cash budget is an exercise in forecasting for the manager of a small company. The amount of detail, the need to produce alternative budgets, and the frequency of revision all depend on forecasting errors. This simplicity is a luxury that the managers of large domestic corporations and multinationals cannot afford. To prepare their more complex cash budgets, they must formulate corporate policies about cash and loan consolidation and foreign exchange management.

Small Companies. The financial manager of a small company must create only one companywide cash budget. The total time and effort the manager dedicates to its preparation, as well as the amount of detail it includes, depend on the accuracy of previous budgets. The budget may be revised or updated every month, every quarter, or whenever management decides that circumstances have changed so that the underlying assumptions on which the budget is based are no longer valid. The cash budget serves primarily as a standard, a benchmark, against which to judge actual performance.

Large, Domestic Companies. For a large, domestic company, the cash budget is not only a standard; it takes on a control function, as well. Each budget unit prepares its own cash budget and submits the document to company headquarters for review and approval. The parent company consolidates the units' budgets, evaluates their net effect on its cash flows, makes improvements where necessary, and then sends the revised budgets back to the units. The parent then holds the financial managers of these units responsible for their actual performance relative to the budgeted projections. A significant discrepancy may require either a good explanation or a personnel change. Given the consequences of a difference in forecasted versus actual outcomes, cash budgeting is usually an ongoing process for a large company. The proliferation of intercompany computer networks and spreadsheet software has made updates and modifications of cash budgets both routine and continuous.

The financial managers of large companies make more strategic decisions than the managers of small companies. For instance, the parent company may allow each budget unit to implement its own investment policy. Unit financial managers can then choose their own securities and maturities. As a second strategy, the parent company may set general guidelines for managing the units' portfolios and allow the units' financial managers to implement this investment policy as they see fit. The financial manager of a parent company that follows such a strategy seldom attempts to micromanage units' portfolios unless unit mangers show flagrant disregard of the parent company's guidelines. As a third investment policy, the parent company may require units to remit all temporary surplus funds to the parent, where they are combined into one portfolio of securities managed by headquarters personnel. Each budget unit is then credited with its proportionate share of the portfolio's earnings and allocated its fair share of the transaction costs.

The same strategy choices generally apply to short-term debt. The financial managers of budget units may be free to borrow from their own sources at whatever interest rates they can negotiate, or the parent company may set up credit lines and allow the unit managers access to these lines as needed. Alternatively, the parent company may do all the short-term borrowing, and then relend these funds to the budget units as necessary, passing along proportionate interest charges, as well.

Multinational Companies. Like large domestic companies, multinationals consolidate unit budgets. Because the various budgets involve multiple currencies, however, the centralization of cash management decisions becomes more urgent. The parent company must be sure that adequate information is shared among the budget units, that consolidation does not obscure significant opportunities to reduce costs and enhance returns, and that the ultimate standard for evaluating

EXHIBIT 5.3

MNC Inc. Intracompany Payments Matrix (in seller's currency)

Owed to the Subsidiary in	Owed by the Subsidiary in Canada	United States	Mexico
Canada	—	C$50,000	C$80,000
United States	US$60,000	—	US$40,000
Mexico	P108,000	P90,000	—

cash management decisions is the maximization of the parent company's profitability.

netting
A currency-management technique that minimizes currency conversion costs by reducing the amounts and frequency of currency conversions to pay for transactions between subsidiaries.

One currency-management technique used by most multinationals is called **netting**. This technique minimizes currency conversion costs by reducing the amounts and frequency of currency conversions to pay for transactions between budget units. The best way to explain this concept is with an illustration.

Suppose that MNC Inc. has a subsidiary in Canada, another in the United States, and a third in Mexico. Each subsidiary produces a different product, but each sells all three products in its own country. This arrangement leads to considerable buying and selling among them. To allow these transactions:

1. The Canadian subsidiary needs both U.S. dollars and Mexican pesos.
2. The U.S. subsidiary needs both Canadian dollars and Mexican pesos.
3. The Mexican subsidiary needs both Canadian and U.S. dollars.

Without parental currency management, each transaction between two subsidiaries would require the buyer to obtain the seller's currency. Suppose that the intracompany payments matrix for MNC Inc. in a particular month looks like Exhibit 5.3. At the end of the month, the Mexican subsidiary owes the Canadian subsidiary 80,000 Canadian dollars and the U.S. subsidiary owes the Mexican subsidiary 90,000 pesos.

Suppose also that the exchange rates at the end of the month are forecasted to be C$1.25/US$ and P3/US$. (This implies reverse conversion ratios of US$0.80/C$ and US$0.333/P, and cross rates of P2.4/C$ and C$0.42/P. See Chapter 2.)

Exhibit 5.3 indicates that the Mexican subsidiary has to convert 80,000 times 2.4, or 192,000 pesos into 80,000 Canadian dollars during the month, while the Canadian subsidiary has to convert 108,000 times 0.42, or 45,360 Canadian dollars into 108,000 Mexican pesos. Restating Exhibit 5.3 in a uniform currency reveals an opportunity for MNC Inc. to cut its total currency conversion costs.

Exhibit 5.4 restates Exhibit 5.3 in U.S dollars. The Mexican subsidiary needs $64,000 to pay the Canadian subsidiary during the month, while the Canadian subsidiary needs $36,000 to pay the Mexican subsidiary. This is a net dollar flow of $28,000 from the Mexican subsidiary to the Canadian one. If these two subsidiaries pay for the transactions as they occur, MNC Inc. has to bear the conversion costs of $64,000 plus $36,000, or $100,000 worth of currency; if the

EXHIBIT 5.4

MNC Inc. Intracompany Payments Matrix (U.S. dollars)

Owed to the Subsidiary in	Owed by the Subsidiary in: Canada	United States	Mexico
Canada	—	$40,000	$64,000
United States	$60,000	—	$40,000
Mexico	$36,000	$30,000	—

transactions are netted and settled at the end of the month, MNC Inc. has to incur conversion costs for exchanging only $28,000 worth of currency.

Exhibit 5.5 calculates the net payments between each pair of subsidiaries in U.S. dollars. If MNC Inc.'s subsidiaries pay for all transactions as they occur, Exhibit 5.4 indicates that they must convert a total of $270,000 worth of currency. If MNC Inc. uses the netting technique and exchanges currency only for the net payments at the end of the month, Exhibit 5.5 indicates that it must convert only $58,000 worth of currency.

If the multinational parent is headquartered in the United States, it may extend the netting technique to require that its Mexican subsidiary pay the Canadian obligation to the U.S. subsidiary in lieu of a transfer of cash to Canada, saving the conversion costs on an additional $20,000. Some countries limit or prohibit netting by placing controls on foreign exchange. This protects profitable currency exchange opportunities for their own banks, but it obviously places a ceiling on the savings a multinational can achieve by netting.

CAPITAL BUDGETS

In academic circles, a capital budget is treated simply as an asset selection plan. For an operating business, however, this definition is not complete if it does not consider the company's plans to finance the assets it selects.

Asset selection is based on an evaluation of the desirability of acquiring long-term assets. This desirability requires consideration of two things: the potential return that the asset will generate and the risk that the asset will fail to generate this return. If the potential return appears to be worth the risk, the firm decides to acquire the asset. If it evaluates more than one asset, the firm chooses those assets with the best returns relative to their risks (or the lowest risks relative to their returns).

The company must then decide how to raise the money to acquire the asset(s). It can raise long-term funds in four ways: by issuing debt, preferred stock, or common stock, or by retaining earnings. The choice of a financing source generally depends on the cost of each type of financing, the proportion of debt already in the company's capital structure, and the effect of the package—the new asset(s) plus the new funds—on the company's earnings per share.

EXHIBIT 5.5

MNC Inc. Net Payments Matrix (U.S. dollars)

Owed to the Subsidiary in	Owed by the Subsidiary in: Canada	United States	Mexico
Canada	—	$0	$28,000
United States	$20,000	—	10,000
Mexico	0	0	—

Specific Issues in Asset Selection

In organizing the asset selection process, the firm must carefully create a list of independent assets, categorized where possible into groups of mutually exclusive assets. **Independent assets**, whether the firm decides to acquire them or not, have no impact on each other's cash flows. Dependent assets, on the other hand, do have some impact on each other, and the nature of this impact determines the type of dependence. **Complementary assets** enhance each other's cash inflows and/or reduce each other's cash outflows. **Competitive assets** reduce each other's cash inflows and/or increase each other's cash outflows. **Supplementary assets** are sometimes called *necessary companion* assets; if the firm acquires one, it must acquire the other.

independent asset
An asset that has no impact on another asset's cash flows, whether the firm decides to acquire it or not.

complementary asset
An asset that enhances another asset's cash inflows and/or reduces another asset's cash outflows.

competitive asset
An asset that reduces another asset's cash inflows and/or increases another asset's cash outflows.

supplementary assets
Sometimes called a *necessary companion asset*, one that cannot be acquired without another.

mutually exclusive asset
An asset that is an alternative to another; if the firm acquires one, it automatically rejects the other.

A manufacturing company might evaluate independent assets like replacing equipment on an assembly line and buying a new limousine for the CEO. Neither asset would have any impact on the cash flows of the other. A manufacturer of industrial lighting might identify complementary assets such as machines to make improved office light bulbs and machines to make light fixtures designed to utilize these bulbs efficiently. Each product, light bulbs and fixtures, would enhance the sales of the other. A brewery would consider machinery for producing light beer as a competitive asset, since the light beer might reduce sales of the company's regular beer, even if it were to increase the company's total sales.

A company considering whether or not to construct a new building, and whether or not to install an air conditioning system, would be making a serious mistake if it were to evaluate these two projects as independent assets. The building is a necessary companion asset for the air conditioning system. If they were evaluated as independent projects, the merits of the building might lead the firm to reject it while the air conditioning system might seem acceptable on its own merits. Where would the company put the air conditioning system?

The analysis must include three options:

1. Construct a new building with air conditioning
2. Construct a new building without air conditioning
3. Do nothing

These three projects are not only independent of each other, they are **mutually exclusive assets**. Management simply chooses the best project, and automatically rejects the others.

abandonment problem
A comparison of expected future benefits over the remaining life of an asset to its expected salvage value if the firm scraps it before the end of its life.

capital rationing problem
The need to choose among assets when a company cannot raise enough money to acquire all profitable assets.

After the firm compiles a list of potential assets that it might acquire, it must consider additional possibilities. First, it can postpone some projects though their rates of return may be different if they begin at different times, and the cost of capital will change with changing economic conditions. Second, some projects can be terminated before completion. The **abandonment problem** compares the expected future benefits over the remaining life of an asset to its expected salvage value if the firm decides to scrap the asset before the end of its life. Thus, an asset with a five-year life can be liquidated at the end of one, two, three, or four years, so management really has to choose among five mutually exclusive alternatives.

Also, the firm faces a **capital rationing problem** whenever it cannot raise enough money to acquire all profitable assets. Suppose that a company were considering four profitable projects with equal lives. Its cost of capital is less than 15 percent, but it cannot raise more than $5 million at any price:

ASSET	RATE OF RETURN	COST	ANNUAL CASH FLOW
F	22%	$1 million	$220,000
G	20	2 million	400,000
H	18	1 million	180,000
I	15	2 million	300,000

Accepting F, G, and H, the three projects with the highest rates of return, would invest only $4 million and produce a total annual cash flow of $800,000. A better decision, accepting, G, H, and I, would invest the whole $5 million and produce a total annual cash flow of $880,000. The best decision, however, is to accept F, G, and I, which would produce a total annual cash flow of $920,000.

The firm must also resolve the reinvestment problem when proposed projects have different lives. Suppose that Asset A will produce a 20 percent annual return but it will last for only two years. The firm can then be replace it with an asset that will produce an annual return of 5 percent for the next 18 years. Asset D, however, will produce a 10 percent annual return for the next 20 years. In the long run, the company would be better off choosing Asset D. It is easy to suggest that, theoretically, Asset A plus its replacement should be compared to Asset D, but in practice, finding a common life for all assets under consideration along with their future replacements is impossible.

Finally, the asset selection decision cannot ignore the concept of risk. Most numerical input for a capital budget requires long-term forecasting. Future materials prices, wage rates, selling prices, demand levels, scrap values, and tax rates have to be projected. As these forecasts stretch further out into the future, the potential for forecasting errors increases. Risk in this context is the probability that the asset will not produce the expected cash flows.

Financial Practice

Financial managers have created various tools to help them reach correct decisions and create optimal cash budgets. The mathematics of these tools will be covered in detail later in this book.

Discounted Cash Flow Analysis. One capital budgeting tool, discounted cash flow analysis, standardizes the asset evaluation process. The financial manager estimates the after-tax cash flows from each asset and the points in time when the firm can expect those cash flows. The manager then chooses a time value of money in the form of a discount rate. In theory, this rate is the company's required rate of return.

In practice, the company has to determine its required rate of return as part of the analysis. This determination can be made in any one of three ways, depending on company policy. If the company assumes that it already has the funds it needs and is looking for the best place to invest them, then the appropriate discount rate is the **opportunity cost** of those funds: the rate of return that the company could earn in its best alternative investment. If the company assumes that it will have to raise the funds, then the appropriate discount rate is its **marginal cost of capital**: the increase in the dollar cost of funds relative to the increase in the dollar amount of funds. If management has some target rate of return that it insists must be achieved to keep the stockholders satisfied or to compensate for risk, then the appropriate discount rate is this **required rate of return**.

opportunity cost

The rate of return that the company could earn in its best alternative investment.

marginal cost of capital

The increase in the dollar cost of funds relative to the increase in the dollar amount of funds.

required rate of return

The target rate of return that management insists must be achieved to keep stockholders satisfied or to compensate for risk.

The financial manager evaluates each asset by discounting its future after-tax cash flows back to the present and comparing the total discounted benefits to the initial cost. This comparison can be expressed as a net dollar amount, or **net present value** (NPV). It can also be expressed as a ratio called a **profitability index** (PI). Alternatively, it can be expressed as a rate of return. The **internal rate of return** (IRR) is the rate that equates the asset's total discounted benefits to its initial cost. An acceptable asset has a positive net present value, a profitability index greater than 1.0, and an internal rate of return greater than the discount rate. Chapter 10 explains the mechanics of these calculations in great detail.

net present value

The discounted future after-tax cash flows from an asset less its initial cost.

profitability index

The ratio of discounted future after-tax cash flows from an asset to its initial cost.

internal rate of return

The rate of return that equates the total discounted benefits of an asset to its initial cost.

If the discount rate has not already been adjusted to reflect an asset's risk, the financial manager's next step is to measure the risk of each proposed project. This requires estimation of the expected variation in each project's future after-tax cash flows (and possibly even in its initial cost). By a variety of statistical methods, the manager can then calculate the probability that each asset will be profitable.

Risk–Return Analysis. A second capital budgeting tool, risk–return analysis, is derived from the theory of portfolio management. To avoid an excessive digression into mathematics, consider Assets *J* through *P*, whose levels of risk and return have been calculated and are indicated on the graph in Exhibit 5.6. All seven assets are desirable, but assume that the company cannot afford to acquire more than three of them. Which assets should it choose?

Asset K produces the same return as Asset J, but has more risk. It is said to be *dominated* by J and can therefore be eliminated from further consideration. Asset M is just as risky as Asset P, but P has a better return. M is dominated by P and therefore M should be eliminated. Asset O has more risk than Asset P and produces less return. Therefore, P dominates O and O should be eliminated. (More generally, Asset K is dominated by J, L, M, N, and P; Asset M is dominated by L, N, and P; Asset O is dominated by both N and P.)

EXHIBIT 5.6

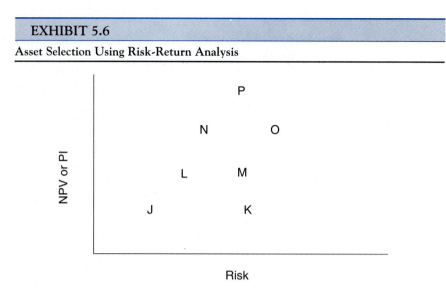

Asset Selection Using Risk-Return Analysis

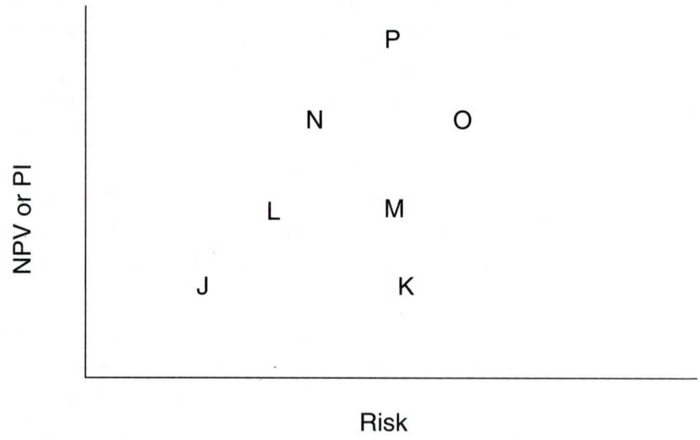

This process leaves Assets J, L, N, and P, none of which dominate the others. The financial manager must then determine if, for instance, the extra return provided by Asset N when compared to Asset L is worth the extra risk associated with N. Which three of the remaining four assets the firm will choose is determined by its risk aversion.

Obviously, the capital budget must be completed before the analyst can complete the *pro forma* financial statements and the cash budget. Since most large companies revise their capital budgets every six months or so, the other statements must also be revised at that time.

Proposals to acquire new assets can be generated within a company from the top down if planning is driven by a desire to meet managerial targets, from the bottom up if employee suggestions are encouraged, or from both directions at once. The size of the company is a major determinant of the routes that capital budgeting proposals take.

Capital Budget and Company Size

The capital budget has one characteristic in common with the three financial statements already considered: it is more complicated and time consuming for a larger company. A small company may view leasing a car for the CEO as a major decision. A multinational may obtain fleets of cars so routinely that guidelines may standardize the decision and authorization for a fleet purchase may require no more than the signature of a junior executive.

Small Companies. A smaller company evaluates fewer proposals for new assets or projects, but each individual proposal becomes more significant. One large new asset may represent a substantial proportion of firm's total capital, increasing the risk of default through the growing burden of debt, or appreciably diluting equity. A single purchase may represent the only new asset the company will be able to afford for years to come. The possibility that the proposed asset will not produce the expected cash inflows, or that it will require greater cash outflows than anticipated, is subject to prolonged deliberation. The firm carefully weighs advantages and disadvantages of alternative proposals, and no matter whether the proposal started as an employee suggestion or management's dream, the analysts spend an enormous amount of time and energy gathering and weighing information. A larger company may spend more time on capital budgeting, and may have one person or a whole department responsible for evaluating proposals, but the smallest companies devote the most attention to specific capital budgeting projects because a single project can make or break such a firm.

Large Domestic Companies. A multidivisional company typically has a two-stage capital budgeting process. Asset selection is done first by each budget unit, which evaluates all potential projects from the point of view of the unit's best interests. The unit then submits the list of desirable projects to company headquarters, to compete for funding with all of the submissions by other company units. After reviewing the cash flow projections and evaluating the underlying assumptions, the parent company approves some proposals, postpones others, and rejects the rest; then it prepares to finance the acceptable projects.

The parent can base its decision on at least three capital budgeting systems. The ideal system would accept any project with a rate of return greater than the company's marginal cost of capital. A long list of acceptable projects may, however, make the parent company unable or unwilling to raise sufficient capital at one time.

Some companies operate reward-and-punishment systems, allocating the largest blocks of funds to their most profitable budget units and rationing funds to their least profitable ones. The rationale for this system is that it is good policy to give the strongest support to those who can use company funds most efficiently. One practical consequence of using this system, however, is that it occasionally deprives a less profitable unit of the improvements it needs to enhance its performance.

Many companies ration funds in a different way. Recognizing that projects undertaken by various subsidiaries embody different degrees of risk, the parent company assigns different target discount rates to its various subsidiaries. A riskier subsidiary must apply a higher discount rate when evaluating proposals. This generally results in less risky subsidiaries submitting longer lists of acceptable projects to the parent company and risky subsidiaries submitting shorter lists.

Multinational Companies. A multinational's capital budgeting process may involve some degree of internal conflict. A proposal that appears to be a good investment to a foreign subsidiary may not increase the wealth of parent company shareholders. Occasionally, the reverse is true. A project may look good from the parent company's perspective, but may be seen as unprofitable by the subsidiary. The parent company's point of view almost always prevails.

FOCUS ON FINANCE

Partial Contents of a Capital McBudget

Corporate capital budgets are not published documents, but some of their contents become public knowledge because they issue press releases about new projects. During 1993, for example, the following news items about McDonald's appeared:

1. In February, the Israeli agriculture ministry announced that Kibbutz Saad would grow a strain of potatoes that McDonald's uses for its french fries. Since this strain cannot be legally imported from the United States and is not grown anywhere in Israel, McDonald's capital budget must include plans for its first franchise in Israel.
2. In March, reports were confirmed that a heavyweight hamburger, the 5.3 ounce Mickey-D, was being test marketed at several dozen restaurants in Illinois, Kentucky, Iowa, Missouri, and Tennessee. Since a Big Mac is only 3.2 ounces, McDonald's capital budget must include plans for equipment and/or packaging needed by this new product.
3. In October, the German government announced that, as a two-year experiment, McDonald's was replacing GermanRail's unprofitable catering service on the 120-m.p.h. train between Berchtesgaden and Hamburg. Hamburgers on the "McTrain" are slightly more expensive than those sold under stationary golden arches, and McDonald's capital budget must include plans for this new approach to selling really fast food.
4. In November, McDonald's announced that it had opened gas-station-based outlets with limited menus in Arkansas, Florida, Indiana, and Massachusetts. Its capital budget must include plans for further test marketing.
5. In December, McDonald's opened its first restaurant in Saudi Arabia. Prince Khaled bin Fahd Al-Faisal owns the franchise in Riyadh. McDonald's announced that a second restaurant in Riyadh and one in Jiddah would open in 1994.

Source: Newsday, various 1993 issues.

Conflicts in evaluations of a proposal can be caused by many factors. A foreign subsidiary may have more confidence in its forecasts of sales volume and revenue, future costs, and the longevity of the project than the parent does. If the subsidiary's managers cannot make a convincing case for their estimates, the project will never get beyond this evaluation stage.

If both parties agree on the projections, conflict may arise over the sources of funding for the project. The initial financing of a project may be raised locally, or the funds may be disbursed by the parent company. The impact of this financing choice may be regarded unfavorably by the multinational, even though the subsidiary evaluates the project as having a rate of return higher than its cost of capital.

Another possible conflict arises if the decision makers at headquarters view the project as having an adverse impact on future cash flows between parent and subsidiary. The project may reduce subsidiary-to-parent remittances or it may require future infusions of working capital from the parent. The subsidiary's management may view these changes in cash flow as passing requirements for increased future profitability; the parent may consider them totally unacceptable.

Finally, the project may indeed be profitable when its cash flows are evaluated in the local currency, but potential changes in host country cross-border currency restrictions, or in taxes on remittances of profits to the parent company, may make the project unprofitable from the multinational's perspective. Prospects for unfavorable changes in exchange rates may also make the project unattractive to the parent company.

Emergency Changes in Plans

Occasionally, unforeseen events make the results predicted by the *pro formas*, the cash budget, or the capital budget impossible to achieve. Natural or man-made disasters, major lawsuits, or sudden changes in technology or consumer demand are a few examples. To the extent that a company can anticipate some of these events, it is wise to prepare contingency plans. These are frequently referred to as "what if?" scenarios, and they give management the flexibility to prepare a defensive strategy.

SUMMARY

Together four financial statements help a company to create its financial plan: the *pro forma* balance sheet, *pro forma* income statement, cash budget, and capital budget. *Pro forma* financial statements project financial data into the future instead of reporting historical records. The amount of detail they contain expands with the size of the company. They can be prepared as either targets or forecasts.

A target *pro forma* balance sheet applies management's desired external or internal growth rate to the company's total assets, then calculates the various components of total assets and total capital that are necessary to reach the target. The short-term debt figure changes to balance the *pro forma* balance sheet. A *pro forma* balance sheet results from an extrapolation of past trends using any of several techniques, and the degree of statistical sophistication is at the discretion of the forecaster.

A target *pro forma* income statement starts with the level of net sales desired by management, deducts expected operating costs, distributes EBIT to creditors, units of government, and stockholders; retained earnings shows whatever is left. A *pro forma* income statement reflects the same forecasting methods that produced the *pro forma* balance sheet.

A small company does less work than a larger company when creating *pro forma* statements, but any significant errors in these projections may have serious consequences for the company. A large domestic company usually prepares *pro forma* statements for each subsidiary and consolidates them—with adjustments—to generate a set of statements for the parent company. A multinational must not only convert the currencies of its subsidiaries to the currency used by the parent, but it must also adjust its bookkeeping practices for international differences in tax laws and rates.

A cash budget projects a company's cash inflows and outflows over the coming months. A firm must plan to finance short-term cash deficits and invest short-term cash surpluses. The assumptions made in preparing the cash budget must be reconciled with those made in preparing the *pro forma* statements.

A small company prepares only one cash budget, revises it as necessary, and uses it as a standard against which to judge the company's actual performance. A large company usually uses subsidiaries' cash budgets as control tools as well as performance standards. Financing decisions are usually based on the parent company's consolidated cash budget. Multinationals can reduce some currency exchange costs by netting cash flows between their subsidiaries.

Capital budgeting requires the company to plan both the selection and financing of desirable long-term assets. Ideally, the company should acquire any asset whose rate of return exceeds the firm's cost of capital. In practice, a firm chooses assets from a list of independent projects, some of which may be mutually exclusive. The firm must evaluate the possibilities of postponing the purchase of an asset or abandoning an asset before the projected end of its useful life. A company may be unwilling or unable to finance every potentially profitable asset, so it must choose the combination of assets that will produce the greatest total wealth for its stockholders. Since not all assets last the same amount of time, the firm must also consider reinvestment rates at the end of assets' lives. Finally, the risk associated with the acquisition of an asset cannot be ignored. Discounted cash flow techniques standardize the asset evaluation process and risk–return analysis facilitates the asset selection process.

A small company may find only limited affordable opportunities to invest in profitable assets, but the selection of a new asset may have a significant impact on the health of the company. A large company requires budgeting units to submit lists of projects thay they expect to be profitable; the firm then chooses those projects that are most likely to give the best return to the parent company. Multinational companies often have to resolve conflicts when assets that appear beneficial to a foreign subsidiary do not appear beneficial from the parent company's viewpoint.

After preparing all four statements, a company may decide to construct a set of contingency statements, as part of a defensive strategy against possible unfavorable events.

Key Terms

abandonment problem
accrual basis
capital rationing problem
cash basis
competitive asset
complementary asset
external growth
independent asset
internal growth
internal rate of return
marginal cost of capital
minority interest
mutually exclusive asset
net present value
netting
opportunity cost
profitability index
pro forma statement
required rate of return
supplementary asset
transfer pricing policy

Self-Study Questions

1. What four financial statements help a company to create its financial plan?
2. Explain the differences among EBIT, EAIBT, and EAT.
3. Why can't a company simply add up all the components of its subsidiaries' balance sheets to get its own balance sheet?
4. What must a multinational corporation do before consolidating its financial statements?
5. Name two ways to prepare *pro forma* statements and explain why they are different.
6. What three bookkeeping changes might a multinational corporation make to compensate for international differences in tax rates?
7. What is a cash budget?
8. What options can a multidivisional domestic corporation choose for its short-term investment strategy?
9. What is a capital budget?
10. Name four ways a company can obtain the money to acquire long-term assets.

Self-Test Problems

1. A multinational corporation has the intracompany payments matrix below. Calculate the net payments matrix. How much currency must the corporation convert with and without netting?

Intracompany Payments Matrix (U.S. dollars)

Owed to the Subsidiary in	Owed by the Subsidiary in: Australia	United States	Brazil
Australia	—	$200,000	$600,000
United States	$900,000	—	$300,000
Brazil	$400,000	$500,000	—

2. A multinational corporation has the intracompany payments matrix below. If the appropriate exchange rates are FF6/US$, NZ$2/US$, and SF1.5/US$ for France, New Zealand, and Switzerland, respectively, calculate the net payments matrix. How much currency conversion would netting eliminate?

Intracompany Payments Matrix (seller's currency, 000)

Owed to the Subsidiary in	Owed by the Subsidiary in: France	New Zealand	Switzerland	United States
France	—	FF450	FF378	FF750
New Zealand	NZ$500	—	NZ$200	NZ$800
Switzerland	SF225	SF405	—	SF660
United States	US$330	US$90	US$860	—

3. A company has only $7 million to invest in new assets. If it requires an 8 percent return, which of the following assets should it choose? (All have the same life expectancy.)

ASSET	RATE OF RETURN	INITIAL COST	ANNUAL CASH FLOW
X	15%	$4 million	$600,000
Y	12	4 million	480,000
Z	10	2 million	200,000

Discussion Questions

1. Explain why stockholders, creditors, and managers find balance sheets and income statements useful.
2. Why would the creditors of a company be more interested in its EBIT than its EAT?
3. Intracompany, short-term loans do not show up on a consolidated balance sheet. Why not?
4. What does the minority interest component of a balance sheet tell a financial analyst?
5. What is the difference between external and internal growth?
6. Name five factors that influence the sizes of the components of a *pro forma* balance sheet for a company that is growing internally.
7. What advantages does a small company have compared to larger companies when preparing *pro forma* financial statements?
8. Why might a company prepare more than one version of its *pro forma* statements?
9. Describe the difference between accrual basis and cash basis accounting.
10. Projections made by small companies are usually conservative. Why?
11. A large company revises its cash budget on an ongoing basis; a small company only makes revisions as needed. Why?
12. Why might a multinational corporation set its transfer pricing policy to reduce the profits of one of its foreign subsidiaries?
13. Give three reasons why the sales figures on a firm's *pro forma* income statement will not match those on its cash budget without reconciliation.
14. What short-term borrowing options does a multidivisional company have?
15. What factors affect the desirability of an asset?
16. Illustrate the difference between independent and dependent projects with an example of each.
17. What is the abandonment problem?
18. What is the capital rationing problem?
19. A company has a marginal cost of capital of 10 percent and a choice between two machines. The first machine has a rate of return of 12 percent and is expected to last ten years. The second machine has a rate of return of

15 percent and is expected to last five years. What other information does the firm need to make a good decision?

20. Why might a foreign subsidiary consider an asset profitable when its parent does not?

Problems

1. The Worldwide Watch Company, headquartered in Delaware, has one subsidiary in Taiwan (exchange rate = T$25/US$) and another in India (exchange rate = R31/US$). With the following intracompany payments matrix, how much currency conversion could be eliminated by netting?

Intracompany Payments Matrix (seller's currency, 000)

OWED TO THE SUBSIDIARY IN	OWED BY THE SUBSIDIARY IN TAIWAN	INDIA	UNITED STATES
Taiwan	—	T$1,040,000	T$525,000
India	R465,000	—	R930,000
United States	$80,000	$100,000	—

2. A U.S. multinational corporation has subsidiaries in Ecuador, Haiti, and Venezuela. The exchange rates are:

   Es2,000/US$ for the Ecuadoran sucre

   Hg12/US$ for the Haitian gourde

   Vb125/US$ for the Venezuelan bolivar

   Given the intracompany payments matrix below, calculate the net payments matrix. How much currency conversion would netting eliminate?

Intracompany Payments Matrix (seller's currency)

OWED TO THE SUBSIDIARY IN	OWED BY THE SUBSIDIARY IN ECUADOR	HAITI	UNITED STATES	VENEZUELA
Ecuador	—	Es2,000,000	Es14,000,000	Es8,000,000
Haiti	Hg12,000	—	Hg108,000	Hg72,000
United States	$15,000	$10,000	—	$5,000
Venezuela	Vb750,000	Vb375,000	Vb1,125,000	—

3. A company has only $50 million to invest in new assets. If its required rate of return is 10 percent, which of the following assets should it choose? (All assets have the same life expectancy.)

ASSET	RATE OF RETURN	INITIAL COST	ANNUAL CASH FLOW
A	20%	$12 million	$4.0 million
B	20	7 million	2.3 million
C	18	10 million	3.2 million
D	15	8 million	2.4 million
E	14	9 million	2.6 million
F	12	11 million	3.1 million
G	12	6 million	1.7 million

Topics for Further Research

1. Obtain copies of the financial statements of three multinational corporations: one originating in the United States, one in Japan, and one in Europe. What differences and similarities are obvious?
2. Choose five well-known U.S. corporations. What proportion of the business of each (sales, profits, assets) comes from foreign operations?
3. Most successful companies grow internally, with occasional spurts of external growth. Choose one company in each of three different industries and review its history in Moody's *Manuals*. What conclusions can be drawn about these firms' growth?

Answers to Self-Test Problems

1.

Net Payments Matrix (U.S. dollars)

OWED TO THE SUBSIDIARY IN	OWED BY THE SUBSIDIARY IN AUSTRALIA	UNITED STATES	BRAZIL
Australia	—	0	$200,000
United States	$700,000	—	0
Brazil	0	$200,000	—

Without netting, $2,900,000 in currency must be converted; with netting, only $1,100,000 must be converted.

2.

Intracompany Payments Matrix (U.S. dollars, 000)

OWED TO THE SUBSIDIARY IN	OWED BY THE SUBSIDIARY IN FRANCE	NEW ZEALAND	SWITZERLAND	UNITED STATES
France	—	$75	$63	$125
New Zealand	$250	—	100	400
Switzerland	150	270	—	440
United States	330	90	860	—

Net Payments Matrix (in U.S. dollars, 000)

Owed to the Subsidiary in	Owed by the Subsidiary in: France	New Zealand	Switzerland	United States
France	—	$0	$0	$0
New Zealand	$175	—	0	310
Switzerland	87	170	—	0
United States	205	0	420	—

Without netting, $3,153,000 in currency must be converted; with netting, only $1,367,000 in currency must be converted. The conversion of $1,786,000 in currency is eliminated.

3. The company can afford to acquire only Z and either X or Y. It cannot afford to acquire both X and Y. The pair (X,Z) has a total annual cash flow of $800,000, and is better than the pair (Y,Z), which has a total annual cash flow of $680,000.

CHAPTER

6

Developing the Cash Budget

LEARNING OBJECTIVES

This chapter explains the mechanics of preparing a cash budget. At the conclusion of this chapter the reader should be able to:

1. *Predict the amount and timing of a company's cash inflows and outflows*
2. *Calculate a company's net cash flows*
3. *Set up a Lotus-type spreadsheet to do these calculations*
4. *Prepare a contingency cash budget*
5. *Choose securities appropriate to the company's short-term investment policy*
6. *Evaluate the various costs of borrowing short-term funds*

A cash budget is a detailed forecast of a company's expected cash inflows and outflows. It is usually prepared by the financial manager based on monthly projections for the forthcoming year. The net impact of these expected cash flows on the company's cash balance is critical.

If the budget projects a temporary cash surplus, the financial manager must formulate a short-term investment strategy, choosing among the various money market instruments' returns and maturities to balance risks against after-tax returns. If the budget projects a temporary cash deficit, the financial manager may be able to take steps to prevent it. If not, forewarning gives the manager time to shop around among various financial institutions to obtain funds on the most favorable terms.

PREPARING A CASH BUDGET

A firm's cash budget is not prepared like the annual report: written, polished, published, and forgotten once a year, every year. The cash budget is a living document, set up in a computer spreadsheet application and frequently revised and updated. The appendix at the end of the chapter illustrates the process of preparing a cash budget.

Cash Budgeting for Small Companies

A small company prepares one cash budget that covers its entire operation. It may, if circumstances warrant, prepare alternative contingency budgets.

The cash budget serves several purposes:

1. It highlights the uncertainties associated with various expected cash flows. This increases the flexibility with which management can react to events that make actual cash flows differ from expected cash flows. This minimizes the potential that the firm will have to cope with excess or insufficient liquidity.
2. It gives the financial manager time to analyze alternative short-term investment and borrowing strategies.
3. It improves working capital management by projecting the cash flow consequences of changes in inventory purchasing policies, credit extension policies, receivables collection policies, and so forth.
4. It enhances management's forecasting ability. Analysis of discrepancies between actual cash flows and budgeted cash flows can point out both inadequate performance and inaccurate forecasting assumptions.

Cash Budgeting for Large Domestic Companies

A large domestic company prepares a cash budget for each operating division and subsidiary. Units submit these subordinate budgets to company headquarters, where they are consolidated to develop an overall corporate cash budget. A diversified company can enhance financial efficiency by evaluating and reacting to the continuous flow of projections from each subsidiary or division to company headquarters. The feedback from top management to the operating units is also useful. Further, the consolidation process can offfset different cash flow patterns among the company's various operating centers which may help it to reduce reliance upon outside financing.

In most cases, the two-way information flows required to construct a cash budget will blend the ideas of the parent company with those of its subsidiaries and subdivisions. Management at company headquarters sets goals and objectives and sends them to the local units. Local managers make preliminary assumptions about sales and expenses and senior management reviews and approves these positions. Local managers prepare budgets based on these assumptions, and the unit budgets are consolidated at the next management level and passed upward to culminate in a total consolidated budget for the whole company. At each management level, the budget is reviewed to ensure consistency with the company's overall objectives.

Cash Budgeting for Multinationals

A large, multinational corporation is usually divided into profit centers either by major product type or by major operating function such as manufacturing, marketing, and distribution. Each center has its own administration; its own accounting, planning, and marketing departments; and its own employee relations staff. These profit centers are sometimes subdivided into local operating units with more detailed structures. If the operations of the multinational are widespread, its profit centers may be grouped by major geographical area such as European, North American, South American, Far Eastern, and African regions.

The company devises a budgeting process to suit its particular organizational structure. Functional units normally prepare budgets within each profit center because the budget serves as an important control tool. Most businesses follow some version of a two-way procedure: The parent company sets objectives and priorities and sends them to the local units. Budgets are built on assumptions formulated by the local units and approved by the parent company. The completed and approved budget helps management to compare actual results with projections. Substantial differences between the two may result in revised budgeting procedures, revised operating practices, or replacement of profit center managers.

Some special, challenging tasks complicate preparation of a cash budget for a multinational corporation. These tasks include:

reporting currency
The currency in which a multinational denominates its accounts.

1. Translating local currency revenues and costs into the multinational's **reporting currency** (the currency in which the parent company denominates its accounts) using forecasted exchange rates
2. Collecting the information required to prepare the budget (The more complicated nature of the multinational's business makes it more difficult to compile all relevant information.)
3. Managing the budgeting process (As the process spreads across more countries, it becomes more complicated.)
4. Reconciling differences between local accounting methods
5. Establishing a multinational cash mobilization system to aid multinational netting, short-term borrowing, and investment policies

The local budgets prepared for head office review and consolidation must be adjusted to conform to the parent company's accounting practices. Once the budget for a local unit is approved, it must be readjusted back into the local accounting system to aid in local control.

Forecasting Sales Internally

A single business unit can predict sales in two ways. It can base projections on the unit's planned selling activities or on a statistical extension of its past sales. Either way, the process requires a reality check to be sure that the predicted level of sales is feasible. Sustainable growth rate models perform this task.

Marketing Forecasts. The budgeting process starts with a monthly forecast of sales revenue. This forecast may be based on projections from the marketing department to reflect the company's planned advertising and other promotional activities, on a survey of the expectations of the company's salespeople, or on purchasing projections made by the company's customers. Both the nature of the business and past experience with different techniques guide this process.

Marketing projections require careful analysis from outside the marketing department. What assumptions do the projections reflect about product pricing, number of units sold, and share of the market? Are the sales predictions reasonable, given the recent history of the company, industry trends, and the expected state of the economy? Are the sales predictions feasible when compared to the company's production capacity? Are the sales projections compatible with management's goals for growth? Finally, how good is the marketing department's track record for accuracy of projections? How large have its forecasting errors been in the past? Have its forecasts consistently overestimated or underestimated actual results? Have forecasting errors been larger in some months or seasons and smaller in others? The whole point of these questions is to adjust the new forecasts to make them as accurate as possible.

The adjustment process still requires great care, however. As the original forecasts move through communications channels in a large company, almost everyone who sees the forecasts may feel obligated to make their own adjustments before forwarding the information. When these forecasts reach their final destination, any resemblance to the original numbers may be purely accidental.

Extrapolation Models. A firm can also forecast sales by using various statistical techniques. A business that has operated for several years can extrapolate sales figures by fitting a straight line or a curve to historical data, and then making subsequent adjustments for seasonal or cyclical variations. Such projections allow measurement of expected forecasting errors, as well.

A company may set a target growth rate, which may or may not correlate well with its historical growth rate. For an annual target, the annual increase in sales will be distributed among the cash budget figures for the months of the year according to historical seasonal patterns. A much more specific—and difficult—technique forecasts sales each month based on a target percentage or amount by which they should exceed the most recent actual sales for the same month. For example, management may target next January's sales to be 5 percent higher than this January's sales. This should fully accommodate future economic conditions, the company's competition, and its internal operations and it should reflect a strategy to produce the desired sales increase. The extra cash inflows and outflows implied by this strategy are presumed to have management's approval.

A large company may have sufficient personnel and computer time available to prepare both marketing forecasts and statistical forecasts. In such a case, an additional step should analyze any large differences between monthly sales predictions made by the two methods and attempt to resolve the discrepancies.

FOCUS ON FINANCE

Illustration of Extrapolation Models

The accompanying graphs illustrate four simple mathematical models. In Graph A, sales are increasing by a fairly constant dollar amount each month, so a straight line is fitted to the points representing monthly sales. This line is then extended to the right to predict sales. In Graph B, sales are growing by a constant percentage each month, so an exponential curve is fitted to historical sales and extended to the right. In Graph C, monthly sales have been growing, but at a decreasing rate, so a modified exponential curve is used. Management does not expect sales to reach Level *b*, but it does not expect sales to decline, either. In Graph D, monthly sales have reached their peak and are beginning to decline, so a polynomial curve is used. The mathematics involved in fitting extrapolation models to actual data and using them to make projections are generally developed in a marketing research course.

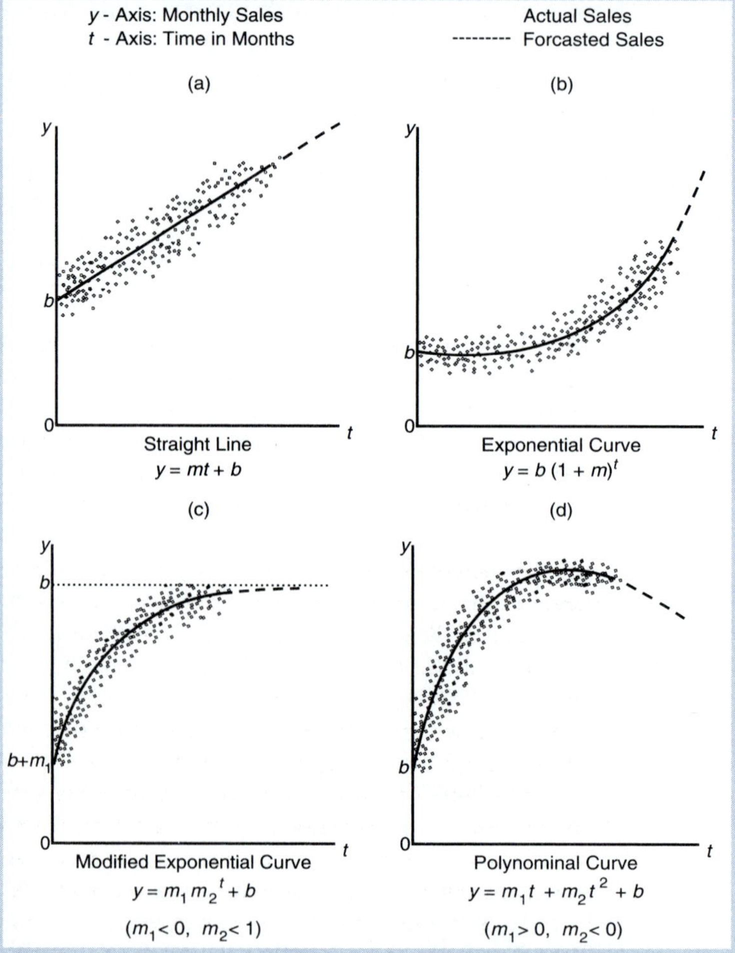

Sustainable Growth Rate Models. Sustainable growth rate models are mathematical equations that relate sales growth to selected variables such as operating efficiency, marketing and promotional resources, profitability, competition, the state of the economy, and/or the company's capital structure. Such models do not produce predictions of future sales; they help the analyst to check the feasibility of predictions made by other methods.

A sustainable growth rate model could calculate the maximum growth rate of sales that a company could expect based on an equation that encompassed all operating aspects of the company—finance, marketing, management, economic conditions, and so forth. Such a model usually does not contain an all-inclusive selection of company variables because it does not predict how much sales *will* grow. The model usually includes a selection of financial variables or marketing variables because it attempts to determine the *upper limit* of sales growth, given the results of a set of financial decisions or marketing decisions.

One sustainable growth rate model based on the financial characteristics of a company is given by the following equation:

$$SGR = \frac{(m)(P/S)[1 + (D/E)]}{(A/S) - (m)(P/S)[1 + (D/E)]} \qquad \textbf{(6.1)}$$

where: SGR = sustainable growth rate

m = earnings retention ratio

S = sales

A = total assets

P = net profit after taxes

D = total debt

E = total equity

A/S measures the company's asset use efficiency.

D/E measures the company's capital structure.

P/S measures the company's profitability.

SGR indicates the maximum growth rate of sales that the company can support, given the levels of the financial variables in the equation. It is not necessarily the growth rate that the company can achieve, because the equation ignores both selling efforts and the availability of buyers, as well as expected economic conditions and management decisions.

For example, if a company's management decides to make a major effort to increase asset efficiency, it can try new procedures that may:

1. Produce more sales by making better use of existing assets
2. Maintain the existing sales level while reducing assets
3. Make sales increase faster than assets increase

Any one of these decisions may raise the upper limit and allow the company's sales to grow more quickly. Without such changes, if the company's forecasting technique predicts that sales will grow at a rate higher than the SGR, the prediction must be adjusted downward.

Equation 6.1 emphasizes the following relationships:

1. If m increases, then SGR increases. As the company retains a larger percentage of its earnings (or, conversely, pays out a smaller percentage of its earnings as dividends), it can grow more quickly.
2. If P and/or P/S increase, then SGR increases. As the company becomes more profitable and generates more internal funds, it can grow more quickly.
3. If D/E increases, then SGR increases. As the company increases the proportion of debt in its capital structure, it can grow more quickly.
4. If A/S decreases, then SGR increases. As the company uses its assets more efficiently to produce sales, it can grow more quickly.

❖ EXAMPLE 6.1

Suppose that a company retains half of its earnings and its profit rate is 5 percent. It is a high technology company, so it needs $1 in assets to generate $1 in sales. If its capital structure is 60 percent debt, then its sustainable growth rate is:

$$\text{SGR} = \frac{(0.5)(0.05)(1 + 0.6)}{(1/1) - (0.5)(0.05)(1+0.6)} = 0.0417 \text{ or } 4.17 \text{ percent}$$

Changing one variable at a time, as in the four suggestions above, may boost the sustainable growth rate above 4.17 percent. For instance:

1. If m increases to 60 percent, the SGR increases to 5.04 percent
2. If P/S increases to 6 percent, the SGR increases to 5.04 percent
3. If D/E increases to 70 percent, the SGR increases to 4.36 percent
4. If A/S decreases to $1/$1.10, the SGR increases to 4.60 percent. ❖

Forecasting Sales Externally

As an alternative to internal forecasting, a firm may follow a top-down procedure. The forecaster starts with predictions about the state of the economy, builds in factors that affect the firm's industry, estimates the company's share of the market, calculates annual sales, and then breaks down the annual figure into a monthly sales pattern.

A very large corporation may employ professional economists who make their own predictions about the state of the economy, but most companies purchase macroeconomic predictions from research or financial institutions. Company personnel may modify this information to reflect their perceptions of the track records of forecasters, or they may accept outside forecasts without change. A firm may purchase updates or complete them in-house.

The overall reaction of an industry to different stages of the economic cycle—growth, prosperity, recession, or stagnation—becomes the next concern of the forecaster. This analysis must also account for legal, environmental, technological, and international changes that affect the demand for and/or pricing of the industry's output.

Next, the forecaster adjusts for the expected strength of competing companies in the industry, the company's plans to counter competitive forces, and special circumstances that affect the specific company. The company's future market share depends on brand loyalty, promotional efforts, legal actions, planned introductions of new products, services, pricing strategies, credit-granting standards, terms of trade, and/or efficiency-enhancing projects. The forecast should also reflect any plans to expand the company's production or add to its facilities. It must also consider plans for external growth by acquisition of other companies or subdivisions of other companies.

The forecaster faces the most difficult challenge in the attempt to predict cash flows associated with diversification into new product lines, new services, new markets (domestic or foreign), or even into new industries. These are usually first-time forecasts, and the company has no historical data on which to base its estimates. The process may depend on information from outside sources of questionable reliability. This portion of a cash budget may be pure guesswork, so a conservative company will prepare two budgets: one based on a most-likely scenario and the other based on a worst-case scenario. Some companies employ statistical techniques to prepare best case, normal case, and worst case sales forecasts, and then assign a subjective probability to each case. This enables the analyst to calculate the expected sales value and base the budget on this calculation.

After forecasting total sales for the period, the analyst can use statistical methods to distribute that total over coming months. Seasonal peaks and valleys can be built into the budget in many ways. Further, the accuracy of past sales forecasts should be reviewed to detect and correct any consistent prediction errors.

A company may prepare both internal and external forecasts, and then attempt to reconcile the two sets of numbers. This task may prove to be easy, hard, or impossible. Still, the attempt will highlight inconsistencies in assumptions and differences in goals, expectations, and information.

BUDGETING CASH FLOWS

A typical company's principal source of cash inflows is payments by customers for goods and services purchased. Still, the cash budget cannot ignore other cash-producing activities. The firm may have small, repetitive inflows caused by business sidelines such as rental of surplus storage space, or it may have large, occasional inflows caused by significant activities like issuing stock or bonds.

The cash budget must also include every part of a company's day-to-day operations that results in a cash outflow. The forecaster must know the timing and amounts of these cash outflows to ensure that the company can meet its obligations. Even if only a handful of the thousands (or millions) of checks a company writes each year bounce, the company's credit rating will suffer, its borrowing

FOCUS ON FINANCE

AN UNANTICIPATED CASH FLOW: CITICORP

Citicorp, the holding company that owns Citibank, miscalculated the unit value (share price) of a balanced investment fund it started in 1985. The error caused the company to overstate returns on the bank's Savings Incentive Plan. When Citicorp acknowledged the error at the end of June 1993, it amounted to $70 million and affected over 8,000 of the bank's employees and retirees. Citicorp did not ask employees who had withdrawn funds from their overstated accounts to return the excess amounts. Instead, it made a voluntary contribution of $30 million to the plan and adjusted the balances of the participants downward.

Source: *Newday*, July 1, 1993.

costs will escalate, its ability to borrow may be impaired, and its profit margin will decline.

Cash Inflows from Sales

After completing a total sales revenue estimate for each period in the budget, the company must predict when the cash proceeds from those sales will become available. If it makes some sales on cash terms, the money will be available immediately.

Retail Credit Sales. If retail customers pay with credit cards, the timing of the cash inflows depends on whether the company issues its own credit card or accepts bank cards such as Visa and MasterCard. The terms of a company's credit card agreement dictate the expected payment schedule; most bank cards reimburse sales proceeds (less service charges) quickly.

Corporate Credit Sales. Cash inflows from sales on credit to other companies generally depend on the terms of trade the company offers. For example, terms of net 30 allow customers to take 30 days to pay. Terms of 2/10, net 30 allow customers to choose between paying in 10 days and deducting 2 percent of the amount on the invoice, or paying the invoice in full in 30 days. The proportions of customers who make 10-day payments and those who make 30-day payments vary seasonally and with the business cycle, and must be projected carefully.

Some percentage of sales revenue will always take longer to turn into cash in hand because the customers take more than the indicated time to pay, or make errors in the paperwork involved in payment. Errors may be accidental or deliberate. Deliberate errors include tricks like sending unsigned checks or mailing checks in the wrong envelopes, which give a dishonest customer a few extra days to get money into the bank to cover the checks, while giving the appearance of payment made in good faith. Obviously, repetition of these tricks will destroy the customer's credit rating.

FOCUS ON FINANCE

MACY'S NEVER-PAY-IN-FULL POLICY

When a store sells large quantities of merchandise, a small percentage of the items it purchases are normally found to be defective. The store customarily pays the manufacturer 100 percent of the amount billed, then sorts out the defective items and returns them to the manufacturer with a request for an appropriate refund.

Macy's decided many years ago that this custom tied up too much cash. The retailer carefully calculated the average percentage of defective merchandise shipped by its suppliers, and, as a matter of policy, simply assumed that each new shipment contained this average. It therefore paid its suppliers the amount billed *less* the anticipated refund for this average percentage of defectives. When the actual defectives were counted, Macy's would request a much smaller refund or make a supplemental payment, depending on the discrepancy between the expected and actual defects. Any supplier who objected to this practice would no longer sell to Macy's.

The availability of spendable cash from customer payments depends on how long it takes the company to process its customers' checks and deposit them. The time required for the banking system to clear the checks has an effect, as well.

Bad Debts. A small percentage of sales never turns into cash because customers get into financial difficulty after making their purchases and cannot pay for them. Long delays and complete failure to pay are directly influenced by the credit-granting standards and collection policies of the seller. Low standards and lax policies tend to increase delayed payments and failures to pay, slowing down cash inflows.

Seasonal and cyclical effects may also cause changes in these percentages; at some times during the year (for example, around tax-due dates) customers are traditionally strapped for cash and they may postpone payment for a few days or weeks. In certain industries with many, small customers, some periods during the economic cycle may induce terminal financial difficulties for some customers and leave them unable to pay their suppliers at all.

A specific company may turn over unpaid accounts receivable to its own collection department or a commercial collection agency. This action may take place when payment is 90 days overdue or six months overdue, or whenever management decides that too much time has passed. A collection agency typically collects about half of the outstanding amount of debt (less during a recession) and it keeps a significant percentage of what it collects as compensation for this service. Still, the cash budget should report whatever amount the company expects to receive, in the month that the company expects to receive it.

Other Cash Inflows

The cash budget must include all cash inflows in their appropriate time periods. It must account for rents on property the company owns, royalty payments, refunds from suppliers and tax authorities, income from investments, and all other non-sales revenues. If the company plans to raise funds by selling securities such as notes, stocks, or bonds, the proceeds from the new issues must appear in the cash budget. If the company plans to sell any of its assets, the analyst most forecast the net cash inflows from these sales and include them in the cash budget.

Even nonrecurring items, such as judgments that the firm may win in lawsuits, should be included. If such nonrecurring items are substantial, the firm may need to prepare two cash budgets: an optimistic budget that assumes that the company wins the lawsuit, and a pessimistic budget that assumes a loss in court. Further, when the court reaches a decision, the company must be ready to create alternative versions of the appropriate cash budget. No lawsuit loser ever pays the initial judgment of the court; its lawyers always negotiate a smaller settlement. If a company cannot negotiate a satisfactory reduction, it may file for protection from the claim under the bankruptcy laws. The cash budget must reflect these uncertainties.

Cash Outflows

The cash budget must attempt to predict the amount and timing of every expenditure of cash by a company in careful detail. This is not the same as recording expenses on the company's income statement. For example, expenses that do not generate cash outflows do not appear in the cash budget. It does not report depreciation and amortization charges or write-offs of the values of worthless assets.

Materials Purchases. Company policy and business practices in the firm's industry dictate whether the firm purchases raw materials and component parts in accordance with planned production cycles or in anticipation of sales. However it schedules purchases, it must estimate payments for them during the preparation of the cash budget. The timing of the actual payments, less any discounts the firm will take, is probably the most difficult part of the estimation process, and historical patterns provide invaluable guidance.

If cash is tight or credit is too expensive, a firm may attempt to ease the situation by stretching the payments, that is, paying after the 30th day if the terms are net 30. The potential gain from stretching due dates is determined by the strictness of the seller who sets the terms; the buyer does not gain any advantage from delaying payment and earning a reputation as a late payer. In fact, such a reputation may cause many suppliers to insist on terms of cash on delivery (COD) or payment in advance—cash before delivery (CBD).

Payments for Labor. For convenience, a textbook illustration of a cash budget may show one line in the cash outflow section labeled "Wages and Salaries," or some equivalent phrase. In a budget for any real business larger than a mom-and-pop operation, there are many budget lines devoted to labor costs. Top management traditionally receives equal monthly payments plus occasional (or annual) bonuses, which may or may not be based on the company's profit performance. Middle managers may receive paychecks biweekly. Clerical workers usually receive constant weekly amounts, possibly supplemented by overtime, while laborers' pay may depend on the production schedule. The firm may contract the services of uniformed workers (such as security forces and janitorial staff) from other companies for a basic monthly charge plus extra help as needed. It may pay consultants on a project-related basis. Since forecasting errors will vary with the type of employee, it is usually prudent to budget each type on a separate line.

In addition to payroll outflows, the labor cost portion of the cash budget must forecast all additional expenses associated with labor. These include taxes such as Social Security taxes; federal, state, and local income taxes withheld; workers' compensation insurance premiums; and unemployment insurance premiums. The cash budget must also include the cash outflows necessary to pay for fringe benefits such as health and life insurance, pension fund contributions, day care, and so forth. Most of these expenses are constant percentages of wages and can be aggregated using so-called *wrap rates* that incorporate them into the direct salary forecast.

The cash budget must estimate irregular labor cost outflows such as tuition reimbursements, training costs, pay raises, vacation pay, and severance pay. Occasional discontinuities in pay schedules caused by negotiations for new contracts for union workers may require the firm to prepare more than one budget. The range of possibilities may include an optimistic budget that assumes settlement in the company's favor, a pessimistic one that assumes settlement in the union's favor with or without a strike, and a compromise budget built on the most likely settlement in between.

Utilities. The forecaster can predict cash outflows for oil, gas, electric, water, waste disposal, telephone, and some computer information services with minimal difficulty, but these figures are subject to major errors when unanticipated changes in technology, politics, taxes, or international relations occur. The sudden availability and popularity of 900 telephone numbers is a case in point. Until access to such numbers could be restricted, outflows for corporate telephone bills suddenly drastically exceeded the amounts budgeted.

Asset Purchases. A company's capital budgeters determine whether or not to purchase new assets. Once they decide to purchase, however, the cash budget must include all cash outflows that the purchases require. Financial managers who prepare the cash budget cannot override capital budgeting decisions, but in well-structured companies they can advise manangement on timing the asset purchases to minimize the cost of borrowing or the loss of investment returns.

Redemption of Securities. Previously issued notes and bonds eventually reach maturity and investors demand cash payment. The firm may simply replace these securities with equivalent amounts of new ones, or management may decide to borrow more or less than the original amount. This decision is based on both prevailing interest rates and the availability of cash.

A debt issue may have a mandatory sinking fund, which means that the company must pay off a part of the debt each year, on the anniversary date of the security's issue. Failure to make these payments can result in bankruptcy.

The firm need not plan to pay off outstanding preferred and common stock because they have no maturity dates. Companies occasionally choose to repurchase some of their outstanding stock, however, for many reasons:

1. The current market price may be too low.
2. Too much stock may be outstanding when the company cannot make profitable use of all of its current funds.
3. The firm may hold the stock for future distribution to satisfy management's or employees' stock option plans.
4. The company's own stock may be a desirable investment for the company's pension plan.
5. The firm may offer its stock in exchange for another company's stock when attempting a takeover.
6. The company may wish to buy out certain shareholders who have become nuisances.
7. The company may choose to distribute capital gain income rather than dividend income.
8. The company may decide to effect a large change in its capital structure without taking on more debt.
9. The company may want to distribute extra one-time income to investors.

The cash budget must reflect any plans to repurchase or pay off outstanding securities. Such a payment is an outflow; if the firm must raise new capital to make the payment, the new capital will appear as a cash inflow.

Investments and Acquisitions. A company's top management may decide to purchase real property, securities, other companies, or divisions of other companies, anticipating a very favorable impact on the company's profits. The cash outflow required for such purchases must appear in the cash budget for the appropriate time period.

Interest and Dividend Payments. The cash budget must show semiannual interest payments on the company's outstanding notes and bonds, and quarterly dividend payments on the company's outstanding preferred and common stock. This portion of the cash budget does not, however, show interest payments on short-term borrowings that the firm arranges in response to the completed cash budget.

Taxes. A corporation is subject to the tax laws of government jurisdictions in which it operates. In the United States, the federal government levies an income tax on corporate profits, which the firm must estimate and pay quarterly (on

March 15, June 15, September 15, and December 15) and reconcile with actual earnings annually. The impact of the reconciliation depends upon the fiscal year under which the company has chosen to operate.

State and local governments also impose taxes on corporate profits; estimation and payment rules generally coincide with federal regulations. In addition, corporations may be required by state and local governments to pay semiannual property taxes, annual franchise taxes, and/or monthly sales taxes.

Foreign governments may tax the profits, remittances of interest and dividends, property, sales, or value added of a company's foreign operations. The regulations and timing of tax payments vary by country. The firm can usually claim the amount of foreign income taxes it pays as a credit against U.S. federal income taxes it owes.

Nonrecurring Items. In a manner similar to the estimation of cash inflows, a company can anticipate nonroutine cash outflows which may or may not materialize. Involvement in a lawsuit with an uncertain outcome may require the firm to prepare alternative cash budgets for win/lose situations, as explained before.

Miscellaneous Outflows. The cash outflow estimates enumerated thus far are common to all going concerns. No business can run without labor and materials costs, capital expenditures, and tax payments, but individual companies or companies in specific industries may face unique cash outflows. Research and development costs are disproportionately large in the drug and aerospace industries. Exploration costs are important in the extractive (oil and mining) industries. Reforestation costs are unique to the lumber/paper industry. Public utilities with nuclear facilities pay exceptionally heavy regulatory compliance costs. Companies that do business in foreign countries may choose to pay disguised or blatant bribery payments and political contributions. The cash budget must include every cash outflow, whether or not it is unique to the company, or even legal in the United States. The budget is an internal management tool, not an audited external report, although company records are subject to subpoena by the U.S. Justice Department. Internal documents must, therefore, carefully disguise foreign payments that might be considered bribes and kickbacks. The only way to avoid this ethical dilemma may be to forego expansion into areas of the world where people expect such practices.

Calculating Net Cash Flows and Cash Balances

After estimating all cash outflows, the forecaster calculates their monthly totals, and subtracts them from total monthly cash inflows to get a monthly net cash flow. There is no reason to expect that every month will show a positive net cash flow. Every business hopes, however, that some months will show positive net cash flows.

Whether the process leads to surplus or deficit, the company's cash position is calculated by taking the company's cash on hand at the start of the period, and accumulating the cash flows it expects over time. In determining how much cash a firm can invest or how much it must borrow, the preparer of a cash budget cannot start with the presumption of zero cash. Top management determines how much cash the company should plan to have on hand throughout the budgeting period. This **minimum cash balance** serves several purposes at once.

minimum cash balance
The amount of cash the company should plan to have on hand throughout the budgeting period.

First, it is a cushion against forecasting errors. The size of this cushion is determined by comparing past cash budgets to actual company cash flows. If the monthly differences show very little fluctuation, the company may simply require a cash cushion equal to the average size of the error. If the error varies a lot from month to month, the changes may exhibit some seasonal pattern that the company can apply to find an appropriate minimum cash balance.

The minimum cash balance also allows for cash deficits within budget periods. A cash budget could predict, for example, that a company will have a net cash inflow of $2 million in March. This means that it will have $2 million more in cash at the end of March than it had at the end of February. This projection gives no guarantee, however, that these cash flows will be evenly distributed throughout March. Some companies increase their minimum cash balances to cover invisible cash deficits that might occur within the month. Others solve the problem by preparing, and constantly updating, daily cash budgets for the coming week, weekly cash budgets for the coming month, and monthly cash budgets for the rest of the coming year.

Finally, the minimum cash balance acknowledges that even with today's technology, a company cannot operate without some cash on hand. The firm still needs a petty cash box when vending machines don't work and the employees want reimbursement, when the boss leaves home without a wallet, when someone needs supplies for an office party, when somebody has to take a taxi, when deliverypersons have to be tipped, when bail money is needed, and so forth.

SELECTING SHORT-TERM INVESTMENTS

When a company expects cash on hand to exceed its minimum balance, it should plan to invest the surplus. Chapter 4 discussed the many types of money and capital market securities available. The selection of securities for short-term investment takes into account risk, return, and diversification issues.

Risk

The company must first define an acceptable level of risk for its short-term investments. The board of directors usually establishes a policy that states how much risk is acceptable, but this leaves a financial manager with a great deal of latitude in determining how much risk to take.

The firm can avoid the risk of default completely by investing only in U.S. Treasury securities. This strategy generates a minimal rate of return because, for any given maturity, the yields on Treasury securities are the lowest taxable rates in the United States.

Most corporations avoid unacceptable levels of illiquidity risk by carefully selecting securities. They do not invest their temporary surplus cash in municipal securities or in small federal agency issues. They also avoid other types of securities that are thinly traded.

To the extent that inflation risk cannot be avoided, it is generally ignored. It adds to a financial manager's incentive to seek higher rates of return, but it usually has no bearing on the specific choice of securities.

Choosing securities with unacceptably high levels of market risk can lead directly to the unemployment of the financial manager. This keeps most temporary corporate cash out of the stock market, the corporate bond market, the options market, and most commodities futures contracts. However, if a company is familiar with the price behavior of a specific commodity because it constitutes some portion of the firm's inventory, the financial manager may hold futures contracts in that commodity as short-term investments. A soft drink company, for instance, might trade futures contracts in sugar and orange juice concentrate, but it would avoid precious metals contracts. Companies with subsidiaries in the major industrial nations might invest in currency futures contracts, but a small domestic company would not.

Selection of securities with appropriate maturities can minimize a company's exposure to interest rate risk. Exhibit 6.1 illustrates a hypothetical company's pattern of temporary cash surpluses, based on the following data from its cash budget:

MONTH	NET CASH FLOW ($000)	ACCUMULATED CASH SURPLUS ($000)
April	$ 0	$ 0
May	1,200	1,200
June	600	1,800
July	300	2,100
August	1,000	3,100
September	–2,500	1,600
October	–600	1,000
November	–1,000	0
December	0	0
January	500	500
February	0	500
March	–500	0

If the company expects interest rates to rise while it holds short-term securities, it must expect the market prices of these securities to fall. To avoid these losses, it should choose securities that will mature when it expects to need the money.

Of the $1.2 million cash inflow in May, the company can invest $1 million knowing that it will not have to liquidate the investment until November. Therefore, it can invest this money in securities that mature in about 180 days. If it needs the money a few days before maturity, the securities will have market prices very close to their face (or maturity) values, and the company will lose little by selling them before maturity. If the money will still be available a few days after the

EXHIBIT 6.1

Accumulated Cash Surplus

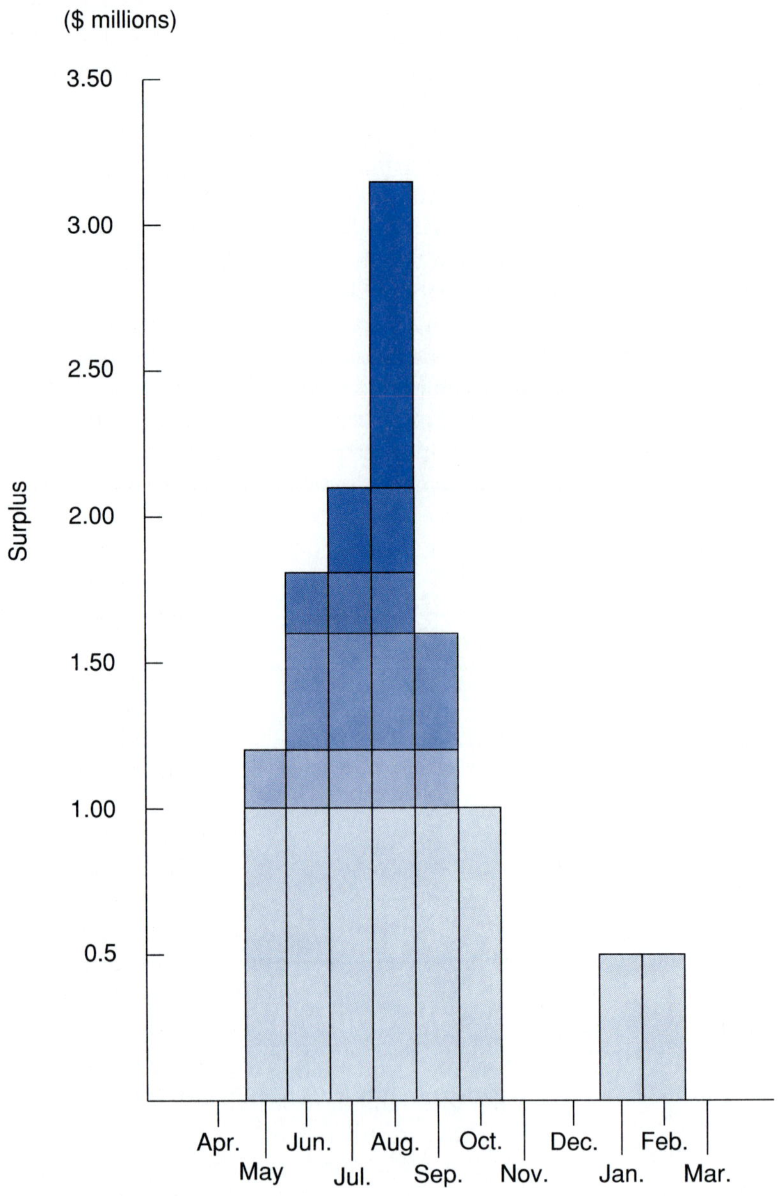

EXHIBIT 6.2

Investment Plan

MONTH OF INFLOW	AMOUNT ($000)	DAYS TO MATURITY
May	$1,000	180
May	200	150
June	400	120
June	200	90
July	300	60
August	1,000	30
January	500	60

securities mature, the firm can be reinvest it in T-bills or repurchase agreements, a choice that it can evaluate at that time.

The firm can invest the remaining $200,000 of the May cash inflow in securities that will mature in about 150 days, since it will need these funds to meet part of the $600,000 liquidation in October.

Following the same logic, the firm can invest the amounts listed in Exhibit 6.2 for the appropriate periods of time. It must remembered, however, that this plan is based on uncertain forecasts. The plan is subject to change as emerging information causes the financial manager to revise expectations. Treating this investment strategy as if it were engraved on stone tablets could be ruinous.

At first glance, a policy of investing only in securities that mature in 30 days may seem appealing. The company would receive full face value and could reinvest at the new, higher rate each month. Two additional factors affect the analysis, however.

First, by repeatedly reinvesting, the company would have to buy a total of $10.8 million in securities, and it would pay commissions on that total. Investing each amount once—as it comes in—and holding the purchased securities to their various maturities would involve buying only $3.6 million in securities and paying commissions on this smaller total.

Second, the original investment strategy suits the normal, upward sloping market yield curve. By investing for the longest maturity possible, the investor gets the highest yield available at the time.

If interest rates are expected to decline while the company is holding short-term securities, the market prices of these securities will rise. To maximize these gains, the following principles should guide the choice of securities: (1) The longer the time period until a security matures, the greater the change in market price in response to a change in interest rates. (2) The higher the face rate on a security, the greater the change in market price in response to a change in interest rates. Therefore, if interest rates are expected to fall, the hypothetical company in Exhibit 6.1 should invest the $1.2, $0.6, $0.3, $1.0, and $0.5 million cash inflows in the longest-lasting, highest-coupon securities it can find.

EXHIBIT 6.3

Yields on 30-Day Securities

	3/29/94	3/29/92	3/29/90
Treasury bills	3.36%	4.04%	8.10%
Treasury bonds	3.04	3.06	7.39
Fannie Mae	2.98	3.38	6.01
Freddie Mac	2.25	2.79	6.37
Sallie Mae	3.20	3.30	7.83
Certificates of deposit	2.96	3.71	7.76
Bankers' acceptances	3.57	4.16	8.28
Commercial (dealer) paper	3.67	4.25	8.35
Eurodollars	3.63	4.25	8.63

Source: "Money Rates," "Treasury Bonds, Notes & Bills," and "Government Agency & Similar Issues," *The Wall Street Journal*, various issues.

Return

Because financial managers generally try to minimize risk first and maximize return second when selecting short-term investments, most companies restrict their lists of acceptable money market instruments to Treasury securities, three or four federal agency securities, certificates of deposit, bankers' acceptances, commercial paper, repurchase agreements, and Eurodollars.

Exhibit 6.3 illustrates that the yields on these six types of securities vary only by fractions of percent, and they have maintained this relationship for years. A difference of ¼ percent (0.25 percent) on $1 million invested for 30 days is $208.33 in interest before taxes. The interest on all of the securities listed in Exhibit 6.3 is subject to federal corporate income tax in the United States. The interest on the Treasury securities is free of state and local income taxes in most states, which enhances their attractiveness to companies headquartered in high-tax states. Still, corporations tend to invest much more than $1 million in money market instruments. Since the invested sums can be so large, anything the financial manager can do to increase the company's investment returns is significant. Buying new issues of securities eliminates the need to pay commissions. Buying Treasury tax anticipations bills (and sometimes municipal tax anticipation notes) produces a few days' extra interest.

Diversification

U.S. money market rates show a very close correlation, so when interest rates on Treasury securities rise (or fall), the rates on other money market instruments rise (or fall) proportionately. Therefore, financial managers are constantly tempted to seek investments outside the United States, where they can usually find securities with much higher yields, and rates that move on different cycles than U.S. Treasury rates. This international diversification, however, adds foreign exchange rate risk to a company's short-term portfolio.

For many years, firms found Canadian Treasury bills to be attractive at peaks in U.S. interest rates, because the Canadian business cycle tends to follow the U.S. business cycle with approximately a six-month time lag. This strategy entails accepting a degree of foreign exchange risk because of the fluctuations in the exchange rate between the U.S. and Canadian dollars. Until the separatist movement in Quebec became internationally recognized, U.S. investors considered Canada to be without country risk.

On the whole, financial managers are conservative investors. Most view foreign opportunities to earn spectacular returns with great suspicion; they opt instead for foreign securities whose returns are countercyclical to those available in the United States.

SHORT-TERM BORROWING

A company can cover a short-term cash deficit by borrowing from a financial institution, from another corporation, or from the public. These loans may be secured by some of the borrower's assets, or unsecured. When a lender makes a loan without any company assets pledged as collateral, the loan is based on the lender's faith in the borrower's ability to earn a profit and repay the loan.

Unsecured Loans

Commercial banks are the primary sources of short-term loans for most corporations. Banks make unsecured loans of two kinds: credit lines and revolving credit agreements. They can also assist a company when it issues commercial paper.

Credit Lines. When a bank opens a credit line for a corporation, it fixes the maximum amount a company can borrow during a future time period, usually one year. The bank bases this amount on its perception of the company's cash needs as projected in its cash budget and *pro formas*, and on the company's expected ability to generate an adequate cash flow to repay the loan, plus interest. The variable interest rate on a credit line is usually defined as some published money market rate (frequently, the prime rate or the one-year T-bill rate) plus X percent. The size of X depends on the creditworthiness of the borrower and how anxiously the bank wants to make loans. The bank charges interest only on the amount the company actually borrows. Almost all credit lines require the borrower to clean up the line (i.e., to pay it off completely) at least 1 month out of 12. For most companies, the clean-up clause is not a problem; they simply obtain credit lines from more than one bank.

The bank sees a credit line as a commitment to deposit money into a company's checking account immediately upon request, up to the preset limit. This commitment can be reduced, however, when economic conditions deteriorate. When the supply of loanable funds gets tight, banks respond by cutting back the credit lines they have extended.

FOCUS ON CAREERS

CASH MANAGER

The cash manager oversees the flow of cash and financial assets and develops information to assess the present and future cash positions of the firm. Specifically, the cash manager is responsible for the quality of the cash budget, the credit arrangements negotiated with banks, and the management of the company's portfolio of money market instruments.

Generally the cash manager reports to the corporate controller who in turn reports to the CFO. One or more junior executives report to the cash manager. They are responsible for analyzing lock box operations, bank relationships, and money market opportunities. Other junior executives interface with the company's various domestic and foreign subsidiaries and subdivisions, implementing the CFO's financial policies and the cash manager's operating strategies. This management team has appropriate support staff, the size of which varies based on the frequency of cash budget updating and the number of local cash budgets to be consolidated into the parent company's budget.

A bachelor's degree in accounting or finance is the minimum level of education necessary for a cash manager. Three to five years experience in the junior management ranks is also expected. This middle management position usually commands a salary of $40,000 to $60,000, depending upon the level of responsibility, the number of departmental employees, and the size of the corporation.

Revolving Credit Agreements. If a corporation wants a guarantee that a specific amount of funds will be available when needed, it obtains a revolving credit agreement from a bank. To ensure that it can provide the money when the company needs it, the bank invests the agreed-upon amount in T-bills, which it can liquidate on demand. To compensate the bank for tying up funds in this low-yielding money market security, the company pays both interest on whatever it borrows and a commitment fee on the unborrowed balance. The variable interest rate is tied to the prime rate or the one-year Treasury rate. The commitment fee is a fixed percentage per month. In the 1990s, some banks began to institute policies of charging commitment fees on the entire amounts specified in revolving credit agreements. Revolving credit agreements can be written for terms of up to 18 months, and do not require clean-up periods.

Direct Loans. If a company requires financing for a specific project for a known duration (six months, two years, or whatever), it can arrange a direct loan from a bank. It may repay this loan in monthly installments or all at once at maturity. Interest charges are calculated on the outstanding balance of the loan, not on the original amount borrowed. If the loan is repaid in installments, it is said to be an **amortized loan**. If the loan stretches over more than a year, the bank may require the borrower to pledge some asset as security.

amortized loan
A loan repaid in monthly installments. The interest is calculated on the outstanding balance of the loan, not on the original amount borrowed.

Commercial Paper. If a company expects to need large amounts of money for a short time, and it is willing to borrow on a discounted basis while paying a bank or dealer a fee or commission to make the arrangements, it may issue commercial paper to raise funds. Only a financially strong company can borrow from the public at rates lower than bank rates by issuing dealer paper. (The direct placement of commercial paper by finance companies was discussed in Chapter 4.)

Euronotes and Euro-Commercial Paper. Euronotes are short-term debt instruments sold outside the country in whose currency they are denominated. They resemble U.S. commercial paper, but differ in two respects: they are usually underwritten by banks and their average maturities are longer than those of U.S. commercial paper. Euronotes that are not underwritten are called *Euro-commercial paper*. Multinational corporations with good name recognition can usually raise short-term funds by issuing Euronotes and Euro-commercial paper. These debt instruments expand the financing options of multinational corporations and they improve flexibility by allowing firms to raise funds in a variety of currencies. Moreover, the Euronote and Euro-commercial paper markets do not demand credit quality as high as the U.S. commercial paper market requires. This has made Eurofinancing accessible to corporations that find it hard to raise money in the U.S. commercial paper market.

Cost. The nominal rate at which a company borrows is usually lower than the effective cost of the loan. Traditionally, all of the following terms have the same meaning: *nominal rate*, *stated rate*, *face rate*, *coupon rate*, and *interest rate* all refer to the percentage charge that a lender imposes to make a loan. On the other hand, the following terms share a meaning that is different from the first group: *effective rate*, *effective cost*, *annual percentage rate*, and *yield* all refer to the percentage charge that the borrower actually incurs. The nominal rate does not differ from the effective rate because somebody is lying; the discrepancy usually reflects other terms of the loan that prevent the borrower from getting full use of the total amount of money it borrows.

collect loan
A loan that gives the borrower the full amount on Day 1, to be repaid on Day 365, plus interest.

discounted loan
A loan that gives the borrower the full amount on Day 1, but requires payment of the interest on Day 1, with the full amount borrowed to be repaid on Day 365.

compensating balance
A requirement that a borrower deposit a percentage of a loan in a noninterest-bearing checking account, and leave it there while the loan remains outstanding.

Consider a **collect loan** of $100,000 for one year. A nominal 10 percent rate to the lender is an effective 10 percent rate to the borrower if the terms dictate that the borrower gets the full $100,000 on Day 1 and pays back the full $100,000 on Day 365, plus $10,000 interest. Alternatively, the terms of a **discounted loan** require that the borrower gets the full $100,000 on Day 1, pays the $10,000 interest on Day 1, and pays back the full $100,000 on Day 365. Thus, the company gets the use of only $90,000 for the year, raising the effective rate to $10,000/$90,000, or 11.1 percent, although the nominal rate is still $10,000/$100,000, or 10 percent.

A collect loan with a **compensating balance** requires that on Day 1, the borrower must deposit a percentage of the loan in a noninterest-bearing checking account and leave it there for the duration of the loan. Compensating balance requirements vary from 10 percent to 20 percent of the amount borrowed. From a collect $100,000 loan with a 10 percent nominal rate and a 20 percent compensating balance, the borrowing company gets $100,000 and deposits $20,000 into its checking account on Day 1. On Day 365, it withdraws the $20,000, adds $80,000 to it, and repays the $100,000 plus $10,000 interest. The company has the use of only \$80,000 during the year, so the effective rate is \$10,000/\$80,000, or 12.5 percent.

When a bank or dealer charges a fee or commission to arrange a commercial paper issue, it deducts this amount from the proceeds of the loan on Day 1. Commercial paper is a discounted security, so the interest is also deducted on Day 1. While \$100,000 is an unrealistic total for a one-year commercial paper issue (since the amount is too small and the maturity is too long), these terms make the example comparable with examples assumed in the preceding paragraphs. Further, assume that the bank charges a 10 percent nominal rate and a normal dealer's commission of 1⁄12 of 1 percent (0.08333 percent). The proceeds to the issuing company on Day 1 would be:

$$\$100,000 - \$10,000 - \$83.33 = \$89,916.67$$

The borrower would repay \$100,000 on Day 365, so the effective rate would be \$10,083.33/\$89,916.67, or 11.2 percent.

Despite these large discrepancies between nominal and effective rates, the Truth in Lending Law does not require lenders to disclose them for commercial loans. Lenders are under no obligation to tell a borrowing company anything but the nominal rate. Congress maintains that business managers should be able to recognize the significant difference between nominal and effective rates without government interference.

Calculation of effective rates is not merely an academic exercise. If the borrower actually needs the full \$100,000, then it must borrow more than \$100,000. A bigger difference between the nominal rate and the effective rate requires a larger loan. The following equation gives the amount that this company must borrow:

$$Y = X - rX - bX - c \tag{6.2}$$

where Y = amount of money the borrower needs
X = amount of money that it must borrow
r = interest rate for a discounted loan
b = percentage compensating balance, if any
c = commission or fee, if any

For the 10 percent discounted loan with no compensating balance, the firm would need to borrow \$111,111.11 to get the use of \$100,000:

$$\$100,000.00 = X - 0.1X - 0X - 0$$
$$\$100,000.00 = 0.9X$$
$$\$111,111.11 = X$$

For a collect loan with a 20 percent compensating balance, the firm would have to borrow \$125,000 to get the use of \$100,000:

$$\$100{,}000 = X - 0X - 0.2X - 0$$
$$\$100{,}000 = 0.8X$$
$$\$125{,}000 = X$$

For a commercial paper issue with a 10 percent interest rate and an $83.33 commission, the firm would have to sell $111,203.70 of paper to get the use of $100,000:

$$\$100{,}000.00 = X - 0.1X - 0X - \$83.33$$
$$\$100{,}083.33 = 0.9X$$
$$\$111{,}203.70 = X$$

The terms of a loan have their own impact on the cash budget. The timing of interest payments depends on whether a short-term loan is a discounted or collect loan. The firm that pays commissions or fees to issue commercial paper must add an additional line to the cash budget to record these cash outflows. The amount of a compensating balance can be lumped into the cash balance line or entered on a separate line to help management control.

Asset-Based Loans

A potential borrower comparing costs will usually find a secured loan to be cheaper than an unsecured loan. The lender can claim the assets pledged as collateral if the borrower defaults; hence, the lender bears a smaller risk and should get less compensation. However, most corporate financial managers prefer not to encumber company assets, and will pay higher rates for unsecured loans as long as these loans are available. Only when a company exhausts its unsecured borrowing power will management consider pledging short-term assets such as inventories and accounts receivable as collateral.

Loans Secured by Inventory. To continue normal operations, a company must hold sufficient amounts of raw materials, work in process, and finished goods to function efficiently. Only two of these three kinds of inventory have any value as security for a loan: raw materials and finished goods. A lender that claims title to a company's inventory hopes never to take physical possession of it or to auction it off to get an outstanding loan repaid. Lenders are totally unwilling to take on the completion of work-in-process to get their money back, so this portion of a company's inventory has no value as collateral.

A lender appraises the market value of a company's raw materials and finished goods, then agrees to lend the company some percentage of that value, usually no more than 70 percent. The exact percentage depends on various characteristics of the inventory, such as perishability, securability, price stability, and marketability.

Perishability can result from both fragile condition and obsolescence. Food requires huge storage costs. Explosives and drugs mandate high insurance coverage. Items tied to the latest hit movie may become unmarketable in a matter of months. None of these would have much, if any, value to a lender as collateral for a loan.

FOCUS ON FINANCE

DIAMONDS AS COLLATERAL

♦ ♦ ♦

Cut, faceted, unset diamonds would seem to meet the criteria for good collateral. They are nonperishable; in fact, diamond is one of the hardest natural substances. Higher quality of a stone, based on cut, color, and clarity, makes it less likely to go out of fashion. Diamonds are identifiable; cut diamonds produce X-ray portraits as unique as human fingerprints. They are price-protected to some extent; the members of the diamond cartel manage the supply of stones so that prices rarely fall.

Diamonds are not securable, however, because they are relatively tiny and lightweight. Further, if a cut stone is recut, there is no way to identify it by its previous X-ray. In addition, recutting a stone reduces its size and value. Finally, a diamond has no set market value; appraisals can vary from one jeweler to another.

Securability refers to the lender's ability to make sure the collateral exists, in the specified location, for the duration of the obligation. Large, secured inventory items have unremovable and unalterable identification numbers. For smaller or liquid items, the safety of the storage facility is paramount.

Price stability has a great impact on the value of inventory as collateral. Possible downward fluctuations in price frighten lenders.

Marketability is different from perishability. It refers to the skills and techniques necessary to sell collateral that the lender must seize upon the default of a loan. If the lender needs higher academic qualifications to sell the collateral (e.g., an advanced degree in electrical engineering or rocket science), the value of the inventory declines as collateral for a loan.

Loans Secured by Accounts Receivable. When pledged as collateral in a manner similar to inventory, the quality levels of accounts receivable affect the amounts of loans that they can secure. The maximum loan can be as high as 80 percent of the value of the accounts receivable, depending on their quality characteristics, such as:

1. Overall creditworthiness of the borrower's customers
2. Sizes of individual accounts
3. Length of time for which the borrowing company extends credit to its customers

SUMMARY

A cash budget projects monthly cash inflows and outflows for the coming year. It is the basis for planning short-term investments and negotiating short-term borrowing arrangements. The budget is a useful management tool for planning and controlling the company's financial condition. This process is much more complicated for multinational corporations.

Cash budgeting starts with a forecast of sales, which can be made internally by the company's marketing department, by statistical extrapolation of past data, or by reconciling target and sustainable growth rates. The forecast of sales can also be made externally by superimposing specific company and industry expectations on macroeconomic predictions.

Given a sales forecast, the analyst projects monthly cash inflows and outflows. The bulk of the inflows usually represents collections from sales; a large proportion of the cash outflows derive from the production and sale of goods and services. The cash budget projects the amounts and timing of these cash flows as accurately as possible. Great attention to detail is required.

Comparing estimates of inflows and outflows reveals the net expected cash flow each month. These net cash flows form the basis for planning short-term borrowing and investing.

The company's cash budget maintains a minimum cash balance to protect the company against forecasting errors and disruptions in timing of cash flows within budget periods, and because a company cannot operate without any cash on hand. The firm invests cash that accumulates above the minimum balance in specific types of securities that minimize its exposure to default, illiquidity, and market risk; these include U.S. Treasury securities, some federal agency securities, certificates of deposit, bankers' acceptances, and commercial paper. Careful selection of maturity dates can minimize the company's exposure to interest rate risk. International diversification of securities can balance the interest rate cycle that affects all U.S. money market instruments, but it subjects the investor to foreign exchange rate risk and country risk.

A company can borrow from commercial banks in the form of credit lines, revolving credit agreements, or direct loans when it needs to cover short-term cash deficits. It can also borrow from the public at home or abroad by issuing commercial paper, Euronotes, or Euro-commercial paper. All such loans are usually unsecured. When it exhausts its unsecured borrowing power, a company may be able to pledge its inventory or accounts receivable as collateral for a secured loan.

The cost of a loan can be calculated two ways: the nominal rate stated by the lender or the effective cost experienced by the borrower. The difference between the two reflects other terms of the loan that prevent the borrower from getting full use of the total amount of money borrowed.

Key Terms

amortized loan
collect loan
compensating balance
discounted loan
minimum cash balance
reporting currency

Self-Study Questions

1. Give five reasons for preparing a cash budget.
2. Explain several ways in which a company's marketing department can supply a monthly forecast of sales.
3. Explain some influences on the timing of cash inflows from sales.
4. Name some cash inflows that a company might predict but that are not related to sales.
5. Why do depreciation and amortization charges affect the cash budget indirectly?
6. What can cause major forecasting errors in the utilities section of a cash budget?
7. The minimum cash balance serves several purposes. Name two.
8. How can a company minimize default risk in its short-term investments? Illiquidity risk? Market risk?
9. How is a credit line different from a revolving credit agreement?
10. What factors affect the value of a company's inventory as collateral for a loan?

Self-Test Problems

1. A company pays out half of its earnings in the form of dividends, has a 6 percent net profit margin, a 40 percent debt ratio, and $1 in sales for every $0.20 in assets. What is the maximum growth rate of sales that the company can sustain?
2. The following statistics are available for L. J. Hill Corporation: sales = $800 million, total assets = $400 million, net profit after taxes = $25 million, retained earnings = $10 million, total debt = $100 million, total equity = $300 million. What is the fastest rate at which L. J. Hill can grow?
3. A bank offers the Ibert Company an 8 percent discounted loan with no compensating balance. If the Ibert Company needs $250,000, how much does it have to borrow?
4. The Von Ent Corporation needs $50 million and wants to issue 180-day commercial paper. The dealer informs Von Ent that the paper will have to pay interest at an annual rate of 12 percent, and that the dealer's commission will be 1⁄12 of 1 percent. How much commercial paper will the company have to issue?

Discussion Questions

1. Why do people call a cash budget a *living document*?
2. How are cash budgets for small companies, large domestic companies, and multinationals different?
3. If management sets a target growth rate of sales, what impact does this have on a company's cash budget?
4. Should a marketing forecast and a statistical forecast be expected to project exactly the same amount of sales?
5. How does a top-down forecast arrive at final values?

6. How do economic and industry conditions affect an external sales forecast?
7. Why are first-time cash flow forecasts the most difficult to predict?
8. Discuss at least two reasons why a company's accounting expenses and cash outflows might differ.
9. Why should the section of a cash budget that reports payments for labor contain more than one line?
10. Discuss five reasons why a company might repurchase some of its outstanding stock.
11. Discuss three reasons why a company might prepare alternative cash budgets.
12. How does the capital budget influence the cash budget?
13. A company's cash budget shows negative cash flows in 6 months out of 12, and positive cash flows in the other 6 months. Explain why you would or would not expect the company to have financial difficulties during the year.
14. Why wouldn't a financial manager always invest a company's temporary cash surpluses in 180-day Treasury bills as a matter of policy?
15. How can a company minimize interest rate risk if it expects interest rates to rise while it is holding short-term investments?
16. Why would a financial manager consider diversifying a company's portfolio of short-term securities internationally?
17. Under what conditions would a company prefer to borrow on a revolving credit agreement rather than a credit line?
18. How do Euronotes differ from U.S. commercial paper?
19. If you were a banker, how would you evaluate a publisher's inventories of blank paper and textbooks as collateral for a loan?
20. What factors affect the value of a company's accounts receivable as collateral for a loan?

Problems

1. Engineered Mice, Inc. has a 75 percent earnings retention ratio. Its net profit after taxes is 5 percent of sales. Half of its capital structure consists of debt, and it generates $1.25 in sales for every $1 of assets it owns.
   (a) What is its sustainable growth rate?
   (b) What would happen to the SGR if the earnings retention ratio were increased to 85 percent while all the other variables remained the same?
2. How would a company's sustainable growth rate behave if the company had no debt in its capital structure ($D/E = 0$) and it paid no dividends ($m = 1.0$)?

3. General Specific Corp.'s pattern of temporary cash surpluses is based on the following projections obtained from its cash budget:

Month	Net Cash Flow ($000)	Accumulated Cash Surplus ($000)
November	$1,000	$1,000
December	3,000	4,000
January	(2,000)	2,000
February	1,000	3,000
March	3,000	6,000
April	(5,000)	1,000
May	1,000	2,000
June	(2,000)	0
July	0	0
August	4,000	4,000
September	(4,000)	0
October	0	0

As in Exhibit 6.1, graph the accumulated cash surplus. Plan a maturity schedule for GSC's investments if interest rates are expected to rise.

4. Golden Garbage Company needs to borrow $1 million for one year. It can borrow from Safe Bank, which offers a collect loan at a 12 percent nominal rate or from Secure Bank, which offers a discounted loan at an 11 percent nominal rate. Alternatively, it can issue commercial paper at a 10 percent nominal rate, and the dealer will charge 1/12 of 1 percent to bring the issue to market. How should Golden Garbage raise $1 million if it is determined to incur the lowest effective cost?
5. A company needs $2.5 million. Bank A offers a collect loan with a 7.5 percent nominal rate and a 20 percent compensating balance. Bank B offers a discounted loan with an 8.75 percent nominal rate and no compensating balance.
   (a) What is the effective cost of each loan?
   (b) How much will the company have to borrow if it chooses Bank A?
   (c) How much will the company have to borrow if it chooses Bank B?
   (d) Explain the impact of each of these loans on the company's cash budget.

Topics for Further Research

1. Construct your own personal monthly cash budget for the coming year. (Remember, use of a credit card is a short-term loan, not a cash outflow.) Decompose next month's data into four weekly budgets, then decompose next week's data into seven daily budgets.
   (a) Explain the factors you considered when determining your minimum cash balance.
   (b) At the end of next week, compare your actual cash flows to your budgeted cash flows. How would you use your analysis of the discrepancies to improve the following week's budget?

2. Prepare your own personal income statement and balance sheet as of last December 31, then prepare *pro forma* statements as of next December 31. Are you more certain about some estimates than others?
3. List at least ten assets that you might include in your own personal capital budget. Estimate the cash inflows and outflows for each of these assets. Remember that since they are personal assets, they are not depreciable.

Answers to Self-Test Problems

1.
$$SGR = \frac{(0.5)(0.06)(1 + 0.40)}{0.2 - (0.5)(0.06)(1 + 0.40)}$$
$$= 0.042/0.158$$
$$= 0.266, \text{ or } 26.6 \text{ percent}$$

2.
$$SGR = \frac{(10/25)(25/800)[1 + (100/300)]}{(400/500) - (10/25)(25/800)[1 + (100/300)]}$$
$$= \frac{(0.4)(0.03125)(1.33)}{(0.8) - (0.4)(0.03125)(1.33)}$$
$$= 0.01666/0.06334$$
$$= 0.263, \text{ or } 26.3 \text{ percent}$$

3.
$$\$250{,}000 = X - 0.08X$$
$$\$250{,}000 = 0.92X$$
$$\$271{,}739.13 = X$$

4. Because this is 180-day (half-year) paper, the interest charge will reflect half of the annual rate, or 6 percent. The commission will be:

$$\$50{,}000{,}000 \times (0.01/12) = \$41{,}667$$
$$\$50{,}000{,}000 = X - 0.06X - \$41{,}667$$
$$\$50{,}041{,}667 = 0.94X$$
$$\$53{,}235{,}815 = X$$

APPENDIX 6A

Cash Budget Illustration

It is September 199X. SMH Company has just prepared its cash budget, which is the spreadsheet in Exhibit 6A.1. The spreadsheet in Exhibit 6A.2 shows the *Lotus 1-2-3* formulas used to construct the cash budget. The explanations below describe one spreadsheet line (or row) at a time. Column A holds the labels for each row, and Row 1 contains the labels for each month.

The budget preparer was given a sales forecast of $15 million for the next 12 months.

Average Sales (Row 2). Without any adjustments, the sales per month equal $15,000,000/12, or $1,250,000. This amount is entered directly into each column in Row 2, from Cell B2 to Cell M2.

Seasonal (Row 3). The company's historic seasonal pattern has been calculated as a percentage of average monthly sales. (Like all seasonal indices, these 12 percentages sum to 1,200 percent and average 100 percent.) October sales, for instance, have typically equaled 104 percent of average. These seasonal percentages have been typed directly into each column in Row 3, from Cell B3 to Cell M3.

Sales (Row 4). The monthly sales projections are calculated by multiplying the seasonal percentages by the average monthly sales. The formula +B2*B3 is entered into Cell B4 and copied into Cells C4 through M4. The *Lotus* /COPY command automatically changes cell references from +B2*B3 to +C2*C3 when copying from Column B to Column C.

Discounted (Row 5). SMH Company sells on terms of 2/10 net 30. An examination of the sales history shows that in October, November, and December, 12 percent of sales are discounted. During the other nine months of the year, only 10 percent of the sales are discounted. These percentages are entered directly into Cells B5 through M5 in decimal form.

Collections (Row 6). To facilitate reading the budget, this line is left blank.

Disc. Now (Row 7). Cell B4 times Cell B5 is the amount of October's sales that will be discounted. The discount is 2 percent, so the budget projects that only 98 percent of the sales amount will be collected as cash from customers who take the discount. Since these customers will pay in ten days, only sales made in the first 20 days of October produce a cash inflow in that month. Since 20 days are approximately 0.67 of a month, Cell B7, the October cash inflow from October's discounted sales, contains the formula +B4*B5*.98*.67. This is shortened to +B4*B5*.6566 and copied into Cells C7 through M7.

Disc. Later (Row 8). Discounted sales made during the last ten days of October are paid during the first ten days of November. Ten days are approximately 0.33 of a month, so Cell C8, the November cash inflow from October's discounted sales, contains the formula +B4*B5*.98*.33. This is shortened to +B4*B5*.3283 and copied into Cells D8 through M8. Cell B8 will contain the discounted sales from the last ten days of September. This number is entered directly based on prior budgets.

Full Later (Row 9). Historically, a constant 1 percent of the remaining customers fail to pay at all, 5 percent pay a week or so late, and the balance pay on time on the 30th day. For October, November, and December, 100 percent minus 12 percent minus 1 percent minus 5 percent, or 82 percent pay in full the following month. For the other months, 100 percent minus 10 percent minus 1 percent minus 5 percent, or 84 percent pay in full the following month. Cell C9 contains the formula +B4*.82, which is copied into cells D9 and E9. Cell F9 contains the formula +E4*.84, which is copied into cells G9 through M9. Cell B9 is known to be 84 percent of September's sales, and the number is entered directly.

Late (Row 10). Each month, customers pay for 5 percent of sales after the 30th day; so the cash from 5 percent of October's sales will be received in December. Cell D10 contains the formula +B4*.05, which is copied into Cells E10 through M10. Cell B10 contains 5 percent of August's sales and Cell C10 contains 5 percent of September's sales. These two numbers are entered directly.

Bad Debt (Row 11). When a customer defaults on an account receivable, SMH Company turns the account over to bill collection agencies. These agencies have usually collected 40 percent of delinquent accounts in the past. The company's contract allows the agencies to keep half of what they collect. Thus, the company expects to get a net cash inflow of 20 percent of the bad debt, which is 1 percent of sales. This inflow happens six months after the sale was made. Therefore, sales of $1,300,000 in October will produce a cash inflow in March of:

$$\$1{,}300{,}000 \times 0.01 \times 0.20 = \$2{,}600$$

Cell G11 contains the formula +B4*.01*.2, which is shortened to +B4*.002 and copied into Cells H11 through M11. Cells B11 through F11 reflect 20 percent of 1 percent of sales from May to September. These numbers are entered directly.

Leases (Row 12). The company leases some of its assets to other companies. It requires the lessees to pay $500 per month. This amount is entered directly into Cell B12 and copied into cells C12 through M12.

Asset Sales (Row 13). The company anticipates a cash inflow of $6,000 in January from the sale of some old machinery. This number is entered in Cell E13. The other cells in Row 13 contain zeroes because the company does not plan to sell any other assets.

EXHIBIT 6A.1

SMH Company Cash Budget

Row	A	B	C	D	E	F
1	Month	October	November	December	January	February
2	Average Sales	1250000	1250000	1250000	1250000	1250000
3	Seasonal	1.04	1.09	1.12	0.91	0.85
4	Sales	1300000	1362500	1400000	1137500	1062500
5	Discounted	0.12	0.12	0.12	0.10	0.10
6	Collections:					
7	Disc. Now	102430	107354	110309	74688	69764
8	Disc. Later	49375	50450	52876	54331	36787
9	Full Later	924000	1066000	1117250	1148000	955500
10	Late	53500	55000	65000	68125	70000
11	Bad Debt	2100	1980	2000	2140	2200
12	Leases	500	500	500	500	500
13	Asset Sales	0	0	0	6000	0
14	Dividends	0	450	0	0	450
15	Total Inflow	1131905	1281734	1347935	1353784	1135201
16						
17	Purchases	420000	341250	318750	367500	382500
18	Payments	390000	408750	420000	341250	318750
19	Labor	545000	560000	455000	425000	490000
20	Utilities	130000	136250	140000	113750	106250
21	Buy Assets	0	0	25000	0	0
22	Interest	0	0	0	0	0
23	Dividends	16000	0	0	18500	0
24	Taxes	0	0	450000	125000	0
25	Total Outflow	1081000	1105000	1490000	1023500	915000
26						
27	Net Cash Flow	50905	176734	−142065	330284	220201
28	Investment	50000	177000	−142000	330000	221000
29	Total Invested	50000	227000	85000	415000	636000
30	Loans	0	0	0	0	0
31	Total Loans	0	0	0	0	0
32	Cash Balance	100905	100639	100574	100858	100059

Dividends (Row 14). The company owns some stock in another company. This stock pays dividends of $450 in November, February, May, and August, so $450 is typed into Cells C14, F14, I14, and L14. The rest of the cells in Row 14 are filled with zeroes because the company does not own any other stock.

Total Inflow (Row 15). The company's total cash inflows are the sums of the amounts in Rows 7 through 14. For October, the formula for Cell B15 is +B7+B8+B9+B10+B11+B12+B13+B14. However, this can be shortened to @SUM(B7 . . . B14) and then copied into Cells C15 through M15. Because of space limitations, the spreadsheet shows only @SUM(B7.B14).

G	H	I	J	K	L	M
March	April	May	June	July	August	September
1250000	1250000	1250000	1250000	1250000	1250000	1250000
0.98	1.02	1.01	1.00	0.99	0.99	1.00
1225000	1275000	1262500	1250000	1237500	1237500	1250000
0.10	0.10	0.10	0.10	0.10	0.10	0.10
80434	83717	82896	82075	81254	81254	82075
34361	39617	40829	40425	40021	40021	40425
892500	1029000	1071000	1060500	1050000	1039500	1039500
56875	53125	61250	63750	63125	62500	61875
2600	2725	2800	2275	2125	2450	2550
500	500	500	500	500	500	500
0	0	0	0	0	0	0
0	0	450	0	0	450	0
1067270	1208684	1259725	1249525	1237025	1226675	1226925
378750	375000	371250	371250	375000	400000	410000
367500	382500	378750	375000	371250	371250	375000
510000	505000	500000	495000	495000	500000	533333
122500	127500	126250	125000	123750	123750	125000
0	0	0	0	0	0	0
100000	0	0	0	0	0	100000
0	18500	0	0	18500	0	0
450000	0	125000	450000	0	0	450000
1550000	1033500	1130000	1445000	1008500	995000	1583333
−482730	175184	129725	−195475	228525	231675	−356408
−483000	175000	130000	−196000	229000	231000	−356000
153000	328000	458000	262000	491000	722000	366000
0	0	0	0	0	0	0
0	0	0	0	0	0	0
100329	100513	100238	100763	100288	100963	100555

Blank (Row 16). To separate cash inflows from cash outflows, this row has deliberately been left blank.

Purchases (Row 17). As a matter of policy, the company buys its raw materials as it needs them, approximately two months before the sale of its finished product. Its raw materials costs are 30 percent of sales, so October's purchases are 30 percent of December's sales. Cell B17 contains the formula +D4*.3, which is copied into cells C17 through K17. Cells L17 and M17 are 30 percent of next October's and November's sales. While these sales numbers do not appear in the current budget, the purchases are estimated to be $400,000 and $410,000, and are entered directly.

EXHIBIT 6A.2

***Lotus* Spreadsheet**

Row	A	B	C	D	E	F	G
1	Month	October	November	December	January	February	March
2	Average Sales	1250000	1250000	1250000	1250000	1250000	1250000
3	Seasonal	1.04	1.09	1.12	0.91	0.85	0.98
4	Sales	+B2*B3	+C2*C3	+D2*D3	+E2*E3	+F2*F3	+G2*G3
5	Discounted	0.12	0.12	0.12	0.10	0.10	0.10
6	Collections:						
7	Disc. Now	+B4*B5*.6566	+C4*C5*.6566	+D4*D5*.6566	+E4*E5*.6566	+F4*F5*.6566	+G4*G5*.6566
8	Disc. Later	49375	+B4*B5*.3283	+C4*C5*.3283	+D4*D5*.3283	+E4*E5*.3283	+F4*F5*.3283
9	Full Later	924000	+B4*.82	+C4*.82	+D4*.82	+E4*.84	+F4*.84
10	Late	53500	55000	+B4*.05	+C4*.05	+D4*.05	+E4*.05
11	Bad Debt	2100	1980	2000	2140	2200	+B4*.002
12	Leases	500	500	500	500	500	500
13	Asset Sales	0	0	0	6000	0	0
14	Dividends	0	450	0	0	450	0
15	Total Inflow	@SUM(B7.B14)	@SUM(C7.C14)	@SUM(D7.D14)	@SUM(E7.E14)	@SUM(F7.F14)	@SUM(G7.G14)
16							
17	Purchases	+D4*.3	+E4*.3	+F4*.3	+G4*.3	+H4*.3	+I4*.3
18	Payments	+B4*.3	+C4*.3	+B17	+C17	+D17	+E17
19	Labor	+C4*.4	+D4*.4	+E4*.4	+F4*.4	+G4*.4	+H4*.4
20	Utilities	+B4*.1	+C4*.1	+D4*.1	+E4*.1	+F4*.1	+G4*.1
21	Buy Assets	0	0	25000	0	0	0
22	Interest	0	0	0	0	0	100000
23	Dividends	16000	0	0	18500	0	0
24	Taxes	0	0	450000	125000	0	450000
25	Total Outflow	@SUM(B18.B24)	@SUM(C18.C24)	@SUM(D18.D24)	@SUM(E18.E24)	@SUM(F18.F24)	@SUM(G18.G24)
26							
27	Net Cash Flow	+B15–B25	+C15–C25	+D15–D25	+E15–E25	+F15–F25	+G15–G25
28							

Payments (Row 18). The purchases do not constitute cash outflows, just as sales did not constitute cash inflow. It is necessary to plan for when SMH Company will pay for its purchases. The suppliers of its raw materials offer terms of 1/10 net 60, and the financial manager has decided that this discount is not worth taking. Therefore, the company will pay in 60 days. It will pay for October's purchases in December, so Cell D18 contains the cell reference +B17. This is copied into Cells E18 through M18. Cells B18 and C18 contain the payments for purchases made in August and September, which are 30 percent of sales in October and November. Cell B18 contains the formula +B4*.3 which is copied into Cell C18.

Labor (Row 19). The text indicates that labor payments should be entered in a multitude of lines because labor costs have many components whose cash flow patterns differ significantly. It is sufficient for our purposes, however, to make the simplifying assumption that total labor costs constitute 40 percent of sales, and are incurred and paid in the month prior to the sales. October's labor costs will be 40

H	I	J	K	L	M
April	May	June	July	August	September
1250000	1250000	1250000	1250000	1250000	1250000
1.02	1.01	1.00	0.99	0.99	1.00
+H2*H3	+I2*I3	+J2*J3	+K2*K3	+L2*L3	+M2*M3
0.10	0.10	0.10	0.10	0.10	0.10
+H4*H5*.6566	+I4*I5*.6566	+J4*J5*.6566	+K4*K5*.6566	+L4*L5*.6566	+M4*M5*.6566
+G4*G5*.3283	+H4*H5*.3283	+I4*I5*.3283	+J4*J5*.3283	+K4*K5*.3283	+L4*L5*.3283
+G4*.84	+H4*.84	+I4*.84	+J4*.84	+K4*.84	+L4*.84
+F4*.05	+G4*.05	+H4*.05	+I4*.05	+J4*.05	+K4*.05
+C4*.002	+D4*.002	+E4*.002	+F4*.002	+G4*.002	+H4*.002
500	500	500	500	500	500
0	0	0	0	0	0
0	450	0	0	450	0
@SUM(H7.H14)	@SUM(I7.I14)	@SUM(J7.J14)	@SUM(K7.K14)	@SUM(L7.L14)	@SUM(M7.M14)
+J4*.3	+K4*.3	+L4*.3	+M4*.3	400000	410000
+F17	+G17	+H17	+I17	+J17	+K17
+I4*.4	+J4*.4	+K4*.4	+L4*.4	+M4*.4	533333
+H4*.1	+I4*.1	+J4*.1	+K4*.1	+L4*.1	+M4*.1
0	0	0	0	0	0
0	0	0	0	0	100000
18500	0	0	18500	0	0
0	125000	450000	0	0	450000
@SUM(H18.H24)	@SUM(I18.I24)	@SUM(J18.J24)	@SUM(K18.K24)	@SUM(L18.L24)	@SUM(M18.M24)
+H15–H25	+I15–I25	+J15–J25	+K15–K25	+L15–L25	+M15–M25

percent of November's sales, so Cell B19 contains the formula +C4*.4. This is copied into Cells C19 through L19. September's labor costs (40 percent of next October's sales), $533,333, are typed directly into Cell M19.

Utilities (Row 20). Another simplifying assumption combines oil, gas, electric, water, waste disposal, telephone, and other services into one row. Assuming that, together, they constitute a so-called *wrap rate* of 10 percent of the current month's sales, Cell B20 contains the formula +B4*.1, which is copied into Cells C20 through M20. It is worth repeating that real life could never work out this simply.

Buy Assets (Row 21). The cash inflows section of the cash budget shows that SMH Company expects to sell $6,000 of old machinery in January. This is because it will buy $25,000 of new machinery in December. The $25,000 cost is typed directly into Cell D21. All the other cells in Row 21 contain zeroes because this is the only asset purchase in the budget for the next 12 months.

Interest (Row 22). The company is obligated to pay $100,000 in interest on its outstanding bonds every March and September. Cells G22 and M22 contain $100,000; the other cells in this row contain zeroes. All numbers are entered directly.

Dividends (Row 23). The company plans to pay $16,000 in dividends to its common stockholders in October. It expects this payment to rise to $18,500 for January, April, and July. Cell B23 contains $16,000. Cells E23, H23, and K23 contain $18,500. All other cells in Row 23 contain zeroes. All numbers are entered directly.

Taxes (Row 24). Federal and state estimated tax payments are budgeted at $450,000 for March, June, September, and December. Local property taxes are budgeted at $125,000 in January and May. These payments are entered directly into the appropriate cells. All other cells in Row 24 contain zeroes.

Total Outflow (Row 25). The company expects no nonrecurring cash outflows, so its total cash outflows are the sums of the amounts in Rows 18 through 24. Row 17, Purchases, is not included in this total because it does not reflect cash outflows. For October, the formula for Cell B25 is @SUM(B18. . . B24). This formula is copied into Cells C25 through M25.

Blank (Row 26). To separate cash outflows from net cash flow, this row has deliberately been left blank.

Net Cash Flow (Row 27). Total cash inflows minus total cash outflows equal net cash flow. Cell B27 for October contains the formula +B15–B25. This formula is copied into Cells C27 through M27.

Completing the Cash Budget

From this point on, the *Lotus* spreadsheet in Exhibit 6A.2 serves only a record-keeping function, so there will be no further references to it. The cash budget spreadsheet in Exhibit 6A.1 becomes the working spreadsheet and is completed one column (month) at a time.

Assume, for the sake of simplicity, that at the end of September (which is also the beginning of October) the SMH Company will have no short-term debt outstanding, no short-term investments, and a cash balance of exactly $100,000. Company policy dictates a minimum cash balance of $100,000 every month for budgeting purposes. Assume that investments can be bought and sold in multiples of $1,000, and loans can be obtained and repaid in any denomination.

In practice, the portion of the cash budget below the Net Cash Flow line (Row 27) would be much more detailed. If company policy allowed investments in various types of securities, one line would correspond to each type. Even if the financial manager were restricted to investing in T-bills only, the budget should list 30-day bills, 60-day bills, and so forth on different lines. Additionally, a row should report interest rate forecasts, and another row should record interest received.

The loan forecasts would also need more than the two rows indicated. Loan activity involving different lenders should be recorded in different rows. Other rows should show compensating balances, factor fees, commitment fees, and any other cash flows arising from the loans.

Finally, if the company's cash balance is not all kept in one account, separate lines should indicate this fact. The financial manager must keep tight control over the company's cash on hand. Exhibit 6A.1 uses a simplified format because the variety of detailed structures available makes choosing one for illustration almost meaningless.

October. By the end of October, the company expects a net cash inflow of $50,905. It can invest $50,000 of this amount in securities. The $905 balance increases the cash account.

November. By the end of November, the company expects to experience a net cash inflow of $176,734. It can withdraw $266 from the cash balance, leaving $100,639. The inflow plus the cash will allow it to invest $177,000. The total amount of securities it holds will rise to $227,000.

December. By the end of December, the company will experience a net cash outflow of $142,065. It can cover this by selling $142,000 of securities and drawing down the cash balance by $65. The company is left with $85,000 invested and $100,574 in cash.

Examination of the last six lines of the cash budget reveals that, despite net cash outflows in December, March, June, and September, the company will not have to borrow at all. Its security holdings will form the pattern displayed in Exhibit 6A.3. The investment strategy the company will follow will depend on whether it expects interest rates to be stable, to rise, or to fall during the period covered by the budget, and on the company's aversion to different types of risk.

EXHIBIT 6A.3

Security Holdings of SMH Company

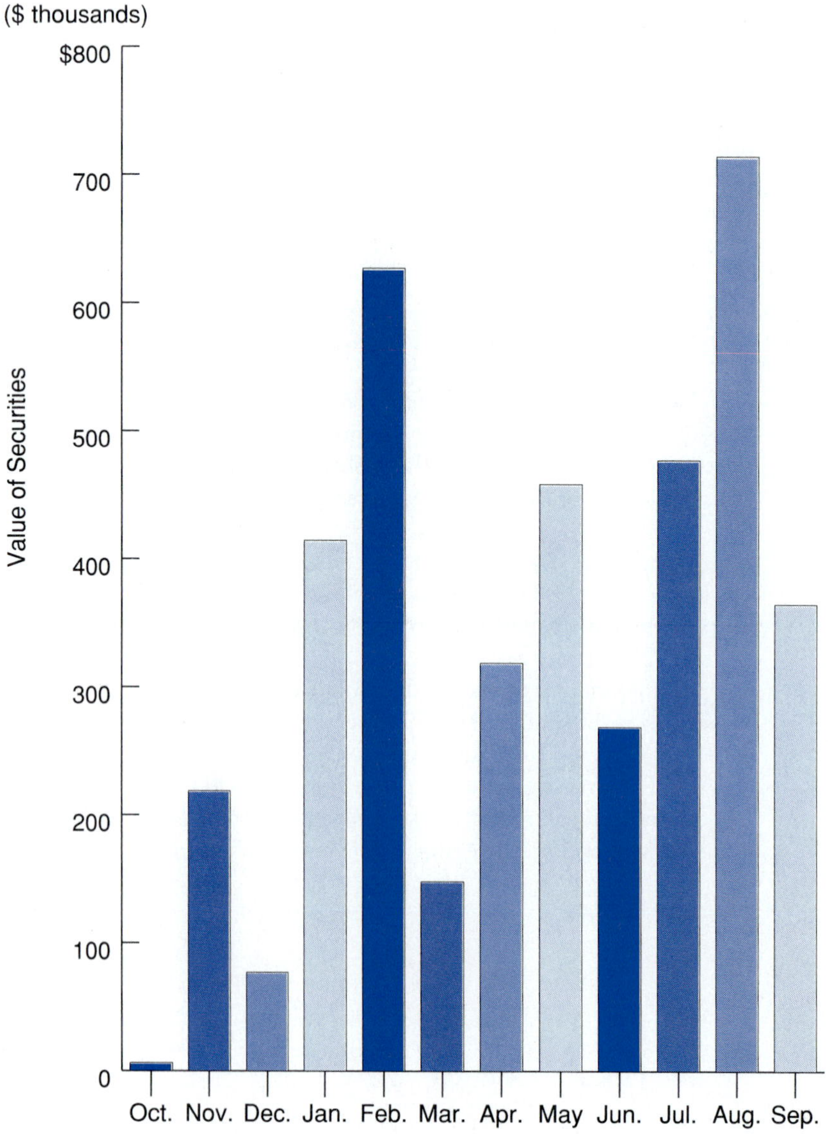

CHAPTER

7

Working Capital Management

LEARNING OBJECTIVES

This chapter examines the details of financial decision making for the major components of working capital. It also scrutinizes the impacts of these decisions on the company's financial plans. At the conclusion of this chapter, the reader should be able to:

1. *Describe how a cash microbudget enhances the management of cash and float*
2. *Explain which methods of float management are illegal or unethical*
3. *Calculate the cost of missing discounts offered as part of a supplier's terms of trade*
4. *Make cost-effective decisions about paying foreign suppliers*
5. *Evaluate the cash budget implications of the various terms of trade a company can offer its customers*
6. *Judge the desirability of factoring accounts receivable*
7. *Evaluate the cost consequences for the company's financial plans of inventory decisions made by production and marketing managers.*

The four components of working capital analyzed in this chapter are cash, accounts payable, accounts receivable, and inventory. Many people have common experiences that can give them some degree of familiarity with the concepts of working capital management, yet they do not recognize the connection.

A college student may occasionally write home for money and be delighted when a check arrives in the mail; another may call home for money and plead that cash be wired to the nearest Western Union office. These requests both result from cash management decisions. Anyone who possesses a credit card and has paid the minimum amount due instead of the outstanding balance at least once has been introduced to accounts payable management decisions. Everyone who ever had a paper route or provided baby sitting for regular customers knows the basics of accounts receivable management. Any driver who has ever bought gasoline after deliberating how much to buy ("Can I get where I want to go on $2 worth?") appreciates the basics of inventory management.

WORKING CAPITAL COMPONENTS

A company's *net working capital* is defined as the difference between its current assets and current liabilities. For nonfinancial U.S. corporations, current assets average about 40 percent of total assets. Current liabilities are somewhat smaller; on average, they amount to about 30 percent of total assets. Net working capital thus averages 10 percent of total assets.

A more detailed breakdown of working capital includes six major components: cash, marketable securities, accounts payable, inventory, accounts receivable, and short-term debt. Chapter 6 covered the management of two components in depth, marketable securities and short-term debt, in conjunction with cash budgeting. This chapter analyzes the management of the remaining four components. Some minor components of working capital include prepaid expenses, accruals for taxes and other expenses, and the current portion of long-term debt. Financial managers must continually reassess the balance between these components, taking into consideration alternative investment opportunities, tax consequences, and overall financial plans.

The financial manager has different degrees of authority over the various components of working capital. Decisions that affect cash, marketable securities, accounts payable, and short-term debt are strictly financial. Decisions that involve accounts receivable require consultation with the company's marketing managers, however, and financial decisions that involve inventory are subordinate to decisions made by the company's production and marketing managers.

Still, financial managers bear some responsibility for the management of every component of working capital. Their responsibilities include:

1. Accelerating cash inflows and slowing down cash outflows
2. Ensuring that the company holds minimal amounts of nonearning assets
3. Evaluating the effects of working capital decisions on the company's cash budget and *pro forma* statements

The goal of working capital management, therefore, is to maximize profitability by minimizing the costs of the company's current liabilities and maximizing the returns from the company's current assets.

These responsibilities are essentially the same for small companies; large domestic companies; and multinationals. The dollar amounts are different, and a few special factors affect decisions that involve international elements.

EXHIBIT 7.1

Cash Budget Spreadsheet Columns

Column	Spreadsheet Dated Friday, August 1, 199X	Spreadsheet Dated Friday, August 8, 199X
B	Monday 8/4/9X	Monday 8/11/9X
C	Tuesday 8/5/9X	Tuesday 8/12/9X
D	Wednesday 8/6/9X	Wednesday 8/13/9X
E	Thursday 8/7/9X	Thursday 8/14/9X
F	Friday 8/8/9X	Friday 8/15/9X
G	Week 2 8/11–8/17	Week 2 8/18–8/24
H	Week 3 8/18–8/24	Week 3 8/25–8/31
I	Week 4 8/25–8/31	Week 4 9/1–9/7
J	September 199X	September 199X
K	October 199X	October 199X
L	November 199X	November 199X
M	December 199X	December 199X
N	January 199X+1	January 199X+1
O	February 199X+1	February 199X+1
P	March 199X+1	March 199X+1
Q	April 199X+1	April 199X+1
R	May 199X+1	May 199X+1
S	June 199X+1	June 199X+1
T	July 199X+1	July 199X+1

MANAGING CASH

The primary goal of cash management is to accelerate cash inflows and slow down cash outflows, while holding a minimum amount of idle cash. Collecting cash due more quickly and delaying paying out cash longer allow the firm to borrow less and/or invest more. This reduces the amount of interest the firm pays, increases the amount of interest it earns, and enhances its overall profitability. Investing idle cash has the same effect.

Microbudgeting

The cash budget problem introduced in the Appendix to Chapter 6 projects monthly cash inflows and outflows for the next 12 months. Breaking down the nearest month's data into weekly data, and the data for the nearest week into daily data, makes cash management more effective. Any company large enough to have a financial manager usually has cash balances that require daily management. To do this, a typical firm uses a multicolumn budgeting spreadsheet and revises it weekly.

To understand how this works, imagine the 12-column spreadsheet in Appendix 6A broken down into the 19-column spreadsheet whose column headings are shown in Exhibit 7.1. The exhibit replaces column B (August 199X) in the Appendix 6A spreadsheet with the eight columns, B through I. This additional detail breaks down all the cash inflows and outflows for August into daily projections for the first week and weekly projections for the rest of the month. The exhibit breaks down the net cash flows and the investment, loan, and cash balances into the same format. (Columns J through T in Exhibit 7.1 are exactly the same as Columns C through M in the Appendix 6A spreadsheets; they have simply moved to the right.) The budget's expanded detail for near-future data makes it possible to micromanage the company's finances and minimizes forecasting errors.

Exhibit 7.1 also illustrates how the budget would be revised after a week had passed. Every week, the microbudgeter makes daily projections for the following week, and revises the weekly projections and extends them for another week. Every fourth week or so, the budgeter revises the monthly projections and extends them an additional month into the future.

Minimum Cash Balances. The microbudget's weekly minimum cash balances are smaller than the monthly minimums, and the daily minimum cash balances are smaller than the weekly ones. There are several reasons for this:

1. Forecasts for shorter periods in the near future are more accurate, reducing the size of the cushion needed to protect the company against forecasting errors.
2. The shorter budgeting period (a week instead of a month) reduces the amounts and probabilities of cash flow imbalances within the period.
3. A nearer and shorter budgeting period increases the financial manager's ability to control the company's cash flows.

The microbudget changes other items along with the minimum cash balances. For instance, Chapter 6 implied that an entire compensating balance had to be on deposit every day that a loan remained outstanding. This is not necessarily true; some banks may impose different requirements. Consider some popular variations:

1. The borrower's *average* deposit balance for the month (or week) cannot fall below the required compensating balance.
2. The borrower must have the required compensating balance on deposit at the end of one specific day every week.
3. If the borrower already maintains a substantial average deposit balance in the bank, part or all of it may be counted as part of the compensating balance.

float
The dollar value of checks both written by and received by a company that have not yet cleared through the banking system.

Float. One item that is invisible in monthly budgets, but becomes important in microbudgets, is called **float**. It is the dollar value of checks both written by and received by the company that have not yet cleared through the banking system.

When a company writes a check to pay for a purchase, its ledgers show an immediate reduction in its bank balance. Time passes as the seller receives the check and deposits it. The amount of money the company has on deposit at the bank does not decrease until the seller's bank presents the check to the buyer's bank for payment. Until this happens, the company's records show a bank balance

disbursement float
The positive difference between the bank balance shown on the company's records and its actual bank balance, because a check that the company has written has not yet cleared.

collection float
The negative difference between the bank balance shown on the company's records and its actual bank balance, because a check that the company has received has not yet cleared.

net float
Disbursement float minus collection float at a point in time.

lower than the actual balance at the bank. This difference is called **disbursement float**.

Conversely, when a company receives a check from a customer, its ledgers show an immediate increase in its bank balance. Sooner or later, the company deposits the check, but the amount of money the company has on deposit does not increase until its bank presents the check to the customer's bank for payment. Until this happens, the company's records show a balance higher than its actual bank balance. This difference is called **collection float**.

Net float at any point in time equals disbursement float minus collection float. Net float can be positive or negative. If a company anticipates positive net float, it can reduce its cash balance at the bank with an overnight repurchase agreement, or repo. The company buys Treasury bills from the bank and sells them back to the bank the next day. The purchase and sale prices are agreed upon in advance, and set so that the company earns a yield that is a little less than the expected market yield on a T-bill held overnight. In exchange for a fixed fee and the expected yield differential, the bank accepts the exposure to interest rate risk and market risk. If a company already owns T-bills and anticipates negative net float, it can increase its cash balance at the bank with a reverse repo: it can sell T-bills to the bank and buy them back the next day, at prices agreed upon in advance. The yield to the bank on a reverse repo is a little higher than the expected market yield on an overnight T-bill, but the cost to the company is lower than the effective cost of using its credit line or other loan arrangements.

Float can be attributed to the three parts of the collection and disbursement process:

1. Mailing time, which is the time from the moment the payer writes a check until the payee receives it
2. Processing time, which is the time from the moment the payee receives the check until it deposits the check in its bank
3. Clearing time, which is the time from the moment the payee's bank receives the check until the payer's bank honors it

Cash Flow Timing

Most cash management techniques seek to reduce the time during which financial managers do not have control over company funds. Speeding up collections or delaying disbursements by one day may substantially increase the profits a company earns on its short-term investments. If the company is cash-short, holding onto cash can significantly reduce the need to borrow, and the interest that the firm must pay, again increasing profits. Financial managers use three tools to manage cash: float management, zero-balance accounts, and concentration banking.

Float Management. Float management tries to minimize at least one component of the time required to collect funds and to increase at least one component of the time before the firm disburses funds. There are legal and illegal, as well as ethical and unethical, ways to do this.

FOCUS ON FINANCE

DEBIT TELEPHONE CARDS

Debit telephone cards are common in Europe and Japan, where most phones are equipped with insertion slots and the cards are magnetically imprinted with the user's personal code. In the United States, the use of debit phone cards is slowly but surely expanding.

The user buys a card representing from $5 to $500 worth of calling credit (perhaps charging the purchase to Visa or MasterCard), and the price of each call is automatically deducted from the prepaid balance. Phone services usually impose surcharges of $0.75 per call for credit card calls, but debit card calls have no surcharge. The per-minute rate for debit card calls is also usually lower than for credit card calls, and additional discounts kick in when the customer subsequently buys more calling time. Rates are the same regardless of distance or time of day, but some cards can't be used for international calls.

A lockbox system attempts to reduce mailing and processing time. A company sets up post office boxes in strategic locations near its customers because mail can reach the boxes more quickly than company headquarters. The company opens an account at a local bank, which empties the box at least once a day, opens the mail, deposits the checks, and forwards the documents that accompany the checks to the company. To maximize float, a payment can be made by draft or with a check drawn on a bank that is a long distance from the payer.

Lockbox systems are widely used by large companies with geographically dispersed customers. They are also used by multinationals, although lockboxes are not available in every country. Some foreign banking systems do not service lockboxes.

While faxing checks has not yet become acceptable because no adequate security system has been devised, there are other electronic ways to minimize float. Firms have transferred large payments by wire for years, although it is an expensive way to move money. Payments from retail customers who use bank debit cards are available to the seller on the same day, but the availability of this system is limited outside the United States.

check kiting
An illegal and unethical practice of writing checks against bank float.

Ethical and legal problems arise when a company tries to exploit the float caused by the time required to clear checks within the banking system. Writing checks for amounts greater than the checkwriter's bank balance is a felony. Writing checks against bank float amounts to using the same dollar twice; practiced systematically, this practice can lead to prosecution for **check kiting**. To illustrate check kiting, assume that a company draws a $1 million check on its $1 million account at Bank A and it deposits this check in its own account at Bank B. It simultaneously draws a $1 million check on Bank B and deposits the new check in a third account at Bank C. Until both checks clear, the company appears to have a total of $3 million in its bank accounts. If the checks take at least one day to clear, the company can invest $3 million in overnight repos ($1 million at each bank), tripling the yield on its $1 million cash balance.

Check kiting is not always illegal in other countries. Some foreign banking systems do not yet appreciate the value of minimizing clearing time, and a multinational faces great temptation to "play the float" created by these slow-moving banks. The terminology—the word *playing* for instance—suggests that the practice in not considered unethical by those who engage in it.

Zero-Balance Accounts. Commercial banks in the United States and some other industrialized countries have developed zero-balance accounts to help corporations free up some of their cash balances. A company establishes a master bank account and a set of special-purpose, local bank accounts. These subaccounts remain empty and are used only for disbursements. To pay a check written on one of these local banks, the primary bank immediately and automatically transfers the necessary funds from the master account, usually a revolving loan account. Thus, only the master account requires a minimum cash balance. This balance is lower than the sum of the balances in each of the subaccounts if they were to function independently and required minimum balances of their own. The zero-balance account reduces the amount of money the company has in no-yield checking account balances.

Concentration Banking. Another banking service available in the United States and some other industrialized countries is known as *concentration banking*. To accelerate cash receipts, the company arranges for checks written to it to be deposited in local banks, minimizing processing time. A concentration bank then pools the funds from these bank accounts into one master account. This movement of deposits involves a wire transfer that is essentially instantaneous.

A multinational corporation may attempt to copy the advantages of concentration banking by closely monitoring its deposits in banks in different locations and transferring money as quickly as possible into a self-designated master account. The transfer time varies with the efficiency of foreign banking systems. Also, the technique requires many currency exchanges to accommodate the currencies handled by the master bank.

The profitability of this strategy depends in part on the profitability of holding a portfolio of currencies. A multinational can generate profits from the foreign currencies it accumulates either by investing them in local securities or by trading them whenever it finds favorable cross rates. Currency portfolio managers must use the same techniques as managers of stock and bond portfolios. They must consider expected returns, expected variability of these returns (risk), and interrelationships of return patterns on the assets in their portfolios. For example, a currency portfolio manager must know whether to expect a loss, a gain, or no significant change in French francs whenever a loss on German marks is expected.

MANAGING ACCOUNTS PAYABLE

A company incurs an account payable when it purchases materials and supplies on credit. The buyer may consider different credit terms offered by potential suppliers as part of the decision to choose a specific supplier. After it selects a supplier, however, the purchasing company usually has no role in determining the credit terms it is offered. Sellers must offer the same credit terms to all creditworthy customers, or they can be sued for discriminatory selling practices. The amount of credit a seller grants can vary with the size, financial condition, and prior credit history of the customer, but the credit terms cannot.

Credit Terms

If a seller sets terms of 1/10 net 30, the buyer has a choice: to pay in 10 days and get a discount of 1 percent of the amount of the invoice, or to pay the full amount of the invoice in 30 days. In order to make this decision, the buyer must recognize that the amount listed on the invoice has two components:

1. The purchase price of the merchandise, which is 99 percent of the invoice amount
2. The interest charge for a 20-day loan, which is 1 percent of the invoice amount

When it sends a $100 invoice, the seller grants the buyer a 10-day, interest-free loan of $99 and, if the buyer wants it, an additional 20-day loan at an effective cost of $1/$99, or 1.01 percent for the 20-day period.

Buyer's Cost of Trade Credit. To compare the cost of this loan from the supplier to the costs of other short-term sources of funds, it is necessary to calculate the *annual* cost of borrowing from the supplier. This cost is not simply 12 times the discount rate because, if the customer were to place 12 consecutive orders a year, the seller would lend money interest-free for 12 x 10, or 120 days per year and at 1.01 percent for 12 x 20, or 240 days per year.

To calculate the annual cost of trade credit correctly, assume that the customer places 365/20, or 18.25 consecutive orders in a year. This assumption means that the customer owes the supplier interest every day during the year. This overlap is illustrated in Exhibit 7.2. The annual cost of borrowing from a supplier selling on terms of 1/10 net 30 is therefore:

$$18.25 \times 1.01\% = 18.4325 \text{ percent}$$

The annual cost of paying at the end of the net period and consistently passing up the discount is:

$$C = [d/(1 - d) \times (365/p) \qquad \textbf{(7.1)}$$

where: C = annual cost

d = discount rate

p = time period during which interest is charged

EXHIBIT 7.2

Consecutive Interest-Bearing Accounts Payable

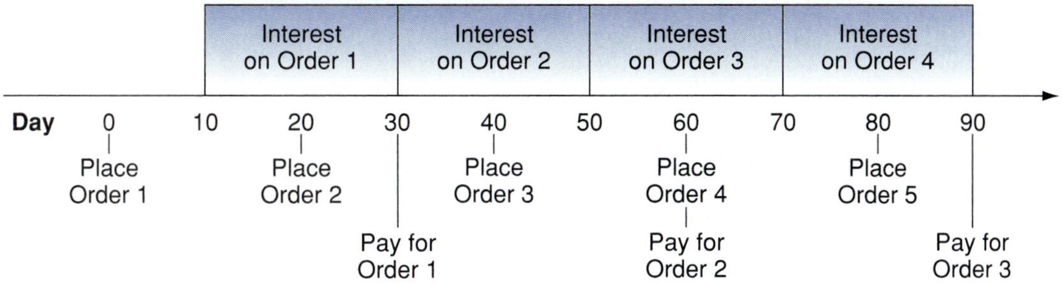

❖ EXAMPLE 7.1

The annual cost of not paying for 60 days when a supplier offers terms of 2/10 net 60 is:

$$(0.02/0.98) \times (365/50) = 14.9 \text{ percent}$$

In this case, interest of 2.04 percent is charged for 50 days, the difference between the 10-day interest-free period and the net period of 60 days. ❖

Availability of Trade Credit. If the purchaser can borrow elsewhere at a lower rate than the supplier offers, it is better to arrange the loan and pay the supplier on the tenth day. Some financial managers, however, look upon accounts payable as spontaneous financing; they see trade credit as a loan granted automatically without the time and trouble of filling out a loan application, waiting for the lender's approval, and repeating the process elsewhere if the application is rejected. Also, the seller has an incentive to grant credit that a lender does not: the sale of the merchandise at a profit. Once a customer has approval to make credit purchases, this approval is rarely rescinded if the buyer makes timely payments. In fact, increased amounts of credit may be available with one phone call if the buyer has a good credit history, and the supplier's sales personnel will usually be eager to help the buyer obtain approval.

Management Decisions

Even though a buyer has no control over the credit terms a seller offers, decisions still need to be made, such as the decision to take a discount or pay at the end of the credit period.

Payment Date. If a company purchases supplies on terms of 1/10 net 30, and it decides not to take the discount, it has no reason to pay before the 30th day; it incurs the 1 percent interest charge of the 11th day. A company that consistently paid on the 11th day would be borrowing for one day at an annual effective cost of:

$$(0.01/0.99) \times (365/1) = 368.65 \text{ percent}$$

Paying consistently on the 12th day would represent a series of two-day loans at an annual effective cost of:

$$(0.01/0.99) \times (365/2) = 184.33 \text{ percent}$$

Paying consistently on the 13th day would have an annual effective cost of 122.9 percent; paying on the 14th day would cost 92.2 percent; paying on the 15th day would cost 73.7 percent, and so on.

Pursuing this line of reasoning, some financial managers have become aware of the annual effective cost curve associated with trade credit. This curve is illustrated in Exhibit 7.3. The scale of the Y-axis is appropriate for terms of 1/10 net xx, but the shape of the curve remains the same if Y is scaled for 2/10 net xx, 3/10 net xx, or whatever discount the seller offers.

stretching the terms of trade
Paying suppliers a day or a few days late to lower the effective annual cost of trade credit.

The downward slope of this cost curve tempts some financial managers. They reason that their suppliers will not object to payments that are just a little late. **Stretching the terms of trade** by paying a day later or a few days late, lowers the annual effective cost of this credit. Paying on the 31st day instead of the 30th reduces the cost of not taking a 1 percent discount from 18.4 percent to 17.6 percent; paying on the 32nd day reduces the cost to 16.8 percent. The reductions continue indefinitely, although they get smaller and smaller. The cost of paying on the 60th day, for example, was calculated previously as 7.4 percent.

In practice, those who employ this technique begin by paying their accounts on time. Having established a good track record, the firm then dates the next check on time, and mails it one day late. If the seller does not object, the next time the firm dates the check on time, but mails it two days late. This process continues until the seller responds. Most companies send polite reminders that bills are overdue, followed by more demanding notices, and finally by threats to turn the account over to their collection departments for legal action. Those who stretch the terms of trade have no intention of pressing the issue this far, however. Having determined the length of time it takes to stimulate the seller's first response, such a firm pays just before that limit, to avoid getting a reputation as a slow payer.

monopsony
A large company that is the principal or only customer of another company.

A few companies practice a more callous version of stretching. A buyer may be a **monopsony;** that is, it may be a small company's principal—or worse, only—customer. Such buyers have been known to pay whenever they please, taking discounts whether or not sellers offered them. Sellers that object too vigorously are reminded that without the slow-paying customer's orders, the sellers may be forced to go out of business.

Foreign Accounts. Accounts payable that must be settled in a foreign currency require more complicated management than domestic transactions because the exchange rate when payment is due may differ from the exchange rate at the time the sale takes place. This can produce either a gain or a loss, but the

EXHIBIT 7.3

Annual Effective Cost Curve for Terms of 1/10 net xx

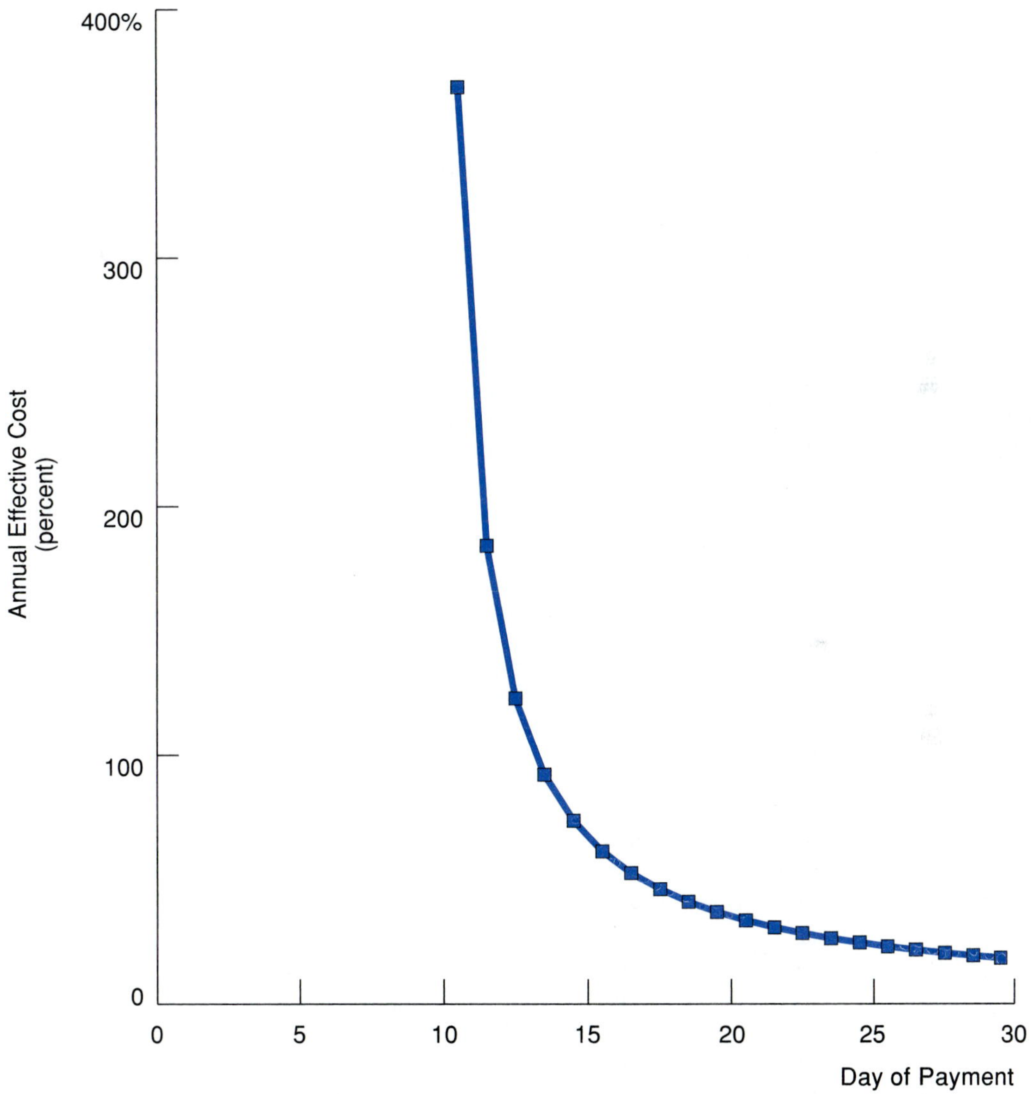

buyer is really concerned only that the U.S. dollar will buy fewer units of a foreign currency when the account payable is due.

The buyer has two choices: to hedge the payable against exchange risk and lock in the dollar cost of settling the payable, or to remain unhedged and settle the account payable at the prevailing exchange rate 30 days after the sale. There are many hedging instruments available in the currency and money markets.

❖ EXAMPLE 7.2

Suppose that a U.S. department store purchases P250,000 worth of embroidered blouses made in the Philippines. The sales terms require payment net 30 in Philippine pesos, and the current exchange rate is P25/US$. If the buyer were to pay on the day of the sale, the blouses would cost P250,000/25, or $10,000. Suppose further that the financial manager of the department store believes that the exchange rate will be P22/US$ in 30 days.

The buyer has to choose a strategy that will minimize the dollar cost of settling the payable in 30 days.

1. Remaining unhedged would raise the purchaser's cost to P250,000/22, or $11,364 if the exchange rate forecast is correct.
2. Hedging with a **forward contract** would lock in the exchange rate at which a bank would deliver P250,000 in 30 days. As long as the contract costs less than $11,364, this strategy is better than the unhedged strategy.
3. Hedging with money market instruments requires several steps. The buyer must borrow dollars in the U.S. market, convert them into pesos, invest the pesos in Philippine securities maturing in 30 days, and use the proceeds to pay off the P250,000 debt.

forward contract
An agreement that locks in the exchange rate at which a bank will deliver a specified amount of foreign currency on a specified date.

The steps required for hedging have to be calculated in reverse order:

1. The amount of pesos the buyer would need on the day of sale would depend on the interest rate available in the Philippines. Assume that the Philippine rate were 8 percent per year, or 0.67 percent for 30 days. The amount of pesos needed would be P250,000/1.0067, or P248,336.
2. The dollar cost of obtaining P248,336 on the day of sale would be P248,336/25, or $9,933.33.
3. If the U.S. interest rate available to the buyer were 12 percent per year, or 1 percent for 30 days, the dollar cost of settling the account payable using this strategy would be $9,933.33 × 1.01, or $10,033.33.

If the forward contract would cost more than $10,033.33, then this third strategy would be best.

If this transaction had involved one of the developed nations' currencies, a fourth strategy would have been available: buying a currency futures contract for delivery in 30 days. (No futures contracts for Philippine pesos trade in the U.S. markets.) If the buyer is a multinational corporation, it may have sufficient expertise to locate a futures contract in the Tokyo, Hong Kong, or Singapore markets, as well as sufficient Japanese yen, Hong Kong dollars, or Singapore dollars with which to buy it. ❖

Cash Budget Impact. The credit terms that suppliers offer and the payment dates that buyers choose directly influence the cash outflows section of the buyers' cash budgets. If a U.S. firm must pay in foreign currency, its cash budget must record the timing and amount of the outflow of U.S. dollars.

After a firm's budget has been completed and reviewed, the financial manager may evaluate the company's policies on payment dates or conversion of dollars into foreign currencies to determine whether changes would improve the company's cash position or profitability. Such policy changes would then be incorporated into a revised cash budget.

MANAGING ACCOUNTS RECEIVABLE

When a company sells its goods or services to a customer on credit, it creates an account receivable. Company policy dictates:

1. The terms under which the firm will extend credit
2. The type of customer to which it will extend credit
3. The timing and nature of collection activity it will take against delinquent accounts
4. How to handle foreign accounts

On occasion, a firm may consider changes in credit terms or credit-granting standards. The financial manager must evaluate the impact of these changes on the company's profitability and cash budget.

Credit Policy

A seller can decide to offer credit terms as simple as net 30, or as complicated as 1.75/10 net 45, 1 pm. Stating terms of *net 30* means that the seller is willing to offer a 30-day loan without charging interest. Credit terms like these are marketing tools; they may be necessary to meet the credit terms offered by competitors.

Stating terms of *1.75/10 net 45, 1 pm* means that the buyer has three choices:

1. Deduct 1.75 percent of the amount of the invoice and pay for the merchandise within 10 days
2. Pay the full amount of the invoice in 45 days
3. Stretch payment beyond the 45th day and pay the invoice amount plus 1 percent interest per month (for each month or fraction of a month)

Credit terms like these are financial tools; they are intended to speed up cash inflows from customers that are perceived to be slow payers. The seller can offer other variations of these terms, as well. For instance, *net 30 EOM* means that customers have 30 days after the end of the month to pay for the merchandise received during that month. An invoice received on September 10 would not have to be paid until October 30. These terms are convenient for customers who make frequent, small purchases. Sales of gift items to large retail stores in November and

December may be made on terms stated *net 30 EOY*. These buyers do not have to pay until January 30, 30 days after the end of the year.

Seller's Cost of Trade Credit. If a company offers credit terms that include a discount for prompt payment, it must be sure to set its prices at levels to cover its costs and produce its normal profit with the discounted payments. When a customer chooses to forego a discount and pay at the end of the net period, the extra payment represents interest on a short-term loan from the seller to the buyer. Unless competitive factors prevent it, this interest rate should be higher than the seller's cost of borrowing short-term funds.

Terms of 1/10 net 60, for example, represent an annual effective rate of:

$$(0.01/0.99) \times (365/50) = 7.37 \text{ percent}$$

The seller that offers these terms should be able to borrow at less than 7.37 percent itself. Suppose, though, that its borrowing costs are 10 percent. Obviously, its profits diminish every time a customer takes 60 days to pay. The solution to this problem is to raise the selling prices of its merchandise across the board, then raise the discount rate available to those who pay in 10 days, so they do not have to pay the price increase. (The seller's problem, remember, is with the rate it can charge those who get both the merchandise and the 50-day loan.)

The seller cannot break even with a price increase of 1 percent and an increase in the discount of 1 percent. To see why, consider a $1 million purchase. A 1 percent price increase would raise the cost of this purchase to $1,010,000. A 1 percent discount at this new price would reduce the transaction's cost by $10,100, to $999,900, which is below the original price. To keep prices the same for those who pay in ten days, the seller must raise the price by a larger percentage than the increase in the discount rate. It must raise price by:

$$(1.00/0.99) - 1.00 = 1.0101 \text{ percent}$$

This would boost the transaction's cost to $1,010,101; a 1 percent discount would bring this price back to $1 million. A higher discount magnifies this effect: a seller must raise prices by 2.0408 percent for a 2 percent discount to restore the original price, and by 3.0927 percent for a 3 percent discount to restore the original price.

Recall the company with the 1/10 net 60 problem; it need not add 1 percent to the discount rate to change its credit-granting loss to a profit. Even a 0.5 percent change would turn the loss to a profit. Terms of 1.5/10 net 60 would have an annual cost of 11.12 percent for buyers who took 60 days to pay. This would produce an 11.12 minus 10, or 1.12 percent change in the profit rate for the seller. To keep prices the same for those who paid in 10 days, it would increase prices across the board by:

$$(0.99/0.985) - 1.00 = 0.508 \text{ percent}$$

Customers who used to pay $990 for $1,000 of merchandise in 10 days would still pay $990 for the same merchandise, but the invoice value would be $1,005.08 before they deducted the 1.5 percent discount.

FOCUS ON CAREERS

CREDIT MANAGER

The role and responsibilities of a credit manager can vary widely depending upon whether the position is in a financial institution, a retail or wholesale establishment, or a manufacturing company. However, all credit managers pursue several common objectives. The credit manager must maintain and update all pertinent data relating to borrowers, create new borrower relationships, prepare reports for internal and external audits, and provide assistance and information to other areas of the organization. A retail credit manager must approve customer credit just as a commercial bank credit manager does, but the retail credit manager deals with individuals while the bank credit manager generally deals with corporate borrowers.

While a college degree in business administration, economics, or accounting is preferred, a liberal arts graduate with good communications skills and a concentration in business may qualify, as well. Generally the entry level position is that of a management trainee and promotion to credit manager generally requires five or more years of experience.

Salary, as always, depends upon experience and responsibility. The credit manager of a financial institution with a staff of ten or more professionals would command a salary around $55,000. Positions in nonfinancial companies generally pay less.

Future prospects, particularly at the retail level, are dismal. The use of bank credit cards rather than store credit, factoring of receivables, and centralization of credit information will result in the downsizing of most retail credit departments.

Credit Standards. A typical company makes two types of credit decisions. When a new customer places an order, it must decide whether or not to extend credit. Second, when it judges a new customer to be creditworthy or an old customer requests expanded credit, the firm must decide how much credit to grant.

Traditionally, financial managers have based these decisions on the five Cs of credit—character, capacity, capital, collateral, and conditions:

1. *Character* refers to the customer's willingness to pay. The financial manager judges character by comparing the customer's credit history with other companies. Information sources such as Dun & Bradstreet, TRW, and banks that subscribe to credit reports by Robert Morris Associates can generally provide information such as:
   (a) How many suppliers report extending credit to this customer
   (b) How much credit the customer has outstanding
   (c) Whether or not the customer usually takes discounts
   (d) How often the customer has paid promptly, or slowly, or how often other firms have had difficulty collecting from the customer
2. *Capacity* refers to the customer's ability to pay. A company may ask a potential customer to submit copies of its financial statements to evaluate the customer's ability to pay for the merchandise on time. Small, nonpublic companies with unaudited statements pose problems for credit analysts.

3. *Capital* refers to the seller's ability to collect. Analysis focuses special attention on the customer's balance sheet to predict the probable outcome of litigation if the customer does not pay on time.
4. *Collateral* refers to the seller's desire to make a secured loan. The customer may want to place a large order, or the customer may be expected to do a significant amount of repeat business. If the seller has some doubt about the customer's willingness or ability to pay, it may seek a pledge of assets in case of default on the credit extended.
5. *Conditions* refers to the state of the economy, the health of the seller's and buyer's industries, and the degree of competition the seller faces. All may influence the credit-granting decision.

Collection Policy. Managers frequently fail to appreciate the seriousness of delinquent accounts receivable until they face major financial problems that require a cost-cutting binge. To appreciate the gravity of this problem, it is necessary to examine a sale's contribution to net profit.

Suppose that a company's taxable income (EAIBT) is 7.5 percent of sales, its tax rate is 33.3 percent, and its net profit margin is 5 percent. From the proceeds of a $1,000 sale, then:

$$\$1{,}000 \times (1 - 0.075) = \$925 \text{ pays operating costs}$$
$$(\$1{,}000 - \$925) \times 0.333 = \$25 \text{ pays taxes}$$
$$\$1{,}000 - \$925 - \$25 = \$50 \text{ is the company's profit}$$

If the firm fails to collect anything on the account, it has $925 in unreimbursed costs and owes no taxes. It will take the after-tax profits from $925/0.05, or $18,500 in successful sales just to break even.

Thus, even if a buyer cannot pay an account in full, every dollar the seller salvages from a partial collection is significant. Whether the company has in-house bill collectors or contracts with an outside agency, the normal costs of the collection process are part of the $925 operating costs. Recovery rates vary with economic conditions, the size and financial quality of the company's customers, and how quickly the firm starts the collection process. A company that actively pursues a delinquent account more quickly will enjoy a higher recovery rate.

The collection process itself is expensive. Outside bill collectors usually earn a small fee plus half of whatever they recover. The net proceeds of an efficient in-house collection department are only marginally higher.

Immediate pursuit of past-due accounts is far more effective than waiting in reducing a company's losses. In the above illustration, the company can afford to spend $75 (its tax on the sale plus its net profit) specifically attempting to collect the $1,000, and still break even on the sale. This $75 can buy significant amounts of stationery and postage, phone calls, personnel effort, and computer time, above and beyond the normal operating costs of the collection department.

Foreign Accounts. Collections from domestic corporate customers depend mostly on the willingness and ability of the customer to pay, but collections from foreign corporate customers depend heavily on intermediation by commercial banks, as well. There are six different methods of payment for international transactions. The last three listed below create accounts receivable; the first three do not.

1. A seller may ask first-time customers and customers in a noncompetitive market to pay for goods in advance of shipment.
2. The seller may ship goods under a **sight draft**, which is a document drawn by the seller that instructs the customer to pay the face amount of the draft "on sight," that is, when it is presented to the customer. The seller ships the goods and presents the sight draft for payment through its bank. This bank will allow the customer to take possession of the goods only after the customer pays the draft.
3. A customer can obtain a letter of credit from its bank, which assures the seller of payment when the bank is satisfied that the shipment has been made.
4. The seller may ship goods under a **time draft**, which is a document drawn by the seller instructing the customer to pay the face amount of the draft at a specified future date. The seller's bank, working through its local correspondent bank, will allow the customer to take possession of the goods only after the customer has signed the draft, thereby creating a **trade acceptance**. If the buyer fails to pay the draft at maturity, the collecting bank is not obligated to honor it and make payment. A trade acceptance is different from the banker's acceptance discussed in Chapter 4; the latter is a time draft accepted by a bank, and the bank is obliged to honor it.
5. The seller may ship merchandise to a customer under **consignment**. The customer does not have to pay until it sells the merchandise.
6. **Open account transactions** are the same as credit sales to domestic corporate customers. The seller ships the goods, creates an account receivable, and relies on the willingness and ability of the customer to pay when due.

sight draft
A document drawn by the seller that instructs the customer to pay the face amount of the draft when presented with it.

time draft
A document drawn by a seller instructing the customer to pay the face amount at a specified future date.

trade acceptance
A time draft signed by the customer to indicate acceptance of the obligation.

consignment
An agreement that a customer does not have to pay for a shipment until it sells the merchandise.

open account transaction
A transaction in which the seller ships goods, creates an account receivable, and relies on the willingness and ability of the customer to pay when due.

Receivables Management Techniques

An attempt to change the cash inflow patterns from sales in any significant way involves major managerial decisions. Should the company enlist the help of a **factor** to speed up its cash flow? A factor is a financial company that lends money to corporations, which pledge their accounts receivable as collateral for the loans; the factor may also buy accounts receivable outright. Will factoring produce benefits worth its costs and the changes that the company will undergo?

If management is not prepared for such a drastic move, then perhaps the company should change its credit terms. How will its customers react? How will its competitors react? What will happen to sales? To the timing of cash inflows? To the amount of cash inflows?

factor
A financial company that lends money to corporations, which pledge their accounts receivable as collateral for the loans.

Factoring. From the beginning of the 20th century until the 1960s, factoring in the United States involved finance companies located in New York City whose sole purpose was to help corporations turn their accounts receivable into cash.

They were a company's last legal resort for funds, and they frequently agreed to arrangements that would keep a company's customers from learning that the company was utilizing the services of a factor. Employment by a factor generally meant working in the most economically run office environments in the United States.

When a company initially approached a factor, it had to decide whether it wanted to borrow against its receivables or sell the accounts outright to the factor. (Not all factors performed both services; those willing to buy receivables were called *old-line factors*.) Either way, the factor would examine all of the company's accounts, approving some and rejecting others.

If the company and the factor could come to terms on the nature of their relationship, the company would agree to clear all future credit sales with the factor before finalizing them. Based on the creditworthiness of a potential customer, the factor determined how much credit the seller could extend. The company then made the sale. The factor recorded the account receivable and handled all subsequent paperwork and collections activity until the customer paid, or until the account was conclusively written off as a bad debt.

A company that used a factor was free to dismantle its billing and collections department, redeploy or dismiss its employees, and terminate any agreements it had with collection agencies. These cost savings helped defray the cost of the factor's services, but the company essentially became "married" to the factor. The company could make credit sales only with the approval of the factor, because it had no means of processing the bills or monitoring their collection. Terminating a relationship with a factor required a company to reconstruct its billing and collections department or find another factor.

As compensation for its services, the factor would assess a percentage factor fee on all of the company's receivables. The size of this fee depended on the credit terms the company offered, the general creditworthiness of the company's customers, and whether it had factored its receivables with or without recourse. A longer net period and riskier customers both increased the factor's fee. In a factoring agreement with recourse, if the receivable proved to be uncollectible, the company took the loss even though the factor had approved the extension of credit. In an agreement without recourse, the factor absorbed the loss. Since this amounted to insuring accounts receivable, the factor fee was higher because it included an insurance premium. Factoring without recourse agreements generally led to fewer credit sale approvals.

If a company wanted to borrow against its receivables, the factor might lend the company up to 90 percent of the net value of each receivable. The net value was the amount of the invoice less the factor fee and less any discount the seller's credit terms offered the customer. The company did not have to borrow the maximum amount the factor was willing to lend. The factor charged interest on whatever amount the firm borrowed, at a rate between 1 percent and 7 percent higher than commercial banks were charging on secured, short-term loans. When the customer paid off the account, the factor deducted the factor fee and any principal and interest, and forwarded the balance to the company. If a company sold its accounts

FOCUS ON FINANCE

NationsBanc Commercial Corp.

♦ ♦ ♦

NationsBanc Commercial Corp. (NBCC), the third largest U.S. factor, purchased $7.3 billion in accounts receivable during 1993, earning $74 million in gross, noninterest income. Its clients include U.S. manufacturers of such diverse products as apparel, textiles, footwear, and furniture, Chinese producers of Christmas tree lights, sake brewers in Japan, growers of sheep embryos in Australia, and manufacturers of chemical war detection devices in Norway.

NBCC is a member of Factors Chain International, the world's largest trade association of factors, with 98 members in 30 countries. These member factors do credit research for each other in their domestic markets, which facilitates international trade. They can relieve importers of the cumbersome and time-consuming process of getting letters of credit to ensure payment.

Globally, factors take the credit risks and collection responsibilities for $225 billion in international credit sales. Over $32 billion of this amount is handled by the five largest U.S. factors:

CIT Group Holdings, Inc. (New Jersey)

BNY Financial Co. (New York)

NationsBanc Commercial Corp. (Georgia)

Heller Financial Inc. (Illinois)

Barclays Commercial Corp. (North Carolina)

Source: Kenneth Cline, "NationsBanc Has Global Ambitions for Its Big Factoring Subsidiary," *American Banker*, March 30, 1994, pp. 4-5.

receivable to a factor, the procedure was essentially the same, but the title to the accounts changed hands.

In the chronically cash-starved apparel industry, factoring was almost universal. Factors also supported the toy industry. Toy manufacturers accumulated net cash outflows to develop new designs in early spring, to manufacture the goods in summer, to promote them in fall, and to pay for preholiday shipments. These firms depended heavily on their massive postholiday net cash inflows. In other industries, however, resorting to a factor was considered to be an indication that a company had exhausted its borrowing power and was on the brink of insolvency.

In the 1960s, the rest of the financial world widely recognized the lucrative profits of factoring. Commercial banks and conglomerates such as ITT began buying factors, and the credit crunch during the 1970s eliminated the remaining independent factors; they either sold out or were wiped out by the failures of such retail giants as W. T. Grant, E. J. Korvette, and S. Klein. The new owners of factoring subsidiaries positioned themselves as respectable financiers; they dropped the use of the word *factor* and ended the practice of buying accounts receivable. They would only lend against receivables, but they continued to perform the credit-approving, billing, and collections functions.

Ten years later, the first inexpensive advertisements began to appear throughout the United States for small factoring businesses located in Entrepreneur's Square (Nevada, Arizona, Utah, and New Mexico). Today, almost another decade later, such companies are scattered all over the nation. They usually offer services besides factoring, such as bill collecting, legal advice, tax advice, or processing of medical accounts receivable. Most will buy accounts receivable as well as lend against them.

cross-border factoring

A network of factors in different countries who share information about the creditworthiness of importers and handle collections of local receivables for each other.

Factors that service exporters generally buy foreign accounts receivable without recourse. **Cross-border factoring** involves a network of factors in different countries. They share information about the creditworthiness of importers and handle collections on local receivables for each other. These factors are usually subsidiaries of commercial banks and other financial institutions.

Changing Credit Terms. Occasionally, a suggestion from a nonfinancial department about a change in credit terms will filter up a company's chain of command. It usually takes one of two forms:

1. "We are currently selling on credit terms of 2/10 net 45. We could boost sales significantly by changing the terms to 3/10 net 60."
2. "We are currently selling on terms of 2/10 net 45. We could increase profits or speed up cash flow significantly by changing the credit terms to 1/10 net 30."

To judge these proposals on their financial merits alone, assume that the company's product is identical to those of all of its competitors and that no price/service/location differential distinguishes them. Suppose that all companies offer terms of 2/10 net 45 and brand loyalty is insignificant. (If you think there is no such product in the real world, identify the brand name of the next loose rubber band or paper clip you encounter.)

The company can divide its customers into three groups: Group A always takes the discount, Group B always pays on time at the end of the net period, and Group C always pays a little late, but not so late that the company will refuse to extend credit in the future. Each of these groups has its own line in the cash inflows section of the cash budget.

The annual cost of missing a discount when the terms are 2/10 net 45 is 21.3 percent. Group A customers can borrow elsewhere at less than 21.3 percent; they do so and pay the company in 10 days. Group B customers cannot borrow elsewhere for less than 21.3 percent, so they borrow from the seller at that rate for 35 days. Group C customers are either in such tight financial constraints that they cannot borrow elsewhere and cannot pay the company on time, or they are stretching the terms of trade. Each competitor's customers fit these same three descriptions.

Changing the credit terms to 3/10 net 60 would raise customers' annual cost of foregoing discounts to 22.6 percent. It would reduce the cash inflow from all of the company's Group A customers by $1 per $100 invoice. This price cut would attract all of the Group A customers from all of the company's competitors.

Some of the company's Group B customers could borrow money elsewhere for less than 22.6 percent (but more than 21.2 percent), so they would move into Group A and start taking the discount. This would reduce the cash inflow from them by $3 per $100 invoice, but would speed up this inflow from 45 days to 10 days. The rest of the company's Group B customers could not borrow money elsewhere for less than 22.6 percent, so they would stay with the company as Group B customers and pay in 60 days. This would not change the amount of their cash inflow, but it would slow the inflow down by 15 days. Either way, the change in terms would be advantageous to Group B customers, so it would attract them from all of the firm's competitors.

Some of the company's Group C customers could pay on time if they were given 15 more days, so they would move into Group B. Whether these customers had been paying on the 46th day or the 59th day, they would all begin to pay on Day 60. The rest of Group C, those who were stretching the terms of trade, would continue to stretch them. If they had paid on Day 48 under terms of net 45, they would begin to pay on Day 63 under terms of net 60. As a whole, the total cash inflow from Group C does not change, but it would slow down. The chance to improve their credit reputations or stretch the terms of trade further would attract all of the Group C customers from all competitors.

If the company were to make this change and its competitors did not, it would destroy them. Obviously, the competitors would have to change their credit terms to 3/10 net 60 immediately to remove any incentive for their customers to leave them. The net effect of such a change on the originating company would be, therefore, *no increase* in sales, but a slower, smaller cash inflow.

The other credit change suggestion, changing from 2/10 net 45 to 1/10 net 30, can be analyzed in the same way. The change would reduce the annual cost of foregoing discounts from 21.3 percent to 18.4 percent. Those customers in Group A who could borrow elsewhere at less than 18.4 percent would continue to do so, but they would leave the company and go to the competition because the company's new terms would represent a $1 per $100 invoice price increase to them. The remaining customers in Group A could borrow elsewhere at rates between 18.4 percent and 21.3 percent. If the company had no competition, they would stay and become Group B customers. It would be cheaper for them to go to the competition, however, as Group A customers. The company's new terms would not attract any of the competition's Group A customers.

If the company's Group B customers were to stay, they would have to pay in 30 days. The competition would give them 45 days to pay, so they would go. The company's Group C customers couldn't or wouldn't pay in 45 days, so they could not or would not pay in 30 days. They would move to any competitor who would sell to them. The new terms would attract none of the competition's Group B and C customers. Thus, if the company were to make this change and its competitors did not, the company would wipe itself out, definitely not the result intended.

Financial managers must address other variations of these two suggestions. For example, the terms could be changed to 1/10 net 60 or 3/10 net 30. Because the analytical process is the same, these possibilities have been incorporated into the questions at the end of the chapter.

Cash Budget Impact. The credit terms that a company offers to its customers function partially as marketing tools that can increase or decrease its total sales. However, the size of the discount and the net period offered also affect the company's cash flows. A larger discount produces a smaller and faster cash inflow. A longer net period produces a slower cash inflow and larger opportunity costs and collection costs. The financial manager must verify that the company lends funds at a rate higher than its own short-term borrowing costs.

The standards by which a company grants credit determine how much cash will actually flow into it at a given level of sales. They also have an impact on processing costs: stricter standards increase the expense of processing an application for credit. The costs of obtaining credit histories and ratings increase; the time spent analyzing this data also increases.

The same statement can be made about the aggressiveness of a company's efforts to collect delinquent accounts. More effort to collect raises collection costs and reduces bad debt losses. Repeated cost/benefit analyses of all standards and practices are necessary parts of managing a company's accounts receivable.

If a company is profitable but its cash budget is tight, factoring may ease the problem. Factors limit the amount of credit a company can extend, forcing it to forego sales to some marginal customers. The high cost of this source of credit also reduces the profits the firm earns on every credit sale, but the bulk of the proceeds from these sales are available to the seller immediately.

When a company considers changing its credit terms, it must evaluate the changes in the amounts and timing of the cash inflows it expects from various types of customers. The change will affect each cash inflow line on the cash budget. In the real world, these consequences are mitigated somewhat by differences in quality, service, and dependability between the company and its competitors.

INVENTORY COST MANAGEMENT

Decisions concerning the acquisition, storage, processing, and selling of inventory are the joint responsibility of several company officials. Purchasing, production, marketing, and financial managers must all have input into these decisions. Failure to coordinate these planning activities can prevent the company's significant investment in inventory from producing a satisfactory profit. The following discussion is concerned primarily with the financial manager's input: controlling costs.

Components of Inventory Cost

Managers divide inventory costs into four basic types: acquisition or purchasing costs, carrying costs, stock-out or shortage costs, and disposal costs. The financial manager seeks to minimize the total cost of inventory. Unfortunately, the interrelationships among the four costs frequently cause actions that reduce one type of cost but increase another type of cost.

FOCUS ON FINANCE

SAFETY STOCK LEVELS

If a firm could obtain inventory instantaneously upon placing an order, and if the need for inventory were known with certainty, then no firm would need to carry safety stocks.

Suppose that a company needs 100,000 reams of paper per year, and it calculates the EOQ as 5,480 reams. If paper usage is a constant 100,000/365, or 274 reams per day, then the company will use up an order 5,480/274, or 20 days after receiving it.

Assuming instantaneous delivery, the company's inventory will fit the following pattern:

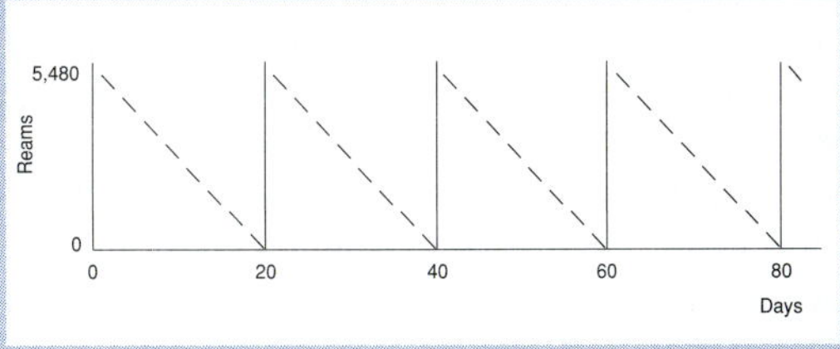

If, however, delivery takes three days, the company has to calculate a new order point as 3 x 274, or 822 reams. If the firm places an order when its inventory falls to 822 reams on the 17th day, the paper will be delivered just as the firm exhausts its inventory on the 20th day.

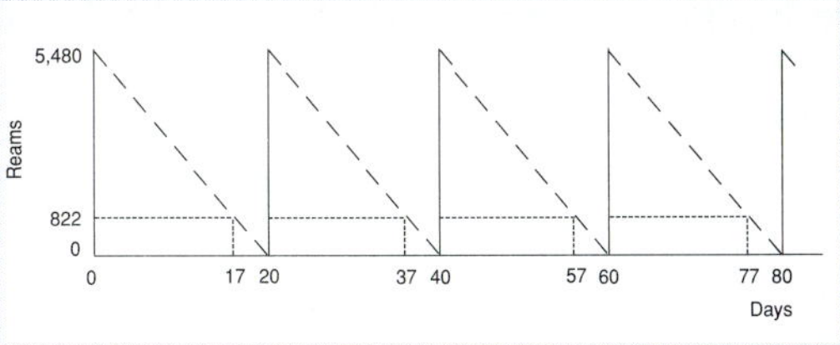

If the delivery time is uncertain, the firm can increase the lead time. This will create a slowly rising safety stock. Suppose the firm raises its order point to four days' supply: 4 x 274, or 1,096 reams. Suppose further that the four deliveries scheduled in the illustration take four, three, three, and four days, respectively. The firm will maintain a one-day safety stock from Day 39 through Day 76. The company's inventory pattern then becomes:

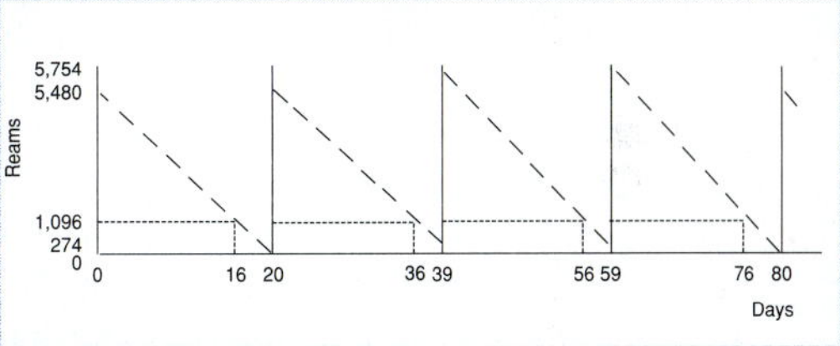

If inventory usage is uncertain, the company should develop a policy of carrying permanent safety stocks. It can do this either by raising the order point or by making a one-time purchase. The appropriate amount of safety stock to carry depends on:

1. Degree of uncertainty—Less certain forecasted inventory needs require larger safety stocks.
2. Variation in delivery time—Greater variation requires a larger safety stock.
3. Stock-out cost—A higher cost for lost production time or sales requires a larger safety stock.
4. Carrying cost—A smaller carrying cost requires a larger safety stock.

Purchasing Costs. Acquisition cost, or purchasing cost, equals the number of units purchased times the price per unit, plus shipping or freight costs. Several considerations can affect purchasing cost.

1. Quantity discounts reduce the per-unit purchase price and shipping costs for larger orders. However, these larger quantities cost more to store and insure, and they tie up a lot of company funds.

2. The supplier that offers the lowest selling prices may not offer favorable terms of trade.
3. The lowest purchase prices may reflect unsatisfactory quality, unreliable delivery, or temporarily favorable exchange rates. Shopping around for the best prices for every order increases the cost of placing orders.
4. International suppliers may be able to offer low selling prices because their local governments do not prohibit environmental damage, child labor, wages below livable minimums, or other unethical practices. Most buyers relish trips at company expense to inspect a potential supplier's facilities or to "dot the *is* and cross the *ts*" on a contract negotiated over a great distance. For such buyers to claim ignorance of conditions that would be unacceptable in their home countries is indefensible.

Carrying Costs. Carrying costs include all the direct and hidden costs of owning inventory, from raw materials through work in process to finished goods. Carrying costs increase when inventories increase. These costs include:

1. Storage expenses, and the costs of manual or computerized record keeping systems
2. Insurance premiums and taxes
3. Losses on unsellable or unusable inventories (Inventories lose value for several reasons: inappropriate specifications, damage, obsolescence, regulatory changes, deterioration, storage in unfindable locations, and shrinkage, which is a euphemism for employee or customer theft.)
4. Interest or opportunity cost of funds invested in inventories.

Stock-out Costs. A company incurs stock-out or shortage costs when it lacks sufficient inventory to meet its needs. Carrying inadequate stocks of finished goods can lead to lost sales, both currently and in the future. Carrying inadequate stocks of raw materials may force the firm to operate in inefficient production runs, or even to shut down production temporarily while purchasers buy emergency supplies, possibly at premium prices. Stock-out costs decrease when inventory levels increase. However, any attempt to avoid stock-outs by holding safety stocks of critical components increases carrying costs.

Disposal Costs. A company's normal marketing and promotional costs are not part of inventory costs. Disposal costs cover extra efforts needed to "clean out the attic," to get rid of raw materials, work-in-process, or finished goods that the firm cannot sell like normal merchandise. Some retailers, like Fortunoff and Macy's, open special warehouse clearance outlets to dispose of damaged, shop-worn, or remainder merchandise. Under legal duress, some manufacturers pay enormous sums to dispose of toxic or hazardous components or by-products that they have stored for years. Other suppliers search the world for markets where they can dump technologically obsolete products at prices that will allow them to recoup at least some of their costs. Almost every Latin American government has a fleet of obsolete U.S. planes obtained at bargain prices; in almost every African nation, citizens try to squeeze the last mile out of obsolete U.S. and European cars.

Minimizing Inventory Cost

Scholars have devoted enormous effort to apply mathematical models to inventory control. Academic majors such as operations management, production engineering, and management information systems offer many courses in inventory modeling. The five models introduced below are intended to highlight the interface between financial management and inventory management.

ABC Model. This crude approach to inventory management divides a company's inventory into three categories. Category A includes essential raw materials and component parts whose levels the firm must monitor closely. This kind of inventory may be extremely expensive, hard to obtain, or crucial to the production process. This category may also include finished goods with high profit margins, or those that the firm must offer immediately to avoid permanent loss of important customers. Category C includes raw materials that are inexpensive, quick and easy to obtain, or free of the risk of obsolescence. It may also include finished goods with low markups and selling prices, those that can be easily substituted for another of the company's products, those sold on impulse at store registers, or those carried for the convenience of customers buying other things. Category C takes little management time; the company may carry a large supply and/or reorder whenever somebody notices a low stock level. Category B includes all other inventory items; this category demands management effort less than Category A but greater than Category C.

Two-Bin Model. Delivery time is crucial for a two-bin model. The company estimates how long it must wait for delivery of each inventory item. It then calculates how many units of an item it will use during the time it must wait for delivery. It orders twice that number of units and divides them into two bins. When the first bin is emptied, purchasers place a new order. By the time the order arrives, the second bin should be empty. The order refills both bins, and the process is repeated. This system, sometimes called the *JIT (just-in-time) model*, is attributed to Japanese manufacturers.

If delivery times or usage rates vary significantly, the company may use a three-bin system in which a third bin holds a small safety stock. Management specifies an acceptable probability that this bin might also be emptied before delivery of a new order. Statistical models can then indicate just how small this bin should be.

Complete Count Model. Many supermarket chains and large home improvement centers rely on computer systems that are supposed to keep exact counts of all items these firms hold in inventory. As clerks scan customer purchases at the checkout register, the computer subtracts sold items from the store's inventory. Based on automatic reorder points, the computer program prints out daily lists of inventory items that should be replenished. The program also allows

FOCUS ON FINANCE

MORE THAN THE PRICES WERE INSANE!

Crazy Eddie's, a 43-store consumer-electronics discount chain with a notorious TV commercial, declared bankruptcy in 1987. In 1993, its founder, Eddie Antar, was tried along with his brothers Mitchell and Allen in federal court in New Jersey on charges of securities fraud and racketeering. The Securities and Exchange Commission recovered $1.04 million from Antar's bank account in Montreal and froze approximately $13 million in other accounts in Britain, Liechtenstein, and Israel. Prosecutors never found $45 million in inventory "that could have filled a line of tractor trailers nine miles long," according to trial testimony. The three brothers were accused of defrauding investors of more than $80 million by selling stock whose worth they artificially boosted by inflating the value of their inventory.

Source: Newsday, various 1993 issues.

for deliveries and shrinkage rates. These systems' accuracy levels have proved to be less than perfect; which the owners generally attribute this to human error at the registers.

EOQ Model. The economic order quantity model focuses on carrying costs and ordering costs. It assumes fixed acquisition costs, given the number of units the firm expects to sell per year. These costs are unaffected by the sizes of the orders the company places. The model also assumes that the company uses up its inventory at a constant rate per time period (day or week) until it exhausts its inventory. At exactly that point, the company takes delivery on a new order, and this process repeats all year. As the company orders larger quantities, its carrying costs and the time interval between orders increases. Thus, larger quantities reduce total ordering costs. The EOQ model totals these two costs and calculates the minimum total cost. The EOQ is the size of the order a company should place to achieve this minimum total cost. See Exhibit 7.4. As this exhibit illustrates, the firm can minimize the total cost where the ordering cost line intersects the carrying cost line. At that point, these two costs are equal.

To work with the EOQ model, the following definitions will prove useful:

Y = number of units the company needs during one year

Q = number of units the company orders at one time

C = carrying cost per unit for a year, in dollars

P = cost of placing one order, in dollars

EXHIBIT 7.4

Relationship Between Order Quantity and Cost

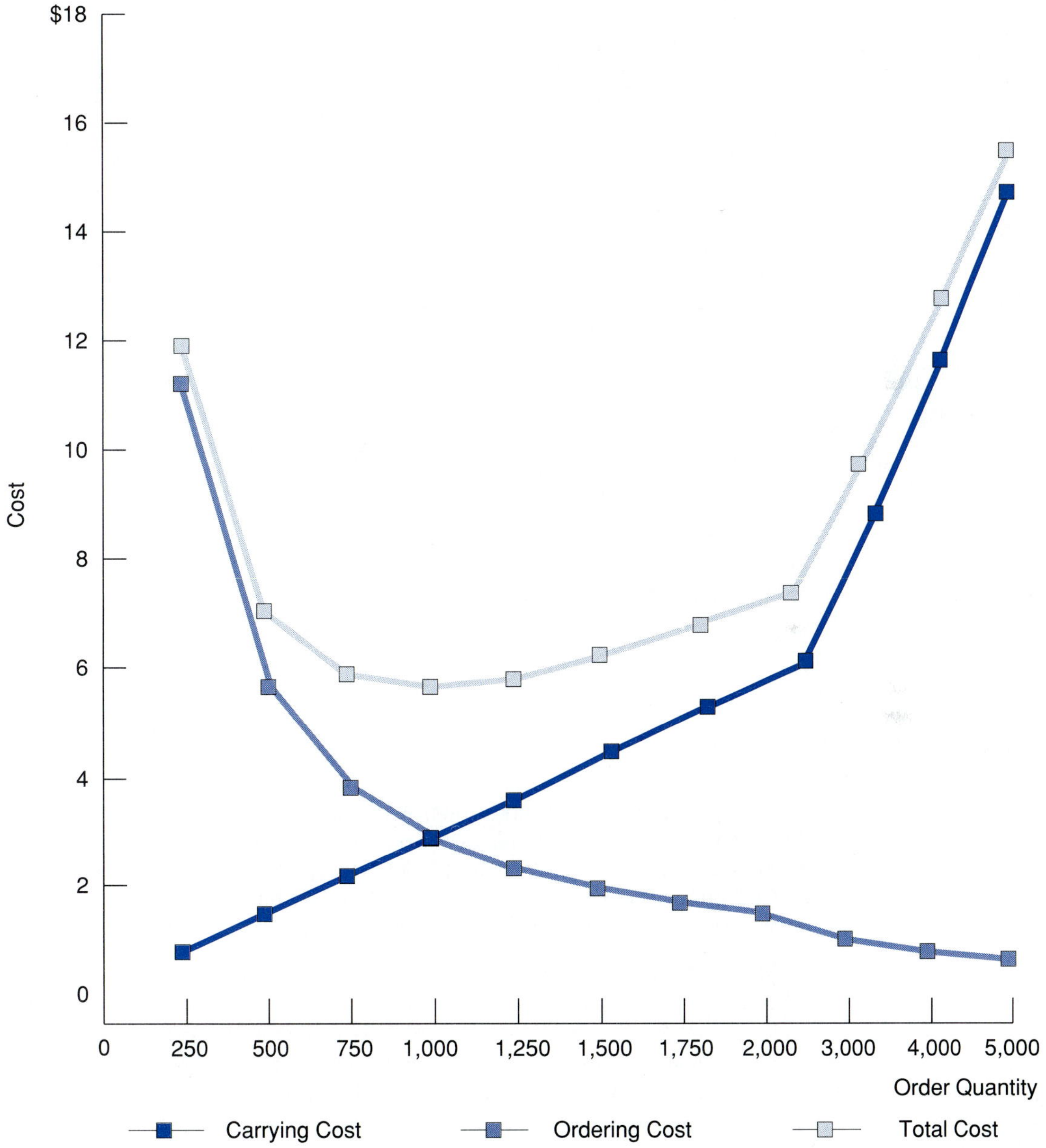

These variables then become part of several calculations:

$Q/2$ = average inventory held during the year

$CQ/2$ = total carrying costs (ascending in Exhibit 7.4)

Y/Q = number of orders placed per year

PY/Q = total ordering costs (descending in Exhibit 7.4)

The firm can express its total ordering and carrying costs as:

$$\text{Total cost} = CQ/2 + PY/Q \tag{7.2}$$

This is the U-shaped curve in Exhibit 7.4.

Setting carrying cost equal to ordering cost and solving for Q produces the EOQ, the amount that the firm should order to minimize total cost:

$$CQ/2 = PY/Q$$

Multiplying both sides of the equation by $2Q/C$ produces:

$$Q^2 = 2PY/C$$

Taking the square root of both sides of the equation produces the EOQ:

$$Q = \sqrt{2PY/C} \tag{7.3}$$

❖ EXAMPLE 7.3

Suppose that a company uses 100,000 sacks of sugar a year. Its carrying cost is $6 per sack per year and it spends $30 to place an order. The quantity of sugar it should order at one time is:

$$EOQ = \sqrt{(2)(\$30)(100{,}000)/\$6}$$
$$= \sqrt{1{,}000{,}000}$$
$$= 1{,}000 \text{ sacks}$$

The company will place 100,000/1,000, or 100 orders per year. Its total ordering cost will be $30 × 100, or $3,000. Its total carrying cost will be $6 × 1,000/2, or $3,000, so its total cost will be $3,000 plus $3,000, or $6,000. Placing orders of any other size will produce a higher total cost, as shown in Exhibit 7.5. ❖

MRP Models. In industries that can schedule production runs months in advance, production managers have been able to estimate their raw materials and components needs and the timing of these requirements. Various computerized materials requirements planning (MRP) models have been developed to assist in this back-scheduling. Based on these models, the company's purchasing agents schedule orders so that suppliers will make deliveries as needed. This is another method of minimizing carrying costs and disposal costs.

EXHIBIT 7.5

Inventory Costs for Different Order Sizes

Quantity Ordered	Carrying Cost	Ordering Cost	Total Cost
250	$ 750	$12,000	$12,750
500	1,500	6,000	7,500
750	2,250	4,000	6,250
1,000	**3,000**	**3,000**	**6,000**
1,250	3,750	2,400	6,150
1,500	4,500	2,000	6,500
1,750	5,250	1,714	6,964
2,000	6,000	1,500	7,500
3,000	9,000	1,000	10,000
4,000	12,000	750	12,750
5,000	15,000	600	15,600

SUMMARY

Cash management seeks to accelerate cash inflows and slow down cash outflows, while holding minimal idle cash balances. Microbudgeting breaks down the nearest month's cash budget data into data for daily and weekly budgeting periods. This gives the financial manager more detailed information to guide efforts to control checking account balances, and to reduce the float attributable to mailing and processing times. Except for banks' systems to reduce check-clearing times, most attempts to squeeze advantages from check-clearing float are illegal or unethical. As part of their cash management programs, banks have developed zero-balance accounts to minimize company cash balances, and concentration banking to accelerate cash receipts.

Accounts payable management seeks to choose a payment date that minimizes the company's short-term borrowing costs without risking insolvency or earning a reputation as a slow payer. Currency exchange rates complicate the decision making process for a company with foreign suppliers. A buyer must evaluate a credit offer based, in part, on possible changes in exchange rates before it must make payment. If the rates are expected to change in the seller's favor, the buyer may have to decide whether to:

1. Delay converting of dollars into the foreign currency
2. Convert immediately and invest the foreign currency in securities denominated in that currency until the payment date
3. Buy a forward contract from a bank for future delivery of the foreign currency
4. Buy a currency futures contract, if one is available

Accounts receivable management seeks to offer competitive terms of trade to creditworthy domestic and foreign customers to maximize profits without impairing the seller's present and future cash flows. To achieve this goal, the firm can vary:

1. The discount rate it offers
2. The length of time it allows the customer to wait before paying
3. The strictness of the standards that guide its decision to extend credit, and, if so, how much credit to extend
4. The aggressiveness of its attempts to collect delinquent accounts

Companies rely heavily on the services of commercial banks when they extend credit to foreign customers. A few companies obtain financing from factors when they nearly exhaust their borrowing ability from cheaper sources. When a company considers changing the terms of trade it offers, it must anticipate the reactions of its various types of customers. The desirability of the proposed change depends on its impact on the amount and timing of the company's cash inflows.

In inventory management, the financial manager seeks to control total costs. This can be difficult because attempts to reduce purchasing costs drive up carrying costs, reduce stock-out costs, and increase disposal costs. Many mathematical models have been developed to manage inventories. The nature of a business determines which model is most useful.

Key Terms

check kiting
collection float
consignment
cross-border factoring
disbursement float
factor
float
forward contract
monopsony
net float
open account transaction
sight draft
stretching the terms of trade
time draft
trade acceptance

Self-Study Questions

1. What is the primary goal of cash management?
2. What is float? Name three causes of float.
3. Name three legal, ethical ways to manage float.
4. What is meant by *stretching the terms of trade*?
5. A seller offers terms of 2/10 net 30. One customer buys $1,000 of merchandise, while another buys $2,500. If they both pay on Day 30, why do both incur the same annual percentage cost of foregoing the discount?
6. Explain the five Cs of credit.
7. What are the six different methods of payment for international transactions? Which three produce accounts receivable?
8. What does a factor do for a company?
9. Your company and its competitors sell on terms of 2/10 net 30. An employee suggests that terms of 1/10 net 30 would be more profitable. Explain to

the employee why your competitors would send a thank-you card if you took this advice.

10. What are the four types of inventory costs?

Self-Test Problems

1. A company can borrow from its bank at an effective rate of 12 percent. One of its suppliers offers terms of 3/10 net 90. Should the company borrow from the bank and pay the supplier in ten days?
2. Quick Co. has two potential suppliers that can provide merchandise of identical quality. Speedy, Inc. sells on terms of 1/10 net 45 and Jiffy Bros. sells on terms of 2/10 net 60. If Quick Co. can borrow from its bank at 13 percent, what should it do to minimize its costs?
3. A U.S. importer purchases I£30,000 worth of knit sweaters on credit in Ireland when the exchange rate is US$1.50/I£. The Irish punt (pound) is expected to rise in value to US$1.60/I£ when the account must be settled. How much can the buyer afford to pay a bank for a forward contract on Irish punts?
4. A U.S. jeweler purchases Tb25 million worth of sapphires in Thailand on terms of net 60. The exchange rate is Tb25/US$, but the Thai baht is expected to rise in value to Tb21/US$ when the account must be settled. To hedge this account, the jeweler can invest in Thai government securities at 10 percent and borrow in the United States at 15 percent. A forward contract for Thai bahts costs $1,005,000. What should the jeweler do?
5. The Blue Angel Nursery sells 10,000 hydrangea bushes every year. It costs $10 to carry one bush in inventory for a year, and $45 to place an order for more bushes. What is the EOQ?
6. A shoe store sells 64,000 pairs of sneakers a year. It costs $4 to carry a pair of sneakers in inventory for a year, and $5 to place an order for more sneakers. What is the EOQ? Suppose that the sneakers manufacturer offers the shoe store a one-cent reduction in purchase price if the store orders 500 pairs of sneakers at a time. Should the shoe store owner stick to the EOQ? (Hint: Calculate the total cost using the EOQ and the total cost using an order of 500 sneakers.)

Discussion Questions

1. Which items change when the financial manager breaks down data for the first month of a cash budget to create a microbudget?
2. The text lists four variations of compensating balance requirements. What are they and which one would a corporation prefer?
3. Why would a company prefer positive net float to negative net float?
4. Rank the different kinds of float according to the company's ability to reduce them and explain your reasoning.
5. What is check kiting and why is it illegal?
6. What is the difference between a lockbox system and a concentration banking service? Can they be combined?

7. If a seller offers terms of net 30, can it make a profit by extending this credit?
8. Suppose that banks are lending at a rate lower than the annual effective rate a firm would incur by not taking discounts. Under what circumstances might a buyer borrow from suppliers instead of banks?
9. Is it unethical for a company in a monopsony position to take a discount that was not offered? Why or why not?
10. A company buys its supplies on terms of 1/10 net 60 and sells its finished goods on terms of 2/10 net 30. What additional information do you need to determine if it is making a profit operating on these credit terms?
11. A company and its competitors sell on terms of 2/10 net 45. An employee suggests that 3/10 net 30 would be an improvement. Explain what might happen if the company made the change, but its competitors did not.
12. How much can a company afford to spend attempting to collect a delinquent account?
13. Of the six methods of payment for international transactions, which methods represent extensions of credit to importers? Who extends this credit?
14. How does factoring reduce a company's profits while speeding up its cash inflows?
15. Why is it difficult to end a factoring arrangement?
16. Explain how attempts to reduce inventory carrying costs might drive up other inventory costs.
17. When a company increases its inventories, which costs rise? Why?
18. If the ABC inventory model were applied to a fried chicken franchise, identify some A-type, B-type, and C-type inventory items.
19. Suppose a local hardware store uses a two-bin inventory model. How might a forecast of extremely bad weather (not the weather itself) wreck this system?
20. Would a complete count inventory model be worth installing in a household appliance store? Why or why not?

Problems

1. A company can borrow from its bank at an effective rate of 10 percent. One of its suppliers offers terms of 2/10 net 60, but the company believes it can stretch the terms of trade to pay after 75 days without damaging its credit reputation. Should it borrow from the bank and pay the supplier in ten days or just pay the supplier in 75 days?
2. Automated Systems, Inc. (ASI) has two potential suppliers for the same electronic components. ASI knows that the components are identical in every way, except for the terms of trade. Supplier A sells on terms of 2/10 net 30 and Supplier B sells on terms of 1/10 net 60. ASI's bank is willing to lend at 0.8 percent per month. What should ASI do?
3. A U.S. buyer purchases Nn2.2 million worth of African art on credit in Nigeria when the exchange rate is Nn22/US$. The Nigerian naira is expected to rise in value to Nn20/US$ when the account must be settled.

The buyer waits until payment is due. If the expected exchange rate turns out to be accurate, how much extra will it cost the buyer to settle the account?

4. A U.S buyer purchases Dk180,000 worth of skis in Denmark on terms of net 30. The exchange rate is Dk6/US$, but the Danish krone is expected to rise in value to Dk5/US$ when the account must be settled. To hedge, the buyer can invest in Denmark at 6 percent and borrow in the United States at 9 percent. A forward contract for Danish krones costs $31,000. Which of the three alternatives should the buyer choose?
5. The Candun Toy Co. sells 2.5 million yo-yos a year. It costs 25 cents to carry a yo-yo in inventory for a year, and $20 to place an order for more yo-yos. What is the EOQ?
6. A store sells 12,000 hand-carved portrait frames a year. It costs $6 to carry a frame in inventory for a year and $10 to place an order for more frames. What is the EOQ? How many orders would the store place a year? What is its total inventory cost?

Topics for Further Research

1. Construct a cash microbudget for yourself for the next month. State your daily cash inflows and outflows for the next week and weekly cash flows for the following three weeks. Use a credit card rate of 18 percent as your annual borrowing rate (this equals 1.5 percent per month or 0.05 percent per day). Use the rate your bank offers on money market accounts as your investment rate.
2. Is the need to hedge foreign accounts payable a realistic problem?
   (a) To get a recent answer to this question, locate the "World Value of the Dollar" data in a Monday issue of *The Wall Street Journal.* Compare the exchange rates to those listed in an issue of the *Journal* about 30 days previously. How many of the approximately 200 exchange rates moved unfavorably for U.S. buyers? (Note that the exchange rates for Cyprus, the Falkland Islands, Gibraltar, Ireland, Malta, Saint Helena, and the United Kingdom are quoted as US$ per foreign currency unit, while all other rates are quoted as foreign currency unit per US$.)
   (b) Since many foreign accounts extend credit for more than 30 days, repeat the above comparison using issues of *The Wall Street Journal* that are 90 days apart.
3. Arrange a visit to a local business at the convenience of the manager. Ask how the firm keeps track of its inventory.
   (a) Do not expect anyone in the business to recognize the titles of the inventory control methods mentioned in this or any other textbook. It does not matter what their method is called; you are interested only in how they do it.
   (b) Ask only about item counts. *Any* questions about money or inventory value will make you look like a potential thief or an undercover agent for some tax department—in short, an object of suspicion.

Answers to Self-Test Problems

1. Yes. Foregoing the discount and paying the supplier on the 90th day has an annual cost of:

$$(3/97) \times (365/80) = 0.1411, \text{ or } 14.11 \text{ percent}$$

The bank loan is less expensive.

2. The annual cost of borrowing from Speedy for 45 days is:

$$(1/99) \times (365/35) = 0.1053, \text{ or } 10.53 \text{ percent}$$

The annual cost of borrowing from Jiffy for 60 days:

$$(2/98) \times (365/50) = 0.1490, \text{ or } 14.9 \text{ percent}$$

Quick Co. should buy from Speedy and pay in 45 days. The annual cost of borrowing from Speedy is lower than the annual cost of borrowing from either Jiffy or the bank.

3. The account payable is worth I£30,000 x $1.50, or $45,000 now. At an exchange rate of US$1.60/I£, it will cost 30,000 x $1.60, or $48,000 to settle the account. The importer can afford to pay the bank any price up to $48,000 for a forward contract.
4. The account payable is worth Tb25,000,000/25, or $1 million now. Unhedged, it could cost 25,000,000/21, or $1,190,476 to settle the account in 60 days. To hedge the account:
   (a) Buy Tb25,000,000/(1 + 0.10/6), or Tb24,589,357 now.
   (b) Borrow Tb24,589,357/25, or $983,574.28 in the United States now.
   (c) Pay $983,574.28 x (0.15/6), or $24,589.36 interest.
   The total cost of this transaction is $983,574.28 plus $24,589.36, or $1,008,163.64. Hedging will be cheaper than taking an unhedged position if the exchange rate forecast turns out to be accurate. However, the forward contract is even less expensive and should be purchased instead.

5.

$$Q = \sqrt{(2)(10{,}000)(45)/10}$$
$$= \sqrt{90{,}000}$$

6.

$$Q = \sqrt{(2)(64{,}000)(5)/4}$$
$$= \sqrt{160{,}000}$$
$$= 400 \text{ pairs of sneakers}$$

$$\text{Total Cost for 400} = (\$4)(400/2) + (\$5)(64{,}000/400)$$
$$= \$800 + \$800$$
$$= \$1{,}600$$
$$\text{Total cost for 500} = (\$4)(500/2) + (\$5)(64{,}000/500) - (\$0.01)(64{,}000)$$
$$= \$1{,}000 + \$640 - \$640$$
$$= \$1{,}000$$

No, the shoe store owner should not stick to the EOQ.

CHAPTER

8

The Time Value of Money

LEARNING OBJECTIVES

This chapter introduces the time value of money, a fundamental concept in finance, and the principles of compounding and discounting. The chapter develops mathematical formulas for computing future values and present values of both a single cash flow and a series of cash flows and it discusses the applications of these formulas. Appendices to the chapter illustrate calculations of future and present values using *Lotus* spreadsheets and an HP12C financial calculator. At the conclusion of this chapter, the reader should be able to:

1. *Define the term* time value of money *and explain why money has a time value*
2. *Explain how the time value of money is the basis for the payment of interest*
3. *Explain interest rate differences among various types of loans*
4. *Define the terms* annual percentage rate (*APR*), stated annual rate, *and* effective annual rate (*EAR*)
5. *Show how the timing of cash flows is critical in finance*
6. *Use mathematical formulas to compute the future values and present values of cash flows*
7. *Discuss the importance of the present value concept in valuation*
8. *Demonstrate such practical skills as calculating payment schedules for installment and mortgage loans and comparing investments with different cash flow patterns*

Financial decisions involve cash flows—both inflows and outflows. Cash outflows represent expenditures and cash inflows represent receipts. Some cash flows may occur immediately, and others may be spread over a period of time.

Consider the decision to get a full-time job. It typically requires an immediate, lump sum expenditure to prepare and print resumes, and pay for new clothes or at least hair styling, followed by a series of small cash outflows for postage, phone calls, and transportation to job interviews; the total may even include a large employment agency fee. The job search ultimately results in a series of cash inflows—paychecks. The decision to attend college involves the same pattern of cash flows, but the amounts are much larger and spread over a longer period of time.

Corporations make financial decisions such as investing in a new product, financing a pension plan, and acquiring a new company, which have their own cash inflows and outflows. However, corporate cash flows are usually measured in hundreds of millions or even billions of dollars. These cash flows are estimated with the greatest of care and are analyzed with mathematical procedures that have become fully developed and accepted over decades.

The cash flow analysis is complicated by the fact that most decisions involve comparing cash flows that occur in different time periods. Generally outflows occur first and inflows occur later. Simply subtracting total cash outflows from total cash inflows could produce a poor decision because a dollar has different values at different times; a dollar today is worth more than a dollar tomorrow. In short, money has a time value.

The correct procedure for comparing cash flows that occur in different time periods is to convert them all into either present values (today's values) or future values (values at a future date) before making the comparison. Either procedure provides a scientific basis for financial decision making by making the cash flows time equivalent.

TIME VALUE OF MONEY

time value of money
The idea that a dollar tomorrow is worth less than a dollar today.

Discussing the **time value of money** and using phrases like "money has time value" refers to the fact that a dollar obtained today is worth more than a dollar obtained at a future date. Stated differently, a dollar obtained in the future is less valuable than a dollar obtained today. This principle has enormous implications for financial decision making. Consider, for example, a simple investment that costs $1,100 today and promises to pay $500 in the first year and $700 in the second year. This investment cannot be considered worthwhile simply because the total of the cash inflows exceeds the cash outflow. Similarly, it is incorrect to conclude that an offer of $200 in the first year and $400 in the second year is identical to an offer of $400 in the first year and $200 in the second year. Cash flows in different time periods cannot be simply added together without violating the principle of the time value of money.

Why does money have a time value? People prefer the present use of money to its future use because of uncertainties and inflation. First, they tend to discount the future because they are not sure of their ability to enjoy a dollar in the future as much as, or in the same way as, a dollar today. The future is uncertain; hence a

FOCUS ON FINANCE

INVESTORS WANTED MORE!

In the early 1980s, Campeau Corporation (a Canadian firm) offered 14 percent on its bond issue to finance the purchase of Federated Department Stores. Investors rejected the offer. Only when the offer was raised to 17 percent could Campeau Corporation find interested buyers for its bonds. Why did investors turn down a 14 percent offer by Campeau Corporation? At that time, they thought that the 14 percent sounded low considering the market's perception of the default risk associated with the investment.

dollar expected in the future cannot have the same value to an individual as a dollar today.

Second, money loses purchasing power under conditions of inflation. In an inflationary environment, money will lose its purchasing power (or value) over time, making a future dollar less valuable to an individual than a present dollar.

Today's value of a future dollar declines as people wonder more about the future, anticipate higher inflation, or both. A decline in today's value means an increase in the time value of money. Thus, the time value of money at any given time depends on people's perception of the future and their inflation expectation.

Time Value and Interest Rates

Giving up the present use of money in exchange for its future use, as in lending and investing, involves:

1. A sacrifice in the form of postponing consumption (because people prefer present consumption to future consumption)
2. The possibility of a reduction in purchasing power (inflation risk)
3. Exposure to risks such as default risk and liquidity risk

Recall that default risk refers to uncertainty about the payment itself. A future dollar becomes more and more uncertain as the possibility of being deprived of that dollar increases. As a dollar becomes more distant, default risk rises. Liquidity risk is the possibility that one will be unable to convert an investment to cash easily and without substantial loss.

People who lend and invest expect compensation for their sacrifice and risk exposure. For financial assets, this compensation takes the form of interest, dividends, and/or capital appreciation. Compensation for postponing consumption is often referred to as *pure interest*. Amounts that compensate for inflation and other types of risk are called *risk premiums*. (Some prefer the Latinized term, *risk premia.*)

The total compensation received by a lender or an investor can be considered the sum of separate amounts to compensate for sacrifice of current consumption, inflation risk, and other types of risk. If a bank pays 5 percent on a savings deposit

EXHIBIT 8.1

Key Interest Rates (Annualized)[a]

Prime rate (The base rate charged by banks on corporate loans)	6.25%
Federal funds rate (The rate for overnight borrowing of reserves among commercial banks)	3.37
Commercial paper rate (The rate on 90-day, high-grade, unsecured notes sold through dealers by major corporations)	3.95
Treasury bill rate (90 day)	3.63
Bankers' acceptance rate (90 day)	3.80
Eurodollar deposit rate (90 day)	4.00
Certificate of deposit rate (90 day)	3.38
Treasury bond rate (30 year)	7.26

[a]As of Monday, April 11, 1994

and 7 percent on a certificate of deposit, the 2 percent differential is compensation for liquidity risk. The 5 percent constitutes compensation for sacrifice, inflation, and default risk.

The fact that lenders and investors demand and receive compensation is itself evidence that money has a time value. Practically, therefore, money has time value because it can earn interest. The size of the compensation (that is, the rate of return) in a specific case depends on investors' perception of the risks associated with the investment. Investors generally demand higher compensation on higher-risk investments, and historical return data confirm the positive association between risk and return. Financial markets provide information on all aspects of the returns and risks associated with investments and help individuals make their lending and investment decisions.

Why Do Interest Rates Differ?

Interest rate differences associated with various types of loan transactions can be explained easily in terms of the ideas discussed above. In a given country, one can assume that all loan transactions are exposed to the same time preference of consumption and inflation risk. They may differ, however, in terms of tax liability and degree of exposure to other types of risk. By evaluating the time preference, risk exposure, and tax liability of a given loan transaction, lenders determine the interest they must earn.

For a longer time to maturity and greater risk, lenders demand a higher interest rate. For example, lenders accept much lower interest rates on Treasury bills than on commercial paper because the bills are less risky and have a tax advantage. For the same reasons, they settle for lower interest rates on Treasury bonds than on corporate bonds of the same maturities. Exhibit 8.1 highlights the extent of differences in interest rates on common types of loan transactions.

FUTURE VALUE AND COMPOUNDING

future value
The amount to which a payment or payments will grow by a future date compounded at a stated interest rate.

present value
The present worth of a future amount or series of amounts.

The ideas of the time value of money and interest rates have generated a number of concepts to aid market participants in their decision making. Two of these concepts are **future value** and **present value**. Students develop many practical skills from studying these concepts, including the ability to:

1. Determine the amount that must be invested today to obtain a specific amount at a future date
2. Determine the expected rate of return on an investment whose future cash flows are known or estimated in advance
3. Determine the number of years needed to accumulate a certain amount or pay off a loan
4. Determine the periodic payment on an amortized loan
5. Compare investment opportunities with different cash flow characteristics

Money loaned or invested today will usually grow into a larger amount over time; this amount is called the *future value*. Perhaps the simplest case is the accumulation in a bank account at a future point in time when neither principal nor interest has been withdrawn. Suppose that someone deposits $10,000 in a savings account that pays an annual interest rate of 5 percent. The principal plus interest accumulated in that account in six years is the future value of $10,000 six years from now.

It is important to note that future value includes interest on accumulated interest because the concept assumes that interest earned in each period is reinvested to become part of the principal for the next period. This means that in each successive period, the amount on which interest is calculated increases. The process of leaving accumulated interest to earn more interest is known as **interest compounding**. By definition, the future value calculation involves interest compounding.

interest compounding
A process by which accumulated interest earns more interest.

Now, contrast interest compounding with the principle of simple interest, where the interest is not accumulated and reinvested. With simple interest, interest is calculated and paid on the same principal for each period. Therefore, the principal plus the simple interest earned on a given amount will always be less than the future value of that amount. The principle of interest compounding is illustrated and contrasted with simple interest as part of the study of the future value of a dollar below.

Future Value of a Dollar

The future value of a dollar is the accumulation in an account a year later, two years later, or *n* years later, of a dollar deposited (or invested) today at a given interest rate. To illustrate the calculation of the future value of a dollar, assume that someone deposits a dollar in a savings account that pays 5 percent annual interest; the money remains in the account for ten years. The dollar grows at the rate of 5 percent per year, and the accumulation at the end of each successive year is its future value for that year. Exhibit 8.2 describes the process of determining the future value.

EXHIBIT 8.2

Accumulation under Interest Compounding

	AFTER A YEAR A DOLLAR BECOMES			
YEAR	PRINCIPAL	INTEREST	TOTAL ACCUMULATION	
1	\$1.0000	\$0.0500	\$1.0500	
2	1.0500	0.0525	1.1025	$(1+0.05)^2$
3	1.1025	0.0551	1.1576	$(1+0.05)^3$
4	1.1576	0.0579	1.2155	$(1+0.05)^4$
5	1.2155	0.0608	1.2763	$(1+0.05)^5$
6	1.2763	0.0638	1.3401	$(1+0.05)^6$
7	1.3401	0.0670	1.4071	$(1+0.05)^7$
8	1.4071	0.0704	1.4775	$(1+0.05)^8$
9	1.4775	0.0739	1.5513	$(1+0.05)^9$
10	1.5513	0.0776	1.6289	$(1+0.05)^{10}$

EXHIBIT 8.3

Accumulation under Simple Interest

	AFTER A YEAR A DOLLAR BECOMES		
YEAR	PRINCIPAL	INTEREST	TOTAL ACCUMULATION
1	\$1	\$0.05	\$1.05
2	1	0.05	1.10
3	1	0.05	1.15
4	1	0.05	1.20
5	1	0.05	1.25
6	1	0.05	1.30
7	1	0.05	1.35
8	1	0.05	1.40
9	1	0.05	1.45
10	1	0.05	1.50

The total interest earned on \$1 in ten years at 5 percent is \$0.6289. Note that each year starts with a new principal amount which is equal to the previous year's principal plus the interest on it. Now compare this process with the simple interest calculation illustrated in Exhibit 8.3.

Simple interest gives a smaller amount of total interest earned on \$1 than interest compounding gives. At the end of three years, for example, simple interest generates total interest on \$1 of \$0.15 (3 × \$0.05), while interest compounding generates \$0.1576. Exhibit 8.4 illustrates the difference graphically.

Compounding gives a future value composed of three elements: the initial amount (the principal), interest earned on the principal at the stated rate (simple interest), and interest earned on accumulated interest (compound interest). To illustrate this, consider the future value of \$1 at the end of the second year in the previous example: \$1.1025. The future value at the end of the second year includes

EXHIBIT 8.4

Investor's Wealth Under Simple and Compound Interest

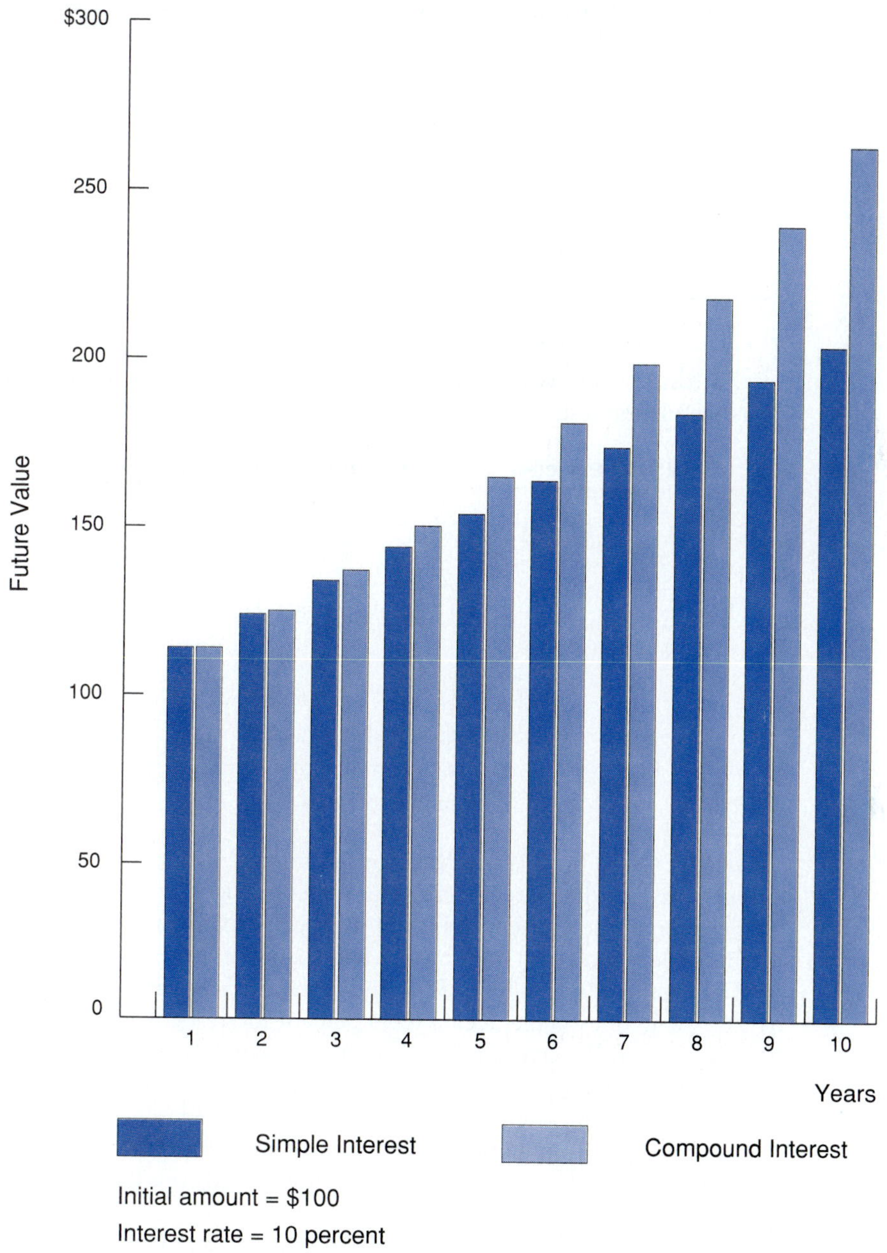

EXHIBIT 8.5

Future Value Interest Factors

	INTEREST RATE (i)				
PERIOD(n)	1 PERCENT	5 PERCENT	10 PERCENT	15 PERCENT	20 PERCENT
1	1.0100	1.0500	1.1000	1.1500	1.2000
2	1.0201	1.1025	1.2100	1.3225	1.4400
3	1.0303	1.1576	1.3310	1.5208	1.7280
4	1.0406	1.2155	1.4641	1.7490	2.0736
5	1.0510	1.2763	1.6105	2.0114	2.4883
.	.	.	.	.	.
.	.	.	.	.	.
.	.	.	.	.	.
10	1.1046	1.6289	2.5937	4.0456	6.1917

interest on the first year's interest, in addition to the initial amount and two years' simple interest.

Future value at the end of second year	=	Principal	+ two years of simple interest	+ interest on first year's interest
$1.1025	=	$1.00	+ $0.10	+ $0.0025

Using symbols, a generalized formula for calculating the future value of a dollar can be written as:

$$FV\{\$1\} = \$1(1+i)^n \text{ or simply } \$(1+i)^n \tag{8.1}$$

where FV = future value

i = stated annual interest rate

n = number of years

The expression $(1+i)^n$ is the future value interest factor ($FVIF_{n,i}$) and i is the annual compounding rate. Future value tables provide the values of *FVIF* for various combinations of i and n. Table C.1 in Appendix C is an *FVIF* table. A segment of this table is presented in Exhibit 8.5 to explain its use.

To find the future value of $1 in ten years at a 5 percent annual interest rate ($FVIF_{10,5\%}$), for example, locate the 5 percent interest column and follow down that column until you reach the row that corresponds to ten periods. This reveals the *FVIF*, 1.6289, which is identical to the result shown in Exhibit 8.2.

The future value interest factor can also be obtained using a hand-held calculator with a power function key, labeled y^x. Most calculators make this procedure very simple. Enter $(1+i)$, press the y^x key, enter n, and press the equal key. Try this procedure to obtain the $FVIF_{10,5\%}$.

Appendix 8A illustrates the use of *Lotus* spreadsheets to solve future value problems. Appendix 8.B provides step-by-step instructions for the same tasks using the HP12C financial calculator.

Future Value of a Single Amount

To obtain the future value of a single amount, multiply the amount by the future value of a dollar, or the $FVIF_{n,i}$.

$$FV\{P_0\} = P_0(1+i)^n = P_0(FVIF_{n,i}) = P_n \quad (8.2)$$

where P_0 = amount today

P_n = future value in n years

The subscript of P is the time subscript; zero indicates the amount now, 1 indicates the amount one period from now, 2 indicates the amount two periods from now, and so on.

❖ EXAMPLE 8.1

Find the future value of $2,000 at the end of five years if the annual interest rate is 10 percent. By how much would this amount differ if the interest were withdrawn each year?

$$\begin{aligned} FV\{P_0=\$2{,}000\} &= \$2{,}000(1+0.10)^5 \\ &= \$2{,}000(1.10)^5 \\ &= \$2{,}000(1.6105) \\ &= \$3{,}221 \end{aligned}$$

If interest were withdrawn each year, the interest earned in five years would total $200 × 5, or $1,000. The interest plus the principal at the end of six years is, therefore, $2,000 plus $1,000, or $3,000. The difference between the future value and this amount is $221 ($3,221 – $3,000). (Note that the future value interest factor of 1.6105 could have been obtained directly from the *FVIF* table, Exhibit 8.5, at the intersection of the column that corresponds to 10 percent interest and the row that corresponds to five periods.) ❖

Future Value and Compounding Periods

Previous illustrations of the future value calculation involved once-a-year compounding using annual interest rates. In the future value interest factor of Equation 8.1, n represented years as the number of **compounding periods** and i, the annual **compounding rate**. These specifications may not fit all real-life situations. In fact, interest compounding more frequently than once a year (i.e. interest periods are shorter) is quite common these days. For example, credit card companies calculate interest on monthly balances. Some banks calculate interest daily on certain types of deposits.

compounding period
A time period specified for calculating and reinvesting interest.

compounding rate
The annual interest rate used in interest compounding.

How does more frequent interest compounding affect the future value of an amount? If interest on interest is calculated and reinvested more frequently, money should grow more quickly to a larger future value. Consider, for example, the future value of $2,000 deposited for six years at an annual interest rate of 8 percent, compounded quarterly. The interest period in this case is three months. Since interest is calculated every three months, a quarterly interest rate of 2 percent is

FOCUS ON CAREERS

Mortgage Closing Specialist

Mortgage closing specialists are the central points of contact for customers after their loans have been approved. A mortgage closing is a formal meeting between the borrower, the lender, and attorneys for both sides. During this meeting, both parties must agree to every word, phrase, and penny in the mortgage contract; when they finally resolve all questions and differences, both parties sign the mortgage contract.

A closing specialist works to facilitate the closing process by counseling customers on the documentation required for closing and by working with the closing attorneys to ensure compliance with Federal National Mortgage Association regulations and the firm's own closing requirements.

Commercial banks, thrift institutions, and mortgage banks offer employment opportunities. Since the position involves frequent, stressful contact with customers and attorneys, good communications skills and patience are essential. Strong time management and organizational skills are also required, combined with a careful eye for detail. Academic requirements are fairly broad based, and junior college graduates have excellent employment opportunities. Generally the entry level position is clerical in nature. One to three years of experience in mortgages qualifies a candidate for the specialist position. Advancement opportunities exist within the mortgage department as an employee can assume greater managerial responsibilities.

Given the minimal management responsibilities associated with the entry level position, the starting salary is generally between \$20,000 and \$25,000.

obtained by dividing the annual rate by 4. Compounding at 2 percent over 24 periods (6 years times 4 quarters per year) gives the future value of this amount. Thus, the future value of \$2,000 with quarterly compounding is:

$$\begin{aligned} FV\{\$2{,}000\} &= \$2{,}000(1 + 0.02)^{24} \\ &= \$2{,}000(1.6084) \\ &= \$3{,}216.80 \end{aligned}$$

To obtain the appropriate *FVIF* from the future value table, locate the 2 percent interest rate column and follow it down until you reach the row that corresponds to 24 periods.

This amount is greater than \$3,173.74, the future value of \$2,000 at 8 percent for six years with annual compounding. The future value gets larger as the compounding period becomes shorter. Equation 8.1 can be modified easily to deal with compounding more frequent than once a year. Representing the frequency of compounding by f, the modified formula can be written as:

$$FVIF_{nf,i} = [1 + (i/f)]^{nf} \tag{8.3}$$

where i/f = interest rate for the compounding period

nf = number of compounding periods

EXHIBIT 8.6

Series Summary

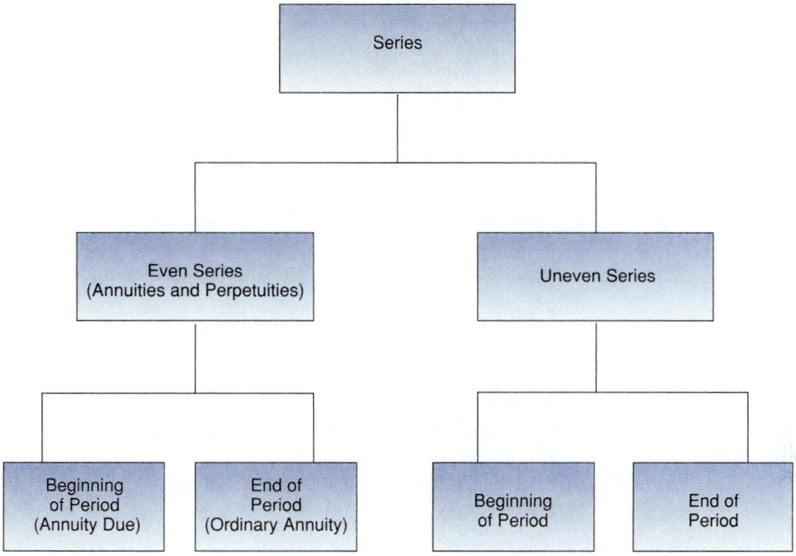

Future Value of a Series of Cash Flows

annuity

A series of periodic, equal cash flows (payments or receipts) over a fixed length of time.

perpetuity

An annuity with cash flows that continue forever.

annuity due

An annuity with cash flows that occur at the beginning of each period.

ordinary annuity

An annuity with cash flows that occur at the end of each period.

So far, the discussion has been confined to the future value of a single amount with annual and more frequent compounding. Financial deals often involve series of amounts or cash flows over considerable periods of time. A series consists of several cash flows that represent individual payments or receipts. To obtain the future value of a series, one can sum the future values of the individual amounts. Before looking at the future value of a series, it will be useful to get acquainted with different types of series.

A real-world series may be an even series (a string of equal amounts) or an uneven series (a string containing unequal amounts). The cash flows of a series may occur at the beginning or at the end of each period. An even series with periodic cash flows over a fixed number of periods is known as **annuity**. In other words, an annuity is a set of periodic, equal payments; the period may be a month, a year, or any other defined length of time. (The dictionary meaning of *annuity*—the annual payment of an allowance or income—emphasizes the connection to this word *annual*. In finance, however, it has been common practice to refer to any series of equal payments, annual or otherwise, as an annuity.

An annuity with cash flows that continue forever is called a **perpetuity**. An annuity with beginning-of-period cash flows is called an **annuity due**, and an annuity with end-of-period cash flows is called an **ordinary annuity**. The diagram in Exhibit 8.6 summarizes the various types of series.

Future Value of an Uneven Series. Let $P_1, P_2, P_3, P_4, \ldots P_n$ be a series (P_t) of annual payments that occur at the beginning of each year for n years. The future value of this series at the end of nth year is given by:

$$
\begin{aligned}
FV\{P_t\} &= FV\{P_1\} + FV\{P_2\} + \ldots + FV\{P_n\} \\
&= P_1(1+i)^n + P_2(1+i)^{n-1} + \ldots + Pn(1+i)^1 \\
&= P_1(FVIF_{n,i}) + P_2(FVIF_{n-1,i}) + \ldots + P_n(FVIF_{1,i}) \qquad (8.4)
\end{aligned}
$$

Note that the first payment earns interest for n years, the second payment for n–1 years, the third payment for n–2 years, and so on.

If the timing of the payments changes to the end of each year, then the expression for the future value changes to:

$$FV\{P_t\} = P_1(1+i)^{n-1} + P_2(1+i)^{n-2} + \ldots + P_n(1+i)^0 \qquad (8.5)$$

Note the difference. In this case, the first payment earns interest for n–1 years, the second payment for n–2 years, and so on. The last payment does not earn any interest. In other words, end-of-period payments earn interest for one less period than beginning-of-period payments.

❖ EXAMPLE 8.2

What balance will an account hold at the end of four years, if the amounts given below are deposited at the beginning of each year and the account pays an annual interest rate of 10 percent?

YEAR	AMOUNT
1	\$2,000
2	3,000
3	2,500
4	1,500

$$
\begin{aligned}
FV\{P_t\} &= \$2,000(1.1)^4 + \$3,000(1.1)^3 + \$2,500(1.1)^2 + \$1,500(1.1)^1 \\
&= \$2,000(1.4641) + \$3,000(1.331) + \$2,500(1.21) + \$1,500(1.1) \\
&= \$2,928.20 + \$3,993 + \$3,025 + \$1,650 \\
&= \$11,596.20
\end{aligned}
$$

This represents total savings of \$9,000 plus accumulated interest of \$2,596.20. Presenting these results on a time line,

YEARS:	1	2	3	4	FV
Deposits:	\$2,000	\$3,000	\$2,500	\$1,500	
					$\$1,500(1.1)^1 = 1,650.00$
					$\$2,500(1.1)^2 = 3,025.00$
					$\$3,000(1.1)^3 = 3,993.00$
					$\$2,000(1.1)^4 = 2,928.20$
					\$11,596.20 ❖

❖ EXAMPLE 8.3

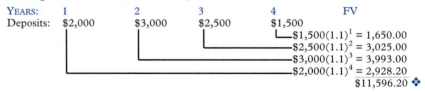

If the amounts in Example 8.2 are deposited at the end of each year, instead of at the beginning, what will be the future value of the series?

$$FV\{P_t\} = \$2{,}000(1.1)^3 + \$3{,}000(1.1)^2 + \$2{,}500(1.1)^1 + \$1{,}500(1.1)^0$$
$$= \$2{,}000(1.331) + \$3{,}000(1.21) + \$2{,}500(1.1) + \$1{,}500(1)$$
$$= \$2{,}662 + \$3{,}630 + \$2{,}750 + \$1{,}500$$
$$= \$10{,}542$$ ❖

Future Value of an Annuity (A). Suppose that someone deposits \$1 at the end of every year for four years, and the annual interest rate is 10 percent. This is an ordinary \$1 annuity (A_O=\$1), and its future value at the end of four years is given by:

$$FV\{A_O=\$1\} = \$1(1+0.1)^3 + \$1(1+0.1)^2 + \$1(1+0.1)^1 + \$1(1+0.1)^0$$
$$= \$1.331 + \$1.210 + \$1.100 + \$1.000$$
$$= \$4.641$$

Using summation notation, the future value of a \$1 ordinary annuity can be written as:

$$FV\{A_O = \$1\} = \$1\sum_{t=1}^{n}(1+0.1)^{t-1} \quad (8.6)$$

where t is the time index.

The right-hand side of Equation 8.6 is mathematically equivalent to $\$1\{[(1+0.1)^4 - 1]/0.1\}$. Replacing the right-hand side,

$$FV\{A_O=\$1\} = \$1\{[(1+0.1)^4 - 1]/0.1\}$$
$$= \$1(4.641)$$
$$= \$4.641$$

Generalizing this expression to any interest rate and any number of years, the future value of a \$1 ordinary annuity can be written as:

$$FV\{A_O = \$1\} = \$1\sum_{t=1}^{n}(1+i)^{t-1}$$
$$= \$1\left[\frac{(1+i)^n - 1}{i}\right] \quad (8.7)$$

Instead of evaluating the future value of each amount separately and then summing the individual future values, Equation 8.7 provides a shortcut to the calculation of the future value of an ordinary dollar annuity.

The expression:

$$\sum_{t=1}^{n}(1+i)^{t-1}$$

or its equivalent expression $\{[(1+i)^n - 1]/i\}$ is known as the *future value interest factor for an ordinary annuity* ($FVIFA_{O\,n,i}$). The $FVIFA_{O\,n,i}$ for a given n and i can be obtained from either a FVIFA table or a calculator. Table C.2 in Appendix C provides values of $FVIFA_O$ for various combinations of i and n.

If someone deposits a dollar at the beginning of each year, this creates an annuity due. The future value of a \$1 annuity due (A_D=\$1) in four years at 10 percent interest is given by:

$$\begin{aligned} FV\{A_D=\$1\} &= \$1(1+0.1)^4 + \$1(1+0.1)^3 + \$1(1+0.1)^2 + \$1(1+0.1)^1 \\ &= \$1.4641 + \$1.331 + \$1.210 + \$1.10 \\ &= \$5.1051 \end{aligned}$$

In summation notation, the expression can be written as:

$$FV\{A_D = \$1\} = \$1\sum_{t=1}^{4}(1+0.1)^t \tag{8.8}$$

The right-hand side of Equation 8.8 is mathematically equivalent to $\$1[[(1+0.1)^n - 1]/0.1](1+0.1)$. By replacing it:

$$\begin{aligned} FV\{A_D=\$1\} &= \$1[[(1+0.1)^4 - 1]/0.1](1+0.1) \\ &= \$1(5.1051) \\ &= \$5.1051 \end{aligned}$$

Generalizing to any interest rate and any number of years, the future value of a \$1 annuity due can be expressed as:

$$\begin{aligned} FV\{A_D = \$1\} &= \$1\sum_{t=1}^{n}(1+i)^t \\ &= \$1\left\{\left[(1+i)^n - 1\right]/i\right\}(1+i) \end{aligned} \tag{8.9}$$

The expression:

$$\sum_{t=1}^{n}(1+i)^t$$

or its equivalent expression $\$1[[(1+i)^n - 1]/i](1+i)$ is called the *future value interest factor for an annuity due* ($FVIFA_{D\,n,i}$). Note that the future value of a dollar annuity due is greater than that of an ordinary dollar annuity by the factor $(1+i)$. This is explained by the fact that dollar payments in an annuity due earn interest for an additional period compared to dollar payments in an ordinary annuity. To obtain the $FVIFA_D$, multiply the $FVIFA_O$ from Table C.2 in Appendix C by $(1+i)$.

To obtain the future value of an annuity of any amount, multiply that amount by the corresponding FVIFA.

1. When A is an ordinary annuity:

$$FV\{A_O\} = A_O \sum_{t=1}^{n} (1+i)^{t-1}$$
$$= A_O \left[\frac{(1+i)^n - 1}{i} \right]$$
$$= A_O (FVIFA_{O\,n,i}) \quad (8.10)$$

❖ EXAMPLE 8.4

Twin brothers Joseph and John open savings accounts at a bank that pays 6 percent annual interest. Joseph deposits $120 at the end of every year for four years, and John deposits $10 at the end of every month for four years. The bank compounds interest monthly on John's deposits and annually on Joseph's deposits. Which brother has more money at the end of four years?

Joseph's account represents an ordinary annuity of $120 deposited every year. The total of four payments plus interest is:

$$FV\{A_O = \$120\} = \$120(FVIFA_{O\,4,6\%})$$
$$= \$120\{[(1+0.06)^4 - 1]/0.06\} = \$120(4.3746)$$
$$= \$524.95$$

This amount includes total deposits of $480 plus accumulated interest of $44.96.

John's account represents an ordinary annuity of $10 deposited every month for four years. The compounding period is a month, and the monthly interest rate is 0.5 percent. This gives a total of 48 compounding periods.

$$FV\{A_O = \$10\} = \$10(FVIFA_{O\,48,0.5\%})$$
$$= \$10\{[(1+0.005)^{48} - 1]/0.005\}$$
$$= \$10(54.0978)$$
$$= \$540.98$$

This amount includes total deposits of $480 plus accumulated interest of $60.98. ❖

2. When A is an annuity due:

$$FV\{A_D\} = A_D \sum_{t=1}^{n} (1+i)^t = A(FVIFA_{D\,n,i})$$
$$= A_D \left[\frac{(1-i)^n - 1}{i} \right] (1+i)$$
$$= A_D (FVIFA_{O\,n,1})(1+i) \quad (8.11)$$

❖ EXAMPLE 8.5

Assume that Joseph and John from Example 8.4 make deposits at the beginning of each period. Calculate the future values of their accounts.

For Joseph's Account:

$$FV\{A_D = \$120\} = \$120(FVIFA_{D\,4,6\%})$$
$$= \$120(FVIFA_{O\,4,6\%})(1+0.06)$$

$$= \$120\big[[(1+0.06)^4 - 1]/0.06\big](1.06)$$
$$= \$120(4.3746)(1.06)$$
$$= \$556.45$$

This represents total deposits of $480 plus accumulated interest of $76.46.

For John's account:

$$FV\{A_D=\$10\} = \$10(FVIFA_{D,\,48,0.5\%})$$
$$= \$10(FVIFA_{O,\,48,0.5\%})(1+0.005)$$
$$= \$10\big[[(1+0.005)^{48} - 1]/0.005\big](1.005)^{12}$$
$$= \$10(54.0978)(1.005)$$
$$= \$543.68$$

This represents total deposits of $480 plus accumulated interest of $63.68. ❖

Stated Rate, Annual Percentage Rate, and Effective Annual Rate

The way an interest rate is quoted (or stated) makes a difference in the amount actually received or paid. We have seen that a rate quoted as 12 percent compounded quarterly is not the same as 12 percent per year. Therefore, it is important to understand the implications of the various ways that interest rates are quoted.

In interest rate quotations such as 12 percent compounded quarterly or 1 percent per month, the 12 percent and the 1 percent are known as *stated rates*. An **annual percentage rate** (APR) is the periodic (stated) rate multiplied by the number of periods in a year. For example, if a stated monthly rate is 1 percent, then the APR is 12 percent (1 percent times 12). When the stated interest rate is annual, the stated rate and the APR are the same.

annual percentage rate (APR)
The annual interest rate obtained by multiplying a stated, periodic rate by the number of periods in a year.

The interest rate that one actually ends up paying or receiving is called the **effective annual rate** (EAR). If the interest rate is quoted for a period shorter than one year, the effective annual rate will be higher than the APR. The expression "12 percent compounded quarterly," for example, implies an effective annual rate of 12.68 percent. The EAR is higher because quarterly compounding pays interest quarterly on accumulated interest. A formula for determining the effective annual rate implied in a stated annual rate is given by:

effective annual rate
The annual interest rate that one actually receives or pays. Also known as the *actual interest rate*.

$$EAR = (1 + i/f)^f - 1 \qquad \textbf{(8.12)}$$

where f = frequency of compounding

i = stated annual rate

For any stated annual rate, the effective annual rate gets larger as the frequency of compounding increases.

EARs have proven to provide effective criteria for comparing different types of interest compounding arrangements that banks offer on deposits. Suppose that Bank A offers a deposit rate of 12 percent compounded monthly and Bank B offers 12.25 percent compounded semiannually. Which offer would pay you more for a deposit account? Comparing the EARs of the two offers is the most effective way of finding the answer. The EAR of Bank A's offer is 12.68 percent and that of Bank B's offer is 12.62 percent.

FOCUS ON FINANCE

TRUTH-IN-LENDING LAWS

If a lender quotes interest rates for a period shorter than one year, truth-in-lending laws in the United States require that the lender disclose the corresponding annual percentage rate (APR) on all consumer loans. These laws also specify the minimum size of type in documents and prohibit important disclosures in footnotes.

❖ EXAMPLE 8.6

If a bank charges monthly interest of 1.4 percent on a loan, what are the APR and EAR?

$$\begin{aligned} \text{APR} &= 1.4\% \times 12 \\ &= 16.8 \text{ percent} \\ \text{EAR} &= (1 + 0.014)^{12} - 1 \\ &= 1.1816 - 1 \\ &= 0.1816 \text{ or } 18.16 \text{ percent} \end{aligned}$$

The APR on the loan is 16.8 percent, but the borrower would pay actual interest (an EAR) of 18.16 percent. ❖

To sum up, there are three things to remember about future value:

1. Future value increases with an increase in the interest rate, the number of years, and the frequency of compounding.
2. Doubling the interest rate more than doubles the amount of interest earned.
3. Compounding more frequently than once a year boosts the effective interest rate above both the stated annual rate and the annual percentage rate.

PRESENT VALUE AND DISCOUNTING

The concept of future value deals with questions like: How much will a $1,000 current deposit be worth ten years from now if it earns 6 percent interest every year? Another type of question comes up quite often in financial management: How much should we pay for a deal that promises certain cash flow(s) in the future? This is the same as asking the question, how much is a deal that promises certain cash flow(s) in the future worth today?

The answer to this type of question involves the concept of present value. Present value refers to today's value (expressed in current dollars) of some future amount(s). It essentially reverses the questions of future value.

Present value can be defined as the maximum that one is willing to pay today, given the current interest rate, for an amount or a series of amounts promised in the future. This definition is based on the assumption that no one will pay more today for future cash flows than they are worth today. A formula for calculating the present value of a future amount is easily derived from this definition.

Consider, for example, a promise to pay \$10,000 in ten years. What is the present value of this promise, or the maximum that one is willing to pay for it, if the interest rate is 6 percent? Since money has a time value, the maximum one will pay for this promise today has to be less than \$10,000. Will anyone pay, say, \$6,000 today for this promise? If \$6,000 were invested elsewhere at 6 percent, its future value in ten years would be \$10,745.10 [$\$6{,}000(1.06)^{10}$]. Therefore, no one would pay \$6,000 for a promise of \$10,000 because they could earn more with this money elsewhere.

The maximum that one should pay today is that amount whose future value is equal to \$10,000, the amount promised. Let X represent this maximum:

$$X(FVIF_{10,6\%}) = \$10{,}000$$

Solving this equation for X,

$$\begin{aligned} X &= \$10{,}000(1/FVIF_{10,6\%}) \\ &= \$10{,}000[1/(1+0.06)^{10}] \\ &= \$5{,}584 \end{aligned}$$

The promise of \$10,000 in ten years is worth only \$5,584 in today's dollars when the interest rate is 6 percent. This is the same as saying that the present value of \$10,000 in ten years is \$5,584 when the interest rate is 6 percent.

Present Value of a Future Dollar

The effort to devise a general formula for calculating present value begins with the present value of a future dollar. How much is a dollar to be received in four years worth today, if the interest rate is 5 percent per year? To answer this question, let X be the present value of \$1 in four years. According to the definition of present value:

$$\$X(FVIF_{4,5\%}) = X(1+0.05)^4 = \$1$$

Solving the equation for X:

$$\begin{aligned} X &= \$1[1/(1+0.05)^4] \\ &= \$1[1/(1+0.05)]^4 \\ &= \$0.83 \end{aligned}$$

The present value of \$1 to be received in four years with an interest rate of 5 percent is 83 cents. Because the interest rate is in the denominator of this calculation, an interest rate higher than 5 percent will give a present value smaller than \$0.83. A higher interest rate reduces present value.

EXHIBIT 8.7

Present Value Interest Factors

PERIOD (n)	INTEREST RATE (i)				
	1 PERCENT	2 PERCENT	5 PERCENT	10 PERCENT	15 PERCENT
1	0.9900	0.9804	0.9524	0.9091	0.8695
2	0.9803	0.9612	0.9070	0.8264	0.7561
3	0.9706	0.9423	0.8638	0.7513	0.6575
4	0.9609	0.9238	0.8227	0.6830	0.5717
5	0.9515	0.9057	0.7835	0.6209	0.4972
.	.	.	.	.	.
.	.	.	.	.	.
.	.	.	.	.	.
10	0.9053	0.8203	0.6139	0.3855	0.2472

Using the usual symbols, i for interest rate and n for the number of years, the formula for calculating the present value of a future dollar can be expressed as:

$$PV\{\$1\} = \$1[1/(1+i)^n] \text{ or } \$1[1/(1+i)]^n \quad \textbf{(8.13)}$$

The expression $1/(1+i)^n$ is known as the *present value interest factor* ($PVIF_{n,i}$). Present value tables provide the values of *PVIF* for various combinations of i and n. Table C.3 in Appendix C is one such table, and a segment of this table appears in Exhibit 8.7.

Use this table to find the *PVIF* for a given period and rate. For example, when $n = 5$ and $i = 10$ percent, select the column headed 10 percent and follow down until you reach the row that corresponds to Period 5. The *PVIF* in this case is 0.6209.

A hand-held calculator with inverse and exponential function keys can also give the *PVIF*. To find the *PVIF* using a calculator, follow these steps:

1. Enter 1 plus the interest rate.
2. Press the key marked y^x and enter the number of periods.
3. Press the equal (=) key.
4. Press the inverse key, marked $1/x$.

Appendix 8A presents *Lotus* spreadsheet applications for solving present value problems. Appendix 8B illustrates steps for using the HP12C financial calculator.

Present Value of a Single Amount

To find the present value of an amount other than \$1, multiply the amount by the relevant PVIF:

$$PV\{P_n\} = P_n[1/(1+i)^n]$$
$$= P_n(PVIF_{n,i}) \quad \textbf{(8.14)}$$

where P_n = amount at period n

❖ EXAMPLE 8.7

If an investment promises a single cash flow of $20,000 in 20 years and the interest rate is 8 percent, what is the maximum price one should pay for this investment?

$$\begin{aligned} PV\{P_{20}=\$20{,}000\} &= \$20{,}000(PVIF_{n,i}) \\ &= \$20{,}000[1/(1.08)^{20}] \\ &= \$20{,}000(0.2145) \\ &= \$4{,}290 \end{aligned}$$ ❖

discounting
A process of reducing value.

discount rate
The interest rate that reduces a future cash flow to its present value.

discount factor
The factor that converts a future dollar into its present value.

Calculating a present value is also known as **discounting**. Discounting is a process of reducing. It is the exact opposite of compounding. A future value calculation compounds a current amount or a series of amounts of money forward into the future; a present value calculation discounts a future sum or a series of future amounts back to the present. Because present value implies discounting, the interest rate used in a present value calculation is known as the **discount rate**, and the *PVIF* is known as the **discount factor.**

Future value and present value are related concepts. At a given interest rate, if Amount A represents the future value of Amount B, then B is the present value of A. For example, $110.25 is the future value of $100 in two years compounded annually at 5 percent; $100 is the present value of $110.25 in two years discounted at 5 percent. The *PVIF* is the inverse of *FVIF*.

$$PVIF_{n,i} = 1/(1+i)^n = 1/FVIF_{n,i}$$

Like compounding periods, discounting periods can be shorter than a year. Shorter discounting periods make the present value smaller.

❖ EXAMPLE 8.8

Discount $2,000 monthly over two years at an annual interest rate of 12 percent. Compare this result with the result of discounting $2,000 annually over the same period.

With the discounting period of one month, the stated annual rate gives a monthly discount rate of 1 percent for 24 discounting periods. The present value of $2,000 discounted monthly at an annual rate of 12 percent is:

$$\begin{aligned} PV\{\$2{,}000\} &= \$2{,}000[1/(1+0.01)^{24}] \\ &= \$2{,}000(0.7876) \\ &= \$1{,}575.20 \end{aligned}$$

Discounting $2,000 annually gives a present value of:

$$\begin{aligned} PV\{\$2{,}000\} &= \$2{,}000[1/(1+0.12)^{2}] \\ &= \$2{,}000(0.7972) \\ &= \$1{,}594.40 \end{aligned}$$

Monthly discounting results in a smaller present value than yearly discounting at the same annual rate. ❖

The *PVIF* can be modified easily to accommodate shorter discounting periods. A modified *PVIF* formula is given by:

$$PVIF_{nf,i} = 1/[1+(i/f)]^{nf} \quad (8.15)$$

where i/f = discount rate for the period

nf = number of discounting periods

Present Value of a Series of Cash Flows

Most real decision-making situations involve series of cash flows. This makes the present value of a series of cash flows a useful concept. Consider, for example, an offer of a series of payments of $12,000 per year for the next 15 years in exchange for a single payment of $92,250 today. Would you accept this offer if you had the money? The offer is definitely worthwhile if its present value exceeds its cost. The present value of the offer is given by the present value of the promised cash flows, discounted at an interest rate that is equal to the opportunity cost (i.e., the interest rate that the money can earn elsewhere in a similar investment).

Present Value of an Uneven Series. The present value of a series is determined by calculating the present value of each amount separately and then summing these present values. Let $P_1, P_2, P_3, \ldots P_n$ be an uneven series (P_t) of n amounts occurring at the end of each year; let i be the discount rate. The present value of the series is given by:

$$PV\{P_t\} = P_1(PVIF_{1,i}) + P_2(PVIF_{2,i}) + \ldots + P_n(PVIF_{n,i})$$

$$PV\{P_t\} = P_1[1/(1+i)^1] + P_2[1/(1+i)^2] + \ldots + P_n[1/(1+i)^n] \quad (8.16)$$

If payments occur at the beginning of each year, the present value will change to:

$$PV\{P_t\} = P_1[1/(1+i)^0] + P_2[1/(1+i)^1] + \ldots + P_n[1/(1+i)^{n-1}] \quad (8.17)$$

The reason for the change is the fact that the beginning-of-period payments will be discounted over one less period. The present value of a series with beginning-of-period payments is always larger than the present value of the same series with end-of-period payments.

❖ EXAMPLE 8.9

Find the present value of the following end-of-period cash flows when i = 12 percent.

YEAR	DOLLAR AMOUNT (P_t)
1	1,250
2	960
3	1,350
4	1,350

$$PV\{P_t\} = \$1,250[1/(1.12)^1] + \$960[1/(1.12)^2] + \$1,350[1/(1.12)^3] + \$1,350[1/(1.12)^4]$$

$$= \$1{,}250(0.8929) + \$960(0.7972) + \$1{,}350(0.7118) + \$1{,}350(0.6355)$$
$$= \$1{,}116.12 + \$765.31 + \$960.93 + \$857.92$$
$$= \$3{,}700.28$$

Presenting these results on a time-line of cash flows gives:

	PV	YEARS 1	2	3	4
	CASH FLOWS:	$1,250	$960	$1,350	$1,350
$\$1{,}250[1/(1.12)^1] =$	$1,116.00	←			
$960[1/(1.12)^2] =$	765.31		←		
$1{,}350[1/(1.12)^3] =$	960.93			←	
$1{,}350[1/(1.12)^4] =$	857.92				←
	$3,700.16				

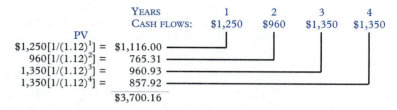

If the cash flows were to occur at the beginning of each period, the present value would be:

$$PV\{P_t\} = \$1{,}250[1/(1.12)^0] + \$960[1/(1.12)^1] + \$1{,}350[1/(1.12)^2] + \$1{,}350[1/(1.12)^3]$$
$$= \$1{,}250(1.000) + \$960(0.8929) + \$1{,}350(0.7972) + \$1{,}350(0.7118)$$
$$= \$1{,}250.00 + \$857.18 + \$1{,}076.22 + \$960.93$$
$$= \$4{,}144.33$$ ❖

Present Value of an Annuity. Suppose that someone deposits $1 at the end of every year for four years. What is the present value of this annuity if the annual interest rate is 10 percent? It is an ordinary annuity (A_O), and its present value is given by:

$$PV\{A_O = \$1\} = \$1[1/(1+0.1)^1] + \$1[1/(1+0.1)^2] + \$1[1/(1+0.1)^3] + \$1[1/(1+0.1)^4]$$
$$= \$0.9090 + \$0.8264 + \$0.7513 + \$0.6830$$
$$= \$3.1698$$

Writing this series in summation notation:

$$PV\{A_O = \$1\} = \$1\sum_{t=1}^{4}\left[1/(1+0.1)^t\right] \qquad \textbf{(8.18)}$$

The right-hand side of Equation 8.18 is mathematically equivalent to $\$1[[1 - 1/(1+0.1)^4]/0.1]$. Replacing it:

$$PV\{A_O = \$1\} = \$1\{[1 - 1/(1+0.1)^4]/0.1\}$$
$$= \$1(3.1698)$$
$$= \$3.1698$$

To complete the derivation, generalize this expression to any interest rate and any number of years:

$$PV\{A_O = \$1\} = \$1\sum_{t=1}^{n}\left[1/(1+i)^t\right] = \$1\left[\frac{1-1/(1+i)^n}{i}\right] \quad (8.19)$$

Equation 8.19 provides a shortcut to calculate the present value of an ordinary $1 annuity.

The expression:

$$\sum_{t=1}^{n}\left[1/(1+i)^t\right]$$

or its equivalent expression $[[1-1/(1+i)^n]/i]$ is known as the *present value interest factor for an ordinary annuity* ($PVIFA_O$). The values of $PVIFA_O$ for various combinations of i and n can be obtained from a *PVIFA* table (refer to Table C.4 in Appendix C) or using a calculator.

If the dollar deposits are made at the beginning of each year (which makes the series an annuity due, A_D), the present value of the annuity will change to:

$$\begin{aligned} PV\{A_D=\$1\} &= \$1[1/(1+0.1)^0] + \$1[1/(1+0.1)^1] + \$1[1/(1+0.1)^2] + \$1[1/(1+0.1)^3] \\ &= \$1.0000 + \$0.9091 + \$0.8264 + \$0.7513 \\ &= \$3.4868 \end{aligned}$$

Using summation notation, the expression can be written as:

$$PV\{A_D = \$1\} = \$1\sum_{t=1}^{4}\left[1/(1+0.1)^{t-1}\right] \quad (8.20)$$

The right-hand side of Equation 8.20 is mathematically equivalent to $\$1[[1-1/(1+0.1)^4]/0.1](1+0.1)$. Replacing it:

$$\begin{aligned} PV\{A_D=\$1\} &= \$1[[1-1/(1+0.1)^4]/0.1](1+0.1) \\ &= \$1(3.1698)(1+0.1) \\ &= \$3.4868 \end{aligned}$$

Generalize this expression to any interest rate and any number of years:

$$PV\{A_D = \$1\} = \$1\sum_{t=1}^{n}1(1+i)^{t-1} = \$1\left[\frac{1-1/(1+i)^n}{i}\right](1+i) \quad (8.21)$$

The expression:

$$\sum_{t=1}^{n}(1+i)^{t-1}$$

or its equivalent expression $\$1[[1-1/(1+i)^n]/i](1+i)$ is called the *present value interest factor for an annuity due* ($PVIFA_D$). The value of $PVIFA_D$ is determined by multiplying the $PVIFA_O$ by $(1+i)$. Note that the value of this factor is higher than the value of the present value factor for an ordinary annuity, again because it discounts the earlier payments over one less period.

The present value of any annuity (A) is easily defined by multiplying the amount of the annuity by the appropriate *PVIFA*.

1. When A is an ordinary annuity:

$$\begin{aligned} PV\{A_O\} &= \$A \sum_{t=1}^{n} \left[1/(1+i)^t \right] \\ &= \$A_O \left[\frac{1-1(1+i)^n}{i} \right] \\ &= \$A_O \left(PVIFA_{O\,n,i} \right) \end{aligned} \tag{8.22}$$

❖ EXAMPLE 8.10

Find the present value of a business opportunity that promises \$12,000 at the end of each year for the next 15 years, if the annual interest rate is 8 percent.

$$\begin{aligned} PV\{A_O = \$12{,}000\} &= \$12{,}000\ (PVIFA_O) \\ &= \$12{,}000\{[1-1/(1+0.08)^{15}]/0.08\} \\ &= \$12{,}000(8.5595) \\ &= \$102{,}714.00 \end{aligned}$$ ❖

2. When A is an annuity due:

$$\begin{aligned} PV\{A_D\} &= \$A_D \sum_{t=1}^{n} \left[1/(1+i)^{t-1} \right] \\ &= \$A_D \left[\frac{1-1/(1+i)^n}{i} \right](1+i) \\ &= \$A_D \left(PVIFA_{D\,n,i} \right) \end{aligned} \tag{8.23}$$

❖ EXAMPLE 8.11

Assuming that the annual payments in Example 8.10 occur at the beginning of each year instead of at the end, determine the present value of the annuity.

$$\begin{aligned} PV\{A_D = \$12{,}000\} &= \$12{,}000(PVIFA_O)(1+0.08) \\ &= \$12{,}000[[1-1/(1+0.08)^{15}]/0.08](1+0.08) \\ &= \$12{,}000(8.5595)(1.08) \\ &= \$110{,}931.12 \end{aligned}$$ ❖

Present value interest factors for annuities can be obtained from annuity present value tables or determined with the help of a calculator. Most annuity present value tables provide values for the ordinary annuity only. To determine the present

FOCUS ON FINANCE

PRESENT VALUE OF A PERPETUITY

A perpetuity is a special kind of annuity with cash flows that continue forever. A good example of a perpetuity is preferred stock, which promises a fixed dividend forever. Since perpetuities have infinite cash flows, they defy the valuation procedure of discounting each cash flow separately and then adding the discounted values. Fortunately, the formula for determining the present value of a perpetuity turns out to be a simple one, thanks to the mathematical rule for finding the sum of an infinite series.

Representing a perpetuity by the symbol *PT* and the periodic cash flow by *A*, and using the sum of an infinite series rule, the present value of a perpetuity can be expressed as:

$$PV\{PT\} = \$A[1/(1+i)] + A[1/(1+i)^2] + \ldots$$
$$= \$A(1/i)$$

Example:

A preferred stock promises a \$4 dividend. What is the present value (that is, the price) of this stock if the discount rate is 8 percent?

$$PV\{PT\} = \$4(1/0.08)$$
$$= \$50$$

Note that \$50 may not be the exact market price of this stock because changes in investors' perceptions continually modify the appropriate discount rate.

value interest factor for an annuity due, as mentioned before, multiply the present value interest factor of an ordinary annuity by the factor $(1+i)$.

The present value of an amount or a series of amounts depends on three factors:

1. Annual discount rate
2. Length of time (or number of years) of discounting
3. Frequency of discounting in a year

The present value decreases with an increase in each of these factors.

FUTURE VALUE AND PRESENT VALUE APPLICATIONS

The illustrative examples presented so far have emphasized finding the *FV* or the *PV* of a single amount or a series of amounts. The future value and present value formulas can help a financial manager answer a number of other problems, such as finding the interest rate, the number of periods, and the annuity amount when other variables are given.

Finding the Interest Rate

One can find the implied interest (or growth) rate for a known *FV* or *PV*, number of years, and frequency of compounding or discounting.

❖ EXAMPLE 8.12

Ms. Jefferson sold a stock for $2,261 after buying it ten years ago for $1,000. What annual rate of interest did she earn from this investment?

The future value of Ms. Jefferson's $1,000 investment in ten years is $2,261. To find the implied annual interest rate, either solve the future value equation for *i* or use the future value table. The future value equation for this problem is:

$$\$1{,}000(1+i)^{10} = \$2{,}261$$
$$(1+i)^{10} = \$2{,}261/1{,}000$$
$$= 2.261$$

The $FVIF_{10,i}$ is 2.261. To determine the implied interest rate from the future value table, locate the row that corresponds to Period 10, and move along that row until you reach the column with the number 2.261, or a number close to it. Identify the interest rate that corresponds to that column.

If the implied interest rate involves a fraction, the interest factor tables will not provide exact answers, as most tables give factors only for whole number interest rates. Solving the future value equation for *i* produces the exact answer. To solve the future value equation for *i* in this case, one must eliminate the exponential expression on the left-hand side. One way to do this is to raise both sides of the equation to the $^1/_{10}$ or 0.1 power. Most business calculators can handle this operation. Solving the equation for *i*, results in:

$$[(1+i)^{10}]^{0.1} = 2.261^{0.1}$$
$$1+i = 1.085$$
$$i = 1.085 - 1$$
$$= 0.085 \text{ or } 8.5 \text{ percent}$$

One can also use the present value equation to answer this problem. Write the present value equation of the problem and follow the above steps. Try it—the answer should be the same. ❖

❖ EXAMPLE 8.13

A $10,000, four-year car loan obtained by Maria Lopez carries a monthly installment payment of $263.34. How much interest (measured by annual percentage rate) is she paying on this loan?

Installment loan payments are ordinarily end-of-period payments. Since the amount of the loan represents the present value of future payments, the present value of 48 monthly installments is $10,000.

$$PV\{A_O=\$263.34\} = \$263.34\left[1-1/[1+(i/12)]^{48}\right]/(i/12) = \$10{,}000$$
$$\{1-1/[1+(i/12)]^{48}\}/(i/12) = \$10{,}000/\$263.34$$
$$= 37.974$$

The *PVIFA* is 37.974. As in the previous example, one can either solve the present value equation for *i* or use the present value annuity table to obtain the implied interest rate. This equation is not easy to solve. To obtain the answer from the annuity table, locate the *PVIFA* of 37.974 on the row that corresponds to 48 periods. The interest rate for the column with the *PVIFA* of 37.974 is 1 percent; this is a monthly interest rate. The implied annual percentage rate is, therefore, 12 percent. ❖

FOCUS ON FINANCE

RULE OF 72

There is a back-of-the-envelope approach to determining the interest rate or the number of periods that are required to double an amount. This approach is known as the *rule of 72*. The rule of 72 states: for a given i, $n = 72/i$ and for a given n, $i = 72/n$. This rule provides a fairly accurate answer for interest rates between 5 and 20 percent.

Example:

Using the rule of 72, find:

1. The number of years required to double $2,000 if the interest rate is 8 percent
2. The interest rate the money must earn to double in six years

1. The rule gives n as approximately 72/8, or nine years.
2. It gives i as approximately 72/6, or 12 percent.

Note that the exact answers are $n = 9.007$ years and $i = 12.25$ percent.

Determining the Number of Years

Often a financial manager needs to find the number of years it takes for an amount to reach a desired level at a future date, given the interest rate. Consider, for example, a simple question like "How many years will it take to double an amount if it grows at an annual rate of 5 percent?" To answer this question, select a hypothetical value of $30,000, set its future value as double that amount, or $60,000, and solve the future value equation for the *FVIF*.

$$
\begin{aligned}
FV(\$30{,}000) &= \$60{,}000 \\
\$30{,}000(1+0.05)^n &= \$60{,}000 \\
(1+0.05)^n &= \$60{,}000/30{,}000 \\
&= 2
\end{aligned}
$$

The $FVIF_{n,5\%}$ in this case is 2 and n is unknown. To find the value of n from the FVIF table, follow down the column that corresponds to the 5 percent interest rate until you see an *FVIF* equal to or close to 2. The number of periods that corresponds to the row with an *FVIF* of 2 is the value of n. The value of n in this case is a little over 14 years.

Solving the future value equation for n provides an exact answer. To solve the equation for n, eliminate the exponential expression by taking the logarithm of both sides of the equation. Again most business calculators can handle this operation. The result of this operation is:

$$
\begin{aligned}
\ln[(1+0.05)^n] &= \ln 2 \\
n[\ln(1+0.05)] &= \ln 2 \\
n(0.0488) &= 0.6931 \\
n &= 14.2 \text{ years}
\end{aligned}
$$

The exact number of years it will take for money to double when the interest rate is 5 percent is 14.2 years, or 14 years and 73 days.

Determining Annuity Payments

One can use the future value formula to determine the annuity payment required to accumulate a specific amount at a future date. The present value formula can determine the annuity payment that an investment today will generate in the future.

❖ EXAMPLE 8.14

Ronald and Nancy Walsh are planning to celebrate their 25th wedding anniversary on a cruise ship three years from now. They expect the trip to cost $5,000, and they want to make a fixed payment every month to an interest-bearing account to cover the cost. If the account pays 6 percent per year, what monthly payment should they make?

The future value that they plan to accumulate is $5,000. They can make 36 payments during the three years that remain before the trip. Since this payment is a fixed amount, it amounts to an annuity payment. The monthly interest rate is 0.5 percent. Assuming that the Walshes make payments at the end of each month, the problem can be expressed as:

$$FV\{A_O\} = A_O(FVIFA_{O\,36,0.5\%})$$
$$= \$5{,}000$$

Solving for A_O:

$$A_O = \$5{,}000/FVIFA_{O\,36,0.5\%}$$
$$= \$5{,}000/39.3361$$
$$= \$127.11$$

The monthly payment needed to generate $5,000 in three years at a 6 percent annual interest rate is $127.11. ❖

❖ EXAMPLE 8.15

John Coulter took early retirement and received $75,000 as an incentive payment. If he invests this amount in an annuity that earns 8 percent and promises end-of-period annual payments for the next 20 years, what would be the amount of each payment?

The present value of the annuity (A_O) over the 20-year period is $75,000. Using the present value of an annuity equation,

$$PV\{A_O\} = A_O(PVIFA_{O\,20,\,8\%}) = \$75{,}000$$

Solving for A_O:

$$A_O = \$75{,}000/PVIFA_{O\,20,\,8\%}$$
$$= \$75{,}000/9.8181$$
$$= \$7{,}638.95$$

John Coulter can expect to receive $7,638.95 every year for 20 years from his investment. ❖

Amortizing a Loan

amortization
Liquidation of a debt by installment payments.

amortization schedule
A table that describes beginning-of-period balances, installment payments, and the breakdown of each installment payment into its interest and principal components.

The PV formula is used to determine the periodic payments in certain types of amortization plans. **Amortization** is the liquidation of a debt by making periodic payments, each including an interest amount and a partial payment of principal. An **amortization schedule** is prepared as part of the amortization plan. This schedule describes the amount of the periodic payments and the breakdown of each payment into interest and principal components.

A debt can be amortized in a number of ways. For one way, the borrower can pay a fixed amount toward the principal plus the interest on the outstanding balance every period. In this method, the borrower will pay a different amount every period. This method is commonly found in medium-term business loans made by banks. Credit card accounts also use this method.

In the most widely used method of loan amortization, the borrower pays a fixed amount every period until the loan is liquidated. This method is commonly used for home mortgages. As the fixed payments represent an annuity, the calculation of the periodic payment for a particular loan amount can use the present value of an annuity formula. The steps below lead to construction of an amortization schedule for a loan account with fixed payments:

1. Determine the fixed periodic payment on the loan using the PVIFA formula. The PVIFA formula is used because the loan amount represents the present value of the future payments to the lender. The payment is calculated by setting the present value of these payments equal to the amount of the loan.
2. Determine the outstanding balance of the loan at the beginning of each period and calculate the interest on that amount. This amount is the interest component of the periodic payment.
3. Determine the amount of principal that is included in the periodic payment by subtracting the interest from the amount of each payment.
4. Determine the remaining loan balance at the end of each period by subtracting the principal component of each payment from the loan balance at the beginning of the period.
5. Complete the following amortization schedule:

1 Period	2 Beginning Balance	3 Payment Amount	4 Interest	5 Principal Repayment (3-4)	6 Ending Balance (2-5)
1					
2					
3					
4					
.					
.					
.					
n					

❖ EXAMPLE 8.16

O'Connor's Delivery Service takes out a $10,000 loan. The loan carries a 9 percent annual interest rate and it will be amortized with fixed monthly payments over a four-year period. Construct the amortization schedule for this loan.

Since the lender is exchanging $10,000 today for a 48-month annuity, the present value of those payments to the lender must equal the amount of the loan. The discounting period is a month and the monthly interest rate is 0.09/12, or 0.75 percent. Assuming that the borrower makes payments at the end of every month, this is an ordinary annuity and A_O is the monthly payment.

$$PV\{A_O\} = A_O(PVIFA_{O\,48,0.75\%}) = \$10{,}000$$
$$A_O[[1 - 1/(1.0075)^{48}]/0.0075] = \$10{,}000$$
$$A_O(40.1848) = \$10{,}000$$
$$A_O = \$248.85$$

1 Period	2 Beginning Balance	3 Payment Amount	4 Interest	5 Principal Repayment	6 Ending Balance
1	$10,000.00	$248.85	$75.00	$173.85	$9,826.15
2	9,826.15	248.85	73.70	175.15	9,651.00
3	9,651.00	248.85	72.38	176.47	9,474.53
4	9,474.53	248.85	71.06	177.79	9,296.74
5	9,296.74	248.85	69.73	179.12	9,117.62
.	.	.	.	.	.
.	.	.	.	.	.
.	.	.	.	.	.
48	246.99	248.85	1.86	246.99	0.00

Due to rounding, the last payment may not quite cover the last period's beginning balance and the interest on it. This discrepancy is ignored in the amortization schedule because the standard commercial practice is to increase the last payment by the few dollars needed to bring the ending balance to zero. ❖

Note two interesting facts about amortization payments: (1) the interest component of the payment declines, and (2) the principal component increases. Since residential mortgages are amortized this way, each mortgage payment adds more to the homeowner's equity than the previous payment.

Valuation

discounted cash flow approach
The method of determining the value of an asset by discounting its future cash flows using an appropriate discount rate.

Valuation is a basic theme in financial management. The term *valuation* refers to the process of determining the monetary value of an asset or a collection of assets (such as a firm). In finance, valuation is generally based on the future cash flows (net of taxes) that the asset can generate. The present value of these cash flows represents the value of the asset. This approach to valuation, known as the **discounted cash flow approach**, is considered to be the most scientific of all valuation approaches.

The value of an asset expressed in monetary terms represents its price. Therefore, valuation amounts to asset pricing. To attract a buyer, the price of an asset must reflect its present worth. The present worth of an asset is the present value of the future cash flows that the asset is expected to generate. If the seller asks a price greater than the present value of the asset to the buyer, no transaction will take place. Therefore, the market price at which a transaction takes place must reflect the present value of the asset. Hence, the discounted cash flow approach is the most appropriate way to derive a value of an asset.

To value an asset using the discounted cash flow approach, the analyst estimates the future cash flows of the asset and discounts them using an appropriate discount rate. The appropriate discount rate must reflect the buyer's (or investor's) time value of money.

❖ EXAMPLE 8.17

Suppose that an investment opportunity offers the following end-of-period annual payments for five years:

YEAR	PAYMENTS
1	$460
2	$650
3	$750
4	$750
5	$800

What will be the price (or value) of this opportunity if the investor's time value of money is 12 percent?

Under the discounted cash flow approach, the value of the opportunity is given by the present value of its cash flows:

YEAR	PAYMENTS	PV OF PAYMENTS		
1	$460	$460(PVIF_{1,12\%})$	$460(0.8928)	$ 410.68
2	650	$650(PVIF_{2,12\%})$	650(0.7972)	518.18
3	750	$750(PVIF_{3,12\%})$	750(0.7118)	533.85
4	750	$750(PVIF_{4,12\%})$	750(0.6355)	476.62
5	800	$800(PVIF_{5,12\%})$	800(0.5674)	453.92
				$ 2,393.25

The present value of the opportunity is $2,393.25. This is the maximum price an investor would pay when the time value of money is 12 percent. ❖

Net Present Value

net present value

The present value of cash inflows from an asset minus the present value of its cash outflows (costs).

A concept closely related to present value is **net present value** (NPV). This concept is widely used as a criterion for investment decision making. The net present value of an asset or investment is the present value of its (expected) cash inflows minus its cost. If acquiring the asset exposes the buyer to costs over many years, the present value of the costs is used to calculate the NPV. An asset with a positive NPV is worth the investment. This means that, after converting all cash flows to today's dollars, the firm will take in more than it pays out. An asset with a negative NPV is not worth the investment.

❖ EXAMPLE 8.18

Nash Associates, a real estate firm, has an opportunity to buy a piece of land today for \$40,000. The firm expects the land to appreciate to \$45,000 by next year. If the interest rate at which money can be borrowed or lent is 10 percent, should the firm invest in the land?

The NPV of this investment opportunity is given by:

$$\begin{aligned} NPV &= PV(\text{Cash inflow}) - \text{Cost} \\ &= \$45{,}000(PVIF_{1,10\%}) - \$40{,}000 \\ &= \$45{,}000(0.9091) - \$40{,}000 \\ &= \$40{,}909.50 - \$40{,}000 \\ &= \$909.50 \end{aligned}$$

Since the NPV is positive, the land is worth buying. ❖

The logic of NPV analysis is very simple. If the firm in Example 8.18 has \$40,000, it can do one of two things: buy the piece of land or lend the money at 10 percent. Investing in the land is expected to convert the \$40,000 investment into \$45,000 in one year. This means that \$45,000 is the future value of \$40,000 one year from now. This implies an interest rate, or growth rate of money, of:

$$\begin{aligned} FV\{\$40{,}000\} &= \$45{,}000 \\ \$40{,}000(1+i) &= \$45{,}000 \\ (1+i) &= \$45{,}000/\$40{,}000 \\ (1+i) &= 1.125 \\ i &= 1.125 - 1 \\ &= 0.125 \text{ or } 12.5 \text{ percent} \end{aligned}$$

The investment in land earns 12.5 percent, a rate higher than the 10 percent lending rate. A positive NPV always implies that the return from the investment is higher than the return the money could earn in an alternative opportunity.

If the firm does not have the \$40,000, it could borrow the amount at 10 percent and generate a 12.5 percent return from investing in the land. This would provide the firm with a gain of 2.5 percent. Note that the NPV of \$905 is 2.5 percent of \$40,000.

Comparing Assets

The future and present value concepts can simplify comparisons of assets with different features.

❖ EXAMPLE 8.19

Asset A promises end-of-period payments of \$1,000 per year for ten years and Asset B promises \$11,000 at the end of the tenth year. If the interest rate is 6 percent, which asset is the better investment?

The difference in the timing of the cash flows prevents comparing the two assets by looking only at their total cash flows. A meaningful comparison is possible only if the assets are represented by their present values or future values.

Assuming an interest rate of 6 percent, the present values of A and B are given by:

$$PV\{A\} = \$1{,}000(PVIFA_{O\ 10,6\%}) = \$7{,}360.10$$
$$PV\{B\} = \$11{,}000(PVIF_{10,6\%}) = \$6{,}142.40$$

Asset A is the better asset. Comparing the future values gives the same conclusion. The future values of A and B are given by:

$$FV\{A\} = \$1{,}000(FVIFA_{O\ 10,6\%}) = \$13{,}180.80$$
$$FV\{B\} = \$11{,}000.00$$ ❖

Funding Future Obligations

sinking fund
A fund created by annual contributions to pay off a debt.

When a firm borrows long-term, it may make periodic (usually annual) payments into a fund, called a **sinking fund**, in order to accumulate enough money to pay back the loan on schedule. Sinking funds are commonly associated with borrowing through bond issues. Similar funds may be created to provide for other future obligations such as a need to retire preferred stock or to pay for employees' future health benefits.

❖ EXAMPLE 8.20

Funtoys Corporation borrows $10 million through a 15-year bond issue. The firm makes annual payments to a sinking fund over the life of the bond to accumulate enough funds to retire the bond at maturity. If the firm can earn 7 percent on its money, what should be the amount of the sinking fund payment?

The annual payment is a fixed amount (or annuity) which compounds at 7 percent per year. It should have a future value of $10 million in 15 years. Assuming end-of-period payments, the annual payment is given by:

$$A_O(FVIFA_{O\ 15,7\%}) = \$10{,}000{,}000$$
$$A_O(25.129) = \$10{,}000{,}000$$
$$A_O = \$10{,}000{,}000/25.129$$
$$A_O = \$397{,}946.60$$ ❖

SUMMARY

One of the most important concepts in finance is the time value of money. The time value of money plays a key role in the determination of interest rates and the valuation of assets. *Valuation* refers to the determination of how much something is worth today; it is fundamental to all financial decision making.

The concept of time value of money refers to the fact that a future dollar is worth less than a present dollar. The reason that money has a time value, and how much time value it has, are explained by factors such as people's tendency to discount the future, inflation risk, and default risk. The interest rate (or the rate of return) that lenders (or investors) receive reflects the time value of money.

Several concepts based on the time value of money have been devised to aid the financial decision making process. Two of these concepts are future value and present value. Future value is the amount to which a single amount or a series of amounts will grow at a future date when compounded at a given interest rate. Present value is the present worth of a single amount or a series of amounts in the future discounted at a given interest rate.

The formulas and shortcuts for calculating future and present values are listed below. The symbols *i*, *n*, and *f* refer to the interest rate, the number of years, and the frequency of compounding or discounting, respectively.

Future value of a dollar:

$$FV\{\$1\} = \$1(1+i)^n = FVIF_{n,i}$$

Future value of an amount (P_0):

$$FV\{P_0\} = P_0(1+i)^n = P_0(FVIF_{n,i})$$

Future value of an ordinary annuity:

$$FV\{A_O\} = A_O \sum_{t=1}^{n} (1+i)^{t-1} = A(FVIFA_{O\,n,i})$$

$$= A_O\left[\frac{(1+i)^n - 1}{i}\right]$$

Future value of an annuity due:

$$FV\{A_D\} = A_D \sum_{t=1}^{n} (1+i)^t = A(FVIFA_{D\,n,i}) = A(FVIFA_{O\,n,i})(1+i)$$

$$= A_D\left[\frac{(1+i)^n - 1}{i}\right](1+i)$$

Effective annual rate of interest (EAR):

$$EAR = [1 + (i/f)]^f - 1$$

Present value of a dollar:

$$PV\{\$1\} = \$1[1/(1+i)^n] = PVIF_{n,i}$$

Present value of an amount (P_n):

$$PV\{P_n\} = \$P_n[1/(1+i)^n] = \$P_n(PVIF_{n,i})$$

Present value of an ordinary annuity:

$$PV\{A_O\} = \$A_O \sum_{t=1}^{n} \left[1/(1+i)^t\right] = \$A(PVIFA_{O\,n,i})$$

$$= \$A_O\left[\frac{1 - 1/(1+i)^n}{i}\right]$$

Present value of an annuity due:

$$PV\{A_D\} = \$A_D \sum_{t=1}^{n} \left[1/(1+i)^{t-1}\right] = \$A(PVIFA_{O\,n,i})(1+i)$$

$$= \$A_D \left[\frac{1-1(1+i)^n}{i}\right](1+i)$$

Future value depends on the stated interest rate, the number of years, and the frequency of compounding. Present value depends on the stated interest rate, the number of years, and the frequency of discounting.

Present value and future value concepts have uses in a wide range of problem-solving situations. They include:

1. Determining the interest rate when *FV*, *PV*, and the number of years are known
2. Determining the number of years it will take for an amount to reach a specific sum at a future date growing at a given interest rate
3. Finding an annuity amount, given the future value or present value
4. Comparing assets with different characteristics
5. Amortizing loans
6. Performing asset valuation
7. Selecting assets based on their net present values
8. Calculating funding for future obligations

Key Terms

amortization
amortization schedule
annual percentage rate
annuity
annuity due
compounding period
compounding rate
discounted cash flow approach
discount factor
discount rate
discounting
effective annual rate
future value
interest compounding
ordinary annuity
net present value
perpetuity
present value
sinking fund
time value of money

Self-Study Questions

1. Why does money have a time value?
2. How is the time value of money related to the interest rate?
3. Why do different loan transactions have different interest rates?
4. Why is the future value computation called *compounding* and the present value computation called *discounting*?
5. If you deposit money in an account, would you prefer monthly compounding or annual compounding of interest? Why?
6. What is an annuity? Give an example.

7. How does the frequency of compounding affect future and present values and why?
8. What is the effective annual rate (EAR)?
9. Explain the effects of time to maturity, discount rate, and frequency of discounting on present values.
10. What is amortization? Explain the use of the present value concept in determining the periodic payment.

Self-Test Problems

1. A bank offers an 8 percent annual interest rate on a five-year fixed deposit. What is the future value of a deposit of $10,000:
   (a) If interest is compounded annually?
   (b) If interest is compounded quarterly?
2. A sum of $8,000 is invested in a certificate of deposit that matures in ten years and pays 8 percent annually.
   (a) How much interest will the CD earn in ten years if the interest is left to accumulate in the account?
   (b) How much interest will it earn in ten years if the interest is withdrawn each year?
3. A recently advertised investment deal offers to double your money in nine years. What is the implied rate of return (interest rate) in this deal, assuming annual compounding?
4. A sum of $1,000 is deposited in an account that pays 9 percent per annum. How many years will it take to increase this amount to $3,642.50?
5. If you sold a rare coin for $1,500 after buying it five years earlier for $500, what annual rate of return did you earn on your investment?
6. Mr. Swanson anticipates an expenditure of $25,000 in ten years, and he wants to start a savings account to generate this sum. He can either deposit a lump sum in the account today or make annual deposits of equal amounts into the account for ten years. The savings account pays 6 percent interest.
   (a) What is the lump sum that Mr. Swanson must deposit?
   (b) What is the amount of the annual deposits that Mr. Swanson must make?
7. Investment A offers to pay a lump sum of $850 at the end of five years and Investment B offers to pay $150 per year for five years. If the interest rate is 8 percent, which is the better investment?
8. The table below summarizes the cash flows promised by Investments X, Y, and Z:

YEAR	INVESTMENT X	INVESTMENT Y	INVESTMENT Z
1	$300	$400	$250
2	350	250	350
3	450	350	500

(a) Compute the present values of the investments using a discount rate of 8 percent.
(b) If the cost of each investment is $900, which of these investments will be worthwhile?

9. What is the present worth of an end-of-year annuity of $2,000, given a 6 percent interest rate, if the first payment is due 2 years from today and the last payment is due 20 years from today?
10. If you take a 30-year mortgage for $200,000 at 9 percent interest, what will your monthly payment be? Construct an amortization schedule for the first two periods.

Discussion Questions

1. Why does the present value of a dollar decrease more if you have to wait longer to receive it?
2. If there is no inflation and no risk of default, will a present dollar be preferred to a future dollar? Explain your answer.
3. What is interest compounding? How does interest compounding change the future value of an investment as compared to simple interest?
4. What are future value and present value interest factors?
5. Explain why the present value interest factor for a future amount will always be less than 1.0.
6. How do increases in the following variables affect (a) the future value of a present amount and (b) the present value of a future amount?
   (i) interest rate
   (ii) frequency of compounding
   (iii) number of years
7. Distinguish between the stated annual rate, annual percentage rate, and effective annual rate.
8. Discuss the difference between an ordinary annuity and an annuity due.
9. What would happen to the future and present values of an annuity if the interest rate were suddenly to fall?
10. Why is the future value of a $100 annuity due larger than that of a $100 ordinary annuity?
11. What is the difference between an annuity and a perpetuity?
12. What is amortization? Explain how the present value concept underlies the construction of an amortization table.

Problems

1. Compute the future values of the following amounts:

AMOUNT	YEAR	INTEREST RATE	FUTURE VALUE
$ 100	5	9.0%	
1,250	4	8.5	
2,500	9	8.0	

2. Compute the present value of the following amounts:

AMOUNT	YEAR	INTEREST RATE	FUTURE VALUE
$ 1,200	6	8.0%	
10,500	10	6.0	
100	20	10.0	
125,650	10	7.5	

3. Someone deposits $2,000 in an account that earns a 9 percent annual rate of interest. What will be the amount in this account at the end of five years if interest compounds:
   (a) annually?
   (b) semiannually?
   (c) monthly?
4. Mrs. Appleton deposits $10,000 in an account that earns 8 percent. How much interest will she earn at the end of four years if (a) she leaves the interest to accumulate and (b) she withdraws the interest each year?
5. If you want your salary to double in eight years, at what annual rate must your salary increase?
6. A house bought for $140,000 five years ago is sold for $210,000. What is the annual rate of appreciation in the value of the house?
7. A bank offers two deposit accounts. One pays 9 percent compounded monthly and another pays 9.10 percent compounded quarterly. Which account is better?
8. If a bank charges interest at a monthly rate of 1.25 percent, what is the APR? What is the EAR?
9. You need $55,000 in 20 years and your money can earn 9 percent. How much should you invest today to achieve your goal?
10. An investment opportunity offers $20,000 in ten years. What is the present value of the opportunity if the interest rate is 8 percent?
11. Ms. Turnipseed will receive $50,000 in five years from a financial settlement. She needs the cash now and wants to borrow against this future cash flow. How much can she borrow if the lender wants 9 percent on the loan?
12. Two investors, A and B, have 8 percent and 9 percent time values of money, respectively. An investment opportunity that promises $10,000 in one year is priced at $9,217. Which of the two investors will buy this investment?
13. Calculate the future value and the present value of the following series of end-of-period cash flows. Assume a 6 percent annual interest rate.

YEAR	AMOUNT	FUTURE VALUE	PRESENT VALUE
1	$ 600		
2	750		
3	1,000		
4	850		
5	950		

14. If an investment opportunity offers $2,000 at the end of every year for ten years, what is the present value of this opportunity if the interest rate is 8 percent?
15. If you were to set aside a certain amount each year to achieve a goal of saving $55,000 in 20 years, what amount should you save annually if the current interest rate is 9 percent?
16. If $150 is deposited at the beginning of each month, how much will be in the account at the end of four years if the interest rate is 9 percent?
17. How much will be in an account at the end of four years if $150 is deposited at the end of each month at an annual interest rate of 9 percent?
18. Annual deposits of $3,600 are made into a retirement account for a period of 15 years. How much will the account have at the end of 25 years if it pays 6 percent interest?
19. Monthly deposits of $300 are made into a retirement account for a period of 15 years. How much will the account have at the end of 25 years if it pays 6 percent interest?
20. What is the present value of an end-of-year annuity of $1,200 that lasts for ten years, if the interest rate is 8 percent?
21. What is the present value of a beginning-of-period annuity of $1,200 that lasts for ten years with an interest rate of 8 percent?
22. An investment costs $6,710 today and promises $1,000 per year for the next 10 years. What is the rate of return on this investment?
23. The winner of a lottery is given the following payment options for the prize:

	YEAR			
OPTION	1	2	3	4
A	$10,000	$ 0	$ 0	$ 0
B	5,000	0	0	6,000
C	3,000	3,000	3,000	3,000
D	0	0	6,400	6,400

Which option should the winner accept if the time value of money is 8 percent?

24. A firm must pay off a debt obligation of $500,000 at the end of 15 years. The firm wants to pay into a sinking fund every year starting five years from now to liquidate the debt. What annual contribution should it make to the sinking fund if the interest rate is 6 percent?
25. A company is considering the introduction of a new toy that promises the following annual cash flows:

YEAR	CASH FLOW
1	$250,000
2	300,000
3	350,000
4	200,000
5	150,000

If the cost of introducing the toy is \$1,000,000 and the cost of financing is 10 percent, should the company undertake this investment?

Topics for Further Research

1. (a) Determine the fixed monthly payment for a 15-year mortgage if the loan amount is \$150,000 and the interest rate is 9 percent.
   (b) Construct an amortization schedule.
2. The Utopia State Lottery has a game that promises to pay a million-dollar winner \$50,000 a year for 20 years "to minimize the tax bite." Discuss the consequences of this arrangement for the winner.
3. Karen Kline is 30 years old and plans to retire at age 60. She wants to make fixed annual payments to a pension plan that would pay \$15,000 each year for 20 years after retirement.
   (a) How much must Karen contribute annually to the pension plan if the interest rate is 7 percent and contributions are made until retirement?
   (b) What is her annual contribution if she stops making payments at age 50 and the interest rate is 7 percent?
   (c) What is her annual contribution if the interest rate is 7 percent until retirement and 6 percent thereafter, and payments are made until retirement?

Answers to Self-Test Problems

1. (a)

$$\begin{aligned}\$10{,}000(FVIF_{5,8\%}) &= \$10{,}000(1.08)^5 \\ &= \$10{,}000(1.4693) \\ &= \$14{,}693\end{aligned}$$

   (b)

$$\begin{aligned}\$10{,}000(FVIF_{20,2\%}) &= \$10{,}000(1.02)^{20} \\ &= \$10{,}000(1.4859) \\ &= \$14{,}859\end{aligned}$$

2. (a) Compound interest:

$$\begin{aligned}\$8{,}000(FVIF_{10,8\%}) &= \$8{,}000(1.08)^{10} \\ &= \$8{,}000(2.1589) \\ &= \$17{,}271.2 \\ \text{Interest amount} &= \$17{,}271.2 - \$8{,}000 \\ &= \$9{,}271.2\end{aligned}$$

   (b) Simple interest:

$$\text{Interest amount} = \$8{,}000(0.08)\text{x}10 = \$6{,}400$$

3. Assume that the amount is \$100:

$$\begin{aligned}FV\{\$100\} &= \$200 \\ \$100(1+i)^9 &= \$200 \\ (1+i)^9 &= \$200/100 = 2\end{aligned}$$

From the *FV* table, *i* is approximately 8 percent. Solving the equation, *i* equals 8.005 percent.

4.
$$\$1{,}000(1.09)^n = \$3{,}642.50$$
$$(1.09)^n = \$3{,}642.5/1{,}000) = 3.6425$$

From the *FV* table, *n* equals 15 years.

5. This problem can be solved either (a) by treating \$1,500 as the future value of \$500 or (b) by treating \$500 as the present value of \$1,500.

(a)
$$FV\{\$500\} = \$1{,}500$$
$$\$500(FVIF_{5,i}) = \$1{,}500$$
$$FVIF_{5,i} = \$1{,}500/500 = 3$$
$$(1+i)^5 = 3$$

From the *FV* table, *i* is approximately 24 percent. Solving the equation, *i* equals 24.57 percent.

(b)
$$PV\{\$1{,}500\} = \$500$$
$$\$1{,}500(PVIF_{5,i}) = \$500$$
$$(PVIF_{5,i}) = \$500/1{,}500 = 0.3333$$
$$[1/(1+i)]^5 = 0.3333$$

From the *FV* table, *i* is approximately 24 percent. Solving the equation, *i* =equals 24.57 percent.

6. (a) The lump sum deposit is the present value of \$25,000:

$$PV\{\$25{,}000\} = \$25{,}000(PVIF_{10,6\%})$$
$$= \$25{,}000[1/(1.06)]^{10}$$
$$= \$25{,}000(0.5584)$$
$$= \$13{,}960$$

(b) The annual deposit is the annuity whose future value is \$25,000. Assume that all annuities make end-of-period payments unless mentioned otherwise.

$$FV\{A_O=?\} = \$25{,}000$$
$$A_O\{[(1.06)^{10} - 1]/0.10\} = \$25{,}000$$
$$A_O(13.1808) = \$25{,}000$$
$$A_O = \$25{,}000/13.1808$$
$$= \$1{,}896.69$$

7. Compare the investments based on their future values or present values. *PV* of Investment A:

$$PV\{\$850\} = \$850(PVIF_{5,8\%})$$
$$= \$850[1/(1.08)]^5$$
$$= \$850(0.6806)$$
$$= \$578.51$$

PV of Investment *B*:

$$PV\{A_O=\$150\} = \$150(PVIFA_{O\,5,8\%})$$
$$= \$150\{[1-(1/1.08)^5]/0.08\}$$
$$= \$150(3.9927)$$
$$= \$598.90$$

Investment B is better.

8. (a)

Year	PVIF	Investment X	Investment Y	Investment Z
1	0.9259	$277.77	$370.36	$231.47
2	0.8573	300.05	214.32	300.05
3	0.7938	357.21	277.83	396.90
PV		$935.03	$862.51	$928.42

(b) Investments X and Z will be worthwhile.

9. This requires a two-step calculation. First, find the present value of 18 payments of $2,000 each. In the next step, calculate the present value of the amount obtained in the first step for the two-year period.

$$PV\{A_O=\$2{,}000\} = \$2{,}000(PVIFA_{O\,18,6\%})$$
$$= \$2{,}000\left[[1-1/(1.06)]^{18}/0.06\right]$$
$$= \$2{,}000(10.8276)$$
$$= \$21{,}655.20$$
$$PV\{\$21{,}655.20\} = \$21{,}655.20(PVIF_{2,6\%})$$
$$= \$21{,}655.20(1/1.06)^2$$
$$= \$21{,}655.20(0.8900)$$
$$= \$19{,}273.13$$

10. The present value of 360 monthly payments (12 months times 30 years) is $200,000. The monthly interest rate is 0.09/12, or 0.0075.

$$PV\{A_O\} = \$200{,}000$$
$$A_O(PVIFA_{O\,360,0.75\%}) = \$200{,}000$$
$$A_O\left[[1-(1/1.0075)^{360}]/0.0075\right] = \$200{,}000$$
$$A_O(124.2819) = \$200{,}000$$
$$A_O = 200{,}000/124.2819$$
$$= \$1{,}609.24$$

Period	Beginning Balance	Installment Amount	Interest	Principal Repayment	End-of-period Balance
1	$200,000.00	$1,609.27	$1,500.00	$ 109.27	$199,890.73
2	$199,890.73	1,609.27	1,499.18	110.09	199,780.64

APPENDIX 8A

Example Solutions Using Lotus 1-2-3

The solutions given below for the examples in Chapter 8 utilize the @functions in *Lotus 1-2-3* when they are available. If predefined functions do not generate the desired solutions, the formulas necessary to solve the examples are given. These formulas should be copied *exactly*; no commas, dollar signs, or blank spaces are to be inserted. Also, remember the sequence of mathematical operations as they are performed (unless parentheses in the formula change the order):

1. Exponents (^) are calculated first.
2. Multiplication (*) and division (/) are performed next.
3. Addition (+) and subtraction (–) are performed last.

❖ EXAMPLE 8.1

Enter in Cell A1: 2000*1.1^5
Answer in Cell A1: 3221.02
Enter in Cell A2: +A1-5*200-2000
Answer in Cell A2: 221.02 ❖

❖ EXAMPLE 8.2

Enter in Cell A1: 2000*1.1^4+3000*1.1^3+2500*1.1^2+1500*1.1^1
(Note that the ^1 ending on the formula is optional.)
Answer in Cell A1: 11596.2, or $11,596.20 ❖

❖ EXAMPLE 8.3

Enter in Cell A1: 2000*1.1^3+3000*1.1^2+2500*1.1^1+1500*1.1^0
(Note that the *1.1^1 ending on the formula is optional.)
Answer in Cell A1: 10542, or $10,542 ❖

❖ EXAMPLE 8.4

1. Enter in Cell A1: @FV(120,.06,4)
   Answer in Cell A1: 524.9539, or $524.95
2. Use the F2 function key to edit the entry in Cell A1:
   Enter in Cell A1: @FV(10,.005,48)
   Answer in Cell A1: 540.9783, or $540.98 ❖

❖ EXAMPLE 8.5

1. Enter in Cell A1: 120*((1.06^4-1)/.06)*1.06
   Answer in Cell A1: 556.4512, or $556.45
2. Enter in Cell A1: @FV(10,.005,48)
   Answer in Cell A1: 540.9783
   Enter in Cell A2: +A1*1.005
   Answer in Cell A2: 543.6832, or $543.68 ❖

❖ EXAMPLE 8.6

1. Enter in Cell A1: 1.4*12
   Answer in Cell A1: 16.8
2. Enter in Cell A1: 1.014^12-1
   Answer in Cell A1: .181554, or 18.16% ❖

❖ EXAMPLE 8.7

Enter in Cells A1 through A19: 0
Enter in Cell A20: 20000
Enter in Cell A21: @NPV(.08,A1..A20)
Answer in Cell A21: 4290.964, or $4,290.96 ❖

❖ EXAMPLE 8.8

If discounted monthly:
Enter in Cells A1 through A23: 0
Enter in Cell A24: 2000
Enter in Cell A25: @NPV(.01,A1..A24)
Answer in Cell A25: 1575.132, or $1,575.13
If discounted annually:
Enter in Cell A1: 0
Enter in Cell A2: 2000
Enter in Cell A3: @NPV(.12,A1..A2)
Answer in Cell A3: 1594.388, or $1,594.39 ❖

❖ EXAMPLE 8.9

Enter in Cell A1: 1250
Enter in Cell A2: 960
Enter in Cell A3: 1350
Enter in Cell A4: 1350
Enter in Cell A5: @NPV(.12,A1..A4)
Answer in Cell A5: 3700.23, or $3,700.23
If the cash flows occur at the beginning of each period,use the F2 function key to edit the entry in Cell A5.
Enter in Cell A5: @NPV(.12,A2..A4)
Answer in Cell A5: 2894.258
Enter in Cell A6: +A1+A5
Answer in Cell A6: 4144.258, or $4,144.26 ❖

❖ EXAMPLE 8.10

Enter in Cell A1: @PV(12000,.08,15)
Answer in Cell A1: 102713.7, or $102,713.70 ❖

❖ EXAMPLE 8.11

Enter in Cell A1: @PV(12000,.08,14)
Answer in Cell A1: 98930.84
Enter in Cell A2: +A1+12000
Answer in Cell A2: 110930.8, or $110,930.80 ❖

❖ EXAMPLE 8.12

Enter in Cell A1: @RATE(2261,1000,10)
Answer in Cell A1: .085001, or 8.5% ❖

❖ EXAMPLE 8.13

Enter in Cell A1: -10000
Enter in Cell A2: 263.34
Enter in Cell A3: /c from A2 to A3..A49
Enter in Cell A50: @IRR(0.01,A1..A49)
Answer in Cell A50: 0.01
Enter in Cell A51: +A50*12
Answer in Cell A51: 0.12 ❖

❖ EXAMPLE 8.14

Enter in Cell A1: 5000/((1.005^36-1)/.005)
Answer in Cell A1: 127.1097, or $127.11 ❖

❖ EXAMPLE 8.15

Enter in Cell A1: @PMT(75000,.08,20)
Answer in Cell A1: 7638.916, or $7,638.92 ❖

❖ EXAMPLE 8.16

Enter in Cell A1: @PMT(10000,.0075,48)
Answer in Cell A1: 248.8504, or $248.85 ❖

❖ EXAMPLE 8.17

Enter in Cell A1: 460
Enter in Cell A2: 650
Enter in Cell A3: 750
Enter in Cell A4: 750
Enter in Cell A5: 800
Enter in Cell A6: @NPV(.12,A1..A5)
Answer in Cell A6: 2393.306, or $2,393.31 ❖

❖ EXAMPLE 8.18

Enter in Cell A1: 45000/1.1-40000
Answer in Cell A1: 909.0909, or $909.09 ❖

❖ EXAMPLE 8.19

Enter in Cells A1 through A10: 1000
Enter in Cell A11: @NPV(0.06,A1..A10)
Answer in Cell A11: 7360.087, or $7,360.09
Enter in Cells B1 through B9: 0

Enter in Cell B10: 11000
Enter in Cell B11: @NPV(0.06,B1..B10)
Answer in Cell B11: 6142.342, or $6,142.34 ❖

❖ EXAMPLE 8.20

Enter in Cell A1: 10000000/((1.07^15-1)/.07)
Answer in Cell A1: 397946.2, or $397,946.20 ❖

APPENDIX 8B

Example Solutions Using the HP12C Financial Calculator

The underlined keystrokes represent function keys on the HP12C. Please note that each key may have up to three functions, depending on the register used. Numerals and the +, –, ×, ÷ symbols are not underlined. Before beginning a problem, clear all registers.

❖ EXAMPLE 8.1

KEYSTROKE	DISPLAY
(a) CLX	0.0
(b) 5 n	5.0
(c) 10 i	10.0
(d) 2000 CHS PV	–2,000.0
(e) FV	3,221.02 ❖

❖ EXAMPLE 8.2

KEYSTROKE	DISPLAY
(a) CLX	0.0
(b) 4 n	4.0
(c) 10 *i*	10.0
(d) 2000 CHS PV	–2,000.0
(e) FV	2,928.2
(f) STO 1	2,928.2
(g) 3 n	3.0
(h) 10 i	10.0
(i) 3000 CHS PV	–3,000.0
(j) FV	3,993.0
(k) STO 2	3,993.0
(l) 2 n	2.0
(m) 10 i	10.0
(n) 2500 CHS PV	–2,500.0
(o) FV	3,025.0
(p) STO 3	3,025.0
(q) 1 n	1.0
(r) 10 i	10.0
(s) 1500 CHS PV	–1,500.0
(t) FV	1,650.0
(u) RCL 1 +	2,928.2
(v) RCL 2 +	3,993.0
(w) RCL 3 +	3,025.0
	11,596.2 ❖

❖ EXAMPLE 8.3

KEYSTROKE	DISPLAY
(a) CLX	0.0
(b) 3 n	3.0
(c) 10 i	10.0
(d) 2000 CHS PV	–2,000.0
(e) FV	2,662.0
(f) STO 1	2,662.0
(g) 2 n	2.0
(h) 10 i	10.0
(i) 3000 CHS PV	–3,000.0
(j) FV	3,630.0
(k) STO 2	3,630.0
(l) 1 n	1.0
(m) 10 i	10.0
(n) 2500 CHS PV	–2,500.0
(o) FV	2,750.0
(p) STO 3	2,750.0
(q) 1500 ENTER	1,500.0
(r) RCL 1 +	2,662.0
(s) RCL 2 +	3,630.0
(t) RCL 3 +	2,750.0
	10,542.0 ❖

❖ EXAMPLE 8.4

1. Joseph

KEYSTROKE	DISPLAY
(a) CLX	0.0
(b) 4 n	4.0
(c) 6 i	6.0
(d) 120 CHS PMT	–120.0
(e) FV	524.95

2. John

(a) CLX	0.0
(b) 4 g 12×	48.0
(c) 6 g 12÷	0.5
(d) 10 CHS PMT	-10.0
(e) FV	540.98 ❖

❖ EXAMPLE 8.5

1. Joseph

KEYSTROKE	DISPLAY
(a) CLX	0.0
(b) 4 n	4.0
(c) 6 i	6.0
(d) 120 CHS PMT	–120.0
(e) g beg	
(f) FV	556.45

2. John

KEYSTROKE	DISPLAY
(a) CLX	0.0
(b) 4 g 12×	48.0
(c) 6 g 12÷	0.5
(d) 10 CHS PMT	–10.0
(e) g beg	
(f) FV	543.68 ❖

❖ EXAMPLE 8.6

KEYSTROKE	DISPLAY
(a) CLX	0.0
APR:	
(b) 1.4 ENTER	1.4
(c) 12 ×	16.80
EAR:	
(a) 16.80 ENTER	16.8
(b) 12 n ÷ i	1.4
(c) 100 CHS ENTER PV	–100.0
(d) FV +	18.16 ❖

❖ EXAMPLE 8.7

KEYSTROKE	DISPLAY
(a) CLX	0.0
(b) 20000 FV	20,000.0
(c) 20 n	20.0
(d) 8 i	8.0
(e) PV	–4,290.96

Note: The minus sign represents a cash outflow. ❖

❖ EXAMPLE 8.8

KEYSTROKE	DISPLAY
1. Monthly discounting	
(a) CLX	0.0

(b) 2000 FV	2,000.0
(c) 12 g 12÷	1.0
(d) 2 g 12×	24.0
(e) PV	−1575.13
2. Annual compounding	
(a) CLX	2.0
(b) 2000 FV	2,000
(c) 12 i	12.0
(d) 2 n	2.0
(e) PV	−1,594.39

Note: The minus signs represent cash outflows.❖

❖ EXAMPLE 8.9

KEYSTROKE	DISPLAY
1. End-of-period cash flows	
(a) f CLX	0.0
(b) 0 g CFo	0.0
(c) 1250 g CFj	1,250.0
(d) 960 g CFj	960.0
(e) 1350 g CFj	1,350.0
(f) 2 g Nj	2.0
(g) 12 i	12.0
(h) f NPV	3,700.23
2. Beginning-of-period cash flows	
(a) f CLX	0.0
(b) 1250 g CFo	1,250.0
(c) 960 g CFj	960.0
(d) 1350 g CFj	1,350.0
(e) 2 g Nj	2.0
(f) RCL n	2.0
(g) 12 i	12.0
(h) f NPV	4,144.26 ❖

❖ EXAMPLE 8.10

KEYSTROKE	DISPLAY
(a) f CLX	0.0
(b) 12000 PMT	12,000.0
(d) 15 n	15.0
(e) 8 i	8.0
(f) PV	−102,713.74

Note: The minus sign represents a cash outflow. ❖

❖ EXAMPLE 8.11

KEYSTROKE	DISPLAY
(a) f CLX	0.0
(b) g beg	
(c) 12000 PMT	12,000.0
(d) 15 n	15.0
(e) 8 i	8.0
(f) PV	–110,930.84

Note: The minus sign represents a cash outflow. ❖

❖ EXAMPLE 8.12

KEYSTROKE	DISPLAY
(a) f CLX	0.0
(b) 2261 FV	2,261.0
(c) 10 n	10.0
(d) 1000 CHS PV	–1,000.0
(e) i	8.5 ❖

❖ EXAMPLE 8.13

KEYSTROKE	DISPLAY
(a) f CLX	0.0
(b) 4 g n	48.0
(c) 10000 PV	10,000.0
(d) 263.33 CHS PMT	–263.34
(e) i	1.0
(f) 12 ×	12.0 ❖

❖ EXAMPLE 8.14

KEYSTROKE	DISPLAY
(a) f CLX	0.0
(b) 3 g 12×	36.0
(c) 6 g 12÷	0.5
(d) 5000 FV	5,000.0
(e) PMT	–127.10

Note: The minus sign represents a cash outflow. ❖

❖ EXAMPLE 8.15

KEYSTROKE	DISPLAY
(a) f CLX	0.0
(b) 75000 PV	75,000.0
(c) 8 i	8.0
(d) 20 n	20.0

(e) PMT	–7,638.92

Note: The minus sign represents a cash outflow. ❖

❖ EXAMPLE 8.16

KEYSTROKE	DISPLAY
(a) f CLX	0.0
(b) 10000 PV	10,000.0
(c) 9 g 12÷	0.75
(d) 4 g 12×	48.0
(e) PMT	–248.85

Note: The minus sign represents a cash outflow. ❖

❖ EXAMPLE 8.17

KEYSTROKE	DISPLAY
(a) g CLX	0.0
(b) 0 g CFo	0.0
(c) 460 g CFj	460.0
(d) 650 g CFj	650.0
(e) 750 g CFj	750.0
(f) 2 g nj	2.0
(g) 800 g CFj	800.0
(h) 12 i	12.0
(i) f NPV	2,393.30 ❖

❖ EXAMPLE 8.18

KEYSTROKE	DISPLAY
(a) f CLX	0.0
(b) 40000 CHS g CFo	40,000.0
(c) 45000 g CFj	45,000.0
(d) 10 i	10.0
(e) 1 n	1.0
(f) f NPV	909.09
(g) f IRR	12.5 ❖

❖ EXAMPLE 8.19

KEYSTROKE	DISPLAY
1. Asset A Present Value	
(a) f CLX	0.0
(b) 1000 PMT	1,000.0
(d) 10 n	10.0
(e) 6 i	6.0
(f) PV	–7,360.09

2. Asset B Present Value

(a) f CLX	0.0
(b) 11000 FV	11,000.0
(c) 10 n	10.0
(d) 6 i	6.0
(e) PV	−6,142.40

3. Asset A Future Value

(a) f CLX	0.0
(b) 1000 CHS PMT	−1,000.0
(c) 10 n	10.0
(d) 6 i	6.0
(e) FV	13,180.79

Note: The minus signs represent cash outflows. ❖

❖ EXAMPLE 8.20

KEYSTROKE	DISPLAY
(a) f CLX	0.0
(b) 10000000 FV	10,000,000.0
(c) 7 i	7.0
(d) 15 n	15.0
(e) PMT	−397,946.24

Note: The minus sign represents a cash outflow. ❖

CHAPTER

9

Return, Risk, and Valuation

LEARNING OBJECTIVES

The primary objectives of this chapter are to discuss the return and risk characteristics of investments and to examine the basics of asset valuation. At the conclusion of this chapter, the reader should be able to:

1. *Identify the sources of returns and measure them*
2. *Define and compare three variants of the return concept: expected return, required return, and realized return*
3. *Form expectations and determine required rates of return*
4. *Define* investment risk, *explain why it exists, and measure it using familiar techniques*
5. *Explain how portfolio diversification can reduce risk*
6. *Explain why some components of risk can be eliminated by diversification and others cannot*
7. *Explain the basics of asset valuation*
8. *Value bonds and stocks using the discounted cash flow approach*

Investors commit funds to acquire assets that promise future cash flows in excess of the amounts they initially commit. These excess amounts constitute investors' expected returns. Such a return is usually expressed as a percentage of the amount committed or invested. For example, interest promised on a commonplace investment, such as a bank certificate of deposit, constitutes the investor's expected return. Depending on the type of investment, the actual return may differ from the expected return.

Assets may be classed as financial or real. Financial assets, which represent claims to real assets, include stocks, bonds, mortgages, commercial paper, bank deposits, and other securities. Real assets include such tangible items as precious metals, diamonds, paintings, plant and equipment, and real estate. This chapter applies return, risk, and valuation concepts to financial assets. The next chapter applies these concepts to real assets.

RELATIONSHIP BETWEEN RETURN, RISK, AND VALUATION

Investors make investment decisions on the basis of the returns that they expect. Investors want to make sure that the expected returns of chosen investments at least equal the returns they require to commit their funds. In a world of unpredictable events, investors' expectations are rarely fulfilled exactly. A particular return may turn out better or worse than an investor expected at the time of investment. The possibility that a return will be different from the expected return is known as return uncertainty or **investment risk**.

investment risk
The possibility that an actual return will differ from the expected return.

Investment risk forces an investor to evaluate the return and risk characteristics of every investment opportunity before making a decision. Investors may differ in their attitudes toward risk. Some may like taking risk, while others may make explicit efforts to avoid or minimize it. Risk-averse investors include risk premiums in the required rates of return they demand to invest in risky assets. When estimating the net present value of a risky asset, such an investor uses a risk-adjusted rate of return as the discount rate.

To deal with investment risk effectively, it must be measured. Two widely used measures of investment risk are the standard deviation of investment returns and beta. The former measures the total risk of an investment; the latter measures only the risk attributable to changes in the overall market. An investor may buy more than one security in an attempt to minimize risk through diversification. Careful selection of securities can reduce risks attributable to specific companies, but the investment portfolio will still be exposed to market risk. International diversification can help increase a portfolio's return and reduce its risk.

Valuation of assets is part of the investment process. Assets traded in the market are routinely valued by both buyers and sellers. *Valuation* refers to the determination of an asset's value, hence its price, at a given time. The discounted cash flow approach is the most intuitive and forward-looking technique for the valuation of assets. It determines asset values on the basis of the future benefits (cash flows) that they promise to investors and investors' required rates of return. Finance also measures asset value by book value and liquidation value.

RETURN

The return on an investment is the difference between the funds committed to it and the cash flows received from it. This difference may be positive or negative, resulting in a gain or loss. To measure return, one must first specify an investment period. Returns are usually measured and reported on an annual basis. Most investment returns consist of two types of cash flows: income flows (interest and dividend payments) during the investment periods and capital gains or losses (increases or decreases in the values of the assets). For example, money invested in a bond will produce periodic interest payments and a capital gain or loss when the bondholder sells or redeems the security.

The returns on some assets (both real and financial) consist of either capital gains (and no income flows) or income flows (and no capital gains or losses). Treasury bills fall into the first category. An investor pays one amount to buy a Treasury bill and receives another amount upon selling it; the bill pays nothing while the investor owns it. The difference between the purchase price and sale price represents the return on the Treasury bill. Investments in gold share these return characteristics. An example of the second category of assets is a savings account. It generates interest payments during the deposit period and the deposited amount is returned when the period ends.

Measuring Return

Returns on investments are measured either in currency amounts or as percentages. A dollar measure of return includes the sum of all income flows and the capital gain or loss during the investment period.

❖ EXAMPLE 9.1

Suppose that an investor acquired 100 shares of Dixie Corporation stock at $20 each last year. If the investor receives $0.50 per share in dividends during the year and sells the shares at year-end for $21 each, the dollar return from this investment amounts to:

$$\text{Dollar return} = \text{Dividend income} + \text{Capital gain (loss)} \quad (9.1)$$

$$= (\text{Dividend} \times 100) + (\text{Sale price}-\text{Purchase price}) \times 100$$

$$= (\$0.50 \times 100) + (\$21 - \$20)(100)$$

$$= \$50 + \$100$$

$$= \$150 ❖$$

Another way of describing the dollar return is to represent it as the difference between the cash inflows and cash outflows of the investment:

$$\text{Dollar return} = \text{Cash inflows} - \text{Cash outflows} \quad (9.2)$$

$$= (\text{Dividend flows} + \text{Sale price}) - \text{Purchase price}$$

$$= [(\$0.50 \times 100) + (\$21 \times 100)] - (\$20 \times 100)$$

$$= \$50 + \$2{,}100 - \$2{,}000$$

$$= \$150$$

If the investor decides not to sell the shares this year, putting off realizing the capital gain or loss, the total dollar return on the investment for one year remains $150. The return calculation does not depend on whether or not all relevant cash flows are realized. Even for shares held for many years, the annual return calculation is still based on yearly dividend flows, the beginning-of-year market value, and the end-of-year market value of the shares:

EXHIBIT 9.1

Comparison of Asset Returns

Assets	Amount Invested	Annual Dollar Return	Annual Percentage Return
A	$ 6,500	$550	8.46%
B	10,000	780	7.80

Annual dollar return on stock = Dividend flows during the year + (End-of-year market value – Beginning-of-year market value)

This is sometimes called the *paper return.*

Measuring and reporting returns in percentage terms is more common and convenient than dollar returns. It also has some advantages. The percentage measure represents the return as a percentage of the amount invested or the market value of the asset at the beginning of the investment period. It measures the return per dollar invested.

Annual percentage return = Annual dollar return/Amount invested or Beginning-of-year market price **(9.3)**

= $150/$2,000

= 0.075 or 7.5 percent

An alternative way of calculating this percentage is:

Annual percentage return = [(Annual dividend flows + End-of-year market value)/Beginning-of-year market value] – 1 **(9.3A)**

= [($150 + $2,000)/$2,000] – 1

= $2,150/$2,000 – 1

= 1.075 – 1

= 0.075 or 7.5 percent

The most important advantage of representing returns in percentage terms is that it allows easy and meaningful comparisons of returns among investments of different sizes. To illustrate this point, consider Assets A and B described in Exhibit 9.1. Comparing percentage returns makes Asset A look like the better investment. Based on dollar returns, Asset B looks better. This contradiction is caused by the different amounts of money invested in Assets A and B. Though the total return on Asset B is higher at $780, this represents a return per dollar invested of only 7.8 cents. Asset A generates 8.46 cents per dollar invested, so if it were as large as Asset B, its total dollar return would be $846. Asset A is, in fact, the better investment. Therefore, the basis for comparing the profitability of assets should be the return per dollar invested and not total dollar return.

Investments occasionally produce negative returns (losses). Negative returns may result from payment defaults and/or declines in asset values. If the sale price of the Dixie shares in Example 9.1 had been $19 instead of $21, the investor would have suffered a loss, that is, received a negative return. Reworking Example 9.1 with a sale price of $19 produces:

$$\begin{aligned} \text{Dollar return} &= \text{Dividend income} + \text{Capital gain (loss)} \\ &= \$50 + (-\$100) \\ &= -\$50 \\ \text{Percentage return} &= -\$50/\$2{,}000 \\ &= -2.5 \text{ percent} \end{aligned}$$

Return on a Foreign Investment

An attempt to determine the return on a foreign investment must consider changes in the exchange rate. Income flows and asset price appreciation or depreciation for a foreign investment are denominated in a foreign currency. To find the investor's return they must be converted into his or her domestic currency. Income flows to a U.S. investor have to be converted into dollars at the exchange rates that prevail when the flows occur. Any capital gain or loss must be adjusted for any change in the exchange rate since the investment was made. Even if the price of the asset appreciates, the investor may actually suffer a capital loss if the domestic currency appreciates against the foreign currency. The relevant return on a foreign investment is the dollar return or percentage return adjusted for exchange rate changes.

❖ EXAMPLE 9.2

A U.S. resident bought 100 shares of KLM at a price of 36 guilders per share a year ago on the Amsterdam Stock Exchange. At that time, the guilder–dollar exchange rate was 1.90 guilders per dollar. The exchange rate now is 2.00 guilders per dollar. The shares paid 1.5 guilders in dividends during the year and are selling today for 37 guilders per share.

1. What is the dollar investment in KLM shares?
2. What is the dollar return to the investor?
3. What is the percentage return to the investor?

$$\begin{aligned} \text{Dollar investment in KLM shares} &= (100 \times 36)/1.90 \\ &= \$1{,}894.74 \\ \text{Total dividend in guilders} &= 100 \times 1.5 \\ &= 150 \\ \text{Total dividend in dollars} &= 150/[(2.00 + 1.90)/2] \\ &= \$76.92 \\ \text{Proceeds from the stock sale in guilders} &= 100 \times 37 \\ &= 3{,}700 \end{aligned}$$

$$\begin{aligned}
\text{Proceeds from the stock sale in dollars} &= 3{,}700/2 \\
&= \$1{,}850.00 \\
\text{Capital gain in guilders} &= 3{,}700 - 3{,}600 \\
&= 100 \\
\text{Capital loss in dollars} &= \$1{,}894.74 - \$1{,}850.00 \\
&= -\$44.74 \\
\text{Total dollar return on the investment} &= \$76.92 - \$44.74 \\
&= \$32.18 \\
\text{Percentage return} &= \$32.18/\$1{,}894.74 \\
&= 0.017\text{, or } 1.7 \text{ percent.}
\end{aligned}$$

❖

Nominal and Real Returns

nominal return
The return on an investment before adjusting for inflation.

real return
The inflation-adjusted return, on an investment, or the nominal return minus the inflation rate.

Nominal return refers to the returns in current dollars on an investment. This does not take into consideration any gain or loss caused by a change in the purchasing power of money during the time investors' funds remain committed. For example, if $100 invested last year comes to be worth $110 this year, the investment has produced a 10 percent nominal return. This does not necessarily mean that the investor has gained 10 percent in purchasing power. The **real return** reflects any gain or loss in purchasing power. If inflation were to reduce the purchasing power of a dollar during the time an investment were held, the investors' real return would be less than 10 percent.

To determine the real return on an investment, adjust the nominal return for the effects of inflation. To find the real return that corresponds to the 10 percent nominal return in the above example, convert $110 into its real value today and then compare it to the original investment of $100. For the purpose of this illustration, assume that the inflation rate during the year was 5 percent.

The nominal amount divided by (1 + Inflation rate) equals the real value of that amount. The real value of $110 after 5 percent inflation is:

$$\begin{aligned}
\text{Real value} &= \$110/(1+0.05) \\
&= \$104.77
\end{aligned}$$

The real return in dollar terms is $104.77 minus $100, or $4.77. In percentage terms, the real return is:

$$\begin{aligned}
\text{Real percentage return} &= (\$104.77 - \$100)/\$100 \\
&= 0.0477\text{, or } 4.77 \text{ percent}
\end{aligned}$$

Thus, when the inflation rate is 5 percent, a nominal return of 10 percent equals a real return of 4.77 percent. This means that investors gain only 4.77 percent in purchasing power for their investments.

A formal expression of the real rate of return is given by:

$$r = (1 + R)/(1 + q) - 1 \qquad \textbf{(9.4)}$$

FOCUS ON FINANCE

Fisher Effect

The relationship between the nominal and real returns is known as the **Fisher Effect.** Irving Fisher, a prominent U.S. economist at the turn of the century, pointed out this relationship by expressing the nominal rate as the sum of the real rate and the expected inflation rate:

$$r = (1 + R)/(1 + q) - 1$$

$$1 + r = (1 + R)/(1 + q)$$

$$(1 + r)(1 + q) = 1 + R$$

$$1 + r + q + rq = 1 + R$$

$$r = 1 + R - 1 - q - rq$$

$$r = R - q - rq$$

When inflation is moderate, the cross-product term, rq, is small and usually ignored. The result is the famous Fisher effect:

$$R = r + q$$

The Fisher effect says that a 1 percent increase or decrease in the expected inflation rate will cause the nominal interest rate to increase or decrease by 1 percent, if the real rate remains constant.

where r = real return

R = nominal return

q = inflation rate

❖ EXAMPLE 9.3

Find the real rate of return when the nominal rate is 12 percent and the inflation rate is 6 percent.

$$r = (1 + 0.12)/(1 + 0.06) - 1$$

$$= 1.0566 - 1$$

$$= 0.0566, \text{ or } 5.66 \text{ percent}$$ ❖

expected return
The return that an investor expects when initiating an investment.

realized (or actual) return
The return than an investor actually receives.

required return
The return that an investor requires to invest in an asset.

Variants of the Return Concept

Three variants of the return concept frequently arise in investment analysis and decision making contexts. They are **expected return** (R^e), **realized** or **actual return** (R^a), and **required return** (R^r). Note that the e, a, and r superscripts simply identify the symbols; they are not exponents.

Expected Return. The expected return is the return that an investor expects when initiating an investment. Return expectations are based on forecasted or anticipated income flows and capital gains or losses, which depend on future economic conditions and company performance. If an investor foresees different possibilities for the return on an investment because of uncertain future economic

expected value
The statistical calculation of an average value from a list of possible outcomes.

conditions and company performance, then the expected return is the average of these possibilities. Statisticians refer to this average as the **expected value**, and symbolize it as $E(R)$. In an uncertain world, it is realistic to assume that an investment has many possible return outcomes.

❖ EXAMPLE 9.4

Consider a simple investment situation with three possible outcomes:

1. A 25 percent chance that economic conditions will improve, causing stock in the BLT Company to generate a 12 percent return
2. A 50 percent chance that economic conditions will not change, in which case BLT stock will generate an 8 percent return
3. A 25 percent chance that economic conditions will deteriorate and BLT stock will generate only a 5 percent return

A statistician would present these possibilities in the form of a probability distribution of returns:

Probability Distribution

STATE OF THE ECONOMY	PROBABILITY	INVESTMENT RETURN
Improving	0.25	12%
Stable	0.50	8
Deteriorating	0.25	5

The expected return on BLT stock, which can be symbolized as either $E(R)$ or R^e, is the average of the three possibilities. It is calculated by multiplying each possible return by its probability and then adding the products.

$$E(R) = R^e = 0.25(12\%) + 0.50(8\%) + 0.25(5\%) \quad (9.5)$$

$$= 3\% + 4\% + 1.25\%$$

$$= 8.25 \text{ percent}$$ ❖

Realized Return. The realized return is the return the investor actually receives, in contrast to the return that he or she expects. The realized return could be any rate because it depends on innumerable market forces. Any of three rates mentioned in the probability distribution of return in Example 9.4 could be the realized rate of return for BLT. If economic conditions improve, the investor will receive a 12 percent return. If economic conditions do not change, the realized rate of return will be 8 percent. If economic conditions deteriorate, BLT stock will produce a 5 percent return.

Required Return. The required return is the return that an investor demands. Alternatively, it can be defined as the return that is necessary to induce an investor to commit funds. Therefore, it is the minimum expected return that would induce an investor to acquire an asset. For example, an investor who requires a 9 percent return from assets as risky as the stock of the BLT Company will not be interested in the stock.

The required rate of return is generally defined as the sum of two elements:

1. Compensation for giving up the use of funds and inflation, which is given by the rate an investor can obtain from a risk-free investment (the **risk-free rate**)
2. Compensation for bearing the risk associated with a specific investment (the **risk premium**).

risk-free rate
The rate of return on a risk-free asset.

risk premium
A mark-up on the risk-free rate that a risk averse investor demands to invest in risky assets.

$$\text{Required return } (R^r) = \text{Risk-free rate } (R_f) + \text{Risk premium } (RP) \quad \textbf{(9.6)}$$

The risk premium element provides a crucial contribution to the explanation of why required rates of return differ for different types of assets. Specifying a required rate of return for a given investment involves:

1. Identifying a risk-free rate
2. Measuring risk
3. Determining a risk premium

INVESTMENT RISK

Every investment is undertaken with the expectation of a return, which the investor may or may not actually realize. If the investment presents a broad range of possible returns, it is very unlikely that the expectation will be exactly realized. This element of uncertainty about return outcome represents the investment risk, and it has implications for financial decision making.

Investment risk is generally defined as the probability that an asset's actual return will differ from its expected return. It is tempting to restrict the definition of investment risk to the possibility on an actual return below the expected return because investors are obviously concerned about adverse outcomes. However, if an actual return exceeds the expected return, the investor may regret not having committed a larger percentage of funds to this asset. The definition of risk should, therefore, consider any deviation of actual return from expected return. Investment risk ceases to exist once the return (favorable or unfavorable) is realized.

If an investment is certain to exactly realize its expected return, then it has no investment risk. To be free of investment risk, a security must produce expected cash flows whether or not economic conditions change. Treasury bills and certificates of deposit for $100,000 or less, if held to maturity, are generally considered to be free of investment risk. The short-term nature of these assets also minimizes interest rate risk and default risk.

Sources of Investment Risk

The reasons for return uncertainty lie in the unpredictable nature of the future events that shape the performance of companies that issue securities. Two sets of events (factors) have been identified as sources of investment risk:

FOCUS ON FINANCE

NEW FOCUS AT KODAK

In October 1993, Kodak hired George M. C. Fisher, a technology wizard from Motorola, as CEO three months after firing its chairman, Kay R. Whitmore. With Mr. Fisher on board, Kodak planned to move ahead with two bold programs: a vigorous cost-cutting and restructuring program and a new focus on high-technology methods of capturing images and information on film, digitizing them, and communicating them instantly over the airways. Kodak was thus positioning itself to play a part in the information superhighway of the future.

Mr. Fisher brought to Kodak much needed talents: innovative manufacturing methods and product designs, a willingness to take chances on the technology of the future, and the ability to deal effectively with foreign competition. This last talent was especially desirable since Kodak's share of the international film market dropped drastically during the 1980s.

The stock market responded positively to the news by pushing up the price of Kodak's stock by \$4.875 to \$63.625 per share, an 8.3 percent jump in one day.

The Kodak story is just one of many examples of how a change in management produces a stock market reaction. The market treats such management changes as specific risk factors and reacts accordingly.

Source: Wall Street Journal, October 29, 1993, p. A1.

1. Changes in general economic conditions (in both domestic and foreign markets) that affect the security market as a whole
2. Changes in specific firms' operating and financial conditions that affect only the securities of those firms

The first set of factors includes changes in domestic and foreign inflation and interest rates, exchange rates, broad-based technology developments, and the business cycle. Because these factors affect the performance and the return-generating ability of all firms, they are known as *market* (or *systematic*) sources of risk. They may affect various firms differently but few firms can escape their impact.

Security prices are systematically related to each of the market sources of risk. Bond and stock prices generally move together; they react to changes in interest rates and inflation rates by moving in the opposite direction. An appreciating dollar, on the other hand, attracts foreign investors and causes security prices to rise; a depreciating dollar does the opposite. Changes in systematic factors usually directly influence the capital gain (or loss) component of the return. They may also indirectly affect the income flow component. The return uncertainty caused by these factors is often referred to as **systematic** (or **market**) **risk**.

systematic risk
Return uncertainty caused by economywide developments.

The second set of risk factors include firm-specific developments such as new inventions, changes in management, changes in financial structure, and changes in the prices of the firm's inputs and products. Such factors affect the fortunes of an individual firm without affecting the overall market. Positive changes may improve returns and negative changes may cause deterioration in returns. For example, if a computer software firm such as Microsoft Corporation were to develop a new software package that outperforms all competing packages, this firm-specific development would increase the return-generating ability of Microsoft. The departure of a key executive for a more lucrative position at another company would constitute a firm-specific event that would affect the return-generating abilities of both firms.

unsystematic risk Return uncertainty caused by firm-specific developments.

Firm-specific risk factors are known as *unsystematic* (or *specific*) sources of investment risk. The return uncertainty caused by these sources is called **unsystematic** (or **specific**) **risk**. Unsystematic risk is often treated as the sum of financial risk, risk that arises from changes in financial structure, and business risk, risk that arises from changes in operating conditions.

$$\text{Total risk} = \text{Systematic risk} + \text{Unsystematic risk} \tag{9.7}$$

$$\text{Total risk} = \text{Systematic risk} + \text{Business risk} + \text{Financial risk} \tag{9.7A}$$

Using the concepts of systematic and unsystematic risks, the realized return on any asset, *i*, can be expressed as:

$$R^a_i = R^e_i + M + E_i \tag{9.8}$$

where R^a_i = realized return on Asset *i*

R^e_i = expected return on Asset *i*

M = deviation of the realized return from the expected return due to systematic factors

E_i = deviation of the realized return from the expected due to unsystematic factors

Investor Behavior toward Risk

Given that most investment opportunities are risky, how do investors react to risk in investments? Investors' behavior can be summarized in terms of their available options. They can:

1. Avoid risk entirely by investing only in risk-free assets
2. Accept risk, but insist on compensation in the form of a risk premium
3. Prefer taking risk
4. Remain indifferent to risk

risk aversion An investor attitude that demands compensation to bear risk.

The first option is highly restrictive because it sharply reduces the number of acceptable assets. The second option makes all available investment opportunities acceptable, provided they pay financial rewards for taking risk in the form of risk premiums. The first two options reflect investor behavior known as **risk aversion**. The third option exposes the investor to great financial uncertainty; it amounts to gambling. In the fourth option, investors do not distinguish between risk-free and risky investments.

Risk aversion simply means that investors require higher returns on investments with higher risk. Given a choice between two assets with equal returns and different risk levels, a risk-averse investor will select the asset with the lower risk.

Ample empirical evidence confirms that investors are generally risk averse. Risk aversion is manifested in people's willingness to buy car, life, hospital, and accident insurance. By incurring a small cost to buy insurance, people protect themselves against large financial losses that result from uncertain events. Risk-averse behavior is also evident in the pricing of securities in the market. Historical studies of security prices and rates of return have revealed that riskier securities generally sell at lower prices and produce higher returns than less risky ones.

Not all investors exhibit risk-averse behavior in all of their financial commitments all the time. Casino gambling, buying lottery tickets, and other types of wagering amount to risk preference. Gamblers incur small costs while pursuing large financial gains. The odds of winning are usually very small.

Since risk-averse investors demand higher risk premiums on riskier assets, they must promise higher minimum expected returns to induce investors to commit funds. To determine the risk premium for an investment, investors should know the amount of risk it involves and the price of risk. They need a way to quantify investment risk and determine its price.

Measuring Investment Risk

Risk analysis focuses on describing and measuring return uncertainties associated with investments. Investors need this information to compare investment risks and determine appropriate risk premiums. Two widely used measures of risk are the standard deviation of returns and beta.

Standard Deviation. Investment risk reflects the uncertainty of returns. This uncertainty is the result of the variability of returns. A statistical measure of variability can be adapted to measure return uncertainty, or investment risk. Standard deviation, the most popular statistical measure of variability, has become a widely accepted measure of investment risk.

The standard deviation of returns measures the average deviation of returns from the expected return. If return possibilities are widely distributed, the variability of return is large, resulting in a high standard deviation. Thus a large standard deviation indicates high investment risk. A narrower distribution of returns means less variation, giving a low standard deviation. This is interpreted to indicate low investment risk.

To calculate the standard deviations of returns:

1. Calculate the expected (average) return
2. Subtract this expected return from the individual returns
3. Square these differences
4. Multiply each squared difference by its probability
5. Add these products and take the square root of the sum

❖ EXAMPLE 9.5

Calculate the standard deviation of returns for BLT Corporation's stock, based on the distribution of returns described in Example 9.4. The expected return of this stock is 8.25 percent.

FOCUS ON FINANCE

DEFINITIONS OF MEAN AND STANDARD DEVIATION OF RETURNS

The formal definitions of the mean and the standard deviation of returns differ for frequency and probability distributions.

It is usually assumed that the probability distribution of returns is normal, that is, the plot of the probabilities against the returns is bell-shaped and symmetrical. The expected value lies in the center of a normal distribution and the left side of the distribution is the mirror image of the right side. This means that the probability of a return being *x* percent greater than expected is the same as the probability of a return being *x* percent less than expected. Other features of a normal distribution include:

1. The probability of a return being within 1 standard deviation of the expected return is about 68 percent.
2. The probability of a return being within 2 standard deviations of the expected return is about 95 percent.
3. The probability of a return being more than 3 standard deviations away from the expected return is less than 1 percent.

Expected Return

$$R^e = E(R) = (1/n)\sum_{j=1}^{n} R_j f_j \qquad \text{For a frequency distribution}$$

$$= \sum_{j=1}^{n} R_j p_j \qquad \text{For a probability distribution}$$

Standard Deviation of Returns

$$S = \sqrt{1/(n)\sum_{j=1}^{n}\left[R_j - E(R)\right]^2 f_j} \qquad \text{For a frequency distribution}$$

$$= \sqrt{\sum_{j=1}^{n}\left[R_j - E(R)\right]^2 p_j} \qquad \text{For a probability distribution}$$

where Rj = jth return (observed or expected)

p_j = probability of jth return

f_j = frequency of jth return

n = number of possible returns

RETURN	STEP 2	STEP 3	PROBABILITY	STEP 5
12%	12–8.25	$(3.75)^2 = 14.0625$	0.25	3.515625
8	8–8.25	$(-0.75)^2 = 0.5625$	0.50	0.281250
5	5–8.25	$(-3.25)^2 = 10.5625$	0.25	2.640625

$$S = \sqrt{(3.515625 + 0.281250 + 2.640625}$$

$$= \sqrt{6.4375}$$

$$= 2.54 \text{ percent}$$

The standard deviation of returns for BLT is 2.54 percent. This means that if this investment could be repeated many times, and if the distribution of the returns is normal, the actual return will be between 5.71 percent and 10.79 percent (i.e., 8.25 percent ± 2.54 percent) two-thirds of the time. ❖

The future return possibilities of an investment are difficult to determine. Therefore, investors usually estimate the standard deviation measure of risk from historical return data. Since the estimator generally uses only a recent sample of returns rather than all existing historical data, the formula to estimate the standard deviation is given by:

$$S = \sqrt{1/(n-1)\left[\left[R_1 - E(R)\right]^2 + \left[R_2 - E(R)\right]^2 + \ldots + \left[R_n - E(R)\right]^2\right]} \qquad \textbf{(9.9)}$$

where n = number of observations in the sample

R_j = actual historical return in the jth period

❖ EXAMPLE 9.6

Bonds A and B have generated the historical returns for eight years listed below:

YEAR	RETURN ON BOND A	RETURN ON BOND B
1	6%	4%
2	8	12
3	4	5
4	1	2
5	−6	−10
6	4	5
7	5	4
8	2	2

Determine the expected returns and the standard deviations of returns for these bonds. Which bond is riskier? (Note: The transition from history to future possibilities assumes that each year's historical return is equally probable. The probability of each return, therefore, is $1/n$, or $1/8$. This assumption simplifies the calculations considerably.)

$$E(R_A) = R^e(A) = (6+8+4+1-6+4+5+2)/8$$
$$= 3 \text{ percent}$$
$$E(R_B) = R^e(B) = (4+12+5+2-10+5+4+2)/8$$
$$= 3 \text{ percent}$$
$$S(A) = \sqrt{\begin{array}{l} 1/7\big[(6-3)^2+(8-3)^2+(4-3)^2+(1-3)^2 \\ +(-6-3)^2+(4-3)^2+(5-3)^2+(2-3)^2\big] \end{array}}$$
$$= \sqrt{(1/7)(9+25+1+4+81+1+4+1)}$$
$$= \sqrt{126/7}$$
$$= 4.24 \text{ percent}$$
$$S(B) = \sqrt{\begin{array}{l} 1/7\big[(4-3)^2+(12-3)^2+(5-3)^2+(2-3)^2 \\ +(-10-3)^2+(5-3)^2+(4-3)^2+(2-3)^2\big] \end{array}}$$
$$= \sqrt{(1/7)(1+81+4+1+169+4+1+1)}$$
$$= \sqrt{262/7}$$
$$= 6.12 \text{ percent}$$

Bonds A and B have the same expected value for the return, but different standard deviations. Asset B has a larger standard deviation, hence it is riskier. ❖

coefficient of variation
The standard deviation divided by the mean. It standardizes variability by measuring variation relative to the mean.

In Example 9.6, how would one determine which bond is riskier if either (1) both the expected returns and standard deviations of returns were different, or (2) the expected returns were different, but the standard deviations of returns were the same? In such cases, a scaled measure of variability known as the **coefficient of variation** (CV) can allow the comparison. The coefficient of variation is calculated by dividing the standard deviation by the mean. It measures the variability relative to the mean; that is, it standardizes the variability. Bond A's CV equals 4.24%/3%, or 1.41. Bond B's CV equals 6.12%/3%, or 2.04. This suggests that an investor in Bond A would incur only about three-quarters of the risk that an investor in Bond B would face.

Risk measured by standard deviation represents the total risk (systematic risk plus unsystematic risk) associated with an investment. In practice, it is difficult to measure the two components separately, but it is not impossible.

Portfolio Diversification and Risk Reduction. Most investors invest in multiple assets, creating portfolios of assets. A portfolio can include real assets or

portfolio diversification

Combining assets with different risk–return characteristics.

financial assets or both. Portfolios managed by mutual funds and other institutional investors usually contain large numbers of assets. Selection of assets with diverse risk–return characteristics is called **portfolio diversification**. For example, a diversified portfolio might consist of securities issued by firms in unrelated industries such as automobile, pharmaceutical, and financial services. A portfolio of bonds, stocks, commodities futures contracts, and index options would also be considered diversified.

Portfolio diversification can reduce overall risk. The ability of the technique to reduce risk depends on correlations between the returns on various assets in the portfolio. One asset may have a high return while another has a low return under given economic conditions; often, the positions of such assets reverse when economic conditions change. These two assets' returns are negatively correlated. If it combines assets with negatively correlated returns, portfolio diversification can reduce risk substantially. The reason for this is simple. While some securities in a well-diversified portfolio may lose money, chances are that other securities in that portfolio will make money at the same time. This minimizes the impact of the money-losing securities on the overall performance of the portfolio. It is important to note that portfolio diversification can reduce only the unsystematic component of total risk.

Portfolio diversification can do little to reduce systematic risk because most assets are more or less equally exposed to systematic risk. Therefore, systematic risk is also known as *nondiversifiable risk*, and unsystematic risk is also known as *diversifiable risk*.

International Diversification. Forming portfolios of domestic and foreign securities with contrasting risk–return characteristics may increase portfolio returns and lower both unsystematic and systematic risk. The outcome of international diversification depends, however, on a number of factors:

1. Timing of changes in economic conditions in each country
2. Risk–free rate and the degree of risk-aversion in each country's market
3. Changes in exchange rates

If similar changes in economic conditions were to occur in all countries at the same time, international diversification would do little to reduce risk. Fortunately, national business cycles show some significant differences, which knowledgeable portfolio managers can use to their advantage. Further, an entire foreign market need not move countercyclically to the U.S. market. If a portfolio manager can locate a number of firms with opposite risk–return characteristics in foreign markets, it may help to reduce the unsystematic risk of a portfolio's U.S. securities.

Differences in the risk-free rates and the degrees of risk aversion in foreign markets may contribute to higher portfolio returns. When a foreign market has a higher risk-free rate and degree of risk aversion, foreign investors will have higher required rates of return. This means that the expected returns on foreign securities will be higher.

FOCUS ON CAREERS

GLOBAL FUND MANAGER

The job of a fund manager is complex. The manager must research diverse securities markets and competing funds, identify new investment opportunities, prepare investment strategies and supervise their implementation, and undertake appropriate and timely asset selection. A global fund manager must develop adequately diversified portfolios that span the international markets so as to maximize return relative to acceptable levels of risk. A global fund manager has an added responsibility—to be acutely aware of international events continuously.

Qualifications include an advanced degree and/or CFA certification with a minimum of five years experience in fund sales or client relationship arrangements. A proven track record in portfolio management and fluency in at least one language in addition to English are both required. An exceptional individual with all of these qualifications can look forward to a six-figure salary with significant bonus potential.

Exchange rate changes can play havoc with any anticipated gains from international diversification. Consider, for example, a foreign market that experiences business cycle changes opposite to those in the U.S. market and is characterized by a higher risk-free rate and greater risk aversion. U.S. investors stand to gain from diversifying by acquiring investments in that market. However, if the foreign currency depreciates during that period against the dollar, the exchange rate change can wipe out much of the benefit of investing in that market. Therefore, the gain from international diversification must be assessed after adjusting for exchange rates. The exchange rate risk associated with international investment can be hedged in the forward and futures markets for currencies, but unfortunately, for many countries' currencies such hedging facilities are not available.

correlation coefficient
A statistical measure of the relationship between changes in two variables.

Calculation of Portfolio Return and Risk. A portfolio's expected return and standard deviation can be calculated from the expected returns and standard deviations of the assets in the portfolio. This calculation requires the proportion (weight) of each asset in the portfolio and the **correlation coefficients** of the asset returns. The correlation coefficient is a statistical measure of the relationship between the returns of two assets. The coefficient can be any value between +1.00 and −1.00, inclusive. A correlation coefficient of +1.00 means that changes in the returns of two assets are perfectly synchronized; when one asset's return increases, so does the other's. A correlation coefficient of −1.00 means that changes in the returns of the two assets are perfectly opposite; when one asset's return increases, the other's return decreases. A correlation coefficient of zero indicates no relationship between the changes in the returns of the two assets.

To keep the mathematics of calculating a portfolio's return and risk simple, assume a two-asset portfolio. The expected return and standard deviation of returns for the portfolio of two assets are:

$$E(R_p) = w_A E(R_A) + w_B E(R_B) \tag{9.10}$$

$$S_p = \sqrt{w_A{}^2 S_A{}^2 + w_B{}^2 S_B{}^2 + 2w_A w_B S_A S_B \text{Corr}(R_A, R_B)} \tag{9.11}$$

where $E(R_p)$ = expected return of the portfolio
$E(R_A)$ = expected return of Asset A
$E(R_B)$ = expected return of Asset B
R_A = return of Asset A
R_B = return of Asset B
S_A = standard deviation of Asset A
S_B = standard deviation of Asset B
S_p = standard deviation of the portfolio
w_A = proportion of the portfolio invested in Asset A
w_B = proportion of the portfolio invested in Asset B
$\text{Corr}(R_A,R_B)$ = correlation coefficient for returns on Assets A and B

❖ EXAMPLE 9.7

A U.S. stock has an expected return of 6 percent and a standard deviation of 2 percent. A Canadian stock has an expected return of 8 percent and a standard deviation of 4 percent. The correlation coefficient for their returns is +0.7. Find the expected return and the standard deviation of a portfolio invested 40 percent in the U.S. stock and 60 percent in the Canadian stock.

$$E(R_p) = 0.4(6\%) + 0.6(8\%)$$

$$= 2.4\% + 4.8\%$$

$$= 7.2 \text{ percent}$$

$$S_p = \sqrt{(0.4)^2(2\%)^2 + (0.6)^2(4\%)^2 + 2(0.4)(0.6)(4\%)(2\%)(0.7)}$$

$$= \sqrt{0.64\% + 5.76\% + 2.69\%}$$

$$= 3.01 \text{ percent}$$

If the correlation coefficient between the stocks, returns were −0.6 instead of +0.7, the portfolio's standard deviation would be substantially less than 3.01 percent. Recalculating the standard deviation of the portfolio with a correlation coefficient of −0.6 produces:

$$S_p = \sqrt{(0.4)^2(2\%)^2 + (0.6)^2(4\%)^2 + 2(0.4)(0.6)(4\%)(2\%)(-0.6)}$$

$$= \sqrt{0.64\% + 5.76\% + 2.30\%}$$

$$= 2.02 \text{ percent}$$ ❖

Note that the portfolio's standard deviation with negatively correlated returns is less than the weighted average of the standard deviations of the individual stocks ($0.4 \times 2\% + 0.6 \times 4\% = 3.2$ percent). This illustrates the substantial reduction in risk that a portfolio can achieve by combining assets with negatively correlated returns. A stronger negative correlation produces greater risk reduction.

beta
A measure of a security's systematic risk relative to the market.

market portfolio
A portfolio that consists of all securities traded in the market in proportion to their shares of the total market value.

regression coefficient
A measure of how much and in what direction a security's return changes in response to a change in the return on the market portfolio.

Beta. The standard deviation of returns is a measure of the absolute variability of returns, and, therefore, of total risk. Investors also use another measure of risk known as **beta**, usually represented by the Greek symbol β. A security's beta measures the variability of its return relative to the variability of the return on the **market portfolio**. Therefore, beta is considered a measure of relative risk.

The market portfolio consists of all risky securities traded in the market. By its very nature, the market portfolio is a well-diversified portfolio; as such, it is free from unsystematic risk. The variability of returns for the market portfolio is due entirely to systematic (marketwide) factors. By measuring a security's variability relative to that of the market portfolio, beta measures only the systematic risks or market risk, of a security.

To estimate the beta of a security, plot its historical returns against the historical returns on the market portfolio and fit a straight line through those points. The slope of the line that best fits the plot of returns is called the **regression coefficient.** The regression coefficient is a measure of how much and in what direction the security's return changes in response to a change in the return on the market portfolio. Hence, it is an estimate of beta.

$$R_i = \alpha_i + \beta_i R_M + u_i \tag{9.12}$$

where R_i = historical return on Asset i

R_M = historical returns on a market portfolio

β_i = slope of the regression equation (beta of Asset i)

α_i = intercept of the regression equation

u_i = regression error term (to measure the effects of firm-specific events)

If β equals zero, the security's return is not affected by the changes in the return on the market portfolio. A β of 0.5 implies that a security is half as risky as the market portfolio. A β of 1.0 implies that a security is just as risky as the market portfolio. A β of 1.5 implies that a security is one and a half times as risky as the market portfolio. A β of -1.5 implies that a security's return and the market return move in opposite directions, and the security is one and a half times as risky as the market portfolio.

The Standard & Poor's Index of the stock prices of the 500 largest publicly held corporations, usually called the *S&P 500*, is the most popular proxy for the market portfolio in beta calculations. To use beta, remember several things:

1. Beta for the market portfolio is always 1.0.
2. Beta measures only the systematic risk associated with a security.

3. A higher beta indicates greater systematic risk.
4. Beta may be either positive or negative.
5. Beta coefficients are not stable over time.
6. Estimating beta over a longer time period brings the value closer to 1.0.
7. Beta varies among securities.
8. The beta of a portfolio is given by the weighted average of the betas of individual securities in the portfolio.
9. Betas of thousands of stocks are routinely calculated and published by Merrill Lynch, Value Line, Standard & Poor's, Moody's, and many other organizations.

Beta, Risk Premium, and Required Rate of Return

In a market where most investors are risk averse, risky investments command risk premiums. Earlier, the chapter defined *risk premium* as the mark-up that risk-averse investors add to the risk-free rate when determining their required rates of return. Therefore, the risk premium on any asset, *i*, can be expressed as:

$$RP_i = R_i^r - R_f \quad \textbf{(9.13)}$$

where RP_i = risk premium on Asset *i*

R^r_i = required rate of return on Asset *i*

R_f = risk-free rate

The size of the risk premium varies with the level of risk and the price of risk. The price of risk is determined by the prevailing degree of risk aversion in the market.

The market does not reward risk that is borne unnecessarily. Since investors can eliminate unsystematic risk through diversification at no cost, the market offers compensation only for risk that investors cannot diversify away: systematic risk. Therefore, in determining the risk premium component of an investor's required rate of return for a security, the relevant risk should be the systematic risk represented by the security's beta.

The price of systematic risk is inferred from past market results, just as the value of beta is inferred, in the absence of certain knowledge of the future. The price of systematic risk is given by the return on the market portfolio in excess of the risk-free rate divided by the market beta.

$$\text{Price of systematic risk} = (R_M - R_f)/\beta_M \quad \textbf{(9.14)}$$

where R_M = return on the market portfolio

β_M = market beta

Since the market beta is always 1.00, the price of systematic risk is the market risk premium, $R_M - R_f$.

As mentioned before, the price of systematic risk reflects the degree of risk aversion in the market. Greater risk aversion increases the price of risk. Using this definition of the price of systematic risk, one can define the risk premium for Security *i* as the product of the level of the security's risk (β_i) and the price of risk (RP_M).

EXHIBIT 9.2

Betas for Selected Securities

Cygnus Therapeutic	2.45	N.Y. Times	1.05
Promus Cos.	2.05	Hershey Foods	1.00
Intelligent Electronics	2.00	AT&T	0.95
Clothestime	1.95	Ralston Purina	0.90
Micropolis Corp.	1.85	La-Z-Boy Chair	0.85
Charles Schwab	1.80	Ohio Edison	0.80
Filene's Basement	1.75	U.S. Trust	0.75
Ann Taylor Stores	1.70	Pennzoil	0.70
Spiegel Inc.	1.65	Mobil Corp.	0.65
Harley Davidson	1.60	Allegheny Power Sys.	0.60
Home Depot	1.55	Consumers Water	0.55
Caldor	1.50	WD-40 Co.	0.50
Fruit of the Loom	1.45	GWC Corp.	0.45
Hilton Hotels	1.40	Hecla Mining	0.40
Phillips-Van Heusen	1.35	Newmont Mining	0.35
Pier 1 Imports	1.30	Placer Dome	0.30
Woolworth	1.25	Lac Minerals	0.25
Loews Corp.	1.20	Homestake Mining	0.15
Ford Motor	1.15	Pegasus Gold	0.10
Borden Inc.	1.10	Free State Consolidated	0.05

Source: "Summary & Index," *Value Line Investment Survey*, April 1, 1994.

$$RP_i = \beta_i(RP_M) = \beta_i(R_M - R_f) \tag{9.15}$$

where RP_i = risk premium for Security i

RP_M = market risk premium

The required rate of return for Security i is the risk-free rate plus the security's risk premium:

$$R_i^r = R_f + \beta_i(R_M - R_f) \tag{9.16}$$

Based on estimates of R_f, R_M, and β_i, Equation 9.16 will determine the required rate of return on any Security i. Exhibit 9.2 lists estimated betas for selected securities.

❖ EXAMPLE 9.8

What is the required rate of return on a security with a beta of 0.80, if the risk-free rate is 6 percent and the return on the market portfolio is 10 percent?

$$R_i^r = R_f + \beta_i(R_M - R_f)$$

$$R^r = 6\% + 0.80(10\% - 6\%)$$

$$= 6\% + 3.2\%$$

$$= 9.2 \text{ percent}$$ ❖

Securities' beta coefficients can be compared with measures of their total risk. Consider two securities, A and B, whose standard deviations and betas are given below:

	Security A	Security B
Standard deviation	15%	25%
Beta	1.30	0.75

Which security will have to pay a higher risk premium in the market? Security B has greater total risk, but less systematic risk than Security A. Since total risk is the sum of systematic and unsystematic risk, Security B will have the higher unsystematic risk. Therefore, Security A will have to pay a higher risk premium.

The market process maintains the same reward (risk premium) for systematic risk for all securities, including the market portfolio. If these risk premiums get out of line, competition brings them to equality. This means that the reward–risk ratio (or the price of systematic risk) is the same for all securities. If a security carries twice as much systematic risk as another security, then its reward will be twice as large. The reward–risk ratio for Security *i* can be expressed as:

$$[E(R_i) - R_f]/\beta_i \tag{9.17}$$

Since the market process ensures that the reward–risk ratio in Equation 9.17 is the same for all securities, as well as the market portfolio:

$$[E(R_i) - R_f]/\beta_i = [E(R_m - R_f] \tag{9.18}$$

where $E(R_i)$ = expected return on Security *i*

$E(R_m)$ = expected return on the market portfolio

Security Market Line

A graphical representation of the relationship between securities' expected rates of return and their betas.

Capital Asset Pricing Model

A mathematical model that relates the expected return on a security to the risk-free rate and the market price of risk.

Rearranging the terms in Equation 9.18 gives:

$$E(R_i) = R_f + [E(R_m) - R_f]\beta_i \tag{9.19}$$

Equation 9.19 expresses the expected return on a security as the sum of the risk-free rate and the expected risk premium. Note that the risk premium here is the mark-up for bearing systematic risk.

Equation 9.19 defines the **Security Market Line** (SML) illustrated in Exhibit 9.3. The horizontal axis measures a security's beta, and the vertical axis its expected return. The slope of the SML is given by $E(R_M) - R_f$, or the price of systematic risk. In practice, $E(R_M)$ is assumed to be a historic measurement. Since the price of risk is the same for all securities, all securities will lie on this line, hence the name *Security Market Line*. Equation 9.19 represents the same relationship as the **Capital Asset Pricing Model** (CAPM), a security pricing technique whose derivation is based on a complex set of assumptions.

VALUATION OF BONDS, COMMON STOCKS, AND PREFERRED STOCKS

The issue of valuation is important to both investors and financial managers. Investors need to value assets to make sure that the price they are paying for an

EXHIBIT 9.3

Security Market Line

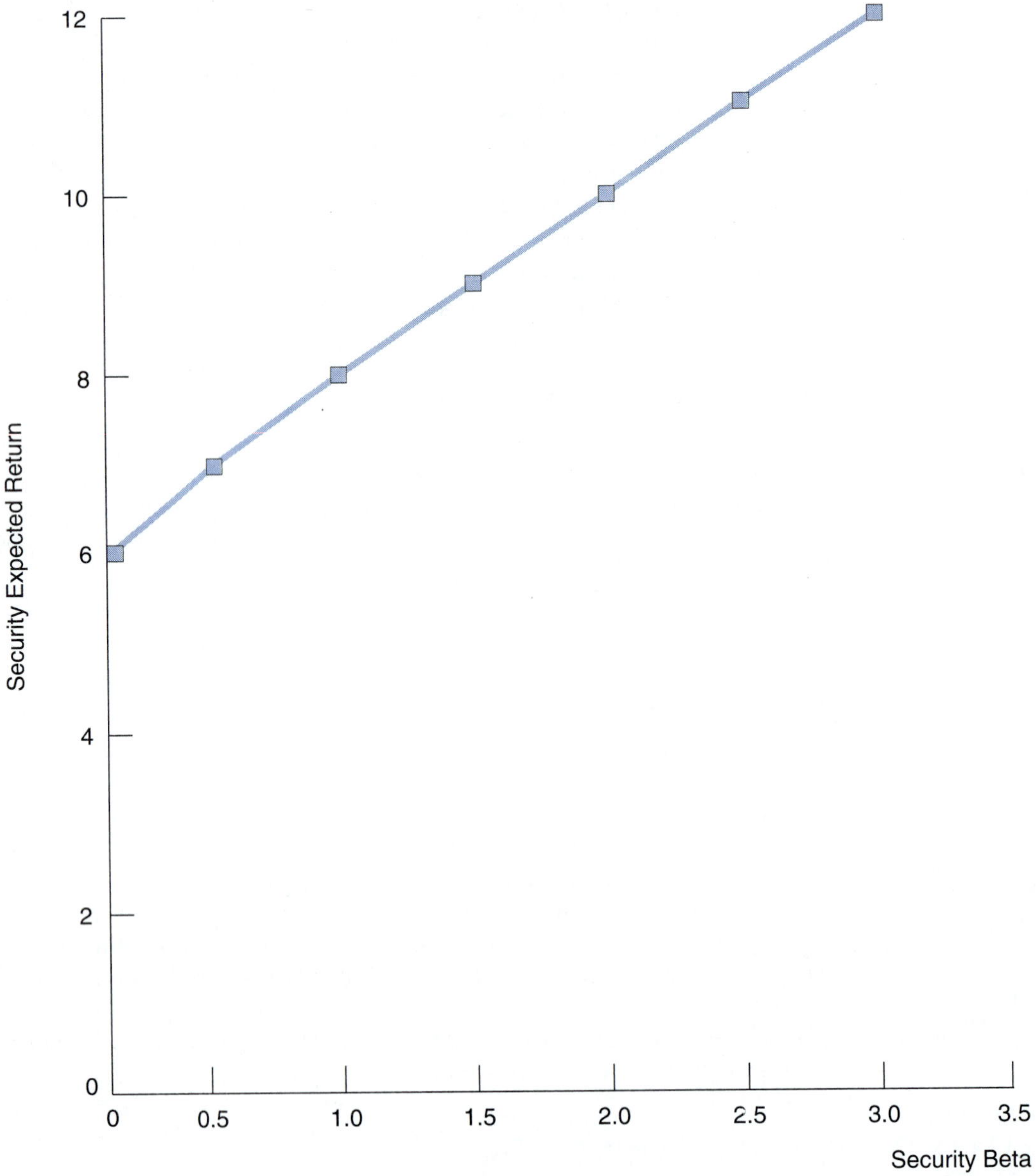

Risk-free rate = 6 percent
Expected return on market portfolio = 8 percent

asset is not more than what it is worth. A financial manager is concerned about the value of the firm's stock because every financial decision is judged by its effect on the price of the firm's stock. Often, the financial manager is also a stockholder of the firm. The financial manager is also concerned about the value of the firm's bonds because this determines the cost of debt financing.

Investors value assets based on those assets' potential cash flows. Since investment involves a commitment of funds (i.e., paying a price) in anticipation of cash flows, investors value an asset (or determine the maximum price to pay for them) at a level that will ensure them their required rates of return.

This approach to valuation involves the present value concept. The value of an asset is given by the present value of its expected future cash flows discounted at the investors' required rate of return. This is known as the *discounted cash-flow approach*, as explained in Chapter 8. Valuation uses the required rate of return as the discount rate because the asset's future cash flows must produce a rate of return equal to the investor's required rate of return. The stock and bond valuation models discussed in this chapter are specific cases of the generalized technique of discounting cash flows.

Applying the discounted cash flow approach involves:

1. Estimating net cash flows and their time patterns
2. Determining a required rate of return that reflects the investment's risk
3. Calculating the present value of the expected cash flows using the required rate of return as the discount rate

The market price of a security is its value in exchange. Since the present value of an asset is the maximum price one is willing to pay for that asset, an investor seeks to buy a financial asset when its market price is less than or equal to its present value. Therefore, in a competitive market, the price of an asset should reflect its present value.

Valuation of Bonds

The value of a bond to an investor is the present value of the future cash flows that the bond promises. This present value is the maximum price that an investor should pay for the bond. In a market that processes information efficiently, the price of a bond will reflect its present value. The present value, and the price, will change with time as interest rates and investor expectations change.

face value
The redemption value of a bond.

coupon rate
The rate of interest promised on a bond.

yield to maturity
The annualized rate of return on a bond when held to maturity.

The cash flows investors expect of a bond at any given time depend on its **face value**, its time to maturity, and the **coupon rate** (or interest rate) it promises. The discount rate used to calculate the present value of all of the bond's cash flows until maturity is the investors' required rate of return for the bond. The required rate of return may be different for different bonds depending on the risk that the issuer will default on coupon and principal payments. This discount rate is also called the **yield to maturity** or *bond yield*, for short. Investors often use the yield to maturity available on a class of similar bonds as the required rate of return for a given bond. When a bond's price and future cash flows are known, its yield to maturity can be calculated by finding the discount rate that makes the present value of the cash flows equal its price.

❖ EXAMPLE 9.9

Exel Corporation issues a bond with a \$1,000 face value, ten years to maturity, and a 9 percent coupon rate. All cash flows are end-of-period payments. If a bond with similar features currently yields 10 percent, what is the value of Excel's bond?

The cash flows expected from this bond are ten annual interest payments \$90 (9 percent of \$1,000) and a principal payment of \$1,000 at the end of the tenth year. The value of this bond is calculated below using a time line of cash flows:

Time Line of Exel Bond's Cash Flows

					YEARS					
	1	2	3	4	5	6	7	8	9	10
Cash Flows										
Coupon	\$90	\$90	\$90	\$90	\$90	\$90	\$90	\$90	\$90	\$90
Face value										\$1,000
Total	\$90	\$90	\$90	\$90	\$90	\$90	\$90	\$90	\$90	\$1,090
PVIF	0.9091	0.8264	0.7513	0.6830	0.6209	0.5645	0.5132	0.4665	0.4241	0.3855
PV	81.82	74.38	67.62	61.47	55.88	50.80	46.19	41.98	38.17	420.19

Bond value = Sum of the present values of the cash flows

= \$938.50 ❖

Note that the cash flows of a bond have an annuity component that consists of equal interest payments. To simplify a bond value calculation, find the present value of the annuity component separately and then add it to the present value of the face value repayment.

$$\begin{aligned}
\text{Bond value} &= PV \text{ of coupon payments} + PV \text{ of face value} \\
&= \$90(PVIFA_{10,10\%}) + \$1{,}000(PVIF_{10,10\%}) \\
&= \$90(6.1446) + \$1{,}000(0.3855) \\
&= \$553.01 + \$385.50 \\
&= \$938.51
\end{aligned}$$

Using symbols and generalizing the process, the bond valuation model can be written as:

$$\begin{aligned}
V_B &= C\left(PVIFA_{n,i}\right) + F\left(PVIF_{n,i}\right) \\
&= C\sum_{t=1}^{n}\left[1/(1+i)^t\right] + F\left[1/(1+i)^n\right] \\
&= C\left[\frac{1-\left[1/(1+i)^2\right]}{i}\right] + F\left[1/(1+i)^n\right] \qquad (9.20)
\end{aligned}$$

where V_B = present value of a bond
F = face value
i = discount rate (interest rate)
C = coupon amount
n = years to maturity

The bond valuation model in Equation 9.20 assumes that bond makes a coupon payment once a year. Since semiannual payments are customary among corporate and government issuers, the valuation model needs to be modified to accommodate semiannual cash flows. The modification involves reducing the coupon amount and the discount rate by half and doubling the number of discounting periods.

$$\begin{aligned} V_B &= (C/2)(PVIFA_{2n,i/2}) + F(PVIF_{2n,i/2}) \\ &= (C/2)\sum_{t=1}^{2n}\left[1/(1+i/2)^t\right] + F\left[1/(1+i/2)^{2n}\right] \\ &= (C/2)\left[\frac{1-\left[1/(1+i/2)^{2n}\right]}{i/2}\right] + F\left[1/(1+i/2)^{2n}\right] \end{aligned} \tag{9.21}$$

The semiannual interest payment on the bond in Example 9.9 is \$45. Equation 9.21 gives a present value for the bond that is \$0.81 less than the original calculation.

$$\begin{aligned} V_B &= \$90/2\{1-[1/(1+0.10/2)^{20}]/(0.10/2)\} + \$1{,}000[1/(1+0.10/2)^{20}] \\ &= \$45[1-[1/(1+0.05)^{20}]/0.05] + \$1{,}000[1/(1+0.05)^{20}] \\ &= \$45(12.4622) + \$1{,}000(0.3769) \\ &= \$560.80 + \$376.90 \\ &= \$937.70 \end{aligned}$$

The value of a bond may be higher than, equal to, or lower than its face value depending on the size of the coupon rate relative to the market interest (discount) rate. Example 9.9 values the bond below its \$1,000 face value because its coupon rate is lower than the currently prevailing discount rate. The coupon rate determines the amount of the buyer's periodic interest receipts. The discount rate represents the buyer's required rate of return. When the coupon rate is lower than the discount rate, the only way the investor can earn the required rate of return is by paying a price below the face value.

If the coupon rate is higher than the market discount rate, the value of the bond rises above its face value. Since the higher coupon bond will pay the investor more than the required rate of return, the investor will be willing to pay a price that is higher than the face value. If the coupon rate and the discount rate are the same, the value of the bond will equal its face value, for the same reasons. A bond that sells for a price above its face value is called a **premium bond**; a bond that sells for a price below its face value is called a **discount bond**; a bond that sells exactly at its face value is called a **par-value bond**.

premium bond
A bond selling at a price that exceeds its face value.

discount bond
A bond selling at a price below its face value.

par-value bond
A bond selling at a price equal to its face value.

Any change in the market interest rates, and hence the discount rate, causes bond values to move in the opposite direction. This inverse relationship between bond prices and interest rates explains why bond prices change so frequently, despite their fixed cash flows. If the discount rate on Exel Corporation's bond in Example 9.9 were to decline from 10 percent to 8 percent as a result of a decline in the market interest rate, the value of the bond would increase from \$937.70 to:

$$\begin{aligned} V_b &= \$90/2[1-[1/(1+0.08/2)^{20}]/(0.08/2)] + \$1{,}000[1/(1+0.08/2)^{20}] \\ &= \$45\{1-[1/(1+0.04)^{20}]/0.04\} + \$1{,}000[1/(1+0.04)^{20}] \\ &= \$45(13.5903) + \$1{,}000(0.4564) \\ &= \$611.56 + \$456.40 \\ &= \$1{,}067.96 \end{aligned}$$

Discount rates do not drop so precipitously overnight, however. As the rate slowly (and probably erratically) declines from 10 percent to 8 percent over time, the value of Exel's bond will slowly (and equally erratically) climb from \$937.70 to \$1,067.96. The current market price of this bond will hover near its value, responding to momentary changes in buying and selling pressures as individual and institutional investors enter the market.

interest rate risk
The probability of bond prices falling due to an increase in the interest rate.

bond duration
A measure of the interest rate risk on bonds that takes into account the effects of both the coupon rate and the time to maturity.

The response of bond prices to changes in interest rates, and the sensitivity of this response, characterize the **interest rate risk** of bond investment. Interest rate risk is defined as the possibility that the market interest rate will rise causing bond prices to fall. The sensitivity of bond prices to changes in interest rates is measured by **bond duration**, a sophisticated measure of interest rate risk.

Remember, however, that an investor who holds a bond to maturity need not fear interest rate risk. The price of a bond will always approach its face value as the maturity date approaches. The price of a premium bond will fall and that of a discount bond will rise. On the day of maturity, the bond price will be \$1,000, its face value.

Valuation of Common Stock

Corporations issue common stock as their fundamental means of raising long-term capital. All corporations have common stock outstanding, although it may or may not be available to the general public for investment. Some corporations also issue preferred stock. The value of either type of stock to investors depends on its expected cash flows: a stream of quarterly dividend payments plus the price the investor expects to receive from the sale of the stock.

The cash flow pattern of preferred stock is different from that of common stock because preferred usually pays dividends of a constant dollar amount. This amount is fixed when the stock is first issued. Common stock promises no specific dividend so valuation calculations must consider this uncertainty.

Valuation of stock, in general, is more complicated than valuation of bonds because:

1. Stock has no maturity date, so its cash flows do not span any finite period.
2. The required rate of return on a stock is not easy to set.

Since neither dividend payments nor the expected selling price are known in advance, the valuation of a common stock must rely on forecasts of these cash flows. Cash flow forecasting needs depend on the investor's time horizon. Someone who intends to hold the investment only for one year must forecast only two cash flows: the dividend for the year and the expected price of the stock at the end of the year. An investment period of two years would require forecasts of three cash flows: dividends for each of two years and the expected price at the end of the two-year period. To value an investment for an infinite period (i.e., a common stock that someone expects to hold forever), one must forecast the infinite series of dividend flows.

The value of common stock for different investment horizons can be expressed as the sum of the present values of the individual cash flows. For stock held for one year:

$$V_{CS} = D_1[1/(1+k)] + P_1[1/(1+k)] \qquad \textbf{(9.22A)}$$

For an investment period of two years:

$$V_{CS} = D_1[1/(1+k)] + D_2[1/(1+k)^2] + P_2[1/(1+k)^2] \qquad \textbf{(9.22B)}$$

In general, for an investment period of n years:

$$V_{CS} = D_1[1/(1+k)] + D_2[1/(1+k)^2] + \ldots + D_n[1/(1+k)^n] + P_n[1/(1+k)^n] \quad \textbf{(9.22C)}$$

Finally, for an infinite investment period:

$$V_{CS} = D_1\left[1/(1+k)\right] + D_2\left[1/(1+k)^2\right] + \ldots$$

$$= \sum_{t=1}^{\infty} D_t\left[1/(1+k)^t\right] \qquad \textbf{(9.22D)}$$

where D_t = expected dividend in Period t
P_t = expected price at the end of Period t
k = required rate of return on common stock
V_{CS} = value of common stock

dividend discount model

A stock valuation model that bases stock value on discounted future dividend flows.

These models are called **dividend discount models** for the obvious reason that they value common stock by discounting its dividend flows.

❖ EXAMPLE 9.10

Jennifer Sloans is considering investing in stock which she plans to hold for two years. She expects the stock to pay dividends of \$1.50 per share in each of the two years and to sell for \$20 at the end of two years. If she requires an 8 percent return on this stock, how much should she pay for it?

The discounted cash flow approach gives a value of this stock today of:

$$V_{CS} = \$1.50[1/(1.08)] + \$1.50[1/(1.08)^2] + \$20[1/(1.08)^2]$$
$$= \$1.39 + \$1.28 + \$17.15$$
$$= \$19.82$$ ❖

Whether or not Sloans can actually buy this stock for $19.82 depends on market conditions at the time she places the call to her broker. If other investors who are active at that moment have different expectations or require different rates of return, the market price may be above or below $19.82.

How do investors form expectations of future dividends and future prices? They base dividend expectations on companies' forecasted future performance. They base expectations of future prices on forecasts of the amounts that future buyers will pay for the stock. These future prices depend on buyers' forecasts of dividend flows and selling prices beyond their own purchase date. For example, a stock's expected price at the end of two years reflects its expected dividend flows and its expected price beyond the two-year period.

Investors usually forecast common stock dividends under certain assumptions about the future performance of the issuing company. These assumptions provide enormous help to simplify the present value calculation. Some of the assumptions and their contributions to simplify the valuation models are discussed below.

zero-growth model
A dividend discount stock valuation model that assumes zero growth in dividends.

Zero-Growth Model. The **zero-growth model** model assumes that dividends will remain constant at the current level. This assumption is relevant for companies which are expected to remain stable with little or no growth. Since the dividends constitute an infinite series of equal payments, their present value can be calculated in the same way as the present value of a perpetuity (introduced in Chapter 8):

$$V_{CS} = D_1\left[1/(1+k)\right] + D_2\left[1/(1+k)^2\right] + \ldots$$

$$= \sum_{t=1}^{\infty} D_t\left[1/(1+k)^t\right]$$

Since all the D factors equal the current level of the dividend, D_0, it can be placed in front of the summation notation.

$$V_{CS} = D_0 \sum_{t=1}^{\infty}\left[1/(1+k)^t\right]$$

The summation factor (everything after D_0) is an infinite series whose sum is equal to $1/k$. This allows investors to express the value of a zero-growth stock as:

$$V_{CS} = D_0/k$$

❖ EXAMPLE 9.11

Meadville Manufacturing Company (MMC) has paid a per-share dividend of $2.50 on its common stock recently, and the future dividend is expected to remain at this level forever. If the required rate of return on MMC's equity is 8 percent, at what price should its common shares trade?

$$V_{CS} = \$2.50/0.08 = \$31.25$$ ❖

EXHIBIT 9.4

Time Line for Dividends Growing at a Constant Rate

Let the current dividend, D_0, be $2 per share, and the growth rate, g, be 8 percent.

	YEARS				
	0	1	2	n	∞
CFs	D_0	$D_1=D_0(1+g)$	$D_2=D_0(1+g)^2$	$D_n=D_0(1+g)^n$	$D_\infty=D_0(1+g)^\infty$
	$2	$2(1.08)	$2(1.08)^2$	$2(1.08)^n$	$2(1.08)^\infty$

Constant-Growth Model. This model assumes that a firm's dividend will grow at a constant rate, g. The assumption applies to companies which are expected to grow at a constant rate, and many companies do plan explicitly for such growth. Dividend flows expected from such a company have the characteristics of a growing perpetuity. Exhibit 9.4 illustrates a time line of dividend flows with constant growth.

The value of a common stock with constant dividend growth is defined as:

$$V_{CS} = D_1\left[1/(1+k)\right] + D_2\left[1/(1+k)^2\right] + \ldots$$

$$= D_0(1+g)\left[1/(1+k)\right] + D_0/(1+g)^2\left[1/(1+k)^2\right] + \ldots$$

$$= \sum_{t=1}^{\infty} D_0(1+g)^t\left[1/(1+k)^t\right]$$

$$= D_0 \sum_{t=1}^{\infty} (1+g)^t\left[1/(1+k)^t\right] \quad (9.23)$$

The summation factor (as before, everything after D_0) is an infinite series whose sum equals $(1+g)/(k-g)$. This simplifies Equation 9.23 to:

$$V_{CS} = D_0(1+g)/(k-g) \text{ or } D_1/(k-g) \quad (9.24)$$

constant-growth model

A dividend discount stock valuation model that assumes that dividends will grow at a constant rate.

Equation 9.24 is known as the **constant-growth dividend discount model**, or the Gordon model, named after Myron J. Gordon who popularized it. The application of this model is restricted to growth rates below the discount rate. For growth rates greater than or equal to the discount rate, the model does not provide a sensible answer.

❖ EXAMPLE 9.12

The New Image Construction Company has just paid a $3 dividend on its common stock, and the dividend is expected to grow at a constant rate of 6 percent per year.

1. What is the expected dividend on the company's stock four years from now?
2. What is the value of the stock today, if the required rate of return is 10 percent?

FOCUS ON FINANCE

A Nonconstant Growth Model

It is realistic to assume that growth rates of dividends will not be constant. Most companies go through life cycles of growth characterized by high growth rates in the early stages of their cycles; growth rates generally level off as the corporation matures. Let g_1 and g_2 be two growth rates, g_1 lasting for n_1 years and g_2 persisting beyond the n_1 years. The valuation model of a common stock with two dividend growth rates is:

$$V_{CS} = \sum_{t=1}^{n1} D_0(1+g_1)^t\left[1/(1+k)^t\right]$$

$$+D_0(1+g_1)^{n1}(1+g_2)/(k-g_2)\left[1/(1+k)^{n1}\right]$$

The first term on the right-hand side of the equation represents the present value of the dividend flows during the n_1 periods, and the second term represents the present value of dividend flows beyond the n_1 periods.

Example

The Marshall Creek Manufacturing Company has recently paid a \$2 dividend on its common stock, and the dividend is expected to grow at 25 percent a year for the next three years. Thereafter, it will grow more slowly, at 8 percent. How much should an investor pay for this stock today if the discount rate is 10 percent?

The present value of the expected dividend flows during the first three years is:

$$PV = \$2(1.25)[1/(1.10)] + \$2(1.25)^2[1/(1.10)^2] + \$2(1.25)^3[1/(1.10)^3]$$
$$= \$2.2727 + \$2.5828 + \$2.9347$$
$$= \$7.79$$

The present value of the expected dividend flows beyond the first three years is the same as the present value of the expected price of the stock at the end of the third year. Using the Gordon model, the expected price at the end of the third year is:

$$\$2(1.25)^3(1.08)/(0.10 - 0.08) = \$210.93$$

Note that the amount $\$2(1.25)^3(1.08)$, or \$4.22, is the expected dividend for the fourth year, which corresponds to D_1 in the Gordon model.

The present value of the expected price is:

$$\$210.93[1/(1.10)^3] = \$158.47$$

Adding the two present values together gives the value of the stock:

$$V_{CS} = \$7.79 + \$158.47$$
$$= \$166.26$$

a. Expected dividend in four years $= \$3(1 + 0.06)^4$
$= \$3.79$

b. $V_{CS} = \$3(1 + 0.06)/(0.10 - 0.06)$
$= \$79.50$ ❖

The dividend discount models discussed above rely on information about the current dividend, from which they forecast future dividend flows. This does not, however, mean that the dividend discount model cannot give a value for stock of a company that has not paid any dividend in the past. A firm that has not paid any dividends in the past may pay a dividend in the future. Growing companies often postpone paying dividends, even when they are profitable. They retain their profits to finance growth. The dividend discount model focuses on the expectation of future dividend flows.

Valuation of Preferred Stock

Preferred stock usually promises investors a fixed dividend, much like the periodic interest payment on a bond. Unlike a bond, preferred dividend payments do not terminate at a specified future date. The expected dividend payment stream from preferred stock has the characteristics of a perpetuity. Therefore, the present value of preferred stock can be calculated using the formula for the present value of a perpetuity.

Note, however, that investors' required rate of return for preferred stock is not the same as that for common stock or bonds of the same company. Preferred stock exposes the investor to less risk than the same firm's common stock and more risk than its bonds. Therefore, investors require a lower rate of return on a company's preferred stock than on its common stock, and a higher rate than on its bonds.

The value of preferred stock is given by:

$$V_{PS} = D_1\left[1/(1+k)\right] + D_2\left[1/(1+k)^2\right] + \ldots$$

$$= \sum_{t=1}^{\infty} D_t\left[1/(1+k)^t\right]$$

where D_t = expected dividend in Year t
k = required rate of return
V_{PS} = value of preferred stock

Since all of the D factors are the same:

$$V_{PS} = D\sum_{t=1}^{\infty}\left[1/(1+k)^t\right]$$

$$= D/k \qquad \textbf{(9.25)}$$

❖ EXAMPLE 9.13

How much is a preferred stock worth today if it promises \$2 per year in dividends and the required rate of return is 10 percent?

$$V_{PS} = \$2/0.10$$
$$= \$20.00$$ ❖

book value
A measure of the value of a share of stock based on the accounting values of assets and liabilities.

liquidation value
The value that stockholders could realize per share by breaking up the firm and selling its assets.

Other Definitions of Stock Value

So far, the discussion on stock valuation has been confined to the intrinsic or present value of a stock. It has also been noted that the market price of a stock (or any asset, for that matter) reflects its intrinsic value. However, some other concepts of stock value have specific uses in financial management. Two of these concepts are **book value** and **liquidation value**.

Book Value. The book value of a stock is based on the net worth of the company as shown on its balance sheet. To obtain book value divide the firm's net worth by the number of common shares it has outstanding. Since net worth is an accounting concept based on the accounting values of assets and liabilities, the book value of a stock is essentially an accounting concept. The book value may be higher, lower, or equal to the market value of a stock.

Liquidation Value. The amount of money that stockholders could realize per share by breaking up the firm, selling its assets, and paying off its debt is the liquidation value of the stock. If the market price of a firm's stock falls below its liquidation value, the stockholders could earn more by breaking up the firm and selling its assets. Such a firm often becomes a takeover target. The liquidation value is generally considered to be a floor for the stock price.

SUMMARY

People commit funds to assets or invest with the expectation of a return. In most cases, the return comes in the form of both an income flow and a capital gain/loss. The return can be negative.

Investors measure returns either in dollar terms or in percentage terms. Percentages allow more useful comparisons of returns among investments of different sizes.

The real return on an investment is the gain or loss in the purchasing power of the invested money. Inflation always reduces real returns below nominal (dollar) returns; real returns can be negative.

Investment analysis employs three variants of the return concept: expected return, required return, and realized return. In a given investment situation, all three can have different values because of the uncertainty of investment outcomes. The required return is the return investors must earn to compensate for risk and loss of use of their funds. Therefore, it is defined as the minimum expected return that is necessary to induce investors to invest in an asset. Investors determine their required rates of return by adding risk premium mark-ups to the risk-free rate.

Investment risk is the possibility that the actual return on an investment will be different from its expected return. It reflects the variability of returns, or return uncertainty. Investment risk is caused by two sets of factors: systematic (market) factors and unsystematic (firm-specific) factors.

Investors are generally risk averse. They deal with investment risk by avoiding it, or by demanding risk premiums (mark-ups above the risk-free rate) on risky assets. The risk premium they demand on a given asset depends on the amount of risk and the price of risk. The price of risk, in turn, depends on the degree of risk aversion among investors. Investment risk is measured by the standard deviation of returns and by beta.

Standard deviation measures total risk, including both unsystematic and systematic risk; beta measures systematic risk relative to the market. Portfolio diversification can reduce and even eliminate unsystematic risk. Systematic risk cannot be diversified away. The securities market rewards only nondiversifiable (systematic) risk. Therefore, the relevant measure of risk for determining a risk premium is beta.

The discounted cash flow approach to valuation bases the value of an asset on its future expected cash flows. This approach defines the value of a bond as the present value of the repayment of the face value at maturity and periodic coupon payments, if any. The investor's required rate of return serves as the discount rate for the present value calculation. Bond values and interest rates are inversely related, and this relationship defines the interest rate risk of investing in bonds.

The discounted cash flow approach defines the value of a stock as the present value of its expected dividend flows. The investor's required rate of return serves as the discount rate for the present value calculation. Since the expected dividend flows of stocks are not finite, simplifying assumptions about future dividend flows facilitate the determination of stock values.

Two additional concepts of stock value used in finance are book value and liquidation value.

Bond Valuation Models

When interest is paid annually:

$$V_B = C\left[\frac{1-\left[1/(1+i)^n\right]}{i}\right] + F\left[1/(1+i)^n\right]$$

When interest is paid semiannually:

$$V_B = (C/2)\left[\frac{1+\left[1/(1+i/2)^{2n}\right]}{i/2}\right] + F\left[1/(1+i/2)^{2n}\right]$$

Stock Valuation Models

Zero-growth model for common stock:

$$V_{CS} = D_0/k$$

Constant-growth model for common stock:

$$V_{CS} = D_0(1+g)/(k-g) \text{ or } D_1/(k-g)$$

Nonconstant-growth model for common stock:

$$V_{CS} = \sum_{t=1}^{n1} D_0(1+g_1)^t\left[1/(1+k)^t\right] + D_0(1+g_1)^{n1}(1+g_2)/(k-g_2)\left[1/(1+k)^{n1}\right]$$

Perpetuity model for preferred stock:

$$V_{PS} = D\sum_{t=1}^{\infty}\left[1/(1+k)^t\right] = D/k$$

Key Terms

beta
bond duration
book value
Capital Asset Pricing Model
coefficient of variation
constant-growth model
correlation coefficient
coupon rate
discount bond
dividend discount model
expected return
expected value
face value
interest rate risk
investment risk
liquidation value
market portfolio
nominal return
par-value bond
portfolio diversification
premium bond
real return
realized (or actual) return
regression coefficient
required return
risk aversion
risk premium
risk-free rate
Security Market Line
systematic risk
unsystematic risk
yield to maturity
zero-growth model

Self-Study Questions

1. What is the significance of computing returns in percentage terms as opposed to dollar terms?
2. Define *real return* on an investment. Is it always less than the nominal return?
3. What are expected, required, and realized returns?
4. Define *investment risk* and discuss its sources.
5. How do risk-averse investors deal with risky investments?
6. What is portfolio diversification? How does it affect investment risk?
7. Discuss the features of the standard deviation of returns as a measure of investment risk.
8. What is the Security Market Line?
9. Describe the discounted cash flow approach to valuation.
10. How do the present value, the book value, and the liquidation value of a stock differ?

Self-Test Problems

1. Philip Dunsmore bought 50 shares of Ivy Chemicals stock a year ago at $42 a share. He has received dividends of $0.50 per share. The price of Ivy Chemicals stock today is $44.50. If he sells the shares today, what is the return on his investment? Calculate the return using all three return definitions discussed in the text.
2. Asset A promises a $1,200 annual return on an investment of $10,000, and Asset B promises a $1,600 annual return on an investment of $16,000. Which investment is better? Why?

3. What will be the real return on an investment that promises a nominal return of 12 percent if the expected inflation rate is 8 percent?
4. The historical returns on Assets A and B for ten years are:

YEARS	1	2	3	4	5	6	7	8	9	10
Asset A	6	–4	8	4	7	9	3	5	8	–6
Asset B	7	–2	7	6	4	7	8	6	4	3

Calculate the mean and the standard deviation of returns for both assets. Which asset is riskier?

5. Using the assets in Self-Test Problem 4, calculate the average return and the standard deviation of returns for a two-asset portfolio assuming that 30 percent is invested in Asset A and 70 percent in Asset B. The correlation coefficient of the returns on Assets A and B is 0.50.
6. Determine the required rate of return on a stock with a beta of 1.5, if the risk-free rate is 5 percent and the return on the market portfolio is 8 percent.
7. If investors require a 12 percent rate of return on a security with a beta of 1.2 and the risk-free rate is 6 percent, what is the market price of risk?
8. Find the value of a bond that pays an 8 percent coupon and matures in 12 years. Assume that investors' required rate of return is 10 percent and the bond pays interest semiannually.
9. The preferred stock of Empire Electric Corporation pays a $4 dividend annually. How much should Nancy O'Connor pay for it if her required rate of return is 8 percent?
10. The United States Transportation Company has just paid a $1.50 dividend on its common stock. Analysis of the company indicates that the dividend should grow at an 8 percent annual rate. If investors require a 12 percent rate of return, how much is this stock worth?

Discussion Questions

1. Define *investment return* and identify its sources.
2. What is the required rate of return? How do investors determine this rate?
3. One of the main concerns of investors is the uncertainty of returns. Why are returns on investments uncertain? How do investors deal with it?
4. Describe investors' behavior toward risk.
5. Why are some risks diversifiable while others are not?
6. The chapter states that the securities market will not reward investors for bearing diversifiable risk. Why?
7. What is the beta of a security? How would you interpret a beta of 1.5? –0.5?
8. Discuss the dividend discount model of stock valuation.
9. What cash flows does a typical bond promise to investors?
10. What is the interest rate risk of investing in bonds? On what does it depend?

Problems

1. Jeremy Kline invested $450,000 in an apartment building three years ago. The building produces net rental income of $40,000 per year and has been appreciating in value at the rate of 5 percent a year.
   (a) Calculate the yearly rates of return (paper return) on this investment.
   (b) If Kline sells the building at the end of this year, what is the annualized rate of return?
2. If the expected annual inflation rate is 4 percent, what is the real rate of return on an investment that earns a 9 percent nominal rate?
3. If one wants to earn a 3 percent real rate, what nominal rate should one demand when the inflation rate is 2.5 percent?
4. Based on the following historical returns, calculate the means and the standard deviations for the two securities:

YEAR	SECURITY A	SECURITY B
1	6%	4%
2	–4	1
3	2	5
4	7	3
5	4	–1
6	8	5

5. Construct a portfolio of Securities A and B described in Problem 4 with equal amounts invested in each security.
   (a) What is the expected return on the portfolio?
   (b) If the correlation coefficient between the securities' returns is 0.6, what is the standard deviation of the portfolio return?
6. A portfolio is formed with 40 shares of one stock priced at $15 per share and 50 shares of another stock priced at $25 per share.
   (a) What are the portfolio weights?
   (b) What happens to the portfolio weights if share prices change?
7. What is the required rate of return for a stock with a beta of 0.80 if the return on the market portfolio is 12 percent and the risk-free rate is 7 percent?
8. What is the price of systematic risk if the return on the market portfolio is 10 percent and the risk-free rate is 6 percent?
9. Should Maggie Johnson pay $890 for a ten-year bond with an 8 percent annual coupon when the present market rate is 10 percent?
10. Bonds issued by International Freight Company (IFC) pay a 9 percent coupon rate, have a face value of $1,000, and mature in 20 years. If the rate of return on similar bonds is 12 percent and IFC's bonds pay interest annually, at what price should they trade?
11. What price should investors pay for IFC's bonds in Problem 10 if they were to pay interest semiannually?

12. Global Insurance Company has paid $2.00 in annual dividends on its common stock recently, and this dividend is expected to grow at an annual rate of 5 percent. If investors require a 10 percent return to invest in this stock, what is its current value?
13. At what price should a security sell if it pays $1.50 annually forever when investors require an 8 percent return?
14. Ms. Geisinger invests in foreign stocks. She bought 100 shares of a French company, AGF, at FF500 last year when the exchange rate between the French franc and the U.S. dollar was FF5/$. The company has not paid any dividends during the past year. The price of the stock today is FF650 and the exchange rate is FF6.25/$. If Ms. Geisinger sells the stock today, what is the rate of return on her investment?

Topics for Further Research

1. Global Insurance Company has two bonds outstanding, each with a face value of $1,000. One bond pays an 8 percent coupon rate and has ten years to maturity. The other bond pays a 9 percent coupon rate and has eight years to maturity. Which bond carries greater interest rate risk? (Calculate the changes in the bond prices in response to a change in the interest rate to substantiate your answer.)
2. Using *Value Line*, pick two firms from different industry groups and collect earnings and dividend data (including forecasts of future growth). Estimate the stock values for these firms using the dividend discount stock valuation model and compare the results with their current market prices.

Answers to Self-Test Problems

1.

Dollar return = Dividend income + Capital gain (loss)
= $0.50(50) + ($44.50–$42.00)50
= $25 + $125
= $150

Dollar return = Cash inflow + Cash outflow
= [$0.50(50) + $44.50(50)] – $42.00(50)
= ($25 + $2,225) – $2,100
= $2,250 – $2,100
= $150

Annual percentage return = Annual dollar return/Amount invested
= $150/$2,100
= 0.071, or 7.1 percent

2. Annual percentage return on Asset A:

$1,200/10,000 = 0.12, or 12 percent

Annual percentage return on Asset B:

$1,600/16,000 = 0.10, or 10 percent

Asset A is the better investment because it promises a higher rate of return.

3. Real rate of return, $r = (1 + R)/(1 + q) - 1$

$$= (1.12)/(1.08) - 1$$
$$= 1.037 - 1$$
$$= 0.037, \text{ or } 3.7 \text{ percent}$$

4. Average returns:

$$E(R_A) = (6 - 4 + 8 + 4 + 7 + 9 + 3 + 5 + 8 - 6)/10$$
$$= 4.00 \text{ percent}$$

$$E(R_B) = (7 - 2 + 7 + 6 + 4 + 7 + 8 + 6 + 4 + 3)/10$$
$$= 5.00 \text{ percent}$$

Standard deviations:

$$S(A) = \sqrt{\begin{aligned}&(1/9)\Big[(6-4)^2 + (-4-4)^2 + (8-4)^2 + (4-4)^2 + (7-4)^2 \\ &+ (9-4)^2 + (3-4)^2 + (5-4)^2 + (8-4)^2 + (-6-4)^2\Big]\end{aligned}}$$
$$= \sqrt{(1/9)(9 + 64 + 16 + 0 + 9 + 25 + 1 + 1 + 16 + 100)}$$
$$= \sqrt{(1/9)(241)}$$
$$= \sqrt{27.78}$$
$$= 5.17 \text{ percent}$$

$$S(B) = \sqrt{\begin{aligned}&(1/9)\Big[(7-5)^2 + (-2-5)^2 + (7-5)^2 + (6-5)^2 + (4-5)^2 \\ &+ (7-5)^2 + (8-5)^2 + (6-5)^2 + (4-5)^2 + (3-5)^2\Big]\end{aligned}}$$
$$= \sqrt{(1/9)(4 + 49 + 4 + 1 + 1 + 4 + 9 + 1 + 1 + 4)}$$
$$= \sqrt{(1/9)(78)}$$
$$= \sqrt{8.67}$$
$$= 2.94 \text{ percent}$$

Coefficients of variation:

Asset A = 5.15/4 = 1.2925

Asset B = 2.94/5 = 0.588

Asset A is riskier.

5. Portfolio's expected return:

$$E(R_p) = 0.3(4\%) + 0.5(5\%)$$
$$= 1.2\% + 3.5\%$$
$$= 4.7 \text{ percent}$$

$$S(P) = \sqrt{(0.3)^2(5.17)^2 + (0.7)^2(2.94)^2 + 2(0.3)(0.7)(5.17)(2.94)(0.5)}$$

$$= \sqrt{(0.09)(26.72) + (0.49)(8.64) + 3.19}$$

$$= \sqrt{2.40 + 2.23 + 3.19}$$

$$= \sqrt{7.82}$$

$$= 2.80$$

6.

$$\begin{aligned} R^r &= R_f + (R_M - R_f)\beta \\ &= 5\% + (8\% - 5\%)1.5 \\ &= 5\% + 4.5\% \\ &= 9.5 \text{ percent} \end{aligned}$$

7.

$$\begin{aligned} R^r &= R_f + (R_M - R_f)\beta \\ 12\% &= 6\% + (R_M - R_f)1.2 \\ R_M - R_f &= 5 \text{ percent, the market price of risk} \end{aligned}$$

8.

$$\begin{aligned} V_b &= PV\{\text{Coupon payments}\} + PV\{\text{Face Value}\} \\ &= C(PVIFA_{O\,24,5\%}) + F(PVIF_{24,5\%}) \\ &= \$40[1\text{-}(1/1.05)^{24}/0.05] + \$1{,}000(1/1.05)^{24} \\ &= \$40(13.7986) + \$1{,}000(0.3100) \\ &= \$551.94 + \$310.00 \\ &= \$861.94 \end{aligned}$$

9.

$$\begin{aligned} V_{ps} &= D/k \\ &= \$4/0.08 \\ &= \$50.00 \end{aligned}$$

10.

$$\begin{aligned} V_{cs} &= D_0(1+g)/(k-g) \\ &= \$1.50(1.08)/(0.12-0.08) \\ &= \$1.62/0.04 \\ &= \$40.50 \end{aligned}$$

APPENDIX 9A

Example Solutions Using Lotus 1-2-3

The solutions given below for the examples in Chapter 9 utilize the @functions in *Lotus 1-2-3* when they are available. If predefined functions do not generate the desired solutions, the formulas necessary to solve the examples are given. These formulas should be copied *exactly*; no extra commas, dollar signs, or blank spaces are to be inserted. The notation <RET> instructs you to press the enter or return key. Also, remember the sequence of mathematical operations as they are performed (unless parentheses in the formula change the order):

1. Exponents (^) are calculated first.
2. Multiplication (*) and division (/) are performed next.
3. Addition (+) and subtraction (–) are performed last.

❖ EXAMPLE 9.1

Enter in Cell A1: .50*100+(21–20)*100

Answer in Cell A1: 150

The alternative calculation requires:
Enter in Cell A1: .50*100+21*100–20*100

Answer in Cell A1: 150

❖ EXAMPLE 9.2

1. Dollar investment
Enter in Cell A1: 100*36/1.9

Answer in Cell A1: 1894.74

2. Dollar return
Enter in Cell A1: 1894.74+100*1.5/2–100*37/2

Answer in Cell A1: 30.26

3. Percentage return
Enter in Cell A1: 30.26/1894.74

Answer in Cell A1: .015971, or 1.6 percent

❖ EXAMPLE 9.3

Enter in Cell A1: 1.12/1.06–1

Answer in Cell A1: .056604

❖ EXAMPLE 9.4

Enter in Cell A1: .25

Enter in Cell A2: .5

Enter in Cell A3: .25

Enter in Cell B1: 12

Enter in Cell B2: 8

Enter in Cell B3: 5

Enter in Cell A4: @SUMPRODUCT(A1..A3,B1..B3)

Answer in Cell A4: 8.25

❖ EXAMPLE 9.5

Enter in Cell A1: 12–8.25

Enter in Cell A2: 8–8.25

Enter in Cell A3: 5–8.25

Enter in Cell B1: +A1^2

Enter in Cell B2: +A2^2

Enter in Cell B3: +A3^2

Enter in Cell C1: +B1*.25

Enter in Cell C2: +B2*.5

Enter in Cell C3: +B3*.25

Enter in Cell C4: @SUM(C1..C3)

Answer in Cell C4: 6.4375

Enter in Cell C5: +C4^.5

Answer in Cell C5: 2.537223

❖ EXAMPLE 9.6

For Bond A:
Enter in Cell A1: 6

Enter in Cell A2: 8

Enter in Cell A3: 4

Enter in Cell A4: 1

Enter in Cell A5: –6

Enter in Cell A6: 4

Enter in Cell A7: 5

Enter in Cell A8: 2

Enter in Cell A9: @AVG(A1..A8)

Answer in Cell A9: 3

Enter in Cell A10: @STDS(A1..A8)

Answer in Cell A10: 4.242641

For Bond B, replace the numbers in Cells A1 through B8. The answers in Cells A9 and A10 will change to 3 and 6.117889 automatically.

❖ EXAMPLE 9.7

Enter in Cell A1: .4

Enter in Cell A2: .6

Enter in Cell A3: 6

Enter in Cell A4: 8

Enter in Cell A5: 2

Enter in Cell A6: 4

Enter in Cell A7: +A1*A3+A2*A4

Answer in Cell A7: 7.2

Enter in Cell A8: .7

Enter in Cell A9: (+A1^2*A5^2+A2^2*A6^2+2*A1*A2*A5*A6*A8)^.5

Answer in Cell A9: 3.014631, or 3.01 percent

If the correlation coefficient were –0.6, the entry Cell A8 would change to –0.6. Cell A9 would then show the answer 2.023858, or 2.02 percent automatically.

❖ EXAMPLE 9.8

Enter in Cell A1: 6+.8*(10–6)

Answer in Cell A1: 9.2

❖ EXAMPLE 9.9

Enter in Cells A1 through A9: 90

Enter in Cell A10: 1090

Enter in Cell A11: @NPV(.1,A1..A10)

Answer in Cell A11: 938.5543, or $938.55

❖ EXAMPLE 9.10

Enter in Cell A1: 1.5

Enter in Cell A2: 21.5

Enter in Cell A3: @NPV(.08,A1..A2)

Answer in Cell A3: 19.82167, or $19.82

❖ EXAMPLE 9.11

Enter in Cell A1: 2.5/.08

Answer in Cell A1: 31.25

❖ EXAMPLE 9.12

1. Expected dividend
Enter in Cell A1: 3*1.06^4

Answer in Cell A1: 3.787431, or $3.79

2. Present value
Enter in Cell A1: 3*1.06/(.1–.08)

Answer in Cell A1: 79.5, or $79.50

❖ EXAMPLE 9.13

Enter in Cell A1: 2/.1

Answer in Cell A1: 20

CHAPTER 10

Capital Budgeting

LEARNING OBJECTIVES

This chapter identifies the long-term investment needs of a typical firm and examines the various capital budgeting methods (techniques) by which managers evaluate investment projects. The objective of the chapter is to outline the essentials of the capital budgeting process and to highlight the advantages and disadvantages of each technique. At the conclusion of this chapter, the reader should be able to:

1. *Outline the capital budgeting process*
2. *Distinguish between mutually exclusive and independent investment projects*
3. *Identify and estimate cash flows as part of capital budgeting*
4. *Discuss various methods of project evaluation and selection*
5. *Compare evaluation methods and discuss the possibility of decision conflict*
6. *Explain why company executives prefer certain methods.*

Part of every firm's total investment provides for fixed (long-term) assets such as plant and equipment. These investments are also known as *capital goods investments*. Firm's fixed asset needs vary with the natures of their businesses. For example, transportation companies use different fixed assets than pharmaceutical manufacturers.

A firm typically invests in fixed assets when it starts its business and when it wants to expand or to replace some existing assets. Firms constantly review their needs for fixed assets. Management must decide which fixed assets the firm should acquire and determine how much to invest in fixed assets.

Investing in fixed assets is an important decision because:

1. The firm ties up scarce funds in these assets and it cannot liquidate them easily.

2. These investments define the line of business for the firm.
3. These investments affect the firm's profitability and success for many years.
4. These investments convey the firm's earnings growth potential to investors.

A bad capital spending decision may set the stage for a firm's downfall. Hence, managers must carefully evaluate proposed projects, using appropriate evaluation methods, before making any investment decision.

CAPITAL BUDGETING CONCEPTS

Investing in fixed assets involves current spending in anticipation of future cash flows, just like any other investment. Because of the long-term nature of these assets, the cash flows are spread over many years. Some assets do not realize their full cash-flow potentials until the later years of their economic lives.

An on-going business may need to invest in fixed assets in any of the following situations:

1. The firm plans to market a new line of products.
2. The firm plans to expand its existing product lines.
3. The firm is considering replacing some of its equipment to reduce on maintenance requirements or otherwise reduce costs.
4. The firm is considering investing in new physical property such as an office building.
5. The firm is required to invest in projects to improve safety, health, and environmental effects of its operations.
6. The firm is considering making some foreign direct investment.

Investment projects typically result from the firm's strategic planning process. Sometimes ideas for new products or new markets come from individual employees or divisions of the corporation. Many corporations encourage employees to make suggestions and reward them when their suggestions improve the profitability of the company. The financial manager's task is to analyze proposed projects to determine their profitability and, therefore, their ability to add value to the company's stock.

If a firm is considering an investment in new product lines, it will evaluate various alternatives and select those deemed acceptable by its chosen evaluation method. If it is considering replacing existing equipment, then the firm will compare alternatives to existing equipment. If a proposed project adds additional capacity by increasing plant size, equipment, or staff, then the evaluation will focus on the contribution of the project to the firm's profits. Whatever the nature of a project, the underlying objective of the financial manager in capital budgeting analysis is to determine its economic desirability or value to the firm.

Sometimes firms make capital investments for social and environmental reasons. Examples include investments in day-care facilities and pollution-control devices. The firm cannot analyze these projects in terms of value added to the company within a specified period. Investments in pollution control are often mandated by the government; the financial manager must determine the least costly way to satisfy regulators.

Capital Budget

capital budget
An outline of planned capital spending.

Capital budgeting is the process of evaluating and selecting long-term assets for investment. The **capital budget** is an outline of the projects a firm selects for investment. It represents the firm's planned expenditures on fixed assets, or its capital spending.

The basic objective of capital budgeting is to undertake only the most profitable investments, those that enhance the value of the firm the most. The analysis and selection process typically involves:

1. Identifying and estimating the future cash flows each project will generate
2. Evaluating and ranking proposed projects
3. Establishing a decision rule for the chosen evaluation method
4. Making a decision

Finance has developed several methods by which to evaluate and rank investment projects. The most commonly used methods are:

1. Payback period (PBP)
2. Accounting rate of return (ARR)
3. Net present value (NPV)
4. Internal rate of return (IRR)
5. Profitability index (PI)

Capital Budgeting versus Security Valuation

Capital budgeting is concerned with investments in physical assets whereas security valuation is concerned with investments in financial assets. Both require calculating present values for the respective assets on which to base investment decisions. Security valuation tries to ensure a rate of return that at least equals the investor's required rate of return. Capital budgeting tries to ensure that the firm invests in physical assets whose present values exceed their costs, or whose rates of return exceed the cost of financing them, thereby increasing the value of the firm's stock.

mutually exclusive project
A project whose selection depends on whether or not another project is selected.

independent project
A project whose selection does not depend on whether or not other projects are accepted. Such a project is judged on its merits alone.

Valuation of physical assets is perhaps more complicated than valuation of financial assets because their cash flows are more complex and difficult to estimate. This fact will become evident as this chapter explores the details of the capital budgeting process.

Mutually Exclusive and Independent Projects

Capital budgeting analysis of projects proposed for investment must carefully designate them as either **mutually exclusive projects** or **independent projects**. Projects are mutually exclusive when the firm is interested only in one of them.

Hence, the selection of one automatically excludes all others even if all are acceptable under a given evaluation criterion. Mutually exclusive projects typically arise when there are alternative methods or equipment which can perform the same task. For example, a firm that is considering computerizing its billing procedure may evaluate computer systems supplied by several companies before making a selection.

Projects are independent when accepting one does not depend upon whether or not others are accepted. Each project is judged on its own merit, and the firm accepts all projects that pass the decision rule, subject to the availability of funds. For example, Pizza Hut might evaluate projects to open restaurants in China and Thailand. These two are independent projects because opening restaurants in China would not preclude opening restaurants in Thailand, if both were profitable and if Pizza Hut could afford to do both.

capital rationing
Allocation of available funds to the highest-ranked projects.

Capital budgeting analysis confronts three situations: mutually exclusive projects, independent projects with capital rationing, and independent projects with no capital rationing. **Capital rationing** becomes necessary when a firm cannot invest in all acceptable projects because of insufficient funds. The firm is forced to ration available funds by rejecting some otherwise acceptable projects.

Project Cash Flows versus Accounting Cash Flows

Capital budgeting analysis focuses on project cash flows rather than accounting cash flows. Project cash flows represent the actual costs and benefits associated with investing in a project. For example, accountants subtract noncash charges such as depreciation from revenue when calculating taxes and net income. Capital budgeting requires, however, that the analyst add back these noncash charges to net income to calculate project cash flows.

CASH FLOW ESTIMATION

Estimating future cash flows is perhaps the most difficult and demanding task in capital budgeting. The cash flows used in capital budgeting are generally classified as:

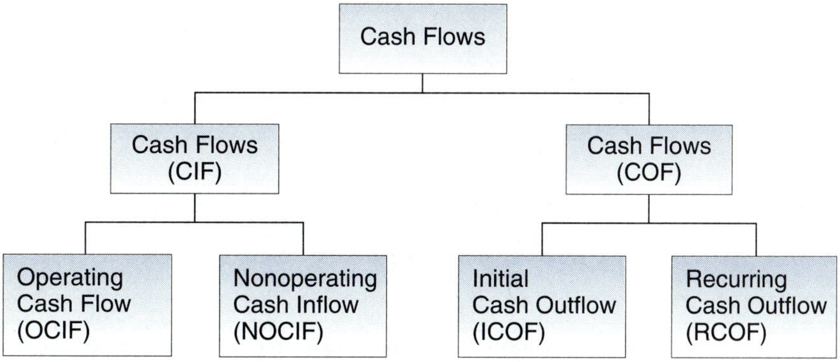

Cash Inflows

Cash inflows (CIF) represent a project's earnings, net of costs and taxes. The operating cash inflow (OCIF) is the net earnings that the project is expected to generate. It is defined as:

$$OCIF = (R - C - AD)(1 - T) + AD \quad \text{or} \tag{10.1a}$$

$$OCIF = EBIT(1 - T) + AD \tag{10.1b}$$

where R = sales revenue

C = operating costs

AD = asset depreciation charge

T = corporate tax rate

$EBIT$ = earnings before interest and taxes

Nonoperating cash inflows (NOCIF) usually consist of the after-tax proceeds from resales of old equipment. This kind of inflow may occur both at the beginning and at the end of the capital budgeting period for a project that involves replacement of a long-term asset. It will occur only at the end of the capital budgeting period if the project involves new assets rather than replacement of old ones. Because the depreciable life of an asset, as established by the current rules of depreciation, is generally shorter than its economic life, most assets retain some value after their depreciable lives end. They can be resold to generate income. The current rules of depreciation are discussed later in this chapter.

Another potential NOCIF consists of tax benefits such as an investment tax credit. To encourage investment and stimulate the economy, a country suffering from recession may amend its tax laws to allow companies to reduce their tax bills by some small percentage of the values of any new assets they acquire. The law may restrict the types of assets that qualify for this tax credit, and/or the percentage may vary for different types of assets.

Cash Outflows

The cash outflows (COF) are costs other than operating costs. The initial cash outflow (ICOF) consists of the expenditures required to acquire and install an asset; this may also include an investment in net working capital. Recurring cash outflows (RCOF) include on-going costs such as subsequent investments in net working capital and expenditures related to safety and environmental protection.

❖ EXAMPLE 10.1

The Dixon Company has been shipping its merchandise to its customers by mail, rail, UPS, and Federal Express. Management has been considering buying trucks and hiring drivers to deliver the company's products instead. Identify the various cash flows attributable to the project.

The OCIF will consist of the after-tax savings in shipping costs and the tax reduction from the depreciation charges on the trucks. The savings in shipping costs will represent the difference between the current delivery costs and the costs of licensing, insuring, maintaining, and fueling the trucks, paying the drivers' salaries and fringe benefits, and paying highway use taxes and tolls.

The NOCIF will be the after-tax scrap or trade-in value of the trucks when the company ultimately disposes of them. If the firm plans to fire the drivers at that time, this figure must also include severance pay.

The ICOF will consist of the purchase price of the trucks, their registration fees, and the cost of advertising for qualified drivers. The RCOF will include such items as replacement tires, repairs not covered by insurance, and any costs associated with scheduling deliveries efficiently. ❖

Depreciation Accounting

Accounting rules allow investors to depreciate the values of long-term assets. Depreciation charges the cost of an asset against the revenue it earns over a period of time. The rationale for depreciation is that the cost of goods produced by an asset must include a charge to recover the cost of the asset.

Depreciation is a noncash charge because it is not an actual expenditure or cash outflow. It is also tax deductible, like other elements of a firm's costs. The firm actually retains cash for the depreciation amounts listed on the income statement. This cash becomes part of the operating cash flows of the asset.

straight-line depreciation
A method of calculating depreciation that divides the cost of an asset into equal annual amounts.

The rules for depreciation appear in the IRS Tax Code. Historically, U.S. firms have used two depreciation methods: straight-line depreciation and accelerated depreciation. The **straight-line depreciation** method spreads the cost of an asset equally over its useful (economic) life. For example, if an asset costs $10,000 and has a useful life of 10 years, the annual depreciation charge is $10,000/10, or $1,000. The accelerated method follows a different principle. It lets a firm set aside larger percentages of the cost in the early years of an asset's useful life.

Accelerated Cost Recovery System
A capital asset depreciation method introduced into tax law in 1981 and modified by the Tax Reform Act of 1986.

Until 1954, tax law required U.S. businesses to follow the straight-line method for depreciation accounting. In 1954, it introduced two accelerated methods, known as *double-declining balance* and *sum-of-years'-digits*. For a review of these methods, see Appendix A. Congress replaced these methods with a simpler procedure known as the **Accelerated Cost Recovery System** (ACRS) in 1981. The Tax Reform Act of 1986 introduced a modified ACRS (MACRS) that changed the manner in which firms use the ACRS method.

The MACRS method divides the depreciable assets into several property classes with different cost-recovery periods. Exhibit 10.1 describes the MACRS property classes. The cost recovery period of each class is set at the midpoint of the range of the economic lives of assets included in that class. The depreciable amount for an asset in each class is calculated by multiplying the cost of the asset by a percentage calculated on the basis of a declining-balance method, with a switch to the straight-line method when it becomes advantageous.

half-year convention
IRS rule which treats all property as if it were placed in service at midyear.

The determination of depreciable amounts also follows the **half-year convention** rule which assumes that all assets are placed in service in the middle of the first year. As a result, the firm will depreciate each asset over one more year than its class specifies. The depreciation calculation ignores the expected salvage value of

EXHIBIT 10.1

MACRS Property Classes

PROPERTY CLASS	TYPES OF PROPERTY
3-year	Equipment used in research
5-year	Automobiles, trucks, computers, and certain special manufacturing tools
7-year	Furniture, fixtures, and most industrial equipment
10-year	Certain longer-lived equipment such as barges, tug vessels, and other water-related transportation equipment
15-year	Telephone distribution equipment, data communications equipment, and other specialized items
20-year	Farm buildings, sewer pipe, and other long-lived assets
27½-year	Residential rental property
31½-year	Nonresidential real property

the asset; that is, the asset is depreciated assuming a zero value at the end of its MACRS life.

The cost recovery percentages for three-year, five-year, seven-year, and ten-year property classes are based on a 200 percent declining balance method with a switch to the straight-line method at a specified point. The percentages for 15-year and 20-year classes are based on a 150 percent declining balance method with a switch to the straight-line method at a specified point. The percentages for real estate, the 27½-year and 31½-year classes, are based on the straight-line method. Exhibit 10.2 provides the annual cost recovery percentages for some property classes under MACRS.

Current tax laws allow the firm to use the straight-line method in place of the MACRS for any asset. However, only rarely would a taxpayer find the straight-line method advantageous because the MACRS provides tax savings earlier.

Book Value versus Market Value

Depreciation charges are calculated on the basis of the historical cost or the book value of the asset. Each year the book value of the asset declines by the amount of the depreciation. The useful life of an asset depreciated under MACRS generally exceeds its depreciable life. The price at which an asset can be sold, its market value, can differ from its book value at any time. The market value at the end of an asset's depreciable life is known as its **salvage value**. If the market value differs from the book value when the asset is sold, the firm must determine the tax consequences of this sale and adjust the cash flow estimates.

salvage value
The resale or scrap value of an asset.

EXHIBIT 10.2

Percentages of Annual Cost Recovery under MACRS

	Property Class					
Year	3-Year	5-Year	7-Year	10-Year	15-Year	20-Year
1	33.33%	20.00%	14.29%	10.00%	5.00%	3.75%
2	44.45	32.00	24.49	18.00	9.50	7.22
3	14.81	19.20	17.49	14.40	8.55	6.68
4	7.41	11.52	12.49	11.52	7.70	6.18
5		11.52	8.93	9.22	6.93	5.71
6		5.76	8.92	7.37	6.23	5.29
7			8.93	6.55	5.90	4.89
8			4.46	6.55	5.90	4.52
9				6.56	5.91	4.46
10				6.55	5.90	4.46
11				3.28	5.91	4.46
12					5.90	4.46
13					5.91	4.46
14					5.90	4.46
15					5.91	4.46
16					2.95	4.46
17						4.46
18						4.46
19						4.46
20						4.46
21						2.23

Relevant Cash Flows

To estimate a project's revenues and costs, the firm must carefully identify cash flows. It is easy to overlook relevant cash flows, and to include others that should be omitted.

incremental cash flow

Cash flows specific to a project. To identify them, subtract the firm's cash flows without the project from its cash flows with the project.

sunk cost

A previously incurred expenditure on a project independent of whether or not the project is accepted. Hence it is not part of the project's cash flows.

Incremental Cash Flows. Capital budgeting should focus on cash flows that are specific to the project being analyzed. These are its **incremental cash flows**. If it is an expansion project, the analysis must meticulously separate project-specific cash flows from the general cash flows of the business. Project-specific cash flows can be defined as the net changes in the firm's cash flows that the project would produce. These changes may consist of enhanced revenues and/or reduced costs. To identify them, subtract the cash flows of the firm without the project from its cash flows with the project. Evaluating a project on the basis of project-specific or incremental cash flows is known as the *stand-alone principle*.

Sunk Costs. Sunk costs are not part of a project's incremental cash flows. Firms often incur costs in connection with a project that do not have any bearing on the decision to accept or reject a project. These costs are treated as **sunk costs**. Examples of such costs include expenditures on marketing studies prior to introducing a new product, consultants' fees, and expenditures on basic research

EXHIBIT 10.3

Determination of Incremental Net Working Capital

Year	Accounts Receivable	Accounts Payable	Net Working Capital	Incremental Net Working Capital
1	$ 650	$480	$170	$170
2	800	600	200	30
3	1,000	750	250	50

that lead to the development of new products. Since the firm has incurred these costs in the past, it cannot change them whether it decides to accept or reject the project. Therefore, they are not considered part of the incremental costs of the project.

Costs of Existing Assets. A firm may use assets that it already owns in a new project. The costs of such assets must be part of the incremental costs of the project. Suppose that a manufacturing firm plans to construct a retail outlet on an open plot of land it already owns. The cost of the open plot of land should be included in the incremental costs of the project. The relevant cost of this land for capital budgeting is not its book value, but its opportunity cost. The opportunity cost of an asset is the value of the asset in its next best use; this is generally reflected in the market price of the asset.

Changes in Net Working Capital. A project may require additional investment in net working capital every year. Such additions become necessary, for example, when the project-related accounts receivable increase faster than the project-related accounts payable. A hypothetical example of the need for additional investment in net working capital is illustrated in Exhibit 10.3.

Expansion is another situation which calls for additional investment in working capital. The firm recovers all incremental investments in net working capital at the end of the project's life. In the last year of the project, a cash inflow item will represent the recovery of past investments in net working capital. Exhibit 10.3 shows the net working capital recovered in the third year (the terminal year of the project) as the sum of incremental net working capital investments, which is $250 ($170 + $30 + $50).

Financing Costs. The cost of debt or equity that the firm expects to incur in financing a project is not considered to be part of its incremental cash flows. It is excluded because the project evaluation is concerned only with the cash outflows and inflows that are directly related to the project. The firm makes interest and dividend payments to creditors and stockholders, but they depend on how the firm chooses to finance the project. They are independent of project selection. Some project evaluation methods do incorporate financing cost, however. This will be explained later when considering the evaluation methods.

EXHIBIT 10.4

Determining After-Tax Cash Flows

	CASE A	CASE B	CASE C	CASE D	CASE E	CASE F
Salvage value	$125,000	$ 15,000	$ 10,000	$ 12,000	$ 6,000	–$ 5,000
Book value	10,000	10,000	10,000	0	10,000	10,000
Original cost	100,000	100,000	100,000	100,000	100,000	100,000
Taxable at 36 percent	90,000	5,000	0	12,000	–4,000	–15,000
Taxable at 28 percent	25,000	0	0	0	0	0
After-tax cash flow	85,600	13,200	10,000	7,680	7,440	400

Taxes. Taxes are project-related expenses, and hence part of the incremental cash flows. The firm must pay taxes on both operating and nonoperating income. Therefore, capital budgeting must consider after-tax cash flows.

After-Tax Salvage Values. When a company finishes using an asset, it may sell it, trade it in, or throw it away. Whatever it does, the choice will probably have some cash flow and tax consequences. Thus, the financial manager must forecast the future of the asset, and how much cash the company will receive or spend. This terminal cash flow is referred to as the *after-tax salvage value* of an asset. Exhibit 10.4 illustrates the determination of after-tax salvage value in six different cases.

In Case A in Exhibit 10.4, the expected salvage value exceeds the original cost of the project. The difference between the original cost and the book value ($100,000 minus $10,000, or $90,000) is taxed at the corporate income tax rate, assumed to be 36 percent in the exhibit. The difference between the salvage value and the original cost ($125,000 minus $100,000, or $25,000) is a capital gain and is subject to capital gains tax. The exhibit assumes a tax rate on capital gains of 28 percent. The total tax bill is $32,400 plus $7,000, or $39,400, and the after-tax cash flow is $125,000 minus $39,400, or $85,600.

If the firm sells an asset before the end of its depreciable life and the estimated salvage value exceeds the book value (leaving unrecovered depreciation), then the difference between salvage value and book value is subject to taxation at the corporate income tax rate. This situation is illustrated in Case B in Exhibit 10.4. The tax due is:

$$(\$15{,}000 - \$10{,}000) \times 36\% = \$1{,}800$$

The after-tax cash flow is $15,000 minus $1,800, or $13,200.

Case C in Exhibit 10.4 illustrates the consequences of selling an asset before the end of its depreciable life when its estimated salvage value just equals its book value. There is no taxable difference and the after-tax cash flow is $10,000.

If the firm sells an asset at the end of its depreciable life, its book value under MACRS is always zero. Thus, the entire salvage value is subject to taxation. This situation is illustrated in Case D in Exhibit 10.4. The tax due is $12,000 × 36 percent, or $4,320 and the after-tax cash flow is $12,000 minus $4,320, or $7,680.

Changes in technology may accelerate the obsolescence of an asset. In such a situation, an asset sold before the end of its depreciable life may have a salvage value less than its book value. The difference between the two constitutes a tax-deductible loss. This generates a tax saving, which is an additional cash inflow. Case E in Exhibit 10.4 involves an asset sale that causes a writeoff of $4,000 in book value. The tax saving is $4,000 × 36 percent, or $1,440 and the after-tax cash flow is $6,000 plus $1,440, or $7,440.

In an extreme variation of Case F, the firm may dispose of an asset before the end of its depreciable life when it has no salvage value. In fact, the company may have to pay someone to take it away. Case F in Exhibit 10.4 involves just such a situation. To the writeoff of $10,000 in book value, the company must add the $5,000 disposal expense, creating a loss of $15,000. This reduces its tax bill by $15,000 × 36 percent, or $5,400 and produces an after-tax cash flow of $5,400 minus $5,000, or $400.

Foreign Projects

Estimating and evaluating cash flows for a foreign project are generally more complicated than they are for a domestic project. Complications arise from three main sources:

1. Exchange rate uncertainty.
2. Political and economic uncertainty.
3. The project's cash flows to the parent company may differ from the project's cash flows to the foreign subsidiary.

Though all three problems are common to every foreign project, their relative severity may vary. Consider exchange rate uncertainty. The company must translate all cash flows associated with a foreign project into its reporting currency for purposes of capital budgeting. The estimated cash flows of the project must allow for the effects of expected changes in the exchange rate. The quality of the estimates depends on the accuracy of the currency forecasts.

Political and economic uncertainty (also known as *country risk*) can lead to changes in a project's cash flows due to political, regulatory, or economic policy changes. The firm must evaluate the possibilities of these changes and their impact on cash flows and incorporate these effects in the project's cash flow estimate.

For various reasons, a parent company may realize different cash flows from a project than its foreign subsidiary. Among the most common reasons:

1. The foreign subsidiary may be required to make payments to its parent company for such items as interest on loans, dividends on equity investments, and licensing or royalty fees.
2. The parent company may supply inputs, including management services, to the foreign subsidiary.
3. Domestic tax rates may differ from foreign tax rates.
4. The parent company may suffer losses in its exports as a result of newly introduced foreign projects. This is known as **cannibalization**.

cannibalization

A situation when a new product takes sales away from existing products, or when a foreign project substitutes for a company's export.

EXHIBIT 10.5

Time Line of Cash Flows

YEARS	0	1	2	3	4	5
Initial investment	(ICOF)					
Initial NWC investment	(ICOF)					
Operating cash flows		OCIF	OCIF	OCIF	OCIF	OCIF
Addition to NWC		(RCOF)	(RCOF)	(RCOF)	(RCOF)	NOCIF
Salvage value						NOCIF
Total cash flow	(COF)	CIF	CIF	CIF	CIF	CIF

If the parent company expects to suffer export losses whether or not it invests in the foreign project because of competition from other firms, then it should not attribute such losses to the project. They are not the result of cannibalization.

These differences between parent and subsidiary cash flows raise the issue of which project cash flows, the parent's or the subsidiary's, should form the basis for project evaluation. The choice affects the accept–reject decision, since a project that is acceptable to the subsidiary may not be acceptable to the parent. In practice, multinational corporations tend to evaluate foreign projects from both viewpoints before making final selections. The final selection should, however, reflect the stockholders' best interests.

Cash Flow Time Line

Cash flow estimates for a project are usually presented in the form of a time line of cash flows. Exhibit 10.5 illustrates this time line format.

❖ EXAMPLE 10.2

Exotic Fragrance Inc. is considering an addition to its existing family of fragrances. The new product will call for an initial investment of $1 million in equipment and $100,000 in working capital. The equipment will be depreciated under MACRS; it falls in the 5-year property class. The equipment has an expected resale value at the end of the sixth year of $150,000. The company expects to sell 100,000 ounces of this fragrance per year at a price of $10 per ounce. The variable and fixed costs of production are estimated to be $500,000 per year. The company expects to lose sales on its existing line of fragrances, producing an expected reduction in EBIT from the existing products of $100,000 per year. The company falls in the 34 percent tax bracket.

1. What is the initial investment in this project?
2. Calculate the project's annual OCF.
3. Determine the terminal cash flows of the project.
4. Prepare a time line of expected cash flows for the project.

1. The initial investment:

Investment in fixed assets	$1,000,000
Investment in net working capital	100,000
ICOF	$1,100,000

2. The new scent will produce revenue of 100,000 × $10, or $1,000,000. Its annual operating cash flows (in thousands of dollars) will be:

YEAR	1	2	3	4	5	6
Depreciation						
Cost of equipment	$1,000	$1,000	$1,000	$1,000	$1,000$	1,000
MACRS percentage	×0.2	×0.32	×0.19	×0.12	×0.11	×0.06
Depreciation	200	320	190	120	110	60
Operating cash flows						
Revenue	$1,000.0	$1,000.0	$1,000.0	$1,000.0	$1,000.0	$1,000.0
Cost	−500.0	−500.0	−500.0	−500.0	−500.0	−500.0
Depreciation	−200.0	−320.0	−190.0	−120.0	−110.0	−60.0
EBIT	$ 300.0	$ 180.0	$ 310.0	$ 380.0	$ 390.0	$ 440.0
Existing EBIT Reduction	−100.0	−100.0	−100.0	−100.0	−100.0	−100.0
Net EBIT	$ 200.0	$ 80.0	$ 210.0	$ 280.0	$ 290.0	$ 340.0
Tax (34%)	−68.0	−27.2	−71.4	−95.2	−98.6	−115.6
After-tax EBIT	$ 132.0	$ 52.8	$ 138.6	$ 184.8	$ 191.4	$ 224.4
Depreciation	+200.0	+320.0	+190.0	+120.0	+110.0	+60.0
OCIF	$ 332.0	$ 372.8	$ 328.6	$ 304.8	$ 301.4	$ 284.4

3. Terminal cash flows: Since the equipment is fully depreciated, the proceeds are subject to taxation, as in Case D of Exhibit 10.4.

Salvage value	$ 150,000
Tax (34%)	−51,000
After-tax cash flow	$ 99,000
Recovery of NWC investment	+100,000
NOCIF	$ 199,000

4. The time line of cash flows for the project:

YEAR	0	1	2	3	4	5	6
ICOF	−$1,100	—	—	—	—	—	—
OCIF	—	$332.0	$372.8	$328.6	$304.8	$301.4	$284.4
NOCIF	—	—	—	—	—	—	199.0
Total cash flows	−$1,100	$332.0	$372.8	$328.6	$304.8	$301.4	$483.4 ❖

To identify and evaluate project cash flows, remember:

1. All cash flow estimates are net of taxes.
2. Only project-specific (incremental) cash flows are relevant.
3. Analysis generally assumes that all cash flows occur at the end of the year.
4. The analysis excludes sunk costs such as consulting fees and the cost of research that precedes the project.
5. The analysis must include any increase in net working capital investment that the project requires as a cash outflow.
6. The after-tax difference between the resale value and the book value of the project represents a cash inflow.

FOCUS ON CAREERS

Budget Officer

The budget officer is responsible for directing and coordinating the activities associated with formulating, monitoring, and presenting budgets. This involves assigning personnel and resources. The budget officer develops the timetable required for the budgeting process and establishes policies for carrying out the budget directives of the board of directors. The budget officer must consult with unit heads to ensure that adjustments are made in accordance with the long-term planning objectives of the firm. Furthermore, the budget officer is responsible for presenting the budget to management.

This position requires a minimum of five years experience in budgeting, excellent communication and organizational skills, and the ability to work with numbers. An undergraduate degree with a major in finance or accounting is essential.

Many financial firms use the budget preparation department as an in-house training center since it gives those who work on the budget the opportunity to investigate all phases of the corporation. The budget officer thus needs good interpersonal skills and the patience to train new employees. The rewards for an experienced budget officer include a salary in the $60,000 range combined with bonus or profit-sharing opportunities.

PROJECT EVALUATION METHODS

After estimating cash flows, the next step in capital budgeting is to evaluate these estimated cash flows to allow for selection of acceptable projects. Many evaluation methods have been devised, and several have been frequently used by financial managers. These methods fall into two broad groups: those that use a discounted cash flow (DCF) approach and those that do not.

Each capital budgeting method defines some criterion for evaluating projects. Project selection is made using a decision rule based on the evaluation criterion. A decision rule is an accept–reject rule to separate financially acceptable projects from unacceptable ones. The decision rule for an evaluation method may differ from situation to situation. For example, the decision rule for mutually exclusive projects is different from the one for independent projects.

Nondiscounted Cash Flow Methods

Nondiscounted cash flow methods evaluate projects without calculating the present values of their cash flows. Two common non-DCF methods are the payback period (PBP) and the accounting rate of return (ARR).

payback period
The number of years that the firm expects a project to take to recover its cost.

Payback Period. **Payback period** (PBP), the best-known nondiscounted cash flow method for project evaluation, uses a project's payback period as the criterion for evaluation and comparison. The payback period is the number of years a firm expects a project to take to recover its initial investment. Managers rank investment projects by their payback periods and set up a decision rule based on a target or cutoff payback period. The target payback period is the maximum PBP acceptable to the firm. All projects that meet the target PBP are acceptable for investment.

One way of determining the PBP of a project is by accumulating its annual cash inflows until the sum equals the initial investment. The number of years required to make these two amounts equal is the PBP of the project.

❖ EXAMPLE 10.3

Consider a project with the following initial investment and estimated annual cash inflows:

YEAR	ANNUAL CASH FLOWS
0	($1,500)
1	500
2	700
3	600
4	400

What is the PBP for the project?

The accumulated cash inflows are as follows:

YEAR	ACCUMULATED CASH FLOWS
1	$500
2	1,200
3	1,800
4	2,200

Comparing the initial cost of $1,500 and the accumulated cash inflows indicates that the project will require between two and three years to recover its initial investment. ❖

At the end of the second year, $1,500 minus $1,200, or $300, remains unrecovered. Assuming that the project generates cash flows uniformly throughout the year, it will take only one-half of the third year ($300/$600) to recover the remainder. The PBP for this project is thus two and one-half years. Exhibit 10.6 descibes the decision rules for payback period analysis.

❖ EXAMPLE 10.4

Transamerica Transportation Company is considering three projects for investment. Cost and cash flow estimates for the projects appear in the table below. The projects are evaluated using the payback period method. The company will consider only those projects that recover their investments in two and one-half years or less. Calculate the payback periods for the projects and set up a decision rule. Which project(s) should Transamerica choose?

EXHIBIT 10.6

PBP Decision Rules

	DECISION RULE	
	Accept	**Reject**
Mutually exclusive projects	The project with the lowest PBP that is ≤ the target PBP	All others
Independent projects and no capital rationing	All projects with PBP ≤ the target PBP	Others
Independent projects and capital rationing	The projects with PBP ≤ the target PBP. Choose them by rank (smallest PBP first) until capital is exhausted	All others

Project Cash Flows

	A		B		C	
Project Year	**Annual Cash Flow**	**Accumulated Cash Flow**	**Annual Cash Flow**	**Accumulated Cash Flow**	**Annual Cash Flow**	**Accumulated Cash Flow**
0	−$1,000	—	−$1,500	—	−$1,200	—
1	400	$ 400	200	$ 200	600	$ 600
2	400	800	400	600	400	1,000
3	400	1,200	800	1,400	300	1,300
4	400	1,600	1,000	2,400	600	1,900
PBP (years):		2.50		3.10		2.67

Decision rule: Accept any project with a PBP ≤ 2.5 years.
Decision: Accept only Project A. ❖

The payback period method has many deficiencies. First, while adding the cash flows of different years to determine the time required to recover a project's cost, it pays no attention to the time value of money. This is a serious drawback. A dollar to be received a year from now is worth more now than a dollar to be received two years from now.

Second, PBP does not pay attention to the cash flows that occur beyond the payback period. In Example 10.4, the $600 inflow in Period 4 for Project C has no impact on the evaluation of the project because it already has recovered the initial cash outflow of $1,200. Project B is rejected in spite of having the largest total expected cash inflows of all the projects, because most of its cash flows occur after it has recouped its initial cash outflow.

Third, PBP ignores the differences in cash flow patterns. Though Project C accumulates a larger cash inflow than Project A in every one of the four years, it ranks second to Project A because the only number that matters is the time each takes to recover the initial outlay.

Fourth, PBP uses an arbitrary target payback period in its accept–reject decision rule. No rationale other than management prerogative supports requiring a payback period of two and one-half years in Example 10.4.

Despite its deficiencies, the payback period method has remained quite popular among financial managers. Even large and sophisticated corporations are known to use this method to choose among small projects and as a preliminary screening device for larger projects. It owes its popularity to several attractive features:

1. It is easy to understand and use.
2. It does not require elaborate analysis of the entire life of the project.
3. Its emphasis on early cash flows makes it particularly useful for projects whose cash flows become more uncertain beyond a few years. This is critically important when evaluating foreign projects in politically unstable countries.
4. Its bias toward liquidity (shorter PBP) makes it particularly attractive to small firms that cannot afford to wait long and who must focus on the liquidity of the investment.
5. It can be used as a rough screening device to identify larger projects that seem worthy of sophisticated analysis.

Accounting Rate of Return. This method evaluates projects in terms of the net income they produce and the amount of funds invested in them. It uses the **average accounting return** (AAR) as its criterion for evaluating and ranking projects. A common definition of the average accounting return is:

average accounting return
A rate of return obtained by dividing the average annual accounting profit by the average book value of the asset.

$$ARR = \frac{\text{Average annual accounting profit}}{\text{Average book value}} \qquad (10.2)$$

Suppose that a project costs $20,000 and its assets are depreciated fully over a five-year period using the straight-line method. The project is expected to produce an average annual accounting profit (net income) of $3,000 over its depreciable life. Since the project will be fully depreciated, the average book value of this investment is:

$$(\$20{,}000 - 0)/2 = \$10{,}000$$

The expected average accounting return of this investment is $3,000/$10,000, or 0.3, which is equivalent to 30 percent.

This method ranks projects by their average accounting returns. The choice hinges on a decision rule based on an arbitrarily chosen target average accounting return. Exhibit 10.7 describes the ARR decision rules.

❖ EXAMPLE 10.5

The initial costs and annual accounting profits (AAPs) of three mutually exclusive projects, X, Y, and Z, are given in the following table. All projects will be depreciated over a five-year period using the straight-line method. Calculate the average accounting returns and rank the projects. If the target ARR for the firm is 14 percent, which investment should it accept?

EXHIBIT 10.7

ARR Decision Rules

	DECISION RULE	
	ACCEPT	REJECT
Mutually exclusive projects	The project with the highest AAR that is ≥ the target AAR	All others
Independent projects and no capital rationing	All projects with AAR ≥ the target AAR	Others
Independent projects and capital rationing	The projects with AAR ≥ the target AAR. Choose them by rank (largest AAR first) until capital is exhausted.	All others

PROJECTS	X	Y	Z
Initial Cost	$1,000	$1,500	$1,200
AAP in Year 1	100	80	95
AAP in Year 2	90	75	70
AAP in Year 3	150	100	115
AAP in Year 4	120	85	75
AAP in Year 5	175	110	100

Average annual accounting profit

For X: ($100 + $90 + $150 + $120 + $175)/5 = $127
For Y: ($80 + $75 + $100 + $85 + $110)/5 = $90
For Z: ($95 + $70 + $115 + $75 + $100)/5 = $91

Average book value

For X: ($1,000 - 0)/2 = $500
For Y: ($1,500 - 0)/2 = $750
For Z: ($1,200 - 0)/2 = $600

Average accounting return

For X: $127/$500 = 0.25 Rank = 1
For Y: $90/$750 = 0.12 Rank = 3
For Z: $91/$600 = 0.15 Rank = 2

Decision rule: Accept the project with the highest average accounting return if it is higher than the target ARR.
Decision: Accept Project X. ❖

Like the payback period method, average accounting return suffers from many drawbacks, some of them similar to those of the payback period. First, it ignores the time value of money when adding the net incomes of different years.

Second, it ignores the differences in the time patterns of net income by averaging them. One project may generate most of its net income in later years and another project in earlier years, yet both projects may end up with the same average accounting profit.

Third, ARR does not focus on the right factors when it uses accounting profit and book value to calculate a return on investment. A return based on these measures (instead of cash flows and market values) is not a true economic return, and it is inconsistent with the corporate goal of value maximization.

Fourth, the target accounting rate of return in the decision rule is not based on any generally accepted criteria. It can change at the whim of management.

The advantages of the ARR method include its simplicity and the familiarity of management with its concepts. Moreover, ARR makes it easy to monitor the performance of a new project over time, because accounting reports routinely provide data for both existing and new investments.

Discounted Cash Flow Methods

Discounted cash flow methods are more scientific and theoretically valid than the nondiscounted cash flow methods because they evaluate projects in light of the time value of money, the effect of cash flow patterns, and all cash flows. Frequently used DCF methods include net present value (NPV), internal rate of return (IRR), and profitability ratio (PI).

net present value
The present value of a project's cash flows, net of costs.

Net Present Value. The **net present value** (NPV) of a project is the measure of value it adds to the firm (or the wealth it creates). To illustrate the concept of net present value, consider a car dealer who buys used cars, fixes them up, and resells them. Suppose the dealer pays $1,200 for a car that needs work and spends an additional $800 painting the car and fixing its mechanical problems. The dealer's total investment in this car is now $2,000. The dealer sells the refurbished car for $2,600 after six months. The value added to the car is the difference between the cost and resale price (market value), which is $2,600 minus $2,000, or $600.

When analyzing a project for investment, the present value of the value added (or simply, the net present value) is the relevant concept. Since the car dealer took six months to generate a cash inflow of $2,600 from an investment of $2,000, the present value of the value added is obtained by discounting $2,600 over the six-month period, using the dealer's time value of money as the discount rate, and then subtracting the cost from this discounted amount. Assuming a 10 percent time value of money for the dealer, the present value of the value added is given by:

$$\begin{aligned} NPV &= PV\{\$2{,}600\} - \$2{,}000 \\ &= \$2{,}600[1/(1 + 0.10/2)] - \$2{,}000 \\ &= (\$2{,}600/1.05) - \$2{,}000 \\ &= \$2{,}476 - \$2{,}000 \\ &= \$476 \end{aligned}$$

Using symbols, the equation for the NPV of a project can be written as:

$$NPV = PV\{\text{Cash inflows}\} - \text{Cost}$$
$$= CIF_1(PVIF_{1,k}) + CIF_2(PVIF_{2,k}) + \ldots CIF_n(PVIF_{n,k}) - \text{Cost}$$
$$= \sum_{t=1}^{n} CIF_t\left[1/(1+k)^t\right] - \text{Cost} \tag{10.3}$$

where CIF_t = expected net cash inflow
k = discount rate
n = number of periods the project will last
t = time index

Equation 10.3 assumes that all investments in the project occur at the beginning, which is correct for many projects. If a project involves capital expenditures in later years, then the NPV equation should be modified as follows:

$$NPV = PV\{\text{Cash inflows}\} - PV\{\text{Cash outflows}\} \tag{10.4a}$$
$$NPV = PV\{\text{Net cash inflows}\} \tag{10.4b}$$

The firm's (marginal) cost of capital (its cost of financing the project) serves as the discount rate in calculating the NPV of a project. The firm's cost of capital makes the appropriate discount rate because the firm must earn at least as much as it spends to finance the project. Otherwise, it should reject the project. The cost of capital for a firm is determined by the rates of return required by the suppliers of funds, as discussed in Chapter 13.

Since the goal of capital budgeting is to select only those investments that add value or create wealth for stockholders, managers should undertake only projects with positive NPVs. This method ranks projects by their NPVs and selects them based on a decision rule that reflects the positive NPV requirement. Exhibit 10.8 describes the decision rules of the NPV method.

A project with a positive NPV is expected to make a profit. It should produce enough cash inflows to pay for all expenses, including the cost of debt or equity financing, and generate a surplus to contribute to the stockholders' wealth.

❖ EXAMPLE 10.6

Cash flow estimates of two mutually exclusive projects, P and Q, are given in the table below. The firm's cost of capital is 10 percent. Calculate the NPVs for the projects and determine which project the firm should accept.

YEAR	PROJECT P	PROJECT Q
0	($2,800)	($3,000)
1	200	2,000
2	500	1,100
3	800	600
4	1,300	290
5	1,970	100

EXHIBIT 10.8

NPV Decision Rules

	DECISION RULE Accept	Reject
Mutually exclusive projects	The project with the highest NPV that is ≥ 0	All others
Independent projects and no capital rationing	All projects with NPV ≥ 0	Others
Independent projects and capital rationing	The projects with NPV ≥ 0. Choose them by rank (largest NPV first) until capital is exhausted	All others

$$
\begin{aligned}
NPV(P) &= \$200(PVIF_{1,10\%}) + \$500(PVIF_{2,10\%}) + \$800(PVIF_{3,10\%}) \\
&\quad + \$1{,}300(PVIF_{4,10\%}) + \$1{,}970(PVIF_{5,10\%}) - \$2{,}800 \\
&= \$200(0.9090) + \$500(0.8264) + \$800(0.7513) \\
&\quad + \$1{,}300(0.6830) + \$1{,}970(0.6209) - \$2{,}800 \\
&= \$181.80 + \$413.20 + \$601.04 + \$887.90 + \$1{,}223.17 \\
&\quad - \$2{,}800 \\
&= \$507.11
\end{aligned}
$$

$$
\begin{aligned}
NPV(Q) &= \$2{,}000(PVIF_{1,10\%}) + \$1{,}100(PVIF_{2,10\%}) + \$600(PVIF_{3,10\%}) \\
&\quad + \$290(PVIF_{4,10\%}) + \$100(PVIF_{5,10\%}) - \$3{,}000 \\
&= \$2{,}000(0.9090) + \$1{,}100(0.8264) + \$600(0.7513) \\
&\quad + \$290(0.6830) + \$100(0.6209) - \$3{,}000 \\
&= \$1{,}818.00 + \$909.04 + \$450.78 + \$198.07 + \$62.09 \\
&\quad - \$3{,}000 \\
&= \$437.98
\end{aligned}
$$

NPV ranks Project P ahead of Project Q:

Decision rule: Accept the project with the highest positive NPV.

Decision: Accept Project P. ❖

internal rate of return
The annual rate of return implied by the cash flows of an investment. It also gives the growth rate of the invested money.

The NPV method overcomes all of the drawbacks of the PBP and ARR methods. It is a theoretically valid method for analyzing the profitability of projects. It is the preferred method in principle, if not in practice.

Internal Rate of Return. This method evaluates and compares projects based on their expected internal rates of return. The **internal rate of return**

(IRR) is the annualized rate of return that a project generates on the funds invested in it. Unlike the ARR, it discounts the salvage value and cash flows of a project. Determining an internal rate of return is the same as finding a discount rate (the interest rate) when the present value and the future value (or future cash flows) are given, as discussed in Chapter 8.

When an amount invested today generates future cash flows, some discount rate will make the present value of these cash flows equal to the amount invested. This discount rate is the rate of growth of the money invested, or the annualized return on the investment. Following this reasoning, the IRR of a project can be defined as the discount rate that equates the present value of its future cash inflows with the initial investment. The IRR of a project is obtained by solving the following equation for the discount rate, k:

$$\text{Cost}(ICOF) = PV\{CIF\}$$

$$= \sum_{t=1}^{n} CIF_t\left[1/(1+k)^t\right] \quad (10.5)$$

The IRR can also be defined as the discount rate that makes a project's NPV equal zero. To see this, rearrange the terms in Equation 10.5 as

$$PV\{CIF\} - \text{Cost} = 0 \quad (10.6A)$$

If the project involves capital expenditure in later years, then Equation 10.6A should be written as:

$$PV\{CIF\} - PV\{COF\} = 0 \quad (10.6B)$$

❖ EXAMPLE 10.7

Consider two investments. Investment A costs \$1,000 today and is expected to pay back \$1,150 in one year and nothing thereafter. Investment B costs \$1,000 today and is expected to pay back \$700 in the first year, \$650 in the second year, and nothing thereafter.

To find the IRR of Investment A:

$$\$1{,}000 = PV\{\$1{,}150\}$$
$$= \$1{,}150(PVIF_{1,k\%})$$
$$= \$1{,}150[1/(1+k)]$$
$$\$1{,}000(1+k) = \$1{,}150$$
$$\$1{,}000k = \$1{,}150 - \$1{,}000$$
$$\$1{,}000k = \$150$$
$$k = \$150/\$1{,}000$$
$$= 0.15, \text{ or } 15 \text{ percent}$$

To find the IRR of Investment B:

$$\$1{,}000 = PV\{\$700\} + PV\{\$650\}$$
$$= \$700(PVIF_{1,k\%}) + \$650(PVIF_{2,k\%})$$
$$= \$700[1/(1+k)] + \$650[1/(1+k)^2]$$

$$= [\$700(1 + k) + \$650]/(1 + k)^2$$
$$\$1{,}000(1 + k)^2 = \$700(1 + k) + \$650$$
$$0 = \$1{,}000(1 + 2k + k^2) - 700(1 + k) - \$650$$
$$0 = \$1{,}000 + \$2{,}000k + \$1{,}000k^2 - \$700 - \$700k - \$650$$
$$0 = \$1{,}000k^2 + \$1{,}300k - \$350$$

Using the quadratic rule:

$$k = \left[-\$1{,}300 \pm [(\$1{,}300)^2 + 4(\$1{,}000)(\$350)]^{1/2}\right]/\$2{,}000$$
$$= (-\$1{,}300 + \$1{,}757.84)/\$2{,}000 \text{ or}$$
$$(-\$1{,}300 - \$1{,}757.84)/\$2{,}000$$
$$= +\ 0.229 \text{ or}$$
$$-\ 1.53$$

Since a discount rate cannot be negative, k equals 22.9 percent. ❖

Determining IRR gets more complicated for a longer investment period. Therefore, IRRs for investment periods longer than two years are determined by trial and error. The trial and error method locates the discount rate that makes the NPV of the investment equal zero by systematically trying different discount rates. Many business calculators and spreadsheet programs are programmed to calculate IRR.

net present value profile

A plot of the NPVs of a project at different discount rates.

The trial and error method generates a schedule of discount rates and corresponding NPVs known as a **net present value profile**. By plotting the net present value profile of a project on a graph, with the X-axis representing discount rates and the Y-axis representing NPVs, the IRR of a project can be located as the point where the profile intersects the X-axis. This point identifies the discount rate that makes the NPV equal to zero. This discount rate is the IRR of the project. Exhibit 10.9 illustrates the NPV profile of Investment B from Example 10.7.

Projects are ranked by their IRRs. The decision rule for selection uses a cutoff IRR, which is usually set equal to the firm's cost of capital. This enables the firm to compare a project's internal rate of return with the firm's cost of capital. Exhibit 10.10 describes the IRR decision rules.

❖ EXAMPLE 10.8

Construct NPV profiles and locate IRRs for the projects described in Example 10.6 and rank the projects. Which project is acceptable if the firm's cutoff IRR is 14 percent?

YEAR	PROJECT P	PROJECT Q
0	($2,800)	($3,000)
1	200	2,000
2	500	1,100
3	800	600
4	1,300	290
5	1,970	100

EXHIBIT 10.9

NPV Profile of Investment B

DISCOUNT RATE	NPV
0.0%	$350.0
5.0	256.2
10.0	173.6
15.0	100.2
20.0	34.7
22.9	0.0
25.0	−24.0
30.0	−76.9

EXHIBIT 10.10

IRR Decision Rules

	DECISION RULE	
	ACCEPT	REJECT
Mutually exclusive projects	The project with the highest IRR that is ≥ the target IRR	All others
Independent projects and no capital rationing	All projects with IRR ≥ the target IRR	Others
Independent projects and capital rationing	The projects with IRR ≥ the target IRR. Choose them by rank (highest IRR first) until capital is exhausted.	All others

The NPV profiles of Projects P and Q are:

DISCOUNT RATE	NPV(P)	NPV(Q)
0%	$1,970.00	$1,090.00
5	1,148.10	737.70
10	507.11	437.98
11	396.40	383.70
12	290.60	330.70
13	189.60	279.30
14	93.14	229.50
15	0.79	180.95
16	−87.51	133.91
17	−172.00	88.00
18	−252.89	43.47
19	−330.38	0.02
20	−404.52	−42.28
22	−543.90	−123.30

The IRR of Investment P is approximately 15 percent, and the IRR of Investment Q is approximately 19 percent. IRR ranks Project Q ahead of Project P.

Decision rule: Choose the project with the highest IRR that exceeds the target IRR.

Decision: Choose Project Q. ❖

The IRR ranking and decision do not match those of the NPV method. The reasons for this conflict between decision outcomes are explained in the last section of this chapter.

The IRR method has some good features. Its use of an annualized rate of return appeals to most analysts and financial managers more than the dollar measure of the NPV method. Analysts and financial managers find it easy to represent their project evaluations in terms of rates of return because most people are more familiar with the concept of return than with NPV. A number of capital budgeting surveys have confirmed that the IRR is, in fact, the most favored method among financial managers.

IRR does, however, have some problems. One problem arises from nonconventional cash flows. Project cash flows are nonconventional when the series contains more than one negative cash flow. In other words, the project is expected to incur one or more net cash outflows in later years, in addition to the initial cash investment. Conventional cash flows begin with one negative cash flow in the initial period, and all of the rest of the cash flows are positive. Classic examples of projects that may produce more than one negative cash flow include oil-well pumping, strip mining, and nuclear power plants. In these cases, resource depletion can cause future outputs to decline and net operating cash flows to turn negative. Projects that produce air and water pollution may also face negative cash flows in later years if the companies are required to pay for clean-up activities.

Nonconventional cash flows may generate multiple IRR values. In such a situation, it is preferable to use the NPV method instead of going through a lengthy calculation to determine whether or not the IRR has multiple values. The NPV is unambiguous; it produces a single, correct decision. Calculating IRRs by computer usually obscures this problem. Software packages written in the last 20 years suppress the display of all but the lowest positive IRR.

profitability index
An index that measures a project's benefits in current dollars per dollar invested.

Profitability Index. This method evaluates projects using an index of profitability. The **profitability index** is constructed by dividing the present value of the project's expected cash inflows by the cost of the project:

$$PI = PV\{CIFs\}/ICOF$$

$$= \sum_{t=1}^{n} CIF_t\left[1/(1+k)^t\right]/\text{Initial investment} \tag{10.7}$$

The profitability index is also known as the *benefit/cost ratio* because it measures a project's benefit in present value terms per dollar invested. Suppose that the pre-

EXHIBIT 10.11

PI Decision Rules

	DECISION RULE	
	ACCEPT	REJECT
Mutually exclusive projects	The project with the highest PI that is ≥ 1.0	All others
Independent projects and no capital rationing.	All projects with PI ≥ 1.0	Others
Independent projects and capital rationing	The projects with PI ≥ 1.0 Choose them by rank (the highest PI first) until capital is exhausted.	All others

sent value of a project's expected cash inflows is $1,150 and its cost is $1,000. The PI for this project is $1,150/$1,000, or 1.15. The PI of 1.15 means that a dollar invested in the project is expected to generate $1.15 worth of benefits, measured in current dollars.

The concepts of PI and NPV are connected. The NPV is obtained by subtracting the cost from the PV{CIF}, whereas the PI is obtained by dividing the PV{CIF} by the cost. Because both derive measures from the same cash flows, one might expect the selection outcomes to be the same under both methods. This is not so. In some situations, the selection outcomes may differ, as will be discussed later in this chapter.

The PI method ranks projects by their indices. Its decision rule comes from the idea that an acceptable project must produce benefits with a present value at least equal to its cost. Exhibit 10.11 describes the PI decision rules.

❖ EXAMPLE 10.9

Calculate the PIs for the projects described in Example 10.6 and rank the projects. Which project should the firm accept?

PROJECT	PV{CIF}	COST	PI
P	$3,307.11	$2,800	1.18
Q	3,437.98	3,000	1.15

PI ranks Project P ahead of Project Q.

Decision rule: Accept the project with the highest PI greater than 1.0.

Decision: Accept Project P. ❖

DCF METHODS AND DECISION CONFLICTS

Evaluating only one project can produce no conflict among the three DCF methods because each method is based on the discounted cash flow concept:

1. If NPV > 0, then IRR > the discount rate, and PI > 1.0
2. If NPV < 0, then IRR < the discount rate, and PI < 1.0
3. If NPV = 0, then IRR = the discount rate, and PI = 1.0

When evaluating more than one project, however, the DCF methods may not produce the same accept–reject decision. It is useful to identify at the outset the situations where accept–reject decision conflict may arise, and then explain the reasons for the conflict. Suppose the firm evaluates three projects.

1. When the projects are mutually exclusive, each method may recommend accepting a different project.
2. When projects are independent and the firm faces no capital constraint (capital rationing), all three methods will produce identical accept–reject decisions.
3. When projects are independent and the firm must operate under a capital constraint, the accept–reject decisions depend on the conditions encountered.

The sources of decision conflict for mutually exclusive projects can be traced to two features of the projects: the time pattern of their cash flows and their sizes. Two projects differ in the time patterns of their cash flows if one project generates most of its cash flows in the early years and the other weights its cash flows toward the later years. Two projects differ in size when the amounts invested in them are different. Either condition can give rise to decision conflicts under DCF methods.

The connection between the time pattern of cash flows and the decision conflict is illustrated by Projects P and Q in Examples 10.6, 10.8, and 10.9. Project P generates most of its cash flows in the later years, whereas Project Q generates most of its cash flows in the early years. The project rankings and the decision outcome of NPV analysis are different from those of IRR analysis but the same as those of PI analysis.

Exhibit 10.12 illustrates the conflict between NPV and IRR by plotting the NPV profiles of Projects P and Q, as calculated in Example 10.8. Project P has an IRR of 15 percent and Project Q's IRR is 19 percent, as indicated by the intersection points of the respective NPV profiles with the *X*-axis. If the firm is using the IRR method and projects are mutually exclusive, it will select Project Q for any discount rate below 19 percent. If the firm uses the NPV method, its selection will be different depending on the discount rate. If the discount rate is below 11.5 percent (the point where the NPV profiles intersect each other), the firm will choose project P as it has a higher NPV in this range of discount rates. If the discount rate is above 11.5 percent, the firm will choose Project Q as it has a higher NPV in this range of discount rates. Thus, the decision conflict will arise only when the discount rate is below 11.5 percent.

EXHIBIT 10.12

NPV Profiles for Projects P and Q

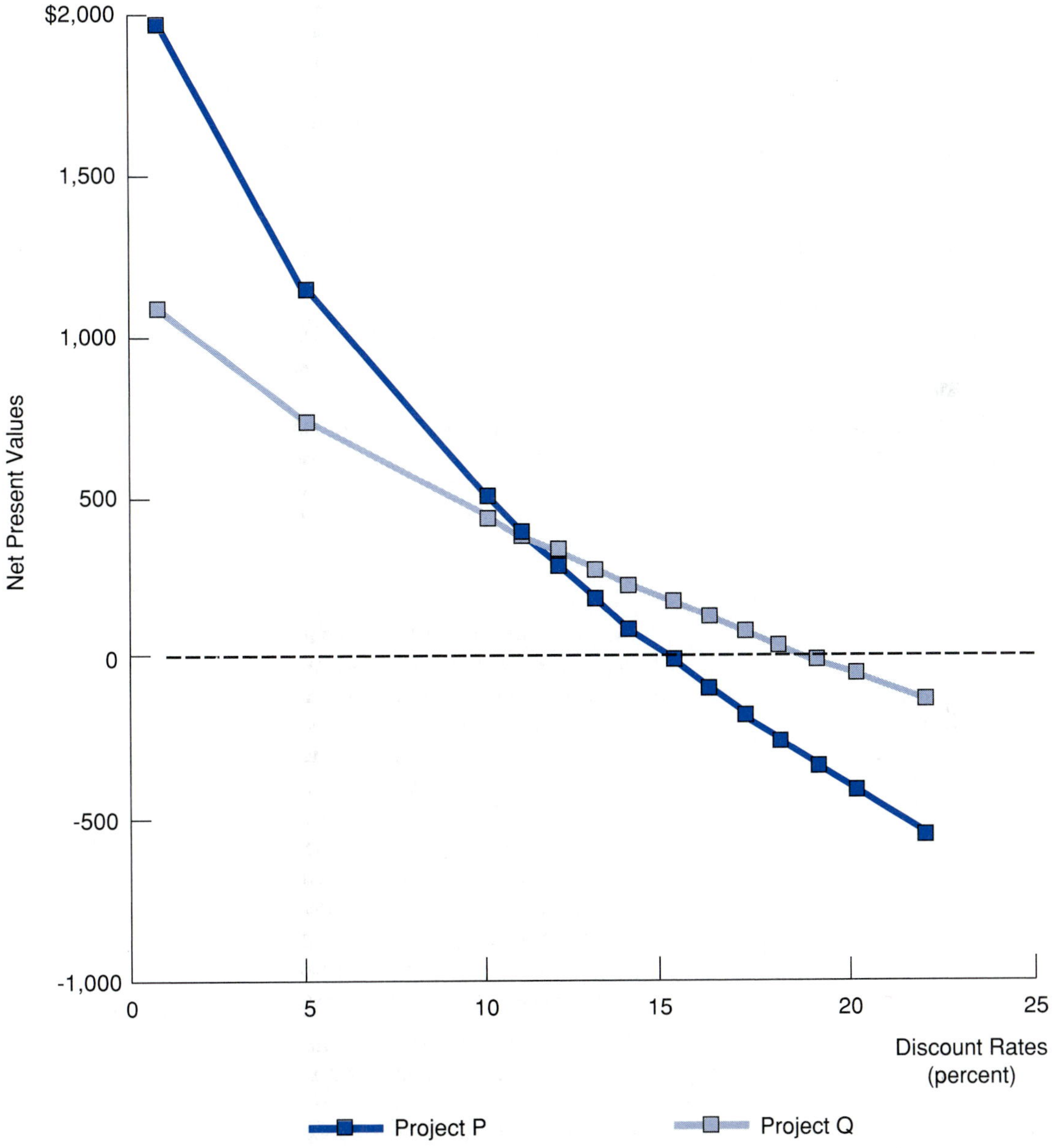

The NPV and IRR decision conflict arises from the reinvestment rates that these methods assume. The cash flows of a project occur periodically, and the NPV and IRR calculation considers them to be reinvested as they occur. In both situations, the firm will have different amounts to reinvest. For example, if a firm accepts a project with larger early cash flows, it will have more to reinvest in the early years than if it had chosen the alternative project.

The NPV method uses the cost of capital as the discount rate to determine the NPV, and implicitly assumes reinvestment of the cash flows at this rate. The IRR method assumes that the reinvestment rate for all cash flows is the IRR itself. Thus, IRR gives a project with large, early cash flows an advantage over a project with large, later cash flows.

Since the IRR of a project can differ from the firm's cost of capital, both methods cannot be right about the firm's reinvestment rate. It is both more realistic and more conservative to assume the cost of capital rather than the internal rate of return as a firm's reinvestment rate. For example, if the IRR of a project is 25 percent and the firm's cost of capital is 12 percent, it is less likely that the firm will be able to reinvest the cash flows from the project for a 25 percent return.

The main source of conflict between the NPV and PI is the size difference, and not the difference in cash flow patterns. Even if the cash flows have the same time pattern, a difference in size can give rise to decision conflict. The reason for this lies in the way these two methods calculate the benefits of investing in projects. NPV expresses the benefits in absolute terms as dollar benefits, and the PI expresses them in relative terms. Because of the difference in the way these two methods express project benefits, a higher-cost project with a higher NPV can have a lower PI and vice versa. To illustrate this point, consider two mutually exclusive projects whose cash flows, NPVs, and PIs are described in Exhibit 10.13. The calculations assume a discount rate of 10 percent.

The NPV method will lead a financial manager to choose Project K, whereas a financial manager using the PI method will choose Project L. The NPV method sees \$365 in benefits from Project K as better than \$195 in benefits from Project L. When these benefits are considered as inflows per dollar invested, the PI viewpoint, Project L promises a larger return than Project K. Therefore, PI favors Project L. Note that the time patterns of the cash flows are similar. Both generate most of their cash inflows in the early years.

For independent projects, NPV and IRR produce the same accept–reject decision. The explanation is simple. Since IRR corresponds to an NPV of zero, projects with IRRs greater than k (the cost of capital) also have NPVs greater than zero. Hence accepting projects with IRRs greater than k also means accepting projects with NPVs greater than zero.

NPV and PI agree in evaluations of independent projects when the firm faces no capital constraint. However, a capital constraint may lead NPV's accept–reject decision to differ from PI's. Under this condition, PI can prove to be a superior ranking criterion to NPV. This possibility is illustrated in Exhibit 10.14.

EXHIBIT 10.13

Comparison of NPV and PI

	Project K		Project L	
Year	Cash Flow	PV{CF}	Cash Flow	PV{CF}
0	–$1,000	–$1,000	–$500	–$500
1	800	727	350	318
2	500	413	275	227
3	300	225	200	150
NPV		$365		$195
PI	$1,365/$1,000 = 1.36		$695/$500 = 1.39	

EXHIBIT 10.14

Comparison of NPV and PI under Capital Rationing

Project	Cost	PV{CIF}	NPV	PI
S	$3,000	$3,570	$570	1.19
T	2,000	2,200	200	1.10
U	1,000	1,180	180	1.18
V	600	720	120	1.20
W	400	460	60	1.15

Exhibit 10.14 ranks projects by their NPVs. Suppose that a firm can invest only $5,000, and it has to allocate this amount among its acceptable projects. The NPV method would lead the firm to select Projects S and T, and the investment of $5,000 would produce a total NPV of $770. The PI method would give rankings of V, S, U, W, and T. With $5,000 to invest, the firm could afford to select V, S, U, and W, producing a total NPV of $930. PI yields a larger NPV, and, therefore, it is a superior method of project selection under capital rationing.

If the firm faces no capital rationing, no conflict arises between NPV and PI. The reason again is simple. Every project with a PI greater than 1.0 will also have a NPV greater than zero, so both criteria will give the same accept–reject signal for any given project.

Projects with Different Lives

Until now, discussions of mutually exclusive projects have assumed that the projects under consideration had the same economic life. This assumption may not hold in all cases. Firms must often choose investment projects from competing alternatives that have different economic lives. The reinvestment rate that the analysis assumes will be available after the termination of the project with the shorter life becomes a critical element of the decision. A simple illustration will suffice.

❖ EXAMPLE 10.10

Consider a firm that provides copying services. It invests in high-speed copiers, replacing them as they wear out. The firm is now comparing two copiers that have the same initial cost, but different lives. Copier I is expected to last six years, and Copier X is expected to last three years. The cost of capital for the firm is 12 percent.

	COPIER I			COPIER X		
YEAR	CASH FLOWS	DISCOUNT FACTOR	PRESENT VALUE	CASH FLOWS	DISCOUNT FACTOR	PRESENT VALUE
0	−$20,000	1.0000	−$20,000	−$20,000	1.0000	−$20,000
1	5,000	0.8929	4,465	9,000	0.8929	8,036
2	6,000	0.7972	4,783	10,000	0.7972	7,972
3	7,000	0.7118	4,983	9,000	0.7118	6,406
4	6,000	0.6355	3,813			
5	5,000	0.5674	2,837			
6	4,000	0.5066	2,026			

	COPIER I	COPIER X
NPV	$2,907	$2,414
PI	$22,907/$20,000 = 1.145	$22,414/$20,000 = 1.121
IRR	17.14%	18.89% ❖

Although the NPV and PI favor Copier I, IRR favors Copier X. This conflict arises because the analysis is incomplete. It ignores the difference between the lives of the projects. It ignores the fact that the firm will have to repeat the investment in Copier X along with its cash flows after three years. Therefore, the comparison of projects must adjust the figures to identify a common life. Two well-known alternative approaches for dealing with this type of problem are the **replacement chain** approach and the **equivalent annual annuity** (EAA) approach.

replacement chain
Replications of a project to define equal lives for the purpose of capital budgeting analysis.

equivalent annual annuity
An annual annuity with the same NPV as the cash flows of a project.

The replacement chain method theoretically extends the lives of the projects by repeating them (i.e., creating a replacement chain) until all projects have the same life. For example, the replacement chain method would extend the life of short-lived Copier X to six years by replicating the project once. If the life of Copier I were nine years, then Copier X would require two replications to establish a common life with Copier I.

The replacement chain procedure makes three key assumptions. First, it assumes that the firm will replace the projects as they wear out. Second, it assumes that the costs and cash flows of the projects will remain the same in every replication. Third, it assumes that the firm's cost of capital (the discount rate) remains unchanged throughout all replications.

One way of calculating the NPV of a replicated project is to:

1. Calculate the NPV of each replication (chain) separately.
2. Discount the NPV of each replication back to the present using the cost of capital as the discount rate.
3. Add the discounted NPVs of all replications.

Following this procedure, Copier X becomes the acceptable investment according to NPV.

1. Copier X has an NPV of $2,414 in Year 0 and another NPV of $2,414 in Year 3. (The $20,000 investment is made in Year 3 and the cash inflows of $9,000, $10,000, and $9,000 occur in Years 4, 5, and 6, respectively.)
2. The present value of $2,414 in Year 3 is $2,414 × 0.7118, or $1,718 in Year 0.
3. The NPV of buying one Copier X now and another in Year 3 is $2,414 plus $1,718, or $4,132.

Another way to accomplish the same thing is to set up the cash flows assuming automatic replacement. Thus, for Copier X, the net cash flow in Year 3 is –$11,000. This number is obtained by adding the last cash inflow of $9,000 from the original copier to the outflow of $20,000 for the replacement copier. The calculations are as follows:

	COPIER I			COPIER X		
YEAR	CASH FLOWS	DISCOUNT FACTOR	PRESENT VALUE	CASH FLOWS	DISCOUNT FACTOR	PRESENT VALUE
0	–$20,000	1.0000	–$20,000	–$20,000	1.0000	–$20,000
1	5,000	0.8929	4,465	9,000	0.8929	8,036
2	6,000	0.7972	4,783	10,000	0.7972	7,972
3	7,000	0.7118	4,983	–11,000	0.7118	–7,830
4	6,000	0.6355	3,813	9,000	0.6355	5,720
5	5,000	0.5674	2,837	10,000	0.5674	5,674
6	4,000	0.5066	2,026	9,000	0.5066	4,559

	COPIER I	COPIER X
NPV	$2,907	$4,131
PI	$22,907/$20,000 = 1.145	$24,131/$20,000 = 1.207
IRR	17.14%	18.89%

When the replacement chain procedure is employed all three methods, NPV, PI, and IRR, agree that Copier X is the better investment.

The replication process can, however, become very cumbersome if the lives of the projects are far apart and not exact multiples of each other. Consider, for example, three projects with expected lives of three, five, and seven years. The replacement chain method would extend each project to 3 × 5 × 7, or 105 years to arrive at a common life. The three-year project would have to be replicated another 34 times; the five-year project would have to be replicated another 20 times; the seven-year project would have to be replicated another 14 times. In such situations, it is easier to use the equivalent annual annuity (EAA) approach.

The EAA approach compares the annual annuities implied by the NPVs of projects with different lives. It assumes that the projects are replicated to a common life or indefinitely, and that the cost of capital remains the same. It does not, however, require calculating NPVs for all of the replications. To determine the EAA of a project:

1. Calculate the NPV of the project over its economic life.
2. Determine the annual annuity (the series of annual equal cash flows) that has the same NPV as the project.

The project with the higher EAA is the better project. The EAAs for the copiers in Example 10.9 are calculated below:

COPIER I		COPIER X	
PV{EAA}	\$2,907	PV{EAA}	\$2,414
EAA($PVIFA_{6,12\%}$)	\$2,907	EAA($PVIFA_{3,12\%}$)	\$2,414
EAA(4.1114)	\$2,907	EAA(2.4018)	\$2,414
EAA	\$2,907/4.1114	EAA	\$2,414/2.4018
EAA	\$707	EAA	\$1,005

Copier X has the higher EAA and is the better project.

The problem with unequal lives does not affect independent projects because selection among them is based on individual merit; the firm makes no either–or decision. The NPV selection procedure automatically considers differences in the lives of the projects.

SUMMARY

Firms need to invest in fixed assets. This need arises when a new business is started, an existing business is expanded, aging equipment is replaced to improve efficiency or reduce costs, and regulations require more strict environmental protection. All fixed asset investments are subjected to capital budgeting analysis to determine the value they will add and their overall acceptability. The proposed investment projects may be mutually exclusive or independent.

Capital budgeting involves estimating the cash flows that the proposed investment projects will generate, analyzing these cash flows, ranking projects, and selecting those that meet the firm's criteria. Each evaluation method uses a unique criterion for analyzing project cash flows and comparing projects. Using its criterion, each method sets up a decision rule for project selection. A capital budget, the result of the capital budgeting process, is an outline of the firm's planned capital spending.

Estimating cash flows is perhaps the most difficult part of capital budgeting. Project cash flows are different from accounting cash flows. The relevant cash flows of a project are its incremental after-tax cash outflows and inflows. Cash flow estimation for foreign projects is complicated by such factors as exchange rate uncertainty, economic and political risk, and the difference between project cash flows to the parent and the subsidiary.

Evaluation methods fall into two broad groups: discounted cash flow (DCF) methods and non-DCF methods. The first group uses the discounted cash flow approach to analyze projects, and the second uses other methods. The most popular methods in the first group are NPV, IRR, and PI. The PBP and ARR fall in the second group. DCF methods are considered theoretically superior to non-DCF methods because they allow for the time value of money, the time patterns of cash flows, and all cash flows.

Differences in project sizes, lives, and the time patterns of the projects' cash flows can give rise to conflicting accept–reject decisions under different DCF methods. For mutually exclusive projects, the three evaluation methods can result in conflicting accept–reject decisions if the above differences are present. For independent projects, the size difference alone is sufficient to cause a conflict between the NPV and PI decisions under capital rationing.

If mutually exclusive projects have unequal lives, the replacement chain and the equivalent annual annuity approaches will analyze them correctly on a common life basis.

Key Terms

Accelerated Cost Recovery System
average accounting return
cannibalization
capital budget
capital rationing
equivalent annual annuity
half-year convention
incremental cash flow
independent project
internal rate of return
mutually exclusive project
net present value
net present value profile
payback period
profitability index
replacement chain
salvage value
straight-line depreciation
sunk cost

Self-Study Questions

1. What is capital budgeting?
2. How is capital budgeting similar to security valuation?
3. What are mutually exclusive and independent projects?
4. Define *operating cash flows* and *nonoperating cash flows* and give some examples.
5. Why should a sunk cost like expenditures on market research be ignored when evaluating the cash flows of a new product?
6. What is a payback period?
7. Define *average accounting return*. What is wrong with this measure as a criterion for project evaluation?
8. Describe the concept of a net present value.
9. Define *internal rate of return*.
10. What are the similarities and dissimilarities between the NPV and PI methods?

Self-Test Problems

1. A firm sells a fully depreciated machine for $30,000. The original cost of the machine was $225,000. What is the after-tax cash flow of this transaction to the firm, if the firm falls in the 36 percent tax bracket? How would

the answer change if the machine had a book value of $15,000 at the time of resale?

2. Olympus Rental Company will add ten Lexuses to its fleet. The cars cost $35,000 each, and fall into the five-year MACRS depreciation class. Each car is expected to generate $20,000 in rental revenue per year. The operating cost for each car is 40 percent of its revenue. The company falls in the 34 percent tax bracket and has a cost of capital of 8 percent. What are the expected annual operating cash inflows of this investment?
3. What is the payback period of an investment that costs $45,000 and is expected to generate the following cash inflows?

YEAR	CASH INFLOWS
1	$15,000
2	12,000
3	10,500
4	6,500
5	4,000

4. Compute the internal rate of return for the following two investments and rank them. Which is the better investment?

YEAR	ASSET A	ASSET B
0	–$ 1,200	–$ 1,200
1	600	700
2	450	350
3	300	250
4	250	100

5. A firm is considering three projects, P, Q, and R, for investment. The cash flow estimates of the projects are as follows:

YEAR	PROJECT P	PROJECT Q	PROJECT R
0	–$5,000	–$5,000	–$5,000
1	3,000	1,000	0
2	2,000	2,500	3,500
3	1,500	3,000	3,500

The firm's cost of capital is 12 percent.

(a) Compute the NPV, IRR, and PI for each project and rank them under each criterion.

(b) If the projects are mutually exclusive, which project will the firm accept?

(c) If the projects are independent and the firm has funds of $10,000, which projects should it choose?

6. A firm plans to purchase electronic equipment that costs $75,000. It will depreciate the equipment over five years using the straight-line method. Prepare a schedule of end-of-year book values for this asset.

Discussion Questions

1. Distinguish between capital budgeting and a capital budget.
2. Name some investments that are subject to capital budgeting analysis.
3. Explain why a company might have to be forced to dispose of its toxic wastes safely. Frame your answer in the context of the company's capital budget.
4. What is the significance of distinguishing between mutually exclusive and independent projects in capital budgeting?
5. What is the basic objective of capital budgeting?
6. Why is cash flow estimation more complicated for a foreign project than for a domestic project?
7. Explain the concept of incremental cash flows. How are they determined?
8. Many employees of the Short Island Aerospace Co. (SIACO) live in suburban communities near the company. SIACO is considering buying vans to drive these workers from home to job and back. This will reduce the number of single-occupant vehicles on the road, traffic congestion, and air pollution. List as many of the relevant cash flows attributable to this project as you can.
9. What are the drawbacks and redeeming features of the non-DCF methods?
10. Explain the discounted cash flow approach.
11. State the NPV decision rule for mutually exclusive projects.
12. What should a firm use as the discount rate when calculating NPV?
13. What is an NPV profile?
14. State the IRR decision rule for mutually exclusive projects.
15. Why is the IRR method of project evaluation so popular?
16. State the PI decision rule for mutually exclusive projects.
17. In spite of their common approach, the DCF methods may not produce the same accept–reject decision in a given case. Why?
18. What is capital rationing? Why does the PI method prove superior to the NPV method in situations of capital rationing?
19. What is a reinvestment rate? How does it figure in the decision conflict among the DCF methods?
20. Describe the replacement chain solution to the problem of evaluating projects with unequal lives.

Problems

1. A proposed project is expected to increase sales revenue by $2 million and add $800,000 to operating costs. The project costs $2.5 million and falls in the MACRS five-year property class. If the project is depreciated using MACRS and the firm's tax rate is 34 percent, what are the annual expected operating cash flows from this project?

2. An asset costs $250,000 and is depreciated over five years. Construct depreciation schedules for the asset using both the straight-line and MACRS methods.
3. A firm sells equipment for $40,000. The book value of the equipment at the time of the sale is $60,000. What is the after-tax cash inflow from this transaction if the firm is in the 30 percent tax bracket?
4. If it costs $10,000 to dispose of equipment that still has a book value of $5,000, what is the after-tax cash inflow from this transaction to a firm that falls in the 34 percent tax bracket?
5. Nature's Delight manufactures soft drinks from fruit juices. The firm is evaluating the introduction of a new drink using a mixture of fruit juices. The production facilities for this product will be located in an unused section of the existing plant. The estimated cost of renovating this section is $150,000. Machinery will cost $800,000 and an additional $40,000 to install. The project will also call for an investment of $30,000 in working capital. The machinery, including the installation cost, will be depreciated by the straight-line method over seven years to zero book value and has an expected salvage value of $75,000. Management expects to sell 2 million bottles of the new drink per year at a price of $0.50 each. Each bottle will cost $0.37 to produce. The firm is in the 34 percent tax bracket. Define incremental cash flows and construct a time line of cash flows for the project.
6. Construction equipment costs $250,000 and it falls in the seven-year MACRS property class.
   (a) Prepare a schedule of end-of-year book values for the machinery.
   (b) If this machinery is sold for $100,000 in the third year of its depreciable life and the firm is in the 36 percent tax bracket, what is the after-tax cash flow associated with this transaction?
7. A project that costs $10,000 is depreciated by the straight-line method to zero over a five-year period. The project is expected to generate annual accounting profits of $800, $1,000, $600, $1,000, and $900, respectively, during this period. Calculate the project's average accounting return.
8. The Hudson Processing Company is considering two mutually exclusive projects whose expected cash inflows and initial costs are given below. If the company uses the PBP method and has a target PBP of three years, which project will it accept?

YEAR	PROJECTS A	PROJECT B
0	–$5,000	–$6,000
1	2,500	1,200
2	2,000	1,800
3	1,000	2,000
4	500	4,000

9. Will Nature's Delight accept the project evaluated in Problem 5 if its cost of capital is 10 percent?
10. John Myers, the president of Emit Enterprises, is considering two mutually exclusive projects. Myers believes in the IRR technique of project evaluation. The estimated cash flows for the projects are given below:

YEAR	PROJECT A	PROJECT B
0	–$800	–$1,000
1	400	600
2	300	400
3	300	300

Determine the IRR for each project. At what cost of capital will neither project be acceptable?
11. Calculate the NPV of a project with the following cash flows:

YEAR	CASH FLOWS
0	–$18,000
1	6,000
2	7,000
3	5,000
4	3,000

The firm's cost of capital is 12 percent.
12. Projects X and Y have the estimated cash flows given below:

YEAR	PROJECT X	PROJECT Y
0	–$10,000	–$14,000
1	5,000	7,000
2	4,000	5,500
3	3,500	3,700
4	2,000	1,500

(a) Evaluate and rank the projects using the PBP method.
(b) Which project(s) will be acceptable if the firm's target PBP is three years?
13. Consider the following cash flow estimates on three projects:

YEAR	PROJECT P	PROJECT Q	PROJECT R
0	–$10,000	–$8,000	–$10,000
1	6,000	1,000	1,500
2	3,500	2,500	3,500
3	2,000	3,000	4,000
4	1,000	3,500	5,000

The firm's cost of capital (or required rate of return) is 9 percent.
(a) Calculate the NPV, IRR, and PI of each project and rank them.
(b) If projects are mutually exclusive, which one will be selected?
14. A commercial ice cream maker costs $8,540. The project is estimated to produce operating cash flows (OCFs) of $2,500 each year for four years. Calculate the NPV for the project at discount rates of 0 percent, 5 percent,

10 percent, and 12 percent. Sketch the project's NPV profile using these numbers.

15. Costs and present values of the cash inflows of five projects under consideration are given below:

PROJECTS	COSTS	PV{CIF}
A	$10,000	$10,750
B	15,000	15,900
C	8,000	9,200
D	7,000	7,800
E	5,000	5,500

(a) Calculate the NPVs and PIs for the projects and rank them under both methods.
(b) If funds available to the firm are limited to $30,000, which projects will it select under the NPV and PI methods?
(c) If selections under the two methods differ, which method should the firm use? Why?

16. A firm is evaluating two investments with unequal lives. The firm's cost of capital is 9 percent. The estimated cash flows on the project are given below:

YEAR	PROJECT X	PROJECT Y
0	–$80,000	–$80,000
1	50,000	26,500
2	50,000	26,500
3		26,500
4		26,500

(a) Calculate each project's NPV.
(b) Applying the replacement chain and equivalent annual annuity approaches, rank the projects. Which project should the firm choose?

Topics for Further Research

1. Greenville Water Supply Company is considering replacing its pumping system with a new, high-efficiency model. The new system costs $250,000 and an additional $10,000 for installation and testing. The installation and testing cost will be added to the cost of equipment for depreciation. The new system will be depreciated using the straight-line method over seven years. The existing system has been in operation for four years and is being depreciated on the straight-line basis over seven years. The annual depreciation charge on the old system is $30,000 and it has a resale value of $50,000. It is estimated that the yearly savings in operating costs will amount to $50,000. The firm's cost of capital is 8 percent and its tax rate is 34 percent. Should the firm go ahead with the replacement?

2. Elgin Corporation manufactures lawn mowers and other garden tools. It is considering a new lawn mower that is quieter and less expensive to operate, and that cuts down on pollution. The marketing department predicts good demand for a such a mower in view of the growing concern about noise and air pollution. The government is also considering imposing pollution standards for garden equipment. The firm estimates that sales of the new mowers will reach 400,000 units the first year and grow at 10 percent per annum thereafter. It is assumed that the sale of the new lawn mowers will cut into the sale of existing models and cost the company $200,000 per year in pre-tax earnings. The new mower will sell for $200. Per unit operating costs (variable plus fixed costs) are estimated at $120. The machinery to build the new mower will cost $2 million and will be depreciated over seven years. Furthermore, the working capital needs of the firm will increase by $300,000. Given the firm's cost of capital at 8 percent and a tax rate of 34 percent, develop a capital budgeting schedule that evaluates this project.
3. General Instruments Company is proposing to manufacture cable boxes. The company thinks that it can sell 200,000 units per year at $45 each. The variable cost of manufacturing these boxes is estimated at $30 each and the total fixed cost should be $300,000 per year. The equipment cost is $1.5 million and it will be depreciated by the straight-line method over a five-year period. After five years the equipment is expected to have a market value of $200,000. The project also needs a NWC investment of $200,000 in the first year. The company is in the 34 percent tax bracket, and its required rate of return (cost of capital) is 12 percent. Calculate NPV, PI, and IRR. Should the company go ahead with this proposal?

Answers to Self-Test Problems

1. If the machine is fully depreciated, the entire resale value is taxable. The after-tax cash flow to the firm is:

$$\$30{,}000(1 - 0.36) = \$19{,}200$$

If the machine has a book value at the time of the sale, only the difference between the resale price and the book value is taxed. The after-tax cash flow to the firm is:

$$(\$30{,}000 - \$15{,}000)(1 - 0.36) = \$9{,}600$$

2. $$OCF = (R - C - D)(1 - T) + D$$

Time line of cash inflows:

	Year					
	1	2	3	4	5	6
Depreciation Calculation:						
Cost	$350,000	$350,000	$350,000	$350,000	$350,000	$350,000
MACRS %	0.20	0.32	0.19	0.12	0.11	0.06
Dep.	$70,000	112,000	66,500	42,000	38,500	21,000
Operating cash flows:						
Revenue	$200,000	$200,000	$200,000	$200,000	$200,000	$200,000
Cost(60%)	120,000	120,000	120,000	120,000	120,000	120,000
Dep.	70,000	112,000	66,500	42,000	38,500	21,000
EBIT	10,000	−32,000	13,500	38,000	41,500	59,000
Tax(34%)	3,400	−10,880	4,590	12,920	14,110	20,060
EBIT(1−*T*)	6,600	−21,120	8,910	25,080	27,390	38,940
Add Dep.	70,000	112,000	66,500	42,000	38,500	21,000
Salvage						100,000
OCIF	$76,600	$90,880	$75,410	$67,080	$65,890	$159,940
PVIF	0.9090	0.8264	0.7513	0.6830	0.6209	0.5644
PVs	$69,629	$75,103	$56,655	$45,815	$40,911	$90,270

PV of all cash inflows: $378,383.

3.

Year	Cash Flow	Accumulated Cash Inflow
0	−$45,000	
1	15,000	$15,000
2	12,000	27,000
3	10,500	37,500
4	6,500	44,000
5	4,000	48,000

PBP = 4.25 years.

4. Project A :

$\$1{,}200 = \$600[1/(1+IRR_A)] + \$450[1/(1+IRR_A)^2] + \$300[1/(1+IRR_A)^3]$
$+ \$250[1/(1+IRR_A)^4)$

IRR_A = 15 percent.

Project B:

$\$1{,}200 = \$700[1/(1+IRR_B)] + \$350[1/(1+IRR_B)^2)] + \$250[1/(1+IRR_B)^3]$
$+ \$100[1/(1+IRR_A)^4]$

IRR_B = 9 percent.
IRR ranks Project A ahead of Project B.

5. (a) Present value at 12 percent discount rate:

YEAR	PVIF	PROJECT P	PROJECT Q	PROJECT R
0	1.0000	–$5,000.00	–$5,000.00	–$5,000.00
1	0.8928	2,678.40	1,339.10	0.00
2	0.7972	1,594.40	1,594.40	2,790.20
3	0.7118	1,067.70	2,135.40	2,491.30
NPV		$ 340.50	$ 69.00	$ 281.50

Internal rate of return:

$$\$5,000 = \$3,000[1/(1+IRR_P)] + \$2,000[1/(1+IRR_P)^2] + \$1,500[1/(1+IRR_P)^3]$$

IRR_P = 16.5 percent.

$$\$5,000 = \$1,500[1/(1+IRR_Q)] + \$2,000[1/(1+IRR_Q)^2] + \$3,000[1/(1+IRR_Q)^3]$$

IRR_Q = 12.7 percent.

$$\$5,000 = \$3,500[1/(1+IRR_R)^2] + \$3,500[1/(1+IRR_R)^3]$$

IRR_R = 14.5 percent.

Profitability index:

$$PI_P = \$5,340.5/5,000 = 1.068$$
$$PI_Q = \$5,069.0/5,000 = 1.014$$
$$PI_R = \$5,281.5/5,000 = 1.056$$

Project ranks:

PROJECTS	NPV	IRR	PI
P	1	1	1
Q	3	3	3
R	2	2	2

(b) Project P will be chosen under all methods.
(c) Projects P and R will be chosen under all methods.

6. The depreciation amount is $75,000/5, or $15,000.
The book value is cost minus accumulated depreciation.

YEAR	DEPRECIATION	ACCUMULATED DEPRECIATION	END-OF-YEAR BOOK VALUE
1	$15,000	$15,000	$60,000
2	15,000	30,000	45,000
3	15,000	45,000	30,000
4	15,000	60,000	15,000
5	15,000	75,000	0

APPENDIX 10A

Example Solutions Using Lotus 1-2-3

The solutions given below for the examples in Chapter 10 utilize the @functions in *Lotus 1-2-3* when they are available. If predefined functions do not generate the desired solutions, the formulas necessary to solve the examples are given. These formulas should be copied *exactly*; no extra commas, dollar signs, or blank spaces are to be inserted. The notation <RET> instructs you to press the enter or return key. Also, remember the sequence of mathematical operations as they are performed (unless parentheses in the formula change the order):

1. Exponents (^) are calculated first.
2. Multiplication (*) and division (/) are performed next.
3. Addition (+) and subtraction (–) are performed last.

Examples 10.1, 10.3, and 10.4 do not require computer assistance.

❖ EXAMPLE 10.2

Enter in Cell A1: ICOF,t=0

Enter in Cell A2: -1000000-100000

Leave Cell A3 blank.

Enter in Cell A4: MACRS

Enter in Cell A5: 1000000*.2

Enter in Cell A6: 1000000*.32

Enter in Cell A7: 1000000*.19

Enter in Cell A8: 1000000*.12

Enter in Cell A9: 1000000*.11

Enter in Cell A10: 1000000*.06

Leave Cell A11 blank.

Enter in Cell A12: After tax

Enter in Cell A13: 1–.34

Leave Cell A14 blank.

Enter in Cell A15: RCIF

Enter in Cell A16: 1000000–500000–100000

Leave Cell A17 blank.

Enter in Cell A18: NOCIF

Enter in Cell A19: 150000*A13+100000

Enter in Cell B1: t=1

Enter in Cell B2: +A13*(A16-A5)+A5

Enter in Cell C1: t=2

Enter in Cell C2: +A13*(A16–A6)+A6

Enter in Cell D1: t=3

Enter in Cell D2: +A13*(A16–A7)+A7

Enter in Cell E1: t=4

Enter in Cell E2: +A13*(A16–A8)+A8

Enter in Cell F1: t=5

Enter in Cell F2: +A13*(A16–A9)+A9

Enter in Cell G1: t=6

Enter in Cell G2: +A13*(A16–A10)+A10+A19

The row of Cells A2 . . G2 should be identical to the time line.

❖ EXAMPLE 10.5

Enter Initial Cost in Cell A1: 1000

Enter First AAP in Cell A2: 100

Enter Second AAP in Cell A3: 90

Enter Third AAP in Cell A4: 150

Enter Fourth AAP in Cell A5: 120

Enter Fifth AAP in Cell A6: 175

Enter Book Value in Cell A7: 0

Enter in Cell A8: @AVG(A2..A6)

Enter in Cell A9: (A1+A7)/2

Enter in Cell A10: +A8/A9

Answer in Cell A10: 0.254

The numbers in Cells A1 . . A6 can be replaced with the numbers for Project Y, and the answer in Cell A10 will change to 0.120. The numbers in Cells A1 . . A6 can be replaced with the numbers for Project Z, and the answer in Cell A10 will change to 0.15167.

❖ EXAMPLE 10.6

Enter in Cell A1: –2800

Enter in Cell A2: 200

Enter in Cell A3: 500

Enter in Cell A4: 800

Enter in Cell A5: 1300

Enter in Cell A6: 1970

Enter in Cell A7: @NPV(.1,A2..A6)

Enter in Cell A8: +A7+A1

Answer in Cell A8: 507.23

Enter in Cell B1: –3000

Enter in Cell B2: 2000

Enter in Cell B3: 1100

Enter in Cell B4: 600

Enter in Cell B5: 290

Enter in Cell B6: 100

Enter in Cell B7: /CA7 <RET> <RET>

Enter in Cell B8: +B7+B1

Answer in Cell B8: 438.23

❖ EXAMPLE 10.7

Enter in Cell A1: –1000

Enter in Cell A2: 1150

Enter in Cell A3: @IRR(.15,A1..A2)

Answer in Cell A3: .15

Enter in Cell B1: –1000

Enter in Cell B2: 700

Enter in Cell B3: 650

Enter in Cell B4: @IRR(.20,B1..B3)

Answer in Cell B4: .228919

❖ EXAMPLE 10.8

Cells A1 . . B6 are the same as in Example 10.6.

Enter in Cell A7: @IRR(.14,A1..A6)

Answer in Cell A7: 0.190005, or 19 percent

Enter in Cell B7: /CA7 <RET> <RET>

Answer in Cell B7: 0.143693, or 14 percent

❖ EXAMPLE 10.9

Cells A1 . . B7 are the same as they were in Example 10.6.

Enter in Cell A8: +A7/–A1

Answer in Cell A8: 1.181152

Enter in Cell B8: +B7/–B1

Answer in Cell B8: 1.146076

❖ EXAMPLE 10.10

(a)

Enter in Cell A1: –20000

Enter in Cell A2: 5000

Enter in Cell A3: 6000

Enter in Cell A4: 7000

Enter in Cell A5: 6000

Enter in Cell A6: 5000

Enter in Cell A7: 4000

Enter in Cell A8: @NPV(.12,A2..A7)

Enter in Cell A9: +A8+A1

Answer in Cell A9: 2906.678

Enter in Cell A10: +A8/-A1

Answer in Cell A10: 1.145334

Enter in Cell A11: @IRR(.12,A1..A7)

Answer in Cell A11: 0.171355, or 17.14 percent

Enter in Cell B1: –20000

Enter in Cell B2: 9000

Enter in Cell B3: 10000

Enter in Cell B4: 9000

Enter in Cell B5: 0

Enter in Cell B6: 0

Enter in Cell B7: 0

Enter in Cell B8: /CA8 <RET> <RET>

Enter in Cell B9: /CA9 <RET> <RET>

Answer in Cell B9: 2413.675

Enter in Cell B10: /CA10 <RET> <RET>

Answer in Cell B10: 1.120684

Enter in Cell B11: /CA11 <RET> <RET>

Answer in Cell B11: 0.18891, or 18.89 percent

(b) Cells A1 . . A11, B1 . . B3, and B8 . . B11 are the same as in Example 10.10(a).

Change Cell B4 to: –11000

Change Cell B5 to: 9000

Change Cell B6 to: 10000

Change Cell B7 to: 9000

Answer in Cell B9: 4131.682

Answer in Cell B10: 1.206584

Answer in Cell B11: 0.18891, or 18.89 percent

(c)

Enter in Cell A1: @PMT(2907,.12,6)

Answer in Cell A1: 707.0572

Enter in Cell A2: @PMT(2414,.12,3)

Answer in Cell A2: 1005.066

CHAPTER

11

Debt and Preferred Stock as Long-Term Sources of Funds

LEARNING OBJECTIVES

This chapter examines the characteristics of debt and preferred stock. At the conclusion of this chapter, the reader should be able to:

1. *Explain how a company can repay its debt early*
2. *Compare the consequences of issuing securities with different priorities of claims in case of bankruptcy*
3. *Analyze the impact of restrictive covenants on the freedom of management to make financial decisions*
4. *Evaluate the influence of the terms of an outstanding security on its cost*
5. *Calculate the costs of debt and preferred stock*
6. *Discuss the scope of the international markets for debt securities*
7. *Evaluate the relative advantages and disadvantages of debt and preferred stock*
8. *Explain the characteristics of convertible securities and the consequences of issuing them*

In deciding how to raise long-term funds, a company has to consider many factors. For example, it must decide whether it wants to pay back the money or not. If it does, it considers issuing debt; if not, it considers issuing stock.

A company that decides to issue debt must pick a maturity date and determine under what circumstances it might want to pay off the debt early. It must decide whether to issue secured or unsecured debt. It must consider whether the market will expect it to accept restrictions on management's freedom to make financial decisions. It must estimate how external analysts will evaluate the quality of its debt issues because higher-quality debt bears a lower interest rate. It must decide whether to sell the debt issue in its home country or in foreign markets, and in which currencies.

A company that decides to issue preferred stock must determine under what circumstances it might want to retire that stock. It must also consider whether the market will expect it to accept restrictions on management's freedom to make financial decisions. It must decide whether or not to pay professionals to evaluate the quality of its preferred stock; higher-quality preferred bears a lower dividend rate. Above all, it must decide on the terms of its dividend commitment.

Finally, the company must decide whether or not to make the new issue of either debt or preferred stock convertible into its common stock at the discretion of the investor. Convertibility would make the issue less expensive, but it would ultimately increase the number of common shares outstanding. Analysts measure the potential dilution of earnings per share from the day a firm issues a convertible security.

LONG-TERM DEBT

public offering
A sale of registered securities to the general public.

trustee
A financial institution, usually a commercial bank, that monitors a bond issuer's performance as long as the bond is outstanding, to ensure that the company fulfills its obligations to bondholders.

private placement
A sale of unregistered securities to fewer than 20 investors, usually financial institutions.

prospectus
A document that condenses the information in an indenture; the firm must offer it to potential investors.

Corporations raise intermediate and long-term funds from financial institutions and from the public by issuing notes and bonds, among other securities. If a company borrows by means of a **public offering**, it issues bonds, usually in denominations of $1,000, to anyone who is willing to buy them. This transaction requires that the firm register the bond issue with the Securities and Exchange Commission (SEC), and it must appoint a **trustee**. A trustee is a financial institution, usually a commercial bank, that monitors the company's performance as long as the bond is outstanding to ensure that it fulfills its obligations to the bondholders. If a company has more than one bond issue outstanding, each issue may have a different trustee. Alternatively, if the company borrows by issuing notes or bonds to a few (legally, less than 20) financial institutions, the issue is a **private placement** and does not have to be registered.

Whether it borrows publicly or privately, the company must prepare an indenture agreement, a document that fully describes all the terms of the bond issue and details the company's current and recent financial condition. Terms in the indenture can change only with the approval of most of the bondholders. To prevent collusion between the company and one large investor, approval of a change is often required from 66⅔ percent of the bondholders, and from the holders of 66⅔ percent of the amount of bonds outstanding. When a firm sells bonds through a public offering, it must also condense the information in the indenture into a **prospectus**, a document that it must offer to potential investors.

Maturity

The standard corporate bond issue matures in 20, 25, or 30 years. During the 1990s, more than a dozen corporations have taken advantage of historically low interest

EXHIBIT 11.1

Bonds with Exceptionally Long Maturities

ISSUER	RATE	ISSUED	MATURITY	AMOUNT (000)
1,000 years				
Toronto, Grey & Bruce Railway[a]	4.000%	1883	2883	£719
100 years				
Walt Disney Company	7.550	1993	2093	$ 300,000
Coca-Cola Company	7.375	1993	2093	150,000
50 years				
Boeing Corp.	7.350	1992	2042	100,000
Boeing Corp.	6.875	1993	2043	125,000
Boeing Corp.	7.875	1993	2043	175,000
Consolidated Rail Corp.	7.875	1993	2043	250,000
Ford Motor Company	7.750	1993	2043	200,000
Pacific Bell Corp.	7.375	1993	2043	300,000
Tennessee Valley Authority	8.250	1992	2042	1,000,000
Tennessee Valley Authority	7.250	1993	2043	750,000
Texaco Capital Corp.	7.500	1993	2043	200,000

[a]Denomination = £100 with coupon payable in gold in London; denomination and coupon equivalents in Canadian currency for bondholders in Canada.

rates and issued bonds with 40 years to maturity. Some bonds with exceptionally long maturities are listed in Exhibit 11.1. The 100-year bond of the Walt Disney Company created quite a stir when it was issued, and market wits dubbed it the *Sleeping Beauty Bond.*

The issuer of a standard bond agrees to pay a fixed amount of simple interest every six months and to repay the principal at maturity. This interest is usually expressed as a percentage of the bond's denomination (also called *face value*, *par value*, or *maturity value*). The interest rate is also referred to as the *coupon rate* or the *face rate*. Thus, an 8 percent bond with a 25 year maturity issued on October 10, 1990, would pay $1,000 × 8 percent × ½, or $40 in interest every April 10 and October 10 from 1991 through 2015. It would repay the $1,000 principal on October 10, 2015. Occasionally, corporate borrowers have attempted to issue innovative debt securities such as **variable rate bonds**, whose interest rates change with market rates, or **baby bonds**, with face values of $500 or $100. These innovations generally have been unpopular with investors.

variable rate bond

A bond whose interest rate changes with market rates.

baby bond

A bond with a face value of $500 or $100.

For various reasons, a corporate borrower may want to pay off a bond before maturity. It can do so by several different methods. Some early repayment methods must be specified in the indenture; others need not be mentioned.

Call Feature. A company may include a call feature in a bond's indenture for four reasons; two of them involve cost. If a company issues a bond at a time when interest rates are above cyclical lows, it may plan to replace this issue with a less costly bond when interest rates fall. Second, a company may need to borrow when its financial condition is below optimum, leading investors to demand a high risk premium as part of the bond's interest rate. It may plan on replacing this issue with a less costly bond when its financial condition improves. Third, a company may not be sure that it will need the borrowed funds for the entire amount of time until maturity. Finally, current conditions in the bond market or within the company may force the firm to include terms in the bond indenture that it does not want to tolerate until the bond matures.

A call feature allows the company to "call a bond in" and pay it off before maturity. The indenture specifies four conditions for a call:

1. The minimum time that must elapse before a bond can be called. The customary alternatives are immediately, after three years, or after five years. The company bases this decision on its estimate of the amount of time until interest rates will fall, or until its financial condition will improve.
2. The call premium, usually one year's interest if the bond is called during the first year during which the company can call it. This premium is a bonus payment to the bondholders to compensate for the forced liquidation of their investment at a time when they cannot replace the same level of income without accepting additional risk.
3. The rate of decline of the call premium. The call premium decreases each year the bond remains outstanding, and it disappears before maturity. An investor who must surrender a 30-year bond after, say, 19 years does not deserve as much compensation as an investor who must surrender a 30-year bond after only four years.
4. The amount of time that must pass between the **announcement date of the call**, the date on which the company announces that it is calling a bond, and the **effective call date**, the date on which the call actually happens. This is usually a choice between a four-week to six-week period or a 30-day to 60-day period. If the company has decided to replace a called bond with a new issue, it sells the replacement bond during this period. Also during this period, investors who are unwilling to accept the call will sell the bond, even though its market price jumps to its approximate call value on the announcement date and stays there until the effective date.

announcement date of a call
The date on which a company announces that it is calling a bond.

effective call date
The date on which a bond call actually happens.

On the announcement date, the company must place a notice in the financial press and the bond's trustee writes to all bondholders, requesting that they turn in their bonds. On the effective date, the company must deliver to the trustee enough money to pay the interest due to that date, the call premium, and the principal of $1,000 per bond. The trustee then sends the appropriate payments to investors who have turned in their bonds. It holds any balance in escrow for those who have retained them. An investor who delivers a called bond a month or two (or even ten years) later will get the same amount of money as those who sent their bonds in on time; no interest is paid on the amount held in escrow. As far as the company is concerned, the bond ceases to exist on the effective date.

In deciding whether to issue a callable or a noncallable bond, a company weighs the benefits of early retirement against the higher interest rate that the

FOCUS ON FINANCE

Available Information about a Bond

RJR Nabisco has an $8^5/8$ percent sinking fund debenture outstanding. The following information, rephrased in layman's terms, was obtained from Moody's *Industrial Manual*, vol. 2 (1993), p. 3,453.

Debenture Features

The issue is rated Baa3, the lowest rating a bond can have and still be considered of investment quality. The firm sold $500 million to the public on March 23, 1987. As of December 31, 1992, $440,650,000 was still outstanding. The bond matures on March 15, 2017. Each year, the company pays $43.12 interest per bond on March 15 and $43.13 on September 15 to bondholders who were registered as owners on the previous March 1 and September 1, respectively. The company picked Connecticut National Bank as this bond's trustee.

This is a fully registered bond, sold in denominations of $1,000 or any whole-number multiple. It is not possible to buy a fraction of a bond. The bond can be transferred (sold) and exchanged for larger or smaller denominations without any service charge being imposed by RJR Nabisco.

This bond is callable on at least 30, but not more than 60, days' notice. The call may retire the bond partially or completely at the following prices:

Up to March 14	Call Price
1994	$1,056.06
1995	1,051.75
1996	1,047.44
1997	1,043.13
1998	1,038.81
1999	1,034.50
2000	1,030.19
2001	1,025.88
2002	1,021.56
2003	1,017.25
2004	1,012.94
2005	1,008.63
2006	1,004.31
Thereafter	1,000.00

If the bond is called, the bondholder is also entitled to accrued interest to date. The bond may not be called before March 15, 1997, however, if the company intends to replace it with debt that costs less than 8.75 percent annually.

The bond has a $25 million sinking fund requirement that must be satisfied every March 15 from 1998 to 2016. The company has the option of paying off more than this amount. Bonds called to satisfy the sinking fund also require 30 to 60 days' notice, but holders of such bonds receive $1,000. The sinking fund is designed to retire 95 percent of the bonds before maturity.

Restrictive Covenants

This is a senior, unsecured debenture and its indenture does not limit the firm's debt. However, if the company and its subsidiaries issue secured debt that exceeds 10 percent of consolidated net tangible assets, a negative pledge clause applies. This clause prohibits the company from issuing new debt that would take priority over these debentures.

Neither the company nor its subsidiaries may sell assets and lease them back through a lease that lasts more than three years, unless such a transaction is allowed under the negative pledge clause, or the net proceeds from the sale of the assets at least equal the assets' fair market value, and the proceeds are used to retire debt.

The indenture may be modified with the consent of the holders of $66^2/3$ percent of the debentures outstanding. The trustee, or the holders of 25 percent of the outstanding bonds, may declare the principal due and payable if the company defaults on the indenture provisions. The company has 30 days' grace for the payment of interest.

The proceeds from the sale of the debenture will be used for general corporate purposes, including working capital, reduction of short-term debt, repurchases of the company's outstanding securities, and capital expenditures.

Bond History

The debenture was offered to the public at $986.75 per $1,000 bond on March 13, 1987, through a syndicate managed by Shearson Lehman Brothers, Inc. Dillon, Read & Co., Inc. was a major participant in the syndicate. The company received $978 from the sale of each $1,000 bond.

market demands of callable securities. From the market's point of view, higher probability of an early call increases the interest rate differential.

Sinking Funds. Accounting standards require the issuer to maintain a sinking fund on the books for every outstanding bond. This entry recognizes that a prudent company should put aside some money every year to accumulate the funds necessary to pay off the bond at maturity. Accounting standards are, however, based on the assumption that corporations are "going concerns." Therefore, the company is not actually required to accumulate cash to retire the debt. A going concern will not reduce its assets to eliminate debt; it will issue a new bond to pay off the old one.

A sinking fund provision in a bond indenture is *not* an accounting requirement. It is the result of a recommendation made by the investment banker that helps a company plan a new bond issue. If the company lacks financial strength, the investment banker may suggest that the company actually pay off part of the new bond each year. This gradual reduction in outstanding debt improves the company's financial condition and the safety of the remaining bonds. Such a sinking fund can be fixed or variable. A **fixed sinking fund** requires the firm to retire the same amount of debt each year, on the anniversary date of the bond. A **variable sinking fund** requires the firm to retire an increasing amount of debt each year on the premise that, as time passes, the company's increasing cash flow will enhance its ability to repay loans.

fixed sinking fund
The retirement of the same amount of debt each year, on the anniversary date of the bond.

variable sinking fund
The retirement of an increasing amount of debt each year, on the anniversary date of the bond.

The sinking fund may or may not completely retire the issue by maturity. If it does not, the obligation for the remaining principal is referred to as a *balloon payment*. For instance, a $100 million, 25-year bond with a fixed $3 million annual sinking fund would have a $25 million balloon. If the annual sinking fund were $4 million, the bond would have no balloon.

Suppose that the indenture of a 10 percent corporate bond requires a $2 million sinking fund. Each year, on the bond's anniversary, the company turns over $2 million to the bond's trustee. The trustee then randomly selects $2,000,000/$1,000, or 2,000 bonds and notifies the holders that their bonds have been called to satisfy sinking fund requirements. The bondholders send their bonds to the trustee, which then remits $1,000 plus the interest due. The former bondholders receive no call premium. Further, as time passes, the outstanding bonds' risk of illiquidity increases because fewer of them remain outstanding and the market for them gets thinner.

The sinking fund clause in an indenture agreement almost always specifies that the annual payment is to be made "in cash or in bonds." This has advantages for both the company and the bondholders. If market interest rates rise above the bond's coupon rate, its market price falls below par. The term "in cash or in bonds" allows the company to buy its own bonds in the open market and turn them over to the trustee to satisfy the sinking fund requirement. If the company were to buy 2,000 bonds at a cost of $950 per bond (commission included), it would save $100,000 while satisfying its obligation. This arrangement is also satisfactory to bondholders, because the bonds that the firm acquires in the market are those that investors were willing to sell. Investors who wish to hold their bonds do not lose them to a random call.

Sometimes, if interest rates rise substantially and the market price of a bond falls far below $1,000, a company that has the necessary cash buys as many bonds as it can get, accumulating enough to satisfy the sinking fund for several years. Not only does the company retire some of its debt at a discount, it also avoids paying interest on bonds it holds to satisfy future sinking fund requirements.

Put Bonds. A call feature allows early bond repayment at the company's option. A sinking fund feature makes the early retirement of specific bonds a matter of chance. A put feature gives the bondholder the right to demand early repayment. Put bonds have yet to develop a strong appeal to U.S. investors; they are found more frequently in foreign bond markets.

Tender Offers. If a bond indenture includes no provision for early retirement, a company that wishes to pay off its debt early has only one alternative: it can buy as many of its bonds as possible on the open market and then make a **tender offer** for any that remain outstanding. A tender offer is a public announcement that the company is willing to purchase all outstanding bonds in an issue at a price higher than the current market price. To discourage a shrewd bondholder or two from holding out for an even better price, most companies make their tender offers two-tiered. In a **two-tiered tender offer** the company announces that it will pay a high price for the bond until a certain date and a lower price after that date; both prices are higher than the current market price. For example, a company may have an outstanding bond, maturing in January 2003, currently trading in the market around $1,010. It can make a tender offer to buy back this bond for $1,050 during the next six months, and for $1,030 thereafter.

tender offer
A public announcement that a company is willing to purchase all outstanding bonds in an issue at a price above the current market price.

two-tiered tender offer
A bond issuer's offer to buy its outstanding bonds at a high price until a certain date and a lower price after that date; both prices are higher than the current market price.

Claims on Assets

The general public, Wall Street professionals, and the financial press refer to all long-term corporate debt issues as *bonds*. Lawyers, however, recognize an important distinction between two types of corporate debt: debentures and bonds.

Debentures. A company may borrow long term without offering any of its assets as collateral for the loan. Such a security is technically a debenture, although the financial world will refer to it as a *bond*. The market trusts that the company will be able to generate future cash flows large enough to pay the debenture's interest when due and repay its principal at maturity.

The indenture agreement identifies the debt issue as either a **senior debenture** or a **subordinate debenture**. The distinction is important in case of bankruptcy. A debenture holder has a claim to interest due up to the date of bankruptcy plus the security's $1,000 face value that ranks with those of other unsecured creditors. The claims of senior debenture holders must be satisfied in full, however, before the claims of subordinate debenture holders can be paid. When a company has a choice between issuing senior or subordinate debentures, it always decides to

senior debenture
An unsecured debt issue with claims against the company in case of bankruptcy ranked with the claims of other unsecured creditors.

subordinate debenture
An unsecured debt issue that can be paid off in case of bankruptcy only when claims of all senior debentures have been paid in full.

issue senior securities because they require lower interest rates than the subordinate securities. Investors who buy subordinate debentures expect higher compensation to accept greater risk.

mortgage bond
A long-term debt security with a mortgage note attached that pledges some or all of the borrower's assets as collateral for the loan.

Bonds. A company may also borrow long term and pledge some or all of its assets as collateral for the loan. This pledge is contained in a mortgage note attached to the bond issue. Common usage shortens the name of such debt issues to **mortgage bonds**. The assets that secure the debt are identified and fully described in the indenture. In case of bankruptcy, the proceeds from liquidation of the mortgaged assets are used to pay the claims of the mortgage bondholders: interest due up to the date of the bankruptcy plus the $1,000 face value of the bond.

The fair market value of physical assets pledged as collateral must always exceed the amount that the firm borrows against them. The first time an issuer pledges an asset as collateral, the resulting security is a first mortgage bond; it may represent 65 percent to 90 percent of the asset's fair market value. If the asset appreciates in value, or the issuer partially pays off the first mortgage, the unpledged portion of the fair market value of the asset may be pledged as collateral for another secured loan, a second mortgage bond. In case of bankruptcy, the claims of the first mortgage holders must be paid in full before the second mortgage holders can be paid anything.

If a company has a choice between issuing a debenture or a mortgage bond, it usually decides to issue the debenture. The mortgage bond would carry a lower interest rate, but U.S. managers generally prefer unsecured debt. They are reluctant to encumber assets other than real estate.

Priority of Claims in Bankruptcy Proceedings. If a company goes bankrupt with both debentures and mortgage bonds outstanding, several conditional rules govern repayment of these obligations. First, prior claims such as unpaid wages, unpaid taxes, and the court costs of the bankruptcy process must be paid. Then the proceeds from the mortgaged assets are used to pay the claims of the mortgage holders. If these proceeds are insufficient, the unpaid claims of the mortgage holders are treated like the claims of unsecured creditors. On the other hand, if these proceeds exceed the mortgage holders' claims, any balance is distributed to the unsecured creditors.

A few examples, all based on the same balance sheet, will make these principles clear. Suppose that a company goes bankrupt with the following balance sheet:

ASSETS		LIABILITIES AND EQUITY	
Mortgaged assets	$200 million	General creditors	$ 50 million
Other assets	300 million	First mortgage	120 million
		Second mortgage	40 million
		Senior debenture	60 million
		Subordinate debenture	30 million
		Common stock	210 million
		Retained earnings	−10 million
Total assets	$500 million	Total capital	$500 million

❖ EXAMPLE 11.1

chattel mortgage bond

A debt secured by movable property.

After the prior claims are settled, the proceeds from the liquidation of the mortgaged assets yields $100 million. These mortgaged assets are not necessarily real estate; a **chattel mortgage bond** can pledge moveable property such as machinery and equipment as collateral. Such assets do not normally produce their book values on the auction block, though. Liquidation of the other assets (primarily accounts receivable and inventory) yields $120 million. How is the total $220 million in cash distributed?

The $100 million proceeds of the mortgaged assets go to the first-mortgage holders; the second-mortgage holders get nothing from the proceeds of the mortgaged assets. The remaining claims against the company are categorized by class and totaled:

General creditors	$ 50 million
Mortgages ($20 million + $40 million)	60 million
Debentures ($60 million + $30 million)	90 million
Total claims	$200 million

Since $120 million is available to settle claims of $200 million, each class will get $120 million/$200 million, or 60 percent of its claim. The general creditors will get 0.6 × $50 million, or $30 million. The mortgage holders will get 0.6 × $60 million, or $36 million. Since the first mortgage holders still have an unpaid claim of $20 million, they get this amount and the second mortgage holders get the remaining $16 million. The debenture holders get 0.6 × $90 million, or $54 million, all of which goes to the senior debenture holders. The subordinate debenture holders, like the stockholders, get nothing. ❖

Example 11.1 may give an unpleasant shock to those whose only experience with mortgages comes from debt secured by real estate. Unsecured creditors may get a better payoff in bankruptcy proceedings than secured creditors. In the example, the senior debenture holders received $54 million to settle their $60 million claim (90 cents on the dollar), while the second mortgage holders received only $16 million to settle their $40 million claim (40 cents on the dollar). This legally required distribution may still seem disproportionate when the liquidation produces a greater sum of cash.

❖ EXAMPLE 11.2

Suppose now that the liquidation of the mortgaged assets yields $150 million, while the liquidation of the other assets yields $100 million. How is the total of $250 million in cash distributed?

The first-mortgage holders receive $120 million of the $150 million proceeds from the mortgaged assets. The second-mortgage holders get the remaining $30 million. The unsatisfied claims against the company are categorized by class and totaled:

General creditors	$50 million
Mortgages	10 million
Debentures	90 million
Total claims	$150 million

Since $100 million is available to settle claims of $150 million, each class gets $100 million/$150 million, or two-thirds of what the firm owes. The general creditors get two-thirds of $50 million, or $33,333,333. The second mortgage holders get two-thirds of $10 million, or $6,666,667, giving them a total reimbursement of $36,666,667 on their $40 million claim. The debenture holders get two-thirds of $90 million, or $60 million, all of which goes to the senior debenture holders. Again, the subordinate debenture holders and the stockholders get nothing. ❖

While Example 11.2 distributes $30 million more than Example 11.1, the proportions may seem skewed to the bankruptcy novice. Example 11.2 pays the senior debenture holders in full, while the second-mortgage holders receive less than 92 cents on each dollar of their claim.

Bankruptcy distribution laws allow only two ways in which second-mortgage holders can be paid in full:

1. The proceeds from the liquidation of the mortgaged assets must produce enough cash to settle all mortgage holders' claims in full.
2. The proceeds of the liquidation of all the assets must produce enough cash to settle all creditors' claims in full.

❖ EXAMPLE 11.3

The liquidation of mortgaged assets yields $160 million; the liquidation of the other assets yields $100 million.

The first-mortgage holders receive $120 million of the $160 million proceeds of the liquidation of the mortgaged assets; the remaining $40 million goes to the second-mortgage holders. The $100 million from the sale of the other assets pays off the other creditors. The remaining claims against the company are categorized by class and totaled:

General creditors	$ 50 million
Debentures	90 million
Total claims	$140 million

Since $100 million remains to settle claims of $140 million, each class of creditors gets $100 million/$140 million, or 71.429 percent of its claim. The general creditors get 0.71429 × $50 million, or $35,714,000. The debenture holders get 0.71429 × $90 million, or $64,286,000; of this amount, $60 million goes to the senior debenture holders. The subordinate debenture holders get the remaining $4,286,000. The stockholders get nothing. ❖

Equipment Trust Certificates. Another type of security that pledges assets to secure debt, equipment trust certificates are primarily used by railroads and airlines (and sometimes by other types of businesses such as oil companies and trucking companies) to finance expensive equipment. The manufacturer transfers title of the equipment to a trust company or the trust department of a commercial bank. The trustee pays for the equipment and leases it to the user company. This user makes a large first lease payment to the trustee, usually 20 to 25 percent of the purchase price of the equipment. The trustee recoups the balance of the purchase

FOCUS ON FINANCE

BOMB-PROOF RATINGS

The Port Authority of New York and New Jersey owns the World Trade Center in New York City. On February 26, 1993, the Trade Center was subjected to a terrorist bomb attack. Its electronic systems were badly damaged and a substantial portion of its office space became unusable pending major repairs. The Trade Center accounts for 44 percent of the Port Authority's net annual revenues.

By the end of the following week, the financial world had completed its analysis of the situation. The Port Authority announced that it expected its $600 million in property damage insurance and $400 million in liability insurance to cover its losses. Moody's Investors Service confirmed its A1 rating on the Port Authority's $4.3 billion in outstanding bonds. Standard & Poor's and Fitch's Investors Services confirmed their AA- ratings on them as well.

An underwriting syndicate managed by Merrill Lynch bought the Port Authority's new $100 million bond issue on March 3 by bidding an interest rate of 5.44 percent. This was touted as a vote of confidence in the Port Authority by investors, because before the explosion, the market had been expecting the bonds to carry a 5.46 percent rate.

Source: Newsday, March 4, 1993, p. 43.

price by selling equipment trust certificates to investors, pledging the equipment as collateral.

The user of the equipment makes periodic lease payments in amounts carefully calculated to enable the trustee to pay interest on the outstanding certificates and gradually retire them. After paying off the certificates, the trustee sells the equipment to the company for some nominal price and the lease is terminated. While the trustee holds title to the equipment, however, the user must maintain the equipment properly, keep the trustee informed of its location and condition, and pay all taxes and insurance charges.

Bond Quality

restrictive covenant
A limitation on a company's actions specified in an indenture that management agrees to observe as long as the bonds are outstanding.

The quality levels of corporate bonds vary from company to company, and sometimes among the bonds issued by the same company. Individual investors often ignore one determinant of bond quality, the package of **restrictive covenants** written into the bond indenture. Few professional investment managers make this mistake. Restrictive covenants are limitations on the company's actions that management agrees to observe as long as the bonds are outstanding. The trustee monitors the company's compliance with these covenants. If a company ignores the trustee's warnings and persistently violates one or more of the covenants, the trustee will reluctantly haul the company into bankruptcy court.

Bond indentures may include some common restrictive covenants and some unusual ones. Of the following list of common restrictive covenants, only the first one is universal. It is found in all bond indentures.

1. The company cannot pay dividends on stock if the payment reduces accumu-

lated retained earnings to a level below the amount shown on the balance sheet when the bonds are issued. By restricting future dividend payments to after-tax income earned after the bonds are issued, this covenant attempts to preserve whatever equity cushion the bonds have when they are issued.

2. The company cannot borrow in the future if the amount borrowed will raise the company's debt–equity ratio above a specified ceiling. A variation of this covenant may limit future dollar amounts of debt.
3. The company cannot issue bonds equal in rank to the current issue as long as this bond is outstanding. The presence of this covenant forces companies to issue subordinate debentures if they must borrow before this issue terminates.
4. A **negative pledge clause** is a variation of the preceding covenant. It prevents the company from issuing new debt that will take priority over the issue whose indenture contains this clause. This covenant usually restricts a company's freedom to mortgage its assets.
5. Management cannot allow the company's current ratio (current assets/current liabilities) to fall below a specified floor as long as the bond issue is outstanding. A variation of this covenant establishes a floor below which the company's net working capital (current assets minus current liabilities) cannot fall.
6. Management cannot sell and lease back any of the company's assets as long as the bond is outstanding. This covenant protects the bondholders from an owner–manager arranging an asset sale and leaseback, then distributing the cash from the sale to stockholders in the form of a huge dividend before declaring bankruptcy.

negative pledge clause
A provision in a bond indenture that prevents the company from issuing new debt that will take priority over the bonds covered by the indenture.

Risk. Corporate bonds are affected by inflation risk, market risk, and interest rate risk, regardless of which company issues them. Inflation risk affects all corporate bonds the same way: an unexpectedly large increase in the general price level will deprive all bondholders of some purchasing power. Market risk also has a universal effect on bonds: an unanticipated news event or change in the mood of investors will affect the bond market as a whole and the prices of all corporate bonds traded that day.

Interest rate risk results from the movement of bond prices in a direction opposite to any movement of interest rates. How much risk an investor faces depends on the sensitivity of bond prices to changes in interest rates. The sensitivity of a bond price, defined as the ratio of percentage change in bond price to percentage change in the interest rate, in turn, depends on two characteristics of the bond: time to maturity and coupon rate.

1. At a given coupon rate, the longer the time to maturity, the greater the dollar change as well as the percentage change in price. Hence, long-term bonds are riskier.
2. At a given maturity, the higher the coupon rate on a bond, the greater the dollar change in price and the smaller the percentage change in price. Hence, lower coupon bonds are riskier.

EXHIBIT 11.2

Interest Rate Risk

	Bond Prices					
Coupon Rate		**6 percent**			**12 percent**	
Market Rates	**5 percent**	**6 percent**	**7 percent**	**5 percent**	**6 percent**	**7 percent**
Maturity						
10-year	$1,077.20	$1,000.00	$929.72	$1,540.50	$1,441.60	$1,351.13
20-year	1,124.63	1,000.00	894.04	1,872.36	1,688.18	1,529.68

	Price Changes					
Coupon Rate		**6 percent**			**12 percent**	
Market Rates	**5 percent**	**6 percent**	**7 percent**	**5 percent**	**6 percent**	**7 percent**
Maturity						
10-year	$ 77.20		–$ 70.28	$ 98.90		–$ 91.47
	(7.72%)		(–7.02%)	(6.86%)		(–6.34%)
20-year	$124.63		–$105.96	$184.18		–$158.50
	(12.46%)		(–10.59%)	(10.90%)		(–9.38%)

These principles can be illustrated by comparing how the prices of four $1,000 face-value bonds react when interest rates change. The four bonds are:

1. A 6 percent bond with 10 years to maturity,
2. A 6 percent bond with 20 years to maturity,
3. A 12 percent bond with 10 years to maturity,
4. A 12 percent bond with 20 years to maturity.

To evaluate the price changes and the nature of interest rate risk, consider a starting interest rate of, say, 6 percent and calculate the prices of the four bonds described above. Then recalculate bond prices by increasing and decreasing the interest rate by one percentage point. Finally calculate the changes in bond prices both in dollar terms and percentage terms and compare the results.

Exhibit 11.2 contains the results of these calculations. Bond prices are obtained by using the bond valuation model developed in Chapter 9 (see Equation 9.20). The model assumes that coupon payments are made annually.

$$V_B = C(PVIFA_{n,i}) + F(PVIF_{n,i})$$

$$= C\left[\frac{1-1/(1+i)^n}{i}\right] + F\left[1/(1+i)^n\right]$$

where C = annual coupon amount
F = face value
i = interest rate
n = years to maturity

To illustrate the first principle of interest rate risk, compare the price changes of the 10-year bonds to those of the 20-year bonds. The longer the time to maturity, the greater the dollar changes as well as percentage changes in price. To illustrate the

EXHIBIT 11.3

Moody's Bond Ratings

RATING	DESCRIPTION
Aaa	Judged to be of the best quality. They carry the smallest degree of investment risk and are generally referred to as "gilt edge." Interest payments are protected by a large or by an exceptionally stable margin and principal is secure. While the various protective elements are likely to change, such changes as can be visualized are most unlikely to impair the fundamentally strong position of such issues.
Aa	Judged to be of high quality by all standards. They are rated lower than the best bonds because margins of protection may not be as large as in Aaa securities, or fluctuation of protective elements may be of greater amplitude, or there may be other elements present which make the long-term risks appear somewhat larger than in Aaa securities.
A	Possess many favorable investment attributes and are to be considered as upper-medium grade obligations. Factors giving security to principal and interest are considered adequate but elements may be present which suggest a susceptibility to impairment some time in the future.
Baa	Considered as medium-grade obligations, i.e., they are neither highly protected nor poorly secured. Interest payment and principal security appear adequate for the present but certain protective elements may be lacking or may be characteristically unreliable over any great length of time. Such bonds lack outstanding investment characteristics and in fact have speculative characteristics as well.
Ba	Judged to have speculative elements; their future cannot be considered as well assured. Often the protection of interest and principal payments may be very moderate and thereby not well safeguarded during both good and bad times over the future. Uncertainty of position characterizes bonds in this class.
B	Generally lack characteristics of the desirable investments. Assurance of interest and principal payments or of maintenance of other terms of the contract over any long period of time may be small.
Caa	Are of poor standing. Such issues may be in default or there may be present elements of danger with respect to principal or interest.
Ca	Obligations which are speculative in a high degree. Such issues are often in default or have other marked shortcomings.
C	The lowest rated class of bonds and issues so rated can be regarded as having extremely poor prospects of ever attaining any real investment standing.

Moody's applies numerical modifiers, 1, 2, and 3 in each rating classification from Aa through B. The modifier 1 indicates that the security ranks in the higher end of its rating category; the modifier 2 indicates a mid-range ranking; the modifier 3 indicates that the issue ranks in the lower end of its rating category.

Source: Moody's *Industrial Manual*, 1993, pp. vi – vii.

second principle of interest rate risk, compare the price changes of the 6 percent bonds with those of the 12 percent bonds. The higher the coupon rate, the greater the dollar changes in price and the smaller the percentage changes in price.

The risk of illiquidity is company-specific. Illiquidity risk increases for a company with fewer bonds outstanding, and for a company with less actively traded bonds. An investor who buys a relatively illiquid bond may push up its price that day; an investor who sells such a bond may depress its price.

Default risk is bond-specific. The terms of the bond and the present and future financial condition of the company all affect the probability that an investor will not receive interest or principal repayment when due. This risk is evaluated by companies such as Moody's and Standard & Poor's, who are paid by corporate bond issuers to publish their bond ratings. Exhibits 11.3 and 11.4 list these companies' ratings classes and their descriptions. Bonds rated triple-A have the least default

EXHIBIT 11.4

Standard & Poor's Bond Ratings

Rating	Description
AAA	Has the highest rating assigned by Standard & Poor's. Capacity to pay interest and repay principal is extremely strong.
AA	Has a very strong capacity to pay interest and repay principal and differs from the higher-rated issues only in small degree.
A	Has a strong capacity to pay interest and repay principal although it is somewhat more susceptible to the adverse effects of changes in circumstances and economic conditions than debt in higher-rated categories.
BBB	Is regarded as having an adequate capacity to pay interest and repay principal. Whereas it normally exhibits adequate protection parameters, adverse economic conditions or changing circumstances are more likely to lead to a weakened capacity to pay interest and repay principal for debt in this category than in higher-rated categories.
BB	Has less near-term vulnerability to default than other speculative issues. However, it faces major ongoing uncertainties or exposure to adverse business, financial or economic conditions which could lead to inadequate capacity to meet timely interest and principal payments. This rating is also used for debt subordinated to senior debt that is assigned an actual or implied BBB– rating.
B	Has a greater vulnerability to default but currently has the capacity to meet interest payments and principal repayments. Adverse business, financial, or economic conditions will likely impair capacity or willingness to pay interest and repay principal. This rating is also used for debt subordinated to senior debt that is assigned an actual or implied BB or BB– rating.
CCC	Has a currently identifiable vulnerability to default, and is dependent upon favorable business, financial, and economic conditions to meet timely payment of interest and repayment of principal. In the event of adverse business, financial, or economic conditions, it is not likely to have the capacity to pay interest and repay principal. The CCC rating is also used for debt subordinated to senior debt that is assigned an actual or implied B or B– rating.
CC	Typically applied to debt subordinated to senior debt that is assigned an actual or implied CCC rating.
C	Typically applied to debt subordinated to senior debt which is assigned an actual or implied CCC– rating. The C rating may be used to cover a situation where a bankruptcy petition has been filed, but debt service payments are continued.
CI	Reserved for income bonds on which no interest is being paid.
D	Is in payment default. This rating is used when interest payments or principal payments are not made on the date due even if the applicable grace period has not expired, unless S&P believes that such payments will be made during such grace period. This rating also will be used upon the filing of a bankruptcy petition if debt service payments are jeopardized.

Standard & Poor's ratings from AA to CCC may be modified by the addition of plus (+) or minus (–) signs to show relative standing within the major rating categories.

Source: *Standard & Poor's Manual*, 1993, p. 2,681.

risk and pay the lowest interest rates that corporate bonds can pay at the time they are issued. As a general rule, subordinate debentures are rated one level below senior debentures issued by the same company. Second-mortgage bonds are rated one level below first-mortgage bonds that pledge the same assets as collateral.

On any given bond, Moody's ratings usually match Standard & Poor's. Ratings that differ are almost never more than one level apart. (If they were, one rating would be wrong.) Differences in ratings are usually temporary. Both rating companies may upgrade or downgrade a rating simultaneously, but frequently they change their evaluations within a few weeks of each other. Standard & Poor's pub-

FOCUS ON FINANCE

JUNK BOND KING

In 1970, Michael R. Milken joined the Wall Street firm that ultimately became known as Drexel Burnham Lambert, Inc. To find his own niche in the investment banking world, he meticulously researched the securities market. He discovered that junk bonds—he prefers the term *securitized business loans*—were actually high yielding securities with minimal default risk under most economic conditions.

Blessed with a genius for salesmanship, Milken popularized investment in junk bonds. With demand for low-grade securities growing, he increased the supply by facilitating leveraged buyouts (LBOs). In an LBO deal, a company borrows huge sums of cash from banks and the public in order to buy a majority or all of the outstanding stock of another corporation. When the managers of these takeover targets were hostile, their efforts to prevent the acquisitions were usually futile because the junk bond issuers could offer to pay high cash prices for the target stocks.

In what was probably Milken's most crucial deal, he raised $1.7 billion almost overnight to help T. Boone Pickens take over Gulf Oil. This deal, and his assistance to Kohlberg Kravis Roberts in the takeover of RJR Nabisco, made the public aware of corporate raiders and predatory capital. Investment bankers began to routinely help identify, buy, and dismember companies whose stock prices were too low because their assets were undervalued. Fear of becoming the next takeover target prompted large corporations to seek curbs on takeovers financed by junk bonds.

In 1986, an employee of Drexel, Dennis Levine, was arrested for insider trading. To lighten his sentence, Levine informed on Ivan Boesky, who made it possible for the federal government to hit Milken with a 98-count indictment.

Milken confessed to six counts of securities fraud, paid more than $1 billion in penalties and settlements, and spent 22 months in a federal prison camp in California. He has been permanently barred from securities trading and is currently performing three years of court-mandated, full-time community service. He is also guest lecturing at UCLA and has started a new enterprise, EEN Communications Network, to develop and market interactive educational software.

Sources: Francis X. Clines, "An Unfettered Milken Has Lessons to Teach," *New York Times*, October 16, 1993, pp. 1 – 2; "Doing good by being bad," *Economist*, July 24, 1993, p. 87 (a review of Robert Sobel, *Dangerous Dreamers*, New York: John Wiley & Sons, 1993); Amy Barrett, "Freedom Is No Picnic for Mike Milken," *Business Week*, December 13, 1993, p. 48.

lishes *CreditWatch*, a list of borrowers whose bond ratings it is reviewing for possible change.

investment quality bond
A bond rated Baa or higher by Moody's, or BBB or higher by Standard & Poor's.

speculative quality bond
A bond rated Ba or lower by Moody's, or BB or lower by Standard & Poor's.

Bonds rated Baa or higher by Moody's, or BBB or higher by Standard & Poor's, are classified as **investment quality**. A rating of Ba or lower from Moody's, or BB or lower from Standard & Poor's, classifies an issue as a **speculative quality bond**. The distinction is important because state laws forbid financial intermediaries that act as **fiduciaries** (institutions trusted to manage the investment portfolios of others) from buying speculative grade securities for the investors whose funds they manage. This prohibition sharply reduces the demand for speculative securities, depressing their prices, increasing their yields, and magnifying their illiquidity risk.

fiduciary

A financial institution trusted to manage the investment portfolios of others.

If a company chooses not to have its securities rated, the market assumes that the rating would not have been high enough to satisfy management. Junk bonds issued in the 1970s and 1980s were usually unrated, although the manipulations of a few greedy financiers turned some investment-grade bonds to junk.

Cost

An important consideration in any financing decision is the cost of the issued securities. The customary way to calculate cost is to compare out-of-pocket expenses with the amount of money raised.

Coupon Rate. Until 1983, corporate bonds were issued in two forms: registered bonds and coupon (bearer) bonds. A registered bond had a serial number and the trustee kept track of who owned it. Every six months, the trustee mailed an interest check to the investor. If the check was large enough, the trustee reported this income to the Internal Revenue Service.

A coupon bond, also known as a *bearer bond*, actually had coupons attached to it and stated "Pay to Bearer" on its face. A 25-year coupon bond had 50 coupons attached. Every six months when the interest payment fell due, the bondholder cut off a coupon and deposited it in a bank account like cash. The bank collected the interest payment without charging for this service, and it did not report such deposits to the Internal Revenue Service.

Holders of coupon bonds were legally required to report their interest as taxable income, but the IRS had no way of knowing who owned coupon bonds. Widespread failure to report coupon interest brought about legislation which made the issuance of bearer bonds illegal after January 1, 1983. At about the same time, as a result of the elimination of free clearinghouse services, banks were forced to pass the cost of coupon redemption (presently $3 per coupon at most commercial banks in New York) on to their depositors. This made the old coupon bonds expensive to own and encouraged their holders to request the companies that had issued them to exchange them for registered bonds.

The terminology remains, however. The coupon yield on a bond is the annual dollar interest payments divided by the $1,000 denomination of the bond. A registered bond issued on January 8 with a coupon yield of 8⅞ percent pays $88.75 interest per year. The trustee mails out two checks to the bondholder of record: one for $44.37 every July 8 and one for $44.38 every January 8. These payments are reported to the Internal Revenue Service on Form 1099.

flotation cost

The expenses incurred to sell a new security to the public.

Specific Cost. From the perspective of a company's financial manager, the cost of borrowing is mitigated by the fact that interest is a tax-deductible expense for the corporation. Further, the size of a bond issue is not necessarily the same as the amount of funds the company receives because it costs money to float a bond issue. This **flotation cost** includes a long list of expenses. The largest item on this list is the amount paid to the investment banker, whose services include:

1. Providing advice about the terms and timing of the issue to enhance its mar-

ketability to the public
2. Preparing the indenture and prospectus
3. Filing the SEC registration forms
4. Purchasing the security from the company and reselling it to the general public

Other expenses included in the flotation cost are legal fees, accounting fees, printing and engraving fees, the SEC registration fee, and the cost to have the bonds rated by Moody's and/or Standard & Poor's. In addition, the price of the bond may change as the issuing date approaches. If the coupon rate and terms become highly desirable in the eyes of the market, the bond will sell at a premium. If they become undesirable, it will sell at a discount. The investment banker's expertise keeps these price changes small, but cannot eliminate them completely.

The specific cost of a debt issue is therefore calculated as the after-tax interest cost on the net proceeds to the company. By convention, the cost of capital is denoted by k and a specific source of capital is indicated by a subscripted k. The cost of debt will be denoted by k_D, and if a company had two bond issues outstanding, their costs would be calculated separately and identified as k_{D1} and k_{D2}.

$$k_D = \frac{\$1{,}000(c)(1-T)}{\$B(1-f)} \quad (11.1)$$

where k_D = specific cost of debt
c = coupon rate
T = company's tax rate
f = flotation cost as a percentage of bond price
B = price of bond

❖ EXAMPLE 11.4

The Conservative Hatrack Company issues 50,000 callable 7 percent 30-year bonds at $992. It has a tax rate of 36 percent and incurs 2 percent of the price as flotation cost. What is the specific cost of this debt issue?

The specific cost of debt is:

$$k_D = \frac{\$1{,}000(.07)(1-.36)}{\$992(1-0.02)} = \frac{\$44.80}{\$972.16} = 0.0461\text{, or 4.61 percent}$$

This calculation was done on a per-bond basis. It could also have been calculated on a per-issue basis. The answer will be the same, but the calculation involves many zeroes:

$$k_D = \frac{\$50{,}000{,}000(0.07)(1-0.36)}{\$49{,}600{,}000(1-0.02)} = \frac{\$2{,}240{,}000}{\$48{,}608{,}000} = 0.0461\text{, or 4.61 percent}$$ ❖

Equation 11.1 divides the after-tax coupon payment by the net proceeds from the sale of the bond to arrive at the specific cost of debt. This way of measuring the cost of debt may not produce the same annual cost for all the years of a bond's life. In the last year, the numerator of the formula will include a capital gain (or loss) to the bond holder if the bond was originally sold at a discount (or a premium). This will produce a different cost of debt for the last year. If a bond was sold at face value, the specific cost obtained from Equation 11.1 will be the same for all years, including the last year.

Since Equation 11.1 cannot produce a constant annual cost (or annual average cost) of debt in all situations, it is not an adequate formula for calculating the specific cost of debt when determining the firm's overall cost of capital. The firm's overall cost of capital is used as the discount rate in capital budgeting and other financial decision making, and it should be an annual average rate calculated for the entire life of the debt. A more general formula is needed, and such a formula can be devised using the concept of *yield to maturity*, or YTM for short.

An investor in a coupon bond receives annual coupon payments and the principal at maturity in return for the price paid or the amount invested in the bond. If it is a zero-coupon bond, the only cash flow will be the return of the principal at maturity. The YTM is defined as the annualized rate of return (or the annual average rate of return) these cash flows will generate for the investor on the amount invested in a bond if it is held to maturity. It is the same as the internal rate of return discussed in Chapter 10 in the context of capital budgeting. In effect, the discount rate i equates the present value of all of the bond's cash flows with its price. To find the YTM, the bond valuation model discussed in Chapter 9 (see Equation 9.20) is solved for i.

$$V_B = C\left[\frac{1-1/(1+i)^n}{i}\right] + F\left[1/(1+i)^n\right]$$

As in the case of IRR, YTM is calculated by trial and error. It can be approximated by calculating the YTM as

$$YTM = \frac{\$1{,}000(c) + (\$1{,}000 - B)/n}{(\$1{,}000 + B)/2} \qquad (11.2)$$

where YTM = the yield to maturity

c = coupon rate

B = price of bond (cost to the investor)

n = number of years to maturity

Since YTM is the annualized rate of return on the price paid for a bond, it is also the bond investors' required rate of return.

❖ EXAMPLE 11.5

Calculate both the approximate and the exact YTM at the time of issue for the Conservative Hatrack Company's callable 7 percent 30-year bonds sold at $992. Assume annual coupon payments are made.

The approximate yield to maturity is:

$$\text{YTM} = \frac{\$1{,}000(0.07) + (\$1{,}000 - \$992)/30}{(\$1{,}000 + \$992)/2}$$
$$= \frac{\$70 + \$0.27}{\$996}$$
$$= .0705, \text{ or } 7.05 \text{ percent}$$

Using the HP12C, the @IRR function in Lotus 1-2-3, or trial and error, the exact yield to maturity is 0.070655, or 7.07 percent. ❖

Since the cash inflows to the bond investors are the cash outflows of the bond issuer, a general formula for computing the specific cost of debt can be obtained by adjusting YTM for the tax benefits and flotation cost.

$$\text{Specific Cost of Debt} = \text{YTM}(1-T)/(1-f) \qquad (11.3)$$

❖ EXAMPLE 11.6

Calculate the specific cost of debt for Conservative Hatrack Company's bond issue in Example 11.5 using its YTM.

$$\text{Specific cost of debt} = \text{YTM}(1-T)/(1-f)$$
$$= 0.0707(1 - 0.36)/(1 - 0.02)$$
$$= 0.04617 \text{ or } 4.62 \text{ percent}$$ ❖

From the investor's point of view, a more relevant concept of YTM is the one that also takes into consideration that

1. The investor can buy the bond at any time, not just when it is first sold to the public.
2. If an investor buys a bond in the secondary market, it will be necessary to pay a commission to a broker.

❖ EXAMPLE 11.7

An investor pays a $30 commission to a broker to buy one Conservative Hatrack Company callable 7 percent 30-year bond for $992. The bond was issued one year ago. What is the yield to maturity to the investor?

The after-commission cost is $992 + $30 = $1,022. (There is no commission charged for cashing in a bond at maturity.) The approximate yield to maturity is:

$$\text{YTM} = \frac{\$1{,}000(.07) + (\$1{,}000 - \$1{,}022)/29}{(\$1{,}000 + \$1{,}022)/2}$$

$$= \frac{\$70 - \$0.76}{\$1,011}$$

$$= 0.06849, \text{ or } 6.85 \text{ percent}$$ ❖

The market has developed other concepts of bond yield such as *current yield* and *yield to first call*. The current yield of a bond is obtained by dividing the coupon amount by the price of the bond. It is not equal to the bond's YTM unless the bond sells at its face value. Both current yield and YTM change with a change in the bond price.

Yield to first call is considered by investors instead of yield to maturity when *both* of the following conditions exist:

1. A bond has not been outstanding long enough for the company to be able to call it yet.
2. Interest rates are expected to fall so much that, when the bond can be called, it is likely to be called.

The approximate yield to first call can be calculated as:

$$\text{YTFC} = \frac{\$1{,}000(c) + (\$1{,}000 + P - B')/n'}{(\$1{,}000 + P + B')/2} \qquad \textbf{(11.4)}$$

where YTFC = yield to first call
c = coupon rate
P = call premium
B' = after-commission bond cost to the investor
n' = number of years until the bond can be called

❖ EXAMPLE 11.8

The Conservative Hatrack Company's callable 7 percent 30-year bonds, issued two years ago, are currently selling in the market for $950. The bond is callable five years after issue and the call premium is 7 percent. Interest rates are expected to fall significantly during the next three years. An investor buys a CHC bond and pays a broker $30 commission. What are the current yield and yield to first call?

The after-commission cost is $950 + $30 = $980. Current yield is:

$$\text{CY} = \frac{\$70}{\$980}$$

$$= 0.714 \text{ or } 7.14 \text{ percent}$$

If the bond is called in three years, the investor will receive $1,070.

The yield to first call is:

$$\text{YTFC} = \frac{\$1{,}000(.07) + (\$1{,}000 + \$70 - \$980)/3}{(\$1{,}000 + 70 + 980)/2}$$

$$= \frac{\$70 + \$30}{\$1025}$$

$$= .0976, \text{ or } 9.76 \text{ percent}$$ ❖

Access to International Debt Markets

foreign bond

A debt security sold in a foreign country with the face value, principal, and interest denominated in that country's currency.

Most free-market economies allow corporations to venture outside the bond markets of their home countries to raise debt capital. They can issue bonds in the capital markets of other countries that permit foreign debt issues. Such issues are called **foreign bonds**, and their face values, principals, and interest payments are denominated in the currencies of the countries where they are issued. Such a bond must offer an interest rate appropriate for that market. Corporations can thus save on interest expenses by choosing low-cost markets. If the prime rate is 6 percent in the United States and 3.5 percent in Japan, a U.S. corporate borrower can save a substantial amount of interest by issuing bonds in Japan. However, if the borrower has no cash inflows in Japanese yen, it will be exposed to exchange rate risk every time it must convert U.S. dollars to yen to make interest or principal payments.

The most important capital markets for foreign bond issues are Zurich, New York, Frankfurt, London, Amsterdam, and Tokyo. Bonds issued in foreign markets are often known by nicknames such as *Yankee bonds* in New York, *Samurai bonds* in Tokyo, *Rembrandt bonds* in Amsterdam, and *Bulldog bonds* in London. Foreign bonds can be issued in several countries simultaneously.

Governments usually regulate some aspects of foreign bonds issued or sold in their jurisdictions. They may require issuers to register foreign bonds before offering them for sale. They may also establish financial disclosure standards, and/or impose timing requirements and size limitations.

Corporations can also issue another type of bond denominated in a foreign currency and sold in foreign capital markets. Known as *Eurobonds*, these securities were discussed as potential investments in Chapter 4. Eurobonds differ from foreign bonds in that countries that allow firms to issue them do not require preoffering registrations, set disclosure standards, or regulate the amount and timing of such issues. Bonds denominated in U.S. dollars dominate the Eurobond market, accounting for more than half of outstanding Eurobonds. Other popular currencies in the Eurobond market include the Deutschemark, French franc, Canadian dollar, British pound, Japanese yen, and Dutch guilder.

Eurobonds are bearer bonds. They usually pay interest once a year, have few restrictive covenants, and are always callable. The interest on Eurobonds is free of all foreign taxes, but a U.S. citizen must pay U.S. federal and state income tax on the interest income. Eurobonds can be floating rate, zero-coupon, convertible, or mortgage-backed securities.

currency cocktail bond

A Eurobond denominated in a mixture of currencies.

Some Eurobonds are known as **currency cocktail bonds** because they are denominated in various mixtures of currencies. The mixture is a weighted average, and is frequently referred to as a *basket* of currencies. The most favored cocktail bonds are bonds denominated in European Currency Units (ECUs), a basket of the currencies of the European Community, and in Special Drawing Rights (SDRs), a basket of five major currencies. Denomination in multiple currencies protects the payments of interest and principal against the vagaries of changes in the value of a single currency. Cocktail bonds are particularly useful to corporations that have cash inflows in many currencies.

A corporation can also issue a security called a *dual-currency bond* by denominating the sale price and the coupon payments in one currency and the principal redemption value in another currency. This allows the firm to match the currency composition of its cash outflows and inflows. Suppose that a U.S. multinational with operations in Japan needs long-term funds in Japanese yen, and it expects to be able to pay back the debt in U.S. dollars. If long-term interest rates in the Japanese market are lower than U.S. rates, the firm can issue a dual-currency bond with the issue price and interest payable in yen and the principal redeemable in U.S. dollars. This benefits the firm in two ways. It pays a lower interest rate, and it avoids exposure to exchange risk when it redeems the bond. This bond will be particularly attractive to investors who think the exchange rate might move in their favor when the principal repayment comes due.

To illustrate the advantages of this bond, assume that when it is issued the interest rate in Japan is lower than the U.S. rate, and that the yen–dollar exchange rate is ¥100/$. The multinational issues a bond with a par value of ¥100,000 and sets the redemption value at $1,030. The exchange rate implied by the redemption price is then ¥100,000/$1,030, or ¥97.09/$. Now, if the exchange rate remains unchanged at ¥100/$, a Japanese investor will realize $1,030 × ¥100, or ¥103,000 when the bond matures. As long as the exchange rate is higher than the implied rate at maturity, the investor will get back more than the face value at maturity. If the exchange rate falls below ¥97.09/$, the investor will lose. The redemption liability of the firm, however, remains at $1,030, whatever happens to the exchange rate.

Dual-currency bonds became popular in the 1980s, and U.S. corporations such as GMAC, Sears, and Shearson/American Express have made use of this market. Further innovation in dual-currency issues led to the creation of reverse dual-currency bonds, with interest payable in a high-interest-rate currency and the principal payable in a low-interest-rate currency.

Swaps

Recent developments in world capital markets have resulted in the creation of two very useful financial instruments: currency swaps and interest rate swaps. Corporate borrowers have used swap markets to:

1. Create debt liabilities to suit their cash flow patterns
2. Reduce the cost of borrowing
3. Share the exchange rate risk associated with international borrowing

currency swap
An agreement negotiated between two borrowers who wish to make payments in a currency other than those that they borrowed.

Currency Swaps. Financial managers have developed various types of **currency swap** contracts. One common type is a contract between two borrowers who wish to make payments in a currency other than the one that they borrowed. Suppose that a U.S. company can get the best loan terms by issuing bonds in the U.S. market, but it has a Swiss subsidiary that generates a large cash flow in Swiss francs. At the same time, a Swiss company finds its cheapest available loan in Switzerland, but its U.S. subsidiary generates a large cash flow in U.S. dollars.

These two companies can avoid exchange risk by assuming each other's obligations to make interest payments and principal repayments. The U.S. company receives dollar payments from the U.S. subsidiary of the Swiss company and passes them along to its creditors. The Swiss company receives franc payments from the Swiss subsidiary of the U.S. company and passes them along to its creditors. If these two companies can find each other easily, they may negotiate such a contract between themselves. If not, they may rely on the services of a swap broker, usually a bank, to locate each other.

The World Bank has frequently used currency swaps. Its best-known transaction was with IBM as the counterparty and Salomon Brothers as the intermediary in 1981. In this deal, the World Bank swapped newly created, dollar-denominated debt obligations for IBM's already outstanding Swiss franc and Deutschemark debt obligations. To match the deal, the World Bank had to issue two separate Eurodollar bonds.

Interest Rate Swaps. This type of swap transaction involves an exchange between two borrowers of interest payment streams of different character, such as fixed rate payments for floating rate payments. Suppose that Company X can find only a fixed-rate loan at 8 percent, but it would really have preferred to borrow at a floating rate, which it perceives as having a comparative cost advantage. Company Y has an adjustable rate mortgage with an interest rate calculated as the one-year Treasury bill rate plus 3 percent. If Company Y would rather have a fixed rate, the two companies can negotiate an **interest rate swap** contract. Company X agrees to make Company Y's floating-rate payments when they are due, and Company Y agrees to make Company X's fixed-rate payments when they are due.

interest rate swap
An agreement between two borrowers to exchange interest payments.

When the interest rate swap market was developing, commercial banks played the role of intermediaries, locating and bringing together counterparties for a fee. In today's swap market, most large commercial banks act exclusively as counterparties to swap deals. Each borrower enters into a swap contract with a commercial bank. The bank, in turn, tries to make an offsetting swap contract with another borrower to avoid interest rate risk.

A swap arrangement between Companies X and Y, using a commercial bank as a counterparty, might work as follows:

1. Company X agrees to make payments to the commercial bank at the one-year Treasury bill rate plus 3.25 percent.
2. The commercial bank agrees to make the 8 percent, fixed-rate payments for Company X.
3. Company Y agrees to make payments to the commercial bank at a fixed rate of 8.5 percent.
4. The commercial bank agrees to make the mortgage payments at the one-year T-bill rate plus 3 percent for Company Y.

FOCUS ON CAREERS

CORPORATE SECURITIES ATTORNEY

Many professionals such as accountants, lawyers, psychologists, and health care specialists work for large corporations, or for firms that cater to such corporations, rather than in individual practice. Lawyers, for instance, can find employment in financial institutions that handle a myriad of issues from mortgage closings to defending the institutions against litigation. If the corporation is actively issuing new securities, then it needs specialized legal services. Very few corporations can afford to have a staff attorney who specializes in securities law, thus, they turn to large law firms that specialize in this practice.

The corporate securities attorney will participate in writing/reviewing bond indentures and securities prospectuses, negotiating privately placed securities contracts, and all other issues relating to corporate capitalization. Additionally, such attorneys are adept at handling the intricacies of mergers, acquisitions, leveraged buyouts, bankruptcies, and the creation of new corporations. To serve corporations with operations that are international in scope, additional expertise in international securities law is essential.

Securities law is a specialty within the legal profession and generally commands a very respectable salary. Compensation generally is in the area of several thousand dollars per hour and often includes opportunities to invest in new issues. Such attorneys live very well and may be able to retire very early.

cross-currency interest rate swap

A contract through which a company exchanges floating-rate financing in one currency for fixed-rate financing in another currency.

Company X has its floating-rate loan, Company Y has its fixed-rate mortgage, and the commercial bank has a 0.5 percent profit on the fixed-rate loan combined with a 0.25 percent profit on the variable-rate loan.

Interest rate swaps and currency swaps can be combined easily. A company can obtain floating-rate financing in one currency and exchange it for fixed-rate financing in another currency. This type of contract is known as **cross-currency interest-rate swap**. Unless arranged between the subsidiaries of a multinational, this type of contract almost always employs the services of a swap dealer.

PREFERRED STOCK

Preferred stock has some characteristics of debt and some characteristics of common stock. As a general rule, the dividend on preferred stock is fixed when the stock is issued; the issuer pays one-fourth of this constant amount to the stockholders of record every third month. Each time, the company's board of directors must meet and declare that the dividend should be paid. Once the board has declared a dividend, it is a legal obligation of the company and failure to pay it results in bankruptcy proceedings. If the board decides not to declare a dividend, however, the firm has no legal obligation to pay one.

The dividend yield on preferred stock is generally higher than the interest rate that the company would have to pay if it issued bonds. Further, income tax laws allow the firm to deduct the interest expense of bonds from taxable

FOCUS ON FINANCE

SPECIAL CASE OF PUBLIC UTILITIES

Electric utilities are investor-owned, regulated monopolies. The rates they can charge their customers, their allowed returns on equity, their capital spending, their acquisition of new subsidiaries or other expansion plans, their depreciation rates, their capital structures, and their costs of capital all require approval by the public utilities commissions of the states in which they operate. Over the years, these commissions have been almost unanimous in their opinions that utilities should have some preferred stock in their capital structures.

Water utilities are in a similar situation. Although most suppliers of water are municipal systems, many local government officials have recently become anxious to get out of the water supply business. They face enormous upgrading costs to comply with the federal Clean Water Act and the Safe Drinking Water Act. This recent trend to privatization in the industry has been held back by the necessity of investor-owned water utilities to obtain approval of every significant decision they make.

Preferred stock is almost always more expensive than debt. In terms of the specific costs, $k_P > k_D$. This tends to restrain unregulated companies from issuing preferred stock. As shown in the table below, however, almost all electric and water utilities have some preferred stock in their capital structures. On average, only one out of five companies in 18 selected nonregulated industries has chosen to issue preferred stock.

Industry	Number of Companies	Companies with Preferred Stock: Number	Companies with Preferred Stock: Percentage
Electric utilities (regulated)	95	93	97.9%
Water utilities (regulated)	7	6	85.7
Natural gas utilities (partially regulated)	47	31	66.0
Paper and forest products	30	13	43.3
Telecommunications	25	10	40.0
Petroleum and oil-field services	64	25	39.1
Building materials	21	7	33.3
Diversified companies	49	14	28.6
Apparel, textiles and shoes	31	8	25.8
Aerospace/defense	38	9	23.7
Chemicals	59	13	22.0
Food, beverages and groceries	84	18	21.4
Machinery and machine tools	52	10	19.2
Precision instruments	22	4	18.2
Retail stores	89	14	17.5
Publishing and newspapers	32	5	15.6
Medical supplies and drugs	69	10	14.5
Computers, peripherals, software, and semiconductors	82	11	13.4
Electronics and electrical equipment	55	7	12.7
Recreation, hotels, and gaming	35	4	11.4
Office equipment and supplies, industrial services	46	4	8.7
Total of nonregulated companies	893	186	20.8

income, but those laws prohibit the deduction of dividend payments. These two facts cause preferred stock to be much more expensive than bonds. Consequently, corporations have raised far more money by selling bonds than by selling preferred stock.

cumulative preferred stock
Preferred stock on which the firm owes an undeclared dividend to the stockholders until it is declared and paid.

noncumulative preferred stock
Preferred stock on which the firm owes an undeclared dividend to the stockholders for one year, after which it is lost forever.

Preferred stock can be cumulative or noncumulative. On **cumulative preferred stock**, the firm owes an undeclared dividend to the stockholders until it is declared and paid. Undeclared dividends on **noncumulative preferred stock** are lost after one year. The board does feel pressure to declare dividends. It can pay no dividends on common stock as long as the firm owes any undeclared dividends on preferred stock.

If a company has a choice between issuing cumulative or noncumulative preferred stock, it will usually choose the former because its dividend rate is lower. Some companies have tried issuing preferred stock without specifying a type. They hoped to get the lower dividend rate of cumulative preferred without losing the right to erase undeclared dividends after one year. The courts have ruled, however, that if the type is not stated, the stock is cumulative.

Because the dividend is fixed, the market price of preferred stock behaves like the market price of bonds. It reacts to changes in interest rates, rising when they fall and vice versa.

participating preferred stock
Stock that entitled preferred stockholders to receive larger dividends in an exceptionally profitable year.

Historically, some companies have issued **participating preferred stock**. If the company were to enjoy an exceptionally profitable year, the preferred stockholders were entitled to participate in this good fortune by receiving a larger dividend. The indenture for a participating preferred issue specified several special conditions:

1. It carefully defined the determinants of an exceptionally profitable year.
2. It limited the amount of any bonus dividend.
3. It required that the common stockholders be paid an equivalent bonus.

After World War II, labor union negotiators who understood accounting demanded that employees also benefit from "exceptionally profitable years" by receiving higher salaries or better fringe benefits. These became permanent arrangements, not one-year bonuses. Corporate executives responded by adjusting bookkeeping methods to avoid displays of exceptional profits, eliminating the advantages of participating preferred stock. No such stock has been issued in recent years.

Substantial fluctuations in interest rates over the last 30 years have induced some companies to issue adjustable-rate preferred stock. The indenture for such an issue defines the relationship between preferred dividends and some specific interest rate. This linkage effectively stabilizes the market price of preferred stock. Adjustable-rate preferred stock has met a more favorable reception than adjustable-rate bonds by investors.

Maturity

Preferred stock has no maturity date. It remains outstanding as long as the company operates unless management decides to buy it back. A preferred stock issue may have a call feature that makes it analogous to a callable bond. Preferred stock can be made callable immediately, after three years, or after five years. The call premium usually amounts to one year's dividend payments, and this amount declines over time.

Accounting rules mandate no sinking fund for preferred stock because the company is not obligated to pay it off or buy it back. The stock can have a real sinking fund, however, if management wishes to retire it gradually. This sinking fund works the same way as a sinking fund on a bond, but it can leave no balloon payment.

If preferred stock is not callable and has no sinking fund, it can be retired only by means of a market repurchase and a tender offer. Again, a two-tiered tender offer is usually made as a protection against holdouts.

Historically, the boards of a few companies with cumulative preferred stock outstanding have not declared dividends for a decade or more. The cash drain on such a company to rectify the situation would have been unbearable. To solve the problem, these companies have made tender offers to preferred stockholders that combined cash with common stock. Suppose that a company's preferred stock is worth $100 per share and it has accumulated undeclared dividends of $72 per share. The company might offer preferred stockholders a combination of cash and common stock worth $185. The incentives for the preferred stockholders to accept this tender offer would be the $13 profit, plus the realization that if they did not accept the offer, the undeclared dividends would just keep accumulating.

Claim on Assets

In case of bankruptcy, all creditors must be paid in full before the preferred stockholders can receive anything. If the proceeds from liquidation of the company's assets exceed the creditors' claims, the preferred stockholders are entitled to the par value of their stock, any surplus amount that the company received when it initially sold the stock, and all undeclared dividends it owed. If the firm has declared a dividend but not paid it, the stockholders' claim for that amount is treated as a general creditor's claim. While there are no senior and subordinated issues of preferred stock, a corporation may issue different classes of preferred stock. Each class would have a unique combination of restrictive covenants.

Quality

Preferred stock may be issued with a long list of restrictive covenants, just like bonds. The universal prohibition against any reduction of the existing accumulated retained earnings, however, is replaced with a covenant meant to protect preferred stockholders. This covenant usually states that if the board of directors fails to declare a dividend for six consecutive quarters, the preferred stockholders have the right to elect two members of the board. These two directors are an addition to the normal number of directors, and they serve until the company is no longer in arrears on preferred dividends. These two directors are supposed to encourage the board to consider the effects of company decisions on the preferred stockholders, but their influence varies inversely with the original size of the board.

Moody's and Standard & Poor's rate preferred stock with the same alphanumeric system they use for bonds, if the company is willing to pay for the service. These agencies usually rate a company's preferred stock one step lower than its outstanding senior debentures.

Cost

The dividend yield on preferred stock is the equivalent of the coupon rate on bonds. If a share of stock costs $40 and pays a $4 annual dividend, the yield is $4/$40, or 10 percent. Because the preferred dividend is a perpetuity, this yield is also the equivalent compound rate.

Because preferred dividends are not tax deductible for the issuer, the specific cost of capital for preferred stock is calculated as:

$$k_p = D/(S - F) \tag{11.5}$$

where k_p = specific cost of preferred stock
D = annual dividend in dollars
S = initial selling price of the stock
F = flotation cost per share

❖ EXAMPLE 11.8

Montague Mining Company issues $50-par preferred stock that promises to pay a $4 dividend per share. If the stock sells for $51 and the flotation cost is $3 per share, what is the specific cost?

$$k_p = \$4/(\$51 - \$3)$$
$$= \$4/\$48$$
$$= 0.833\text{, or } 8.33 \text{ percent}$$ ❖

CONVERTIBLE SECURITIES

A company can build a conversion feature into bond and preferred stock issues. This feature allows investors, at their discretion, to convert their securities into specified numbers of shares of the company's common stock. The bonds of a multinational's subsidiary may be convertible into the common shares of the parent company.

Convertible Bonds

Companies usually issue convertible bonds when they plan to invest the funds in profitable assets that will not enhance earnings in the near future. They do not wish to be saddled with long-term debt for decades, nor do they wish to dilute earnings per share by issuing common stock immediately. If the number of outstanding shares of common stock were to increase, without a proportionate rise in net income after taxes, the company's earnings per share would decline. This dilution of earnings per share would depress the stock price.

Convertible bonds are a compromise. The company raises the necessary funds by issuing relatively inexpensive debt. Later, as the new assets begin to generate increased after-tax income, the bonds can be exchanged for common stock without reducing earnings per share and depressing the market price of the stock. In theory, this compromise works.

conversion ratio
The number of shares of common stock for which one convertible bond can be exchanged.

conversion price
The price of a share of common stock, calculated as the face value of a convertible bond divided by the conversion ratio.

Suppose that Parks Entertainment Company's common stock is selling for $22 a share. In order to expand, Parks issues bonds, each of which can be converted into 40 shares of common stock. This is known as the **conversion ratio**. It means that the **conversion price** of the stock is $1,000/40, or $25 per share. The conversion price is usually set 10 to 15 percent higher than the stock's current market price. If Parks chooses a larger spread, it runs the risk of being perceived as overly optimistic. The market will ignore the conversion feature if it does not expect the conversion price in a reasonable period of time. If Parks chooses a smaller spread, the market price may exceed the conversion price before the new assets have had a chance to increase earnings, causing the higher market price to be unstable.

A convertible bond buyer would not immediately convert the bond into stock. Conversion would reduce the value of the investment from $1,000 to $22 × 40, or $880, generating an immediate loss of $120. Rather, the investor waits for the stock price to rise above $25 per share. If, after a few years, Parks' earnings rise and the stock price increases to $27, the $1,000 bond can be converted into common stock worth $27× 40, or $1,080. The investor could then realize a profit of $80 by converting the bond and selling the stock. Because convertible bonds offer this potential for capital gains, convertibles pay lower interest rates than straight (nonconvertible) bonds.

In practice, as long as the market price of the common stock is below the conversion price, the market will value the convertible bond like a straight bond. Its market price will fall when interest rates rise, and it will rise when interest rates decline. When the market price of the common stock is above the conversion price, however, the relationship between the market price of the convertible bond and interest rates ends. The market price of Parks' convertible bond will then be 40 times the market price of the common stock. If the stock price rises by $1, the bond price will rise by $40. There is no ceiling on the market price of the bond.

Because of this price mechanism, the bondholders will negate the compromise inherent in the convertible bond. They will not convert it into stock until the day before it matures for several reasons:

1. The coupon rate on the bond is usually higher than the dividend yield on the common stock.
2. Both coupon and dividend payments are taxed at the same rate, so the bonds will give the investor more after-tax income.

FOCUS ON FINANCE

Bausch & Lomb: Soft Lens and Convertibles

When Wall Street realized that Bausch & Lomb had invented a soft contact lens that was both successful and without competition, it quadrupled the value of the company's stock during 1971. At that time, Bausch & Lomb had two convertible debentures outstanding. Both securities broke all previous records for price increases.

One issue was a convertible subordinated debenture rated Baa that paid 4.5 percent interest. The firm had sold $8,542,600 of these bonds on June 1, 1959 with a maturity date of June 1, 1979. They were convertible into common stock at $18 per share; one $1,000 bond could be converted into 55 shares of stock plus $10 cash. This conversion ratio was fully protected against dilution; after the stock split 2-for-1 in 1966, a bond could be converted into 111 shares of stock (at $9 per share) plus $1. The bond had a sinking fund that forced some conversions every year, and so it was fully converted/retired by May 31, 1973.

The other issue was a convertible subordinated debenture also rated Baa that paid 4.75 percent interest. The firm had sold $7,038,600 of these bonds on June 28, 1960 with a maturity date of July 1, 1980. They were convertible into common stock at $26.75 per share; one $1,000 bond could be converted into 37 shares of stock plus $10.75 cash. This ratio was also fully protected against dilution. After the 2-for-1 split, a bond could be converted into 74 shares of stock (at $13.375 per share) plus $10.75 cash. The bond had a sinking fund that forced some conversions every year, and so it was fully converted/retired by June 30, 1973.

	Common Stock Price		4.5 Percent Debenture Price		4.75 Percent Debenture Price	
	Low	High	Low	High	Low	High
1960	$70.00	$ 71.00	$1,080.00	$ 1,600.00	$ 980.00	$1,140.00
1961	70.00	75.50	1,130.00	1,320.00	1,040.00	1,125.00
1962	75.00	78.50	980.00	1,175.00	990.00	1,100.00
1963	78.00	81.00	1,040.00	1,185.00	1,010.00	1,100.00
1964	81.00	82.00	1,110.00	1,295.00	1,040.00	1,120.00
1965	82.00	140.00	1,230.00	1,880.00	1,041.00	1,300.00
1966[a]	66.38	123.00	1,770.00	3,379.00	1,160.00	2,254.00
1967	109.75	163.50	3,000.00	4,361.00	1,900.00	2,910.00
1968	85.50	150.00	1,930.00	4,330.00	1,700.00	2,800.00
1969	102.00	163.25	2,820.00	4,380.00	1,070.00	2,920.00
1970	54.25	159.50	1,550.00	3,940.00	1,040.00	2,630.00
1971	92.75	382.50	2,576.00	10,625.00	1,750.00	7,218.00
1972[b]	84.50	389.50	2,730.00	10,100.00	1,850.00	7,000.00

[a]Stock split 2-for-1 on April 8, 1966. Subsequent stock prices are quoted for two postsplit shares.
[b]Stock split 2-for-1 on May 26, 1972. Stock price quoted for 1972 high is for two presplit shares;.the quote for the 1972 low is for four postsplit shares.

3. The market price of the bond will equal the conversion ratio times the market price of the stock, so the investor will get the same capital gain from either security.
4. The commission on a bond transaction is usually less than the commission on a common stock transaction involving an equivalent dollar amount, so the investor will keep more of the capital gain by selling bonds instead of stock.

To make a convertible bond work the way it is supposed to work in theory, the company must supplement the conversion feature in one of two ways. It can either make the bond callable and convertible, or it can set up a varying conversion ratio.

If a bond is both callable and convertible, the company can force the bondholders to convert. Suppose that when Parks Entertainment Company's stock reaches $30 a share in the market, the call premium on the bond is 9 percent. If Parks calls the bond, its market price should fall on the announcement date from $30 × 40, or $1,200, to $1,090, and remain at approximately that figure until the effective date. During that interval, the only way the investor can recover $1,200 is by converting the bond into stock and selling the stock. On the effective date, the bondholder is entitled to $1,090 and there is no way to recoup the lost $110.

The terms of a bond with a varying conversion ratio may state that Parks' bond can be converted into 40 shares of stock during the first five years, into 39 shares during the next five years, and into 38 shares from the eleventh year until maturity. Determined (or ignorant) investors may hold onto the bond until maturity, sacrificing a share or two as time passes. If the market price of the stock is higher than the conversion price, however, a substantial proportion of the bondholders will convert before the end of the fifth year. Most of the remaining bondholders will convert before the end of the tenth year. At least one investor will always continue to hold the bond, no matter how many shares will be lost.

If a company wants to completely eliminate a convertible bond issue, it must make the bond callable. If a company is satisfied with a significant reduction in the number of bonds outstanding, it can set up a varying conversion ratio. A company may want to postpone making such a decision for a few years by incorporating both alternatives into one bond. This does not increase the bond's market value.

Convertible Preferred Stock

Everything discussed above about the conversion feature of a bond applies to preferred stock, as well, with one exception. Convertible preferred stock is issued when a nonfinancial corporation wants to take over another company by buying most or all of its outstanding common stock. The acquirer could offer the shareholders of the target company four things in exchange for their common stock:

1. *Cash.* The acquirer would have to make an offer that is higher than the current market price. It may not have this much cash.
2. *The acquiring company's bonds.* The shareholders of the target company are

not likely to be willing to exchange their ownership status for creditor status, even if the exchange is profitable for them.

3. *The acquiring company's common stock.* The acquisition may take some time to digest, so the acquirer's profits may not increase immediately. Issuing additional shares to finance the acquisition would therefore only dilute the acquirer's earnings per share.
4. *The acquiring company's convertible preferred stock.* There are two elements to consider here:
   (a) If conditions are right, the fixed dividend on the acquirer's preferred stock will be greater than the fluctuating dividend on the target company's common stock, so the target company's shareholders can increase their income by accepting the exchange offer.
   (b) If the target company can be absorbed profitably, the market price of the acquiring company will eventually exceed the conversion price, giving the target shareholders a capital gain whether they sell the preferred stock or convert it to common.

A company that issues convertible preferred stock has the same decision to make as a company that issues convertible bonds. Making the preferred stock callable guarantees the issuing company that it can eliminate the preferred stock at some future time. A varying conversion ratio will eventually reduce the number of outstanding preferred shares, but probably without ever eliminating the issue completely.

One major advantage of issuing convertible securities is diminished by the customary practices of financial analysts and accountants. Convertible securities avoid the immediate dilution of earnings per share that would occur if the firm were to issue common stock instead. Analysts and accountants have learned to calculate the potential dilution that new convertibles represent. The calculation of earnings per share divides net income after taxes by the number of shares of common stock outstanding. The calculation of **fully diluted earnings per share** divides post-conversion net income after taxes by the number of shares of common stock that would be outstanding if every security that could be converted into common stock were actually converted and every option outstanding were exercised. As the discrepancy between earnings per share and fully diluted earnings per share rises, analysts see more risk in the company's common stock.

fully diluted earnings per share
Net income after taxes divided by the number of shares of common stock that would be outstanding after conversion of every security that could be converted into common stock.

SUMMARY

Companies can borrow long-term funds by issuing bonds that mature in 20, 25, or 30 years, or even longer. The issuer can make provisions to retire the bonds early by incorporating a call feature, a sinking fund feature, or a put feature into the indenture. Lacking these provisions, the company has to make a tender offer to buy back the bonds.

The debt may be unsecured, in the form of senior or subordinate debentures, or secured, in the form of first or second mortgage bonds. These distinctions affect the interest rate because they determine the priority of the lenders' claims in case the borrower goes bankrupt. Detailed rules govern the distribution of proceeds from liquidated assets.

Restrictive covenants in a bond indenture are limitations on the company's actions that management agrees to observe as long as the bonds are outstanding. Common covenants affect a company's dividend payout, borrowing ability, financial condition, and ability to dispose of assets. These covenants, coupled with analysis of the company's current financial condition and future prospects, determine the rating that Moody's and Standard & Poor's assign to the company's bonds. A lower rating forces the issuer to pay a higher interest rate.

The cost of bonds can be calculated in several ways. The coupon rate compares the dollars of interest paid to the face value of the bond. The specific cost of debt compares the after-tax cash flows to the net proceeds from the sale of the bond. The approximate yield to maturity compares a bond's annual interest and eventual capital gain or loss to its average investment value. The yield to first call takes the same approach as the approximate YTM, but assumes that the issuer will call the bond as soon as it can.

A corporate borrower can sell bonds at home or abroad. A bond sold outside the home country of the borrower is called a *foreign bond.* Its face value, principal, and interest are denominated in the currency of the country where it is issued. Eurobonds are locally tax-free bearer bonds. They usually pay interest once a year and have few restrictive covenants; they are always callable. A Eurobond can be denominated in one or two currencies, or in a weighted average of several currencies.

If a company borrows money at a fixed rate, but prefers a floating rate, it can swap interest payments with a company that has borrowed money at a floating rate, but prefers a fixed rate. Two borrowers who wish to make payments in currencies other than those they borrowed can also exchange their obligations. These transactions may or may not require the expertise of a swap dealer.

Preferred stock is a hybrid security that has some characteristics of both debt and common stock. Preferred dividend payments are generally fixed, and accrue if undeclared. Preferred stock has no maturity date, but it can have a call feature or a sinking fund. In case of bankruptcy, all creditors must be paid in full before the preferred stockholders can claim their paid-in capital. Preferred stock can have restrictive covenants and can be rated by Moody's and Standard & Poor's with the same alphanumeric system these agencies use for bonds.

Because dividends are not a tax-deductible expense, the cost of preferred compares the dividend either to the current preferred stock price (to calculate the yield) or to the proceeds from the original sale (to get the specific cost).

Issuers can make bonds and preferred stock convertible into common stock. This feature terminates or minimizes the long-term, fixed cash outflow of bonds while avoiding the immediate dilution of earnings per share that a common stock issue would cause. A company can design a convertible security with a varying conversion ratio to encourage conversion, or with a call feature to force conversion. Convertible bonds are issued to acquire assets that will take a few years to boost earnings. Convertible preferred stock is issued to acquire other companies.

Key Terms

announcement date of a call
baby bond
chattel mortgage bond
conversion price
conversion ratio
cross-currency interest rate swap
cumulative preferred stock
currency cocktail bond
currency swap
effective call date
fiduciary
fixed sinking fund
flotation cost
foreign bond
fully diluted earnings per share
interest rate swap
investment quality bond
mortgage bond
negative pledge clause
noncumulative preferred stock
participating preferred stock
private placement
prospectus
public offering
restrictive covenant
senior debenture
speculative quality bond
subordinate debenture
tender offer
trustee
two-tiered tender offer
variable-rate bond
variable sinking fund

Self-Study Questions

1. What is a call feature?
2. Explain what happens to the market price of a bond when a company announces that it is calling the bond.
3. What is a put bond?
4. List three differences between senior and subordinated debentures.
5. What is the universal restrictive covenant for bonds?
6. Bonds rated BBB and BB differ in quality, as do bonds rated AAA and AA. Are these two differences equally significant?
7. Name six factors that affect a company's specific cost of debt.
8. Why might a U.S. corporation issue a foreign bond?
9. What is an interest rate swap?
10. What is the universal restrictive covenant for preferred stock?

Self-Test Problems

1. A company goes bankrupt. The proceeds from the liquidation of mortgaged assets pay off the mortgage holders in full, leaving \$1 million more. The liquidation of other assets produces \$8 million. If the firm owes general creditors \$5 million, and senior and subordinated debentures remain outstanding worth \$6 million each, how much do the subordinated debenture holders get?
2. When Ballistic Airlines went bankrupt, its balance sheet showed that it had (in millions of dollars):

ASSETS		LIABILITIES AND EQUITY	
Mortgaged assets	$100	General creditors	$20
Other assets	100	First mortgage	60
		Second mortgage	10
		Senior debenture	50
		Subordinated debenture	10
		Total equity	50
Total assets	$200	Total capital	$200

After liquidation of Ballistic's assets and settlement of the prior claims, the proceeds of the other assets were $70 million and the proceeds of the mortgaged assets were $65 million. How was the $135 million distributed?

3. The Dandy Denture Company issues $80 million in callable, 6 percent, 20-year bonds at $990 per bond. It has a tax rate of 30 percent and incurs a 2 percent after-tax flotation cost. Calculate the approximate YTM, the exact YTM, and the specific cost of debt.
4. Quartz Clock Co. issues $250 million in callable, 9 percent, 25-year bonds. It has a 40 percent tax rate. The flotation costs are 5 percent and the bonds sell for $975 each. Calculate the approximate YTM, the exact YTM, and the specific cost of debt.
5. Bluejay Books, Inc. has callable 8.5 percent 20-year bonds currently selling in the market for $1,050. They were issued four years ago and are callable five years after issue. The call premium the first year is 8.5 percent. Interest rates are expected to fall significantly during the next two years. If an investor buys a Bluejay bond and pays the broker a $9 commission, what is the investment's yield to first call?
6. The Last National Bank of Memphis has $50 million in callable 12 percent bonds outstanding. They were issued last year and are callable five years after issue. The call premium starts at 12 percent and declines annually. Interest rates are expected to fall significantly. If an investor buys one of these bonds for $950 now and pays a broker a $10 commission, what is the investment's yield to first call?
7. Bloopsie Cola issues $100-par preferred stock that promises to pay a $7.50 dividend per share. If the stock sells for $102 and the flotation cost is $5 per share, what is the specific cost?
8. The Hol-D-Fone Co. issues $4.75 no-par preferred stock that nets the company $48.50 after flotation costs. What is the specific cost of the stock?
9. If a corporate bond can be converted into 16 shares of common stock, what is the conversion price of the stock?
10. A bond can be converted into common stock at $20 per share. If the market price of the common stock has risen to $32, what is the market price of the bond?

Discussion Questions

1. Why would a company make a bond callable?
2. How can a call feature work to the disadvantage of an investor?
3. Why would a sinking fund improve a bond issue?
4. Why does the sinking fund phrase "in cash or in bonds" work as an advantage to both the company and the bondholders?
5. What phenomenon led to the concept of two-tiered tender offers?
6. Why might a tender offer fail?
7. Explain the priorities of debt securities in bankruptcy.
8. Why do companies issue subordinated debentures?
9. Why would bondholders favor a restrictive covenant establishing a floor under net working capital?
10. Explain one bond-specific risk and one company-specific risk.
11. Explain the difference between investment quality and speculative quality bonds.
12. Under what conditions would investors focus on yield to first call?
13. If the prime rate in Germany is 8 percent when the U.S. prime rate is 6 percent, in which country would companies try to issue foreign bonds?
14. When would a company want to engage in a cross-currency interest rate swap?
15. Why would the services of a swap dealer be unnecessary if two subsidiaries of the same company wanted to do a currency swap?
16. What characteristics do bonds and preferred stock issues have in common? How are they different?
17. Why does cumulative preferred stock pay a lower dividend than noncumulative preferred stock?
18. If a company goes bankrupt without paying a declared dividend, how are the stockholders' claims treated?
19. Why would adjustable-rate preferred stock have a relatively stable market price?
20. If a convertible bond is not callable and has a fixed conversion ratio, why would investors wait until the day before it matures to convert it?

Problems

1. A company with no second mortgages or subordinate debentures outstanding goes bankrupt. The proceeds from the liquidation of mortgaged assets are distributed to the mortgage holders, leaving \$100 million of their claims unsatisfied. The liquidation of the company's other assets produces \$500 million. If the firm owes \$300 million to general creditors and \$400 million to debenture holders, how is the \$500 million distributed?
2. Tropical Avians, Inc. goes bankrupt when its balance sheet shows the following amounts (in millions of dollars):

ASSETS		LIABILITIES AND EQUITY	
Mortgaged assets	$10	General creditors	$22
Other assets	90	First mortgage	6
		Second mortgage	2
		Senior debenture	40
		Subordinated debenture	10
		Total equity	20
Total assets	$100	Total capital	$100

After the assets are liquidated and the prior claims are paid, the court has $5.0 million from the mortgaged assets and $42.5 million from the other assets. How does it distribute this $47.5 million?

3. Nationwide Florists, Inc. issues an 11 percent, 25-year bond at $998 per bond and a 4.5 percent flotation cost. Nationwide's tax rate is 35 percent. What are the bond's approximate YTM, exact YTM, and specific cost?
4. The Kamanur Corp. issues $350 million in 9⅜ percent, 30-year bonds. The issue sells at $1,005, less a 2.8 percent flotation cost. Kamanur's tax rate is 34 percent. What is the bond's approximate YTM, exact YTM, and specific cost?
5. An investor buys an 8 percent, one-year-old bond for $940. It is callable three years after issue with an 8 percent premium. If interest rates are expected to decline substantially over the next few years, what is the bond's yield to first call?
6. A 7 percent bond has been outstanding for two years, and it now sells for $1,100. It is callable five years after issue with a 7 percent premium. If interest rates are expected to decline substantially over the next few years, what is the bond's yield to first call?
7. The Silver Rose Company has an issue of preferred stock outstanding that pays an annual dividend of $6.50. If the stock sold to net the company $52 per share, what was its specific cost?
8. The Quadratic Company has an issue of preferred stock outstanding that pays an annual dividend of $14. If the stock sold for $100 per share before deducting a flotation cost of $4 per share, what was its specific cost?
9. If a corporate bond can be converted into common stock at $40 per share, what is its conversion ratio?
10. A corporate bond can be converted into common stock at $50 per share. If the market price of the common stock has risen to $53, what is the market price of the bond?

Topics for Further Research

1. Find ten companies in Moody's *Industrial Manual* with publicly held bonds. Be sure they do not all have the same rating. Determine whether or not these bonds are callable. If they are, compare the terms of the call features.
2. Select two companies from Moody's *Industrial Manual* and two companies from Moody's *Utilities Manual* with outstanding preferred stock. Compare the terms of the issues. Do they share any restrictive covenants? Are the

public utility preferred stocks noticeably different from the industrial preferred stocks?

3. Select a convertible bond that is selling for more than $1,000 because the market price of the issuer's common stock is greater than the conversion price. Compare the daily closing price of the bond with the daily closing price of the stock for ten trading days. How close is the relationship between the two security prices?

Answers to Self-Test Problems

1.

$$\begin{aligned}
\text{Total claims} &= \$5{,}000{,}000 + \$6{,}000{,}000 + \$6{,}000{,}000 \\
&= \$17{,}000{,}000 \\
\text{Total available} &= \$1{,}000{,}000 + \$8{,}000{,}000 \\
&= \$9{,}000{,}000 \\
\text{Distribution percentage} &= \$9{,}000{,}000/\$17{,}000{,}000 \\
&= 0.5294, \text{ or } 52.94 \text{ cents per dollar} \\
\text{Distributed to general creditors} &= \$5{,}000{,}000 \times 0.5294 \\
&= \$2{,}647{,}060 \\
\text{Distributed to debenture holders} &= \$12{,}000{,}000 \times 0.5294 \\
&= \$6{,}352{,}940 \\
\text{Distributed to senior debenture holders} &= \$6{,}000{,}000 \\
\text{Distributed to subordinate debenture holders} &= \$352{,}940
\end{aligned}$$

2. The proceeds of the mortgaged assets were distributed $60 million to the first-mortgage holders and $5 million to the second-mortgage holders.

$$\begin{aligned}
\text{Remaining claims} &= \$20{,}000{,}000 + \$5{,}000{,}000 + \$50{,}000{,}000 \\
&\quad + \$10{,}000{,}000 \\
&= \$85{,}000{,}000 \\
\text{Total available} &= \$70{,}000{,}000 \\
\text{Distribution percentage} &= \$70{,}000{,}000/\$85{,}000{,}000 \\
&= 0.8235, \text{ or } 82.35 \text{ cents per dollar} \\
\text{Distributed to general creditors} &= \$20{,}000{,}000 \times 0.8235 \\
&= \$16{,}470{,}000 \\
\text{Distributed to second-mortgage holders} &= \$5{,}000{,}000 \times 0.8235 \\
&= \$4{,}120{,}000 \\
\text{Distributed to debenture holders} &= \$60{,}000{,}000 \times 0.8235 \\
&= \$49{,}410{,}000 \text{ (all to senior debenture holders)} \\
\text{Distributed to subordinate debenture holders} &= \$0
\end{aligned}$$

3. The approximate YTM is:

$$\text{YTM} = \frac{\$1{,}000(0.06) + (\$1{,}000 - \$990)/20}{(\$1{,}000 + \$990)/2}$$

$$= \frac{\$60.00 + \$0.50}{\$995}$$
$$= 0.06080, \text{ or } 6.09 \text{ percent}$$

The exact YTM is 0.06087, or 6.09 percent.
The specific cost of debt is:

$$k_D = 0.06087(1 - 0.3)/(1 - 0.02)$$
$$= 0.04348, \text{ or } 4.35 \text{ percent}$$

4. The approximate YTM is:

$$\text{YTM} = \frac{\$1{,}000(0.09) + (\$1{,}000 - \$975)/25}{(\$1{,}000 + \$975)/2}$$
$$= \frac{\$90 + \$1}{\$987.50}$$
$$= 0.09215, \text{ or } 9.22 \text{ percent}$$

The exact YTM is 0.092598, or 9.26 percent.
The specific cost of debt is:

$$k_D = 0.092598(1 - 0.4)/(1 - 0.05)$$
$$= 0.05848, \text{ or } 5.85 \text{ percent}$$

5.
$$YTFC = \frac{\$85 - (\$1{,}059 - \$1{,}085)/1}{(\$1{,}059 + \$1{,}085)/2}$$
$$= \$111/\$1{,}072$$
$$= 0.1035, \text{ or } 10.35 \text{ percent}$$

6.
$$YTFC = \frac{\$120 - (\$960 - \$1{,}120)/4}{(\$960 + \$1{,}120)/2}$$
$$= \$160/\$1{,}040$$
$$= 0.1538, \text{ or } 15.38 \text{ percent}$$

7.
$$k_P = \$7.50/(\$102.00 - \$5.00)$$
$$= \$7.50/\$97.00$$
$$= 0.0773, \text{ or } 7.73 \text{ percent}$$

8.
$$k_P = \$4.75/\$48.50$$
$$= 0.0979, \text{ or } 9.79 \text{ percent}$$

9. $\$1{,}000.00/16 = \$62.50$

10. $\$1{,}000.00/\$20 = 50$ shares
$50 \times \$32 = \$1{,}600$, the market price of the bond

CHAPTER 12

Leases, Common Stock, and Retained Earnings as Long-Term Sources of Funds

LEARNING OBJECTIVES

This chapter examines three additional sources of long-term funds for corporations. At the conclusion of this chapter, the reader should be able to:

1. *Justify leasing as a source of financing*
2. *Calculate the cost of a lease*
3. *Determine whether to lease a desirable asset or purchase it with borrowed funds*
4. *Define the characteristics of common stock*
5. *Outline the rights of a common stockholder*
6. *Calculate a company's cost of common stock*
7. *Explain the various uses of treasury stock*

In addition to issuing bonds and preferred stock, as discussed in Chapter 11, corporations can also finance new assets by leasing them, by selling common stock, or by retaining profits instead of paying them out in the form of dividends.

Financial managers must understand the different types of leases. They must also know how to calculate the cost of a lease, and how to decide whether to lease an asset or buy it.

Investors in common stock are the owners of the company that issues the stock. Policy decisions that affect the value of the stock are made by a company's board of directors, whose members are elected by the stockholders. Financial managers implement many of the board's policy decisions. They must analyze the possible consequences of the board's decisions, as well as their own. They must also be able to calculate the cost of common stock, which requires an understanding of the desires and expectations of stockholders, as well as the value of the company.

Dividend policy decisions directly affect the amount of retained earnings a corporation accumulates. Since retained earnings are also common stockholders' money, they must be managed just as carefully as the proceeds from common stock sales.

LEASES

lessee

The party to a lease contract who borrows an asset and makes periodic payments in exchange for the right to use it.

lessor

The party to a lease contract who owns the asset and agrees to let the lessee use it in exchange for periodic payments.

operating (service) leases

A relatively short-term, cancelable contract that does not show up on a company's balance sheet.

financial (capital) lease

A non-cancelable, long-term contract whose present value usually must be reported on the lessee's balance sheet.

Leasing is a form of financing because the **lessee** effectively borrows the asset instead of borrowing cash to buy the asset. The **lessor** owns the asset and agrees to let the lessee use it in exchange for periodic payments. Lessors may be equipment manufacturers, commercial banks, independent leasing companies, or wealthy individuals. There are many different leasing arrangements, although almost all lease contracts fit into one of two distinct categories. A financial manager needs to know how to deal with two separate leasing issues: calculating the cost of a lease, and deciding whether to lease or buy an asset.

Types of Leases

Lease contracts can be categorized as either **operating** or **service leases** and **financial** or **capital leases**. Operating leases are relatively short-term agreements. The lease payments normally do not fully cover the cost of the asset to the lessor, and the lessee may lease the asset again when the first lease terminates. The lessor services the asset, pays any taxes owed, and buys any insurance required. The lessee frequently has the right to cancel the lease contract before the expiration date and return the asset without penalty. Operating leases do not show up on a company's balance sheet.

Financial leases usually last as long as the economic life of the asset. The lease payments plus the expected salvage value of the asset together usually cover the cost of the asset to the lessor and generate a return on the investment. The lessee is normally responsible for any required service, taxes, and insurance on the asset. The lease cannot be canceled without a significant penalty. The present value of the lease payments usually must be calculated and reported on both sides of the lessee's balance sheet because it represents both an asset and a liability.

Cost of a Lease

When leasing an asset, the lessee agrees to make periodic (usually monthly) payments to the lessor. These payments are ordinarily fixed at the time the lease is signed, but if the contract covers a long period of time, a clause may permit occasional increases to compensate for inflation. If the lease meets IRS standards and is not a disguised installment purchase, then the lease payments are tax deductible. If the IRS determines that a lease contract does not meet the criteria for a true lease, then the firm may deduct only that portion of the lease payment that represents interest.

FOCUS ON FINANCE

LEASE/BUY A CADDY?

A full-page advertisement in *The Wall Street Journal* on May 9, 1994 detailed the cost of driving around in a 1994 Cadillac DeVille. The manufacturer's suggested retail price, including the destination charge, was $34,903. Leasing the same car would require a down payment of $2,400 plus a $425 refundable security deposit. Lease payments of $399 a month for 24 months would begin immediately. The customer would have the option of purchasing the car at the end of the lease for $26,107.

The same issue of the *Journal* indicated that a two-year certificate of deposit would yield 4.25 percent before taxes. Suppose that Lillian Ibert has $35,000, is in the 38 percent tax bracket, has never damaged a car in her life, and doesn't expect to do so in the next two years. Her after-tax opportunity cost per month is:

$$0.0425 \times (1 - 0.38)/12 = 0.002195, \text{ or } 0.2195 \text{ percent}$$

If Lillian were to lease the DeVille, her initial cash outflow would be $2,400 plus $425 plus $399, or $3,224. Her recurring cash outflows would be $399 a month for 23 months. If she returns the car undamaged, she will get a cash inflow of $425 in the 24th month. The net present value of this lease contract, discounted at 0.2195 percent, is $11,734.66.

If Lillian were to lease the DeVille and then buy it at the end of the lease, she would have a cash outflow of $26,107 minus $425, or $25,682 in the 24th month. The other cash outflows would remain the same. The net present value of this arrangement, discounted at 0.2195 percent, is $36,449.12. Obviously, buying the Caddy now is better than buying it after leasing it for two years.

Should Lillian lease the Caddy or buy it now? Which would you do?

The Internal Revenue Service has established five criteria to determine the true nature of a lease contract:

1. If a lease includes a purchase option at its termination, it must require payment of the asset's fair market value at that time.
2. The lease must terminate while at least 20 percent of the asset's economic life remains.
3. The lease payments cannot decline during the life of the lease, unless they are specifically tied to a price index that actually declines during the term of the lease.
4. The lease payments must provide the lessor with a fair market rate of return.
5. Renewal options must reflect the fair market value of the asset at the time of renewal.

To calculate the cost of a lease it is necessary to estimate all cash flows that result from leasing the asset and then find the internal rate of return of these cash flows. Since leasing is a form of financing, this internal rate of return multiplied by -1 is the specific cost of a lease, k_L.

Ordinarily, the first lease payment is made immediately and the last payment is made one period before the end of the lease. All such payments are cash outflows. To calculate k_L, one must also identify a cash inflow. A lease does not give the lessee a cash inflow, but it does prevent a cash outflow to purchase the asset instead of leasing it. To calculate the cost of the lease, treat this averted cash outflow as a cash inflow.

The cash flows associated with a lease are:

Time Period	Cash Flow
0	Fair market value of the asset – Lease payment after tax
1	– Lease payment after tax
2	– Lease payment after tax
.	.
.	.
.	.
n–1	– Lease payment after tax
n	0

❖ EXAMPLE 12.1

Mike's Auto Parts, Inc. leases a snow removal machine from Lorna's Leasing Co. for five years. If Mike's had purchased the machine, it would have cost $2,500. The lease contract calls for monthly payments of $80 and specifies that after five years Mike's will return the machine to Lorna's. The lease does not include an option to purchase the machine. Mike's has a 30 percent tax rate.

To find the cost of the lease, solve the following equation for k_L:

$$\$2500 - \$80(1-0.3) = \sum_{t=1}^{59} \frac{-\$80(1-0.3)}{(1+k_L)^t}$$

$$\$2,444 = (-\$56)(PVIFA_{k,59})$$

$$-43.64286 = PVIFA_{k,59}$$

$$k_L = 1.124 \text{ percent monthly}$$

$$k_L = 13.49 \text{ percent annually}$$ ❖

The cost of the lease for Mike's Auto Parts, 13.49 percent, is not necessarily the rate of return for Lorna's Leasing. They differ for several reasons:

1. Lorna's may be able to buy snow removal machines in quantity and negotiate a better price than $2,500 each.
2. As the owner, Lorna's is entitled to depreciate the machine. The depreciation tax shield is an additional cash inflow.
3. Lorna's Leasing Co. may have a different tax rate than Mike's Auto Parts.
4. Lorna's still owns the machine at the end of five years and can lease it again or sell it, thus deriving additional cash benefits from it.

EXHIBIT 12.1

Structuring the Lease/Buy Decision

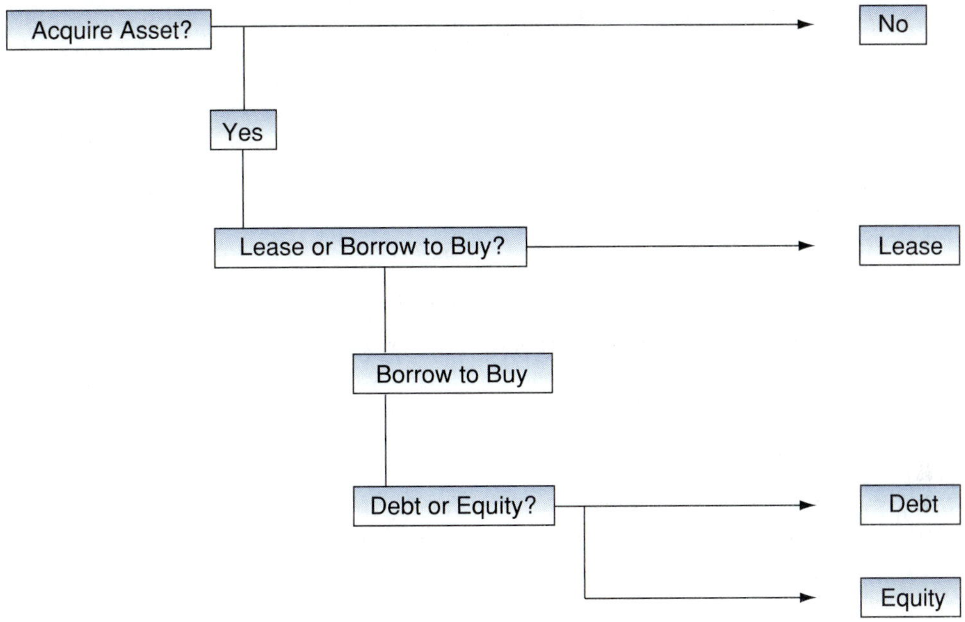

Leasing versus Buying

When deciding whether to lease or purchase an asset, great care must be taken to structure the problem correctly. As Exhibit 12.1 illustrates, three questions may need answers.

First, determine that the asset itself is desirable. This entails finding the asset's net present value, profitability index, or internal rate of return without giving any consideration to the method of financing. The asset must appear to be desirable solely on the basis of its own cash flows.

If the asset is desirable, compare the cash flows associated with a lease and the cash flows associated with a loan. The type of loan doesn't matter. It could be a note payable to a bank, a mortgage, an installment loan, publicly issued bonds, or any other form of debt. It must be debt—and not equity—for several reasons:

1. The interest cost of debt is tax deductible, as are the lease payments.
2. The debt has a maturity date that can be negotiated to match the termination date of the lease.
3. The financial risk of borrowing is the same as the financial risk of leasing: failure to meet, or satisfactorily renegotiate, payment schedules will drive the lessor/borrower into bankruptcy proceedings.

EXHIBIT 12.2

Spreadsheet Loan Columns for a Term Loan or Bond

(1) Time Period	(2) Interest	(3) Principal	(4) Total Payment	(5) Outstanding Balance
0	0	0	0	$40,000
1	$2,000	0	$ 2,000	40,000
2	2,000	0	2,000	40,000
3	2,000	0	2,000	40,000
4	2,000	$40,000	42,000	0

Finally, if the firm decides to buy rather than lease, it can subsequently decide how to finance the purchase. The choice between borrowing and using equity funds involves evaluating the differences in cost and risk attributable to issuing bonds and stocks.

The lease versus borrow-to-buy decision is best set up as a spreadsheet; it can then be solved manually, with a hand calculator, or by any spreadsheet program. This format is adaptable to all lease/buy problems and minimizes the chance that the analysis will ignore a relevant cash flow or consider an irrelevant cash flow. To solve a lease/buy problem, create an $n \times 15$ matrix with n equal to the number of time periods over which the lease extends. The 15 columns contain either the relevant cash flows or data needed to calculate the cash flows.

To facilitate explanation, these 15 columns can be grouped into several categories. They should contain projections of cash flows associated with the loan, with the purchase, with the calculation of the borrow-to-buy cash flows, with the lease, and with the present value of the difference in cash flows between the two financing methods. Since the timing of the cash flows is critical, the first column indicates the time period t, starting with $t = 0$. (These columns are discussed by category and illustrated in Exhibit 12.5.)

Loan Columns. Four columns are necessary to evaluate the cash flow implications of a loan: the interest payment in each period, the principal payment in each period (if required), the total payment made by the borrower, and the outstanding balance of the loan after the payment is made. The outstanding balance is not a cash flow, but including this column facilitates the calculation of interest for certain types of loans. To illustrate how different types of loans would fit this format, consider a four-period loan of $40,000 with an interest rate of 5 percent per period. Exhibit 12.2 illustrates the cash flows for a term loan or bond.

Exhibit 12.3 details the cash flows for an amortized (mortgage) loan with a fixed payment of $11,280. For an amortized loan, the borrower pays interest on the outstanding balance of the loan for each payment period. The difference between the fixed payment and the interest constitutes a repayment of principal. The interest portion of the payment decreases every period and the principal repayment por-

EXHIBIT 12.3

Spreadsheet Loan Columns for an Amortized Loan

(1) Time Period	(2) Interest	(3) Principal	(4) Total Payment	(5) Outstanding Balance
0	0	0	0	$40,000
1	$2,000	$ 9,280	$11,280	30,720
2	1,536	9,744	11,280	20,976
3	1,049	10,231	11,280	10,745
4	537	10,745	11,282	0

EXHIBIT 12.4

Spreadsheet Loan Columns for an Installment Loan

(1) Time Period	(2) Interest	(3) Principal	(4) Total Payment	(5) Outstanding Balance
0	0	0	0	$40,000
1	$2,000	$10,000	$12,000	30,000
2	2,000	10,000	12,000	20,000
3	2,000	10,000	12,000	10,000
4	2,000	10,000	12,000	0

tion increases. Note that the last payment contains an extra $2 to complete payment in full. An amount this small is usually attributed to rounding. A large amount would be called a balloon payment. Most commercial mortgages include balloons; most residential mortgages do not.

Exhibit 12.4 details the cash flows for a loan that requires repayment of principal in equal installments of $10,000. An installment loan calculates interest on the amount borrowed, not on the amount outstanding, so the effective rate is approximately double the stated rate.

Purchase Columns. Three columns (Columns 6, 7, and 10 of the spreadsheet) report figures attributable to the purchase of the asset. One column lists depreciation charges that appear quarterly on the company's books. These charges are not cash flows, but they do affect the taxes that the purchaser has to pay. The next column gives the service or maintenance costs that the purchaser expects to encounter; these may reflect direct expenses or periodic payments for a service contract. If the lease contract requires the lessee to pay these costs, this column can be left blank.

Column 10 allows the decision maker to adjust the beginning and/or ending cash flows if circumstances require such adjustments. The two possible adjustments are:

1. The after-tax salvage value of the asset if it is to be sold. If the sale will pro-

duce a cash inflow, the amount is entered in the appropriate row of Column 10 as a negative number.

2. The investment tax credit, if and when the federal government reinstates it. This credit has been a political football for decades and is not available at the time of this writing. When available, the amount is entered in the first row of Column 10 as a negative number.

Cash Flow Calculation Columns. Some of the cash flows in the preceding columns represent tax-deductible expenses. They are: interest (Column 2), depreciation (Column 6), and service or maintenance costs (Column 7). The spreadsheet must sum these three columns and enter the total for each period in the deductible column (Column 8). The tax shield is calculated in Column 9 by multiplying the sum of the deductible items by the company's tax rate.

The expected after-tax cash flows from borrowing to buy the asset are then calculated and the result is entered in Column 11. This amount equals the loan payment (Column 4), plus the service costs (Column 7), plus the adjustments (Column 10), minus the tax shield (Column 9). If these net cash outflows are larger than the expected after-tax net cash outflows from leasing the asset, then the firm should lease the asset.

Lease Columns. Normally, only two columns are necessary: Column 12 lists the lease payments from time zero to time $n-1$, and Column 13 states the after-tax lease payment. Column 12 is multiplied by 1.0 minus the lessee's tax rate to get the after-tax lease payment, found in Column 13.

Present Value of the Difference Column. The after-tax cash flows of the lease (Column 13) are subtracted from the after-tax cash flows generated by borrowing the money and buying the asset (Column 11). If the difference is positive, the purchase requires a larger cash outflow. If the difference is negative, the lease requires a larger cash outflow. Whatever the sign, the difference for each period is recorded in Column 14.

These differences must be discounted to their present values. Each number in the column of differences must be divided by $(1 + k_D)^t$ to get its present value (Column 15). The company's after-tax cost of long-term debt serves as the discount rate. If the company has more than one debt issue outstanding, k_D is a weighted average of the costs of these issues. Note that k_D does not include the cost of the debt being considered in Columns 2 through 5.

Lease Decision. Column 15 is totaled. If the sum is negative, the borrow-to-buy decision is better; if the sum is positive, the decision to lease is better.

❖ EXAMPLE 12.2

The Pennsyltucky Corporation has decided to acquire a $1 million machine for its research laboratory. The machinery has an expected life of three years and the manufacturer has offered to lease it to the company for $30,000 per month. The terms of the lease include service at the manufacturer's expense.

Alternatively, a bank has offered Pennsyltucky a 12 percent, $1 million loan, to be amortized over three years with a fixed monthly payment of $33,000 and a balloon payment of $9,231.80 at the end of the loan term. If the company chooses to buy the machinery, the manufacturer offers a service contract for $1,000 per month.

The MACRS method gives depreciation figures on this machine of $333,300 the first year, $444,400 the second year, $148,200 the third year, and $74,100 the fourth year. These figures are recognized quarterly. Pennsyltucky plans to sell the machinery for its book value at the end of the third year.

The company has a 40 percent tax rate and its average after-tax cost of debt is 7.2 percent annually. Should it lease the machine or borrow the money and buy it?

The values in the spreadsheet in Exhibit 12.5 show columns calculated as described above. The following details relate specifically to Example 12.2:

1. The 12 percent interest rate equals 1 percent per month. Each number in the outstanding balance column is multiplied by 1 percent to get the interest payment in the subsequent period.
2. Since corporate taxes are paid quarterly, the annual depreciation charge is divided by four and entered every third month in the column labeled *Depreciation*.
3. The tax shield amounts to 40 percent of the deductible expenses.
4. Since Pennsyltucky plans to sell the machine for its book value at the end of three years, the *Adjustments* column shows a $74,100 cash inflow in Period 36.
5. The *After-Tax Lease Cash Flow* column is 60 percent of the *Lease Payment* column.
6. The present values of the differences are calculated using a discount rate of 0.6 percent (7.2 percent/12).

The positive net present value of $40,201.31 indicates that Pennsyltucky should lease the machine. ❖

International Leasing

International leasing is complicated by several factors. If the firm must make lease payments in a foreign currency, exchange rate fluctuations can significantly affect the cash flows associated with the lease. Since the lease payments are fixed by contract, the financial manager is in the best possible situation to hedge the payment liabilities against exchange rate risk, but the hedging strategy itself involves an additional cost to reduce risk exposure.

The myriad international borrowing possibilities can complicate the borrow-and-buy portion of the decision. The analyst must evaluate loan arrangements in different countries and choose the best one for comparison to the lease. This lease/buy analysis may now involve three currencies: the lender's, the lessor's, and the lessee's. Possible government restrictions on cross-border currency flows may complicate matters even further.

EXHIBIT 12.5

Pennsyltucky Corporation Lease or Buy Spreadsheet

Time	Interest	Principal Repayment	Total Payment	Outstanding Balance	MACRS Depreciation	Service Contract
0	0.00	0.00	0.00	1,000,000.00	0.00	1,000.00
1	10,000.00	23,000.00	33,000.00	977,000.00	0.00	1,000.00
2	9,770.00	23,230.00	33,000.00	953,770.00	0.00	1,000.00
3	9,537.70	23,462.30	33,000.00	930,307.70	83,325.00	1,000.00
4	9,303.08	23,696.92	33,000.00	906,610.78	0.00	1,000.00
5	9,066.11	23,933.89	33,000.00	882,676.88	0.00	1,000.00
6	8,826.77	24,173.23	33,000.00	858,503.65	83,325.00	1,000.00
7	8,585.04	24,414.96	33,000.00	834,088.69	0.00	1,000.00
8	8,340.89	24,659.11	33,000.00	809,429.58	0.00	1,000.00
9	8,094.30	24,905.70	33,000.00	784,523.87	83,325.00	1,000.00
10	7,845.24	25,154.76	33,000.00	759,369.11	0.00	1,000.00
11	7,593.69	25,406.31	33,000.00	733,962.80	0.00	1,000.00
12	7,339.63	25,660.37	33,000.00	708,302.43	83,325.00	1,000.00
13	7,083.02	25,916.98	33,000.00	682,385.46	0.00	1,000.00
14	6,823.85	26,176.15	33,000.00	656,209.31	0.00	1,000.00
15	6,562.09	26,437.91	33,000.00	629,771.40	111,100.00	1,000.00
16	6,297.71	26,702.29	33,000.00	603,069.12	0.00	1,000.00
17	6,030.69	26,969.31	33,000.00	576,099.81	0.00	1,000.00
18	5,761.00	27,239.00	33,000.00	548,860.81	111,100.00	1,000.00
19	5,448.61	27,511.39	33,000.00	521,349.41	0.00	1,000.00
20	5,213.49	27,786.51	33,000.00	493,562.91	0.00	1,000.00
21	4,935.63	28,064.37	33,000.00	465,498.54	111,100.00	1,000.00
22	4,654.99	28,345.01	33,000.00	437,153.52	0.00	1,000.00
23	4,371.54	28,628.46	33,000.00	408,525.06	0.00	1,000.00
24	4,085.25	28,914.75	33,000.00	379,610.31	111,100.00	1,000.00
25	3,796.10	29,203.90	33,000.00	350,406.41	0.00	1,000.00
26	3,504.06	29,495.94	33,000.00	320,910.48	0.00	1,000.00
27	3,209.10	29,790.90	33,000.00	291,119.58	37,050.00	1,000.00
28	2,911.20	30,088.80	33,000.00	261,030.78	0.00	1,000.00
29	2,610.31	30,389.69	33,000.00	230,641.08	0.00	1,000.00
30	2,306.41	30,693.59	33,000.00	199,947.49	37,050.00	1,000.00
31	1,999.47	31,000.53	33,000.00	168,946.97	0.00	1,000.00
32	1,689.47	31,310.53	33,000.00	137,636.44	0.00	1,000.00
33	1,376.36	31,623.64	33,000.00	106,012.80	37,050.00	1,000.00
34	1,060.13	31,939.87	33,000.00	74,072.93	0.00	1,000.00
35	740.73	32,259.27	33,000.00	41,813.66	0.00	1,000.00
36	418.14	41,813.66	42,231.80	0.00	37,050.00	0.00

COMMON STOCK

Ownership of a corporation resides in the common stockholders, but their control over management varies from company to company. Common stock cannot be callable or convertible, nor can it have a sinking fund. If a company buys back

Total Deductible	Tax Shield	Adjustments	Purchase Cash Flow	Lease Payment	After-Tax Lease Cash Flow	Cash Flow Difference	Present Value of Difference
1,000.00	400.00	0.00	600.00	30,000.00	18,000.00	–17,400.00	–17,400.00
11,000.00	4,400.00	0.00	29,600.00	30,000.00	18,000.00	11,600.00	11,530.82
10,770.00	4,308.00	0.00	29,692.00	30,000.00	18,000.00	11,692.00	11,552.95
93,862.70	37,545.08	0.00	–3,545.08	30,000.00	18,000.00	–21,545.08	–21,161.88
10,303.08	4,121.23	0.00	29,878.77	30,000.00	18,000.00	11,878.77	11,597.90
10,066.11	4,026.44	0.00	29,973.56	30,000.00	18,000.00	11,973.56	11,620.73
93,151.77	37,260.71	0.00	–3,260.71	30,000.00	18,000.00	–21,260.71	–20,511.14
9,585.04	3,834.01	0.00	30,165.99	30,000.00	18,000.00	12,165.99	11,667.06
9,340.89	3,736.35	0.00	30,263.65	30,000.00	18,000.00	12,263.65	11,690.57
92,419.30	36,967.72	0.00	–2,967.72	30,000.00	18,000.00	–20,967.72	–19,868.70
8,845.24	3,538.10	0.00	30,461.90	30,000.00	18,000.00	12,461.90	11,738.28
8,593.69	3,437.48	0.00	30,562.52	30,000.00	18,000.00	12,562.52	11,762.49
91,664.63	36,665.85	0.00	–2,665.85	30,000.00	18,000.00	–20,665.85	–19,234.35
8,083.02	3,233.21	0.00	30,766.79	30,000.00	18,000.00	12,766.79	11,811.58
7,823.85	3,129.54	0.00	30,870.46	30,000.00	18,000.00	12,870.46	11,836.47
118,662.09	47,464.84	0.00	–13,464.84	30,000.00	18,000.00	–31,464.84	–28,764.43
7,297.71	2,919.09	0.00	31,080.91	30,000.00	18,000.00	13,080.91	11,886.95
7,030.69	2,812.28	0.00	31,187.72	30,000.00	18,000.00	13,187.72	11,912.53
117,861.00	47,144.40	0.00	–13,144.40	30,000.00	18,000.00	–31,144.40	–27,965.10
6,488.61	2,595.44	0.00	31,404.56	30,000.00	18,000.00	13,404.56	11,964.40
6,213.49	2,485.40	0.00	31,514.60	30,000.00	18,000.00	13,514.60	11,990.68
117,035.63	46,814.25	0.00	–12,814.25	30,000.00	18,000.00	–30,814.25	–27,176.53
5,654.99	2,261.99	0.00	31,738.01	30,000.00	18,000.00	13,738.01	12,043.93
5,371.54	2,148.61	0.00	31,851.39	30,000.00	18,000.00	13,851.39	12,070.90
116,185.25	46,474.10	0.00	–12,474.10	30,000.00	18,000.00	–31,474.10	–26,398.51
4,796.10	1,918.44	0.00	32,081.56	30,000.00	18,000.00	14,081.56	12,125.54
4,504.06	1,801.63	0.00	32,198.37	30,000.00	18,000.00	14,198.37	12,153.21
41,259.10	16,503.64	0.00	17,496.36	30,000.00	18,000.00	–503.64	–428.53
3,911.20	1,564.48	0.00	32,435.52	30,000.00	18,000.00	14,435.52	12,209.25
3,610.31	1,444.12	0.00	32,555.88	30,000.00	18,000.00	14,555.88	12,237.62
40,356.41	16,142.56	0.00	17,857.44	30,000.00	18,000.00	–142.56	–119.14
2,999.47	1,199.79	0.00	32,800.21	30,000.00	18,000.00	14,800.21	12,295.06
2,689.47	1,075.79	0.00	32,924.21	30,000.00	18,000.00	14,924.21	12,324.12
39,426.36	15,770.55	0.00	18,229.45	30,000.00	18,000.00	229.45	188.35
2,060.13	824.05	0.00	33,175.95	30,000.00	18,000.00	15,175.95	12,382.96
1,740.73	696.29	0.00	33,303.71	30,000.00	18,000.00	15,303.71	12,412.73
37,468.14	14,987.25	–74,100.00	–46,855.45	0.00	0.00	–46,855.45	–37,777.47
							NPV = 40,201.31

some of its common stock on the open market, it cannot resell the stock to the public at a later date without risking charges of illegal price manipulation. Common stock is not rated, but an almost infinite number of investment advisors are anxious to sell lists of stocks that they view as good investments.

FOCUS ON CAREERS

SECURITIES ANALYST

A securities analyst evaluates financial and economic information in an effort to forecast business, industry, and economic conditions. The analyst gathers information from company financial statements, industry publications, and financial periodicals and newspapers. Interpreting data concerning price, yield, stability, and future trends occupies a significant percentage of the hours spent at work. The analyst then summarizes the information and either reports it to upper management or presents it to investors via investment newsletters. If the analyst is employed by a life insurance company, a pension fund, or any institution with a large investment portfolio, then the evaluation is integrated into company portfolio decisions. If the analyst works for a brokerage house, then the evaluation will form part of the brokerage house's overall investment recommendations to its clients.

A securities analyst needs a strong quantitative background in accounting or finance. Brokerage houses frequently seek individuals with strong mathematical skills (such as engineers) or specialized industry experience to serve as part of investment analysis teams. Analysts frequently need advanced degrees, such as an MBA. Firms offer them little training and advancement opportunities are limited. However, a salary level of $50,000 to $75,000 is common. Performance is generally rewarded with bonuses which may well equal three to six months' salary. Exceptional performance may attract the attention of the media, which can produce contacts for lucrative consulting contracts.

Common stock is neither cumulative nor noncumulative. A dividend, if declared, must be paid, and any dividend not declared is lost forever. The amount of dividends paid to common stockholders is not fixed.

Claim on Assets

As owners of the company, common stockholders have a residual claim against its assets. Rarely do they receive anything when company assets are liquidated in Bankruptcy Court proceedings. If any liquidation value remains after the creditors and preferred stockholders have been paid in full, this remainder is divided among the common stockholders on a per share basis.

Some investors mistakenly believe that if a company is liquidated, they are entitled to the **book value** of their shares. This book value is the total of the par value of the stock, the **capital surplus** (the price paid in excess of the par value when the stock was first sold to the public), and the per-share value of accumulated retained earnings. This represents the conventional way to record the amount of money contributed to the company by its owners, but book value has nothing to do with the amount of money the owners will receive if the company fails and its assets are auctioned.

book value
The total of the par value of a firm's stock, its capital surplus, and the per-share value of its accumulated retained earnings.

capital surplus
The price that buyers pay in excess of par value when stock is first sold to the public.

Book value is normally much lower than market value. However, the market price of the common stock may fall below book value when the market has a very low opinion of the company's ability to continue operating.

Voice in Management

Common stockholders are the legal owners of a corporation. As such, they have the right to elect the members of the board of directors, which theoretically hires the managers of the company. The board makes the major policy decisions for the company; management implements these policies.

Directors are elected at a company's annual shareholders' meeting. Before the meeting, management sends a ballot to each common stockholder, who is usually entitled to one vote for each share of stock he or she owns. This ballot usually contains only one name per position to be filled, but the name(s) of person(s) other than those listed may be written in. Unless they are part of an organized effort to elect another slate of candidates, these write-in votes are doomed to failure. To win a corporate election, a candidate for director must obtain a majority of votes cast.

proxy statement
A statement giving someone who will attend a company's annual shareholders' meeting the right to cast a stockholder's votes.

Stockholders do not have to be present at the meeting in order to vote. They can submit their votes by **proxy statements**, which means that they sign their ballots and a statement giving someone who will attend the meeting the right to cast their votes for them. By custom, shareholders who do not attend the meeting delegate their voting authority to management. Many individual investors do not bother to attend the meeting or to send in their proxy statements.

In recent years, some of the major brokerage houses that hold common stock in custody for their clients have found an easy way to obtain this proxy power. The corporation sends the ballots to the broker to forward to the stockholders. The broker sends the ballots to the stockholders along with a letter stating that the stockholders should send their signed ballots and proxy statements back to the broker. The letter adds that if the stockholders do not respond, the broker will construe this lack of response as authorization to vote the stockholders' shares *as the broker sees fit*.

straight voting
A procedure that gives the stockholder one vote for each share of common stock he or she owns for each position to be filled.

Voting Rights. A corporation may use either of two voting procedures. **Straight voting** is a procedure that gives the stockholder one vote for each share he or she owns for each position to be filled. If six directors are to be elected, a stockholder who owns 100 shares of common stock can cast 600 votes, 100 for each director. Suppose that 70 voting stockholders own 100 shares each. A total of 42,000 votes are cast (7,000 for each position), and each winning director must get at least 3,501 votes. In this illustration, at least 36 stockholders, a majority, must agree on each director elected.

cumulative voting
A procedure that gives the stockholder one vote for each common share he or she owns, times the number of positions to be filled; the shareholder can distribute those votes at will.

Cumulative voting, in contrast, gives the stockholder one vote for each share he or she owns times the number of positions to be filled; the shareholder can distribute those votes at will. The shareholder in the illustration above could cast all 600 votes for one director, or 300 votes each for two directors, or any other combination. The six candidates who get the most votes will win. If the stockholders must elect x directors, any director who receives $1/(x + 1)$ of the vote plus one vote will win. Since $1/(6 + 1) = 1/7$, any director who gets at least $(1/7)(42,000) + 1$, or 6,001 votes will be elected. In this illustration, only 11 stockholders have to agree in order to guarantee that they will get one director elected. Thus, shareholders

FOCUS ON FINANCE

FORD'S CLASS A AND B STOCKS

As of September 30, 1993, the Ford Motor Company had 455.9 million shares of Class A common stock and 35.4 million shares of Class B common stock outstanding. The Class A stock is owned by the general public; the Class B stock is owned by members of the Ford family, their trusts or corporations, and the Edison Institute. Certificates for shares of Class B stock may be transferred only among investors entitled to own them.

Class A stock is entitled to one vote per share. Class B stock is entitled to as many votes per share as necessary to give the B holders 40 percent of the number of votes cast on any matter. If the corporation ever has fewer than 5,625,000 Class B shares outstanding, the Class B shareholders will be reduced to one vote per share.

Class A and Class B shares entitle their owners to share equally in dividends. However, stock dividends must be paid to each class only in stock of that class. If Ford Motor Company is liquidated, Classes A and B will share equally in the distribution of assets.

Class A stock has no preemptive rights. Class B stockholders have preemptive rights to purchase any Class B stock issued by the company. If the firm offers common stock to holders of Class A shares, then holders of Class B shares must be offered shares of Class B stock on a ratable basis and at the same price per share.

A holder of Class B stock is entitled at any time to convert any or all shares into an equal number of shares of Class A stock. Class B stock acquired by the company or converted into Class A stock cannot be reissued as Class B stock.

with relatively small amounts of stock can get representation on the board of directors if they cooperate. Many states in the United States have made cumulative voting mandatory for corporations chartered within their boundaries.

To protect the company from takeover attempts, which cumulative voting can encourage, most corporations stagger the terms of the directors. Only a fraction of the board is elected each year, so it may take several years to vote in a majority of new directors.

Multiple Classes of Stock. Some corporations have more than one class of common stock outstanding. The different classes have different voting rights and may receive different dividend payments. When a company has Class A and Class B common stock outstanding, the Class B stock is usually held by representatives of the company's founding family and has disproportionately large voting power. The media have dubbed such stock **killer *B*s**. The stock exchanges generally frown on failure to comply with the one share, one vote rule, but they do not automatically exclude noncompliers from being listed.

killer *B*s
Classes of common stock that offer disproportionately large voting power.

Other Shareholder Rights. One significant advantage of the corporate form of business organization is the limited liability of the owners. Because a corporation is a distinct entity under the law, a stockholder is not liable for the company's debts.

Stockholders have the right to sell their shares without permission from the company's management or other shareholders. They also have the right to obtain information from management about the company's operations and financial condition, to the extent that releasing the information will not adversely affect the competitive position of the firm. This right is usually satisfied by the company's publication of quarterly and annual reports.

preemptive right
The right of a firm's current stockholders to maintain their proportion of ownership by purchasing any new shares issued by the corporation before it offers them to the public.

A **preemptive right** is the right of a firm's current stockholders to maintain their proportion of ownership by purchasing any new shares issued by the corporation before it offers them to the public. Some states prohibit the preemptive right unless it is specifically included in the corporate charter; in other states it automatically exists unless specifically denied in the corporate charter. This right applies to common stock and to securities that are convertible into common stock. It does not apply to common stock issued as payment in a corporate takeover or to employees under a stock option plan. Without this right, management could issue new stock to an investor or a select group of investors who could affect the outcome of any issue that required a majority vote by the shareholders.

Dividend Policy

The memory and logic of the market dictate corporate dividend policy to some extent. Before the credibility of information disclosed by corporations was regulated, standardized, and fully accepted, dividends were valuable as the only proof that a stock certificate represented ownership of a solvent, profitable company. Early statistical studies, as primitive as Fred Flintstone's car, demonstrated that $1 of dividends had as much impact on the market price of a stock as $3 or $4 in reported earnings per share. The visitors' galleries in the major stock exchanges still display exhibits by corporations boasting of their records for paying continuous dividends for many decades.

This tradition inhibits the financial decisions of U.S. corporations, making it difficult for them to cut their dividends. Even when a company can do better for its stockholders by reinvesting retained earnings than the stockholders can do for themselves by reinvesting dividends, the company's board of directors will hesitate to reduce or omit a dividend payment. It is a fact of the market that when a company cuts its dividend, for a good reason or a bad one, its stock price falls.

Exhibit 12.6 illustrates a desirable dividend history for a U.S. company. It has several notable characteristics:

1. Since the firm paid its first dividend at Time A, it has never cut that dividend. The market interprets this as a sign that the company has not been strapped for cash since Time A.
2. The dividend has increased rapidly on occasion, such as the period between Time B and Time C. During that period, the market would have interpreted these increases as a signal that the board of directors was optimistic about the company's future profits and cash flows. Directors raise dividends only when they believe that the firm can sustain the increase in the future.
3. The dividend did not increase at all during the period between Time C and

EXHIBIT 12.6

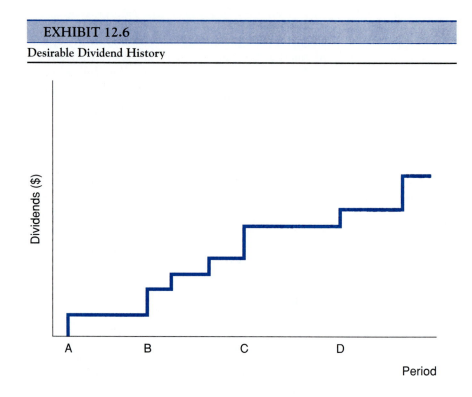

Desirable Dividend History

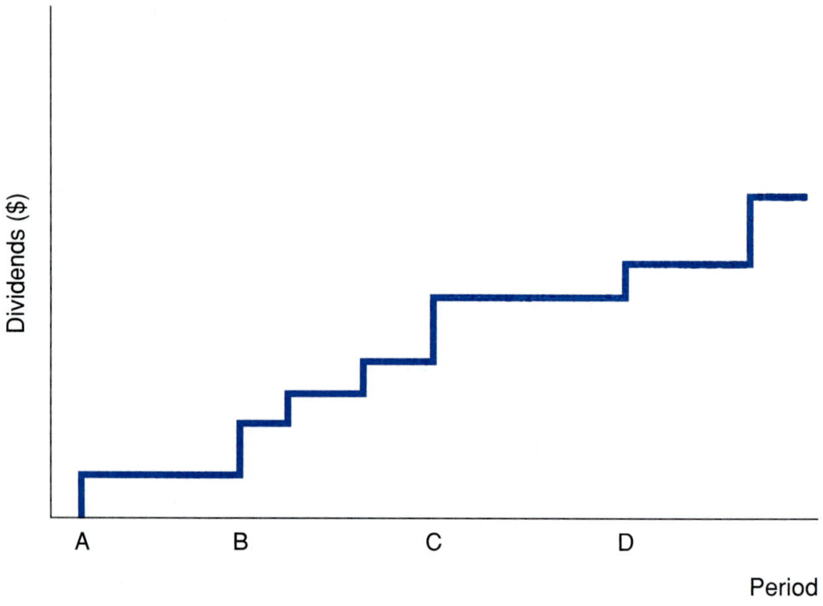

Time D. During that period, the market would have interpreted this stability as a signal that the directors were pessimistic about the company's ability to sustain a higher dividend.

4. The directors slowly became more optimistic about the company's future after Time D.

Specific Cost

The cost of common stock cannot be calculated in the same manner as the specific costs of other securities. Comparing the company's payment, the annual dividend, to the net proceeds from the sale of the stock presents two difficulties that other securities do not.

First, when a company issues bonds or preferred stock, each new issue is an individual security and has its own specific cost. When a company issues additional shares of common stock, however, the new issues become indistinguishable from the already outstanding shares. Stock issued 50 years ago at $10 a share is no different from stock issued yesterday at $90 a share. If stock prices did not inflate over time, this problem could be solved by calculating a weighted average of the net proceeds of all of a company's common stock sales in its lifetime. As the sample of well-known companies in Exhibit 12.7 illustrates, however, stock prices have increased tremendously over time. A $10,000 investment, made when each firm

EXHIBIT 12.7

Price Appreciation of $10,000 Invested in Newly Issued Stocks

Company	When Issued	Value of the Investment, April 19, 1994
Sherwin Williams	1884	$6,127,616
Xerox	1906	5,238,000
Black & Decker	1910	1,385,319
Coca-Cola	1919	9,216,000
PPG Industries	1920	2,277,600
Kellogg	1922	1,556,000
Dun & Bradstreet	1930	2,918,400
Reynolds Metals	1937	640,623
McDonald's	1965	4,626,346
Bally Manufacturing	1968	98,824

EXHIBIT 12.8

Effect of a 5 Percent Stock Dividend ($000)

Before the stock dividend	
Common stock (par $1; 10 million shares)	$ 10,000
Paid-in capital	150,000
Retained earnings	600,000
Total equity	$760,000
After the stock dividend	
Common stock (par $1; 10.5 million shares)	$ 10,500
Paid-in capital	157,500
Retained earnings	592,000
Total equity	$760,000

first offered shares to the public in the year indicated, would have grown in value to the amount shown as of April 19, 1994.

The specific cost calculation is complicated for another reason: comparing a company's current dividend to the net proceeds from the original sale of stock to the public many years ago produces numbers that have no economic usefulness. As the company grows, its dividend payout also grows, so the current dividend related to a long-ago stock price yields an astronomically high percentage, even when the company has not issued new stock in the interim.

Stock Dividends. When a company's board of directors declares a stock dividend, it gives existing shareholders additional shares of common stock instead of a cash distribution. The declaration is usually expressed as a percentage. A 2 percent stock dividend would give a shareholder 2 shares for every 100 shares of stock he or she held. A stock dividend affects only the equity portion of the company's balance sheet, as shown in Exhibit 12.8.

FOCUS ON FINANCE

MORE VALUE AND MORE PAPER

The companies listed in Exhibit 12.7 have paid many stock dividends and split their stocks many times. An investor who purchased 100 shares of stock in one of these firms when it was first issued to the public would be holding the following number of shares as of April 19, 1994:

Sherwin Williams	191,488
Xerox	54,000
Black & Decker	71,042
Coca-Cola	230,400
PPG Industries	31,200
Kellogg	32,000
Dun & Bradstreet	51,200
Reynolds Metals	2,593
McDonald's	18,588
Bally Manufacturing	2,400

To illustrate how this happens, consider the history of Sherwin Williams, North America's largest producer of paints and varnishes. It was incorporated on July 16, 1884 in Ohio. The company declared the following stock dividends and splits in the 110 years between 1884 and 1994.

Stock Dividend	Year	Stock Split	Date
5%	1886	4 for 1	August 1920
5	1887	2 for 1	August 1947
10	1889	2 for 1	December 1959
$33\frac{1}{3}$	1901	2 for 1	December 1964
$33\frac{1}{3}$	1903	2 for 1	March 1981
20	1906	2 for 1	March 1983
$33\frac{1}{3}$	1909	2 for 1	March 1986
$33\frac{1}{3}$	1911		
10	1915		
50	1920		

Suppose that an investor bought 100 shares during 1885 and took the cash value of any fractional shares whenever the firm paid stock dividends. By July 1920, that investor held 748 shares of stock. This number quadrupled in August 1920, then doubled six times in subsequent years. If that investor were alive today, he or she would possess 191,488 shares of Sherwin Williams common stock.

Because a stock dividend increases the number of shares of outstanding stock, all per-share amounts decrease. If the company in Exhibit 12.8 had net income of \$20 million, for example, its earnings per share before the stock dividend were \$20 million/10 million, or \$2; its earnings per share after the stock dividend would be \$20 million/10.5 million, or \$1.90. Theoretically, if the market price of a share of stock was \$40 (20 times earnings per share) before the dividend, it should be \$38 afterward. Since:

$$\$40 \times 100 = \$38 \times 105 = \$4{,}000 \text{ (The \$1 difference is a rounding discrepancy.)}$$

the investor should gain or lose nothing because of a stock dividend. In effect, the company simply prints extra stock certificates and distributes them proportionately to the shareholders. Each investor's fraction of ownership of the company has not changed, so the market value of this position should not change.

However, dividends send a signal to the market. Paying a stock dividend instead of a cash dividend tells the world that the company has a cash flow problem. Thus, the stock dividend will probably cause the stock price to decline. A

EXHIBIT 12.9

Results of Various Hypothetical Stock Splits

	Before Split	After a 2–1 Split	After a 3–2 Split	After a 4–1 Split
Company				
Number of shares outstanding	12 million	24 million	18 million	48 million
Par value	$36	$18	$24	$9
Owners' equity	$432 million	$432 million	$432 million	$432 million
Investor				
Shares held	100	200	150	400
Market price	$60	$30	$40	$15
Value	$6,000	$6,000	$6,000	$6,000
Dividend/share	$3.00	$1.50	$2.00	$0.75
Earnings/share	$6	$3	$4	$1.50

stock dividend paid in addition to a regular cash dividend (a rare event) tells the world that the company sees itself as a possible takeover target, and the stock price may rise in anticipation.

Under generally accepted accounting principles, a stock dividend is a distribution of 20 percent or less. A stock distribution that exceeds 25 percent is a stock split. A distribution between 20 percent and 25 percent can be treated either way.

Stock Splits. As time passes and a stock's value increases, the company may find its shares priced out of reach of individual investors. To correct that situation, the company may decide to split the stock. In a 2-for-1 split, the company simply notifies the shareholders that for every share they previously held, they now have two shares. Investors whose stocks are in the custody of their brokers need do nothing; those who possess stock certificates can send them to the company for replacement if they so desire. They can sell old certificates just as easily as the new ones, but some investors prefer to keep all of their paperwork up-to-date. Other investors may be interested in liquidating fractions of their holdings from time to time; to do this, they may have to exchange the old certificates for new ones.

A stock split has a few notable consequences. Exhibit 12.9 illustrates the various effects of different split ratios. The post-split market prices in Exhibit 12.9 reflect instantaneous changes. If management correctly determines that the firm's stock has become prohibitively expensive, then its post-split market price will rise as pent-up demand for this newly affordable stock is satisfied. Since investors normally purchase stock in round lots of 100 shares, smaller investors are more attracted to a stock selling for $30 a share ($3,000 for a round lot) than to a stock selling for $60 a share ($6,000 for a round lot). Also, most brokers charge slightly higher commissions on odd lot trades than on round lot trades.

FOCUS ON FINANCE

REVERSE SPLITS

A company may decide to reduce the number of shares of common stock outstanding by declaring a reverse split. A 1-for-3 reverse split, for example, would leave the shareholders owning one share for every three they had previously owned. This may happen after a company's stock has declined in price substantially over a long period of time. An element of speculation influences investing in very low-priced stocks, and the company's management may wish to avoid association with such an image.

A reverse split does not change the fraction of ownership of the company that each investor holds, nor does it affect the total value of any investor's holdings automatically. The announcement of a reverse split may signal the market that management is not optimistic about the company's ability to raise its stock price by growing earnings. This may depress the stock price a little further.

Calculating Cost. Calculating the cost of outstanding common stock to a company requires a different method than that presented earlier for bonds and preferred stock. The specific cost of outstanding common stock can be defined as the rate of return required by the firm's common stockholders. Granted, not all stockholders require the same rate of return. Dissatisfied investors have two alternatives if the stock produces a return below their expected return:

1. They can communicate their dissatisfaction to management. If they own large blocks of stock or are influential in the marketplace, management will respond.
2. They can sell their shares and invest elsewhere. If a significant number of small investors take such action, the stock price will decline and management will be forced to take corrective action. Either way, management must please the stockholders.

Calculating the company's specific cost of common stock is not an easy task as there is no direct way to observe the stockholders' required rate of return. It must be estimated. The estimator must use the company's price, earnings, dividend, and risk data to infer the stockholders' required rate of return. These variables are linked directly or indirectly to what investors want. There are two approaches for using these variables to determine stockholders' required rate of return: the Dividend Discount Model of Stock Valuation and the Capital Asset Pricing Model (CAPM). Both are discussed in Chapter 9.

In the dividend discount model, the value of common stock is the present value of its expected dividend flows discounted at the stockholders' required rate of return. For a common stock whose dividend flows are expected to grow at a constant rate, g, its value (or price) is given by Equation 9.24:

$$P_0 = D_1/(k_C - g_D)$$

where k_C = stockholders' required rate of return (or the specific cost of common equity)

D_1 = next-year's expected dividend per share

g_D = expected growth rate of dividends

P_0 = current stock price per share

The current dividend and its expected growth rate can be used to forecast D_1. Then the price of common stock is determined entirely by the stockholders' required rate of return. For a given price and expected dividend, the implied stockholders' required rate of return (or the specific cost of equity) can be obtained by solving the model for k_C.

$$k_C = D_1/P_0 + g_D \quad (12.1)$$

where D_1/P_0 = the expected dividend yield

In the United States, stock prices increase when corporate earnings grow. The amount of the increase is directly (but not perfectly) related to the expected rate of growth. A growing company can pay out increasing dividends, although it is not obliged to do so. Therefore, the specific cost of common stock equation derived from the dividend discount model can be modified by replacing the dividend term with an earnings term. This way of defining the specific cost of common stock is particularly useful for companies that do not have any dividend record.

$$k_C = E_1/P_0 + g_E \quad (12.2)$$

where k_C = specific cost of common stock

P_0 = current stock price per share

E_1 = next-years' expected earnings per share

g_E = expected growth rate of earnings

E_1/P_0 = expected earnings-price ratio

If most of a company's stockholders (or the influential ones) are seeking income, Equation 12.1 is appropriate. As a general rule, the dividend yield on common stock should be approximately 60 percent of the prevailing rates offered to depositors by commercial banks, although this relationship varies, as Exhibit 12.10 illustrates. If the banks are paying 5 percent, the dividend yield on common stocks should be about $5 \times 0.6 = 3$ percent. Companies whose dividend yields are noticeably higher than 3 percent will attract income-seeking investors. Companies with dividend yields of 3 percent or less will attract investors who are seeking price appreciation through earnings growth.

If the stockholders are interested in realizing their return through price appreciation, Equation 12.2 is appropriate. The earnings-price ratio in this equation is the reciprocal of the price-earnings multiple, a barometer of investors' demand for a stock. Ignoring many academic controversies and real-world aberrations, one can assume that a normal long-run price-earnings multiple is in the 8× to 13× range.

EXHIBIT 12.10

Dividend Yields and Interest Rates

	Dividend Yield on Dow Jones Industrial Average	Interest Rate on 183-Day to 1-Year Time Deposits	Dividend Yield as a Percentage of Interest Rate
1962	3.60	4.00	0.90
1963	3.30	4.00	0.83
1964	3.70	4.50	0.82
1965	3.10	5.50	0.56
1966	3.70	5.00	0.74
1967	3.40	5.00	0.68
1968	3.50	5.00	0.70
1969	3.90	5.34	0.73
1970	4.20	5.34	0.79
1971	3.50	5.75	0.61
1972	3.40	5.75	0.59
1973	3.80	5.50	0.69
1974	5.00	5.50	0.91
1975	4.70	5.50	0.85
1976	4.20	5.50	0.76
1977	5.10	5.48	0.93
1978	5.90	5.49	1.07
1979	6.00	5.47	1.10
1980	6.10	5.65	1.08
1981	6.00	5.58	1.08
1982	6.10	8.89	0.69
1983	4.70	9.56	0.49
1984	5.10	9.11	0.56
1985	4.70	7.77	0.60
1986	3.70	7.54	0.40
1987	3.10	7.14	0.43
1988	3.90	8.19	0.48
1989	4.10	7.86	0.52
1990	3.60	7.33	0.49
1991	3.30	5.49	0.60

Sources: "A Long-Term Perspective: Dow Jones Industrial Average, 1920–1991," Supplement to *Value Line Investment Survey*, (1992); and *Statistical Abstract of the United States* (Washington, D.C.: U.S. Government Printing Office, various years).

This implies that a normal earnings-price ratio is in the 12.5 percent to 8 percent range. If investors are very anxious to buy a stock, they will push the price-earnings multiple up, lowering the earnings-price ratio. This does not mean that a company's specific cost of common stock will go down. A high price-earnings multiple is associated with a high expected rate of growth in earnings, so there is a balancing act going on within the k_C equation.

If investors are avoiding a stock or selling it off, they will push the price-earnings multiple down. This avoidance, however, will be the result of low or declining expectations about the company's long-term growth in earnings. Again, k_C will be more stable than the stock price.

❖ EXAMPLE 12.3

The Farina Way Company's common stock is currently selling for $24 a share. The company is expected to pay a $2 dividend next year, and future dividends are expected to grow at a long-term rate of $6\frac{2}{3}$ percent. The company's earnings per share are expected to be $3 and are expected to grow at a long-term rate of 7 percent. If the current rates being offered to commercial bank depositors are approximately 8 percent, calculate k_C.

Farina Way is paying out more than half of its earnings instead of reinvesting them, and the growth rates of dividends and earnings are almost the same. These are not characteristics of a company that will produce substantial price appreciation through reinvestment of growing earnings. Investors are only willing to pay $24/$3 = 8× the earnings of the company, which means they do not perceive Farina Way to be a rapidly growing company. Furthermore, bank rates of 8 percent imply dividend yields of about 8 × 0.6 = 4.8 percent. Farina Way's dividend yield is $2/$24 = $8\frac{1}{3}$ percent. Equation 12.1 should be used.

$$\begin{aligned} k_C &= 8\tfrac{1}{3} \text{ percent} + 6\tfrac{2}{3} \text{ percent} \\ &= 15 \text{ percent} \end{aligned}$$ ❖

❖ EXAMPLE 12.4

Backyard Computer Corp.'s common stock is currently trading at about $40 a share in the market. BCC has been paying 60 cents a year in dividends per share since it went public and is expected to continue this payment for the foreseeable future. Earnings per share are expected to be $3 next year, and are expected to grow at a long-term rate of 7 percent. If the current rates being offered by commercial banks to their depositors are approximately 6 percent, calculate k_C.

BCC is reinvesting most of its earnings to sustain its growth. Investors are willing to pay $40/$3 = 13.3× the earnings of the company, which means they are optimistic about BCC's future growth in earnings. Bank rates of 6 percent imply dividend yields of about 6 × 0.6 = 3.6 percent. BCC's dividend yield is $0.60/$40 = 1.5 percent. Equation 12.2 should be used.

$$\begin{aligned} k_C &= \$3/\$40 + 7 \text{ percent} \\ &= 14.5 \text{ percent} \end{aligned}$$ ❖

The second approach, the Capital Asset Pricing Model, defines investors' expected (or required) rate of return from a security in terms of a risk-free rate and a risk premium. See Equation 9.19. Using the symbol k in place of the R in this equation to make the expression consistent with the dividend discount model, the CAPM can be stated as:

$$E(k_i) = k_f + [E(k_m) - k_f]\beta_i$$

where $E(k_i)$ = expected return on security i
k_f = risk-free rate
$E(k_m)$ = expected return on the market portfolio
β_i = a measure of security's relative risk
$E(k_m) - k_f$ = market risk premium

The risk-free rate represents compensation for the time value of money, and the risk premium is compensation for systematic risk.

Since $E(k_i)$ is the risk-adjusted rate of return investors expect from the company, it is the specific cost of common equity for the company.

$$k_C = k_f + [E(k_m) - k_f]\beta_i \tag{12.3}$$

The specific cost of equity, defined in this way, depends on the prevailing risk-free rate, the market risk premium, and the stock's beta risk. The risk-free rate is observed and the market risk premium and the security's beta can be estimated.

❖ EXAMPLE 12.5

Newport Trading Co.'s stock has a beta of 1.5. If the expected return on the market portfolio is 8 percent and the risk-free rate is 5 percent, what is Newport's cost of equity capital?

Using the CAPM approach,

$$\begin{aligned} k_C &= 0.05 + 1.5(0.08 - 0.05) \\ &= 0.05 + 0.045 \\ &= 0.095, \text{ or } 9.5 \text{ percent} \end{aligned}$$ ❖

The two approaches to calculating the stockholders' required rate of return, the dividend discount model and the Capital Asset Pricing Model, may not produce the same required rate of return as they depend on different (though related) sets of data. The choice of an approach is left to the individual doing the calculation who should consider how easy each approach is to use in a particular case.

The dividend discount model is easy to understand and requires estimating only the dividend growth rate. The stock price is observed. The CAPM, on the other hand, is more complex and requires estimating the market risk premium and beta. Only the risk-free rate is observed. Errors in the estimation result in inaccurate measures of the cost of equity.

The dividend discount model, however, has one major disadvantage. As mentioned before, it can be applied only to those companies that pay dividends. Since the CAPM is based on market-generated information, it can be applied to all companies whose stocks are traded. The CAPM also treats investment risk explicitly.

Treasury Stock

treasury stock
Common stock that a company repurchases and holds.

Common stock that a company has repurchased to hold out of public hands is referred to as **treasury stock**. The firm pays no dividends on treasury stock. It has no cost or voting rights, and it is worthless in a bankruptcy liquidation. The company's acquisition of treasury stock reduces both the outstanding stock and paid-in capital items on its balance sheet. This pool of stock has several possible uses for a profitable corporation.

stock options
Fringe benefits that allow option holders to buy stock below market prices. Firms award them as part of employee compensation to encourage or reward performance.

The firm can distribute treasury stock when management or employees exercise their **stock options**. These stock options are not the puts and calls discussed in an earlier chapter. They are fringe benefits which allow holders to buy the company's stock below its current market price. Companies award stock options as part of employee compensation to encourage or reward performance. If the manager or employee has an incentive to be more productive, the company's earnings will grow, its stock price will rise, and the incentive will increase in value. The manager or employee may or may not be allowed to sell stock acquired in this way before leaving the company, depending on the terms of the specific options.

A company can also use treasury stock when it plans to acquire another company. Suppose that Company A, whose stock is selling at $25 per share, wants to acquire Company B, whose stock is selling at $46 per share. Company A may offer the stockholders of Company B two shares of A for every share of B that they own. If Company B has 1 million shares of stock outstanding, then Company A must hold 2 million of its own shares in order to make this offer. If it does not have 2 million shares of treasury stock available, it has to issue new shares and incur flotation costs.

If a company is short on cash, it can distribute treasury stock as a stock dividend instead of a cash dividend. This action may generate a flurry of odd-lot trading as some investors sell their new shares to get the cash.

The firm can contribute treasury stock instead of cash to its employee pension plan. Such contributions usually have no effect on the market price of the outstanding stock.

If the company cannot foresee using treasury stock for any of these purposes, it can hold it indefinitely or retire it. Firms rarely retire treasury stock because if they need to issue new stock at a later date the market will view the flotation cost that could have been avoided as wasted money.

Warrants

Sometimes, a corporation may expect difficulty selling a new bond issue. The company may not be in great financial shape, it may have turned down an uncomfortable number of the investment banker's suggestions while designing the bond, or it may consider the current state of the bond market to be unfavorable. In order to encourage investors to accept and buy its bonds, the company may attach warrants to them. A warrant is a security that gives the holder the right to buy shares of common stock from the company at a fixed price for a stated amount of time.

Firms may also issue warrants to sweeten stock issues. Whether they accompany stock or bonds, warrants can make issuing new securities easier and/or cheaper. They have an added bonus for the company at a later date, as well. If the stock price rises and the warrants are exercised, the company will receive an additional cash inflow. The firm can distribute treasury stock for this kind of transaction, as well, without fear of violating any security laws.

❖ EXAMPLE 12.6

Suppose that the L. L. Moppett Corporation has common stock trading in the market between \$31 and \$32 a share. The company issues a new bond with warrants attached. Each warrant allows the holder to buy three shares of common stock for \$100 during the coming six months. The warrants are worthless when the firm issues them. Anyone could buy three shares of Moppett for \$93 to \$96 in the market, so a warrant holder would be foolish to exercise the warrant and pay \$100 to buy three shares.

However, if Moppett stock were expected to rise to \$35 within the coming six months, the warrant would then be worth:

$$(3 \times \$35) - \$100 = \$5$$

In the expectation that Moppett stock might rise, the warrant will have a positive market value at issue. Greater expectations for a price increase would boost this value higher. Further, if Moppett stock were to reach \$35 within six months, the market price of the warrant would be greater than \$5, reflecting expectations that Moppett stock could go even higher. ❖

A bond's indenture specifies whether or not the warrants can be detached from the bond. Detachable warrants are usually issued to sweeten a new issue for the investment banker, which commits to buy the new bonds from the company and resell them to the public. The investment bank can detach the warrants and hold them or sell them separately if it expects the price of the company's stock to rise. Alternatively, the investment banker can leave the warrants attached to the bonds and sell both for a slightly higher price than the issue would otherwise command. Nondetachable warrants are usually issued to make a bond issue more attractive to the investing public.

A warrant can give rights to any number of shares, and a bond can have any number of warrants attached to it. Further, the company can set the expiration date on the warrants as far into the future as it wishes. One-year and four-year warrants are not uncommon, and some warrants are issued with no expiration date at all.

RETAINED EARNINGS

The profits that a company earns, but does not pay out in the form of dividends also constitute common stockholders' money. In a world without double taxation, a company could pay out 100 percent of its net income after taxes and then sell additional shares of stock to investors to increase its equity base. In the United States, however, corporations pay taxes on profits, then they pay out some after-tax profits to stockholders in the form of dividends. The government taxes these distributions again as income to the investors at the same rates they pay on their salaries. Theoretically, investors should require a rate of return on retained earn-

FOCUS ON FINANCE

WORTHLESS WARRANTS

Some companies have carried the concept of warrants to ridiculous extremes. In an attempt to substitute sweetness for quality, companies have been known to issue so many perpetual warrants that, if all of them were exercised, it would triple the number of shares of common stock outstanding. The market value of such warrants is usually a fraction of a penny apiece; the smallest price any of the authors remembers seeing is 1/256th of a dollar. These securities can depress the market value of the underlying stock because of the enormous spread between earnings per share and fully diluted earnings per share.

These warrants do attract some speculators because, with such tiny prices, any significant increase in demand can easily cause the price to double. These warrants also attract the attention of regulators when prices move. Speculators have been known to trade the warrants back and forth between themselves to give the market the false impression that demand for the warrants is increasing and spectacular rates of return are imminent. The SEC and the exchanges prohibit such artificial enhancement of trading volume, but charges of price manipulation have not been easy to prove.

ings (k_R) that is equivalent to the rate of return they could earn from reinvesting their after-tax dividends.

❖ EXAMPLE 12.7

Tompkins Inc. is earning 10 percent on money it has raised by selling common stock, and it pays a $1 annual dividend per share. Suppose that an investor must pay $0.39 in income tax on that dollar, leaving $0.61 to reinvest. What return could the investor expect on this money?

Assuming that the investor is satisfied with the risk–return combination available from Tompkins Inc., he or she can spend the 61 cents to purchase additional Tompkins common shares. The investor will earn 10 percent on this reinvested capital, generating a return of $0.61× 0.1, or $0.061 per dollar. This is the most satisfactory return available to this investor. ❖

If the company retains the dollar instead of paying it out as a dividend, the investor should be satisfied as long as the firm reinvests the dollar in any project that earns at least 6.1 percent. Tompkins Inc. would then do just as well for its investors as they could do for themselves. The specific cost of retained earnings should, therefore, be:

$$k_R = k_C(1 - \tau) \tag{12.4}$$

where k_R = specific cost of retained earnings

k_C = specific cost of common stock

τ = investor's personal income tax rate

Every Wall Street professional knows that if Tompkins were to retain that dollar and reinvest it at 6.1 percent, investors would sell their common stock holdings and the stock price would fall. In one of the irrationalities of the real world market, an investor who cannot earn 10 percent on a dollar of dividends still demands that the company continue earning 10 percent on every dollar it retains. For all practical purposes, then, the cost of retained earnings is:

$$k_R = k_C \tag{12.5}$$

SUMMARY

A lease is a form of financing that enables a company to acquire assets without first raising a large block of cash. The cost of financing an asset acquisition through a lease is calculated as the internal rate of return on the series of after-tax cash flows associated with the lease. Making a lease/buy decision involves comparing relevant cash flows; the spreadsheet format does this best. The lease/buy decision gets more complicated when the comparison must accommodate international financial arrangements.

Common stock is a security that represents an ownership share in a corporation. It cannot be callable, convertible, or cumulative. Its market price cannot legally be manipulated by the issuing company. Its dividend is not fixed or guaranteed. Established corporations are, to some extent, captives of their historic dividend payment policies. Reducing or omitting a dividend sends a strong signal to the market that the company may be on the verge of insolvency.

In case of bankruptcy, common stockholders are entitled to the residual value of the corporation. If any cash remains after the creditors and preferred stockholders have been paid in full, this remainder is divided among the common stockholders on a per-share basis.

Common stockholders elect members of their company's board of directors at the annual shareholders' meeting. They can vote by proxy if they do not attend the meeting in person. In straight voting, each shareholder has one vote per share for each position; in cumulative voting, these votes can be allocated as the stockholder wishes. Cumulative voting procedures magnify the power of small stockholders, but they may also facilitate takeover attempts.

Some corporations have more than one class of common stock outstanding. Each class may have different voting rights and receive different dividend payments.

Common stock prices generally appreciate in the long run. In order to keep their shares affordable, companies split their stocks when the shares become too expensive. Stock splits change the number of shares outstanding, the number of shares held by investors, the par value, and the market value of the shares. Splits do not change the value of investors' holdings or the value of the company's owners' equity.

The long-term increase in stock prices has another effect. It prevents the analyst from calculating the specific cost of common stock like the specific costs of bonds and preferred stock. To derive the cost of common stock, it is necessary to determine what sort of return the common stockholders require. If they want income, then the cost of capital formula should be based on dividends; if they want price appreciation, then the calculation of k_C should focus on earnings. An alternative approach, the CAPM model, defines the cost of equity in terms of a risk-free rate and a risk premium.

Common stock that a company repurchases and holds is called *treasury stock.* The company cannot resell it in the market without risking accusations that it is manipulating its own stock price. A firm can distribute treasury stock when:

1. Managers or employees exercise stock options
2. It wants to acquire a company through a stock-for-stock transaction
3. It pays a stock dividend in lieu of a cash dividend
4. It does not want to contribute cash to its pension fund
5. Warrantholders exercise their rights to buy stock from the firm

A warrant is a security that gives the holder the right to buy shares of common stock from the issuing company at a fixed price for a stated period of time. It can be attached to a new bond or stock issue to enhance the attractiveness of the new security.

The final source of long-term funds available to a company is its retained earnings. Since these funds belong to the common stockholders, the cost of retained earnings is the same as the cost of common stock.

Key Terms

book value
capital surplus
cumulative voting
financial (capital) lease
killer *B*s
lessee
lessor
operating (service) lease
preemptive right
proxy statement
stock option
straight voting
treasury stock

Self-Study Questions

1. Which type of lease shows up on a company's balance sheet?
2. What three steps are part of the decision to lease or purchase an asset?
3. How might an international lease involve three currencies?
4. If a company's board of directors decides not to declare a dividend on its common stock, what alternatives do the common stockholders have?
5. If a company's board of directors cuts the dividend on a firm's outstanding stock, what signal does the market perceive?
6. What is the difference between straight voting and cumulative voting?
7. Why might a company have more than one class of common stock outstanding?
8. Name three things a company can do with its treasury stock.
9. What is a warrant?

10. If a company's cost of common stock is 16 percent, what is the cost of its retained earnings? Why?

Self-Test Problems

1. A restaurant leases a $35,000 commercial oven for three years. After taxes, the lease payments are $1,100 per month. What is k_L, the cost of the lease?
2. The Spayce Sprocket Co. leases its employee parking lot for ten years. Spayce could have purchased the land for $100,000. The lease contract calls for monthly payments of $1,400 and specifies that, at termination, Spayce can renew the lease, but it cannot purchase the land. If Spayce has a 40 percent tax rate, find the annual cost of leasing.
3. Spacetoy Inc. is considering leasing a machine that it could buy for $600,000. If it were to borrow the money to buy the machine, it could get a six-year term loan at 8 percent. The interest would be payable every six months. If Spacetoy Inc. were to buy the machine, it would also have to buy annual service contracts, which it estimates would cost $10,000 at the beginning of each year. The machine belongs in the five-year MACRS property class for depreciation purposes. It will be depreciated semiannually and will have no salvage value at the end of its sixth year. If Spacetoy Inc. leases the machine, it must make semiannual lease payments of $55,000. Spacetoy Inc. has a 30 percent tax rate and an average after-tax cost of debt of 5 percent. Should Spacetoy Inc. lease the machine or buy it?
4. EZ Travel Agency is considering leasing or buying a $7.5 million touring bus. It could get a three-year mortgage loan at 10 percent; the monthly payment of $242,000 would leave no balloon. Ownership of the bus would cost EZ $1,000 a month in maintenance, an expense that it would not incur if it were to lease the bus. The bus would fall in the seven-year MACRS property class for depreciation purposes, and EZ can sell it for its book value any time during its life. Depreciation would be charged quarterly. EZ could lease the bus for a monthly payment of $200,000. The company has a 36 percent tax rate and its after-tax cost of debt is 7 percent. Should the firm purchase the bus or lease it?
5. Four of a company's directors are to be elected. If stockholders can cast 1 million votes in a cumulative voting system, how many votes does any one director need in order to get elected?
6. One director is to be elected. Stockholders will cast 80,000 votes in a cumulative voting system. How many votes does a candidate need in order to get elected? How many votes would one need in a straight voting system?
7. What effect would a 4-for-3 stock split have on a stock with a par value of $26 and a market price of $50?
8. What effect would a 5-for-2 stock split have on a stock with earnings per share of $7.50 and a market price of $120?
9. A company that pays no dividends reports earnings per share of $2. Over the last ten years, its earnings per share have grown at a compound rate of 6

percent. If the current stock price is $25 a share, what is the cost of this common stock?

10. Outstanding stock of the Grand Canyon Lighting Co. trades at $30 a share. If GCL has been paying a $3 dividend since 1975 and the current bank rate is 5 percent, what is GCL's cost of common stock?
11. Ritter and Renwick, Inc. has stock outstanding with a beta of 1.15. If the expected return on the S&P 500 is 12 percent and the risk-free rate is 3 percent, what is the company's cost of equity capital?
12. The Gruber Corporation's stock has a beta of 0.80. The market portfolio is expected to produce a return of 10 percent, and the risk-free rate is 4 percent. What is Gruber's cost of equity capital?

Discussion Questions

1. How does an operating lease differ from a financial lease?
2. Give two reasons why a financial lease does not meet the IRS criteria for a true lease.
3. Why might a lease contract contain a clause allowing future lease payments to vary?
4. When comparing the costs of leasing and purchasing an asset, why must the analyst assume that the purchase would be financed with debt?
5. Why are exchange rate fluctuations an important factor in international leasing arrangements?
6. Why can't common stock be callable or convertible?
7. If a company that has paid a slowly but steadily growing dividend for years institutes a policy of paying out one-third of its earnings in the form of dividends, how will the stock market react?
8. What do common stockholders get if their company goes bankrupt?
9. What is meant by the one share, one vote rule?
10. Explain voting by proxy.
11. Explain one way a corporation can protect itself from takeover attempts.
12. Give two reasons why the cost of common stock cannot be calculated the same way as k_D and k_P.
13. Jack Daniels bought 100 shares of stock in Sharp Axe Co. many years ago. While he has held it, the stock split 2-for-1, 3-for-2, and then 2-for-1 again. How many shares does Jack have now?
14. Suppose that banks currently pay interest rates of 7 percent. Would a common stock with a 5 percent dividend yield attract investors who wanted income or price appreciation?
15. Explain a preemptive right and what advantage it gives to existing shareholders.
16. Why do stock dividends normally depress the price of outstanding common stock?
17. How can treasury stock provide a profit incentive?
18. Why do companies issue warrants?

19. How does a company decide whether to make its warrants detachable or nondetachable?
20. Why does double taxation give a company an incentive to retain its earnings?

Problems

1. A company leases a machine worth $185,000 for five years. The lease payment is $5,000 per month and the company has a 30 percent tax rate. Find k_L.
2. A company leases a communications system worth $1 million for two years. The lease payment is $66,000 per month and the company has a 33 percent tax rate. Find k_L.
3. A manufacturer is considering whether to lease a new machine or buy it for $250,000. The machine's producer offers a two-year installment loan at 9 percent with interest payable monthly. Purchasing the machine would add $300 per month to the company's maintenance costs. The machine would fall in the three-year property class for MACRS depreciation purposes, but the firm could sell it for its book value at any time. Alternatively, the firm could lease the machine for $12,000 per month. If the company has a 33 percent tax rate and an after-tax cost of debt of 6 percent, should it lease or buy the machine?
4. The Dandy Dipper Co. is facing a lease/purchase decision on $400,000 of dipping equipment. The manufacturer offers a four-year mortgage note at 7⅜ percent. The monthly payment will be $9,648.24. Because of rounding, the final payment (in the 48th month) will be $9,648.46. Ownership of the equipment will cost Dandy Dipper $500 a month for cleaning and servicing. The firm would avoid this expense if it were to lease the equipment. Dipping equipment belongs in the seven-year property class for depreciation purposes. Dandy Dipper calculates depreciation monthly and assumes that at any point in time, the equipment's book value equals its salvage value. If the firm were to lease the equipment, the monthly lease payment would be $8,000. Dandy Dipper has a 35 percent tax rate and its after-tax cost of debt is 8 percent. Should it purchase or lease the equipment?
5. Eight of a company's 24 directors are to be elected. If stockholders will cast 45,676,789 votes in a cumulative system, how many votes does any one director need in order to get elected?
6. Two of a company's 24 directors are to be elected. If stockholders will cast 45,676,789 votes in a cumulative voting system, how many votes does any one director need in order to get elected?
7. What effect would a 2-for-1 stock split have on a stock with a par value of $50, a market price of $108, and earnings per share of $21?
8. What effect would a 10 percent stock dividend have on a stock with a par value of $50, a market price of $108, and earnings per share of $21?

9. If a stock has a dividend yield of 5 percent and the dividend is expected to grow at an annual rate of 6 percent, what is k_C?
10. If a stock is selling for ten times earnings and the earnings are growing at 8 percent annually, what is k_C?
11. Hobart Car Company's stock has a beta of 1.3. The S&P 500 is expected to produce a 9 percent return, and the risk-free rate is 4.5 percent. What is k_C for Hobart?
12. The Kast Iron Co. has stock outstanding with a beta of 0.75. If the market portfolio is expected to return 15 percent and the risk-free rate is 5 percent, what is the Kast Iron Company's cost of equity?

Topics for Further Research

1. Visit your favorite car dealer. Describe the car you want, then determine the cash flows associated with leasing it. Also determine the cash flows associated with buying it. Use your least expensive credit card rate as your discount rate, and determine whether it is cheaper to lease or buy your car.
2. Examine a copy of the *Value Line Investment Survey*, Part 3, "Ratings and Reports." The last page of each report shows a list with the title "Stock Dividends Declared." First, determine which listings are stock splits and which are true stock dividends. Look up each company on the list that has an ex-date. How did the price of each company's stock behave before and after that ex-date?
3. Examine the oldest copies of Moody's *Bond Survey* available to you. Find a bond or preferred stock that was issued with warrants (the listing will show "w/wts"). Examine subsequent newspaper reports to determine the market price of the warrants. Examine the appropriate Moody's *Manual* to determine the terms of the warrant. Is it a worthless warrant?

Answers to Self-Test Problems

1.

$$
\begin{aligned}
0 &= \$1{,}100(PVIFA_{k,36}) - \$35{,}000 \\
PVIFA_{k,36} &= \$35{,}000/\$1{,}100 \\
&= 31.81818 \\
k_L &= 0.006833 \text{ per month} \\
&= 0.081996, \text{ or } 8.2 \text{ percent per year}
\end{aligned}
$$

2.

$$
\begin{aligned}
0 &= \$1{,}400(1 - 0.4)(PVIFA_{k,120}) - \$100{,}000 \\
PVIFA_{k,120} &= \$100{,}000/\$840 \\
&= 119.0476
\end{aligned}
$$

An annuity that lasts as long as 120 periods can be treated as a perpetuity, so $119.0476 = 1/k$.

$$
\begin{aligned}
k_L &= 0.0084 \text{ per month} \\
&= 0.1008, \text{ or } 10.08 \text{ percent per year}
\end{aligned}
$$

3. Exhibit 12.11 displays the necessary calculations. The interest would be $48,000 per year and the $600,000 loan would be repaid in full at the end

EXHIBIT 12.11

Spacetoy Inc. Lease or Buy Spreadsheet

Time	Interest	Principal Repayment	Total Payment	Outstanding Balance	MACRS Depreciation	Service Contract
0	0.00	0.00	0.00	600,000.00	0.00	10,000.00
1	24,000.00	0.00	24,000.00	600,000.00	60,000.00	0.00
2	24,000.00	0.00	24,000.00	600,000.00	60,000.00	10,000.00
3	24,000.00	0.00	24,000.00	600,000.00	96,000.00	0.00
4	24,000.00	0.00	24,000.00	600,000.00	96,000.00	10,000.00
5	24,000.00	0.00	24,000.00	600,000.00	57,600.00	0.00
6	24,000.00	0.00	24,000.00	600,000.00	57,600.00	10,000.00
7	24,000.00	0.00	24,000.00	600,000.00	34,560.00	0.00
8	24,000.00	0.00	24,000.00	600,000.00	34,560.00	10,000.00
9	24,000.00	0.00	24,000.00	600,000.00	34,560.00	0.00
10	24,000.00	0.00	24,000.00	600,000.00	34,560.00	10,000.00
11	24,000.00	0.00	24,000.00	600,000.00	34,560.00	0.00
12	24,000.00	600,000.00	624,000.00	0.00	0.00	0.00
					Depreciation = 600,000.00	
					Book Value = 0.00	

of the sixth year. The MACRS depreciation schedule would charge 20 percent of the value of the asset in Year 1; 32 percent in Year 2; 19.2 percent in Year 3; 11.52 percent each in Years 4 and 5; and 5.76 percent (the half-year convention) in Year 6. The interest, service contract, and depreciation would be tax deductible. The discount rate would be 2.5 percent semiannually. Since the NPV is positive, the company should lease the machine.

4. Exhibit 12.12 illustrates the necessary calculations. The MACRS depreciation schedule would charge 14.29% of the value of the bus in Year 1, 24.49 percent in Year 2, and 17.49 percent in Year 3. At the end of three years, the total depreciation taken would amount to $4,220,250 and the bus could be sold for $7.5 million less that amount, or $3,279,750. The discount rate would be 0.583 percent per month. Since the NPV is negative, the company should buy the bus.

5. $1{,}000{,}000 \times 1/(4 + 1) + 1 = 200{,}001$ votes

6. $80{,}000 \times 1/(1 + 1) + 1 = 40{,}001$ votes, the same as for a straight voting system

7. New par value $= \$26 \times 3/4 = \$19.50$

   New market price $= \$50.00 \times 3/4 = \$37.50$

8. New earnings per share $= \$7.50 \times 2/5 = \$3.00$

   New market price $= \$120 \times 2/5 = \$48$

TOTAL DEDUCTIBLE	TAX SHIELD	PURCHASE CASH FLOW	LEASE PAYMENT	AFTER-TAX LEASE CASH FLOW	CASH FLOW DIFFERENCE	PRESENT VALUE OF DIFFERENCE
10,000.00	3,000.00	7,000.00	55,000.00	38,500.00	–31,500.00	–31,500.00
84,000.00	25,200.00	–1,200.00	55,000.00	38,500.00	–39,700.00	–38,731.71
94,000.00	28,200.00	5,800.00	55,000.00	38,500.00	–32,700.00	–31,124.33
120,000.00	36,000.00	–12,000.00	55,000.00	38,500.00	–50,500.00	–46,894.27
130,000.00	39,000.00	–5,000.00	55,000.00	38,500.00	–43,500.00	–39,408.85
81,600.00	24,480.00	–480.00	55,000.00	38,500.00	–38,980.00	–34,452.64
91,600.00	27,480.00	6,520.00	55,000.00	38,500.00	–31,980.00	–27,576.25
58,560.00	17,568.00	6,432.00	55,000.00	38,500.00	–32,068.00	–26,977.69
68,560.00	20,568.00	13,432.00	55,000.00	38,500.00	–25,068.00	–20,574.48
58,560.00	17,568.00	6,432.00	55,000.00	38,500.00	–32,068.00	–25,677.76
68,560.00	20,568.00	13,432.00	55,000.00	38,500.00	–25,068.00	–19,583.08
58,560.00	17,568.00	6,432.00	55,000.00	38,500.00	–32,068.00	–24,440.46
24,000.00	7,200.00	616,800.00	0.00	0.00	616,800.00	458,625.27
						NPV = 91,683.75

9. $$k_C = \$2/\$25 + 6\%$$
$$= 14 \text{ percent}$$

10. $$k_C = \$3/\$30 + 0\%$$
$$= 10 \text{ percent}$$

11. $$k_C = 0.03 + 1.15(0.12 - 0.03)$$
$$= 0.03 + 0.1035$$
$$= 0.1335, \text{ or } 13.4 \text{ percent}$$

12. $$k_C = 0.04 + 0.8(0.10 - 0.04)$$
$$= 0.04 + 0.048$$
$$= 0.088, \text{ or } 8.8 \text{ percent}$$

EXHIBIT 12.12

EZ Travel Agency Lease or Buy Spreadsheet

Time	Interest	Principal Repayment	Total Payment	Outstanding Balance	MACRS Depreciation	Service Contract
0	0.00	0.00	0.00	7,500,000.00	0.00	10,000.00
1	62,500.00	179,500.00	242,000.00	7,320,500.00	0.00	10,000.00
2	61,004.17	180,995.83	242,000.00	7,139,504.17	0.00	10,000.00
3	59,495.87	182,504.13	242,000.00	6,957,000.03	267,937.50	10,000.00
4	57,975.00	184,025.00	242,000.00	6,772,975.04	0.00	10,000.00
5	56,441.46	185,558.54	242,000.00	6,587,416.49	0.00	10,000.00
6	54,895.14	187,104.86	242,000.00	6,400,311.63	267,937.50	10,000.00
7	53,335.93	188,664.07	242,000.00	6,211,647.56	0.00	10,000.00
8	51,763.73	190,236.27	242,000.00	6,021,411.29	0.00	10,000.00
9	50,178.43	191,821.57	242,000.00	5,829,589.72	267,937.50	10,000.00
10	48,579.91	193,420.09	242,000.00	5,636,169.63	0.00	10,000.00
11	46,968.08	195,031.92	242,000.00	5,441,137.71	0.00	10,000.00
12	45,342.81	196,657.19	242,000.00	5,244,480.53	267,937.50	10,000.00
13	43,704.00	198,296.00	242,000.00	5,046,184.53	0.00	10,000.00
14	42,051.54	199,948.46	242,000.00	4,846,236.07	0.00	10,000.00
15	40,385.30	201,614.70	242,000.00	4,644,621.37	459,187.50	10,000.00
16	38,705.18	203,294.82	242,000.00	4,441,326.55	0.00	10,000.00
17	37,011.05	204,988.95	242,000.00	4,236,337.60	0.00	10,000.00
18	35,302.81	206,697.19	242,000.00	4,029,640.42	459,187.50	10,000.00
19	33,580.34	208,419.66	242,000.00	3,821,220.75	0.00	10,000.00
20	31,843.51	210,156.49	242,000.00	3,611,064.26	0.00	10,000.00
21	30,092.20	211,907.80	242,000.00	3,399,156.46	459,187.50	10,000.00
22	28,326.30	213,673.70	242,000.00	3,185,482.77	0.00	10,000.00
23	26,545.69	215,454.31	242,000.00	2,970,028.45	0.00	10,000.00
24	24,750.24	217,249.76	242,000.00	2,752,778.69	459,187.50	10,000.00
25	22,939.82	219,060.18	242,000.00	2,533,718.51	0.00	10,000.00
26	21,114.32	220,885.68	242,000.00	2,312,832.84	0.00	10,000.00
27	19,273.61	222,726.39	242,000.00	2,090,106.44	327,937.50	10,000.00
28	17,417.55	224,582.45	242,000.00	1,865,524.00	0.00	10,000.00
29	15,546.03	226,453.97	242,000.00	1,639,070.03	0.00	10,000.00
30	13,658.92	228,341.08	242,000.00	1,410,728.95	327,937.50	10,000.00
31	11,756.07	230,243.93	242,000.00	1,180,485.02	0.00	10,000.00
32	9,837.38	232,162.62	242,000.00	948,322.40	0.00	10,000.00
33	7,902.69	234,097.31	242,000.00	714,225.08	327,937.50	10,000.00
34	5,951.88	236,048.12	242,000.00	478,176.96	0.00	10,000.00
35	3,984.81	238,015.19	242,000.00	240,161.77	0.00	10,000.00
36	2,001.35	240,161.77	242,163.12	0.00	327,937.50	0.00
				Depreciation =	4,220,250.00	
				Book Value =	3,279,750.00	

Total Deductible	Tax Shield	Purchase Cash Flow	Lease Payment	After-Tax Lease Cash Flow	Cash Flow Difference	Present Value of Difference
10,000.00	3,600.00	6,400.00	200,000.00	128,000.00	−121,600.00	−121,600.00
72,500.00	26,100.00	225,900.00	200,000.00	128,000.00	97,900.00	97,332.23
71,004.17	25,561.50	226,438.50	200,000.00	128,000.00	98,438.50	97,300.02
337,433.37	121,476.01	130,523.99	200,000.00	128,000.00	2,523.99	2,480.33
67,975.00	24,471.00	227,529.00	200,000.00	128,000.00	99,529.00	97,240.13
66,441.46	23,918.93	228,081.07	200,000.00	128,000.00	100,081.07	97,212.44
332,832.64	119,819.75	132,180.25	200,000.00	128,000.00	4,180.25	4,036.88
63,335.93	22,800.93	229,199.07	200,000.00	128,000.00	101,199.07	97,161.53
61,763.73	22,234.94	229,765.06	200,000.00	128,000.00	101,765.06	97,138.30
328,115.93	118,121.73	133,878.27	200,000.00	128,000.00	5,878.27	5,578.47
58,579.91	21,088.77	230,911.23	200,000.00	128,000.00	102,911.23	97,096.27
56,968.08	20,508.51	231,491.49	200,000.00	128,000.00	103,491.49	97,077.45
323,280.31	116,380.91	135,619.09	200,000.00	128,000.00	7,619.09	7,105.43
53,704.00	19,333.44	232,666.56	200,000.00	128,000.00	104,666.56	97,044.21
52,051.54	18,738.55	233,261.45	200,000.00	128,000.00	105,261.45	97,029.77
509,572.80	183,446.21	68,553.79	200,000.00	128,000.00	−59,446.21	−54,479.59
48,705.18	17,533.86	234,466.14	200,000.00	128,000.00	106,466.14	97,005.22
47,011.05	16,923.98	235,076.02	200,000.00	128,000.00	107,076.02	96,995.10
504,490.31	181,616.51	70,383.49	200,000.00	128,000.00	−57,616.51	−51,889.39
43,580.34	15,688.92	236,311.08	200,000.00	128,000.00	108,311.08	96,979.16
41,843.51	15,063.66	236,936.34	200,000.00	128,000.00	108,936.34	96,973.33
499,279.70	179,740.69	72,259.31	200,000.00	128,000.00	−55,740.69	−49,331.67
38,326.30	13,797.47	238,202.53	200,000.00	128,000.00	110,202.53	96,965.90
36,545.69	13,156.45	238,843.55	200,000.00	128,000.00	110,843.55	96,964.30
493,937.74	177,817.59	74,182.41	200,000.00	128,000.00	−53,817.59	−46,805.80
32,939.82	11,858.34	240,141.66	200,000.00	128,000.00	112,141.66	96,965.31
31,114.32	11,201.16	240,798.84	200,000.00	128,000.00	112,798.84	96,967.91
357,211.11	128,596.00	123,404.00	200,000.00	128,000.00	−4,596.00	−3,928.05
27,417.55	9,870.32	242,129.68	200,000.00	128,000.00	114,129.68	96,977.26
25,546.03	9,196.57	242,803.43	200,000.00	128,000.00	114,803.43	96,984.01
351,596.42	126,574.71	125,425.29	200,000.00	128,000.00	−2,574.71	−2,162.46
21,756.07	7,832.19	244,167.81	200,000.00	128,000.00	116,167.81	97,001.64
19,837.38	7,141.46	244,858.54	200,000.00	128,000.00	116,858.54	97,012.50
345,840.19	124,502.47	127,497.53	200,000.00	128,000.00	−502.47	−414.71
15,951.88	5,742.68	246,257.32	200,000.00	128,000.00	118,257.32	97,038.31
13,984.81	5,034.53	24,695.47	200,000.00	128,000.00	118,965.47	97,053.25
329,938.85	118,777.99	−3,156,364.87	0.00	0.00	−3,156,364.87	−2,560,061.13
						NPV = −541,956.11

APPENDIX 12A

Example Solutions Using Lotus 1-2-3

The solutions given below for the examples in Chapter 12 use @functions in *Lotus 1-2-3* when they are available. If the predefined functions do not generate the desired solutions, the formulas necessary to solve the examples are given. These formulas should be copied *exactly*; insert no extra commas, dollar signs, or blank spaces. The notation <RET> indicates that you should press the enter or return key. Remember the sequence of mathematical operations (unless parentheses in the formula change it):

1. Exponents (^) are calculated first.
2. Multiplication (*) and division (/) are performed next.
3. Addition (+) and subtraction (–) are performed last.

❖ EXAMPLE 12.1

Enter in Cell A1: –2444
Enter in Cell A2: 56
Enter in Cell A3: /CA2 <RET> A3..A60
Enter in Cell A61: @IRR(.01,A1..A60)
Answer in Cell A61: 0.010647, or 1.06 percent
Enter in Cell A62: +A61*12
Answer in Cell A62: 0.127758, or 12.78 percent

❖ EXAMPLE 12.2

Loan Columns

Leave Cell A1 blank.
Enter in Cell A2: Time
Enter in Cell A3: 0
Enter in Cell A4: +A3+1
Enter in Cell A5: /CA4 <RET> A5..A39
Leave Cell B1 blank.
Enter in Cell B2: Interest
Enter in Cell B3: 0
Enter in Cell B4: +E3*.01
Enter in Cell B5: /CB4 <RET> B5..B39
Enter in Cell D1: Total
Enter in Cell D2: Payment
Enter in Cell D3: 0
Enter in Cell D4: 33000
Enter in Cell D5: /CD4 <RET> D5..D38

Enter in Cell C1: Principal
Enter in Cell C2: Repayment
Enter in Cell C3: 0
Enter in Cell C4: +D4–B4
Enter in Cell C5: /CC4 <RET> C5..C38
Enter in Cell E1: Outstanding
Enter in Cell E2: Balance
Enter in Cell E3: 1000000
Enter in Cell E4: +E3–C4
Enter in Cell E5: /CE4 <RET> E5..E38
Enter in Cell E39: 0
Enter in Cell C39: +E38
Enter in Cell D39: +B39+C39

Purchase Columns

Enter in Cell F1: MACRS
Enter in Cell F2: Depreciation
Enter in Cell F3: 0
Enter in Cell F4: /CF3 <RET> F4..F39
Enter in Cells F6, F9, F12, and F15: 333300/4
Enter in Cells F18, F21, F24, and F27: 444400/4
Enter in Cells F30, F33, F36, and F39: 148200/4
Enter in Cell G1: Service
Enter in Cell G2: Contract
Enter in Cell G3: 1000
Enter in Cell G4: /CG3 <RET> G4..G38
Enter in Cell G39: 0
Leave Cell J1 blank.
Enter in Cell J2: Adjustments
Enter in Cell J3: 0
Enter in Cell J4: /CJ3 <RET> J4..J38
Enter in Cell J39 –74100

Cash Flow Calculation Columns

Enter in Cell H1: Total
Enter in Cell H2: Deductible
Enter in Cell H3: +B3+F3+G3
Enter in Cell H4: /CH3 <RET> H4..H39
Leave Cell I1 blank.
Enter in Cell I2: Tax Shield
Enter in Cell I3: +H3*.4
Enter in Cell I4: /CI3 <RET> I4..I39
Enter in Cell K1: Purchase
Enter in Cell K2: Cash Flow
Enter in Cell K3: +D3+G3–H3+J3

Enter in Cell K4: /CK3 <RET> K4..K39

Lease Columns

Enter in Cell L1: Lease
Enter in Cell L2: Payment
Enter in Cell L3: 30000
Enter in Cell L4: /CL3 <RET> L4..L38
Enter in Cell L39: 0
Enter in Cell M1: Lease
Enter in Cell M2: Cash Flow
Enter in Cell M3: +L3*(1–.4)
Enter in Cell M4: /CM3 <RET> M4..M39

Present Value of the Difference Columns

Enter in Cell N1: Cash Flow
Enter in Cell N2: Difference
Enter in Cell N3: +K3–M3
Enter in Cell N4: /CN3 <RET> N4..N39
Enter in Cell O1: Present Value
Enter in Cell O2: of Difference
Enter in Cell O3: +N3
Enter in Cell O4: +N4/(1 + .006)^1
Enter in Cell O5: +N5/(1 + .006)^2

Repeat this sequence until you reach Cell O39.

Enter in Cell O39: +N39/(1 + .006)^36
Enter in Cell O41: @SUM(O3..O39)

CHAPTER

13

Cost of Capital and Capital Structure Policy

LEARNING OBJECTIVES

This chapter examines the weighted average and marginal costs of capital, and the theories relating capital costs to capital structure. At the conclusion of this chapter, the reader should be able to:

1. *Calculate a company's weighted average cost of capital*
2. *Describe how a financial analyst outside the company could measure and evaluate a company's capital structure*
3. *Explain the relationship between a company's cost of capital and its capital structure*
4. *Choose the best way to raise additional long-term funds for a company that needs external capital*
5. *Calculate a company's marginal cost of capital, whether it raises funds domestically or from foreign sources*
6. *Explain the implications of the marginal cost of capital*

The weighted average of the specific costs of captial of a company's financing sources sets a minimum performance standard for its assets. They must produce a return at least as high as the cost of the funds that the firm spends to obtain them.

Theories have evolved and changed substantially over the past 40 years to explain the behavior of this weighted average cost. Originally, it was believed that the cost of capital depended on a company's capital structure, that is, the proportions of debt and equity financing it used. Classic theory held that each company could identify one optimal (minimum cost) debt ratio. In the 1950s, empirical research suggested that the cost of capital was not affected by the debt ratio at all. This research later brought its authors Nobel prizes. Subsequent statistical analyses have shown, however, that to minimize its cost of capital a firm should keep its debt ratio within a certain range. The range varies depending on the type of business as well as the stage of the economic cycle.

A company whose debt ratio is within its optimal range can raise funds by issuing bonds, preferred stock, or common stock. It should choose whichever security maximizes the earnings per share available for distribution to the common shareholders. In other words, the method of financing should maximize shareholder wealth.

Whenever a company obtains substantial external funds, it must recalculate its weighted average cost of capital. This suggests that the firm can calculate a marginal cost of capital, one of several criteria by which it can select new assets.

WEIGHTED AVERAGE COST OF CAPITAL

After determining the cost of each specific source of a firm's capital, an analyst will calculate the weighted average cost of capital, k. The company's assets should produce a rate of return higher than k, and one of the financial manager's responsibilities is to keep the average cost of capital as low as possible. The weights in this calculation are the proportions of each specific source of capital. This average is defined by the equation:

$$k = w_D k_D + w_L k_L + w_P k_P + w_C k_C + w_R k_R \qquad (13.1)$$

where w_i = weight of the specific source of capital
k_i = cost of the specific source of capital
D = debt
L = lease
P = preferred stock
C = common stock
R = retained earnings

Chapter 12 explained that $k_C = k_R$, so equity can be defined as common stock plus retained earnings. The cost of equity becomes $k_E = k_C = k_R$ and the weight of equity can be calculated as $w_E = w_C + w_R$. This reduces Equation 13.1 to:

$$k = w_D k_D + w_L k_L + w_P k_P + w_E k_E \qquad (13.2)$$

❖ EXAMPLE 13.1

Suppose that Trixie Industries' total capital consists of $300 million in debt, $100 million in leased assets, no outstanding preferred stock, $400 million in common stock, and $200 million in retained earnings. Its after-tax specific costs are 6 percent for the debt, 8 percent for the leases, and 10 percent for the equity.

$$
\begin{aligned}
\text{Total capital} &= (\$300 + \$100 + \$400 + \$200) \text{ million} \\
&= \$1{,}000 \text{ million, or } \$1 \text{ billion} \\
w_D &= \$300 \text{ million}/\$1 \text{ billion} \\
&= 0.3 \\
w_L &= \$100 \text{ million}/\$1 \text{ billion} \\
&= 0.1 \\
w_P &= 0 \\
w_E &= (\$400 \text{ million} + \$200 \text{ million})/\$1 \text{ billion} \\
&= 0.6 \\
k &= (0.3)(6\%) + (0.1)(8\%) + (0.6)(10\%) \\
&= 8.6 \text{ percent}
\end{aligned}
$$

A company must generate a return on its assets at least equal to its weighted average cost of capital in order to justify its existence economically. If the return on assets is less than the cost of the funds used to obtain those assets, then management must take remedial action to either raise the rate of return or lower the cost of funds, or both.

Variations in Calculating k

Some financial authorities have claimed that no two people would calculate exactly the same cost of capital for a company unless they were in direct communication and detailed agreement with each other. While this statement probably exaggerates the variation of methods, it contains some truth, for several reasons.

Book Weights versus Market Weights. Analysts can calculate and use the weighted average cost of capital for two different reasons. The first purpose is historical; this figure is the only information that potential investors and financial analysts outside the company can find to evaluate the company's recent performance. They derive the weights of the various sources of funds from book values (the amounts shown on the firm's balance sheet). When k is calculated this way, it is compared to the company's return on existing assets. This return equals net income after taxes, expressed as a percentage of the book value of the company's assets.

The relevance of this historical value comes from the fact that a company has financed its existing assets by a pool of funds. No one can look at a company's balance sheet and identify individual assets that it financed by specific funds it borrowed, retained, or raised by selling preferred or common stock. Dollars invested in a company and subsequently circulating within it are **fungible dollars**, which means that no one can identify their specific origins. A company's balance sheet does not even identify large blocks of land, buildings, and/or machinery acquired by specific forms of financing. To obtain such information, one must search through a company's past quarterly and annual financial reports and press releases.

fungible dollar
Money circulating in a corporation that cannot be connected to a specific origin.

Besides a historical value, one can calculate a current value for the weighted average cost of capital. This method is used by a company's financial manager as part of financial decision making. The current value assigns weights to the various sources of funds based on the market values of outstanding issues, (taking the exact number of outstanding bonds or stock shares multiplied by their current market prices). The manager uses k calculated in this way to derive the company's marginal cost of capital, which then functions as a discount rate when selecting assets by the NPV, PI, and IRR methods (as described in Chapter 10).

Some finance theorists have attempted to label the current and historical cost of capital calculations as "true" and "biased," but such a judgmental appraisal is unnecessary. These two calculations can coexist peacefully because:

1. They serve two different purposes: current decision making and evaluation of past performance.
2. They are used by two different groups: internal managers and external analysts.

Arbitrary Security Pricing. Calculated costs of capital can also vary because both the market weights and the specific costs of securities rely on those securities' current market prices. This is a problem because the definition of *current* is arbitrary. The current price could be the closing price on the last day of the week, the month, or the quarter. It could be the average price at which the security traded yesterday or last week or over the last ten days. It could be the price at which the financial manager expects the security to trade in the near future, but how near?

In fact, the cost of capital depends on the price at which the CEO or CFO thinks the security should trade. Whether or not this executive's opinion is realistic, it is the source of the number used in the company's internal calculations. Given the enormous capitalization of most corporations, a difference of even a dollar in the choice of a current market price can significantly affect the company's weighted average cost of capital.

Different Sources of Information. The data that an analyst gathers determines the calculated cost of capital. One easily accessible source of data that can help the general public to evaluate the recent performance of a company is the *Value Line Investment Survey*. This publication makes the calculation of a company's weighted average cost of capital relatively quick and painless. Exhibit 13.1 shows Value Line data for American Brands as of December 24, 1993.

❖ EXAMPLE 13.2

Exhibit 13.1 provides information to calculate the weighted average cost of capital for American Brands.

EXHIBIT 13.1

Value Line Data on American Brands

AMERICAN BRANDS NYSE-AMB | RECENT PRICE **33** | P/E RATIO **11.1** (Trailing: 8.8 Median: 9.5) | RELATIVE P/E RATIO **0.70** | DIV'D YLD **6.0%** | VALUE LINE **313**

TIMELINESS 4 Below Average (Relative Price Performance Next 12 Mos.)
SAFETY 2 Above Average (Scale: 1 Highest to 5 Lowest)
BETA 1.10 (1.00 = Market)

High:	12.8	15.1	16.3	17.5	26.3	30.0	35.9	40.9	41.6	47.6	49.9	40.6
Low:	8.8	10.8	13.2	13.3	15.7	18.3	21.1	30.6	30.9	35.6	39.0	28.5

1996-98 PROJECTIONS

	Price	Gain	Ann'l Total Return
High	60	(+80%)	20%
Low	45	(+35%)	13%

Insider Decisions

	M	A	M	J	J	A	S	O	N
to Buy	0	0	0	0	0	0	0	0	0
Options	2	0	0	0	0	0	0	0	0
to Sell	2	0	0	0	0	0	0	0	0

Institutional Decisions

	1Q'93	2Q'93	3Q'93
to Buy	139	115	108
to Sell	172	172	151
Hld's(000)	99077	96882	98682

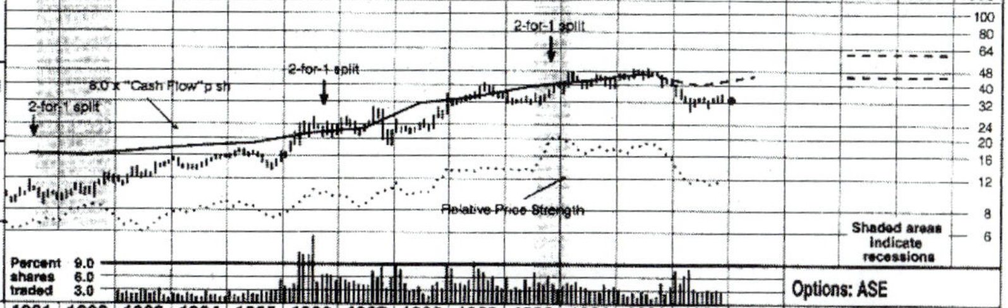

Options: ASE

1977	1978	1979	1980	1981	1982	1983	1984	1985	1986	1987	1988	1989	1990	1991	1992	1993	1994	© VALUE LINE PUB., INC.	96-98
22.17	24.69	27.47	31.33	29.83	29.48	32.27	31.75	33.37	38.55	41.57	64.13	62.24	68.78	68.97	72.19	*66.00*	*70.00*	Revenues per sh A	*88.70*
1.01	1.29	1.84	2.09	2.06	2.01	2.14	2.26	2.35	2.67	2.85	3.95	4.29	4.90	5.26	5.82	*4.75*	*5.15*	"Cash Flow" per sh	*7.45*
.73	.99	1.50	1.75	1.67	1.64	1.69	1.80	1.84	2.09	2.21	2.72	3.26	3.76	3.91	4.29	*3.30*	*3.50*	Earnings per sh B	*5.20*
.37	.45	.58	.74	.80	.88	.89	.93	.98	1.02	1.06	1.13	1.26	1.40	1.59	1.81	*1.97*	*2.10*	Div'ds Decl'd per sh C ■	*2.70*
.36	.48	.58	.86	.74	.67	.62	.74	.77	1.16	.83	1.26	1.34	1.48	1.15	1.42	*1.45*	*1.65*	Cap'l Spending per sh	*1.90*
5.63	6.22	6.78	7.88	8.33	8.72	9.22	9.60	10.86	11.56	13.32	13.34	15.34	18.13	20.42	20.38	*22.70*	*24.15*	Book Value per sh D	*30.25*
208.21	209.69	212.79	217.10	219.19	220.66	219.79	220.34	219.00	219.71	220.18	186.80	191.54	200.36	203.92	202.58	*200.00*	*200.00*	Common Shs Outst'g E	*195.00*
7.7	6.1	4.9	5.3	5.8	6.4	7.6	8.1	8.6	10.3	10.8	9.0	10.7	9.2	10.7	10.5	*Bold figures are Value Line estimates*		Avg Ann'l P/E Ratio	*10.0*
1.01	.83	.71	.70	.70	.71	.64	.75	.70	.70	.72	.75	.81	.68	.68	.64			Relative P/E Ratio	*.75*
6.6%	7.5%	7.8%	8.0%	8.3%	8.3%	6.9%	6.3%	6.2%	4.8%	4.4%	4.6%	3.6%	4.1%	3.8%	4.0%			Avg Ann'l Div'd Yield	*5.2%*

CAPITAL STRUCTURE as of 9/30/93
Total Debt $2987.9 mill. **Due in 5 Yrs** $1700 mill.
LT Debt $2145.6 mill. **LT Interest** $199.1 mill.
(LT interest earned: 7.1x; total interest coverage: 5.5x) (34% of Cap'l)
Leases, Uncapitalized Annual rentals $82.9 mill.
Pension Liability None

Pfd Stock $17.5 mill. **Pfd Div'd** $1.6 mill.
Incl. 588,000 shs. of $2.67 cum. preferred (no par), each conv. into 4.08 com. shs. (less than 1% of Cap'l)
Common Stock 201,706,052 shs. (66% of Cap'l) **as of 10/29/93**

1983	1984	1985	1986	1987	1988	1989	1990	1991	1992	1993	1994	© VALUE LINE PUB., INC.	96-98
7093.4	6995.2	7308.3	8469.6	9152.9	11980	11921	13781	14064	14624	*13200*	*14000*	Revenues ($mill) A	*17300*
11.2%	11.4%	11.0%	10.7%	10.8%	12.0%	12.8%	12.4%	12.6%	13.5%	*12.0%*	*12.0%*	Operating Margin	*13.0%*
99.1	102.9	110.2	128.9	141.0	211.9	206.0	250.5	281.2	304.1	*295*	*330*	Depreciation ($mill)	*440*
390.3	414.1	420.9	474.3	502.7	540.8	630.8	745.1	806.1	885.0	*660*	*700*	Net Profit ($mill)	*1015*
46.5%	44.5%	43.9%	42.8%	41.2%	45.1%	40.6%	37.0%	34.9%	36.8%	*37.0%*	*37.0%*	Income Tax Rate	*37.0%*
5.5%	5.9%	5.8%	5.6%	5.5%	4.5%	5.3%	5.4%	5.7%	6.1%	*5.0%*	*5.0%*	Net Profit Margin	*5.9%*
792.8	729.9	773.4	534.3	924.1	417.1	457.8	525.8	463.1	531.2	*540*	*675*	Working Cap'l ($mill)	*1500*
602.7	732.3	740.5	693.2	1631.5	2359.2	1717.4	2433.8	2551.9	2406.8	*2150*	*2000*	Long-Term Debt ($mill)	*1800*
2237.9	2304.8	2562.9	2715.9	3103.9	2660.7	3101.5	3790.0	4316.0	4282.5	*4560*	*4640*	Net Worth ($mill)	*5900*
14.8%	15.0%	13.8%	14.9%	11.9%	12.8%	15.2%	13.6%	13.3%	14.7%	*11.5%*	*12.0%*	% Earned Total Cap'l	*14.5%*
17.4%	18.0%	16.4%	17.5%	16.2%	20.3%	20.3%	19.7%	18.7%	20.7%	*14.5%*	*14.5%*	% Earned Net Worth	*17.0%*
8.7%	9.1%	8.0%	9.2%	8.7%	12.2%	12.9%	12.6%	11.3%	12.0%	*6.0%*	*6.0%*	% Retained to Comm Eq	*8.5%*
55%	54%	55%	51%	49%	44%	40%	39%	42%	44%	*60%*	*60%*	% All Div'ds to Net Prof	*52%*

CURRENT POSITION ($MILL.)	1991	1992	9/30/93
Cash Assets	82.3	54.8	81.0
Receivables	1340.7	1255.3	1118.2
Inventory (FIFO)	2141.0	1810.2	1743.5
Other	356.8	376.1	272.5
Current Assets	3920.8	3496.4	3215.2
Accounts Payable	346.8	339.6	974.2
Debt Due	730.6	824.7	842.3
Other	2380.3	1800.9	955.6
Current Liab.	3457.7	2965.2	2772.1

ANNUAL RATES of change (per sh)	Past 10 Yrs.	Past 5 Yrs.	Est'd '90-'92 to '96-'98
Revenues	8.5%	14.0%	*4.0%*
"Cash Flow"	9.0%	14.5%	*6.0%*
Earnings	8.5%	14.0%	*4.5%*
Dividends	7.0%	8.0%	*9.0%*
Book Value	9.0%	11.0%	*7.5%*

Calendar	QUARTERLY REVENUES ($ mill.) A Mar.31	Jun.30	Sep.30	Dec.31	Full Year
1990	3203	2952	3866	3760	13781
1991	3857	2937	3473	3797	14064
1992	3834	3245	3773	3772	14624
1993	3738	2846	3302	*3314*	*13200*
1994	*3400*	*3000*	*3750*	*3850*	*14000*

Calendar	EARNINGS PER SHARE B Mar.31	Jun.30	Sep.30	Dec.31	Full Year
1990	.97	.79	.97	1.03	3.76
1991	1.06	.90	.91	1.04	3.91
1992	1.18	.98	.98	1.15	4.29
1993	1.22	.75	.51	*.82*	*3.30*
1994	*.90*	*.73*	*.80*	*1.07*	*3.50*

Calendar	QUARTERLY DIVIDENDS PAID C ■ Mar.31	Jun.30	Sep.30	Dec.31	Full Year
1989	.305	.305	.305	.34	1.26
1990	.34	.34	.34	.385	1.41
1991	.385	.385	.385	.438	1.59
1992	.438	.438	.438	.493	1.81
1993	.493	.493	.493	.493	

BUSINESS: American Brands, Inc. is a consumer products holding company with a focus on cigarettes. U.S. tobacco operations account for 12% of '92 revenues, and 31% of operating profits. U.S. brands include *Pall Mall, Tareyton, Lucky Strike, Carlton, Montclair, Malibu,* and *Misty.* Gallaher Tobacco Ltd. subsidiary is the market leader in the U.K. with about a 41.5% market share (44%, 32%). Other segments: liquor (9%, 11%), life insurance (7%, 9%), hardware and home improvement (7%, 9%), office products (6%, 3%), and speciality products (15%, 5%). Has about 47,000 employees; 69,385 shareholders. Chairman & C.E.O.: W. Alley. Pres. & C.O.O.: T. Hays. Inc.: DE. Address: 1700 E. Putnam Ave., Old Greenwich, CT. 06870. Tel.: 203-698-5000.

American Brands' earnings picture remains troubled. The company's British cigarette division, Gallaher Tobacco, is performing well, but currency adjustments are preventing year-to-year segment earnings gains. Moreover, the company's U.S. tobacco profits have declined substantially since competitor Philip Morris tipped off a cigarette price war by lowering *Marlboro* prices by 40¢ per pack this past April. While that battle appears to be abating somewhat, as cigarette producers, including American, recently enacted a 4¢-per-pack price increase, we don't envision a return to past profit levels anytime soon, and as a result, we expect the fourth-quarter tally to lag well behind last year's mark.

We think the bottom line will regain some lost ground in 1994. In response to the competitive pressures plaguing its tobacco divisions, the company has continued to cut costs, taking charges totalling 11¢ a share in the third quarter to cover further workforce reductions. (The company also took a one-time, 9¢-a-share charge, excluded from our earnings presentation, to reduce trade inventories.) This will augment previously enacted cost-cutting measures, partially offsetting margin weakness arising from lower cigarette prices next year. Meanwhile, American's other businesses, which have accounted for some 50% of operating profits this year, should continue to improve through 1994 as the U.S. economy picks up steam, although increased competition may pressure earnings at its distilled spirits unit. All told, domestic tobacco profits are apt to remain lean for a while, but lower costs and improved results elsewhere should permit some share-net expansion next year, to $3.50.

These shares aren't a particularly compelling choice for now. Near-term prospects for this untimely stock are further clouded by the threat of an increase in cigarette excise taxes, likely sometime in 1994. And the possibility of negative litigation outcomes in coming years adds to this equity's risk. Although this good-quality issue offers worthwhile total returns out to 1996-98, we would advise investors to defer purchase until better earnings momentum is present.

Paul J. Travers *December 24, 1993*

(A) Incl. Franklin Life,'79; Pinkerton's,'83-'87; Southland Life Insurance, 1/84 thru 3/89. Excl. Sunshine Biscuits and Jergens, '88. (B) Primary earnings. Excl. nonrecurring items: '86, 49¢; '90, (77¢); '92, (99¢); '93 ($1.08); excl. gain from discontinued operations: '87, 9¢; '88, 20¢. Next earnings report due late Jan. (C) Next div'd meeting about Jan. 26. Goes ex about Feb. 5. Div'd payment dates: Mar. 1, June 1, Sept. 1, Dec. 1. ■ Div'd reinvestment plan available. (D) Incl. intangibles. In '92, $3.1 billion, $15.32/sh. (E) In mill., adj. for splits.

Company's Financial Strength	A+
Stock's Price Stability	75
Price Growth Persistence	75
Earnings Predictability	95

Source: *The Value Line Investment Survey*, December 24, 1993, p. 313. Copyright 1993 by Value Line Publishing, Inc. Reprinted by permission; all rights reserved

From the Capital Structure box:

1. Long-term interest paid: $199,100,000
2. Long-term debt outstanding: $2,145,600,000
3. w_D: 0.34
4. Preferred dividends paid: $1,600,000
5. Preferred stock outstanding: $17,500,000
6. w_P: 0.01
7. w_E: 0.65

From the top line of the page:

1. Recent price: $33 per share
2. Dividend yield: 6.0 percent

From the Annual Rates box:

1. Estimated growth rate for earnings: 4.5 percent
2. Estimated growth rate for dividends: 9.0 percent

From the data tables, 1993 column:

1. Earnings per share: $3.30
2. Income tax rate: 37 percent
3. Rate of return earned on total capital: 11.5 percent

$$k_D = [\$199{,}100{,}000 \times (1 - 0.37)]/\$2{,}145{,}600{,}000$$
$$= 5.8 \text{ percent}$$
$$k_P = \$1{,}600{,}000/\$17{,}500{,}000$$
$$= 9.1 \text{ percent}$$

The prevailing interest rate on bank deposits in December 1993 was about 3 percent. Dividend yields on common stock should therefore have been about 0.6 × 3 percent, or 1.8 percent. Since American Brands' dividend yield of 6.0 percent far exceeded the norm, the dividend formula should be used to calculate the cost of equity:

$$k_E = 6.0 \text{ percent} + 9.0 \text{ percent}$$
$$= 15.0 \text{ percent}$$
$$k = (0.34)(5.8\%) + (0.01)(9.1\%) + (0.65)(15.0\%)$$
$$= 11.81 \text{ percent}$$ ❖

Value Line estimated American Brands' rate of return on assets at 11.5 percent in 1993. Its weighted average cost of capital of 11.81 percent suggests that the company is marginally unprofitable. This calculation, however, is less useful to American Brands' management than the weighted average cost of capital based on the current values of American Brands' outstanding securities.

capital structure

The proportions of debt and equity by which a company has financed its asset acquistions.

Capital Structure Theory

However it is calculated, a company's weighted average cost of capital depends on its **capital structure**, the proportions of debt and equity by which it has financed

FOCUS ON FINANCE

American Brands Inc.: Capital Structure Details

An alternative source for information about a company's capital structure is available from Moody's. The following information was taken from the 1993 edition of Moody's *Industrial Manual*, pp. 2,558–2,562. The information is dated December 31, 1992.

It is impossible to calculate all the specific costs of capital for these securities (k_{D1} through k_{D14}, k_P, and k_C) because of the missing information. It is also impossible to calculate the weighted average cost of capital using either book weights or market weights, for the same reason. Further, the American Brands report indicates that the firm has additional long-term debt outstanding in the amount of $995,287,000 (38 percent of the total detailed above). The entry notes that this debt is composed of:

1. $200,000,000 notes payable
2. $376,500,000 other notes
3. $237,500,000 revolving credit notes
4. $45,400,000 in 12.5 percent Sterling loan stock due 2009
5. $22,300,000 miscellaneous debt
6. $113,587,000 in 9.75 percent Eurosterling notes that mature on May 15, 1993

If an analyst wants details about the outstanding securities, Moody's *Manuals* are the first place to look. For a debt issue, the entry lists the amount authorized, the amount outstanding, the date issued, the maturity date, the dates of interest payments, the trustee, the available denomination(s), the terms of the call feature (if any), the restrictive covenants, the debt holder's rights on default, where the security is listed (if it is), the purpose for which the firm issued the debt, the offering price and syndicate manager, the proceeds to the company from the sale (if available), and the market price range for the last three years.

For an equity issue, the entry lists the number of shares authorized, outstanding, in the company's treasury, and reserved; dividend rights, reinvestment plans, and payment records; preemptive rights (if any); call, conversion, and sinking fund features and restrictive covenants (for preferred stock); voting rights (for common stock); where the security is listed and its ticker symbol, the registrar, the transfer agent, and the annual price ranges for the last five years.

Security Type	Maturity	Outstanding	Proceeds	1992 Price Range
9.500% Es. note[a]	1994	$ 75,725,000	n.a.	n.a.
5.250% note	1995	200,000,000	$997.26	$1,012.50–$985.00
12.000% Es. note	1995	60,580,000	n.a.	n.a.
9.250% Es. note	1998	75,725,000	n.a.	n.a.
7.500% Note	1999	150,000,000	991.40	1,035.00–1,002.50
9.000% Note	1999	100,000,000	991.75	1,058.75–1,055.00
7.625% Euronote	2001	150,000,000	n.a.	n.a.
7.750% E.C.D.[b]	2002	39,960,000	n.a.	n.a.
8.500% Note	2003	200,000,000	990.25	1,110.00–1,012.50
5.375% E.C.D.	2003	3,425,000	n.a.	n.a.
E.C.D. (rate n.a.)	2005	200,000,000	n.a.	n.a.
9.125% Debenture	2016	150,000,000	n.a.	1,078.75–1,010.00
8.625% Debenture	2021	150,000,000	962.30	1,020.00–990.00
7.875% Debenture	2023	150,000,000	n.a.	n.a.
$2.67 Convertible Preferred	—	19,060,456	n.a.	200.25–166.75
Common stock	—	895,300,000	n.a.	49.875–39.00
Total outstanding		$2,619,775,456		

[a]An Es. note is a Eurosterling note; it is denominated in British pounds sterling.
[b]An E.C.D. is a Eurodollar convertible debenture.

EXHIBIT 13.2

Classical Capital Structure Theory

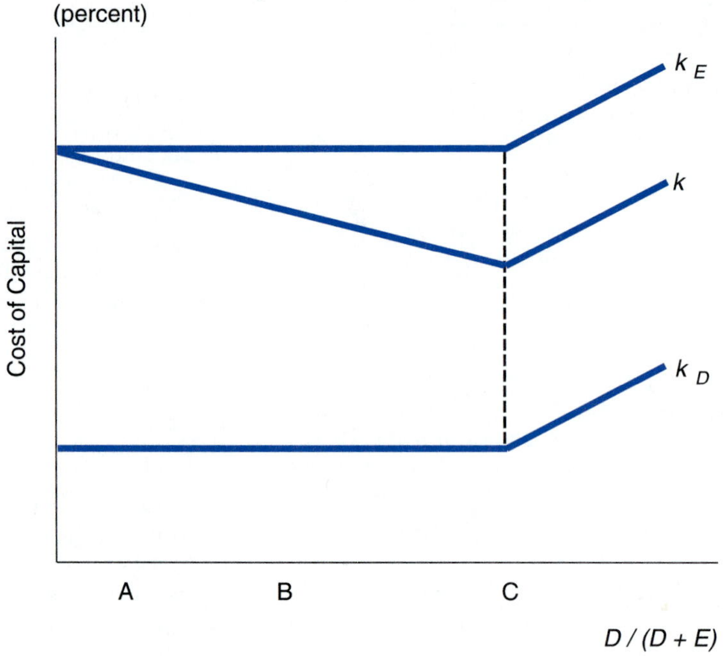

its asset acquisitions. The nature of this relationship has been investigated and debated thoroughly.

Classical or Traditional Theory. The early theory of the relationship between a company's cost of capital and its capital structure was developed while finance was still a subdivision of economics. This theory proposed the relationship illustrated in Exhibit 13.2.

A company's debt ratio can be calculated as the proportion of its debt to its total capital (debt plus equity). This ratio is measured along the X-axis of the graph in Exhibit 13.2. A company's specific costs of capital are related to this ratio, as measured on the Y-axis. The specific cost of debt is indicated by the line labeled k_D. It does not touch the Y-axis because at the axis the firm could have no debt; the ratio would be zero. As the company's debt ratio increases, its cost of debt remains constant as long as the creditors do not perceive any exposure to significantly increased default risk. At some point C, however, the creditors will feel that the company's debt has reached a critical proportion. Additional borrowing will raise the debt ratio above (to the right of) Point C, significantly increasing default risk.

The creditors will demand greater compensation for taking this higher risk, and the cost of additional debt will rise.

The specific cost of equity is indicated by the line labeled k_E in Exhibit 13.2. It lies above the cost of debt line everywhere on the graph because equity is always more expensive than debt. Equity holders demand more compensation than creditors because they bear more risk. This increase in risk comes from two sources:

1. A solvent company must pay interest on its debt, but it need not declare dividends on its stock if it wants to conserve cash.
2. If a company goes bankrupt, its creditors must be paid in full before anything can be distributed to equity holders.

Classical capital structure theory holds that a company's stockholders share the creditors' apprehension about borrowing too much. Again, when the debt ratio rises above Point C, the cost of equity rises to compensate the stockholders for their increased exposure to default risk.

The weighted average cost of capital curve, labeled k in Exhibit 13.2, is derived from these two specific cost lines. At the Y-axis, the company has no debt, so the weighted average cost of capital is 100 percent of the cost of equity. At Point A, the company has a little debt and a lot of equity. Because it can borrow funds more cheaply, the weighted average cost declines a little. At Point B, the company uses more debt and less equity. The weighted average cost (composed of a larger proportion of cheap funds and a smaller proportion of expensive funds) is even lower than at Point A. This decline in the weighted average continues up to Point C, but to the right of that point, where the costs of both types of financing begin to rise, the weighted average cost also rises. Therefore, at Point C:

1. The weighted average cost of capital is at a minimum
2. The company's capital structure is at its optimum point
3. The debt ratio is at its best level

Classical theory has some significant consequences. First, it implies that the financial manager must manage the company's debt ratio to keep the capital structure at its optimal point. At this optimal point, the company minimizes its financing costs. The theory does not help the financial manager to identify this optimal point; this requires a process of trial and error. Further theoretical elaboration on the topic of capital structure indicates that the location of a firm's optimal point can vary from industry to industry, and changes as the economy goes through the phases of a business cycle.

As another consequence, the classical theory implies that the company must raise new funds in proportions that will maintain its optimal capital structure. For example, suppose that a company needs external financing of $100 million and its optimal debt ratio is 35 percent. It must sell a combination of $35 million in bonds and $65 million in stock. Selling such a package of securities has never been a common practice in the United States. When a company needs external funds, it raises the money by selling one type of security at a time: either stock or bonds. The next time it needs funds, it repeats the either/or decision. The theory implies that, for approximately 100 years, financial managers have deliberately incurred excessive costs of capital whenever they have obtained funds from the public.

As a third consequence, strict adherence to the principle of cost minimization would require that, whenever a company retained some or all of its earnings, the financial manager would immediately have to borrow additional funds. Suppose that a company were positioned exactly at Point C. Retaining any profit would increase the company's equity and, therefore, reduce its debt ratio. This would move the company to the left of Point C, where its weighted average would be higher than necessary. In order to reduce costs, the company would have to borrow money (whether it needed the funds or not) in order to raise its debt ratio back to Point C. Conversely, if a company positioned exactly at Point C incurred a loss, it would have to repay some of its debt. The loss would decrease the company's equity, increasing its debt ratio and moving it to the right of Point C. Again, its weighted average cost of capital would be higher than necessary. In order to reduce the cost of capital, it would have to reduce its outstanding debt.

M&M Theory. In 1958, Franco Modigliani and Merton Miller published an article called "The Cost of Capital, Corporation Finance, and the Theory of Investment" in the *American Economic Review*. The article presented a new theory of capital structure to explain the results of the authors' research on the relationship between the cost of capital and capital structure. They examined the electric utility and oil industries in both a recession year and a year of prosperity. All four data sets led them to conclude that the nature of the relationship resembled Exhibit 13.3.

Notice that some things have not changed. The cost of debt behaves exactly as it does in classical theory. The cost of equity is still always higher than the cost of debt. M&M claimed, however, that their statistical evidence indicated that the weighted average cost of capital was a straight line that neither rose nor declined. In order for the weighted average to remain flat, the cost of equity must rise. (As the proportion of less expensive debt increases and the proportion of more expensive equity decreases, the average cost declines unless the cost of equity rises.) A rising cost of equity line implies that stockholders demand more compensation for exposure to default risk as soon as the company starts to borrow.

The graph in Exhibit 13.3 presents the cost curves as published by M&M. Subsequent research by other academicians has completed the picture, and Exhibit 13.4 illustrates their conclusions. If the weighted average cost of capital remains flat when the cost of debt rises, then the cost of equity must decline when the company borrows too much. This implies that when the creditors (the first in line in case of bankruptcy) are worrying about increased risk of default, the stockholders (the last in line at a bankruptcy) are so happy that they are satisfied with a declining return on their investment in the company.

Expressed in these terms, the M&M theory defies common sense, but M&M did not express their hypothesis in these terms. They reasoned that the value of a firm depends on its net operating income (sales revenues minus operating costs), not on net income after taxes (sales revenues minus operating costs, financing costs,

EXHIBIT 13.3

M&M's Capital Structure Theory

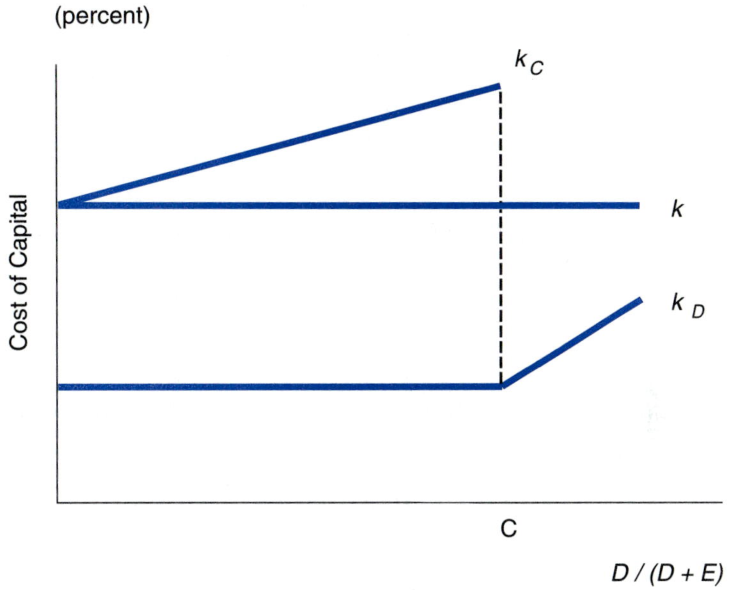

and taxes). Therefore, the debt ratio has no effect on the value of the firm because it does not affect the weighted average cost of capital.

In building their theory, M&M made several assumptions:

1. Investors are all rational and equally well-informed.
2. Transaction costs for trading securities are inconsequential.
3. All firms with equivalent business risk should have the same expected return and, therefore, the same weighted average cost of capital.
4. Income taxes are irrelevant.
5. Investors can substitute their personal debt (by borrowing to buy stock) for corporate debt when they are not satisfied with the level of corporate debt.
6. The stock and bond markets are perfect.

In the theoretical world M&M created with these assumptions, the relationship between cost of capital and capital structure illustrated in Exhibits 13.3 and 13.4 is valid. Scholars spent the next decade investigating the nature of this relationship in the real world, where the assumptions do not hold. For their work and the voluminous research they inspired, Modigliani and Miller have been individually awarded Nobel prizes in economics.

EXHIBIT 13.4

Completed Form of M&M's Capital Structure Theory

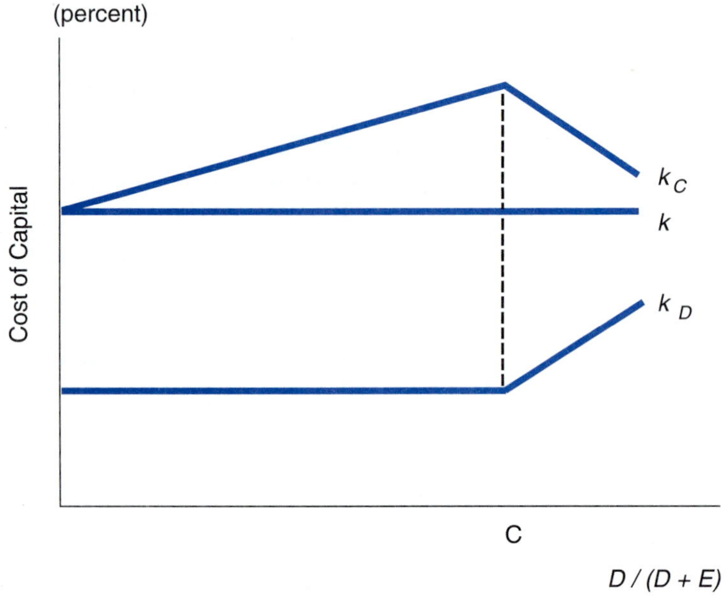

Modern Theory. The earliest research inspired by M&M investigated the relationship between cost of capital and capital structure in other industries. These industries proved to have more diverse debt ratios than the oil and electric utility industries. The additional data led to the relationships illustrated in Exhibit 13.5.

The behavior of the cost of debt remains unchanged. The cost of equity curve, however, indicates that stockholders accept a small amount of debt without worrying about a significant increase in the risk of default. As long as they do not demand additional compensation, the cost of equity remains flat and the weighted average cost of capital declines. However, the stockholders begin to worry that the company has too much debt when the debt ratio rises above Point F. They seek additional compensation from that point on, and the weighted average flattens out. When the creditors begin to worry and the cost of debt starts to rise, the weighted average also rises. This defines an optimal range—all the debt ratios between Point F and Point C—where the weighted average cost of capital is minimal. The financial manager's job is to keep the company's capital structure within this optimal range.

EXHIBIT 13.5

Modern Capital Structure Theory

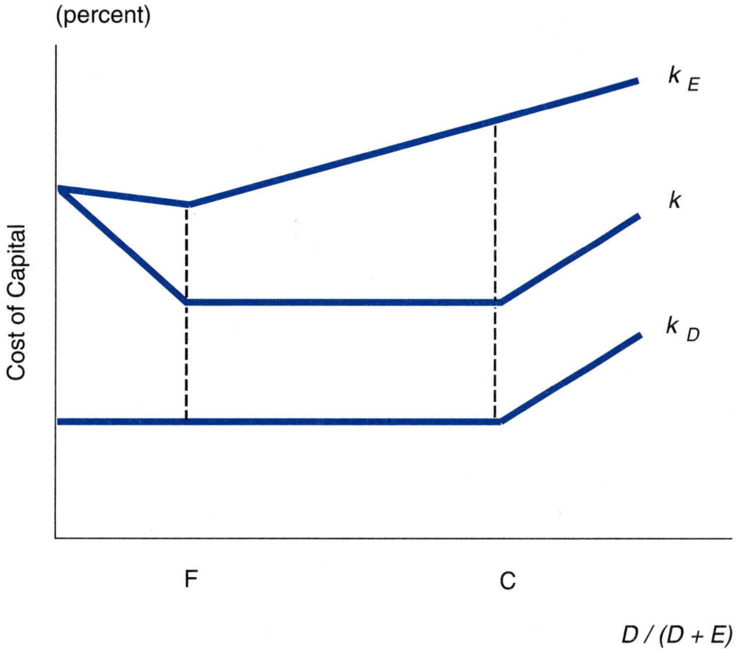

This flat-segment phenomenon explains why Modigliani and Miller got the empirical results that they published. M&M chose two industries in which companies had debt ratios between Point F and Point C. Extrapolating this flat segment of the weighted average cost of capital curve from 0 percent debt to 100 percent debt was not a good statistical procedure, but it led them to create their net operating income hypothesis.

The implications of the modern theory are compatible with actual corporate practices. First, the financial manager can identify other corporations with similar business risks, calculate their debt ratios and costs of capital, and determine the shape of the weighted average cost of capital curve that is appropriate for a particular company.

Second, a company can raise external funds by issuing only one type of security at a time if its debt ratio lies between Point F and Point C. Companies with debt ratios at or close to Point F must raise funds by issuing bonds. Companies with debt ratios at or near Point C must raise funds by selling common stock. Companies with debt ratios well within the optimal range can issue either bonds or common stock. It is never necessary to sell two types of securities at once.

EXHIBIT 13.6

Effect of Business Risk on the Optimal Range

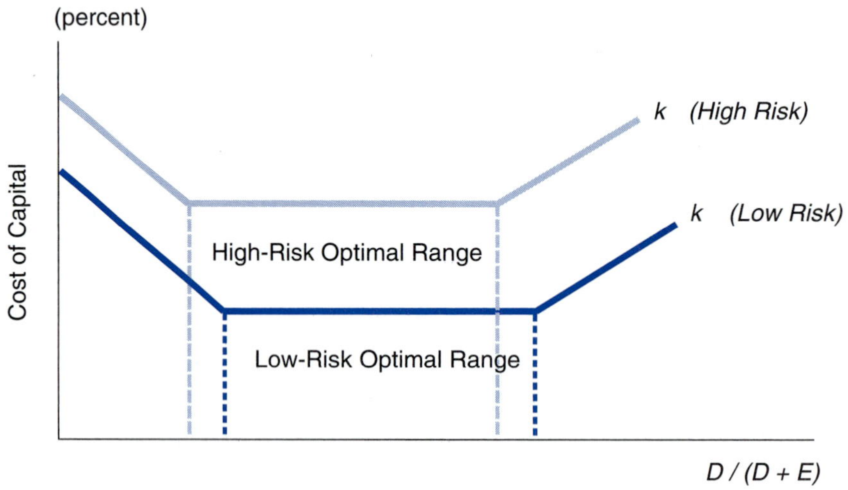

Third, there is no need to borrow when a profitable company pays out less than 100 percent of its earnings as dividends. In the absence of new financing, its balance sheets show annual increases in equity because its retained earnings account increases. When it needs new external financing, this phenomenon and the tax-deductibility of interest payments almost always drive it to issue debt.

The modern theory of capital structure overcomes the practical problems encountered by the classical theory. It also avoids the M&M theory's need for unrealistic assumptions.

None of the graphs in Exhibits 13.2 through 13.5 indicated scale because there are no permanent, universal limits on the optimal range. Industries with higher levels of business risk usually have lower optimal ranges than less risky industries. See Exhibit 13.6. When recessionary periods bring lower interest rates and more frequent business failures, the optimal ranges for all businesses are lower than the optimal ranges in periods of economic expansion. See Exhibit 13.7.

CHOOSING THE NEW SECURITY TO ISSUE

Capital structure theory sets limits on the financial manager's freedom to choose which type of security to issue. If the company's debt ratio is at or near a limit of the optimal range, it must issue the type of new security that will minimize its

EXHIBIT 13.7

Effect of Economic Conditions on the Optimal Range for Any Company

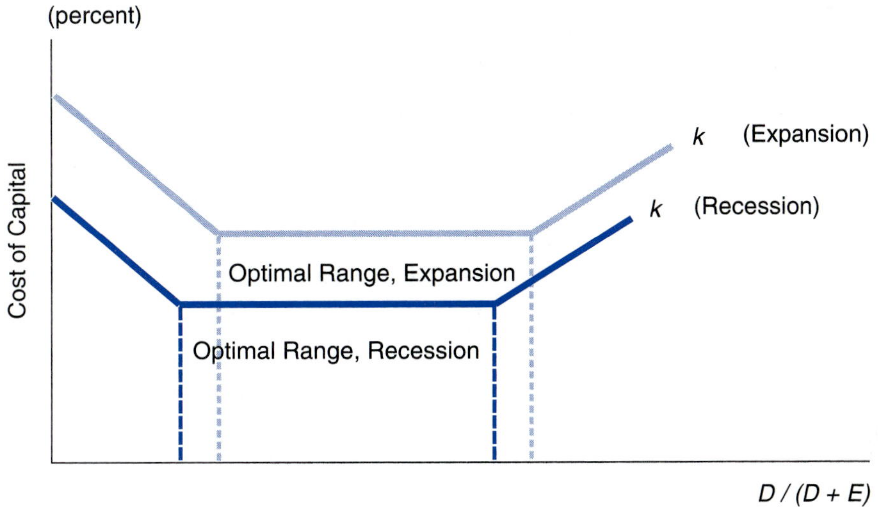

weighted average cost of capital. If the firm's debt ratio is between the limits of the optimal range, however, and at a considerable distance from both limits, the company is free to issue either bonds or stock. Deciding which security to issue requires another tool.

EBIT–EAPS Solution

earnings available per share
The amount of after-tax profit that the company has available to distribute to common stockholders and/or to retain for its own use.

earnings before interest and taxes
Another name for net operating income, this is the amount left after subtracting labor, materials, overhead, and depreciation from sales revenue.

Earnings available per share (EAPS) is the amount of after-tax profit that the firm has available to distribute to common stockholders and/or to retain for its own use. EAPS is also the driving force behind the company's stock price. The amount an investor is willing to pay for a share of stock in the company depends on the investor's perception of the company's ability to generate EAPS.

EAPS is affected by the form of financing a company chooses. Therefore, when it must choose among bonds, preferred stock, and common stock, the company should issue the type of security that it expects will produce the highest EAPS. This choice will maximize shareholder wealth.

Earnings before interest and taxes (EBIT) is another name for net operating income. It is the amount left after subtracting labor, materials, overhead, and depreciation from sales revenue. This amount is not affected by the type of financing a company chooses. It provides an appropriate starting point from which to build an estimate of EAPS.

❖ EXAMPLE 13.3

Tickel Corporation needs to raise $50 million to buy additional machinery. When this equipment is installed and operating efficiently, Tickel expects to generate EBIT of $200 million a year from the combination of its old and new assets. The investment banker informed Tickel's financial manager that the company can tap alternative sources of funds. It can issue bonds with a 12 percent coupon rate, $100-par preferred stock that will pay a dividend of $15 per share, or common stock at $40 per share. Tickel Corporation already has $100 million in long-term debt, on which it pays 10 percent interest. It also has 20 million shares of common stock outstanding. It has no preferred stock outstanding, and its tax rate is 30 percent. Which type of security should it issue?

To answer the question, Tickel's financial manager must estimate EAPS for each type of security. Some preliminary calculations are necessary:

$$\text{Interest on old debt} = \$100 \text{ million} \times 10\%$$
$$= \$10 \text{ million}$$
$$\text{Interest on new debt} = 50 \text{ million} \times 12\%$$
$$= \$6 \text{ million}$$
$$\text{New preferred dividend} = (\$50 \text{ million}/\$100) \times \$15$$
$$= \$7.5 \text{ million}$$
$$\text{New common shares} = \$50 \text{ million}/\$40$$
$$= 1.25 \text{ million}$$

	Bonds	Preferred Stock	Common Stock
EBIT	$200,000,000	$200,000,000	$200,000,000
Old interest	−10,000,000	−10,000,000	−10,000,000
New interest	−6,000,000	0	0
Taxable income	$184,000,000	$190,000,000	$190,000,000
Tax (30 percent)	−55,200,000	−57,000,000	−57,000,000
Income after tax	$128,800,000	$133,000,000	$133,000,000
Preferred dividend	0	−7,500,000	0
Earnings available	$128,800,000	$125,500,000	$133,000,000
Number of common shares	20,000,000	20,000,000	21,250,000
EAPS	$6.44	$6.28	$6.26

Tickel should issue bonds because they are expected to produce the highest EAPS, $6.44. ❖

Breakeven EBIT

When using EBIT, remember that it is a forecast. It projects the operating profit that the firm's old and new assets will produce. Since this amount is not guaranteed, a different EBIT may actually result from the company's operations. The financial manager needs to assess whether bonds would remain the best choice under different circumstances. Rather than develop new estimates of EAPS with alternative EBITs, it is more efficient to work backward and calculate the breakeven EBIT for each type of security. This means answering the question, what level of EBIT will produce an EAPS of zero for each type of security?

❖ EXAMPLE 13.4

Find the breakeven EBIT for each type of security available to Tickel Corporation in Example 13.3.

	Bonds	Preferred Stock	Common Stock
EAPS	$0	$0	$0
Number of common shares	×20,000,000	×20,000,000	×21,250,000
Earnings available	$0	$0	$0
Preferred dividend	0	+$7,500,000	0
Income after tax	$0	$7,500,000	$0
Taxable income	$0	$10,714,285[a]	$0
New interest	+6,000,000	0	0
Old interest	+10,000,000	+10,000,000	+10,000,000
Breakeven EBIT	$16,000,000	$20,714,285	$10,000,000

[a]70% of Taxable income = Income after tax
Taxable income = Income after tax/0.7
Taxable income = $7,500,000/0.7
= $10,714,285 ❖

If the company were to issue common stock, an EBIT greater than $10 million would leave some earnings for the common stockholders. If it were to issue bonds, an EBIT greater than $16 million would leave some earnings for the common stockholders. If it were to issue preferred stock, EBIT would have to exceed $20,714,285 to leave some earnings for the common stockholders. If EBIT turns out to be very small, the firm must consider the option not to invest at all and forego issuing any new securities.

Generalized EBIT–EAPS Relationship

Suppose that there are equally reasonable alternative forecasts of EBIT. The analyst need not recalculate EAPS. For any EAPS greater than zero, a linear relationship holds between EAPS and EBIT for each type of security. A graph can display this relationship, as Exhibit 13.8 shows.

Point H (on the bond line) corresponds to the relationship in Example 13.3: an EBIT of $200 million gives an EAPS of $6.44. Point G corresponds to the relationship in Example 13.4: an EBIT of $16 million gives a zero EAPS. The EAPS that corresponds to any other amount of EBIT can be read directly from the bond line that connects these two points.

The same process reveals the effects of a preferred stock issue. At Point K, based on Example 13.3, an EBIT of $200 million gives an EAPS of $6.28. Point J corresponds to the relationship in Example 13.4: an EBIT of $20.7 million gives a zero

EXHIBIT 13.8

EBIT–EAPS Relationship for Bonds and Preferred Stock

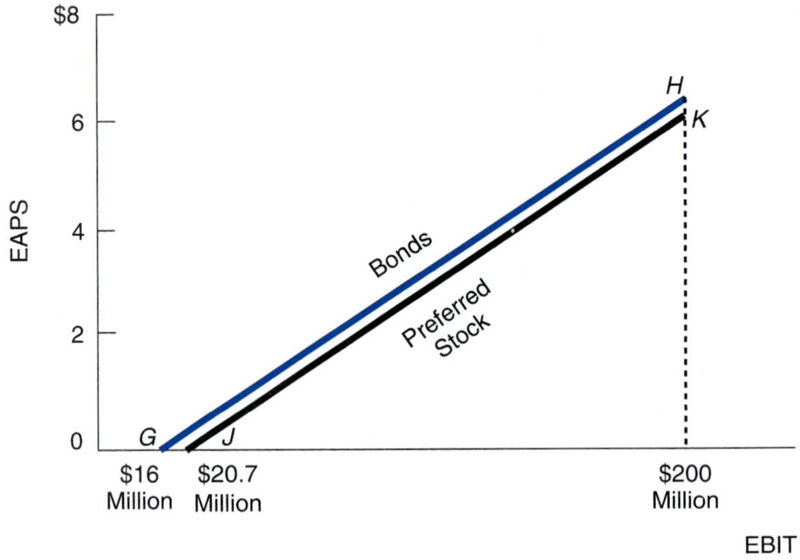

EAPS. It is not a coincidence that the preferred stock line connecting these two points runs parallel to the bond line and below it. For any given level of EBIT, a bond issue will always leave a higher EAPS than a preferred stock issue. There are two reasons for this. First, the interest rate on the bond issue is always lower than the dividend rate on preferred stock because the bondholder takes less risk. Second, interest is a tax-deductible expense; dividends are not. Therefore, if they were to base their decisions only on cost, companies would always choose to issue bonds rather than preferred stock.

The choice between bonds and common stock, however, requires more complex analysis. As Exhibit 13.9 shows, common stock produces higher values for EAPS at low levels of EBIT. Bonds generate higher values for EAPS at high levels of EBIT.

Points G and H (on the bond line) are the same as in Exhibit 13.8. Point M (on the common stock line) corresponds to the relationship in Example 13.3: an EBIT of $200 million gives an EAPS of $6.26. Point L corresponds to the relationship in Example 13.4: an EBIT of $10 million gives a zero EAPS.

The bond and common stock lines are not parallel; they intersect at an EBIT of approximately $110 million. Since it is important to know the exact point of intersection, it must be calculated algebraically. At the point of intersection for a specific EBIT, the EAPS after a bond issue ($EAPS_B$) equals the EAPS after a common stock issue ($EAPS_C$).

EXHIBIT 13.9

EBIT–EAPS Relationship for Bonds and Common Stock

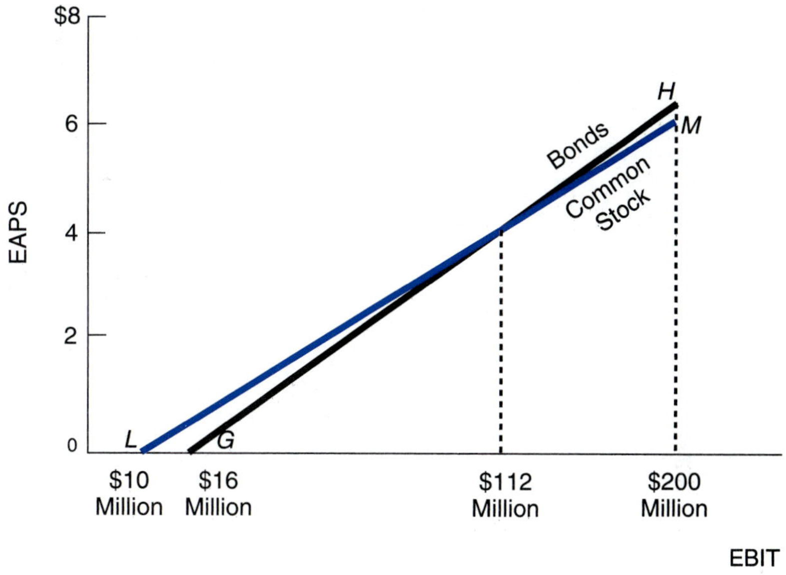

Referring back to Example 13.3, EAPS can be defined as:

$$EAPS = [(EBIT - I)(1 - T) - PD]/N \tag{13.4}$$

where $EBIT$ = earnings before interest and taxes
I = total interest
T = tax rate
PD = preferred stock dividends
N = number of common stock shares outstanding

If Tickel Corporation were to issue bonds:

$$\begin{aligned} EAPS_B &= [(EBIT - \$16 \text{ million})(1 - 0.3) - 0]/20 \text{ million} \\ &= (0.7EBIT - \$11.2 \text{ million})/20 \text{ million} \end{aligned}$$

If Tickel Corporation were to issue common stock:

$$\begin{aligned} EAPS_C &= [(EBIT - \$10 \text{ million})(1 - 0.3) - 0]/21.25 \text{ million} \\ &= (0.7EBIT - \$7 \text{ million})/21.25 \text{ million} \end{aligned}$$

At the point of intersection, $EAPS_B = EAPS_C$. Therefore,

$$\frac{0.7EBIT - \$11.2 \text{ million}}{20 \text{ million}} = \frac{0.7EBIT - \$7 \text{ million}}{21.25 \text{ million}}$$

FOCUS ON CAREERS

LOAN OFFICER

Employed primarily by depository financial institutions, the loan officer interviews potential borrowers, evaluates their financial conditions, and recommends approval for credit lines or extensions of credit in the form of commercial loans, real estate loans, consumer credit loans, or credit cards. Given the breadth of the field, loan officers generally specialize in a single area such as commercial lending, mortgage lending, consumer lending, or international lending.

The commercial loan officer must review the financial documentation presented by the applicant, evaluate the potential of the business, and judge the appropriateness of the application. The type of lending may vary from revolving credit agreements to term loans to letters of credit. Generally the loan officer has a working knowledge of the borrower's business and conducts frequent on-site visits.

While an accounting degree is not essential, a financial institution expects a prospective loan officer to have a strong background in finance and accounting. Since the position involves extensive customer contact, interpersonal and communications skills are essential. A starting salary in a commercial bank is around $25,000. Semi-annual reviews of work performance can rapidly generate a salary above $50,000.

This equation contains only one unknown, so it can be simplified and solved as follows:

$$21.25(0.7EBIT - \$11.2 \text{ million}) = 20(0.7EBIT - \$7 \text{ million})$$
$$14.875EBIT - \$238 \text{ million} = 14EBIT - \$140 \text{ million}$$
$$0.875EBIT = \$98 \text{ million}$$
$$EBIT = \$112 \text{ million}$$

These results indicate that, if Tickel Corp. expects its net operating revenue (EBIT) to exceed $112 million when the new assets are operating efficiently, it should finance those assets with bonds. Debt financing will provide the greatest EAPS. On the other hand, if Tickel expects its EBIT to fall short of $112 million with the new assets, then it should finance those assets with common stock. Equity financing will provide the greatest EAPS.

If Tickel expects EBIT of exactly $112 million, then either bonds or common stock will produce an EAPS of $3.36. (The proof is left to the reader.) Mathematically, it makes no difference which security the firm issues.

Because the actual EBIT may fall short of the expected EBIT of $112 million, issuing new equity might be a better choice since it exposes the stockholders to less risk; they would face no possibility of default if the firm could not pay its dividend. If Tickel were to issue bonds and the new project were to produce disappointing revenues, the inability to pay interest could bring on corporate failure and liquidation.

Despite this argument, U.S. financial managers have demonstrated a preference for debt securities. If Tickel expected an EBIT close to $112 million, its financial manager would probably choose to issue bonds.

MARGINAL COST OF CAPITAL

marginal cost of capital
The cost of raising additional funds to finance new investment opportunities.

The **marginal cost of capital,** k', is the cost of raising additional funds to finance new investment opportunities. It is the weighted average of the cost of additional funds (or of the last dollar raised by the firm) if more than one source of funds is used. The relevant concept of capital when making an investment or a financial decision is the marginal cost of capital, not the existing weighted average cost of capital, k.

The marginal cost of capital for a firm is affected by the

1. Size of additional financing needed
2. Capital structure (the debt ratio)
3. Responses of specific costs as more funds are raised

Marginal Cost of Domestic Financing

The marginal cost of capital for a firm is commonly analyzed by holding its capital structure constant at the optimal level and varying the amounts of additional funds to be raised and their specific costs. Keeping the capital structure constant means that long-term capital is to be raised in the same proportion of debt to equity as the existing capital structure. For example, assume that the existing (optimal) capital structure of a firm is 40 percent debt and 60 percent equity, and the firm is planning to raise $2 million in additional long-term capital. Under the constant capital structure assumption, it will have to raise $800,000 by borrowing and the balance of $1.2 million by selling new shares of common stock.

The specific cost of equity from the sale of new shares of common stock will always be higher than the cost of existing equity because of the flotation cost. However, if the equity component of the additional funds is obtained entirely as an increase in retained earnings, the specific cost of equity will not change because there is no flotation cost. On the other hand, the cost of equity may be even higher if investors demand a higher rate of return because of any additional risk involved in the firm's proposed investment.

The cost of raising additional debt may go up if creditors demand a higher risk premium to compensate for any perceived increase in financial risk. It is reasonable to assume that for most firms, there are limits on the amount of borrowing that can be done without affecting the cost of debt. In other words, a firm can borrow at the same cost within a given range for its debt ratio, but when its borrowing moves on to a higher range, a higher cost will kick in. For example, a firm with a capital structure of 40 percent debt and 60 percent equity may find that its cost of borrowing additional amounts will change in the following manner:

COST OF DEBT	RANGE OF ADDITIONAL BORROWING
6 percent	$1,000,000 to $3,000,000
7 percent	$3,000,001 to $4,000,000
8 percent	$4,000,001 to $4,500,000

Similar ranges may also exist for the cost of new equity.

These observations about the behavior of specific costs suggest that the marginal cost of capital will increase as more and more long-term capital is raised. If constant cost ranges for each source of capital exist, then the marginal cost will not rise smoothly.

❖ EXAMPLE 13.5

Germino Industries has 7 5/8 percent bonds which sold at par, no leased assets or preferred stock, and 125 million shares of common stock outstanding. The bonds are currently trading at $982.50 in the market, and there are one million bonds outstanding. The stock price is $22, the dividend is $1.10 per share, the earnings are $2 per share, and both are projected to grow at a long-term rate of 9 percent. Germino has a tax rate of 36 percent and $767.5 million in retained earnings. At the present time, banks are paying 4 percent interest.

1. Find the weights of the various types of capital used by Germino Industries and calculate the weighed average cost of capital.
2. Construct a marginal cost of capital schedule if Germino Industries is considering raising $100 million in additional long-term capital under the following assumptions:

a. Funds will be obtained in the same proportion as the existing capital structure.
b. Projects targeted for investment by Germino have the same risk as the average risk of its existing assets and the firm will continue to pay the same dividends per share as before. This means that the firm will be able to sell new shares of common equity at the existing price of $22.
c. The floatation cost is 4 percent of the security price.
d. Germino Industries can raise up to $20 million in new debt without causing any increase in the specific cost of debt. Borrowing above this limit will raise the creditors' required rate of return (YTM) by one percentage point.
e. Germino Industries expects to retain $30 million of its earnings.

1. First, it is necessary to determine market values.

$$\begin{aligned}\text{Value of existing bonds} &= 1 \text{ million} \times \$982.50\\ &= \$982{,}500{,}000\\ \text{Current value of common stock} &= 125 \text{ million} \times \$22\\ &= \$2{,}750 \text{ million}\\ \text{Total capital} &= \$982.5 \text{ million} + \$2{,}750 \text{ million} + \$767.5 \text{ million}\\ &= \$4{,}500 \text{ million}\end{aligned}$$

The specific capital weights are:

$$\begin{aligned}w_D &= \$982.5 \text{ million} / \$4{,}500 \text{ million}\\ &= 0.218\\ w_C &= \$2{,}750 \text{ million} / \$4{,}500 \text{ million}\\ &= 0.611\\ w_R &= \$767.5 \text{ million} / \$4{,}500 \text{ million}\\ &= 0.171\end{aligned}$$

Next, the specific costs need to be determined. Since bonds were sold at par and carried a coupon rate of 7⅝ (7.625) percent, the YTM or the return to the investor is the same as the coupon rate, 7.625 percent. The cost of debt to the firm is the YTM adjusted for tax benefits and floatation cost:

$$k_D = \$7.625(1 - 0.36)/(1 - 0.04)$$
$$= 5.08 \text{ percent}$$

The dividend yield is \$1.10/\$22 = 5 percent, which is greater than 60 percent of the current bank rate of 4 percent, so the dividend version of the cost of common stock is utilized:

$$k_C = (\$1.10/\$22) + 9\%$$
$$= 14 \text{ percent}$$

The weighted average cost of capital for the existing assets is:

$$k = (0.218)(5.08\%) + (0.611)(14\%) + (0.171)(14\%)$$
$$= 1.107 + 8.554 + 2.394$$
$$= 12.06 \text{ percent}$$

2. Since Germino expects to provide \$30 million from retained earnings, the specific cost of equity will not rise (i.e., it will stay at the current level of 14 percent) until a total of \$38,363,171 in additional funds is raised. This amount is found by dividing the available retained earnings by the current proportion of equity capital in Germino's capital structure.

The proportion of equity is:

$$w_C + w_R = 0.611 + 0.171$$
$$= 0.782$$

Thus, the maximum amount of additional funds is:

$$\$30 \text{ million}/0.782 = \$38,363,171$$

The firm can raise up to \$38,363,171 in new capital without resorting to the sale of new shares or changing its debt ratio. In other words, \$30 million in additional retained earnings will support \$8,363,171 in additional debt without changing Germino's debt ratio of 0.218.

Since new debt up to \$20 million can be raised without causing the specific cost of debt to go up, the marginal cost of capital for the additional amount of \$38,363,171 (\$30,000,000 in retained earnings plus \$8,363,171 in debt) will remain equal to the existing weighted average cost of capital.

$$k'_1 = k$$
$$k'_1 = w_D k'_D + w_C k'_C + w_R k'_R$$
$$= 0.218(5.08\%) + (0.611 + 0.171)(14\%)$$
$$= 12.06 \text{ percent}$$

To raise more than \$38,363,171, the firm needs to sell new shares of common stock. Under the assumptions, the firm can sell new shares at the old price of \$22 per share, but there will be a flotation cost of \$0.88 per share. The new specific cost of equity will, therefore, be:

$$k'_C = \$1.10/(\$22.00 - \$0.88) + 9\%$$
$$= 14.21 \text{ percent}$$

To calculate the cost of the debt component of the new capital above \$38,363,171, Germino must first determine the maximum new capital that can be raised without increasing the cost of its debt component. This maximum is obtained by dividing \$20 million (the amount of debt that can be obtained without affecting cost) by the proportion of debt in Germino's capital structure, w_D.

$$\$20 \text{ million}/0.218 = \$91{,}743{,}119$$

Germino Industries can raise up to \$91,743,119 in new capital without affecting the cost of its debt component. The marginal cost of raising new capital between \$38,363,171 and \$91,743,119 will be:

$$k'_2 = w_D k'_D + w_C k'_C + w_R k'_R$$
$$= 0.218(5.08\%) + (0.611 + 0.171)(14.21\%)$$
$$= 1.1074 + 11.1122$$
$$= 12.22 \text{ percent}$$

Any borrowing beyond \$20 million will cost 1 percent more than 7.625 percent, as assumed in the problem. The new specific cost of this additional debt will be:

$$k'_D = 8.625(1 - 0.36)/(1 - 0.04)$$
$$= 5.75 \text{ percent.}$$

The marginal cost of raising new capital above \$91,743,119 will be:

$$k'_3 = w_D k'_D + w_C k'_C + w_R k'_R$$
$$= 0.218(5.75\%) + (0.611 + 0.171)(14.21\%)$$
$$= 1.2535 + 11.1122$$
$$= 12.37 \text{ percent}$$ ❖

Exhibit 13.10 summarizes these results in the form of a marginal cost of capital schedule.

The end of each range of new capital is known as the break point in the cost of capital (k') schedule. These break points refer to the total financing at which a specific cost of capital rises. For Germino Industries, there are two break points: \$38,363,171 and \$91,743,171. At the first break point, the cost of equity financing rises and at the second break point, the cost of debt financing rises. Exhibit 13.11 presents a graph of the MCC schedule.

As mentioned before, the k' schedule is a useful tool for investment and financial decision making. The marginal cost of capital is compared to the rate of return (or the IRR) expected from the investment being financed. To enhance

EXHIBIT 13.10

Marginal Cost of Capital Schedule
Germino Industries

The Range of New Capital	k'
\$1 – \$38,363,171	12.05 percent
\$38,363,172 – \$91,743,191	12.22 percent
\$91,743,192 – \$100,000,000	12.35 percent

stockholder wealth, returns from investments must exceed their marginal cost of capital.

If a firm's optimal capital structure consists of a range of debt ratios instead of a single optimal ratio (the optimal point in Classical Capital Structure Theory), it has the flexibility of choosing among different capital structures within the optimal range when obtaining new funds. This complicates the calculation of marginal cost of capital because it relaxes the assumption that a firm will raise new funds in the same proportion as the funds in its present (optimal) capital structure. Therefore, construction of the marginal cost of capital schedule may involve different weights and different specific costs.

Marginal Cost of Foreign Financing

The marginal cost of financing a foreign project is likely to differ from the cost of financing a domestic project. A firm's ability to raise funds in foreign capital markets, including the market where its foreign affiliate is located, can make a substantial difference in the specific costs of various sources of capital. Involvement in foreign projects may give a company easier access to local and international capital markets. Financing possibilities may differ among markets, and interest rates surely will vary.

Some foreign markets are more liquid and their investors require much lower rates of return. Exchange rate changes also affect the cost of capital from foreign sources. Calculating the marginal cost of capital in such a situation must incorporate anticipated changes in exchange rates.

The parent company's shareholders may provide capital at a lower cost if they view foreign investments by the firm as a substitute for their own international portfolio diversification and risk-reduction efforts. When a foreign economy is not perfectly synchronized with the home country's economy, international diversification into that country should help the firm to reduce the variability of its cash flows. Reducing the variability of cash flows lowers the firm's financial risk, and therefore the risk premium demanded by investors.

The cost of capital for a foreign project must also take into account the political risk associated with that project. Political risk reflects the possibility that political events in the host country may affect a firm's cash flows from its subsidiary. The analyst may add a premium to the calculated cost of capital to account for politi-

EXHIBIT 13.11

Marginal Cost of Capital Schedule for Germino Industries

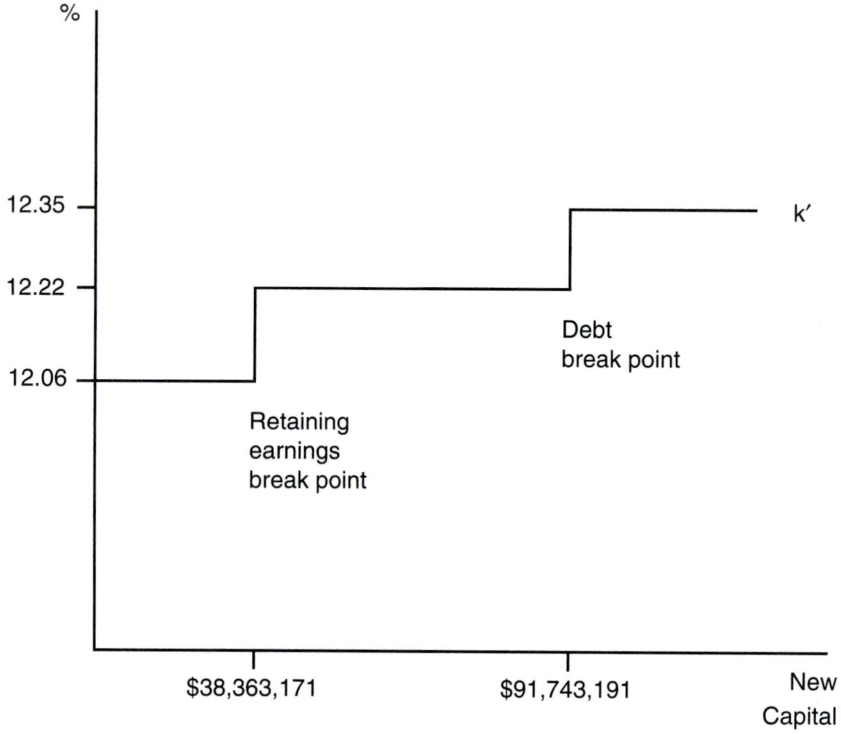

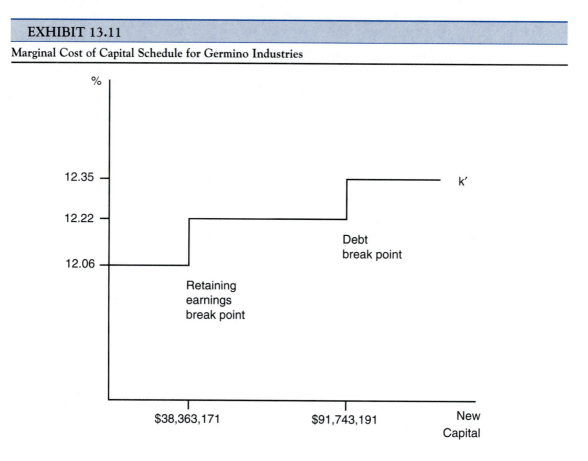

cal risk. Since any evaluation of political risk is subjective, the political risk premium added to the cost of capital is essentially arbitrary.

Multinational firms can often raise capital more cheaply through debt or equity issues in Euromarkets and foreign markets because of their multinational status and name recognition. Standardizing financial disclosure practices and the increasing international importance of credit ratings also help multinational firms to raise capital at lower costs in international capital markets.

Multinational firms are taxed by both their home and host countries, though. The tax policies of the home and host countries can affect the cost of financing a foreign project in a number of ways. Consider equity financing first. Earnings retained by the subsidiaries of a U.S. multinational are not subject to U.S. corporate income tax and foreign withholding tax until they are repatriated. Moreover, the firm can tap these funds without any flotation or transfer costs. A U.S. firm should be able to reduce its cost of capital by using its foreign subsidiary's retained earnings as a source of capital for a foreign investment.

A multinational corporation may manage to defer or even avoid paying taxes on cash flows other than retained earnings. Firms have found many ways to control the flow of cash between subsidiary and parent companies to reduce or avoid tax liabilities. These methods include transfer pricing, leads and lags, royalties and fees, and intracompany loans, as discussed in previous chapters. The firm's ability to avoid or reduce its tax liabilities affects its after-tax cost of equity financing.

The effect of taxes on the cost of debt financing is determined by the tax status of interest payments in the countries where the firm borrows. If a firm borrows from a local source to finance a foreign project, and the interest is not tax deductible in the host country, then the cost of debt financing will be higher. For example, Great Britain does not allow firms to deduct interest paid to a foreign affiliate from taxable income.

❖ EXAMPLE 13.6

Earth Movers Inc. (EMI), a U.S. manufacturer of heavy equipment, is considering investing in a manufacturing subsidiary in Spain. The project does not change the overall risk of the parent company. The following information is available:

Current debt ratio: 0.5

After-tax cost of debt: 6 percent

Cost of equity: 10 percent

Cost of new equity raised in the United States: 9 percent

Cost of new equity raised in Spain: 8.5 percent

After-tax cost of new debt raised in the United States: 6 percent

Cost of new debt raised in Spain: 8 percent

Spanish tax rate: 25 percent

Assume that the interest on debt is tax deductible in Spain and the local currency, the peseta, is expected to lose value against the U.S. dollar at an annual rate of 4 percent.

1. If the parent finances the project entirely with its own funds, what is the marginal cost of capital for the project?

If the risk characteristics of the proposed project match those of the parent company, then the parent's cost of equity does not change. Earth Movers' weighted average cost of capital is the marginal cost of capital for this project:

$$k' = w_D k_D + w_E k_E$$
$$= 0.5(6\%) + 0.5(10\%)$$
$$= 8 \text{ percent}$$

2. If the parent finances the project 60 percent with its own funds and 40 percent with debt raised in Spain, what is the marginal cost of capital for the project?
The project's marginal cost of capital is a weighted average:

$$k'^{*} = wk + w_{D^*} k_{D^*}$$

where w = weight of the parent's capital

w_{D*} = weight of the Spanish debt

k = the cost of the parent's capital

k_{D*} = after-tax cost of the Spanish debt

The U.S. parent can calculate the after-tax cost of the Spanish debt from the following equation:

$$k_{D*} = i^*(1 - t^*)(1 + d) + d$$

where i^* = Spanish interest rate

t^* = Spanish tax rate

d = percentage change in the exchange value of the peseta

Note that if the Spanish currency is expected to appreciate against the U.S. dollar, d is positive; if the Spanish currency is expected to depreciate against the dollar, d is negative.

$$\begin{aligned} k_D^* &= 8\%(1 - 0.25)(1 - 0.04) - 0.04 \\ &= 1.76 \text{ percent} \\ k'^* &= 0.6(8\%) + 0.4(1.76\%) \\ &= 4.8\% + 0.07\% \\ &= 4.87 \text{ percent} \end{aligned}$$

3. If the parent finances the project entirely with new equity and debt raised in Spain, what is the marginal cost of capital of the project?

The parent's marginal cost of financing the project is:

$$\begin{aligned} k'^* &= w_{D*}k_{D*} + w_{E*}k_{E*} \\ &= 0.5(1.76\%) + 0.5(8.5\%) \\ &= 0.88\% + 4.25\% \\ &= 5.13 \text{ percent} \end{aligned}$$ ❖

SUMMARY

A company's weighted average cost of capital includes all of the specific costs of the funds it has raised, weighted according to their individual proportions of total capital. The company's assets must earn a rate of return greater than this weighted average to keep the company viable in the long run.

External analysts and investors usually weight the specific costs based on the book values of the various sources of capital. Management uses market values to calculate those weights to keep its decision making parameters current.

Classical capital structure theory holds that each firm can identify one optimal debt ratio that minimizes the company's weighted average cost of capital; the financial

FOCUS ON FINANCE

DOLLAR COST OF BORROWING ABROAD

The dollar cost of borrowing in a foreign market is given by the after-tax interest expenses adjusted for any exchange gain or loss. To illustrate how to determine this cost, assume that one unit of foreign currency is borrowed locally at an annual interest rate of i^*. Let t^* be the local tax rate and S_0 and S_1 be the current and one-year expected exchange rates expressed as the dollar value of the foreign currency.

The after-tax cost of repaying one dollar of the loan at the end of one year is given by:

$$[1 + i^*(1 - t^*)](S_1)$$

The value of $1 of the loan today is $1(S_0)$. To find the effective cost of the local debt, expressed as a percentage (k_{D*}), subtract $1(S_0)$ from $[1 + i^*(1 - t^*)](S_1)$ and divide the difference by $1(S_0)$.

$$\begin{aligned} k_{D*} &= \{[1 + i^*(1 - t^*)](S_1) - 1(S_0)\}/1(S_0) \\ &= [1 + i^*(1 - t^*)](S_1/S_0) - 1 \end{aligned}$$

Let d be the percentage change in the value of the foreign currency. It must be less than the local interest rate, i^*. Then:

$$\begin{aligned} d &= (S_1 - S_0)/S_0 \\ &= S_1/S_0 - 1 \\ 1 + d &= S_1/S_0 \end{aligned}$$

If the currency is expected to appreciate against the dollar, d is positive; if it is expected to depreciate, d is negative.

Substituting the equation above into the previous one produces:

$$\begin{aligned} k_{D*} &= [1 + i^*(1 - t^*)](1 + d) - 1 \\ &= (1 + d) + i^*(1 - t^*)(1 + d) - 1 \\ &= i^*(1 - t^*)(1 + d) + d \end{aligned}$$

The first term on the right-hand side of this equation is the after-tax cost of local debt, adjusted for any exchange rate change. The second term is the exchange gain or loss. When d is positive, it will cost more dollars to service the debt; this represents an exchange loss to the borrower. When d is negative, it will cost fewer dollars to service the debt; this represents an exchange gain to the borrower.

It can be shown that the dollar cost of long-term borrowing in a foreign market is the same as the cost of one-period borrowing, provided that the expected rate of change in the foreign currency value remains steady.

manager has the job of keeping the company at that optimal capital structure. The implications of this theory contradict actual financial practices in the United States.

Based on their groundbreaking statistical studies, Modigliani and Miller reasoned that the value of a firm depends on net operating income, not on net income after taxes. Therefore, a company's debt ratio has no effect on its weighted average cost of capital. They built their theory on assumptions that did not correspond to real-world conditions.

Subsequent research has produced the current, generally accepted capital structure theory. This theory proposes an optimal range of debt ratios; within this range, the weighted average cost of capital is a constant, minimal rate. It is the financial manager's job to keep the company within its optimal range. The consequences of this theory are compatible with practices in the real financial world.

When its capital structure is within the optimal range, a company can raise external funds by issuing whatever type of security it pleases: debt, preferred stock, or common stock. To maximize shareholder wealth, however, the company should choose whichever security will produce the greatest earnings available for distribution to the stockholders (EAPS).

At any level of operating income (EBIT), issuing bonds will produce more earnings available per share than issuing preferred stock because of differences in tax laws and risk levels. The desirability of bonds compared to common stock, however, varies with EBIT. A lower EBIT makes common stock more desirable; a higher EBIT makes bonds more desirable.

The marginal cost of capital is the cost of raising additional funds to finance new investment opportunities. It is affected by the size of the additional financing, the company's debt ratio, and any changes in specific costs as more funds are raised. The marginal cost of capital generally increases as more and more long-term capital is raised.

Key Terms

capital structure
earnings available per share
earnings before interest and taxes
fungible dollar
marginal cost of capital

Self-Study Questions

1. Name five sources of funds that may be included in the weighted average cost of capital.
2. Explain the two different methods which can be used to calculate weights for the weighted average cost of capital.
3. What is the nature of the relationship between k_D and the debt ratio?
4. Why is k_C always higher than k_D, regardless of the level of the debt ratio?
5. According to classic capital structure theory, what is the relationship between a company's weighted average cost of capital and its debt ratio?
6. According to Modigliani and Miller, what is the relationship between a company's weighted average cost of capital and its debt ratio?
7. According to modern capital structure theory, what is the relationship between a company's weighted average cost of capital and its debt ratio?
8. Why does EAPS react differently from EBIT based upon the type of financing a company chooses?
9. For a relatively low level of EBIT, will EAPS be higher if a firm issues bonds or preferred stock? Why?
10. How might a financial manager use the marginal cost of capital?

Self-Test Problems

1. Bisch & Co. has $250 million in bonds outstanding, with a specific cost of 6 percent. It leases no assets. It has $250 million in preferred stock outstanding, with a specific cost of 10 percent. It has also issued $500 million in equity with a specific cost of 15 percent. Find Bisch's weighted average cost of capital.
2. The market value of Abend Company's outstanding bonds is $80 million, and their specific cost is 7 percent. Abend leases $50 million of machinery at an after-tax cost of 8 percent. The market value of the company's preferred stock is $20 million, and its specific cost is 10 percent. The market value of the company's common stock is $150 million, and k_C is 12 percent. If Abend Company has $100 million in retained earnings, what is its weighted average cost of capital?
3. Format Foto, Inc. needs to raise $20 million externally. It can sell bonds with a 10 percent coupon rate, preferred stock with a 12 percent dividend, or common stock at $40 per share. Format Foto expects EBIT of $10 million with the new asset. It is already paying $1 million interest on outstanding debt. It has a tax rate of 30 percent and 2 million shares of common stock outstanding. How should the company raise the $20 million?
4. At what level of EBIT do the bond and common stock lines for Format Foto (described in Problem 3) intersect?
5. McKenzie Corp. has $2 billion in capital and the following capital structure:

SOURCE	w_i	k_i
Debt	0.30	6%
Common Stock	0.40	12%
Retained Earnings	0.30	12%

McKenzie is considering raising $125 million in additional capital in the same proportions as its existing capital structure. It expects to retain $50 million of its earnings. It currently calculates k_C as $3/$50 + 0.06, and expects to be able to raise at least $100 million by selling common stock at $50 per share. The flotation cost will probably be 3 percent of the market price. McKenzie does not expect to be able to borrow more than $30 million at 6 percent, however. Any debt beyond that limit is expected to cost 8 percent.

Calculate McKenzie Corp.'s weighted average cost of capital and construct a marginal cost of capital schedule for the $125 million.

6. Agami Oil International (AOI) has $1.1 billion in capital, 45 percent of which is borrowed at a specific cost of 5.5 percent. Equity consists of 30 percent common stock and 25 percent retained earnings. AOI pays a $1 per share dividend and its expected long-term growth rate is 10 percent. The stock price fluctuates around $25 per share.

AOI wants to raise $300 million in additional capital in the same proportions as its existing capital structure. It expects to retain $100 million of its earnings. Investment bankers have advised AOI that it probably cannot sell more than $200 million in common stock without depressing the price. The flotation cost will be 2 percent. They have also warned AOI that it can only raise another $100 million by borrowing at 5.5 percent. Every additional $100 million borrowed therefore will raise the specific cost 1 percent.

Calculate AOI's weighted average cost of capital and construct a marginal cost of capital schedule for the $300 million.

7. MTM Inc. is considering investing in a manufacturing subsidiary in Mexico. MTM's weighted average cost of capital is 8.5 percent. If MTM borrows in Mexico, its cost of debt will be 7.5 percent and the interest on that debt will be tax deductible in Mexico. The Mexican tax rate is 40 percent. Assume that the Mexican peso is expected to lose value against the U.S. dollar at an annual rate of 2 percent. If the project has the same risk characteristics as the parent company and is financed half-and-half with MTM's funds and Mexican debt, what is its marginal cost of capital?
8. Hip Hop Hair, Inc. (HHH), a manufacturer of styled extensions, needs to expand its factory in Hong Kong. The following current data are available:

Current debt ratio: 0.25

After-tax cost of debt: 8 percent

Cost of equity: 12 percent

Cost of new equity raised in the United States: 14 percent

Cost of new equity raised in Hong Kong: 12 percent

After-tax cost of new debt raised in the United States: 10 percent

Cost of new debt raised in Hong Kong: 9 percent

Hong Kong tax rate: 30 percent

Assume that the interest on debt is tax deductible in Hong Kong, and the Hong Kong dollar is expected to appreciate against the U.S. dollar at an annual rate of 1 percent.

(a) If HHH finances the expansion entirely with funds raised in the United States, what is the project's marginal cost of capital?

(b) If the expansion has the same risk characteristics as the parent company, and HHH finances it with 25 percent U.S. financing and 75 percent debt raised in Hong Kong, what is the project's marginal cost of capital?

(c) If the project has the same risk characteristics as the parent company, and HHH finances it with new debt and equity raised in Hong Kong, what is the project's marginal cost of capital?

Discussion Questions

1. How are a company's rate of return on assets and weighted average cost of capital related?
2. Why might some people calculate *k* using book values as weights while others use market values as weights?
3. Explain how a company's weighted average cost of capital reacts to a change in the proportion of debt it uses according to classical capital structure theory.
4. To follow the classical theory of capital structure, which financial practices would a modern firm have to change?
5. Which cost of capital behaves the same way in all three capital structure theories?
6. Explain how Modigliani and Miller's theory differs from classical capital structure theory.
7. If the weighted average cost of capital is a straight, flat line, how should a company determine the best type of security to issue to generate external funds?
8. To follow Modigliani and Miller's theory of capital structure, which financial practices would a modern firm have to change?
9. Why would industries with high levels of business risk have lower optimal ranges than less risky industries?
10. Identify two financial practices that are consistent with the modern theory of capital structure.
11. What effect does a recession have on weighted average cost of capital curves?
12. If a company's debt ratio is at or near the lower limit of its optimal range and the company needs external financing, which type of security should it issue?
13. What is a breakeven EBIT?
14. Why do the bond line and the preferred stock line fail to intersect on an EBIT–EAPS graph?
15. Why is EAPS with preferred stock always lower than EAPS with bonds for a given level of EBIT?
16. Do the preferred stock line and the common stock line intersect on an EBIT–EAPS graph? Under what condition(s) would this information be important?
17. What effect would higher interest rates have on an EBIT–EAPS graph?
18. What effect would higher tax rates have on an EBIT–EAPS graph.
19. Explain the significance of break points in the marginal cost of capital schedule.
20. Explain why a firm might be able to reduce its weighted average cost of capital if it includes some foreign financing in its capital structure.

Problems

1. The market values of MeisterBrand Company's outstanding bonds and common stock are $333 million and $225 million, respectively. The company also has $442 million in retained earnings. If k_D is 9 percent and k_C is 12 percent, what is MeisterBrand's weighted average cost of capital?
2. I. S. Clock Company has $300 million in bonds outstanding, with k_D equal to 8 percent. It leases $200 million in assets, and estimates k_L at 12 percent. It has $100 million in preferred stock outstanding, on which it pays $12 million in annual dividends. It has also issued $600 million in equity, and calculates that k_E is 14 percent. What is the Clock Company's weighted average cost of capital?
3. A company needs to raise $10 million to buy assets. It expects EBIT of $75 million. The company has no debt or preferred stock outstanding, but it has 7 million shares of common stock outstanding. Its tax rate is 35 percent. Should it issue 8 percent bonds or common stock at $10 a share? What is the breakeven EBIT?
4. General Uniforms, Inc. estimates that it can borrow $40 million at 10 percent interest. It already has $100 million in 7 percent debt outstanding. Alternatively, the company could raise the $40 million by selling 1 million shares of common stock. It has 6 million shares of common stock outstanding. General Uniforms has no preferred stock outstanding, and its tax rate is 36 percent. At what level of EBIT will the company generate the same EAPS from the bonds and the stock?
5. Philippatos Publishing Corp. (PPC) has the following capital structure:

SOURCE	w_i	k_i
Debt	0.25	10%
Common Stock	0.25	15%
Retained Earnings	0.50	15%

PPC is considering raising $400 million in additional capital in the same proportions as its existing capital structure. It expects to retain $200 million of its earnings. It currently calculates k_C as $2.40/$40 + 0.09, and expects to be able to raise at least $300 million by selling common stock at $40 per share. The flotation cost will probably be 2 percent of the market price. PPC does not expect to be able to borrow more than $75 million at 10 percent, however. Any debt beyond that limit is expected to cost 12 percent.

Calculate PPC's weighted average cost of capital and construct a marginal cost of capital schedule for the $400 million.

6. Engemann Engines, Inc. (EEI) has $800 million in capital, 10 percent of which is borrowed at a specific cost of 4.9 percent. Equity consists of 60 percent common stock and 30 percent retained earnings. EEI pays a $0.40 per share dividend and its expected long-term growth rate is 17.5 percent. The stock price is about $16 per share.

EEI wants to raise $80 million in additional capital in the same proportions as its existing capital structure. It expects to retain $20 million of its earnings. Investment bankers have advised EEI that it probably cannot sell more than $50 million in common stock without depressing the price. The flotation cost will be 5 percent. They have also warned EEI that it can only raise another $5 million by borrowing at 4.9 percent. The next $5 million borrowed will have a specific cost of 6 percent.

Calculate EEI's weighted average cost of capital and construct a marginal cost of capital schedule for the $80 million.

7. Hagar & Browne, Inc. (HBI) is considering investing in a manufacturing subsidiary in Sweden. HBI's weighted average cost of capital is 15 percent. If HBI borrows in Sweden, its cost of debt will be 10 percent and the interest on that debt will be tax deductible in Sweden. The Swedish tax rate is 16 percent. Assume that the Swedish krona is expected to appreciate against the U.S. dollar at an annual rate of 5 percent. If the project has the same risk characteristics as the parent company and is financed one-third with HBI's funds and two-thirds with Swedish debt, what is the project's marginal cost of capital?
8. New Order Airlines (NOA) is based in the United States, but it plans to open facilities in the Ukraine. The following current data are available:

   Current debt ratio: 0.28

   After-tax cost of debt: 10 percent

   Cost of equity: 16 percent

   Cost of new equity raised in the United States: 18 percent

   Cost of new equity raised in the Ukraine: 15 percent

   After-tax cost of new debt raised in the United States: 12 percent

   Cost of new debt raised in the Ukraine: 11 percent

   Ukrainian tax rate: 45 percent

   Assume that the interest on debt is tax deductible in the Ukraine, and that the Ukrainian karbovanet is expected to lose value against the U.S. dollar at an annual rate of 3 percent.

   (a) If NOA finances the expansion entirely with funds raised in the United States, what is the marginal cost of capital?
   (b) If the expansion has the same risk characteristics as the parent company, and NOA finances it with 20 percent U.S. financing and 80 percent debt raised in the Ukraine, what is the project's marginal cost of capital?
   (c) If the project has the same risk characteristics as the parent company and NOA finances it with new debt and equity raised in the Ukraine, what is its marginal cost of capital?

Topics for Further Research

1. Look up Home Depot and McDonald's in the *Value Line Investment Survey*. Refer to Example 13.2 in the text and calculate k for each company. Compare these costs to "Percentage Earned on Total Capital."
2. Choose an electric utility company from Moody's *Public Utilities Manual*. For all of the listed bonds it has outstanding, note their rates, maturities, and the exchange(s) where they are listed. Observe the market prices for these bonds in the newspaper for ten consecutive trading days. Do the bonds move in the same direction as the Dow Jones Utilities Index each day? For any bonds that appear in the newspaper listings every day, calculate the percentage change in price each day. Calculate the daily percentage change in the Utilities Index. Based on your sample, do you think that the bonds have betas greater than, equal to, or less than 1.0?
3. Choose an industry from the *Value Line Investment Survey* that includes at least 12 companies. Examine the debt ratios of all companies in the industry. Calculate k for each company and plot the points on a capital structure graph. Can you identify the limits of the optimal range for that industry?

Answers to Self-Test Problems

1.

$$\begin{aligned} \text{Total capital} &= \$250 \text{ million} + \$250 \text{ million} + \$500 \text{ million} \\ &= \$1 \text{ billion} \end{aligned}$$

$$\begin{aligned} w_D = w_P &= \$250 \text{ million}/\$1 \text{ billion} \\ &= 0.25 \end{aligned}$$

$$\begin{aligned} w_E &= \$500 \text{ million}/\$1 \text{ billion} \\ &= 0.50 \end{aligned}$$

$$\begin{aligned} k &= (0.25)(6\%) + (0.25)(10\%) + (0.50)(15\%) \\ &= 11.5 \text{ percent} \end{aligned}$$

2.

$$\begin{aligned} \text{Total Capital} &= \$80 \text{ million} + \$50 \text{ million} + \$20 \text{ million} \\ &\quad + \$150 \text{ million} + \$100 \text{ million} \\ &= \$400 \text{ million} \end{aligned}$$

$$\begin{aligned} w_D &= \$80 \text{ million}/\$400 \text{ million} \\ &= 0.2 \end{aligned}$$

$$\begin{aligned} w_L &= \$50 \text{ million}/\$400 \text{ million} \\ &= 0.125 \end{aligned}$$

$$\begin{aligned} w_P &= \$20 \text{ million}/\$400 \text{ million} \\ &= 0.05 \end{aligned}$$

$$\begin{aligned} w_E &= (\$150 \text{ million} + \$100 \text{ million})/\$400 \text{ million} \\ &= 0.625 \end{aligned}$$

$$\begin{aligned} k &= (0.2)(7\%) + (0.125)(8\%) + (0.05)(10\%) + (0.625)(12\%) \\ &= 10.4 \text{ percent} \end{aligned}$$

3. The firm should issue common stock because it produces the highest EAPS.

	BONDS[a]	PREFERRED STOCK[a]	COMMON STOCK[a]
EBIT	$10,000	$10,000	$10,000
Old interest	1,000	1,000	1,000
New interest	2,000	0	0
Taxable income	$ 7,000	$ 9,000	$ 9,000
Tax (30%)	2,100	2,700	2,700
Income after taxes	$ 4,900	$ 6,300	$ 6,300
Preferred dividend	0	2,400	0
Earnings available	$ 4,900	$ 3,900	$ 6,300
Number of common shares	2,000	2,000	2,500
EAPS	$2.45	$1.95	$2.52

[a]Amounts in thousands, except per-share data.

4.
$$\frac{(EBIT - \$3 \text{ million})(0.30)}{2 \text{ million}} = \frac{(EBIT - \$1 \text{ million})(0.30)}{2.5 \text{ million}}$$
$$(2.5)(EBIT - \$3 \text{ million}) = (2.0)(EBIT - \$1 \text{ million})$$
$$2.5EBIT - \$7.5 \text{ million} = 2.0EBIT - \$2 \text{ million}$$
$$0.5EBIT = \$5.5 \text{ million}$$
$$EBIT = \$11 \text{ million}$$

5. The weighted average cost of capital is:

$$k = (0.3)(6\%) + (0.4)(12\%) + (0.3)(12\%)$$
$$= 10.2 \text{ percent}$$

The specific cost of equity will not rise until a total of \$50 million/(0.4 + 0.3) = \$71,428,571 in new capital is raised, because \$50 million in retained earnings will support \$21,428,571 in new debt. Since McKenzie can borrow up to \$40 million without an increase in k_D, the marginal cost of capital up to the \$71,428,571 breakpoint (k_1') will equal the existing weighted average cost of capital, 10.2 percent.

To raise more than this, McKenzie will have to sell new shares of common stock at \$50 less the flotation cost of \$1.50 per share. This will raise the specific cost of equity to:

$$k_C' = [\$3/(\$50.00 - \$1.50)] + 0.06$$
$$= 12.2 \text{ percent}$$

The amount of borrowing that can be done at McKenzie's current 6 percent cost is \$30 million. Therefore, the maximum new capital that can be raised without increasing the cost of debt is \$30 million/0.3 = \$100 million. This is McKenzie's second breakpoint. The marginal cost of raising new capital between the first and second breakpoints will be:

$$k_2' = (0.3)(6\%) + (0.7)(12.2\%)$$
$$= 10.34 \text{ percent}$$

Any borrowing beyond \$30 million is expected to cost 8 percent, so the marginal cost of raising the remaining \$25 million will be:

$$k_3' = (0.3)(8\%) + (0.7)(12.2\%)$$
$$= 10.94 \text{ percent}$$

MARGINAL COST OF CAPITAL SCHEDULE

MCKENZIE CORP.

THE RANGE OF NEW CAPITAL	k'
\$1 to \$71,428,571	10.20 percent
\$71,428,572 to \$100,000,000	10.34 percent
\$100,000,001 to \$125,000,000	10.94 percent

6.

$$k_C' = \$1/\$25 + 0.10$$
$$= 14 \text{ percent}$$

The weighted average cost of capital is:

$$k = (0.45)(5.5\%) + (0.3)(14\%) + (0.25)(14\%)$$
$$= 10.18 \text{ percent}$$

\$100 million in retained earnings will support \$181,818,182 in new capital.

$$\$100 \text{ million}/0.55 = \$181,818,182$$

The \$81,818,182 in new debt will still cost 5.5 percent.

$$k_1' = 10.18 \text{ percent}$$

Because the flotation cost is 50 cents per share, the sale of new common stock will raise the specific cost of equity to:

$$k_C' = [\$1/(\$25.00 - \$0.50)] + 0.10$$
$$= 14.41 \text{ percent}$$

The maximum new capital that can be raised without increasing the cost of debt is \$100 million/0.45 = \$222,222,222.

$$k_2' = (0.45)(5.5\%) + (0.55)(14.41\%)$$
$$= 10.40 \text{ percent}$$

Any borrowing between \$100 million and \$200 million is expected to cost 6.5 percent, so the marginal cost of raising the remaining \$77,777,778 will be:

$$k_3' = (0.45)(6.5\%) + (0.55)(14.41\%)$$
$$= 10.85 \text{ percent}$$

Marginal Cost of Capital Schedule
Agami Oil International

The Range of New Capital	k'
\$1 to \$181,818,182	10.18 percent
\$181,818,183 to \$222,222,222	10.40 percent
\$222,222,223 to \$300,000,000	10.85 percent

7.
$$k_{D^*} = 7.5\%(1 - 0.4)(1 - 0.02) - 0.02$$
$$= 0.0241, \text{ or } 2.41 \text{ percent}$$

$$k'^* = (0.5)(8.5\%) + (0.5)(2.41\%)$$
$$= 0.0666, \text{ or } 6.66 \text{ percent}$$

8. (a)
$$k' = (0.25)(8\%) + (0.75)(12\%)$$
$$= 0.11, \text{ or } 11 \text{ percent}$$

(b)
$$k_{D^*} = 9\%(1 - 0.3)(1 + 0.01) + 0.01$$
$$= 0.07363, \text{ or } 7.363 \text{ percent}$$

$$k'^* = (0.25)(11\%) + (0.75)(7.363\%)$$
$$= 0.0827, \text{ or } 8.27 \text{ percent}$$

(c)
$$k'^* = (0.25)(8.27\%) + (0.75)(12\%)$$
$$= 0.110675, \text{ or } 11.07 \text{ percent}$$

CHAPTER

14

Investment Banks and Their Services

LEARNING OBJECTIVES

This chapter examines the primary markets, both public and private, and their participants. At the conclusion of this chapter, the reader should be able to:

1. *Explain the many decisions necessary to plan a new security issue*
2. *Describe the services offered by an investment banker*
3. *Compare the different methods by which a firm can sell a new issue of securities*
4. *Calculate the value of a preemptive right*
5. *Define the term private placement*
6. *Explain the need for and role of venture capital*

When a corporation or local government needs to raise external funds, it utilizes some or all of the services of an investment bank. These specialized financial functions include designing the terms of the security, preparing the documents necessary to register, promote, and sell it, organizing the sales effort; and supporting the security in the aftermarket. Investment bankers have the talent, experience, and contacts to perform most or all of these functions better than their corporate clients.

The life of an investment banker is not easy. The industry has gotten competitive, the market for financial services has become global, and some customers' new security offerings have become too risky for routine underwriting procedures. Compensation for risk taking and services rendered has to be shared with other participants in most transactions that bring new securities to the market.

Investment banks can market their services to corporations in a variety of ways. They can serve as consultants and advisors in a preemptive rights offering, when a company offers new shares of common stock to its existing stockholders. The investment banker may help negotiate a private placement, when a company sells its securities to one or a few investors. A new company seeking start-up or expansion funds needs venture capital; the investment bank can provide contacts and help prepare the paperwork.

ISSUING NEW SECURITIES

public offering
A sale of new securities by a publicly held company.

investment bank
A financial institution with the primary function of distributing new securities for publicly held companies.

initial public offering
A sale of a company's new securities for the first time.

underwriting
The basic service of an investment bank, which consists of buying a new security from a company and then reselling it to investors.

A **public offering** is a sale of new securities. It is said to take place in the *primary market*, although this market is a mechanism with no physical location. Financial institutions called **investment banks** (IBs) are the major players in this market. Their expertise in the procedures necessary to issue new securities leads almost all issuers to use their services. An investment bank has the experienced financial advisors, the legal talent, and the sales contacts to perform this function far more efficiently than its corporate clients could perform it themselves. Investment banks earn compensation commensurate with the services they perform. Their services are slightly different for public offerings and **initial public offerings** (IPOs), sales of a company's new securities for the first time.

Public Offerings

An investment bank's basic service consists of buying a new security issue from a company or municipal government and then reselling it to investors. This service is called **underwriting** a security. Plans for an underwriting may begin with either the issuer that will raise the external financing or the investment bank.

Underwriting Initiated by an Issuer. A potential issuer can use the services of an investment bank at almost any stage in the planning process for a new security. The issuer may simply decide how much external capital it needs and then announce that it requires the services of an underwriter to raise the money. In this situation, the investment bank participates fully in planning and designing the new issue, does the paperwork necessary to comply with federal and state legal requirements, brings the new security to the public's attention, buys it from the issuing company or government, and resells it to investors.

Designing a new issue includes a range of related tasks:

1. Determining whether a corporation should sell bonds, preferred stock, or common stock
2. Selecting the features of the issue, such as callability, convertibility, and restrictive covenants. If the issuer is a municipal government, the structure of the issue (redemption clauses, tax exemption, purpose, and so forth) must be decided. If the issuer is a corporation, sweeteners such as warrants may be added.
3. Pinpointing the date when the issue should hit the market, based on the issuer's needs, forecasted market conditions, and a knowledge of how much financing other users of funds plan to do.

FOCUS ON FINANCE

New Municipal Underwriting Ethics

In October 1993, SEC Chairman Arthur Levitt Jr. announced that the nation's largest investment banks had agreed to a self-imposed ban on political contributions intended to influence state and local government officials. According to the agreement, each firm would:

1. Cease making political donations itself
2. Prohibit political donations by any employees involved in municipal finance at the state and local level
3. Permit other employees to donate to political campaigns, as long as the donations were not intended to influence awards of new or continuing municipal business
4. Formulate guidelines regarding gifts of lunches, limousine services, expense-paid travel, personal items, and other favors to municipal employees who were in positions to determine which investment banks would underwrite municipal issues

Merrill Lynch, Smith Barney Shearson, Bear Sterns, Donaldson Lufkin & Jenrette, Salomon Brothers, and Paine Webber Group were among the 17 firms that agreed to the ban.

4. Estimating the bond coupon rate or stock price that will satisfy the market, given the previous decisions, the issuer's financial condition, and the size of the new issue
5. Evaluating the need for and cost of **making a market** in the issue after the initial sale. When an IB makes a market in a security, it commits itself to buy the security from sellers and to sell its own holdings of the security to buyers, in order to stabilize the price for a limited time.

making a market
A commitment by an investment bank to buy a security from sellers and to sell its own holdings of the security to buyers, in order to stabilize the price for a limited time.

For most of this century, market tradition compelled an issuer to use the same investment bank to bring all its new securities to market. Changing underwriters was a public declaration that the former IB had performed unsatisfactorily. Only in the past quarter-century has securities underwriting become a competitive industry. Some companies have modified the old custom, issuing domestic bonds through one investment bank, issuing stock in the U.S. market through another, and selling securities in foreign markets through a third. Other issuers have abandoned the concept of institutional loyalty completely, requiring IBs to compete for every new security issue.

Each major step in the security issuing process requires the approval of the company's board of directors: determining the need for external financing, selecting an investment bank, and finalizing the details of the security's provisions. The board must also either approve or select a trustee for a fixed income security.

Meeting Legal Requirements. After the security's design satisfies both the issuing company and the underwriter, they evaluate its compliance with the legal requirements for a public offering. The Securities Act of 1933 requires that an issuer make full disclosure of information on a new security to the public. Almost all new issues must be registered with the SEC, with four exceptions:

1. Short-term issues with less than 270 days to maturity
2. Small issues that involve no more than $1.5 million in a single year
3. Issues by railroads, which are regulated by the Interstate Commerce Commission (although federal legislation is being prepared to shift railroad issues to the SEC's jurisdiction)
4. Issues of companies that sell their securities to residents of a single state

The issuer must file a registration statement with the SEC that contains detailed information on the company, the nature of its business, its history, its financial statements, its management and their holdings of the company's securities, and its competitive environment. The statement must also disclose all relevant information about the new security, including its terms and conditions, the issuer's use of the proceeds from the issue, legal opinions, and whatever risks the investor might have to bear.

prospectus

A summary of all the significant information about an issuing company and its new security gathered from the SEC registration statement.

red herring

A prospectus circulated to promote interest in a forthcoming issue before SEC approval. The face of the prospectus indicates this preapproval status in red lettering.

In addition, the company must file a **prospectus**, which summarizes the significant information in the registration statement. It will be distributed to dealers, brokers, and prospective investors, as well as to others who request it, after the security's registration has been approved. If it is distributed before SEC approval, the face of the prospectus must indicate this fact in red lettering. Such preapproval prospectuses that contain blanks or price ranges instead of final prices circulate to promote interest in the forthcoming issue. They are known in the trade as **red herrings**. The investment bank usually pays the legal and accounting costs to prepare all of these documents, as well as the printing costs and registration fees; it charges them back to the issuing company as "legal and administrative expenses."

The financial press informs the public of these filings. *The Wall Street Journal* lists recent SEC filings in a daily column called "Financing Business." As Exhibit 14.1 shows, for a debt issue filing , the news report identifies the dollar amount and the investment bank(s). For an equity issue filing, the news report identifies the number of shares and the investment bank.

The SEC reviews the registration statement and the prospectus to verify that they disclose complete information free of any indication of fraud. This review can take anywhere from three weeks to six months, depending on the volume of new issues being registered. Generally, the process takes 40 to 60 days. If the statements appear to be complete and accurate, the SEC approves the registration and the security can be sold. If the statements appear to be incomplete or fraudulent, the SEC issues a stop order, which prevents the securities from being sold until the issuer corrects the deficiencies.

SEC approval does *not* indicate that the security will be a good investment. It says only that the information in the registration documents appears to be complete and accurate. If the SEC learns otherwise after it has approved the registration, it can go to court and get an injunction to halt trading in the security.

After the SEC approves the registration statement, the company and the investment bank tentatively schedule the date to sell the security. A list of cor-

EXHIBIT 14.1

Report of Recent SEC Filings

Recent SEC Filings

WASHINGTON – The following issues were recently filed with the Securities and Exchange Commission:

Equity Residential Properties Trust, an offering of 5.5 million common shares of beneficial interest, with a 30-day overallotment option for 825,000 additional shares, via Merrill Lynch & Co.

GeneMedicine Inc., an initial offering of 2,125,000 common shares, at an estimated $7 to $9 a share, with an overallotment option for an additional 281,250 shares, via D. Blech & Co.

Geon Co., a shelf offering of up to $150 million of debt securities.

Orion Network Systems Inc., an initial offering of three million common shares, at an expected $18 to $20 a share, with an overallotment option for 450,000 additional shares, via Merrill Lynch and Salomon Brothers Inc.

Parker & Parsley Petroleum Co., an amended offering of 2,360,000 common shares, with an overallotment option for 354,000 additional shares, via Goldman, Sachs & Co.

Province of Quebec, a shelf offering of about $2.2 billion of debt securities.

Teck Corp., an offering of $150 million of convertible subordinated debentures, with an overallotment option for $20 million of additional debentures, via Merrill Lynch, Goldman Sachs and S.G. Warburg & Co.

U.S. Delivery Systems Inc., a shelf offering of three million common shares.

Source: The Wall Street Journal, May 31, 1994, p. C27.

porate issues and other securities scheduled for sale in the coming week appears in each Monday's edition of *The Wall Street Journal* and other papers that carry detailed business news. If Monday is a holiday, the column appears in Tuesday's edition. As Exhibit 14.2 illustrates, a column labeled "Securities Offering Calendar" details the issuer, the size and type of issue, the investment bank (if any), and the exact day (if known), for each upcoming new issue.

When the issue has been priced and offered, the press publishes the details of the offering. *The Wall Street Journal* carries this information in a daily column called "New Securities Issues," as shown in Exhibit 14.3. At about the same time, the investment bank places an advertisement, called a *tombstone* because of its shape and format, intended to alert investors that the security is being offered for sale. The tombstone must carry a notice that it does not represent an offer to sell the security. The tombstone for the ANTEC Corporation stock issue shown in Exhibit 14.4 indicates that the security is being offered for sale in the United States, Canada, and Europe.

shelf registration

An SEC procedure that allows a large corporation to register at one time all of the stocks or bonds it intends to issue in the following two years.

A large corporation that already has securities listed on a stock exchange can take advantage of **shelf registration** procedures. SEC Rule 415 allows the company to register all of the stocks or bonds it intends to issue in the following two years at one time. Upon approval, the firm sells a fraction of the registered issue to the public and places the remainder "on a shelf." Whenever it wants to raise additional funds by selling a portion of these securities, it files a brief amendment to the original registration statement, and the SEC grants approval in a matter of days. The total cost of issuing securities via shelf registration has been estimated as approx-

EXHIBIT 14.2

Weekly Schedule of Securities Offerings

SECURITIES OFFERING CALENDAR

The following U.S. Treasury, corporate and municipal offerings are tentatively scheduled for sale this week, according to Dow Jones Capital Markets Report and Dow Jones News Service:

TREASURY

Today

$24 billion of three and six-month bills.

Tomorrow

$17 billion of two-year notes.

Wednesday

$11 billion of five-year notes.

Thursday

$16.5 billion of 52-week bills.

CORPORATES

Today

JPS Automotive Products Corp.—$180 million of seven-year senior notes via Donaldson, Lufkin & Jenrette Securities Corp.

Wednesday

Federal National Mortgage Association – $1.5 billion of 10-year global notes via Merrill Lynch & Co. and J.P. Morgan Securities Inc.

Presley Cos. – $200 million of 10-year senior notes via Donaldson, Lufkin & Jenrette.

One Day In The Week

Agco Corp.—3.3 million shares, via CS First Boston Inc.

Atmel Corp. – 2.2 million shares, via Alex. Brown & Sons Inc.

Bell Microproducts Inc. – 2.4 million shares, via Bear, Stearns & Co.

Charles E. Smith Residential Realty – initial 12.2 million shares, via Goldman, Sachs & Co.

Collins & Aikman Holdings – initial 20 million shares, via Goldman Sachs.

Capstone Capital Trust Inc. – initial 5.8 million shares, via Smith Barney Shearson Inc.

Dominion Resources Inc. – initial 6.9 million units, via Smith Barney Shearson.

Empire Gas Corp. – $121 million of 10-year senior secured notes via Morgan Stanley & Co.

Geoworks – initial 2.5 million shares, via Robertson Stephens & Co.

Gerrity Oil & Gas Corp. – $100 million of 10-year senior subordinated notes via Morgan Stanley.

Intelcom Group Inc.—five million shares, via PaineWebber Inc.

Multicare Cos. – three million shares, via Lehman Brothers.

Network Peripherals Inc. – initial three million shares, via Lehman Brothers.

PT Indah Kiat Pulp & Power Corp. – $50 million of five-year secured notes, $100 million of eight-year guaranteed secured -notes and $100 million of 12-year guaranteed secured notes via Morgan Stanley.

Riverwood International Corp. – $100 million of 10-year senior notes via J.P. Morgan.

Surgical Health Corp. – $75 million of 10-year senior notes via Smith Barney Shearson.

Tesoro Pete Corp. – five million shares, via CS First Boston.

Theratex – initial four million shares, via Robertson Stephens & Co.

Trend Lines Inc. – initial two million shares, via Prudential Securities Inc.

Wabash National Corp. – one million shares, via Alex. Brown & Sons.

Welcome Homes Inc. – initial three million shares, via Donaldson, Lufkin & Jenrette.

Xenova Group PLC - initial three million American depositary shares, via PaineWebber.

MUNICIPALS

Tomorrow

Clark County, Nev. – $102.2 million of various transportation-improvement bonds, via competitive bid.

Los Angeles Department of Water & Power – $50 million of waterworks revenue bonds, via competitive bid.

San Francisco – $175 million of 1994-95 tax and revenue anticipation notes, via competitive bid.

Wednesday

Dallas – $99.9 million of series 1994 general obligation bonds, via competitive bid.

Houston – $110 million of series 1994 tax and revenue anticipation notes, via competitive bid.

Rhode Island – $125 million of tax anticipation notes, via competitive bid.

Santa Cruz County, Calif. – $50 million of 1994-95 tax and revenue anticipation notes, via competitive bid.

Wisconsin—$350 million of 1994 operating notes, via competitive bid.

Thursday

New Hampshire Municipal Bond Bank – $75.3 million of various series 1994 bonds, via competitive bid.

One Day In The Week

Alabama Power Co. – $53.7 million of pollution control revenue refunding bonds, via a J.P. Morgan group.

Alaska Student Loan Corp. – $50 million of student-loan revenue bonds, via a Smith Barney Shearson group.

Minnesota Housing Finance Agency—$60 million of single-family mortgage revenue bonds, via a PaineWebber group.

New Jersey Health Care Facilities Financing Authority—$71 million of bonds, via a Bear, Stearns group.

New York City Industrial Development Agency – $419 million of series 1994A special-facility revenue bonds, via a Smith Barney Shearson group.

New York State Medical Care Facilities Finance Agency—$170 million of bonds, via a Merrill Lynch group.

Philadelphia – $157 million of refunding and new-money general obligation bonds, via a Bear Stearns group.

San Diego County – $345 million of notes, including $60 million of taxable short-term securities, via a Merrill Lynch group.

Santa Margarita Water Control District, Calif. – $200 million of bonds, via a PaineWebber group.

Source: The Wall Street Journal, May 31, 1994, p. C27.

imately half of the cost that the issuer would incur to register and issue each block of securities separately.

For example, Chemical Banking Corp. filed a shelf registration statement with the SEC in August 1993 to issue up to $2.5 billion of securities. The single regis-

EXHIBIT 14.3

Securities Offerings and Prices

NEW SECURITIES ISSUES

The following were among yesterday's offerings and pricings in U.S. and non-U.S. capital markets, with terms and syndicate manager, as compiled by Dow Jones Capital Markets Report:

CORPORATE

El Al Airlines—$274 million of guaranteed trade certificates due June 26, 2006, priced at par to yield 7.39%, according to MCM CorporateWatch. The certificates were sold through Guaranteed Trade Trust 1994-A, a special-purpose vehicle. The issue was priced at a spread of 47 basis points above the interpolated five-year and 10-year Treasurys. Rated triple-A by Moody's Investors Service Inc. and Standard & Poor's Ratings Group, the issue will be sold through underwriters led by Citicorp Securities Inc.

Federal Home Loan Bank System—$104 million of notes due June 30, 1997, priced initially at par to yield 6.37%, according to MCM CorporateWatch. The noncallable issue was priced at a spread of seven basis points above Treasurys in a competitive bid won by Goldman, Sachs & Co.

EQUITY

Duracraft Corp. – 1.4 million common shares priced at $38 each through underwriters led by Adams Harkness & Hill Inc. and First Albany Corp.

Multicare Cos. – three million common shares priced at $16 each through underwriters led by Lehman Brothers Inc.

MUNICIPAL

Alaska Student Loan Corp. – $50 million 1994 Series A student-loan revenue bonds priced by a Smith Barney Inc. group. This issue is subject to the federal alternative-minimum tax. Yields range from 4.8% in 1997 to 6.07% in 2007. The bonds are insured by Ambac Indemnity Corp. and carry triple-A ratings from Moody's and S&P.

Clark County, Nev. – $103.7 million various transportation improvement bonds apparently won by a Smith Barney Inc. group. The bonds, rated an insured triple-A by Moody's and triple-A by S&P, were priced for reoffering to yield from 4.6% in 1998 to 6.2% in 2019.

Hillsborough County, Fla.—$121.8 million Series 1994 solid-waste and resource-recovery bonds apparently won by a Merrill Lynch & Co. group. Yields for reoffered bonds range from 4.2% in 1996 to 5.8% in 2008. This refunding-revenue offering is insured by the Municipal Bond Investors Assurance Corp. and carries triple-A ratings from Moody's and S&P.

Minnesota Housing Finance Agency—$62.3 million single-family mortgage bonds priced by a PaineWebber Inc. group. Included are $24 million Series K bonds priced to yield from 4.3% in 1996 to 6.4% in 2015. The $15.7 million Series L bonds and the $22.7 million Series M bonds are subject to the federal alternative-minimum tax. The Series L bonds have a 6.7% coupon and are priced at par to yield 6.7% July 1, 2020. The Series M bonds also have a 6.7% coupon and are priced at par to yield 6.7% July 1, 2026. Moody's is expected to rate the issue double-A, and S&P is expected to assign a double-A-plus rating.

New York State Medical Care Facilities Finance Agency—$168.8 million 1994 Series B bonds priced by a Merrill Lynch & Co. group. The hospital and nursing-home mortgage revenue bonds are insured by the Federal Housing Administration. Yields range from 3.5% in August 1995 to 6.3% in 2024. S&P has rated the offering triple-A.

San Francisco – $175 million 1994-95 tax and revenue anticipation notes won by Goldman, Sachs & Co. The notes have a 4.25% coupon and are priced to yield 3.65% July 15, 1995. Moody's has rated the issue MIG-1, and S&P has assigned an SP-1-plus rating.

ASSET-BACKED

Alliance Funding Corp. – $100 million of home-equity loan asset-backed certificates priced in two parts through underwriters led by Merrill Lynch & Co. The certificates were sold through AFC Mortgage Loan Trust 1994-2, a special-purpose vehicle. The $76 million Class A-1 certificates were priced as 6.95s at 99.75 to yield 6.93%, 92.5 basis points above the two-year when-issued Treasury note. The $24 million Class A-2 certificates were priced as 7.95s at 99.125 to yield 8.145%, 115 basis points above the 7.5-year interpolated Treasury. Both tranches are rated triple-A by Moody's and S&P.

General Motors Acceptance Corp. – $1.08 billion of senior auto-receivables asset-backed certificates priced through underwriters led by CS First Boston Inc., according to MCM CorporateWatch. The securities were sold through GMAC 1994-A Grantor Trust, a special-purpose vehicle. General Motors Acceptance Corp. is a unit of **General Motors** Corp. The certificates are rated triple-A by Moody's and S&P and were priced as 6.3s at 99.9375 to yield 6.424%, a spread of 58 basis points above the Treasury's 5.125% coupon notes due March 1996.

EUROBOND

Australian Industry Development Corp. (Australian agency) – 15 billion yen of three-year, callable, step-up Eurobonds due July 18, 1997, at issue price 100.15 via CS First Boston and Tokai Bank Europe Ltd. Fees 0.15. Coupon 2.9% in the first year, 3.5% in the second year and 4.1% until maturity. Callable at each coupon date.

Compagnie Generale Des Eaux (France) – one billion French francs of 8.125% Eurobonds due August 2, 2004, at issue price 100.977 via Banque National de Paris. Reoffered at 99.402 to yield 8.215% annually, a spread of 38 basis points over the interpolated yield curve between the 5.5% OAT due April 2004 and the 6.75% OAT due October 2004. Fees 2%.

Industrial Development Bank of India (India)—$100 million of Eurobonds due July 7, 1999, at issue and reoffer price 99.73 via JP Morgan Securities Ltd. Coupon set at 100 basis points over three-month London Interbank Offered Rate to yield 110 basis points over three-month Libor. Put option exercisable after three years and on every coupon date thereafter. Fees 0.375.

Landeskreditbank Baden-Wurttemberg (Germany) – 129 million Australian dollars of debt due Dec. 29, 1998, and priced at par via Nomura International PLC. First tranche bears coupon of 20% for first year and 4% for years two to four. Thereafter, coupon will be six-month Australian dollar British bankers' rate less 45 basis points with minimum of 6% and maximum of 9%. Second tranche bears coupon of 20% for first year and 4% for years two to four. Thereafter, coupon will be six-month Australian dollar British bankers' rate less 88 basis points with minimum of 6% and maximum of 10%. Fees undisclosed.

World Bank (supranational)-100 billion yen of zero-coupon Eurobonds due Sept. 20, 1999, at issue and fixed reoffer price 14.22 via Nikko Europe PLC. Fees 0.45.

Source: *The Wall Street Journal*, May 25, 1994, p. C19.

tration allowed the firm to issue debt instruments, preferred stock, and common stock. It brought Chemical's total unused shelf filings up to $4.25 billion. Chemical would say only that it planned to use the funds for general corporate purposes.

A small corporation that sells securities to residents of a single state can escape SEC scrutiny. However, each of the 50 states has a Securities Commission that regulates new securities issued within that state. States created these commissions to

EXHIBIT 14.4

Tombstone Ad

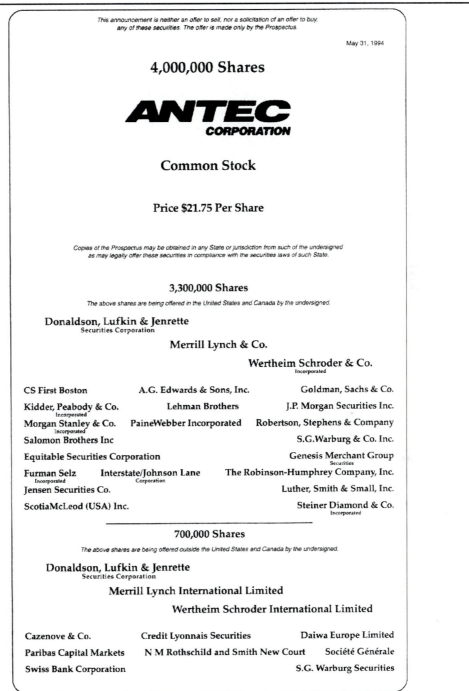

This announcement is neither an offer to sell, nor a solicitation of an offer to buy, any of these securities. The offer is made only by the Prospectus.

May 31, 1994

4,000,000 Shares

ANTEC
CORPORATION

Common Stock

Price $21.75 Per Share

Copies of the Prospectus may be obtained in any State or jurisdiction from such of the undersigned as may legally offer these securities in compliance with the securities laws of such State.

3,300,000 Shares

The above shares are being offered in the United States and Canada by the undersigned.

Donaldson, Lufkin & Jenrette
Securities Corporation

Merrill Lynch & Co.

Wertheim Schroder & Co.
Incorporated

CS First Boston — A.G. Edwards & Sons, Inc. — Goldman, Sachs & Co.

Kidder, Peabody & Co. Incorporated — Lehman Brothers — J.P. Morgan Securities Inc.

Morgan Stanley & Co. Incorporated — PaineWebber Incorporated — Robertson, Stephens & Company

Salomon Brothers Inc — S.G.Warburg & Co. Inc.

Equitable Securities Corporation — Genesis Merchant Group Securities

Furman Selz Incorporated — Interstate/Johnson Lane Corporation — The Robinson-Humphrey Company, Inc.

Jensen Securities Co. — Luther, Smith & Small, Inc.

ScotiaMcLeod (USA) Inc. — Steiner Diamond & Co. Incorporated

700,000 Shares

The above shares are being offered outside the United States and Canada by the undersigned.

Donaldson, Lufkin & Jenrette
Securities Corporation

Merrill Lynch International Limited

Wertheim Schroder International Limited

Cazenove & Co. — Credit Lyonnais Securities — Daiwa Europe Limited

Paribas Capital Markets — N M Rothschild and Smith New Court — Société Générale

Swiss Bank Corporation — S.G. Warburg Securities

Source: The Wall Street Journal, May 31, 1994, p. C22.

prevent fraudulent sales of securities, but they vary greatly in their effectiveness. State laws that govern the issuing and trading of securities are referred to as **blue sky laws** because they were passed to prevent unscrupulous financiers from selling securities worth no more than "a piece of blue sky."

blue sky law
A state law that governs issuing and trading securities within a state, to prevent unscrupulous financiers from selling fraudulent securities.

Competitive Bidding. Some corporations prefer to design their new securities themselves, then hire investment banks to do the legal and marketing work. These companies downplay the advisory services of the IBs and usually work with the institutions that cost them the least. A large corporation may hire its traditional investment bank to complete an initial shelf registration, and then award subsequent off-the-shelf securities sales to the lowest-cost bank.

In either case, the issuing company announces the planned sale and invites sealed bids. Competing investment banks submit their bids at the specified time and place, and the issuer awards the underwriting work to the least-cost bidder. Since an underwriter buys the securities from the company and resells them, the least-cost bidder is usually the one that offers to pay the highest price for the securities.

Best Efforts Sales. Sometimes investment banks doubt that the market will welcome a security that a company has designed or previously registered. The yield may be too low, the restrictive covenants may be inappropriate, or the security may be too risky, given the company's financial condition. If the company cannot or will not make adjustments that investment banks consider necessary for a successful underwriting, none will submit a bid. Large investment banking firms are simply not interested in such issues.

A smaller investment bank may, however, offer to handle a **best efforts sale**. The investment bank, acting as an agent for the company, attempts to sell the issue directly to the public, making its best efforts to find buyers for the issue. Such an agreement always includes a cutoff percentage; if, for example, 90 percent of the issue is not sold by a specific date, the issue will be canceled. The percentage is determined by the company's ability to get alternative (usually short-term) financing to cover the shortfall.

best efforts sale
An investment bank, acting as an agent for an issuing company, attempts to sell a new issue directly to the public, making its best efforts to find buyers for the entire issue.

Underwritings Initiated by Investment Banks. The investment banking industry has become highly competitive during the last quarter-century. As one competitive tactic, IBs began to research lists of publicly held corporations, seeking those who had not issued any new securities lately. They assigned analysts to study these companies, to determine how much external capital they could raise, in what form, and at what price. Armed with this information, the investment banks attempted to convince the CFOs of these companies that they could benefit substantially from issuing new securities.

This tactic was so successful that the IBs extended it and began predicting which companies were likely to issue securities in the near future. They developed similar packages of information for such companies and used them to preempt the companies' internal decision making about sales of new securities. This further

FOCUS ON FINANCE

WALL STREET ZOO

In October 1991, Merrill Lynch produced a new security, the LYNX, for Schering-Plough Corporation. The name is an acronym for a ***L**iquid **Y**ield **N**ote e**X**change*. The LYNX was a zero coupon note due in five years, yielding 6.5 percent, with warrants attached that gave the holder the right to buy Schering stock for $90 in 1996. The LYNX sold to net approximately $775 million. While the LYNX is outstanding, Schering pays no interest on it, but the company will have to report $226 million in interest charges over five years. This saves the company $77 million in federal income taxes.

In 1996, Schering will have to pay off the notes for $801 million. However, if the firm's stock price is greater than $90 at that time, the warrant holders will exercise them and buy 8.8 million new shares at $90 each. This will give Schering $792 million, enough to pay off almost all of the notes. In addition, Schering will have avoided paying nondeductible dividends of at least $66 million.

The LYNX is not the only security with an animal acronym. Merrill Lynch started the concept when it invented the TIGR in 1982. An acronym for ***T**reasury **I**ncome **G**rowth **R**eceipt*, Merrill creates this security by stripping a Treasury bond of its semiannual interest payments and selling each payment as a separate security. Thus, a 30-year Treasury bond could beget 60 little TIGRs.

Other beastly securities are:

1. CATS—**C**ertificates of **A**ccrual on **T**reasury **S**ecurities—are Salomon Brothers' version of TIGRs.
2. COGRs, pronounced "cougars"—**C**ertificates **O**f **G**overnment **R**eceipts—are A. G. Becker's version of TIGRs.
3. COLTS—**C**ontinuously **O**ffered **L**onger-**T**erm **S**ecurities—were invented by Merrill Lynch, Salomon Brothers, First Boston, and Morgan Stanley together, on behalf of the World Bank. The holder gets a medium-term yield on a short-term investment.
4. LIONs—**L**ehman **I**nvestment **O**pportunity **N**otes—are Lehman Brothers' version of TIGRs.
5. LYONs—**L**iquid **Y**ield **O**ption **N**otes—are another Merrill Lynch invention. These callable, zero-coupon securities allow the investor to convert both principal and interest into common stock. The investor can also redeem the security for cash every few years, in case the stock price hasn't risen enough to make conversion attractive.
6. OPPOSSMS—**OP**tions to **P**urchase **O**r **S**ell **S**pecified **M**ortgage-backed **S**ecurities—were also invented by Merrill Lynch. The name is a definition.
7. SPDRs, pronounced "spiders"—**S**tandard & **P**oor's **D**epository **R**eceipts—were invented by the American Stock Exchange. These are shares in a trust fund that owns stock in the 500 firms that make up the S&P 500 Index. They differ from shares in an index fund because they:
   (a) Are priced at one-tenth the value of the S&P Index, so their price changes continuously throughout the day
   (b) Can be bought on margin
   (c) Can be traded with stop orders to limit losses
   (d) Can be sold short when the index is expected to drop
   (e) Have no minimum purchase requirement
   (f) Incur the same brokerage commissions as common stock
   (g) Have a market maker, Spear Leeds & Kellogg, to ensure liquidity

Sources: Allan Sloan, "New Slick Critter Joins Wall St. Zoo," *Newsday*, October 13, 1991, p. 104; and Jerry Morgan, "'Spiders' Hit Amex," *Newsday*, January 29, 1993, pp. 45–46.

weakened the traditional ties between companies and the investment banks with whom they had always dealt. Fragmentary evidence indicates that, as usual, increased competition has reduced the cost of external financing.

The aggressiveness of today's investment bankers knows no bounds. If traditional securities do not appeal to investors or issuers, they invent new ones. This usually involves the creation of a new type of security which represents a legal claim to one or more cash flows from a traditional security. For instance, an investment bank may purchase a firm's new bonds and then create and sell some securities that represent the discounted principal and other securities that give buyers rights to one or more interest payments.

Initial Public Offerings (IPOs)

going public
Selling common stock to the public in an initial public offering.

When a company sells common stock to the public for the first time, it is said to be **going public**. Such an initial public offering (IPO) depends especially heavily on investment bankers because the issuer has no stock outstanding to indicate an appropriate market price. The underwriter has to estimate a correct offering price and how soon after registration to offer the issue. A typical IPO "bounces," that is, increases substantially on the first day of trading. A good example of this is the IPO of Esmor Correctional Services Inc., an operator and builder of halfway houses and private prisons. At the end of January 1994, the firm's investment bank priced its first stock offering of 833,333 shares at $6.25 each. The next day, the stock began trading at $7.50, climbing as high as $9 before closing at $8.25.

Some underwriters believe that a successful IPO generates a self-fulfilling prophecy. If an underwriter deliberately underprices an IPO, it will bounce and give the firm a reputation for handling successful IPOs. Each success will make investors more likely to expect the underwriter's next IPO to bounce; their anxiety to buy it will make that next bounce happen.

Timing is critical for an IPO, though. At the seasonal peak for IPOs—late March to early May—issuers may register 100 or so IPOs with the SEC; these issues will all come to market within six weeks. Professional analysts believe that stock market conditions must be just right to generate strong demand for IPOs. They look for several market characteristics:

midcap
A company whose shares of common stock have a total market value (capitalization) between $250 million and $1 billion.

small cap
A company whose shares of common stock have a total market value (capitalization) less than $250 million.

1. The major stock indices must be steadily appreciating.
2. Year-to-date returns for **midcaps** must be positive. A midcap is a company whose shares of common stock have a total market value (i.e., capitalization) between $250 million and $1 billion. The NASDAQ Composite Index consists mostly of midcaps.
3. **Small caps** (stocks with capitalizations below $250 million) must be outperforming the S&P 500. This means that the Russell 2000 Index (an index of 2,000 small caps and midcaps) must be increasing faster than the S&P 500 Index (an index of the 500 companies with the largest capitalizations).

If the IPO does not sell out immediately, its price may decline in subsequent trading. The underwriter can legally stabilize the price of the issue by buying shares back for up to 30 days or until the issue sells out, whichever comes first. The

FOCUS ON FINANCE

Buy an IPO Only at the Offering Price!

Investors may be lured to IPOs when they hear reports of the best performers, or repelled when they hear of the worst. For instance, Lone Star Steakhouse & Saloon stock was offered on March 12, 1992 at $13.50 a share; by December 31 it was at $37.63, almost triple its offering price. On the other hand, Cellcor Inc. was offered on March 13, 1992 at $11.00 a share; by December 31 it was at $2.50.

Prudential Securities, Inc. studied 1,500 IPOs that came to market in 1991, 1992, and 1993. The average IPO's price increase beat the NASDAQ Composite Index (NCI) by 10.9 percent on its first day of trading. However, IPOs are not suitable for a long-term investor because these issues peaked with a 15 percent return over the NCI after three months. The difference in return between the IPOs and the NCI decreased steadily for the next 21 months.

IPOs bought at the close of the first trading day peak with a 3.3 percent return over the NCI after three months, and return less than the NCI after one year.

Source: William Power, "Your Money Matters," *The Wall Street Journal*, March 17, 1994, pp. C1, C18.

underwriter must, however, announce its intention to support the price before the offering.

INVESTMENT BANKING MECHANICS

Investment banks earn compensation for all of the services they render: advice, legal and administrative services, risk bearing, and market making. Issuers pay fees for the first two that vary little among investment banks of equivalent financial status, but differ significantly between status classes. Compensation for risk bearing is unique to each situation.

Syndication

Under normal conditions, one investment banking firm does not act alone to sell a new security to the public. To spread the risk and facilitate distribution of the bonds or shares, the investment bank that negotiates with the issuing company invites other investment banks to participate in the purchase and sale of the security. This group of participating firms is called an underwriting **syndicate**. The originating bank, usually known as a *lead bank* or *managing house*, usually manages the issue, sells the largest portion of the securities, and receives the greatest percentage of the underwriting profit. The security's tombstone advertisement lists this firm first.

syndicate
A group of investment banks formed to participate in the purchase and sale of a new security to spread the risk and facilitate the distribution of the bonds or shares.

Each participant in the syndicate is allocated a percentage of the issue, based on the amount of securities it expects to sell to the public. Sometimes each participant is obliged to sell its share of securities without help; any that cannot sell

EXHIBIT 14.5

Top Underwriters in 1993

	Underwritings Booked ($ billions)	Share of Market	Fees Earned ($ billions)
Merrill Lynch & Co.	$174	16.4%	$1.8
Goldman, Sachs & Co.	127	12.0	1.1
Lehman Brothers	116	10.9	1.0

all their shares or bonds are stuck holding the remainder. Sometimes a member of a syndicate may farm out part of its portion of the issue to brokers and dealers, giving them commissions for the securities that they sell. Thus, a selling group may consist of more than just the syndicate members.

In still other arrangements, the syndicate pools any unsold securities and then divides the pool among all the participants for sale. Whatever the arrangements, at the end of the transaction, the syndicate ceases to exist.

An investment bank may participate in more than one syndicate at a time. It may even be a managing participant in more than one syndicate at a time. A managing underwriter invites a particular investment bank to join a syndicate based on the invitee's demonstrated ability to sell all of its allocated securities. Predictably, the largest investment banks underwrite the largest proportion of new issues. Exhibit 14.5 lists the top underwriters for 1993. In that year, total underwriting fees earned by the industry amounted to $9.11 billion, an increase of 34 percent over 1992, which was a record year.

Compensation

gross underwriting spread
The difference between the price underwriters pay for a security and the price at which they resell the security to the public.

Compensation for underwriting an issue consists of the **gross underwriting spread** on the security. This spread is the difference between the price the underwriters pay for the security and the price at which they resell the security to the public. It has several components:

1. The legal and administrative expenses discussed earlier in this chapter
2. The manager's fee
3. The selling concession which is the syndicate participant's payment for each bond it sells
4. The underwriting profit, the balance of the gross underwriting spread, which is distributed to members of the syndicate in the same proportions as their participation.

❖ EXAMPLE 14.1

The Bedrock Broadcasting Company needs to raise $150 million and has decided to sell bonds to the public. Able Banking Corp. (ABC), has formed a syndicate to underwrite the issue. ABC itself has a 25 percent participation in the syndicate, along with six other participants: DEF with 20 percent; GHI with 15 percent; and JKL, MNO, PQR, and STU with 10 percent each.

The syndicate buys the bonds, with $1,000 face values, from the company at $989.25. It sells them to the public for $999.75 each. The selling concession amounts to $6 per bond; the issue generates administrative expenses of $250,000. ABC requires a manager's fee of 15 percent of the gross spread.

1. What is the gross underwriting spread?
2. What is the flotation cost as a percentage of the bond issue?
3. How much does each investment bank receive?

1.

$$\begin{aligned}\text{Gross underwriting spread per bond} &= \$999.75 - \$989.25\\ &= \$10.50\\ \text{Number of bonds issued} &= \$150\text{ million}/\$1{,}000\\ &= 150{,}000\\ \text{Gross underwriting spread} &= 150{,}000 \times \$10.50\\ &= \$1.575\text{ million}\end{aligned}$$

2.

$$\begin{aligned}\text{Flotation cost} &= \$1.575\text{ million}/(150{,}000 \times \$989.25)\\ &= 0.0106\text{, or }1.06\text{ percent}\end{aligned}$$

3.

$$\begin{aligned}\text{Selling concession} &= 150{,}000 \times \$6\\ &= \$900{,}000\\ \text{Manager's fee} &= \$1.575\text{ million} \times 0.15\\ &= \$236{,}250\\ \text{Underwriting profit} &= \$1.575\text{ million} - \$900{,}000 - \$250{,}000 - \$236{,}250\\ &= \$188{,}750\end{aligned}$$

Assuming that each member of the syndicate sells all of its share of the 150,000 bonds, they earn the following compensation:

$$\begin{aligned}\text{ABC} &= \$236{,}250 + [(\$188{,}750 + \$900{,}000) \times 0.25]\\ &= \$508{,}437.50\\ \text{DEF} &= (\$188{,}750 + \$900{,}000) \times 0.20\\ &= \$217{,}750\\ \text{GHI} &= (\$188{,}750 + \$900{,}000) \times 0.15\\ &= \$163{,}312.50\\ \text{JKL} &= \text{MNO} = \text{PQR} = \text{STU}\\ &= (\$188{,}750 + \$900{,}000) \times 0.10\\ &= \$108{,}875\end{aligned}$$

❖

Making a Market

During the initial negotiations between a common stock issuer and the underwriter, the company may be concerned about the behavior of its stock price after the new issue is sold. The promotional efforts of the investment banker may produce a good price when the stock is initially sold to the public, but when the excitement dies down, the price of the company's outstanding shares may decline. To prevent this, the underwriter may agree to make a market in the stock for a limited amount of time, usually 30 days to 6 months.

While making a market, the investment bank holds some of the stock in its own portfolio. It quotes bid and ask prices at which it is willing to buy or sell shares of the stock. Unless the company, or the stock market itself, suffers dramatic price changes caused by unforseen events, the investment bank keeps the company's stock price stable. Knowledge that an IB will manage a new stock issue in the aftermarket enhances the issue's appeal to investors.

International Activities of U.S. Investment Banks

U.S. investment banks can enter the international financial markets from two different directions. They can help U.S. corporations sell new securities abroad, and they can help foreign corporations sell securities in the United States. In recent years, they have added a new line of business: assisting in the privatization of state-run enterprises.

Underwriting U.S. Securities Abroad. A U.S. corporation with a subsidiary in a foreign country may choose to issue bonds or stock in that country to finance the subsidiary's operations. The U.S. parent may locate an investment bank in that country to underwrite the new security, or it may turn to its familiar U.S. investment bank for help. If it chooses a U.S. IB, that underwriter usually forms a cross-border syndicate. The syndicate relies on the expertise of the foreign investment bank to comply with foreign registration and distribution practices and to facilitate the sale of the issue. If the U.S. investment bank foresees sufficient business in a specific foreign market, it may open its own branch office or subsidiary in that country to enhance its profits.

A U.S. corporation with a more global perspective may decide to issue Eurobonds to avoid the registration delays and disclosure requirements of the SEC. This market may offer an additional cost advantage because recent research indicates that dollar-denominated Eurobonds can sell to produce significantly lower yields than similar U.S. bonds, except those rated triple-A. A U.S. investment bank may form an international syndicate to assist in the global distribution of a Eurobond issue.

A U.S.-based multinational corporation may float a new issue of securities in a foreign market to:

1. Avoid registration delays and disclosure requirements
2. Take advantage of cheaper sources of financing, if that market offers lower interest or dividend rates

3. Improve its relationship with a foreign government
4. Enhance its ability to finance foreign takeovers with stock
5. Cover dividend payments with the foreign currency generated by subsidiaries

In May 1993, New York City sold $200 million in yen-denominated bonds to Japanese institutional investors such as life insurance companies and banks. These Samurai bonds, sold through Nikko Securities Company, were said to be the largest issue ever sold in Japan from an American state or local debtor. The bonds are saving the city about $380,000 in interest payments every year.

An issuer must balance the advantages of selling securities in a foreign market against several disadvantages, such as:

1. The costs of preparing multiple financial statements that comply with different local formats
2. Coping with various restrictions on foreign stocks imposed by local governments
3. Possible increases in the multinational's cost of capital
4. Reporting foreign exchange losses on the multinational's U.S. financial statements

Investment banks have reacted to this multimarket strategy by forming global syndicates to distribute securities across several or many countries efficiently.

Underwriting Foreign Securities. The U.S. dollar is the most popular currency in which to denominate Eurobonds. Foreign corporations that issue dollar-denominated Eurobonds depend on multinational syndicates of investment banks to distribute their bonds in many countries. U.S. investment banks may join these syndicates. They may also help foreign corporations to raise money in the United States by selling Yankee bonds.

Foreign corporations and multinationals trying to sell large common stock issues usually desire access to the U.S. primary market because of its size, efficiency, and liquidity. U.S. investment banks must participate in such an underwriting because they can provide essential expertise in the disclosure requirements for SEC registration and stock exchange listing.

privatization
Sale of a majority or minority stake in a state-run enterprise either to multinational companies through a bidding process, or to the public through a new stock issue.

Privatization. A new source of stock issues has engaged the efforts of investment banks in recent years. The **privatization** of state-run enterprises in developing countries, former communist countries, and some members of the European Community has led to global searches for equity capital.

The privatization process has taken different forms in different countries. Developing countries have sold majority or minority stakes in state-run enterprises, either to multinational companies through bidding processes, or to the public through new stock issues. Mexico has been the front-runner among the developing countries and has one of the most successful privatization programs. Between 1988 and 1991, the Mexican government sold 160 companies for about $13 billion. Argentina is another developing country that has privatized almost all of its state-run enterprises. The privatization trend is also gathering strength in Asian countries. Among the European countries, privatization of state-run enterprises has reached historic proportions in Great Britain, France, Italy, and Greece.

In the former communist countries, the process has been more complex, involving both foreign and local participation. These governments have supported local participation by providing vouchers and subsidized loans. Hungary has chosen to rely heavily on foreign private capital; in 1992 alone, almost 60 percent of its privatized capital came from foreign sources. Russia has set a target of privatizing 80 percent of its industrial capacity by July 1994. The Czech government planned to sell 770 companies in 1994 through a voucher system.

Investment banks participate in almost all privatization efforts. They function as consultants, program designers, and advisors. Further, whenever a privatization deal requires issuing stock to the public, they are involved in underwriting and related responsibilities.

INVESTMENT BANKS AS ADVISORS

The financial, legal, and sales experience that an investment banker acquires in the underwriting function can serve corporations in other situations, as well. An investment bank can serve as a consultant, an advisor, and even a safety net for a rights offering, private placement, or venture capital deal.

Rights Offerings

Instead of selling new shares of common stock, or securities that are convertible into common stock, to the general public through an investment bank, a company may offer a new issue directly to existing shareholders on a preemptive subscription basis. This offering can be voluntary, but the state in which the company is chartered may require it. A **preemptive right** gives existing common stockholders the right to preserve their proportionate ownership in the corporation whenever it issues new shares of common stock.

preemptive right
A legal requirement that existing common stockholders have the chance to preserve their proportionate ownership in the corporation when it issues new shares of common stock.

❖ EXAMPLE 14.2

The Tropical Ice Company has 1 million shares of common stock outstanding, and its shareholders have a preemptive right. Mr. and Mrs. Carey own 20,000 shares of TIC common stock. If the company decides to issue 100,000 new shares of stock, it must give the Careys the option to buy 2 percent, or 2,000 of them, to preserve their proportionate ownership of the company (20,000/1 million = 2 percent). ❖

When a company sells securities by privileged subscription, it gives its stockholders one right for each share of stock they own. The company specifies how many rights a stockholder needs to subscribe to an additional share of stock, the subscription price per share, and the expiration date of the right. It may hire an investment banker as a consultant when making these decisions, but it has no need for underwriting services. Issue costs for a rights offering may amount to 35 to 50 percent of the issuing costs of a normal public offering.

rights on

A share of stock and its preemptive right are inseparable and must trade together until the close of a rights offering's date of record.

***ex* rights**

A share of stock and its preemptive right can trade separately between a rights offering's date of record and expiration date.

The company's board of directors establishes a date of record for a rights offering. The stock trades **rights on** until the close of the date of record; the share of the stock and the right are inseparable during that time. After the date of record, the stock trades ***ex* rights** (the share of stock and the right can trade separately). This means that investors who buy the stock before the date of record receive the right to subscribe to the new issue. Investors who buy the stock after the date of record receive no right to subscribe to additional stock.

The theoretical value of a right before the date of record is:

$$R = (P - S)/(N + 1) \qquad \textbf{(14.1)}$$

where R = theoretical value of one right

P = market price of one share of stock selling rights on

S = subscription price per share

N = number of rights needed to buy one share of stock

❖ EXAMPLE 14.3

The Karcic Company's stock is trading for $85 per share. The company issues rights with a subscription price of $60 per share. If it takes nine rights to buy a share of stock, what is the theoretical value of one right?

$$R = (\$85.00 - \$60.00)/(9 + 1)$$

$$= \$2.50$$ ❖

When a stock goes *ex* rights, its market price theoretically declines by the value of one right. In effect, after the date of record, the right and the stock trade separately. In Example 14.3, when Karcic Company's stock goes *ex* rights, its market price should decline to $82.50 and its right should retain its theoretical value of $2.50.

Investors with rights have three alternatives:

1. They can exercise the rights and buy additional shares of common stock.
2. They can sell the rights after the date of record.
3. They can do nothing and let the rights expire.

❖ EXAMPLE 14.4

The Happy Valley Corporation has common stock outstanding that is trading at $50 per share. The company issues new stock at a subscription price of $45 a share; it takes three rights to buy an additional share. Donald, Mickey, and Goofy each own 100 shares of Happy Valley stock. After the date of record, Donald sells his rights, Mickey exercises his rights, and Goofy lets his rights expire. What happens to the value of each stockholder's portfolio?

$$\text{Value of a right} = (\$50.00 - \$45.00)/(3 + 1)$$

$$= \$1.25$$

$$\text{Stock price after date of record} = \$50.00 - \$1.25$$
$$= \$48.75$$
$$\text{Original value of all three portfolios} = \$50.00 \times 100$$
$$= \$5,000.00$$

After selling the rights, Donald holds $48.75 × 100, or $4,875 in stock and $1.25 × 100, or $125 in cash. Since this totals $5,000, the value of Donald's portfolio is unchanged.

Mickey exercises his rights and buys 100/3, or 33 additional shares of stock at a cost of $45.00 × 33, or $1,485.00. He has one right left, which he sells for $1.25. His total investment is $6,485. The value of his portfolio is $48.75 × 133, or $6,483.75 in stock and $1.25 in cash. This totals $6,485, exactly equal to Mickey's total investment.

After letting his rights expire, Goofy holds $48.75 × 100, or $4,875 in stock. He has lost $125. ❖

Theoretically, if the rights have any value, it does not matter whether stockholders sell their rights or exercise them; the only choice that produces a loss is letting the rights expire. In practice, however, each alternative produces a slightly different result. Selling the rights obligates the seller to pay a brokerage commission. Further, the cost basis of the original stock is reduced by the proceeds of the rights sale, resulting in a higher tax bill when the owner eventually sells the stock. Exercising the rights requires an additional investment of $1,485. The stockholder will also have to pay commissions and higher taxes eventually. Letting the rights expire produces a tax-deductible loss of $125 when the shares are sold.

The actual market prices of the stock and the rights may differ from their theoretical values. Day-to-day trading pressures will make the stock price fluctuate around $48.75 and the price of the right will vary a bit above and below $1.25. Further, a major change in the stock market could have a drastic effect on both the market and theoretical prices of the stock and the right.

Suppose, for example, that during the interval before the stock trades *ex* rights, the stock market rises and pulls the price of Happy Valley stock up to $60.00 a share. The value of Donald's portfolio rises to $6,375.00 ($6,000.00 in stock and $375.00 in cash). Mickey still has to spend $1,485 to buy 33 shares of stock, but the value of his portfolio rises to $7,983.75 ($7,980.00 in stock and $3.75 in cash). Goofy holds $6,000.00 in stock.

Alternatively, suppose that during the same time interval, the stock market falls, depressing the price of Happy Valley stock to $40.00. Donald holds $4,000.00 in stock and no cash because his rights have lost their market value. Mickey would be foolish to spend $1,485.00 to exercise his rights; he could buy 33 shares of stock on the market for $1,320.00. Goofy would be holding $4,000.00 in stock, the same as Donald.

The level of the subscription price an issuer chooses has important implications. A higher subscription price increases the probability that the market price will fall below it, preventing stockholders from exercising their rights. A lower subscription price increases the probability that stockholders will exercise their rights and the firm will complete a successful stock sale. To manage these opposing forces, a company can protect itself by obtaining a **standby commitment** from an investment bank or syndicate to underwrite the unsold shares of stock. To make such a commitment, the IB usually asks for a flat fee plus a charge for each unsold share of stock that it buys. As the IB sees a greater need for a standby commitment, its fee rises.

standby commitment
An agreement with an investment bank or syndicate to underwrite any unsold shares of stock when a rights offering expires.

Another consideration compels the issuer to set the subscription price carefully. A lower subscription price forces the firm to issue more new shares to produce the amount of funds that it requires. This dilutes earnings per share and may damage the stock price. It also increases the company's quarterly cash outflow if it intends to maintain the dividend per share at its most recent level. Most rights offerings set subscription prices between 10 and 20 percent less than the stocks' market prices. For this reason, most issuers find a preemptive rights offering more expensive than an underwritten new stock issue.

Another major disadvantage of a preemptive rights offering is its failure to broaden the stockholder base. A broader base is essential for a small company that aspires to be listed on one of the national exchanges. A broader stockholder base is also helpful if a company's managers want to reduce the volatility of the stock price, or if they want to fight a takeover by another company.

Private Placements

Corporations raise a substantial amount of external capital without undertaking public offerings. A company can sell a multimillion dollar bond or preferred stock issue to a single financial institution or to a small group of large investors (individuals and/or institutions). An investment banker can serve as a source of contacts, as an advisor on the terms of placement, and as a negotiator if the issuing corporation so desires.

Corporations tap many large, private sources of capital. One such source is the Teachers Insurance and Annuity Association, whose advertisement appears in Exhibit 14.6.

A company with publicly held common stock cannot sell additional common stock of the same class privately. However, a privately owned company can sell new stock to investors who understand that no market exists, and none may ever exist, in which they can liquidate their investment.

Advantages. A private placement of new securities can give an issuer many advantages:

1. Since it need not register the security with the SEC, or prepare and print a prospectus, it can issue a privately placed security quickly.
2. Private placement avoids the public disclosure of information necessary to register a public offering. The investor or small group of investors who will buy a private placement may demand to know more about the company than the SEC would, but information shared with them does not become a matter of public record.

EXHIBIT 14.6

Private Source of Capital

TIAA

Private placements for flexible financing

With a $68 billion portfolio, Teachers Insurance has the resources and experience needed for successful private placement lending. We finance loans of all sizes to public and private companies in nearly every business sector. Flexible terms and structures meet the special needs of borrowers.

Our parameters are broad:

- *Senior, subordinated, convertible, secondaries, asset-backed, leveraged leases, and LBOs*
- *Loan amounts from $10 million to $100 million*
- *Maturities of 7 to 20 years*

We work through brokers or directly. Let's talk about your needs.

This announcement appears as a matter of record only.

Deer Park Refining Limited Partnership

$42,000,000

Senior Notes
Due 2008

TIAA

This announcement appears as a matter of record only

Double Diamond Funding Limited Partnership

$23,358,260

Fixed-Rate Mortgage-Backed Notes
Due 2006

TIAA

This announcement appears as a matter of record only.

Hutchinson Technology Incorporated

$20,000,000

Senior Notes
Due 2004

TIAA

This announcement appears as a matter of record only

Universal Forest Products, Inc.

$20,000,000

Senior Notes
Due 2004

TIAA

Northeast	South/Southeast	Midwest	West	Structured Finance
Larry Archibald	Steve Brausa	Kip Thompson	Rod Eaton	Mike O'Kane
(212) 916-4308	(212) 916-4322	(212) 916-4335	(212) 916-4347	(212) 916-4345

Teachers Insurance and Annuity Association
730 Third Avenue, New York, NY 10017-3206
Securities Division

Source: *The Wall Street Journal*, May 25, 1994, p. C18.

3. Negotiating the terms of the issue directly with the investor allows the issuer to design them to meet its needs. For example, a bond placed with one or two insurance companies might give the issuer the option to delay or omit interest payments for a limited time in exchange for a higher coupon rate. A bond offered to the general public would require payment of interest every six months to avoid bankruptcy court.
4. If the company's needs change over time, it can renegotiate the terms of a privately placed security much more easily than the terms of a publicly held security. Publicly held bonds frequently require approval of any change in terms by 66⅔ percent of bondholders as well as holders of 66⅔ percent of the firm's outstanding bonds. A simple illustration will clarify this point: consider a \$300 million bond issue held by 90 investors. Any change in terms would have to be approved by at least 60 investors, who owned at least \$200 million of the bonds.
5. A privately placed financing arrangement is more flexible than a public offering of stock or bonds. Suppose, for example, that a company needs new funds to finance a \$60 million construction project. Contractors are customarily paid on a percentage-of-completion basis; the construction firm would receive one-third of the cost (\$20 million) up front, another \$20 million when it had completed one-third of the construction, and the final \$20 million when it finished two-thirds of the construction. A private placement would allow the company to borrow the money as needed, \$20 million at a time. A public sale of bonds or stock would give the company the entire \$60 million at once. Because it needs only \$20 million immediately, it would have to invest the remaining \$40 million temporarily. The normal (upward-sloping) yield curve almost guarantees that the company's short-term investments would yield less than the cost of its long-term bond. It could avoid this net loss on the \$40 million by borrowing as needed through flexible, privately placed debt.
6. Private placement allows small companies to sell securities that would be prohibitively expensive in a public offering. Many institutional investors are willing to buy a bond issue as small as \$1 million, but the flotation costs of a publicly issued \$1 million bond could easily total one year's interest on the debt.
7. A private placement avoids most of the initial underwriting or selling expenses of offering an issue to the public. A company may hire an investment banker as a consultant to help plan and negotiate a private placement, but this cost is usually a small fraction of underwriting costs.

Disadvantages. Private placements also have a few disadvantages:

1. A single investor or a small group of financial institutions may monitor the issuing company's performance much more closely than the trustee for investors in a public offering. The company may be forced to comply much more strictly with whatever restrictive covenants it has accepted.
2. The interest/dividend cost of a private placement is usually higher than the

FOCUS ON CAREERS

VENTURE CAPITALIST

A venture capitalist provides money in exchange for securities representing or potentially representing partial ownership in unseasoned companies. These securities may be shares of common stock, convertible bonds, convertible preferred stock, or bonds with detachable warrants. Venture capitalists may invest before a company has produced its first profit; some are even willing to invest before a company begins to operate. They are attracted to the prospect of rapid growth and the expectation of healthy profits within three to five years.

While friends, family, and even potential customers may provide funds to start up a new enterprise, the true venture capitalist is a wealthy individual who may have first-hand knowledge of the product or the entrepreneur that justifies tolerating high risk in hopes of a high return. While many organized venture capital corporations and partnerships have established capital bases and professional management, they generally are unwilling to fund start-up enterprises.

The typical venture capitalist, often referred to as an *angel*, has an income in excess of $100,000 and a net worth of more than $1 million. The venture capitalist may well be a doctor, dentist, lawyer, accountant, or sports figure. What they all have in common is faith in either a product or an individual entrepreneur. While few make their livings from their venture capital activities, they all expect to be compensated grandly for taking risk.

interest/dividend cost of a public offering. This balances against the speed and flexibility that make private placements so desirable.

3. The interest cost of privately placed debt may vary over time. Publicly issued bonds almost always pay fixed coupon rates; the interest rates on privately placed bonds frequently adjust to market conditions. Debt placed while interest rates are low will become progressively more expensive over time.
4. Institutional investors sometimes require initial enticements, such as warrants to purchase common stock, to invest in a private placement. The warrants, if exercised, will provide additional funds to the company at a later date, but they add to the cost of the privately placed issue.

Venture Capital

A new business may obtain venture capital financing by selling stock to institutions and wealthy individuals willing to accept large risks in exchange for potentially great returns. An entrepreneur with an innovative idea must prepare a business plan describing the venture, its management team, the necessary financing, and any conditions that could impede its growth. If possible, the plan should name key personnel with knowledge and experience in the areas of marketing, finance, operations, and research and development. It should include *pro forma* financial statements, along with the information that would normally appear on an SEC registration statement.

The owners of a firm with a short history and a need for operating capital may also seek venture capital, even before becoming profitable. The firm must provide

FOCUS ON FINANCE

Fouled Out!

♦ ♦ ♦

Wilt Chamberlain's Restaurant Inc. operates a sports bar and restaurant in Boca Raton, Florida. The former basketball star is the company's chairman and largest stockholder. The company planned to sell 1.4 million shares of common stock and use the proceeds to open several more bar–restaurant establishments.

Following custom, the underwriter, Meyers Pollock Robbins Inc., priced the company's initial public offering after the market closed on February 11, 1993 and offered it for sale at $7 a share the next day. Instead of bouncing, the stock closed at $4.63 on February 12. Angry investors called the underwriter and threatened to take legal action if their purchases weren't rescinded. Chamberlain and the underwriters agreed to withdraw the IPO.

Financial analysts blamed the investment bankers for the debacle. They said the company was "virtually a start-up" and should have sought venture capital instead of trying to sell stock to the public. It was Meyers Pollock Robbins' first stock underwriting.

Source: Newsday; February 17, 1993, p. 35.

recent, audited financial statements, *pro forma* financial statements, cash and capital budgets, and operating plans.

Few venture capitalists want to actively manage companies; they want to buy a significant percentage of the firm's common stock, and possibly provide financial, marketing, accounting, or technical advice. Some venture capitalists invest only in new, start-up companies, others prefer going concerns. Some demand majority ownership in the venture; others are satisfied with smaller percentages. Most ask for options that allow them to buy more shares at the original price if the venture succeeds.

Investment bankers can direct entrepreneurs to venture capitalists who are likely to be interested in their proposals. IBs can also help going concerns prepare business plans or financial documentation. The larger investment banks may even provide some of the venture capital themselves. In addition to compensation for services rendered, these firms attempt to secure future business (IPOs and underwritings) for themselves.

SUMMARY

The primary market is the mechanism through which companies sell new securities. The principal financial institution in this market is the investment bank. Its major function is underwriting, which means buying new securities from the issuer and reselling them to the public.

Investment banks may help to plan new securities from their inception. They provide valuable expertise in designing, pricing, registering, promoting, and selling a new security. Registering almost any new security requires the legal talents of an investment bank.

Large corporations may complete shelf registrations, registering a large block of securities all at once and then selling portions of it as needed. Investment banks may bid competitively to handle these subsequent sales.

If investment bankers doubt that a new security will sell well, they may refuse to underwrite it. They hesitate to buy new issues if they expect difficulty selling them to the public. In such a case, an investment bank may act as the company's agent during a best efforts sale.

The investment banking industry has become increasingly competitive, with banks seeking out corporations that they think might need external funds in the near future. They are especially enthusiastic about bringing initial public offerings (IPOs) to market.

Investment banks usually form syndicates to underwrite new security issues. Individual IBs do not participate equally in the distribution of securities and profits; they participate in proportion to their estimated ability to sell the new securities.

In addition to their advisory function, legal expertise, and marketing skills, investment banks may serve issuers by stabilizing security prices in the aftermarket. They also help U.S. corporations to sell new securities abroad, and they underwrite foreign securities in the United States. The most recent addition to this range of functions has been assisting in the privatization of state-run enterprises.

Investment bankers can advise corporations that make rights offerings. Instead of selling common stock to the general public with the help of an investment bank, some companies offer it to existing shareholders at prices discounted from the current market prices of their outstanding shares. This practice gives existing shareholders the opportunity to maintain their proportionate ownership in the corporation.

Instead of raising external capital from the public, corporations may attempt to place a new security privately by negotiating its sale directly to one or more institutional or wealthy investors. The issuer must weigh the advantages of speed, privacy, flexibility, and low flotation costs against the disadvantages of higher interest and dividend yields and closer monitoring. Again, the investment bank can serve in an advisory capacity.

Entrepreneurs that need start-up capital and new companies that need funds for expansion may seek investment by venture capitalists. Investment bankers can help by providing contacts, assisting in documentation, or even investing some of their own funds.

Key Terms

best efforts sale
blue sky laws
ex rights
going public
gross underwriting spread
initial public offering
investment bank
making a market
midcap
preemptive right
privatization
prospectus
public offering
red herring

rights on	standby commitment
shelf registration	syndicate
small cap	underwriting

Self-Study Questions

1. What is the primary function of an investment bank?
2. List the five decision areas that govern the design of a new security issue.
3. What information appears in the registration statement filed with the SEC for a new security?
4. What is the difference between a prospectus and a red herring?
5. What is a shelf registration?
6. What is an underwriting syndicate?
7. How does privatization involve investment banks?
8. An investor has stock that will go *ex* rights tomorrow. What alternatives does the investor have today? If the investor does nothing today, what alternatives will remain tomorrow?
9. List four advantages and four disadvantages of a private placement.
10. What is the difference between an IPO and a venture capital opportunity?

Self-Test Problems

1. Tigerbrands, Inc. is selling $50 million in new bonds. Clavin and Hubbes, Inc., the managing underwriter, has a 40 percent participation in the syndicate it has formed. The syndicate will buy the bonds from the company at $986 per $1,000 bond and sell them to the public for $996 each. The selling concession will be $5 per bond; the issue will generate administrative expenses of $100,000. Clavin and Hubbes requires a manager's fee of 12 percent of the gross spread. How much will Clavin and Hubbes receive if this issue is a sellout?
2. Brucker Bros., Inc. needs to raise $200 million and has decided to sell bonds to the public. Weisman, Cioffari, and Romeo, Inc. (WCR), has formed a syndicate to underwrite the issue. WCR has a 45 percent participation in the syndicate, leaving the balance for two other participants: Miller Inc. with 30 percent, and The Polysius Bank with 25 percent. The syndicate will buy the bonds, with $1,000 face values, from the company at $991.50 each; it will sell them to the public for $999.50 each. The selling concession will be $4 per bond; the issue will generate administrative expenses of $300,000. WCR requires a manager's fee of 15 percent of the gross spread.
   (a) What is the flotation cost as a percentage of the bond issue?
   (b) How much does each investment bank receive?
3. Stock in Dowd's Dairy Products, Inc. is trading for $60 per share. The company issues rights with a subscription price of $50 per share. If a buyer needs

four rights to buy one share of stock, what is the theoretical value of one right?

4. A corporation has common stock outstanding that is trading at $23 per share. The subscription price of a rights offering is $20 a share, and it takes two rights to buy an additional share. An investor owns 100 shares of this stock. What will happen to the value of these shares if, after the date of record, the investor:
   (a) Sells the rights?
   (b) Exercises the rights?
   (c) Lets the rights expire?

Discussion Questions

1. Why do almost all corporations hire investment banks to help issue securities instead of selling the securities to the public themselves?
2. If the SEC approves the registration statement for a new security, does this mean that the security is a good investment for everybody?
3. When would the SEC go to court to get an injunction to halt trading in a new security?
4. Why do large corporations use shelf registrations?
5. Why do underwriters face frequent accusations of underpricing IPOs?
6. Why would investors prefer that an investment banker make a market in a stock it underwrites?
7. If the SEC is performing efficiently, why do all 50 states have blue sky laws and their own Securities Commissions?
8. Why might an investment bank insist on a best efforts sale instead of an underwriting?
9. What happens if the subscriptions to a security sold on a best efforts basis fail to reach the cutoff percentage?
10. Why do investment banks form syndicates?
11. What is a cross-border syndicate and why would one be formed?
12. Why might U.S. multinationals float new issues of securities in foreign markets? What disadvantages do these issues face?
13. Why might U.S. investment banks help to underwrite foreign stocks in the United States?
14. Why do investment banks fear setting subscription prices too high or too low?
15. The actual market price of a stock and its rights may differ from their theoretical values. Why?
16. How might the terms of a privately placed bond be more flexible than those of a public offering?
17. Why might a small company see more advantage in issuing a privately placed bond than a public offering?
18. Some privately placed bonds have adjustable interest rates. Explain how this might be either an advantage or a disadvantage.

19. What is a standby commitment and why might it be necessary?
20. What types of businesses utilize the venture capital market?

Problems

1. Ibert, Inc. is issuing $400 million in new bonds. Lillian, Agnes, and Veronica, Inc. (LAV), the managing underwriter, has a one-third participation in the syndicate it has formed. The syndicate will buy the bonds from the company at $992 per $1,000 bond, and sell them to the public for $999 each. The selling concession will be $3.50 per bond; the issue will generate administrative expenses of $250,000. LAV requires a manager's fee of 14 percent of the gross spread. How much will LAV receive if it sells out this issue?
2. Consolidated Transnational is selling $800 million in bonds. Berg, Bourg, and Burke, Inc. (BBB), has formed a syndicate to underwrite the issue, in which it has a 60 percent participation. Two other participants divide the remainder: CCC and DDD have 20 percent each. The syndicate will buy the bonds (with $1,000 face value) from the company at $988 each and sell them to the public for $997 each. The selling concession will be $6 per bond; the issue will generate administrative expenses of $350,000. BBB requires a manager's fee of 15 percent of the gross spread.
   (a) What is the flotation cost as a percentage of the bond issue?
   (b) How much does each investment bank receive?
3. M. Butler Co. stock is trading for $39 per share. The company issues rights with a subscription price of $24 per share. If it takes five rights to buy one share of stock, what is the theoretical value of one right?
4. Ritter Corporation's common stock is trading at $85 per share. The subscription price is $60 a share, and it takes four rights to buy an additional share. An investor owns 100 shares of this stock. What will happen to the value of these shares if, after the date of record, the investor:
   (a) Sells the rights?
   (b) Exercises the rights?
   (c) Lets the rights expire?

Topics for Further Research

1. Find a listing for an IPO in *The Wall Street Journal*. Follow the price of the security in the NASDAQ listings for two weeks. Did the stock bounce? What happened after that?
2. Choose a tombstone for a large issue by a well-known corporation. Backtrack in *The Wall Street Journal* to identify when the issue appeared in the calendar. When was it offered or priced? When did the SEC filing take place?
3. Choose a full-service securities dealer from the *Value Line Investment Service*. Examine the information available in Moody's *Banking and Finance Manual* about the dealer. How significant is the dealer's investment banking operation?

Answers to Self-Test Problems

1. Gross underwriting spread

$$\begin{aligned}
\text{per bond} &= \$996 - \$986 \\
&= \$10 \\[1ex]
\text{Number of bonds issued} &= \$50 \text{ million}/\$1{,}000 \\
&= 50{,}000 \\[1ex]
\text{Gross underwriting spread} &= 50{,}000 \times \$10 \\
&= \$500{,}000 \\[1ex]
\text{Selling concession} &= 50{,}000 \times \$5 \\
&= \$250{,}000 \\[1ex]
\text{Manager's fee} &= \$500{,}000 \times 0.12 \\
&= \$60{,}000 \\[1ex]
\text{Underwriting profit} &= \$500{,}000 - \$250{,}000 - \$60{,}000 - \$100{,}000 \\
&= \$90{,}000 \\[1ex]
\text{Clavin \& Hubbes} &= \$60{,}000 + [(\$90{,}000 + \$250{,}000) \times 0.4] \\
&= \$196{,}000
\end{aligned}$$

2. Gross underwriting spread

$$\begin{aligned}
\text{per bond} &= \$999.50 - \$991.50 \\
&= \$8 \\[1ex]
\text{Number of bonds issued} &= \$200 \text{ million}/\$1{,}000 \\
&= 200{,}000 \\[1ex]
\text{Gross underwriting spread} &= 200{,}000 \times \$8 \\
&= \$1.6 \text{ million} \\[1ex]
\text{Flotation cost} &= \$1.6 \text{ million}/(200{,}000 \times \$991.50) \\
&= 0.81\% \\[1ex]
\text{Selling concession} &= 200{,}000 \times \$4 \\
&= \$800{,}000 \\[1ex]
\text{Manager's fee} &= \$1.6 \text{ million} \times 0.15 \\
&= \$240{,}000 \\[1ex]
\text{Underwriting profit} &= \$1.6 \text{ million} - \$800{,}000 - \$240{,}000 - \$300{,}000 \\
&= \$260{,}000 \\[1ex]
\text{WCR} &= \$240{,}000 + [(\$260{,}000 + \$800{,}000) \times 0.45] \\
&= \$717{,}000 \\[1ex]
\text{Miller Inc.} &= (\$260{,}000 + \$800{,}000) \times 0.30 \\
&= \$318{,}000 \\[1ex]
\text{Polysius Bank} &= (\$260{,}000 + \$800{,}000) \times 0.25 \\
&= \$265{,}000
\end{aligned}$$

3.
$$R = (\$60 - \$50)/(4 + 1)$$
$$= \$2$$

4. Before the stock goes *ex* rights, the portfolio is worth 100 × \$23, or \$2,300.

$$R = (\$23 - \$20)/(2 + 1)$$
$$= \$1$$

After selling the rights, the portfolio is worth 100 × \$22 + \$100, or \$2,300

Exercising the rights allows the investor to buy 100/2, or 50 additional shares at \$20, for an additional investment of \$1,000. After exercising the rights, the portfolio will be worth 150 × \$22, or \$3,300. After the rights expire, the portfolio will be worth 100 × \$22, or \$2,200

CHAPTER

15

Secondary Markets for Securities

LEARNING OBJECTIVES

This chapter concentrates on the secondary securities markets, emphasizing the stock markets, their participants, and measures of their activity. At the conclusion of this chapter, the reader should be able to:

1. *Explain the role of a secondary market*
2. *Identify the similarities of secondary markets around the globe*
3. *Describe a stock exchange, its listed securities, its method of functioning, and its membership*
4. *Distinguish an OTC market from a stock exchange*
5. *Describe the operations of stock, bond, options, and futures markets*
6. *Outline characteristics of the fundamental and technical analysis methods*
7. *Describe the range of decisions that face institutional and individual investors*

After an issuer sells a security in the primary market through an underwriter, it trades among investors in the secondary market. A high-quality secondary market attracts investors who help it to function efficiently.

Secondary markets are either organized trading places (securities exchanges) or electronic networks (over-the-counter markets). The principal financial institutions are brokerage houses, which function as exchange members, dealers, and agents for investors trading securities.

Various secondary markets trade stocks, bonds, options, and futures contracts all over the globe. Each market follows the same general principles and relies on the active participation of investors for its growth and sustenance. Advancements in communications and data processing technology have given rise to sophisticated markets, even in less developed nations.

Techniques to analyze security price and volume data have been around a long time. The combination of on-line databases and powerful personal computers has only recently allowed investors to exploit these techniques fully to choose appropriate securities and time their trades judiciously.

SECONDARY MARKETS

outstanding securities

A security that was originally sold to the public in the primary market.

A secondary market is a mechanism to help investors trade **outstanding securities** among themselves. The proceeds of security sales in secondary markets do not go to the securities' issuers; they go to the investors who liquidate their investments.

Without a secondary market, the corresponding primary market would be a mere fraction of its current size. It would be difficult to issue new securities for several reasons:

1. The securities would be illiquid. Once a company sold them to investors, the security holders could not terminate their investments except by requesting the issuer to return the funds they originally provided. If the issuer lacked available cash to buy back its securities, the investors would have to hold their securities permanently.
2. There would be no way to determine the current market value of a security. The one value of a security to the only owner it could ever have would be its historical cost.
3. Regardless of the returns investors initially expected, they would be at the mercy of the issuer once they owned the securities. If a security represented a legal claim against the company (for example, interest payments), an investor could force payment of that return only by threatening the company with bankruptcy proceedings. If the security represented no legal claim (for example, dividends), investors could do nothing to force payment.

This scenario suggests several characteristics of a high-quality secondary market. First, the market should present current, readily accessible, and credible information to all investors about:

1. The issuer of a security—the company, its history, its business, and its managers
2. The terms of a security—all of the legal features that determine the amount, timing, and uncertainty of the cash flows that investors expect
3. A security's trading activity—its price and volume
4. The number and type of investors attracted to each security

Second, the market should be efficient. In an efficient market, security prices reflect currently available information. Also, prices adjust quickly as new information becomes available.

Third, a high-quality market should have price continuity. Security prices should not fluctuate substantially from trade to trade unless:

1. Significant new information becomes available
2. Something causes a change in the factors that affect the supply of or demand for investment funds

EXHIBIT 15.1

National and Regional Stock Exchanges

	United States	Canada	Germany	Japan
National exchanges	New York American	Toronto	Frankfurt	Tokyo
Regional exchanges	Boston Cincinnati Philadelphia Chicago Salt Lake City Spokane Pacific (San Francisco and Los Angeles)	Vancouver Montreal	Munich Dusseldorf Hamburg Berlin Stuttgart Hanover Bremen	Hiroshima Kyoto Osaka Niigata Fukuoto Uagoya Sapporo

Fourth, a high-quality market is deep. It should bring together an adequate number of potential buyers and sellers who are willing to act when a security's price falls below or rises above its current market price. A lack of price continuity often plagues a thin market.

Fifth, transaction costs should be low. Investors are attracted to markets with low transaction costs for a given dollar amount of trading. Low transaction costs encourage greater trader participation and increase market depth.

Many secondary markets trade securities on this planet, and their quality varies enormously. Secondary securities markets can be classified by the types of securities they trade (bonds, stocks, options, and futures contracts), by trading systems, and by geography.

STOCK MARKET

The stock markets in the United States, Canada, Germany, and Japan consist of a system of national stock exchanges, regional stock exchanges, and over-the-counter trading networks. Exhibit 15.1 lists the national and regional exchanges of these nations.

A developed country typically has at least a national stock exchange and an over-the-counter market. Less developed countries' stock markets vary greatly in quality. Some, like Singapore, consider the establishment of an internationally respected stock exchange to be a national priority. Others, like Russia and China, are content to provide some physical place labeled "stock exchange" in case enough economic growth occurs to support an active stock market.

Stock Exchanges

A stock exchange is a legal organization formed to facilitate the trading of a specific list of stocks (hence the term *listed stocks*) by its members. A national stock exchange lists many large, high-quality companies; a regional stock exchange lists smaller, local companies. Some countries allow dual listing on both national and regional exchanges; others do not.

auction system
A method of trading shares of stock in which the highest bidder buys from the seller with the lowest asking price.

Stock Exchange Listings. The United States has two national stock exchanges, the New York Stock Exchange (also called the *NYSE* or the *Big Board)* and the American Stock Exchange (called the AMEX), located six blocks from each other in New York City. Trades in all listed stocks on both exchanges take place in cavernous areas called *trading floors*, where traders and brokers who represent buyers and sellers meet. Trading employs an **auction system**: the highest bidder buys shares of stock from the seller with the lowest asking price. The exchange reports every floor trade and its price to the world electronically. The financial press reports the total number of shares traded and the highest, lowest, and last trading prices for every listed stock daily.

About 2,400 domestic and foreign companies have shares listed on the NYSE. A company must meet the following requirements, among others, to be listed there:

1. It must have generated income before taxes of at least $2.5 million in the most recent year or $2 million in each of the two preceding years.
2. It must have net tangible assets of at least $18 million.
3. The market value of its public shares must be at least $18 million.
4. It must have at least 1.1 million publicly held shares of common stock.
5. At least 2,000 stockholders must own at least 100 shares of its stock each.

About 1,000 domestic and foreign companies have stock listed on the AMEX. Its listing requirements are less rigorous:

1. The firm must have generated income before taxes of at least $750,000 in the most recent year, or at least $750,000 in two of the preceding three years.
2. It must have stockholders' equity of at least $4 million.
3. It must have at least 500,000 publicly held shares of common stock.
4. At least 800 stockholders must own at least 100 shares each.
5. The current stock price must be at least $3 per share.
6. The total market value of its public float (shares) must be at least $3 million.

Between 1950 and 1970, for every $1 in stock value traded on the AMEX, approximately $3 in stock value was traded on the NYSE. During those 20 years, the average daily dollar volume of trading on both exchanges grew at about the same rate, increasing six-fold. However, the daily dollar trading volume on the NYSE grew much faster than on the AMEX during the next 20 years. By 1990, shares worth an average of $157 million changed hands daily on the Big Board while only $13 million traded daily on the AMEX.

In Japan, the Tokyo Stock Exchange (TSE) lists both domestic and foreign stocks for about 1,600 companies. Traders buy and sell the 150 most actively traded Japanese stocks on the exchange's trading floor; members trade all others over computer terminals in their offices. All trades use the auction process.

In the United Kingdom, the London Stock Exchange (LSE) lists about 2,000 domestic companies and 600 foreign companies. All trades in the 65 most actively traded stocks (the Alpha List) are reported to the public. The next 500 most active stocks comprise the Beta List. Alpha and Beta stocks trade in an auction system. The remaining stocks, more than 2,000 issues, comprise the Gamma List. They are traded through market-makers in **negotiated transactions.** Traders buy these securities from or sell them to dealers, who set their bid and asking prices individually. The LSE has no trading floor; all transactions occur on a computer network. Moreover, instead of regional exchanges, the LSE maintains operating units across England (in Birmingham, Manchester, Bristol, and Liverpool), in Northern Ireland (Belfast), and in Scotland (Glasgow).

negotiated transaction
Traders buy securities from or sell them to market makers, who set their bid and asking prices individually.

Stock Exchange Membership. Stock exchanges may restrict membership to citizens, residents of the country, or corporations, or they may open it to anyone who can meet their membership requirements. Exchanges usually require potential members to produce evidence that demonstrates their competence, integrity, and access to adequate capital.

In the United States, stock exchange members fall into several classes:

1. **Commission brokers**, who buy or sell securities for their customers
2. **Floor brokers**, who execute orders for commission brokers who experience excessive volume
3. **Registered traders**, who buy and sell securities for their own accounts
4. **Specialists**, who conduct auctions and serve as both brokers and dealers. A specialist handles a dozen stocks, more or less, matching buy and sell orders from brokers and traders. They are also expected to buy and sell their assigned stocks using their own money to promote price continuity and maintain orderly markets.

commission broker
A stock exchange member who acts as an agent to buy or sell securities for customers.

floor broker
A stock exchange member who executes trades for commission brokers who have too much work to handle.

registered trader
A stock exchange member who buys and sells securities for his or her own account.

specialists
A stock exchange member who conducts auctions and serves as both a broker and a dealer to maintain an orderly market in an assigned group of stocks.

A stock exchange requires members to "buy seats" on the exchange. This seat, or membership, can be sold when the membership is no longer wanted at a price that varies with the profit expected from being an exchange member. This profit is directly related to stock market activity. Since 1960, a seat on the NYSE has varied in price from $55,000 in 1975 to $1.15 million in 1987 (before the October crash). In 1994 seats were selling for $750,000. During the same period, seats on the AMEX ranged from $34,000 to $420,000, with a 1994 sale price around $163,000. Currently, a seat on the Tokyo Stock Exchange costs about US$7 million.

The NYSE has 1,366 seats available; 400 are for specialists on the trading floor. The AMEX has 900 seats available; 23 are for specialists.

The Tokyo Stock Exchange operates slightly differently. It has 124 regular members and four specialists, called *Saitori.* Firms that buy memberships are allowed to place several employees per membership on the trading floor. Regular members have an average of 20 employees each on the floor; *Saitori* members have

FOCUS ON CAREERS

SECURITIES TRADER

A number of different individuals carry out trading on the floor of the NYSE: the commission broker, the floor broker, the registered trader, and the specialist. Before being allowed to purchase a seat, an individual must demonstrate an understanding of the stock market, secure sponsorship by a member of the exchange, and prove access to adequate capital. Brokerage houses can provide the necessary training, and are willing to sponsor individuals in whom they see integrity and trading talent.

Generally some college experience is required, but more important is a personality capable of handling the mayhem of exchange trading. While starting salaries for commission brokers are generally in the low $20s plus commissions, an experienced trader usually earns four to five times that amount.

an average of 90 employees per membership. *Saitori* members do not act as dealers to maintain orderly markets.

London Stock Exchange members are either brokers or jobbers; the LSE has no specialists. The brokers are allowed to make markets in stocks and bonds. Jobbers buy and sell securities for their customers. Security trading firms buy memberships on the LSE, but the firms' individual employees are the actual members of the exchange. During the first year, a firm pays a membership fee based on the number of members it has. Thereafter, the annual membership fee is 1 percent of the firm's gross revenue.

Worldwide, 24-Hour Trading. Together, the New York, Tokyo, Hong Kong, Singapore, and London stock markets comprise the major focal points of a trading network that allows internationally minded investors to trade stocks 24 hours a day. Additionally, they can trade 10,000 U.S. and European stocks whenever the NYSE is closed through Instinet, a private, electronic trading system owned by Reuters.

third market
The mechanism through which an investor buys a listed security from a seller without going through the exchange on which it is listed.

fourth market
The mechanism through which a financial institution buys a block of securities from another financial institution without using the services of a broker.

The OTC Market

Stocks that are not listed on a stock exchange are said to trade in the *over-the-counter (OTC) market*. This expression dates back to the previous century, when traders bought securities in brokerage offices much as they bought sugar in a grocery store.

Theoretically, investors can trade any security—listed or not—over the counter. The only necessities are a buyer, a seller, and knowledge of how to do the legal paperwork. When an investor buys a listed security from a seller without going through the exchange, the trade is said to occur in the **third market**. When a financial institution buys a block of securities from another financial institution without using the services of a broker, the trade is said to occur in the **fourth market**.

In the United States, about 8,000 stocks trade on the OTC market. The National Association of Securities Dealers (NASD) has facilitated trading over the counter by creating an electronic network that allows all OTC companies to participate at some level. The top tier of the electronic network is the National Market System (NMS), a listing of about 3,000 stocks that meet the following criteria:

1. The company has net tangible assets of at least $2 million.
2. The company has capital and surplus of at least $1 million.
3. The company has at least 500,000 shares of common stock outstanding.
4. The stock's trading volume averages at least 600,000 shares per month or 30,000 shares per day for six months.
5. The stock is distributed among at least 300 stockholders.
6. The bid price of the stock has been at least $10 per share for at least five business days.
7. The stock has attracted at least five market makers for at least five business days.

The NASD Automated Quotation (NASDAQ) System allows brokers and dealers to obtain current stock price, trading volume, and market maker information. For companies in the NMS listing, the system reports stock price and volume data for the most recent sale, as well as daily total volume traded and daily high, low, and closing prices. See Exhibit 15.2 for an excerpt from the NASDAQ/NMS quotations in *The Wall Street Journal.*

An additional 5,000 stocks are included in the NASDAQ System outside the NMS. About 1,300 stocks are classified as small caps. The issuers lack sufficient equity to meet NMS requirements, but the stocks are actively traded by investors. For the remaining stocks, a broker can obtain current bid and asking price quotations by specific market makers from the NASD Bulletin Board, and then execute the customer's order at the best available price.

In the United Kingdom, OTC trades are reported on the Stock Exchange Automated Quotations International (SEAQ) system. U.S. investors can find daily information on various international securities in the *Financial Times*. For some U.S. brokers, potential customer cross-border securities trades may justify the cost of going on line for various foreign quotation systems.

Brokerage Houses

Brokerage houses function as department stores for financial services. At one extreme, a full-service brokerage house may perform all of the functions indicated in Exhibit 15.3. At the other extreme, a discount brokerage house performs only one service: trading securities in the secondary market in response to customers' orders.

A full-service broker allocates all of its overhead to its profit centers and negotiates its commissions and fees with its larger clients. Consequently, it charges individual investors relatively high commissions. A discount broker minimizes overhead expenses, so it can keep commissions relatively low, whether charged per dollar, per share, or as a flat fee. Exhibit 15.4 presents some representative commission charges.

EXHIBIT 15.2

NASDAQ/NMS Quotations

NASDAQ NATIONAL MARKET ISSUES

	52 Weeks Hi	Lo	Stock	Sym	Div	Yld %	PE	Vol 100s	Hi	Lo	Close	Net Chg
	41¼	26½	EatonVance	EAVN	.60f	2.1	9	130	28½	27½	28	-⅝
	8⅜	4 13/16	Ecogen	EECN		...	dd	286	7⅞	7¾	7⅞	...
n	3⅝	1⅜	Ecogen wt			...	...	339	2⅞	2¾	2¾	...
	10½	4¼	EcoSci	ECSC		...	dd	232	5½	5	5	...
	8⅛	2⅞	EdisnCtrl	EDCO		...	...	32	4½	4½	4½	...
	48¾	9¾	EducatnAlt	EAIN		...	37	2439	12¼	11	11¾	-5/16
	7¼	2⅝	EducDev	EDUC		...	25	17	6	5¾	6	+⅛
n	11	8	EducInsght	EDIN		...	...	5	9	9	9	-¼
	14	4⅛	Edunetics	EDNTF		...	...	82	4⅝	4¼	4⅝	+⅜
	19	6¼	Edusoft	EDUSF		...	21	422	9½	8¾	8 13/16	-1 1/16
n	8⅜	4¾	EffectMgt	EMSI		...	13	91	5¾	5	5¼	-⅜
	11	6⅝	Egghead	EGGS		...	dd	529	7¼	6¾	6⅞	-¼
	17¾	9½	ElChico	ELCH		...	dd	5	14¾	14¾	14¾	-⅛
	3⅜	2 7/16	vjElPasoElec	ELPAQ		...	...	355	2 9/16	2½	2½	...
▼	45½	23	Elbit	ELBTF	.21e	.9	12	43	23	22½	22¾	-2
	21¼	14	ElcoInd	ELCN	.52	2.9	12	12	17¾	17¾	17¾	-¼
	7 1/16	1 15/16	ElecGasTech	ELGT		...	dd	134	2 5/16	2	2 5/16	...
n	14¼	7½	ElecFuel	EFCX		...	...	223	8¼	7½	7½	-1
	17	9⅛	ElectroSci	ESIO		...	9	308	10	9⅝	10	-⅜
s	15	9 21/32	ElectroRent	ELRC		...	11	80	13¾	13¼	13½	-¾
	5	3½	ElectroSensr	ELSE	.10	2.5	14	10	4	4	4	-3/16
n	36	13¾	Electroglas	EGLS		...	13	171	30¾	30	30¾	+¼
	56⅛	26½	Electrolux	ELUXY	1.56e	3.5	...	20	45½	45	45	-1½
	9⅜	5¾	ElectrmgSc	ELMG		...	40	180	8⅞	8¾	8¾	-⅛
▼	42	14¾	ElectrArts	ERTS		...	17	14043	15¾	14	15⅜	+⅜
n	8⅝	6¾	ElectroFab	EFTC		...	...	60	8⅛	8⅛	8⅛	-½
	14	5	ElectroRtl	ERSI		...	dd	3	8	7	8	+½
	20½	13¼	EFII	EFII		...	15	899	17¼	16¼	17	...
n	19	9¼	ElekTek	ELEK		...	17	18	12½	12	12	-½
	17½	7¼	EllettBros	ELET	.14e	1.1	17	151	14¼	13¼	13¼	-⅝
▼	22½	11	ElronElec	ELRNF		...	21	206	10⅞	10⅜	10⅜	-1½
n	9	6½	EltronInt	ELTN		...	...	102	8¼	7¾	8	-⅛
	8¾	4¼	Embrex	EMBX		...	...	35	4⅞	4⅝	4⅞	+⅛
	2¾	¾	Embrex wt			...	...	15	1	1	1	-⅛
	17¼	3⅝	EmisphereTch	EMIS		...	dd	514	5⅛	4¾	5	-¼
n	16½	11	EmmisBdcst A	EMMS		...	...	22	14½	13¾	14½	-¼
	34¼	9⅛	Empi	EMPI		...	12	229	12¼	11¾	11⅞	-⅛
s	12⅛	3⅛	Emulex	EMLX		...	dd	193	7¼	6⅞	6⅞	...
n	11⅜	4 21/32	ENCAD	ENCD		...	...	768	10	9⅛	9¼	-9/16
n	6⅜	3⅛	EncoreCptr	ENCC		...	...	2223	4¼	3⅞	4	-⅛
	17	7½	EncoreWire	WIRE		...	25	55	17	16	17	+½
	8¼	5¼	Endosonic	ESON		...	dd	8	5¼	5¼	5¼	-½
	14¼	6¾	EngyBioSys	ENBC		...	...	61	7¾	7¾	7¾	-¼
	10½	7¼	EnexRes	ENEX	.20	2.1	12	29	9½	9½	9½	-⅜
	4⅝	2⅛	EngrSupprt	EASI		...	18	40	4	4	4	-1/16
	3 15/16	1¾	EngrgMeas	EMCO		...	13	20	3¼	3¼	3¼	-⅛
▼	17½	9¼	EngleHome	ENGL	.16	1.7	8	344	9¾	9	9¼	-¾
	9¾	3¾	EnhancImag	EITI		...	dd	34	6	5½	5½	...
n	10½	5	EnSysEnvr	ENSY		...	...	11	5	5	5	...
	5⅜	2⅝	Envirogen	ENVG		...	...	98	3⅝	3⅜	3⅝	+3/16
	8⅛	4¾	EnvrTch	EVTC		...	...	80	8⅛	7¾	7¾	-⅛
	2⅞	⅞	EnvrTch wt			...	...	129	2	1 15/16	1 15/16	-⅛
n	3⅝	2	Enviropur	EPUR		...	...	409	2 7/16	2 5/16	2 7/16	+⅛
	4⅝	2½	Envrsource	ENSO		...	dd	638	3⅛	2 15/16	3⅛	+1/16
	28½	8¼	Envirotest A	ENVI		...	56	450	19½	18½	18½	-1
	23	12½	EnvoyCp	ENVY		...	47	973	22	21	21⅛	-¾
	6⅜	2⅝	Enzon	ENZN		...	...	301	3⅛	2⅞	3	+⅛
	24¼	15¾	EquiCredit	EQCC		...	7	34	17⅜	17	17	-½
	7¾	3¾	EquinoxSys	EQNX		...	24	674	5	4½	4¾	+¼
	4 1/16	2	Equitex	EQTX		...	...	71	2 7/16	2¼	2 7/16	+⅛
n	14½	12¼	EquityInns	ENNS	.06p	...	...	21	13½	13	13	...
n	6½	3¾	EquityMktg	EMAK		...	...	420	4⅛	3¾	4⅛	...
	9	3½	EqityOil	EQTY	.05j	...	dd	67	3⅞	3¾	3⅞	...
	60¼	35⅞	EricsnTel	ERICY	.62e	1.2	...	5548	50⅞	49⅞	50⅜	-⅛
s	9⅛	6½	Escalade	ESCA		...	14	31	7½	7¼	7½	+¼
	24¼	19⅞	ESELCO	EDSE	1.00b	4.3	...	1	23½	23½	23½	-½
	21½	14¾	EskimoPie	EPIE	.20	1.1	14	75	19⅜	19	19	-¼
n	10¼	6½	EsmorCorrect	ESMR		...	...	212	10¼	9¾	10	-¼
	18¼	10½	EsselCp	ESSF		...	12	11	15	15	15	-⅛
▼	14¼	7	EthicalHldg	ETHCY		...	...	101	6 29/32	6⅝	6 29/32	-3/32
s	18⅝	12⅝	EvanSuthrld	ESCC		...	40	33	15½	15½	15½	...
	4½	3⅛	EvansInc	EVAN		...	39	5	3⅛	3⅛	3⅛	-⅜
n	12¾	4½	EvansSys	EVSI		...	16	2	6½	6½	6½	+½
	18	12	EvergrnBcp	EVGN		...	dd	25	16½	15¾	16⅛	-⅛
s	19½	12⅜	Expeditor	EXPD	.10	.5	25	226	19⅛	19	19	...
	12¾	6⅝	ExpressAm	EXAM		...	dd	331	10¼	9¼	9¼	-1
	66¼	27	ExpresScrpt	ESRX		...	45	29	57½	55½	55⅝	-1⅞
	14¼	7	ExstarFnl	EXTR		...	22	36	8	8	8	+½
	4¾	2⅛	Ezcony	EZCOF		...	dd	32	4¼	3⅞	4	...
	22¾	10¼	Ezcorp	EZPW		...	22	147	13¾	13	13½	+½
			-F-F-F-									
	24½	20	F&M Bcp	FMBN	.80b	3.3	13	1	24¼	24¼	24¼	+1
	23¾	17½	F&M BcpInc	FMBK	.48	2.2	15	100	22¾	22	22	-1
	22¼	16½	F&C Bnshr	FSCC	.60a	2.8	20	157	21¾	21¼	21¾	+¼
	14½	3¾	F&M Distrib	FMDD		...	55	408	4⅝	4⅜	4⅜	-⅛
x	18¼	14¼	F&M Ntl	FMNT	.58	3.3	13	97	17¾	17½	17½	+¼
	5½	3⅞	FDP	FDPC		...	55	1	5½	5½	5½	...
s	14¾	11¼	FF Bncp	FFSB	.56	3.9	9	2	14½	14½	14½	...
n	17¼	12¾	FFLC Bcp	FFLC	.24	1.4	...	28	17¼	16½	17¼	+⅜
n	15⅝	12¼	FFY Fnl	FFYF	.30e	2.0	...	168	15⅝	15¼	15¼	...
n	15½	8½	FLIR Sys	FLIR		...	16	140	13⅛	12½	13⅛	-⅛
	6¼	3⅜	FM Prop	FMPO		...	dd	750	3 9/16	3⅜	3½	-1/16
n▼	23	22½	FNB CpNC	FNBN		...	...	5	21	21	21	-2
	7⅛	5	FNB Rochstr	FNBR		...	22	207	6 3/16	6⅛	6 3/16	...
	15¾	8½	FSI Int	FSII		...	14	54	12	11½	12	+¼
n▼	31¼	13¾	FTP Sftwr	FTPS		...	...	2215	14⅛	12½	13⅜	-1
▼	9⅞	6½	FahnestkVnr	FAHNF		...	4	5	6 15/32	6 15/32	6 15/32	-1/32
	7¾	4½	FailureGp	FAIL		...	...	118	5¼	5	5¼	+¼
	30¼	16	FairIsaac	FICI	.14	.5	25	11	30¼	29	30¼	...
n	6½	2¾	FairldCmunty	FFCI		...	...	63	6⅛	5⅞	6⅛	+1/16
	3⅛	1	FalcnOil	FLOGE		...	dd	17	1 9/16	1⅛	1⅛	-⅛
	15¾	8½	FalcnPdt	FLCP	.03e	.3	17	567	10½	10¼	10½	+¼
	24½	12½	FamilyBcp	FMLY	.50	2.1	10	91	24	23¼	23¾	...
	1	⅛	FamStkHse	RYFL		...	dd	212	11/32	¼	21/64	+5/64
s	36	17	FarmHmFnl	FAHS	.32	1.0	20	324	33⅜	32¾	32 13/16	-11/16
n	15¾	9¼	FarmrsMechan	FMCT		...	...	50	15¾	15	15½	...
	8⅜	4⅛	Farr	FARC		...	39	12	4⅝	4⅝	4⅝	-⅜
	8¼	3⅝	Farrel	FARL	.04e	.7	cc	40	6⅛	6	6⅛	-⅝
	18¼	4⅞	FastComm	FSCX		...	dd	443	6⅛	5⅞	5⅞	...
	39½	21¾	Fastenal	FAST	.04e	.1	47	3767	34	32¼	32½	-1⅜
n	15	13¼	FCB Fnl	FCBF	.21e	1.4	...	16	15	14½	14½	+⅛
	18½	15¼	FedlScrw	FSCR	.40a	2.2	7	20	18	17½	18	+1⅛
	16¼	3¾	Ferofluid	FERO		...	dd	66	5¾	5⅜	5⅜	...
	30	18¼	FHP Int	FHPC		...	15	2106	24¾	24	24¾	+¼
n▼	24⅝	24⅛	FHP Int pfA			...	...	3141	24½	24	24¼	-¼
	20	14¼	FidltyBcp	FSBI	.28	1.8	10	55	15⅞	15¾	15⅞	-1⅛
n	13	10¼	FidelityBcpIL	FBCI		...	...	136	12¾	12¼	12¾	...
	11½	8¼	FideltySvVa	FFRV	.12	1.3	7	2	9½	9½	9½	-¾
n	14¾	11¾	FidltyFSB FL	FFFL	.08p	...	...	275	14¼	14	14	-½
	24⅞	12⅞	FidelityNY	FDNY		...	...	703	24⅝	23¾	24	-⅝
	55	45	FfthThrd	FITB	1.08	2.0	16	1258	54¾	54½	54⅝	+⅛
	9⅝	2¾	FftyOffStrs	FOFF		...	dd	472	3¾	3⅜	3½	-¼
	20	7¼	Figgie B	FIGI	.19j	...	dd	12	10¾	10¼	10¾	...
	18¼	7⅞	Figgie A	FIGIA	.31j	...	dd	155	11⅛	10¾	11 1/16	+3/16
	12⅜	6¾	FileneBsmt	BSMT		...	dd	717	10⅛	9¾	9⅞	-1/16
	29¼	11	Filenet	FILE		...	23	2123	21¼	20	20	-1½
	5	2 1/32	FnlBenft A	FBGIA	.21t	6.5	3	7	3¼	3¼	3¼	+⅛
s	14¾	11	FnlInstit	FIRE	.26	1.9	...	20	13½	13¼	13½	+1
n	6¾	5⅝	FinForSci	FFSI		...	...	253	6⅝	6⅜	6½	+⅛
n	⅞	¼	FinForSci wt			...	...	1259	⅝	7/16	½	-⅛
	11½	5⅝	FinishLine	FINL		...	9	97	7¼	6½	6¾	-½
n	11⅝	8¾	FinishMaster	FMST		...	...	10	9¾	9¾	9¾	...
	8¾	6⅛	FstAlbny	FACT	.20b	2.6	6	3	7⅝	7⅝	7⅝	+⅛
n	27¼	17½	FstAlert	ALRT		...	...	615	27¼	26¼	27	-⅛
	34¾	28	FstAmCp	FATN	.84	2.6	8	1038	32½	31¾	32	-¾
s	30¾	22⅛	FstBcpOh	FBOH	1.00f	3.9	11	107	25½	24¾	25½	+½
	28½	26	FstBks pf		2.25	8.5	...	2	26½	26½	26½	+½
	4¾	3⅛	FstCash	PAWN		...	17	6	4⅛	4⅛	4⅛	...
n	8	3½	FstChartrBk	FCBK		...	...	45	7⅛	7	7	...
	50	40	FstCtzBk A	FCNCA	.70	1.6	8	2	43	43	43	+½
	15	9 1/32	FstCtzFnl	FCIT	.65t	4.9	8	2	13⅜	13⅜	13⅜	+⅜
	26	15¾	FstColonl	FCOLA	.60	2.6	20	57	24¼	23½	23½	-¼
	35¼	28	FstColonial dep	FCOLZ	1.75	5.4	...	13	32½	32¼	32¼	-1¾
n	19 3/64	15 15/16	FirstColonl	FTCG	.68b	3.9	...	2	17¼	17¼	17¼	-⅜
s	31 51/64	23½	FstCmmrc	FCOM	1.00	3.4	8	1689	29¾	28¾	29¼	-½
	41¼	31½	FstCmmrc pf		1.81	5.0	...	11	36½	35¾	36½	+½
	5½	2¾	FstCmrclBcp	FCOB		...	dd	93	3½	3¼	3½	

Source: *The Wall Street Journal*, June 3, 1994, p. C7.

EXHIBIT 15.3

Functions of a Brokerage House

Regulatory Protection

The Securities and Exchange Commission has the power to regulate the sale of securities in both the primary and secondary markets. It also oversees the activities of the stock exchanges, the OTC market, brokers and dealers, the NASD, and investment companies. It requires periodic reports from all participants in the secondary markets except individual investors who do not qualify as insiders, and who do not own 5 percent or more of the outstanding stock of any company. Most of the information in these SEC reports is available to the public.

In addition, the SEC enforces numerous regulations aimed at preventing price manipulation and fraudulent practices by financial institutions and the officers and directors of publicly held corporations. A corporation must file an 8-K report

EXHIBIT 15.4

Brokerage House Commissions

Brokerage House	Type	Commission on 100 Shares at $40 per Share	Commission on 1,000 Shares at $20 per Share
Merrill Lynch	Full-service	$100	$374
Smith Barney	Full-service	98	432
Charles Schwab	Discount	55	144
Quick & Reilly	Discount	49	109
Brown & Co.	Discount	29	29

each month to reveal any action that might materially affect the value of its bonds or stock. The corporation must also file a 9-K report every six months to present an unaudited report of revenues, expenses, and extraordinary items. Further, the SEC requires an annual 10-K report from every corporation; this document contains more detailed information for the whole year. Any interested person can go to the SEC's offices and examine these reports; photocopies are available for a nominal fee.

OTHER SECONDARY MARKETS

Secondary markets for most other securities operate in the same manner as the stock market, although they are not as large or as meticulously regulated. Various segments of the bond market, the options market, and the futures market are efficient and deep, and their transaction costs are not exorbitant.

The Bond Market

The U.S. secondary bond market can be subdivided into markets for government, municipal, and corporate issues. Bond dealers trade U.S. Treasury bonds and federal agency notes and bonds over the counter, primarily as a service to financial institutions. The dealers (market makers) in these government issues include large banks and major brokerage houses. An individual investor who wishes to trade outstanding Treasury or agency bonds can go to a dealer or broker, or to a local commercial bank, which will go to a dealer in turn. All major newspapers report daily price quotations for government issues, but they omit trading volume. Brokers negotiate commission schedules for large investors. Fees generally vary inversely with the dollar amount of bonds traded. Small investors usually pay non-negotiable per-bond or per-transaction fees.

gilt market
The market for government securities in the United Kingdom.

In the United Kingdom, the market for British government securities has been restructured along the lines of the U.S. market. It is called the **gilt market** because the securities used to have golden (gilded or gilt) edges. This extravagance has been discontinued, but the terminology remains.

Municipal Bonds. Commercial banks and investment bankers make active markets in municipal issues. They commit substantial portions of their own portfolios to municipal issues (shortened to *munis*) since they serve as the underwriters when the issues are sold in the primary market. The commercial press offers very little information about the daily prices and trading volume of munis because individual issues trade in thin markets. *Barron's*, for instance, allots only a small space to statistics on selected municipal bonds, as shown by Exhibit 15.5.

Moody's annually updates information about the states, cities, agencies, and other government units that issue munis, and publishes it in its *Municipal and Government Manual*. However, state laws governing municipal accounting practices vary enormously. Further, most local governments use the fund accounting method, which is generally rather unfamiliar to investors. For these two reasons, many potential buyers of munis ignore the detailed information on the government unit that issues the security and rely instead on the ratings assigned to the security by Moody's and Standard & Poor's. In addition, investors can choose among a significant number of unrated municipal bonds. The commission structure for municipals resembles that for U.S. government bonds, but fees are slightly higher.

Corporate Bonds. The secondary market for corporate bonds in the United States is organized exactly like the stock market. The bond exchange operated by the NYSE lists corporate bonds issued by more than a 1,000 different domestic and foreign corporations. The American Stock Exchange lists nearly 300 bonds. All other bonds trade over the counter. Trades involving large blocks of listed corporate bonds are usually negotiated in the OTC market, bypassing the exchanges' trading floors.

The financial press reports daily price and trading volume information on listed corporate bonds. *The Wall Street Journal* prints selected information on OTC corporate bond transactions daily and a complete listing appears weekly in *Barron's*. Commissions for bonds generally vary inversely with the dollar amounts traded, but they are almost always less than the commissions charged for stock trading.

Almost all Eurobonds, foreign bonds, and local bonds trade in their home countries over the counter. Investment banks usually function as market makers, although the foreign branches of multinational brokerage houses may choose to make markets in certain bonds that seem likely to appeal to substantial numbers of investors. This market is subject to far less regulation than the U.S. bond market, and commissions vary substantially.

Options Market

As explained in an earlier chapter, traders exchange two types of publicly traded stock option contracts: calls and puts. A call gives the contract owner the right, but not the obligation, to buy 100 shares of stock at a specified price (called the *strike price* or *exercise price*) for a limited time. A put gives the contract owner the right, but not the obligation, to sell 100 shares of stock at a specified strike price for a limited time.

EXHIBIT 15.5

Selected Municipal Bond Listings

Muni Issues

Friday, June 10, 1994

Obligations issued by a state or municipality whose interest payments are exempt from Federal, and possibly from local taxation as well.

Issue	Coupon	Mat.	Price	YTM
Anne Arundel Md Ser94	6.000	04-01-24	97½	6.18
Atlanta Ga Airpt 94B	6.000	01-01-21	97⅜	6.20
Brazos River Auth	5.600	12-01-17	94	6.08
Calif Health Fac	5.550	08-15-25	89½	6.32
Fla Mun Pwr Agy Ser93	5.100	10-01-25	86½	6.07
Florida St Bd Ed	5.125	06-01-22	88¼	5.99
Fulton Co Sch Dist Ga	5.625	01-01-21	95⅜	5.97
Ga Muni Elec Auth	6.500	01-01-26	103	6.28
Harris Co Tex	6.125	08-15-20	100⅞	6.06
Hawaii Dept Budgt&Fin	5.450	11-01-23	89¾	6.21
Hawaii Hsng Fin & Dev	6.000	07-01-26	93½	6.48
humphreys idb tenn swdi	6.700	05-01-24	102⅝	6.50
Ill Regional TA	6.250	06-01-24	100¼	6.23
Kansas City Util Sys	6.375	09-01-23	103	6.15
L.A. Co. Pub Wks Fin Au	6.000	10-01-15	98¼	6.15
Lehigh Co Pa. Ind Dvl	5.500	02-15-27	91	6.14
Martin Co Indus Fac	6.800	05-01-24	103	6.57
Mo Hlth & Ed Facs	5.250	05-15-21	86⅞	6.26
N.J. Econ Dev Auth PCR	6.400	05-01-32	100	6.40
NYC Lcl Govt Asst Cp	5.500	04-01-18	91½	6.18
NYC Muni Water Fin	5.500	06-15-23	92¾	6.03
NYS Dorm Auth Mt Sinai	5.000	07-01-21	86¼	6.03
NYS Environmental	5.875	06-15-14	98	6.05
NYS Med Care Fac	6.125	02-15-14	100¼	6.10
NYS Med Care Facil	5.250	08-15-14	90⅜	6.08
NYS Power Auth Ser C	5.250	01-01-18	89⅝	6.08
Orange Co Fla	6.000	10-01-24	99⅝	6.03
Orlando-Orange co Fla	5.125	07-01-20	90½	5.83
P R Elec Pwr Auth	6.375	07-01-24	101¾	6.24
PuertoRico pub im go 94	6.450	07-01-17	103⅛	6.20
PuertoRico pub im go 94	6.500	07-01-23	103⅜	6.25
Reedy Creed Fla	5.000	10-01-14	89¼	5.91
S.F. Cal. Sewr Ref Rev	5.375	10-01-22	90¼	6.10
Salem Co Pol Ctrl	5.450	02-01-32	88	6.29
Salt Riv Proj Ariz	5.000	01-01-16	87⅜	6.04
San Ant Tex El Gas	5.000	02-01-14	88⅝	5.98
TBTA NY	5.000	01-01-24	84½	6.13
Univ of Calif	6.375	09-01-19	101¼	6.28
Univ of Calif	6.375	09-01-24	101⅛	6.29
Valdez Al Marine Term	5.650	12-01-28	90½	6.33

Source: *Barron's*, June 11, 1994, p. MW59.

Stock Options. About 19 million puts and calls are traded on the New York, American, Philadelphia, and Pacific Stock Exchanges and on the Chicago Board Options Exchange annually. These contracts usually have expiration dates within the following six months. In addition, approximately 2.5 million long-term options contracts (LEAPS) are traded over the counter. LEAPS can have expiration dates up to two years away.

Daily trading volumes and closing prices for both types of contracts are listed in the financial press. The commission usually starts at a minimum of $30 per transaction and increases at a decreasing rate as the size of the trade increases.

Index Options. Many investors hesitate to predict price movements in individual stocks given time limitations; they may predict the general direction of the market as a whole in the near future with more confidence. This willingness to speculate has fertilized the creation of **index options**.

index options
Contracts that allow the contract holder to buy (if the contract is a call) or sell (if it is a put) a specific stock market index at a specific price for a limited amount of time.

Puts and calls on stock market indices follow the same principles as puts and calls on individual stocks. Exercising such an option does not involve the purchase or sale of a basket of stocks. Instead, if the contract holder chooses to exercise the option, the parties settle in cash. The settlement equals the difference between the exercise price of the option and the market value of the index.

The major index options are:

1. The OEX contracts, listed on the Chicago Board Options Exchange represent options on the largest 100 companies in the Standard & Poor's 500 Index.
2. The SPX contracts, listed on the Chicago Board Options Exchange represent options on all 500 companies in the Standard & Poor's 500 Index.
3. The RUT contracts, listed on the Chicago Board Options Exchange represent options on all of the stocks in the Russell 2000 Index.
4. The Major Market contracts, listed on the AMEX represent options on 20 blue-chip stocks, 15 of which are in the Dow Jones Industrial Average.
5. The Value Line Composite contracts, listed on the Philadelphia Stock Exchange represent options on the 1,700 stocks covered by the Value Line Investment Service.
6. The XOC contracts, traded on the Philadelphia Exchange represent options on the 100 largest OTC companies.
7. The WSX contracts, traded on the Pacific Exchange represent options on all of the stocks included in the Wilshire 5000 Index.

Other index options cover certain segments of the stock market, such as pharmaceuticals, utilities, banks, and gold and silver mines. Options on selected European and Japanese indices are also traded on U.S. exchanges.

Futures Market

Futures contracts promise future deliveries of specific quantities of agricultural products, metals, oil, domestic and foreign debt instruments, foreign currencies, and securities indices. Most investors who trade futures contracts do not have or want the underlying commodities. However, they expect the prices of the commodities and, therefore, the values of the contracts to change before the delivery date. These investors are really **speculators**. They attempt to profit by buying and selling contracts within short periods of time.

speculators
A trader who seeks profits by trading futures contracts or other derivative instruments over short periods of time.

hedger

A trader who uses a futures contract or other derivative instrument to protect a position in the underlying commodity or security.

The few investors who trade commodities futures contracts because their interest in the underlying commodities are not speculators. They are called **hedgers**, and they usually take positions in the futures markets that counter their positions in the commodities. A few examples will clarify the concept of hedging.

❖ EXAMPLE 15.1

Quaker Oats may have many square miles of its farmland planted with oats. Assume for simplicity that the company plants enough to provide a harvest that matches its need for oats exactly. Suppose, however, that the crop benefits from spectacularly good weather. Quaker's new estimate projects an oat harvest much larger than necessary; the firm decides to sell the surplus.

Quaker has two possibilities: (1) it can wait until the harvest, then sell its extra oats at the prevailing market price, or (2) it can sell as many futures contracts as necessary now, promising delivery of the oats at harvest time. Quaker would calculate the net present value (NPV) of selling the surplus harvest and compare it to the NPV of selling the futures contracts. It would choose the action with the larger NPV. If it were to decide to sell oat futures contracts, Quaker would be hedging its position in oats. ❖

❖ EXAMPLE 15.2

Suppose that Poland Springs, the Maine bottled water company, sells some of its spring water to Canadian customers and accumulates Canadian dollars. Further suppose that the company does a major promotional campaign in Canada once a year, spending many of those Canadian dollars. Afterward, it converts the unspent balance into American dollars.

Because the exchange rate between Canadian and American dollars fluctuates, Poland Springs' CFO could establish a policy of selling Canadian dollar futures contracts with delivery dates near the end of the promotional campaign. This hedge would stabilize the American dollar value of the unspent balance. ❖

❖ EXAMPLE 15.3

Suppose that a mutual fund has some of its portfolio invested in the stocks of large Japanese companies. The fund faces the risk of sudden, major declines in the value of this portion of its portfolio when the Japanese market drops or the exchange rate of the Japanese yen changes. To protect against this risk, it could sell Nikkei 225 Index futures and Japanese yen futures on the Chicago Mercantile Exchange. Hedges like these are also called *portfolio insurance*. ❖

U.S. investors can choose among almost 100 different futures contracts on 11 different exchanges in the United States. Exhibit 15.6 displays the list of exchanges and the commodities that underlie their futures contracts. In addition, U.S. investors regularly trade barley, wheat, canola, and flaxseed contracts on the Winnipeg Commodity Exchange, as well as Canadian bankers' acceptances and ten-year Canadian government bond contracts on the Montreal Exchange. The most recent expansion of investors' horizons involves the London International Financial Futures Exchange, where traders exchange futures contracts for Eurodollars, Euromarks, Euroswiss franks, British sterling, gilt bonds, German

EXHIBIT 15.6

Commodities Exchanges and Their Futures Contracts

Chicago Board of Trade: Corn, oats, soybeans, wheat, silver, gold, U.S. Treasury notes and bonds, federal funds, the *Bond Buyer* Municipal Bond Index, anhydrous ammonia, and diammonium phosphate

Chicago Mercantile Exchange: Cattle, hogs, lumber, U.S. Treasury bills, the 30-day London InterBank Offered Rate (LIBOR), Eurodollars, Euromarks, the Japanese yen, the Deutschemark, the Canadian dollar, the British pound, the Swiss franc, the Australian dollar, the French franc, the S&P 500 Index, the S&P MidCap 400 Index, the Russell 2000 Index, the Major Market Index, and the Nikkei 225 Index

Coffee, Sugar & Cocoa Exchange (New York): Cocoa, coffee, world (cane) sugar, and domestic (beet) sugar

COMEX (New York): Copper, gold, silver, and the Eurotop 100 Index

International Petroleum Exchange (New York): Brent crude oil and gas oil

Kansas City Board of Trade: Wheat, the Mini Value Line Index, and the Value Line Index

MidAmerica Commodity Exchange (Chicago): Rice, corn, oats, soybeans, wheat, cattle, hogs, gold, silver, platinum, U.S. Treasury bonds and ten-year notes, the British pound, the Deutschemark, the Japanese yen, the Swiss franc, and Eurodollars

Minneapolis Grain Exchange: Wheat and white wheat

New York Cotton Exchange: Cotton and orange juice concentrate

New York Futures Exchange: The NYSE Composite Index and the Commodities Research Bureau Index

New York Mercantile Exchange: Platinum, palladium, crude oil, heating oil, unleaded gasoline, natural gas, and propane

government bonds, Italian government bonds, and the *Financial Times'* London Stock Exchange Index (the "FooTSiE").

Brokerage houses set per-contract commission rates, which differ significantly between discount and full-service houses. Of course, for large enough trades, all commissions are negotiable. Futures contracts are very volatile and many investors are wary of holding them overnight. Therefore, most brokerage houses have two different commission rates: a lower rate for a day trade, and a higher rate for a long-term trade (overnight or longer).

round turn
The commission charged for a commodity futures contract purchase: it covers both the immediate purchase and the later sale of the contract.

Unlike commissions on stocks, bonds, and options, commissions for purchases and sales of futures contracts are both charged at once when the purchase is made. This is called a **round turn**, and its rationale reflects market practices. Many investors buy bonds and hold them until they mature or are called. In either case, no commission can be charged for selling the bond. Investors who buy stocks can hold them for a lifetime and pass them down from generation to generation. Until the shares are sold, no commission can be charged. Investors who buy options may allow the contracts to expire worthless, and again no commission can be charged for their sale. For stocks, bonds, and options, therefore, brokers cannot be sure they will earn a commission on the sale. They must wait until the securities are sold to collect the commission on the sale. When investors buy futures contracts, howev-

FOCUS ON FINANCE

CREATING A NEW FUTURES CONTRACT

The New York Mercantile Exchange (Nymex) is planning to offer a futures contract on electricity that could begin trading early in 1995. Developing and listing new futures contracts is a lengthy, difficult, and often expensive process, with no guarantee of success. It can take as long as two years to establish the trading history and liquidity demanded by most commodity funds and speculators.

Still-unresolved difficulties in designing the contract include:

1. Establishing a national delivery point—Deregulation of the generating industry is more advanced in some states than in others, and the nature of the commodity makes the delivery point a tricky choice.
2. Some potential contract users would prefer cash settlements rather than delivery.
3. Utility companies are bickering over whether the contract should specify firm delivery or interruptible supplies.

Utility companies that generate and distribute electricity to their customers are interested in hedging their prices, as are corporations that use huge amounts of power, such as steel manufacturers. Some fund managers whose portfolios are heavily weighted with financial futures are interested in electricity futures contracts for diversification. Energy futures contracts in general have been very popular with speculators, and electricity futures are a similar product.

Additionally, the Nymex is interested in launching aluminum, zinc, and nickel futures contracts to compete with the London Metal Exchange. It is also considering futures contracts on computer chips, junk bonds, and the Consumer Price Index. The CPI is an intangible commodity, but that does not have any effect on the exchange's ability to create a futures contract. The Chicago Board of Trade is considering trading clean-air and clean-water futures, also based on intangibles.

Source: Wall Street Journal, April 28, 1994, p. C1.

er, the brokers *know* that more than 90 percent of them will sell the contracts in the near future, so the selling commission can be collected up front. An investor who holds a futures contract when it expires takes delivery of the commodity and pays for it, be it 5,000 bushels of corn or 100,000 Canadian dollars.

spot (cash) price
The current market price of the commody that underlies a futures contract.

The financial press publishes current market prices (called **spot prices** or *cash prices*) for underlying commodities, as well as selected information on the futures contracts. As explained in Chapter 4, the following data are available for actively traded futures contracts:

settle price
The last price of the day for a commodity futures contract.

open interest
The number of futures contracts outstanding for a particular commodity.

1. The first price at the opening of the trading day, the day's high and low prices, and the **settle** (closing) **price**
2. The highest and lowest prices the contract has reached while it has been outstanding
3. The number of contracts outstanding (**open interest**) on the previous day (i.e., the trading day before the day for which the quotes are supplied)
4. The trading volume for the day

Those who buy futures contracts do not pay for them in full. Traditionally, a futures trader pays the broker about 10 percent of the value of a futures contract.

A contract holder who wants to take delivery of the commodity waits until the delivery date, pays the broker the remaining 90 percent of the original contract value, and takes possession of the commodity. This does not work for conceptual, financial commodities such as stock and bond indices, because there is no way the commodity (the index) can be delivered. Instead, the cash value of the index on the delivery date is calculated, the broker's 90 percent is subtracted, and the balance of the cash is paid to the contract holder.

To complicate matters, it is possible to trade options contracts (puts and calls) on futures contracts. This involves buying a contract that allows the owner, at a fixed price for a limited time, to buy or sell a contract that promises future delivery of a commodity at a specified future date.

MEASURING MARKET ACTIVITY

The SEC, the states, the exchanges, and the NASD have created regulations and set standards to protect investors from fraud by the issuers of securities and from unethical practices by brokers and dealers. Brokerage houses themselves have created ethics committees to oversee the practices of their employees. No amount of regulation or oversight can protect investors, however, if the prices of the securities they have chosen move unfavorably.

Securities Indices

Charles Dow constructed the first stock market index to indicate the behavior of stock prices in general. Innocent of statistical training, Dow chose twelve stocks that he considered to be typical of the market, added their prices, and divided by 12. By doing the same thing day after day, he produced an average price which, investors were led to believe, rose when stock prices in general were going up and declined when most stock prices were falling. The first problem Dow encountered was mechanical, a stock split, and he solved it by reducing the divisor.

The next problem he encountered was a selection problem. One of the stocks began to behave "atypically." Dow solved this problem by splicing in a replacement stock that was behaving typically, and the splicing required more fiddling with the divisor. The third problem cropped up in 1911—competition from other suppliers of market information. To answer the charge that the list was too small, the Dow Jones Industrial Average (DJIA) was expanded to 20 stocks in 1912 and to 30 stocks in 1928; it has remained that size for more than 65 years. By June 28, 1994, the initial divisor of 30 had been reduced to 0.3861073.

Criticisms of the DJIA have been plentiful:

1. Its sample of stocks reflects the Dow Jones Company's judgment instead of a random sample, so the index doesn't represent the whole market.
2. Its stocks are the bluest of the blue chips, so the index represents only what is happening to large, successful, mature companies.
3. The weighting system is flawed; adding up the prices of 30 stocks and dividing means that a 1 percent movement in the most expensive stock will have

FOCUS ON FINANCE

CORRECTING AN INDEX FOR SPLITS

Suppose that an index is constructed for a sample of three stocks, A, B, and C. On the first day, the stock prices are \$10, \$15, and \$20, respectively. An index structured like the Dow Jones Industrial Average would be calculated as:

$$I_1 = (\$10 + \$15 + \$20)/3$$
$$= 15.00$$

Suppose that on the second day the stock prices are \$11, \$15, and \$22, respectively. The index is recalculated as:

$$I_2 = (\$11 + \$15 + \$22)/3$$
$$= 16.00$$

If, on the second day, Stock C were to split 2-for-1, an attempt to adjust for the split in either of the following ways would produce misleading results:

1. Entering Stock C at its post-split price would depress the index:

$$I_2' = (\$11 + \$15 + \$11)/3$$
$$= 12.33$$

2. Recognizing that the \$22 value of Stock C represents the price of two shares would also depress the index:

$$I_2'' = (\$11 + \$15 + \$22)/4$$
$$= 12.00$$

The Dow Jones Industrial Average solves this problem by using one share of Stock C at the post-split price, then adjusting the denominator to force I_2 to equal 16.00.

$$I_2 = 16.00 = (\$11 + \$15 + \$11)/X$$
$$X = 2.3125$$

This new denominator, 2.3125, is used until another stock in the index splits, when the recalculation process is repeated.

much more impact on the index than a 1 percent movement in the cheapest stock.

4. The sample is much too small to represent all listed stocks.
5. The procedure introduces a built-in downsize bias related to stock splits.

Vindication of the DJIA came from its most powerful competitor, Standard & Poor's. S&P created a market value index of 425 industrial stocks. Analysts first compute market value, the market price per share times the number of shares outstanding, for each stock in the index. They total the 425 market values, and then repeat the same set of calculations for a base period. Dividing the current sum of market values by the base sum, and multiplying by 100, gives an index value. The numerator changes daily while the denominator (the base period sum) remains stable, so an increase in the ratio must reflect rising stock values.

Both the Dow Jones Industrial Average and the Standard & Poor's Industrials Index have companions. Both companies have created separate indexes for the stock prices of transportation companies and public utilities. S&P also has an index for financial institutions. Each company has combined its indices; the Dow Jones Composite Index contains 65 companies and the S&P Composite Index contains

500 companies. Oddly enough, the market refers most often to the "Dow Jones 30" (the Industrial Average), and the S&P 500 (the Composite Index), and compares their performances while ignoring the discrepancy in their definitions.

Comparisons and statistical measurements of these two indices have established that:

1. If stocks in general are trending upward or downward, both the DJIA and the S&P500 will reflect this.
2. Both stock indices indicate market turns at the same time.
3. The S&P500 grows a little faster than the DJIA.
4. The S&P500 is a little more volatile than the DJIA.
5. The statistical correlation between the two indices is always greater than 90 percent, regardless of the time period or number of observations used in the calculation.

A very strong correlation has also been found between these two indices and a market value index of all stocks listed on the New York Stock Exchange. Exhibit 15.7 compares the performances of major indices in the U.S. stock market. Observe the timing of the turning points and the growth rates.

Investors in the 1990s do not feel restricted to the U.S. stock market. They roam the world seeking higher returns and/or lower risks. They need to observe the performances of stock market indices for other countries. Exhibit 15.8 compares the performances of major foreign indices, as published by *The Wall Street Journal*. Observe that different markets have different trends and different turning points.

Investment Analysis Techniques

Investing profitably involves two elements: choosing appropriate securities and timing buy and sell orders correctly. Many professional investors select securities based on **fundamental analysis** and time their trades based on **technical analysis**. Fundamental analysis seeks to evaluate the condition of the company that issues a security (or, for a futures contract, the condition of the underlying commodity). Technical analysis tries to evaluate supply and demand for a security and the price and trading volume patterns produced by changes in supply and demand.

fundamental analysis
Evaluation of the condition of the company that issues a security (or, for a futures contract, the condition of the underlying commodity).

technical analysis
Evaluation of supply and demand for a security and the price and trading volume patterns produced by changes in supply and demand.

Fundamental Analysis. Fundamentalists begin their analysis by examining the current state of the economy and trying to forecast what will happen next. They rely on government economic indicators such as production, employment, capital spending, interest rates, inflation, and foreign trade, and on commercial economic indicators such as consumer confidence, relative yields, and stock market indices. They then deduce the consequences of their economic projections for various industries, taking into consideration the leading, concurrent, or lagging relationships between those industries and the overall economy.

Having forecasted the state of an industry, a fundamentalist will then appraise the actions of corporations in that industry to determine if they are likely to increase, maintain, or lose market share. This analysis extends to other factors that affect a company's profitability, such as financing, adaptation to technological

EXHIBIT 15.7

Performances of Various U.S. Stock Market Indices

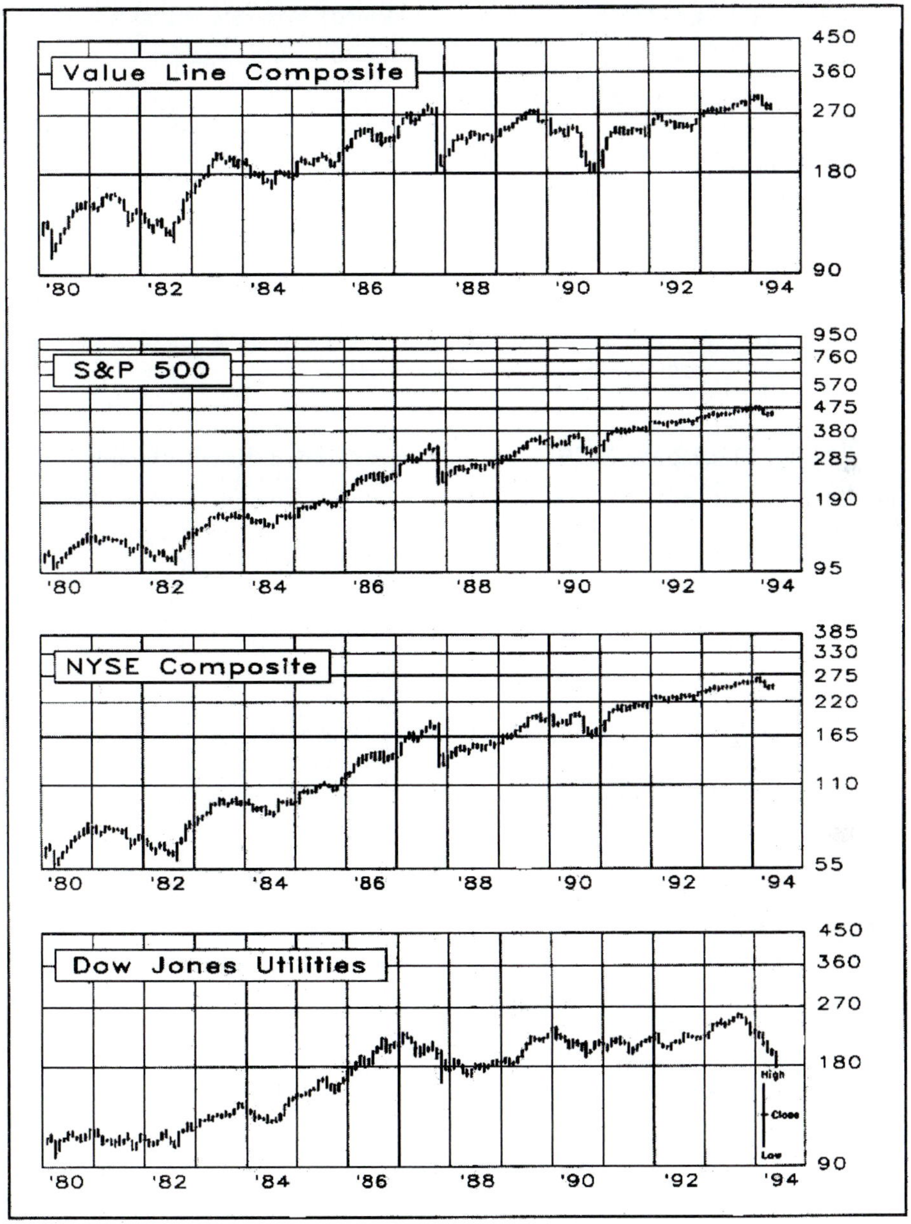

Source: Value Line Investment Survey, May 27,1994, p. 40. Copyright 1994 by Value Line Publishing, Inc. Reprinted by permission; all rights reserved.

EXHIBIT 15.8

Performances of Various Foreign Market Indices

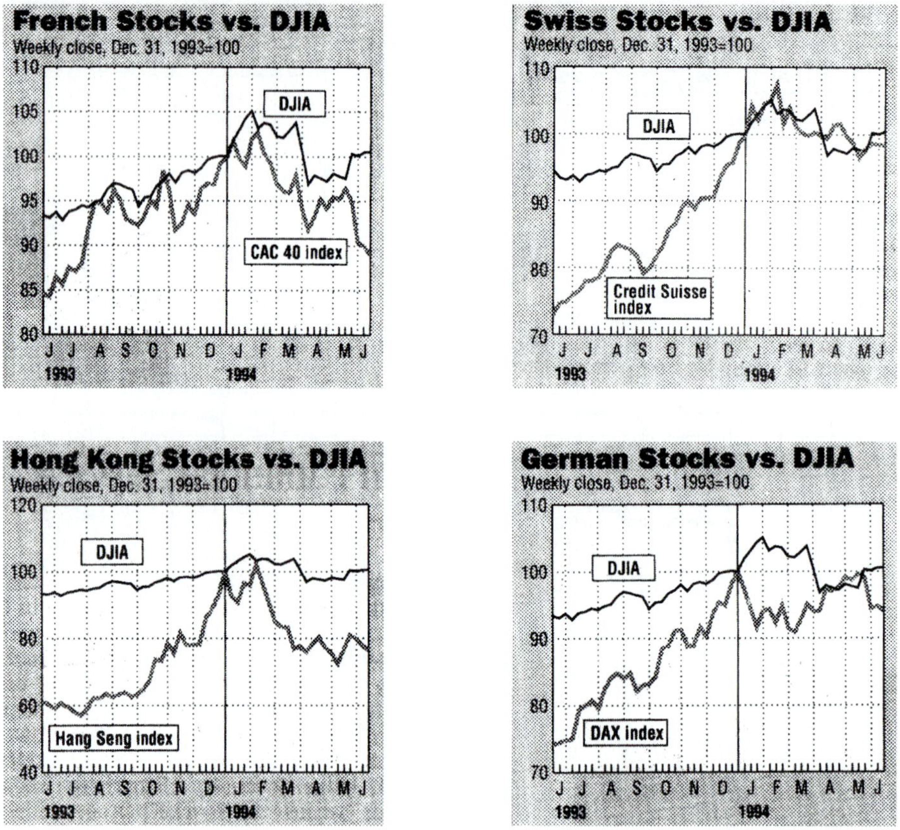

Source: The Wall Street Journal, various issues.

advances, and changes in management. All of this work enables the analyst to project corporate earnings and dividends.

The final step in fundamental analysis involves predicting prices for each company's securities. This requires projecting securities price trends in general and understanding how each company's securities react to changes in the market.

Technical Analysis. Market technicians (also called *chartists*) are not concerned with the condition of the company that issues a security. Instead, they focus on the actions of security traders and the impact of these actions on security prices. They believe that most investors "run with the herd," and a small minority (called *contrarians*) will take positions opposite to the general consensus. Such activity produces patterns in security prices and trading volume statistics.

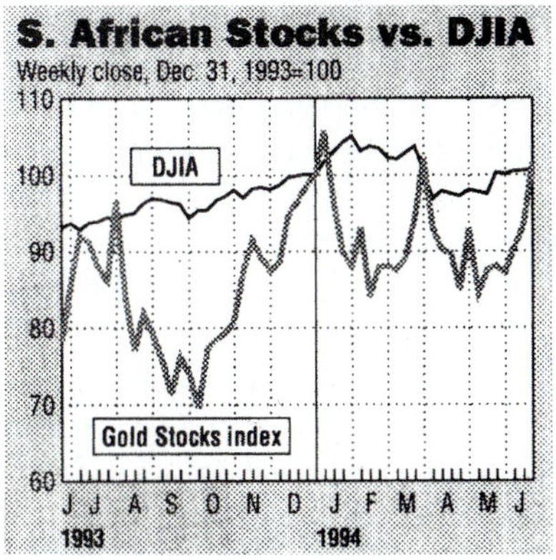

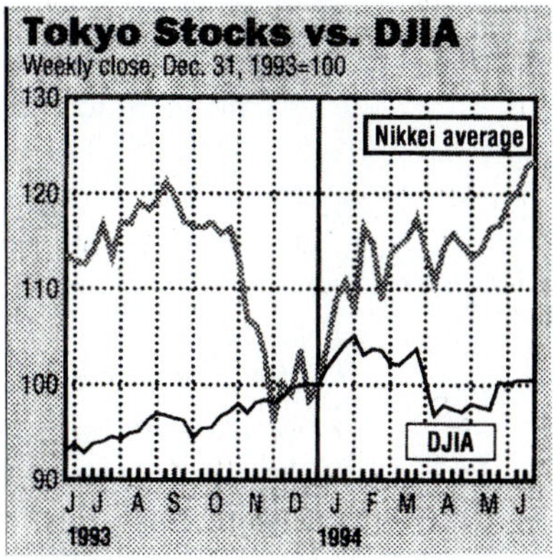

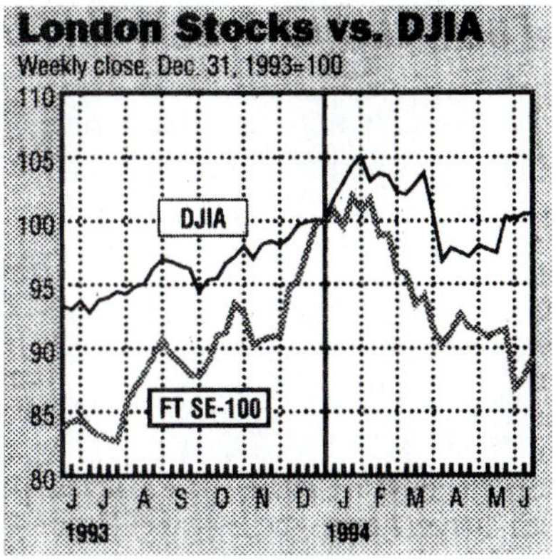

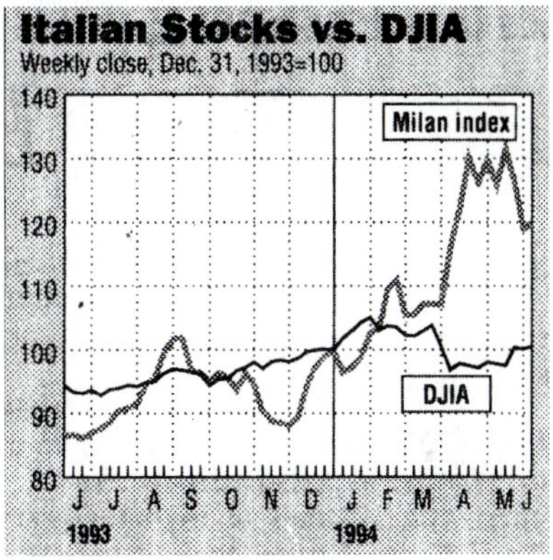

These patterns result from recurring activities, so recognizing a specific pattern makes it relatively easy to forecast the security's price behavior in the near future. Technicians watch for continuation patterns, indicators that a security's price will continue to do what it has been doing, and reversal patterns, indicators that a security's price will move in a new direction.

These technical patterns appear in bar charts. Exhibit 15.9 shows a typical daily bar chart. A vertical bar represents the spread in price during a specific time period. The bar connects the highest price (the top of the bar) at which a security was traded during the chosen period with the lowest price (the bottom of the bar) during the same period. A horizontal mark can be made across the bar to indicate the last trading price for the period. The period can be an hour, a day, a week, or a month. Bars on most paper charts represent one day; bars on most computer-generated charts represent 15-minute intervals. Because the behavior of trading volume is an integral part of the technical analysis of price patterns, the number of shares traded during a specific period always appears at the bottom of the chart. Without the volume bars, the chart is worthless for timing the purchase or sale of investments.

Some technicians choose stocks based on their projections of price movements. They will buy, or recommend that others buy, stocks whose charts suggest price increases sufficiently large to cover commissions and still produce profits. Alternatively, they will sell short, or recommend that others sell short, stocks whose charts suggest price declines sufficiently large to cover commissions and still produce profits. This practice is controversial.

Technical analysis can examine the market as a whole, as well as individual stocks. Chartists believe that patterns displayed by the stock of a specific company are also displayed by indices of stock prices. Technical analysis of the market, however, is usually reinforced by evaluating various published statistics on market activity. These **technical indicators** serve to verify projections based on bar charts.

technical indicator
A statistic on market activity that can support technical analysis of the market.

Technicians follow three technical indicators very carefully: market breadth indicators, short sale statistics, and margin balances. Breadth of market statistics reveal how comprehensive a perceived market movement really is. Breadth indicators compare the number of stocks that have increased to the number of stocks that have declined. The comparison may take the form of a ratio, an index, or a cumulative series of differences (usually, net advances). Technicians see extreme levels in these indicators as predictions of a reversal in the trend of the market. The breadth indicators turn before stock price indices do.

short sale
A market transaction in which an investor sells borrowed securities in anticipation of a price decline.

Short sales statistics emphasize short-run market activity. In a short sale, an investor borrows a security from a broker and sells it because its price is expected to decline. Later, the investor buys the stock back and returns it to the broker. If the price paid was less than the price received (the expectation proved to be correct), the investor has a profit. If the price paid was more than the price received (the expectation proved to be incorrect), the investor has a loss. Many technicians believe that small investors make terrible decisions as a group. They have historically bought when the market has approached peaks and sold when the market neared its bottoms. **Odd-lot trades**, those that involve less than 100 shares, are usually made by small investors. Therefore, technicians look at odd-lot short sales as a percentage of odd-lot trading. An increasing ratio indicates that small investors are pessimistic, which, in turn, suggests that the market should be improving soon.

odd-lot trade
A trade that involves less than 100 shares of stock.

Another near-term indicator that can be constructed from short sales statistics is the short-interest ratio. This is the total number of shares that have been sold short to date, divided by the average number of shares traded in a day. (Such a ratio can be constructed for each of the exchanges and for the NASDAQ/NMS list.) A higher ratio makes technicians more optimistic because every short sale has to be covered, and these purchases should add to demand in the near future.

buying on margin
Borrowing money from a broker to buy securities; the current margin requirement on stocks and bonds (the minimum cash deposit) is 50 percent of the purchase price.

Technicians follow margin account balances at brokerage houses as a smart-money indicator. When an investor **buys on margin**, he or she borrows a per-

EXHIBIT 15.9

Typical Technician's Bar Chart

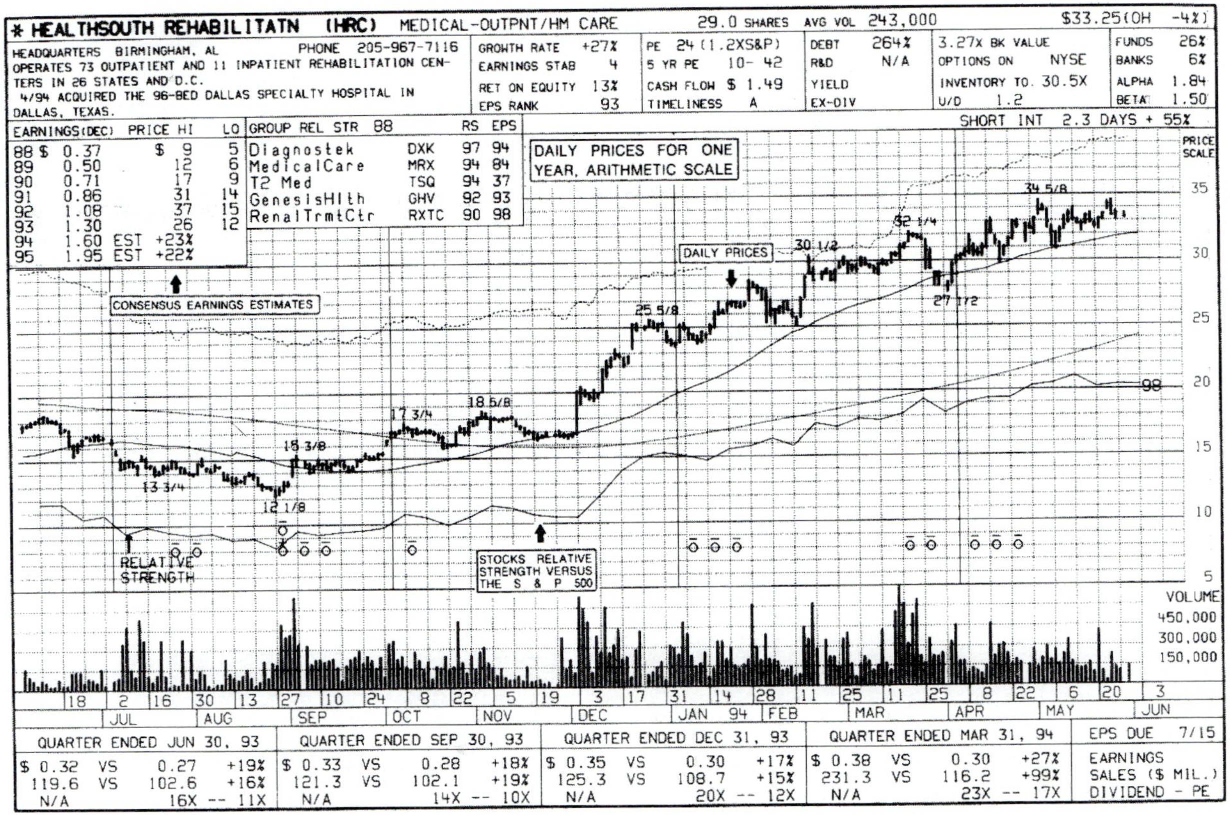

Source: *Investor's Business Daily*, June 2, 1994, p. B12. Reprinted by permission of Investor's Business Daily, ©1994, Investor's Business Daily.

centage of the purchase price from the broker. The maximum percentage is set by the Federal Reserve Bank. The current margin requirement of 50 percent has remained stable for many years. Because technicians believe that only relatively sophisticated investors buy securities on margin, they view an increase in margin borrowing as an optimistic indicator; they see a decrease as pessimistic.

Analysts follow many other technical indicators, such as:

1. The amount of cash held by mutual funds
2. Net redemptions of mutual fund shares by investors
3. The price of a stock exchange seat
4. The ratio of NASDAQ/NMS trading volume to NYSE trading volume
5. The volume of institutional buying and selling of large blocks of stock
6. The ratio of put trades to call trades
7. The spreads between the yields on different quality bonds
8. The spread between the yields on U.S. Treasury bills and Eurodollars
9. The spreads between exchange rates, usually involving the Japanese yen, the British pound, and the U.S. dollar
10. The percentage of stocks near their historic highs
11. The market price–earnings ratio
12. The ratio of market price to book value

INVESTORS

All of the organizations, information networks, and analytical techniques described previously have one purpose. They are designed to induce investors to part with their money. To be effective, they must convince investors that the markets offer future rewards high enough to compensate for foregoing current consumption and accepting the risks associated with investing.

Institutional Investors

Financial institutions accumulate large pools of cash, which they can invest for indefinitely long periods. They can afford to diversify efficiently, choosing many issues, many types of securities, and even many national markets. Exhibit 15.10 shows the percentage of all publicly traded shares held by various types of institutions at the end of the third quarter of 1992. Chapter 3 described the various types of financial institutions. The following section discusses their investment objectives.

Pension Funds. Pension funds have constant cash inflows and predictable cash outflows. They need not search the world for high-risk, high-return investments. In fact, if a defined-benefit pension plan achieves too high a return, the employers, unions, or government units that contribute funds will demand lower future contributions.

EXHIBIT 15.10

Stock Holdings of Institutional Investors

Private pension funds	20.2%
Public pension funds	9.0
Mutual funds	9.0
Foreign institutions	6.3
Life insurance companies	2.5
Other insurance companies	2.5
Miscellaneous institutions	0.7
Total for all institutions	50.2%[a]

[a]Institutional investors held more than half of all publicly traded shares of stock in the United States at the end of the third quarter of 1992.
Source: *Newsday*, January 31, 1993, p. 73.

Life Insurance Companies. Life insurance companies face essentially the same situation as pension funds. Both financial institutions can project the timing and amounts of their cash outflows using highly accurate actuarial tables. These tables are statistical databases that project how long different groups of people (classified by age, gender, education level, type of employment, unhealthy habits, and so forth) will live. Such accurate information helps investment portfolio managers for pension funds and life insurance companies to calculate the returns they need. They calculate how much annual or monthly income their investments will have to produce in the form of interest and dividends and how much in capital gains. They then search for securities that will provide those returns with the least possible risk.

Fire and Casualty Insurance Companies. Fire and casualty insurance companies face much more difficulty in projecting their cash outflows. Since they never know when disaster will strike, they must keep part of their investment portfolios in lower-yielding, more liquid securities. To balance this, they invest the remainder of their portfolios in riskier, higher-yielding securities. Such securities require active management; portfolio managers must quickly replace those that do not appear to be performing according to expectations. These institutions use derivative securities extensively in hedging strategies.

Investment Companies. Investment companies serve different needs and employ different methods. They define their investment goals, choosing from a broad spectrum. At one extreme, new stocks from small companies can provide high growth, great risk, and negligible income. At the other extreme, junk bonds can provide high income, great risk, and no growth. Whatever goal an investment company chooses, it can count on many competing funds attempting the same feat, and this generates great pressure to outperform the competition. Companies that produce the largest growth or the greatest income can expect to attract the most investors.

closed end investment company
An investment company that authorizes and issues a fixed number of shares of its own common stock, which trades in the secondary market.

open end investment company
An investment company that issues shares whenever a potential investor wants to buy them and buys back shares whenever a current investor wants to sell them. Also called a *mutual fund*.

net asset value
The market price of shares in a mutual fund, calculated as the market value of the fund's assets divided by the number of shares the fund has outstanding.

Further discussion of the factors that affect investment company policies must recognize an important distinction among investment companies. **Closed end investment companies** authorize and issue fixed numbers of shares of their own common stock, which trades in the secondary market. A potential investor can buy shares in a closed end investment company only from a current shareholder. **Open end investment companies**, also called *mutual funds*, issue new shares whenever potential investors want to buy them, and they buy back shares whenever current investors want to sell them. The market price of a mutual fund's shares is always the value of the fund's assets divided by the number of fund shares outstanding; this is the **net asset value** per share. Funds calculate this value twice a day.

Mutual funds must plan for relatively unpredictable, potentially massive cash inflows if the investing public rushes to buy them because other investment media do not provide acceptable returns. They also face massive cash outflows when the investing public loses its confidence, or worse, its employment. Given the uncertainty of these cash flows, a mutual fund portfolio manager seeks to balance liquidity, income, growth, and risk. Some very active portfolio managers search the world for a tiny, undiscovered advantage. Hedging mutual fund portfolios against market movements, interest rate changes, and currency risks necessitates the extensive use of puts and calls.

Mutual fund managers cope with an ironic truth that the top-performing fund in any given year can seldom repeat its stellar performance. Outstanding performance attracts so many investors that the fund accumulates too much cash. Having invested to the limit in all of the promising securities the manager can find, the fund has no place to put all of the additional cash, unless the fund is willing to invest in inferior securities. To prevent this, some funds close their doors to new investors when they announce spectacular results.

Individual Investors

Individual investors must choose between attempting to go it alone, trading securities that they think will perform to meet their needs, or investing in financial institutions that will manage their investment money for them. Research has demonstrated that individual investors (who also have jobs and families) cannot manage portfolios much larger than 15 different securities without making serious mistakes, both of omission and commission. However, investors in mutual funds must always pay management fees and, depending on the choice of funds, perhaps entry and exit fees (called *loads* and *back loads*).

SUMMARY

A secondary market is a mechanism for trading in outstanding securities. A high-quality market must ensure that investors have access to sufficient, credible information. It must be efficient, and have price continuity, depth, and minimal transaction costs.

The U.S. stock market has two components: exchanges that trade listed securities and an over-the-counter market. Listed securities change hands in an auction process; dealers make markets in OTC securities and set the prices themselves. Both components are also present in the secondary markets in London and Tokyo. In the United States, stock exchange members function as brokers, traders, or specialists (who also serve as dealers). The Tokyo exchange does not let its specialists act as dealers, and no specialists operate on the London Exchange.

A 24-hour market has developed with the proliferation of national markets and exchanges. Investors trade trade securities 24 hours a day by moving from one market to another, or via electronic networks.

In the United States, about 6,000 stocks trade over the counter. The National Association of Securities Dealers has created an electronic network to facilitate trading in OTC stocks.

Brokerage houses handle the buying and selling of securities for all investors except large financial institutions. A discount broker charges lower commissions than a full-service brokerage house because it has less overhead.

Other securities markets operate like the stock market. U.S. exchanges list over 1,000 corporate bonds. The international bond market and the remaining portions of the U.S. bond market are OTC operations.

Various U.S. exchanges handle trades of puts and calls on both stocks and stock indices that are due to expire within the following six months. Long-term options contracts (LEAPS) are traded OTC.

The 11 futures exchanges in the United States, the two exchanges in Canada, and the London International Financial Futures Exchange accommodate trading in 100 commodities futures contracts. Traders pay round turn commission rates per contract. They can also trade options on futures contracts.

The Dow Jones Industrial Average is the granddaddy of all stock price indices. Although its sample is composed of only 30 blue chip stocks chosen by subjective judgement, it indicates market trends and turning points just as well as the Standard & Poor's 500 Index and the index of all stocks listed on the NYSE. Other indices track various foreign stock markets; they display different trends and turning points than the U.S. indices. The rates of return available to investors in different stock markets vary considerably.

Professional investors may use fundamental analysis to select securities and technical analysis to select the best times to trade. Fundamental analysis evaluates the profit potential of a company, given economic, industry, competitive, and stock market conditions. Technical analysis looks for patterns in price-and-volume bar charts for individual stocks and for stock indices. Technicians forecast stock prices based on repeating patterns, reinforced with analysis of technical indicators.

All of the organizations, information sources, and analytical techniques in the securities markets are designed to induce potential investors to invest. Financial institutions make investment decisions based on their expected cash flow patterns. Individual investors can either select their own securities or choose financial institutions to invest for them.

Key Terms

auction system
buying on margin
closed end investment company
commission broker
floor broker
fourth market
fundamental analysis
gilt market
hedger
index option
negotiated transaction
net asset value
odd-lot trade
open end investment company
open interest
outstanding security
registered trader
round turn
settle price
short sale
specialist
speculator
spot (cash) price
technical analysis
technical indicator
third market

Self-Study Questions

1. Name five characteristics of a high-quality secondary market.
2. What does it mean when a market is said to have depth?
3. What is the difference between auction trading and negotiated trading?
4. Explain the third and fourth markets.
5. What is the NASDAQ System?
6. Explain the difference between a hedger and a speculator in commodity futures contracts.
7. What is the difference between a call contract on a stock and a call contract on an index?
8. What is fundamental analysis?
9. What is technical analysis?
10. What is a mutual fund?

Discussion Questions

1. If secondary markets did not exist, why would it be difficult to issue new securities?
2. How are national and regional stock exchanges different?
3. What information becomes available to the public when a stock is bought and sold on the trading floor of an exchange?
4. Snap-On Tools Corporation has $136 million in income before taxes, 42.5 million shares of common stock outstanding, and 9,173 stockholders. Would you expect it to be listed on the NYSE or the AMEX?
5. What are the similarities and differences between a U.S. specialist and a Japanese *saitori*?
6. How are NASDAQ/NMS and NASDAQ Small-Cap companies different?
7. If an investor needs current information about a stock before buying, would a full-service broker offer any advantage over a discount broker?
8. How are 8-K, 9-K, and 10-K corporate reports different?

9. Is the U.S. muni market a high-quality market? Why or why not?
10. Wilma and Fred bought a February Coca Cola call with a strike price of 40 when Coke was trading at 42⅞. Explain exactly what they bought.
11. Barney and Betty bought a February Coca Cola put with a strike price of 45 when Coke was trading at 42⅞. Explain exactly what they bought.
12. Why do brokers charge round turn commissions on futures contract trades?
13. What is a futures option?
14. How does a futures contract differ from an option contract?
15. A manufacturer knows that it will need 25,000 pounds of copper in six months. What data must it have to decide whether to buy the copper or a copper futures contract?
16. Look at the graph in Exhibit 15.9. If an investor had wanted to invest in two markets that generally moved in opposite directions, which stock markets seem attractive?
17. Why is fundamental analysis a better technique than technical analysis for selecting securities?
18. Why is technical analysis a better technique than fundamental analysis for determining the time to buy securities?
19. Which of the following data would be important to a fundamental analyst and which would a technical analyst gather?
    (a) The unemployment rate
    (b) The number of shares traded daily
    (c) Corporate borrowing
    (d) The number of shares sold short
    (e) A company's EBIT
20. A mutual fund that outperforms other mutual funds of its type is not likely to repeat its victory over the next year. Why not?

Topics for Further Research

1. Collect weekly or monthly data (one or the other; do not mix them) for at least four different stock market indices. Run the data through a statistical package and obtain the correlation matrix. Which indices are the most highly correlated?
2. Research the facts on futures contracts for the commodity of your choice. Check books on the commodities market, brokerage house brochures, and above all, the commodities exchange where the contract is traded.
3. Obtain a copy of *The Dow Jones-Irwin Mutual Fund Yearbook*. Find the best-performing fund in each category and compare the returns these funds produced.

CHAPTER

16

Financial Analysis

LEARNING OBJECTIVES

At the conclusion of this chapter, the reader should be able to:

1. *Describe how different users undertake financial analysis for different purposes*
2. *Evaluate how economy-wide and industry-specific factors may impact the behavior of the individual firm*
3. *Identify the various sources of public information about a particular corporation*
4. *Develop common-size and common-base financial statements and understand their importance in financial analysis*
5. *Define the nature of ratio analysis and the problems associated with it*
6. *Select appropriate ratios to use to evaluate a corporation's financial statements, given the intention of the analyst*

Investors, lenders, and others who need to evaluate the financial integrity of firms can make more informed decisions by applying standardized quantitative techniques. Financial analysis is the process of applying standardized analytical tools and techniques to a firm's financial statements to develop useful decision-making measurements and relationships.

The first step in financial analysis is to obtain the relevant information, and analysts devote much of their time and effort to accumulating corporate data. Some data may be internal to the firm and, thus, available only to its own management. The law requires firms to make other data publicly available. This publicly disclosed information, combined with knowledge about the economy and the industry, provides the basis of most external analysis. However, when a corporation wishes to sell additional debt, it will hire analytical services such as Moody's or Standard & Poor's to evaluate its credit rating. Management must then release significant internal information in order to obtain the most favorable rating possible.

The most frequently used technique of financial analysis involves evaluating appropriate ratios. After compiling these ratios, the analyst compares them with past ratios of the same corporation or with ratios derived for its competitors. Often such analysis involves comparisons with industry norms. In spite of the wealth of information that ratio analysis provides, it is not without its weaknesses. The analyst must be certain not to consider industry norms as absolutes; remember, also, that any ratio analysis, no matter how thorough, focuses on past events, not future trends.

FINANCIAL ANALYSIS AND ITS PURPOSE

The commercial banker deciding whether or not to grant a loan, the CEO evaluating the impact of a corporate acquisition, and the investor speculating in the marketplace, all need to analyze the company's financial condition. Each, however, has different objectives and, thus, each would apply financial analysis differently.

Users of Financial Analysis

Every stakeholder in a company—management, the investors, the employees, the government, and the affected public—has an interest in the success or failure of the business. Consequently, each of the stakeholders has an interest in the financial soundness of the enterprise. While these groups view the business differently and they need different information about the business, they all must use financial analysis.

Managers may use financial analysis most extensively. They need it to evaluate the operational efficiency and the short-term and long-term profitability of the enterprise. Their resource deployment, method of financing, and use of capital are all evaluated using some form of financial analysis.

Investors, including both current and potential stockholders, are particularly concerned about profitability. Consequently, they use financial analysis to evaluate earnings potential, return on equity, and future dividend growth. They are concerned about anything that may affect share value.

Short-term creditors, principally banks and commercial credit lenders, are more interested in a firm's liquidity. Bondholders and other long-term creditors worry about the firm's ability to meet its contractual obligations. Hence, both groups of creditors rely on financial analysis, hoping to identify impending crises in time to avoid them.

Local government officials and employees, especially participants in an ESOP (an employee stock option plan) are interested in the firm's longevity and its potential as a takeover target. After all, their individual interests are best served by maintaining the status quo. Employees keep their jobs and local governments keep their tax bases. Proper application of financial analysis may well provide insight and guidance.

Firm, Industry, and Economy

The prevailing state of economic activity has a significant effect upon most firms, especially those that are sensitive to the business cycle. Cyclically sensitive firms generally prosper in an expanding economy, with rising sales and profit margins. When the economy contracts, cyclically sensitive firms likewise share in the distress. An automotive company generally sells more cars and generates larger profit margins during cyclical expansions than during cyclical contractions.

Some firms scarcely notice the business cycle. A regional telephone company, for example, may experience only slightly slower business during a recession. Similarly, when economic activity improves, this company will experience only a slight increase in its activity.

The impact of changes in economic activity is first felt by the industry, and through the industry, by the individual firm. Sometimes, however, industry-specific events occur that have nothing to do with the overall economy and affect only a small group of firms. For instance, if the United Mine Workers were to strike, coal mining companies would experience significant reductions in sales and profit margins. Only a prolonged strike affects other industries.

Because economywide or industry-specific events can affect an individual firm's performance, financial analysts must be aware of them when making their evaluations. Specifically, an analyst must judge how, and to what extent, an industry contraction or a threat of inflation would affect the firm under investigation. Regression analysis and other forecasting techniques may help the investigator to quantify these relationships.

SOURCES OF FINANCIAL INFORMATION

The availability and reliability of information is quite different for management, government regulators, external analysts, or investors who examine a firm. Since management can generate information about the firm, it has the best access. A firm in a regulated industry must provide much the same information to regulators.

External analysts may perform their analysis with or without the cooperation of the firm. If the firm cooperates, it may offer the analyst much of the information available to management. If management does not cooperate in supplying information, then even a professional analyst is no better off than the average investor. Investors can access only publicly available information; their ability to evaluate the firm depends on how successfully they interpret the available information.

Inside Information

Business publications such as *The Wall Street Journal* serve as sources for much of the publicly available information about a firm. These media outlets identify

FOCUS ON FINANCE

Advance Information

Prepublication knowledge of the contents of the investment advice columns of a business publication can provide a competitive edge to a stock trader. For this reason, publications such as *The Wall Street Journal* and *Business Week* take precautions to avoid leaks.

Still, leaks happen. A classic case came to light in August 1988. William Dillon, a young broker with Merrill Lynch, had convinced an assistant pressman at the R. R. Donnelley & Sons printing plant in Old Saybrook, Connecticut, to supply him with copies of *Business Week* prior to public distribution. Dillon then entered orders for the *Business Week* stock picks as soon as the market opened. It was estimated that in a good week he made several thousand dollars from these trades.

During the investigation of Dillon, the Securities and Exchange Commission uncovered evidence that this was not an isolated incident. Not only was the same thing occurring at other printing plants, but fellow brokers, seeing the insider's profit, were mimicking their trades and profiting as well.

important economic factors and trends, analyze industry conditions, and report relevant factors that affect the firm. The financial pages of most newspapers report firm-specific information relating to sales, earnings, and dividends. Likewise, changes in management, acquisitions, and the firm's entry into the bond and stock markets quickly become public knowledge.

inside information Firm-specific information known to individuals before its public announcement.

Should any of the firm-specific information be known to individuals before its public announcement, it is considered to be **inside information**. Individuals who possess such insider information could potentially benefit from this knowledge by trading in the company's stock ahead of the public announcement. Since this would give the possessor of the information an unfair advantage, the Securities and Exchange Commission (SEC) has declared trading based on insider information illegal. Yet, price movements prior to announcement dates often appear to reflect influence of insider information on individual stocks. Whether such price movements result from speculation or other factors is difficult to ascertain. After the stock market scandals of the 1980s, however, few doubt that some insider trading does take place.

The SEC defines an insider as anyone who meets one of three criteria:

1. An owner of 10 percent or more of a firm's outstanding shares
2. A member of senior management
3. Someone who, by contractual arrangement with the company, has access to information that is not available to the public

Not all those who possess inside information should be considered potential felons. After all, the managers of a corporation possess intimate knowledge of its circumstances. They are, however, expected to use this information to maximize profits for the common stockholders and not for their own personal gain. Thus, all

FOCUS ON FINANCE

AND THE WINNER IS . . .

Since 1940, *Financial World* has conducted an annual report competition. Recognizing that the annual report is a company's most visible document because it is distributed to shareholders, analysts, employees, and the media, *FW* seeks to honor companies that strive for quality and thoroughness. While the reports are judged primarily on their usefulness to shareholders, the needs of the professional analyst are also considered. The Gold Award, *FW*'s highest award, is given to "the best report [that] not only states where a company's strengths and weaknesses lie, but also sketches the impact of economic and social factors on the business and presents a focused view of the company's strengths and goals for the future."

A second award named in honor of Louis Guenther, the founder of the *Financial World* Annual Report Survey, focuses attention on financial writing and reporting. The judging for this award considers not only the thoroughness and detail of the required financial statements, but also the textual interpretation and narrative documentation of the company's financial status.

Silver Awards are given for other corporate publications, such as:

1. Analyst yearbooks, which contain much more detailed information than annual reports (These are reference tools for individual and institutional investors.)
2. Annual meeting reports, which should contain the chairman's remarks, the results of the voting, and an account of the give and take (These should also offer pictures of the companies in action.)
3. Corporate annual reviews, which focus on companies' people, products, and processes instead of their financial results
4. Corporate newsletters, which are published by companies for the information, education, and entertainment of their employees
5. Interim reports, which are quarterly publications that detail industry trends, update strategy forecasts made in annual reports, and document companies' growth or decline
6. Summary annual reports, which present just financial and operating results
7. Video annual reports, which are honored for their combination of visual effects and narrative quality

With almost 1,000 companies entering the competition each year, these awards are highly prized by corporate America.

Source: Financial World, November 9, 1993, p. 97.

---

owners of more than 5 percent of the stock in a firm and all managers of a corporation are required to report all of their market activity in the firm's securities to the SEC.

annual report
A report sent to every shareholder summarizing the year's financial activity for the firm and containing management's assessment of the previous year's performance as well as its outlook for the coming fiscal year.

Company Publications

The single most widely disseminated document relating to the firm is its **annual report**. This report is sent to every shareholder, as well as all potential investors who request information. It generally contains a simplified income statement, balance sheet, and cash flow statement. In addition, it provides management's assessment of the previous year's performance as well as its outlook for the coming fiscal year. Often this report reviews financial and operational highlights for the previous five years and presents a detailed accounting of shareholder equity changes. Not all annual reports are equally useful. Some contain the bare minimum required by SEC reporting rules, while others provide essentially the same information the firm files with the SEC in its annual 10-K report.

As the previous chapter explained, the SEC requires every public corporation to file a 10-K report annually, along with its quarterly version, the 10-Q. Unlike the annual report, this filing omits the glitz, the glossy pages, and the upbeat tempo of the annual report. It is primarily composed of the required financial statements and direct comments about all relevant events affecting the firm's immediate past or future performance. For the sake of convenience, to reduce expenses, and to show that they have nothing to hide, some firms distribute the 10-Ks as their annual reports, merely adding a fancy cover and a message from the CEO.

Analytical and Advisory Services

Numerous analytical and financial services are available both in print and on line to those willing to pay the price. These services range from publications of industry ratios to presentations of virtually every known fact about a given corporation.

Moody's *Industrial, Bond and Finance, Transportation, Public Utility, International,* and *Municipal and Government Manuals.* Moody's *Manuals* provide financial information such as balance sheet and income statement data, and details on outstanding securities. The listings for larger corporations also include basic ratios. In addition, the information generally includes a comparative earnings report. These publications seek to provide all of the basic information an investor could require.

Standard & Poor's *Corporation Records.* Very similar to Moody's *Manuals*, *Corporation Records* generally serves much the same purpose. Its listings, however, generally are not as extensive.

Industry Norms and Key Business Ratios. *Industry Norms*, published by Dun & Bradstreet, provides 14 ratios for each of over 800 different industrial classifications. Since it reports the upper and lower quartiles as well as the median industry value for each ratio, it permits firms to evaluate their relative positions within their industries for these ratios.

Statement Studies. Published by Robert Morris Associates, an association of bank loan and credit officers, *Statement Studies* provides common-size financial statements and 16 ratios for firms in each of approximately 200 industrial classifications. It is generally considered the best source of comparative information for smaller firms, since it includes only firms with less than $250 million in assets.

Almanac of Business and Industrial Financial Ratios. Prentice-Hall's *Almanac of Business and Industrial Financial Ratios* is another source of information about industry norms. It provides a broad ratio base, 24 ratios, but its industry coverage is limited. It categorizes firms by asset size, using 12 groupings, and provides the industry average for each grouping.

Value Line/Value Screen. Available both in print and on line, Value Line publications are designed for the investor. Value Line produces summaries for about 1,700 firms and includes each firm's history and recent activity, financial statistics, and projections for the next five years. It also reports beta, a measure of risk, for each firm.

Compustat. Compiled by Standard & Poor's, *Compustat* provides up to 30 years of financial history for each of 11,000 covered firms. The database provides both stock price movements and dividend information. This is truly the analyst's dream source of financial information, provided one can afford and access it.

TOOLS OF FINANCIAL ANALYSIS

As the descriptions of information sources have implied, financial analysts frequently rely heavily on financial ratios. Depending upon the purpose of the analysis, the ratios employed may differ. For instance, to review the firm's performance, managers often concentrate on developing ratios related to operational issues and then comparing them to the firm's past ratios. While an external analyst may proceed similarly, the choice of ratios will certainly differ and the comparison will most likely focus on industry norms. An investor would also be concerned with ratios, especially those relating to resource use, but would want a mixture of both time-series and cross-sectional analysis. Users of financial analysis have their own objectives and their own tools for achieving these objectives.

Common-Size and Common-Base Financial Statements

One of the most difficult aspects of financial analysis is comparing corporations in the same industry that are vastly different in size. How does one know if the millions of dollars in profit earned by AT&T amount to truly exceptional performance as compared to smaller competitors such as MCI? Absolute numbers have little meaning to the user of financial information.

One method by which analysts produce more meaningful comparisons of corporations of different sizes is to generate **common-size financial statements**. This conversion recasts a balance sheet as a series of percentages. Restatement of the balance sheet items in Exhibit 16.1 gives the common-size statement shown in Exhibit 16.2. This statement expresses all of the assets, liabilities, and equity values as percentages of total assets. These balance sheet percentages allow for meaningful comparisons with other common-size corporate balance sheets or with industry norms.

common-size financial statements
Restructured financial statements that report all balance sheet entries as percentages of total assets and all income statement entries as percentages of sales.

Analysts also generate common-size income statements. This process expresses each entry as a percentage of sales. Expressed in this form, the income statement

EXHIBIT 16.1

Hypothetical Balance Sheet

Grinch, Inc.
Balance Sheet as of December 31, 19X1
($000)

Current assets	
Cash	$ 25
Marketable securities	38
Accounts receivable (net)	143
Notes receivable	63
Inventory	275
Total current assets	$544
Fixed assets	
Land	60
Plant and equipment	568
Less accumulated depreciation	329
Net plant and equipment	$239
Total fixed assets	$299
Other assets	88
Total assets	$931
Current liabilities	
Accounts payable	$164
Notes payable	250
Accrued expenses	28
Total current liabilities	$392
Long-term debt	
Secured notes payable	150
Net worth	
Common stock	105
Capital surplus	190
Retained earnings	94
Total liabilities and net worth	$931

explains what the firm did with each dollar of sales. At a glance, one can tell how much of each sales dollar went for taxes, administrative expenses, advertising, and raw materials. Such figures, while useful in themselves, are even more meaningful for inter-industry comparisons. Restating the income statement in Exhibit 16.3 gives the common-size income statement in Exhibit 16.4.

One can also compare common-size financial statements for the same company over different years. Such comparisons can reveal the percentage changes in various entries and, thus, help the analyst track the firm's progress over time. This can highlight deterioration in financial soundness that absolute values might obscure. For example, the dollar amount for cost of goods sold may be declining, while its percentage of sales rises.

EXHIBIT 16.2

Common-Size Balance Sheet

Grinch, Inc.
Balance Sheet as of December 31, 19X1
(Percentage of Total)

Current assets	
Cash	2.7%
Marketable securities	4.1
Accounts receivable (net)	15.4
Notes receivable	6.8
Inventory	29.5
Total current assets	58.4
Fixed assets	
Land	6.4
Net plant and equipment	25.7
Total fixed assets	32.1
Other assets	9.5
Total assets	100.0%
Current liabilities	
Accounts payable	17.6%
Notes payable	26.9
Accrued expenses	3.0
Total current liabilities	42.1
Long-term debt	
Secured notes payable	16.1
Net worth	
Common stock	11.3
Capital surplus	20.4
Retained earnings	10.1
Total liabilities and net worth	100.0%

Analysts can standardize a company's financial statements in another way by converting them to a common base-year. This method identifies a starting point, or base-year, and then compares subsequent years' financial statements to the base-year statements. Such a procedure, which is really a form of trend analysis, permits the user to determine the growth of each line item. One can also compare graphs of the trend patterns of different corporations.

Sometimes an analyst may both common size and common base the data. The common-sizing must be done first in order to eliminate the effects of growth, then the common-base adjustment gives the change in each item as a percentage of its base-year value. For example, suppose that the ABC Corporation's inventory increased from $150, or 3.6 percent of assets, in 19X1 to $175, or 3.7 percent of assets, in 19X2. While the absolute increase in inventory was $25/$150, or 16.7 percent, only 0.001/0.036, or 2.8 percent of this growth reflected on inventory

EXHIBIT 16.3

Hypothetical Income Statement

Grinch, Inc.
Income Statement for 19X1
($000)

Sales	$2,342
Cost of goods sold	
Material	655
Labor	907
Depreciation	50
Total cost of goods sold	$1,612
Gross profit	730
Expenses	
Selling and administrative expenses	563
Earnings before interest and taxes (EBIT)	$ 149
Interest	18
Income taxes	72
Net income	$ 77

EXHIBIT 16.4

Common-Size Income Statement

Grinch, Inc.
Income Statement for 19X1
(Percentage of Sales)

Sales	100.0%
Cost of goods sold	
Material	28.0
Labor	38.7
Depreciation	2.1
Total cost of goods sold	68.8
Gross profit	31.2
Expenses	
Selling and administrative expenses	24.0
Earnings before interest and taxes (EBIT)	6.4
Interest	0.8
Income taxes	3.1
Net income	3.3%

increased relative to assets. The remainder of the increase in inventory can be attributed to asset growth.

Ratio Analysis

A ratio measures the relationship between two variables. In financial analysis, ratios express relationships between items in a corporation's financial statements. Theoretically, a ratio can relate any two items. However, only certain ratios produce meaningful information about the corporation. Precisely which ratios are meaningful depends in part upon who is doing the analysis and for what purpose.

Certain ratios point out changes in financial conditions while others appraise operating performance. The CEO and the portfolio manager may well consider different ratios to be meaningful. The usefulness of any particular ratio is dictated by the specific objectives of the analyst. Consequently, it is not necessary to compile every ratio possible to analyze a corporation; the user merely selects those ratios that contribute to a particular objective.

Two points are worth noting about ratio analysis. First, ratios are not meant to be definitive rules that govern the operations of the firm. Ratios are intended to point out changes in performance or to identify trends, not to brand a corporation. Second, ratios reflect historical patterns and, thus, may not accurately indicate the future financial condition of the corporation.

Analysts generally classify ratios in five groups based on their purposes:

1. Liquidity ratios analyze a firm's ability to meet its short-term obligations.
2. Activity ratios measure how effectively a firm uses its assets to generate sales.
3. Leverage ratios indicate a firm's ability to meet its long-term obligations.
4. Profitability ratios measure how well a firm generates profits from its sales, assets, and equity investment.
5. Market-based ratios use market data to evaluate a firm's performance.

Exhibit 16.5 lists the ratios discussed in the following sections and their classifications. The alphanumeric coding shown in Exhibit 16.5 is referenced in the text discussion. All numerical illustrations of ratios use data derived from Exhibits 16.1 and 16.3, the hypothetical balance sheet and income statement, respectively, for Grinch, Inc.

Management Analysis. To evaluate the ability of management, an analyst will perform a broad-based appraisal of the company. Such an appraisal typically encompasses operations, profitability, and resource use. Therefore, it generally involves many ratios, with a series of ratios reflecting each purpose. For example, profitability review requires ratios that reflect return on assets and return on equity. Analysis of resource management relies on the activity ratios that relate to asset utilization. Knowing this, management seeks to tailor ratio results to demonstrate superior performance.

The gross profit margin ratio (D1) highlights the ability of management to price the product relative to their ability to control production costs. It is defined as:

$$\text{Gross profit margin} = (\text{Sales} - \text{Cost of goods sold})/\text{Sales}$$

This ratio may be influenced by many factors including product pricing, production costs, sales volume, and inventory accounting methods. Consequently, the analyst must conduct additional investigation if it deviates significantly from the industry norm.

EXHIBIT 16.5

Ratios Classified by Purpose and User

	Management	Creditor	Investor
Liquidity ratios			
(A1)		Current ratio	
(A2)		Quick ratio	
Leverage ratios			
(B1)		Interest coverage ratio	
(B2)		Fixed charges coverage ratio	
(B3)		Debt ratio	Debt ratio
(B4)		Debt-equity ratio	
Activity ratios			
(C1)	Inventory turnover		
(C2)	Receivables turnover		
(C3)	Total asset turnover		
Profitability ratios			
(D1)	Gross profit margin		
(D2)	Net profit margin		
(D3)	ROA		
(D4)	ROE		ROE
Market value ratios			
(E1)			P/E ratio
(E2)			P/BV ratio
(E3)			Payout rate
(E4)			Dividend yield
(E5)			Dividend coverage

Note: The ratios listed under each user's column indicate the primary interests of that user. This does not mean that the user does not evaluate the other ratios.

For Grinch, Inc., the gross profit margin equals:

$$(\$2{,}342 - \$1{,}612)/\$2{,}342 = 0.312, \text{ or } 31.2 \text{ percent}$$

If the industry in which Grinch, Inc. competes averages around 25 percent, then Grinch seems quite effective either in controlling costs or in pricing its product. However, since the use of substandard materials can keep cost of goods sold low, the analyst must carefully evaluate whether or not Grinch, Inc. is maintaining the quality of its output. Without an adequate gross profit margin, the firm may find itself unable to finance such essential discretionary expenditures as advertising and research and development.

Many firms consider the only important margin to be the net profit margin (D2). This ratio measures the profitability of the firm's sales after deducting all expenses. From a different perspective, it identifies how much profit the firm generates for every dollar in sales. The net profit margin is defined as:

$$\text{Net profit margin} = \text{Net income/Sales}$$

FOCUS ON FINANCE

How Much Financial Information?

In this age of stakeholder involvement and demands for greater disclosure, financial statement experts have devised the single-step income statement. This statement combines all items of revenue into one entry and all items of expense into a second entry. The expense line is frequently divided into cost of goods sold, selling and other expense, and interest and debt expense. The only other information presented are entries for EBT, tax, and net income. How much analysis is possible with a five-line or, at most, eight-line statement? The income statement of Scana Corporation is fairly typical:

	Twelve Months Ended			
	March 31,	December 31,		
	1993	1992	1991	1990
Income Statement Data				
Operating revenues				
Electric	$ 840.4	$ 829.5	$ 867.2	$ 851.2
Gas	319.0	305.3	276.7	292.4
Transit	3.4	3.6	3.9	4.0
Total operating revenues	$1,162.8	$1,138.4	$1,147.8	$1,147.6
Operating expenses	946.3	928.6	925.4	921.6
Operating income	$ 216.5	$ 209.8	$ 222.4	$ 226.0
Net income	128.6	117.6	135.9	181.6

Competition, capital structure, and operating characteristics cause the net profit margin to vary within and among industries. Supermarkets have a median net profit margin of 0.8 percent, telephone and other communication service firms have a median of 4.7 percent, and pharmaceutical firms have a median of 12.2 percent. Grinch, Inc. has a low net profit margin, only 3.3 percent or $0.03 per $1 of sales.

$$\$77/\$2{,}372 = 0.033, \text{ or } 3.3 \text{ percent}$$

Given Grinch, Inc.'s relatively high gross profit margin, the extremely low net profit margin may indicate excessive selling and administrative expenses.

Sometimes referred to as the *return on investment ratio,* the return on assets (D3) measures the percentage return earned on the total accounting value of the firm:

$$\text{Return on assets (ROA)} = \text{Net income/Total assets}$$

This ratio can be misleading because different financing methods produce different results. Consequently, EBIT values often replace net income in the ROA computation. Using the original form of this ratio, Grinch, Inc. has generated a return of 8.3 percent on its assets:

$$\$77/\$931 = 0.083, \text{ or } 8.3 \text{ percent}$$

For a service corporation, this return would be low; for a heavy manufacturing firm, an ROA of 8 percent would be reasonable. Some analysts prefer to use an average total asset value, (1980 assets – 1981 assets)/2, since the ratio is intended to measure performance over a period of time and the average asset value better reflects the value of assets on which the firm earned the return.

The primary concern of shareholders, the return on equity ratio (D4) is also important to management. Any substantive change in this value will tend to generate immediate investor response as it is the most frequently cited measure of performance of the firm. It is defined as:

Return on equity (ROE) = Net income/Equity

This ratio is affected by debt financing and tax considerations, as well as the current stage of the business cycle. Consequently, it should be judged relative to economic conditions and the degree of financial leverage a firm employes.

General building contractors, for example, may have negative ROEs during economic contractions and then rebound to average 12 percent or more during normal times. The best performers among the tobacco product firms consistently have ROEs in excess of 50 percent, as do amusement and recreation enterprises.

Although one could find many possible explanations, the almost 20 percent return for Grinch, Inc., while it could be considered good, may well indicate insufficient use of financial leverage in a period of prosperity:

$77/$389 = 0.198, or 19.8 percent

The inventory turnover ratio (C1) is intended to measure the volume of inventory a firm maintains relative to the volume of sales. It is defined as:

Inventory turnover = Cost of goods sold/Average inventory

If the ratio is a value in line with industry norms, then the analysis is complete. However, if it is out of line in either direction, then the deviation must be explained; it could be either good or bad. A low value indicates a large inventory, which may well be desirable if the firm faces high **stockout costs** (the profit foregone due to lost sales and customers if the firm is unable to fill orders on time) relative to its inventory carrying costs. However, a low inventory turnover value more often indicates an excessive stock of often obsolete merchandise.

stockout costs
Profits foregone due to lost sales and customers when the firm is unable to fill orders out of inventory.

On the other hand, an unusually high inventory turnover ratio might well indicate inadequate inventory, perhaps constantly forcing customers onto backorder, generating poor customer relations. The trend toward just-in-time inventory processing, however, has led many firms to deliberately keep their inventories minimal. Thus, it may well be that only the most recent historical norms support relevant comparisons.

The inventory turnover ratio requires the analyst to compute the average inventory for the year. Normally this means adding the beginning and ending inventory values and dividing by 2, but if the firm experiences a seasonal product demand, then this method may well be inadequate and end-of-month averaging may be best. Moreover, if the analyst has only the current year's financial statements, then the lack of data may further distort the figure. In this case a sales-to-inventory ratio may measure inventory turnover more effectively. This measure presents a good picture of single-company trends, but it depends heavily on the firm's markup methodology.

Stretching a point, and using only the available ending inventory data, Grinch, Inc. has an inventory turnover of:

$$\$1{,}612/\$275 = 5.9 \text{ times}$$

Dividing the inventory turnover into 365 shows how long the average dollar remains in inventory. For Grinch, Inc. this is approximately 62 days:

$$365 \text{ days}/5.9 = 61.9 \text{ days}$$

Assuming that the firm's sales would continue at the current average rate, it could meet all demand out of inventory for 62 days before depleting stocks. Having determined the inventory turnover period, the firm must now decide just how profitable it is to tie up funds for 62 days.

The industry norm for heating and air conditioning manufacturers ranges from less than 30 days for the better performers to over 105 days for the weaker firms. Manufacturers of motor vehicle parts fare little better, averaging 44 and 101 days, respectively. The fast food industry, in contrast, has an industry norm between 7 and 14 days.

The relationship of accounts receivable to sales is referred to as the receivables turnover ratio (C2). Analysts frequently divide the ratio into 365 to determine the number of days an average receivable remains outstanding, the firm's average collection period. The average collection period can then be compared with the firm's **terms of trade credit** (the credit terms it offers to its customers).

terms of trade credit
The credit terms offered by a firm to its customers, including the period that it allows before payment on credit sales, the amount of any cash discount, and any other conditions.

Several factors can increase a firm's collection period:

1. An increase in the proportion of credit sales to cash sales
2. A lax collection policy
3. A more liberal credit granting policy
4. Longer terms of trade credit

An average collection period significantly longer than the firm's terms of trade indicates a need for the firm to reexamine its credit policy. An average collection period shorter than what is customary in the industry could mean the loss of customers because of a too restrictive credit policy. Management must set a policy based on relative costs, balancing the potential loss of customers against the cost of offering credit.

The receivables turnover ratio is defined as:

$$\text{Receivables turnover} = \text{Sales}/\text{Accounts receivable}$$

The ratio's illustrative power would be much improved by limiting the numerator to credit sales. While this figure is available to management, it is seldom published.

The better performers in the cable and other pay television industry have receivables turnover ratios around 68, with average payment periods less than five

FOCUS ON CAREERS

FINANCIAL ANALYST

Financial analysts select, evaluate, and interpret financial, economic, and other relevant data as part of an investment or financial decision-making process. They conduct ratio and statistical analyses of available data in an attempt to identify trends and project future prospects.

Financial analysts are employed by banks, insurance companies, and brokerage and investment houses. Some, especially those employed by brokerage houses, are responsible for analyzing individual industries and recommending investment opportunities. Others, primarily those employed by banks, analyze several industries and evaluate only those firms that apply for bank credit. Their role thus involves evaluation of the stability of the industry, as well as the liquidity of the borrower.

An entry-level position requires a bachelor's degree with a strong concentration in finance or economics. Engineers, with their strong mathematical backgrounds, are actively pursued by brokerage firms. Advancement comes fairly quickly, leading to the title of senior financial analyst after seven to ten years. Entry-level salary is normally around $30,000 per year, and a senior analyst earns $75,000 to $100,000. Managers of financial analysis units generally earn $150,000.

Accreditation and recognition of achievement is offered to those who qualify as Chartered Financial Analysts (CFA). This distinction requires the successful completion of three levels of examinations encompassing some 350 hours of study and a total of 18 hours of testing over three years, employer sponsorship, and a minimum of three years of experience in investment decision making.

days. In the wholesale photographic industry, the normal turnover ratio is around 12, with an average pay period of 31 days. For Grinch, Inc. the ratio is 16.4 and the average collection period is approximately 22 days:

$$\$2{,}342/\$143 = 16.4 \text{ times}$$

$$365 \text{ days}/16.4 = 22.3 \text{ days}$$

The sum of the firm's average collection period and its days-in-inventory constitutes its **cash cycle**. This is the number of days it takes to turn a dollar of inventory into a dollar of available cash.

cash cycle
The sum of the firm's average collection period and days-in-inventory. This gives the number of days it takes to turn a dollar of inventory into a dollar of available cash.

Analysts often measure how effectively management is using all available assets to generate sales based on the total asset turnover (C3) ratio. It is defined as:

$$\text{Total asset turnover} = \text{Sales/Total assets}$$

This ratio specifies how many dollars of sales (revenue) the firm generates for every dollar of assets. Grinch, Inc. generates $2.52 in sales for every dollar of assets:

$$\$2{,}342/\$931 = 2.52$$

Again, any evaluation of this number depends on the firm's industry and the firm's stage in its life cycle. A start-up, high-tech firm may well consider $2.52 in sales per dollar on assets to be low.

Creditor Analysis. Short-term creditors look primarily for adequate cash, or the ability to obtain cash to pay creditors. Consequently, they concentrate on the firm's cash flow and factors that affect cash flow. Two ratios, the current ratio and the quick ratio, are commonly used to measure a firm's liquidity. Each of these ratios concentrates on the availability of selected near-cash assets to meet the impending obligations facing the firm.

The broadest of the two liquidity measures, the current ratio (A1) is defined as:

Current ratio = Current assets/Current liabilities

Current assets include cash, marketable securities, and all other assets that can technically be turned into cash within a 12-month period. This list covers inventory, accounts receivable, notes receivable, and prepaid expenses. Current liabilities are defined as cash outlays the firm must make within the next 12 months. Thus, current liabilities include accounts payable, notes payable, the current portion of long-term debt, and any accrued wages and taxes.

The current ratio for Grinch, Inc. is:

$544/$392 = 1.39 times

This number can be interpreted to mean that for every $1.00 of current liabilities the firm has $1.39 in current assets. Put differently, the firm must be able to convert 72 cents of every asset dollar into cash to meet its current obligations. However, a company would do so only under duress.

While industry norms differ significantly depending on the nature of the enterprise, most industries tend to cover current liabilities 2.0 or more times. In children's apparel manufacturing, for example, the better performers generally attain current ratios of 2.3 or better. In the funeral service and crematories industry the industry median is 2.0, while the better performers operate with current ratios exceeding 3.5. Restaurants and fast food retailers, however, seldom operate with current ratios in excess of 1.1; the weaker performers' ratios do not exceed 0.3.

The quick ratio (A2) provides a more conservative test of liquidity. This ratio is intended to identify only those assets that the firm can quickly convert into cash and relate them to current liabilities. This ratio, sometimes termed the *acid test*, is defined as:

Quick ratio = (Cash + Cash equivalents + Accounts and notes receivable)/Current liabilities

More commonly, it is calculated as:

Quick ratio = (Current assets – Inventory)/Current liabilities

For Grinch, Inc. this ratio works out to 0.7:

($25 + $38 + $143 + $63)/$392 = 0.69 times

The quick ratio differs from the current ratio primarily in its omission of inventory. Inventory may not be a very liquid asset, especially in times of distress. The same, however, could be said for at least a portion of the accounts receivable, especially those that are many days past due; this undermines the effectiveness of the quick ratio. Notes receivable that arise at the time of original sale are generally considered more negotiable than accounts receivable and, thus, qualify for inclusion in the quick ratio. Prepaid expenses are usually insignificant in relation to other current assets.

In industries with fairly regular and guaranteed income streams, such as public utilities, quick ratios below 1.0 are acceptable. Most other industries should feature quick ratios of at least 1.0. Again, Grinch, Inc. comes up short.

A low value may indicate that the firm holds too much of its assets in the form of inventory, especially if the current ratio compares favorably to industry norms. However, this practice may not be a problem if the inventory is generic in nature and has a ready market. The combination of a low current ratio and a low quick ratio may well give cause for alarm. This would require more detailed analysis of the current assets.

A high value for the quick ratio may point out the opposite problem—insufficient inventory and a risk of stockouts. This seldom concerns creditors, although it should concern management.

Long-term creditors have two concerns—the firm's ability to make current debt service payments, and their exposure to default risk. The current year's debt service payments, either to repay part of the principal, to meet mandatory sinking fund payments, or simply to pay interest as promised, are included as part of the firm's current liabilities. Consequently, long-term creditors need to examine the current ratio and the quick ratio.

However, several additional ratios are specially designed to highlight the interests of long-term creditors. These include the interest coverage ratio, the fixed-charge coverage ratio, the debt ratio, and the debt-to-equity ratio, among others. Such specialized, long-term creditor ratios are generally termed *financial leverage ratios* and *coverage ratios*.

Instead of relying on end-of-period balance sheet entries to judge the firm's ability to meet its debt obligations, the interest coverage ratio (B1) employs current earnings data from the income statement. It is defined as:

$$\text{Interest coverage} = \text{EBIT/Interest charges}$$

The ratio, sometimes called the *times interest earned ratio*, identifies the number of times the firm's current earnings cover its interest obligations. This ratio also serves as an indicator of a firm's capacity to take on additional debt.

For Grinch, Inc., this ratio indicates that EBIT covers interest charges more than 8.0 times:

$$\$149/\$18 = 8.28 \text{ times}$$

Bondholders for firms in most medium-risk industries would generally consider this to be good. In the industrial chemical manufacturing industry, for example, the better performers have interest coverage ratios in excess of 7.0, while the industry median approximates 3.5. However, one must analyze whether these numbers result from current economic conditions or represent normal industry relationships.

To make this judgment, one must look at this ratio over a number of years. In general, a ratio below 2.0 indicates an impending crisis. Such low values may be unavoidable during a severe recession, however, even for the best of firms.

For a firm with large fixed charges such as lease payments, sinking fund payments, and preferred dividend payments, the interest coverage ratio fails to fully gauge ability to pay. Consequently, one needs a broader ratio to evaluate a firm with such a wide assortment of fixed charges. The fixed-charge coverage ratio (B2) does this:

Fixed-charge coverage = (EBIT + Lease payments)/(Interest + Lease payments + Preferred stock dividends + Sinking fund payments)

Since neither preferred dividends nor sinking fund payments are tax deductible, these items must be adjusted to reflect their before-tax values. This adjustment is achieved by dividing the after-tax payments by $(1 - T)$, where T is the tax rate. For Grinch, Inc. this ratio is not relevant since the firm has a fairly simple capital structure.

To measure the percentage of a firm's assets that it finances with borrowed money analysts refer to the debt ratio (B3), also called the *debt-to-assets ratio*. This ratio is expressed as:

Debt ratio = Total debt/Total assets

Grinch, Inc. has a debt ratio in excess of 58 percent:

$542/$931 = 0.582, or 58.2 percent

Grinch, Inc. is using borrowed money to fund nearly 60 percent of its enterprise. While this may seem high, remember that during the 1980s, corporations commonly borrowed up to 80 percent of their asset values.

Additionally, the nature of the industry influences this ratio; public utilities can assume heavy leverage without undue risk because of their steady income flows, while manufacturing firms need to exercise caution. Whether or not a firm's debt ratio is excessive depends on the projections for growth and stability of future earnings and cash flows. A firm with a high debt ratio must exercise greater care during periods of economic contraction because its debt service will not contract along with its earnings. A high debt ratio may prevent a firm from borrowing more in the market.

A low debt ratio can indicate a problem, as well. A conservative firm, one that uses little debt financing, may well forego opportunities to grow because of its reluctance to increase its debt ratio. Such firms often become prime takeover targets.

In order to isolate the relationship between creditors and shareholders, some analysts use the debt–equity ratio (B4). Defined as:

Debt–equity = Total debt/Total equity

This ratio gives a more direct comparison than the debt ratio of how much funding comes from debt and how much from equity. Simply stated, this ratio measures the degree of protection that the firm's owners offer to the creditors. A higher ratio suggests that creditors assume more risk. A lower ratio indicates more flexibility to borrow in the future.

Calculating the debt–equity ratio for Grinch, Inc., results in a value of 139 percent:

$542/$389 = 1.39, or 139 percent

This means that for every $1.00 supplied by the shareholders, creditors supplied $1.39. Since a good norm for the debt–equity ratio is 100 percent, Grinch, Inc. may have overextended its borrowing capacity. While this would be considered imprudent by today's norms, it was certainly not excessive for the 1980s.

Often, analysts present the debt–equity ratio in a slightly different form. Rather than total debt, the numerator includes only long-term debt. In this form, the equation highlights the relationship between long-term providers of funds. Similarly, the ratio can be converted into a total capitalization ratio by dividing the long-term debt by the total of long-term debt plus equity.

Investor Analysis. In addition to a keen appreciation for the firm's profitability ratios, especially the return on equity (ROE), investors tend to focus primarily on market-based ratios. Consequently, while investor analysis may include a review of economic and industry conditions, along with analysis of the performance of management and the profitability of the enterprise, investors also display keen interest in factors that directly affect them. They pay particular attention to the price–earnings ratio and the market to book value ratio. Investors are also concerned about the disposition of earnings, so they are interested in dividend payout rates, dividend yields, and dividend coverage ratios.

One method of gauging investor confidence in the future prospects of a corporation is to examine the firm's price–earnings (P/E) ratio (E1). If investors see good potential for growth and reasonable risks, then this ratio should be high. It is defined as:

P/E = Market price per share/Current earnings per share

Generally a value in excess of 30 characterizes a speculative stock. However, a value under 5 or 6 may indicate that the market believes that the firm faces too much risk or has little future growth potential. The P/E ratio does fluctuate with the market cycle, rising during bull markets, and falling during bear markets, so the analyst must evaluate it carefully to isolate the effect of the company's individual fortunes.

While book value is meaningless except to the accountant, many investors still use it to evaluate the merits of investing in a firm. Dividing total common stockholders' equity by the number of shares of common stock outstanding (usually on a fully diluted basis) gives book value per share. The market to book value (P/BV) ratio (E2) is the current market price divided by the book value per share:

P/BV = Market price per share/Book value per share

A value below 1 is generally considered bad. It means that investors are unwilling to buy the stock at a price equal to what the company appears to be worth on paper. The firm may well be dying.

The dividend ratio or payout rate (E3) indicates the percentage of its earnings that a firm distributes to shareholders. This percentage may fluctuate from year to year as management attempts to keep the dollar dividends per share constant. However, this ratio can foretell management's reinvestment intentions because mature, stable corporations tend to have high payout rates, while high-growth corporations tend to keep their ratios relatively low or zero. The ratio is expressed as:

$$\text{Payout ratio} = \text{Cash dividends per share/Net income per share}$$

The annualized amount of dividends paid by the corporation, expressed as a percentage of the market price of the firm's stock, is the dividend yield (E4). Since some investors are interested in generating income (quarterly dollar payments) rather than capital gains (stock price appreciation), the dividend yield is important. It is defined as:

$$\text{Dividend yield} = \text{Annual dividend per share/Market price}$$

Like bondholders, stock investors are interested in how well the firm's cash flows cover their returns. They tend to use the dividend coverage ratio (E5) for this purpose. It is defined as:

$$\text{Dividend coverage} = (\text{Net income} + \text{Depreciation})/\text{Expected dividend}$$

While the board of directors must declare any dividend, a higher dividend coverage ratio increases the chance that they will do so. If the dividend coverage ratio remains stable, shareholders can reasonably expect that their current dividend payout will continue to be declared and paid.

DuPont Identity

While financial analysts generally calculate ratios to analyze specific relationships between two independent variables, some financial ratios can be viewed as composites. One such example involves the return on equity (ROE) ratio. As stated earlier in this chapter, this ratio expresses the relationship between net income and total equity in order to evaluate the return that the firm earns per dollar of shareholder equity. However, ROE can also be viewed as a composite of three ratios: an operating efficiency ratio, an asset efficiency ratio, and a financial leverage ratio.

The combination of an operating efficiency ratio and an asset efficiency ratio is equivalent to ROA (net income/assets) as discussed previously. Thus, ROE can also be considered a composite of the ROA and a financial leverage ratio. Specifically, ROE may be expressed as:

$$ROE = \frac{\text{Net income}}{\text{Sales}} \times \frac{\text{Sales}}{\text{Assets}} \times \frac{\text{Assets}}{\text{Equity}}$$

$$= (\text{Net profit margin})(\text{Total asset turnover})(\text{Equity multiplier})$$

When presented in this form, it is called the *DuPont identity*.

The purpose of the DuPont identity is to highlight the cause of any weakness in ROE. It does this by focusing attention on the ratio's components. Thus, the net profit margin component highlights corporate profitability; total asset turnover reports on asset utilization; equity to total assets [1/(1 – Debt ratio)] characterizes the capital structure. Having identified any area of weakness, the analyst can then conduct a more specific analysis to identify and isolate the problem.

For Grinch, Inc. the DuPont identity is:

$$
\begin{aligned}
ROE &= (\$77/\$2{,}342)\ (\$2{,}342/\$931)\ (\$931/\$389)\\
&= (0.033)\ (2.52)\ (2.39)\\
&= 0.198, \text{ or } 19.8 \text{ percent}
\end{aligned}
$$

An evaluation of these DuPont identity components for Grinch, Inc. reveals profitability and capital structure concerns, which the analyst needs to address by more specific ratio analysis.

Time Series versus Cross-Sectional Analysis

Having decided which ratios to calculate, the analyst proceeds to evaluate them. Each ratio must be compared with some standard in order to draw conclusions. The standard of comparison may be either the past performance of the firm in question or, as explained previously, an industry norm.

If the standard of comparison is the past performance of the same firm, then the process is termed *time series analysis*. By comparing the firm's performance on each of the selected ratios over a period of time, the analyst can identify changes in the ratios that indicate areas of weakness or improvement. It may or may not be possible to gather enough information to identify the cause of a specific change.

Cross-sectional analysis compares a firm's ratios to industry norms, or to the ratios of a selected peer group. The analyst wants to identify how well an individual firm has performed relative to other firms in the selected group. Most analysts find their industry norms in sources produced by services such as Robert Morris Associates or Dun & Bradstreet, which specialize in this work.

Cross-sectional analysis may encounter difficulty in placing a firm into an industry classification for comparison. To whom does the analyst compare a highly diversified firm? Since the norms differ by industry, the evaluation of the firm may well be prejudiced by its industry classification. To avoid this problem, an analyst may create a peer group composed of five leading competitors for whom public information is available, or of five firms that sell product mixes similar to that of the firm in question. The analyst then calculates group averages for the appropriate ratios and compares them with the firm's ratios.

Financial Analysis Problems

The greatest difficulty with financial analysis relates to the quality of the data. While most U.S. corporations prepare their financial statements according to GAAP (generally accepted accounting principles), they have wide latitude when accounting for depreciation, inventory values, pension fund contributions, long-term leases, retiree medical benefits, and numerous other items. Differences in accounting methods limit the usefulness of cross-sectional comparisons.

Industry norms generally reflect mean values based upon the top 20 or so firms in an industry classification. The analyst may find little information for firms that do not fall in this upper echelon. Furthermore, no available information indicates just how closely the norm represents the sample of firms. Dispersion information is just not available.

Industry norms also suffer from the disadvantage that they are, by definition, historical averages. Even though the publishers of the norms keep their data as current as possible, changing economic conditions limit their value. Industry averages developed during a recession are not relevant once a recovery begins. Analysts may develop their own norms constructed during similar economic circumstances, but these norms still reflect results for a past period and may not be relevant when evaluating the current or future performance of the firm.

Just because a firm's ratio differs from an industry norm, analysts should not conclude that the firm is having a problem. The difference merely indicates an area that requires further study. Additionally, just because a firm compares favorably with the industry doesn't guarantee that the firm is doing well. Industrywide circumstances, such as technological changes, are likely to affect all firms in an industry, but to different degrees.

FOREIGN FINANCIAL STATEMENT ANALYSIS

International Financial Standards, published by the International Accounting Standards Committee, are accepted in many countries, and they have resulted in disclosure of the accounting principles on which firms prepare their financial statements. Even so, these standards have not resulted in a uniform set of accounting principles.

Consequently, investors in foreign securities and lenders to foreign companies must complete their analysis under the severe handicap of nonuniform standards for the preparation of financial statements, disclosure requirements, and auditing practices across countries. Even when they do understand foreign financial accounting practices, analysts can easily misinterpret financial ratios because of differences in underlying economic, social, and political environments.

Differences in countries' approaches to accounting explain why they follow different accounting systems. Some countries, like Sweden, follow a macroeconomic approach that assumes that the accounting system functions primarily to facilitate government administration of the economy. Another group of countries, represented by the Netherlands, follows a microeconomic approach that focuses on the firm and the preservation of its real assets.

A third group of countries, including the United States, Canada, and the United Kingdom, follow an independent approach. These countries believe that business is an art and involves the independent judgments of its practitioners. The accounting system, therefore, evolves from existing business practices and experience. A fourth group of countries use a uniform accounting system characterized by a set of identical accounting concepts and classifications for all firms to follow. Countries that use this system in various forms include France, Germany, and Argentina.

Past studies of international accounting practices have revealed several areas where differences in the treatment of accounting variables are quite common. Consider two examples: the treatment of goodwill and deferred taxes. In some countries, goodwill is fully amortized; in others, it is not amortized at all. Similar discrepancies are observed with regard to the treatment of deferred taxes. Some countries, such as Italy and Belgium, account for deferred taxes; others do not.

Financial statement disclosure standards also vary. An income statement may start with gross profit without disclosing sales or cost of goods sold. A balance sheet may not disclose how the accountant has valued assets or determined depreciation expenses.

Auditing functions and procedures also vary widely across countries. For example, in Europe, auditing normally does not require counting physical inventory or confirmation of accounts receivable. Some countries commonly permit sampling and statistical methods to verify accounts. In Latin American countries, auditors do not have access to canceled checks to verify disbursements as these checks become the property of the banks.

U.S. analysts generally restate foreign financial statements to conform to GAAP before analyzing, interpreting, or comparing financial ratios. This may resolve the difficulties created by different accounting standards, but it does not always result in an accurate interpretation of financial ratios. The problem arises because of differences in the economic, social, and political environments within which foreign firms operate. Suppose for instance, that a Japanese firm has a debt ratio of 80 percent compared to a 50 percent ratio for a U.S. firm. Other factors being equal, it would be inaccurate to characterize the Japanese firm as being more risky because Japanese enterprises are protected through a system of high-level interdependence between borrowers and their creditor banks. Japanese banks do not consider themselves outsiders; consequently, they are more willing to accommodate troubled businesses than to enforce collection. Moreover, because of a traditional system of issuing new shares, it costs substantially more to raise equity capital in Japan. Thus, Japanese corporations favor debt financing and their debt ratios often seem high by U.S. standards.

SUMMARY

Financial analysis, or the application of analytical tools and techniques to the financial statements of a firm, is generally carried out by management, creditors, investors, and independent analysts. While each group may have different objectives, their underlying methods are similar. First, they must obtain the clearest and most detailed financial information available on the firm, the industry, and the economy. Next, they may need to restate this information in usable form. This may mean creating common-size and common-base financial statements, constructing ratios, and developing time series and cross-sectional statistics. Once this is completed, the analysis can proceed.

The financial analyst generally evaluates ratios relative to industry norms and compares trends in both the ratios and the common-size, common-base statements. This analysis must keep in mind problems inherent in the process. Even perfect analysis would refer only to the past performance of the firm.

A common-size balance sheet relates all line items to total assets, and a common-size income statement relates all entries to net sales. This process permits the analyst to compare firms of unequal size. Common-base financial statements require systematic recalculation of every income statement and balance sheet entry as a percentage of its value in a given base year. Common-base statements permit the analyst to identify the percentage of growth from the base year by line item.

Financial ratios can be classified as liquidity, activity, leverage, profitability, or market-based ratios. Each group is intended to measure a specific attribute of the corporation. Specific users concentrate their analysis on a particular class of ratios. For example, the activity or turnover ratios are designed to measure how effectively a firm uses its assets to generate sales. This information interests management and those who wish to evaluate the effectiveness of management. Liquidity and leverage ratios are most important to short-term and long-term creditors, respectively. Investors are primarily interested in the market value ratios and the profitability ratios.

Because GAAP leaves accountants substantial discretion in developing financial statements, cross-sectional comparisons are sometimes difficult. Furthermore, industry norms are not always suitable reference points since they are generally based upon, or heavily weighted in favor of, the largest firms in an industry. Furthermore, some firms, because of their diversity of products, are difficult to classify and, thus, generally end up being compared to dissimilar firms. Finally, the analyst must allow for the individual idiosyncrasies of specific firms when referencing industry norms.

Analyzing foreign financial statements raises several new issues. Financial statements and accounting principles show little uniformity among nations. Furthermore, differences in economic, social, and political environments complicate attempts to interpret the results of financial analysis.

Summary of Ratios

(A1) Current ratio = Current assets/Current liabilities

(A2) Quick ratio = (Current assets − Inventory)/Current liabilities

(B1) Interest coverage = EBIT/Interest charges

(B2) Fixed-charge coverage = (EBIT + Lease payments)/(Interest + Lease payments + Preferred stock dividends + Sinking fund payments)

(B3) Debt ratio = Total debt/Total assets

(B4) Debt–equity = Total debt/Total equity

(C1) Inventory turnover = Cost of goods sold/Average inventory

Days-in-inventory = 365/Inventory turnover

(C2) Receivables turnover = Sales/Accounts receivable

Average collection period = 365/Receivables turnover

(C3) Total asset turnover = Sales/Total assets

(D1) Gross profit margin = (Sales - Cost of goods sold)/Sales

(D2) Net profit margin = Net income/Sales

(D3) Return on assets (ROA) = Net income/Total assets

(D4) Return on equity (ROE) = Net income/Equity

(E1) Price–earnings (P/E) ratio = Market price per share/Current earnings per share

(E2) Market to book value (P/BV) ratio = Market price per share/Book value per share

(E3) Payout ratio = Cash dividends per share/Net income per share

(E4) Dividend yield = Annual dividend per share/Market price

(E5) Dividend coverage = (Net income + Depreciation)/Expected dividend

Key Terms

annual report
cash cycle
common-size financial statements
inside information
stockout costs
terms of trade credit

Self-Study Questions

1. What is the purpose of financial analysis?
2. Who does the SEC identify as an insider?
3. What company-published sources of information are available to the public?
4. Explain what is meant by common-size financial statements.
5. Classify financial ratios according to their purposes.
6. Identify two liquidity ratios and explain what they are intended to measure.
7. What is the purpose of employing leverage ratios?
8. Where does one obtain data to calculate the market-based ratios?
9. Why is ROE significant to stockholders?
10. What is the purpose of employing the DuPont identity?

EXHIBIT 16.6

Airun Company
Balance Sheet, December 31, 19XX
($ millions)

Current assets		
Cash		$ 500
Marketable securities		2,000
Notes and accounts receivable		2,000
Inventories		1,000
Total current assets		$ 5,500
Fixed assets		
Land		5,000
Plant and Equipment	19,975	
Less accumulated depreciation	475	
Plant and Equipment (net)		19,500
Total fixed assets		$24,500
Other assets		
Prepaid expenses		1,000
Total assets		$31,000
Current liabilities		
Accounts payable		$ 9,000
Notes payable		2,000
Accrued expenses		3,000
Total current liabilities		$14,000
Long-term liabilities		
Secured notes payable		1,000
Net worth		16,000
Total liabilities and net worth		$31,000

Airun Company
Income Statement, December 31, 19XX
($ millions)

Net sales	$48,365
Cost of goods sold	
Depreciation	200
Labor	10,000
Material	15,000
Overhead	5,000
Total cost of goods sold	$30,200
Gross profit	18,165
Selling and administrative expense	8,000
Operating income (EBIT)	$10,165
Interest on debt	100
Income before taxes	$10,065
Income taxes	6,421
Net income	$ 3,644

Self-Test Problems

These problems are based on the financial statement in Exhibit 16.6.

1. Calculate the current ratio and the quick ratio for Airun.
2. What is the inventory turnover ratio for Airun?
3. What is the firm's cash cycle?
4. Calculate ROA for Airun.
5. Calculate ROE for Airun.
6. Determine Airun's debt ratio.
7. Calculate the firm's net profit margin.
8. Construct a common-size balance sheet.
9. Construct a common-size income statement.
10. Assume that Airun has 16 million shares outstanding, and that the stock is selling for $1.75 per share. What is the firm's P/E ratio?

Discussion Questions

1. Numerous stakeholders have an interest in the financial health of a specific business. Who are the stakeholders and what are their concerns?
2. Why is the general level of economic activity an important consideration in any financial analysis?
3. Why would managers be interested in performing financial analysis on their own firms?
4. Why is the information available to management superior to that available to the analyst?
5. What is inside information?
6. Why is the SEC concerned about the dissemination of inside information?
7. What is the relationship between a firm's annual report and its 10-K report?
8. How does the analyst construct common-size financial statements?
9. Why would an analyst want to develop common-base financial statements?
10. If an analyst were to contruct both common-size and common-base financial statements, what would the end products highlight?
11. Why do different groups of stakeholders focus on certain ratios over others?
12. Why would a corporation want to compare its average collection period with its terms of trade credit?
13. Why would an analyst want to calculate more than one turnover ratio to examine a corporation?
14. How do the interests of short-term and long-term creditors differ when they analyze a firm's financial statements?
15. What is the significance of the P/E ratio for the investor?
16. Should the DuPont identity be considered the ultimate ratio, capable of identifying the financial condition of the corporation by itself? Why or why not?
17. Why would an analyst employ time series analysis to examine the financial condition of a firm?
18. What is the difference between cross-sectional analysis and time series analysis?

EXHIBIT 16.7

Frosty and Co.
Balance Sheet as of December 31, 19X1
($000)

Current assets	
Cash and marketable securities	$ 2,520
Accounts receivable	32,340
Inventory	34,860
Total current assets	$ 69,720
Fixed assets	
Net plant and equipment	45,360
Total assets	$115,080
Current liabilities	
Accounts payable	$ 10,710
Notes payable	16,170
Accrued expenses	7,560
Total current liabilities	34,440
Total long-term debt	12,810
Net worth	
Common stock	$ 25,200
Retained earnings	42,630
Total net worth	$ 67,830
Total liabilities and net worth	$115,080

Frosty and Co.
Income Statement for 19X1
($000)

Sales	$171,780
Cost of goods sold	114,240
Selling and administrative costs	35,700
Earnings before interest and taxes (EBIT)	$ 21,840
Interest on debt	13,020
Earnings before taxes (EBT)	$ 8,820
Taxes	3,570
Net income	$ 5,250
Net income per common share	$ 20.83

19. What are some of the problems associated with financial analysis?
20. Since comparison to industry norms requires the classification of a firm in a particular industry, what options does the analyst have when dealing with a diversified manufacturing firm?

Problems

These problems are based on the financial statements of Frosty and Co. in Exhibit 16.7.

1. Calculate two liquidity ratios for the firm.
2. Calculate the inventory turnover and receivables turnover ratios for the firm.
3. What is the firm's cash cycle?
4. Calculate two leverage ratios for the firm.
5. Calculate the ROA and ROE for the firm.
6. What is the difference between the firm's gross and net profit margins?
7. Construct a common-size balance sheet for Frosty and Co.
8. Construct a common-size income statement for Frosty and Co.
9. Assuming a market price of $43.25 per share, what is the firm's P/E ratio?
10. How many shares of Frosty and Co. common stock are outstanding?

Topics for Further Research

1. Pick a Fortune 500 company, obtain its annual report, and construct key financial ratios. Compare the ratios with the appropriate industry norms.
2. Obtain the financial statements for two publicly held corporations of different sizes, but within the same industry. Convert the income statements and balance sheets into common-size statements and comment upon any obvious differences.
3. Using the most recent edition of Moody's *Industrial Manual*, select a corporation for which five or more years of financial data are given. Using the earliest year, develop common-base values for the remaining years. Identify any significant trends.

Answers to Self-Test Problems

1.

$$\text{Current ratio} = \$5{,}500/\$14{,}000$$
$$= 0.39$$
$$\text{Quick ratio} = (\$5{,}500 - \$1{,}000)/\$14{,}000$$
$$= 0.32$$

2.

$$\text{Inventory turnover ratio} = \$48{,}365/\$1{,}000$$
$$= 48.37$$

3.

$$\text{Receivables turnover ratio} = \$48{,}365/\$2{,}000$$
$$= 24.18$$
$$\text{Average collection period} = 365/24.18$$
$$= 15.09$$
$$\text{Days in inventory} = 365/48.37$$
$$= 7.55$$
$$\text{Cash cycle} = \text{Average collection period} + \text{Days in inventory}$$
$$= 15.09 + 7.55$$
$$= 22.64$$

4. $$ROA = \$3{,}644/\$31{,}000 = 0.18$$

5. $$ROE = \$3{,}644/\$16{,}000 = 0.23$$

6. $$\text{Debt ratio} = \$15{,}000/\$31{,}000 = 0.48$$

7. $$\text{Net profit margin} = \$3{,}644/\$46{,}365 = 0.075$$

8. See the top part of Exhibit 16.8.

EXHIBIT 16.8

Airun Company
Common-Size Balance Sheet, December 31, 19XX
(Percentage of Total)

Current assets		
Cash		1.61%
Marketable securities		6.45
Notes and accounts receivable		6.45
Inventories		3.23
Total current assets		17.74%
Fixed assets		
Land		16.13%
Plant and equipment	64.44%	
Less Accumulated Depreciation	1.53	
Plant and equipment (net)		62.90
Total Fixed Assets		79.03%
Other assets		
Prepaid expenses		3.23
Total assets		100.00%
Current liabilities		
Accounts payable		29.03%
Notes payable		6.45
Accrued expenses		9.68%
Total current liabilities		45.16%
Long-term liabilities		
Secured notes payable		3.23
Net worth		51.61
Total liabilities and net worth		100.00%

9. See the bottom part of Exhibit 16.8.

10. $$\text{Earnings per share} = \$3{,}644{,}000/16{,}000{,}000 = \$0.22775$$

$$P/E = \$1.75/\$0.22775 = 7.68$$

EXHIBIT 16.8 *continued*

Airun Company
Common-Size Income Statement, December 31, 19XX
(Percentage of Net Sales)

Net sales	100.00%
Cost of goods sold	
Depreciation	0.4
Labor	20.7
Material	31.0
Overhead	10.3
Total cost of goods sold	62.4%
Gross profit	37.6%
Selling and administrative expense	16.5
Operating income	21.0%
Interest on debt	0.2
Income before taxes	20.8%
Income taxes	13.3
Net income	7.5%

CHAPTER

17

Strategic Interventions in the Corporate Life Cycle

LEARNING OBJECTIVES

This chapter examines mergers, acquisitions, divestitures, reorganizations, and bankruptcies. At the end of this chapter, the reader should be able to:

1. *Explain the difference between a merger and an acquisition*
2. *Describe various ways to prevent undesirable takeovers*
3. *Identify some of the reasons why mergers and acquisitions take place*
4. *Calculate the exchange ratios between companies' stocks in complete and partial acquisitions*
5. *Explain the three steps in formulating a reorganization plan*
6. *Determine the sequence in which claims against a bankrupt company will be satisfied*

The life cycle of a successful corporation is perceived as following a predictable pattern. After conquering its start-up problems, a company grows rapidly. As it thrives, competitors proliferate and saturate the market. The company's growth rate slows down and eventually ceases completely. Unless management finds ways to encourage growth through innovation, the company declines and ultimately dies.

The histories of many major corporations illustrate that this life cycle can turn into a thrilling roller-coaster ride for stockholders as decades pass. By making skillful and/or lucky decisions to restructure, by combining with other companies, or by eliminating selected parts of the existing company, managers can postpone their company's decline and death indefinitely. By making unwise and/or unfortunate decisions of this nature, they can destroy their companies almost overnight.

UPSIZING A CORPORATION

rightsizing

A management decision to deliberately and immediately expand (upsize) or contract (downsize) a company and the scale of its operations.

merger

Two companies combine to produce a new corporate entity. Stockholders exchange outstanding shares of common stock in both companies for shares in the new company.

acquisition

One company takes over another company. The acquirer keeps its identity, and its common stock remains outstanding.

tender offer

A public announcement by an acquiring company that it will buy a majority or all of the outstanding common stock of a target company at a premium over the target's current market price.

Spin doctors are public relations professionals who are highly paid to find appealing ways to describe or explain appalling events or decisions. They have developed the concept of **rightsizing**, which refers to decisions to deliberately and immediately expand (upsize) or contract (downsize) a company and the scale of its operations.

There is only one way to upsize a company internally. The company must sell the right product, in the right package, at the right price, to the right group of customers. There are two ways to upsize a company externally: through mergers and acquisitions.

A **merger** combines two companies to produce a new corporate entity. Both of the original companies lose their identities, and their outstanding shares of common stock are exchanged for shares in the new company. In an **acquisition**, one company takes over another company. The acquirer keeps its identity, and its common stock remains outstanding.

Acquisition Techniques

One company may acquire another by purchasing either its assets or its common stock. Both methods require approval by the target company's shareholders.

Asset Acquisition. If the acquirer wants to buy some or all of the assets of its target company, it negotiates a price with the target company's management. Payment may be in the form of cash, notes, or stock in the acquiring company.

If the acquirer purchases all of the assets, the cash or stock it gives in payment is usually distributed to the target company's shareholders as a liquidating dividend, and the target company ceases to exist. If the acquirer purchases only a portion of the assets, paying with its own stock, the target company may:

1. Hold the stock as an investment
2. Distribute the stock to its shareholders
3. Sell the stock and use the proceeds to buy new assets

If the acquirer purchases only a portion of the assets, paying with cash, the target company may distribute the cash to its stockholders, which would reduce the market value of the target company's stock. The target company may also invest the cash in new assets, which may reduce, maintain, or enhance its market value.

Stock Acquisition. An acquiring company usually makes a public announcement of its offer to buy a majority or all of the outstanding common stock of the target company at a premium over the stock's current market price. This is a **tender offer**. Since the offer is made directly to the stockholders of the target

FOCUS ON FINANCE

Atlantic Richfield Company

The merger of the Atlantic Refining Company and the Richfield Oil Corporation on January 3, 1966, produced a company that was renamed the Atlantic Richfield Company on May 3, 1966.

Before that merger, however, the Atlantic Refining Co. had made the following acquisitions without any need to change its name:

1. Standard Oil Co. of Pittsburgh (1892)
2. Eclipse Lubrication Co. Ltd. (1892)
3. Imperial Refining Co. Ltd. (1892)
4. Acme Oil Co. (1892)
5. The Electric Light Oil Co. (1892)
6. Houston Oil Co. (1956)
7. J. P. Frank Chemical & Plastic Corp. (1961)
8. Buckley & Scott Co. (1961)
9. Argo Oil Corp. (1961)
10. Massachusetts Plastics Corp. (1962)
11. Hondo Oil & Gas Co. (1963)

company, it does not matter whether its management is in favor of, indifferent to, or opposed to the acquisition. If the target company's managers are hostile to the takeover (usually because they expect it to cost them their jobs), they must convince their shareholders to reject the acquisition offer.

Antitakeover Strategies and Devices

If the target company has not taken antiacquisition measures before an actual takeover attempt, management has a hard time stopping a potential takeover. They must convince stockholders that an acquirer's offer is not in their best interests, even though it involves an immediate profit. Management usually argues that the true, long-term value of the stock is higher than the price the acquirer has offered.

Some companies may raise their cash dividends or declare stock splits to increase the market value of their outstanding stock, making a takeover more expensive. When the market knows that a company is a takeover target, such actions raise the stock price because they signal management's intention to resist the takeover attempt. Other companies institute legal actions against the acquiring company as a delaying technique. In both cases, the managers of the target companies may try to merge with a company they perceive to be more friendly, a **white knight**.

white knight
An alternative acquiring company perceived to be more friendly to the target company in a hostile takeover situation.

Some companies try to scare the shareholders—and the general public—by branding the acquirer a malevolent being who will ultimately destroy the shareholders' wealth. Obviously, this tactic can succeed only against a stock-for-stock offer; the threat is meaningless against a cash-for-stock offer.

A few companies pay **greenmail**. When a potential acquirer has already accumulated a block of stock, the target company negotiates an agreement under which it buys back the stock at a premium price in exchange for a promise that the acquirer will cease its attempt to acquire the company.

greenmail
A target company pays a premium price to buy back a block of its stock held by a potential acquirer, who promises to stop trying to acquire the company.

A takeover attempt does not emerge instantly as a rude surprise. An investor who acquires 5 percent or more of a company's outstanding stock must file **Form 13-D** with the SEC. This form identifies the investor and requires disclosure of the investor's total holdings in the company. Each time the investor acquires an additional 1 percent of the stock, an amendment to the 13-D must disclose the change.

Form 13-D
A form filed with the SEC by an investor who acquires 5 percent or more of a company's outstanding stock.

If a company's managers fear a takeover attempt and they oppose acquisition by *any* other company, they usually do not wait until a suitor acts. Instead, they amend the company's charter to put barriers to acquisition in place ahead of time. These barriers are known as **shark repellent devices**. Some of the most popular shark repellents include:

shark repellent device
A barrier to acquisition entered into a corporate charter before the need arises.

1. Staggered terms for the board of directors. For example, a company might require shareholders to elect one-fifth of its board each year. Even though a "shark" could acquire a majority of the common stock in a matter of weeks, it would take three years to replace a majority of the board members.
2. Super-majority merger approval provisions. Approval of a merger may require approval by anywhere from two-thirds to 80 percent of the stockholders instead of a simple majority. This provision is illegal in some states.
3. Fair merger price provisions. A firm may try to set a minimum price (either a dollar amount or a multiple of earnings per share) that any potential acquirer must offer.
4. **Poison pills**. This provision distributes rights to stockholders, allowing them to purchase a new series of securities, such as a new class of common stock with special voting rights, or convertible preferred stock or convertible debentures with a low conversion price. The firm makes this rights offering only when a potential acquirer accumulates a significant percentage of its outstanding stock. The company's board of directors reserves authority to redeem the rights at any time for a token amount. Some types of poison pills are illegal in some states.
5. Lock-up provisions. An acquirer might be able to obtain enough shares to overcome a super-majority merger approval provision if it can buy stock quickly enough. To prevent this, a lock-up provision requires super-majority stockholder approval to modify the corporate charter and any previously passed shark repellent provisions. This provision assumes that some of the remaining shareholders might approve a merger, but would resist charter modifications.

poison pill
A distribution of rights to stockholders that allows them to purchase a new series of securities in an attempt to stop a corporate takeover.

Most companies specify employment conditions for their top managers in contracts. These contracts often have provisions, known as **golden parachutes**, that guarantee the top managers very generous compensation if the company is acquired and they are forced to leave. These contracts do not deter acquisitions, but they do impose extra costs on the remaining stockholders.

golden parachute
A contract provision that guarantees top managers very generous compensation if the company is acquired and they are forced to leave.

Benefits of Mergers and Acquisitions

Except during periodic takeover frenzies, few merger and acquisition attempts are hostile. Companies can and do combine to increase the wealth of their owners.

FOCUS ON FINANCE

GOLDEN HANDSHAKES

Golden parachutes are generous compensation packages for executives forced out of a company after a takeover. Golden handshakes are generous compensation packages for executives who leave "under pressure." Executives who quit to take better jobs elsewhere forfeit their compensation packages, but they usually get even better deals from their new companies. Three recent examples of golden handshakes are:

1. James D. Robinson III, chairman and CEO of American Express Co., received $1,125,000 in severance pay, $825,000 over two years in exchange for agreeing not to compete with AmEx or to try to lure away employees or customers; a $730,000 annual pension, medical and insurance benefits for life; $1.7 million in stock options; and use of his office, secretary, and company cars from February 1993 until September 1994 or until he found a full-time job (whichever came first). He was denied his request for a consultant's contract and use of a company jet.
2. John Sculley, chairman and CEO of Apple Computer, Inc., received $1 million in severance pay; a $750,000, one-year consulting contract; the $180,000 remainder of his annual salary; a $412,000 bonus; and $2.24 million in stock options. In addition, Apple bought his home in Woodside, California, for "fair market value," paid his moving expenses to Greenwich, Connecticut, and agreed to buy his Lear 55 jet for an undisclosed price.
3. Paul Lego, chairman and CEO of Westinghouse Electric Co., received $800,000 in severance pay; a $1.2 million, two-year consulting contract; a $910,000 annual pension; and options to buy 50,000 shares of Westinghouse stock at $16.25. He was eligible for a $1.1 million performance bonus in 1995, even though the company lost $2.38 billion during the last two years of his leadership.

Source: *Newsday*, March 10, 1993, p. 43.

Vertical Integration. When a company merges with or acquires one of its suppliers or customers, it can expect two types of benefits. First, it ensures its supply lines or locks in a market for its finished products. Second, it controls the pricing of products that move between the two segments of the new company. Profits that used to flow to an outside company now remain in-house.

Horizontal Integration. A combination of competitors, if it does not violate antitrust laws, can achieve operating economies and economies of scale. The larger firm can eliminate duplicate facilities and personnel. It can handle larger orders and schedule more efficient production runs. Increases in volume may permit more effective use of marketing, accounting, financial, and managerial resources. The new firm can gain access to foreign markets with minimal cost or risk.

Improved Management. To the extent that an acquirer can manage the combined firm better than the entrenched officers of the target company, a takeover may improve a target company's rate of return. When this improvement

FOCUS ON FINANCE

TO MERGE OR NOT TO MERGE?

On October 13, 1993, Bell Atlantic Corporation announced the largest corporate takeover in U.S. history. It was going to purchase Tele-Communications Inc. (TCI) and its Liberty Media Corporation (LMC) affiliate for $31.4 billion without spending a penny in cash.

Bell is a regional telephone company whose existing common stock was worth about $27.0 billion when the deal was announced. Its chairman, Raymond Smith, said that Bell was planning to issue $21.8 billion in new stock and would offer these shares in exchange for all of the outstanding shares of TCI and LMC, which was in the process of being absorbed into TCI. In addition, Bell would assume about $9.6 billion in TCI–LMC debt. Future interest payments on this debt constituted the only cash outflows facing Bell as a result of the takeover. The new stock would not require any additional cash outflows because it would be a special class that would not pay any dividends.

TCI claimed to be the largest cable TV provider in the world, and LMC provides cable programs and owns a variety of cable channels. Current customers of the companies wouldn't see changes in services offered until 1995 because interactive technology is not yet ready for commercial use. The first new products of Bell-TCI were expected to be a video library available on demand, home shopping, banking, news, and educational programs, and a video version of the Yellow Pages. At the press conference, Smith predicted that most of the revenues attributable to the deal would come from products not yet invented.

Both the Justice Department and a congressional subcommittee were planning to investigate how the deal would affect competition and consumers. In anticipation of such problems, the terms of the deal included a promise to spin off to shareholders those assets that competed with one another.

Four months later, Bell Atlantic and TCI announced that they were unable to reach a final agreement and had terminated merger negotiations. Media analysts discussed several possible reasons for the cancellation.

1. Bell Atlantic's stock soared to nearly $68 a share when the deal was announced, then wiggled its way down to $52.75 by February 23, 1994, the day the deal was terminated. This depressed price meant that Bell Atlantic would have to issue many more shares of stock than initially planned to acquire TCI.
2. Some colleagues of John Malone, the forceful head of TCI, were skeptical of his ability to function as the No. 2 man in any company. (When Vail, Colorado, rejected the fees his cable company demanded, he broadcast nothing but the home phone numbers of city officials all weekend. He got his fees.)
3. In January 1994, Malone publicly suggested that Bell Atlantic should cut or eliminate its $0.67 per share quarterly dividend (almost $1.1 billion per year) and plow the cash back into the company to help build a nationwide telecommunications network. Smith publicly said no.
4. As expected, the Federal Communications Commission mandated a cut in cable television rates on February 22, 1994. These rate controls would reduce TCI's expected $1.95 billion cash flow by an estimated 2 percent.

Whatever the reason or combination of reasons for the failed merger, the market was not surprised. When the termination of negotiations was announced, Atlantic Bell's stock price fell just 50 cents.

To date, the largest successful mergers and acquisitions in the United States were:

Warner Communications and Time, Inc. (1990)	$14.1 billion
RJR Nabisco and Kohlberg Kravis Roberts (1989)	29.5 billion
Squibb and Bristol Myers (1989)	12.1 billion
Kraft and Philip Morris (1988)	13.4 billion
Gulf Corporation and Standard Oil (1984)	13.4 billion
Getty Oil and Texaco (1984)	10.1 billion

exceeds the acquisition costs, the deal increases the wealth of the acquirer's shareholders. To achieve this kind of gain, the acquirer must appraise the target's potential for improvement fairly accurately. The acquirer's managers must also possess the time and skill necessary to upgrade the target's operations.

Synergy. By merging, manufacturers with complementary products may be able to increase the demand for their combined product line. When technology companies merge, each component may derive benefits from sudden access to the other component's recent R&D efforts. In a horizontal merger, each component may derive unexpected benefits from the other's market research or distribution channels. For synergistic companies, the value of the combination exceeds the sum of the companies' individual values.

Last Resort Access. When one company wants access to the tangible, human, or intangible assets of another company, and that access is denied, it may have to acquire the whole company to get what it wants. If, for example, Company A has a patent or copyright for something that Company B could use very profitably, and Company A will not part with its monopoly for any price, it may be worthwhile for Company B to buy Company A.

Diversification. A company may be able to reduce the instability of its sales, earnings, and/or cash flows by acquiring or merging with a company in a different line of business, subject to different government or tax regulations, located in a different geographical area, or with a different financial structure. This reduction in risk should improve the acquirer's stock price. Some doubt the possibility of this gain to stockholders because professional investors have the time and information necessary to create a portfolio of stocks that would diversify away the same amount of risk. Individual investors usually lack this ability, however. If many individual investors see an apparent diversification advantage in a specific merger, their buying will push the stock price up.

Financial Arrangements

When two companies combine in a stock-for-stock deal, it is necessary to calculate the **exchange ratio** between them. This ratio determines how many shares of the target company can be exchanged for one share of the acquiring company.

exchange ratio
The number of shares of a target company that can be exchanged for one share of an acquiring company.

Complete Acquisition. To start with the simplest illustration, assume that Man Company is considering the acquisition of 100 percent of Mouse Company through an exchange of stock. The acquisition would create no synergistic effects, earnings are not expected to grow or to decline, no accounting loopholes affect the data, there are no hidden tax implications, and the stock market ignores the news of the impending takeover. Exhibit 17.1 presents financial data for the two companies.

If Man Company intends to make an acceptable offer to the shareholders of Mouse Company, the exchange ratio must exceed $30/$9, or 3.33:1. In other

EXHIBIT 17.1

Financial Data for Two Hypothetical Companies

	MAN COMPANY	MOUSE COMPANY
Net income	$50 million	$9 million
Shares outstanding	$25 million	$10 million
Earnings per share	$2.00	$0.90
Price–earnings ratio	15×	10×
Stock price	$30.00	$9.00

words, if Man Company were to offer to exchange 1 share of its stock for 3⅓ shares of Mouse Company, the shareholders of Mouse Company would have no incentive to accept the offer. They would see themselves as holding paper worth $30 either way.

Suppose that Man Company were to offer an exchange ratio of 3:1. Mouse Company stockholders could exchange three shares worth $27 for one share of Man Company worth $30. This would give them an apparent profit of $1 per share on their Mouse Company stock.

Would the shareholders of Mouse Company accept the offer? Would the shareholders of Man Company rise in revolt because their managers were giving away $1 per share for Mouse Company (a total of $10 million)? To answer these questions, it is necessary to calculate some data for Man Company after the acquisition:

$$\text{Net income} = \$50 \text{ million} + \$9 \text{ million}$$
$$= \$59 \text{ million}$$

Man Company would have to issue 3.33 million new shares to acquire all 10 million shares of Mouse Company (10,000,000/3). After the acquisition, Man Company would have 25 million plus 3.33 million, or 28.33 million shares outstanding.

$$\text{Earnings per share} = \$59 \text{ million}/28.3 \text{ million}$$
$$= \$2.08$$

Since Man Company would retain its identity, the demand for its stock should not change. Therefore, its price–earnings ratio, which reflects demand, should remain at 15×. In a normal situation, the price–earnings ratio reflects the discount rate investors use to determine the present value of a company's expected earnings per share. In a takeover situation such as this one, however, an additional element affects the analysis: greed.

Maintaining a high P/E ratio benefits everyone concerned—the investment bankers, the managers of Man Co., the stockholders of both companies, and even the managers of Mouse Co. if they have stock options or golden parachutes. The investment bankers expend enormous time and effort diplomatically pointing out this fact to the market. Participants in the market have seen the happy consequences of this game so frequently that they are perfectly willing to cooperate.

FOCUS ON FINANCE

EXTRAVAGANT PRICE–EARNINGS RATIOS

The market saw a major merger movement during the late 1960s and early 1970s. Managers of companies with high price–earnings ratios aggressively sought to acquire companies with lower price–earnings ratios to boost their own share prices. These managers generally did not concern themselves with good management of the conglomerates they were building. Some did not even care that the wildly diversified companies they were assembling could not possibly be managed well. The all-important criterion was the price–earnings ratio.

This merger mania fed on itself, because when companies acquired others with lower price–earnings ratios, their own stock prices rose. These increases attracted investors seeking rapid price appreciation. Greater demand for their stock raised the price–earnings ratios of the acquirers, giving them whole new levels of takeover targets, which increased their own stock prices yet again.

If an economic recession had not terminated this spiral, investment analysis would have degenerated to the single rule: "Invest in the company with the highest price–earnings ratio today." Which company might have won such a contest? The following list of 33 companies, compiled from the *Value Line Investment Survey*, October–December 1974, suggests some likely candidates. However, only the nine companies whose names are followed by asterisks (*) are recognizable in the *Value Line Investment Survey* of January–March 1994. The other 24 have either failed, been acquired, or changed their names over the years.

COMPANY	INDUSTRY	AVERAGE ANNUAL P/E	YEAR
Moore McCormack	Maritime	98.3	1969
Springs Mills*	Textiles	98.2	1968
Keene	Building/construction	97.5	1967
H&R Block*	Personal service	96.3	1967
MCA	Recreation	95.8	1969
High Volt. Engineering	Electronics	95.0	1965
Welbilt	Electronics	94.4	1967
Simmonds Precision	Instruments	94.4	1969
Bunker-Ramo	Electronics	93.9	1967
Curtiss-Wright*	Aerospace/diversified	93.9	1971
Polaroid*	Precision instruments	93.5	1972
Bobbie Brooks	Apparel	93.0	1968
American Standard	Building/construction	92.9	1971
Savin Business Machines	Computer/office equipment	92.0	1966
Potlatch*	Building/construction	91.8	1970
ICN Pharmaceuticals	Ethical drugs	91.7	1967
Molycorp	Metals and mining	91.6	1964
Marquette Cement	Building/construction	91.4	1971
Madison Square Garden	Recreation	90.9	1968
Electronic Memories & Magnetics	Computer/office equipment	90.0	1972
Monarch Machine*	Tools	89.6	1971
National Industries	Conglomerate	88.6	1970

continued on following page

Company	Industry	Average Annual P/E	Year
Calahan Mining	Metals and mining	87.5	1967
United Brands	Food processing	87.4	1970
Victor Comptometer	Computer/office equipment	87.1	1971
Boeing*	Aerospace/diversified	86.2	1969
Cowles Communications	Publishing/advertising	84.6	1971
Memorex	Computer/office equipment	84.0	1972
Sundstrand*	Aerospace/diversified	80.9	1971
LFE	Electronics	80.8	1968
Talley Industries*	Conglomerate	80.7	1969
Braniff International	Air transport	80.3	1967
City Stores	Retail stores	80.0	1971

In fact, rumors of an impending takeover usually cause the price–earnings ratios of *both* companies to rise. This illustration is actually being conservative by assuming that Man Company's P/E ratio would remain at 15×.

$$\text{Post-acquisition stock price} = 15 \times \$2.08$$
$$= \$31.20$$
$$\text{Realized gain per share of Mouse Company} = (\$31.20 - \$27.00)/3$$
$$= \$1.40$$
$$\text{Realized gain per share of Man Company} = \$31.20 - \$30.00$$
$$= \$1.20$$

Thus, the stockholders of both companies should be pleased.

The human urge to optimize prompts another question, though. Does a better exchange ratio exist? Suppose that the managers of Man Company were to offer a 2.5:1 exchange ratio. Stockholders could exchange 2½ shares of Mouse Company stock worth $22.50 for one share of Man Company worth $30.00. This would give them an apparent profit of ($30.00 – $22.50)/2.5, or $3.00 per share on their Mouse Company stock.

This alternative offer would not affect the firm's post-acquisition net income of $59 million. However, it would require Man Company to issue 10 million/2.5, or 4 million new shares to exchange for all of the outstanding shares of Mouse Company. As a result, Man Company would have 25 million plus 4 million, or 29 million shares outstanding.

$$\text{Earnings Per Share} = \$59 \text{ million}/29 \text{ million}$$
$$= \$2.03$$

Again, assuming no change in demand, the price–earnings ratios should remain at 15×.

$$\begin{aligned}
\text{Post-acquisition stock price} &= 15 \times \$2.03 \\
&= \$30.45 \\
\text{Realized gain per share of Mouse Company} &= (\$30.45 - \$22.50)/2.5 \\
&= \$3.18 \\
\text{Realized gain per share of Man Company} &= \$30.45 - \$30 \\
&= \$0.45
\end{aligned}$$

Obviously, Mouse Company shareholders would prefer an exchange ratio of 2.5:1 and Man Company shareholders would prefer an exchange ratio of 3.0:1. These preferences consistently apply to all levels of the exchange ratio. A higher ratio would make Man Company shareholders happier and Mouse Company shareholders less happy.

The upper limit on this exchange ratio was previously established as 3.33:1. There is also a lower limit. The shareholders of Man Company would disapprove of an exchange ratio that would drive the market price of their stock below \$30. Four calculations give the exchange ratio that would make the price exactly equal to \$30:

$$\begin{aligned}
\text{EPS} &= \text{Price/Price–earnings ratio} \\
&= \$30/15 \\
&= \$2 \\
\text{Outstanding Man Co. shares} &= \text{Net income/EPS} \\
&= \$59 \text{ million}/\$2 \\
&= 29.5 \text{ million shares} \\
\text{New Man Co. shares} &= \text{Outstanding shares} - \text{Original shares} \\
&= 29.5 \text{ million} - 25 \text{ million} \\
&= 4.5 \text{ million shares} \\
\text{Exchange ratio} &= \text{Number of Mouse Co. shares/New Man Co. shares} \\
&= 10 \text{ million}/4.5 \text{ million} \\
&= 2.20{:}1
\end{aligned}$$

The lower limit on the exchange ratio is 2.20:1. The shareholders of Man Company would be dissatisfied if management offered to exchange one share of Man Company for fewer than 2.2 shares of Mouse Company.

The acquisition would require an offer between 3.33:1 and 2.20:1. The specific ratio within this range would depend on current market conditions, the recent share price histories of the two companies, and the strength of Man Company's desire to acquire Mouse Company.

Partial Acquisition. As explained in Appendix A, when a company acquires a majority of the outstanding stock of another company, it can report the combined net income of both companies as its own. Assume that Man Company desires to

EXHIBIT 17.2

Complete versus Partial Acquisition of Mouse Company

	100 PERCENT ACQUISITION		51 PERCENT ACQUISITION	
Exchange ratio	3.0:1	2.5:1	3.0:1	2.5:1
Net income	$59 million	$59 million	$59 million	$59 million
New shares	$3.33 million	$4 million	$1.7 million	$2.04 million
Outstanding stock	$28.33 million	$29 million	$26.7 million	$27.04 million
EPS	$2.08	$2.03	$2.21	$2.18
Price–earnings ratio	15×		15×	
Price of Man Co.	$31.20	$30.45	$33.15	$32.70
Gain per share—Mouse	$1.40	$3.18	$2.05	$4.08
Gain per share—Man	$1.20	$0.45	$3.15	$2.70

acquire only 51 percent of the outstanding shares of Mouse Company (5.1 million shares) instead of all of them. The post-acquisition net income of Man Company is still $59 million and the upper limit on the exchange ratio remains at 3.33:1. The lower limit changes, though.

To find the new lower limit, three of the four calculations do not change: EPS is still $2, the number of outstanding shares is still 29.5 million, and the number of new shares is still 4.5 million, but the exchange ratio is now 5.1 million/4.5 million, or 1.13:1.

The lower limit on the exchange ratio drops considerably. This suggests that Man Company would have a different stock price following a partial acquisition than it would have following a complete acquisition. Exhibit 17.2 illustrates the accuracy of this suggestion. The shareholders of both companies gain more per share under a partial acquisition than under a complete acquisition. This is true for any exchange ratio between the limits of 3.33:1 and 1.13:1.

Serial Acquisition. As one consequence of successful acquisitions, each takeover facilitates the next one. The illustration above can be expanded to introduce a third company, Cat Company, that has exactly the same financial data as Mouse Company before the acquisition. Further assume that Man Company had offered an exchange ratio of 2.5:1 for Mouse Company, and that its offer was accepted. Exhibit 17.3 presents the financial data for Man Company after acquiring 100 percent of Mouse Company, Man Company after acquiring 51 percent of Mouse Company, and Cat Company.

To simplify the illustration, assume that if Man Company completely acquires Mouse Company, it will also completely acquire Cat Company. If Man Company acquires only 51 percent of Mouse Company, then it will acquire only 51 percent of Cat Company. The second acquisition will have the same exchange ratio, 2.5:1, although it appears to favor the shareholders of Cat Company more than it did the shareholders of Mouse Company. Exhibit 17.4 displays the results of these two takeovers. Notice that the shareholders and former shareholders of all three companies experience gains. Further, partial acquisitions provide larger gains to all parties.

EXHIBIT 17.3

Financial Data for Three Hypothetical Companies

	Man Company (+100% Mouse)	Man Company (+51% Mouse)	Cat Company
Net income	$59 million	$59 million	$9 million
Shares outstanding	$29 million	$27.04 million	$10 million
Earnings per share	$2.03	$2.18	$0.90
Price–earnings ratio	15×	15×	10×
Stock price	$30.45	$32.70	$9.00

EXHIBIT 17.4

Complete versus Partial Acquisition of Cat Company

	100 Percent Acquisition	51 Percent Acquisition
Exchange ratio	2.5:1	2.5:1
Net income	$68 million	$68 million
New shares	4 million	2.04 million
Outstanding stock	33 million	29.08 million
EPS	$2.06	$2.34
Price–earnings ratio	15×	15×
Price of Man Co.	$30.90	$35.10
Gain per share—Cat	$3.36	$5.04
Gain per share—Mouse	$3.36	$5.04
Gain per share—Man	$0.90	$5.10

A successful acquisition results in a gain for all shareholders involved. The acquisitions of Mouse Company and Cat Company were obviously successful, but this whole illustration was designed to turn out successfully; it is necessary to examine the design.

The assumption of identical data for Cat Company and Mouse Company was a mere convenience. It demonstrates the point, however, that subsequent acquisitions benefit both the original shareholders of Man Company and the former shareholders of Mouse Company.

The assumption that Cat Company and Mouse Company were smaller than Man Company had nothing to do with the successful outcome. To prove this point, consider Dog Company. It has $90 million in net income and 100 million shares outstanding, so it is bigger than Man Company. Dog Company has EPS of $0.90, a price–earnings ratio of 10×, and a stock price of $9. If the original Man Company had acquired Dog Company instead of Mouse Company, the results of the takeover would be as shown in Exhibit 17.5. Obviously, the acquisition was successful. Exhibit 17.5 also illustrates an important principle: a bigger target makes for a better outcome.

The critical element in the design of this illustration is the assumption that Man Company has a larger price–earnings ratio than any of its target companies. If Man Company's P/E ratio had been smaller than those of its targets, no

EXHIBIT 17.5

Complete versus Partial Acquisition of Dog Company

	100 PERCENT ACQUISITION		51 PERCENT ACQUISITION	
Exchange ratio	3.0:1	2.5:1	3.0:1	2.5:1
Net income	$140 million	$140 million	$140 million	$140 million
New shares	33.33 million	40 million	17 million	20.4 million
Outstanding stock	58.33 million	65 million	42 million	45.4 million
EPS	$2.40	$2.15	$3.33	$3.08
Price–earnings ratio	15×	15×	15×	15×
Price of Man Co.	$36.00	$32.25	$49.95	$46.20
Gain per share—Dog	$3.00	$2.10	$7.65	$9.48
Gain per share—Man	$6.00	$2.25	$19.95	$16.20

exchange ratio would result in a post-acquisition gain in the price of Man Company stock.

If all of the outlined acquisition principles are true, why doesn't the real-world company with the highest price–earnings ratio in the market acquire all of the other companies? There are two major reasons why this doesn't happen:

1. When a company is recognized as a takeover target (when it is "in play"), its stock price climbs to whatever price the market expects the potential acquirer to offer. This raises the target's price–earnings ratio, sometimes to a point where the post-acquisition gain per share amounts to pennies. In fact, expectations may outpace the actual offer, leading the acquirer to withdraw the offer because the deal would produce no gain.
2. The illustration was concerned only with the immediate impact of the acquisition. After a company is acquired, the acquirer must synchronize the target's operations with its own existing operations. The acquisition has to be managed just as meticulously as the original company. As a parent firm acquires more companies, the work of good management becomes more difficult.

Current EPS is just one variable that can be used to determine exchange ratios. There are other possibilities; analysts have used future earnings, future cash flows, asset levels, and even sales in the past.

The acquiring company may see a takeover target as an asset that promises a desirable rate of growth in profitability or cash flows for the foreseeable future. (The target may have a lower expected growth rate if the merger does not take place, i.e., if the target does not get the benefit of the acquirer's managerial talents.) The acquirer discounts these projected earnings or cash flows to obtain a present value for the target. It then compares this present value per share to the target company's current market price. If the acquirer values the target company's future performance more highly than the market does, it may make an appropriate offer to the target's shareholders. An acceptable offer should fall somewhere between the acquirer's valuation and the market's.

FOCUS ON FINANCE

EXPENSIVE BABY

In May 1994, Sandoz Ltd., a Swiss drug maker, bought Gerber Products Co. for $3.7 billion, or $53 per share. The price was below $30 per share before rumors about the acquisition started flying. Analysts estimate that it will take Sandoz about five years to break even on the deal, since the purchase price was 29 times Gerber's earnings per share.

Gerber appeared attractive to Sandoz because it has 73 percent of the U.S. baby food market and its after-tax profit margin is 11 percent. The Swiss franc is strong against the dollar, which makes investment in the United States look good to Swiss investors. Also, international accounting standards allow Sandoz to write off against earnings $3.2 billion in goodwill (86 percent of the purchase price). Some analysts think that proceeds from the sale of duplicate equipment and buildings, plus Gerber's $165 million cash flow, will be sufficient to prevent dilution of Sandoz's earnings in 1994.

The downside risks of the deal are geographic. Sandoz's sales and distribution networks are in western Europe, which is both a fragmented and saturated market. H. J. Heinz has 25 percent of European baby food sales, and contests the market fiercely with Nestlé and Danone, a French multinational. Unfortunately, Sandoz has no experience selling baby food. Eastern Europe is the market with expansion potential. Polish babies eat an average of less than 144 jars of baby food a year. By comparison, French babies eat an average of 660 jars of baby food a year; American babies eat an average of 600.

Gerber, for its part, may have trouble marketing Sandoz's products in the United States. It has had little success with products aimed at both children and adults:

Source: "Strained Peas, Strained Profits?" *Business Week*, June 6, 1994, p. 30.

Accounting rules specify how to record the takeover of a company. They offer two alternatives, the purchase method and the pooling of interests method. If the acquisition involves an exchange of cash, notes, bonds, or preferred stock, the purchase method must be used. If the acquisition involves an exchange of common stock, either method can be used. The pooling of interests method does impose two other requirements, though.

1. The acquirer must retain most or all of the target's assets for at least two years.
2. The takeover must be accomplished in a single transaction; it can involve no subsequent contingency payments.

The differences between the two accounting techniques are highlighted in Exhibit 17.6.

Holding Companies

Instead of acquiring the majority of another company's stock, a corporation may purchase a significantly smaller percentage and still obtain a controlling interest in the company. If the common stock of a company is widely distributed among

EXHIBIT 17.6

Accounting Method Differences

	Purchase Method	Pooling Method
Acquired assets go on acquirer's books	At the price paid	At target's book value
Acquirer records acquired income	From merger date on	Retroactively
Premium paid above fair market value of target's assets	Goodwill is amortized	No goodwill

investors, an owner may acquire effective control with, say, 20 percent of the stock. The advantages of operating as a holding company are:

1. The holding company can control another company with a much smaller investment than majority ownership would require.
2. The acquirer can buy stock in the open market gradually, without making a tender offer or paying a premium over market price.
3. The holding company can often achieve operating economies by centralizing the management of all companies under its control.

The greatest disadvantage of a holding company is that 20 percent of the dividends paid by the controlled companies are subject to some income taxes. The effective tax rate on intercorporate dividends is lower than the normal tax rate, but the dividends are taxed again when the holding company pays them out to its own stockholders.

pyramid
A holding company with a controlling interest in other holding companies.

A holding company forms a **pyramid** when it obtains a controlling interest in other holding companies. Suppose that Holding Company X purchases 20 percent of the outstanding stock of Holding Companies Y and Z. Holding Company Y, in turn, owns 20 percent of the outstanding stock of Companies A and B. Holding Company Z owns 20 percent of the outstanding stock of Companies C, D, and E. This arrangement is illustrated in Exhibit 17.7.

Holding Company Y can obtain control of Companies A and B with an investment of:

$$(\$40 \text{ million} \times 0.2) + (\$50 \text{ million} \times 0.2) = \$18 \text{ million}$$

Partial acquisition of A and B, on the other hand, would require an investment of:

$$(\$40 \text{ million} + \$50 \text{ million}) \times 0.51 = \$45.9 \text{ million}$$

Complete acquisition would cost \$90 million. Similarly, Holding Company Z can obtain control of Companies C, D, and E with an investment of \$12 million.

Holding Company X can obtain control of Companies A, B, C, D, and E with an investment of:

EXHIBIT 17.7

Holding Company Pyramid ($millions)

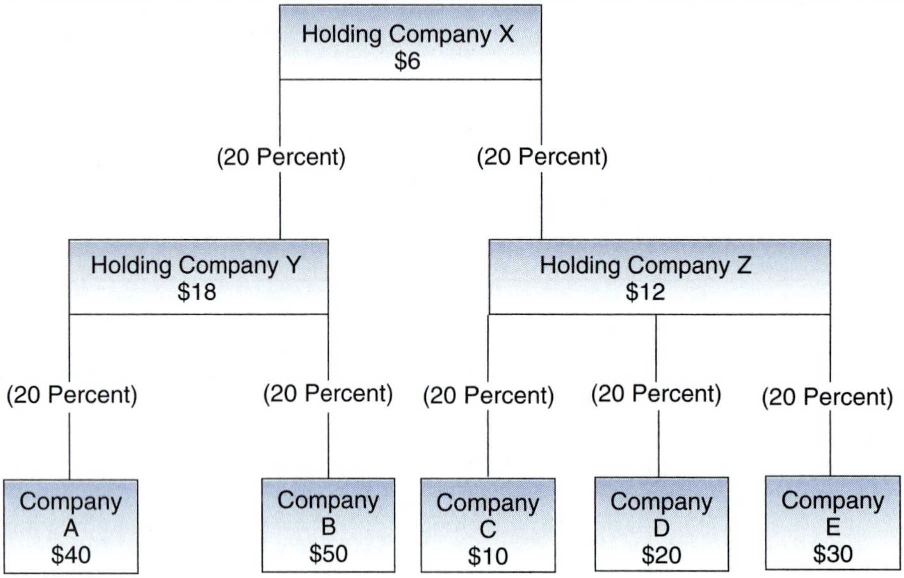

$$(\$18 \text{ million} \times 0.2) + (\$12 \text{ million} \times 0.2) = \$6 \text{ million}$$

Direct partial acquisition of these five companies would require an investment of $150 million × 0.51, or $76.5 million.

As long as A, B, C, D, and E are profitable, their earnings are growing, and they are paying dividends, the shareholders of Holding Company X will be very pleased with the magnified returns on X's tiny investment. The problem with pyramids becomes apparent in difficult economic times. The high degree of leverage necessary to build the pyramid magnifies the losses that X will experience.

DOWNSIZING A CORPORATION

Because a successful business enterprise is expected to grow, corporate downsizing is generally considered undesirable. The contraction of a company does not necessarily decrease its shareholders' wealth, however, because firms downsize for many different reasons and they accomplish it in many ways.

Divestiture

A corporation can divest itself of any part of the enterprise. It can eliminate assets, personnel, activities, product lines, divisions, or subsidiaries. Any or all of these segments of the company can be thrown away, given away, or sold for cash or stock.

Assets. The simplest divestiture decision is whether or not to abandon capital assets—property, plant, and equipment—as discussed in Chapter 5. This decision simply requires the calculation and evaluation of alternative cash flows. If the NPV of the cash flows from an abandonment decision exceeds the NPV of the cash flows from a decision to continue using the asset, then the company should divest itself of the asset. Decisions to jettison assets require careful consideration of the impact of this move on the environment. Companies have spent large sums restoring sites (turning former strip mines into golf courses, for instance) and removing pollutants they have dumped into land and sea.

Personnel. A more complicated downsizing decision involves a reduction of personnel. In addition to analyzing the cash flow consequences of a sizable reduction in its work force, a company must consider:

1. The morale of remaining employees
2. The appropriate redistribution of work among remaining employees
3. The effect of a substantial increase in unemployment on the communities in which the former employees live
4. The possibility of unpleasant reactions to the decision by any affected trade unions
5. Adverse publicity in the media
6. A decline in the market price of the company's stock because the decision may be seen as a negative signal by the market

attrition

A policy of reducing the work force by not replacing most of those who leave a company voluntarily during a specified time period.

For all of these reasons, corporations usually decide to begin personnel reduction programs by **attrition**. This means that a firm does not replace most employees who leave the company voluntarily during a specified time period. This approach may work reasonably well for a company that plans to dismiss a relatively small percentage of its employees, and for a company with a high employee turnover ratio. If a company has a significant number of older workers, an early retirement program coupled with an attrition policy may achieve the desired personnel reduction. These methods are not adequate, however, for a company with substantial numbers of middle-aged workers who have accumulated significant seniority. Such a firm must contemplate direct dismissal, with all of its hazards.

Fruit of the Loom, Inc. has developed an alternative approach: It instituted a four-day, 32-hour workweek for the first quarter of 1994. It also shut down all of its U.S. plants during the first week in January to curtail production and keep inventories in line with demand.

Activities. A company may decide to downsize by subcontracting some of the functions or operations that it previously performed itself. Firms may divest security, pension fund management, cafeteria services, packaging and shipping, product assembly, and even accounts receivable. Such decisions usually involve

FOCUS ON FINANCE

ANYTHING CAN BE DIVESTED

Corporations can divest themselves of anything they wish. Some notable recent divestitures have included:

1. A manufacturing division sold by Westinghouse to obtain funds to reduce its $6.3 billion debt. The seller received $1.1 billion from Eaton Corp., which also assumed $200 million in liabilities attributable to the division.
2. Five million square feet of floor space, eliminated by Pratt & Whitney, manufacturers of aircraft engines. This change accompanied an announcement that the firm would trim its work force of 40,664 people to 30,000 people by the end of 1994.
3. Production facilities for all of the snack food Borden Co. sells in North America. These foods, which include Wise Potato Chips, represent 20 percent of Borden's revenues. The sale will reduce costs by $125 million annually, and reduce fourth quarter earnings for 1993 by $650 million. Borden cut its 1994 dividend to $0.30 a share, half of the 1993 dividend. The announcement drove the stock price down from $18.25 to $15.875 per share.
4. One-half of the rights to "The Flintstones," "The Jetsons," and "Yogi Bear" by Great American Entertainment Co. The Turner Broadcasting System already owned half of the rights to the Hanna-Barbera cartoon library and paid $255 million for the other half.
5. Headquarters staff of 200 people by General Dynamics, which sold its tactical military aircraft business to Lockheed, its missile systems business to Hughes Aircraft, its electronics division to Carlyle Group, and its Amsea sealift unit to International Shipbuilding. General Dynamics announced a special dividend of $20 per share ($100 million) to start divesting itself of $2 billion in cash that it accumulated from the sales, and that it cannot reinvest profitably in the defense industry.

reductions in both assets and personnel. Since they eliminate specific duties, an attrition policy will not work. The company may attempt to relocate valuable employees or to retrain employees who are anxious to continue working for the company. However, if the divestiture decision were intended to cut costs, most of the employees associated with the divested activity will have to be dismissed.

Product Lines. Periodically, most companies conduct thorough reviews of their long-term goals and objectives, and then examine their current operations to evaluate the feasibility of achieving those goals and meeting those objectives. Such an evaluation may identify an inappropriate product line that absorbs a disproportionate share of the company's assets, talent, or funds, or puts the company at a competitive disadvantage.

The decision to divest such a product line must be followed by a decision about the method of divestiture. Can another company, domestic or foreign, produce a satisfactory profit if the divesting company licenses it to make the product line? If so, the firm can sell off the line. If not, it must discard the line.

Divisions and Subsidiaries. One particular operating unit of a company may be more valuable to another company than to the the unit's owner. Consequently, an acquisition-minded company may be willing to pay more for that unit than its present value to the company. If the buying company pays in cash, the divesting company may:

1. Use the cash to pay down its debt
2. Distribute the cash to its stockholders
3. Use the cash to purchase new assets or a new operating unit

If the acquiring company pays for the operating unit by exchanging its own securities, the divesting company usually either holds the securities for a while as an investment or distributes them to its stockholders. Individual investors tend to resent such distributions, believing that the company could have provided higher net proceeds by selling the stock itself and distributing the cash. They often believe that the company could have negotiated a better price in a block trade than they can get in the open market, and they know that the company would have paid less in commissions on the sale.

spin-off
Distribution to stockholders of a divesting company of new common stock to give a division or subsidiary an independent identity.

If the business unit being divested can stand alone as an operating entity, the owner can spin it off instead of selling it. A **spin-off** gives the division or subsidiary an independent identity and distributes its common stock to the stockholders of the divesting company on a pro rata basis. After the spin-off, the business unit is a completely separate, publicly traded company. The stockholders incur no tax liability from the spin-off until they sell the new stock. The market value of the spun-off stock reflects the projected profitability of the new company.

equity carve-out
A divestiture in which the parent company sells the public some stock in a division or subsidiary, making it an independent identity, while keeping a controlling interest.

If the business unit to be divested can stand alone, but the divesting company does not want to relinquish ownership and control, it may divest the unit through an **equity carve-out**. This technique gives the division or subsidiary an independent identity, but instead of giving away all of the new stock, the divesting company sells some of it to the public and keeps a controlling interest for itself.

Reorganization

technical insolvency
The temporary condition of a firm that cannot meet its current obligations.

A company is **technically insolvent** when it cannot meet its current obligations. This condition may be temporary or incurable. Many technically insolvent companies can be rehabilitated, with or without some losses to their creditors and stockholders. To rehabilitate itself, a firm can work voluntarily with its creditors to develop an extension or composition agreement, or it can reorganize under supervision by the Bankruptcy Court.

extension
An agreement between a company and its creditors to postpone the due dates on the balances it owes.

Voluntary Remedies. When a company cannot pay its bills on time, its simplest strategy is to work out some agreement with its creditors to prevent them from taking any legal actions. An **extension** is an agreement between the company and its creditors to postpone the due dates on the balances it owes. The company's major creditors may form a committee to design a plan that schedules payments and institutes some controls over management to support the company's financial recovery. Dissenting creditors may be paid off first, if their claims are small. An extension avoids the time and expense of legal proceedings if the company is basically sound and it cooperates with the creditors' plan. An extension is not a legally enforceable document, but if the company shows bad faith, the creditors can initiate bankruptcy proceedings against it and force it into liquidation.

composition
An agreement for a proportionate settlement of creditors' claims in cash or in a combination of cash and promissory notes.

A **composition** involves a proportionate settlement of creditors' claims in cash or in a combination of cash and promissory notes. The company may propose a settlement of, say, 75 cents on the dollar. The creditors will not accept an offer that appears to be less than their potential net proceeds from liquidation of the company. They may accept the initial 75 percent payoff offer or ask for a slightly higher percentage; all creditors must agree to the final percentage. The plan must pay off dissenting creditors in full, or they can force the company into bankruptcy. Recent IRS rulings have declared that almost all of the forgiven debt is taxable income for the debtor.

Legal Reorganization. Chapter 11 of the Bankruptcy Reform Act of 1978 governs the rehabilitation of a company by reorganizing its capital structure. Voluntary proceedings begin when a company in financial trouble files a petition in Bankruptcy Court. Involuntary proceedings begin when three or more unsecured creditors file the petition. After it accepts the petition, the court issues an order of relief. This order restrains creditors from collecting on their claims until a reorganization plan is approved.

To keep the business going while the parties work out a plan, the company needs credit. Chapter 11 gives priority to claims of creditors who extend credit to the company during this protected time over creditors who were owed money before the case came to court.

Company managers or a trustee appointed by the court must draw up a reorganization plan that is fair, equitable, and feasible. The process for formulating such a plan involves three steps:

1. Determine the total value of the company. This is the present value of its future annual earnings.
2. Establish a new capital structure. The reorganization reduces the total debt of the company by giving some bondholders preferred or common stock. Also, the new debt may have a longer maturity than the company's original debt obligations.
3. Value the company's old securities and exchange them for new securities. The **absolute priority rule** specifies that claims must be settled in the order of their legal priority. In a harsh reorganization, the holders of the company's old current liabilities may receive bonds from the reorganized company, the former bondholders may receive common stock from the reorganized company, and the former stockholders may get nothing.

absolute priority rule
A provision in Chapter 11 of the bankruptcy law that mandates settling claims in the order of their legal priority.

The reorganization plan has to be filed with the court within 120 days unless the judge extends the time period. If it is not filed on time, other parties can draw up reorganization plans and file them, including the creditor's committee, individual creditors, a trustee, and the company itself. More than one plan can be filed. All plans must be submitted to the creditors and stockholders for approval. If the company is publicly held, the plan must also be submitted to the SEC to verify full disclosure.

Each class of claimants must vote on the plans. More than half of the claimants and holders of two-thirds of the amount of the claims in each class must approve a plan to make it acceptable. Claimholders can accept more than one plan, in which case the court chooses among the accepted plans. The company and all of its creditors and stockholders are bound by the plan once it is confirmed by the court.

Firms have filed voluntarily for protection under Chapter 11 of the bankruptcy law for reasons other than technical insolvency. In 1983, Continental Airlines tried to reduce its labor costs by using a filing to break its employees' unions. The Johns Manville Company used such a filing to get a six-year postponement of its liabilities for the asbestos-related injuries or deaths of thousands of its mining and manufacturing employees. A. H. Robins Co. used a bankruptcy filing to minimize the damage claims attributable to its sales of the Dalkon Shield. Union Carbide hid behind Chapter 11 to deny the claims of the Indian government for compensation to its citizens injured by an accidental release of toxic gases in Bhopal.

Texaco used the power of the Bankruptcy Court to minimize an antitrust award. Pennzoil sued Texaco for acquiring Getty Oil at $128.00 a share after Pennzoil thought it had negotiated a firm deal with Getty for $112.50 per share. Pennzoil received an award of $7.5 billion plus $3 billion in punitive damages. Texaco filed for protection under Chapter 11 and ultimately settled with Pennzoil for $3 billion.

LIQUIDATING A CORPORATION

When a corporation cannot afford to continue operating, it is terminated. Again, this can be done voluntarily or involuntarily. It can also be done with or without the supervision of the Bankruptcy Court. The limited liability that corporations offer their owners protects shareholders from loss of their personal assets in a liquidation, but both owners and managers can expect litigation from unhappy creditors. Any stockholders or managers who can be found may have to prove in some court or other that they do not possess former company assets that have been relabeled as personal assets.

Voluntary Liquidation

The owners of a small, incurably insolvent company can simply close the doors of the business and walk away. Creditors are left to fight over whatever they can scavenge from the remains of the business.

If an insolvent corporation has some assets of value, the owners may choose to liquidate them without the intervention of Bankruptcy Court. They sell the assets by auction or negotiation, and distribute the proceeds to the creditors. If they can liquidate the assets quickly enough, the owners can distribute the proceeds as they prefer. When nothing worth the cost of litigation is left, the business ceases to exist. If the liquidation takes too long, three or more unhappy creditors will file petitions with Bankruptcy Court, making voluntary termination impossible.

Liquidation under Legal Supervision

In England, France, Canada, and most of the rest of the world, bankruptcy proceedings have long been considered methods to collect creditors' money and punish failure. In the United States, however, bankruptcy laws have been written and rewritten to encourage entrepreneurship by giving a failed debtor a fresh start. They are based on the assumption that a company has more value as a going concern than as the sum of its failed parts. Hence, Chapter 7 of the Bankruptcy Code applies only when it is certain that a company cannot be resuscitated.

After a bankruptcy petition is filed by either the debtor or the creditors, the court appoints a referee who arranges a creditors' meeting. The creditors bring proof of their claims against the company to the meeting. They also elect a trustee to liquidate the company's assets and distribute the proceeds. The trustee has the assets appraised and sold, some at auction and others after an active search for buyers. Because the assets are liquidated at distress prices, the proceeds from the sale are seldom sufficient to satisfy all of the creditors' claims.

Even if the proceeds were adequate, creditors do not get the first distribution. Chapter 7 establishes the priority of claims and requires settlement of the highest priority claims first.

Administrative Expenses. The fees and costs associated with the bankruptcy must be paid first. These include filing fees with the Bankruptcy Court, referee and trustee fees, attorneys' fees, asset appraisal fees, accounting fees, auctioneer and other liquidators' fees, and customary court costs for recording and transcribing the proceedings. These fees vary with the location of the court; the southern district in New York is known to be especially generous to lawyers.

Postpetition Unsecured Creditors. Companies rarely file bankruptcy petitions and then cease operating immediately. They continue to function for months, sometimes years. This means that they need trade credit and short-term loans as in their normal course of business. To encourage the extension of such credit, Chapter 7 gives second priority in liquidation to unsecured claims that arise after the petition is filed, but before the trustee is appointed.

Labor Claims. To maintain an ongoing concern, and even to complete the liquidation, company employees must continue to work. Since wages, salaries, and commissions always accrue instead of being paid for as incurred, Chapter 7 gives the employees third priority. It imposes a cap on these claims, however; they are not to exceed $2,000 per employee and they must have been earned no more than 90 days before the bankruptcy petition was filed. Claims beyond these limits are settled with all other unsecured creditors' claims.

FOCUS ON CAREERS

COMMERCIAL REAL ESTATE APPRAISER

A commercial real estate appraiser is responsible for estimating the value of commercial properties for commercial buyers and sellers, mortgage lenders, insurance underwriters, bankruptcy proceedings, and government agencies. The appraiser may also testify in zoning hearings or in property-related litigation. A commercial real estate appraiser may be self-employed or an employee of a bank, an insurance company, or a government agency such as the Resolution Trust Corporation or the Department of Housing and Urban Development.

The entry-level position is typically as an assistant to an experienced appraiser. Initial assignments are generally limited to field work and report preparation while studying to pass the necessary examinations to be certified by one or more of the accrediting agencies. The American Institute of Real Estate Appraisers (AIREA), perhaps the most influential of the accrediting boards, requires a candidate for their MAI designation to possess a four-year college degree, pass a series of five appraisal examinations, and have a minimum of five years of creditable appraisal experience. Other accrediting bodies include the American Society of Appraisers, the Society of Real Estate Appraisers, and the International Association of Assessing Officers. Entry-level salaries for commercial real estate appraisers are in the low to mid-twenties. Senior appraisers can earn $100,000 or more per year.

Pension Liabilities. Contributions that the company should have made to its pension plan but did not, must be paid next. As indicated earlier in the text, this distribution is complicated by federal insurance of pension funds.

Consumer Claims. Unsatisfied consumer claims for refunds of deposits to purchase, lease, or rent the company's goods or services have fifth priority. Chapter 7 limits these claims to $900 each.

Taxes. Income tax claims for three tax years prior to the petition and property tax claims for one year prior to the petition must be satisfied next. If the company failed to remit withholding taxes from its employees, these payments must also be made.

Secured Claims. The proceeds from the sale of assets pledged as collateral for loans are paid to the lenders. As illustrated in an earlier chapter, first mortgage holders must be paid in full before second mortgage holders receive anything. Senior debenture holders must be paid in full before subordinate debenture holders receive anything.

If the proceeds from the sale of collateral are insufficient to repay the secured debt in full, the unpaid balance is treated as unsecured debt. If the proceeds from the sale of collateral exceed the secured creditors' claims, the surplus is distributed to lower-priority classes of claimants.

Unsecured Claims. The unsecured claims that creditors documented at the meeting with the referee are paid next. Any claims that were filed after that meeting are paid at the same time, if the tardy creditors can establish that they did not know of the bankruptcy. Unsecured claims include the balances of the claims of secured creditors, if the proceeds from the sales of secured assets were insufficient to pay their claims in full. Accumulated unpaid dividends on preferred stock and declared but unpaid dividends on common stock are also paid at this point. After all of these claims are paid in full, the trustee satisfies the claims of unsecured creditors who knew about the bankruptcy, but filed late.

Miscellaneous. Unpaid fines and punitive damages assessed by other courts in legal actions resolved prior to the filing of the bankruptcy petition are paid next. Interest that has accrued on certain claims after the petition was filed also receives consideration at this stage.

Termination. Claims in each of the above classes must be paid in full before any payment can be made to claimants in the next class. If anything remains after all of these claims are paid in full, the preferred stockholders get the par plus paid-in value of their shares of stock. If anything is left after that (a highly unlikely event), a liquidating dividend is paid to the common stockholders. The residual is divided by the number of outstanding shares and distributed. At this point, the debtor is discharged and relieved of any further claims.

SUMMARY

A merger combines two companies into a new entity; in an acquisition, one company takes over another. An acquisition may involve the purchase of another company's assets or its stock. A company that does not want to be acquired and has no shark repellent devices in place may seek a white knight, pay greenmail, or take legal action against the potential acquirer.

Mergers and acquisitions are expected to increase the wealth of owners by producing economic benefits, improving management, or opening access to assets that the firms could not otherwise acquire. For a synergistic merger, the value of the combined firms exceeds the sum of the individual companies' values. By diversifying, a company may be able to reduce the variability inherent in its operations.

The exchange ratio determines how many shares of the target company to exchange for one share of the acquiring company. The target company's shareholders set an upper limit on this ratio; they will not exchange their shares at a loss. The acquiring company's shareholders set a lower limit on this ratio; they do not want the takeover to reduce the market price of their stock. Since the two groups of shareholders have conflicting interests, management must select an exchange ratio between the limits. The price–earnings ratio of the acquirer must be greater than the price–earnings ratio of the target to find a satisfactory exchange ratio.

A holding company obtains effective control of other companies without acquiring majority positions in their outstanding stocks. A holding company can form a pyramid by acquiring other holding companies; this structure magnifies both profits and losses.

A company can divest itself of assets, personnel, activities, product lines, divisions, or whole subsidiaries. It can accomplish these divestitures by abandoning, selling, or distributing assets. This may or may not enhance the value of the company's stock.

A technically insolvent company that can be rehabilitated must work out some arrangement with its creditors. It may do so through voluntary arrangements such as extensions and compositions, or it may reorganize its capital structure with Bankruptcy Court supervision and approval. Chapter 11 of the Bankruptcy Code regulates reorganizations; Chapter 7 regulates liquidations. When a company's financial problems are terminal, its assets are liquidated and the proceeds are distributed according to priorities established by federal law.

Key Terms

absolute priority rule
acquisition
attrition
composition
equity carve-out
exchange ratio
extension
Form 13-D
golden parachute
greenmail
merger
poison pill
pyramid
rightsizing
shark repellent device
spin-off
technical insolvency
tender offer
white knight

Self-Study Questions

1. List three shark repellent devices.
2. Give five reasons why companies may combine.
3. What is an exchange ratio?
4. What is a holding company? How does it become a pyramid?
5. What is the difference between a spin-off and an equity carve-out?
6. What is technical insolvency?
7. What is the difference between an extension and a composition agreement?
8. What different purposes do Chapter 7 and Chapter 11 of the Bankruptcy Act serve?
9. What three qualities must a reorganization plan have?
10. What is the first claim on the proceeds from the liquidation of a bankrupt company's assets?

Self-Test Problems

1. Curtis Co. is considering taking over Rivers Co. Find the upper and lower limits of the exchange ratio for the stock of these two companies:

	Curtis Co.	Rivers Co.
Net income	$37.5 million	$20 million
Shares outstanding	12.5 million	16 million
Earnings per share	$3.00	$1.25
Price–earnings ratio	12×	6×
Stock price	$36.00	$7.50

2. Curtis Co. is considering purchasing only 51 percent of Rivers Co. Using the information supplied in Problem 1, find the new lower limit to the exchange ratio.

Discussion Questions

1. Explain the difference between a merger and an acquisition.
2. What are the various ways in which one company can acquire the assets of another company?
3. If a company becomes a takeover target and has no shark repellents in place, what can its managers do to stop a takeover attempt?
4. Explain how a poison pill works.
5. If a company's managers have golden parachutes, why might they resist a takeover?
6. What is vertical integration? Why is it beneficial?
7. What is horizontal integration? Why is it beneficial?
8. What is synergy? Why is it beneficial?
9. Which of the many benefits of corporate combination did PepsiCo seek when it acquired KFC?
10. If a company with a high price–earnings ratio takes over a company with a low price–earnings ratio, the stockholders of both companies are usually pleased. Why?
11. Why would a company acquire only 51 percent of another company instead of 100 percent?
12. Pyramids are often subject to antitrust investigations. Why?
13. Why does downsizing become more difficult when personnel are involved instead of just assets?
14. How is a spin-off different from a sell-off? Which do stockholders prefer?
15. Explain how an extension works.
16. Explain how a composition works.
17. Explain the absolute priority rule.
18. Can stockholders' ownership ever be taken from them?
19. In the 1950s, investors who bought stock in the Dole Pineapple Company were told to "wish real hard that something bad happens to those pineapples." The company was carrying its Hawaiian real estate holdings on its

books at cost; some plantations were valued at $0.25 per acre. Is there a financial connection between these two bits of information?

20. In bankruptcy proceedings, which claims have priority over those of unsecured creditors?

Problems

1. Red Co. wants to take over Blue Co. Find the upper and lower limits of the exchange ratio for the stock of these two companies:

	RED CO.	BLUE CO.
Net income	$80 million	$16 million
Shares outstanding	50 million	8 million
Earnings per share	$1.60	$2.00
Price–earnings ratio	14×	9×
Stock price	$22.40	$18.00

2. Red Co. is considering purchasing only 51 percent of Blue Co. Using the information supplied in Problem 1, find the new lower limit.

Topics for Further Research

1. Grumman Corporation was the subject of a bidding war between Northrop and Martin Marietta in 1994. Look up the headlines about this episode in either the *New York Times Index* or *The Wall Street Journal Index*. Check the stock listings for all three companies. Write a report of the story based on all of the headlines.
2. What happened to the stock prices of R. J. Reynolds and Nabisco when RJR Nabisco was formed?
3. Macy's has been trying to reorganize under Chapter 11 proceedings for a long time. Explain the difficulties it has faced, beginning with the leveraged buyout by its management.

Answers to Self-Test Problems

1.

$$\text{Upper limit} = \$36.00/\$7.50 = 4.8{:}1$$

$$\text{Outstanding shares of Curtis Co.} = \$57.5\text{ million}/\$3 = 19{,}166{,}667$$

$$\text{New shares of Curtis Co.} = 19{,}166{,}667 - 12.5\text{ million} = 6{,}666{,}667$$

$$\text{lower limit} = 16\text{ million}/6{,}666{,}667 = 2.44{:}1$$

2.

$$\text{New lower limit} = (16\text{ million} \times 0.51)/6{,}666{,}667 = 1.22{:}1$$

APPENDIX

A

Review of Financial Statements and Accounting Principles

Financial reports present information on the financial position and performance of a business enterprise. These reports are prepared periodically by the firm, and include financial statements (the balance sheet, income statement, statement of retained earnings, and statement of cash flows), reports filed with the Securities and Exchange Commission, tax returns filed with various tax authorities, and special reports prepared for internal use.

Financial statements are the primary sources of public information about a firm. They summarize the firm's financial position and cover various aspects of its operation in some detail. They contain information on many financial characteristics, including the amount invested in the business, the division of this total investment into specific asset groups, short-term and long-term liabilities, net worth, profitability, and cash flow patterns. To use the financial data effectively, an analyst must know how they are determined, what information they reveal, what they do not reveal, and how to reorganize them to obtain specific, desired information.

Financial statements reflect accounting data maintained by the firm's accounting system. The accounting system consists of methods and devices to keep track of the firm's financial activities and to summarize them in a manner that is useful to management. The collection of data and the preparation of financial statements must follow certain ground rules to keep them relevant, reliable, comparable, and understandable, the characteristics that are considered to be essential to financial statements.

Every nation has its own particular set of rules governing financial statement development. In the United States, these ground rules (or accounting principles) are given by generally accepted accounting principles (GAAP). GAAP is a product of joint efforts between private sector organizations and the government to standardize financial reporting practices. The two private sector organizations directly involved in the development of accounting principles are the American Institute of Certified Public Accountants (AICPA) and the Financial Accounting Standards Board (FASB). Together they represent public accountants, accountants in industry, and accounting educators.

EXHIBIT A.1

Balance Sheet Format

Results of Past Investing Decisions	Results of Past Financing and Dividend Policy Decisions
Current assets	Current liabilities
Fixed assets	Long-term debt
	Minority interest
	Owner's equity
Total assets	Total liabilities and equity

The Securities and Exchange Commission (SEC) represents the government in this effort. It has the power to set accounting policies and disclosure requirements for U.S. companies that raise capital by issuing securities to the public. The SEC is not generally involved in formulating accounting principles. It provides official support and approval for the principles developed by the FASB.

The purpose of GAAP is to standardize the concepts and procedures for maintaining accounting data and preparing financial statements. Within the conceptual framework that GAAP provides for the preparation of financial statements, it allows considerable discretion. GAAP is a collection of assumptions (such as the going-concern and stable-dollar assumptions) and principles (such as revenue recognition, matching, and consistency) that set standards for financial reporting. The principles contained in GAAP are based on tradition, practice, and experience. They are reviewed periodically, and necessary changes are incorporated to reflect the changing business environment and developing reporting needs.

BALANCE SHEET

The balance sheet states a firm's financial position at a point in time, usually at the end of the firm's accounting year. It is often described as a snapshot of the firm's finances. The balance sheet shows the cumulative effects of the firm's past financial decisions on its investment, financing, and dividend policy. Results of investment activities appear divided between current (short-term) assets and fixed (long-term) assets. Results of financing activities and dividend policy appear divided among three categories: current (short-term) liabilities, long-term debt, and equity. Exhibit A.1 describes the balance sheet format.

The left side of the balance sheet records the firm's total investment or uses of funds; the right side records how the firm financed investments using debt and equity sources. Since the total investment cannot exceed the finances obtained, the two sides of the balance sheet must necessarily be equal. Hence, the following identity always holds.

Assets = Liabilities (current and long-term) + Stockholders' equity

This identity can also be expressed in another way:

Assets - Liabilities = Stockholders' equity

The balance sheet format is designed to facilitate understanding of the financial position of a business. It lists assets according to the speed with which the firm can use them or convert them into cash, that is, according to their liquidity. This means that the assets listed near the top of the balance sheet can be converted into cash more quickly than those listed toward the bottom.

Current assets include cash and cash equivalents, accounts receivable, and inventory. These short-term items are *current* because the firm expects to use them up or produce cash in one year or one operating cycle, whichever is longer. The operating cycle of a firm is the time required to purchase (or manufacture) inputs, convert the inputs into finished products, sell the finished products, and collect cash. Most business operations have operating cycles of less than a year, but they can be longer, as in distilling and tobacco processing.

Fixed assets include tangible assets such as plant and equipment, as well as intangible assets such as patents and goodwill. The firm uses up these assets over a longer time, and it does not expect to convert them into cash within one year or one operating cycle.

The balance sheet lists liabilities in order of how quickly the firm needs to pay them. Current liabilities include accounts payable, bank borrowing, accrued expenses, and current amounts due on long-term debt. These short-term debts are *current* because the firm must pay them within one year or one operating cycle. Long-term debt consists of outstanding bond issues and long-term loans that the company repays over many years.

Equity generally consists of stock issues and retained earnings, however, it may include additional entries such as treasury shares and a cumulative translation adjustment. The total represents the funds supplied by stockholders and it is worth noting that a firm never has to pay its stockholders except in liquidation. The balance sheet of a fictitious firm, ZeeTec Corporation, is illustrated in Exhibit A.2.

Users of financial statements should recognize that balance sheets of different companies may not be directly comparable because:

1. GAAP allows substantial discretion in the preparation of balance sheets.
2. Accountants use professional judgment in determining the treatment of situations not specifically covered by GAAP.

Cash and Cash Equivalents

Cash and cash equivalents represent the funds held by the firm as of the balance sheet date. A firm usually invests cash that it does not immediately need in short-term, interest-bearing securities that it can reconvert into cash quickly. Known as *cash equivalents*, these include securities such as Treasury bills, negotiable certificates of deposit, and prime commercial paper. These securities are shown on the

EXHIBIT A.2

Sample Balance Sheet

ZeeTec Corporation
Consolidated Balance Sheet
For Years 19X1 and 19X2
($millions)

	19X2	19X1
Current assets		
Cash and cash equivalents	$82.00	$80.50
Accounts receivable	152.00	145.50
Inventories	210.00	206.00
Total current assets	$444.00	$432.00
Fixed assets		
Property, plant, and equipment (net of depreciation)	375.50	356.00
Other fixed assets	84.50	62.00
Total fixed assets	$460.00	$418.00
Total assets	$904.00	$850.00

	19X2	19X1
Current liabilities:		
Accounts payable	$ 95.00	$ 92.00
Notes payable (bank loans)	110.50	102.00
Accrued liabilities	45.00	38.50
Other	22.50	20.50
Total current liabilities	$273.00	$253.00
Long-term debt	285.00	264.00
Minority interest	65.00	65.00
Stockholders' equity		
Capital stock		
Common stock ($2 per share, authorized 15 million, issued and outstanding 15 million)	$ 30.00	$ 30.00
Additional paid-in capital	152.50	150.00
Retained earnings	140.40	120.00
Treasury shares	(25.50)	(21.50)
Cumulative translation adjustment	(16.40)	(10.50)
Total stockholders' equity	$281.00	$268.00
Total liabilities and stockholder's equity	$904.00	$850.00

balance sheet at cost or market value, whichever is lower; the basis of measurement must be disclosed. If a firm has short-term investments in other marketable securities, such as bonds, it lists them in a separate item after this account.

Accounts Receivable

When a business sells goods and services on credit, it creates accounts receivable. Accounts receivable are payment obligations of the firm's customers. These assets of the firm are treated as current assets because they are usually paid within 30 to 60 days. Sometimes, the terms of credit sales may specify longer payment periods (even longer than one year), reflecting a longer operating cycle. Accounts receivable follow just after cash and cash equivalents in order of liquidity. The value reported in this account is the outstanding balance on credit sales as of the balance sheet date. It is common practice to present this value net of any estimates of doubtful and uncollectible amounts.

Inventory

The inventory account measures the value of raw materials, goods in process, and finished goods held by the firm as of the balance sheet date. For a retail store, inventory would consist of only finished goods held for sale. A manufacturer's inventory would consist of all three types of goods. Inventory flows through the operating cycle of a business. It declines with sales and increases with new purchases. This characteristic creates complications for inventory valuation.

The cost principle mandates that a firm carry inventory on its balance sheet at cost. Accounting principles also require that the cost of goods sold match the revenue generated by selling the same goods. If the company acquires inventories at different periods of time and at different costs, then matching cost with revenue and determining the value of end-of-period inventory can become a challenging task for a firm with an inventory of hundreds of items. This job becomes difficult because the flow of inventory seldom corresponds to the actual order in which products are sold.

There are several acceptable methods of determining the cost of end-of-period inventory. The most commonly used methods are:

1. Specific identification method
2. Average cost method
3. First-in, first-out method
4. Last-in, first-out method

The method by which a firm chooses to determine the cost of end-of-period inventory may result in an understatement or an overstatement of its value. This will affect the value of the inventory on the balance sheet as well as the cost of goods sold, the net income, and the taxes reported on the income statement.

The value of end-of-period inventory and the cost of goods sold during the year are related. Determining one determines the other. This relationship is expressed as:

$$\begin{matrix}\text{Cost of goods} \\ \text{available for sale}\end{matrix} - \begin{matrix}\text{Value of} \\ \text{ending inventory}\end{matrix} = \begin{matrix}\text{Cost of goods} \\ \text{sold}\end{matrix}$$

The cost of goods available for sale is the sum of the cost of beginning inventory and the cost of new purchases during the period.

Given the income statement structure, net income is affected by the cost of goods sold. Thus, the inventory valuation method chosen also affects the firm's net income. The following statements help summarize the effects of the inventory valuation method on balance sheet and income statement figures:

1. If the inventory valuation method overstates the value of ending inventory, this will understate the cost of goods sold and overstate net income for the period.
2. If the inventory valuation method understates the value of ending inventory, this will overstate the cost of goods sold and understate the net income for the period.

Specific Identification Method. The specific identification method matches each sale with a specific item in the firm's inventory. Every item in the firm's ending inventory is identified with a specific purchase. The cost of goods sold and the value of the ending inventory are determined accordingly. This method is easy to apply and a logical choice to account for inventory items that differ from each other, have high prices, or low volumes. Inventories of items such as paintings, rare coins, real estate, and heavy equipment fall into this category.

Average Cost Method. The average cost method ignores any differences in the prices paid for inventory at different times. It simply calculates the average cost of all inventory items and uses this average cost to determine the cost of goods sold and the value of the ending inventory. The value of the ending inventory and the cost of goods sold under this method will differ from those determined under the specific identification method.

First-in, First-out (FIFO) Method. The FIFO method assumes that the firm sells its oldest stock first. The ending inventory of any item, therefore, consists of the most recently purchased units. Under this method, the value of the ending inventory reflects the prices of recent purchases, and the cost of goods sold reflects the prices of older units. During a period of inflation, this method prices inventory at a higher value and gives a lower cost of goods sold than the average cost method.

Last-in, First-out (LIFO) Method. The LIFO method assumes that the firm sells its newest stock first. This method assumes that ending inventory consists of older units, hence its value will reflect the prices paid for the older units. During an inflationary period, this method prices inventory at a lower value and gives a higher cost of goods sold than the average cost method. This method does conform to the matching principle of accounting, but it undervalues inventory on the balance sheet, with respect to its replacement cost, during an inflationary period.

All four methods of inventory valuation are acceptable for financial reporting and for reporting taxable income. Firms may use different methods for different types of inventory or for inventories in different geographic regions. The selection of a method (or methods) is a managerial decision, but the balance sheet must disclose the selection. During inflationary periods, the LIFO method becomes the popular choice because it can reduce taxable income. Many U.S. firms switched to LIFO during the inflationary periods of the 1970s and the early 1980s. Note, however, that if a firm uses the LIFO method for tax purposes, it is required to use the same method to report net income.

Fixed Assets

As mentioned before, this account may consist of both tangible and intangible assets. Tangible assets are useful physical objects, generally summarized under the title *property, plant, and equipment* (PP&E). Intangible assets are nonmaterial assets such as patents, copyrights, trademarks, goodwill, and franchises. The balance sheet value of fixed assets represents the cost of acquiring them, net of any accumulated depreciation and amortization. The cost of PP&E is the total expenditures necessary to acquire them and place them in use. It does not include any expenditures for ordinary maintenance and repairs.

Fixed asset costs are allocated against revenues based on their contributions to production and sales. Tangible assets, except land, are depreciated while intangible assets are amortized over their estimated useful lives. The remaining, undepreciated or unamortized value appears in the balance sheet.

Management has considerable discretion in choosing the method by which to depreciate fixed assets. Depreciation involves estimating an asset's economic (useful) life, estimating its residual (salvage) value, and selecting a cost allocation method. Management's decisions on these matters determines annual allocations for fixed asset costs (depreciation expenses), which, in turn, affect the firm's taxes and net income. Management can use one method of depreciation for tax purposes and another method to report net income. The notes to the financial statements should disclose the method.

Prior to 1981, management could use any one of three depreciation methods: straight-line, units-of-output, and accelerated depreciation. The straight-line method spreads the cost of the asset evenly over its useful life. This method is most appropriate when the usage of the asset is uniform over its useful life. This method computes the annual depreciation expense by subtracting the estimated residual value from the cost and dividing this depreciable basis by the estimated useful life. In practice, however, the residual value is often ignored, and the annual depreciation expense is just the cost divided by the number of years of the asset's useful life.

The units-of-output method calculates the annual depreciation expense based on an asset's estimated units of output. The first step divides the depreciable basis (the cost minus the estimated residual value) by the estimated units of output for the life of the asset to arrive at the depreciation expense per unit of output. Multiplying the depreciation expense per unit of output by the number of units of output per year gives the annual depreciation expense.

Each of several different accelerated depreciation methods allocates a larger portion of the cost of an asset to the earlier years of its life. This means that they transfer the cost of an asset to the depreciation expense more rapidly than the straight-line method. The underlying assumption of these methods is that many types of plant and equipment work most efficiently when they are new. Therefore, following the matching principle, a larger portion of an asset's cost should be allocated to its early years. The preferred methods for reporting income to tax authorities reduce the firm's taxable income in the early years of an asset's life and give the firm the benefit of the time value of money.

The accelerated methods include the double-declining-balance approach and the sum-of-the-years'-digits approach. The first allocates the largest portion of the asset's cost to the early years of its life by doubling the straight-line depreciation rate and applying this accelerated rate to a declining base to calculate the annual depreciation expense. This method eliminates the need to subtract the estimated residual value from the cost to determine the depreciable basis, as it automatically generates a residual value.

The sum-of-the-years'-digits method sets yearly depreciation rates by dividing the remaining years of the asset's useful life (as of the beginning of the year) by the sum of the years of useful life. Applying these rates to the depreciable basis of the asset gives the yearly depreciation expense. For example, if an asset has six years of useful life, then the depreciation rates are:

YEAR	DEPRECIATION RATE
1	6/(6+5+4+3+2+1) = 6/21 = 0.2857
2	5/(6+5+4+3+2+1) = 5/21 = 0.2381
3	4/(6+5+4+3+2+1) = 4/21 = 0.1905
4	3/(6+5+4+3+2+1) = 3/21 = 0.1429
5	2/(6+5+4+3+2+1) = 2/21 = 0.0952
6	1/(6+5+4+3+2+1) = 1/21 = 0.0476
	1.0000

In 1981, Congress introduced a new approach for depreciation, the Accelerated Cost Recovery System (ACRS); it modified this method in 1986 as part of the Tax Reform Act. This modified system is commonly referred to as MACRS. The current tax laws require that taxpayers use either MACRS or the straight-line method to compute depreciation expenses.

MACRS does not adjust the cost of an asset for estimated residual value to determine its depreciable basis. The calculation of the depreciation expense follows the double-declining-balance method with a change to the straight-line method when it begins to give a larger depreciation expense. MACRS allocates the largest portion of the asset's cost to its early years, as does the double-declining-balance approach. There is no need to calculate the depreciation rates under MACRS as the IRS provides tables for each class of assets.

The Tax Reform Act of 1986 introduced several other changes regarding depreciation. It defined the depreciable lives of assets by classifying them into depreciable-life classes. Prior to 1986, the depreciable life estimate for an asset could differ from firm to firm. MACRS has eliminated this possibility. Every firm now depreciates similar assets over the same number of years.

The 1986 tax rules on depreciation assume that the firm places all assets in use or disposes of them in the middle of a year. This is known as the *half-year convention*. The half-year convention affects the first year's depreciation expense, calculating the initial expense for only six months. The half-year convention also increases the period over which the asset is depreciated by a half year.

Exhibit A.3 illustrates cost allocation under both MACRS and the straight-line method for a copier that costs $10,000 and is placed in service in February. The copier falls into the MACRS five-year property class.

The choice of depreciation method is the responsibility of management. Past surveys of corporate managers have indicated that they prefer the straight-line method for financial reporting because it allows them to report higher net income. The consistency principle of accounting requires that firms maintain the same

EXHIBIT A.3

Depreciation Schedules

Straight-Line Method: Depreciable basis = $10,000

Year	Depreciation Rate	Computation	Depreciation Expense	Accumulated Depreciation	Book Value
1	20%(0.5)	$10,000(0.1)	$1,000	$1,000	$9,000
2	20	10,000(0.2)	2,000	3,000	7,000
3	20	10,000(0.2)	2,000	5,000	5,000
4	20	10,000(0.2)	2,000	7,000	3,000
5	20	10,000(0.2)	2,000	9,000	1,000
6	20(0.5)	10,000(0.1)	1,000	10,000	0

MACRS: Depreciable basis = $10,000

Year	Depreciation Rate from IRS Table	Depreciation Expense	Accumulated Depreciation	Book Value
1	20.00%	$2,000	$2,000	$8,000
2	32.00	3,200	5,200	4,800
3	19.20	1,920	7,120	2,880
4	11.52	1,152	8,272	1,728
5	11.52	1,152	9,424	576
6	5.76	576	10,000	0

method of depreciation from year to year. This does not, however, prevent them from using different methods for different assets, and different methods for financial statements and tax returns.

Accounts Payable

Accounts payable are short-term obligations that arise from trade credit provided by suppliers of merchandise and services. This account reports the amount outstanding as of the date of the balance sheet.

Notes Payable

Notes payable measures the outstanding balance on short-term bank loans obtained by the firm. It may also include notes payable that arise from transactions such as purchases of real estate and expensive equipment.

Accrued Liabilities

Accrued liabilities represent expenses recognized in the accounting records for which the firm has not yet made cash payments. Payroll, rent, insurance premiums, taxes, lease payments, and interest payments are some examples. The amount on the balance sheet measures the amount owed (accrued), but not yet paid as of the balance sheet date.

Current Portion of Long-Term Debt

The current portion of long-term debt measures the portion of long-term debt that the firm must pay in the current year. This includes any repayments of principal on maturing bonds and the principal portions of mortgage obligations and other long-term debt.

Long-Term Debt

Long-term debt reports outstanding long-term obligations of the firm. It includes bond issues, long-term notes, mortgages, obligations under leases, and other long-term liabilities.

Minority Interest

When a company acquires a controlling interest (more than 50 percent equity) in another company, the consolidation of the statements of the two companies combines the assets of both on the asset side of a single balance sheet. The minority interest represents the portion of the acquired business that the parent firm does not own. It is carried on the liability side of the balance sheet, although it is not a true liability like a debt obligation that would require periodic payments.

Stockholders' Equity

Stockholders' equity represents the firm's ownership interest. It is a residual item determined by subtracting total liabilities from total assets. This classification consists of several subaccounts: capital stock, additional paid-in capital, retained earnings, treasury shares, and a cumulative translation adjustment for any foreign operations.

The capital stock account measures the par value of the common and preferred stock issues of the firm. The additional paid-in capital account shows the difference between the par value and the price obtained when the firm issued the stock. The sum of the capital stock and the additional paid-in capital constitutes the total paid-in capital.

The retained earnings account represents the sum of past, undistributed profits. Retained earnings should not be confused with the firm's cash balances. There is no connection between the two. Retained earnings represent internally generated earnings that the firm has reinvested in the business rather than paying them out as dividends. Year-to-year changes in the retained earnings account are detailed in a separate statement known as the *statement of retained earnings*.

The treasury stock account represents the value (at cost) of the firm's own shares that it reacquires after issue. Firms frequently purchase shares of their own stock in the open market. They may do this to meet the requirements of employee stock option and retirement plans, as a use for excess cash, and to raise reported earnings per share by reducing the number of outstanding shares. When the firm pays cash to acquire these shares, its assets and stockholders' equity decline by the same amount. Therefore, this subaccount is a negative entry in the equity section of the balance sheet.

The cumulative translation adjustment account is the accumulated foreign exchange gain or loss resulting from translation of accounts from the balance sheets of foreign subsidiaries. To prepare a consolidated balance sheet that must account for foreign operations, the firm must convert the accounts of its foreign subsidiaries into its reporting currency, which is the dollar for a U.S. corporation. The conversion or translation may raise or reduce the dollar value of the assets and liabilities of foreign subsidiaries, depending on the direction of the changes in exchange rates since the last balance sheet date. FASB Statement 52 requires that the firm report the net effect of these changes (translation gains or losses) in the equity section of the consolidated balance sheet on a cumulative basis.

INCOME STATEMENT

The purpose of the income statement is to present the operating results of a business by matching the revenue earned during a period with the expenses incurred in earning that revenue. Analysts judge the performance of a firm in terms of its earnings. The income statement presents several measures of earnings. One of these measures, net income, represents the pure profit of the firm. The income statement is structured on the identity:

$$\text{Revenue} - \text{Expenses} = \text{Income}$$

Users of an income statement must recognize that the information that it provides is the product of a wide range of accounting choices, estimates, and judgments made by management. Income and expenditures are measured on an accrual basis, not on a cash basis (i.e., income is recognized when due and expenses when incurred, not when cash changes hands).

The income statement consists of three sections: the operating, nonoperating, and income sections. The operating section contains information on revenue and expenditures directly related to its operations; the nonoperating section contains information on net interest, taxes, and income from other sources; the income section contains information on net income and earnings per common share. The income statement is also known by other titles: the *earnings statement*, the *statement of operations*, and the *profit and loss* (P&L) *statement*.

Income statements are presented in two common formats—multiple-step and single-step. A multiple-step statement reports individual revenue and expense items and provides several intermediate earnings measures. This format is widely used for preparing the monthly income statements used by financial managers of large corporations. A single-step sums all revenue items to show a single revenue total, and all expense items to show a single expense total. The single-step format is usually used in income statements distributed to stockholders. Multiple-step and single-step income statements of the fictitious company, ZeeTec Corporation, are illustrated in Exhibits A.4 and A.5.

EXHIBIT A.4

Multiple-Step Income Statement

ZeeTec Corporation
Consolidated Statement of Income
for the Years Ended 19X1 and 19X2
($ millions)

	19X2	19X1
Sales revenue		
Sales	$235.00	$210.00
Less: returns, allowances, and discounts	2.00	1.50
Net sales	$233.00	$208.50
Cost of goods sold	140.00	135.50
Gross profit	$93.00	$73.00
Operating expenses		
Selling	8.50	7.00
General and administrative	35.00	33.00
Depreciation	9.00	8.00
Total operating expenses	$52.50	$48.00
Operating profit	$40.50	$25.00
Other income and expenses		
Interest income	0.60	0.50
Interest expenses	(2.60)	(2.00)
Net other income	(2.00)	(1.50)
Earnings before taxes	$38.50	$23.50
Taxes	13.09	7.99
Net income	$25.41	$15.51
Earnings per common share	$1.69	1.03
(Average shares outstanding: 15 million)		

Sales Revenue

The sales revenue entry reports the firm's total revenue from cash and credit sales during the accounting period, net of returns, allowances, and discounts. A sales return is a cancelled sale in which the customer returns merchandise. A sales allowance is a price reduction offered to customers for damaged and display merchandise. A sales discount is a cash discount offered on credit sales for early payment. A quantity discount is a cash discount offered to customers who purchase large quantities of merchandise at one time.

Cost of Goods Sold

The cost of goods sold value comes from the inventory accounting system. As mentioned before, the firm's inventory valuation method has a significant impact on this amount.

EXHIBIT A.5

Single-Step Income Statement

ZeeTec Corporation
Consolidated Statement of Income
for the Years Ended 19X1 and 19X2
($ millions)

	19X2	19X1
Revenue		
Net sales	$233.00	$208.50
Interest income	0.60	0.50
Total revenue	$233.60	$209.00
Expenses		
Cost of goods sold	140.00	135.50
Selling	8.50	7.00
General and administrative	35.00	33.00
Depreciation	9.00	8.00
Interest	2.60	2.00
Total expenses	$195.10	$185.50
Income before taxes	$38.50	$23.50
Taxes	13.09	7.99
Net income	$25.41	$15.51
Earnings per common share	$ 1.69	1.03
(Average shares outstanding: 15 million)		

Gross Profit

Gross profit is the difference between the net revenue and the cost of goods sold. It is used in the calculation of the gross profit margin, a measure of efficiency.

Operating Expenses

Operating expenses cover a broad area. They include operating costs for selling, insurance, advertising, rent, administration, repairs and maintenance, utilities, lease obligations (if any), and depreciation.

Operating Profit

Operating profit represents the firm's profit from its operations. As such, this is a measure of the overall performance of the firm. It is also termed *gross margin.*

Other Income and Expenses

The other income and expenses entry includes revenues and expenses from non-operating activities. Typical nonoperating income and expenses are interest received and paid, dividends received, management fees, royalties, gains and losses on securities transactions, and capital gains or losses on the sales of fixed assets.

Earnings before Tax (EBT)

EBT represents earnings before deducting corporate taxes owed to units of federal, state, and local government. Tax is calculated on this amount using an appropriate tax rate. The tax amount reported on the income statement may not equal the amount the firm actually pays if it uses a different depreciation method in reporting income to the tax authorities. Furthermore, the tax amount reported may include more than just income tax. It may be the total of federal, state, and local income taxes, property taxes, excise taxes, foreign taxes (frequently value-added taxes), capital gains taxes, and transfer taxes.

Net Income

Net income is often referred to as the *bottom line*. It represents the firm's profit after deducting all expenses, including taxes.

Earnings per Common Share (EPS)

Every publicly owned business must report EPS. It is the most widely used measure of a firm's performance. EPS is calculated by dividing net income by the number of outstanding common shares, when the firm has only common shares outstanding. If it has preferred stock outstanding, EPS is calculated after subtracting preferred dividends from net income. This is sometimes referred to as *earnings available per common share* (EAPS).

When a firm has convertible preferred stock, warrants, and/or convertible bonds outstanding, it must calculate EPS twice, once on the basis of outstanding common shares (called *primary EPS*) and again on the basis of the common shares that would be outstanding if the holders of all convertible securities and warrants were to convert them into common shares (called *fully diluted EPS* or FDEPS). FDEPS reflects the impact of potential conversion. It is smaller than primary EPS when the firm has convertible securities or warrants outstanding. If the potential dilution reduces the primary EPS by 3 percent or more, then the firm must report both measures of earnings per share.

STATEMENT OF RETAINED EARNINGS

The statement of retained earnings is the least complicated of the financial statements prepared by a firm. It reports changes in the retained earnings account on the balance sheet between two reporting dates. Exhibit A.6 illustrates the structure of the statement of retained earnings using the numbers of the fictitious ZeeTec Corporation.

ZeeTec Corporation has no preferred shares outstanding, so this statement shows no cash dividends on preferred stock. The company pays $5.01 million in cash dividends on common stock. With 15 million common shares outstanding, this amounts to a $0.334 dividend per share. The remaining profit of $20.4 million ($25,410,000 – $5,010,000) is added to the beginning-of-period retained earnings to obtain the end-of-period retained earnings.

EXHIBIT A.6

Sample Statement of Retained Earnings

ZeeTec Corporation
Statement of Consolidated Retained Earnings
for the Year 19X2
($ millions)

		19X2
Retained earnings at the beginning of the accounting period		$120.00
Net income for the year		25.41
Subtotal		$145.41
Less Cash dividends on preferred stock	(0.00)	
Cash dividends on common stock	(5.01)	
Stock dividend	(0.00)	
Subtotal		(5.01)
Retained earnings at the end of the accounting period		$140.40

ZeeTec paid no stock dividends. If it had, the accounting treatment would depend on their size. When stock dividends are small (less than 20 percent) and the firm holds no treasury stock, the market value of the new shares allocated as dividends is transferred from the retained earnings account to the capital stock and additional paid-in capital accounts. This process is called *capitalization of retained earnings*. The payment of these stock dividends does not alter total stockholders' equity.

Large stock dividends, however, are treated differently. Only the par value portion of the price of the new shares is transferred from the retained earnings account to the capital stock account.

STATEMENT OF CASH FLOWS

The statement of cash flows summarizes the firm's cash transactions during the accounting period. It reports cash inflows and outflows relating to various aspects of the firm's operations, categorized by their related activities. Three broad categories in the statement are: cash flows from operating activities, cash flows from investing activities, and cash flows from financing activities.

Cash Flows from Operating Activities

Operating activities include activities connected with the production and delivery of goods for sale. The cash flows that generally result from these activities are:

CASH INFLOWS	CASH OUTFLOWS
Collections from customers	Cash paid to suppliers
Interest and dividend receipts	Cash paid to employees
Other receipts of cash from operations	Interest paid
	Taxes paid
	Other payments relating to operations

Cash Flows from Investing Activities

Investing activities include acquiring and disposing of securities and fixed assets. The cash flows resulting from these activities are:

CASH INFLOWS	CASH OUTFLOWS
Cash from selling securities (of other firms)	Payments for fixed assets
Cash from selling fixed assets	Payments for debt and equity securities of other firms
Cash from collecting loan principal payments	Loans advanced

Cash Flows from Financing Activities

Financing activities include borrowing, raising capital by issuing debt and equity securities, redeeming debt, and paying dividends to stockholders. The cash flows resulting from these activities are:

CASH INFLOWS	CASH OUTFLOWS
Proceeds from short-term and long-term borrowing	Repayment of loan principal (excluding interest)
Cash from selling stock	Payments of cash dividends
	Purchases of the firm's own shares.

The statement of cash flows represents changes in the balance sheet accounts between two periods. Since the balance sheet always balances, these changes should also balance. In the balancing process, the cash account absorbs the net effect of changes in other balance sheet accounts.

The importance of the statement of cash flows lies in supplying information that the income statement does not provide. The income statement accounts for income and expenses on an accrual basis, whereas the statement of cash flows presents the cash effects of operating and nonoperating activities to a firm on a cash basis. A company may have a positive net income, but it can still go bankrupt if it does not have enough cash.

Exhibit A.7 illustrates the structure of the statement of cash flows using the 19X2 statement for the fictitious ZeeTec Corporation. The net increase (decrease) in cash shown in Exhibit A.7 will be absorbed by the cash account on the 19X2 balance sheet. Since it is a net increase, the 19X2 cash account will be larger by that amount.

EXHIBIT A.7

Sample Statement of Cash Flows

ZeeTec Corporation
Statement of Cash Flows
for the Year 19X2
($millions)

	19X2
Cash flows from operating activities:	
Cash received from customers	$186.90
Interest and dividends received	2.60
Cash paid to suppliers of inventory	(80.40)
Cash paid to employees	(45.50)
Cash paid for other operating expenditures	(33.40)
Interest paid on loans	(2.00)
Taxes paid	(13.09)
Net cash flow	$15.11
Cash flows from investing activities	
Purchases of securities	$(4.50)
Purchases of fixed assets	(56.10)
Proceeds from sales of securities	5.90
Proceeds from sales of fixed assets	5.10
Net cash flow	$(49.60)
Cash flows from financing activities	
Cash dividends paid	$(5.01)
Repayments of short-term and long-term debts	(10.60)
Proceeds from short-term and long-term borrowing	51.60
Net cash flow	35.99
Net increase (decrease) in cash	$1.50

Discussion Questions

1. Why must firms prepare financial statements according to certain ground rules?
2. What is GAAP? What does the Financial Accounting Standards Board have to do with it?
3. Why does a balance sheet always have to balance?
4. What is current about current assets and liabilities?
5. How are cost of goods sold, inventory value, and net income related?
6. Compare and contrast the FIFO, LIFO, and average cost methods of inventory valuation.
7. Why are certain assets depreciated or amortized and not treated as expenses in the year of their acquisition? Name the methods of depreciation discussed in the text.
8. Why is accelerated depreciation the preferred method for reporting taxable income?
9. How do the multiple-step and single-step income statement formats differ?

EXHIBIT A.8

Montegu Corp. Financial Statements

Montegu Corporation
Consolidated Balance Sheet
For Years 19X1 and 19X2
($ millions)

	19X2	19X1		19X2	19X1
Current assets			Current liabilities		
Cash and cash equivalents	$10.00	$12.50	Accounts payable	$16.00	$18.00
Accounts receivable	55.50	50.00	Notes payable	63.00	65.50
Inventories	70.00	80.00	Accrued liabilities	4.00	4.50
Total current assets	$135.50	$142.50	Total current liabilities	$83.00	$88.00
Total fixed assets	150.00	140.00	Long-term debt	87.00	82.00
			Stockholders' equity		
			Capital stock		
			Common stock	5.00	5.00
			Additional paid-in capital	65.00	65.00
			Retained earnings	45.50	42.50
			Total stockholders' equity	115.50	112.50
Total assets	$285.50	$282.50	Total liabilities and stockholders' equity	$285.50	$282.50

Montegu Corporation
Consolidated Income Statement
For the Years Ended 19X1 and 19X2
($ millions)

	19X2	19X1
Net sales revenue	$180.00	$190.00
Cost of goods sold	115.50	125.00
Gross profit	$64.50	$65.00
Total operating expenses	42.50	44.50
Operating profit	$22.00	$20.50
Other income and expenses		
Interest income	0.40	0.35
Interest expenses	(1.50)	(1.60)
Net other income	(1.10)	(1.25)
Earnings before taxes	$20.90	$19.25
Taxes	7.11	6.54
Net income	$13.79	$12.71

10. What does the statement of cash flows report? What are the major differences between the statement of cash flows and the income statement?

Problems

1. Excel Corporation, a construction company, acquires a tractor at a cost of \$300,000. This equipment falls into the MACRS five-year property class. Calculate the depreciation schedule for this equipment under both the MACRS and the straight-line methods.

   Note: Problems 2 through 5 are based on the income statement and balance sheet of Montegu Corporation in Exhibit A.8.
2. Present Montegu's income statement in single-step format.
3. Construct a statement of retained earnings for Montegu Corporation for 19X2. Assume that Montegu paid cash dividends of \$10.79 million to common stockholders during the year.
4. Identify Montegu's cash flows from operating activities during 19X2.
5. Construct a statement of cash flows for Montegu Corporation for 19X2.

APPENDIX

B

Forms of Business Organization

Businesses are generally organized in one of three principal forms: proprietorship, partnership, or corporation. Businesses also organize themselves in other ways as joint ventures, trusts, syndicates, and joint stock companies, but these forms are significantly less important in the United States.

Each of the principal business organizational forms has its advantages and disadvantages; consequently, they tend to coexist. The most popular form of business organization in the United States is the sole proprietorship. It is estimated that more than 70 percent of all firms operate under this legal form. However, larger entities prefer the corporate form. Nearly 90 percent of all business revenues are generated by corporations, although they constitute less than 20 percent of all firms.

SOLE PROPRIETORSHIPS

A sole proprietorship is a business owned, and frequently operated, by one individual. Perhaps its greatest advantage is its ease of formation. Any individual can start a business. All that is necessary is the desire to do so.

Although the IRS requires every firm to obtain a tax identification number and many states license various business activities, there are no real constraints on establishing a sole proprietorship. It isn't even necessary to open an office; many entrepreneurs operate directly from their homes.

Sole proprietors make up a significant portion of the service industry in the U.S. Such services as dressmaking, housecleaning, textbook editing and financial planning are normally performed by individuals under the proprietorship form of organization. The proprietorship is also the common form of business organization in retail trade, personal transportation, and home repair.

Since the business is individually owned, the proprietor is solely responsible for all decisions. This may be beneficial since it permits a business to react rapidly to a changing environment. It may also be a disadvantage because the owner may lack expertise in all areas of the company's operations. Consequently, the proprietor

EXHIBIT B.1

Federal Personal Income Taxes (1993—Married Filing Jointly)

INCOME	TAX[a]	MIDRANGE AVERAGE TAX RATE
$ 0–36,900	15%	15.00%
36,900–89,150	$5,535.00 + 28%	20.39
89,150–140,000	20,165.00 + 31%	24.48
140,000–250,000	35,928.50 + 36%	28.58
over 250,000	75,528.50 + 39.6%	34.91[b]

[a]The tax rate applies to any income in excess of the base amount. If taxable income were $50,000, the tax on this income would be $5,535 plus 28 percent of all income in excess of $36,900, for a total tax of $9,203.

[b]On $500,000

Source: Your Federal Income Tax, For Individuals (1993), Washington, D.C., Internal Revenue Service, 1993.

may be forced to incur additional expenses to obtain the expert advice necessary to manage a successful enterprise.

Being the sole owner also means that the individual is personally liable for all of the firm's debts. Should the proprietorship incur a business loss or be sued for a business problem, all of the proprietor's personal assets, not just the assets used in the business, are at risk. While insurance can mitigate some of the risk from legal action, there is no protection from the effects of bad business judgment.

Other disadvantages of the sole proprietorship include the difficulty of obtaining large sums of capital and the limited life of the firm. The capital available to the enterprise is limited to funds the owner can raise, usually from personal savings, family, and (occasionally) friends. Some aggressive banks offer credit cards for sole proprietorships, but their credit lines are not especially generous.

The life of the enterprise ceases at the owner's death, although family members may continue the firm's operations. Family members seldom have the desire, drive, or decision making experience necessary to keep the enterprise profitable. Additionally, the termination of the business may have important tax consequences.

The tax authorities treat the proprietorship's income as belonging to the individual. Thus, the individual tax rates as shown in Exhibit B.1 apply to all business income. Given the individual's tax bracket and the amount of earnings reinvested in the business, this may or may not be an advantage. Cash withdrawn from the business, however, is not subject to double taxation as are corporate dividends.

PARTNERSHIPS

A partnership is a business owned by two or more individuals. Except for the number of owners, the partnership form of organization closely resembles the proprietorship. For instance, liability for business losses now extends to all owners and their personal assets. Technically this is termed *joint and several liability*.

Specifically, this means that any one of the partners can be held liable for all of the firm's losses. The partner who incurs the loss then must collect from the others. Note, also, that should one of the partners incur nonbusiness losses, the business assets of that partner are at risk.

Like the proprietorship, the life of the partnership is also limited. Should any of the partners die, the firm is considered terminated. To avoid the consequences of such an event, most partnership agreements transfer the business assets to the remaining partners in exchange for specified compensation. Generally that compensation is limited to the proceeds of a partnership life insurance policy. The existence of such a partnership agreement permits the operations of the firm to continue uninterrupted under a new partnership agreement.

Many of the advantages of the proprietorship remain in the partnership form. For example, a partnership is relatively easy to form; it can be consummated by a simple handshake among the parties involved without any written agreement or conditions. More often than not, however, a partnership agreement is formally drawn up and filed with the state. Such formality is required when the partners have unequal shares in the firm or when one or more silent partners are involved (as explained further under the heading *Limited Partnership* below). Even if the partners file an agreement, the expenses of formation are relatively low.

The partnership form of organization evolved in an effort to overcome some of the shortcomings associated with sole proprietorships. The most significant advantage of the partnership is its greater access to capital. With more than one individual involved, the wealth and resources of all the partners are potentially available. Furthermore, the potential of greater owner contributions enhances commercial bank borrowing capability.

A partnership also brings greater expertise to the firm. Rather than the limited managerial skill of one individual, the partnership can call upon the services of all of the partners. An ideal partnership brings together managerial talents in different aspects of the business. Thus, lawyers, accountants, real estate brokers, securities brokers and dealers, and other professionals generally organize under this form, with each member of the partnership bringing an area of specialization to the enterprise.

One shortcoming of the partnership is the inability of any of the partners to sell their shares of the business without either the consent of the other partners or dissolving the firm. Partnerships require all participants to agree to a change in the arrangement. Should one of the partners wish to sell out, the other partners must all agree to accept the buyer. If they cannot, then the partnership has to be dissolved and the assets sold to satisfy the retiring partner's claim to the firm.

A unique complication arises with the partnership form. Regardless of any partnership agreement to the contrary, when dealing with the public, each partner has an absolute right to enter into binding contracts for the firm. Thus, although the partners may have agreed among themselves that one will handle sales while another handles acquisitions, should one of the partners enter into a commitment outside of this agreement, the firm is still contractually committed. The partners must handle the conflict among themselves.

Nothing compells partners to own equal shares of a partnership. They can agree among themselves to divide profits and losses, degrees of responsibility, and areas of concern unequally. However, unless the partnership agreement is filed with the state within which the firm operates, the government considers the partners to be equal and, thus, responsible for equal proportions of any taxes on profits.

The tax authorities treat the profits of a partnership similarly to those of a proprietorship, except that they are divided up among the partners. Thus, partnership income is considered personal income (whether or not it is reinvested in the firm) and is taxed accordingly.

Limited Partnerships

A special form of partnership limits the liability of some partners. Provided that at least one general partner assumes unlimited liability, state laws allow for a firm to solicit "silent" or limited partners. Such partners are really nothing more than investors; they are forbidden to take active roles in the firm's decision-making process. In recognition of their noninvolvement in management, state laws limit their liability to the amounts of their investments. Thus, should the firm experience losses, the limited partners need not fear threats to their personal assets.

Some investors welcome opportunities to become limited partners since they permit investors to share in the firm's profits without bearing unlimited risk. The firm views the limited partnership as a source of additional capital without limiting the prerogatives of management, although at the expense of sharing the profits.

CORPORATIONS

A corporation is defined as a legal person, separate and distinct from its owners (stockholders), empowered to carry on business as specified in its certificate of incorporation. The certificate of incorporation states the formal name of the firm, its principal office, and its reason for being.

A corporation must be legally created by a state, so it is subject to the laws of that state. Since each state has its own specific rules concerning incorporation, firms seek to incorporate in states that give the widest latitude of operation and/or the lowest tax rates. Delaware is the favorite state for incorporation.

The corporation provides three distinct advantages over the proprietorship and partnership forms of organization: limited liability, permanence of life, and ease of transferring ownership. Since the corporation is a legal entity apart from its owners, it has the power to enter into binding contracts to acquire resources, organize production, and sell its output. It can also sue and be sued in its own name. Consequently, as the corporation has a life apart from its owners, the owners are shielded from litigation and are liable only to the extent of their investments.

The certificate of incorporation generally grants the new corporation permanent life. As long as the company remains out of bankruptcy, it can exist indefinitely, regardless of the life spans of any of its owners. A corporation could exist for hundreds, even thousands, of years.

Ownership in a corporation is represented by shares of stock. Each owner's proportion of the outstanding shares represents that owner's proportion of ownership of the corporation. To divest themselves of their shares of the corporation, owners must merely find buyers for their stock. The new owners do not need the approval of the remaining owners (as is the case with a partnership). Furthermore, if the corporation is large enough to list its stock on an exchange, the owners can sell their stock through a broker and avoid any direct negotiation between seller and buyer.

Many observers claim that the corporation has a greater ability to raise capital than the other forms of organization. This may be true for large corporations that have access to the stock and bond markets, but the corporate structure actually impedes the ability of small firms to obtain loans. Banks and other lenders to small corporations are leery of limits on owners' liability. In a partnership, lenders can attach the owners' personal assets to collect debts. In a corporation of similar size, the lenders can claim only the business assets; thus, they are reluctant to lend. A small, closely held corporation can overcome this lender reluctance by inducing the stockholders to cosign the corporate loan, thereby incurring unlimited personal liability.

In addition to the disadvantage of the legal expenses associated with formation, corporations also face double taxation. Corporations must pay federal corporate income taxes on their profits (EBT). Exhibit B.2 summarizes the federal corporate income tax structure and average rates of taxation.

Once a corporation's board of directors declares a dividend, that dividend is considered to be personal income for the stockholders, and is taxed at the appropriate federal personal income tax rate. This system of taxation amounts to double taxation since corporate profits are taxed, and any distribution of those profits is taxed again.

If the corporation chooses to retain its after-tax earnings rather than pay out dividends, then the funds are taxed only once. Retaining earnings, however, should produce an appreciation in the value of the firm's stock which, when sold, is then subject to the personal capital gains tax (currently at a maximum rate of 28 percent). Further, if the IRS determines that a firm is retaining earnings for the sole purpose of avoiding personal income taxes on dividends, it assesses tax, penalties, and interest.

S Corporations

Stockholders of a company that distributes most of its earnings in dividends dislike paying taxes at the corporate tax rate and then paying taxes on the dividends at the personal tax rate. The Internal Revenue Code provides relief for closely held corporations in this predicament. Subchapter S of the code allows a corporation with 35 or fewer stockholders, all of whom are U.S. citizens or resident aliens, to choose to be taxed as if the firm were a partnership. Firms that make this choice are called *S Corporations*.

EXHIBIT B.2

Federal Corporate Income Taxes, 1993

INCOME	TAX[a]	MIDRANGE AVERAGE TAX RATE
$ 0–50,000	15%	15.00%
50,000–75,000	$ 7,500 + 25%	17.00
75,000–100,000	13,750 + 34%	20.57
100,000–335,000	22,250 + 39%	31.30
335,000–10 million	113,900 + 34%	34.00
10 million–15 million	3.4 million + 35%	34.20
15 million–18.33 million	5.15 million + 38%	34.70
over $18.33 million	35%	35.00

[a]The tax rate applies to any income in excess of the base amount. If taxable income were $150,000, the tax on this income would be $22,250 plus 39 percent of all income in excess of $100,000, for a total tax of $41,750.

Source: *IRS 1993 Tax Guide for Small Business*. Washington, D.C., Internal Revenue Service, 1993.

The apparent tax benefits come with two cautions. First, the stockholders should realize that they are subject to personal income taxes on all of the company's earnings, even those that the firm retains. Second, once the firm elects to be treated as an S Corporation, the decision is difficult to reverse; the IRS requires a significant turnover in ownership before it approves a change.

OTHER FORMS OF BUSINESS ORGANIZATION

In addition to the proprietorship, partnership, and corporate forms of business organizations, several other organizational forms have evolved. Most of these forms seek to serve specific purposes or to overcome some limitation of the traditional forms. Some, such as syndicates and joint ventures, are used extensively in international business to avoid legal complications that can arise from local regulations and to overcome financial and technological limitations.

Joint Ventures

A joint venture is an association of two or more persons and/or corporations created to promote profitable participation in a limited activity or a single transaction. A joint venture resembles a partnership, except that the scope of its activities is very narrow (e.g., the construction of a particular housing complex). Joint venture arrangements tend to be much more informal than partnerships, often not even operating under a firm name.

Tax treatment of joint ventures also resembles that of partnerships in that the individuals involved declare joint venture income as investment income or other income on their personal tax returns. If the joint venture is incorporated, then the corporate tax laws apply. While it is generally assumed that members of a joint venture have limited powers to bind their coventurers, the liability provisions of partnerships generally apply.

Joint ventures are common in real estate construction, oil and mineral exploration, and scientific research. Quite often, a corporation will make its first entry into a foreign market by establishing a joint venture arrangement with a local corporation to expedite the manufacturing, marketing, and distribution of its products. Entrepreneurs in the former Soviet republics actively seek to form joint ventures with German, U.S., and Canadian firms. These entrepreneurs offer to handle the domestic end of the business; they seek products and capital from their foreign partners.

Business Trusts

Often referred to as the *Massachusetts trust*, the business trust arrangement was developed to avoid restrictions that states imposed upon corporations. Specifically, when Massachusetts restricted corporate dealings in real estate, corporations entered into business trusts to circumvent the law. The business trust is also used to limit investors' liability when the corporate form of organization is not feasible.

A business trust is a written agreement that transfers control of the business and the legal ownership of its assets to a trustee, who operates the business for the benefit of the investors. Investors, the beneficiaries of the trust, hold trust certificates as evidence of their contributions. They can transfer these certificates at will, permitting easy changes of ownership. Additionally, since the beneficiaries do not operate the business, their deaths or bankruptcies do not affect the trust. One danger of the business trust is that several states treat the beneficiaries as partners, eliminating the limited liability advantage.

Business trust income is taxed much like corporate income under federal and many state tax laws, except in the case of a real estate investment trust (REIT). REITs are treated as partnerships for tax purposes.

Syndicates

A syndicate generally brings together a group of individuals or corporations to finance a particular project. In investment banking, this is the common form of organization used to underwrite new issues of stocks and bonds and to finance large projects. For example, a real estate syndicate might provide financing for a shopping center, or an entertainment syndicate might finance the acquisition of a sports franchise. Multinational banks employ syndication to spread risk when underwriting international securities issues or providing large, international loans.

A syndicate may organize as either a corporation or a partnership. Its distinguishing characteristic is its specific purpose—to provide financing.

Joint Stock Companies

A joint stock company resembles a corporation in that its ownership is represented by transferable shares, it has perpetual life, and it is generally professionally managed. Yet, the property of a joint stock company is held in the names of its members, it does not protect its owners from personal liability, and it is not treated as a legal entity in court proceedings. In reality, it is a transitional form of organization between the partnership and the corporation.

Professional Corporations

Doctors, lawyers, accountants, and other professionals were prohibited from forming corporations until the 1960s for two reasons:

1. Many believed that professionals should be held personally liable for their activities, and not be permitted to shield their personal assets under corporate umbrellas.
2. Many feared that professionals would be subject to the directions of corporate owners.

The popularity of malpractice insurance negated the first of these concerns, and the limited ownership of the professional corporation (P.C.) satisfied the second.

Professional corporations are not yet recognized in all states. Moreover, a P.C. charter does not shield the owners from unlimited liability. However, federal tax regulations permit professional corporations to direct substantial portions of pretax corporate income into tax-deferred pension plans; this has encouraged their growth.

Discussion Questions

1. What conditions make the proprietorship form of organization the preferred form?
2. Under what circumstances can an investor take an ownership position in a partnership without incurring unlimited liability?
3. Discuss the pros and cons of the corporate form of organization.
4. What are the benefits of the corporate form of organization relative to the partnership?
5. When would stockholders elect S Corporation status?

Problems

1. Company A generates $40,000 in taxable income. Is it better off being taxed as a sole proprietorship or as a corporation?
2. Company B generates $110,000 in taxable income. Is it better off being taxed as a sole proprietorship or as a corporation?

APPENDIX

C

Time Value of Money Tables

TABLE C.1

Future Value of $1

	INTEREST RATE (PERCENT)									
PERIODS	0.50	0.75	1.00	1.50	2.00	3.00	4.00	5.00	6.00	7.00
1	1.0050	1.0075	1.0100	1.0150	1.0200	1.0300	1.0400	1.0500	1.0600	1.0700
2	1.0100	1.0151	1.0201	1.0302	1.0404	1.0609	1.0816	1.1025	1.1236	1.1449
3	1.0151	1.0227	1.0303	1.0457	1.0612	1.0927	1.1249	1.1576	1.1910	1.2250
4	1.0202	1.0303	1.0406	1.0614	1.0824	1.1255	1.1699	1.2155	1.2625	1.3108
5	1.0253	1.0381	1.0510	1.0773	1.1041	1.1593	1.2167	1.2763	1.3382	1.4026
6	1.0304	1.0459	1.0615	1.0934	1.1262	1.1941	1.2653	1.3401	1.4185	1.5007
7	1.0355	1.0537	1.0721	1.1098	1.1487	1.2299	1.3159	1.4071	1.5036	1.6058
8	1.0407	1.0616	1.0829	1.1265	1.1717	1.2668	1.3686	1.4775	1.5938	1.7182
9	1.0459	1.0696	1.0937	1.1434	1.1951	1.3048	1.4233	1.5513	1.6895	1.8385
10	1.0511	1.0776	1.1046	1.1605	1.2190	1.3439	1.4802	1.6289	1.7908	1.9672
11	1.0564	1.0857	1.1157	1.1779	1.2434	1.3842	1.5395	1.7103	1.8983	2.1049
12	1.0617	1.0938	1.1268	1.1956	1.2682	1.4258	1.6010	1.7959	2.0122	2.2522
13	1.0670	1.1020	1.1381	1.2136	1.2936	1.4685	1.6651	1.8856	2.1329	2.4098
14	1.0723	1.1103	1.1495	1.2318	1.3195	1.5126	1.7317	1.9799	2.2609	2.5785
15	1.0777	1.1186	1.1610	1.2502	1.3459	1.5580	1.8009	2.0789	2.3966	2.7590
16	1.0831	1.1270	1.1726	1.2690	1.3728	1.6047	1.8730	2.1829	2.5404	2.9522
17	1.0885	1.1354	1.1843	1.2880	1.4002	1.6528	1.9479	2.2920	2.6928	3.1588
18	1.0939	1.1440	1.1961	1.3073	1.4282	1.7024	2.0258	2.4066	2.8543	3.3799
19	1.0994	1.1525	1.2081	1.3270	1.4568	1.7535	2.1068	2.5270	3.0256	3.6165
20	1.1049	1.1612	1.2202	1.3469	1.4859	1.8061	2.1911	2.6533	3.2071	3.8697
21	1.1104	1.1699	1.2324	1.3671	1.5157	1.8603	2.2788	2.7860	3.3996	4.1406
22	1.1160	1.1787	1.2447	1.3876	1.5460	1.9161	2.3699	2.9253	3.6035	4.4304
23	1.1216	1.1875	1.2572	1.4084	1.5769	1.9736	2.4647	3.0715	3.8197	4.7405
24	1.1272	1.1964	1.2697	1.4295	1.6084	2.0328	2.5633	3.2251	4.0489	5.0724
25	1.1328	1.2054	1.2824	1.4509	1.6406	2.0938	2.6658	3.3864	4.2919	5.4274
26	1.1385	1.2144	1.2953	1.4727	1.6734	2.1566	2.7725	3.5557	4.5494	5.8074
27	1.1442	1.2235	1.3082	1.4948	1.7069	2.2213	2.8834	3.7335	4.8223	6.2139
28	1.1499	1.2327	1.3213	1.5172	1.7410	2.2879	2.9987	3.9201	5.1117	6.6488
29	1.1556	1.2420	1.3345	1.5400	1.7758	2.3566	3.1187	4.1161	5.4184	7.1143
30	1.1614	1.2513	1.3478	1.5631	1.8114	2.4273	3.2434	4.3219	5.7435	7.6123
36	1.1967	1.3086	1.4308	1.7091	2.0399	2.8983	4.1039	5.7918	8.1473	11.4239
48	1.2705	1.4314	1.6122	2.0435	2.5871	4.1323	6.5705	10.4013	16.3939	25.7289
60	1.3489	1.5657	1.8167	2.4432	3.2810	5.8916	10.5196	18.6792	32.9877	57.9464
72	1.4320	1.7126	2.0471	2.9212	4.1611	8.4000	16.8423	33.5451	66.3777	130.5065
84	1.5204	1.8732	2.3067	3.4926	5.2773	11.9764	26.9650	60.2422	133.5650	293.9255
96	1.6141	2.0489	2.5993	4.1758	6.6929	17.0755	43.1718	108.1864	268.7590	661.9766
100	1.6467	2.1111	2.7048	4.4320	7.2446	19.2186	50.5049	131.5013	339.3021	867.7163
108	1.7137	2.2411	2.9289	4.9927	8.4883	24.3456	69.1195	194.2872	540.7960	1,490.898
120	1.8194	2.4514	3.3004	5.9693	10.7652	34.7110	110.6626	348.9120	1,088.188	3,357.788
180	2.4541	3.8380	5.9958	14.5844	35.3208	204.5034	1,164.129	6,517.392	35,896.80	194,571.8
360	6.0226	14.7306	35.9496	212.7038	1,247.561	41,821.62	1,355,196	42,476,396		

INTEREST RATE (PERCENT)								
8.00	9.00	10.00	11.00	12.00	13.00	14.00	15.00	20.00
1.0800	1.0900	1.1000	1.1100	1.1200	1.1300	1.1400	1.1500	1.2000
1.1664	1.1881	1.2100	1.2321	1.2544	1.2769	1.2996	1.3225	1.4400
1.2597	1.2950	1.3310	1.3676	1.4049	1.4429	1.4815	1.5209	1.7280
1.3605	1.4116	1.4641	1.5181	1.5735	1.6305	1.6890	1.7490	2.0736
1.4693	1.5386	1.6105	1.6851	1.7623	1.8424	1.9254	2.0114	2.4883
1.5869	1.6771	1.7716	1.8704	1.9738	2.0820	2.1950	2.3131	2.9860
1.7138	1.8280	1.9487	2.0762	2.2107	2.3526	2.5023	2.6600	3.5832
1.8509	1.9926	2.1436	2.3045	2.4760	2.6584	2.8526	3.0590	4.2998
1.9990	2.1719	2.3579	2.5580	2.7731	3.0040	3.2519	3.5179	5.1598
2.1589	2.3674	2.5937	2.8394	3.1058	3.3946	3.7072	4.0456	6.1917
2.3316	2.5804	2.8531	3.1518	3.4785	3.8359	4.2262	4.6524	7.4301
2.5182	2.8127	3.1384	3.4985	3.8960	4.3345	4.8179	5.3503	8.9161
2.7196	3.0658	3.4523	3.8833	4.3635	4.8980	5.4924	6.1528	10.6993
2.9372	3.3417	3.7975	4.3104	4.8871	5.5348	6.2613	7.0757	12.8392
3.1722	3.6425	4.1772	4.7846	5.4736	6.2543	7.1379	8.1371	15.4070
3.4259	3.9703	4.5950	5.3109	6.1304	7.0673	8.1372	9.3576	18.4884
3.7000	4.3276	5.0545	5.8951	6.8660	7.9861	9.2765	10.7613	22.1861
3.9960	4.7171	5.5599	6.5436	7.6900	9.0243	10.5752	12.3755	26.6233
4.3157	5.1417	6.1159	7.2633	8.6128	10.1974	12.0557	14.2318	31.9480
4.6610	5.6044	6.7275	8.0623	9.6463	11.5231	13.7435	16.3665	38.3376
5.0338	6.1088	7.4002	8.9492	10.8038	13.0211	15.6676	18.8215	46.0051
5.4365	6.6586	8.1403	9.9336	12.1003	14.7138	17.8610	21.6447	55.2061
5.8715	7.2579	8.9543	11.0263	13.5523	16.6266	20.3616	24.8915	66.2474
6.3412	7.9111	9.8497	12.2392	15.1786	18.7881	23.2122	28.6252	79.4968
6.8485	8.6231	10.8347	13.5855	17.0001	21.2305	26.4619	32.9190	95.3962
7.3964	9.3992	11.9182	15.0799	19.0401	23.9905	30.1666	37.8568	114.4755
7.9881	10.2451	13.1100	16.7386	21.3249	27.1093	34.3899	43.5353	137.3706
8.6271	11.1671	14.4210	18.5799	23.8839	30.6335	39.2045	50.0656	164.8447
9.3173	12.1722	15.8631	20.6237	26.7499	34.6158	44.6931	57.5755	197.8136
10.0627	13.2677	17.4494	22.8923	29.9599	39.1159	50.9502	66.2118	237.3763
15.9682	22.2512	30.9127	42.8181	59.1356	81.4374	111.8342	153.1519	708.8019
40.2106	62.5852	97.0172	149.7970	230.3908	352.9923	538.8065	819.4007	6,319.749
101.2571	176.0313	304.4816	524.0572	897.5969	1,530.053	2,595.919	4,383.999	56,347.51
254.9825	495.1170	955.5938	1,833.388	3,497.016	6,632.052	12,506.89	23,455.49	502,400.1
642.0893	1,392.598	2,999.063	6,414.019	13,624.29	28,746.78	60,257.00	125,492.7	4,479,450
1,616.890	3,916.912	9,412.344	22,439.13	53,079.91	124,603.6	290,312.5	671,417.5	39,939,224
2,199.761	5,529.041	13,780.61	34,064.18	83,522.27	203,162.9	490,326.2	1,174,313	82,817,975
4,071.605	11,016.96	29,539.97	78,502.18	206,798.1	540,097.2	1,398,698	3,592,252	
10,252.99	30,987.02	92,709.07	274,636.0	805,680.3	2,341,064	6,738,794	19,219,445	
1,038,188	5,454,684	28,228,209						

TABLE C.2

Future Value of an Ordinary Annuity of $1

	INTEREST RATE (PERCENT)									
PERIODS	0.50	0.75	1.00	1.50	2.00	3.00	4.00	5.00	6.00	7.00
1	1.0000	1.0000	1.0000	1.0000	1.0000	1.0000	1.0000	1.0000	1.0000	1.0000
2	2.0050	2.0075	2.0100	2.0150	2.0200	2.0300	2.0400	2.0500	2.0600	2.0700
3	3.0150	3.0226	3.0301	3.0452	3.0604	3.0909	3.1216	3.1525	3.1836	3.2149
4	4.0301	4.0452	4.0604	4.0909	4.1216	4.1836	4.2465	4.3101	4.3746	4.4399
5	5.0503	5.0756	5.1010	5.1523	5.2040	5.3091	5.4163	5.5256	5.6371	5.7507
6	6.0755	6.1136	6.1520	6.2296	6.3081	6.4684	6.6330	6.8019	6.9753	7.1533
7	7.1059	7.1595	7.2135	7.3230	7.4343	7.6625	7.8983	8.1420	8.3938	8.6540
8	8.1414	8.2132	8.2857	8.4328	8.5830	8.8923	9.2142	9.5491	9.8975	10.2598
9	9.1821	9.2748	9.3685	9.5593	9.7546	10.1591	10.5828	11.0266	11.4913	11.9780
10	10.2280	10.3443	10.4622	10.7027	10.9497	11.4639	12.0061	12.5779	13.1808	13.8164
11	11.2792	11.4219	11.5668	11.8633	12.1687	12.8078	13.4864	14.2068	14.9716	15.7836
12	12.3356	12.5076	12.6825	13.0412	13.4121	14.1920	15.0258	15.9171	16.8699	17.8885
13	13.3972	13.6014	13.8093	14.2368	14.6803	15.6178	16.6268	17.7130	18.8821	20.1406
14	14.4642	14.7034	14.9474	15.4504	15.9739	17.0863	18.2919	19.5986	21.0151	22.5505
15	15.5365	15.8137	16.0969	16.6821	17.2934	18.5989	20.0236	21.5786	23.2760	25.1290
16	16.6142	16.9323	17.2579	17.9324	18.6393	20.1569	21.8245	23.6575	25.6725	27.8881
17	17.6973	18.0593	18.4304	19.2014	20.0121	21.7616	23.6975	25.8404	28.2129	30.8402
18	18.7858	19.1947	19.6147	20.4894	21.4123	23.4144	25.6454	28.1324	30.9057	33.9990
19	19.8797	20.3387	20.8109	21.7967	22.8406	25.1169	27.6712	30.5390	33.7600	37.3790
20	20.9791	21.4912	22.0190	23.1237	24.2974	26.8704	29.7781	33.0660	36.7856	40.9955
21	22.0840	22.6524	23.2392	24.4705	25.7833	28.6765	31.9692	35.7193	39.9927	44.8652
22	23.1944	23.8223	24.4716	25.8376	27.2990	30.5368	34.2480	38.5052	43.3923	49.0057
23	24.3104	25.0010	25.7163	27.2251	28.8450	32.4529	36.6179	41.4305	46.9958	53.4361
24	25.4320	26.1885	26.9735	28.6335	30.4219	34.4265	39.0826	44.5020	50.8156	58.1767
25	26.5591	27.3849	28.2432	30.0630	32.0303	36.4593	41.6459	47.7271	54.8645	63.2490
26	27.6919	28.5903	29.5256	31.5140	33.6709	38.5530	44.3117	51.1135	59.1564	68.6765
27	28.8304	29.8047	30.8209	32.9867	35.3443	40.7096	47.0842	54.6691	63.7058	74.4838
28	29.9745	31.0282	32.1291	34.4815	37.0512	42.9309	49.9676	58.4026	68.5281	80.6977
29	31.1244	32.2609	33.4504	35.9987	38.7922	45.2189	52.9663	62.3227	73.6398	87.3465
30	32.2800	33.5029	34.7849	37.5387	40.5681	47.5754	56.0849	66.4388	79.0582	94.4608
36	39.3361	41.1527	43.0769	47.2760	51.9944	63.2759	77.5983	95.8363	119.1209	148.9135
48	54.0978	57.5207	61.2226	69.5652	79.3535	104.4084	139.2632	188.0254	256.5645	353.2701
60	69.7700	75.4241	81.6697	96.2147	114.0515	163.0534	237.9907	353.5837	533.1282	813.5204
72	86.4089	95.0070	104.7099	128.0772	158.0570	246.6672	396.0566	650.9027	1,089.629	1,850.092
84	104.0739	116.4269	130.6723	166.1726	213.8666	365.8805	649.1251	1,184.845	2,209.417	4,184.651
96	122.8285	139.8562	159.9273	211.7202	284.6467	535.8502	1,054.296	2,143.728	4,462.651	9,442.523
100	129.3337	148.1445	170.4814	228.8030	312.2323	607.2877	1,237.624	2,610.025	5,638.368	12,381.66
108	142.7399	165.4832	192.8926	266.1778	374.4129	778.1863	1,702.988	3,865.745	8,996.600	21,284.26
120	163.8793	193.5143	230.0387	331.2882	488.2582	1,123.700	2,741.564	6,958.240	18,119.80	47,954.12
180	290.8187	378.4058	499.5802	905.6245	1,716.042	6,783.445	29,078.22	130,327.8	598,263.4	2,779,583
360	1,004.515	1,830.743	3,494.964	14,113.59	62,328.06	1,394,021	33,879,878			

INTEREST RATE (PERCENT)

8.00	9.00	10.00	11.00	12.00	13.00	14.00	15.00	20.00
1.0000	1.0000	1.0000	1.0000	1.0000	1.0000	1.0000	1.0000	1.0000
2.0800	2.0900	2.1000	2.1100	2.1200	2.1300	2.1400	2.1500	2.2000
3.2464	3.2781	3.3100	3.3421	3.3744	3.4069	3.4396	3.4725	3.6400
4.5061	4.5731	4.6410	4.7097	4.7793	4.8498	4.9211	4.9934	5.3680
5.8666	5.9847	6.1051	6.2278	6.3528	6.4803	6.6101	6.7424	7.4416
7.3359	7.5233	7.7156	7.9129	8.1152	8.3227	8.5355	8.7537	9.9299
8.9228	9.2004	9.4872	9.7833	10.0890	10.4047	10.7305	11.0668	12.9159
10.6366	11.0285	11.4359	11.8594	12.2997	12.7573	13.2328	13.7268	16.4991
12.4876	13.0210	13.5795	14.1640	14.7757	15.4157	16.0853	16.7858	20.7989
14.4866	15.1929	15.9374	16.7220	17.5487	18.4197	19.3373	20.3037	25.9587
16.6455	17.5603	18.5312	19.5614	20.6546	21.8143	23.0445	24.3493	32.1504
18.9771	20.1407	21.3843	22.7132	24.1331	25.6502	27.2707	29.0017	39.5805
21.4953	22.9534	24.5227	26.2116	28.0291	29.9847	32.0887	34.3519	48.4966
24.2149	26.0192	27.9750	30.0949	32.3926	34.8827	37.5811	40.5047	59.1959
27.1521	29.3609	31.7725	34.4054	37.2797	40.4175	43.8424	47.5804	72.0351
30.3243	33.0034	35.9497	39.1899	42.7533	46.6717	50.9804	55.7175	87.4421
33.7502	36.9737	40.5447	44.5008	48.8837	53.7391	59.1176	65.0751	105.9306
37.4502	41.3013	45.5992	50.3959	55.7497	61.7251	68.3941	75.8364	128.1167
41.4463	46.0185	51.1591	56.9395	63.4397	70.7494	78.9692	88.2118	154.7400
45.7620	51.1601	57.2750	64.2028	72.0524	80.9468	91.0249	102.4436	186.6880
50.4229	56.7645	64.0025	72.2651	81.6987	92.4699	104.7684	118.8101	225.0256
55.4568	62.8733	71.4027	81.2143	92.5026	105.4910	120.4360	137.6316	271.0307
60.8933	69.5319	79.5430	91.1479	104.6029	120.2048	138.2970	159.2764	326.2369
66.7648	76.7898	88.4973	102.1742	118.1552	136.8315	158.6586	184.1678	392.4842
73.1059	84.7009	98.3471	114.4133	133.3339	155.6196	181.8708	212.7930	471.9811
79.9544	93.3240	109.1818	127.9988	150.3339	176.8501	208.3327	245.7120	567.3773
87.3508	102.7231	121.0999	143.0786	169.3740	200.8406	238.4993	283.5688	681.8528
95.3388	112.9682	134.2099	159.8173	190.6989	227.9499	272.8892	327.1041	819.2233
103.9659	124.1354	148.6309	178.3972	214.5828	258.5834	312.0937	377.1697	984.0680
113.2832	136.3075	164.4940	199.0209	241.3327	293.1992	356.7868	434.7451	1,181.882
187.1021	236.1247	299.1268	380.1644	484.4631	618.7493	791.6729	1,014.346	3,539.009
490.1322	684.2804	960.1723	1,352.700	1,911.590	2,707.633	3,841.475	5,456.005	31,593.74
1,253.213	1,944.792	3,034.816	4,755.066	7,471.641	11,761.95	18,535.13	29,219.99	281,732.6
3,174.781	5,490.189	9,545.938	16,658.08	29,133.47	51,008.09	89,327.78	156,363.3	2,511,995
8,013.617	15,462.20	29,980.63	58,300.17	113,527.4	221,121.4	430,400.0	836,611.6	22,397,244
20,198.63	43,510.13	94,113.44	203,983.0	442,324.2	958,481.5	2,073,654	4,476,110	
27,484.52	61,422.68	137,796.1	309,665.2	696,010.5	1,562,784	3,502,323	7,828,750	
50,882.56	122,399.6	295,389.7	713,647.1	1,723,309	4,154,586	9,990,693	23,948,338	
128,149.9	344,289.1	927,080.7	2,496,682	6,713,994	18,008,174	48,134,233		
12,977,337	60,607,594							

TABLE C.3

Present Value of $1

	INTEREST RATE (PERCENT)								
PERIODS	0.50	0.75	1.00	1.50	2.00	3.00	4.00	5.00	6.00
1	0.9950	0.9926	0.9901	0.9852	0.9804	0.9709	0.9615	0.9524	0.9434
2	0.9901	0.9852	0.9803	0.9707	0.9612	0.9426	0.9246	0.9070	0.8900
3	0.9851	0.9778	0.9706	0.9563	0.9423	0.9151	0.8890	0.8638	0.8396
4	0.9802	0.9706	0.9610	0.9422	0.9238	0.8885	0.8548	0.8227	0.7921
5	0.9754	0.9633	0.9515	0.9283	0.9057	0.8626	0.8219	0.7835	0.7473
6	0.9705	0.9562	0.9420	0.9145	0.8880	0.8375	0.7903	0.7462	0.7050
7	0.9657	0.9490	0.9327	0.9010	0.8706	0.8131	0.7599	0.7107	0.6651
8	0.9609	0.9420	0.9235	0.8877	0.8535	0.7894	0.7307	0.6768	0.6274
9	0.9561	0.9350	0.9143	0.8746	0.8368	0.7664	0.7026	0.6446	0.5919
10	0.9513	0.9280	0.9053	0.8617	0.8203	0.7441	0.6756	0.6139	0.5584
11	0.9466	0.9211	0.8963	0.8489	0.8043	0.7224	0.6496	0.5847	0.5268
12	0.9419	0.9142	0.8874	0.8364	0.7885	0.7014	0.6246	0.5568	0.4970
13	0.9372	0.9074	0.8787	0.8240	0.7730	0.6810	0.6006	0.5303	0.4688
14	0.9326	0.9007	0.8700	0.8118	0.7579	0.6611	0.5775	0.5051	0.4423
15	0.9279	0.8940	0.8613	0.7999	0.7430	0.6419	0.5553	0.4810	0.4173
16	0.9233	0.8873	0.8528	0.7880	0.7284	0.6232	0.5339	0.4581	0.3936
17	0.9187	0.8807	0.8444	0.7764	0.7142	0.6050	0.5134	0.4363	0.3714
18	0.9141	0.8742	0.8360	0.7649	0.7002	0.5874	0.4936	0.4155	0.3503
19	0.9096	0.8676	0.8277	0.7536	0.6864	0.5703	0.4746	0.3957	0.3305
20	0.9051	0.8612	0.8195	0.7425	0.6730	0.5537	0.4564	0.3769	0.3118
21	0.9006	0.8548	0.8114	0.7315	0.6598	0.5375	0.4388	0.3589	0.2942
22	0.8961	0.8484	0.8034	0.7207	0.6468	0.5219	0.4220	0.3418	0.2775
23	0.8916	0.8421	0.7954	0.7100	0.6342	0.5067	0.4057	0.3256	0.2618
24	0.8872	0.8358	0.7876	0.6995	0.6217	0.4919	0.3901	0.3101	0.2470
25	0.8828	0.8296	0.7798	0.6892	0.6095	0.4776	0.3751	0.2953	0.2330
26	0.8784	0.8234	0.7720	0.6790	0.5976	0.4637	0.3607	0.2812	0.2198
27	0.8740	0.8173	0.7644	0.6690	0.5859	0.4502	0.3468	0.2678	0.2074
28	0.8697	0.8112	0.7568	0.6591	0.5744	0.4371	0.3335	0.2551	0.1956
29	0.8653	0.8052	0.7493	0.6494	0.5631	0.4243	0.3207	0.2429	0.1846
30	0.8610	0.7992	0.7419	0.6398	0.5521	0.4120	0.3083	0.2314	0.1741
36	0.8356	0.7641	0.6989	0.5851	0.4902	0.3450	0.2437	0.1727	0.1227
48	0.7871	0.6986	0.6203	0.4894	0.3865	0.2420	0.1522	0.0961	0.0610
60	0.7414	0.6387	0.5504	0.4093	0.3048	0.1697	0.0951	0.0535	0.0303
72	0.6983	0.5839	0.4885	0.3423	0.2403	0.1190	0.0594	0.0298	0.0151
84	0.6577	0.5338	0.4335	0.2863	0.1895	0.0835	0.0371	0.0166	0.0075
96	0.6195	0.4881	0.3847	0.2395	0.1494	0.0586	0.0232	0.0092	0.0037
100	0.6073	0.4737	0.3697	0.2256	0.1380	0.0520	0.0198	0.0076	0.0029
108	0.5835	0.4462	0.3414	0.2003	0.1178	0.0411	0.0145	0.0051	0.0018
120	0.5496	0.4079	0.3030	0.1675	0.0929	0.0288	0.0090	0.0029	0.0009
180	0.4075	0.2605	0.1668	0.0686	0.0283	0.0049	0.0009	0.0002	0.0000
360	0.1660	0.0679	0.0278	0.0047	0.0008	0.0000	0.0000	0.0000	0.0000

INTEREST RATE (PERCENT)

7.00	8.00	9.00	10.00	11.00	12.00	13.00	14.00	15.00	20.00
0.9346	0.9259	0.9174	0.9091	0.9009	0.8929	0.8850	0.8772	0.8696	0.8333
0.8734	0.8573	0.8417	0.8264	0.8116	0.7972	0.7831	0.7695	0.7561	0.6944
0.8163	0.7938	0.7722	0.7513	0.7312	0.7118	0.6931	0.6750	0.6575	0.5787
0.7629	0.7350	0.7084	0.6830	0.6587	0.6355	0.6133	0.5921	0.5718	0.4823
0.7130	0.6806	0.6499	0.6209	0.5935	0.5674	0.5428	0.5194	0.4972	0.4019
0.6663	0.6302	0.5963	0.5645	0.5346	0.5066	0.4803	0.4556	0.4323	0.3349
0.6227	0.5835	0.5470	0.5132	0.4817	0.4523	0.4251	0.3996	0.3759	0.2791
0.5820	0.5403	0.5019	0.4665	0.4339	0.4039	0.3762	0.3506	0.3269	0.2326
0.5439	0.5002	0.4604	0.4241	0.3909	0.3606	0.3329	0.3075	0.2843	0.1938
0.5083	0.4632	0.4224	0.3855	0.3522	0.3220	0.2946	0.2697	0.2472	0.1615
0.4751	0.4289	0.3875	0.3505	0.3173	0.2875	0.2607	0.2366	0.2149	0.1346
0.4440	0.3971	0.3555	0.3186	0.2858	0.2567	0.2307	0.2076	0.1869	0.1122
0.4150	0.3677	0.3262	0.2897	0.2575	0.2292	0.2042	0.1821	0.1625	0.0935
0.3878	0.3405	0.2992	0.2633	0.2320	0.2046	0.1807	0.1597	0.1413	0.0779
0.3624	0.3152	0.2745	0.2394	0.2090	0.1827	0.1599	0.1401	0.1229	0.0649
0.3387	0.2919	0.2519	0.2176	0.1883	0.1631	0.1415	0.1229	0.1069	0.0541
0.3166	0.2703	0.2311	0.1978	0.1696	0.1456	0.1252	0.1078	0.0929	0.0451
0.2959	0.2502	0.2120	0.1799	0.1528	0.1300	0.1108	0.0946	0.0808	0.0376
0.2765	0.2317	0.1945	0.1635	0.1377	0.1161	0.0981	0.0829	0.0703	0.0313
0.2584	0.2145	0.1784	0.1486	0.1240	0.1037	0.0868	0.0728	0.0611	0.0261
0.2415	0.1987	0.1637	0.1351	0.1117	0.0926	0.0768	0.0638	0.0531	0.0217
0.2257	0.1839	0.1502	0.1228	0.1007	0.0826	0.0680	0.0560	0.0462	0.0181
0.2109	0.1703	0.1378	0.1117	0.0907	0.0738	0.0601	0.0491	0.0402	0.0151
0.1971	0.1577	0.1264	0.1015	0.0817	0.0659	0.0532	0.0431	0.0349	0.0126
0.1842	0.1460	0.1160	0.0923	0.0736	0.0588	0.0471	0.0378	0.0304	0.0105
0.1722	0.1352	0.1064	0.0839	0.0663	0.0525	0.0417	0.0331	0.0264	0.0087
0.1609	0.1252	0.0976	0.0763	0.0597	0.0469	0.0369	0.0291	0.0230	0.0073
0.1504	0.1159	0.0895	0.0693	0.0538	0.0419	0.0326	0.0255	0.0200	0.0061
0.1406	0.1073	0.0822	0.0630	0.0485	0.0374	0.0289	0.0224	0.0174	0.0051
0.1314	0.0994	0.0754	0.0573	0.0437	0.0334	0.0256	0.0196	0.0151	0.0042
0.0875	0.0626	0.0449	0.0323	0.0234	0.0169	0.0123	0.0089	0.0065	0.0014
0.0389	0.0249	0.0160	0.0103	0.0067	0.0043	0.0028	0.0019	0.0012	0.0002
0.0173	0.0099	0.0057	0.0033	0.0019	0.0011	0.0007	0.0004	0.0002	0.0000
0.0077	0.0039	0.0020	0.0010	0.0005	0.0003	0.0002	0.0001	0.0000	0.0000
0.0034	0.0016	0.0007	0.0003	0.0002	0.0001	0.0000	0.0000	0.0000	0.0000
0.0015	0.0006	0.0003	0.0001	0.0000	0.0000	0.0000	0.0000	0.0000	0.0000
0.0012	0.0005	0.0002	0.0001	0.0000	0.0000	0.0000	0.0000	0.0000	0.0000
0.0007	0.0002	0.0001	0.0000	0.0000	0.0000	0.0000	0.0000	0.0000	0.0000
0.0003	0.0001	0.0000	0.0000	0.0000	0.0000	0.0000	0.0000	0.0000	0.0000
0.0000	0.0000	0.0000	0.0000	0.0000	0.0000	0.0000	0.0000	0.0000	0.0000
0.0000	0.0000	0.0000	0.0000	0.0000	0.0000	0.0000	0.0000	0.0000	0.0000

TABLE C.4

Present Value of an Ordinary Annuity of $1

	INTEREST RATE (PERCENT)								
PERIODS	0.50	0.75	1.00	1.50	2.00	3.00	4.00	5.00	6.00
1	0.9950	0.9926	0.9901	0.9852	0.9804	0.9709	0.9615	0.9524	0.9434
2	1.9851	1.9777	1.9704	1.9559	1.9416	1.9135	1.8861	1.8594	1.8334
3	2.9702	2.9556	2.9410	2.9122	2.8839	2.8286	2.7751	2.7232	2.6730
4	3.9505	3.9261	3.9020	3.8544	3.8077	3.7171	3.6299	3.5460	3.4651
5	4.9259	4.8894	4.8534	4.7826	4.7135	4.5797	4.4518	4.3295	4.2124
6	5.8964	5.8456	5.7955	5.6972	5.6014	5.4172	5.2421	5.0757	4.9173
7	6.8621	6.7946	6.7282	6.5982	6.4720	6.2303	6.0021	5.7864	5.5824
8	7.8230	7.7366	7.6517	7.4859	7.3255	7.0197	6.7327	6.4632	6.2098
9	8.7791	8.6716	8.5660	8.3605	8.1622	7.7861	7.4353	7.1078	6.8017
10	9.7304	9.5996	9.4713	9.2222	8.9826	8.5302	8.1109	7.7217	7.3601
11	10.6770	10.5207	10.3676	10.0711	9.7868	9.2526	8.7605	8.3064	7.8869
12	11.6189	11.4349	11.2551	10.9075	10.5753	9.9540	9.3851	8.8633	8.3838
13	12.5562	12.3423	12.1337	11.7315	11.3484	10.6350	9.9856	9.3936	8.8527
14	13.4887	13.2430	13.0037	12.5434	12.1062	11.2961	10.5631	9.8986	9.2950
15	14.4166	14.1370	13.8651	13.3432	12.8493	11.9379	11.1184	10.3797	9.7122
16	15.3399	15.0243	14.7179	14.1313	13.5777	12.5611	11.6523	10.8378	10.1059
17	16.2586	15.9050	15.5623	14.9076	14.2919	13.1661	12.1657	11.2741	10.4773
18	17.1728	16.7792	16.3983	15.6726	14.9920	13.7535	12.6593	11.6896	10.8276
19	18.0824	17.6468	17.2260	16.4262	15.6785	14.3238	13.1339	12.0853	11.1581
20	18.9874	18.5080	18.0456	17.1686	16.3514	14.8775	13.5903	12.4622	11.4699
21	19.8880	19.3628	18.8570	17.9001	17.0112	15.4150	14.0292	12.8212	11.7641
22	20.7841	20.2112	19.6604	18.6208	17.6580	15.9369	14.4511	13.1630	12.0416
23	21.6757	21.0533	20.4558	19.3309	18.2922	16.4436	14.8568	13.4886	12.3034
24	22.5629	21.8891	21.2434	20.0304	18.9139	16.9355	15.2470	13.7986	12.5504
25	23.4456	22.7188	22.0232	20.7196	19.5235	17.4131	15.6221	14.0939	12.7834
26	24.3240	23.5422	22.7952	21.3986	20.1210	17.8768	15.9828	14.3752	13.0032
27	25.1980	24.3595	23.5596	22.0676	20.7069	18.3270	16.3296	14.6430	13.2105
28	26.0677	25.1707	24.3164	22.7267	21.2813	18.7641	16.6631	14.8981	13.4062
29	26.9330	25.9759	25.0658	23.3761	21.8444	19.1885	16.9837	15.1411	13.5907
30	27.7941	26.7751	25.8077	24.0158	22.3965	19.6004	17.2920	15.3725	13.7648
36	32.8710	31.4468	30.1075	27.6607	25.4888	21.8323	18.9083	16.5469	14.6210
48	42.5803	40.1848	37.9740	34.0426	30.6731	25.2667	21.1951	18.0772	15.6500
60	51.7256	48.1734	44.9550	39.3803	34.7609	27.6756	22.6235	18.9293	16.1614
72	60.3395	55.4768	51.1504	43.8447	37.9841	29.3651	23.5156	19.4038	16.4156
84	68.4530	62.1540	56.6485	47.5786	40.5255	30.5501	24.0729	19.6680	16.5419
96	76.0952	68.2584	61.5277	50.7017	42.5294	31.3812	24.4209	19.8151	16.6047
100	78.5426	70.1746	63.0289	51.6247	43.0984	31.5989	24.5050	19.8479	16.6175
108	83.2934	73.8394	65.8578	53.3137	44.1095	31.9642	24.6383	19.8971	16.6358
120	90.0735	78.9417	69.7005	55.4985	45.3554	32.3730	24.7741	19.9427	16.6514
180	118.5035	98.5934	83.3217	62.0956	48.5844	33.1703	24.9785	19.9969	16.6662
360	166.7916	124.2819	97.2183	66.3532	49.9599	33.3325	25.0000	20.0000	16.6667

INTEREST RATE (PERCENT)									
7.00	8.00	9.00	10.00	11.00	12.00	13.00	14.00	15.00	20.00
0.9346	0.9259	0.9174	0.9091	0.9009	0.8929	0.8850	0.8772	0.8696	0.8333
1.8080	1.7833	1.7591	1.7355	1.7125	1.6901	1.6681	1.6467	1.6257	1.5278
2.6243	2.5771	2.5313	2.4869	2.4437	2.4018	2.3612	2.3216	2.2832	2.1065
3.3872	3.3121	3.2397	3.1699	3.1024	3.0373	2.9745	2.9137	2.8550	2.5887
4.1002	3.9927	3.8897	3.7908	3.6959	3.6048	3.5172	3.4331	3.3522	2.9906
4.7665	4.6229	4.4859	4.3553	4.2305	4.1114	3.9975	3.8887	3.7845	3.3255
5.3893	5.2064	5.0330	4.8684	4.7122	4.5638	4.4226	4.2883	4.1604	3.6046
5.9713	5.7466	5.5348	5.3349	5.1461	4.9676	4.7988	4.6389	4.4873	3.8372
6.5152	6.2469	5.9952	5.7590	5.5370	5.3282	5.1317	4.9464	4.7716	4.0310
7.0236	6.7101	6.4177	6.1446	5.8892	5.6502	5.4262	5.2161	5.0188	4.1925
7.4987	7.1390	6.8052	6.4951	6.2065	5.9377	5.6869	5.4527	5.2337	4.3271
7.9427	7.5361	7.1607	6.8137	6.4924	6.1944	5.9176	5.6603	5.4206	4.4392
8.3577	7.9038	7.4869	7.1034	6.7499	6.4235	6.1218	5.8424	5.5831	4.5327
8.7455	8.2442	7.7862	7.3667	6.9819	6.6282	6.3025	6.0021	5.7245	4.6106
9.1079	8.5595	8.0607	7.6061	7.1909	6.8109	6.4624	6.1422	5.8474	4.6755
9.4466	8.8514	8.3126	7.8237	7.3792	6.9740	6.6039	6.2651	5.9542	4.7296
9.7632	9.1216	8.5436	8.0216	7.5488	7.1196	6.7291	6.3729	6.0472	4.7746
10.0591	9.3719	8.7556	8.2014	7.7016	7.2497	6.8399	6.4674	6.1280	4.8122
10.3356	9.6036	8.9501	8.3649	7.8393	7.3658	6.9380	6.5504	6.1982	4.8435
10.5940	9.8181	9.1285	8.5136	7.9633	7.4694	7.0248	6.6231	6.2593	4.8696
10.8355	10.0168	9.2922	8.6487	8.0751	7.5620	7.1016	6.6870	6.3125	4.8913
11.0612	10.2007	9.4424	8.7715	8.1757	7.6446	7.1695	6.7429	6.3587	4.9094
11.2722	10.3711	9.5802	8.8832	8.2664	7.7184	7.2297	6.7921	6.3988	4.9245
11.4693	10.5288	9.7066	8.9847	8.3481	7.7843	7.2829	6.8351	6.4338	4.9371
11.6536	10.6748	9.8226	9.0770	8.4217	7.8431	7.3300	6.8729	6.4641	4.9476
11.8258	10.8100	9.9290	9.1609	8.4881	7.8957	7.3717	6.9061	6.4906	4.9563
11.9867	10.9352	10.0266	9.2372	8.5478	7.9426	7.4086	6.9352	6.5135	4.9636
12.1371	11.0511	10.1161	9.3066	8.6016	7.9844	7.4412	6.9607	6.5335	4.9697
12.2777	11.1584	10.1983	9.3696	8.6501	8.0218	7.4701	6.9830	6.5509	4.9747
12.4090	11.2578	10.2737	9.4269	8.6938	8.0552	7.4957	7.0027	6.5660	4.9789
13.0352	11.7172	10.6118	9.6765	8.8786	8.1924	7.5979	7.0790	6.6231	4.9929
13.7305	12.1891	10.9336	9.8969	9.0302	8.2972	7.6705	7.1296	6.6585	4.9992
14.0392	12.3766	11.0480	9.9672	9.0736	8.3240	7.6873	7.1401	6.6651	4.9999
14.1763	12.4510	11.0887	9.9895	9.0860	8.3310	7.6911	7.1423	6.6664	5.0000
14.2371	12.4805	11.1031	9.9967	9.0895	8.3327	7.6920	7.1427	6.6666	5.0000
14.2641	12.4923	11.1083	9.9989	9.0905	8.3332	7.6922	7.1428	6.6667	5.0000
14.2693	12.4943	11.1091	9.9993	9.0906	8.3332	7.6923	7.1428	6.6667	5.0000
14.2761	12.4969	11.1101	9.9997	9.0908	8.3333	7.6923	7.1429	6.6667	5.0000
14.2815	12.4988	11.1108	9.9999	9.0909	8.3333	7.6923	7.1429	6.6667	5.0000
14.2856	12.5000	11.1111	10.0000	9.0909	8.3333	7.6923	7.1429	6.6667	5.0000
14.2857	12.5000	11.1111	10.0000	9.0909	8.3333	7.6923	7.1429	6.6667	5.0000

GLOSSARY

abandonment problem A comparison of expected future benefits over the remaining life of an asset to its expected salvage value if the firm scraps it before the end of its life.

absolute priority rule A provision in Chapter 11 of the bankruptcy law that mandates settling claims in the order of their legal priority.

Accelerated Cost Recovery System A capital asset depreciation method introduced into tax law in 1981 and modified by the Tax Reform Act of 1986.

accrual basis An accounting method that recognizes transactions when they are made, not when their cash consequences are felt.

acquisition One company takes over another company. The acquirer keeps its identity, and its common stock remains outstanding.

agency problem The conflict between managers and stockholders over the firm's objectives and the acceptable level of risk.

American depository receipts (ADRs) Receipts that represent shares of a foreign corporation's stock held in trust by a bank. The receipts then trade alongside domestic stock shares.

American option An option contract that can be exercised on or any time before the expiration date.

American terms A system expressing exchange rates of all foreign currencies in terms of U.S. dollars.

amortization Liquidation of a debt by installment payments.

amortization schedule A table that describes beginning-of-period balances, installment payments, and the breakdown of each installment payment into its interest and principal components.

amortized loan A loan repaid in monthly installments. The interest is calculated on the outstanding balance of the loan, not on the original amount borrowed.

announcement date of a call The date on which a company announces that it is calling a bond.

annual percentage rate (APR) The annual interest rate obtained by multiplying a stated, periodic rate by the number of periods in a year.

annual report A report sent to every shareholder summarizing the year's financial activity for the firm and containing management's assessment of the previous year's performance as well as its outlook for the coming fiscal year.

annuity A series of periodic, equal cash flows (payments or receipts) over a fixed length of time.

annuity due An annuity with cash flows that occur at the beginning of each period.

arbitrager Someone who buys and sells currencies to profit from exchange rate and interest rate differences.

attrition A policy of reducing the work force by not replacing most of those who leave a company voluntarily during a specified time period.

auction system A method of trading shares of stock in which the highest bidder buys from the seller with the lowest asking price.

average accounting return A rate of return obtained by dividing the average annual accounting profit by the average book value of the asset.

baby bond A bond with a face value of $500 or $100.

balance of payments The accounts of a country's transactions in goods, services, and financial assets with the rest of the world.

bank run A panic situation in which large numbers of bank depositors attempt to withdraw their money simultaneously.

bankers' acceptance A time draft drawn on and accepted by a bank.

barter system A system of trade in which goods are exchanged for goods.

best efforts sale The process in which an investment banker acts as an agent, helping to sell a newly issued security to the public.

beta A measure of a security's systematic risk relative to the market.

blue sky law A state law that governs issuing and trading securities within a state, to prevent unscrupulous financiers from selling fraudulent securities.

bond duration A measure of the interest rate risk on bonds that takes into account the effects of both the coupon rate and the time to maturity.

book value The total of the par value of a firm's stock, its capital surplus, and the per-share value of its accumulated retained earnings. A measure of the value of a share of stock based on the accounting values of assets and liabilities.

Bretton Woods system The system of fixed exchange rates that prevailed from 1946 until 1973.

buying on margin Borrowing money from a broker to buy securities; the current margin requirement on stocks and bonds (the minimum cash deposit) is 50 percent of the purchase price.

call option A contract between a buyer and a writer that gives the buyer a right, but not an obligation, to buy a certain quantity of an underlying asset at a predetermined price on (or perhaps before) a certain date.

call risk The probability that an issuer will retire a long-term debt security before its maturity date.

cannibalization A situation when a new product takes sales away from existing products, or when a foreign project substitutes for a company's export.

capital asset pricing model A mathematical model that relates the expected return on a security to the risk-free rate and the market price of risk.

capital budget An outline of planned capital spending.

capital market The market for corporate equity securities and their derivatives, and corporate and government long-term debt securities.

capital rationing problem The need to choose among assets when a company cannot raise enough money to acquire all profitable assets.

capital structure The proportions of debt and equity by which a company has financed its asset acquisitions.

capital surplus The price that buyers pay in excess of par value when stock is first sold to the public.

cash basis An accounting method that recognizes transactions when their cash consequences are felt.

cash cycle The sum of the firm's average collection period and days-in-inventory. This gives the number of days it takes to turn a dollar of inventory into a dollar of available cash.

chattel mortgage bond A debt secured by movable property.

check kiting An illegal and unethical practice of writing checks against bank float.

closed end investment company An investment company that authorizes and issues a fixed number of shares of its own common stock, which trades in the secondary market.

co-financing agreement A combination of two or more lenders to share the costs, risks, and profits of a loan.

coefficient of variation The standard deviation divided by the mean. It standardizes variability by measuring variation relative to the mean.

collect loan A loan that gives the borrower the full amount on Day 1, to be repaid on Day 365, plus interest.

collection float The negative difference between the bank balance shown on the company's records and its actual bank balance, because a check that the company has received has not yet cleared.

commercial paper Unsecured, discounted, corporate debt obligations, that mature in up to 270 days, with no conditions attached to the promise to repay.

commission broker A stock exchange member who acts as an agent to buy or sell securities for customers.

common-size financial statements Restructured financial statements that report all balance sheet entries as percentages of total assets and all income statement entries as percentages of sales.

compensating balance A requirement that a borrower deposit a percentage of a loan in a noninterest-bearing checking account, and leave it there while the loan remains outstanding.

competitive asset An asset that reduces another asset's cash inflows and/or increases another asset's cash outflows.

complementary asset An asset that enhances another asset's cash inflows and/or reduces another asset's cash outflows.

composition An agreement for a proportionate settlement of creditors' claims in cash or in a combination of cash and promissory notes.

compounding period A time period specified for calculating and reinvesting interest.

compounding rate The annual interest rate used in interest compounding.

consignment An agreement that a customer does not have to pay for a shipment until it sells the merchandise.

constant-growth model A dividend discount stock valuation model that assumes that dividends will grow at a constant rate.

consumer price index (CPI) A measure of inflation based on a theoretical market basket of consumer goods. It is compiled by the U.S. Department of Labor and published monthly.

conversion price The price of a share of common stock, calculated as the face value of a convertible bond divided by the conversion ratio.

conversion ratio The number of shares of common stock for which one convertible bond can be exchanged.

correlation coefficient A statistical measure of the relationship between changes in two variables.

cost-push theory A theory that holds institutional factors responsible for inflation.

country risk The probability that an investor will not earn the expected return on a foreign investment because of foreign political, economic, social, accounting, legal, or regulatory changes.

coupon rate The rate of interest promised on a bond.

cross rate The exchange rate between two foreign currencies.

cross-border factoring A network of factors in different countries who share information about the creditworthiness of importers and handle collections of local receivables for each other.

cross-currency interest rate swap A contract through which a company exchanges floating-rate financing in one currency for fixed-rate financing in another currency.

cumulative voting A procedure that gives the stockholder one vote for each common share he or she owns, times the number of positions to be filled; the shareholder can distribute those votes at will.

cumulative preferred stock Preferred stock on which the firm owes an undeclared dividend to the stockholders until it is declared and paid.

currency cocktail bonds A Eurobond denominated in a mixture of currencies.

currency swap An agreement negotiated between two borrowers who wish to make payments in a currency other than those that they borrowed.

default risk The probability that a borrower will not pay interest or repay principal when due.

defined-benefit pension plan The sponsor of the plan promises a fixed benefit to the employee upon retirement or disability. The sponsor's contribution varies.

defined-contribution pension plan The sponsor of the plan makes fixed contributions to the plan. The retiree's benefit varies.

deflation The opposite of inflation, in which the general level of prices declines.

demand-pull theory A theory that identifies excessive demand for goods and services as the primary cause of inflation.

depository institution A company that accepts deposits, makes loans, transfers funds, obtains needed currency supplies, manages investments, and provides custodial services. Such institutions include commercial banks and thrifts.

devaluation A government act to reduce the external value of a currency.

disbursement float The positive difference between the bank balance shown on the company's records and its actual bank balance, because a check that the company has written has not yet cleared.

discount bond A bond selling at a price below its face value.

discount factor The factor that converts a future dollar into its present value.

discount rate The interest rate that reduces a future cash flow to its present value.

discounted cash flow approach The method of determining the value of an asset by discounting its future cash flows using an appropriate discount rate.

discounted loan A loan that gives the borrower the full amount on Day 1, but requires payment of the interest on Day 1, with the full amount borrowed to be repaid on Day 365.

discounting A process of reducing value.

disinflation A falling inflation rate.

dividend discount model A stock valuation model that bases stock value on discounted future dividend flows.

earnings available per share The amount of after-tax profit that the company has available to distribute to common stockholders and/or to retain for its own use.

earnings before interest and taxes Another name for net operating income, this is the amount left after subtracting labor, materials, overhead, and depreciation from sales revenue.

effective annual rate The annual interest rate that one actually receives or pays. Also known as the actual interest rate.

effective call date The date on which a bond call actually happens.

equilibrium interest rate An interest rate established by the interaction of demand and supply forces.

equity carve-out A divestiture in which the parent company sells the public some stock in a division or subsidiary, making it an independent identity, while keeping a controlling interest.

equivalent annual annuity An annual annuity with the same NPV as the cash flows of a project.

Eurobond A bond denominated in the domestic currency of the issuing corporation but generally sold outside its country of origin.

Eurocurrency A time deposit held outside a home country, but denominated in the home country's currency.

European option An option contract that can be exercised only on the expiration date.

European terms A system expressing the exchange rate of the U.S. dollar in terms of all foreign currencies.

ex rights A share of stock and its preemptive right can trade separately between a rights offering's date of record and expiration date.

exchange rate The value of a currency expressed in terms of another currency.

exchange rate risk The possibility that the value of an asset or a liability denominated in a foreign currency will change due to a change in the exchange rate.

exchange ratio The number of shares of a target company that can be exchanged for one share of an acquiring company.

expected return The return that an investor expects when initiating an investment.

expected value The statistical calculation of an average value from a list of possible outcomes.

expiration risk The probability that certain types of securities will expire worthless.

extension An agreement between a company and its creditors to postpone the due dates on the balances it owes.

external growth An increase in assets achieved by acquiring other companies or subdivisions of other companies.

face value The redemption value of a bond.

factor A financial company that lends money to corporations, which pledge their accounts receivable as collateral for the loans.

fiduciary A financial institution trusted to manage the investment portfolios of others.

financial institution A company whose principal business involves selecting, holding, or transferring financial assets. Not all financial institutions are financial intermediaries.

financial intermediary An institution that collects funds from those who have surpluses and channels the funds efficiently to those who have deficits. All financial intermediaries are financial institutions.

financial (capital) lease A non-cancelable, long-term contract whose present value usually must be reported on the lessee's balance sheet.

Fisher effect The incorporation of an anticipated inflation rate into the nominal interest rate.

fixed sinking fund The retirement of the same amount of debt each year, on the anniversary date of issuing the bond.

fixed-rate system A system in which governments fix the exchange rates of their countries' currencies.

flexible-rate (floating-rate) system A system in which exchange rates depend entirely on the forces of demand and supply.

float The dollar value of checks both written by and received by a company that have not yet cleared through the banking system.

floor broker A stock exchange member who executes trades for commission brokers who have too much work to handle.

flotation cost The expenses incurred to sell a new security to the public.

flower bond A treasury bond that pays a very low rate but can be used by an individual investor to pay estate taxes.

foreign bond A debt security sold in a foreign country with the face value, principal, and interest denominated in that country's currency.

foreign exchange (forex) market An institutional and communications network for currency trading.

foreign purchasing power The purchasing power of a currency measured in terms of foreign goods and services.

form 13-D A form filed with the SEC by an investor who acquires 5 percent or more of a company's outstanding stock.

forward contract An agreement that locks in the exchange rate at which a bank will deliver a specified amount of foreign currency on a specified date.

forward rate The exchange rate for delivery of a foreign currency at a future date under a forward contract.

forward transaction Buying and selling currency for delivery at a future date.

fourth market The mechanism through which a financial institution buys a block of securities from another financial institution without using the services of a broker.

fully diluted earnings per share Net income after taxes divided by the number of shares of common stock that would be outstanding after conversion of every security that could be converted into common stock.

fundamental analysis Evaluation of the condition of the company that issues a security (or, for a futures contract, the condition of the underlying commodity).

fungible dollar Money circulating in a corporation that cannot be connected to a specific origin.

future value The amount to which a payment or payments will grow by a future date compounded at a stated interest rate.

futures contract A contract that promises delivery of a standardized quantity and quality of some commodity on the third Friday of a specified month.

futures option A contract that gives its holder the right, but not the obligation, to buy or sell a commodities futures contract at a fixed price for a limited period of time.

futures rate The exchange rate specified for delivery of a foreign currency at a future date under a futures contract.

general obligation security Municipal note or bond backed by a state or local government unit's power to tax.

gilt market The market for government securities in the United Kingdom.

going public Selling common stock to the public in an initial public offering.

golden parachute A contract provision that guarantees top managers very generous compensation if the company is acquired and they are forced to leave.

greenmail A target company pays a premium price to buy back a block of its stock held by a potential acquirer, who promises to stop trying to acquire the company.

gross underwriting spread The difference between the price underwriters pay for a security and the price at which they resell the security to the public.

half-year convention An IRS depreciation rule that assumes all assets are placed in service in the middle of the first year.

hedger A trader who uses a futures contract or other derivative instrument to protect a postition in the underlying commodity or security. A currency hedger is someone who buys and sells currencies to profit from exchange rate and interest rate differences.

hyperinflation A rapidly rising inflation rate, often reaching hundreds of percentage points within a few months.

illiquidity risk The probability that investors cannot buy or sell their securities quickly without disturbing the market price.

incremental cash flow Cash flows specific to a project. To identify them, subtract the firm's cash flows without the project from its cash flows with the project.

independent asset An asset that has no impact on another asset's cash flows, whether the firm decides to acquire it or not.

independent project A project whose selection does not depend on whether or not other projects are accepted. Such a project is judged on its merits alone.

index options Contracts that allow the contract holder to buy (if the contract is a call) or sell (if it is a put) a specific stock market index at a specific price for a limited amount of time.

inflation A persistent rise in the general level of prices.

inflation risk The possibility of the actual inflation rate being different from the expected inflation rate.

initial public offering A sale of a company's new securities for the first time.

inside information Firm-specific information known to individuals before its public announcement.

insurance premium Regular, small payment made to an insurance company to pay for a policy that will compensate the policyholder for an irregular large loss.

interest Compensation paid to the lender for the use of loaned money.

interest compounding A process by which accumulated interest earns more interest.

interest rate risk The probability that current market rates of interest will change, making the prices of outstanding securities change in the opposite direction.

interest rate swap An agreement between two borrowers to exchange interest payments.

internal growth An increase in assets achieved by expanding the market for the company's products, increasing the company's share of the existing market, and/or diversifying into new products or services.

internal rate of return The rate of return that equates the total discounted benefits of an asset to its initial cost.

investment bank A financial institution with the primary function of distributing new securities for publicly held companies.

investment opportunity balance The retention of investment funds as cash in anticipation of better future investment opportunities. Also called speculative balance.

investment quality bond A bond rated Baa or higher by Moody's, or BBB or higher by Standard & Poor's.

investment risk The possibility that an actual return will differ from the expected return.

killer Bs Classes of common stock that offer disproportionately large voting power.

lessee The party to a lease contract who borrows an asset and makes periodic payments in exchange for the right to use it.

lessor The party to a lease contract who owns the asset and agrees to let the lessee use it in exchange for periodic payments.

letter of credit A conditional promise from a bank to pay an exporter at a specified future time, after the bank is assured that the goods have been received by the importer, and their value is verified.

limit order An order for a broker to buy (or sell) a security that sets an upper (or lower) limit on the price to be paid (or accepted).

liquidation value The value that stockholders could realize per share by breaking up the firm and selling its assets.

making a market A function of a brokerage house or investment banker in which it carries an inventory of a company's securities and quotes prices at which it is willing to buy or sell.

managed-float system A system in which governments actively manage market-driven changes in the exchange rates of their currencies.

marginal cost of capital The cost of raising additional funds to finance new investment opportunities.

market order An order for a broker to buy or sell a security at the current market price.

market portfolio A portfolio that consists of all securities traded in the market in proportion to their shares of the total market value.

market risk The probability that news events will depress general market prices on the day an investor wants to sell, or inflate prices on the day an investor wants to buy.

marking to market A procedure that adjusts an account balance for the daily gain or loss from a futures transaction.

merger Two companies combine to produce a new corporate entity. Stockholders exchange outstanding shares of common stock in both companies for shares in the new company.

midcap A company whose shares of common stock have a total market value (capitalization) between $250 million and $1 billion.

minimum cash balance The amount of cash the company should plan to have on hand throughout the budgeting period.

minority interest A balance sheet item reporting the value of that portion of a subsidiary that the parent company does not own.

money market The market for debt instruments with original maturities of less than one year.

money stock The amount of money held by the nonbank public as reported by the Federal Reserve System.

monopsony A large company that is the principal or only customer of another company.

mortgage bond A long-term debt security with a mortgage note attached that pledges some or all of the borrower's assets as collateral for the loan.

municipal security A note or bond issued by a unit of a state or local government or any of its affiliates.

mutually exclusive asset An asset that is an alternative to another; if the firm acquires one, it automatically rejects the other.

mutually exclusive project A project whose selection depends on whether or not another project is selected.

negative pledge clause A provision in a bond indenture that prevents the company from issuing new debt that will take priority over the bonds covered by the indenture.

negotiated transaction Traders buy securities from or sell them to market makers, who set their bid and ask prices individually.

net asset value The market price of shares in a mutual fund, calculated as the market value of the fund's assets divided by the number of shares the fund has outstanding.

net float Disbursement float minus collection float at a point in time.

net present value The present value of cash inflows from an asset minus the present value of its cash outflows (costs).

net present value profile A plot of the NPVs of a project at different discount rates.

netting A currency-management technique that minimizes currency conversion costs by reducing the amounts and frequency of currency conversions to pay for transactions between subsidiaries.

nominal return The return on an investment before adjusting for inflation.

noncumulative preferred stock Preferred stock on which the firm owes an undeclared dividend to the stockholders for one year, after which it is lost forever.

nondepository institution A financial company, such as a life insurance company or an investment company, that pools funds from many participants to fund investments.

odd-lot trade A trade that involves less than 100 shares of stock.

open account transaction A transaction in which the seller ships goods, creates an account receivable, and relies on the willingness and ability of the customer to pay when due.

open end investment companies An investment company that issues shares whenever a potential investor wants to buy them and buys back shares whenever a current investor wants to sell them. Also called a mutual fund.

open interest The number of futures contracts outstanding for a particular commodity.

operating (service) leases A relatively short-term, cancelable contract that does not show up on a company's balance sheet.

opportunity cost The rate of return that the company could earn in its best alternative investment.

optimal portfolio mix The portfolio mix that provides the highest return for the risk the investor is willing to bear.

option premium The market price of an option contract.

ordinary annuity An annuity with cash flows that occurs at the end of each period.

outstanding security A security that was originally sold to the public in the primary market.

par-value bond A bond selling at a price equal to its face value.

participating preferred stock Stock that entitled preferred stockholders to receive larger dividends in an exceptionally profitable year.

payback period The number of years that the firm expects a project to take to recover its cost.

perpetuity An annuity with cash flows that continue forever.

poison pill A distribution of rights to stockholders that allows them to purchase a new series of securities in an attempt to stop a corporate takeover.

portfolio diversification Combining assets with different risk–return characteristics.

precautionary balance Cash balance set aside to meet unexpected needs.

preemptive right The right of a firm's current stockholders to maintain their proportion of ownership by purchasing any new shares issued by the corporation before it offers them to the public.

premium bond A bond selling at a price that exceeds its face value.

present value The present worth of a future amount or series of amounts.

price index A numerical device used to measure changes in prices.

primary market The market where newly issued securities are offered and sold by the issuers or their representatives.

private placement A sale of unregistered securities to fewer than 20 investors, usually financial institutions.

privatization Sale of a majority or minority stake in a state-run enterprise either to multinational companies through a bidding process, or to the public through a new stock issue.

pro forma statement A financial statement that projects future data instead of reporting historical data.

profitability index The ratio of an asset's discounted after-tax cash flows to its initial cost.

prospectus A summary of all the significant information about an issuing company and its new security gathered from the SEC registration statement.

proxy statement A statement giving someone who will attend a company's annual shareholders' meeting the right to cast a stockholder's votes.

public offering A sale of registered securities to the general public.

purchasing power of money The amount of goods and services a unit of money can command in the market.

purchasing power risk The probability that investors can buy less with the principal and interest they receive from an investment than they could have bought with their principal at the time they made the investment.

put option A contract between a buyer and a writer that gives the buyer a right, but not an obligation, to sell a certain quantity of an underlying asset at a predetermined price on (or perhaps before) a certain date.

pyramid A holding company with a controlling interest in other holding companies.

real return The inflation-adjusted return on an investment, or the nominal return minus the inflation rate.

realized (or actual) return The return than an investor actually receives.

red herring A prospectus circulated to promote interest in a forthcoming issue before SEC approval. The face of the prospectus indicates this preapproval status in red lettering.

registered trader A stock exchange member who buys and sells securities for his or her own account.

regression coefficient A measure of how much and in what direction a security's return changes in response to a change in the return on the market portfolio.

replacement chain Replications of a project to define equal lives for the purpose of capital budgeting analysis.

reporting currency The currency in which a multinational denominates its accounts.

repurchase agreement A very short-term contract between an investor and a bank or broker fixing the sale and repurchase prices of T-bills to guarantee the investor a profit.

required reserve ratio The percentage of a deposit that the Federal Reserve requires a bank to hold either as cash or on deposit at the Fed. The current ratio is 10 percent.

required return The return that an investor requires to invest in an asset.

required rate of return The target rate of return that management insists must be achieved to keep stockholders satisfied or to compensate for risk.

restrictive covenant A limitation on a company's actions specified in an indenture that management agrees to observe as long as the bonds are outstanding.

revaluation A government act to raise the external value of a currency.

revenue bond A municipal security issued to pay for a specific project and backed by the revenues from that project.

rights on A share of stock and its preemptive right are inseparable and must trade together until the close of a rights offering's date of record.

rightsizing A management decision to deliberately and immediately expand (upsize) or contract (downsize) a company and the scale of its operations.

risk The probability that an investor will not receive the expected return from an investment for one reason or another.

risk aversion An investor attitude that demands compensation to bear risk.

risk-free rate The rate of return on a risk-free asset.

risk premium A mark-up on the risk-free rate that a risk averse investor demands to invest in risky assets.

round lot A trade involving exactly 100 shares of stock.

round turn The commission charged for a commodity futures contract purchased: it covers both the immediate purchase and the later sale of the contract.

salvage value The resale or scrap value of an asset.

secondary market The market in which holders of outstanding securities offer them for resale.

Security Market Line A graphical representation of the relationship between securities' expected rates of return and their betas.

security A paper or electronic document created as evidence of some financial transaction.

senior debenture An unsecured debt issue with claims against the company in case of bankruptcy ranked with the claims of other unsecured creditors.

settle price The last price of the day for a commodity futures contract.

shark repellent device A barrier to acquisition entered into a corporate charter before the need arises.

shelf registration An SEC procedure that allows a large corporation to register at one time all of the stocks or bonds it intends to issue in the following two years.

short sale A market transaction in which an investor sells borrowed securities in anticipation of a price decline.

sight draft A document drawn by the seller that instructs the customer to pay the face amount of the draft when presented with it.

sinking fund A fund created by annual contributions to pay off a debt.

small cap A company whose shares of common stock have a total market value (capitalization) less than $250 million.

special drawing rights (SDRs) An accounting unit constructed as the weighted average of the U.S. dollar, the German mark, the French franc, the British pound, and the Japanese yen to serve as an international currency standard.

specialist A stock exchange member who conducts auctions and serves as both a broker and a dealer to maintain an orderly market in an assigned group of stocks.

speculative quality bond A bond rated Ba or lower by Moody's, or BB or lower by Standard & Poor's.

speculator A trader who seeks profits by trading contracts or other futures derivative instruments over short periods of time. A currency speculator buys and sells currencies in the hope of profiting from their future changes.

spin-off Distribution to stockholders of a divesting company of new common stock to give a division or subsidiary an independent identity.

spot (cash) price The current market price of the commody that underlies a futures contract.

spot rate The exchange rate charged for the immediate delivery of a foreign currency.

spot transaction Buying or selling a currency for immediate delivery.

stagflation A simultaneous increase in both the inflation rate and the unemployment rate.

stakeholder Anyone affected by a firm's decisions.

standby commitment An agreement with an investment bank or syndicate to underwrite any unsold shares of stock when a rights offering expires.

stock options Fringe benefits that allow option holders to buy stock below market prices. Firms award them as part of employee compensation to encourage or reward performance.

stockout costs Profits foregone due to lost sales and customers when the firm is unable to fill orders out of inventory.

straight voting A procedure that gives the stockholder one vote for each share of common stock he or she owns for each position to be filled.

straight-line depreciation A method of calculating depreciation that divides the cost of an asset into equal annual amounts.

stretching the terms of trade Paying suppliers a day or a few days late to lower the effective annual cost of trade credit.

strike price The price of the underlying asset at which an option contract is exercised.

subordinate debenture An unsecured debt issue that can be paid off in case of bankruptcy only when claims of all senior debentures have been paid in full.

sunk cost A previously incurred expenditure on a project independent of whether or not the project is accepted. Hence it is not part of the project's cash flows.

supplementary assets Sometimes called a necessary companion asset, one that cannot be acquired without another.

syndicate A group of investment banks formed to participate in the purchase and sale of a new security to spread the risk and facilitate distribution of the bonds or shares.

systematic risk Return uncertainty caused by overall economic developments.

technical analysis Evaluation of supply and demand for a security and the price and trading volume patterns produced by changes in supply and demand.

technical indicator A statistic on market activity that can support technical analysis of the market.

technical insolvency The temporary condition of a firm that cannot meet its current obligations.

tender offer A public announcement that a company is willing to purchase all of its own or another company's outstanding securities in an issue at a price above the current market price.

terms of trade credit The credit terms offered by a firm to its customers, including the period that it allows before payment on credit sales, the amount of any cash discount, and any other conditions.

third market The mechanism through which an investor buys a listed security from a seller without going through the exchange on which it is listed.

time draft A document drawn by a seller instructing the customer to pay the face amount at a specified future date.

time value of money The idea that a dollar tomorrow is worth less than a dollar today.

trade acceptance A time draft signed by the customer to indicate acceptance of the obligation.

transactions balance Cash balance kept in anticipation of needs to pay for future purchases of goods and services.

transfer pricing policy The establishment of prices on sales between subsidiaries, which may or may not reflect market prices.

treasury bill A $10,000 discounted security issued by the U.S. Treasury that matures in one year or less.

treasury stock Common stock that a company repurchases and holds.

treasury strip One of the two theoretical securities created when a brokerage house sells the principal and the interest payments on a Treasury note or bond separately.

trustee A financial institution, usually a commercial bank, that monitors a bond issuer's performance as long as a bond is outstanding, to ensure that the company fulfills its obligations to bondholders.

two-tiered tender offer A bond issuer's offer to buy its outstanding bonds at a high price until a certain date and a lower price after that date; both prices are higher than the current market price.

underwriting A process in which an investment banker buys a new security issue from a company and resells it to the public.

unsystematic risk Return uncertainty caused by firm-specific developments.

variable rate bond A bond whose interest rate changes with market rates.

variable sinking fund The retirement of an increasing amount of debt each year, on the anniversary date of the bond.

velocity of money The rate at which money changes hands during a given period or the rate of turnover of money.

vesting Having the right to keep accumulated pension benefits.

warrant A security attached to a bond that allows the holder to buy common stock in the issuing company at a price above the current market price but below the expected future market price.

white knight An alternative acquiring company perceived to be more friendly to the target company in a hostile takeover situation.

yield curve A line that depicts the relationship between a security's time to maturity and its yield (rate of return).

yield to maturity The annualized rate of return on a bond when held to maturity.

zero inflation No change in the general level of prices.

zero-growth model A dividend discount stock valuation model that assumes zero growth in dividends.

Index

Note: Key terms are set bold-face.

B

C

D

E

G

J

K

L

M

S

U

V

W

Y

Z

Future value (FV) of \$1

$$FV\{\$1\} = \$1(1+i)^n \tag{8.1}$$

Future value of a single amount (P_t)

$$FV\{P_0\} = P_0(1+i)^n = P_0\left(FVIF_{n,i}\right) = P_n \tag{8.2}$$

Future value of an uneven series

$$\begin{aligned} FV\{P_t\} &= P_1(1+i)^n + P_2(1+i)^{n-1} + \ldots + P_n(1+i)^1 \\ &= P_1\left(FVIF_{n,i}\right) + P_2\left(FVIF_{n-1,i}\right) + \ldots + P_n\left(FVIF_{1,i}\right) \end{aligned} \tag{8.4}$$

Future value of an ordinary annuity of \$1

$$\begin{aligned} FV\{A_O = \$1\} &= \$1\sum_{t=1}^{n}(1+i)^{t-1} \\ &= \$1\left[\frac{(1+i)^n - 1}{i}\right] \end{aligned} \tag{8.7}$$

Future value of an annuity due of \$1

$$\begin{aligned} FV\{A_D = \$1\} &= \$1\sum_{t=1}^{n}(1+i)^t \\ &= \$1\left[\frac{(1+i)^n - 1}{i}\right](1+i) \end{aligned} \tag{8.9}$$

Present value (PV) of \$1

$$PV\{\$1\} = \$1\left[1/(1+i)^n\right] \tag{8.13}$$

Present value of a single amount (P_t)

$$\begin{aligned} PV\{P_n\} &= P_n\left[1/(1+i)^n\right] \\ &= P_n\left(PVIF_{n,i}\right) \end{aligned}$$

Present value of an uneven series

$$\begin{aligned} PV\{P_t\} &= P_1\left[1/(1+i)^1\right] + P_2\left[1/(1+i)^2\right] + \ldots + P_n\left[1/(1+i)^n\right] \\ &= P_1\left(PVIF_{1,i}\right) + P_2\left(PVIF_{2,i}\right) + \ldots + P_n\left(PVIF_{n,i}\right) \end{aligned} \tag{8.16}$$

Present value of an ordinary annuity of \$1

$$\begin{aligned} PV\{A_O = \$1\} &= \$1\sum_{t=1}^{n}\left[1/(1+i)^t\right] \\ &= \$1\left[\frac{1 - 1/(1+i)^n}{t}\right] \end{aligned} \tag{8.19}$$

Present value of an annuity due of \$1

$$\begin{aligned} PV\{A_D = \$1\} &= \$1\sum_{t=1}^{n}\left[1/(1-i)^{t-1}\right] \\ &= \$1\left[\frac{1 - 1/(1+i)^n}{i}\right](1+i) \end{aligned} \tag{8.21}$$

Currencies of the World

Country	Currency	Symbol
Madagascar Democratic Republic	Franc	FMG
Malawi	Kwacha	MK
Malaysia	Ringgit	M$
Maldive	Rufiyaa	RF
Malta	Lira	Lm
Mauritania	Uuguiya	UM
Mauritius	Rupee	Rs
Mexico	New Peso	NPs
Morocco	Dirham	DH
Mozambique	Metical	MT
Nepal	Rupee	R
Netherlands	Guilder	Dfl *or* Fl
Netherlands Antilles	Guilder	NAf
New Zealand	N.Z. Dollar[7]	NZ$
Nicaragua	Gold Cordoba	₡
Nigeria	Naira	₦ *or* Nn
Norway	Norwegian Krone	NOK
Oman	Rial	RO
Pakistan	Rupee	PRs
Panama	Balboa	B/
Papua New Guinea	Kina	K
Paraguay	Guarani	₲
Philippines	Peso	₱
Poland	Zloty	Zt
Portugal	Escudo	Esc
Puerto Rico	Dollar (U.S.)[8]	$

Country	Currency	Symbol
Qatar	Riyal	QR
Romania	Leu	L
Rwanda	Franc	F
Sao Tom and Principe	Dobra	Db
Saudi Arabia	Riyal	SR
Seychelles	Rupee	R
Sierra Leone	Leone	Le
Singapore	Dollar	S$
South Africa	Rand[3]	R
Solomon Islands	Solomon Dollar	$
Somali Republic	Shilling	ShSo
Spain	Peseta	Ptas
Surinam	Guilder	f
Sweden	Krona	SEK
Switzerland	Franc	SFr
Taiwan	Dollar	NT$
Thailand	Baht	Bht *or* Bt
Tonga Islands	Pa'anga	T$
Trinidad and Tobago	Dollar	TT$
Turkey	Lira	TL
United Arab Emirates	Dirham	DH *or* UD
United Kingdom	Pound Sterling	£
Vanuatu	Vatu	VT
Venezuela	Bolivar	Bs
Western Samoa	Tala	WST
Zaire	New Zaire	Z
Zambia	Kwacha	K *or* ZK
Zimbabwe	Dollar	Z$

[1]Also used in Dominica, Grenada, Montserrat, Saint Christopher, Saint Lucia, Saint Vincent.
[2]Also used in Kiribati, Nauru Islands, Tuvalu.
[3]Also used in Burkina Faso, Cameroon, Central African Republic, Chad, People's Republic of Congo, Equatorial Guinea, Gabon, Ivory Coast, Mali Republic, Niger Republic, Senegal, Togo Republic.
[4]Also used in Faeroe Islands, Greenland.
[5]Also used in Andorra, French Guinea, Guadeloupe, Ile de la Reunion, Martinique, Monaco, Saint Pierre.
[6]Also used in San Marino.
[7]Also used in Pitcairn Islands
[8]Also used in Guam, American Samoa, Turks and Caicos Islands, British Virgin Islands, U.S. Virgin Islands.
[9]Also used in Namibia, Venda
[10]Also used in Falkland Islands, Gibraltar, Saint Helena.